CASES AND MATERIALS

MASS MEDIA LAW

SEVENTH EDITION

by

MARC A. FRANKLIN
Frederick I. Richman Professor of Law
Stanford University

DAVID A. ANDERSON
Fred and Emily Marshall Wulff Centennial Chair in Law
University of Texas

LYRISSA BARNETT LIDSKY
Research Foundation Professor of Law
University of Florida

FOUNDATION PRESS
NEW YORK, NEW YORK
2005

THOMSON
—★—
WEST

Foundation Press, of Thomson/West, has created this publication to provide you with accurate and authoritative information concerning the subject matter covered. However, this publication was not necessarily prepared by persons licensed to practice law in a particular jurisdiction. Foundation Press is not engaged in rendering legal or other professional advice, and this publication is not a substitute for the advice of an attorney. If you require legal or other expert advice, you should seek the services of a competent attorney or other professional.

© 1977, 1982, 1987, 1990, 1995, 2000 FOUNDATION PRESS
© 2005 By FOUNDATION PRESS
     395 Hudson Street
     New York, NY 10014
     Phone Toll Free 1–877–888–1330
     Fax (212) 367–6799
     fdpress.com
Printed in the United States of America

ISBN 1–58778–773–3

TEXT IS PRINTED ON 10% POST
CONSUMER RECYCLED PAPER

*To the memory of Ruth K. Franklin
and
to Karen, Beth, Lynetta and Don*

*

PREFACE TO THE SEVENTH EDITION

Preparing this edition has been a challenge. Since the previous edition in 2000, there have been fewer Supreme Court media cases and important lower court decisions than in the previous intervals between editions, yet it is clear that the field of mass media law has changed significantly. Defamation, once the core of the field and this book, is no longer the dominant concern of media lawyers. The attacks of September 11, 2001, and the subsequent "war on terror" seem to have ushered in a new era of government secrecy and impatience with media claims for access to information and confidentiality of sources, but so far there has not been enough definitive litigation on these matters to outline the contours of the new landscape. Ownership of media outlets has consolidated dramatically; how much regulatory restraint on this process will survive is not yet clear. Capturing this dynamic field in a casebook has proven even more difficult than usual.

We have retained the basic organizational structure of the sixth edition. Part I deals primarily with First Amendment restrictions on governmental action toward media. Part II addresses primarily private civil litigation arising out of publication. Part III deals with restrictions on newsgathering, both governmental and civil. We continue to believe that the essential regulatory aspects of media law ought to be integrated with the rest of the materials rather than segregated in chapters dealing with specific types of media, so we have retained the integrated structure that we adopted with the sixth edition.

The tendency of casebooks, particularly those that have been through seven editions, is to become fatter and fatter, as new developments clamor for space beside the old. To preserve icons that teachers may have come to cherish, authors are tempted to convert old principal cases into notes and to retain matter that has become of little more than historical interest. We have tried to resist that tendency. We have streamlined the defamation chapter, eliminated a good deal of detail from the chapters on access to information and access to judicial proceedings, and deleted a considerable amount of textual material between principal cases throughout the book.

As a result, long-time users of the book should be forewarned that they may find favorite cases, excerpts, quotations, and notes missing from this edition. We believe teachers will conclude that these disappointments are outweighed by the advantages of giving students a more manageable amount of material and a less cluttered view of matters of current importance.

With this edition, we welcome a new co-author, Professor Lyrissa Barnett Lidsky. We express our gratitude to Fred H. Cate, who was a co-author on the sixth edition and whose influence and wisdom can still be seen in this edition.

MARC A. FRANKLIN
DAVID A. ANDERSON
LYRISSA BARNETT LIDSKY

January 2005

ACKNOWLEDGMENTS

The authors wish to thank Cory Andrews, Angela Brayer, Marilyn Henderson, Steve Roberts, Shaun Rogers, and Natasha Self for their assistance in producing this edition. We are also grateful to readers of the previous editions for their criticisms and suggestions.

Thanks are also due to authors and copyright holders who permitted excerpts from the following works to be included in this book:

Anderson, David A., "Tortious Speech," *Washington & Lee Law Review*, Vol. 47 at page 71, copyright ©1990 by Washington & Lee Law Review, reprinted by permission.

Baker, C. Edwin, *Human Liberty and Freedom of Speech* from *Human Liberty and Freedom of Speech* by C. Edwin Baker. Copyright © 1992 by Oxford University Press, Inc. Used by permission of Oxford University Press, Inc.

Emerson, Thomas I., *The System of Freedom of Expression*, copyright © 1970 by Thomas I. Emerson. Reprinted with permission of the author.

Fiss, Owen, "Why the State?," *Harvard Law Review*, Vol. 100 at page 781, copyright © 1987 by the Harvard Law Review Association, reprinted by permission.

Jeffries, John C., Jr. "Rethinking Prior Restraint," copyright © 1983 by The Yale Law Journal. Reprinted by permission of The Yale Law Journal Company and Fred B. Rothman & Company from *The Yale Law Journal*, Vol. 92, pages 409–437.

Lemley, Mark A., and Volokh, Eugene, "Freedom of Speech and Injunctions in Intellectual Property Cases," reprinted with permission of the Duke Law Journal, copyright © 1998, from 48 Duke L.J. 147 (1998).

Meiklejohn, Alexander, "The First Amendment Is an Absolute," copyright © 1961 by The University of Chicago. All Rights Reserved. Reprinted by permission of The University of Chicago Press from *Supreme Court Review* (1961), 245, 255–262.

Netanel, Neil Weinstock, "Market Hierarchy and Copyright in Our System of Free Expression," Vanderbilt Law Review, Vol. 54 at 1879, copyright © 2000 by the *Vanderbilt Law Review*, reprinted by permission.

Powe, Lucas A., Jr., "Scholarship and Markets." Reprinted with the permission of *The George Washington Law Review*, copyright © 1987 from 56 Geo. Wash. L. Rev. 1, (1987), pp. 172, 182–84.

Schauer, Frederick, "The Boundaries of the First Amendment: A Preliminary Exploration of Constitutional Salience," *Harvard Law Review*, Vol. 117 at page 1765, copyright © 2004 by the Harvard Law Review Association, reprinted by permission.

SUMMARY OF CONTENTS

TABLE OF CONTENTS

PART TWO: LEGAL ISSUES ARISING FROM PUBLICATION

PART THREE: LEGAL ISSUES ARISING FROM NEWSGATHERING

*

TABLE OF CASES

*

CASES AND MATERIALS

MASS MEDIA LAW

*

PART ONE

THE FIRST AMENDMENT AND GOVERNMENT REGULATION

CHAPTER I

THE FIRST AMENDMENT AND THE MEDIA

A. INTRODUCTION

This is a book about media law, not a book about the First Amendment. Media law has many sources other than the First Amendment. The law of defamation and invasion of privacy is largely common law. A reporter's privilege to refuse to disclose confidences is controlled in many states by statutes. Open-meetings and open-records statutes determine the outcome of most controversies over press access to governmental information. Broadcast regulation is largely accomplished by federal statutes and Federal Communications Commission regulations.

Conversely, many areas of First Amendment law have little to do with the mass media. The religion, association, and petition clauses of that amendment rarely are invoked by the mass media. Even the speech clause generates much litigation that does not affect the media. Cases involving censorship of libraries and school materials use of streets and parks as public forums, and picketing are First Amendment cases but not media law cases.

Nevertheless, the First Amendment does play a large role in nearly every area of media law. It limits the extent to which states may protect reputation and privacy. It gives the press (and public) rights to attend trials, to publish lawfully obtained information, and to protect their sources. It protects the right to disseminate and advertise pornography. It imposes limits on the government's ability to regulate broadcasting—limits that are shifting as technologies and attitudes toward broadcasting change.

Because the influence of the First Amendment is so pervasive in media law, we begin with a brief and selective treatment of First Amendment theory. Our focus is on those portions of First Amendment theory that are likely to influence the outcome of media law issues. The media lawyer must not forget, however, that judges do not see media First Amendment issues in isolation from other kinds of First Amendment cases. A judge hearing a media law case may be influenced by a picketing case he or she recently decided, even if it did not appear in the Media Law Reporter.

First Amendment jurisprudence as we know it was quite slow to develop. In this connection it is necessary to distinguish between First Amendment law and the common law of free speech and free press. The latter began to diverge from its English heritage quite early and developed throughout the eighteenth and nineteenth centuries. First Amendment jurisprudence, on the other hand, is almost entirely a creation of the twentieth century.

The trial of printer John Peter Zenger in New York in 1735 established the practice of allowing the jury to return a general verdict of "not guilty" in seditious libel cases, in contrast to the practice in England, where the jury was only allowed to decide whether the defendant had published the words in question. For this reason, and because of widespread public resistance to government prosecutions of speech, the common law of seditious libel became generally ineffectual in America in the eighteenth century. The common law prohibition against prior restraints was widely accepted in both England and the United States.

The Sedition Act of 1798—enacted just seven years after the First Amendment was adopted—touched off a controversy that became a defining event in the history of freedom of expression. The Federalist Party passed this statute, together with the Alien Act, in an attempt to keep Thomas Jefferson's Republican Party from winning the election of 1800. The Act made it a crime to print any false, scandalous, and malicious writings about the federal government, the Congress, or the president. It conspicuously omitted the vice presidency, which Jefferson then held, and it expired by its own terms in 1801. The Act was enforced vigorously and effectively against Republican newspapers, which were already vastly outnumbered by the Federalist press. Three Republican editors were convicted and three leading Republican newspapers were forced to cease publication. There were 15 indictments in all, leading to 10 convictions. Despite this virtual silencing of the newspapers that supported him, Jefferson won the election and there was no attempt to renew the Sedition Act.

The Sedition Act was never tested in the Supreme Court, but it touched off the first national debate over the meaning of press freedom. It prompted James Madison and Jefferson to write extended discourses on freedom of speech and press, in which both argued that the First Amendment had been intended to deny the federal government the power to punish seditious libel. In the course of making these arguments, they embraced more comprehensive visions of freedom of expression than had generally been expressed previously. Some contend these were *post hoc* constructions that cannot be trusted as accurate statements of the framers' intentions, but all agree that they were influential interpretations upon which much subsequent doctrine was based. Madison's exegesis was adopted by the Virginia legislature and is known as "The Virginia Report of 1799–80." Jefferson's contribution was "The Kentucky Resolutions of 1798." Both are excerpted in Leonard Levy (ed.), Freedom of the Press From Zenger to Jefferson (1966).

There were many free speech and free press controversies in the nineteenth century, principally over censorship of abolitionist publications in the southern states before the Civil War and censorship of "obscenity" in the industrial states after the war. For reasons that have yet to be fully explained, these conflicts did not generate much development of free speech jurisprudence. Courts seemed to acquiesce in generalizations such as "freedom of speech is protected but abuse of the right is not" and in broad definitions of concepts like obscenity. See generally David M. Rabban, The First Amendment in Its Forgotten Years, 90 Yale L.J. 514 (1981).

One reason for the slow development of the First Amendment was that it applied only to the federal government. That was clear both from its language, which prohibited only Congress, and from its legislative history, which explicitly rejected application to the states. Adoption of the Fourteenth Amendment in 1868 was not understood at the time to require any change in this thinking. Because the scope of federal governmental activity was vastly narrower in the nineteenth century than it is today, there were fewer occasions for federal suppression of speech or press. However, much of the suppression of abolitionist material was done by federal postal officials, and the Comstock Act of 1873, which allowed postal authorities to seize "obscenity" and prosecute its senders, was a federal statute.

In any event, the Supreme Court did not begin to develop a comprehensive First Amendment jurisprudence until after World War I. Prosecutions of anarchists, socialists, and other political radicals under the Espionage Act of 1917 and similar state laws finally forced the Court to consider the conflict between the First Amendment and government power to suppress speech. Throughout the decade following World War I, a majority of the Court consistently rejected First Amendment defenses, but Justices Holmes and Brandeis, in a series of famous dissents, began articulating more expansive views of free speech. Not until 1925 did the Court apply the First Amendment to the states.

First Amendment litigation by the mass media is a relatively recent phenomenon. The press did not win a First Amendment case in the Supreme Court until 1931, and not until 1964 did the Supreme Court hold that the First Amendment imposed any limitations on state tort actions, such as libel. Thus, while the law of free speech and free press has been developing for centuries, First Amendment law has developed comparatively recently. In fact, only in the last few decades have the established media engaged regularly in constitutional confrontations with authorities. In part this reflects changes in journalism and the relationship of the press to the government. During World War II virtually the entire American press voluntarily acquiesced in government censorship of military news. As recently as the late 1940s, the White House was covered only by a handful of reporters who sometimes played poker with President Truman. Reporters and government officials often acted as allies, the latter releasing information as a favor, and receiving favorable publicity in return. The investigation of wrongdoing was largely left to ambitious prosecutors and investigating committees; the press's role primarily was to report and comment upon the activities of government.

In the 1960s the relationship between the press and the government changed dramatically. It began with the civil rights movement, with the press often providing sympathetic coverage of the demonstrators' confrontations with governmental authority, first in the South, then in the cities of the North as the movement exploded across the nation. Hostility grew as the press began to join those challenging the government's pronouncements about the goals and progress of the war in Vietnam. In the meantime, changes in the law of defamation (which we will see in Chapter IV) made it easier for the press to take on a role as investigator of government, in addition to its roles as reporter and commentator. Investigative journalism reached perhaps its apogee with the Watergate scandal, which began with disclosures by the Washington Post of White House activities that eventually forced President Nixon to resign.

From then on, investigations by the media themselves, and enthusiastic media reporting of others' allegations of wrongdoing, have played pivotal roles in many of the major events of the times. Media disclosures forced several presidential candidates to withdraw and led to the defeat of several nominees for high executive or judicial office, and politicians have attempted to make the aggressiveness of the media a political issue. In the present generation, intense media coverage surrounding the death of England's Princess Diana, the disclosures of Monica Lewinsky, the impeachment trial of President Clinton, the rape allegation against Kobe Bryant, and other events have been the subject of significant commentary and criticism. And in the wake of the events of September 11, 2001, some commentators have criticized media aggressiveness as evidence of a lack of patriotism, even as others have decried their failure to examine critically information received from the presidential administration.

While the media were becoming more aggressive journalistically, they were also becoming more assertive in the legal system. Until the 1970s, there was no organized media bar. James Goodale, former general counsel of the New York Times, organized an annual media law seminar under the auspices of the Practising Law Institute in New York. This created a nucleus of experienced First Amendment lawyers who shared ideas and expertise among themselves and with other media lawyers across the country. About the same time, the Media Law Reporter was established, bringing important opinions and legislative developments from all jurisdictions to the attention of media lawyers everywhere.

Armed with more expertise, better information, and a support network, media lawyers began asserting new First Amendment arguments, not only defensively in response to libel suits and subpoenas, but also offensively, to gain access to courtrooms and governmental institutions, to gain new protections for commercial speech, to attack discriminatory taxation, and to force reconsideration of restrictions on broadcast journalism.

More recently, the media industry has gone through upheaval as the number and types of media have proliferated. The United States today has approximately 1,450 daily newspapers, more than 6,700 weeklies,* 800 television stations, and 13,500 radio stations. The "big three" commercial television networks have been joined by Fox, UPN, WB, and 280 national cable networks, 20 of which have more than 86 million subscribers. Ninety-

---

* "2004 Facts About Newspapers: A Statistical Summary of the Newspaper Industry," *Newspaper Association of America* (2004).—eds.

five percent of American homes with televisions are passed by cable; 68 percent of those actually subscribe to cable television.*

Although many media operations are small, a growing number are owned by corporate giants: The Walt Disney Company owns Capital Cities/ABC, General Electric owns NBC, News Corporation owns the FOX network, and Viacom owns CBS and Infinity Broadcasting, which in turn owns 185 radio stations around the country and both UPN and MTV. Many media subsidiaries have been very profitable for their corporate owners: The New York Times Company in 1975 posted earnings of less than $13 million; in 1998 the company reported a profit of $521 million and in 2003 reported a total net income of $303 million. The Washington Post Company's profits rose from $12 million in 1975 to $417 million in 1998, and in 2003 the company reported a net income of $241.1 million.

The average operating margin (defined as before-tax profit divided by revenue) for publicly traded newspaper companies in 1997 was 19.5 percent compared with 7.6 percent for all manufacturing industries. Television stations "often enjoy operating margins of more than 45 percent." See Newspapers Arrive at Economic Crossroads, Nieman Reports Summer 1999 (Special Issue) at 4; Gilbert Cranberg, Randall Bezanson, and John Soloski, Taking Stock: Journalism and the Publicly Traded Newspaper Company (2001).

The demand for scarce audience in an overcrowded marketplace and the growing expectation that media operations will contribute to their parent companies' bottom line have contributed to significant changes in reporting, including the rise of tabloid television, the proliferation of talk shows, and an expanded focus on celebrities, human interest stories, and practical information, while reducing hard news to fewer and shorter segments.

New media, especially digital media, have created even more outlets, while expanding both the number of people who originate content and the pressure for viewers, readers, and listeners. The World Wide Web, first made available to the public in 1992, is used today by an estimated 604 million people worldwide, making the web the fastest growing medium in history. In 2002, 63% of Americans were online. Compare this with the fact that during that same year only 56.6% of Americans read one entire book. Although the Internet threatens the viability of many traditional media outlets, it also offers them new avenues for expansion, which may help explain why more than 1,500 daily newspapers in North America had websites in 2004.

The last third of the twentieth century saw a dramatic increase in First Amendment litigation involving the mass media. More than half of all the press cases decided by the U.S. Supreme Court in its history have been

---

* See "Statistics & Resources," National Cable & Television Ass'n (2003) at http://www.ncta.com/Docs/PageContent.cmf?pageID=86; see also "Tenth Annual Report, In the Matter of Annual Assessment of the Status of Competition in the Market for Delivery of Video Programming," 19 FCC Rcd. 1606, at 1607 (2003).—eds.

decided since 1970. This litigation has changed the nature of American journalism and profoundly altered the relationship between the press and government at all levels, and probably will continue to do so. As that case law matures, we are also witnessing a shift in the nature of First Amendment litigation away from defamation, where the constitutional principles are fairly well settled, to cases involving newsgathering, media liability for harmful (but not defamatory) content, media business activities, and the ownership and control of digital expression.

To better understand how courts resolve these cases, we begin by considering the theory of freedom of expression under the First Amendment.

That amendment reads:

Congress shall make no law respecting an establishment of religion, or prohibiting the free exercise thereof; or abridging the freedom of speech or of the press; or the right of the people peaceably to assemble, and to petition the government for a redress of grievances.

B. VALUES SERVED BY SPEECH*

1. THE LEGACY OF HOLMES AND BRANDEIS

Like most Americans, members of the Supreme Court seem to assume that the value of protecting speech is self-evident. Opinions often contain extended analysis of competing interests that are advanced to justify a restriction on speech, but little discussion of the nature of the interests advanced by the speech itself. Two early exceptions were Justice Oliver Wendell Holmes and Justice Louis Brandeis. In the decades after World War I, Holmes and Brandeis explored various philosophical justifications for protecting free speech in a series of cases brought against war protestors and social radicals. Although they rarely wrote for the majority in these cases, the dissents they filed ultimately became the foundation of modern First Amendment theory.

a. Justice Brandeis, Civic Courage, and Free Speech

A much-quoted articulation of some of the values of speech is Justice Brandeis' concurrence in *Whitney v. California*:

Those who won our independence believed that the final end of the State was to make men free to develop their faculties; and that in its government the deliberative forces should prevail over the arbitrary. They valued liberty both as an end and as a means. They believed liberty to be the secret of happiness and courage to be the secret of liberty. They believed that freedom to think as you will and to speak as

---

* We, like courts and other commentators, sometimes use "speech" as shorthand for "freedom of expression" or "freedom of speech and press."—eds.

you think are means indispensable to the discovery and spread of political truth; that without free speech and assembly discussion would be futile; that with them, discussion affords ordinarily adequate protection against the dissemination of noxious doctrine; that the greatest menace to freedom is an inert people; that public discussion is a political duty; and that this should be a fundamental principle of the American government. They recognized the risks to which all human institutions are subject. But they knew that order cannot be secured merely through fear of punishment for its infraction; that it is hazardous to discourage thought, hope and imagination; that fear breeds repression; that repression breeds hate; that hate menaces stable government; that the path of safety lies in the opportunity to discuss freely supposed grievances and proposed remedies; and that the fitting remedy for evil counsels is good ones. Believing in the power of reason as applied through public discussion, they eschewed silence coerced by law—the argument of force in its worst form. Recognizing the occasional tyrannies of governing majorities, they amended the Constitution so that free speech and assembly should be guaranteed.

Fear of serious injury cannot alone justify suppression of free speech and assembly. Men feared witches and burnt women. It is the function of speech to free men from the bondage of irrational fears. To justify suppression of free speech there must be reasonable ground to fear that serious evil will result if free speech is practiced. There must be reasonable ground to believe that the danger apprehended is imminent. There must be reasonable ground to believe that the evil to be prevented is a serious one. Every denunciation of existing law tends in some measure to increase the probability that there will be violation of it. Condonation of a breach enhances the probability. Expressions of approval add to the probability. Propagation of the criminal state of mind by teaching syndicalism increases it. Advocacy of law-breaking heightens it still further. But even advocacy of violation, however reprehensible morally, is not a justification for denying free speech where the advocacy falls short of incitement and there is nothing to indicate that the advocacy would be immediately acted on. The wide difference between advocacy and incitement, between preparation and attempt, between assembling and conspiracy, must be borne in mind. In order to support a finding of clear and present danger it must be shown either that immediate serious violence was to be expected or was advocated, or that the past conduct furnished reason to believe that such advocacy was then contemplated.

Those who won our independence by revolution were not cowards. They did not fear political change. They did not exalt order at the cost of liberty. To courageous, self-reliant men, with confidence in the power of free and fearless reasoning applied through the processes of popular government, no danger flowing from speech can be deemed clear and present, unless the incidence of the evil apprehended is so imminent that it may befall before there is opportunity for full discussion. If there be time to expose through discussion the falsehood and fallacies, to avert the evil by the processes of education, the remedy to be applied is more speech, not enforced silence. Only an emergency can justify repression. Such must be the rule if authority is to be reconciled with freedom. Such, in my opinion, is the command of the Constitution. It is therefore always open to Americans to challenge a law abridging free speech and assembly by showing that there was no emergency justifying it.

Whitney v. California, 274 U.S. 357, 375–77 (1927) (Brandeis, J., concurring).

———

Professor Blasi calls the Brandeis opinion in *Whitney* "arguably the most important essay ever written, on or off the bench, on the meaning of the first amendment." He sees it as identifying freedom of expression with "the ideal of civic courage":

> . . .* To Brandeis, the measure of courage in the civic realm is the capacity to experience or anticipate change—even rapid and fundamental change—without losing perspective or confidence. Assessment of the benefits and risks of unregulated discussion are certain to be affected by what general disposition the decisionmaker has toward the phenomenon of change. The courageous attitude, Brandeis asserts, is that of receptivity to new arrangements and new ways of thinking. Progress, the value literally at the root of progressive philosophy, depends on receptivity to change. And while speech no doubt contributes directly to change by ventilating grievances and reform proposals, the freedom of speech may be most valuable for its indirect effect, salutary even if subtle, on public attitudes toward change. Those attitudes largely determine how the political community responds to the grievances and reforms that are ventilated. Not just judges but all of us need to be liberated from "the bondage of irrational fears" as we encounter unsettling proposals for political change. The essence of civic courage is a healthy mentality regarding change.

Vincent Blasi, The First Amendment and the Ideal of Civic Courage: The Brandeis Opinion in *Whitney v. California,* 29 Wm. & Mary L. Rev. 653, 690–91 (1988).

b. *Justice Holmes and the Marketplace of Ideas*

Although Justice Brandeis was the most eloquent judicial defender of freedom of expression, it was Justice Holmes who contributed the "marketplace of ideas" metaphor to First Amendment jurisprudence. This meta-

---

* Throughout this book omissions of text, or omissions of text plus citation(s), are indicated by ellipses. Omission of citation(s) only are indicated by [ ]. Footnotes are omitted without indication. When footnotes are included, they are numbered as in the original. Footnotes by the editors are indicated by *.—eds.

phor remains the dominant articulation of the value of free speech, at least in the American experience.

One of the earliest expressions of the "marketplace of ideas" came in 1644 in John Milton's Areopagitica, an essay against the English system of licensing publications: "And though all the winds of doctrine were let loose to play upon the earth, so Truth be in the field, we do injuriously by licensing and prohibiting to misdoubt her strength. Let her and Falsehood grapple; who ever knew Truth put to the worse, in a free and open encounter?"

Two hundred years later, the English philosopher and economist John Stuart Mill embraced the metaphor more broadly, as a reason for denying all government power to suppress speech, even though he recognized that truth sometimes loses:

> [T]he peculiar evil of silencing the expression of an opinion is, that it is robbing the human race: posterity as well as the existing genera-tion; those who dissent from the opinion, still more than those who hold it. If the opinion is right, they are deprived of the opportunity of exchanging error for truth; if wrong, they lose what is almost as great a benefit, the clearer perception and livelier impression of truth, produced by its collision with error.
>
> . . .
>
> [T]he dictum that truth always triumphs over persecution is one of those pleasant falsehoods which men repeat after one another till they pass into commonplaces, but which all experience refutes. History teems with instances of truth put down by persecution. If not sup-pressed forever, it may be thrown back for centuries. . . . It is a piece of idle sentimentality that truth, merely as truth, has any inherent power denied to error of prevailing against the dungeon and the stake.

John Stuart Mill, On Liberty 20, 30–31 (S. Collini, ed. 1989). The market-place metaphor, envisioned by Milton and developed by Mill, entered First Amendment jurisprudence in Justice Holmes' dissenting opinion in Abrams v. United States, 250 U.S. 616 (1919). Abrams and four other socialist immigrants were convicted of sedition for publishing pamphlets that urged workers in munitions plants to strike to protest the deployment of Ameri-can troops to help put down the Russian Revolution. A majority of the Supreme Court upheld the convictions, but Justice Holmes, joined by Justice Brandeis, argued in dissent that the pamphlets were not seditious because they did not attack the form of the U.S. government or cripple it in its war effort. More generally, Holmes wrote:

> Persecution for the expression of opinions seems to me perfectly logical. If you have no doubt of your premises or your power and want a certain result with all your heart you naturally express your wishes in law and sweep away all opposition. To allow opposition by speech seems to indicate that you think the speech impotent, as when a man says that he has squared the circle, or that you do not care whole-heartedly for the result, or that you doubt either your power or your

premises. But when men have realized that time has upset many fighting faiths, they may come to believe even more than they believe the very foundations of their own conduct that the ultimate good desired is better reached by free trade in ideas—that the best test of truth is the power of the thought to get itself accepted in the competition of the market, and that truth is the only ground upon which their wishes safely can be carried out. That at any rate is the theory of our Constitution. It is an experiment, as all life is an experiment.

Judge Learned Hand voice a similar sentiment in an antitrust case brought against the Associated Press. He observed that one of the most "vital of all general interests" is "the dissemination of news from as many different sources, and with as many different facets and colors as is possible. That interest is closely akin to, if indeed it is not the same as, the interest protected by the First Amendment; it presupposes that right conclusions are more likely to be gathered out of a multitude of tongues, than through any kind of authoritative selection. To many this is, and always will be, folly; but we have staked upon it our all." United States v. Associated Press, 52 F. Supp. 362 (S.D.N.Y. 1943).

For an illuminating insight into the views of the First Amendment held by Justice Holmes, Judge Learned Hand, and the influential scholar Zechariah Chafee, see Gerald Gunther, "Learned Hand and the Origins of Modern First Amendment Doctrine: Some Fragments of History," 27 Stan. L. Rev. 719 (1975). See generally Stanley Ingber, The Marketplace of Ideas: A Legitimizing Myth, 15 Duke L.J. 1 (1984); G. Edward White, The Canonization of Holmes and Brandeis: Epistemology and Judicial Reputations, 70 N.Y.U. L. Rev. 576 (1995). For extensive analysis of the application of First Amendment principles during wartime, see Geoffrey Stone, Perilous Times: Free Speech in Wartime from the Sedition Act of 1798 to the War on Terrorism (2004).

———

Critics of the marketplace theory point to the fact that it is an ideal that has never been fully realized. Many citizens are barred from meaningful participation in the marketplace of ideas by poverty or inadequate education, and class, race, or gender may impair the ability of some speakers to make their voices heard. Media corporations sometimes set the parameters of public debate based on what sells rather than on what an informed citizenry needs to know. And even though the Internet gives citizens widespread access to a medium of mass communication, the speakers whose voices are most influential online are often the very same speakers whose voices dominate public debate in the conventional media. A more fundamental critique of the marketplace theory has to do with the limits of human nature. Even if the marketplace of ideas were functioning perfectly, there is still some question whether "Truth" would emerge, as human beings often adhere to irrational beliefs.

Several contemporary critics of the marketplace theory also argue that it prevents democratic reforms that would actually advance free speech interests. Professor Cass Sunstein argues, for example, that adherence to the marketplace metaphor has resulted in "safeguard[ing] speech that has little or no connection with democratic aspirations and that produces serious social harm." Sunstein argues that just as the federal government intervened in the economic marketplace to correct market failures during the New Deal, governmental intervention in the marketplace of ideas is sometimes warranted:

> [It is possible] that government controls on the broadcast media, designed to ensure diversity of view and attention to public affairs, would help the system of free expression. Such controls could promote both political deliberation and political equality. In such reforms, I contend, lies the best hope for keeping faith with time-honored principles of democratic self-government under modern conditions.

Cass R. Sunstein, Democracy and the Problem of Free Speech xviii–xx, 18–19 (1993).

Despite these criticisms, the marketplace theory of free speech remains a powerful force in First Amendment jurisprudence. One explanation might be that judges, at least justices of the U.S. Supreme Court, are less dissatisfied than the critics with the results of marketplace-based jurisprudence. As Professor Sunstein acknowledges, that model has produced a great deal of freedom:

> Over the last forty years, the American law of freedom of speech experienced nothing short of a revolution. The revolution accomplished enormous good. It would be hard to argue that a return to the pre–1950 law of free speech would provide a better understanding of the free speech principle. . . .

> At the same time, a crucial part of that achievement is a dynamic and self-revising free speech tradition. Our liberty of expression owes much of its content to the capacity of each generation to rethink the understandings that were left to it. To the economists' plea that "the perfect is the enemy of the good," we should oppose John Dewey's suggestion that "the better is the enemy of the still better." . . .

Id. at 250.

2.   SCHOLARS AND FIRST AMENDMENT THEORY

Reasons for protecting speech can be divided, crudely, into two groups: those relating to instrumental ends, such as successful operation of the political process, and those relating to personal ends, such as autonomy. Professor Kent Greenawalt draws this distinction more elegantly, between "consequentialist" and "nonconsequentialist" justifications for speech. "A practice has value from a *consequentialist* point of view if it contributes to some desirable state of affairs. . . . A *nonconsequentialist* reason claims that something about a particular practice is right or wrong without regard to the consequences." *See* Kent Greenawalt, Speech, Crime, and the Uses of Language 14 (1989). Did Justices Holmes and Brandeis employ consequentialist or nonconsequentalist justifications for protecting freedom of expression? As you read the writings of the scholars below, consider carefully whether consequentialist or nonconsequentialist justifications underpin their theories of free speech. Are all of these justifications equally applicable to freedom of the press?

The System of Freedom of Expression
Thomas I. Emerson
6–9 (1970).

The system of freedom of expression in a democratic society rests upon four main premises. These may be stated, in capsule form, as follows:

First, freedom of expression is essential as a means of assuring individual self-fulfillment. The proper end of man is the realization of his character and potentialities as a human being. For the achievement of this self-realization the mind must be free. Hence suppression of belief, opinion, or other expression is an affront to the dignity of man, a negation of man's essential nature. Moreover, man in his capacity as a member of society has a right to share in the common decisions that affect him. To cut off his search for truth, or his expression of it, is to elevate society and the state to a despotic command over him and to place him under the arbitrary control of others.

Second, freedom of expression is an essential process for advancing knowledge and discovering truth. An individual who seeks knowledge and truth must hear all sides of the question, consider all alternatives, test his judgment by exposing it to opposition, and make full use of different minds. Discussion must be kept open no matter how certainly true an accepted opinion may seem to be; many of the most widely acknowledged truths have turned out to be erroneous. Conversely, the same principle applies no matter how false or pernicious the new opinion appears to be; for the unaccepted opinion may be true or partially true and, even if wholly false, its presentation and open discussion compel a rethinking and retesting of the accepted opinion. The reasons which make open discussion essential for an intelligent individual judgment likewise make it imperative for rational social judgment.

Third, freedom of expression is essential to provide for participation in decision making by all members of society. This is particularly significant for political decisions. Once one accepts the premise of the Declaration of Independence—that governments "derive their just powers from the consent of the governed"—it follows that the governed must, in order to exercise their right of consent, have full freedom of expression both in forming individual judgments and in forming the common judgment. The principle also carries beyond the political realm. It embraces the right to participate in the building of the whole culture, and includes freedom of expression in religion, literature, art, science, and all areas of human learning and knowledge.

Finally, freedom of expression is a method of achieving a more adaptable and hence a more stable community, of maintaining the precarious balance between healthy cleavage and necessary consensus. This follows because suppression of discussion makes a rational judgment impossible, substituting force for reason; because suppression promotes inflexibility and stultification, preventing society from adjusting to changing circumstances or developing new ideas; and because suppression conceals the real problems confronting a society, diverting public attention from the critical issues. At the same time the process of open discussion promotes greater cohesion in a society because people are more ready to accept decisions that go against them if they have a part in the decision-making process. Moreover, the state at all times retains adequate powers to promote unity and to suppress resort to force. Freedom of expression thus provides a framework in which the conflict necessary to the progress of society can take place without destroying the society. It is an essential mechanism for maintaining the balance between stability and change.

The validity of the foregoing premises has never been proved or disproved, and probably could not be. Nevertheless our society is based upon the faith that they hold true and, in maintaining a system of freedom of expression, we act upon that faith. . . .

Two basic implications of the theory underlying our system of freedom of expression need to be emphasized. The first is that it is not a general measure of the individual's right to freedom of expression that any particular exercise of that right may be thought to promote or retard other goals of the society. The theory asserts that freedom of expression, while not the sole or sufficient end of society, is a good in itself, or at least an essential element in a good society. The society may seek to achieve other or more inclusive ends—such as virtue, justice, equality, or the maximum realization of the potentialities of its members. These are not necessarily gained by accepting the rules for freedom of expression. But, as a general proposition, the society may not seek them by suppressing the beliefs or opinions of individual members. To achieve these other goals it must rely upon other methods: the use of counter-expression and the regulation or control of conduct which is not expression. Hence the right to control individual expression, on the ground that it is judged to promote good or evil, justice or injustice, equality or inequality, is not, speaking generally, within the competence of the good society.

The second implication, in a sense a corollary of the first, is that the theory rests upon a fundamental distinction between belief, opinion, and communication of ideas on the one hand, and different forms of conduct on the other. For shorthand purposes we refer to this distinction hereafter as one between "expression" and "action." As just observed, in order to achieve its desired goals, a society or the state is entitled to exercise control over action—whether by prohibiting or compelling it—on an entirely different and vastly more extensive basis. But expression occupies an especially protected position. In this sector of human conduct, the social right of suppression or compulsion is at its lowest point, in most respects nonexistent. A majority of one has the right to control action, but a minority of one has the right to talk.

———

Why the State?

Owen M. Fiss
100 Harv. L. Rev. 781, 787–88 (1987).

Today, public debate is dominated by the television networks and a number of large newspapers and magazines. The competition among these institutions is far from perfect, and some might argue for state intervention on a theory of market failure. There is a great deal of force to those arguments, but they obscure a deeper truth—a market, even one that is working perfectly, is itself a structure of constraint. A fully competitive market might produce a diversity of programs, formats, and reportage, but, to borrow an image of Renata Adler's, it will be the diversity of "a pack going essentially in one direction."

The market constrains the presentation of matters of public interest and importance in two ways. First, the market privileges select groups, by making programs, journals, and newspapers especially responsive to their needs and desires. One such group consists of those who have the capital to acquire or own a television station, newspaper, or journal; another consists of those who control the advertising budgets of various businesses; and still another consists of those who are most able and most likely to respond enthusiastically to advertising. The number in the last group is no doubt quite large (it probably includes every nine-year-old who can bully his or her parents into purchasing one thing or another), but it is not coextensive with the electorate. To be a consumer, even a sovereign one, is not to be a citizen.

Second, the market brings to bear on editorial and programming decisions factors that might have a great deal to do with profitability or allocative efficiency (to look at matters from a societal point of view) but little to do with the democratic needs of the electorate. For a businessman, the costs of production and the revenue likely to be generated are highly pertinent factors in determining what shows to run and when, or what to feature in a newspaper; a perfectly competitive market will produce shows or publications whose marginal cost equals marginal revenue. Reruns of I Love Lucy are profitable and an efficient use of resources. So is MTV. But there is no necessary, or even probabilistic, relationship between making a profit (or allocating resources efficiently) and supplying the electorate with the information they need to make free and intelligent choices about government policy, the structure of government, or the nature of society. This point was well understood when we freed our educational systems and our universities from the grasp of the market, and it applies with equal force to the media.

None of this is meant to denigrate the market. It is only to recognize its limitations. The issue is not market failure but market reach. The market might be splendid for some purposes but not for others. It might be an effective institution for producing cheap and varied consumer goods and for providing essential services (including entertainment) but not for producing the kind of debate that constantly renews the capacity of a people for self-determination. The state is to act as the much-needed countervailing power, to counteract the skew of public debate attributable to the market and thus preserve the essential conditions of democracy. The purpose of the state is not to supplant the market (as it would under a socialist theory), nor to perfect the market (as it would under a theory of market failure), but rather to supplement it. The state is to act as the corrective *for* the market. The state must put on the agenda issues that are systematically ignored and slighted and allow us to hear voices and viewpoints that would otherwise be silenced or muffled.

Fiss argues that changes in the marketplace since the framing of the speech and press clauses justify governmental intervention. Have changes since Fiss published his article in 1987 weakened or strengthened his argument? Most First Amendment traditionalists reject his argument. Professor Lucas Powe's critique, excerpted below, is particularly scathing:

> . . . [Fiss invokes] a Golden Era, at the founding of the Republic, when the marketplace worked. Ideas were easily interchanged, either face to face at the local tavern or through pamphlets or newspapers. Because entry costs were minimal anyone could participate in the democratic dialogue.
>
> . . .
>
> For Fiss, Jeffersonian democracy was the time when power was evenly dispersed in society. Imagine how great this news would be to the slaves, free blacks, women, and landless white males of Jefferson's America were they not long since dead. Fiss's fleeting, and inaccurate, allusion to Jeffersonian democracy cannot obscure the conclusion that he stands the First Amendment on its head. . . .
>
> . . .
>
> What Fiss leaves unexplained—because it is unexplainable—is how the First Amendment ceased being a bar to government action and instead became the vehicle to justify government regulation. Quite simply, Fiss is asking for an amendment to the Constitution rather than an interpretation of the Constitution. . . .

Lucas A. Powe, Jr., Scholarship and Markets, 56 Geo. Wash. L. Rev. 172, 182–84 (1987).

The First Amendment is an Absolute

Alexander Meiklejohn
1961 Sup. Ct. Rev. 245, 255–262.

. . . The First Amendment does not protect a "freedom to speak." It protects the freedom of those activities of thought and communication by which we "govern." It is concerned, not with a private right, but with a public power, a governmental responsibility.

In the specific language of the Constitution, the governing activities of the people appear only in terms of casting a ballot. But in the deeper meaning of the Constitution, voting is merely the external expression of a wide and diverse number of activities by means of which citizens attempt to meet the responsibilities of making judgments, which that freedom to govern lays upon them. That freedom implies and requires what we call "the dignity of the individual." Self-government can exist only insofar as the voters acquire the intelligence, integrity, sensitivity, and generous devotion to the general welfare that, in theory, casting a ballot is assumed to express.

The responsibilities mentioned are of three kinds. We, the people who govern, must try to understand the issues which, incident by incident, face the nation. We must pass judgment upon the decisions which our agents make upon those issues. And, further, we must share in devising methods by which those decisions can be made wise and effective or, if need be, supplanted by others which promise greater wisdom and effectiveness. Now it is these activities, in all their diversity, whose freedom fills up "the scope of the First Amendment." These are the activities to whose freedom it gives its unqualified protection. . . .

. . .

. . . First of all, the freedom to "vote," the official expression of a self-governing man's judgment on issues of public policy, must be absolutely protected. None of his subordinate agencies may bring pressure upon him to drive his balloting this way or that. None of them may require him to tell how he has voted; none may inquire by compulsory process into his political beliefs or associations. In that area, the citizen has constitutional authority and his agents have not.

Second, there are many forms of thought and expression within the range of human communications from which the voter derives the knowledge, intelligence, sensitivity to human values: the capacity for sane and objective judgment which, so far as possible, a ballot should express. These, too, must suffer no abridgment of their freedom. I list four of them below.

1. Education, in all its phases, is the attempt to so inform and cultivate the mind and will of a citizen that he shall have the wisdom, the independence, and, therefore, the dignity of a governing citizen. Freedom of education is, thus, as we all recognize, a basic postulate in the planning of a free society.

2. The achievements of philosophy and the sciences in creating knowledge and understanding of men and their world must be made available, without abridgment, to every citizen.

3. Literature and the arts must be protected by the First Amendment. They lead the way toward sensitive and informed appreciation and response to the values out of which the riches of the general welfare are created.

4. Public discussions of public issues, together with the spreading of information and opinion bearing on those issues, must have a freedom unabridged by our agents. Though they govern us, we, in a deeper sense, govern them. Over our governing, they have no power. Over their governing we have sovereign power.

. . .

. . . We must recognize that there are many forms of communication which, since they are not being used as activities of governing, are wholly outside the scope of the First Amendment. Mr. Justice Holmes has told us about these, giving such vivid illustrations as "persuasion to murder" and "falsely shouting fire in a theatre and causing a panic." And Mr. Justice Harlan, referring to Holmes and following his lead, gave a more extensive list: "libel, slander, misrepresentation, obscenity, perjury, false advertising, solicitation of crime, complicity by encouragement, conspiracy. . . ." Why are these communications not protected by the First Amendment? Mr. Justice Holmes suggested an explanation when he said of the First Amendment in *Schenck*. "It does not even protect a man from an injunction against uttering words that may have all the effect of force."

Now it may be agreed that the uttering of words cannot be forbidden by legislation, nor punished on conviction, unless damage has been done by them to some individual or to the wider society. But that statement does not justify the imputation that all "words that may have all the effect of force" are denied the First Amendment's protection. The man who falsely shouts "Fire!" in a theatre is subject to prosecution under validly enacted legislation. But the army officer who, in command of a firing squad, shouts "Fire!" and thus ends a life, cannot be prosecuted for murder. He acts as an agent of the government. And, in fact, all governing communications are intended to have, more or less directly, "the effect of force." When a voter casts his ballot for a tax levy, he intends that someone shall be deprived of property. But his voting is not therefore outside the scope of the First Amendment. His voting must be free.

The principle here at stake can be seen in our libel laws. In cases of private defamation, one individual does damage to another by tongue or pen; the person so injured in reputation or property may sue for damages. But, in that case, the First Amendment gives no protection to the person sued. His verbal attack has no relation to the business of governing. If, however, the same verbal attack is made in order to show the unfitness of a candidate for governmental office, the act is properly regarded as a citizen's participation in government. It is, therefore, protected by the First Amendment. And the same principle holds good if a citizen attacks, by words of disapproval and condemnation, the policies of the government, or even the structure of the Constitution. These are "public" issues concerning which, under our form of government, he has authority, and is assumed to have competence, to judge. Though private libel is subject to legislative control, political or seditious libel is not.

. . .

. . . In the current discussions as to whether or not "obscenity" in literature and the arts is protected by the First Amendment, the basic principle is, I think, that literature and the arts are protected because they have a "social importance" which I have called a "governing" importance. For example, the novel is at present a powerful determinative of our views of what human beings are, how they can be influenced, in what directions they should be influenced by many forces, including, especially, their own judgments and appreciations. But the novel, like all the other creations of literature and the arts, may be produced wisely or unwisely, sensitively or coarsely, for the building up of a way of life which we treasure or for tearing it down. Shall the government establish a censorship to distinguish between "good" novels and "bad" ones? And, more specifically, shall it forbid the publication of novels which portray sexual experiences with a frankness that, to the prevailing conventions of our society, seems "obscene"?

The First Amendment seems to me to answer that question with an unequivocal "no." Here, as elsewhere, the authority of citizens to decide what they shall write and, more fundamental, what they shall read and see, has not been delegated to any of the subordinate branches of government. It is "reserved to the people," each deciding for himself to whom he will listen, whom he will read, what portrayal of the human scene he finds worthy of his attention.

. . .

———

Meiklejohn first set forth his view that the First Amendment protected only "political" speech in his 1948 book, Free Speech and Its Relation to Self–Government. There he argued that speech not relevant to self-government was protected only by the due process clause, not the First Amendment. That argument has not been accepted, but the notion that "political speech" lies at the core of the First Amendment is now a cornerstone of First Amendment jurisprudence. His definition of "political" speech seemed to expand significantly between that book and the 1961 excerpt quoted above. Readers of the 1961 article were surprised to learn that speech of "governing" importance includes even obscenity. If the concept extends that far, what kinds of speech does it exclude? If even obscenity helps the citizen participate in democracy, why not private defamation? Does Meiklejohn's line between protected and unprotected speech boil down to a truth-falsity dichotomy? Even if relevance to self-government is not the only basis for full First Amendment protection, might the law still indulge a special solicitude for that kind of speech?

Meiklejohn did not envision a fully participatory model of public discourse. For him, the model of discourse was "the traditional American town meeting," a forum that regulates the speech of participants to attain particular goals. In Free Speech and Its Relation to Self–Government, Meiklejohn contended: "What is essential is not that everyone shall speak, but that everything worth saying shall be said." *Id.* at 22–25. Professor Robert Post has argued that Meiklejohn's "town meeting model" of public discourse "reflects an insufficiently radical conception of the reach of self-determination." Democracy contemplates not just citizen input into the "substance of collective decisions, but also the larger framework of function within which such collective decision-making is necessarily conceived as taking place. . . ." Meiklejohn's Mistake: Individual Autonomy and the Reform of Public Discourse, 64 Colo. L. Rev. 1109, 1117 (1993).

A different function of free speech is identified by Professor Vincent Blasi in The Checking Value in First Amendment Theory, 1977 Am. B. Found. Res. J. 521, 527:

> . . . This is the value that free speech, a free press, and free assembly can serve in checking the abuse of power by public officials. Consider the most important ways in which the First Amendment has made a difference in recent years. But for the peace marches and other protests, the Johnson administration might very well have escalated the war in Vietnam after the Tet offensive and the Nixon administration might have attempted to sustain a wider war after the Cambodian "incursion." But for the tradition of a free press, the crimes and abuses of Watergate might never have been uncovered. These incidents in our recent political experience are so familiar that it is easy to underestimate their importance. In the last decade, the First Amendment has had at least as much impact on American life by facilitating a process by which countervailing forces check the misuse of official power as by protecting the dignity of the individual, maintaining a diverse society in the face of conformist pressures, promoting the quest for scientific and philosophic truth, or fostering a regime of "self-government" in which large numbers of ordinary citizens take an active part in political affairs.

The checking value is distinct from Emerson's and Meiklejohn's self-government value in several respects, most notably because it is not dependent upon active citizen participation in governmental decision-making:

> The checking value is premised upon a different vision—one in which the government is structured in such a way that built-in counterforces make it possible for citizens in most, but not all, periods to have the luxury to concern themselves almost exclusively with private pursuits. This vision does not deny that the survival of humanist values depends in the final instance on the continuing capability of the populace, to mobilize politically in order to forestall the advent of irreversible totalitarianism or to undo damage caused by petty tyrants. But the level of political involvement and awareness necessary to maintain that capability is considerably lower than that required by the vision of self-government.

———

In the excerpt below, Professor Baker places respect for individual autonomy at the core of First Amendment theory. As you read, consider how Baker responds to Meiklejohn's theory of the First Amendment.

Human Liberty and Freedom of Speech
C. Edwin Baker
47–50 (1989).

. . . [ ] I will refer to individual self-fulfillment and participation in change, or self-realization and self-determination as the key first amendment values.

. . .

. . . Collective groups, for example, states, have norms that they claim or assert members have an obligation to obey. They claim the obligation to obey the laws is a matter of legitimacy, not merely force. As noted above, such an assertion must be premised on a relation to the other. Specifically, the assertion must appeal to some aspect of the relationship that justifies the claim that the other should accede. It would be inconsistent with the practice of addressing appeals to others for the collective to expect the other to accede if the other was not being treated with respect as an autonomous agent—that is, as one to whom claims are properly addressed. . . . In other words, reasoned justification of legal obligation may require respect for rights of equality and autonomy and democratic participation.

Elaboration of this core insight of social contract doctrines helps explain both the propriety of, and proper limits on, collective self-definitional or welfare-maximizing decision making. First, the practices of democratic decision making or welfare maximization policies can often be understood as properly implementing equal respect for persons as autonomous agents. Although some people may be more advantaged or disadvantaged by any particular decision or policy, at least the abstract or formal claim of both democratic decision making and utilitarianism is that their procedures do not imply distinctions between the worth of persons but that they do provide a method for choosing collective norms, which are the only alternative to interactions based on raw force. For example, utilitarian theory argues for fulfilling as many of people's desires as possible, weighting the desires (or preferences) of each person equally. Democratic decision making gives each person the same potential say in results, a say that properly would represent the person's autonomous choice or commitment. Thus, democratic decision making manifests, or at least is consistent with, respect for people's autonomy and equality. This respect is important given that its presence is crucial for redeeming the implicit claim that the resulting norms are obligatory.

But if this respect for people's equality and autonomy is crucial, then any collective decision, norm, or practice that denies this equality or autonomy is inconsistent with a necessary aspect of the claim for accepting or according legitimacy to the collective's practices and decisions. This observation leads to the conclusion that the group has no authority to act in ways that deny a person's equality or . . . a person's autonomy. Hence, the same basic considerations crucial for justifying legal obligation both justify collective democratic decision making and require limits on it. Fundamental constitutional restraints on democratic choice are the result.

Historically, not all societies have exhibited the view that these premises of respect for individual autonomy and equality are necessary for a justifiable legal order or for legal obligation. Despite whatever desirable features exist in these societies, from our present perspective, their denial of these premises reflects objectionable hierarchy, closure, and their structural distortion of the possibility of communicative action and discursive will formation. Even putting aside the universalistic aspect of these evaluations, the assumption that respect for people's equality and autonomy is fundamental may still provide the best explanation for the basic commitments of actual liberal democratic states. In other words, we could start with the various commitments that we do in fact seem to accept—democracy, for example. That commitment can surely be explained in various possible ways. Still, as suggested above, a quite persuasive account of that commitment is that it embodies even more fundamental commitments—that is, the commitment to democracy is an implication of the more basic commitment of respect for individual equality and liberty.

This account of democracy as secondary also provides a logical explanation of constitutionalism—that is of foundational restraints on democracy. The normally accepted account of our constitutionalism is that it protects certain rights even from majority override. In other words, this account treats certain values—human dignity, respect for individuals' equality and autonomy—as fundamental and directs that democracy must operate within the constraint of respect for these values. Moreover, many alternative accounts of democracy or of other basic, accepted features of our society as well as interpretations of cultural and legal texts, when discursively pressed, will also seem best defended from perspectives that assume respect for equality and liberty as basic.

Thus, from any of three different perspectives—the abstract nature of communicative action aimed at agreement, the abstract justification of legal obligation, or the historically contingent accounting for legal obligation and the institutional order of our liberal democratic society—we have an account of the legal order or of the collective whole that commits it to respect individual autonomy or a realm of individual liberty that serves the values of self-fulfillment and participation in change. Moreover, this account of the foundational status of this realm of liberty would help explain why utilitarian balancing does not justify limiting first amendment rights.

————

Related to the autonomy arguments made by Professor Baker are arguments that free speech is an aspect of dignity and equality. From this perspective, suppression of speech is objectionable, regardless of any other consequences, because it violates the government's duty to respect the dignity and equality of each citizen. This theory is, of course, subject to the objection that it is not peculiar to speech:

> My impression is that people gain dignity from adequate incomes, interesting jobs, meals on the table, shelter, and economically independent children. . . . If the argument is that personal dignity requires equal respect for individuals in political processes, in the public sphere, then the dignity argument merges with the normative argument for democracy.

Mark G. Yudof, In Search of a Free Speech Principle, 82 Mich. L. Rev. 680, 695 (1984). Others see at least a possibility of a special connection between speech and the interests of dignity and equality:

> Expressions of beliefs and feelings lie closer to the core of our persons than do most actions we perform; restrictions of expression may offend dignity to a greater degree than most other restrictions; and selective restrictions based on the content of our ideas may imply a specially significant inequality.

Kent Greenawalt, Speech, Crime, and the Uses of Language 34 (1989).

———

Autonomy is invaded both when an individual is forbidden from speaking and when the individual is required to speak. The First Amendment sometimes seems to protect this autonomy-based interest. For example, it denies government the power to stop a protester from expressing his thoughts even in a way that others find offensive, see, e.g., Cohen v. California, 403 U.S. 15 (1971) (protecting the right to wear a jacket bearing the words "Fuck the Draft"). It also denies the state power to compel drivers to display on license plates a state motto they find repugnant, see Wooley v. Maynard, 430 U.S. 705 (1977), or to require religious objectors to recite the pledge of allegiance, West Virginia State Board of Education v. Barnette, 319 U.S. 624 (1943). Justice Robert Jackson explained the principle at stake in Barnette as follows:

> If there is any fixed star in our constitutional constellation, it is that no official, high or petty, can prescribe what shall be orthodox in politics, nationalism, religion, or other matters of opinion or force citizens to confess by word or act their faith therein. If there are any circumstances which permit an exception, they do not now occur to us.

Id. Professor Jed Rubenfeld argues that the autonomy-based interest described by Justice Jackson—which he dubs the anti-orthodoxy principle—is the bedrock of the First Amendment. The First Amendment's Purpose, 53 Stan. L. Rev. 767, 818–821 (2001). Rubenfeld points out that the anti-orthodoxy principle, as formulated by Justice Jackson, is "absolutely incompatible with cost-benefit, balancing approaches to the First Amendment." Rubenfeld concedes, however, that "[t]he domain of speech to which the anti-orthodoxy principle applies is not all encompassing. There is a kind of orthodoxy that government can and does enforce every day, even in the sense of prescribing what people must and must not say. I refer to the orthodoxy of true and false facts. While it is true that 'there is no such thing as a false idea' under the First Amendment, there is clearly such a thing as a false fact. The laws of libel, fraud, perjury, and so on, all punish people for speaking falsely on matters of fact."

———

Another aspect of autonomy involves the individual's right to receive information. Denying that right might be thought to interfere with the autonomous individual's right to learn, choose, and decide. This interest also seems to receive some First Amendment protection. For example, the Supreme Court held that consumers had standing to attack a state law forbidding price advertising by pharmacists, because they had a First Amendment right to receive that information in the interest of making informed consumer decisions. See Virginia State Board of Pharmacy v. Virginia Citizens Consumer Council, Inc., 425 U.S. 748, 1 Med. L. Rptr. 1930 (1976) (the Court also recognized an instrumentalist interest in efficient operation of a free market economy).

———

The theories discussed above hold that speech must be protected because of its positive value to self-government. Another possibility is that speech is protected because of the *negative* effects of allowing government to regulate speech:

> . . . Throughout history the process of regulating speech has been marked with what we now see to be fairly plain errors. Whether it be the condemnation of Galileo, religious persecution in the sixteenth and seventeenth centuries, the extensive history of prosecution for expressing seditious views of those now viewed as patriots, or the banning of numerous admittedly great works of art because someone thought them obscene, acts of suppression that have been proved erroneous seem to represent a disproportionate percentage of the governmental mistakes of the past. . . .

> . . .

> Freedom of speech is based in large part on a distrust of the ability of government to make the necessary distinctions, a distrust of governmental determinations of truth and falsity, an appreciation of the fallibility of political leaders, and a somewhat deeper distrust of governmental power in a more general sense. . . .

Frederick Schauer, Free Speech: A Philosophical Enquiry 81–86 (1982).

3.   FIRST AMENDMENT ECLECTICISM

There is no necessity to choose one exclusive justification for protecting speech, of course. Some of those who espouse the self-realization justifications insist that all other arguments are derivative, but most First Amendment theorists are willing to accept a pluralistic notion of purposes. Professor Schauer suggests viewing the First Amendment as an umbrella for a number of more or less distinct principles, each with its own justification, and each directed towards a separate group of problems:

> Under such a view . . . we might in fact have several first amendments. We might have one first amendment directed primarily to the problem of government suppression of its critics. The justifications for this first amendment might be largely of the democratic theory and abuse of governmental power varieties. . . . Another first amendment might be directed primarily towards the problem of open inquiry in the sciences and academic institutions, being based primarily on the heritage of Galileo and the search for truth/marketplace of ideas justifications for the principle of free speech. . . . A third first amendment might be a reaction to an excess of historical censorship of the arts . . . perhaps even based in part on notions of self-realization.

Frederick Schauer, Must Speech Be Special?, 78 Nw. U. L. Rev. 1284, 1303–04 (1983). *See also* Steven Shiffrin, The First Amendment and Economic Regulation: Away From a General Theory of the First Amendment, 78 Nw. U. L. Rev. 1212, 1283 (1983) (arguing that no "single theory could explain, or dictate helpful conclusions in, the vast terrain of speech regulation").

Professor Rubenfeld also criticizes what he terms "giant-sized First Amendment theories," albeit from a different perspective:

> Philosophical approaches to the First Amendment adopt a universalistic approach; the result, ironically, is parochialism. When people derive First Amendment rights from a theory of democracy or individuality, they imply that our freedom of speech—the one guaranteed by the United States Constitution—is in principle applicable to every democratic society or to every society that values individual autonomy. But America's freedom of speech reflects America's distinctive constitutional commitments, which other nations need not and do not share.

Jed Rubenfeld, The Freedom of Imagination: Copyright's Constitutionality, 112 Yale L.J. 1, 30–31 (2002). What are the unique constitutional commitments to which Rubenfeld refers?

4.   THE INTERNET AND FIRST AMENDMENT THEORY

The Internet gives ordinary citizens inexpensive access to a medium of mass communication. The Internet therefore allows more citizens than ever before to participate in public discussion and debate and makes it harder for wealthy or powerful speakers, including the mass media, to dominate the marketplace of ideas. Much of the initial scholarship on the Internet viewed it as having very positive implications for First Amendment values. See Anne Wells Branscomb, Anonymity, Autonomy, and Accountability: Challenges to the First Amendment in Cyberspace, 104 Yale L.J. 1639 (1995); Eugene Volokh, Cheap Speech and What It Will Do, 104 Yale L.J. 1805 (1995).

Yet, the very features of the online world that could make it the embodiment of an accessible marketplace of ideas also pose significant issues. For example, the vast majority of online expression is not scrutinized by editors and producers or other trained intermediaries whose judgment (or lack thereof) has been a feature of the context in which most media law has developed. Because the Internet facilitates anonymous and inexpensive communication, it may be difficult to identify the originator of a defamatory or otherwise harmful message or to recover damages if he or she is identified. Internet access providers—universities, employers, and commercial Internet service providers—find it almost impossible to scrutinize the huge volume of electronic communication that flows through their servers, even if they desired to do so. Because the Internet crosses state and national boundaries, speakers cannot effectively control the geographic dissemination of their digital expression, yet most laws imposing liability for harmful expression vary from state to state (and from country to country).

The following article addresses some implications of the Internet for First Amendment theory.

Market Hierarchy and Copyright in Our System of Free Expression

Neil Weinstock Netanel
53 Vand. L. Rev. 1879, 1888–91, 1919–20 (2000).

Critics of government efforts to promote expressive diversity in mass communication maintain that the abundance of "cheap speech" on the Internet renders government media regulation unnecessary and constitutionally infirm. On the Net, they emphasize, everyone can be a speaker and everyone can find a wealth of diverse expression and information. Concomitantly, they point out, the Internet drastically reduces the control of publishers, broadcasters, newspapers, bookstores, and other private intermediaries over what speakers will say and audiences will hear. In cyberspace, authors can communicate directly to readers, and readers can freely become authors, not only selecting what they read but also responding to it. In this new, richly pluralist information marketplace, critics claim, the speech hierarchy rationale for government regulation and intervention no longer holds.

. . . [T]he critics' portrait of a highly democratic Internet bears scant resemblance to what much of the Internet is rapidly becoming. The Internet, indeed, is poised to change in ways that will bring back many of the structural characteristics of the predigital mass media market. Our communications universe, to be certain, will continue to feature a lively and widely diverse array of virtual street corner podia, including email discussion groups, chat rooms, individual web sites, and other fora heretofore unimagined. But the recent Tsunami wave of telecommunications and media company mergers, capped as of this writing by America Online's acquisition of Time Warner, portend domination by a few corporate behemoths, online as well as off. Akin to today's mass media markets, purveyors of broadband access to high-production-value video and audio content will likely determine who can provide what content through which distribution channels. If current trends continue, indeed, the communications market will exhibit unprecedented levels of vertical as well as horizontal integration, enabling each telecommunications conglomerate to provide and exercise control over a full component of access, distribution, and content.

As a result, those seeking to reach a mass audience will need to do so through conglomerate-controlled outlets. They will have to attempt to license their speech to a conglomerate-owned content provider or purchase communications capacity from a conglomerate-owned portal. In each case, they will compete against conglomerate affiliates, which, for reasons of management predisposition and transaction cost savings, will often enjoy preferential treatment from their corporate partner. Alternatively, like the recent sale of Africana.com to Time Warner, small, independent speakers will seek to be acquired by major media/telecommunications firms, further extending conglomerate reach. In such a world, speaking in virtual street corners will be much like handing out leaflets on an urban street corner and independent web publishing will be akin to small, independent press and book publishing. While continuing to occupy a respected position in our system of free expression, they will largely be lost in the din of Disney–ABC, AT&T–Media One, CBS–Viacom, and AOL–Time Warner.

. . .

Ultimately, like in the offline world, it is the large commercial players who succeed in capturing the lion's share of audience attention. Only they have the financial and organizational resources to advertise their products, exploit product and corporate partner synergies, purchase first position in search engine search results and prominent placement of their icons on portal desktops, populate the Internet with links to their sites, and produce star-studded, attention-grabbing content.

. . .

Individual authors and web site operators lack the resources to fulfill the press' traditional, vital role of watchdog against government myopia and oppression. Nor can individuals adequately expose corporate unlawfulness, labor union corruption, and political party self-aggrandizement. Liberal democratic nations necessarily encompass multiple concentrations of power. Only an equally powerful press—not just the daily press, but also a full array of publishing houses, film studios, and broadcasters—can effectively check other entities' and associations' deployment of their power by exposing it to the light of public opinion. Indeed, only a mass media can both catalyze and, to a degree, embody public opinion in the face of government authority and corporate fiefdom.

Must the Supreme Court adopt a single approach to dealing with First Amendment issues that arise in the Internet context? In Reno v. ACLU, 521 U.S. 844 (1997), the Supreme Court rejected the notion that the Internet as a "medium" receives diminished First Amendment protection. However, as Professor Timothy Wu has pointed out:

> [The] First Amendment meaning of the word "medium" makes an exceptionally poor fit for the full range of existing and possible Internet applications. A radio is pretty much a one trick pony—a good trick, yes, but in essence there's only one way a person can use a radio. But the Internet, to understate the obvious, can be used in more than one way. . . . The constitutional meaning of "medium" is too small for the Internet. It has outgrown its box.

Application–Centered Internet Analysis, 85 Va. L. Rev. 1163, 1163–64, 1170–78 (1999). Professor Wu notes that part of the reasoning of *Reno* rests on the argument that the Internet cannot be regulated as extensively as broadcasting because it is not as "invasive" as radio or television. He points out that this argument is true with regard to some Internet applications but is dubious as applied to others, such as "junk email." He therefore contends that "the invasiveness of the Internet" (and hence the level of constitutional scrutiny to be applied) must be evaluated "at the application level." As a result, there can be no single First Amendment approach to Internet issues.

C.   METHODS OF FIRST AMENDMENT ANALYSIS

Just as there is no single justification for the First Amendment, there is no single model, method, or theory by which courts analyze First Amendment problems. In deciding how to analyze First Amendment issues, courts often take into account a variety of factors, such as the content of the speech, the context in which it was expressed, the type of restraint being employed, and the nature of the harm that the restraint is intended to prevent or punish. Courts may consider these and other factors more than once: for example, when deciding what method of analysis to apply, and then again when actually applying that analysis to the facts before them. Courts are often not explicit or consistent about how they determine which method of analysis to use or, in fact, about which method they are using. As a result, it is often difficult for students of media law to make sense of First Amendment jurisprudence, and it is easy to fall prey to what Justice Stevens called the "hypnotic fascination with the endeavor to explain and to organize that development in rigidly defined compartments." John Paul Stevens, The Freedom of Speech, 102 Yale L.J. 1293 (1992).

In this section, we consider a broad range of methods of First Amendment analysis, including those applicable to most media law cases today. Before beginning, however, it is worth mentioning two methods of analysis that do not receive extensive treatment here, albeit for very different reasons.

The first of these two methods is the literal approach. The literal approach originates in the text of the First Amendment. The First Amendment says Congress can pass "no law" abridging freedom of expression; thus, a literalist would insist that any and every law that abridges freedom of expression is unconstitutional. As Justice Hugo Black, the most famous defender of this approach wrote: "[The First Amendment] says 'no law,' and that is what I believe it means." Edmund Cahn, Justice Black and First Amendment "Absolutes": A Public Interview, 37 N.Y.U. L. Rev. 549, 554 (1962). Thus, the only restrictions that Justice Black believed permissible under the First Amendment were incidental restrictions on the time, place, and manner of an individual's freedom of expression.

Despite its intuitive appeal, the literal approach is rarely used today. Even the most ardent supporter of the literal approach would agree that the First Amendment does not protect perjury or threats of violence; yet the literal approach provides no rational method for explaining why such speech is unprotected. Even Justice Black found himself forced to narrow the scope of what counts as speech in order to reach the "correct" result in a speech case. In Cohen v. California, 403 U.S. 15 (1971), Justice Black's dissent argued that the state could punish one of its citizens for wearing a jacket that said "Fuck the Draft." According to Justice Black, wearing a jacket expressing this sentiment was not speech but physical conduct that a state could legitimately regulate. The literal approach did not allow Justice Black to balance the State's interests against the right to freedom of expression. Thus, he was forced to resort to strained reasoning to avoid what to him was an unacceptable outcome.

Another method of analysis that does not receive extended treatment in this section is the method used for speech restrictions designated as prior restraints. Prior restraints continue to be an important subset of First Amendment analysis; indeed, it is for this reason that prior restraints are treated in detail in Chapter II. For now, it is enough to note that it was in the context of prior restraints that the concept of special protection for expression was first reflected in the common law. And prior restraints continue to be regarded with special hostility by courts today, so much so that litigants frequently seek to claim that government restrictions on their speech act as prior restraints, no matter how dissimilar those restrictions may be to the historic version of that concept.

We now turn to three of the most important methods for analyzing First Amendment problems in a broad range of cases: the balancing approach, the categorical approach, and the clear and present danger approach. The three methods summarized here do not exhaust the possibilities for analyzing First Amendment issues, and there is considerable blurring of the lines between these models. They are presented here only to provide a framework for our continuing effort to understand the many ways courts approach First Amendment issues.

1.   BALANCING

Today the most frequently used method for determining the propriety of such a restraint on freedom of expression is "balancing." This approach involves weighing two interests—the government's concern about protecting a particular interest, such as national security or individual reputation, against the speaker's or writer's (and society's) interests in expression.

Professor Chafee, an early advocate of balancing, expressed the virtues of that approach in his book, Free Speech in the United States 31 (1941):

> Or to put the matter another way, it is useless to define free speech by talk about rights. The agitator asserts his constitutional right to speak, the government asserts its constitutional right to wage war. The result is a deadlock. . . . To find the boundary line of any right, we must get behind rules of law to human facts. In our problem, we must regard the desires and needs of the individual human being who wants to speak and those of the great group of human beings among whom he speaks. That is, in technical language, there are individual interests and social interests, which must be balanced against each other, if they conflict, in order to determine which interest shall be sacrificed under the circumstances and which shall be protected and become the foundation of a legal right. It must never be forgotten that the balancing cannot be properly done unless all the interests involved are adequately ascertained, and the great evil of all this talk about rights is that each side is so busy denying the other's claim to rights that it entirely overlooks the human desires and needs behind that claim.

Balancing has had its champions and its detractors on the Court over the years. Balancing on a case-by-case basis makes it difficult to predict whether a certain exercise of free speech will be protected in a later court test. Despite this and other criticisms, freedom of expression cases are frequently decided by balancing interests. Some decisions focus on the interests at stake in the individual case; this is commonly characterized as "ad hoc" balancing, and the specific interests applicable to the facts of the particular case are considered crucial. Others use a more general process, called "definitional" balancing. Here the interests analyzed transcend the merits of a particular case. Rather than asking, for example, whether the value of speech in a particular case outweighed the arguments for proscribing it, the court might generalize and consider the values of that category of speech, or that category of speaker, and develop a more general analysis. This approach makes it easier to predict outcomes because of the generalized quality of the decision. See Melville B. Nimmer, The Right to Speak from *Times* to *Time:* First Amendment Theory Applied to Libel and Misapplied to Privacy, 56 Cal. L. Rev. 935, 942–45 (1968), and Gerald Gunther, In Search of Judicial Quality on a Changing Court: The Case of Justice Powell, 24 Stan. L. Rev. 1001 (1972).

The balancing process can be and perhaps is made infinitely variable by tilting the scales. In First Amendment cases, the tilt favors the side of speech, so that the competing interest must be not merely weightier, but weightier in some specified degree. This means that a restriction on speech may be unconstitutional, even though the interest the restriction serves is legitimate and even perhaps weightier than the competing speech interest, if it does not outweigh the speech interest *sufficiently.*

Courts often refer to the different balancing tests applied in freedom of expression cases as "levels of scrutiny." These levels of scrutiny have widely varying and inconsistent labels (such as "strict," "exacting," and "intermediate"). The Supreme Court has likewise been inconsistent in describing the state interest required to sustain a statute's validity and in describing the requisite "fit" between the goals or "ends" of a statute and the means chosen to achieve those ends. However, three broad "levels of scrutiny" have emerged.

"Strict scrutiny" requires "the State [to] show that its regulation is necessary to serve a compelling state interest and is narrowly drawn to achieve that end." Arkansas Writers' Project, Inc. v. Ragland, 481 U.S. 221, 231, 13 Med. L. Rptr. 2313, 2317 (1987). As articulated in Minneapolis Star & Tribune Co. v. Minnesota Comm'r of Revenue, 460 U.S. 575, 585, 9 Med. L. Rptr. 1369, 1374 (1983), the test requires that the State assert an interest "of compelling importance that it cannot achieve" without the regulation. Nonetheless, the Court does not always require that the means be the least restrictive available. Strict scrutiny, as we will see, is applied to most "discriminatory restriction[s] or prohibition[s] of speech. . . ." *Arkansas Writers' Project*, 481 U.S. at 236 (Scalia, J., dissenting). Recognizing the Court's propensity for striking down regulations to which it applies strict scrutiny in a different context, Professor Gerald Gunther has characterized the standard of review as " 'strict' in theory, and fatal in fact." Gerald Gunther, The Supreme Court 1971 Term—Foreword: In Search of Evolving Doctrine on a Changing Court: A Model for a Newer Equal Protection, 86 Harv. L. Rev. 1, 8 (1972).

"Intermediate scrutiny" generally requires that a government regulation be closely related to an "important," "significant," or "substantial" governmental interest. In the specific context of the First Amendment, intermediate scrutiny refers to a variety of tests used by the Court to evaluate regulations that affect expression but are not targeted at expression, target only "low-value" expression, or do not discriminate among types of expression. For example, in United States v. O'Brien, 391 U.S. 367, 376–77 (1968), the Court announced a test applicable for regulations that target conduct but incidentally restrict speech: "[W]hen 'speech' and 'non-speech' elements are combined in the same course of conduct," government regulation of that conduct is "sufficiently justified if it is within the constitutional power of the Government; if it furthers an important or substantial governmental interest; if the governmental interest is unrelated to the suppression of free expression; and if the incidental restriction on alleged First Amendment freedoms is no greater than is essential to the furtherance of that interest."

In Perry Education Ass'n v. Perry Local Educators' Ass'n, 460 U.S. 37, 44 (1983), the Court applied a test to evaluate the constitutionality of what have become known as "time, place, and manner" regulations: Regulations of the time, place, and manner of expression are constitutional if they "are content-neutral, are narrowly tailored to serve a significant government interest, and leave open ample alternative channels of communication." And in Central Hudson Gas & Electric Corp. v. Public Service Comm'n, 447 U.S. 557, 566, 6 Med. L. Rptr. 1497, 1501 (1980), and Board of Trustees v. Fox, 492 U.S. 469, 477–481 (1989), the Supreme Court identified a test applicable to commercial speech: the expression at issue "must concern lawful activity and not be misleading"; the asserted governmental interest must be "substantial"; and the regulation must be one that "directly advances the governmental interest asserted" and must be narrowly tailored to achieve the desired ends. We will encounter each of these tests in cases throughout the book.

"Rational basis scrutiny" is the least restrictive scrutiny applied by the Court. Under this level of scrutiny, statutes and other government actions are valid if they bear a rational relation to a legitimate government purpose. Rational basis scrutiny is rarely applied when First Amendment interests are at stake.

More variable, perhaps, than the adjectives used to describe the balancing process is the value that judges assign to various interests. Balancing necessarily requires judges to decide that some legislatively established policies are more important than others. For example, the Supreme Court has held that a state's interest in preventing abuse of the discovery process is sufficient to justify prohibiting a newspaper from disclosing information it obtained through that process, but a state's interest in protecting the privacy and candor of prospective jurors is not sufficient to justify a judge's refusal to release transcripts of the voir dire examination of jurors. Compare Seattle Times Co. v. Rhinehart, 467 U.S. 20, 10 Med. L. Rptr. 1705 (1984), with Press–Enterprise Co. v. Superior Court (I), 464 U.S. 501, 10 Med. L. Rptr. 1161 (1984). (These cases are discussed in Chapter XI).

The cases that follow are the Supreme Court's initial efforts at balancing in media cases. As you read them, try to see how the justices assign weights to the interests being balanced.

Landmark Communications, Inc. v. Virginia

Supreme Court of the United States, 1978.
435 U.S. 829, 98 S. Ct. 1535, 56 L. Ed.2d 1, 3 Med. L. Rptr. 2153.

[The Virginia constitution directed the legislature to create a commission to investigate charges against judges—and decreed that proceedings before the commission "shall be confidential." A statute creating the commission declared that the proceedings were confidential "and shall not be divulged by any person to anyone except the Commission, except that the record of any proceeding filed with the Supreme Court shall lose its confidential character." A proceeding is filed with the Supreme Court only when the commission finds grounds for filing a formal complaint.

Landmark's newspaper, the Virginian Pilot, accurately reported that a named judge was under investigation by the Commission. Landmark was found guilty of a misdemeanor and fined $500 plus costs of prosecution. The Supreme Court of Virginia affirmed. It rejected Landmark's argument that the statute applied only to the participants in the proceedings or to initial disclosure of confidential information. Instead, it concluded that the paper's actions "clearly . . . violated" the statute.

On appeal, the Supreme Court of the United States noted that virtually every state had such a commission, and that all provided for confidentiality. The accepted reasons for confidentiality were (1) it is thought to encourage the filing of complaints and willing participation of witnesses; (2) judges are protected from injury by publication of unexamined complaints until the meritorious can be separated from the unjustified; and (3) confidence in the judiciary is maintained by avoiding announcement of groundless claims. In addition, when removal is justified judges are more likely to resign voluntarily or retire if publicity can be avoided.

But even accepting the value of confidentiality, the Court considered this "only the beginning of the inquiry." Landmark was not attacking the confidentiality requirement. It was objecting to making it a crime to divulge or publish the information—a step taken by only Virginia and Hawaii.]

MR. CHIEF JUSTICE BURGER delivered the opinion of the Court.

. . .

The narrow and limited question presented, then, is whether the First Amendment permits the criminal punishment of third persons who are strangers to the inquiry, including the news media, for divulging or publishing truthful information regarding confidential proceedings of the Judicial Inquiry and Review Commission. We are not here concerned with the possible applicability of the statute to one who secures the information by illegal means and thereafter divulges it. We do not have before us any constitutional challenge to a State's power to keep the Commission's proceedings confidential or to punish participants for breach of this mandate.[10] [ ] Nor does Landmark argue for any constitutionally compelled right of access for the press to those proceedings. [ ] Finally, as the Supreme Court of Virginia held, and appellant does not dispute, the challenged statute does not constitute a prior restraint or attempt by the State to censor the news media.

Landmark urges as the dispositive answer to the question presented that truthful reporting about public officials in connection with their public duties is always insulated from the imposition of criminal sanctions by the First Amendment. It points to the solicitude accorded even untruthful

---

10. At least two categories of "participants" come to mind: Commission members and staff employees, and witnesses or putative witnesses not officers or employees of the Commonwealth. No issue as to either of these categories is presented by this case.

speech when public officials are its subjects, [ ], and the extension of First Amendment protection to the dissemination of truthful commercial information, [ ] to support its contention. We find it unnecessary to adopt this categorical approach to resolve the issue before us. We conclude that the publication Virginia seeks to punish under its statute lies near the core of the First Amendment, and the Commonwealth's interests advanced by the imposition of criminal sanctions are insufficient to justify the actual and potential encroachments on freedom of speech and of the press which follow therefrom. [ ]

A.

In Mills v. Alabama, 384 U.S. 214, 218 (1966), this Court observed: "Whatever differences may exist about interpretations of the First Amendment, there is practically universal agreement that a major purpose of that Amendment was to protect the free discussion of governmental affairs." . . . The operations of the courts and the judicial conduct of judges are matters of utmost public concern. . . .

. . .

The operation of the Virginia Commission, no less than the operation of the judicial system itself, is a matter of public interest, necessarily engaging the attention of the news media. The article published by Landmark provided accurate factual information about a legislatively authorized inquiry pending before the Judicial Review and Inquiry Commission, and in so doing clearly served those interests in public scrutiny and discussion of governmental affairs which the First Amendment was adopted to protect. [ ]

B.

. . .

The Commonwealth . . . focuses on what it perceives to be the pernicious effects of public discussion of Commission proceedings to support its argument. It contends that the public interest is not served by discussion of unfounded allegations of misconduct which defames honest judges and serves only to demean the administration of justice. The functioning of the Commission itself is also claimed to be impeded by premature disclosure of the complainant, witnesses, and the judge under investigation. Criminal sanctions minimize these harmful consequences, according to the Commonwealth, by ensuring that the guarantee of confidentiality is more than an empty promise.

It can be assumed for purposes of decision that confidentiality of Commission proceedings serves legitimate state interests. The question, however, is whether these interests are sufficient to justify the encroachment on First Amendment guarantees which the imposition of criminal sanctions entails with respect to nonparticipants such as Landmark. The Commonwealth has offered little more than assertion and conjecture to support its claim that without criminal sanctions the objectives of the statutory scheme would be seriously undermined. While not dispositive, we note that more than 40 States having similar commissions have not found it necessary to enforce confidentiality by use of criminal sanctions against nonparticipants.

Moreover, neither the Commonwealth's interest in protecting the reputation of its judges, nor its interest in maintaining the institutional integrity of its courts is sufficient to justify the subsequent punishment of speech at issue here, even on the assumption that criminal sanctions do in fact enhance the guarantee of confidentiality. Admittedly, the Commonwealth has an interest in protecting the good repute of its judges, like that of all other public officials. Our prior cases have firmly established, however, that injury to official reputation is an insufficient reason "for repressing speech that would otherwise be free." [ ]. The remaining interest sought to be protected, the institutional reputation of the courts, is entitled to no greater weight in the constitutional scales. . . . Mr. Justice Frankfurter, in his dissent in *Bridges,* [314 U.S. 252 (1941)] agreed that speech cannot be punished when the purpose is simply "to protect the court as a mystical entity or the judges as individuals or as anointed priests set apart from the community and spared the criticism to which in a democracy other public servants are exposed." [ ]

The Commonwealth has provided no sufficient reason for disregarding these well established principles. We find them controlling and, on this record, dispositive.

. . .

Accordingly, the judgment of the Supreme Court of Virginia is reversed, and the case remanded for further proceedings not inconsistent with this opinion.

MR. JUSTICE BRENNAN and MR. JUSTICE POWELL took no part in the consideration or decision of this case.

MR. JUSTICE STEWART, concurring in the judgment.

Virginia has enacted a law making it a criminal offense for "any person" to divulge confidential information about proceedings before its Judicial Inquiry and Review Commission. I cannot agree with the Court that this Virginia law violates the Constitution.

There could hardly be a higher governmental interest than a State's interest in the quality of its judiciary. Virginia's derivative interest in maintaining the confidentiality of the proceedings of its Judicial Inquiry and Review Commission seems equally clear. Only such confidentiality, the State has determined, will protect upright judges from unjustified harm and at the same time insure the full and fearless airing in Commission proceedings of every complaint of judicial misconduct. I find nothing in the Constitution to prevent Virginia from punishing those who violate this confidentiality. [ ]

But in this case Virginia has extended its law to punish a newspaper, and that it cannot constitutionally do. If the constitutional protection of a free press means anything, it means that government cannot take it upon itself to decide what a newspaper may and may not publish. Though government may deny access to information and punish its theft, government may not prohibit or punish the publication of that information once it falls into the hands of the press, unless the need for secrecy is manifestly overwhelming.

It is on this ground that I concur in the judgment of the Court.

Notes and Questions

1. What is the "categorical" approach that the majority declines to adopt?

2. The majority says prior cases have established that protecting the reputations of judges and courts is not a sufficient interest to justify punishment of the speech at issue here. If that question were not already decided, how would the Court decide whether those interests are "sufficient"?

3. In the majority's view, could a commission employee be prosecuted successfully for leaking information about the proceeding to the press? How do the state's interests differ when the defendant is a state employee?

Smith v. Daily Mail Publishing Co.

Supreme Court of the United States, 1979.
443 U.S. 97, 99 S. Ct. 2667, 61 L. Ed.2d 399, 5 Med. L. Rptr. 1305.

[A West Virginia statute made it a crime for a newspaper to publish the names of juveniles in connection with delinquency proceedings without a written order of the court. The respondent newspapers learned over a police radio about a killing at a junior high school. Reporters went to the scene and obtained the name of the suspect by asking witnesses, the police, and a prosecuting attorney. The name was revealed thereafter in the newspapers and over several broadcasting stations.

After being indicted, the newspapers obtained an order from the state supreme court barring any prosecution on the ground that the statute was unconstitutional.]

MR. CHIEF JUSTICE BURGER delivered the opinion of the Court.

We granted certiorari to consider whether a West Virginia statute violates the First and Fourteenth Amendments of the United States Constitution by making it a crime for a newspaper to publish, without the written approval of the juvenile court, the name of any youth charged as a juvenile offender.

. . .

(2)

Respondents urge this Court to hold that because § 49–7–3 requires court approval prior to publication of the juvenile's name it operates as a "prior restraint" on speech. [ ] Respondents concede that this statute is not in the classic mold of prior restraint, there being no prior injunction against publication. Nonetheless, they contend that the prior approval requirement acts in "operation and effect" like a licensing scheme and thus is another form of prior restraint. See *Near v. Minnesota* [ ]. As such, respondents argue, the statute bears "a 'heavy presumption' against its constitutional validity." [ ] They claim that the State's interest in the anonymity of a juvenile offender is not sufficient to overcome that presumption.

. . .

Petitioners do not dispute that the statute amounts to a prior restraint on speech. Rather, they take the view that even if it is a prior restraint the statute is constitutional because of the significance of the State's interest in protecting the identity of juveniles.

(3)

The resolution of this case does not turn on whether the statutory grant of authority to the juvenile judge to permit publication of the juvenile's name is, in and of itself, a prior restraint. First Amendment protection reaches beyond prior restraints, [ ] and respondents acknowledge that the statutory provision for court approval of disclosure actually may have a less oppressive effect on freedom of the press than a total ban on the publication of the child's name.

Whether we view the statute as a prior restraint or as a penal sanction for publishing lawfully obtained, truthful information is not dispositive because even the latter action requires the highest form of state interest to sustain its validity. Prior restraints have been accorded the most exacting scrutiny in previous cases. [ ]. However, even when a state attempts to punish publication after the event it must nevertheless demonstrate that its punitive action was necessary to further the state interests asserted. [*Landmark*, supra]. Since we conclude that this statute cannot satisfy the constitutional standards defined in *Landmark Communications, Inc.,* we need not decide whether, as argued by respondents, it operated as a prior restraint.

Our recent decisions demonstrate that state action to punish the publication of truthful information seldom can satisfy constitutional standards. In *Landmark Communications* we declared unconstitutional a Virginia statute making it a crime to publish information regarding confidential proceedings before a state judicial review commission that heard complaints about alleged disabilities and misconduct of state-court judges. In declaring that statute unconstitutional, we concluded:

> "[T]he publication Virginia seeks to punish under its statute lies near the core of the First Amendment, and the Commonwealth's interests advanced by the imposition of criminal sanctions are insufficient to justify the actual and potential encroachments on freedom of speech and of the press which follow therefrom." 435 U.S., at 838.

In [Cox Broadcasting Corp. v. Cohn, 420 U.S. 469 (1975)], we held that damages could not be recovered against a newspaper for publishing the name of a rape victim. The suit had been based on a state statute that made it a crime to publish the name of the victim; the purpose of the statute was to protect the privacy right of the individual and the family. The name of the victim had become known to the public through official court records dealing with the trial of the rapist. In declaring the statute unconstitutional, the Court, speaking through Mr. Justice White, reasoned:

> "By placing the information in the public domain on official court records, the State must be presumed to have concluded that the public interest was thereby being served. . . . States may not impose sanctions on the publication of truthful information contained in official court records open to public inspection." 420 U.S., at 495.

One case that involved a classic prior restraint is particularly relevant to our inquiry. In Oklahoma Publishing Co. v. District Court, 430 U.S. 308 (1977), we struck down a state court injunction prohibiting the news media from publishing the name or photograph of an 11–year-old boy who was being tried before a juvenile court. The juvenile judge had permitted reporters and other members of the public to attend a hearing in the case, notwithstanding a state statute closing such trials to the public. The court then attempted to halt publication of the information obtained from that hearing. We held that once the truthful information was "publicly revealed" or "in the public domain" the court could not constitutionally restrain its dissemination.

None of these opinions directly controls this case; however, all suggest strongly that if a newspaper lawfully obtains truthful information about a matter of public significance then state officials may not constitutionally punish publication of the information, absent a need to further a state interest of the highest order. These cases involved situations where the government itself provided or made possible press access to the information. That factor is not controlling. Here respondents relied upon routine newspaper reporting techniques to ascertain the identity of the alleged assailant. A free press cannot be made to rely solely upon the sufferance of government to supply it with information. See Houchins v. KQED, Inc., 438 U.S. 1, 11 (1978) (plurality opinion); Branzburg v. Hayes, 408 U.S. 665, 681 (1972). If the information is lawfully obtained, as it was here, the state may not punish its publication except when necessary to further an interest more substantial than is present here.

(4)

The sole interest advanced by the State to justify its criminal statute is to protect the anonymity of the juvenile offender. It is asserted that confidentiality will further his rehabilitation because publication of the name may encourage further antisocial conduct and also may cause the juvenile to lose future employment or suffer other consequences for this single offense. In Davis v. Alaska, 415 U.S. 308 (1974), similar arguments were advanced by the State to justify not permitting a criminal defendant to impeach a prosecution witness on the basis of his juvenile record. We said there that "[w]e do not and need not challenge the State's interest as a matter of its own policy in the administration of criminal justice to seek to preserve the anonymity of a juvenile offender." [ ] However, we concluded that the State's policy must be subordinated to the defendant's Sixth Amendment right of confrontation. Ibid. The important rights created by the First Amendment must be considered along with the rights of defendants guaranteed by the Sixth Amendment. See *Nebraska Press Assn. v. Stuart*, [ ]. Therefore, the reasoning of *Davis* that the constitutional right must prevail over the state's interest in protecting juveniles applies with equal force here.

The magnitude of the State's interest in this statute is not sufficient to justify application of a criminal penalty to respondents. Moreover, the statute's approach does not satisfy constitutional requirements. The statute does not restrict the electronic media or any form of publication, except "newspapers," from printing the names of youths charged in a juvenile proceeding. In this very case, three radio stations announced the alleged assailant's name before the Daily Mail decided to publish it. Thus, even assuming the statute served a state interest of the highest order, it does not accomplish its stated purpose.

In addition, there is no evidence to demonstrate that the imposition of criminal penalties is necessary to protect the confidentiality of juvenile proceedings. . . . [A]ll 50 states have statutes that provide in some way for confidentiality, but only five, including West Virginia, impose criminal penalties on nonparties for publication of the identity of the juvenile. Although every state has asserted a similar interest, all but a handful have found other ways of accomplishing the objective. See [*Landmark*].[3]

(5)

Our holding in this case is narrow. There is no issue before us of unlawful press access to confidential judicial proceedings, [ ]; there is no issue here of privacy or prejudicial pretrial publicity. At issue is simply the power of a state to punish the truthful publication of an alleged juvenile delinquent's name lawfully obtained by a newspaper.[4] The asserted state interest cannot justify the statute's imposition of criminal sanctions on this type of publication. Accordingly, the judgment of the West Virginia Supreme Court of Appeals is

Affirmed.

3. The approach advocated by the National Council of Juvenile Court Judges is based on cooperation between juvenile court personnel and newspaper editors. It is suggested that if the courts make clear their purpose and methods then the press will exercise discretion and generally decline to publish the juvenile's name without some prior consultation with the juvenile court judge.

4. In light of our disposition of the First and Fourteenth Amendment issue, we need not reach respondents' claim that the statute violates equal protection by being applicable only to newspapers but not other forms of journalistic expression.

MR. JUSTICE POWELL took no part in the consideration or decision of this case.

[Justice Rehnquist, who concurred in the judgment, filed the only separate opinion. He believed that protecting juveniles in this type of case was an interest of the "highest order" and "far outweighs any minimal interference with freedom of the press. . . ." He also noted that the Court's decision "renders nugatory" state expungement laws, because a potential employer may now obtain information on juvenile offenses by visiting the morgue of the local newspaper. Also, in future cases the "press will still be able to obtain the child's name in the same manner as it was acquired in this case. [ ] Thus, the Court's reference to effective alternatives [other than criminal punishment] for accomplishing the State's goal is a mere chimera."

He did concur, however, because the state's statute did not accomplish its stated purpose. Since broadcasters could, and did, identify the juvenile, it was "difficult to take very seriously West Virginia's asserted need to preserve the anonymity of its youthful offenders when it permits other, equally, if not more, effective means of mass communication to distribute this information without fear of punishment."]

Notes and Questions

1. Justice Rehnquist thought the state's interest in protecting juveniles in this case was of the "highest order." The majority apparently did not share his view of the importance of the interest. How are judges supposed to determine whether state interests are sufficiently high to meet this standard? Should the constitutionality of the statute turn on the value assigned to the interest by the state, or by the reviewing judges?

2. Would the result be different if the statute had applied to broadcasters as well as newspapers? To all media? To all unauthorized disclosures of juveniles' names?

3. Does the principle of *Daily Mail* apply when the reporter knows the information has been obtained illegally or made available by mistake? In Bartnicki v. Vopper, 532 U.S. 514 (2001), the Supreme Court considered whether a radio station could constitutionally be held liable for broadcasting the contents of a private telephone conversation that had been illegally intercepted. In that case, the radio station knew that a third party had illegally intercepted a tape of the conversation, but the station itself took no part in the interception. The Supreme Court held, 6–3, that the First Amendment protected the radio station from liability under the facts of the case, although two of the six Justices in the majority wrote a separate concurrence to emphasize that the Court's holding was "narrow" and "limited to the special circumstances present" in the case. *Id.* at 535 (Breyer and O'Connor, J., concurring). The *Bartnicki* decision is discussed more fully in Chapter VIII.

4. What is the "unit of measure" the Court used in balancing the interests at stake in this case? Consider the following:

> Someone says that the First Amendment "interests" associated with pornography are "outweighed" by the resultant violence to and subordination of women. Someone else replies that on the contrary, as far as he is concerned, the First Amendment rights at stake outweigh the harms. Neither of these people will actually be engaged in anything like a real balancing of interests. They will be wholly unable to explain the "calculations" that supposedly went into their "balance." Neither will have the slightest actual idea of the real-world amounts of the "costs" or "benefits" involved, nor of how to measure them, nor even of what would count as a relevant cost or benefit. How then did they know which way, for them, the balance came out? The rhetoric of balancing is a disguise in such contexts. It serves as a conclusory, obfuscatory language masking more fundamental, although frequently very poorly thought-through, instincts about the freedom of speech.

Jed Rubenfeld, The First Amendment's Purpose, 53 Stan. L. Rev. 767, 789 (2001). If Professor Rubenfeld is correct, what is the alternative? Are other methods of analysis more intellectually sound? Professor Rubenfeld argues that the key inquiry in First Amendment cases should be "an open and direct inquiry into the law's purpose." *Id.* at 768. Under this approach, laws whose purpose is to suppress or promote particular content or particular viewpoints violate the First Amendment.

2. THE CATEGORICAL APPROACH

From time to time, the Supreme Court has placed certain categories of words outside the First Amendment's protection. In 1942, the Court indicated, in Chaplinsky v. New Hampshire, 315 U.S. 568 (1942), that certain classes of expression might be subject to legal sanctions after their utterance:

> There are certain well-defined and narrowly limited classes of speech, the prevention and punishment of which have never been thought to raise any Constitutional problem. These include the lewd and obscene, the profane, the libelous, and the insulting or "fighting" words those, which by their very utterance inflict injury or tend to incite an immediate breach of the peace. It has been well observed that such utterances are no essential part of any exposition of ideas, and are of such slight social value as a step to truth that any benefit that may be derived from them is clearly outweighed by the social interest in order and morality.

Chaplinsky was arrested for calling a town marshal (to his face) a "God-damned racketeer and a damned Fascist." The Supreme Court characterized the expression as "fighting words . . . likely to cause violence." The expressive element was not protected because the words invited a violent response by the person to whom they were directed.

Note that protection hinges on the categories of expression and not on the point of view the speaker has expressed on a subject. Indeed, the Court frequently has asserted that government must not encourage or hinder speech based on whether officials like the views being expressed. For instance, a city cannot allow peaceful picketing by union members while prohibiting all other peaceful picketing. Such an ordinance in Chicago, which allowed demonstrations near school buildings only if labor matters were involved, was invalidated by the Court. Chicago Police Dept. v. Mosley, 408 U.S. 92, 96 (1972).

The following case is not a media case, but it has important implications for choice of analytical method in many First Amendment cases.

R.A.V. v. City of St. Paul

Supreme Court of the United States, 1992.
505 U.S. 377, 112 S. Ct. 2538, 120 L. Ed.2d 305.

[Petitioner and several other teenagers allegedly taped together several chair legs to make a crude cross, and then burned it inside the fenced yard of a black family that lived near where petitioner was staying. The city of St. Paul charged petitioner with, among other things, violating the city's "hate crime" ordinance:

> Whoever places on public or private property a symbol, object, appellation, characterization or graffiti, including, but not limited to, a burning cross or Nazi swastika, which one knows or has reasonable grounds to know arouses anger, alarm or resentment in others on the basis of race, color, creed, religion or gender commits disorderly conduct and shall be guilty of a misdemeanor.]

JUSTICE SCALIA delivered the opinion of the Court.

. . .

Petitioner moved to dismiss this count on the ground that the St. Paul ordinance was substantially overbroad and impermissibly content-based and therefore facially invalid under the First Amendment. The trial court granted this motion, but the Minnesota Supreme Court reversed. That court rejected petitioner's overbreadth claim because, as construed in prior Minnesota cases, [ ] the modifying phrase "arouses anger, alarm or resentment in others" limited the reach of the ordinance to conduct that amounts to "fighting words," i.e., "conduct that itself inflicts injury or tends to incite immediate violence . . .," [ ] and therefore the ordinance reached only expression "that the first amendment does not protect." [ ]. The court also concluded that the ordinance was not impermissibly content-based because, in its view, "the ordinance is a narrowly tailored means toward accomplishing the compelling governmental interest in protecting the community against bias-motivated threats to public safety and order." [ ]. We granted certiorari [ ] [and we reverse].

I

In construing the St. Paul ordinance, we are bound by the construction given to it by the Minnesota court. [ ] Accordingly, we accept the Minnesota Supreme Court's authoritative statement that the ordinance reaches only those expressions that constitute "fighting words" within the meaning of *Chaplinsky*. [ ] Petitioner and his amici urge us to modify the scope of the *Chaplinsky* formulation, thereby invalidating the ordinance as "substantially overbroad," [ ]. We find it unnecessary to consider this issue. Assuming, arguendo, that all of the expression reached by the ordinance is proscribable under the "fighting words" doctrine, we nonetheless conclude that the ordinance is facially unconstitutional in that it prohibits otherwise permitted speech solely on the basis of the subjects the speech addresses.

The First Amendment generally prevents government from proscribing speech, [ ] or even expressive conduct, [ ], because of disapproval of the ideas expressed. Content-based regulations are presumptively invalid. *Simon & Schuster, Inc. v. Members of N.Y. State Crime Victims Bd.*, [infra p. 87.] [ ] From 1791 to the present, however, our society, like other free but civilized societies, has permitted restrictions upon the content of speech in a few limited areas, which are "of such slight social value as a step to truth that any benefit that may be derived from them is clearly outweighed by the social interest in order and morality." *Chaplinsky*, [ ]. We have recognized that "the freedom of speech" referred to by the First Amendment does not include a freedom to disregard these traditional limitations. See, e.g., Roth v. United States, 354 U.S. 476 (1957) (obscenity); Beauharnais v. Illinois, 343 U.S. 250 (1952) (defamation); *Chaplinsky v. New Hampshire*, supra, ("fighting words"); [ ]. Our decisions since the 1960s have narrowed the scope of the traditional categorical exceptions for defamation, [ ], and for obscenity, [ ], but a limited categorical approach has remained an important part of our First Amendment jurisprudence.

We have sometimes said that these categories of expression are "not within the area of constitutionally protected speech," [*Roth, Beauharnais, Chaplinsky*]; or that the "protection of the First Amendment does not extend" to them, [ ]. Such statements must be taken in context, however, and are no more literally true than is the occasionally repeated shorthand characterizing obscenity "as not being speech at all," [ ]. What they mean is that these areas of speech can, consistently with the First Amendment, be regulated because of their constitutionally proscribable content (obscenity, defamation, etc.)—not that they are categories of speech entirely invisible to the Constitution, so that they may be made the vehicles for content discrimination unrelated to their distinctively proscribable content. Thus, the government may proscribe libel; but it may not make the further content discrimination of proscribing only libel critical of the government. . . .

. . .

The proposition that a particular instance of speech can be proscribable on the basis of one feature (e.g., obscenity) but not on the basis of another (e.g., opposition to the city government) is commonplace, and has found application in many contexts. We have long held, for example, that nonverbal expressive activity can be banned because of the action it entails, but not because of the ideas it expresses—so that burning a flag in violation of an ordinance against outdoor fires could be punishable, whereas burning a flag in violation of an ordinance against dishonoring the flag is not. [ ]. Similarly, we have upheld reasonable "time, place, or manner" restrictions, but only if they are "justified without reference to the content of the regulated speech." [ ] And just as the power to proscribe particular speech on the basis of a noncontent element (e.g., noise) does not entail the power to proscribe the same speech on the basis of a content element; so also, the power to proscribe it on the basis of one content element (e.g., obscenity) does not entail the power to proscribe it on the basis of other content elements.

In other words, the exclusion of "fighting words" from the scope of the First Amendment simply means that, for purposes of that Amendment, the unprotected features of the words are, despite their verbal character, essentially a "nonspeech" element of communication. Fighting words are thus analogous to a noisy sound truck: Each is, as Justice Frankfurter recognized, a "mode of speech," Niemotko v. Maryland, 340 U.S. 268, 282 (1951) (Frankfurter, J., concurring in result); both can be used to convey an idea; but neither has, in and of itself, a claim upon the First Amendment. As with the sound truck, however, so also with fighting words: The government may not regulate use based on hostility—or favoritism— towards the underlying message expressed. [ ]

. . .

Even the prohibition against content discrimination that we assert the First Amendment requires is not absolute. It applies differently in the context of proscribable speech than in the area of fully protected speech. The rationale of the general prohibition, after all, is that content discrimination "rais[es] the specter that the Government may effectively drive certain ideas or viewpoints from the marketplace." [ ] But content discrimination among various instances of a class of proscribable speech often does not pose this threat.

When the basis for the content discrimination consists entirely of the very reason the entire class of speech at issue is proscribable, no significant danger of idea or viewpoint discrimination exists. Such a reason, having been adjudged neutral enough to support exclusion of the entire class of speech from First Amendment protection, is also neutral enough to form the basis of distinction within the class. To illustrate: A State might choose to prohibit only that obscenity which is the most patently offensive in its prurience—i.e., that which involves the most lascivious displays of sexual activity. But it may not prohibit, for example, only that obscenity which includes offensive political messages. . . .

Another valid basis for according differential treatment to even a content-defined subclass of proscribable speech is that the subclass happens to be associated with particular "secondary effects" of the speech, so that the regulation is "justified without reference to the content of the . . .

speech," [ ]. A State could, for example, permit all obscene live performances except those involving minors. Moreover, since words can in some circumstances violate laws directed not against speech but against conduct (a law against treason, for example, is violated by telling the enemy the nation's defense secrets), a particular content-based subcategory of a proscribable class of speech can be swept up incidentally within the reach of a statute directed at conduct rather than speech. [ ] Thus, for example, sexually derogatory "fighting words," among other words, may produce a violation of Title VII's general prohibition against sexual discrimination in employment practices, [ ]. Where the government does not target conduct on the basis of its expressive content, acts are not shielded from regulation merely because they express a discriminatory idea or philosophy.

These bases for distinction refute the proposition that the selectivity of the restriction is "even arguably 'conditioned upon the sovereign's agreement with what a speaker may intend to say.' " [ ] There may be other such bases as well. Indeed, to validate such selectivity (where totally proscribable speech is at issue) it may not even be necessary to identify any particular "neutral" basis, so long as the nature of the content discrimination is such that there is no realistic possibility that official suppression of ideas is afoot. (We cannot think of any First Amendment interest that would stand in the way of a State's prohibiting only those obscene motion pictures with blue-eyed actresses.) Save for that limitation, the regulation of "fighting words," like the regulation of noisy speech, may address some offensive instances and leave other, equally offensive, instances alone. [ ]

II.

Applying these principles to the St. Paul ordinance, we conclude that, even as narrowly construed by the Minnesota Supreme Court, the ordinance is facially unconstitutional. Although the phrase in the ordinance, "arouses anger, alarm or resentment in others," has been limited by the Minnesota Supreme Court's construction to reach only those symbols or displays that amount to "fighting words," the remaining, unmodified terms make clear that the ordinance applies only to "fighting words," that insult, or provoke violence, "on the basis of race, color, creed, religion or gender." Displays containing abusive invective, no matter how vicious or severe, are permissible unless they are addressed to one of the specified disfavored topics. Those who wish to use "fighting words" in connection with other ideas—to express hostility, for example, on the basis of political affiliation, union membership, or homosexuality—are not covered. The First Amendment does not permit St. Paul to impose special prohibitions on those speakers who express views on disfavored subjects. [ ].

In its practical operation, moreover, the ordinance goes even beyond mere content discrimination, to actual viewpoint discrimination. Displays containing some words—odious racial epithets, for example—would be prohibited to proponents of all views. But "fighting words" that do not themselves invoke race, color, creed, religion, or gender—aspersions upon a person's mother, for example—would seemingly be usable ad libitum in the placards of those arguing in favor of racial, color, etc. tolerance and equality, but could not be used by that speaker's opponents. One could hold up a sign saying, for example, that all "anti-Catholic bigots" are misbegotten; but not that all "papists" are, for that would insult and provoke violence "on the basis of religion." St. Paul has no such authority to license one side of a debate to fight freestyle, while requiring the other to follow Marquis of Queensbury Rules.

What we have here, it must be emphasized, is not a prohibition of fighting words that are directed at certain persons or groups (which would be facially valid if it met the requirements of the Equal Protection Clause); but rather, a prohibition of fighting words that contain (as the Minnesota Supreme Court repeatedly emphasized) messages of "bias-motivated" hatred and in particular, as applied to this case, messages "based on virulent notions of racial supremacy." [ ]. One must wholeheartedly agree with the Minnesota Supreme Court that "[i]t is the responsibility, even the obligation, of diverse communities to confront such notions in whatever form they appear," [ ], but the manner of that confrontation cannot consist of selective limitations upon speech. St. Paul's brief asserts that a general "fighting words" law would not meet the city's needs because only a content-specific measure can communicate to minority groups that the "group hatred" aspect of such speech "is not condoned by the majority." [ ] The point of the First Amendment is that majority preferences must be expressed in some fashion other than silencing speech on the basis of its content.

. . .

The content-based discrimination reflected in the St. Paul ordinance comes within neither any of the specific exceptions of the First Amendment prohibition we discussed earlier, nor within a more general exception for content discrimination that does not threaten censorship of ideas. It assuredly does not fall within the exception for content discrimination based on the very reasons why the particular class of speech at issue (here, fighting words) is proscribable. As explained earlier, [ ], the reason why fighting words are categorically excluded from the protection of the First Amendment is not that their content communicates any particular idea, but their content embodies a particularly intolerable (and socially unnecessary) mode of expressing whatever idea the speaker wishes to convey. St. Paul has not singled out an especially offensive mode of expression—it has not, for example, selected for prohibition only those fighting words that communicate ideas in a threatening (as opposed to a merely obnoxious) manner. Rather, it has proscribed fighting words of whatever manner that communicate messages of racial, gender, or religious intolerance. Selectivity of this sort creates the possibility that the city is seeking to handicap the expression of particular ideas. That possibility would alone be enough to render the ordinance presumptively invalid, but St. Paul's comments and concessions in this case elevate the possibility to a certainty.

. . .

It hardly needs discussion that the ordinance does not fall within some more general exception permitting all selectivity that for any reason is beyond the suspicion of official suppression of ideas. The statements of St. Paul in this very case afford ample basis for, if not full confirmation of, that suspicion.

Finally, St. Paul and its amici defend the conclusion of the Minnesota Supreme Court that, even if the ordinance regulates expression based on hostility towards its protected ideological content, this discrimination is nonetheless justified because it is narrowly tailored to serve compelling state interests. Specifically, they assert that the ordinance helps to ensure the basic human rights of members of groups that have historically been subjected to discrimination, including the right of such group members to live in peace where they wish. We do not doubt that these interests are compelling, and that the ordinance can be said to promote them. But the "danger of censorship" presented by a facially content-based statute, [ ], requires that that weapon be employed only where it is "necessary to serve the asserted [compelling] interest," [ ]. The existence of adequate content-neutral alternatives thus "undercut[s] significantly" any defense of such a statute, [ ] casting considerable doubt on the government's protestations that "the asserted justification is in fact an accurate description of the purpose and effect of the law," [ ]. The dispositive question in this case, therefore, is whether content discrimination is reasonably necessary to achieve St. Paul's compelling interests; it plainly is not. An ordinance not limited to the favored topics, for example, would have precisely the same beneficial effect. In fact the only interest distinctively served by the content limitation is that of displaying the city council's special hostility towards the particular biases thus singled out.

. . .

[Justice White, joined by Justices Blackmun and O'Connor, concurred in the judgment, but only on the ground that the ordinance as construed by the Minnesota Supreme Court criminalized not only fighting words, but also speech that merely causes "anger, alarm or resentment," and therefore was unconstitutionally overbroad. They believed that if the statute had reached only fighting words, it would have been constitutional even if it treated some fighting words differently than others because of their content. Justice White's opinion continued:]

[T]his Court has long held certain discrete categories of expression to be proscribable on the basis of their content. For instance, the Court has held that the individual who falsely shouts "fire" in a crowded theatre may not claim the protection of the First Amendment. [ ] The Court has concluded that neither child pornography, nor obscenity, is protected by the First Amendment. [ ]. And the Court has observed that, "[l]eaving aside the special considerations when public officials [and public figures] are the target, a libelous publication is not protected by the Constitution." [ ].

All of these categories are content based. But the Court has held that the First Amendment does not apply to them because their expressive content is worthless or of de minimis value to society. [*Chaplinsky*]. We have not departed from this principle, emphasizing repeatedly that, "within the confines of [these] given classification[s], the evil to be restricted so overwhelmingly outweighs the expressive interests, if any, at stake, that no process of case-by-case adjudication is required." [ ]. This categorical approach has provided a principled and narrowly focused means for distinguishing between expression that the government may regulate freely and that which it may regulate on the basis of content only upon a showing of compelling need.

Today, however, the Court announces that earlier Courts did not mean their repeated statements that certain categories of expression are "not within the area of constitutionally protected speech." [ ]. The present Court submits that such clear statements "must be taken in context" and are not "literally true." [ ].

To the contrary, those statements meant precisely what they said: The categorical approach is a firmly entrenched part of our First Amendment jurisprudence. Indeed, the Court in [Roth v. United States, 354 U.S. 476, 482–483 (1957)] reviewed the guarantees of freedom of expression in effect at the time of the ratification of the Constitution and concluded, "[i]n light of this history, it is apparent that the unconditional phrasing of the First Amendment was not intended to protect every utterance." [ ]

In its decision today . . . the majority holds that the First Amendment protects those narrow categories of expression long held to be undeserving of First Amendment protection—at least to the extent that lawmakers may not regulate some fighting words more strictly than others because of their content. . . . Should the government want to criminalize certain fighting words, the Court now requires it to criminalize all fighting words.

. . . It is inconsistent to hold that the government may proscribe an entire category of speech because the content of that speech is evil, [ ] but that the government may not treat a subset of that category differently without violating the First Amendment; the content of the subset is by definition worthless and undeserving of constitutional protection.

The majority's observation that fighting words are "quite expressive indeed," [ ], is no answer. Fighting words are not a means of exchanging views, rallying supporters, or registering a protest; they are directed against individuals to provoke violence or to inflict injury. [ ] Therefore, a ban on all fighting words or on a subset of the fighting words category would restrict only the social evil of hate speech, without creating the danger of driving viewpoints from the marketplace. [ ]

Therefore, the Court's insistence on inventing its brand of First Amendment underinclusiveness puzzles me. The overbreadth doctrine has the redeeming virtue of attempting to avoid the chilling of protected expression, [ ], but the Court's new "underbreadth" creation serves no desirable function. Instead, it permits, indeed invites, the continuation of expressive conduct that in this case is evil and worthless in First Amendment terms, [ ], until the city of St. Paul cures the underbreadth by adding to its ordinance a catchall phrase such as "and all other fighting words that may constitutionally be subject to this ordinance."

[Justice Stevens concurred in the judgment on the ground that the statute reached more than fighting words and therefore was overbroad, but disagreed with all the other justices on the merits of categorization, arguing that it "sacrifice[d] subtlety for clarity and is . . . ultimately unsound."]

Notes and Questions

1.   Laws that target expression are subject to challenge on the ground that they are substantially overbroad, that is, that they sweep too far into the realm of expression protected by the First Amendment. First Amendment overbreadth doctrine is an exception to ordinary rules of standing. It allows "someone whose conduct is not constitutionally protected [to] escape a legal sanction on the ground that the statute under which she is threatened would be constitutionally invalid as applied to someone else[.]" Richard H. Fallon, Jr., Making Sense of Overbreadth, 100 Yale L.J. 853 (1991). As the Supreme Court has explained, "the transcendent value to all society of constitutionally protected expression is deemed to justify 'attacks on overly broad statutes with no requirement that the person making the attack demonstrate that his own conduct could not be regulated by a statute drawn with the requisite narrow specificity.' " Gooding v. Wilson, 405 U.S. 518, 520–21 (quoting Dombrowski v. Pfister, 380 U.S. 479, 486 (1965)). How does Justice White describe the justification for overbreadth doctrine? Why does he question the justification for "the Court's new 'underbreadth' doctrine"? What is the justification for invalidating statutes on grounds of underinclusiveness?

2.   Suppose the City of St. Paul had argued for the recognition of a new category of unprotected speech—hate speech. If that were the relevant category, the ordinance presumably would be neither overbroad nor under-inclusive. Is *Chaplinsky*'s listing of categories exhaustive? How would the Court decide whether hate speech is "of such slight value as a step to truth" that it need not be protected?

3.   The most conspicuous categorical exception to the First Amendment is obscenity. Although the problem of deciding what fits the category often seems to defy principled analysis, and although the effort consumes a significant amount of judicial resources, the Court has steadfastly refused to abandon the categorical approach to obscenity. In 1973, after more than two decades of trying to define obscenity, the Court, 5–4, articulated the definition that remains in effect today. Miller v. California, 413 U.S. 15, 1 Med. L. Rptr. 1441 (1973).

Despite the Court's continued adherence to the categorical approach, there is much about the law of obscenity that does not seem categorical at all. Even obscene material receives some First Amendment protection. The state cannot require pre-screening, even of material that meets the test for obscenity, unless it provides special procedures to assure prompt decision and speedy judicial review, see Freedman v. Maryland, 380 U.S. 51, 1 Med.

L. Rptr. 1126 (1965) and the state cannot punish a person for possessing obscene material in a private home, see Stanley v. Georgia, 394 U.S. 557 (1969). Obscenity is examined in greater detail in Chapter III.

4. The *Chaplinsky* concept of "categorization" continues to be relevant today because the Supreme Court continues to treat some categories of speech as wholly outside the protection of the First Amendment. For example, expression meeting the Supreme Court's definition of "incitement"—advocacy that is "directed to inciting or producing imminent lawless action and is likely to incite or produce such action"—receives no First Amendment protection. Brandenburg v. Ohio, 395 U.S. 444, 447 (1969). What other categories of speech might be "adjudged neutral enough to support exclusion of the entire class of speech from First Amendment protection?" Perjury? Solicitation of crime? Offering bribes? Offering sex for money? Enticing a child from custody? Threats of violence?

5. The Supreme Court revisited the matter of hate speech in a case involving a Virginia statute that made it a crime for "any person or persons, with the intent of intimidating any person or group of persons, to burn, or cause to be burned, a cross on the property of another, a highway or other public place." The Supreme Court of Virginia had relied on *R.A.V.* to conclude that the statute discriminated on the basis of content and was therefore unconstitutional. The U.S. Supreme Court disagreed. See Virginia v. Black, 538 U.S. 343 (2003).

The Court distinguished *R.A.V.* on the basis that the Minneapolis ordinance at issue there targeted expressive conduct that would "arouse anger, alarm or resentment in others on the basis of race, color, creed, religion or gender." The Virginia statute, in contrast, applied to all cross burning done with intent to intimidate. As a result, Justice O'Connor wrote for the majority, "the Virginia statute does not single out for opprobrium only that speech directed toward 'one of the specific disfavored topics.' "

Justice O'Connor characterized cross burning as a "particularly virulent form of intimidation." Intimidation is "constitutionally proscribable" when it is a "type of true threat, where a speaker directs a threat to a person or group of persons with the intent of placing the victim in fear of bodily harm or death." The Virginia statute was constitutional because cross burning is one of the forms of intimidation "most likely to inspire fear of bodily harm."

The Court determined, however, that another provision of the Virginia statute, which provided that "[a]ny such burning of a cross shall be prima facie evidence of an intent to intimidate a person or group of persons," was unconstitutional. Consequently, the Court overturned the convictions below in which that provision had been explicitly applied and remanded two other convictions with instructions that the lower court consider what effect, if any, the provision had caused.

Justices Souter, Kennedy, and Ginsburg concurred in the majority's rejection of the "prima facie evidence" provision, but dissented from the decision to otherwise uphold the statute. The dissenters argued that the thrust of *R.A.V.* was to prohibit regulation of expression or expressive conduct unless there was a "high probability that no 'official suppression of ideas [was] afoot.' " According to the dissent, the statute should be read as a whole, and the existence of the "prima facie evidence" language runs the risk of influencing juries to convict and therefore of "skew[ing] the statute toward suppressing ideas."

Is the majority's attempt to distinguish *R.A.V.* convincing? Does the Virginia statute employ permissible content discrimination in the context of "proscribable speech"? For an argument that cross burning should be treated as protected political speech, punishable only under laws that can survive strict scrutiny, see W. Wat Hopkins, Cross Burning Revisited: What the Supreme Court Should Have Done in Virginia v. Black and Why It Didn't, 26 Comm/Ent 269 (2004).

———

Most of the categories of speech included in *Chaplinsky*'s list of "well-defined and narrowly limited classes of speech, the prevention and punishment of which have never been thought to raise any Constitutional problem" are no longer thought to be wholly outside the protection of the First Amendment. Categorization is used not to deny protection altogether, but to single out certain kinds of speech for more or less protection. The Court sometimes suggests, for example, that speech pertaining to elections or government is "close to the core" of the First Amendment and is entitled to special protection. On the other hand, the Court categorizes advertising as a species of speech entitled to something less than the full protection of the First Amendment. As a result, categorization today is almost always linked with balancing, with the choice of category determining the level of scrutiny to be used when balancing the competing interests.

Nonetheless, there are still categories of speech that are not even thought to implicate the First Amendment. For example, the law of criminal solicitation clearly regulates speech, and yet the First Amendment puts no restraints on this body of law. In the article excerpted below, Professor Schauer examines "the speech that the First Amendment ignores." He argues that neither First Amendment theory nor legal doctrine fully explain why such speech is outside "the boundaries of the First Amendment."

The Boundaries of the First Amendment: A Preliminary Exploration of Constitutional Salience

Frederick Schauer
117 Harv. L. Rev. 1765 (2004).

. . .

To set the stage, it will be useful to explain the distinction between the coverage and the protection of the First Amendment. All rules—legal or otherwise—apply only to some facts and only under some circumstances. Even before we see what a rule does, we must make the initial determination of whether it applies at all—whether we are within its scope of operation. So too with the First Amendment, which of course is not infinitely applicable. Though many cases involve the First Amendment, many more do not. The acts, behaviors, and restrictions not encompassed by the First Amendment at all—the events that remain wholly untouched by the First Amendment—are the ones that are simply not covered by the First Amendment. It is not that the speech is not protected. Rather, the entire event—an event that often involves "speech" in the ordinary language sense of the word—does not present a First Amendment issue at all, and the government's action is consequently measured against no First Amendment standard whatsoever. The First Amendment just does not show up.

. . .

. . . [N]o First Amendment-generated level of scrutiny is used to determine whether the content-based advertising restrictions of the Securities Act of 1933 are constitutional, whether corporate executives may be imprisoned under the Sherman Act for exchanging accurate information about proposed prices with their competitors, whether an organized crime leader may be prosecuted for urging that his subordinates murder a mob rival, or whether a chainsaw manufacturer may be held liable in a products liability action for injuries caused by mistakes in the written instructions accompanying the tool. Each of these examples involves some punishment for speech, and each involves liability based both on the content and on the communicative impact of the speech. And yet no First Amendment degree of scrutiny appears. In these and countless other instances, the permissibility of regulation—unlike the control of incitement, libel, and commercial advertising—is not measured against First Amendment-generated standards.

. . .

Now that we have glimpsed part of the vast expanse of human communication that lies beyond the boundaries of the First Amendment, it is tempting to suppose that the line between what is inside and what is outside, even if not explicable in terms of constitutional text or Framers' intent, is nonetheless susceptible of theoretical explanation. Perhaps there exists an organizing principle—a descriptive or positive theory—coherently explaining which speech winds up within the First Amendment and which speech winds up without.

Yet however hard we try to theorize about the First Amendment's boundaries, . . . efforts at anything close to an explanation of the existing terrain of coverage and noncoverage are unavailing. . . . Theories based on self-government or democratic deliberation have a hard time explaining why (except as mistakes, of course) the doctrine now covers pornography, commercial advertising, and art, inter alia—none of which has much to do with political deliberation or self-governance, except under such an attenuated definition of "political" that the justification's core loses much of its power. "Search for truth" or "marketplace of ideas" accounts are similarly at a loss to explain the coverage of utterances without much truth value, including self-expression generally and the self-expressive aspects of most art and literature in particular. Indeed, if we were concerned about actually increasing knowledge and exposing error, it is far from clear that we would so easily protect both communication that is largely emotive and communication that is demonstrably factually false. Personal autonomy and self-expression accounts of the First Amendment are also difficult to justify descriptively. . . .

Not only are existing normative theories substantially narrower in some respects than current doctrine, but in other respects they are also substantially broader. "Distrust of government" theories, for example, cannot explain why that distrust has not been extended to the SEC, the FTC, the FDA, the Justice Department, or judges managing a trial—all of which involve government officials making content-based decisions about speech, and none of which is now covered by the First Amendment.

. . .

[Schauer ultimately argues that a "complex array of factors, some of which are doctrinal but many of which are not" explain why some types of speech lie outside the boundaries of the First Amendment. Amongst these factors are the following.]

One possible nondoctrinal factor helping to explain judicial determinations or social understandings of noncoverage may be the existence of a sympathetic litigant or class of litigants. . . . Although it is true that people you might not invite to lunch have been the major forces in crystallizing and reinforcing First Amendment doctrine, the doctrinal rules seem often to have arisen initially in the context of relatively more sympathetic litigants. By contrast, when arguments for expanding the boundaries of the First Amendment have been surrounded by unsympathetic litigants or classes of litigants—offerors of securities, telemarketers, price fixers, workplace gropers, con artists, terrorists, racist murderers, and indeed even music pirates, for example—the results have been different, and the borders of the First Amendment have not shifted.

. . .

Possibly even more significant is the presence or absence of an existing and well-entrenched regulatory scheme. Most of the domains in which significant content-based regulation of propositional speech has persisted—unimpeded by the First Amendment—have been domains in which an elaborate regulatory scheme, often managed by an agency dedicated to that form of regulation, is already in place. . . . It is one thing to make it harder to regulate a certain type of utterance, but another thing entirely to dismantle a long-standing regulatory structure. . . .

Moreover, the existence of an established regulatory scheme may also produce an environment in which the likely challengers to that scheme have become comfortable with it and have learned how to use it to their advantage. . . .

Finally, we can return to the First Amendment's magnetism and its ability to place some First Amendment issues at the center of public and media attention. As many of the examples here suggest, coverage may often be a function simply of the persistent visibility of First Amendment rhetoric, and noncoverage may conversely be a function of the failure of such rhetoric to take hold. In important respects, public and media attention to First Amendment claims may produce a kind of self-fulfilling prophecy in which First Amendment rhetoric newly applied to topics previously outside the First Amendment creates the visibility that itself helps to bring the entire topic into the domain of the First Amendment. . . .

3.   CLEAR AND PRESENT DANGER

The beginning of serious awareness of First Amendment issues arose out of the litigation provoked by the Espionage Act of 1917 and related state statutes designed to unify the nation during and after World War I. The Espionage Act banned attempts to cause insubordination in the armed forces or to obstruct military recruiting or to conspire to achieve these results. Most of these cases, which confronted the Court from 1919 until the mid–1920s, involved radical speakers who opposed the war effort and criticized the political and economic structure of the country.

From these cases emerged the "clear and present danger" test, first proposed by Justice Holmes, in Schenck v. United States, 249 U.S. 47 (1919). The appellant in *Schenck* had been convicted under the Espionage Act for publishing a leaflet that urged young men to oppose being drafted to fight in the war. Holmes, writing for the majority, upheld the conviction on the grounds that expression could be punished when "the words used are used in such circumstances and are of such a nature as to create a clear and present danger that they will bring about the substantive evils that Congress has a right to prevent. It is a question of proximity and degree."

Justice Brandeis, in a dissenting opinion joined by Justice Holmes, expanded upon the clear and present danger test in Whitney v. California, 274 U.S. 357 (1927). Part of that discussion is excerpted supra at p. 7. Immediately following that passage, Brandeis wrote:

> Moreover, even imminent danger cannot justify resort to prohibition of these functions essential to effective democracy, unless the evil apprehended is relatively serious. Prohibition of free speech and assembly is a measure so stringent that it would be inappropriate as the means for averting a relatively trivial harm to society. . . . [I]t is hardly conceivable that this Court would hold constitutional a statute which punished as a felony the mere voluntary assembly with a society formed to teach that pedestrians had the moral right to cross unenclosed, unposted, waste lands and to advocate their doing so, even if there was imminent danger that advocacy would lead to a trespass.

The Court again upheld the conviction of a radical political speaker. A quarter century later, a plurality of the Court recognized that the Holmes–

Brandeis position had become the majority view—but the plurality then refused to apply it. Dennis v. United States, 341 U.S. 494 (1951), involved prosecution of 11 leading members of the Communist Party for conspiring to advocate the forcible overthrow of the government of the United States.

The plurality noted that each case confronting Justices Holmes and Brandeis involved "a comparatively isolated event, bearing little relation in their minds to any substantial threat to the safety of the community. . . . They were not confronted with any situation comparable to the instant one—the development of an apparatus designed and dedicated to the overthrow of the Government, in the context of world crisis after crisis."

The plurality adopted the test framed by Judge Learned Hand in the lower court: "In each case [courts] must ask whether the gravity of the 'evil,' discounted by its improbability, justifies such invasion of free speech as is necessary to avoid the danger." That statement "takes into consideration those factors which we deem relevant, and relates their significances. More we cannot expect from words."

The plurality found that the requisite danger existed. The formation of a "highly organized conspiracy, with rigidly disciplined members subject to call when the leaders, these petitioners, felt the time had come for action, coupled with the inflammable nature of world conditions, similar uprisings in other countries, and the touch-and-go nature of our relations with countries with whom petitioners were in the very least ideologically attuned, convince us that their convictions were justified on this score. . . . If the ingredients of the reaction are present, we cannot bind the Government to wait until the catalyst is added."

The clear and present danger test was recast in the form of "incitement" in Brandenburg v. Ohio, 395 U.S. 444 (1969), involving prosecution of a Ku Klux Klan member for advocating racial and religious bigotry. The criminal syndicalism statute under which Ohio proceeded bore close similarities to the statute in *Whitney*. "But *Whitney* has been thoroughly discredited by later decisions. See [*Dennis*]. These later decisions have fashioned the principle that the constitutional guarantees of free speech and free press do not permit a State to forbid or proscribe advocacy of the use of force or of law violation except where such advocacy is directed to inciting or producing imminent lawless action and is likely to incite or produce such action."

Since the statute permitted punishment of advocacy without a showing that imminent lawless action was likely to follow, the convictions could not stand. *Whitney* was overruled.

Although the clear and present danger test was once the focal point for debate over the meaning of freedom of expression, its importance and utility must not be overstated. The test itself is rarely used today, though variants of it continue to be employed in several contexts. In Chapter VI, for example, we will see the "incitement" test applied to situations in which media presentations are alleged to have induced persons to physically harm themselves or others.

The clear and present danger test, even in its stronger forms, has not prevented punishment for the content of political speech. John Hart Ely asserted that the problem with this standard and, even more, the balancing approach, was that the First Amendment "simply cannot stand on the shifting foundation of ad hoc evaluations of specific threats." To avoid such evaluations he proposed that whenever content is being regulated the First Amendment "immunizes all expression *save that which falls within a few clearly and narrowly defined categories.*" (Emphasis in original). For Professor Ely, the advantage of this approach is that "the consideration of likely harm takes place at wholesale, in advance, outside the context of specific cases." Once the categories are fixed, "likely effect drops out of the calculation, and expression that does not fall within one of the categories is simply protected, irrespective of the identity of the speaker and the audience." John Hart Ely, Democracy and Distrust 109–10 (1980). Is it feasible to adopt an approach that always excludes considerations based on the perceived urgencies of the moment?

D. THE PRESS CLAUSE

1. HISTORY AND SIGNIFICANCE OF THE PRESS CLAUSE

Up to now we have drawn no distinction between freedom of speech and freedom of the press. Indeed, the courts usually draw no such distinction. In most cases, it seems to make no difference whether the party invoking the protection of the First Amendment is relying on the speech clause or the press clause.

From the outset, the Supreme Court has assumed that the First Amendment protected media corporations as fully as individuals. Giving media the same "free speech" rights as individuals has had several important consequences. One is that it is often unnecessary to consider the press clause as a possible independent source of rights. Another is that rights won through litigation by the media often become rights equally available to everyone. The Court usually uses "speech" and "press" interchangeably, or absorbs both into the phrase "freedom of expression." The Court has never explicitly held that the press clause gives the press rights not available to others.

Occasionally, however, cases arise that may implicate the press clause specifically. We consider examples later in this section. Other cases that seem to implicate the press clause include those in which the press complains about tax schemes that discriminate against (or among) portions of the press (discussed in Chapter III) and those in which reporters claim a privilege against identifying their sources (discussed in Chapter IX).

The possibility that the press clause might protect interests that are not covered by the speech clause has touched off a lively debate. Historically, there is little doubt that the press clause was viewed as having independent significance.

> . . . Freedom of the press—not freedom of speech—was the primary concern of the generation that wrote the Declaration of Indepen-

dence, the Constitution, and the Bill of Rights. Freedom of speech was a late addition to the pantheon of rights; freedom of the press occupied a central position from the very beginning.

. . .

That the press clause has a distinct history does not mean, of course, that it must be given a meaning different from the speech clause today, or even that it had a different meaning in 1791. It is possible that checking government power was also the purpose of the speech clause. My own guess, however, is that the latter was more closely related to the incipient notion of individual autonomy that underlay the religion clauses. But in either event, most modern analysis, by focusing on the speech clause, gets the matter upside down. As a means of checking government power, speech was an afterthought, if it was viewed as serving that function at all; the press was expected to be the primary source of restraint.

David A. Anderson, The Origins of the Press Clause, 30 UCLA L. Rev. 455, 533–34 (1983). Compare C. Edwin Baker, Advertising and a Democratic Press 118 (1994):

Free speech is easily seen as a fundamental personal right, a guarantee of individual liberty, a person's right to be expressive. In contrast, "the press" could refer to an institution or set of humanly created entities. The only persuasive (secular) reasons to give constitutional protection to an institution are instrumental judgments that doing so will serve human values. History, political theory, and the practice of other countries suggest that the Press Clause is best understood as a structural provision designed to protect an institution (or a category of enterprises) because of its contribution to various forms of human good—in particular, the press's contribution to checking governmental abuses and its provision of perspective and information useful to people in their self-defining activities.

The most famous argument for rights arising from the press clause was made by Justice Stewart in a speech a few months after the Watergate scandal, fueled by aggressive investigative reporting, had forced President Nixon to resign. (Most of the cases cited in the footnotes will become familiar as you progress through this book.)

"Or of the Press"[†]

Potter Stewart
26 Hastings L.J. 631 (1975).

I turn this morning to an inquiry into an aspect of constitutional law that has only recently begun to engage the attention of the Supreme Court. Specifically, I shall discuss the role of the organized press—of the daily

---

† Excerpted from an address on November 2, 1974, at the Yale Law School Sesquicentennial Convocation, New Haven, Connecticut. The Hastings Law Journal holds no copyright on this material.—eds.

newspapers and other established news media—in the system of government created by our Constitution.

It was less than a decade ago—during the Vietnam years—that the people of our country began to become aware of the twin phenomena on a national scale of so-called investigative reporting and an adversary press—that is, a press adversary to the Executive Branch of the Federal Government. And only in the two short years that culminated last summer in the resignation of a President did we fully realize the enormous power that an investigative and adversary press can exert.

The public opinion polls that I have seen indicate that some Americans firmly believe that the former Vice President and former President of the United States were hounded out of office by an arrogant and irresponsible press that had outrageously usurped dictatorial power. And it seems clear that many more Americans, while appreciating and even applauding the service performed by the press in exposing official wrongdoing at the highest levels of our national government, are nonetheless deeply disturbed by what they consider to be the illegitimate power of the organized press in the political structure of our society. It is my thesis this morning that, on the contrary, the established American press in the past ten years, and particularly in the past two years, has performed precisely the function it was intended to perform by those who wrote the First Amendment of our Constitution. I further submit that this thesis is supported by the relevant decisions of the Supreme Court.

Surprisingly, despite the importance of newspapers in the political and social life of our country the Supreme Court has not until very recently been called upon to delineate their constitutional role in our structure of government.

. . .

In very recent years cases involving the established press finally have begun to reach the Supreme Court, and they have presented a variety of problems, sometimes arising in complicated factual settings.

In a series of cases, the Court has been called upon to consider the limits imposed by the free press guarantee upon a state's common or statutory law of libel. As a result of those cases, a public figure cannot successfully sue a publisher for libel unless he can show that the publisher maliciously printed a damaging untruth.[1]

The Court has also been called upon to decide whether a newspaper reporter has a First Amendment privilege to refuse to disclose his confidential sources to a grand jury. By a divided vote, the Court found no such privilege to exist in the circumstances of the cases before it.[2]

---

1. See Rosenbloom v. Metromedia, Inc., 403 U.S. 29 (1971); Curtis Publ. Co. v. Butts, 388 U.S. 130 (1967); New York Times Co. v. Sullivan, 376 U.S. 254 (1964).

2. Branzburg v. Hayes, 408 U.S. 665 (1972).

In another noteworthy case, the Court was asked by the Justice Department to restrain publication by the *New York Times* and other newspapers of the so-called Pentagon Papers. The Court declined to do so.[3]

In yet another case, the question to be decided was whether political groups have a First Amendment or statutory right of access to the federally regulated broadcast channels of radio and television. The Court held there was no such right of access.[4]

Last Term the Court confronted a Florida statute that required newspapers to grant a "right of reply" to political candidates they had criticized. The Court unanimously held this statute to be inconsistent with the guarantees of a free press.[5]

It seems to me that the Court's approach to all these cases has uniformly reflected its understanding that the Free Press guarantee is, in essence, a *structural* provision of the Constitution. Most of the other provisions in the Bill of Rights protect specific liberties or specific rights of individuals: freedom of speech, freedom of worship, the right to counsel, the privilege against compulsory self-incrimination, to name a few. In contrast, the Free Press Clause extends protection to an institution. The publishing business is, in short, the only organized private business that is given explicit constitutional protection.

This basic understanding is essential, I think, to avoid an elementary error of constitutional law. It is tempting to suggest that freedom of the press means only that newspaper publishers are guaranteed freedom of expression. They *are* guaranteed that freedom, to be sure, but so are we all, because of the Free Speech Clause. If the Free Press guarantee meant no more than freedom of expression, it would be a constitutional redundancy. Between 1776 and the drafting of our Constitution, many of the state constitutions contained clauses protecting freedom of the press while at the same time recognizing no general freedom of speech. By including both guarantees in the First Amendment, the Founders quite clearly recognized the distinction between the two.

It is also a mistake to suppose that the only purpose of the constitutional guarantee of a free press is to insure that a newspaper will serve as a neutral forum for debate, a "market place for ideas," a kind of Hyde Park corner for the community. A related theory sees the press as a neutral conduit of information between the people and their elected leaders. These theories, in my view, again give insufficient weight to the institutional autonomy of the press that it was the purpose of the Constitution to guarantee.

In setting up the three branches of the Federal Government, the Founders deliberately created an internally competitive system. As Mr.

---

3. New York Times Co. v. United States, 403 U.S. 713 (1971).

4. Columbia Broadcasting Sys., Inc. v. Democratic Nat'l Comm., 412 U.S. 94 (1973).

5. Miami Herald Publ. Co. v. Tornillo, [418 U.S. 241] (1974).

Justice Brandeis once wrote:[6]

> The [Founders'] purpose was, not to avoid friction, but, by means of the inevitable friction incident to the distribution of the governmental powers among three departments, to save the people from autocracy.

The primary purpose of the constitutional guarantee of a free press was a similar one: to create a fourth institution outside the Government as an additional check on the three official branches. Consider the opening words of the Free Press Clause of the Massachusetts Constitution, drafted by John Adams:

> The liberty of the press is essential to the security of the state.

The relevant metaphor, I think, is the metaphor of the Fourth Estate. What Thomas Carlyle wrote about the British Government a century ago has a curiously contemporary ring:

> Burke said there were Three Estates in Parliament; but, in the Reporters' Gallery yonder, there sat a Fourth Estate more important far than they all. It is not a figure of speech or witty saying; it is a literal fact—very momentous to us in these times.

For centuries before our Revolution, the press in England had been licensed, censored, and bedeviled by prosecutions for seditious libel. The British Crown knew that a free press was not just a neutral vehicle for the balanced discussion of diverse ideas. Instead, the free press meant organized, expert scrutiny of government. The press was a conspiracy of the intellect, with the courage of numbers. This formidable check on official power was what the British Crown had feared—and what the American Founders decided to risk.

It is this constitutional understanding, I think, that provides the unifying principle underlying the Supreme Court's recent decisions dealing with the organized press.

Consider first the libel cases. Officials within the three governmental branches are, for all practical purposes, immune from libel and slander suits for statements that they make in the line of duty.[7] This immunity, which has both constitutional and common law origins, aims to insure bold and vigorous prosecution of the public's business. The same basic reasoning applies to the press. By contrast, the Court has never suggested that the constitutional right of free *speech* gives an *individual* any immunity from liability for either libel or slander.

In the cases involving the newspaper reporters' claims that they had a constitutional privilege not to disclose their confidential news sources to a grand jury, the Court rejected the claims by a vote of five to four, or, considering Mr. Justice Powell's concurring opinion, perhaps by a vote of four and a half to four and a half. But if freedom of the press means simply freedom of speech for reporters, this question of a reporter's asserted right

---

6. Myers v. United States, 272 U.S. 52, 293 (1926) (dissenting opinion).

7. See Barr v. Matteo, 360 U.S. 564 (1959).

to withhold information would have answered itself. None of us—as individuals—has a "free speech" right to refuse to tell a grand jury the identity of someone who has given us information relevant to the grand jury's legitimate inquiry. Only if a reporter is a representative of a protected *institution* does the question become a different one. The members of the Court disagreed in answering the question, but the question did not answer itself.

The cases involving the so-called "right of access" to the press raised the issue whether the First Amendment allows government, or indeed *requires* government, to regulate the press so as to make it a genuinely fair and open "market place for ideas." The Court's answer was "no" to both questions. If a newspaper wants to serve as a neutral market place for debate, that is an objective which it is free to choose. And, within limits, that choice is probably necessary to commercially successful journalism. But it is a choice that government cannot constitutionally impose.

Finally the Pentagon Papers case involved the line between secrecy and openness in the affairs of Government. The question, or at least one question, was whether that line is drawn by the Constitution itself. The Justice Department asked the Court to find in the Constitution a basis for prohibiting the publication of allegedly stolen government documents. The Court could find no such prohibition. So far as the Constitution goes, the autonomous press may publish what it knows, and may seek to learn what it can.

But this autonomy cuts both ways. The press is free to do battle against secrecy and deception in government. But the press cannot expect from the Constitution any guarantee that it will succeed. There is no constitutional right to have access to particular government information, or to require openness from the bureaucracy.[8] The public's interest in knowing about its government is protected by the guarantee of a Free Press, but the protection is indirect. The Constitution itself is neither a Freedom of Information Act nor an Official Secrets Act.

. . .

It is quite possible to conceive of the survival of our Republic without an autonomous press. For openness and honesty in government, for an adequate flow of information between the people and their representatives, for a sufficient check on autocracy and despotism, the traditional competition between the three branches of government, supplemented by vigorous political activity, might be enough.

The press could be relegated to the status of a public utility. The guarantee of free speech would presumably put some limitation on the regulation to which the press could be subjected. But if there were no guarantee of a Free Press, government could convert the communications media into a neutral "market place of ideas." Newspapers and television

8. Cf. Pell v. Procunier, 417 U.S. 817 (1974); Saxbe v. Washington Post Co., 417 U.S. 843 (1974).

networks could then be required to promote contemporary government policy or current notions of social justice.

Such a constitution is possible; it might work reasonably well. But it is not the Constitution the Founders wrote. It is not the Constitution that has carried us through nearly two centuries of national life. Perhaps our liberties might survive without an independent established press. But the Founders doubted it, and, in the year 1974, I think we can all be thankful for their doubts.

2.   WHAT IS "THE PRESS"?

Chief Justice Burger responded to Justice Stewart in a concurring opinion a few years later. The case struck down a Massachusetts statute, forbidding corporations from making expenditures or contributions to influence the outcome of referenda on matters not directly affecting the business of the corporation. The Court held that the statute violated the First Amendment rights of corporations. Chief Justice Burger wrote separately to emphasize his view that banks and other business corporations could not be accorded less protection under the First Amendment than media corporations. He identified two "fundamental difficulties" with giving media corporations special protection under the press clause. First, he argued that the historical record showed that the authors of the First Amendment did not contemplate extending a "special" privilege to the institutional press. (Most scholars would contest this reading of history.) Chief Justice Burger then wrote:

> The second fundamental difficulty with interpreting the Press Clause as conferring special status on a limited group is one of definition. [ ] The very task of including some entities within the "institutional press" while excluding others, whether undertaken by legislature, court, or administrative agency, is reminiscent of the abhorred licensing system of Tudor and Stuart England—a system the First Amendment was intended to ban from this country. [ ] Further, the officials undertaking that task would be required to distinguish the protected from the unprotected on the basis of such variables as content of expression, frequency or fervor of expression, or ownership of the technological means of dissemination. Yet nothing in this Court's opinions supports such a confining approach to the scope of Press Clause protection.[6] . . .

First National Bank v. Bellotti, 435 U.S. 765, 797–802, 3 Med. L. Rptr. 2105, 2118–2120 (1978) (Burger, C.J., concurring) (citations omitted).

The logic of this analysis led Chief Justice Burger to advocate a functional definition of the press: anyone who publishes is a member of the press for constitutional purposes, and the press clause simply protects the right to disseminate one's "speech" to a wide audience. The problem with

---

6. Near v. Minnesota ex rel. Olson, 283 U.S. 697 (1931), which examined the meaning of freedom of the press, did not involve a traditional institutionalized newspaper but rather an occasional publication (nine issues) more nearly approximating the product of a pamphleteer than the traditional newspaper.

this argument, of course, is that it makes the press clause a redundancy, to which Chief Justice Burger responded that freedom of the press "merited special attention simply because it had been more often the object of official restraints." *Id.*

———

The problem of defining "the press" for constitutional purposes seems formidable. The possibility that it includes all written communication is almost universally rejected. Professor Nimmer asserts that defining press to mean "written communication" is too narrow, because it excludes broadcasting, and too broad because it includes even writings that are not distributed to others. Melville B. Nimmer, "Introduction—Is Freedom of the Press a Redundancy: What Does It Add to Freedom of Speech?" 26 Hastings L.J. 639, 651–52 (1975).

Professor David Lange sees a similar problem: "If the press is defined broadly enough to include the pamphleteer and the underground, the definition also will have to approach speech so closely that the exclusion of speech will often seem arbitrary and unjustified. We will have, in Justice Stewart's words, 'a structural provision,' but with no distinct structure. If, on the other hand, the pamphleteer and the underground are excluded, the result is perverse; these are two elements in the contemporary press which the Framers themselves would have recognized." David Lange, The Speech and Debate Clauses, 23 UCLA L. Rev. 77, 106 (1975).

Recent economic and technological developments have raised even more vexing questions in identifying the "intended beneficiaries" of the press clause: "Are Internet service providers press? Databases such as Nexis or Westlaw? Online chat rooms or bulletin boards? Purveyors of Hollywood or Washington gossip? Online magazines or news services? Websites maintained by conventional media? Radio (or TV) talk shows? How about investment and financial services or credit-reporting agencies? Companies that compile, index, and deliver public records? Is there a difference between 'the press' and 'the media'?" David A. Anderson, Freedom of the Press, 80 Tex. L. Rev. 429, 435–36 (2002). Professor Anderson further notes that "[t]o the extent that existing law defines 'the press' at all, it does so mostly in terms of specific media forms." He argues that courts should try to avoid invoking the press clause in ways that would require a constitutional definition of the press, leaving the dispensation of special press protections to the political branches.

Does the problem of defining the press make it impossible to justify giving the press special constitutional protection? Even if we could reach consensus in defining the press, do media corporations need special protections?

3.   CAN MEDIA CORPORATIONS BE GIVEN SPECIAL PROTECTION?

Chief Justice Burger's insistence that business corporations have the same First Amendment rights as media corporations was cast into doubt by McConnell v. Federal Election Comm'n, 540 U.S. 93, 124 S.Ct. 619 (2003).

McConnell is a complex decision addressing the constitutionality of the Bipartisan Campaign Reform Act of 2002 (BCRA), which sought to overhaul campaign finance law. In *McConnell*, the Supreme Court upheld several portions of the BCRA, among them a provision prohibiting corporations (including most non-profit corporations) and unions from using general treasury funds to pay for "electioneering communications" while leaving media free to editorialize for or against candidates. The prohibition includes TV ads that (1) refer to a clearly identified candidate for Federal office; (2) are made within 30 days before a primary or within 60 days before a general election; and (3) are "targeted to the relevant electorate."

This provision was enacted to close a loophole in the Federal Election Campaign Act (FECA). Previously the FECA had prohibited corporations and unions from using general treasury funds to expressly advocate the election or defeat of candidates for federal office. Corporations and unions had circumvented around this provision by running ads that discussed general political issues and referred to a particular candidate's stance on those issues, without explicitly advocating voting for or against the candidate. The BCRA was intended to prevent corporations and unions from running such "sham" issue ads.

In upholding this provision, the Supreme Court viewed it as regulating expression by corporations and unions rather than banning it completely. *McConnell*, 124 S.Ct. at 694. Corporations and unions remained free to use PAC funds—funds specifically approved for that purpose by shareholders or union members—for electioneering communications.* The Court held that the State had a compelling interest in mitigating " 'the corrosive and distorting effects of immense aggregations of wealth' " on the political process, and preventing circumvention of valid limits on campaign contributions. Id. at 695.

The Court then rejected arguments that the regulation was both overbroad and underinclusive. The overbreadth argument failed because even if the regulation "inhibit[ed] some constitutionally protected corporate and union speech," its effect on such speech was not substantial " 'relative to the scope of the law's plainly legitimate applications.' " The Court rejected the argument that the regulation was underinclusive because it did not regulate electioneering communications in the print media or on the Internet, reasoning that Congress was entitled to reform the campaign finance system " 'one step at a time,' " addressing the most acute problems first. Id. at 697.

Finally, the Court rejected the argument that the regulation was unconstitutional because it exempted media corporations from its reach.

> FECA's § 304(f)(3)(B)(i) excludes from the definition of electioneering communications any "communication appearing in a news story, commentary, or editorial distributed through the facilities of any broadcast station, unless such facilities are owned by any political party, political

---

* These segregated funds are commonly known as Political Action Committees, or PACs.—eds.

committee or candidate." [ ] Plaintiffs argue this provision gives free rein to media companies to engage in speech without resort to PAC money. [The section's] effect, however, is much narrower than plaintiffs suggest. The provision excepts news items and commentary only; it does not afford carte blanche to media companies generally to ignore FECA's provisions. That statute's narrow exception is wholly consistent with First Amendment principles. "A valid distinction . . . exists between corporations that are part of the media industry and other corporations that are not involved in the regular business of imparting news to the public." [ ] Numerous federal statutes have drawn this distinction to ensure that the law "does not hinder or prevent the institutional press from reporting on, and publishing editorials about, newsworthy events." [ ] . . .

Id. at 697–98.

For Justice Scalia, who dissented, the answer was to give business corporations the same First Amendment Rights as the media. *McConnell*, 124 S.Ct. at 725. He criticized the majority's assumption that "a corporation does not enjoy full First Amendment protection":

[T]he text of the First Amendment does not limit its application in this fashion, even though '[b]y the end of the eighteenth century the corporation was a familiar figure in American economic life.' [ ] Nor is there any basis in reason why First Amendment rights should not attach to corporate associations—and we have said so. [Here, Justice Scalia cited several Supreme Court decisions protecting the speech rights of corporations, including *Bellotti*, supra p. 62.]

   . . . In the modern world, giving the government power to exclude corporations from the political debate enables it effectively to muffle the voices that best represent the most significant segments of the economy and the most passionately held social and political views. People who associate—who pool their financial resources—for purposes of economic enterprise overwhelmingly do so in the corporate form; and with increasing frequency, incorporation is chosen by those who associate to defend and promote particular ideas—such as the American Civil Liberties Union and the National Rifle Association, parties to these cases. Imagine, then, a government that wished to suppress nuclear power—or oil and gas exploration, or automobile manufacturing, or gun ownership, or civil liberties—and that had the power to prohibit corporate advertising against its proposals. To be sure, the individuals involved in, or benefited by, those industries, or interested in those causes, could (given enough time) form political action committees or other associations to make their case. But the organizational form in which those enterprises already *exist*, and in which they can most quickly and most effectively get their message across, is the corporate form. The First Amendment does not in my view permit the restriction of that political speech. And the same holds true for corporate electoral speech: A candidate should not be insulated from the most effective speech that the major participants in the economy and major incorporated interest groups can generate.

But what about the danger to the political system posed by "amassed wealth"? The most direct threat from that source comes in the form of undisclosed favors and payoffs to elected officials—which have already been criminalized. . . . The use of corporate wealth (like individual wealth) to speak to the electorate is unlikely to "distort" elections—*especially* if disclosure requirements *tell* the people where the speech is coming from. The premise of the First Amendment is that the American people are neither sheep nor fools, and hence fully capable of considering both the substance of the speech presented to them and its proximate and ultimate source. If that premise is wrong, our democracy has a much greater problem to overcome than merely the influence of amassed wealth. Given the premises of democracy, there is no such thing as *too much* speech.

Id. at 725–26 (emphasis provided).

In a separate dissent, Justice Thomas criticized the majority's distinction between media and nonmedia corporations. Justice Thomas argued that the logic of the majority's decision in *McConnell* supported "outright regulation of the press":

. . . None of the rationales offered by the defendants, and none of the reasoning employed by the Court [for regulating corporate speech], exempts the press. "This is so because of the difficulty, and perhaps impossibility, of distinguishing, either as a matter of fact or constitutional law, media corporations from [nonmedia] corporations." Bellotti, 435 U.S., at 796, 98 S.Ct. 1407 (Burger, C.J., concurring). Media companies can run procandidate editorials as easily as nonmedia corporations can pay for advertisements. Candidates can be just as grateful to media companies as they can be to corporations and unions. In terms of "the corrosive and distorting effects" of wealth accumulated by corporations that has "little or no correlation to the public's support for the corporation's political ideas," [ ], there is no distinction between a media corporation and a nonmedia corporation. Media corporations are influential. There is little doubt that the editorials and commentary they run can affect elections. Nor is there any doubt that media companies often wish to influence elections. One would think that the New York Times fervently hopes that its endorsement of Presidential candidates will actually influence people. What is to stop a future Congress from determining that the press is "too influential," and that the "appearance of corruption" is significant when media organizations endorse candidates or run "slanted" or "biased" news stories in favor of candidates or parties? Or, even easier, what is to stop a future Congress from concluding that the availability of unregulated media corporations creates a loophole that allows for easy "circumvention" of the limitations of the current campaign finance laws?

. . .

Id. at 740–41.

Professor Steven Shiffrin has offered additional objections to giving the media more First Amendment protection than others receive—at least in the area of tort law:

> . . . The idea that first amendment protections should be consciously divvied out in more generous doses to those with knowledge, wealth, and capacity to cause damage is indefensible. . . .
>
> Affording non-media defendants less first amendment protection than media defendants would deter non-media contributions to the democratic dialogue (and thus would weaken the media's contribution), would favor those with greater capacity to cause damage and with greater ability to compensate for that damage (by spreading the risk), would require difficult determinations as to which communications would and would not merit the label "press" or "media," would strain basic principles of first amendment equality, and would diminish respect for the democratic process.

Steven Shiffrin, Defamatory Non–Media Speech and First Amendment Methodology 25 UCLA L. Rev. 915, 934–35 (1978). Are the "non-media contributions to democratic dialogue" envisioned by Shiffrin the same as those envisioned by Justice Scalia? Is there a difference between the argument that the media should receive no more protection than individual speakers and the argument that media corporations should receive no more protection than other corporations?

Notes and Questions

1. After *McConnell*, may the government prevent media corporations from expressly advocating the election of a particular candidate in the weeks before an election? During the 2004 presidential election, a conservative advocacy group petitioned the Federal Election Commission to stop television ads for Michael Moore's documentary *Fahrenheit 9/11* on the grounds that the ads were "electioneering communications" forbidden by the BCRA. The documentary was released in the summer before the presidential election and was sharply critical of the Bush administration. The documentary explicitly advocated the defeat of President George W. Bush in the November elections. The FEC found that the ads for the documentary, which did not explicitly mention any presidential candidates, did not violate the BCRA. See "The Race to the White House; FEC Dismisses Complaint Against 'Fahrenheit' Ads," The Los Angeles Times, August 6, 2004, at A25. Would televising the documentary before the election have been a violation of the BCRA?

2. What might the media gain from a substantive Press Clause? The press at various times has claimed immunity from "gag" orders and prior restraints; a privilege not to respond to questions about reporters' and editors' states of mind; special protection against searches and seizures, at least when the press is not suspected of criminal activity; and general freedom from government regulations, such as those designed to promote fairness, diversity of press ownership, or other economic or social policies.

3. Might the press lose something from a substantive press clause? Several commentators have worried that if the media gain special rights because of their status as the public's eyes and ears, special responsibilities might follow. See Anthony Lewis, A Preferred Position for Journalism?, 7 Hofstra L. Rev. 595, 605 (1979); William W. Van Alstyne, The Hazards to the Press of Claiming a "Preferred Position," 28 Hastings L.J. 761 (1977).

For a different argument that a substantive Press Clause might result in less protection for the press, see David A. Anderson, Freedom of the Press, 80 Tex. L. Rev. at 510 (2002). After surveying both the constitutional and nonconstitutional sources of preferential treatment of the press, Anderson concludes: "The paradox of the Press Clause is this: giving the press special constitutional protection inevitably diminishes the ability to give the press special protection by nonconstitutional means." If the Supreme Court recognizes special constitutional press rights that must be accorded to anyone who meets the definition of press, other government entities may forego creating statutory or administrative protections because fighting over who gets them is too difficult or too costly: "The prospect of litigating these issues, or just the burden of devising policies to avoid litigation, might dissuade agencies from attempting to accommodate the press when doing so entails the exclusion of someone else."

> The media themselves are likely to disagree about the value of constitutionalizing decisions about the press. Established media have little to gain from it. They are the entities best protected by existing arrangements, they have the power and influence to retain those advantages, and because they are the beneficiaries of the status quo, they have that always helpful ally: inertia. The likely result of providing others with a basis for challenging these arrangements would be a dilution of the advantages enjoyed by the established media. . . . But whether to constitutionalize press protection ought not to be decided by choosing sides among the media. The question is whether it better serves the public's interest in freedom of the press.

Id. at 511–512.

4. FREEDOM OF SPEECH AND FREEDOM OF PRESS IN CONFLICT?

As noted earlier, sometimes the freedoms of speech and press may be in tension. In the following case that issue is framed in the context of a would-be speaker who would like to use a newspaper's space to respond to the paper's criticism of him—and a newspaper that does not want its facilities used in that manner.

It may be helpful in considering this problem to know about a strain of criticism of the marketplace of ideas. This has come from people who believe that concentration of ownership in the media industries has destroyed whatever marketplace may have existed when the First Amendment was adopted. In the mid 1940s, the nongovernmental Commission on Freedom of the Press (the Hutchins Commission), concluded that the press, despite the enforcement of antitrust laws, had become increasingly concentrated in the hands of fewer individuals. Media owners were reasonably free from government interference, but the First Amendment had little direct application to most people. The Commission therefore argued that publishers and broadcasters should be more socially responsible, treating each media outlet as a means of disseminating a wide range of viewpoints. It further suggested that the government finance new communications outlets and that an independent government agency oversee the press's performance.

Professor William Ernest Hocking expanded on the Commission's work in his book, Freedom of the Press (1947), which argued that the government may regulate to ensure the press fulfills its public responsibility to provide citizens with "adequate" news and information, an admittedly "indefinite standard," but one which implies giving the public a breadth of news coverage and viewpoints. Another commission member, Professor Zechariah Chafee, stated that the press could not play its proper part in society in the "mere absence of governmental restrictions." Rather, "affirmative action by the government or others" would be needed. Chafee argued that "just as a free market for goods needs law against monopoly," the government should regulate the marketplace of ideas to "promote rather than restrict free speech." Such laws might require "essential facilities accessible to all," methods to assure that communication channels remain open, and measures directed at particular communication industries "intended to promote freedom, improve content, or otherwise make them perform their proper function in a free society." 2 Zechariah Chafee, Government and Mass Communications 471 (1947).

A more recent advocate of the Commission's approach is Professor Jerome A. Barron. He believes the marketplace of ideas is an antiquated concept because the media and society have changed so much since 1791. It is difficult for a person to begin a newspaper because of the prohibitive cost or to begin a broadcast service because of licensing restrictions. Barron sees the media as censors because they limit the views they disseminate and permit few new or unpopular ideas to be heard widely. Barron concludes that those who do not control media should be able to express their views through the mass media. "At the very minimum," Barron writes, "the creation of two remedies is essential—(1) a nondiscriminating right to purchase editorial advertisements in daily newspapers, and (2) a right of reply for public figures and public officers defamed in newspapers." Jerome A. Barron, Freedom of the Press for Whom? 6 (1973). See also Jerome A. Barron, Access to the Press—A New First Amendment Right, 80 Harv. L. Rev. 1641 (1967).

Barron had an opportunity to try to persuade the Supreme Court to make his ideas the law. He represented Pat Tornillo, the litigant seeking access to the press, in the case that follows.

Miami Herald Publishing Co. v. Tornillo

Supreme Court of the United States, 1974.
418 U.S. 241, 94 S. Ct. 2831, 41 L. Ed.2d 730, 1 Med. L. Rptr. 1898.

MR. CHIEF JUSTICE BURGER delivered the opinion of the Court.

The issue in this case is whether a state statute granting a political candidate a right to equal space to reply to criticism and attacks on his record by a newspaper, violates the guarantees of a free press.

I.

In the fall of 1972, appellee, Executive Director of the Classroom Teachers Association, apparently a teachers' collective bargaining agent, was a candidate for the Florida House of Representatives. On September 20, 1972, and again on September 29, 1972, appellant printed editorials critical of appellee's candidacy. In response to these editorials appellee demanded that appellant print verbatim his replies, defending the role of the Classroom Teachers Association and the organization's accomplishments for the citizens of Dade County. Appellant declined to print the appellee's replies, and appellee brought suit in Circuit Court, Dade County, seeking declaratory and injunctive relief and actual and punitive damages in excess of $5,000. The action was premised on Florida Statute § 104.38 (1973), a "right of reply" statute. . . .[2]

[Appellant sought a declaration that § 104.38 was unconstitutional. The Circuit Court held that the section violated both the state and federal constitutions. On direct appeal, the Florida Supreme Court reversed, holding that the statute furthered the "broad societal interest in the free flow of information to the public." It also held that the statute is not impermissibly vague because it informs "those who are subject to it as to what conduct on their part will render them liable to its penalties." Civil remedies, including damages, were held to be available under this statute. The state supreme court narrowed the statute by construing "any reply" to mean a reply "wholly responsive to the charge made." Moreover, the reply must be "neither libelous nor slanderous of the publication nor anyone else, nor vulgar nor profane." The case was remanded for further proceedings accordingly.]

III.

A.

The challenged statute creates a right to reply to press criticism of a candidate for nomination or election. The statute was enacted in 1913, and this is only the second recorded case decided under its provisions.

---

2. "104.38 *Newspaper Assailing Candidate in an Election; Space for Reply.* If any newspaper in its columns assails the personal character of any candidate for nomination or for election in any election, or charges said candidate with malfeasance or misfeasance in office, or otherwise attacks his official record, or gives to another free space for such purpose, such newspaper shall upon request of such candidate immediately publish free of cost any reply he may make thereto in as conspicuous a place and in the same kind of type as the matter that calls for such reply, provided such reply does not take up more space than the matter replied to. Any person or firm failing to comply with the provisions of this section shall be guilty of a misdemeanor of the first degree, punishable as provided in § 775.082 or § 775.083."

Appellant contends the statute is void on its face because it purports to regulate the content of a newspaper in violation of the First Amendment. Alternatively it is urged that the statute is void for vagueness since no editor could know exactly what words would call the statute into operation. It is also contended that the statute fails to distinguish between critical comment which is and which is not defamatory.

B.

[In this section the Court "set out in some detail" virtually every argument made by proponents of access to the media. The Court noted that access advocates argued that in 1791 "[a] true marketplace of ideas existed in which there was relatively easy access to the channels of communication" but at the time *Tornillo* came before the Court concentration of ownership in the media industry, the "elimination of competing newspapers in most of our large cities," and other technological and economic developments had "place[d] in a few hands the power to inform the American people and shape public opinion." The increasing power and influence of the media had also deprived the public of meaningful participation in public debate. The Court summarized the historical and economic arguments of access advocates as follows:]

It is urged that the claim of newspapers to be "surrogates for the public" carries with it a concomitant fiduciary obligation to account for that stewardship. From this premise it is reasoned that the only effective way to insure fairness and accuracy and to provide for some accountability is for government to take affirmative action.

[The Court then reviewed legal arguments supporting enforced access:

—Associated Press v. United States, 326 U.S. 1 (1945) (upholding enforcement of antitrust laws against news service, and noting that the First Amendment "rests on the assumption that the widest possible dissemination of information from diverse and antagonistic sources is essential to the welfare of the public"; freedom of the press "does not sanction repression of that freedom by private interests").

—New York Times Co. v. Sullivan, 376 U.S. 254 (1964) (in limiting state libel law the Court spoke of a "profound national commitment to the principle that debate on public issues should be uninhibited, robust, and wide-open").

—Rosenbloom v. Metromedia, Inc., 403 U.S. 29 (1971) (plurality opinion in libel case asserts that if states "fear that private citizens will not be able to respond adequately to publicity involving them, the solution lies in the direction of ensuring their ability to respond, rather than in stifling public discussion of matters of public concern"—and observing that "some states have adopted retraction statutes or right-of-reply statutes").

—Passages from books or articles by Justice Douglas (expressing "deep concern" regarding the effects of newspaper monopolies), Professor Barron (his previously cited writings) and Professor Emerson (contending that a "limited right of access to the press can be safely enforced," but preferring "[g]overnment measures to encourage a multiplicity of outlets, rather than compelling a few outlets to represent everybody").]

IV.

However much validity may be found in these arguments, at each point the implementation of a remedy such as an enforceable right of access necessarily calls for some mechanism, either governmental or consensual. If it is governmental coercion, this at once brings about a confrontation with the express provisions of the First Amendment and the judicial gloss on that Amendment developed over the years.

The Court foresaw the problems relating to government-enforced access as early as its decision in *Associated Press v. United States*, supra. There it carefully contrasted the private "compulsion to print" called for by the Association's bylaws with the provisions of the District Court decree against appellants which "does not compel AP or its members to permit publication of anything which their 'reason' tells them should not be published." 326 U.S., at 20 n. 18. In Branzburg v. Hayes, 408 U.S. 665, 681 (1972), we emphasized that the cases then before us "involve no intrusions upon speech or assembly, no prior restraint or restriction on what the press may publish, and no express or implied command that the press publish what it prefers to withhold." In Columbia Broadcasting System, Inc. v. Democratic National Committee, 412 U.S. 94, 117 (1973), the plurality opinion as to Part III noted:

> "The power of a privately owned newspaper to advance its own political, social, and economic views is bounded by only two factors: first, the acceptance of a sufficient number of readers—and hence advertisers—to assure financial success; and, second, the journalistic integrity of its editors and publishers."

An attitude strongly adverse to any attempt to extend a right of access to newspapers was echoed by several Members of this Court in their separate opinions in that case. Id., at 145 (Stewart, J., concurring); id., at 182 n. 12 (Brennan, J., dissenting). Recently, while approving a bar against employment advertising specifying "male" or "female" preference, the Court's opinion in Pittsburgh Press Co. v. Human Relations Comm'n, 413 U.S. 376, 391 (1973), took pains to limit its holding within narrow bounds:

> "Nor, *a fortiori,* does our decision authorize any restriction whatever, whether of content or layout, on stories or commentary originated by Pittsburgh Press, its columnists, or its contributors. On the contrary, we reaffirm unequivocally the protection afforded to editorial judgment and to the free expression of views on these and other issues, however controversial."

Dissenting in *Pittsburgh Press,* Mr. Justice Stewart, joined by Mr. Justice Douglas, expressed the view that no "government agency—local, state, or federal—can tell a newspaper in advance what it can print and what it cannot." [ ]

We see that beginning with *Associated Press,* supra, the Court has expressed sensitivity as to whether a restriction or requirement constituted the compulsion exerted by government on a newspaper to print that which it would not otherwise print. The clear implication has been that any such compulsion to publish that which " 'reason' tells them should not be published" is unconstitutional. A responsible press is an undoubtedly desirable goal, but press responsibility is not mandated by the Constitution and like many other virtues it cannot be legislated.

Appellee's argument that the Florida statute does not amount to a restriction of appellant's right to speak because "the statute in question here has not prevented the Miami Herald from saying anything it wished" begs the core question. Compelling editors or publishers to publish that which " 'reason' tells them should not be published" is what is at issue in this case. The Florida statute operates as a command in the same sense as a statute or regulation forbidding appellant to publish specified matter. Governmental restraint on publishing need not fall into familiar or traditional patterns to be subject to constitutional limitations on governmental powers. Grosjean v. American Press Co., 297 U.S. 233, 244–45 (1936). The Florida statute exacts a penalty on the basis of the content of a newspaper. The first phase of the penalty resulting from the compelled printing of a reply is exacted in terms of the cost in printing and composing time and materials and in taking up space that could be devoted to other material the newspaper may have preferred to print. It is correct, as appellee contends, that a newspaper is not subject to the finite technological limitations of time that confront a broadcaster but it is not correct to say that, as an economic reality, a newspaper can proceed to infinite expansion of its column space to accommodate the replies that a government agency determines or a statute commands the readers should have available.

Faced with the penalties that would accrue to any newspaper that published news or commentary arguably within the reach of the right-of-access statute, editors might well conclude that the safe course is to avoid controversy. Therefore, under the operation of the Florida statute, political and electoral coverage would be blunted or reduced. Government-enforced right of access inescapably "dampens the vigor and limits the variety of public debate," New York Times Co. v. Sullivan, supra, 376 U.S. at 279. The Court, in Mills v. Alabama, 384 U.S. 214, 218 (1966) stated:

"[T]here is practically universal agreement that a major purpose of [the First] Amendment was to protect the free discussion of governmental affairs. This of course includes discussions of candidates. . . ."

Even if a newspaper would face no additional costs to comply with a compulsory access law and would not be forced to forgo publication of news or opinion by the inclusion of a reply, the Florida statute fails to clear the barriers of the First Amendment because of its intrusion into the function of editors. A newspaper is more than a passive receptacle or conduit for news, comment, and advertising. The choice of material to go into a newspaper, and the decisions made as to limitations on the size and content of the paper, and treatment of public issues and public officials—whether fair or unfair—constitute the exercise of editorial control and judgment. It has yet to be demonstrated how governmental regulation of this crucial process can be exercised consistent with First Amendment guarantees of a free press as they have evolved to this time. Accordingly, the judgment of the Supreme Court of Florida is reversed.

It is so ordered.

MR. JUSTICE BRENNAN, with whom MR. JUSTICE REHNQUIST joins, concurring.

I join the Court's opinion which, as I understand it, addresses only "right of reply" statutes and implies no view upon the constitutionality of "retraction" statutes affording plaintiffs able to prove defamatory falsehoods a statutory action to require publication of a retraction. See generally Note, Vindication of the Reputation of a Public Official, 80 Harv. L. Rev. 1730, 1739–1747 (1967).

MR. JUSTICE WHITE, concurring.

. . . A newspaper or magazine is not a public utility subject to "reasonable" governmental regulation in matters affecting the exercise of journalistic judgment as to what shall be printed. [ ]. We have learned, and continue to learn, from what we view as the unhappy experiences of other nations where government has been allowed to meddle in the internal editorial affairs of newspapers. Regardless of how beneficent-sounding the purposes of controlling the press might be, we prefer "the power of reason as applied through public discussion" and remain intensely skeptical about those measures that would allow government to insinuate itself into the editorial rooms of this Nation's press.

. . .

To justify this statute, Florida advances a concededly important interest of ensuring free and fair elections by means of an electorate informed about the issues. But prior compulsion by government in matters going to the very nerve center of a newspaper—the decision as to what copy will or will not be included in any given edition—collides with the First Amendment. Woven into the fabric of the First Amendment is the unexceptionable, but nonetheless timeless, sentiment that "liberty of the press is in peril as soon as the government tries to compel what is to go into a newspaper." 2 Z. Chafee, Government and Mass Communications 633 (1947).

. . . [T]his law runs afoul of the elementary First Amendment proposition that government may not force a newspaper to print copy which, in its journalistic discretion, it chooses to leave on the newsroom floor. . . .

Notes and Questions

1.   The Court says the statute penalizes newspapers that publish material that might trigger a right of reply. What is that penalty? Assume that the statute in Tornillo required the newspaper to accept Tornillo's reply as a paid advertisement at prevailing rates. Most papers try to maintain a

certain ratio of advertising to news, so in the aggregate an increase in advertising generates an increase in news space. If the likely effect of the statute would be to increase the newspaper's revenues and allow it to increase the amount of space dedicated to news, would the statute still be unconstitutional? Is the "intrusion into the function of editors" an independent ground of decision?

2.   Is the case for a right-of-reply stronger or weaker when it is limited to a pending election? Professor Cass Sunstein, who questions the outcome or at least the rationale in *Tornillo*, suggests that the Court may have suspected that the "special problem with [the statute] was that it was limited to candidates for office," which gave the Court reason "to suspect that the law was an effort by political candidates to insulate themselves from attack." Cass R. Sunstein, Democracy and the Problem of Free Speech 271 n.20 (1993). Might incumbents reasonably think that they would benefit more from this type of statute than would challengers? Recall Professor Schauer's argument that one reason for according speech special protection is distrust of government, including "an appreciation of the fallibility of political leaders." Schauer, Free Speech: A Philosophical Enquiry, supra p. 24.

On the other hand, the Florida Supreme Court thought the statute's limited application to electoral situations strengthened the argument for the statute:

> The public *"need to know"* is most critical during an election campaign. By enactment of [this statute] our legislature responded to the need for insuring free and fair elections. . . . The Legislature in 1913 decided that owners of the printing press had already achieved such political clout that when they engaged in character assailings, the victim's electoral chances were unduly and improperly diminished. To assure fairness in campaigns, the assailed candidate had to be provided opportunity to respond: otherwise not only the candidate would be hurt *but also* the people would be deprived of both sides of the controversy. (287 So.2d 78).

3.   On another point, Professor Sunstein observes that the reason he cannot write for the New York Times is that the paper "is given the legal power to exclude people who want to write for it. . . . [I]f I am stopped from doing so, it is in significant part because the *Times* is able to invoke the law of trespass to back up its exclusionary decision. Without the law of trespass, we would be in the state of nature. . . . The system [of protection for speech] in a regime of property rights may well be fine or even wonderful; but it should be assessed in terms of its consequences for speech." Sunstein notes that legal entitlements like trespass law "enable some private actors but not others to speak and be heard." If Sunstein is correct that the media's power to exclude derives largely from legal entitlements, should free speech law be used to offset the benefits conferred by these entitlements? From what other sources does the media's power to exclude derive?

4. Access proponents argued that a right of access to media could be implied from the First Amendment itself. In *Tornillo,* the right had been created by the legislature—and the judiciary was being asked to uphold the statute rather than to create a new right at the constitutional level. Does one situation present a stronger case than the other?

5. Can *Tornillo* be seen as a "right not to speak" case?

E. ARE ELECTRONIC MEDIA DIFFERENT?

In the previous section we considered whether the press might be treated differently from other speakers for some First Amendment purposes. We now consider whether the nature of the medium might warrant differential treatment under the First Amendment. This issue has been most commonly raised in the context of television and radio broadcasting, and has often focused on the technical characteristics of the electromagnetic spectrum used by those media.

The electromagnetic spectrum is a unique natural resource in many different ways. Utilization does not use it up or wear it out. It does not require continual maintenance to remain usable. It is subject to pollution (interference), but once the interference is removed the pollution and its effects disappear totally. It is everywhere, in the sense that it surrounds us whether we are in a building or outside, and it is intangible, in that we cannot touch it, but it has very distinct properties and, as we discuss below, is almost always scarce. It has many characteristics of a public resource, like a park, not only because of its omnipresence but also because it can be used by many people, but, like private property, it can be occupied to the exclusion of others.

Use of the electromagnetic spectrum is governed by five properties: space, time, frequency, power, and antenna height. For example, two broadcasters can broadcast on the same frequency at the same time if they are far enough apart, operating at low enough power, or their antennae are sufficiently low or separated by mountains that are sufficiently high. Where two users of spectrum are not sufficiently separated by space, time, frequency, power, or height, they interfere with each other. A particularly powerful signal may drown out a weaker one or, as is more commonly the case, the signals will be of less quality or even unintelligible as a result of their interference with each other.

The technological characteristics and potential uses of the broadcast media led to regulation of these media unlike that applicable to print media. During the 1920s, hundreds of radio stations began broadcasting with little or no government oversight. The Supreme Court described the situation thus: "the allocation of frequencies was left entirely to the private sector, and the result was chaos." Red Lion Broadcasting Co. v. Federal Communications Comm'n, 395 U.S. 367, 1 Med. L. Rptr. 2053 (1969). Competing stations broadcast at the same frequency in the same geographic location, and signal interference made it impossible for them to reach their listeners. It soon became apparent that governmental regulation was necessary in order for the broadcasting system to function. Indeed, both broadcasters and government regulators turned to Congress for help.

Congress responded with the Radio Act of 1927. The Act created the Federal Radio Commission, which became the Federal Communications Commission in 1934, to allocate the electromagnetic spectrum available for commercial and public broadcasting. Broadcast licenses were issued for a limited term, and licenses were to be granted and renewed as dictated by "public interest, convenience, or necessity." Broadcast licensees that carried the advertisements of one political candidate were required to give or sell equal time to opposing candidates. The Act forbade censorship of broadcast programming while it banned obscene, indecent, or profane language.

The Communications Act of 1934 soon replaced the Radio Act, although it maintained the provisions governing broadcasters virtually intact. The 1934 Act centralized federal authority for overseeing the conduct of common carriers (telephone and telegraph operators) and broadcasters in the Federal Communications Commission. The rules promulgated and enforced by the FCC under the Communications Act have given rise to extensive litigation about the First Amendment rights of broadcasters and the application of the amendment to broadcasting. Although the Communications Act was substantially amended by the Telecommunications Competition and Deregulation Act of 1996, the FCC today continues to issue licenses to broadcasters, renew licenses periodically, insure that broadcasters comply with technical and operations rules, and develop rules to regulate broadcasting.

Red Lion. One of the most important cases regarding broadcasters' First Amendment rights addressed issues similar to those presented by *Tornillo* in the context of radio broadcasting. In Red Lion Broadcasting Co. v. Federal Communications Comm'n, 395 U.S. 367, 1 Med. L. Rptr. 2053 (1969), the FCC was in the process of creating a rule out of its common law practice of insisting that when " 'during the presentation of views on a controversial issue of public importance, an attack is made upon the honesty, character, integrity or like personal qualities of an identified person or group, the licensee shall, within a reasonable time, [no longer than a week] after the attack' " send that person or group a script or tape of the attack and " 'an offer of a reasonable opportunity to respond over the licensee's facilities.' " During the mid 1960s two cases arose challenging the "personal attack rule." The Supreme Court addressed both cases in *Red Lion* and unanimously upheld the rule. Justice White, writing for the Court, began by noting that:

> [D]ifferences in the characteristics of new media justify differences in the First Amendment standard applied to them.
>
> Just as the Government may limit the use of sound-amplifying equipment potentially so noisy that it drowns out civilized private speech, so may the Government limit the use of broadcast equipment. The risk of free speech of a broadcaster, the user of a sound truck, or

any other individual does not embrace a right to snuff out the free speech of others.

When two people converse face to face, both should not speak at once if either is to be clearly understood. But the range of the human voice is so limited that there could be meaningful communications if half the people in the United States were talking and the other half listening. Just as clearly, half the people might publish and the other half read. But the reach of radio signals is incomparably greater than the range of the human voice and the problem of interference is a massive reality. The lack of know-how and equipment may keep many from the air, but only a tiny fraction of those with resources and intelligence can hope to communicate by radio at the same time if intelligible communication is to be had, even if the entire radio spectrum is utilized in the present state of commercially acceptable technology.

The Court noted that it was this chaos in the early days that led Congress to develop a licensing system. Then:

Where there are substantially more individuals who want to broadcast than there are frequencies to allocate, it is idle to posit an unabridgeable First Amendment right to broadcast comparable to the right of every individual to speak, write, or publish. If 100 persons want broadcast licenses but there are only 10 frequencies to allocate, all of them may have the same "right" to a license; but if there is to be any effective communication by radio, only a few can be licensed and the rest must be barred from the airwaves. It would be strange if the First Amendment, aimed at protecting and furthering communications, prevented the Government from making radio communication possible by requiring licenses to broadcast and by limiting the number of licenses so as not to overcrowd the spectrum.

. . .

By the same token, as far as the First Amendment is concerned those who are licensed stand no better than those to whom licenses are refused. A license permits broadcasting, but the licensee has no constitutional right to be the one who holds the license or to monopolize a radio frequency to the exclusion of his fellow citizens. There is nothing in the First Amendment which prevents the Government from requiring a licensee to share his frequency with others and to conduct himself as a proxy or fiduciary with obligations to present those views and voices which are representative of his community and which would otherwise, by necessity, be barred from the airwaves.

This is not to say that the First Amendment is irrelevant to public broadcasting. On the contrary, it has a major role to play as the Congress itself recognized in § 326, which forbids FCC interference with "the right of free speech by means of radio communication." Because of the scarcity of radio frequencies, the Government is permitted to put restraints on licensees in favor of others whose views should be expressed on this unique medium. But the people as a whole retain their interest in free speech by radio and their collective right to have the medium function consistently with the ends and purposes of the First Amendment. It is the right of the viewers and listeners, not the right of the broadcasters, which is paramount. [ ] It is the purpose of the First Amendment to preserve an uninhibited marketplace of ideas in which truth will ultimately prevail, rather than to countenance monopolization of that market, whether it be by the Government itself or a private licensee. [ ]; [*Times v. Sullivan*]; Abrams v. United States, 250 U.S. 616, 630 (1919) (Holmes, J., dissenting). "[S]peech concerning public affairs is more than self-expression; it is the essence of self-government." [*Garrison v. Louisiana*]. See Brennan, The Supreme Court and the Meiklejohn Interpretation of the First Amendment, 79 Harv. L. Rev. 1 (1965). It is the right of the public to receive suitable access to social, political, esthetic, moral, and other ideas and experiences which is crucial here. That right may not constitutionally be abridged either by Congress or by the FCC.

The Court then turned to the specific constraint in the case. Justice White observed that the "Government could surely have decreed that each frequency should be shared among all or some of those who wish to use it, each being assigned a portion of the broadcast day or the broadcast week." Nor could the personal attack rule be distinguished from the requirement that broadcasters must give or sell time to political candidates if the station has given or sold time to their opponents—a provision that had never been questioned. Then:

> Nor can we say that it is inconsistent with the First Amendment goal of producing an informed public capable of conducting its own affairs to require a broadcaster to permit answers to personal attacks occurring in the course of discussing controversial issues, or to require that the political opponents of those endorsed by the station be given a chance to communicate with the public. Otherwise, station owners and a few networks would have unfettered power to make time available only to the highest bidders, to communicate only their own views on public issues, people and candidates, and to permit on the air only those with whom they agreed. There is no sanctuary in the First Amendment for unlimited private censorship operating in a medium not open to all.

The Court then rejected the claim that if this type of obligation is imposed, licensees will eliminate coverage of important political issues. The opinion noted that broadcasters had not aired bland programming in the past and "even now they do not assert that they intend to abandon their efforts in this regard. It would be better if the FCC's encouragement were never necessary to induce the broadcasters to meet their responsibility. And if experience with the administration of those doctrines indicates that they have the net effect of reducing rather than enhancing the volume and quality of coverage, there will be time enough to reconsider the constitutional implications. The fairness doctrine in the past has had no such overall effect." If licensees "should suddenly prove timorous, the Commission is not powerless to insist that they give adequate and fair attention to public issues. It does not violate the First Amendment to treat licensees given the privilege of using scarce radio frequencies as proxies for the entire community, obligated to give suitable time and attention to matters of great public concern. . . . Congress need not stand idly by and permit those with licenses to ignore the problems which beset the people or to exclude from the airways anything but their own views of fundamental questions. The statute, long administrative practice, and cases are to this effect."

After rejecting claims of "vagueness," the Court also rejected the claim that even if past scarcity justified this rule current conditions no longer did so:

> Scarcity is not entirely a thing of the past. Advances in technology, such as microwave transmission, have led to more efficient utilization of the frequency spectrum, but uses for that spectrum have also grown apace. Portions of the spectrum must be reserved for vital uses unconnected with human communication, such as radio-navigational aids used by aircraft and vessels. Conflicts have even emerged between such vital functions as defense preparedness and experimentation in methods of averting midair collisions through radio warning devices. "Land mobile services" such as police, ambulance, fire department, public utility, and other communications systems have been occupying an increasingly crowded portion of the frequency spectrum and there are, apart from licensed amateur radio operators' equipment, 5,000,000 transmitters operated on the "citizens' band" which is also increasingly congested. Among the various uses for radio frequency space, including marine, aviation, amateur, military, and common carrier users, there are easily enough claimants to permit use of the whole with an even smaller allocation to broadcast radio and television uses than now exists.

The opinion noted that the "very high frequency television spectrum is, in the country's major markets, almost entirely occupied, although space reserved for ultra high frequency television transmission, which is a relatively recent development as a commercially viable alternative, has not yet been completely filled."

> The rapidity with which technological advances succeed one another to create more efficient use of spectrum space on the one hand, and to create new uses for that space by ever growing numbers of people on the other, makes it unwise to speculate on the future allocation of that space. It is enough to say that the resource is one of considerable and growing importance whose scarcity impelled its regulation by an agency authorized by Congress. Nothing in this record, or in our own researches, convinces us that the resource is no longer one for which there are more immediate and potential uses than can be accommodated, and for which wise planning is essential. This does not mean, of

course, that every possible wavelength must be occupied at every hour by some vital use in order to sustain the congressional judgment.

Even where gaps existed, Justice White's opinion for the Court noted that:

> existing broadcasters have often attained their present position because of their initial government selection in competition with others before new technological advances opened new opportunities for further uses. Long experience in broadcasting, confirmed habits of listeners and viewers, network affiliation, and other advantages in program procurement give existing broadcasters a substantial advantage over new entrants, even where new entry is technologically possible. These advantages are the fruit of a preferred position conferred by the Government. Some present possibility for new entry by competing stations is not enough, in itself, to render unconstitutional the Government's effort to assure that a broadcaster's programming ranges widely enough to serve the public interest.

> In view of the scarcity of broadcast frequencies, the Government's role in allocating those frequencies, and the legitimate claims of those unable without governmental assistance to gain access to those frequencies for expression of their views, we hold the regulations and ruling at issue here are both authorized by statute and constitutional.

––––––

The personal attack rule is no longer in effect. See Radio–Television News Directors Ass'n v. FCC, 229 F.3d 269 (2000) (issuing writ of mandamus vacating the personal attack and political editorial rules). However, the paradigm of broadcast regulation outlined in *Red Lion* continues to have validity. For now, the important point is to see how differently the Court treated broadcasting in 1969 and print media in 1974. Many expected that in *Tornillo* the Court would focus on the relationship to *Red Lion,* but the Court did not mention the case.

Whether the technologies of certain media justify differential First Amendment treatment has arisen in the context of the Internet, cable, and direct broadcast satellite. In Reno v. ACLU, 521 U.S. 844, 868–70 (1997), the Supreme Court refused to apply the *Red Lion* paradigm to the Internet because it had not historically been subject to regulation and is not characterized by scarcity; thus, the Court held that there is "no basis of qualifying the level of First Amendment scrutiny that should be applied to this medium." As we shall see in Chapter III, the Supreme Court in Turner Broadcasting System, Inc. v. Federal Communications Commission ("Turner I"), infra p. 202, also refused to apply the "relaxed standard of scrutiny" from *Red Lion* to cable on the ground that it is not characterized by physical scarcity. The Court observed that "given the rapid advances in fiber optics and digital compression technology, soon there may be no practical limitation on the number of speakers who can use the cable medium. Nor is there any danger of physical interference between two cable speakers attempting to share the same channel." The Court rejected the argument that "market dysfunction" (or what might be termed economic scarcity) justified applying *Red Lion* to cable television because "the special physical characteristics of broadcast transmissions, not the economic characteristics of the broadcast market, are what underlies our broadcast jurisprudence," However, the Court also refused to apply *Tornillo* to the cable regulations at issue in the case, basing its refusal in part on the "technological differences between newspapers and cable television." These differences, particulary the "bottleneck" control that cable operators can exercise over their broadcast competitors, are discussed in *Turner I*, infra pp. 206. The District of Columbia Circuit Court of Appeals did apply *Red Lion*'s "relaxed standard of scrutiny" to direct broadcast satellite due to the "finite number of satellite positions available for DBS use." Time Warner Entertainment Co. v. Federal Communications Comm'n, 93 F.3d 957 (D.C. Cir. 1996), discussed in Chapter II, *infra* p. 218.

In *Red Lion*, the Court focused on the scarcity of electromagnetic spectrum as a justification for treating broadcast media differently than print media. Other, often related, justifications that have enjoyed varying degrees of success include:

Public ownership. Under the Communications Act of 1934, the public retains ownership of the airwaves, and broadcasters receive a license for a limited period of time to use the airwaves in the public interest. See 47 U.S.C. § 301. Although the Telecommunications Act of 1996, 47 U.S.C. § 309(1) (2000), revised the licensing criteria to be employed by the FCC, the Act still requires the FCC to base license renewal in part on the public interest. The Supreme Court invoked the FCC's " 'broad' mandate to assure broadcasters operate in the public interest" as a justification for a requirement that broadcasters maintain records of "politically related broadcasting requests" to aid the government in policing campaign finance restrictions. McConnell v. Federal Communications Comm'n, supra 63, at p. 712.

Intrusiveness. Broadcasting, which comes into the home in a way that print media do not, is often said to be intrusive. In essence, the argument is that some affirmative act is required before a newspaper or magazine enters the house. Although it is true that a similar affirmative act is required before a radio or television set is brought into the home, the homeowner does not know the content of the program that will come out of that set when it is turned on or when the dial or remote control is activated. In Federal Communications Comm'n v. Pacifica Foundation, 438 U.S. 726, 3 Med. L. Rptr. 2553 (1978), reprinted infra p. 149, involving indecent speech, Justice Stevens for the majority asserted that the way in which broadcasting enters the home is such that "prior warnings cannot completely protect the listener or viewer from unexpected program content."

Pervasiveness. In *Pacifica*, Justice Stevens also observed that "the broadcasting media have established a uniquely pervasive presence in the lives of all Americans." Others have tied the "uniquely pervasive" theme to the large number of radios (five per household) and television sets in the country (at least one in 98.2 percent of all households), and the number of hours per days that the average television set is on (seven hours).

Inability to control access. Related to the intrusiveness and pervasiveness points is the notion that broadcasters cannot control the reach of their messages. Unlike movie house and bookstore proprietors (and cable programmers), who can control access, the broadcaster's message is available to anyone with access to a set. Although the same is true of newspaper, magazine and book publishers as well, in each of these cases the physical copy still must be delivered or sold by someone who has the opportunity to prevent individuals or members of identifiable groups from acquiring the copy.

Power. The fact that more people say they get their news and information from television than from print media has led some to suggest that the "power" of the broadcast media alone justifies the imposition of some content regulation. When the print media were the most powerful in the country, would this same argument have justified various types of regulation of those media? If so, what types of regulation would be justified by a "power" analysis?

Vividness. It is often claimed that because broadcasting uses more of the senses than does the print medium, or at least uses more vivid senses, the influence of broadcasting is greater. Some have argued that the high-tech reporting of the Gulf War may have contributed to motivating public opinion in favor of Operation Desert Storm, just as vivid field reporting of the Vietnam War may have been a strong factor in shifting public attitude against that war, both of which were beyond the potential of print journalism. What effect did the footage obtained by "embedded" reporters who accompanied troops in the Iraq war have on support for the war at its inception?

Glorification of violence. There is now much concern that television might be particularly powerful in its capacity to induce some viewers to emulate antisocial behavior that these viewers see on the screen. Is this more likely to occur with television than with radio? Than with print media? Than with movies viewed in a theater? Than with a DVD viewed on a television screen at home?

Impact on children. The impact of broadcasting on children is said to be different from that of the print media because broadcasting reaches children who are too young to read, and also is said to reach them in a more influential way. Is this equally true of both radio and television? Would this justify special regulation of the content of programming? Would this justify regulation of the Internet?

Combinations of characteristics. As potent as some observers think each of these individual factors may be, it is clear that in combination they may be even more potent. Which groupings seem most likely to appear together? Do groupings necessarily exacerbate the problems that exist singly?

––––––

The FCC, the U.S. Court of Appeals for the District of Columbia, many scholars, and Justices Douglas and Stewart have argued that the scarcity doctrine no longer justifies special constitutional treatment of government restrictions on broadcast expression. See Columbia Broad. Sys., Inc. v. Democratic Nat'l Comm., 412 U.S. 94, 144 (1973) (Stewart, J., concurring); *id.* at 149 (Douglas, J., concurring); Telecommunications Research & Action Center v. Fed. Communications Comm'n, 801 F.2d 501 (D.C. Cir. 1986); In re Complaint of Syracuse Peace Council against Television Station WTVH Syracuse, New York, 2 FCC Rcd. 5043, 5048 (1987) (mem. opinion and order).

Opponents of the scarcity justification have advanced a variety of arguments for their position. Five of the most prominent are:

a. There isn't any scarcity. There have always been unallocated frequencies for some spectrum use, for example, unallocated AM, FM, or VHF frequencies in markets thought too small to support commercial service; UHF frequencies where broadcasters preferred VHF frequencies; and AM frequencies where broadcasters were holding out for FM stereo.

In 1950 only 87 percent of television broadcasting stations authorized by the FCC were in operation; only 93 percent of authorized AM and FM radio stations were in operation. By 1990, the total usage of authorized frequencies was even smaller. Only 85 percent of television broadcasting stations authorized by the FCC were in operation; 95 percent of authorized AM radio stations were in operation; and 84 percent of authorized FM radio stations were in operation. The total number of commercial and public broadcasters holding licenses from the FCC in 2004 was 17,033.

b. The government created any scarcity that exists. The government regulates how much frequency to assign to broadcasters, how long they can broadcast, how much power they can use, and where and how high they can locate their transmission facilities. If there were qualified applicants who were denied the opportunity to broadcast, the government could have accommodated them by allocating less bandwidth to other broadcasters or by restricting the time of day at which they could broadcast, or how much power or how tall an antenna they could use.

c. Scarcity isn't necessarily bad or unusual. Market demand often results in scarcity as service and product providers gear up to respond to that demand. Scarcity often contributes to innovation. If there aren't enough 6 KHz VHF broadcast frequencies, broadcasters will develop technologies for broadcasting in 4 KHz. If there isn't enough newsprint, newspapers will begin recycling and look for alternatives to wood fiber paper. Scarcity is common in many markets, and in many communications markets. As we will see in Chapter II, the Supreme Court refuses to consider economic scarcity as a justification for treating cable differently for constitutional purposes. And *Tornillo* seemed to firmly reject economic scarcity as a basis for government-enforced access to newspapers.

d. Scarcity should not require a different constitutional standard for reviewing government restraints on broadcasters, but instead should affect the way in which traditional standards are applied. For example, rather than reduce the level of scrutiny in *Red Lion*, critics of scarcity argue that the Court should have applied the same standard of review as the Court used in *Miami Herald* (strict scrutiny), but found that because of scarcity a right of reply requirement was necessary to serve a compelling interest.

e. Technology is quickly making scarcity a thing of the past. As Professor Yoo points out, "[t]he impending arrival of a series of new broadcast technologies, including digital transmission, program storage, video-on-demand, spread spectrum, and packet switching, holds the promise of elimination of the spectrum as a physical constraint even if broadcasting is viewed in isolation from other media." Christopher S. Yoo, The Rise and Demise of the Technology–Specific Approach to the First Amendment, 91 Georgetown L. J. 245 (2003). Even the FCC has conceded "the dramatic transformation in the telecommunications marketplace provides a basis for the [Supreme] Court to reconsider its application of diminished First Amendment protection to the electronic media." In re Complaint of Syracuse Peace Council, 2 FCC Rcd. 5043, 5058 (1987) (citing FCC v. League of Women Voters, 468 U.S. 364 (1984)).

For a more extended critique of the scarcity rationale, see Lee C. Bollinger, Images of a Free Press 87–90 (1991); Lucas A. Powe, American Broadcasting and the First Amendment 197–209 (1987); Fred H. Cate, The First Amendment and the National Information Infrastructure, 30 Wake Forest L. Rev. 1 (1995); Mark S. Fowler and Daniel L. Brenner, A Marketplace Approach to Broadcast Regulation, 60 Tex. L. Rev. 207 (1982); David L. Bazelon, FCC Regulation of the Telecommunications Press, 1975 Duke L.J. 213; Ronald Coase, The Federal Communications Commission, 2 J. L. & Econ.1, 12–27 (1959).

CHAPTER II

CONTENT–BASED REGULATION OF MEDIA

Organizationally, we begin by distinguishing between situations in which the government itself seeks to restrict media speech and situations in which a private party seeks the restriction and the government, through the courts or otherwise, is principally a referee. A statute forbidding broadcasters from declaring winners in elections until the polls have closed would be an example of the former. A libel suit is an example of the latter. The distinction is imperfect, of course. Direct governmental action to restrict speech may be instigated by a private person, as when a citizen's complaint leads the local prosecutor to initiate an obscenity prosecution. And the private lawsuit implicates governmental decisions, either by statute or judicial decision, to protect such interests as reputation and privacy.

Nonetheless, the distinction is useful because historically, at least, courts have thought that direct governmental restriction of media posed First Amendment problems different from those raised by private lawsuits. This has produced different analytical approaches to the two kinds of problems. Defamation, for example, is the subject of a completely different First Amendment methodology from that used to analyze statutes restricting exit polling. In other areas these differences seem to be blurring, as the Supreme Court extends some sort of balancing test to more and more situations, but underlying assumptions about the dangers to a free press posed by direct governmental regulation, on the one hand, and private litigation, on the other, are still important. This chapter and the next deal with direct governmental regulation; the following five chapters deal principally with private litigation.

Within the sphere of direct governmental regulation, courts draw an important distinction between content-based and content-neutral regulations. We have already seen several examples of content-based regulation, in *Landmark Communications, Daily Mail, R.A.V.,* and *Tornillo.* In those cases we saw various approaches to content-based regulations. Media are also subject to a wide variety of content-neutral regulations. Some of those apply to businesses of all forms; some apply to media alone, but without regard for the content those media carry. The dividing line between content-based and content-neutral restrictions is so significant that it often has the effect of determining the constitutionality of the government's action, even though the classification of restrictions as content-based or content-neutral is not always easy or consistent. We use this dividing line to organize the next two chapters.

Most discussion of the distinction between content-based and content-neutral restrictions occurs in cases in which the government argues that its regulation should be subjected to lesser scrutiny because it is content-neutral. For that reason, we defer detailed consideration of the distinction until the next chapter. In the cases in this chapter, there is little discussion of the matter because the restrictions are conceded to be content-based.

Whereas content-neutral regulations only occasionally involve First Amendment issues, and even then are usually subject to only moderate constitutional review, content-based regulations always raise significant First Amendment issues. The importance of the determination that a regulation is "content-based" is clearly reflected in the Supreme Court's opinion in Simon & Schuster, Inc. v. New York State Crime Victims Board, 502 U.S. 105 (1991). In that case, the Court upheld a challenge to a New York statute requiring "that an accused or convicted criminal's income from works describing his crime be deposited in an escrow account. These funds are then made available to the victims of the crime and the criminal's other creditors." The statute had been inspired by fears that "Son of Sam" serial killer David Berkowitz might reap a windfall profit by selling his story. The statute, rarely used since its enactment in 1977, was one of several ways in which the state sought to obtain compensation for crime victims and their families.

Justice O'Connor, writing for the Court, began by noting that "[a] statute is presumptively inconsistent with the First Amendment if it imposes a financial burden on speakers because of the content of their speech."

> This is a notion so engrained in our First Amendment jurisprudence that last Term we found it so "obvious" as to not require explanation. [*Leathers v. Medlock,* infra 225] It is but one manifestation of a far broader principle: "Regulations which permit the Government to discriminate on the basis of the content of the message cannot be tolerated under the First Amendment." Regan v. Time, Inc., 468 U.S. 641, 648–649 (1984). . . . As we reiterated in *Leathers,* " 'The constitutional right of free expression is . . . intended to remove governmental restraints from the arena of public discussion, putting the decision as to what views shall be voiced largely into the hands of each of us . . . in the belief that no other approach would comport with the premise of individual dignity and choice upon which our political system rests.' " [ ] (quoting Cohen v. California, 403 U.S. 15, 24 (1971)).

Justice O'Connor found the New York statute to be content-based, rejecting the State's claims that content-based laws raised constitutional concerns only when they reflected a legislative intent to discriminate or applied only to the media:

> [The statute] singles out income derived from expressive activity for a burden the State places on no other income, and it is directed only at works with a specified content. Whether the First Amendment "speaker" is considered to be [the author], whose income the statute

places in escrow because of the story he has told, or [the publisher], which can publish books about crime with the assistance of only those criminals willing to forgo remuneration for at least five years, the statute plainly imposes a financial disincentive only on speech of a particular content.

"In order to justify such differential treatment," Justice O'Connor wrote, " 'the State must show that its regulation is necessary to serve a compelling state interest and is narrowly drawn to achieve that end.' "

The State had argued that the statute served three interests: (1) depriving criminals of the profits of their crimes; (2) compensating victims; and (3) "ensuring that criminals do not profit from storytelling about their crimes before their victims have a meaningful opportunity to be compensated for their injuries." The Court found that the first two interests were compelling, but that the statute was broader than necessary to serve those interests. The third interest—which the statute arguably served more narrowly—the Court found to be

> on far shakier ground. The Board cannot explain why the State should have any greater interest in compensating victims from the proceeds of such 'storytelling' than from any of the criminal's other assets. Nor can the Board offer any justification for a distinction between this expressive activity and any other activity in connection with its interest in transferring the fruits of crime from criminals to their victims. Thus even if the State can be said to have an interest in classifying a criminal's assets in this manner, that interest is hardly compelling.

Justice Kennedy concurred in the judgment, but argued that the Court should not have applied a balancing test in this context:

> The New York statute we now consider imposes severe restrictions on authors and publishers, using as its sole criterion the content of what is written. The regulated content has the full protection of the First Amendment and this, I submit, is itself a full and sufficient reason for holding the statute unconstitutional. In my view it is both unnecessary and incorrect to ask whether the State can show that the statute " 'is necessary to serve a compelling state interest and is narrowly drawn to achieve that end.' " [ ] That test or formulation derives from our equal protection jurisprudence, [ ] and has no real or legitimate place when the Court considers the straightforward question whether the State may enact a burdensome restriction of speech based on content only, apart from any considerations of time, place, and manner or the use of public forums.
>
> Here a law is directed to speech alone where the speech in question is not obscene, not defamatory, not words tantamount to an act otherwise criminal, not an impairment of some other constitutional right, not an incitement to lawless action, and not calculated or likely to bring about imminent harm the State has the substantive power to prevent. No further inquiry is necessary to reject the State's argument that the statute should be upheld.

Borrowing the compelling interest and narrow tailoring analysis is ill-advised when all that is at issue is a content-based restriction, for resort to the test might be read as a concession that States may censor speech whenever they believe there is a compelling justification for doing so. Our precedents and traditions allow no such inference.

Justice Kennedy went on to lament the Court's increasing use of the "compelling interest inquiry . . . even where the sole question is, or ought to be, whether the restriction is in fact content based." He concluded:

The inapplicability of the compelling interest test to content-based restrictions on speech is demonstrated by our repeated statement that "above all else, the First Amendment means that government has no power to restrict expression because of its message, its ideas, its subject matter, or its content." Police Dept. of Chicago v. Mosley, 408 U.S. 92, 95 (1972). [ ] These general statements about the government's lack of power to engage in content-discrimination reflect a surer basis for protecting speech than does the test used by the Court today.

There are a few legal categories in which content-based regulation has been permitted or at least contemplated. These include obscenity, [ ], defamation, [ ], incitement, [ ], or situations presenting some grave and imminent danger the government has the power to prevent [ ]. These are, however, historic and traditional categories long familiar to the bar, although with respect to the last category it is most difficult for the government to prevail. [ ] While it cannot be said with certainty that the foregoing types of expression are or will remain the only ones that are without First Amendment protection, as evidenced by the proscription of some visual depictions of sexual conduct by children, see New York v. Ferber, 458 U.S. 747 (1982), the use of these traditional legal categories is preferable to the sort of ad hoc balancing that the Court henceforth must perform in every case if the analysis here used becomes our standard test.

As you read the cases in this chapter, keep in mind this colloquy between Justices O'Connor and Kennedy about the proper evaluation of content-based restrictions.

A.   PRIOR RESTRAINTS

The invention of a commercially viable printing press in the late fifteenth century prompted many governments to attempt to control its use. In England, the government pursued a variety of strategies for controlling the press, including prohibiting printers from publishing works that had not been licensed by government officials, who could censor objectionable passages or deny a license altogether. The licensure requirement was codified by Parliament in a series of acts making it a criminal offense to print a work without a license; it was in response to the first of these that John Milton wrote his *Areopagitica* in 1644. See supra p. 10. The last licensing legislation expired in 1693 and was not renewed. Even before the First Amendment was adopted, it was understood in both England and

America that "prior restraints" were inconsistent with freedom of speech. Blackstone wrote in 1769:

> The liberty of the press is indeed essential to the nature of a free state; but this consists in laying no previous restraints on publications, and not in freedom from censure for criminal matter when published. Every freeman has an undoubted right to lay what sentiments he pleases before the public; to forbid this is to destroy the freedom of the press; but if he publishes what is improper, mischievous or illegal, he must take the consequence of his own temerity.

4 William Blackstone, Commentaries 151, 152. It seems unlikely that the framers of the First Amendment shared Blackstone's view that freedom of the press meant *only* freedom from prior restraint. The historical evidence suggests that the framers saw that a free press would be essential to their vision of democracy and understood that it would have to mean more than freedom from prior restraint. See, e.g., David A. Anderson, The Origins of the Press Clause, 30 UCLA L. Rev. 455 (1983). Leonard Levy once held the contrary view but he retreated from that position. See Leonard Levy, Emergence of a Free Press xi (1985).

The Supreme Court once did embrace Blackstone's view, however. See Patterson v. Colorado, 205 U.S. 454 (1907). The publisher of the Rocky Mountain News had been fined $1,000 for contempt for publishing editorials attributing improper political motives to several members of the Colorado Supreme Court. When he appealed his conviction to the U.S. Supreme Court, the majority, in an opinion by Justice Holmes, held that the First Amendment was not violated because there was no prior restraint. Even if Patterson's statements were true, the First Amendment did not forbid punishing the publication. "The preliminary freedom extends to the false as well as the true; the subsequent punishment may extend as well to the true as to the false."

The Court began to recede from this view after World War I. In cases involving criminal prosecutions of anarchists and other political radicals, the majority of the Court upheld the convictions, but not on the ground that the First Amendment forbade only prior restraints. That notion was finally repudiated explicitly in Grosjean v. American Press Co., 297 U.S. 233, 248 (1936).

In any event, it has never been doubted that the First Amendment was intended *at least* to forbid prior restraints. The common law's hostility to prior restraints did not necessarily extend to injunctions, however. That hostility grew out of the English experience with licensing of the press, and what Blackstone meant by "prior restraint" was an administrative system giving some agency of government power to grant or deny permission to publish. Only later, with the expansion of equity jurisdiction and the emergence of injunctive relief as a common remedy, was the concept of prior restraint applied to judicial prohibitions against publication.

The leading cases have involved restraints imposed because of the content of the speech. Restrictions that may operate as a prior restraints but that are not content-based (such as city ordinances requiring a permit before parading or protesting) are usually not subjected to the full rigor of prior restraint analysis. On the other hand, it is hard to imagine that an injunction ordering a newspaper not to publish on Sundays, though content-neutral, would not be analyzed as a prior restraint. We treat prior restraints in this chapter as a species of content-based regulation, recognizing that the same principles may apply to at least some content-neutral restraints.

1.   THE PRESUMPTION OF UNCONSTITUTIONALITY

Near v. Minnesota
Supreme Court of the United States, 1931.
283 U.S. 697, 51 S.Ct. 625, 75 L.Ed. 1357, 1 Med.L.Rptr. 1001.

[A Minnesota law authorized abatement, as a public nuisance, of a "malicious, scandalous and defamatory newspaper, or other periodical." In the abatement action the defendant had available the defense "that the truth was published with good motives and for justifiable ends." A Minneapolis prosecutor sought to abate publication of The Saturday Press for publishing material allegedly violating the Minnesota statute on nine separate occasions. The Press had published articles charging in substance "that a Jewish gangster was in control of gambling, bootlegging and racketeering in Minneapolis, and that law enforcing officers and agencies were not energetically performing their duties." After summarizing the nature of the charges, the Court concluded that "[t]here is no question but that the articles made serious accusations against the public officials named and others in connection with the prevalence of crimes and the failure to expose and punish them." After the prosecutor presented his evidence, the defendant rested without offering evidence contending that the statute authorizing the abatement was unconstitutional. The state court "abated" the Press and perpetually enjoined the defendants from publishing or circulating "any publication whatsoever which is a malicious, scandalous or defamatory newspaper." The state supreme court affirmed, adding that it saw no reason for "defendants to construe the judgment as restraining them from operating a newspaper in harmony with the public welfare, to which all must yield" and that defendants had not indicated a desire "to conduct their business in the usual and legitimate manner."]

MR. CHIEF JUSTICE HUGHES delivered the opinion of the Court.

. . .

This statute, for the suppression as a public nuisance of a newspaper or periodical, is unusual, if not unique, and raises questions of grave importance transcending the local interests involved in the particular action. It is no longer open to doubt that the liberty of the press, and of speech, is within the liberty safeguarded by the due process clause of the Fourteenth Amendment from invasion by state action. . . . Liberty of speech, and of the press, is also not an absolute right, and the State may punish its abuse. *Whitney v. California*, [ ]. Liberty, in each of its phases, has its history and connotation and, in the present instance, the inquiry is as to the historic conception of the liberty of the press and whether the statute under review violates the essential attributes of that liberty.

. . .

If we cut through mere details of procedure, the operation and effect of the statute in substance is that public authorities may bring the owner or publisher of a newspaper or periodical before a judge upon a charge of conducting a business of publishing scandalous and defamatory matter—in particular that the matter consists of charges against public officers of official dereliction—and unless the owner or publisher is able and disposed to bring competent evidence to satisfy the judge that the charges are true and are published with good motives and for justifiable ends, his newspaper or periodical is suppressed and further publication is made punishable as a contempt. This is of the essence of censorship.

The question is whether a statute authorizing such proceedings in restraint of publication is consistent with the conception of the liberty of the press as historically conceived and guaranteed. In determining the extent of the constitutional protection, it has been generally, if not universally, considered that it is the chief purpose of the guaranty to prevent previous restraints upon publication. The struggle in England, directed against the legislative power of the licenser, resulted in renunciation of the censorship of the press. The liberty deemed to be established was thus described by Blackstone: "The liberty of the press is indeed essential to the nature of a free state; but this consists in laying no *previous* restraints upon publications, and not in freedom from censure for criminal matter when published. Every freeman has an undoubted right to lay what sentiments he pleases before the public; to forbid this, is to destroy the freedom of the press; but if he publishes what is improper, mischievous or illegal, he must take the consequence of his own temerity." 4 Bl. Com. 151, 152; [ ]. The distinction was early pointed out between the extent of the freedom with respect to censorship under our constitutional system and that enjoyed in England. Here, as Madison said, "the great and essential rights of the people are secured against legislative as well as against executive ambition. They are secured, not by laws paramount to prerogative, but by constitutions paramount to laws. This security of the freedom of the press requires that it should be exempt not only from previous restraints by the Executive, as in Great Britain, but from legislative restraint also." Report on the Virginia Resolutions, Madison's Works, vol. IV, p. 543. . . .

The criticism upon Blackstone's statement has not been because immunity from previous restraint upon publication has not been regarded as deserving of special emphasis, but chiefly because that immunity cannot be deemed to exhaust the conception of the liberty guaranteed by state and federal constitutions. The point of criticism has been "that the mere exemption from previous restraint cannot be all that is secured by the constitutional provisions"; and that "the liberty of the press might be rendered a mockery and a delusion, and the phrase itself a by-word, if, while every man was at liberty to publish what he pleased, the public authorities might nevertheless punish him for harmless publications." 2 Cooley, Const. Lim., 8th ed., p. 885. But it is recognized that punishment for the abuse of the liberty accorded to the press is essential to the protection of the public, and that the common law rules that subject the libeler to responsibility for the public offense, as well as for the private injury, are not abolished by the protection extended in our constitutions. [ ] The law of criminal libel rests upon that secure foundation. . . . In the present case we have no occasion to inquire as to the permissible scope of subsequent punishment [because the statute provides no punishment except contempt for violating the injunction, and appellant had not done so]. . . .

The objection has also been made that the principle as to immunity from previous restraint is stated too broadly, if every such restraint is deemed to be prohibited. That is undoubtedly true; the protection even as to previous restraint is not absolutely unlimited. But the limitation has been recognized only in exceptional cases: "When a nation is at war many things that might be said in time of peace are such a hindrance to its effort that their utterance will not be endured so long as men fight and that no Court could regard them as protected by any constitutional right." Schenck v. United States, 249 U.S. 47, 52. No one would question but that a government might prevent actual obstruction to its recruiting service or the publication of the sailing dates of transports or the number and location of troops. On similar grounds, the primary requirements of decency may be enforced against obscene publications. The security of the community life may be protected against incitements to acts of violence and the overthrow by force of orderly government. The constitutional guaranty of free speech does not "protect a man from an injunction against uttering words that may have all the effect of force. Gompers v. Bucks Stove & Range Co., 221 U.S. 418, 439." *Schenck v. United States*, supra. These limitations are not applicable here. Nor are we now concerned with questions as to the extent of authority to prevent publications in order to protect private rights according to the principles governing the exercise of the jurisdiction of courts of equity.

The exceptional nature of its limitations places in a strong light the general conception that liberty of the press, historically considered and taken up by the Federal Constitution, has meant, principally although not exclusively, immunity from previous restraints or censorship. The conception of the liberty of the press in this country had broadened with the exigencies of the colonial period and with the efforts to secure freedom from oppressive administration. That liberty was especially cherished for the immunity it afforded from previous restraint of the publication of censure of public officers and charges of official misconduct. . . . Madison, who was the leading spirit in the preparation of the First Amendment of the Federal Constitution, thus described the practice and sentiment which led to the guaranties of liberty of the press in state constitutions:

"In every State, probably, in the Union, the press has exerted a freedom in canvassing the merits and measures of public men of every description which has not been confined to the strict limits of the common law. On this footing the freedom of the press has stood; on this footing it yet stands. . . . Some degree of abuse is inseparable from the proper use of everything, and in no instance is this more true than in that of the press. It has accordingly been decided by the practice of the States, that it is better to leave a few of its noxious branches to their luxuriant growth, than, by pruning them away, to injure the vigour of those yielding the proper fruits. . . ."[10]

The fact that for approximately one hundred and fifty years there has been almost an entire absence of attempts to impose previous restraints upon publications relating to the malfeasance of public officers is significant of the deep-seated conviction that such restraints would violate constitutional right. . . .

The importance of this immunity has not lessened. . . . [T]he administration of government has become more complex, the opportunities for malfeasance and corruption have multiplied, crime has grown to most serious proportions, and the danger of its protection by unfaithful officials and of the impairment of the fundamental security of life and property by criminal alliances and official neglect, emphasizes the primary need of a vigilant and courageous press, especially in great cities. The fact that the liberty of the press may be abused by miscreant purveyors of scandal does not make any the less necessary the immunity of the press from previous restraint in dealing with official misconduct. Subsequent punishment for such abuses as may exist is the appropriate remedy, consistent with constitutional privilege.

In attempted justification of the statute, it is said that it deals not with publication *per se,* but with the "business" of publishing defamation. If, however, the publisher has a constitutional right to publish, without previous restraint, an edition of his newspaper charging official derelictions, it cannot be denied that he may publish subsequent editions for the same purpose. He does not lose his right by exercising it. . . .

Nor can it be said that the constitutional freedom from previous restraint is lost because charges are made of derelictions which constitute crimes. . . . Historically, there is no such limitation; it is inconsistent with the reason which underlies the privilege, as the privilege so limited would be of slight value for the purposes for which it came to be established.

The statute in question cannot be justified by reason of the fact that the publisher is permitted to show, before injunction issues, that the matter published is true and is published with good motives and for justifiable ends. If such a statute, authorizing suppression and injunction on such a basis, is constitutionally valid, it would be equally permissible for the legislature to provide that at any time the publisher of any newspaper could be brought before a court, or even an administrative officer (as the

---

10. Report on the Virginia Resolutions, Madison's Works, vol. iv, 544.

constitutional protection may not be regarded as resting on mere procedural details) and required to produce proof of the truth of his publication, or of what he intended to publish, and of his motives, or stand enjoined. If this can be done, the legislature may provide machinery for determining in the complete exercise of its discretion what are justifiable ends and restrain publication accordingly. And it would be but a step to a complete system of censorship. . . .

. . .

For these reasons we hold the statute, so far as it authorized the proceedings in this action . . . to be an infringement of the liberty of the press guaranteed by the Fourteenth Amendment. . . .

MR. JUSTICE BUTLER, dissenting.

. . .

The Minnesota statute does not operate as a *previous* restraint on publication within the proper meaning of that phrase. It does not authorize administrative control in advance such as was formerly exercised by the licensers and censors but prescribes a remedy to be enforced by a suit in equity. In this case there was previous publication made in the course of the business of regularly producing malicious, scandalous and defamatory periodicals. The business and publications unquestionably constitute an abuse of the right of free press. The statute denounces the things done as a nuisance on the ground, as stated by the state supreme court, that they threaten morals, peace and good order. . . . It is fanciful to suggest similarity between the granting or enforcement of the decree authorized by this statute to prevent *further* publication of malicious, scandalous and defamatory articles and the *previous restraint* upon the press by licensers as referred to by Blackstone and described in the history of the times to which he alludes.

. . .

MR. JUSTICE VAN DEVANTER, MR. JUSTICE McREYNOLDS, and MR. JUSTICE SUTHERLAND concur in this opinion.

Notes and Questions

1. As we discuss further below, much of the special hostility to traditional prior restraints has concerned the context in which they historically operated: one was prohibited from publishing without the approval of a professional censor who usually operated in secret and with great discretion. *Near*, by contrast, involved a specific statute that required the government to apply to a court for an injunction against "malicious, scandalous and defamatory" material, and gave the publisher the opportunity to challenge the injunction by showing that such material was true and "published with good motives and for justifiable ends." Moreover, the injunction only prevented Near from publishing additional "malicious, scandalous and defamatory" material. Should the Court have applied its special hostility to traditional prior restraints to these provisions?

2. While the *Near* case was making its way from the Minnesota Supreme Court to the U.S. Supreme Court, Chief Justice Taft and Justice Sanford died. Both had usually voted with the group that dissented in *Near*. They were replaced by Chief Justice Hughes and Justice Roberts, both of whom voted with the majority. "If Taft was still Chief Justice and Sanford was still sitting, there would have been at least five votes, perhaps even six, for the Minnesota law." Fred Friendly, Minnesota Rag 119 (1981). Friendly's book is a lively account of the case, the politics and journalism of the time, and the personalities involved in the litigation.

3. *Near* was the first case ever in which the Court invoked the First Amendment to invalidate any type of state restriction on the press. If it had gone the other way, how might that have changed the course of free speech jurisprudence?

––––––

Defining prior restraint. Was the injunction in *Near* really a prior restraint? What is it that distinguishes prior restraints from other kinds of prohibitions on speech? And what is the distinctively pernicious characteristic of prior restraints? Litigators, aware of the preemptive power of the phrase "this is a prior restraint," attempt to apply the label to many different kinds of disputes. One recurring argument might be called the "de facto prior restraint" argument: the restriction in question is not in form a licensing scheme or an injunction, but the challenger claims it will have the same effect.

The Supreme Court rejected such an argument in Alexander v. United States, 509 U.S. 544 (1993). Alexander, operator of numerous "adult entertainment" businesses in Minnesota, was convicted of transporting multiple copies of four obscene magazines and three videos in interstate commerce and engaging in the business of selling obscene material. Those convictions provided the basis for a finding that he had engaged in a "pattern of racketeering" for purposes of the Racketeer Influenced and Corrupt Organizations Act (RICO), and under the forfeiture provisions of RICO the government seized all of Alexander's thirty-one businesses, confiscated $9 million in profits, and destroyed all of the inventory found in his stores, which included millions of dollars worth of books and videos, most of which had never been found to be legally obscene and were therefore presumptively protected by the First Amendment.

The Supreme Court held, 6–3, that the forfeiture should not be analyzed as a prior restraint. Viewing it as a subsequent punishment, the Court said the seizure was no more likely to chill speech than the six-year prison sentence and $100,000 fine that Alexander did not challenge on First Amendment grounds. The Court remanded, however, for further consideration of Alexander's claim that the forfeiture was an "excessive fine" under the Eighth Amendment. Excerpts from the majority and dissenting opinions on the prior restraint issue follow. Chief Justice Rehnquist, for the Court:

[P]etitioner's proposed definition of the term "prior restraint" would undermine the time-honored distinction between barring speech in the future and penalizing past speech. The doctrine of prior restraint originated in the common law of England, where prior restraints of the press were not permitted, but punishment after publication was. This very limited application of the principle of freedom of speech was held inconsistent with our First Amendment as long ago as Grosjean v. American Press Co., 297 U.S. 233, 246 (1936). While we may have given a broader definition to the term "prior restraint" than was given to it in English common law, our decisions have steadfastly preserved the distinction between prior restraints and subsequent punishments. Though petitioner tries to dismiss this distinction as "neither meaningful nor useful," [ ] we think it is critical to our First Amendment jurisprudence. Because we have interpreted the First Amendment as providing greater protection from prior restraints than from subsequent punishments, [ ] it is important for us to delineate with some precision the defining characteristics of a prior restraint. To hold that the forfeiture order in this case constituted a prior restraint would have the exact opposite effect: it would blur the line separating prior restraints from subsequent punishments to such a degree that it would be impossible to determine with any certainty whether a particular measure is a prior restraint or not.

Despite Chief Justice Rehnquist's statement that "it is important for us to delineate with some precision the defining characteristics of a prior restraint," his opinion contains nothing more specific than the excerpt quoted above.

Justice Kennedy, joined by Justices Blackmun and Stevens, dissented:

The majority tries to occupy the high ground by assuming the role of the defender of the doctrine of prior restraint. It warns that we disparage the doctrine if we reason from it. But as an analysis of our prior restraint cases reveals, our application of the First Amendment has adjusted to meet new threats to speech. The First Amendment is a rule of substantive protection, not an artifice of categories. The admitted design and the overt purpose of the forfeiture in this case are to destroy an entire speech business and all its protected titles, thus depriving the public of access to lawful expression. This is restraint in more than theory. It is censorship all too real.

. . .

As our First Amendment law has developed, we have not confined the application of the prior restraint doctrine to its simpler forms, outright licensing or censorship before speech takes place. In considering governmental measures deviating from the classic form of a prior restraint yet posing many of the same dangers to First Amendment freedoms, we have extended prior restraint protection with some latitude, toward the end of declaring certain governmental actions to fall within the presumption of invalidity. This approach is evident in *Near*. . . .

. . . In one sense the injunctive order [in *Near*], which paralleled the nuisance statute, did nothing more than announce the conditions under which some later punishment might be imposed, for one presumes that contempt could not be found until there was a further violation in contravention of the order. But in *Near* the publisher, because of past wrongs, was subjected to active state intervention for the control of future speech. We found that the scheme was a prior restraint because it embodied "the essence of censorship."

. . .

. . . As governments try new ways to subvert essential freedoms, legal and constitutional systems respond by making more explicit the nature and the extent of the liberty in question. First in *Near*, and later in [other cases], we were faced with official action which did not fall within the traditional meaning of the term prior restraint, yet posed many of the same censorship dangers. Our response was to hold that the doctrine not only includes licensing schemes requiring speech to be submitted to a censor for review prior to dissemination, but also encompasses injunctive systems which threaten or bar future speech based on some past infraction.

Although we consider today a new method of government control with unmistakable dangers of official censorship, the majority concludes that First Amendment freedoms are not endangered because forfeiture follows a lawful conviction for obscenity offenses. But this explanation does not suffice. The rights of free speech and press in their broad and legitimate sphere cannot be defeated by the simple expedient of punishing after in lieu of censoring before. [ ] This is so because in some instances the operation and effect of a particular enforcement scheme, though not in the form of a traditional prior restraint, may be to raise the same concerns which inform all of our prior restraint cases: the evils of state censorship and the unacceptable chilling of protected speech.

Does Justice Kennedy's opinion suggest that anything that "chills speech unacceptably" should be analyzed as a prior restraint?

2.   OVERCOMING THE PRESUMPTION OF UNCONSTITUTIONALITY

Recall that the Supreme Court in *Near* stated that the First Amendment's prohibition against prior restraints could be overcome only in "exceptional cases," such as cases involving dire threats to national security. The first real test of the "national security" exception came in New York Times Co. v. United States, 403 U.S. 713 (1971), which is better known as the "Pentagon Papers" case.

While the war in Vietnam and the domestic controversy surrounding it were at their peak, the New York Times obtained a copy of a classified 47–volume government report that came to be popularly known as the "Pentagon Papers." After several months of intense and highly secret preparations, the Times began publishing a series of articles about the report. The

Justice Department moved to enjoin publication. A district judge in New York denied the injunction, but publication was temporarily restrained pending appeal, and the Court of Appeals for the Second Circuit ordered the injunction granted.

While the Times' case was being litigated, the Washington Post began publishing material from the same report. The Justice Department also moved to enjoin the Post. A district judge in Washington refused to issue a preliminary injunction and the Court of Appeals for the District of Columbia affirmed. The Supreme Court issued stays to prevent publication in both cases, heard oral argument, and five days later issued its decision.

The Court issued a brief per curiam opinion dissolving the injunctions:

> "Any system of prior restraints of expression comes to this Court bearing a heavy presumption against its constitutional validity." Bantam Books, Inc. v. Sullivan, 372 U.S. 58, 70 (1963); see also Near v. Minnesota, 283 U.S. 697 (1931). The Government "thus carries a heavy burden of showing justification for the imposition of such a restraint." Organization for a Better Austin v. Keefe, 402 U.S. 415, 419 (1971). The District Court for the Southern District of New York in the *New York Times* [ ] case and the District Court for the District of Columbia and the Court of Appeals for the District of Columbia Circuit [ ] in the *Washington Post* case held that the Government had not met that burden. We agree.

New York Times Co. v. United States, 403 U.S. 713, 1 Med. L. Rptr. 1031 (1971).

Every member of the Court wrote a separate opinion. Justice Black, concurring, argued that the injunctions were so clearly unconstitutional that the Court should have vacated them without hearing oral argument. Justice Douglas, concurring, also believed the First Amendment was an absolute bar to enjoining publication. Justice Brennan, concurring, noted that the government had only offered "surmise or conjecture" of harmful consequences from publishing the documents and that such speculation did not rise to the level of demonstrating that this case fit within that "single, extremely narrow class of cases in which the First Amendment's ban on prior judicial restraint may be overridden," citing *Schenck* and *Near*. Justice Marshall, concurring, believed the executive branch had no power to ask the courts to enjoin publication when Congress had not authorized such a remedy. Justice Stewart, in a concurring opinion, stressed that "in the cases before us we are asked neither to construe specific regulations nor to apply specific laws. We are asked, instead, to perform a function that the Constitution gave to the Executive, not the Judiciary." Justice White, concurring, noted that Congress had enacted provisions of the Criminal Code that might apply to the newspapers' conduct, but that Congress had not authorized an injunctive remedy.

Chief Justice Burger, in a dissenting opinion, noted that although the Times had delayed publication for three or four months after it obtained the documents, the newspapers were insisting on such fast review that the

Court did not know what it was acting on. He thought the *Times* case should go to trial in the district court before the Supreme Court decided anything on the merits. Justice Blackmun, in another dissent, said the case should be resolved by weighing "the broad right of the press to publish" against "the very narrow right of the government to prevent," but believed the Court had not had time to develop appropriate standards for that balancing.

Justice Harlan also dissented, arguing that "the Court has been almost irresponsibly feverish in dealing with these cases":

> Both the Court of Appeals for the Second Circuit and the Court of Appeals for the District of Columbia Circuit rendered judgment on June 23. The New York Times' petition for certiorari, its motion for accelerated consideration thereof, and its application for interim relief were filed in this Court on June 24 at about 11 a.m. The application of the United States for interim relief in the *Post* case was also filed here on June 24 at about 7:15 p.m. This Court's order setting a hearing before us on June 26 at 11 a.m., a course which I joined only to avoid the possibility of even more peremptory action by the Court, was issued less than 24 hours before. The record in the *Post* case was filed with the Clerk shortly before 1 p.m. on June 25; the record in the *Times* case did not arrive until 7 or 8 o'clock that same night. The briefs of the parties were received less than two hours before argument on June 26.

> This frenzied train of events took place in the name of the presumption against prior restraints created by the First Amendment. Due regard for the extraordinarily important and difficult questions involved in these litigations should have led the Court to shun such a precipitate timetable.

Justice Harlan ultimately dissented on the basis that the Court had exceeded its authority by doing more than assuring that "the subject matter of the dispute does lie within the proper compass of the President's foreign relations power" and that "the determination that disclosure of the subject matter would irreparably impair the national security be made by the head of the Executive Department concerned—here the Secretary of State or the Secretary of Defense—after actual personal consideration by that officer."

Although the government never sought to invoke criminal sanctions against the media in the Pentagon Papers episode, it did file charges against Daniel Ellsberg and Anthony Russo for leaking the papers to the Times. The government dropped the prosecutions after it was revealed that the White House "plumbers," the same group responsible for the Watergate burglary, had burglarized the office of Ellsberg's psychiatrist looking for information to discredit him. The case is discussed in Melville G. Nimmer, National Security Secrets v. Free Speech: The Issues Left Undecided in the Ellsberg Case, 26 Stan. L. Rev. 311 (1974).

One of the few cases upholding a prior restraint on the press in the interest of national security is United States v. The Progressive, Inc., 467 F. Supp. 990, 4 Med. L. Rptr. 2377 (W.D. Wis. 1979). There, the government sought an injunction under the Atomic Energy Act, 42 U.S.C. § 2011 et seq., prohibiting The Progressive magazine from publishing an article entitled "The H Bomb Secret: How We Got It, Why We're Telling It," by Howard Morland. The magazine contended that the projected article merely assembled data already in the public domain and readily available to any diligent seeker. It said it planned to publish the article to "alert the people of this country to the false illusion of security created by the government's futile efforts at secrecy." The government maintained that much of the information was not in the public domain, that the article contained a core of information that had never before been published, and that even if the specific information was in the public domain, publishing it all in one easily accessible article could help enemies who otherwise might not put all the pieces together. The judge wrote:

> Does the article provide a "do-it-yourself" guide for the hydrogen bomb? Probably not. A number of affidavits make quite clear that a *sine qua non* to thermonuclear capability is a large, sophisticated industrial capability coupled with a coterie of imaginative, resourceful scientists and technicians. One does not build a hydrogen bomb in the basement. However, the article could possibly provide sufficient information to allow a medium size nation to move faster in developing a hydrogen weapon. It could provide a ticket to by-pass blind alleys.
>
> . . .
>
> The Secretary of State states that publication will increase thermonuclear proliferation and that this would "irreparably impair the national security of the United States." The Secretary of Defense says that dissemination of the Morland paper will mean a substantial increase in the risk of thermonuclear proliferation and lead to use or threats that would "adversely affect the national security of the United States."
>
> . . .
>
> A mistake in ruling against The Progressive will seriously infringe cherished First Amendment rights. If a preliminary injunction is issued, it will constitute the first instance of prior restraint against a publication in this fashion in the history of this country, to this Court's knowledge. Such notoriety is not to be sought. It will curtail defendants' First Amendment rights in a drastic and substantial fashion. It will infringe upon our right to know and to be informed as well.
>
> A mistake in ruling against the United States could pave the way for thermonuclear annihilation for us all. In that event, our right to life is extinguished and the right to publish becomes moot.
>
> In the *Near* case, the Supreme Court recognized that publication of troop movements in time of war would threaten national security and could therefore be restrained. Times have changed significantly

since 1931 when *Near* was decided. Now war by foot soldiers has been replaced in large part by war by machines and bombs. No longer need there be any advance warning or any preparation time before a nuclear war could be commenced.

In light of these factors, this Court concludes that publication of the technical information on the hydrogen bomb contained in the article is analogous to publication of troop movements or locations in time of war and falls within the extremely narrow exception to the rule against prior restraint.

. . .

The judge distinguished the Pentagon Papers case on the ground that it involved historical matters rather than a future threat to national security, and because in the Progressive case a statute, Section 2274 of the Atomic Energy Act, authorized injunctions against disclosure of restricted data pertaining to nuclear weapons by anyone with reason to believe such data will be used to secure an advantage to any foreign nation.

While the magazine's appeal of the preliminary injunction was pending, a newspaper in Madison, Wisconsin, published a letter containing the information that The Progressive had been enjoined from publishing, and the Chicago Tribune announced that it would publish the same letter. The government then withdrew its complaint and the case was dismissed. See United States v. Progressive, Inc., 467 F. Supp. 990, 4 Med. L. Rptr. 2377 (W.D. Wis. 1979), dismissed as moot, 610 F.2d 819 (7th Cir. 1979). Although the government reserved its right to bring criminal charges, it did not do so.

Although the Progressive decision is a product of the Cold War era, it is easy to transpose its security concerns to a more modern context. After September 11, 2001, it is easy to imagine terrorists using information about weaknesses in our critical infrastructure (such as nuclear power plants) or information about chemical or biological weapons materials to harm thousands, hundreds of thousands, or even millions of Americans. In fact government officials essentially "classified" the Ph.D. dissertation of a George Mason University graduate student for security reasons. Sean Gorman's thesis mapped the U.S. fiber-optic network using publicly available documents. Government officials feared that terrorists could use the information to disrupt the entire business and industrial sector of the American economy. See "9/11 Turned Thesis Into Time Bomb," Pittsburgh Post–Gazette, July 13, 2003, at A11. How would a court view the government's attempt to restrain publication of such information?

Permissible prior restraints. In a few narrow areas of the law, prior restraints are imposed, if not routinely, at least without the rigorous scrutiny seen in the preceding cases. One such area is copyright infringement. Injunctions are expressly authorized by Section 502 of the Copyright Act and are not an uncommon remedy. Another is trade secret law, where a former employee may be enjoined from disclosing matters deemed confidential, either by virtue of the employment contract or the concept of fiduciary obligations imposed by law. See, e.g., Cherne Industrial, Inc. v. Grounds & Associates, Inc., 278 N.W.2d 81 (Minn. 1979) ("Given the public interest in preserving the ability of parties to freely enter contracts and to seek judicial enforcement of such contracts and in providing judicial remedies for breaches of fiduciary duties imposed by law, any infringement by the injunction on defendants' First Amendment rights is tolerable and justified."). But see State ex rel. Sports Management News, Inc. v. Nachtigal, 324 Or. 80, 921 P.2d 1304, 24 Med. L. Rptr. 2327 (1996), in which the Oregon Supreme Court characterized a statute authorizing courts to require parties to obtain prior court approval before disclosing trade secrets as "a classic 'prior restraint' on publication" and held that the statute violated a state constitutional ban on laws "restraining the free expression of opinion." The court went on to hold that since there was no "historical exception for the prior-restraint protection of trade secrets from publication by a third-party publisher who receives information lawfully," the law was unconstitutional. See also Mark A. Lemley & Eugene Volokh, Freedom of Speech and Injunctions in Intellectual Property Cases, 48 Duke L.J. 147 (1998) (arguing that preliminary injunctions should be granted with the same reluctance in intellectual property cases as they are in defamation cases), infra p. 492.

Preclearance of motion pictures. From the invention of motion pictures, the Court permitted states to require that films be cleared by a government official or board before being shown. Failure to submit the film was an offense, even if the board would have had no choice but to approve the film. An effort to declare such a scheme unconstitutional on its face failed in Times Film Corp. v. Chicago, 365 U.S. 43 (1961).

But in *Freedman v. Maryland,* a case involving a criminal prosecution for violation of the Maryland motion-picture censorship statute that made it unlawful to exhibit a motion picture without having obtained a license, the Court noted the dangers in this type of prior restraint and required certain procedural safeguards. First, the censor bore the burden of proving that the film was unprotected expression. Second, because "only a judicial determination in an adversary proceeding ensures the necessary sensitivity to freedom of expression, only a procedure requiring a judicial determination suffices to impose a valid final restraint." This led the Court to require that the state "within a brief period, either issue a license or go to court to restrain showing the film." Any restraint had to be for "the shortest fixed period compatible with sound judicial resolution." Finally, the state had to assure a "prompt final judicial decision, to minimize the deterrent effect of an interim and possibly erroneous denial of a license." Freedman v. Maryland, 380 U.S. 51, 1 Med. L. Rptr. 1126 (1965).

Under *Freedman,* challenges to movie censorship decisions must be heard within one day, and a decision must be rendered within two more days. In Littleton v. Z.J. Gifts, 541 U.S. 774, 124 S. Ct. 2219 (2004), however, the Supreme Court held that the First Amendment does not require courts to expedite review of decisions on licenses for adult businesses in order to satisfy *Freedman's* requirement of a "prompt final judicial decision." The Court explained that licensing of adult businesses is less subjective than movie censorship and therefore less threatening to First Amendment interests. As a result, the "prompt decision" requirement is met by ordinary judicial procedures as long as those are administered with sensitivity to free speech interests. On the role of procedural protections that support freedom of expression, see Henry P. Monaghan, First Amendment "Due Process," 83 Harv. L. Rev. 518 (1970).

3.   DISOBEYING INJUNCTIONS

In *Near*, the Pentagon Papers case, and *The Progressive*, the newspapers opted to comply with the injunction while challenging it in court, instead of disobeying it and challenging it when held in contempt for doing so. Media are sometimes unwilling to delay publication while the courts decide. For one thing, they fear that by the time the courts vindicate their right to publish, the matter will no longer be news because the public's attention will have turned to something else. Second, as soon as one media outlet is enjoined from publishing, its competitors usually attempt to get and publish the same information. As a result, the media do not acquiesce easily in prior restraints, even temporarily.

Of particular concern to media is the so-called "collateral bar." This rule, employed in most jurisdictions, holds that one charged with contempt for disobeying an injunction cannot defend on the ground that the injunction was unconstitutional. The theory is that orderly judicial process requires that injunctions be obeyed until found to be invalid, although a statute may be ignored with impunity by one who successfully gambles that it will be held invalid.

Most prior restraints are ultimately held to be unconstitutional. When a media organization is subjected to a prior restraint that it believes is unconstitutional, must it nevertheless defer publication until the matter is resolved by the courts? In states that recognize the collateral bar, the answer is yes, with some large exceptions.

The Providence Journal case. In 1985 the Providence Journal obtained from the FBI (through the federal Freedom of Information Act) logs of the FBI's electronic surveillance of Raymond Patriarca, a reputed mob leader who had recently died. Patriarca's son sued to enjoin publication on the ground that the FBI had wrongfully released the logs. Over the objections of the Journal and the government, the district court granted a temporary restraining order forbidding publication pending a hearing two days later. The next day the Journal published an article based on information from the logs, together with a statement by the newspaper saying that although it respected the judge, "in this case we are convinced that his order would impose a prior restraint in violation of the Constitution. For that reason we have decided to publish in today's Journal Bulletin the first of a series of stories based on the Patriarca tapes."

The judge appointed a special prosecutor to press criminal contempt charges against the newspaper and its executive editor. The judge convicted them and sentenced the editor to 18 months in jail, suspended on condition he perform 200 hours of community service. The Journal was fined $100,000.

The trial court relied on Walker v. City of Birmingham, 388 U.S. 307 (1967), which affirmed contempt convictions of Dr. Martin Luther King Jr. and others for violating an injunction against parading without a permit, even though the injunction was ultimately held to be unconstitutional. The trial court also cited United States v. Dickinson, 465 F.2d 496, 1 Med. L. Rptr. 1338 (5th Cir. 1972), upholding two reporters' convictions for contempt for publishing in violation of a judge's order, despite the fact that the appellate court found that order unconstitutional.

On appeal by the Journal, a panel of the Court of Appeals for the First Circuit reversed. It held that both *Walker* and *Dickinson* recognized an exception allowing the defendant to ignore a "transparently invalid" injunction. The TRO against the Journal came within this exception because (1) the Supreme Court precedents create a heavy presumption of unconstitutionality, (2) there was no statutory authorization for the injunction against the Journal, (3) the privacy interests invoked by Patriarca's son were not a sufficient basis for a prior restraint, and (4) the FBI had already disseminated the same information to other media outlets, making it unlikely that the injunction would be effective in preventing the alleged harm. "Because the order was transparently invalid, the appellants should have been allowed to challenge its constitutionality at the contempt proceedings." 820 F.2d 1342, 13 Med. L. Rptr. 1945 (1st Cir. 1986).

At the request of the special prosecutor, the case was reheard en banc. The full court did not vacate the panel opinion, but modified it with a brief additional opinion of its own:

> [I]t seems to us that some finer tuning is available to minimize the disharmony between respect for court orders and respect for free speech.
>
> It is not asking much, beyond some additional expense and time, to require a publisher, even when it thinks it is the subject of a transparently unconstitutional order of prior restraint, to make a good faith effort to seek emergency relief from the appellate court. If timely access to the appellate court is not available or if timely decision is not forthcoming, the publisher may then proceed to publish and challenge the constitutionality of the order in the contempt proceedings.

At that point the court inserted the following footnote: "See Goodale, The Press Ungagged: The Practical Effect on Gag Order Litigation of Nebraska Press Association v. Stuart, 29 Stan. L. Rev. 497, 509–10 (1977) (arguing that *Walker v. City of Birmingham* 'may require no more than an attempt to appeal a void restraining order up to the time the constitutionally protected action is planned to take place.')." In re Providence Journal, 820 F.2d 1354, 14 Med. L. Rptr. 1029 (1st Cir. 1987) (en banc). The special prosecutor's petition for certiorari initially was granted by the Supreme Court, then dismissed on the ground that he did not have authority to appeal on behalf of the government without the authorization of the solicitor general. 485 U.S. 693, 15 Med. L. Rptr. 1241 (1988).

After this decision, when would a prior restraint *not* be "transparently invalid"? If the appellate court immediately grants the defendant's request for review, but does not immediately decide the case, may the defendant safely disobey the injunction on the ground it is being denied "timely decision"? Is proof that further delay would have caused defendant to be "scooped" by a competitor sufficient to show that a "timely" decision was not forthcoming?

In *Dickinson,* supra, p. 105, the court said "in the absence of strong indications that the appellate process is being deliberately stalled—certainly not so in this record—violation with impunity does not occur simply because immediate decision is not forthcoming, even though the communication enjoined is 'news.' " If the appellate court agrees to review the restraint in accordance with its usual timetable, rather than grant expedited review, is the process being "deliberately stalled"? Is the defendant being denied "timely decision"?

The Business Week case. In a decision vacating a much-publicized prior restraint against Business Week magazine, the Sixth Circuit articulated standards that would seem to make most prior restraints against media "transparently invalid." In a $100 million lawsuit by Procter & Gamble Co. against Bankers Trust Co., a federal judge signed a broad protective order allowing the parties to seal discovery materials without specific court approval. The magazine obtained copies of sealed documents and prepared a cover story. At the request of both parties and without notice to Business Week or a hearing, the judge issued temporary restraining orders forbidding the magazine from publishing. The magazine complied and unsuccessfully sought stays from the Sixth Circuit and from Justice Stevens at the Supreme Court. After three weeks and several hearings, the district judge determined that the documents should not have been sealed because there was no "substantial governmental interest" in keeping them confidential, but nevertheless permanently enjoined Business Week from using the material on the ground that the magazine knowingly violated the protective order when it obtained the documents.

By a 2–1 vote, a Sixth Circuit panel held that the dispute was not moot and criticized the district court both for issuing the blanket protective order and for enjoining the publication. The district court abdicated its responsibility when it allowed the parties themselves to determine what documents should be sealed; court papers may be sealed only on a showing "that the particular documents justify court-imposed secrecy."

The permanent injunction was "patently invalid," the court said, because "the private litigants' interest in protecting their vanity or their commercial self-interest simply does not qualify as grounds for imposing a prior restraint" under the Pentagon Papers case.

As for the temporary restraining orders, the court said a TRO against pure speech by the press is not to be judged by the usual standards of Rule

65 of the Federal Rules of Civil Procedure, which permits such ex parte orders to prevent irreparable injury to the applicant. *Ex parte* orders forbidding publication violate the First Amendment unless a "showing is made that it is impossible to serve or notify the opposing parties and give them an opportunity to participate." Substantively, the applicant must show not only that the order is necessary to prevent irreparable injury, but also that the interest threatened is "more fundamental than the First Amendment itself." Finally, such a restraint is to be reviewed de novo at the appellate level, rather than under the usual abuse-of-discretion standard. The dissenter agreed with the majority's analysis of the First Amendment issues, dissenting only on the mootness point. See Procter & Gamble Co. v. Bankers Trust Co., 78 F.3d 219, 24 Med. L. Rptr. 1385 (6th Cir. 1996).

In his opinion denying a stay, Justice Stevens had observed that it was disputed whether the magazine's reporter knew about the sealing before learning of the contents of the file. He then said that he understood the magazine to be acknowledging that "the manner in which [the magazine] came into possession of the information it seeks to publish may have a bearing on its right to do so." McGraw–Hill Cos. v. Procter & Gamble Co., 515 U.S. 1309, 23 Med. L. Rptr. 2247 (1995) (Stevens, J.).

4.   WHY ARE PRIOR RESTRAINTS BAD?

Once a court labels a restriction on speech a prior restraint, the court usually will pronounce it unconstitutional with little further analysis. In an influential law review article, Rethinking Prior Restraints, 92 Yale L.J. 409, 426–33 (1983), Professor John Jeffries searched for the "defining characteristics" that make prior restraints distinctively pernicious and concluded that they were hard to find, at least in the case of injunctions.

First, Jeffries noted the difference between historical prior restraints (e.g., requirements for administrative preclearance, such as licenses) and more modern prior restraints (e.g., injunctions):

> Under a regime of injunctions, there is no routine screening of speech and no administrative shortcut to suppression. The government has to shoulder the entire burden of identifying the case for suppression and of demonstrating in court a constitutionally acceptable basis for such action. Moreover, because an injunction must be sought in open court, the character of the government's claims remains subject to public scrutiny and debate. Most important, the decision to suppress is made by a court, not a censor. Of course, judges are not perfect; sometimes they may err on the side of suppression and enjoin speech without sufficient justification. But the fact remains that judges, unlike professional censors, have no vested interest in the suppression of speech. The institution of the judiciary is peculiarly well suited—in personnel, training, ideology, and institutional structure—to implement the ideals of the First Amendment. . . .

Not only are injunctions unlike administrative preclearance, they are also far more like subsequent punishments than the conventional rhetoric would suggest. In both cases the *threat* of punishment comes before publication; in both cases the *fact* of punishment comes after. The apparent distinction in timing is actually only a shift in the focus of attention. The procedures in an action for criminal contempt—the enforcement phase of the injunctive process—are generally the same as those used in ordinary criminal prosecutions. Proof must be had beyond a reasonable doubt, and the right to trial by jury is guaranteed where the sentence exceeds imprisonment for six months.

On examination, the chief difference between the two schemes turns out to be this: Under a system of injunctions, the adjudication of illegality precedes publication; under a system of criminal prosecution, it comes later. This is a difference, and perhaps for some purposes it matters, but why the timing of the adjudication should affect the scope of First Amendment freedoms is not at all clear.

Jeffries rejected three frequently advanced justifications for why the timing of the adjudication is constitutionally relevant:

The first and most common is that an injunction deters speech more effectively than does the threat of criminal prosecution and for that reason should be specially disfavored. . . . The idea has been variously expressed but never so pithily as in Alexander Bickel's remark that, "A criminal statute chills, prior restraint freezes." . . . [However, Jeffries argues, an] injunction may be more effective at stopping the activity at which it is aimed, but it is also more narrowly confined. There is less risk of deterring activities beyond the adjudicated target of suppression—activities plainly outside the injunctive ban but arguably within the necessarily more general prohibition of a penal law. And many find even an uncertain prospect of criminal conviction and punishment sufficient incentive to steer well clear of arguably proscribed activities.

. . .

Two additional reasons for regarding injunctions as especially deleterious to speech are really only variations on the theme of efficient deterrence. One is that suppression by criminal prosecution is preferable to suppression by injunction because the latter characteristically delays publication, at least for several days, even if the ban ultimately is lifted. The result is a loss in the immediacy of speech, and in some cases an accompanying loss in its value. The other contention is that criminal prosecution is preferable because it allows the disputed material to be published at least once and thus to enter the marketplace of ideas. An injunction, by contrast, is said to prevent the information from ever being made public.

Both of these contentions enjoy wide currency, but neither withstands scrutiny. Both are based on the implicit assumption that the deterrent impact of penal statutes is felt in those cases in which prosecution is brought. Of course, the opposite is true. Every violation of the penal law is, by hypothesis, a case of failed deterrence. Effective deterrence occurs when the violation never takes place. And in some cases, deterrence will be effective. Thus, while an injunction may delay publication for several days, the prospect of penal sanctions may delay publication forever. And while those publications that become subjects of criminal prosecution do become part of the marketplace of ideas, those that are deterred by the threat of penal sanctions never do. There is, in short, no necessary or dependable relation between the form of suppression and any identifiable measure of violence to First Amendment interests. . . .

According to Jeffries, "there is only one respect in which injunctions plausibly can be claimed to have a First Amendment impact significantly greater than the threat of subsequent punishment. That argument is based on the traditional rule that the legality of an injunction may not be challenged by disobeying its terms. In its most uncompromising form, the traditional approach would declare that the invalidity or even unconstitutionality of a court order would be no defense in a contempt proceeding based on violation of that order."

However, as we have seen, the collateral bar rule has been significantly curtailed. Moreover, Jeffries argued, "a properly limited collateral bar rule would not be destructive of our system of freedom of expression."

The reasons for the collateral bar rule are obvious and not unimportant. They include the preservation of judicial authority and the orderly settlement of disputes—values evoked by Justice Stewart's reference to "the civilizing hand of law." But it is also clear that, at least in the context of injunctions against speech, the collateral bar rule must be carefully circumscribed. The Supreme Court has recognized the point and limited the rule accordingly. Indeed, in *Walker* [*v. City of Birmingham*, supra p. 105,] itself the Court acknowledged that a different situation would be presented if an injunction were "transparently invalid" or if delay or frustration were encountered in the effort to contest its validity.

The first of these exceptions covers the case of an injunction so palpably contrary to authority that it falls under a kind of "plain error" rule. The limitation is not trivial, for existing First Amendment precedents would render "transparently invalid" a vast range of injunctions against speech. Nevertheless, this formulation does not address the truly close case, however occasionally it may arise. The second exception may be more to the point, for it speaks directly to the central problem of the collateral bar rule—the risk that an injunction against speech, even though ultimately invalidated, will so delay publication as to make the speech untimely and hence valueless for its purpose. The worst case would be an election-eve attempt by the party in power to enjoin publication of politically damaging information. In such circumstances, even the few days necessary to obtain expedited appellate review might prove seriously prejudicial to that system of representative government which the First Amendment, above all else, should be thought to undergird. In my view, therefore, the normal operation of the collateral bar rule can be sustained only so long as expedited appellate review allows an immediate opportunity to test the validity of an injunction against speech and only so long as that opportunity is genuinely effective to allow timely publication should the injunction ultimately be adjudged invalid. In any event, this is, as Professor Blasi put it, only a "controversy over the validity and scope of the collateral bar rule." It should be addressed in those terms and not, in my view, as a remote and usually unarticulated premise underlying a broad and uncritical acceptance of the conventional rhetoric of prior restraint.

Jeffries concluded:

> The conclusion that I draw from all this is embarrassingly modest. It is not that injunctions are preferable to subsequent punishment as a mechanism for suppression of speech, though that may be true in some cases. Nor would I assert that there is never a case in which injunctive relief should be specially disfavored. In some situations (the election-eve gambit comes to mind) an injunction may be differentially destructive of First Amendment values, just as in others (perhaps regulation of obscenity) it may prove differentially protective. My only point is to question the broad and categorical condemnation of injunctions as a form of "prior restraint."

> In my view, a rule of special hostility to administrative preclearance is fully justified, but a rule of special hostility to injunctive relief is not. Lumping both together under the name of "prior restraint" obscures rather than clarifies what is at stake in these cases. . . .

How central to the controversy is the doctrine of collateral bar? In states that do not follow the doctrine and allow challenges to the validity of the injunction after its violation, what are the major arguments in favor of retaining a prior restraint doctrine?

Does the *Providence Journal* case remove the doubt Professor Jeffries expressed about the "continued vitality" of *Walker v. City of Birmingham*?

For further reading, see Martin Redish, The Proper Role of the Prior Restraint Doctrine in First Amendment Theory, 70 Va. L. Rev. 53 (1984); Jeffrey A. Smith, Prior Restraint: Original Intentions and Modern Interpretations, 28 Wm. & Mary L. Rev. 439 (1987).

B. SPEECH ABOUT JUDICIAL PROCEEDINGS

The principal reason for restricting coverage of judicial proceedings is to protect the fairness of the proceeding, although often other interests, such as privacy of victims or jurors, are invoked as well. Concern about the effect of media coverage on the fairness of trials seems to run in cycles fueled by sensational cases that stimulate new heights of publicity. One peak occurred with the trial in 1932 of Bruno Hauptmann for the kidnapping and murder of Charles Lindbergh's son. Nearly 1,000 reporters and photographers covered the trial, and it is said that as many as 20,000 curious observers gathered in the small town in which the trial was held. This prompted the American Bar Association's first effort to control publicity.

Another peak occurred in the 1960s, when the assassination of President Kennedy dramatically illustrated the potential difficulty of securing an impartial jury in notorious cases. When Lee Harvey Oswald was arrested as the assassin, police proclaimed his guilt and detailed the evidence against him on national television. Then two days later Oswald was murdered on live television. The Warren Commission, in its report on the assassination, expressed grave doubts as to whether he could have received a fair trial, and the effects of prejudicial publicity were an issue in subsequent appeals by the man convicted of Oswald's murder, Jack Ruby. These events and other incidents prompted much discussion within the bar and the judiciary about methods of limiting prejudicial pretrial publicity. In many states, joint committees of lawyers and journalists promulgated guidelines intended to lead to voluntary restraint by both sides.

Publicity surrounding the 1995 trial of O.J. Simpson for the murder of his ex-wife, Nicole Brown Simpson, and Ronald Goldman set off another round of debate about the effect of the media on judicial proceedings in sensational cases. This time the concern was not only about the fair trial rights of the defendant, but also about the integrity of the legal system itself when witnesses, jurors, attorneys, and the judge become national celebrities, some of whom were being offered substantial amounts of money to tell their stories to the media. Another round of debate occurred in 2003–04 when basketball star Kobe Bryant was charged with rape in a case that was later dropped at the accuser's request.

The Supreme Court's first cases on prejudicial publicity involved the effect of news coverage on the defendant's rights, rather than the rights of the press to cover trials. These cases established that if the publicity was sufficiently prejudicial, a conviction might be reversed despite jurors' assurances that they could be impartial, without specific proof that the publicity had denied the accused a fair trial.

In Estes v. Texas, 381 U.S. 532, 1 Med. L. Rptr. 1187 (1965), the Court held that televising parts of a sensational trial over the defendant's objections could be presumed to be prejudicial, despite lack of any specific proof of prejudice. The most important reversal came in the following case, which illustrates both the nature of the publicity problem at one of its most egregious extremes, and the Court's initial faith that the problem could be solved by insulating jurors from prejudicial information.

Sheppard v. Maxwell

Supreme Court of the United States, 1966.
384 U.S. 333, 86 S.Ct. 1507, 16 L.Ed.2d 600, 1 Med.L.Rptr. 1220.

[In 1954, Sheppard was charged with murdering his wife. The case attracted great public attention and extensive media coverage beginning shortly after the murder, before any arrest had been made. The publicity continued through the pretrial and trial period. Sheppard was convicted of second-degree murder. After serving several years in prison, he sought habeas corpus in the federal courts. The district court granted the writ, but the court of appeals reversed.]

MR. JUSTICE CLARK delivered the opinion of the Court.

[The opinion traced the facts in great detail and expressed concern about the effect of pretrial publicity, but did not reverse on that ground.]

While we cannot say that Sheppard was denied due process by the judge's refusal to take precautions against the influence of pretrial publicity alone, the court's later rulings must be considered against the setting in which the trial was held. In light of this background, we believe that the arrangements made by the judge with the news media caused Sheppard to be deprived of that "judicial serenity and calm to which [he] was entitled" [quoting *Estes v. Texas*]. The fact is that bedlam reigned at the courthouse during the trial and newsmen took over practically the entire courtroom, hounding most of the participants in the trial, especially Sheppard. . . . Having assigned almost all of the available seats in the courtroom to the news media the judge lost his ability to supervise the environment. The movement of the reporters in and out of the courtroom caused frequent confusion and disruption of the trial.

[The Court then addressed the issue of publicity during the trial.]

Much of the material printed or broadcast during the trial was never heard from the witness stand, such as the charges that Sheppard had purposely impeded the murder investigation and must be guilty since he had hired a prominent criminal lawyer; that Sheppard was a perjurer; that he had sexual relations with numerous women; that his slain wife had characterized him as a "Jekyll–Hyde"; that he was "a bare-faced liar" because of his testimony as to police treatment; and, finally, that a woman convict claimed Sheppard to be the father of her illegitimate child. As the trial progressed, the newspapers summarized and interpreted the evidence, devoting particular attention to the material that incriminated Sheppard, and often drew unwarranted inferences from testimony. At one point, a front-page picture of Mrs. Sheppard's blood-stained pillow was published after being "doctored" to show more clearly an alleged imprint of a surgical instrument.

Nor is there doubt that this deluge of publicity reached at least some of the jury. On the only occasion that the jury was queried, two jurors admitted in open court to hearing the highly inflammatory charge that a prison inmate claimed Sheppard as the father of her illegitimate child. Despite the extent and nature of the publicity to which the jury was exposed during trial, the judge refused defense counsel's other requests that the jurors be asked whether they had read or heard specific prejudicial comment about the case, including the incidents we have previously summarized. In these circumstances, we can assume that some of this material reached members of the jury. [ ]

VII.

The court's fundamental error is compounded by the holding that it lacked power to control the publicity about the trial. From the very inception of the proceedings the judge announced that neither he nor anyone else could restrict prejudicial news accounts. And he reiterated this view on numerous occasions. Since he viewed the news media as his target, the judge never considered other means that are often utilized to reduce the appearance of prejudicial material and to protect the jury from outside influence. We conclude that these procedures would have been sufficient to guarantee Sheppard a fair trial and so do not consider what sanctions might be available against a recalcitrant press nor the charges of bias now made against the state trial judge.

The carnival atmosphere at trial could easily have been avoided since the courtroom and courthouse premises are subject to the control of the court. . . .

Secondly, the court should have insulated the witnesses. All of the newspapers and radio stations apparently interviewed prospective witnesses at will, and in many instances disclosed their testimony. A typical example was the publication of numerous statements by Susan Hayes, before her appearance in court, regarding her love affair with Sheppard. Although the witnesses were barred from the courtroom during the trial the full verbatim testimony was available to them in the press. This completely nullified the judge's imposition of the rule. [ ]

Thirdly, the court should have made some effort to control the release of leads, information, and gossip to the press by police officers, witnesses, and the counsel for both sides. Much of the information thus disclosed was inaccurate, leading to groundless rumors and confusion. . . .

Defense counsel immediately brought to the court's attention the tremendous amount of publicity in the Cleveland press that "misrepresented entirely the testimony" in the case. Under such circumstances, the judge should have at least warned the newspapers to check the accuracy of their accounts. And it is obvious that the judge should have further sought to alleviate this problem by imposing control over the statements made to the news media by counsel, witnesses, and especially the Coroner and police officers. The prosecution repeatedly made evidence available to the news media which was never offered in the trial. Much of the "evidence" disseminated in this fashion was clearly inadmissible. The exclusion of such evidence in court is rendered meaningless when news media make it available to the public. For example, the publicity about Sheppard's refusal to take a lie detector test came directly from police officers and the Coroner. The story that Sheppard had been called a "Jekyll–Hyde" personality by his wife was attributed to a prosecution witness. No such testimony was given. The further report that there was "a 'bombshell witness' on tap" who would testify as to Sheppard's "fiery temper" could only have emanated from the prosecution. Moreover, the newspapers described in detail clues that had been found by the police, but not put into the record.

The fact that many of the prejudicial news items can be traced to the prosecution, as well as the defense, aggravates the judge's failure to take any action. [ ] Effective control of these sources—concededly within the court's power—might well have prevented the divulgence of inaccurate information, rumors, and accusations that made up much of the inflammatory publicity, at least after Sheppard's indictment.

More specifically, the trial court might well have proscribed extrajudicial statements by any lawyer, party, witness, or court official which divulged prejudicial matters, such as the refusal of Sheppard to submit to interrogation or take any lie detector tests; any statement made by Sheppard to officials; the identity of prospective witnesses or their probable testimony; any belief in guilt or innocence; or like statements concerning the merits of the case. . . . Being advised of the great public interest in the case, the mass coverage of the press, and the potential prejudicial impact of publicity, the court could also have requested the appropriate city and county officials to promulgate a regulation with respect to dissemination of information about the case by their employees. . . . Had the judge, the other officers of the court, and the police placed the interest of justice first, the news media would have soon learned to be content with the task of reporting the case as it unfolded in the courtroom—not pieced together from extrajudicial statements.

From the cases coming here we note that unfair and prejudicial news comment on pending trials has become increasingly prevalent. Due process requires that the accused receive a trial by an impartial jury free from outside influences. Given the pervasiveness of modern communications and the difficulty of effacing prejudicial publicity from the minds of the jurors, the trial courts must take strong measures to ensure that the balance is never weighed against the accused. And appellate tribunals have the duty to make an independent evaluation of the circumstances. Of course, there is nothing that proscribes the press from reporting the events that transpire in the courtroom. But where there is a reasonable likelihood that prejudicial news prior to trial will prevent a fair trial, the judge should continue the case until the threat abates, or transfer it to another county not so permeated with publicity. In addition, sequestration of the jury was something the judge should have raised *sua sponte* with counsel. If publicity during the proceedings threatens the fairness of the trial, a new trial should be ordered. But we must remember that reversals are but palliatives; the cure lies in those remedial measures that will prevent the prejudice at its inception. The courts must take such steps by rule and regulation that will protect their processes from prejudicial outside interferences. Neither prosecutors, counsel for defense, the accused, witnesses, court staff nor enforcement officers coming under the jurisdiction of the court should be permitted to frustrate its function. Collaboration between counsel and the press as to information affecting the fairness of a criminal trial is not only subject to regulation, but is highly censurable and worthy of disciplinary measures.

Since the state trial judge did not fulfill his duty to protect Sheppard from the inherently prejudicial publicity which saturated the community and to control disruptive influences in the courtroom, we must reverse the denial of the habeas petition. The case is remanded to the District Court with instructions to issue the writ and order that Sheppard be released from custody unless the State puts him to its charges again within a reasonable time.

It is so ordered.

MR. JUSTICE BLACK dissents.

Notes and Questions

1.   On Sheppard's retrial he was acquitted and released—after having served ten years in prison. He died four years later. The case not only sparked media interest at the time of the original trial; it also led to the television series "The Fugitive" and a 1993 movie by the same name loosely based on the *Sheppard* case. The popularity of those programs helped Sheppard's son continue his efforts to demonstrate his father's innocence. In 1997, Sheppard's body was exhumed and a DNA sample taken from it failed to match DNA taken from evidence collected at the murder scene. In 1998, Sheppard's estate sued the State of Ohio for wrongful imprisonment, but the claim was held to be barred by the statute of limitations. See Murray v. State, No. 78374, 2002 WL 337732 (Ohio App. 8 Dist. 2002).

2.   Most discussion of the fair trial problem focuses on the jury and assumes that judges and lawyers will not be affected by the publicity. But in many states judges and prosecutors are elected, and even where they are not, those who hope to be appointed to higher positions probably are not oblivious to the effects that publicity might have on their careers. In the *Sheppard* case both the prosecutor and judge were candidates for judgeships in a hotly contested election to take place two weeks after the trial began. In a footnote the Supreme Court said the judge should at least have delayed the trial until after the election. Should the debate about trial publicity be expanded to include the effects on judges and prosecutors as well as jurors?

As the *Estes* and *Sheppard* cases indicate, one response to prejudicial publicity is to reverse the defendants' convictions. Not surprisingly, judges would prefer to avoid that by preventing the publicity. The *Sheppard* opinion was widely interpreted as a mandate to indirectly restrict news coverage before and during trials by restricting what the participants could tell the press. Trial judges issued orders restricting comment by attorneys and sometimes also by parties and witnesses, and bar associations promulgated rules limiting what attorneys were allowed to say. But as we shall see, the free speech rights of attorneys and other participants limit the extent to which they can be silenced.

Moreover, the effort to control their disclosures was often ineffective. In sensational cases, the press invariably obtained information of the sort that the rules were designed to suppress. Information that police or prosecutors previously would have announced publicly now was leaked to the press and published without attribution. Defense lawyers responded to leaks of information adverse to their clients by leaking favorable information, and sometimes initiated publicity battles themselves. Occasionally these episodes led to acrimonious battles in which judges attempted to force reporters to identify lawyers who had leaked information in violation of the rules. As violation of the rules became commonplace, attorneys often ignored them, even holding news conferences at which they discussed matters forbidden by the disciplinary rules.

When restraints on trial participants proved ineffective in preventing pretrial publicity, some judges responded by imposing direct restraints on the press itself, prohibiting publication of certain information thought to be especially prejudicial. That strategy faced formidable constitutional obstacles, however.

1.   RESTRAINTS ON MEDIA

Punishing publication as contempt. In England contempt is not merely a sanction for disobedience to judicial orders, but may be used more broadly to criminally punish unauthorized publication. The British press can be held in contempt for publications that create a substantial risk of seriously prejudicing an active judicial proceeding, even if no restrictive order has been issued and even if the publisher is unaware of the risk.

At one time judges in the United States were thought to have similar powers, but such uses of the contempt power were held unconstitutional long ago. See Bridges v. California, 314 U.S. 252, 1 Med. L. Rptr. 1275 (1941); Wood v. Georgia, 370 U.S. 375, 1 Med. L. Rptr. 1322 (1962). The Supreme Court has not upheld a use of the criminal contempt power to suppress publication since *Bridges*. None of the cases involved publicity threatening the impartiality of a jury, however, and an argument has been made that the decisions would not preclude a narrowly drawn statutory prohibition against certain kinds of highly prejudicial disclosures. See Michael Chesterman, OJ and the Dingo: How Media Publicity Relating to Criminal Cases Tried by Jury is Dealt With in Australia and America, 45 Am. J. Comp. Law 109 (1997).

The decisions rejecting an expansive interpretation of the contempt power did not foreclose the possibility that narrower restrictions might be imposed in specific cases, but that alternative quickly ran afoul of the presumption that prior restraints on the press are unconstitutional.

Nebraska Press Association v. Stuart

Supreme Court of the United States, 1976.
427 U.S. 539, 96 S.Ct. 2791, 49 L.Ed.2d 683, 1 Med.L.Rptr. 1064.

[Six members of a family were found murdered in a small Nebraska town. Local, regional, and national media converged to cover the story. A suspect, Simants, was arrested, charged with committing the murders in the course of a sexual assault, and publicly arraigned. Two days after the arraignment, in preparation for a preliminary hearing to determine whether Simants should be bound over to district court for trial, his attorney and the county attorney jointly requested the county judge to restrict "matters that may or may not be publicly reported to the public" to protect Simants' right to a fair trial. The judge granted the request, prohibiting reporting of any testimony or evidence adduced at the hearing. He further ordered members of the press to observe the Nebraska Bar–Press Guidelines, voluntary standards that had been adopted by the state bar and news media to protect suspects' fair trial rights. Reporters attended the preliminary hearing subject to this order. At the conclusion of the hearing the county judge bound Simants over to the district court.

Petitioners—several press and broadcast associations, publishers, and reporters—intervened the next day in the district court, asking Judge Stuart to vacate the county judge's order. He refused to do so, but narrowed the order to specifically prohibit petitioners from reporting five subjects: (1) the existence or contents of a confession Simants had made to law enforcement officers, which had been introduced in open court at arraignment; (2) the fact or nature of statements Simants had made to other persons; (3) the contents of a note he had written the night of the crime; (4) certain aspects of the medical testimony at the preliminary hearing; (5) the identity of the victims of the alleged sexual assault and the nature of the assault. He also forbade reporting the specific prohibitions of the restrictive order and ordered the petitioners to observe the Bar–Press Guidelines.

Petitioners applied to the Nebraska Supreme Court for a stay, a writ of mandamus, and an expedited appeal. They also sought a stay from the U.S. Supreme Court. When the Nebraska Supreme Court did not act promptly, Justice Blackmun, as Circuit Justice, granted a partial stay as to the Bar–Press Guidelines and reporting of some other matters, but left in place the prohibition against reporting the confession and other facts "highly prejudicial" to Simants or "strongly implicative" of his guilt.

Six weeks after the order was first entered, the Nebraska Supreme Court upheld the order, but further narrowed it to prohibit only reporting of the existence and nature of confessions or admissions and other facts "strongly implicative" of the accused. The court remanded to the district court to consider whether further pretrial proceedings should be closed to the press and public. The U.S. Supreme Court granted certiorari but did not stay the order except to the extent that it had already been stayed by Justice Blackmun. In the meantime, Simants was convicted and sentenced to death.

The Supreme Court held that the controversy was not moot because the dispute otherwise was "capable of repetition, yet evading review."]

Mr. Chief Justice Burger delivered the opinion of the Court.

. . .

In Sheppard v. Maxwell, 384 U.S. 333 (1966), the Court focused sharply on the impact of pretrial publicity and a trial court's duty to protect the defendant's constitutional right to a fair trial. With only Mr. Justice Black dissenting, and he without opinion, the Court ordered a new trial for the petitioner, even though the first trial had occurred 12 years before. Beyond doubt the press had shown no responsible concern for the constitutional guarantee of a fair trial; the community from which the jury was drawn had been inundated by publicity hostile to the defendant. But the trial judge "did not fulfill his duty to protect [the defendant] from the inherently prejudicial publicity which saturated the community and to control disruptive influences in the courtroom." [ ]. The Court noted that "unfair and prejudicial news comment on pending trials has become increasingly prevalent," [ ] and issued a strong warning:

> "Due process requires that the accused receive a trial by an impartial jury free from outside influences. Given the pervasiveness of modern communications and the difficulty of effacing prejudicial publicity from the minds of the jurors, *the trial courts must take strong measures to ensure that the balance is never weighed against the accused. . . .* Of course, there is nothing that proscribes the press from reporting events that transpire in the courtroom. But where there is a reasonable likelihood that prejudicial news prior to trial will prevent a fair trial, the judge should *continue the case* until the threat abates, *or transfer it* to another county not so permeated with publicity. In addition, *sequestration of the jury* was something the judge should have raised *sua sponte* with counsel. If publicity during the proceedings threatens the fairness of the trial, a new trial should be ordered. But we must remember that reversals are but palliatives; the cure lies in those remedial measures that will prevent the prejudice at its inception. The courts must take such steps by rule and regulation that will protect their process from prejudicial outside interferences. *Neither prosecutors, counsel for defense, the accused, witnesses, court staff nor enforcement officers coming under the jurisdiction of the court should be permitted to frustrate its function.* Collaboration between counsel and the press as to information affecting the fairness of a criminal trial is not only subject to regulation, but is highly censurable and worthy of disciplinary measures." [ ] (emphasis added).

Because the trial court had failed to use even minimal efforts to insulate the trial and the jurors from the "deluge of publicity," [ ] the Court vacated the judgment of conviction and a new trial followed, in which the accused was acquitted.

. . .

The state trial judge in the case before us acted responsibly, out of a legitimate concern, in an effort to protect the defendant's right to a fair trial. What we must decide is not simply whether the Nebraska courts erred in seeing the possibility of real danger to the defendant's rights, but whether in the circumstances of this case the means employed were foreclosed by another provision of the Constitution.

V.

The First Amendment provides that "Congress shall make no law . . . abridging the freedom . . . of the press," and it is "no longer open to doubt that the liberty of the press, and of speech, is within the liberty safeguarded by the due process clause of the Fourteenth Amendment from invasion by state action." [*Near*]. The Court has interpreted these guarantees to afford special protection against orders that prohibit the publication or broadcast of particular information or commentary—orders that impose a "previous" or "prior" restraint on speech. None of our decided cases on prior restraint involved restrictive orders entered to protect a defendant's right to a fair and impartial jury, but the opinions on prior restraint have a common thread relevant to this case.

[The Court reviewed its prior restraint cases, primarily *Near* and *New York Times v. United States.*]

The thread running through all these cases is that prior restraints on speech and publication are the most serious and the least tolerable infringement on First Amendment rights. A criminal penalty or a judgment in a defamation case is subject to the whole panoply of protections afforded by deferring the impact of the judgment until all avenues of appellate review have been exhausted. Only after judgment has become final, correct or otherwise, does the law's sanction become fully operative.

A prior restraint, by contrast and by definition, has an immediate and irreversible sanction. If it can be said that a threat of criminal or civil sanctions after publication "chills" speech, prior restraint "freezes" it at least for the time.

The damage can be particularly great when the prior restraint falls upon the communication of news and commentary on current events. Truthful reports of public judicial proceedings have been afforded special protection against subsequent punishment. [ ]. For the same reasons the protection against prior restraint should have particular force as applied to reporting of criminal proceedings, whether the crime in question is a single isolated act or a pattern of criminal conduct. . . . The extraordinary protections afforded by the First Amendment carry with them something in the nature of a fiduciary duty to exercise the protected rights responsibly— a duty widely acknowledged but not always observed by editors and publishers. It is not asking too much to suggest that those who exercise First Amendment rights in newspapers or broadcasting enterprises direct some effort to protect the rights of an accused to a fair trial by unbiased jurors.

Of course, the order at issue—like the order requested in *New York Times*—does not prohibit but only postpones publication. Some news can be delayed and most commentary can even more readily be delayed without serious injury, and there often is a self-imposed delay when responsible editors call for verification of information. But such delays are normally slight and they are self-imposed. Delays imposed by governmental authority are a different matter. . . . As a practical matter, moreover, the element of time is not unimportant if press coverage is to fulfill its traditional function of bringing news to the public promptly.

The authors of the Bill of Rights did not undertake to assign priorities as between First Amendment and Sixth Amendment rights, ranking one as superior to the other. In this case, the petitioners would have us declare the right of an accused subordinate to their right to publish in all circumstances. But if the authors of these guarantees, fully aware of the potential conflicts between them, were unwilling or unable to resolve the issue by assigning to one priority over the other, it is not for us to rewrite the Constitution by undertaking what they declined. It is unnecessary, after nearly two centuries, to establish a priority applicable in all circumstances. Yet it is nonetheless clear that the barriers to prior restraint remain high unless we are to abandon what the Court has said for nearly a quarter of our national existence and implied throughout all of it. . . .

. . .

VI.

We turn now to the record in this case to determine whether, as Learned Hand put it, "the gravity of the 'evil,' discounted by its improbability, justifies such invasion of free speech as is necessary to avoid the danger." United States v. Dennis, 183 F.2d 201, 212 (1950), aff'd, 341 U.S. 494 (1951); see also L. Hand, The Bill of Rights 58–61 (1958). To do so, we must examine the evidence before the trial judge when the order was entered to determine (a) the nature and extent of pretrial news coverage; (b) whether other measures would be likely to mitigate the effects of unrestrained pretrial publicity; (c) how effectively a restraining order would operate to prevent the threatened danger. The precise terms of the restraining order are also important. We must then consider whether the record supports the entry of a prior restraint on publication, one of the most extraordinary remedies known to our jurisprudence.

A.

In assessing the probable extent of publicity, the trial judge had before him newspapers demonstrating that the crime had already drawn intensive news coverage, and the testimony of the County Judge, who had entered the initial restraining order based on the local and national attention the case had attracted. The District Judge was required to assess the probable publicity that would be given these shocking crimes prior to the time a jury was selected and sequestered. He then had to examine the probable nature of the publicity and determine how it would affect prospective jurors.

Our review of the pretrial record persuades us that the trial judge was justified in concluding that there would be intense and pervasive pretrial publicity concerning this case. He could also reasonably conclude, based on common human experience, that publicity might impair the defendant's right to a fair trial. He did not purport to say more, for he found only "a clear and present danger that pretrial publicity *could* impinge upon the defendant's right to a fair trial." (Emphasis added.) His conclusion as to the impact of such publicity on prospective jurors was of necessity speculative, dealing as he was with factors unknown and unknowable.

B.

We find little in the record that goes to another aspect of our task, determining whether measures short of an order restraining all publication would have insured the defendant a fair trial. Although the entry of the order might be read as a judicial determination that other measures would not suffice, the trial court made no express findings to that effect; the Nebraska Supreme Court referred to the issue only by implication. [ ]

Most of the alternatives to prior restraint of publication in these circumstances were discussed with obvious approval in *Sheppard v. Maxwell* [ ]: (a) change of trial venue to a place less exposed to the intense publicity that seemed imminent in Lincoln County;[7] (b) postponement of the trial to allow public attention to subside; (c) searching questioning of prospective jurors . . . to screen out those with fixed opinions as to guilt or innocence; (d) the use of emphatic and clear instructions on the sworn duty of each juror to decide the issues only on evidence presented in open court. Sequestration of jurors is, of course, always available. Although that measure insulates jurors only after they are sworn, it also enhances the likelihood of dissipating the impact of pretrial publicity and emphasizes the elements of the jurors' oaths.

This Court has outlined other measures short of prior restraints on publication tending to blunt the impact of pretrial publicity. [ ]. Professional studies have filled out these suggestions, recommending that trial courts in appropriate cases limit what the contending lawyers, the police, and witnesses may say to anyone. See American Bar Association, Standards for Criminal Justice, Fair Trial and Free Press 2–15 (Approved Draft, 1968).[8]

We note that in making its proposals, the American Bar Association recommended strongly against resort to direct restraints on the press to prohibit publication. ABA Standards, at 68–73. Other groups have reached similar conclusions. [ ]

We have noted earlier that pretrial publicity, even if pervasive and concentrated, cannot be regarded as leading automatically and in every kind of criminal case to an unfair trial. The decided cases "cannot be made

---

7. The respondent and intervenors argue here that a change of venue would not have helped, since Nebraska law permits a change only to adjacent counties, which had been as exposed to pretrial publicity in this case as Lincoln County. We have held that state laws restricting venue must on occasion yield to the constitutional requirement that the State afford a fair trial. Groppi v. Wisconsin, 400 U.S. 505 (1971). We note also that the combined population of Lincoln County and the adjacent counties is over 80,000, pro-viding a substantial pool of prospective jurors.

8. Closing of pretrial proceedings with the consent of the defendant when required is also recommended in guidelines that have emerged from various studies. At oral argument petitioners' counsel asserted that judicially imposed restraints on lawyers and others would be subject to challenge as interfering with press rights to news sources. [ ] We are not now confronted with such issues.

to stand for the proposition that juror exposure to information about a state defendant's prior convictions or to news accounts of the crime with which he is charged alone presumptively deprives the defendant of due process." [ ]. Appellate evaluations as to the impact of publicity take into account what other measures were used to mitigate the adverse effects of publicity. The more difficult prospective or predictive assessment that a trial judge must make also calls for a judgment as to whether other precautionary steps will suffice.

We have therefore examined this record to determine the probable efficacy of the measures short of prior restraint on the press and speech. There is no finding that alternative measures would not have protected Simants' rights, and the Nebraska Supreme Court did no more than imply that such measures might not be adequate. Moreover, the record is lacking in evidence to support such a finding.

C.

We must also assess the probable efficacy of prior restraint on publication as a workable method of protecting Simants' right to a fair trial, and we cannot ignore the reality of the problems of managing and enforcing pretrial restraining orders. The territorial jurisdiction of the issuing court is limited by concepts of sovereignty [ ]. The need for *in personam* jurisdiction also presents an obstacle to a restraining order that applies to publication at-large as distinguished from restraining publication within a given jurisdiction. [ ]

The Nebraska Supreme Court narrowed the scope of the restrictive order, and its opinion reflects awareness of the tensions between the need to protect the accused as fully as possible and the need to restrict publication as little as possible. The dilemma posed underscores how difficult it is for trial judges to predict what information will in fact undermine the impartiality of jurors, and the difficulty of drafting an order that will effectively keep prejudicial information from prospective jurors. When a restrictive order is sought, a court can anticipate only part of what will develop that may injure the accused. But information not so obviously prejudicial may emerge, and what may properly be published in these "gray zone" circumstances may not violate the restrictive order and yet be prejudicial.

Finally, we note that the events disclosed by the record took place in a community of 850 people. It is reasonable to assume that, without any news accounts being printed or broadcast, rumors would travel swiftly by word of mouth. One can only speculate on the accuracy of such reports, given the generative propensities of rumors; they could well be more damaging than reasonably accurate news accounts. But plainly a whole community cannot be restrained from discussing a subject intimately affecting life within it.

Given these practical problems, it is far from clear that prior restraint on publication would have protected Simants' rights.

D.

Finally, another feature of this case leads us to conclude that the restrictive order entered here is not supportable. At the outset the County Court entered a very broad restrictive order, the terms of which are not before us; it then held a preliminary hearing open to the public and the press. There was testimony concerning at least two incriminating statements made by Simants to private persons; the statement—evidently a confession—that he gave to law enforcement officials was also introduced. The State District Court's later order was entered after this public hearing and, as modified by the Nebraska Supreme Court, enjoined reporting of (1) "[c]onfessions or admissions against interests made by the accused to law enforcement officials"; (2) "[c]onfessions or admissions against interest, oral or written, if any, made by the accused to third parties, excepting any statements, if any, made by the accused to representatives of the news media"; and (3) all "[o]ther information strongly implicative of the accused as the perpetrator of the slayings." [ ]

To the extent that this order prohibited the reporting of evidence adduced at the open preliminary hearing, it plainly violated settled principles: "[T]here is nothing that proscribes the press from reporting events that transpire in the courtroom." *Sheppard v. Maxwell* [ ]. The County Court could not know that closure of the preliminary hearing was an alternative open to it until the Nebraska Supreme Court so construed state law; but once a public hearing had been held, what transpired there could not be subject to prior restraint.

The third prohibition of the order was defective in another respect as well. As part of a final order, entered after plenary review, this prohibition regarding "implicative" information is too vague and too broad to survive the scrutiny we have given to restraints on First Amendment rights. [ ] The third phase of the order entered falls outside permissible limits.

E.

. . . We cannot say on this record that alternatives to a prior restraint on petitioners would not have sufficiently mitigated the adverse effects of pretrial publicity so as to make prior restraint unnecessary. Nor can we conclude that the restraining order actually entered would serve its intended purpose. Reasonable minds can have few doubts about the gravity of the evil pretrial publicity can work, but the probability that it would do so here was not demonstrated with the degree of certainty our cases on prior restraint require.

Of necessity our holding is confined to the record before us. But our conclusion is not simply a result of assessing the adequacy of the showing made in this case; it results in part from the problems inherent in meeting the heavy burden of demonstrating, in advance of trial, that without prior restraint a fair trial will be denied. The practical problems of managing and enforcing restrictive orders will always be present. In this sense, the record now before us is illustrative rather than exceptional. It is significant that when this Court has reversed a state conviction because of prejudicial publicity, it has carefully noted that some course of action short of prior restraint would have made a critical difference. [ ] However difficult it may be, we need not rule out the possibility of showing the kind of threat to fair trial rights that would possess the requisite degree of certainty to justify restraint. This Court has frequently denied that First Amendment rights are absolute and has consistently rejected the proposition that a prior restraint can never be employed. [ ]

. . . We hold that, with respect to the order entered in this case prohibiting reporting or commentary on judicial proceedings held in public, the barriers have not been overcome; to the extent that this order restrained publication of such material, it is clearly invalid. To the extent that it prohibited publication based on information gained from other sources, we conclude that the heavy burden imposed as a condition to securing a prior restraint was not met and the judgment of the Nebraska Supreme Court is therefore

Reversed.

[Justices Brennan, Stewart, and Marshall concurred in the judgment. They would have held that prior restraints against the press are never a permissible method of protecting the right to a fair trial. Justice Stevens, concurring, said he might well join in this conclusion if forced to face the issue squarely, but preferred to leave open the possibility of enjoining publication of information improperly obtained. Justice White, concurring, doubted that such restraints would ever be permissible, and said that if the result "in case after case is to be similar to our judgment today, we should at some point announce a more general rule and avoid the interminable litigation that our failure to do would necessarily entail." Justice Powell concurred separately, stating that a prior restraint should issue only when the publicity "poses a high likelihood of preventing, directly and irreparably," the impaneling of an impartial jury.]

Notes and Questions

1. Taking into account the concurring opinions, under what circumstances would a prior restraint be permissible to protect fair trial rights? Why might the barrier be lower here than in New York Times v. United States?

2. Would the result be different if a statute made it a criminal offense for the media to publish specified facts considered by the legislature to be "highly prejudicial" to the defendant's right to a fair trial?

3. Since *Nebraska Press Association,* decisions upholding restrictive orders against the press have been rare. One observer doubts that such orders can ever comply with the stringent requirements of that case: "As noted by Justice White in his concurring opinion, it should be highly unlikely that the 'heavy burden' of satisfying the three elements of the Burger test can

ever be met." Floyd Abrams, "Prior Restraints," *in* 3 Communications Law 799, 814 (Practicing Law Institute 1993).

————

Privileged communications. Might the requirements of *Nebraska Press Association* be met if the media threatened to reveal privileged communications between a defendant and his attorney? The question has not been definitively answered, but some courts have indicated the answer might be yes. During the prosecution of Panamanian General Manuel Antonio Noriega on federal drug charges, CNN announced it would broadcast excerpts from tapes the government had made of telephone calls from Noriega to his defense counsel. At the request of Noriega's attorneys, a district judge issued a temporary restraining order prohibiting broadcast of the tapes and directed the network to turn the tapes over to him for in camera review to determine whether they contained privileged communications. CNN refused to turn the tapes over, broadcast one of them, and sought emergency relief in the Court of Appeals. The network argued that under *Nebraska Press Association*, no prior restraint could be issued in the absence of a threshold finding that the information would threaten Noriega's right to a fair trial and that prohibiting broadcast was the only means of protecting that right. But the Court of Appeals held that the network could not insist that such findings be made and at the same time deny the trial court access to the tapes:

> After review of such tapes, it is entirely conceivable that the District Court may determine that the disclosure of only portions of such tapes would threaten the Sixth Amendment rights of Noriega. Under such circumstances the accused's Sixth Amendment right to a fair trial is properly balanced against the First Amendment rights of the press and public. At this juncture, however, we are required to speculate as a result of CNN's refusal to produce the tape recordings.

United States v. Noriega, 917 F.2d 1543, 18 Med. L. Rptr. 1352 (11th Cir. 1990). The Supreme Court denied CNN's application for stay and petition for certiorari, Justices Marshall and O'Connor dissenting. 498 U.S. 976, 18 Med. L. Rptr. 1358 (1990). CNN eventually was held in contempt for broadcasting the first tape in defiance of the temporary restraining order. To avoid paying a "substantial" fine, CNN broadcast an apology and paid $85,000 to cover the government's legal fees.

Does the refusal by the Eleventh Circuit and the Supreme Court to stay the order requiring CNN to turn the tapes over to the judge imply that *Nebraska Press Association* does not preclude enjoining publication of significant privileged communications?

The South Carolina Supreme Court interpreted the *Noriega* case as permitting prior restraints to protect significant privileged communications between attorney and client, at least in instances where the privileged information otherwise would be disclosed before the requisite findings could be made. If *Nebraska Press* precludes this, the Supreme Court should say so, the court said. A dissenter agreed that *Nebraska Press* ought to be reconsidered, but considered it binding. See Ex Parte State–Record Co., 504 S.E. 2d 592, 27 Med. L. Rptr. 1193 (S.C. 1998).

————

In the absence of a statute, where do courts get the power to issue orders against the press to protect fair trial rights? The assumption that this is an inherent judicial power is considered and rejected in Note, Protective Orders Against the Press and the Inherent Powers of the Courts, 87 Yale L.J. 342 (1977).

The same point is made in Hans A. Linde, Fair Trials and Press Freedom—Two Rights Against the State, 13 Willamette L.J. 211 (1977): "I find it striking that no one seems to ask what law authorized issuance of a gag order, before reaching the question of its constitutionality." Beyond that observation, Linde argued that the Supreme Court has been "careful to avoid any suggestion that a court could take any action directed against publication of whatever information the media did obtain or whatever comments they might choose to publish." He doubted that the state could forbid a publication that would otherwise be protected under the First Amendment in order to assure itself of the ability to obtain a conviction without running afoul of the defendant's Sixth Amendment right to a fair trial.

He found no conflict between the two amendments. "The interests of individuals, for instance the interests of suspects and of newspaper reporters, can and often do conflict. But not their constitutional rights." The basic point was that the accused has no constitutional right against the press, only a right to have the government refrain from acting unconstitutionally against the accused.

The existing view, Linde asserted, "transforms the defendant's fair trial claim against the state into a claim against the media. It lets the state turn two constitutional limitations on its powers into a classic example of 'let's you and him fight.' It asks defendants and reporters to trade off their rights between themselves or let a court do it for them. But this is not constitutional law."

What are the implications of accepting Linde's view?

For a wide range of views on *Nebraska Press Association*, see symposia in 20 St. Louis U. L.J. 654 (1976) and 29 Stan. L. Rev. 383 (1977).

2.   RESTRAINTS ON TRIAL PARTICIPANTS

One of the alternatives to restrictions on publication mentioned in *Nebraska Press Association* is to attack prejudicial publicity at its source, by prohibiting attorneys and other participants in the proceedings from making statements that might prejudice a fair trial. Most states have rules regulating what attorneys may say about pending proceedings.

Gentile v. State Bar. The constitutionality of such rules reached the Supreme Court in a case from Nevada, Gentile v. State Bar of Nevada, 501 U.S. 1030 (1991). That state's Rule 177 (patterned, like those of many other states, after Rule 3.6 of the American Bar Association's Model Rules of Professional Conduct) provided in part:

> 1. A lawyer shall not make an extrajudicial statement that a reasonable person would expect to be disseminated by means of public communication if the lawyer knows or reasonably should know that it will have a substantial likelihood of materially prejudicing an adjudicative proceeding.
>
> [Section 2 contained a list of six categories of statements that would "ordinarily" violate Section 1—for example, statements about confessions or test results.]
>
> 3. Notwithstanding subsection 1 and 2(a–f), a lawyer involved in the investigation or litigation of a matter may state without elaboration:
>
> (a) the general nature of the claim or defense. . . .

Gentile was a Nevada lawyer representing a criminal defendant accused of stealing money and drugs from a vault he owned but rented to police. The case was highly publicized locally. The day after his client was indicted Gentile held a news conference at which he maintained that his client was innocent and suggested that a police detective was the likely thief. The State Bar of Nevada reprimanded the lawyer for violating Rule 177 and the Nevada Supreme Court affirmed. The U.S. Supreme Court reversed 5–4 on the narrow ground that subsection 3 made the rule unconstitutionally vague, but held 5–4 that lawyers' speech can be regulated under a less demanding standard than that established in *Nebraska Press Association* for regulation of the press. Chief Justice Rehnquist wrote for the majority on the issue of the appropriate standard for attorney speech:

> Lawyers representing clients in pending cases are key participants in the criminal justice system, and the State may demand some adherence to the precepts of that system in regulating their speech as well as their conduct. As noted by Justice Brennan in his concurring opinion in Nebraska Press, which was joined by Justices Stewart and Marshall, "[a]s officers of the court, court personnel and attorneys have a fiduciary responsibility not to engage in public debate that will redound to the detriment of the accused or that will obstruct the fair administration of justice." [ ] Because lawyers have special access to information through discovery and client communications, their extrajudicial statements pose a threat to the fairness of a pending proceeding since lawyers' statements are likely to be received as especially authoritative. [ ] We agree with the majority of the States that the "substantial likelihood of material prejudice" standard constitutes a constitutionally permissible balance between the First Amendment

rights of attorneys in pending cases and the state's interest in fair trials.

When a state regulation implicates First Amendment rights, the Court must balance those interests against the State's legitimate interest in regulating the activity in question. [ ] The "substantial likelihood" test embodied in Rule 177 is constitutional under this analysis, for it is designed to protect the integrity and fairness of a state's judicial system, and it imposes only narrow and necessary limitations on lawyers' speech. The limitations are aimed at two principal evils: (1) comments that are likely to influence the actual outcome of the trial, and (2) comments that are likely to prejudice the jury venire, even if an untainted panel can ultimately be found. Few, if any, interests under the Constitution are more fundamental than the right to a fair trial by "impartial" jurors, and an outcome affected by extrajudicial statements would violate that fundamental right. [ ] Even if a fair trial can ultimately be ensured through voir dire, change of venue, or some other device, these measures entail serious costs to the system. Extensive voir dire may not be able to filter out all of the effects of pretrial publicity, and with increasingly widespread media coverage of criminal trials, a change of venue may not suffice to undo the effects of statements such as those made by petitioner. The State has a substantial interest in preventing officers of the court, such as lawyers, from imposing such costs on the judicial system and on the litigants.

The restraint on speech is narrowly tailored to achieve those objectives. The regulation of attorneys' speech is limited—it applies only to speech that is substantially likely to have a materially prejudicial effect; it is neutral as to points of view, applying equally to all attorneys participating in a pending case; and it merely postpones the attorney's comments until after the trial. While supported by the substantial state interest in preventing prejudice to an adjudicative proceeding by those who have a duty to protect its integrity, the rule is limited on its face to preventing only speech having a substantial likelihood of materially prejudicing that proceeding.

Justice Kennedy wrote the dissent on this issue, joined by Justices Marshall, Blackmun, and Stevens:

The various bar association and advisory commission reports which resulted in promulgation of ABA Model Rule of Professional Conduct 3.6 (1981), and other regulations of attorney speech, and sources they cite, present no convincing case for restrictions upon the speech of defense attorneys. [ ] The police, the prosecution, other government officials, and the community at large hold innumerable avenues for the dissemination of information adverse to a criminal defendant, many of which are not within the scope of Rule 177 or any other regulation. By contrast, a defendant cannot speak without fear of incriminating himself and prejudicing his defense, and most criminal defendants have insufficient means to retain a public relations team apart from defense counsel for the sole purpose of countering prosecution statements. These factors underscore my conclusion that blanket rules restricting speech of defense attorneys should not be accepted without careful First Amendment scrutiny.

Justice Kennedy rejected the proposition that commenting to the press is inconsistent with the attorney's proper role:

> Because attorneys participate in the criminal justice system and are trained in its complexities, they hold unique qualifications as a source of information about pending cases. "Since lawyers are considered credible in regard to pending litigation in which they are engaged and are in one of the most knowledgeable positions, they are a crucial source of information and opinion." [ ] To the extent the press and public rely upon attorneys for information because attorneys are well-informed, this may prove the value to the public of speech by members of the bar. If the dangers of their speech arise from its persuasiveness, from their ability to explain judicial proceedings, or from the likelihood the speech will be believed, these are not the sort of dangers that can validate restrictions. The First Amendment does not permit suppression of speech because of its power to command assent.

> One may concede the proposition that an attorney's speech about pending cases may present dangers that could not arise from statements by a nonparticipant, and that an attorney's duty to cooperate in the judicial process may prevent him or her from taking actions with an intent to frustrate that process. The role of attorneys in the criminal justice system subjects them to fiduciary obligations to the court and the parties. An attorney's position may result in some added ability to obstruct the proceedings through well-timed statements to the press, though one can debate the extent of an attorney's ability to do so without violating other established duties. A court can require an attorney's cooperation to an extent not possible of nonparticipants. A proper weighing of dangers might consider the harm that occurs when speech about ongoing proceedings forces the court to take burdensome steps such as sequestration, continuance, or change of venue.

Justice Kennedy declined to say what might be the limits of the state's power to regulate attorney speech:

> If as a regular matter speech by an attorney about pending cases raised real dangers of this kind then a substantial governmental interest might support additional regulation of speech. But this case involves the sanction of speech so innocuous, and an application of Rule 177(3)'s safe harbor provision so begrudging, that it is difficult to determine the force these arguments would carry in a different setting. The instant case is a poor vehicle for defining with precision the outer limits under the Constitution of a court's ability to regulate an attorney's statements about ongoing adjudicative proceedings. At the very least, however, we can say that the Rule which punished petitioner's statement represents a limitation of First Amendment freedoms greater than is necessary or essential to the protection of the particular

governmental interest, and does not protect against a danger of the necessary gravity, imminence, or likelihood.

Justice O'Connor joined the Chief Justice to make a majority of five for the proposition that attorney speech can be regulated more stringently than media speech, but joined the Kennedy group on the vagueness issue, and that provided the five votes to reverse Gentile's punishment on the ground that Section 177(3)(a) misled Gentile into thinking he could safely make his statements.

Notes and Questions

1. Do *Near, Nebraska Press Association*, and *Gentile* suggest a hierarchy in prior restraint analysis—those in the interest of national security are hardest to justify, those issued against media to protect fair trial interests are easier, and those against attorneys in the interest of fair trial are easier still? Or do they suggest that prior restraint analysis has devolved into a balancing exercise in which the fact that the restriction takes the form of a prior restraint is just a factor to be put into the balance?

2. After *Gentile* the ABA amended Model Rule 3.6 to read as follows:

Trial Publicity

(a) A lawyer who is participating or has participated in the investigation or litigation of a matter shall not make an extrajudicial statement that a reasonable person would expect to be disseminated by means of public communication if the lawyer knows or reasonably should know that it will have a substantial likelihood of prejudicing an adjudicative proceeding in the matter.

(b) Notwithstanding paragraph (a), a lawyer may state [here follows a long list of routine types of information, such as identity of persons involved, scheduling of proceedings, and facts about arrests].

(c) Notwithstanding paragraph (a), a lawyer may make a statement that a reasonable lawyer would believe is required to protect a client from the substantial undue prejudicial effect of recent publicity not initiated by the lawyer or the lawyer's client. A statement made pursuant to this paragraph shall be limited to such information as is necessary to mitigate the recent adverse publicity.

. . .

Does the new rule meet the constitutional objections identified in *Gentile*? Does section (c) authorize publicity wars between prosecutions and defense? The ABA House of Delegates approved the revised rule over objections of some prosecutors who said it invited a "right of reply free-for-all."

3. Does the right to trial by an impartial jury contemplate jurors who have not been exposed to pretrial publicity? In a footnote, Chief Justice Rehnquist rejects the argument (which he ascribes to Justice Kennedy) that publicity is not prejudicial if it merely responds to publicity favorable to the other side. "A juror who may have been initially swayed from open-

mindedness by publicity favorable to the prosecution is not rendered fit for service by being bombarded by publicity favorable to the defendant. The basic premise of our legal system is that suits should be tried in court, not in the media. . . . The remedy for prosecutorial abuses that violate the rule lies not in self-help in the form of similarly prejudicial comments by defense counsel, but in disciplining the prosecutor."

4. The Second Circuit struck down an order prohibiting any comment by prosecutors or defense lawyers in the case of the 1993 bombing that damaged the basement of the World Trade Center. Attorneys for three of the defendants challenged the order, contending President Clinton, Governor Cuomo, and President Mubarak of Egypt, not to mention anonymous police and prosecution sources, were making prejudicial statements while the defendants were silenced by incarceration and inability to speak English and their lawyers were silenced by the gag order. The Second Circuit held the order unconstitutional because the judge had not explored less restrictive options. "The restraint on the attorneys' speech is not narrowly tailored. Rather, it is a blanket prohibition that extends to any statements that 'have anything to do with this case' or that even '*may* have something to do with the case.' " United States v. Salameh, 992 F.2d 445, 21 Med. L. Rptr. 1376 (2d Cir. 1993). See also State v. Bassett, 911 P.2d 385 (Wash. 1996) (relying on *Salameh* in lifting gag order in murder case).

5. Is the premise that "suits should be tried in court, not in the media" tenable in high-visibility cases? Even when the courts impose significant restraints on pretrial comment by attorneys, they (or investigators, witnesses, or police) often leak information to the press anyway. For reasons we shall see in Chapter IX, courts may be unable to compel the media to reveal the sources so the leakers can be punished. Are courts willing to engage in the amount of enforcement effort that stopping pretrial publicity would entail?

––––––––

Media challenges to gag orders on lawyers. Do news organizations have standing to challenge restraints against attorneys and other trial participants? If so, should such orders be analyzed as prior restraints on the press? In a case arising out of the 1987 Wedtech scandal, involving bribes to high-level Reagan Administration officials in exchange for government contracts, the Second Circuit allowed media to challenge an order forbidding most comment by prosecutors, defendants, and defense counsel, but refused to analyze the order as a prior restraint because it was not directed at the news organizations. The court held that the media had a limited right to receive information, but upheld the restraint on the ground that there was a "reasonable likelihood" that pretrial publicity otherwise would prejudice the fair trial rights of the Wedtech defendants. Application of Dow Jones & Co., 842 F.2d 603 (2d Cir. 1988).

Justice White, joined by Justices Brennan and Marshall, would have granted certiorari in the *Dow Jones* case to resolve a conflict among the courts of appeals as to whether the "reasonable likelihood" test is the appropriate method of analyzing the media claims. He pointed out that the Ninth Circuit uses that test, see Radio & Television News Ass'n v. U.S. Dist. Court, 781 F.2d 1443 (9th Cir. 1986), while the Sixth Circuit holds that such restrictions must meet a clear and present danger standard. See CBS Inc. v. Young, 522 F.2d 234 (6th Cir. 1975).

Grand jury secrecy. Smith, a newspaper reporter, was subpoenaed to testify before a special grand jury investigating allegations of corruption in the local office of the state's attorney. The special prosecutor warned Smith that if he wrote about his appearance before the grand jury he would be in violation of Fla. Stat. § 905.27, which provided in part:

> (1) A grand juror . . . or any other person appearing before the grand jury shall not disclose the testimony of a witness examined before the grand jury . . . except when required by a court. . . .

> (2) It is unlawful for any person knowingly to publish, broadcast, disclose, divulge, or communicate to any other person . . . any testimony of a witness examined before the grand jury, or the content, gist, or import thereof. . . .

Violation was punishable as a misdemeanor and also as criminal contempt. After the grand jury investigation ended, Smith wanted to write a news story and possibly a book about the investigation, including his testimony before the grand jury and his observation of its work. He sued the state for a declaration that the statute violated his First Amendment rights and an injunction prohibiting his prosecution under the statute.

The Supreme Court held unanimously that the reporter had a First Amendment right to disclose matters that he had learned before his appearance before the grand jury, even if those were also the subject of his testimony there. Chief Justice Rehnquist said the case was governed by *Landmark*, supra p. 32, and *Smith v. Daily Mail*, supra p. 36. The state's interests in preventing suspects from learning about grand jury proceedings and in protecting those who might be accused but not indicted were real, he said, but not sufficient to overcome the reporter's First Amendment right to disclose truthful information lawfully obtained.

The Court did not address whether Smith would have a right to disclose matters he learned during his grand jury appearance—the questions that were asked of him or comments by grand jurors or prosecutors, for example. In a concurring opinion, Justice Scalia said the state might well have stronger interests in preventing disclosure of those matters. Scalia said that although Smith had a right to disclose matters he had learned before his grand jury appearance, the state might even be able to punish him for disclosing that he had testified about those matters to the grand jury. Butterworth v. Smith, 494 U.S. 624, 17 Med. L. Rptr. 1569 (1990).

C.   SPEECH CONCERNING ELECTIONS

Legislatures sometimes prohibit or regulate media communications in the interest of protecting the integrity of elections or the citizens' ability to fully participate in them. As we have seen, facilitating self-government is one of the basic purposes of protecting freedom of expression. Although one might argue that that end could justify restricting expression as well as protecting it, courts generally have not analyzed statutes prohibiting expression to protect the political process any differently than laws prohibiting expression for other reasons.

1.   PRINT MEDIA

Mills v. Alabama. The leading case is Mills v. Alabama, 384 U.S. 214, 1 Med. L. Rptr. 1334 (1966). The Alabama Corrupt Practices Act made it a crime to solicit votes for or against any ballot proposition on election day. The Birmingham Post–Herald carried an editorial urging voters to adopt a mayor-council form of government on the day that question was being voted upon. Its editor, Mills, was arrested for violating the statute. The Alabama Supreme Court sustained the constitutionality of the law on the ground that it was a reasonable restriction imposing only a minor limitation on the press for the salutary purpose of protecting the public from last minute charges that cannot be answered until the election is over.

The U.S. Supreme Court reversed. Justice Black, for the Court, defined the question as "whether it abridges freedom of the press for a State to punish a newspaper editor for doing no more than publishing an editorial on election day urging people to vote a particular way in the election." In view of the practically universal agreement that a major purpose of the First Amendment was to protect free discussion of governmental affairs, "It is difficult to conceive of a more obvious and flagrant abridgment of the constitutionally guaranteed freedom of the press."

He rejected the Alabama Supreme Court's argument that the statute was a reasonable means of protecting the public "from confusive last-minute charges and countercharges" that cannot be effectively answered until the election is over, because it left people free to make such charges on the day preceding the election and then forbade answers to those charges on election day. But he indicated that even if the statute were a reasonable means of preventing unanswerable last-minute charges, it would still be unconstitutional: "We hold that no test of reasonableness can save a state law from invalidation as a violation of the First Amendment when that law makes it a crime for a newspaper editor to do no more than urge people to vote one way or another in a publicly held election."

The Federal Election Campaign Act as amended in 1974 contained a provision forbidding any person from giving more than $1,000 in a year to the campaign of a candidate for federal office, or from spending more than $1,000 in a year to advocate the election or defeat of a candidate. The Supreme Court upheld the limit on contributions but held the spending limit unconstitutional:

> [*Mills* and *Tornillo*] held that legislative restrictions on advocacy of the election or defeat of political candidates are wholly at odds with the guarantees of the First Amendment. . . . Yet the prohibition on elec-

tion day editorials invalidated in *Mills* is clearly a lesser intrusion on constitutional freedom than a $1,000 limitation on the amount of money any person or association can spend *during an entire election year* in advocating the election or defeat of a candidate for public office.

Buckley v. Valeo, 424 U.S. 1 (1976). One interest cited by Congress in justifying the spending limit was to help equalize the ability of individuals to influence the outcome of elections.

The contribution limits upheld in *Buckley* did not apply to "soft money"—money given to political parties or other political organizations and not used to directly advocate the election or defeat of specific candidates. Eventually such funds, raised primarily from corporations and labor unions, made the contribution limits largely ineffectual. In the Bipartisan Campaign Reform Act of 2002 Congress amended the FECA to severely restrict the use of soft money, and the Supreme Court upheld the new restrictions. See McConnell v. Federal Election Comm'n, 540 U.S. 93 (2003). The Court rejected arguments that because the restrictions did not apply to editorials, news stories, or commentary, they gave media corporations an unfair advantage over other corporations. The majority said this was a narrow exception similar to many others that protected the right of the institutional press to report on and editorialize about political matters. Justice Thomas, dissenting, said the decision might eventually authorize regulation of media political speech because in his view there was no basis for distinguishing the first amendment rights of media corporations from those of other corporations.

Restricting campaign speech. In an effort to keep their election complaints commissions from being used to generate negative publicity about opponents, some states attempt to keep such complaints confidential. Such a restriction was held unconstitutional in Lind v. Grimmer, 30 F.3d 1115, 22 Med. L. Rptr. 2313 (9th Cir. 1994). Lind filed a complaint with the Hawaii Campaign Spending Commission and disclosed that he had done so in an election newsletter he published. The group whose contributions Lind had complained about then filed a complaint against Lind asserting that he had violated a statute making complaints to the commission confidential.

The Ninth Circuit held the statute unconstitutional as applied and on its face, and upheld an injunction against its enforcement. The court analyzed the statute as a content-based restriction. The state's justification was that the statute "precludes the Commission's credibility from being invoked to buttress scandalous charges in the heat of a campaign." But the court rejected this argument on the ground that "the fact of filing simply cannot signal the State's approval of a complainant's charges." Citing *Landmark Communications,* the court said Hawaii could not restrict speech for the purpose of discouraging scurrilous charges that might deter people from running for office.

It is a crime in several states to publish certain false statements affecting an election campaign. The details of the offense vary, as these examples suggest:

WIS. STAT. ANN. § 12.05 (1998). No person may knowingly make or publish, or cause to be made or published, a false representation pertaining to a candidate which is intended or tends to affect voting at an election.

MISS. CODE ANN. § 23–15–875 (1998). No person, including a candidate, shall publicly or privately make, in a campaign then in progress, any charge or charges reflecting upon the honesty, integrity or moral character of any candidate, so far as his private life is concerned, unless the charge be in fact true and actually capable of proof; and any person who makes any such charge shall have the burden of proof to show the truth thereof when called to account therefor under any affidavit or indictment against him for a violation of this section. And any language deliberately uttered or published which, when fairly and reasonably construed and as commonly understood, would clearly and unmistakably imply any such charge, shall be deemed and held to be the equivalent of a direct charge. And in no event shall any such charge, whether true or untrue, be made on the day of the primary, or within the last five days immediately preceding the date of the primary.

Violation of the statute is a misdemeanor in Mississippi, a felony punishable by three years in prison and a $10,000 fine in Wisconsin.

The Wisconsin statute takes aim only at falsehoods; does that save it from constitutional objection? In Garrison v. Louisiana, 379 U.S. 64, 1 Med. L. Rptr. 1548 (1964), the Court held that a critic who attacked the integrity of judges could not be punished for criminal libel, consistently with the First Amendment, unless he knew his accusations were false or spoke with reckless disregard of their falsity. Generally in libel, this standard applies to candidates as well as public officials. See Chapter IV. Is there any reason to think the election statutes quoted above would not be subjected to this standard?

The Washington Supreme Court struck down a statute providing criminal penalties for falsehoods in political advertising, even though the statute required a showing of knowing or reckless falsity. By 5–4 vote, the court said the First Amendment requires the state to leave matters of truth and falsity to the electorate. The case involved alleged falsehoods circulated in a flier by opponents of a ballot initiative, and two members of the court's majority said a statute aimed only at falsehoods about candidates might be constitutional. The dissenters said the decision was the first "in the history of the Republic to declare First Amendment protection for calculated lies." State ex rel. Public Disclosure Commission v. 119 Vote No! Committee, 957 P.2d 691 (Wash. 1998).

Mississippi also has a statute requiring any newspaper that during a campaign prints any editorial or story reflecting upon a candidate's integrity or honesty (even by quoting statements of another candidate) to publish the attacked candidate's reply verbatim. See Miss. Code Ann. § 23–15–877 (Cum. Supp. 1988). The statute has been construed to apply only to publications that are defamatory. Manasco v. Walley, 216 Miss. 614, 63

So.2d 91 (1953). Does that save it from unconstitutionality under *Tornillo*, supra p. 69?

Newsgathering. Today, conflicts between media and legislatures concerned about protecting electoral integrity occur primarily in connection with newsgathering. In recent years legislators have been particularly concerned about the possibility that voter participation is influenced by exit polling—the surveying of voters as they leave the polls. The practice, which often permits news organizations to project results in presidential elections long before the actual votes are counted, is a source of particular concern in the West, where because of the time difference polls remain open for several hours after those in the East have closed.

The perceived evil of early projection of winners is that those who have not yet voted will either decide not to vote, or will be influenced to vote for the projected "winner." One solution would be to delay projections until the polls have closed. In recent elections the major networks have adhered to a policy of not projecting results for a particular state until the polls closed in that state. That does not solve the problem in presidential elections for the western states or others with late poll closing times, however; their voters might still be influenced by projections from other states. One solution might be a uniform national hour for poll closing. One proposal that has received some support in Congress is to close all polls in presidential elections (except those in Hawaii and Alaska) at 9 p.m. E.S.T.

The leading case is Daily Herald v. Munro, 838 F.2d 380, 14 Med. L. Rptr. 2332 (9th Cir. 1988). A Washington statute passed in 1983 prohibited the conduct of any exit poll or public opinion poll within 300 feet of a polling place. Several newspapers and broadcasting networks challenged the statute, contending that the 300–foot boundary precluded accurate exit polling and thereby violated the First Amendment. Both the district court and the Ninth Circuit agreed, holding the statute unconstitutional on its face.

The court of appeals held that it was a restriction on speech, not merely a restriction on access to news sources, because it restricted both the dissemination of information gathered by the polling and communication between the pollster and the voter. It was content-based, because it restricted only discussion about the voter's choices. The statute therefore was unconstitutional unless it was narrowly tailored to accomplish a compelling governmental interest by the least restrictive means available. The interest advanced by the state was to prevent disruption at the polling place, but the statute banned nondisruptive polling as well. It was not the least restrictive means, because disruption could be prevented by excluding pollsters from a smaller area, or perhaps by requiring them to inform voters that participation in the survey was voluntary. It was not a permissible time, place, and manner restriction because its effect was to preclude exit polling altogether.

More fundamentally, insofar as the purpose of the statute was to protect the integrity of elections, it was unconstitutional because that purpose was not a constitutionally permissible reason for regulating speech.

There was some evidence in the record suggesting that the legislature's true concern was not disruption, but a belief that early projection of results tended to discourage voter participation. Without deciding which was the true motive, the court said "[T]he general interest of protecting voters from outside influences is not sufficient to justify speech regulation. . . ."

For this proposition the court relied heavily on *Mills v. Alabama*, which, you will recall, held unconstitutional a statute making it a crime to publish an editorial taking a position on a ballot proposition on election day. Do you agree that *Mills v. Alabama* precludes the states from preventing exit polling? That preventing exit polling is a restriction on the speech of the pollsters? On the speech of the voters who otherwise would be polled?

After the *Daily Herald* case, similar statutes were held unconstitutional in Minnesota, Florida, and Montana. In Georgia a 250–foot exclusion was held unconstitutional but the judge engaged in a "narrowing construction" of the statute, reducing the limit to 25 feet and holding that constitutional. National Broadcasting Co. v. Cleland, 697 F. Supp. 1204, 15 Med. L. Rptr. 2265 (N.D. Ga. 1988).

The Supreme Court has not directly addressed the question of exit polling, but its decision in Burson v. Freeman, 504 U.S. 191, 20 Med. L. Rptr. 1137 (1992), may have implications for this issue. The Court upheld a state's power to ban campaign leafletting within 100 feet of a polling place on the ground that history has shown the need to restrict speech in that setting to prevent voter intimidation and fraud. Three dissenting justices cited *Daily Herald* and similar cases as showing that such restrictions are not necessary. Does the majority's rejection of this argument cast doubt on the exit polling cases? Does electioneering near the polls threaten the integrity of elections in ways that exit polling does not?

See generally Note, Exit Polls and the First Amendment, 98 Harv. L. Rev. 1927 (1985).

2.   BROADCAST MEDIA

Campaigns for elective office have been regulated differently over radio and television than in print media ever since the Radio Act of 1927. The federal Communications Act imposes several duties on broadcasters. Section 315(b) forbids stations from charging candidates more than their "lowest unit rate," i.e., the best rate they offer other advertisers.

Section 315(e) has long required broadcasters to keep records of requests by political candidates to buy time as an aid in the enforcement of campaign spending regulations. The Bipartisan Campaign Reform Act of 2002 greatly expanded that record-keeping requirement, to include requests from any individual or group to buy time for any message relating to elections, national legislative issues, or any "political matter of national importance." The National Association of Broadcasters and others challenged the expanded record-keeping obligations on the ground that they were burdensome, vague, and overbroad. The Court held in *McConnell*, supra p. 63, that the requirements were not unconstitutional on their face, but said broadcasters might mount an as-applied challenge when the FCC implemented them.

Equal opportunities. The best-known restriction on broadcast speech about elections requires a station that makes time available to one candidate to offer an "equal opportunity" to all other candidates for the same office. This obligation, imposed by Section 315(a), applies to all candidates for public office. It is popularly known as the "equal time" requirement, but what it actually requires is an equal opportunity to persuade voters, not necessarily temporal parity. The station may not censor the reply, and cannot be held liable if the reply defames someone. See Farmers Educ. & Coop. Union v. WDAY, Inc., 360 U.S. 525 (1959).

The equal opportunity rule does not apply to candidate appearances in bona fide newscasts, news interviews, news documentaries if the appearance is incidental to the subject, or on-the-spot coverage of news events, including political conventions. Presidential news conferences have been held to come within the "news events" exception. See Kennedy for President Comm. v. Federal Communications Comm'n, 636 F.2d 417 (D.C. Cir. 1980) (*Kennedy I*) (holding that supporters of Senator Edward M. Kennedy were not entitled to time to reply to statements President Carter made in a press conference carried by the networks on the evening before the New Hampshire primary in 1980). Because of these exceptions, the effects of the rule are confined largely to political advertising, broadcasting personalities who run for public office, and debates.

The FCC interprets "candidate" to include supporters, so a station that grants use of its facilities to supporters of one candidate must treat supporters of the other candidates equally, essentially as it would have had to treat the candidates themselves. Letter to Nicholas Zapple, 23 F.C.C.2d 707, 19 R.R.2d 421 (1970) (the *Zapple* doctrine). Similarly, the focus on licensees has been broadened to allow candidates to press their statutory demands on networks rather than having to go to each individual licensee that carried the program.

The rule applies to "any 'positive' appearance of a candidate by voice or picture," even if the appearance is not authorized by the candidate and even if the candidate deems the appearance harmful because of the identity or affiliation of the endorsers. In the Matter of Codification of the Commission's Political Programming Policies, 9 FCC Rcd. 651, 74 R.R.2d 611 (1994).

Debates. After a series of rulings to the contrary, the FCC in 1983 decided that broadcasters could sponsor debates among major candidates without incurring obligations under section 315(a). Petitions of Henry Geller et al., 95 F.C.C.2d 1236, 54 R.R.2d 1246 (1983), affirmed without opinion in League of Women Voters Educ. Fund v. Federal Communications Comm'n, 731 F.2d 995 (D.C. Cir. 1984).

A complaint by the 1984 Citizens Party candidate for president that the exclusion of minor party candidates restricted "their access to the ballot and impinge[d] upon associational choices protected by the First Amendment" was rejected in Johnson v. Federal Communications Comm'n,

829 F.2d 157 (D.C. Cir. 1987). The court said "we find the First Amendment interests of candidates, broadcasters and the public adequately served by the adjustments made in the Communications Act [by the news exceptions], and perceive no basis for disturbing the Commission's denial" of the complaint.

In the 1996 election, third party candidate Ross Perot mounted several challenges to his exclusion from coverage of the two major party candidates. He was excluded from the debates between President Bill Clinton and Bob Dole on the basis of a determination by the nongovernmental Commission on Presidential Debates on ground that he did not have a realistic chance of winning. Finding that the equities and the public interest weighed against the court's interference, and holding that there was no state action to support the plaintiffs' constitutional claims, the district court denied relief. The court of appeals rejected a claim that the Federal Election Commission (FEC) had unconstitutionally delegated power to the CPD by permitting each debate-holding group to establish its own "pre-established objective criteria" to determine who may participate. Perot v. Federal Election Comm'n, 97 F.3d 553 (D.C. Cir. 1996).

Perot then argued to the FCC that he was entitled to equal opportunity time based on the major networks' coverage of the Democratic and Republican nominating conventions, the presidential debates, and other programming provided by the networks, including appearances by Clinton and Dole on the ABC program 20/20. The FCC denied Perot's complaint on the ground that all of the programs complained of qualified as bona fide news programming under section 315(a). In re Complaint of Ross Perot v. ABC, CBS, NBC, and Fox Broadcasting Co., 11 FCC Rcd. 13109 (1996). In the last days of the campaign several networks offered free time to the two major candidates and Perot again sought equal opportunity time The FCC again ruled that the broadcasts fell within the bona fide news event exemption. In re Requests of Fox Broadcasting Co., Public Broadcasting Service, and Capital Cities/ABC, Inc., 11 FCC Rcd. 11101 (1996).

Requirements similar to the equal opportunities provision and the equivalent lowest-unit-rate provision are applicable to origination cablecasting. See 47 C.F.R. §§ 76.205, 76.209. Cable operators are not responsible under these rules for secondary transmissions or mandated access channels.

Reasonable access. The second major statute imposing duties on broadcasters in connection with political campaigns applies only to campaigns for federal office—Congress and the presidency. Section 312(a)(7) of the Communications Act requires licensees to give federal candidates "reasonable access" to the airwaves. How to determine what that requires is the issue in the following case.

CBS, Inc. v. Federal Communications Commission
Supreme Court of the United States, 1981.
453 U.S. 367, 101 S.Ct. 2813, 69 L.Ed.2d 706, 7 Med.L.Rptr. 1563.

CHIEF JUSTICE BURGER delivered the opinion of the Court.

[In late 1979 the Carter–Mondale Committee sought to buy 30 minutes of prime time for use in December in order to begin the 1980 campaign.

CBS feared that such a sale would require it to sell time under section 315 to all other announced candidates. ABC responded that it had not yet decided when to begin selling time for the 1980 campaign. NBC responded that December 1979 was too early. The FCC, 4–3, held the networks in violation of section 312(a)(7). The court of appeals affirmed. The Court agreed with the FCC and the court of appeals that Congress had intended to create "an affirmative, promptly enforceable right of reasonable access to the use of broadcast stations for individual candidates seeking Federal elective office," rather than simply to codify prior policies that the FCC had developed under the general public interest standards.]

III A

Although Congress provided in § 312(a)(7) for greater use of broadcasting stations by federal candidates, it did not give guidance on how the Commission should implement the statute's access requirement. Essentially, Congress adopted a "rule of reason" and charged the Commission with its enforcement. . . . The Commission has issued some general interpretative statements, but its standards implementing § 312(a)(7) have evolved principally on a case-by-case basis and are not embodied in formalized rules. . . .

Broadcasters are free to deny the sale of air time prior to the commencement of a campaign, but once a campaign has begun, they must give reasonable and good-faith attention to access requests from "legally qualified" candidates for federal elective office. Such requests must be considered on an individualized basis, and broadcasters are required to tailor their responses to accommodate, as much as reasonably possible, a candidate's stated purposes in seeking air time. . . . [T]o justify a negative response, the broadcaster must show a realistic danger of substantial program disruption—perhaps caused by insufficient notice to allow adjustments in the schedule—or of an excessive number of equal time requests. Further, in order to facilitate review by the Commission, broadcasters must explain their reasons for refusing time or making a more limited counteroffer. If broadcasters take the appropriate factors into account and act reasonably and in good faith, their decisions will be entitled to deference even if the Commission's analysis would have differed in the first instance. . . .

[The Court held that the Commission properly undertook to determine for itself when an election campaign had in fact commenced, without giving deference to the licensee's views on that subject. "Such a decision is not, and cannot be, purely one of editorial judgment."]

Petitioners also challenge the Commission's requirement that broadcasters evaluate and respond to access requests on an individualized basis. In petitioners' view, the agency has attached inordinate significance to candidates' needs, thereby precluding fair assessment of broadcasters' concerns and prohibiting the adoption of uniform policies regarding requests for access.

[The Court rejected the contention. Although the Commission has admonished broadcasters not to "second-guess" the candidate's wisdom or the effectiveness of the particular format, the request need not be honored. The Commission "mandates careful consideration of, not blind assent to, candidates' desires for air time." Even though uniform policies would be more convenient for broadcasters, that approach "would allow personal campaign strategies and the exigencies of the political process to be ignored." These ground rules were sufficiently clear in late 1979 to permit the FCC to rule that the networks had violated the statute by failing to grant "reasonable access."]

IV

Finally, petitioners assert that § 312(a)(7) as implemented by the Commission violates the First Amendment rights of broadcasters by unduly circumscribing their editorial discretion. In [*CBS v. DNC*, 412 U.S. 94 (1973)], we stated:

> The role of the Government as an "overseer" and ultimate arbiter and guardian of the public interest and the role of the licensee as a journalistic "free agent" call for a delicate balancing of competing interests. The maintenance of this balance for more than 40 years has called on both the regulators and the licensees to walk a "tight-rope" to preserve the First Amendment values written into the Radio Act and its successor, the Communications Act.

Petitioners argue that the Commission's interpretation of § 312(a)(7)'s access requirement disrupts the "delicate balanc[e]" that broadcast regulation must achieve. We disagree.

A licensed broadcaster is "granted the free and exclusive use of a limited and valuable part of the public domain; when he accepts that franchise it is burdened by enforceable public obligations." [ ] This Court has noted the limits on a broadcast license:

> A license permits broadcasting, but the licensee has no constitutional right to be the one who holds the license or to monopolize a . . . frequency to the exclusion of his fellow citizens. There is nothing in the First Amendment which prevents the Government from requiring a licensee to share his frequency with others. . . . [*Red Lion*, supra p. 76]

[ ]. Although the broadcasting industry is entitled under the First Amendment to exercise "the widest journalistic freedom consistent with its public [duties]," [*CBS v. DNC*, supra p. 84], the Court has made clear that:

> *It is the right of the viewers and listeners, not the right of the broadcasters which is paramount.* It is the purpose of the First Amendment to preserve an uninhibited marketplace of ideas in which truth will ultimately prevail, rather than to countenance monopolization of that market. . . . It is the right of the public to receive suitable access

to social, political, esthetic, moral, and other ideas and experience which is crucial here. [*Red Lion*] (emphasis added).

The First Amendment interests of candidates and voters, as well as broadcasters, are implicated by § 312(a)(7). We have recognized that "it is of particular importance that candidates have the . . . opportunity to make their views known so that the electorate may intelligently evaluate the candidates' personal qualities and their positions on vital public issues before choosing among them on election day." [*Buckley v. Valeo*] Indeed, "speech concerning public affairs is . . . the essence of self-government." [*Garrison v. Louisiana*] The First Amendment "has its fullest and most urgent application precisely to the conduct of campaigns for political office." [*Monitor Patriot Co. v. Roy*] Section 312(a)(7) thus makes a significant contribution to freedom of expression by enhancing the ability of candidates to present, and the public to receive, information necessary for the effective operation of the democratic process.

Petitioners are correct that the Court has never approved a *general* right of access to the media. [ ] Nor do we do so today. Section 312(a)(7) creates a *limited* right to "reasonable" access that pertains only to legally qualified federal candidates and may be invoked by them only for the purpose of advancing their candidacies once a campaign has commenced. The Commission has stated that in enforcing the statute, it will "provide leeway to broadcasters and not merely attempt *de novo* to determine the reasonableness of their judgments. . . ." If broadcasters have considered the relevant factors in good faith, the Commission will uphold their decisions. [ ] Further, § 312(a)(7) does not impair the discretion of broadcasters to present their views on any issue or to carry any particular type of programming.

Section 312(a)(7) represents an effort by Congress to assure that an important resource—the airwaves—will be used in the public interest. We hold that the statutory right of access, as defined by the Commission and applied in these cases, properly balances the First Amendment rights of federal candidates, the public, and broadcasters.

The judgment of the Court of Appeals is affirmed.

[Justice White, joined by Justices Rehnquist and Stevens, dissented on the ground that the Commission and the Court had failed to give sufficient weight to a "long-standing statutory policy of deferring to editorial judgments that are not destructive of the goals of the Act." As a result, the Commission had read section 312(a)(7) much too broadly. Congress had intended only "to codify what it conceived to be the preexisting duty of the broadcasters to serve the public interest by presenting political broadcasts."]

[In a separate dissent, Justice Stevens argued that the result created "an impermissible risk that the Commission's evaluation of a given refusal by a licensee will be biased—or will appear to be biased—by the character of the office held by the candidate making the request." He noted that the four Democratic commissioners had voted for the Carter–Mondale request and the three Republicans had dissented.]

Notes and Questions

1.   Unlike access sought under *Tornillo* and *Red Lion*, the access here is not contingent upon the uttering of any other speech. Is that a greater or lesser intrusion upon the editorial function? Is there still any kind of a "chilling-effect" argument to be made?

2.   The Court's opinion refers at one point to the "First Amendment interests of candidates and voters." Later it refers to the "First Amendment rights of federal candidates, the public, and broadcasters." Do federal (or all) candidates have special constitutional speech rights that do not extend to members of the public generally? Is the Court suggesting that some types of speech should be accorded greater protection (here in the form of access) than others? The nature of the candidate's interest is pursued in *Forbes*, infra p. 187.

3.   Could the Court uphold a similar statute demanding that print media offer federal candidates reasonable access? In considering this recall (a) the passage stating that the licensee is "granted the free and exclusive use of a limited and valuable part of the public domain;" and (b) the passage stating that the statute is an "effort by Congress to assure that an important resource—the airwaves—will be used in the public interest." Is it essential to the Court's reasoning that the airwaves are considered a "public" resource?

4.   In discussing the First Amendment's role in elections, the Court concludes that the statute "makes a significant contribution to freedom of expression by enhancing the ability of candidates to present, and the public to receive, information necessary for the effective operation of the democratic process." Might the same have been said of the statute in *Tornillo?*

———

Political ads and indecency. Sections 315(a) and 312(a)(7) may both be invoked in the same case, and sometimes their effect must be considered in light of other requirements, such as federal regulation of broadcast "indecency," which the FCC defined in 1975 to mean broadcast "language that describes, in terms patently offensive as measured by contemporary community standards for the broadcast medium, sexual or excretory activities and organs, at times of the day when there is a reasonable risk that children may be in the audience." In re Citizen's Complaint Against Pacifica Found., 56 F.C.C.2d 94, 32 R.R.2d 1331 (1975). Because indecency is defined with reference to children, the FCC generally requires broadcasters to channel indecent speech to times of the day when the Commission and the courts assume that fewer unsupervised children are in the audience. See infra p. 149.

When anti-abortion candidates began using graphic displays of fetuses in their television spots, broadcasters were unclear whether these spots had to be aired at all under section 312(a)(7) and, if so, whether the presentations had to be at times chosen by the candidate under section 315. Becker, a congressional candidate in Georgia, ran a spot displaying images of aborted fetuses on a station in Atlanta. The station received many complaints from viewers and asked the FCC whether it could channel such commercials in the future to late-night hours. The Commission concluded (1) that Mr. Becker's initial advertisement was not indecent, (2) that there was evidence in the record "indicating that the graphic political advertisements at issue can be psychologically damaging to children," (3) that "nothing in 312(a)(7) precludes a broadcaster's exercise of some discretion with respect to placement of political advertisements so as to protect children," and (4) that channeling would not violate the no-censorship provision of section 315(a). The court of appeals reversed, holding that the ruling violated both section 312(a)(7) and section 315(a). See Becker v. FCC, 95 F.3d 75 (D.C. Cir. 1996).

The court held that refusing to air Becker's commercials in prime time violated the no-censorship provision of section 315 because it inhibited the manner in which he was able to discuss public issues and deprived him of the ability to convey his message when and how he saw fit by forcing him to either change its content or accept a time slot that deprived him of his preferred audience. The court concluded:

> Finally, section 315(a) not only prohibits censorship, it also requires that candidates be given "equal opportunities" to use a broadcaster's facilities. To satisfy this requirement, a broadcaster must "make available periods of approximately equal audience potential to competing candidates to the extent that this is possible." [ ] The FCC claims that the [ruling here] does not involve the equal opportunity provision because there was no equal opportunity request before it. Because the equal opportunity requirements "forbid any kind of discrimination by a station between competing candidates," however, channeling clearly implicates the equal opportunity provision of section 315(a).

> This is so because if a station channels one candidate's message but allows his opponent to broadcast his messages in prime time, the first candidate will have been denied the equal opportunity guaranteed by this section. On the other hand, if the station relegates the opponent's advertisements to the broadcasting Siberia to which the first candidate was assigned, it would be violating the opponent's right of reasonable access under section 312(a)(7). We agree with petitioners that these provisions may not be read to create such a tension.

> We conclude from the above that permitting the content-based channeling of political advertisements thwarts the objectives of both section 312(a)(7) and section 315(a) by restricting candidates' ability to "fully and completely inform the voters," [CBS, Inc. v. FCC] and by inhibiting the "full and unrestricted discussion of political issues by

legally qualified candidates," [*WDAY, Inc.*]. Because the [ruling here] is based on impermissible constructions of the Act to which we owe no deference, [ ], we hold that it is without legal effect.

In light of the above, we decline to address Mr. Becker's argument that channeling a candidate's campaign advertisements violates that candidate's First Amendment rights. [ ]

D. SEXUALLY EXPLICIT SPEECH

Depending on the nature of the content and the reason the state seeks to regulate it, restrictions on speech relating to sex may be subjected to different constitutional analyses. This section is organized to reflect the different First Amendment responses that result from characterizing the speech as obscenity, child pornography, or indecency. The mass media rarely run afoul of restrictions on obscenity or child pornography, so we treat those briefly to provide context. Regulation of indecency, however, is a matter of increasing relevance in broadcasting, cable, and Internet communications, so we treat it more extensively.

1. OBSCENITY

Legislatures and the courts have long wrestled with how to protect public sensibilities about sexually explicit expression without violating the First Amendment. Much of the constitutional law of obscenity reflects a process of refining and elaborating the boundaries of the category. The first step was a narrowing of the concept from "immorality" to explicit sexual depictions. In Joseph Burstyn, Inc. v. Wilson, 343 U.S. 495, 1 Med. L. Rptr. 1357 (1952), the Court held that a movie could not be banned by the state on the ground that it was "sacrilegious." The film version of "Lady Chatterley's Lover" could not be banned on the ground that it endorsed adultery because the First Amendment "protects advocacy of the opinion that adultery may sometimes be proper, no less than advocacy of socialism or the single tax." Kingsley Int. Pictures Corp. v. Regents, 360 U.S. 684 (1959).

The Court first attempted to define obscenity in Roth v. United States, 354 U.S. 476, 1 Med. L. Rptr. 1375 (1957): material was obscene if "to the average person, applying contemporary community standards, the dominant theme of the material taken as a whole appeals to prurient interest." It soon became apparent, however, that even members of the Court could not agree on the application of this definition to specific books or films, leading the late Justice Stewart to write in 1964 that an intelligent definition might be impossible, but "I know it when I see it." Jacobellis v. Ohio, 378 U.S. 184, 197 (1964) (Stewart, J., concurring). On 31 occasions, the Court reviewed purportedly obscene material and rendered a judgment as to its permissibility. Justice Brennan complained that the examination of this material was "hardly a source of edification to the members of this Court," and Chief Justice Burger noted that the Court's case by case determination of obscenity had cast it in the "role of a supreme and unreviewable board of censorship for the 50 states." Paris Adult Theatre I v. Slaton, 413 U.S. 49, 92–93, 1 Med. L. Rptr. 1454 (1973) (Brennan, J., dissenting); Walker v. Ohio, 398 U.S. 434, 434 (1970) (Burger, C.J., dissenting). In 1973 the Court, 5–4, articulated the definition that remains in effect today:

> (a) [W]hether "the average person, applying contemporary community standards" would find that the work, taken as a whole, appeals to the prurient interest [ ], (b) whether the work depicts or describes, in a patently offensive way, sexual conduct specifically defined by the applicable state law; and (c) whether the work, taken as a whole, lacks serious literary, artistic, political, or scientific value.

Miller v. California, 413 U.S. 15, 1 Med. L. Rptr. 1441 (1973). The Court held further that "contemporary standards" were to be determined by juries on the basis of their own perceptions, not by reference to nationwide standards. In *Paris Adult Theatre*, supra, the Court held that as long as the *Miller* test was met, theaters could be enjoined from showing obscene films, even if the evidence showed that no one but consenting adults ever saw them, in the interests of "quality of life and the total community environment, the tone of commerce in the great city centers, and possibly, the public safety itself."

The result of this jurisprudence has been considerable diversity in the treatment of obscenity from one place to another. In some cities prosecutors have abandoned the effort to control hard-core pornography, presumably because they believe juries will not convict under local standards. In other cities authorities continue to prosecute, apparently with some success. In still others, adult theaters and other outlets for hard-core pornography are restricted by zoning ordinances to certain districts.

The distribution or public exhibition of sexually explicit expression that meets the *Miller* definition for obscenity may constitutionally be banned, whether it is printed, broadcast, mailed, distributed by telephone, or made available via the Internet. The medium may not, however, be irrelevant to the operation of obscenity regulations, even if courts act as if it is. Purveyors of sexually explicit material on the Internet complain that the community standards concept chills speech in that medium. So far the courts have rejected their arguments. See United States v. Thomas, 74 F.3d 701, 24 Med. L. Rptr. 1321 (6th Cir. 1996). The defendants and several amici representing bulletin board users also argued that computer technology required a new definition of community based on cyberspace connections rather than geography. They argued that use of conventional community standards would subject all bulletin board operators to the standards of the most restrictive communities. But the court said bulletin board operators are no different in this respect from other interstate communicators and, like them, can tailor their operations to steer clear of the least tolerant communities. That this may impose costs on the operators does not make it unconstitutional, the court said.

However, in Ashcroft v. ACLU [I], 535 U.S. 564, 30 Med. L. Rptr. 1801 (2002), six justices expressed the view that a national community standard, rather than local standards, may be required in regulating indecent speech on the Internet. The posture of the case did not require a decision on that point, but in concurring and dissenting opinions a majority of the Court suggested that the practical effects of subjecting online communicators to the potential of prosecution under most restrictive local standards would impose a burden on Internet speech that might be unconstitutional. As we shall soon see, indecency is treated differently than obscenity, so local standards might be permissible in regulation of obscenity even if they are impermissible in connection with indecency. The justices expressed no view on that. The case involved the Child Online Protection Act, which the Court later held was probably unconstitutional on other grounds. See infra p. 167.

Despite the Court's continued adherence to the categorical approach, there is much about the law of obscenity that does not seem categorical at all. Even obscene material receives some First Amendment protection. The state cannot require pre-screening, even of material that meets the test for obscenity, unless it provides special procedures to assure prompt decision and speedy judicial review, see Freedman v. Maryland, 380 U.S. 51, 1 Media L. Rep. 1126 (1965), and the state cannot punish a person for possessing obscene material in a private home, see Stanley v. Georgia, 394 U.S. 557 (1969). "If the First Amendment means anything," Justice Marshall wrote for the Court in *Stanley*, "it means that a State has no business telling a man, sitting alone in his own house, what books he may read or what films he may watch. Our whole constitutional heritage rebels at the thought of giving government the power to control men's minds."

The basis for regulating obscene content broadcast over radio and television has existed in Congressional legislation since the enactment of the Communications Act of 1934. The current version is now found in the general criminal law, 18 U.S.C. § 1464:

> Whoever utters any obscene, indecent, or profane language by means of radio communications shall be fined [up to $250,000] or imprisoned not more than two years, or both.

The same penalties apply to obscene programming on cable. See 47 U.S.C. § 559.

Because they rarely publish or broadcast material that meets the *Miller* definition, obscenity law is not of great concern to most media. The prohibition against broadcast indecency is of more concern, as we shall see shortly.

2. CHILD PORNOGRAPHY

Where children are involved in the creation or consumption of sexually explicit expression, the Supreme Court has permitted states to enact regulations without requiring that the material fit the *Miller* definition of obscenity. For example, the Supreme Court has found that states may not only criminalize the depiction of children in sexually explicit films and photographs, they may prohibit the distribution, and even the mere possession, of those films and photographs in an effort to eliminate the market for child pornography. See New York v. Ferber, 458 U.S. 747, 8 Med. L. Rptr. 1809 (1982).

The *Ferber* principle does not allow Congress to ban "virtual" child pornography, however. The Child Pornography Protection Act of 1996, 18 U.S.C. § 2252A(a)(5)(b), criminalized the production or distribution of any image that "is, or appears to be, of a minor engaging in sexually explicit conduct" or that is "advertised, promoted, presented, described, or distributed in such a manner that conveys the impression" that it depicts a minor engaged in sexually explicit conduct. The government argued that the ban was necessary to prevent use of electronically-created child pornography to whet the appetites of pedophiles for the real thing, prevent them from using such material to seduce children, and avoid stimulating a market for images of real children.

But the Court, 6–3, said "the Government may not suppress lawful speech as the means to suppress unlawful speech." It held the statute overbroad, noting that because it contained no "redeeming value" element in its definition of child pornography, it could be applied to mainstream movies if the fact-finder thought one of the actors "appeared to be" a minor. The Court distinguished *Ferber* on two grounds: first, that it involved material that created a permanent record of a child's abuse, the continued circulation of which would harm the child who had participated; and second, that banning material that uses actual children has a more "proximate link" to removing the economic motive that leads to its production. See Ashcroft v. The Free Speech Coalition, 535 U.S. 234, 30 Med. L. Rptr. 1673 (2002).

3. INDECENCY

The effort to keep sexually explicit material away from the eyes and ears of children affects all types of media. So far as print media are concerned, the effort is generally confined to federal, state, and local laws requiring proprietors to put opaque covers on sexually explicit magazines and sell pornography only in areas to which minors are denied access. Video sales and rentals are subject to similar restrictions. The constitutionality of these derives from Ginsberg v. New York, 390 U.S. 629, 1 Med. L. Rptr. 1424 (1968), which held that material that is not obscene may nonetheless be harmful for children, and its marketing may therefore be regulated.

Broadcasting, cable and satellite television, and the Internet are subject to numerous regulations based largely on the concept of "indecency." Some of these are addressed specifically to the goal of protecting children. Others purport to shield all audiences from indecency, but those usually are unconstitutional unless they can be shown to be necessary to protect children; attempts to prevent adults from being exposed to nonobscene indecency are difficult to reconcile with the premise that speech cannot be suppressed because of its sexual content unless it meets the *Miller* test of obscenity.

Whether the First Amendment permits regulation of nonobscene indecency reached the Supreme Court in the following case.

a. Broadcast indecency

Federal Communications Commission v. Pacifica Foundation

Supreme Court of the United States, 1978.
438 U.S. 726, 98 S.Ct. 3026, 57 L.Ed.2d 1073, 3 Med.L.Rptr. 2553.

[The humorist George Carlin recorded a 12–minute monologue entitled "Filthy Words" before a live audience in a California theater. The theme was "the words you couldn't say on the public, ah, airwaves. . . ." Carlin used each of the seven words repeatedly, showing their many different uses. Pacifica's FM licensee in New York City played the monologue at 2:00 p.m. on a weekday afternoon during a discussion about society's attitude toward language. The station warned that the monologue included language that might offend some listeners. A man who apparently did not hear the warning tuned into the broadcast while driving with his young son, and complained to the Commission. Apparently, no one else complained about the broadcast.

The Commission ruled that Pacifica's action was subject to administrative sanction. Instead of imposing a formal sanction, it put the order in the file for possible use if subsequent complaints were received. The Commission asserted four reasons for treating broadcasting differently from other media: access by unsupervised children; since radio receivers are in the home, privacy interests are entitled to extra deference; unconsenting adults may tune in without a warning that offensive language is being used; and scarcity of spectrum space requires government to license in the public interest. Further facts are stated in the opinions.]

MR. JUSTICE STEVENS delivered the opinion of the Court (Parts I, II, III and IV–C) and an opinion in which THE CHIEF JUSTICE and MR. JUSTICE REHNQUIST joined (Parts IV–A and IV–B).

This case requires that we decide whether the Federal Communications Commission has any power to regulate a radio broadcast that is indecent but not obscene.

[The Court held that the Commission had power to regulate indecent broadcasting by virtue of 18 U.S.C. § 1464, which forbids uttering "any obscene, indecent, or profane language by means of radio communications," and 47 U.S.C. § 303(g), which requires the Commission to "encourage the larger and more effective use of radio in the public interest." It held that "indecent" did not mean the same thing as "obscene" under § 1464, and it accepted the FCC's conclusion that Carlin's monologue as broadcast was indecent. The Court rejected Pacifica's argument that the anti-censorship provision of § 326 prevented the FCC from imposing sanctions on licensees who engage in obscene, indecent, or profane broadcasting.]

The Commission characterized the language used in the Carlin monologue as "patently offensive," though not necessarily obscene, and expressed the opinion that it should be regulated by principles analogous to those found in the law of nuisance where the "law generally speaks to channeling behavior more than actually prohibiting it. . . . [T]he concept of 'indecent' is intimately connected with the exposure of children to language that describes, in terms patently offensive as measured by contemporary community standards for the broadcast medium, sexual or excretory activities and organs at times of the day when there is a reasonable risk that children may be in the audience." [ ]5

IV

Pacifica makes two constitutional attacks on the Commission's order. First, it argues that the Commission's construction of the statutory language broadly encompasses so much constitutionally protected speech that reversal is required even if Pacifica's broadcast of the "Filthy Words" monologue is not itself protected by the First Amendment. Second, Pacifica argues that inasmuch as the recording is not obscene, the Constitution forbids any abridgment of the right to broadcast it on the radio.

A

The first argument fails because our review is limited to the question whether the Commission has the authority to proscribe this particular broadcast. As the Commission itself emphasized, its order was "issued in a specific factual context." [ ] That approach is appropriate for courts as well as the Commission when regulation of indecency is at stake, for indecency is largely a function of context—it cannot be adequately judged in the abstract.

. . .

It is true that the Commission's order may lead some broadcasters to censor themselves. At most, however, the Commission's definition of indecency will deter only the broadcasting of patently offensive references to excretory and sexual organs and activities.[18] While some of these references may be protected, they surely lie at the periphery of First Amendment concern. [ ] The danger dismissed so summarily in *Red Lion*, in contrast, was that broadcasters would respond to the vagueness of the regulations by refusing to present programs dealing with important social and political controversies. Invalidating any rule on the basis of its hypothetical application to situations not before the Court is "strong medicine" to be applied "sparingly and only as a last resort." [ ] We decline to administer that

---

5. Thus, the Commission suggested, if an offensive broadcast had literary, artistic, political, or scientific value, and were preceded by warnings, it might not be indecent in the late evening, but would be so during the day, when children are in the audience. [ ]

18. A requirement that indecent language be avoided will have its primary effect on the form, rather than the content, of serious communication. There are few, if any, thoughts that cannot be expressed by the use of less offensive language.

medicine to preserve the vigor of patently offensive sexual and excretory speech.

B

When the issue is narrowed to the facts of this case, the question is whether the First Amendment denies government any power to restrict the public broadcast of indecent language in any circumstances. For if the government has any such power, this was an appropriate occasion for its exercise.

The words of the Carlin monologue are unquestionably "speech" within the meaning of the First Amendment. It is equally clear that the Commission's objections to the broadcast were based in part on its content. The order must therefore fall if, as Pacifica argues, the First Amendment prohibits all governmental regulation that depends on the content of speech. Our past cases demonstrate, however, that no such absolute rule is mandated by the Constitution.

[The Court discussed clear-and-present danger cases (*Schenck*), provocation situations (*Chaplinsky*), commercial speech cases, libel cases, obscenity cases, and *Young v. American Mini Theatres*, involving zoning of adult theaters.]

The question in this case is whether a broadcast of patently offensive words dealing with sex and excretion may be regulated because of its content. Obscene materials have been denied the protection of the First Amendment because their content is so offensive to contemporary moral standards. [ ] But the fact that society may find speech offensive is not a sufficient reason for suppressing it. Indeed, if it is the speaker's opinion that gives offense, that consequence is a reason for according it constitutional protection. For it is a central tenet of the First Amendment that the government must remain neutral in the marketplace of ideas. If there were any reason to believe that the Commission's characterization of the Carlin monologue as offensive could be traced to its political content—or even to the fact that it satirized contemporary attitudes about four-letter words—First Amendment protection might be required. But that is simply not this case. These words offend for the same reasons that obscenity offends.[23]

Although these words ordinarily lack literary, political, or scientific value, they are not entirely outside the protection of the First Amendment. Some uses of even the most offensive words are unquestionably protected. [ ] Indeed, we may assume, arguendo, that this monologue would be protected in other contexts. Nonetheless, the constitutional protection accorded to a communication containing such patently offensive sexual and excretory language need not be the same in every context. It is a character-

---

23. The Commission stated: "Obnoxious, gutter language describing these matters has the effect of debasing and brutalizing human beings by reducing them to their mere bodily functions . . ." [ ]. Our society has a tradition of performing certain bodily functions in private, and of severely limiting the public exposure or discussion of such matters. Verbal or physical acts exposing those intimacies are offensive irrespective of any message that may accompany the exposure.

istic of speech such as this that both its capacity to offend and its "social value," to use Mr. Justice Murphy's term, vary with the circumstances. Words that are commonplace in one setting are shocking in another. To paraphrase Mr. Justice Harlan, one occasion's lyric is another's vulgarity. Cf. Cohen v. California, 403 U.S. 15, 25.

In this case it is undisputed that the content of Pacifica's broadcast was "vulgar," "offensive," and "shocking." Because content of that character is not entitled to absolute constitutional protection under all circumstances, we must consider its context in order to determine whether the Commission's action was constitutionally permissible.

C

We have long recognized that each medium of expression presents special First Amendment problems. Joseph Burstyn, Inc. v. Wilson, 343 U.S. 495, 502–503. And of all forms of communication, it is broadcasting that has received the most limited First Amendment protection. Thus, although other speakers cannot be licensed except under laws that carefully define and narrow official discretion, a broadcaster may be deprived of his license and his forum if the Commission decides that such an action would serve "the public interest, convenience, and necessity." [The Court noted the difference between *Tornillo* and *Red Lion*.]

The reasons for these distinctions are complex, but two have relevance to the present case. First, the broadcast media have established a uniquely pervasive presence in the lives of all Americans. Patently offensive, indecent material presented over the airwaves confronts the citizen, not only in public, but also in the privacy of the home, where the individual's right to be left alone plainly outweighs the First Amendment rights of an intruder. Rowan v. Post Office Dept., 397 U.S. 728 [1970]. Because the broadcast audience is constantly tuning in and out, prior warnings cannot completely protect the listener or viewer from unexpected program content. To say that one may avoid further offense by turning off the radio when he hears indecent language is like saying that the remedy for an assault is to run away after the first blow. One may hang up on an indecent phone call, but that option does not give the caller a constitutional immunity or avoid a harm that has already taken place.[27]

Second, broadcasting is uniquely accessible to children, even those too young to read. Although Cohen's written message might have been incomprehensible to a first grader, Pacifica's broadcast could have enlarged a child's vocabulary in an instant. . . .[28] . . .

27. Outside the home, the balance between the offensive speaker and the unwilling audience may sometimes tip in favor of the speaker, requiring the offended listener to turn away. See Erznoznik v. Jacksonville, 422 U.S. 205.

28. The Commission's action does not by any means reduce adults to hearing only what is fit for children. [ ] Adults who feel the need may purchase tapes and records or go to theaters and nightclubs to hear these words. In fact, the Commission has not unequivocally closed even broadcasting to speech of this sort; whether broadcast audiences in the late evening contain so few children that playing this monologue would be

It is appropriate, in conclusion, to emphasize the narrowness of our holding. This case does not involve a two-way radio conversation between a cab driver and a dispatcher, or a telecast of an Elizabethan comedy. We have not decided that an occasional expletive in either setting would justify any sanction or, indeed, that this broadcast would justify a criminal prosecution. The Commission's decision rested entirely on a nuisance rationale under which context is all-important. The concept requires consideration of a host of variables. The time of day was emphasized by the Commission. The content of the program in which the language is used will also affect the composition of the audience,[29] and differences between radio, television, and perhaps closed-circuit transmissions, may also be relevant. As Mr. Justice Sutherland wrote, a "nuisance may be merely a right thing in the wrong place,—like a pig in the parlor instead of the barnyard." Euclid v. Ambler Realty Co., 272 U.S. 365, 388 [1926]. We simply hold that when the Commission finds that a pig has entered the parlor, the exercise of its regulatory power does not depend on proof that the pig is obscene.

The judgment of the Court of Appeals is reversed.

MR. JUSTICE POWELL, with whom MR. JUSTICE BLACKMUN joins, concurring.

I join Parts I, II, III, and IV–C of Mr. Justice Stevens' opinion. . . .

. . . [M]y views are generally in accord with what is said in Part IV–C of Mr. Justice Stevens' opinion. [ ] I therefore join that portion of his opinion. I do not join Part IV–B, however, because I do not subscribe to the theory that the Justices of this Court are free generally to decide on the basis of its content which speech protected by the First Amendment is most "valuable" and hence deserving of the most protection, and which is less "valuable" and hence deserving of less protection. [ ] In my view, the result in this case does not turn on whether Carlin's monologue, viewed as a whole, or the words that constitute it, have more or less "value" than a candidate's campaign speech. . . .

The result turns instead on the unique characteristics of the broadcast media, combined with society's right to protect its children from speech generally agreed to be inappropriate for their years, and with the interest of unwilling adults in not being assaulted by such offensive speech in their homes. . . .

[Justice Stewart, joined by Justices Brennan, White, and Marshall, dissented, arguing that "indecent" should be read as meaning the same thing as "obscene" under § 1464, and that the monologue was not obscene.]

[Justice Brennan, joined by Justice Marshall, dissented on constitutional grounds as well. They conceded that privacy interests in the home

permissible is an issue neither the Commission nor this Court has decided.

29. Even a prime-time recitation of Geoffrey Chaucer's Miller's Tale would not be likely to command the attention of many children who are both old enough to understand and young enough to be adversely affected by passages such as: "And prively he caughte hire by the queynte." The Canterbury Tales, Chaucer's Complete Works (Cambridge ed. 1933), p. 58, *l.* 3276.

are substantial, but said the Court made two errors: "First, it misconceives the nature of the privacy interests involved where an individual voluntarily chooses to admit radio communications into his home. Second, it ignores the constitutionally protected interests of both those who wish to transmit and those who desire to receive broadcasts that many—including the FCC and this Court—might find offensive."

As to the first, although allowing radio into the house does not abrogate all privacy interests, those remaining were "surely no greater than those of the people present in the corridor of the Los Angeles County Courthouse [ ] who bore witness to the words, 'Fuck the Draft' emblazoned across Cohen's jacket." Even if a listener retained stronger privacy interests, they were not invaded by a broadcast since "unlike other intrusive modes of communication, such as sound trucks, 'the radio can be turned off' and with a minimum of effort." The Court's approach "permits majoritarian tastes completely to preclude a protected message from entering the homes of a receptive, unoffended minority. No decision of this Court supports such a result."

They argued that some parents "may actually find Mr. Carlin's unabashed attitude" healthy and want their children to be exposed Carlin's monologue, and said the Court's decision interferes with that right. Although Carlin's message may be disseminated by other means, "this is of little consolation to those broadcasters and listeners who, for a host of reasons, not least among them financial, do not have access to, or cannot take advantage of, those other means."

In a footnote, Justice Brennan said Justice Powell's approach "on its face, permits the Commission to censor even political speech if it is sufficiently offensive to community standards. A result more contrary to rudimentary First Amendment principles is difficult to imagine."]

Notes and Questions

1.   Section IV–C is joined by a majority of the Court. What is the rationale of that section? How does it differ from IV–A and IV–B?

2.   Is the "risk" of tuning in to an offensive program on radio or television any greater than the risk of encountering offensive language on a person's clothing on the streets? See Cohen v. California, 403 U.S. 15 (1971). Or offensive films being shown on an outdoor movie screen that is visible from the street? See Erznoznik v. City of Jacksonville, 422 U.S. 205 (1975). If averting your eyes is an adequate remedy in those cases, why is turning off the radio or television set not adequate here?

3.   Is the location relevant? In *Rowan*, cited in IV–C, the Court upheld a postal regulation permitting a person who had received mail he or she considered to be "a pandering advertisement" to request the post office to require the mailer to remove the addressee's name from the sender's mailing list and stop all further mailings to the addressee:

[Weighing] the highly important right to communicate [against] the very basic right to be free from sights, sounds and tangible matter we do not want, it seems to us that a mailer's right to communicate must stop at the mailbox of an unreceptive addressee. . . . That we are often "captives" outside the sanctuary of the home and subject to objectionable speech and other sound does not mean we must be captives everywhere.

Is it relevant in *Pacifica* that the complaining listener heard the broadcast while driving?

————

Safe harbors. The FCC eventually reacted to pressure from Congress and children's groups by ordering broadcasters to channel indecent programming into a "safe harbor"—late night hours when it could be assumed children would not be in the audience. This approach was upheld in Action for Children's Television v. Federal Communications Comm'n, 58 F.3d 654 (D.C. Cir. 1995). In a 7–4 en banc decision, the majority concluded that the government had a compelling interest in protecting children under 18 from exposure to indecent broadcasts and that the channeling of such broadcasts to the period between 10 p.m. and 6 a.m. did not unduly burden the First Amendment. The court identified three compelling interests: "support for parental supervision of children, a concern for children's well-being, and the protection of the home against intrusion by offensive broadcasts." The majority accepted the first two and did not address the third.

In response to an argument that the ban is not narrowly drawn because it applies during school hours when children are presumably not in the audience, the court responded that the government might also be concerned about children too young to attend school. "But more to the point, even if such fine tuning were feasible, we do not believe that the First Amendment requires that degree of precision." Deciding "where along the bell curves of declining adult and child audiences it is most reasonable to permit indecent broadcasts is the kind of judgment that is better left to Congress, so long as there is evidence to support the legislative judgment." Although the restrictions "burden the rights of many adults, it seems entirely appropriate that the marginal convenience of some adults be made to yield to the imperative needs of the young."

Chief Judge Edwards dissented, arguing that the claimed goal of supporting parental supervision was irreconcilable with the claim that it was necessary for the FCC to protect children. He also said there was no empirical evidence to show that the restriction advanced either of those goals.

Judge Wald, joined by Judges Rogers and Tatel, also dissented. She asserted that *Pacifica* had become dated and deserved reconsideration. Even accepting that case, the safe harbor enacted here was unconstitutional. She was especially concerned about the "chill" that derived from the case-by-case determination of what is indecent. She noted that even the newsworthy nature of material may not be dispositive as to whether it is considered indecent. She also argued that

> Because the government can pursue whatever legitimate interests it has in protecting children by facilitating parental control, I do not believe that it can impose a valid ban during any hours it pleases solely because some children are in the audience. Nor do I believe that we can throw up our hands at the assumed impossibility of parental supervision simply because large numbers of children have television sets in their own room. Either or both of these excuses would justify a 24–hour ban as easily as the current . . . ban. Reasoning along these lines totally ignores the adult First Amendment interest that the majority purportedly recognizes and, effectively, gives the government unharnessed power to censor.

Policing broadcast indecency. The FCC defines broadcast indecency as "language or material that, in context, depicts or describes, in terms patently offensive as measured by contemporary community standards for the broadcast medium, sexual or excretory activities or organs." The phrase "contemporary community standards" refers to "an average broadcast viewer" and is a national standard as opposed to the local standard for obscenity that was used in *Miller.* See Infinity Broadcasting Corp. of Pennsylvania, 2 FCC Rcd. 2705, 62 R.R.2d 1202 (1987). A broadcast can be patently offensive even if it has "merit":

> The merit of a work is also only one of the many variables that make up a work's "context," as the Court implicitly recognized in *Pacifica* when it contrasted the Carlin monologue to Elizabethan comedies and works of Chaucer. But merit is simply one of many variables, and it would give this particular variable undue importance if we were to single it out for greater weight or attention than we give other variables. . . . We must, therefore, reject an approach that would hold that if a work has merit, it is per se not indecent. At the same time, we must reject the notion that a work's "context" can be reviewed in a manner that artificially excludes merit from the host of variables that ordinarily comprise context. The ultimate determinative factor in our analysis, however, is whether the material, when examined in context, is patently offensive. . . .

A licensee's reasonable, good faith judgment that the programming is not indecent is not a full defense, but "it is standard procedure for the Commission, in deciding whether to impose a sanction for violation of the law and, if so, what those sanctions should be, to give weight to the reasonable determinations of licensees endeavoring to comply with the law." Infinity Broadcasting Corp. of Pennsylvania (Indecency Policy Reconsideration), 3 FCC Rcd. 930, 64 R.R.2d 211 (1987). A claim that these standards were unconstitutionally vague was rejected in Action for Children's Television v. Federal Communications Comm'n, 852 F.2d 1332, 15 Med. L. Rptr. 1907 (D.C. Cir. 1988).

The FCC enforces the indecency standards primarily through "forfeitures," which are essentially fines. Several of the major forfeitures, including the two Infinity Broadcasting cases cited above, have involved radio broadcasts of Howard Stern. Eager to get FCC clearance for its acquisition of new stations, Infinity in 1995 paid the FCC a forfeiture of $1.7 million to settle numerous complaints over specific Howard Stern programs. See $1.7 Million to Settle Stern Radio Indecency Case, N.Y. Times, Sept. 2, 1995 at 33. In 2004 Clear Channel Communications paid $1.75 million to settle 13 indecency complaints arising from the Howard Stern show and other programs, dropped the Stern show, and fired several disc jockeys. Infinity promptly announced that it would launch the Stern show in nine additional markets, including four in which Clear Channel had dropped it. See Ready to Rumble, Broadcasting and Cable, July 5, 2004.

In Action for Children's Television v. Federal Communications Comm'n, 59 F.3d 1249 (D.C. Cir. 1995), the court rejected claims that the FCC's forfeiture procedure constituted impermissible prior restraint and censorship.

Indecency in live programming. Soon after *Pacifica*, the FCC announced that it did not mean to restrict coverage of news events in which offensive speech is sometimes uttered without a chance for editing: "Under these circumstances we believe that it would be inequitable for us to hold a licensee responsible for indecent language." Later that was refined into a policy that the Commission would not take action against "fleeting and isolated profanity." But that changed in 2004 after several highly publicized incidents, including one in which a singer uttered an obscenity during the Golden Globes presentations on NBC. Under pressure from outraged members of Congress, the Commission announced that henceforth "any broadcast of the 'F-word or a variation thereof in situations such as that here" would be subject to enforcement action against the broadcaster. In re Complaints Against Various Broadcast Licenses Regarding Their Airing of the "Golden Globes Awards" Program, 2004 WL 540339 (2004).

The Commission imposed forfeitures totaling $550,000 against 20 CBS-owned stations that carried the 2004 Super Bowl halftime show in which singer Janet Jackson's breast was exposed. The FCC did not impose forfeitures against many other stations affiliated with but not owned by CBS that also broadcast the show, explaining that they were not involved in planning the halftime show as CBS was. The FCC said it was also influenced by the long history of indecency violations by Infinity Broadcasting which, like CBS, is a subsidiary of Viacom. See FCC Throws Flag at CBS's Halftime Play; Commissioners Propose $550,000 Indecency Fine, Wash. Post, Sept. 23, 2004, at C1.

Viacom eventually paid $3.5 million to settle indecency complaints, including those against the "Opie and Anthony Show," in which hosts of a radio show conducted a contest requiring contestants to have sex in various public places in New York, including St. Patrick's Cathedral, Rockefeller Center, and FAO Schwarz toy store. The payment disposed of all pending complaints against Viacom and its subsidiaries except that relating to the Super Bowl halftime show, which Viacom said it planned to contest. Viacom also agreed to adopt a "compliance plan" and institute tape-delays to prevent future occurrences. See 32 Med. L. Rptr. No. 47, Dec. 7, 2004.

Pacifica established the framework for numerous subsequent Congressional attacks on indecency, not only in broadcasting but also on cable and the Internet: the regulations are justified by the presumed need to protect children, they generally operate by attempting to channel indecent material into "safe harbors" in which the exposure to children is minimized, and the ease or difficulty with which parents can keep the material away from children without help from the government is an important consideration. But since adults have a constitutional right to see and hear indecent material and the producers of it have a constitutional right to supply it to them, the effort to protect children cannot unduly restrict access by adults.

In the print media context, the Supreme Court long ago held that restrictions must not limit what adults may read to "only what is fit for children." Butler v. Michigan, 352 U.S. 380, 383 (1957). "Regardless of the strength of the government's interest" in protecting children, the Court has written, "the level of discourse reaching the mailbox simply cannot be limited to that which would be suitable for a sandbox." Bolger v. Youngs Drug Products Corp., 463 U.S. 60, 74–75 (1983). But in the electronic media, that is not entirely true: whether limitations on the First Amendment rights of adults are permissible generally depends on whether they are necessary and effective as a means of controlling minors' access. Deciding the extent to which indecent but constitutionally protected speech in different media can be burdened in the interest of protecting children is the central issue in the following materials.

b.   Indecency on cable television

After the courts in the 1980s struck down several attempts by states to regulate indecency on cable, in 1992 Congress undertook to do so. The Supreme Court held unconstitutional the key provision of the 1992 Act, which required cable operators to segregate indecent programming and block it from all except those who specifically ordered it, holding that it was overly restrictive and not narrowly tailored to protect children because less restrictive means (such as scrambling laws and lockboxes) were available to restrict children's access. Denver Area Educ. Telecomm. Consortium, Inc. v. Federal Communications Comm'n, 518 U.S. 727 (1996). The same statute authorized cable operators to refuse to carry indecent programming on the channels they leased to others, and the Court upheld that provision. Cable systems used that authority to insist that cable networks scramble indecent programming, which cable operators then made available to subscribers through unscrambling devices for an additional fee. Scrambling can be imprecise, however; sometimes audio or visual portions of the scrambled programs can be heard or seen by nonsubscribers, a phenomenon known as "signal bleed," which is the subject of the following case.

United States v. Playboy Entertainment Group, Inc.

Supreme Court of the United States, 2000.
529 U.S. 803, 120 S.Ct. 1878, 146 L.Ed.2d 865, 28 Med.L.Rptr. 1801.

[To shield children from hearing or seeing images resulting from signal bleed, Congress added Section 505 to the Telecommunications Act of 1996. It required cable television operators providing channels "primarily dedicated to sexually-oriented programming" either to "fully scramble or otherwise fully block" those channels or to limit their transmission to hours when children are unlikely to be viewing (set by the FCC as 10 p.m. to 6 a.m.). Because fool-proof scrambling was expensive in the pre-digital era, the majority of cable operators responded to § 505 by adopting the "time channeling" approach. That meant that that, for two-thirds of the day, no viewers could receive the programming in question.

Playboy Entertainment Group, a supplier of much of the affected programming, challenged § 505's constitutionality. A three-judge District Court concluded that § 505's content-based restriction on speech violated the First Amendment because the Government might further its interests in less restrictive ways. The less restrictive alternative identified by the court was the provision in § 504 of the Act, which required cable operators to block any channel upon a subscriber's request. The evidence showed that less than one percent of subscribers requested such blocking. The government argued that it therefore was not an effective alternative, but the court said that might be because the option was not sufficiently publicized. The court said the government had the burden of proving the ineffectiveness of voluntary blocking by individual households, and had not discharged it.]

JUSTICE KENNEDY delivered the opinion of the Court.

. . .

Since § 505 is a content-based speech restriction, it can stand only if it satisfies strict scrutiny. *Sable Communications of Cal., Inc. v. FCC*, 492 U.S. 115, 126 (1989) [which held that the feasibility of a technological approach to controlling minors' access to "dial-a-porn" messages required invalidation of a complete statutory ban on telephonic pornography]. If a statute regulates speech based on its content, it must be narrowly tailored to promote a compelling Government interest. *Ibid.* If a less restrictive alternative would serve the Government's purpose, the legislature must use that alternative. [Reno v. ACLU, 521 U.S. 844, 25 Med. L. Rptr. 1833 (1997) (holding that restrictions on Internet indecency were unconstitutional because less restrictive alternatives would protect children at least as effectively.] To do otherwise would be to restrict speech without an adequate justification, a course the First Amendment does not permit.

Our precedents teach these principles. Where the designed benefit of a content-based speech restriction is to shield the sensibilities of listeners, the general rule is that the right of expression prevails, even where no less restrictive alternative exists. We are expected to protect our own sensibilities "simply by averting [our] eyes." *Cohen v. California*, 403 U.S. 15, 21 (1971); accord, *Erznoznik v. Jacksonville*, 422 U.S. 205, 210–211 (1975).

Here, of course, we consider images transmitted to some homes where they are not wanted and where parents often are not present to give immediate guidance. Cable television, like broadcast media, presents unique problems, which inform our assessment of the interests at stake, and which may justify restrictions that would be unacceptable in other contexts. See [DAETC, Pacifica]. No one suggests the Government must be indifferent to unwanted, indecent speech that comes into the home without parental consent. The speech here, all agree, is protected speech; and the question is what standard the Government must meet in order to restrict it. As we consider a content-based regulation, the answer should be clear: The standard is strict scrutiny. This case involves speech alone; and even where speech is indecent and enters the home, the objective of shielding children does not suffice to support a blanket ban if the protection can be accomplished by a less restrictive alternative.

. . .

There is, moreover, a key difference between cable television and the broadcasting media, which is the point on which this case turns: Cable systems have the capacity to block unwanted channels on a household-by-household basis. The option to block reduces the likelihood, so concerning to the Court in *Pacifica* [ ], that traditional First Amendment scrutiny would deprive the Government of all authority to address this sort of problem. The corollary, of course, is that targeted blocking enables the Government to support parental authority without affecting the First Amendment interests of speakers and willing listeners—listeners for whom, if the speech is unpopular or indecent, the privacy of their own homes may be the optimal place of receipt. Simply put, targeted blocking is less restrictive than banning, and the Government cannot ban speech if targeted blocking is a feasible and effective means of furthering its compelling interests. This is not to say that the absence of an effective blocking mechanism will in all cases suffice to support a law restricting the speech in question; but if a less restrictive means is available for the Government to achieve its goals, the Government must use it.

. . .

When a student first encounters our free speech jurisprudence, he or she might think it is influenced by the philosophy that one idea is as good as any other, and that in art and literature objective standards of style, taste, decorum, beauty, and esthetics are deemed by the Constitution to be inappropriate, indeed unattainable. Quite the opposite is true. The Constitution no more enforces a relativistic philosophy or moral nihilism than it does any other point of view. The Constitution exists precisely so that opinions and judgments, including esthetic and moral judgments about art and literature, can be formed, tested, and expressed. What the Constitution says is that these judgments are for the individual to make, not for the Government to decree, even with the mandate or approval of a majority. Technology expands the capacity to choose; and it denies the potential of this revolution if we assume the Government is best positioned to make these choices for us.

. . .

There is little hard evidence of how widespread or how serious the problem of signal bleed is. Indeed, there is no proof as to how likely any child is to view a discernible explicit image, and no proof of the duration of the bleed or the quality of the pictures or sound. To say that millions of children are subject to a risk of viewing signal bleed is one thing; to avoid articulating the true nature and extent of the risk is quite another. Under § 505, sanctionable signal bleed can include instances as fleeting as an image appearing on a screen for just a few seconds. The First Amendment requires a more careful assessment and characterization of an evil in order to justify a regulation as sweeping as this. Although the parties have taken the additional step of lodging with the Court an assortment of videotapes, some of which show quite explicit bleeding and some of which show television static or snow, there is no attempt at explanation or context; there is no discussion, for instance, of the extent to which any particular tape is representative of what appears on screens nationwide.

. . .

It is no response that voluntary blocking requires a consumer to take action, or may be inconvenient, or may not go perfectly every time. A court should not assume a plausible, less restrictive alternative would be ineffective; and a court should not presume parents, given full information, will fail to act. If unresponsive operators are a concern, moreover, a notice statute could give cable operators ample incentive, through fines or other penalties for noncompliance, to respond to blocking requests in prompt and efficient fashion.

[The government argued that many parents would fail to order blocking even if § 504 were well publicized. "There would certainly be parents—perhaps a large number of parents—who out of inertia, indifference, or distraction, simply would take no action to block signal bleed, even if fully informed of the problem and even if offered a relatively easy solution." In those instances, "Section 505 would be the only means to protect society's independent interest."]

Even upon the assumption that the Government has an interest in substituting itself for informed and empowered parents, its interest is not sufficiently compelling to justify this widespread restriction on speech. The Government's argument stems from the idea that parents do not know their children are viewing the material on a scale or frequency to cause concern, or if so, that parents do not want to take affirmative steps to block it and their decisions are to be superseded. The assumptions have not been established; and in any event the assumptions apply only in a regime where the option of blocking has not been explained. The whole point of a publicized § 504 would be to advise parents that indecent material may be shown and to afford them an opportunity to block it at all times, even when they are not at home and even after 10 p.m. Time channeling does not offer this assistance. The regulatory alternative of a publicized § 504, which has the real possibility of promoting more open disclosure and the choice of an effective blocking system, would provide parents the information needed to engage in active supervision. The Government has not shown that this alternative, a regime of added communication and support, would be insufficient to secure its objective, or that any overriding harm justifies its intervention.

There can be little doubt, of course, that under a voluntary blocking regime, even with adequate notice, some children will be exposed to signal bleed; and we need not discount the possibility that a graphic image could have a negative impact on a young child. It must be remembered, however, that children will be exposed to signal bleed under time channeling as well. Time channeling, unlike blocking, does not eliminate signal bleed around the clock. Just as adolescents may be unsupervised outside of their own households, it is hardly unknown for them to be unsupervised in front of the television set after 10 p.m. The record is silent as to the comparative effectiveness of the two alternatives.

Basic speech principles are at stake in this case. When the purpose and design of a statute is to regulate speech by reason of its content, special consideration or latitude is not accorded to the Government merely because the law can somehow be described as a burden rather than outright suppression. We cannot be influenced, moreover, by the perception that the regulation in question is not a major one because the speech is not very important. The history of the law of free expression is one of vindication in cases involving speech that many citizens may find shabby, offensive, or even ugly. It follows that all content-based restrictions on speech must give us more than a moment's pause. If television broadcasts can expose children to the real risk of harmful exposure to indecent materials, even in their own home and without parental consent, there is a problem the Government can address. It must do so, however, in a way consistent with First Amendment principles. Here the Government has not met the burden the First Amendment imposes.

. . .

JUSTICE BREYER, with whom the CHIEF JUSTICE, JUSTICE O'CONNOR, and JUSTICE SCALIA join, dissenting.

. . .

The majority first concludes that the Government failed to prove the seriousness of the problem—receipt of adult channels by children whose parents did not request their broadcast. [ ] This claim is flat-out wrong. For one thing, the parties concede that basic . . . scrambling does not scramble the audio portion of the program. For another, Playboy itself conducted a survey of cable operators who were asked: "Is your system in full compliance with Section 505 (no discernible audio or video bleed)?" To this question, 75% of cable operators answered "no." [ ] Further, the Government's expert took the number of homes subscribing to Playboy or Spice, multiplied by the fraction of cable households with children and the average number of children per household, and found 29 million children are potentially exposed to audio and video bleed from adult programming. [ ] Even discounting by 25% for systems that might be considered in full compliance, this left 22 million children in homes with faulty scrambling systems. [ ] And, of course, the record contains additional anecdotal evidence and the concerns expressed by elected officials, probative of a larger problem. [ ]

. . . *If signal bleed is not a significant empirical problem, then why, in light of the cost of its cure, must so many cable operators switch to nighttime hours?* There is no realistic answer to this question. I do not think it realistic to imagine that signal bleed occurs just enough to make cable operators skittish, without also significantly exposing children to these images. [ ]

If, as the majority suggests, the signal bleed problem is not significant, then there is also no significant burden on speech created by § 505. The majority cannot have this evidence both ways. And if, given this logical difficulty and the quantity of empirical evidence, the majority still believes that the Government has not proved its case, then it imposes a burden upon the Government beyond that suggested in any other First Amendment case of which I am aware.

III

The majority's second claim—that the Government failed to demonstrate the absence of a "less restrictive alternative"—presents a closer question. The specific question is whether § 504's "opt-out" amounts to a "less restrictive," but *similarly* practical and *effective,* way to accomplish § 505's child-protecting objective. As *Reno* tells us, a "less restrictive alternativ[e]" must be "at least as effective in achieving the legitimate purpose that the statute was enacted to serve." [ ]

The words I have just emphasized, "similarly" and "effective," are critical. In an appropriate case they ask a judge not to apply First Amendment rules mechanically, but to decide whether, in light of the benefits and potential alternatives, the statute works speech-related harm (here to adult speech) out of proportion to the benefits that the statute seeks to provide (here, child protection).

These words imply a degree of leeway, however small, for the Legislature when it chooses among possible alternatives in light of predicted comparative effects. Without some such empirical leeway, the undoubted ability of lawyers and judges to imagine *some* kind of slightly less drastic or restrictive an approach would make it impossible to write laws that deal with the harm that called the statute into being. As Justice Blackmun pointed out, a "judge would be unimaginative indeed if he could not come up with something a little less 'drastic' or a little less 'restrictive' in almost any situation, and thereby enable himself to vote to strike legislation down." [ ] Used without a sense of the practical choices that face legislatures, "the test merely announces an inevitable [negative] result, and the test is no test at all." [ ]

I turn then to the major point of disagreement. Unlike the majority, I believe the record makes clear that § 504's opt-out is not a similarly effective alternative. Section 504 (opt-out) and § 505 (opt-in) work differently in order to achieve very different legislative objectives. Section 504 gives parents the power to tell cable operators to keep any channel out of their home. Section 505 does more. Unless parents explicitly consent, it inhibits the transmission of adult cable channels to children whose parents may be unaware of what they are watching, whose parents cannot easily supervise television viewing habits, whose parents do not know of their § 504 "opt-out" rights, or whose parents are simply unavailable at critical times. In this respect, § 505 serves the same interests as the laws that deny children access to adult cabarets or X-rated movies. [ ] These laws, and § 505, all act in the absence of direct parental supervision.

. . . I could not disagree more when the majority implies that the Government's independent interest in offering such protection—preventing, say, an 8-year-old child from watching virulent pornography without parental consent—might not be "compelling." [ ] No previous case in which the protection of children was at issue has suggested any such thing. Indeed, they all say precisely the opposite. [ ] They make clear that Government has a compelling interest in helping parents by preventing Minors from accessing sexually explicit materials in the absence of parental supervision. [ ]

. . .

IV

Section 505 raises the cost of adult channel broadcasting. In doing so, it restricts, but does not ban, adult speech. Adults may continue to watch adult channels, though less conveniently, by watching at night, recording programs with a VCR, or by subscribing to digital cable with better blocking systems. [ ] The Government's justification for imposing this restriction—limiting the access of children to channels that broadcast virtually 100% "sexually explicit" material—is "compelling." The record shows no similarly effective, less restrictive alternative. Consequently § 505's restriction, viewed in light of the proposed alternative, is proportionate to need. That is to say, it restricts speech no more than necessary to further that compelling need. Taken together, these considerations lead to the conclusion that § 505 is lawful.

I repeat that my disagreement with the majority lies in the fact that, in my view, the Government has satisfied its burden of proof. In particular, it has proved both the existence of a serious problem and the comparative ineffectiveness of § 504 in resolving that problem. This disagreement is not about allocation of First Amendment burdens of proof, basic First Amendment principle, nor the importance of that Amendment to our scheme of Government. See *ante,* at 1893. First Amendment standards are rigorous. They safeguard speech. But they also permit Congress to enact a law that increases the costs associated with certain speech, where doing so serves a compelling interest that cannot be served through the adoption of a less restrictive, similarly effective alternative. Those standards at their strictest make it difficult for the Government to prevail. But they do not make it impossible for the Government to prevail.

. . .

Congress has taken seriously the importance of maintaining adult access to the sexually explicit channels here at issue. It has tailored the restrictions to minimize their impact upon adults while offering parents help in keeping unwanted transmissions from their children. By finding "adequate alternatives" where there are none, the Court reduces Congress' protective power to the vanishing point. That is not what the First Amendment demands.

I respectfully dissent.

[Concurring opinions of Justices Stevens and Thomas are omitted].

[In a separate dissenting opinion, Justice Scalia argued that § 505 could be sustained on the "simpler ground" that a business that offers hard-core sexual material as a constant and intentional objective of its business and promotes it as such is not protected by the First Amendment.

Thus, while I agree with Justice BREYER'S child-protection analysis, it leaves me with the same feeling of true-but-inadequate as the conclusion that Al Capone did not accurately report his income. It is not only children who can be protected from occasional uninvited exposure to what appellee calls "adult-oriented programming"; we can all be. Section 505 covers only businesses that engage in the "commercial exploitation of erotica solely for the sake of their prurient appeal," [ ]—which, as Playboy's own advertisements make plain, is what "adult" programming is all about. In most contexts, contemporary American society has chosen to permit such commercial exploitation. That may be a wise democratic choice, if only because of the difficulty in many contexts (though not this one) of identifying the panderer to sex. It is, however, not a course compelled by the Constitution. Since the Government is entirely free to *block* these transmissions, it may certainly take the less drastic step of dictating how, and during what times, they may occur.]

Notes and Questions

1. If Congress still believes that voluntary blocking at the customer's request does not sufficiently protect children, what legislative options does this decision leave open? Would the Court sustain a requirement similar to that of § 505 if Congress marshaled stronger evidence of the exposure of children to signal bleed and the ineffectiveness of voluntary blocking? What kind of evidence might suffice?

2. Will regulation always fail the no-less-restrictive-alternative test if technology provides means by which parents can protect their children? Note that the means must also be "effective." Is regulation permissible if the means is ineffective only because of parental indifference? Does the

government have an interest in protecting children whose parents do not protect them? Is it compelling?

3.   Justice Scalia has long argued, as he does in his dissent here, that harm to children is not the only justification for regulation of indecency. Do cases like *Pacifica* and *Playboy* seize upon protection of children as a pretext for some other interest? What might that be? Preserving a set of attitudes about sex? Maintaining a level of decorum in public discourse? Regulating an industry that may create socially costly externalities? Is this approach just a way of evading the choice that has been made between these values and speech through the narrow definition of obscenity?

c.   *Indecency on the Internet*

Efforts by Congress to shield children from pornography on the Internet have encountered the same kind of constitutional obstacles as regulation of indecency on cable. The same massive Telecommunications Act of 1996 that contained the cable indecency provisions at issue in *Playboy* also contained the Communications Decency Act, which criminalized the use of an "interactive computer system" to knowingly send a minor an indecent or obscene communication or make available to a minor "any comment, request, suggestion, proposal, image, or other communication that, in context, depicts or describes, in terms patently offensive as measured by contemporary community standards, sexual or excretory activities or organs. . . ." 47 U.S.C. § 223(a), (d).

This was held unconstitutional in Reno v. American Civil Liberties Union, 521 U.S. 844, 25 Med. L. Rptr. 1833 (1997). The Court noted that computer users seldom encounter sexually explicit material accidentally because they are confronted by titles and warnings as to content. This aspect differentiated the Internet from radio and television. Private systems to permit parents to block their children from access to certain sites had developed to a point where they adequately served that purpose even though they could not screen for sexually explicit images. The Court rejected contentions that credit card verification and age verification were needed to prevent improper access. The opinion observed that the use of "indecent" created so many ambiguities that it was "problematic for purposes of the First Amendment."

> The breadth of the CDA's coverage is wholly unprecedented. Unlike the regulations upheld in *Ginsberg* and *Pacifica*, the scope of the CDA is not limited to commercial speech or commercial entities. Its open-ended prohibitions embrace all nonprofit entities and individuals posting indecent messages or displaying them on their own computers in the presence of minors. The general, undefined terms "indecent" and "patently offensive" cover large amounts of nonpornographic material with serious educational or other value. Moreover, the "community standards" criterion as applied to the Internet means that any communication available to a nationwide audience will be judged by the standards of the community most likely to be offended by the message. The regulated subject matter includes any of the seven "dirty

words" used in the *Pacifica* monologue, the use of which the Government's expert acknowledged could constitute a felony. [ ] It may also extend to discussions about prison rape or safe sexual practices, artistic images that include nude subjects, and arguably the card catalogue of the Carnegie Library.

For the purposes of our decision, we need neither accept nor reject the Government's submission that the First Amendment does not forbid a blanket prohibition on all "indecent" and "patently offensive" messages communicated to a 17–year-old—no matter how much value the message may contain and regardless of parental approval. [The opinion noted that the statute authorized a "lengthy prison term" for a parent who permitted her 17–year-old to use the family computer to obtain such messages.] Similarly, a parent who sent his 17–year-old freshman information on birth control via e-mail could be incarcerated even though neither he, his child, nor anyone in their home community, found the material "indecent" or "patently offensive," if the college town's community thought otherwise.

Congress responded to the Supreme Court's decision in *ACLU v. Reno* in 1998 by enacting a more limited indecency provision, the Child Online Protection Act (COPA), 47 U.S.C. § 231(1). The new law applied only to persons "engaged in the business" of communicating "material that is harmful to minors," § 231(e)(6), and provided affirmative defenses if the defendant could show that in good faith it had restricted access by requiring use of a credit card, digital certificate that verifies age, or other reasonable available technology. Id. § 231(c). Enforcement of COPA was immediately enjoined, however, and the Supreme Court upheld the preliminary injunction on the ground that it probably would ultimately be held unconstitutional for reasons similar to those in *Playboy* and *Reno*: use of filtering and blocking technologies by recipients was almost certain to be found effective and less restrictive than a ban directed at the purveyors of material "harmful to minors." See Ashcroft v. American Civil Liberties Union [II], __ U.S. __, 124 S. Ct. 2783 (2004).

The 5–4 majority said filters impose restrictions at the receiving end instead of restricting speech at its source, thereby allowing adults to receive information they want without the inconvenience of going through identification procedures and without the chilling effect of criminalizing a particular species of speech. The fact that the government could not compel use of filters did not prevent that from being an effective alternative, the majority said, because the government could provide incentives for schools and libraries to use them and promote their acceptance by parents and industry. As in *Playboy*, the fact that some parents would not avail themselves of the opportunity did not necessarily make filtering an ineffective alternative.

In dissent, Justices Breyer, Rehnquist, and O'Connor argued that filtering could not properly be considered an alternative at all, because it was just the status quo that Congress had found to be an inadequate response to the issue of children's access to online pornography. They believed the majority had construed COPA unnecessarily broadly. Properly construed, it would reach only commercial pornography that borders on obscenity, they said, and therefore would impose only modest burdens on speech.

Dissenting separately, Justice Scalia again argued, as he did in *Playboy*, that the business of pornography enjoys no First Amendment protection. He said COPA applied only to that business and therefore was not unconstitutional.

The Court remanded for trial on the merits and said its decision "does not foreclose the District Court from concluding, upon a proper showing by the Government that meets the Government's constitutional burden as defined in this opinion, that COPA is the least restrictive alternative available to accomplish Congress' goal." But the Court's strong endorsement of the filtering alternative indicated that COPA's approach would be hard to sustain. The Court also noted that technological and legislative developments since the Act was first challenged might make it even harder to defend than it was then. Filtering technology had improved in the interim, the Court said, and Congress had passed at least two further statutes that might qualify as less restrictive alternatives to COPA—a prohibition on misleading domain names, and a statute creating a minors-safe "Dot Kids" domain.

Internet pornography in public libraries. Another federal statute, the Children's Internet Protection Act of 2000 (CIPA), § 1701, 114 Stat. 2763A–335, required public libraries that receive federal subsidies for providing Internet access to employ filtering software designed to block access to pornography. It permitted libraries to unblock computers at the request of adult patrons. The American Library Association challenged the statute, contending it would require libraries to violate the First Amendment by censoring what their patrons could view. The Supreme Court upheld the statute. See United States v. American Library Ass'n, Inc., 539 U.S. 194 (2003).

A four-justice plurality said CIPA was a legitimate exercise of Congress's spending power, not substantially different from the decisions libraries make daily as to what books to purchase for their patrons, and raised no First Amendment issue. Justice Kennedy, concurring in the judgment, said the statute might raise First Amendment issues if the unblocking provisions were administered in a way that made adult access too difficult, but those could not be addressed in the ALA's facial challenge. Justice Breyer thought the statute raised First Amendment issues but survived intermediate scrutiny, which he thought was all that was required. Justice Stevens dissented on the ground that the statute imposed unconstitutional conditions on libraries' eligibility for the federal aid. Justices Souter and Ginsburg agreed with Justice Stevens but dissented on the additional ground that the statute was pure censorship since, unlike book acquisition decisions, it made material unavailable not for resource-allocation reasons but because of disapproval of content.

E.   COMMERCIAL SPEECH

1.   CONSUMERS

Media take a keen interest in commercial speech cases. For one thing, what happens in these cases can affect media revenues. Supreme Court decisions holding that pharmacies, lawyers, and other professionals had a First Amendment right to advertise brought millions of dollars of new ad revenue to media. Decisions upholding federal laws banning broadcast cigarette advertising diverted millions of dollars of ad money from television to print, billboards, and sponsorship of sports events (until that was restricted too). For another, the developing jurisprudence of commercial speech may have implications for First Amendment theory generally. Commercial speech analysis often seems to call into question the assumption that courts may not discriminate among various types of protected speech based on judgments as to its value. For both of these reasons, media companies often may be found among the amici who file briefs arguing that particular advertising restrictions are unconstitutional.

The Court has decided many commercial speech cases in the past thirty-five years, and the results are not easy to summarize. The following case explores some of the major threads of commercial speech jurisprudence.

Lorillard Tobacco Co. v. Reilly

Supreme Court of the United States, 2001.
533 U.S. 525, 121 S.Ct. 2404, 150 L.Ed.2d 532, 29 Med.L.Rptr. 2121.

[The Massachusetts attorney general, pursuant to his authority to prevent unfair or deceptive practices in trade, promulgated comprehensive regulations concerning the marketing of cigarettes, cigars, and smokeless tobacco products. Among other things, they regulated outdoor advertising (billboards) and point-of-sale advertising, such as in-store displays. The attorney general, Reilly, said his objective was to "to eliminate deception and unfairness in the way cigarettes and smokeless tobacco products are marketed, sold and distributed in Massachusetts in order to address the incidence of cigarette smoking and smokeless tobacco use by children under legal age . . . [and] to prevent access to such products by underage consumers."

Tobacco companies and retailers challenged the regulations. Insofar as the advertising restrictions applied to cigarettes, the Court held that they were pre-empted by the Federal Cigarette Labeling and Advertising Act (FCLAA), which prescribes mandatory health warnings for cigarette packaging and advertising, 15 U.S.C. § 1333, and preempts similar state regulations, § 1334(b).]

JUSTICE O'CONNOR delivered the opinion of the Court.

. . .

III

By its terms, the FCLAA's pre-emption provision only applies to cigarettes. Accordingly, we must evaluate the smokeless tobacco and cigar petitioners' First Amendment challenges to the State's outdoor and point-of-sale advertising regulations. . . .

A

For over 25 years, the Court has recognized that commercial speech does not fall outside the purview of the First Amendment. [ ] Instead, the Court has afforded commercial speech a measure of First Amendment protection " 'commensurate' " with its position in relation to other constitutionally guaranteed expression. [ ] In recognition of the "distinction between speech proposing a commercial transaction, which occurs in an area traditionally subject to government regulation, and other varieties of speech," [Central Hudson Gas & Electric Corp. v. Public Service Commission, 447 U.S. 557, 6 Med. L. Rptr. 1497 (1980)], we developed a framework for analyzing regulations of commercial speech that is "substantially similar" to the test for time, place, and manner restrictions, [Board of Trustees v. Fox, 492 U.S. 469 (1989).] The analysis contains four elements:

"At the outset, we must determine whether the expression is protected by the First Amendment. For commercial speech to come within that provision, it at least must concern lawful activity and not be misleading. Next, we ask whether the asserted governmental interest is substantial. If both inquiries yield positive answers, we must determine whether the regulation directly advances the governmental interest asserted, and whether it is not more extensive than is necessary to serve that interest." *Central Hudson,* [ ].

Petitioners urge us to reject the *Central Hudson* analysis and apply strict scrutiny. They are not the first litigants to do so. See, *e.g., Greater New Orleans Broadcasting Assn., Inc. v. United States,* 527 U.S. 173, 184 (1999). Admittedly, several Members of the Court have expressed doubts about the *Central Hudson* analysis and whether it should apply in particular cases. See, *e.g., Greater New Orleans, supra,* [ ] (THOMAS, J., concurring in judgment); *44 Liquormart, Inc. v. Rhode Island,* 517 U.S. 484, 501, 510–514 (1996) (joint opinion of STEVENS, KENNEDY, and GINSBURG, JJ.); *id.,* [ ] SCALIA, J., (concurring in part and concurring in judgment); [ ] (THOMAS, J., concurring in part and concurring in judgment). But here, as in *Greater New Orleans,* we see "no need to break new ground. *Central Hudson,* as applied in our more recent commercial speech cases, provides an adequate basis for decision." [ ]

Only the last two steps of *Central Hudson's* four-part analysis are at issue here. The Attorney General has assumed for purposes of summary judgment that petitioners' speech is entitled to First Amendment protection. [ ] With respect to the second step, none of the petitioners contests the importance of the State's interest in preventing the use of tobacco products by minors. [ ]

The third step of *Central Hudson* concerns the relationship between the harm that underlies the State's interest and the means identified by the State to advance that interest. It requires that "the speech restriction directly and materially advanc[e] the asserted governmental interest. 'This burden is not satisfied by mere speculation or conjecture; rather, a governmental body seeking to sustain a restriction on commercial speech must demonstrate that the harms it recites are real and that its restriction will in fact alleviate them to a material degree.' " *Greater New Orleans, supra,* [ ]

. . .

The last step of the *Central Hudson* analysis "complements" the third step, "asking whether the speech restriction is not more extensive than necessary to serve the interests that support it." *Greater New Orleans, supra,* [ ] We have made it clear that "the least restrictive means" is not the standard; instead, the case law requires a reasonable " 'fit between the legislature's ends and the means chosen to accomplish those ends, . . . a means narrowly tailored to achieve the desired objective.' " [quoting *Board of Trustees v. Fox*]. . . .

B

. . .

1

The smokeless tobacco and cigar petitioners contend that the Attorney General's regulations do not satisfy *Central Hudson's* third step. They maintain that although the Attorney General may have identified a problem with underage cigarette smoking, he has not identified an equally severe problem with respect to underage use of smokeless tobacco or cigars. [They argued that their products have different characteristics and marketing strategies than cigarettes and that there was no proof that limiting advertising would materially alleviate any problem of underage use of their products. But the Court cited numerous studies by the Federal Food and Drug Administration and others indicating that advertising stimulates demand for tobacco products, that use of smokeless tobacco and cigars by young people was increasing, and that there were links between those increases and advertising.]

Our review of the record reveals that the Attorney General has provided ample documentation of the problem with underage use of smokeless tobacco and cigars. In addition, we disagree with petitioners' claim that there is no evidence that preventing targeted campaigns and limiting youth exposure to advertising will decrease underage use of smokeless tobacco and cigars. On this record and in the posture of summary judgment, we are unable to conclude that the Attorney General's decision to regulate advertising of smokeless tobacco and cigars in an effort to combat the use of tobacco products by minors was based on mere "speculation [and] conjecture." [ ].

2

Whatever the strength of the Attorney General's evidence to justify the outdoor advertising regulations, however, we conclude that the regulations do not satisfy the fourth step of the *Central Hudson* analysis. The final step of the *Central Hudson* analysis, the "critical inquiry in this case," requires a reasonable fit between the means and ends of the regulatory scheme. [ ] The Attorney General's regulations do not meet this standard. The broad sweep of the regulations indicates that the Attorney General did not "carefully calculat[e] the costs and benefits associated with the burden on speech imposed" by the regulations. *Cincinnati v. Discovery Network, Inc.,* 507 U.S. 410, 417 (1993).

The outdoor advertising regulations prohibit any smokeless tobacco or cigar advertising within 1,000 feet of schools or playgrounds. In the District Court, petitioners maintained that this prohibition would prevent advertising in 87% to 91% of Boston, Worcester, and Springfield, Massachusetts. [ ] The 87% to 91% figure appears to include not only the effect of the regulations, but also the limitations imposed by other generally applicable zoning restrictions. [ ] The Attorney General disputed petitioners' figures but "concede[d] that the reach of the regulations is substantial." [ ] Thus, the Court of Appeals concluded that the regulations prohibit advertising in a substantial portion of the major metropolitan areas of Massachusetts. [ ]

The substantial geographical reach of the Attorney General's outdoor advertising regulations is compounded by other factors. "Outdoor" advertising includes not only advertising located outside an establishment, but also advertising inside a store if that advertising is visible from outside the store. The regulations restrict advertisements of any size and the term advertisement also includes oral statements. [ ].

In some geographical areas, these regulations would constitute nearly a complete ban on the communication of truthful information about smokeless tobacco and cigars to adult consumers. The breadth and scope of the regulations, and the process by which the Attorney General adopted the regulations, do not demonstrate a careful calculation of the speech interests involved.

First, the Attorney General did not seem to consider the impact of the 1,000–foot restriction on commercial speech in major metropolitan areas. . . . [T]he effect of the Attorney General's speech regulations will vary based on whether a locale is rural, suburban, or urban. The uniformly broad sweep of the geographical limitation demonstrates a lack of tailoring.

In addition, the range of communications restricted seems unduly broad. For instance, it is not clear from the regulatory scheme why a ban on oral communications is necessary to further the State's interest. Apparently that restriction means that a retailer is unable to answer inquiries about its tobacco products if that communication occurs outdoors. Similarly, a ban on all signs of any size seems ill suited to target the problem of highly visible billboards, as opposed to smaller signs. To the extent that studies have identified particular advertising and promotion practices that appeal to youth, tailoring would involve targeting those practices while permitting others. As crafted, the regulations make no distinction among practices on this basis.

. . .

The State's interest in preventing underage tobacco use is substantial, and even compelling, but it is no less true that the sale and use of tobacco products by adults is a legal activity. We must consider that tobacco retailers and manufacturers have an interest in conveying truthful information about their products to adults, and adults have a corresponding interest in receiving truthful information about tobacco products. In a case involving indecent speech on the Internet we explained that "the governmental interest in protecting children from harmful materials . . . does not justify an unnecessarily broad suppression of speech addressed to adults." [Citing *Reno*, supra p. 166, and other cases arising from attempts to regulate indecency.]

. . .

A careful calculation of the costs of a speech regulation does not mean that a State must demonstrate that there is no incursion on legitimate speech interests, but a speech regulation cannot unduly impinge on the speaker's ability to propose a commercial transaction and the adult listener's opportunity to obtain information about products. After reviewing the outdoor advertising regulations, we find the calculation in these cases insufficient for purposes of the First Amendment.

C

Massachusetts has also restricted indoor, point-of-sale advertising for smokeless tobacco and cigars. Advertising cannot be "placed lower than five feet from the floor of any retail establishment which is located within a one thousand foot radius of" any school or playground. . . .

. . .

We conclude that the point-of-sale advertising regulations fail both the third and fourth steps of the *Central Hudson* analysis. A regulation cannot be sustained if it " 'provides only ineffective or remote support for the government's purpose,' " [ ], or if there is "little chance" that the restriction will advance the State's goal. [ ] As outlined above, the State's goal is to prevent minors from using tobacco products and to curb demand for that activity by limiting youth exposure to advertising. The 5–foot rule does not seem to advance that goal. Not all children are less than 5 feet tall, and those who are certainly have the ability to look up and take in their surroundings.

. . .

Massachusetts may wish to target tobacco advertisements and displays that entice children, much like floor-level candy displays in a convenience store, but the blanket height restriction does not constitute a reasonable fit with that goal. The Court of Appeals recognized that the efficacy of the regulation was questionable, but decided that, "[i]n any event, the burden on speech imposed by the provision is very limited." [ ] There is no *de minimis* exception for a speech restriction that lacks sufficient tailoring or justification. We conclude that the restriction on the height of indoor advertising is invalid under *Central Hudson's* third and fourth prongs.

. . .

[Justices Kennedy and Scalia concurred in the judgment on the ground that the outdoor advertising restrictions failed the fourth part of the test in *Central Hudson* and thought it unnecessary to decide whether they also failed the third part. "Neither are we required to consider whether *Central Hudson* should be retained in the face of the substantial objections" that its test "gives insufficient protection to truthful, nonmisleading commercial speech."]

JUSTICE THOMAS, concurring in part and concurring in the judgment.

. . .

A

There was once a time when this Court declined to give any First Amendment protection to commercial speech. In *Valentine v. Chrestensen*, 316 U.S. 52, 62 S. Ct. 920, 86 L. Ed. 1262 (1942), the Court went so far as to say that "the Constitution imposes [no] restraint on government as respects purely commercial advertising." [ ] That position was repudiated in *Virginia Bd. of Pharmacy v. Virginia Citizens Consumer Council, Inc.*, 425 U.S. 748, 96 S. Ct. 1817, 48 L. Ed.2d 346 (1976), which explained that even speech "which does 'no more than propose a commercial transaction'" is protected by the First Amendment. [ ] Since then, the Court has followed an uncertain course—much of the uncertainty being generated by the malleability of the four-part balancing test of *Central Hudson*. [ ]

I have observed previously that there is no "philosophical or historical basis for asserting that 'commercial' speech is of 'lower value' than 'noncommercial' speech." [ ] Indeed, I doubt whether it is even possible to draw a coherent distinction between commercial and noncommercial speech. [Citing indirectly Kozinski & Banner, Who's Afraid of Commercial Speech, 76 Va. L.Rev. 627 (1990)].[2]

It should be clear that if these regulations targeted anything other than advertising for commercial products—if, for example, they were directed at billboards promoting political candidates—all would agree that the restrictions should be subjected to strict scrutiny. In my view, an asserted government interest in keeping people ignorant by suppressing expression "is *per se* illegitimate and can no more justify regulation of 'commercial' speech than it can justify regulation of 'noncommercial'

2. Tobacco advertising provides a good illustration. The sale of tobacco products is the subject of considerable political controversy, and not surprisingly, some tobacco advertisements both promote a product and take a stand in this political debate. [ ] A recent cigarette advertisement, for example, displayed a brand logo next to text reading, "Why do politicians smoke cigars while taxing cigarettes?"

speech." . . . I would subject the Massachusetts regulations to strict scrutiny.

B

Even if one accepts the premise that commercial speech generally is entitled to a lower level of constitutional protection than are other forms of speech, it does not follow that the regulations here deserve anything less than strict scrutiny. Although we have recognized several categories of speech that normally receive reduced First Amendment protection, or no First Amendment protection at all, we have never held that the government may regulate speech within those categories in any way that it wishes. Rather, we have said "that these areas of speech can, consistently with the First Amendment, be regulated *because of their constitutionally proscribable content.*" [*R.A.V.,* supra p. 42]. Even when speech falls into a category of reduced constitutional protection, the government may not engage in content discrimination for reasons unrelated to those characteristics of the speech that place it within the category. For example, a city may ban obscenity (because obscenity is an unprotected category, see, *e.g.,* [*Roth,* supra p. 145], but it may not ban "only those legally obscene works that contain criticism of the city government." [*R.A.V.*]

In explaining the distinction between commercial speech and other forms of speech, we have emphasized that commercial speech is both "more easily verifiable by its disseminator" and less likely to be "chilled by proper regulation." [*Virginia Pharmacy*] These characteristics led us to conclude that, in the context of commercial speech, it is "less necessary to tolerate inaccurate statements for fear of silencing the speaker," and also that it is more "appropriate to require that a commercial message appear in such a form, or include such additional information, warnings, and disclaimers, as are necessary to prevent its being deceptive." *Ibid.* Whatever the validity of this reasoning, it is limited to the peculiarly *commercial* harms that commercial speech can threaten—*i.e.,* the risk of deceptive or misleading advertising. As we observed in *R.A.V.:*

"[A] State may choose to regulate price advertising in one industry but not in others, because the risk of fraud (one of the characteristics of commercial speech that justifies depriving it of full First Amendment protection) is in its view greater there. But a State may not prohibit only that commercial advertising that depicts men in a demeaning fashion." [ ].

. . .

Whatever power the State may have to regulate commercial speech, it may not use that power to limit the content of commercial speech, as it has done here, "for reasons unrelated to the preservation of a fair bargaining process." Such content-discriminatory regulation—like all other content-based regulation of speech—must be subjected to strict scrutiny.

. . .

Underlying many of the arguments of respondents and their *amici* is the idea that tobacco is in some sense *sui generis*—that it is so special, so unlike any other object of regulation, that application of normal First Amendment principles should be suspended. [ ] Smoking poses serious health risks, and advertising may induce children (who lack the judgment to make an intelligent decision about whether to smoke) to begin smoking, which can lead to addiction. The State's assessment of the urgency of the problem posed by tobacco is a policy judgment, and it is not this Court's place to second-guess it. Nevertheless, it seems appropriate to point out that to uphold the Massachusetts tobacco regulations would be to accept a line of reasoning that would permit restrictions on advertising for a host of other products.

Tobacco use is, we are told, "the single leading cause of preventable death in the United States." [ ] The *second* largest contributor to mortality rates in the United States is obesity. [ ]. It is associated with increased incidence of diabetes, hypertension, and coronary artery disease, [ ], and it represents a public health problem that is rapidly growing worse. [ ] Although the growth of obesity over the last few decades has had many causes, a significant factor has been the increased availability of large quantities of high-calorie, high-fat foods. [ ] Such foods, of course, have been aggressively marketed and promoted by fast food companies. [ ]

Respondents say that tobacco companies are covertly targeting children in their advertising. Fast food companies do so openly. [ ] Moreover, there is considerable evidence that they have been successful in changing children's eating behavior. [ ] The effect of advertising on children's eating habits is significant for two reasons. First, childhood obesity is a serious health problem in its own right. [ ] Second, eating preferences formed in childhood tend to persist in adulthood. [ ] So even though fast food is not addictive in the same way tobacco is, children's exposure to fast food advertising can have deleterious consequences that are difficult to reverse.

To take another example, the third largest cause of preventable deaths in the United States is alcohol. [ ] Alcohol use is associated with tens of thousands of deaths each year from cancers and digestive diseases. [ ] And the victims of alcohol use are not limited to those who drink alcohol. In 1996, over 17,000 people were killed, and over 321,000 people were injured, in alcohol-related car accidents. [ ] Each year, alcohol is involved in several million violent crimes, including almost 200,000 sexual assaults. [ ]

. . .

Respondents have identified no principle of law or logic that would preclude the imposition of restrictions on fast food and alcohol advertising similar to those they seek to impose on tobacco advertising. [ ] In effect, they seek a "vice" exception to the First Amendment. No such exception exists. [ ] If it did, it would have almost no limit, for "any product that poses some threat to public health or public morals might reasonably be characterized by a state legislature as relating to 'vice activity.' " [ ] That is why "a 'vice' label that is unaccompanied by a corresponding prohibition against the commercial behavior at issue fails to provide a principled justification for the regulation of commercial speech about that activity." [ ]

No legislature has ever sought to restrict speech about an activity it regarded as harmless and inoffensive. Calls for limits on expression always are made when the specter of some threatened harm is looming. The identity of the harm may vary. People will be inspired by totalitarian dogmas and subvert the Republic. They will be inflamed by racial demagoguery and embrace hatred and bigotry. Or they will be enticed by cigarette advertisements and choose to smoke, risking disease. It is therefore no answer for the State to say that the makers of cigarettes are doing harm: perhaps they are. But in that respect they are no different from the purveyors of other harmful products, or the advocates of harmful ideas. When the State seeks to silence them, they are all entitled to the protection of the First Amendment.

[Justices Stevens, Ginsburg, Breyer, and Souter dissented from the Court's decision that state regulation of cigarette advertising was preempted. They agreed that the state had failed to show that the advertising restrictions met the fourth prong of the *Central Hudson* test, but thought that since the case had been decided on summary judgment motions, it should be remanded for trial on that issue.]

Notes and Questions

1. Does the methodology prescribed by *Central Hudson* and employed in this case produce different results than would occur if the Court merely weighed the state's interest in limiting the advertising against the speech interest in not doing so? Does the four-part test make results any more predictable than ad hoc balancing would?

2. The Court has not altered the explanations given in *Virginia Pharmacy*, cited in the principal case, for according commercial speech only limited protection: statements made in commercial speech are more readily verifiable and are less easily chilled because advertisers have strong economic motivations. If those are valid reasons, should they be taken into account in First Amendment analysis generally? Might criminal punishment for making false statements about a public official's voting record be upheld on the ground that voting records are easily verifiable? Makers of movies and television programming have powerful economic incentives for their expression; should entertainment receive reduced First Amendment protection?

3. If the Court embraced Justice Thomas's view that advertising should receive no less protection than other types of speech, would the long-term result be leveling up or leveling down—i.e., full protection for commercial speech or reduced protection for some (or all) other types of speech?

4. Historically, the First Amendment has often been invoked to protect unpopular speakers from majoritarian impulses. Is it wrong (or unnecessary) to use it to insulate powerful commercial interests from regulation?

———

Regulating the advertising of "vice." In the principal case, Justice Thomas says there is no exception making it easier to regulate advertising of vice. That has not always been clear. For a time the Supreme Court appeared willing to permit more regulation of commercial speech about liquor and gambling than other types of commercial speech. In Posadas de Puerto Rico Associates v. Tourism Co. of Puerto Rico, 478 U.S. 328, 13 Med. L. Rptr. 1033 (1986), a 5–4 majority upheld a restriction on casino advertising in Puerto Rico, where casino gambling was legal but the government wished to discourage its own citizens from participating. The restriction allowed casinos to advertise in local media only if the primary audience was tourists. Then-Justice Rehnquist wrote for the majority that because the government of Puerto Rico could have prohibited casino gambling altogether, it was "free to take the less intrusive step of allowing the conduct but reducing the demand through restrictions on advertising." Another line of cases suggested that First Amendment protection for liquor advertising was reduced by the Twenty-first Amendment. That amendment, ending nationwide Prohibition, gave the states power to prohibit sale or use of alcoholic beverages, and the Court had said this created a presumption of validity favoring state regulation as against a First Amendment challenge. See California v. LaRue, 409 U.S. 109 (1972).

The Court disavowed both of these theories in 44 Liquormart, Inc. v. Rhode Island, 517 U.S. 484, 24 Med. L. Rptr. 1673 (1996), striking down a state prohibition against price advertising of liquor. The Court unanimously rejected the idea that the states have special powers to regulate speech about liquor, all the justices agreeing that the Twenty-first Amendment does not qualify or limit rights under the First Amendment. In various opinions, eight justices questioned or rejected the *Posadas* rationale.

The Court upheld a restriction on "vice" advertising in United States v. Edge Broadcasting Co., 509 U.S. 418, 21 Med. L. Rptr. 1577 (1993), but that decision seemed to have more to do with federalism than with the subject matter of the advertising. The Court, 7–2, upheld a federal statute prohibiting a broadcaster from advertising any lottery unless the station is located in a state that has a lottery. The majority said Congress had a substantial interest in accommodating the conflicting policies of lottery and nonlottery states by allowing the former to advertise their lotteries while allowing the latter to shield their residents from lottery advertising.

That rationale appeared to be limited, however, by Greater New Orleans Broadcasting Ass'n v. United States, 527 U.S. 173, 27 Med. L. Rptr. 1769 (1999). The Court unanimously held the same federal statute unconstitutional insofar as it prohibited broadcast commercials for casino gambling, concluding that this aspect of the statute did not directly and materially advance its goal of minimizing casino gambling because it was "pierced by exemptions and inconsistencies," which allowed print media advertising of private casinos and advertising in all media of casinos operated by Indian tribes and other forms of gambling, such as government-operated or nonprofit lotteries and race track betting.

Identifying commercial speech. Not all advertising is commercial speech. For example, the speech at issue in the famous defamation case, *New York Times v. Sullivan*, infra p. 272, was published in an issue ad purchased by civil rights activists, but the Supreme Court treated it as fully protected speech. As Justice Thomas suggested, commercial speech is not easy to define, and the Court has not been eager to supply an authoritative definition. The Court has described it as "expression related solely to the economic interest of the speaker and its audience," but that seems too broad; it could include much business and consumer news that is treated as fully protected.

The Court has also described it as speech which does "no more than propose a commercial transaction," but it clearly encompasses more than that; the *Central Hudson* case, for example, involved "informational" fliers attempting to encourage electric consumers to reduce demand at peak times. When Nike purchased ads to deny charges that its Asian shoe suppliers employed child labor, the California Supreme Court held that the ads were commercial speech "because the messages in question were directed by a commercial speaker to a commercial audience, and because they made representations of fact about the speaker's own business operations for the purpose of promoting sales of its products." Kasky v. Nike, Inc., 27 Cal. 4th 939, 45 P.3d 243, 31 Med. L. Rptr. 1225 (2002). The Supreme Court agreed to hear the case but then dismissed certiorari as improvidently granted.

Telemarketing as commercial speech. Congress authorized the Federal Trade Commission and the Federal Communications Commission to establish nationwide "no-call" lists. The FTC and FCC adopted regulations forbidding commercial telemarketers from calling the home telephone numbers of people who signed up for the list. Exceptions permitted calls for charitable and political purposes and calls by businesses with which the recipient had an established business relationship. The telemarketing industry challenged the regulations, asserting their First Amendment rights as commercial speakers, but the Tenth Circuit upheld the no-call lists. See Mainstream Marketing Services, Inc. v. FTC, 358 F.3d 1228, 32 Med. L. Rptr. 1357 (10th Cir. 2004).

Telemarketers argued that the restrictions failed the third branch of *Central Hudson* because the exceptions for political and charitable calls would make them ineffective in carrying out the stated purposes of reducing intrusions into personal privacy and preventing the fraud and abuse that were said to often accompany unwanted telephone solicitation. They argued that the regulations also failed the fourth branch because the asserted governmental interests could be served by more limited means, such as allowing consumers to request no-call status one company at a time.

In response to the ineffectiveness argument, the court said the list had already proved enormously effective:

So far, more than 50 million telephone numbers have been registered on the do-not-call list, and the do-not-call regulations protect these households from receiving most unwanted telemarketing calls. According to the telemarketers' own estimate, 2.64 telemarketing calls per week—or more than 137 calls annually—were directed at an average consumer before the do-not-call list came into effect. *Cf.* 68 Fed.Reg. at 44152 (discussing the five-fold increase in the total number of telemarketing calls between 1991 and 2003). Accordingly, absent the do-not-call registry, telemarketers would call those consumers who have already signed up for the registry an estimated total of 6.85 *billion* times each year.

As to the second argument, the court said:

> We hold that the national do-not-call registry is narrowly tailored because it does not over-regulate protected speech; rather, it restricts only calls that are targeted at unwilling recipients. [ ] The do-not-call registry prohibits only telemarketing calls aimed at consumers who have affirmatively indicated that they do not want to receive such calls and for whom such calls would constitute an invasion of privacy. *See* Hill v. Colorado, 530 U.S. 703, 716–17 (2000) (the right of privacy includes an unwilling listener's interest in avoiding unwanted communication).

2.   MARKETS

State and federal securities laws contain many restrictions on speech, requiring some disclosures and forbidding others in the interest of honesty, equality, and public confidence in financial markets. Various state statutes forbid disclosure of information that would enable recipients to defraud banks, utility companies, and other businesses. These laws are routinely enforced against nonmedia violators, but on the rare occasions when media run afoul of them, First Amendment defenses are likely to be raised. The Supreme Court has been sharply divided on these questions and has not yet settled on a consistent First Amendment approach to them. In the following case a lower court struggles with some of the First Amendment issues that the Supreme Court so far has avoided.

Securities & Exchange Commission v. Wall Street Publishing Institute, Inc.

United States Court of Appeals, District of Columbia Circuit, 1988.
851 F.2d 365, certiorari denied 489 U.S. 1066 (1989).

[WSPI, a two-person operation, published Stock Market Magazine 10 times annually. Each issue of the magazine typically included two types of material: independently written financial news, and seven or eight longer feature articles about individual companies. The latter invariably described the featured companies in glowing terms, and according to the SEC, were either written by the companies themselves, by public relations firms hired by the companies, or by freelance writers whose fees were paid by the companies. The magazine's masthead described these feature articles as "based on thorough research and first-hand interviews with company officials, economists, security analysts, tax accountants, and other experts."

The SEC alleged that as consideration for the articles, the featured companies paid the writers' fees mentioned above, provided free office space for the magazine's writers, and bought reprints and advertising in the magazine. The Commission brought suit under section 17(b) of the Securities Act of 1933, 15 U.S.C. § 77q(b), which makes it unlawful for any person, including a newspaper, to describe a security for a consideration offered by the issuer without disclosing the fact and amount of the consideration. The SEC sought to enjoin future publication of articles in violation of this statute.]

Before Silberman and D.H. Ginsburg, Circuit Judges, and McGowan, Senior Circuit Judge.

Opinion for the Court by Circuit Judge Silberman.

. . .

B.

The district court denied the injunction, on grounds that it would operate as a prior restraint, holding that the SEC had failed to satisfy the extraordinary showing of potential danger that must support any such restraint. . . .

The Commission contends that the prior restraint doctrine is the wrong analytical framework for a *disclosure* requirement if imposed only after full judicial review on the merits. We agree. The Supreme Court has never held that all injunctions affecting a newspaper's publication are impermissible, or that all must satisfy the standard applied to prior restraints. "The special vice of a prior restraint is that communication will be suppressed, either directly or by inducing excessive caution in the speaker, before an adequate determination that it is unprotected by the First Amendment." Pittsburgh Press Co. v. Pittsburgh Comm'n on Human Relations, 413 U.S. 376, 390 (1973). Orders that are carefully focused, address a continuing course of speech, and are imposed after an opportunity for full merits consideration are not properly analyzed as prior restraints. . . .

. . .

. . . The SEC characterizes the company articles in Stock Market Magazine as commercial speech, and as such entitled only to the limited protection that the First Amendment extends to such communications. [ ] WSPI contends, on the other hand, that the articles cannot be separated from speech that lies at the core of First Amendment interests.

. . .

[W]e are not convinced that the feature articles under consideration here are commercial speech. The articles are not "conceded" to be advertisements, and in fact, are not in an advertisement format. Generally two or three pages long, they are indistinguishable from run-of-the-mill newspaper or magazine stories. Furthermore, while most of the articles specifically mention the company's stock along with its price history, not all do this, and in none is the reference to the company's stock particularly prominent. So, it would be difficult to draw a doctrinal line between these articles and any article that focuses on a particular company.

In short, we do not see a clear fit between the commercial speech doctrine and the publications that the SEC here seeks to regulate. And, we are mindful of Justice Stevens' warning in his concurring opinion in *Central Hudson* that "it is important that the commercial speech doctrine not be defined too broadly lest speech deserving of greater constitutional protection be inadvertently suppressed." [ ] It is, in our view, difficult to foresee the implications of applying the doctrine here, and, in any event, we do not believe it is necessary in order to justify regulation. We believe instead that the government may have the power to regulate Stock Market Magazine, not because the articles are "commercial speech," but rather because of the federal government's broad powers to regulate the securities industry. Where the federal government extensively regulates a field of economic activity, communication of the regulated parties often bears directly on the particular economic objectives sought by the government, [ ] and regulation of such communication has been upheld. . . .

. . .

. . . Speech relating to the purchase and sale of securities, in our view, forms a distinct category of communications in which the government's power to regulate is at least as broad as with respect to the general rubric of commercial speech. Under the commercial speech doctrine, a court judging whether a particular regulation affecting speech is constitutional must determine, among other issues, "whether the asserted governmental interest is substantial." [ ] Here, however, we do not think it necessary for us to inquire, as we would if only commercial speech were involved, whether the government's specific regulatory objective—disclosure of consideration—is constitutionally permissible. In areas of extensive federal regulation—like securities dealing—we do not believe the Constitution requires the judiciary to weigh the relative merits of particular regulatory objectives that impinge upon communications occurring within the umbrella of an overall regulatory scheme. We note, however, that even if we were so required, disclosure requirements have been upheld in regulation of commercial speech even when the government has not shown that "absent the required disclosure, [the speech would be false or deceptive] or that the disclosure requirement serves some substantial government interest other than preventing deception." Zauderer v. Office of Disciplinary Counsel, 471 U.S. 626, 650 (1985). . . .

Stock Market Magazine's failure to disclose consideration received in return for publication is then, in principle, constitutionally proscribable. Nonetheless, we think we are obliged to consider—no matter how the speech is categorized—whether the government's interpretation of consideration poses the danger that "speech deserving of greater constitutional protection [will] be inadvertently suppressed." [*Central Hudson*] Here is our difficulty, for the SEC contends that providing publishers free text, whether directly through the provision of finished articles or indirectly by paying writers' fees to public relations firms, constitutes "consideration" within the meaning of section 17(b). The SEC argues that Stock Market Magazine publishes the company articles "substantially" as penned by the featured companies or their publicists and that this practice should be disclosed. Conditioning regulation on the extent to which text is used, however, would result in both SEC and court interference with the "crucial process" of editorial control, interference that the Supreme Court has decried as particularly repugnant to core First Amendment concerns. *Miami Herald Publishing Co. v. Tornillo*, [ ].

. . .

The fundamental difficulty with the SEC's interpretation of "consideration" in 17(b) as applied to this case, involving a magazine in many respects similar to one of general circulation, is that one of the objects of its requested injunction, the receipt of free text, inevitably implicates interference with fully protected journalistic activity. In other words, so long as consideration is defined in accordance with the material used in the publication, the very definition of consideration will necessarily constitute the line between the sphere of permitted regulation—disclosure of the omitted fact—and wholly protected speech. The crucial factor that distinguishes the feature articles from the balance of the magazine—and which constitutionally justifies regulation—is not the glowing terms used to describe the companies featured. If that were so, the SEC and the federal judiciary would be propelled into what is very close to content regulation of speech. [ ] Rather, permissibility of the disclosure requirement must necessarily turn solely on whether consideration was paid to the magazine for publication of the article—and not on the content of the publication. Were the government to show, for example, direct cash payments to Brown, the Managing Editor, such transactions might well be distinguishable from writers' fees because the payments might be tantamount to payments to the publisher to *carry* the article. Requiring disclosure of such payments would not interfere with either editorial judgments concerning the content of the feature articles or news gathering practices. If consideration were shown to be paid directly in exchange for publication of the articles, therefore, even if the articles were somewhat more subtle in their favorable portrayal of the subject companies' securities than is the typical Stock Market Magazine feature article, we think the disclosure requirement would apply. . . .

. . . [F]orcing a magazine to label its contents as published in return for consideration received from the subject of its articles carries an inherently pejorative connotation. Indeed, such a label converts the article in the reader's mind into an advertisement and surely would sharply diminish the magazine's attractiveness and circulation. Although section 17(b)'s language is facially broad, all depends on how one defines consideration. The House Report described this section as "particularly designed to meet the evils of the 'tipster sheet' as well as articles in newspapers or periodicals that purport to give an unbiased opinion but which opinions in reality are bought and paid for." [ ] That term "bought and paid for" suggests, particularly in light of the constitutional difficulties we have described, a crisp transaction sharply distinguished from normal journalistic editing or news gathering practices. We think then that section 17(b) may not be interpreted as the SEC would wish nor may an injunction issue that reaches as widely as the SEC requests.

While section 17(b) thus cannot support a disclosure requirement premised on the receipt or use of free text, the language of the statute is sufficiently broad that we believe that district court erred in dismissing the complaint. There was some evidence in the record that consideration other than free text, including the purchase of advertising space and orders for reprints, was a *quid pro quo* (i.e., a tie-in agreement) for publication of the articles that the SEC regards as deceptive. Deciding the case on motions for summary judgment, the district court never determined whether such arrangements existed. If they did exist, we have no doubt that an injunction could be fashioned to require disclosure when consideration is paid in this distinct form, without trammeling fully protected speech or interfering with editorial practices that cannot be separated therefrom.

As long as free text, however provided, is not included among the elements of consideration that must be disclosed under section 17(b), an injunction should be permissible if the SEC can establish the necessary factual predicate at trial. In light of the concerns we have outlined, such an injunction must set forth with particularity the types of consideration that must be disclosed so as to avoid improper encroachment into protected speech.

. . .

Notes and Questions

1. Why is prior restraint doctrine the wrong analytical framework for this case? In an omitted portion of the opinion, the court distinguished *Near v. Minnesota* on the ground that there the injunction "prohibited future conduct after a finding of undesirable present conduct," while here "the SEC is not requesting an injunction against future articles, as yet unconsidered by any court. Rather, it requests an injunction against a continuing practice of publishing feature articles without disclosure of consideration." Is the distinction persuasive? Are there other bases for distinguishing *Near?*

2. If speech about securities matters may be regulated more tightly than other speech "because of the federal government's broad powers to regulate the securities industry," in what other areas might it have similar power? Banking? Broadcasting? Labor relations? Is the securities field somehow different from other businesses that are federally regulated?

3. Recall the Supreme Court's repudiation, in *44 Liquormart*, supra, of the theory that liquor advertising could be more closely regulated because of the long regulatory history of liquor. Does that cast doubt on the

rationale advanced in the principal case for regulation of speech about securities?

———

The Lowe case. The Investment Advisers Act of 1940 requires persons engaging in the investment advice business to register with the Securities and Exchange Commission. The Act contains an exemption for publishers "of any bona fide newspaper, news magazine or business or financial publication of general and regular circulation." The SEC revoked Lowe's registration after his third conviction for what the Court described as "serious misconduct in connection with his investment advisory business." When he continued to publish investment advice newsletters, the SEC sought to enjoin him.

The Supreme Court upheld Lowe's right to publish the newsletters. Lowe v. Securities and Exchange Comm'n, 472 U.S. 181 (1985). After extended analysis, the five-member majority construed the "bona fide" exception in the statute broadly and concluded that it exempted Lowe. "Bona fide" covered the publication and not the publisher. Lowe's newsletters were not "personal communications masquerading in the clothing of newspapers, news magazines, or financial publications. Moreover, there is no suggestion that they contained any false or misleading information, or that they were designed to tout any security in which petitioners had an interest. Further, petitioners' publications are 'of general and regular circulation' ":

> The dangers of fraud, deception, or overreaching that motivated the enactment of the statute are present in personalized communications but are not replicated in publications that are advertised and sold in an open market. . . . As long as the communications between petitioners and their subscribers remain entirely impersonal and do not develop into the kind of fiduciary, person-to-person relationships that were discussed at length in the legislative history of the Act and that are characteristic of investment adviser-client relationships, we believe the publications are, at least presumptively, within the exclusion and thus not subject to registration under the Act.

Justice White, joined by the Chief Justice and Justice Rehnquist, concurred on the ground that Lowe was covered by the statute but that the First Amendment protected his right to publish. The government's justification was that it was regulating a "speaking profession" and that "it may require that investment advisers, like lawyers, evince the qualities of truth-seeking, honor, discretion, and fiduciary responsibility." Justice White responded that this principle of restricting entry to a profession had "never been extended to encompass the licensing of speech per se or of the press. [ ] At some point, a measure is no longer a regulation of a profession but a regulation of speech or of the press; beyond that point, the statute must survive the level of scrutiny demanded by the First Amendment."

Justice White concluded that "Where the personal nexus between professional and client does not exist, and a speaker does not purport to be exercising judgment on behalf of any particular individual with whose circumstances he is directly acquainted, government regulation ceases to function as legitimate regulation of professional practice with only incidental impact on speech; it becomes regulation of speaking or publishing as such," subject to the First Amendment.

Turning finally to what regulation might be permissible here under the First Amendment, Justice White found it unnecessary to decide whether Lowe's speech was "fully protected" or "commercial." Even if the speech was considered commercial, the means chosen to prevent investors from falling into the hands of "scoundrels and swindlers" was "extreme." It cannot "be plausibly maintained that investment advice from a person whose background indicates that he is unreliable is *inherently* misleading or deceptive," nor was it clear that remedies less drastic than outright suppression were inadequate.

The SEC attempts to enforce similar restrictions on the Internet. See http://www.sec.gov/news/speech/speecharchive/1999/spch258.htm (reporting speech by SEC Commissioner Laura S. Unger in which she said the SEC had brought actions against 44 publishers of online investment newsletters for failing to disclose that they were being compensated for touting stock).

For further reading see Burt Neuborne, The First Amendment and Government Regulation of Capital Markets, 55 Brooklyn L. Rev. 5 (1989).

F.   GOVERNMENT-SPONSORED SPEECH

1.   GOVERNMENT-OWNED MEDIA

Government is itself in the communications business. Governmental entities publish high school and college newspapers, publish magazines and newsletters, operate radio and television stations, and support the Public Broadcasting System. Content-neutrality can hardly be expected in these settings; government would not create and support these media if it could not exercise some control over their content. But the courts have refused to give government complete freedom to censor its own media.

Most of the litigation in this area has been generated by attempts to censor student newspapers. At the high school level, the state has considerable power to control content of the publications it sponsors. In Hazelwood School District v. Kuhlmeier, 484 U.S. 260, 14 Med. L. Rptr. 2081 (1988), a principal killed stories written for the high school newspaper on student pregnancies and effects on students of parents' divorces. The newspaper was funded entirely by the school and produced by students in a journalism course. The Supreme Court held, 6–3, that censorship of such a curricular publication would violate the First Amendment only if publication served "no valid educational purpose." The principal's judgment that the stories in question were unsuitable was reasonable, the majority said, and his decision therefore violated no constitutional right of the student writers and editors.

The majority opinion indicates that the decision might well have been different if the newspaper had not been part of a course, but one established by the school as a forum for discussion by all students. College newspapers often fit the latter description, and courts have tended to give them somewhat more protection from censorship by their institutional sponsors. For example, Joyner v. Whiting, 477 F.2d 456 (4th Cir. 1973), held that the president of North Carolina Central University could not withdraw support from the campus newspaper, the Echo, even though the newspaper advocated a segregationist blacks-only policy, which the president believed would violate federal law. The court said in the absence of evidence that the Echo posed a danger of physical violence or disruption, authorities could not restrict the editors' expression even if it advocated unlawful racial segregation. "We need not decide whether the Echo is a state agency; it is enough to say that even if it were, it would not be prohibited from expressing its hostility to racial integration."

The First Amendment is applicable, of course, only if the censorship is imposed by an agent of the state, and editorial decisions by the students themselves may not be considered state action. In Yeo v. Town of Lexington, 131 F.3d 241, 26 Med. L. Rptr. 1193 (1st Cir. 1997) (en banc), editors of the newspaper and the yearbook at a public high school both rejected an advertisement advocating sexual abstinence that had been submitted by the parent of a student. The court observed that "[e]very court of appeals which has considered the state action requirement in the context of attempts to attribute student-controlled editorial decisions in public institutions of higher education to public officials has found no state action." Since the decisions to reject the ad had indeed been made by students without influence or control by school officials, the court applied that principle to the high school newspaper.

Student newspapers may get special solicitude because of their functional similarity to independent newspapers and their traditional role as training grounds for journalists. The free speech rights of other state-owned media usually are determined by public forum analysis—a distinct branch of First Amendment jurisprudence evolved largely from cases involving use of public property for parades, demonstrations, meetings, and the arts. Public forum analysis is intricate, as the following case indicates. The case arises in the context of public broadcasting, which may be something of a special case itself. Public stations may be owned by a private non-profit entity or by some agency of government. They almost always are recipients of public money, but the extent of their dependence on such funds varies. And as broadcasters, they are subject to more regulation than print media. We therefore treat them as a distinct subset of state-sponsored speech.

2.   NONCOMMERCIAL BROADCASTING AND EDITORIAL FREEDOM

Arkansas Educational Television Commission v. Forbes
Supreme Court of the United States, 1998.
523 U.S. 666, 118 S.Ct. 1633, 140 L.Ed.2d 875, 26 Med.L.Rptr. 1673.

JUSTICE KENNEDY delivered the opinion of the Court.

A government-owned public television broadcaster sponsored a candidate debate from which it excluded an independent candidate with little popular support. The issue before us is whether, by reason of its state ownership, the station had a constitutional obligation to allow every candidate access to the debate. We conclude that, unlike most other public television programs, the candidate debate was subject to constitutional constraints applicable to nonpublic fora under our forum precedents. Even so, the broadcaster's decision to exclude the candidate was a reasonable, viewpoint-neutral exercise of journalistic discretion.

I

[AETC was a state agency, run by a board appointed by the governor, that owned and operated a network of five noncommercial television stations. Its staff organized a series of televised debates between candidates for the U.S. Senate and House. Working in close consultation with Bill Simmons, Arkansas Bureau Chief for the Associated Press, the AETC staff developed a debate format and decided to limit participation in the debates to the major party candidates or any other candidate who had strong popular support. Forbes was an independent candidate for one of the congressional seats and was excluded from the debate for that seat on the ground that he had no chance of winning. He sued, claiming his exclusion violated both the First Amendment and 47 U.S.C. § 315, supra p. 138.]

II

Forbes has long since abandoned his statutory claims under 47 U.S.C. § 315, and so the issue is whether his exclusion from the debate was consistent with the First Amendment. The Court of Appeals held it was not, applying our public forum precedents. Appearing as amicus curiae in support of petitioners, the Solicitor General argues that our forum precedents should be of little relevance in the context of television broadcasting. At the outset, then, it is instructive to ask whether public forum principles apply to the case at all.

Having first arisen in the context of streets and parks, the public forum doctrine should not be extended in a mechanical way to the very different context of public television broadcasting. In the case of streets and parks, the open access and viewpoint neutrality commanded by the doctrine is "compatible with the intended purpose of the property." . . . In the case of television broadcasting, however, broad rights of access for outside speakers would be antithetical, as a general rule, to the discretion that stations and their editorial staff must exercise to fulfill their journalistic purpose and statutory obligations.

Congress has rejected the argument that "broadcast facilities should be open on a non-selective basis to all persons wishing to talk about public issues." [*CBS v. DNC*, supra p. 141]. Instead, television broadcasters enjoy the "widest journalistic freedom" consistent with their public responsibilities. [ ] Among the broadcaster's responsibilities is the duty to schedule programming that serves the "public interest, convenience, and necessity."

47 U.S.C. § 309(a). Public and private broadcasters alike are not only permitted, but indeed required, to exercise substantial editorial discretion in the selection and presentation of their programming.

As a general rule, the nature of editorial discretion counsels against subjecting broadcasters to claims of viewpoint discrimination. Programming decisions would be particularly vulnerable to claims of this type because even principled exclusions rooted in sound journalistic judgment can often be characterized as viewpoint-based. To comply with their obligation to air programming that serves the public interest, broadcasters must often choose among speakers expressing different viewpoints. "That editors—newspaper or broadcast—can and do abuse this power is beyond doubt," [*CBS v. DNC*]; but "[c]alculated risks of abuse are taken in order to preserve higher values." [Id.] Much like a university selecting a commencement speaker, a public institution selecting speakers for a lecture series, or a public school prescribing its curriculum, a broadcaster by its nature will facilitate the expression of some viewpoints instead of others. Were the judiciary to require, and so to define and approve, pre-established criteria for access, it would risk implicating the courts in judgments that should be left to the exercise of journalistic discretion.

When a public broadcaster exercises editorial discretion in the selection and presentation of its programming, it engages in speech activity. [ ] Although programming decisions often involve the compilation of the speech of third parties, the decisions nonetheless constitute communicative acts. [ ]

Claims of access under our public forum precedents could obstruct the legitimate purposes of television broadcasters. Were the doctrine given sweeping application in this context, courts "would be required to oversee far more of the day-to-day operations of broadcasters' conduct, deciding such questions as whether a particular individual or group has had sufficient opportunity to present its viewpoint and whether a particular viewpoint has already been sufficiently aired." [*CBS v. DNC*] "The result would be a further erosion of the journalistic discretion of broadcasters," transferring "control over the treatment of public issues from the licensees who are accountable for broadcast performance to private individuals" who bring suit under our forum precedents. [Id.] In effect, we would "exchange 'public trustee' broadcasting, with all its limitations, for a system of self-appointed editorial commentators." [Id.]

In the absence of any congressional command to "[r]egimen[t] broadcasters' in this manner," [id.], we are disinclined to do so through doctrines of our own design. This is not to say the First Amendment would bar the legislative imposition of neutral rules for access to public broadcasting. Instead, we say that, in most cases, the First Amendment of its own force does not compel public broadcasters to allow third parties access to their programming.

Although public broadcasting as a general matter does not lend itself to scrutiny under the forum doctrine, candidate debates present the narrow exception to the rule. For two reasons, a candidate debate like the one at issue here is different from other programming. First, unlike AETC's other broadcasts, the debate was by design a forum for political speech by the candidates. Consistent with the long tradition of candidate debates, the implicit representation of the broadcaster was that the views expressed were those of the candidates, not its own. The very purpose of the debate was to allow the candidates to express their views with minimal intrusion by the broadcaster. In this respect the debate differed even from a political talk show, whose host can express partisan views and then limit the discussion to those ideas.

Second, in our tradition, candidate debates are of exceptional significance in the electoral process. "[I]t is of particular importance that candidates have the opportunity to make their views known so that the electorate may intelligently evaluate the candidates' personal qualities and their positions on vital public issues before choosing among them on election day." *CBS, Inc. v. FCC*, [supra p. 141]. Deliberation on the positions and qualifications of candidates is integral to our system of government, and electoral speech may have its most profound and widespread impact when it is disseminated through televised debates. A majority of the population cites television as its primary source of election information, and debates are regarded as the "only occasion during a campaign when the attention of a large portion of the American public is focused on the election, as well as the only campaign information format which potentially offers sufficient time to explore issues and policies in depth in a neutral forum." [ ]

As we later discuss, in many cases it is not feasible for the broadcaster to allow unlimited access to a candidate debate. Yet the requirement of neutrality remains; a broadcaster cannot grant or deny access to a candidate debate on the basis of whether it agrees with a candidate's views. Viewpoint discrimination in this context would present not a "[c]alculated ris[k]," [*CBS v. DNC*], but an inevitability of skewing the electoral dialogue.

The special characteristics of candidate debates support the conclusion that the AETC debate was a forum of some type. The question of what type must be answered by reference to our public forum precedents, to which we now turn.

III

Forbes argues, and the Court of Appeals held, that the debate was a public forum to which he had a First Amendment right of access. Under our precedents, however, the debate was a nonpublic forum, from which AETC could exclude Forbes in the reasonable, viewpoint-neutral exercise of its journalistic discretion.

A

For our purposes, it will suffice to employ the categories of speech fora already established and discussed in our cases. "[T]he Court [has] identified three types of fora: the traditional public forum, the public forum created by government designation, and the nonpublic forum." Cornelius v.

NAACP Legal Defense & Ed. Fund, Inc., 473 U.S. 788, 802 (1985). Traditional public fora are defined by the objective characteristics of the property, such as whether, "by long tradition or by government fiat," the property has been "devoted to assembly and debate." [ ] The government can exclude a speaker from a traditional public forum "only when the exclusion is necessary to serve a compelling state interest and the exclusion is narrowly drawn to achieve that interest." [ ]

Designated public fora, in contrast, are created by purposeful governmental action. "The government does not create a [designated] public forum by inaction or by permitting limited discourse, but only by intentionally opening a nontraditional public forum for public discourse." [ ] Hence "the Court has looked to the policy and practice of the government to ascertain whether it intended to designate a place not traditionally open to assembly and debate as a public forum." [ ] If the government excludes a speaker who falls within the class to which a designated public forum is made generally available, its action is subject to strict scrutiny. [ ]

Other government properties are either nonpublic fora or not fora at all. [ ] The government can restrict access to a nonpublic forum "as long as the restrictions are reasonable and [are] not an effort to suppress expression merely because public officials oppose the speaker's view." [ ]

In summary, traditional public fora are open for expressive activity regardless of the government's intent. The objective characteristics of these properties require the government to accommodate private speakers. The government is free to open additional properties for expressive use by the general public or by a particular class of speakers, thereby creating designated public fora. Where the property is not a traditional public forum and the government has not chosen to create a designated public forum, the property is either a nonpublic forum or not a forum at all.

B

The parties agree the AETC debate was not a traditional public forum. The Court has rejected the view that traditional public forum status extends beyond its historic confines, [ ]; and even had a more expansive conception of traditional public fora been adopted, [ ], the almost unfettered access of a traditional public forum would be incompatible with the programming dictates a television broadcaster must follow. [ ] The issue, then, is whether the debate was a designated public forum or a nonpublic forum.

Under our precedents, the AETC debate was not a designated public forum. To create a forum of this type, the government must intend to make the property "generally available," Widmar v. Vincent, 454 U. S. 263, 264 (1981), to a class of speakers. [ ]. . . .

A designated public forum is not created when the government allows selective access for individual speakers rather than general access for a class of speakers. . . .

These cases illustrate the distinction between "general access," [ ], which indicates the property is a designated public forum, and "selective access," [ ], which indicates the property is a nonpublic forum. On one hand, the government creates a designated public forum when it makes its property generally available to a certain class of speakers, as the university made its facilities generally available to student groups in [*Widmar*]. On the other hand, the government does not create a designated public forum when it does no more than reserve eligibility for access to the forum to a particular class of speakers, whose members must then, as individuals, "obtain permission," [ ], to use it. . . .

The *Cornelius* distinction between general and selective access furthers First Amendment interests. By recognizing the distinction, we encourage the government to open its property to some expressive activity in cases where, if faced with an all-or-nothing choice, it might not open the property at all. That this distinction turns on governmental intent does not render it unprotective of speech. Rather, it reflects the reality that, with the exception of traditional public fora, the government retains the choice of whether to designate its property as a forum for specified classes of speakers.

Here, the debate did not have an open-microphone format. Contrary to the assertion of the Court of Appeals, AETC did not make its debate generally available to candidates for Arkansas' Third Congressional District seat. . . . AETC made candidate-by-candidate determinations as to which of the eligible candidates would participate in the debate. "Such selective access, unsupported by evidence of a purposeful designation for public use, does not create a public forum." [ ] Thus the debate was a nonpublic forum.

In addition to being a misapplication of our precedents, the Court of Appeals' holding would result in less speech, not more. In ruling that the debate was a public forum open to all ballot-qualified candidates, [ ], the Court of Appeals would place a severe burden upon public broadcasters who air candidates' views. In each of the 1988, 1992, and 1996 Presidential elections, for example, no fewer than 22 candidates appeared on the ballot in at least one State. [ ] In the 1996 congressional elections, it was common for 6 to 11 candidates to qualify for the ballot for a particular seat. [ ] In the 1993 New Jersey gubernatorial election, to illustrate further, sample ballot mailings included the written statements of 19 candidates. [ ] On logistical grounds alone, a public television editor might, with reason, decide that the inclusion of all ballot-qualified candidates would "actually undermine the educational value and quality of debates." [ ]

Were it faced with the prospect of cacophony, on the one hand, and First Amendment liability, on the other, a public television broadcaster might choose not to air candidates' views at all. A broadcaster might decide " 'the safe course is to avoid controversy,' . . . and by so doing diminish the free flow of information and ideas." [ ] In this circumstance, a "[g]overn-ment-enforced right of access inescapably 'dampens the vigor and limits the variety of public debate.' " [ ]

These concerns are more than speculative. As a direct result of the Court of Appeals' decision in this case, the Nebraska Educational Televi-sion Network canceled a scheduled debate between candidates in Nebraska's 1996 United States Senate race. [ ] A First Amendment jurisprudence yielding these results does not promote speech but represses it.

C

The debate's status as a nonpublic forum, however, did not give AETC unfettered power to exclude any candidate it wished. As Justice O'Connor has observed, nonpublic forum status "does not mean that the government can restrict speech in whatever way it likes." [ ] To be consistent with the First Amendment, the exclusion of a speaker from a nonpublic forum must not be based on the speaker's viewpoint and must otherwise be reasonable in light of the purpose of the property. [ ]

In this case, the jury found Forbes' exclusion was not based on "objections or opposition to his views." [ ] The record provides ample support for this finding, demonstrating as well that AETC's decision to exclude him was reasonable.

AETC Executive Director Susan Howarth testified Forbes' views had "absolutely" no role in the decision to exclude him from the debate. [ ] She further testified Forbes was excluded because (1) "the Arkansas voters did not consider him a serious candidate"; (2) "the news organizations also did not consider him a serious candidate"; (3) "the Associated Press and a national election result reporting service did not plan to run his name in results on election night"; (4) Forbes "apparently had little, if any, financial support, failing to report campaign finances to the Secretary of State's office or to the Federal Election Commission"; and (5) "there [was] no 'Forbes for Congress' campaign headquarters other than his house." [ ] Forbes himself described his campaign organization as "bedlam" and the media coverage of his campaign as "zilch." [ ] It is, in short, beyond dispute that Forbes was excluded not because of his viewpoint but because he had generated no appreciable public interest. [ ]

There is no substance to Forbes' suggestion that he was excluded because his views were unpopular or out of the mainstream. His own objective lack of support, not his platform, was the criterion. Indeed, the very premise of Forbes' contention is mistaken. A candidate with unconventional views might well enjoy broad support by virtue of a compelling personality or an exemplary campaign organization. By the same token, a candidate with a traditional platform might enjoy little support due to an inept campaign or any number of other reasons.

Nor did AETC exclude Forbes in an attempted manipulation of the political process. The evidence provided powerful support for the jury's express finding that AETC's exclusion of Forbes was not the result of "political pressure from anyone inside or outside [AETC]." [ ] There is no serious argument that AETC did not act in good faith in this case. AETC excluded Forbes because the voters lacked interest in his candidacy, not because AETC itself did.

The broadcaster's decision to exclude Forbes was a reasonable, viewpoint-neutral exercise of journalistic discretion consistent with the First Amendment. The judgment of the Court of Appeals is

Reversed.

JUSTICE STEVENS, with whom JUSTICE SOUTER and JUSTICE GINSBURG join, dissenting.

The Court has decided that a government-owned television network has no "constitutional obligation to allow every candidate access to" political debates that it sponsors. [ ] I do not challenge that decision. The judgment of the Court of Appeals should nevertheless be affirmed. . . . The ad hoc decision of the staff of the Arkansas Educational Television Commission (AETC) raises precisely the concerns addressed by "the many decisions of this Court over the last 30 years, holding that a law subjecting the exercise of First Amendment freedoms to the prior restraint of a license, without narrow, objective, and definite standards to guide the licensing authority, is unconstitutional." Shuttlesworth v. Birmingham, 394 U.S. 147, 150–151 (1969).

In its discussion of the facts, the Court barely mentions the standardless character of the decision to exclude Forbes from the debate. In its discussion of the law, the Court understates the constitutional importance of the distinction between state ownership and private ownership of broadcast facilities. . . .

I

[Forbes had been] a serious contender for the Republican nomination for Lieutenant Governor in 1986 and again in 1990. Although he was defeated in a run-off election, in the three-way primary race conducted in 1990—just two years before the AETC staff decision—he had received 46.88% of the statewide vote and had carried 15 of the 16 counties within the Third Congressional District by absolute majorities. Nevertheless, the staff concluded that Forbes did not have "strong popular support." [ ]

Given the fact that the Republican winner in the Third Congressional District race in 1992 received only 50.22% of the vote and the Democrat received 47.20%, it would have been necessary for Forbes, who had made a strong showing in recent Republican primaries, to divert only a handful of votes from the Republican candidate to cause his defeat. Thus, even though the AETC staff may have correctly concluded that Forbes was "not a serious candidate," their decision to exclude him from the debate may have determined the outcome of the election in the Third District.

If a comparable decision were made today by a privately owned network, it would be subject to scrutiny under the Federal Election Campaign Act unless the network used "pre-established objective criteria to determine which candidates may participate in [the] debate." [ ] No such criteria governed AETC's refusal to permit Forbes to participate in the debate. Indeed, whether that refusal was based on a judgment about "newsworthiness"—as AETC has argued in this Court—or a judgment about "political viability"—as it argued in the Court of Appeals—the facts in the record presumably would have provided an adequate basis either for a decision to include Forbes in the Third District debate or a decision to exclude him, and might even have required a cancellation of two of the other debates.

The apparent flexibility of AETC's purported standard suggests the extent to which the staff had nearly limitless discretion to exclude Forbes from the debate based on ad hoc justifications. Thus, the Court of Appeals correctly concluded that the staff's appraisal of "political viability" was "so subjective, so arguable, so susceptible of variation in individual opinion, as to provide no secure basis for the exercise of governmental power consistent with the First Amendment." [ ]

. . .

III

. . . The dispositive issue in this case, then, is not whether AETC created a designated public forum or a nonpublic forum, as the Court concludes, but whether AETC defined the contours of the debate forum with sufficient specificity to justify the exclusion of a ballot-qualified candidate.

. . .

AETC's control was comparable to that of a local government official authorized to issue permits to use public facilities for expressive activities. In cases concerning access to a traditional public forum, we have found an analogy between the power to issue permits and the censorial power to impose a prior restraint on speech. Thus, in our review of an ordinance requiring a permit to participate in a parade on city streets, we explained that the ordinance, as written, "fell squarely within the ambit of the many decisions of this Court over the last 30 years, holding that a law subjecting the exercise of First Amendment freedoms to the prior restraint of a license, without narrow, objective, and definite standards to guide the licensing authority, is unconstitutional." [*Shuttlesworth*]. . . . Surely the Constitution demands at least as much from the Government when it takes action that necessarily impacts democratic elections as when local officials issue parade permits.

. . .

Like the Court, I do not endorse the view of the Court of Appeals that all candidates who qualify for a position on the ballot are necessarily entitled to access to any state-sponsored debate. I am convinced, however, that the constitutional imperatives that motivated our decisions in cases like *Shuttlesworth* command that access to political debates planned and managed by state-owned entities be governed by pre-established, objective criteria. Requiring government employees to set out objective criteria by which they choose which candidates will benefit from the significant media exposure that results from state-sponsored political debates would alleviate some of the risk inherent in allowing government agencies—rather than private entities—to stage candidate debates.

Accordingly, I would affirm the judgment of the Court of Appeals.

Notes and Questions

1.   Do the dissent's facts about the political role of Forbes in Arkansas undercut the majority's reasoning? AETC's reasoning? Consider Ralph Nader's role in the presidential election of 2000; if even a candidate who has no chance of winning can affect the outcome of an election, does that argue for or against the exclusion of that candidate from debates?

2.   Was AETC's decision "a reasonable viewpoint-neutral exercise of journalistic discretion" as stated by the majority? Did AETC have "nearly limitless discretion to exclude Forbes from the debate based on ad hoc justifications" as charged by the dissent? Might both be accurate?

3.   The majority expresses concern that were "the judiciary to require, and so to define and approve, pre-established criteria for access, it would risk implicating the courts in judgments that should be left to the exercise of journalistic discretion." What is the dissent's response? Who has the better of it?

4.   The majority offers the possibility that Congress might impose "neutral rules for access to public broadcasting." Would that be a good idea after this case? What might they look like? Is there a difference between access for candidates and access for those who espouse ideas?

5.   Why might the FCC have thought it appropriate to set aside licenses for noncommercial stations? Why might Congress have thought it appropriate to help finance this type of station? Consider how the following station formats might influence your answers:

   a.   A station devoted exclusively to political discussion with regular call-in shows and debates and heavy electoral coverage during election seasons. What content restrictions would apply to such a station?

   b.   A station devoted to the concerns of groups that do not appeal to advertisers—such as the poor and recent immigrants. The format would include extensive programming on basic arithmetic, reading and civics, programs devoted to teaching English as a second language, and programs on how to get jobs and get promotions.

   c.   A station devoted to cultural programming.

The League of Women Voters case. A federal statute prohibiting editorializing by any noncommercial station that receives money from the Corporation for Public Broadcasting was held unconstitutional, 5–4, in Federal Communications Comm'n v. League of Women Voters of California, 468 U.S. 364, 10 Med. L. Rptr. 1937 (1984).

Justice Brennan's majority opinion began by observing that "the expression of editorial opinion . . . lies at the heart of First Amendment protection." Moreover, the ban "is defined solely on the basis of the content of the suppressed speech." Nonetheless, he rejected the "compelling interest" approach because of the "special characteristic" of spectrum scarcity and the unique role of noncommercial broadcasting. The majority concluded that restrictions of the sort imposed in this case could be upheld if the Court were "satisfied that the restriction is narrowly tailored to further a substantial governmental interest, such as ensuring adequate and balanced coverage of public issues."

The Court rejected the two justifications offered by the government: (1) to protect noncommercial stations from being coerced by federal funding into becoming vehicles for government propaganda; and (2) to keep stations from becoming convenient targets for capture by private interest groups seeking to express their own partisan viewpoints.

As to the first, the likelihood of congressional retaliation against licensees was "speculative at best." The stations were much more likely to focus on local matters and it did not seem plausible that such editorializing would put public broadcasting in jeopardy. "Indeed, what is far more likely than local station editorials to pose [these dangers] are the wide variety of programs addressing controversial issues produced, often with substantial CPB funding, for national distribution to local stations."

Nor was the ban "sufficiently tailored to the harms it seeks to prevent." The government had failed to explain how editorials on local parks would infuriate Congress to such an extent as to imperil public broadcasting. Nor had it explained how the "suppression of editorials alone serves to reduce the risk [when] station management is fully able to broadcast controversial views so long as such views are not labeled as its own."

If there is concern about the audience's perception that editorials reflect the official view of the government, "this interest can be fully satisfied by less restrictive means that are readily available. . . . Congress could simply require public broadcasting stations to broadcast a disclaimer every time they editorialize, which would state that the editorial represents only the view of the station's management and does not in any way represent the views of the Federal Government or any of the station's other sources of funding."

As to the government's second concern—keeping the station from becoming an outlet for persons or groups who have gained control of the licensee—the section was patently over- and under-inclusive. If stations remain free to control content through their power to select programs, to select persons to be interviewed, and to determine how news reports will be presented, it was "doubtful that § 399 can fairly be said to advance any genuinely substantial governmental interest in keeping controversial or partisan opinions from being aired by noncommercial stations."

Finally, the Court rejected an argument based on the claim that the government's spending power permitted it to prevent those who accepted money from CPB from editorializing.

Justice Rehnquist's dissent, joined by Chief Justice Burger and Justice White, focused on the spending power point. Congress had "rationally determined that the bulk of the taxpayers whose monies provide the funds for grants by the CPB would prefer not to see the management of local educational stations promulgate its own private views on the air at taxpayer expense. . . . This is not to say that the government may attach *any* condition to its largess; it is only to say that when the government is simply exercising its power to allocate its own public funds, we need only find that the condition imposed has a rational relationship to Congress' purpose in providing the subsidy and that it is not primarily 'aimed at the suppression of dangerous ideas.' "

Justice Stevens also dissented. The "court jester who mocks the King must choose his words with great care. An artist is likely to paint a flattering portrait of his patron. . . . Newspaper publishers have been known to listen to their advertising managers. Elected officials may remember how their elections were financed."

The concerns here rested on a foundation "far stronger than merely 'a rational basis' and it is not weakened by the fact that it is buttressed by other provisions that are also designed to avoid the insidious evils of government propaganda favoring particular points of view." It was particularly important that the ban was "completely neutral in its operation—it prohibits all editorials without any distinction being drawn concerning the subject matter or the point of view that might be expressed."

For Justice Stevens, the majority's "disclaimer" solution "would be laughable were it not so Orwellian: the answer to the fact that there is a real danger that the editorials are really government propaganda is for the government to require the station to tell the audience that it is not propaganda at all!"

Recall that in the *American Library Association* case, supra p. 168, four members of the Court believed that the spending power of Congress allowed it to restrict access to content on library computers as a condition of receiving federal subsidies without triggering any First Amendment scrutiny. If that position were adopted by a majority, would it permit Congress to regulate content on public broadcasting as a condition of receiving funds from CPB?

3.   GOVERNMENT AS ADVERTISER

Governmental entities are not only publishers and broadcasters, they are also important advertisers. The armed services buy time for recruiting commercials. Legal advertising has long been an important source of revenue for small-town weeklies. Recently some national media have secured contracts to carry official notices of federal property forfeitures under drug laws. Media have no constitutional right to receive such advertising revenues, but can the government withdraw them for reasons related to the content of the media? If the publisher can show that the termination is a content-based penalty, it violates the First Amendment. But retaliatory motive is often hard to prove.

In North Mississippi Communications v. Jones, 951 F.2d 652, 19 Med. L. Rptr. 1897 (5th Cir. 1992), the Fifth Circuit eased this burden somewhat. The North Mississippi Times alleged that the county board of supervisors switched most of the county's legal advertising to a competing newspaper in retaliation for stories in the Times criticizing the board. The court held that even if most of the advertising would have been transferred for non-retaliatory reasons, the newspaper was entitled to damages if even one ad was improperly withheld, and the burden was on the board to prove a legitimate reason for withholding each ad. The court also indicated the newspaper would be entitled to attorneys fees if any retaliatory action was found.

A Florida newspaper won a judgment of $22,710 plus attorneys fees against a sheriff who terminated legal advertising in retaliation for the newspaper's reporting about him. See Review Publications Inc. v. Navarro, 943 F.2d 1318 (11th Cir. 1991). A fee award of nearly $250,000 was affirmed, 983 F.2d 236 (11th Cir. 1993).

The unconstitutionality of withdrawing advertising in retaliation for unfavorable coverage is sufficiently "clearly established" that officials who do so lose their qualified immunity from suit under 42 U.S.C. § 1983, the First Circuit held. The newspaper El Dia alleged that 18 government agencies that had routinely advertised in El Dia terminated their contracts the day after the newspaper published an article highly critical of Governor Pedro Rossello's administration. The newspaper sued the governor and other officials. The defendants moved to dismiss on the ground that they were immune. Citing *North Mississippi Communications*, supra, and other precedents involving unconstitutional denial of other types of government benefits, the court rejected the claim. "It would seem obvious that using government funds to punish political speech by members of the press and to attempt to coerce commentary favorable to the government would run afoul of the First Amendment." See El Dia, Inc. v. Rossello, 165 F.3d 106, 27 Med. L. Rptr. 1185 (1st Cir. 1999).

Punishing media for their speech is different from punishing them for their business policies, however. In Alameda Newspapers, Inc. v. City of Oakland, 95 F.3d 1406 (9th Cir. 1996), the court saw no First Amendment issue when the defendant city council passed a resolution urging a boycott of plaintiff newspaper because of its labor policies and practices. The city also cancelled its 13 subscriptions and ordered the staff to place its official advertising in other papers—a loss to plaintiff of some $40,000 per year. "To the extent that ANI is asserting that its First Amendment rights were violated because the City's actions were motivated by the council's opposition to ANI's labor or corporate policies, ANI has not stated a valid cause of action. The First Amendment protects newspapers from retaliation by government agencies on account of articles or views that the newspapers have published (or intend to publish), not against retaliation because of the internal policies or business conduct of their owners."

4.   GOVERNMENT PROPAGANDA

Officials at all levels of government attempt to influence the public through reports, press releases, speeches, and radio and television addresses. Building support for programs they favor or opposition to programs they oppose is an essential function of governing. But their monopoly on the use of public resources to advance their side of the argument sometimes raises issues. These have intensified in recent years as agencies have become more aggressive, innovative—and some say devious—in packaging their messages. Perhaps seizing an opportunity created by staff cutbacks that left many television stations without their own representatives in Washington, some agencies began supplying television stations with videos that looked like news stories, were narrated by individuals who appeared to be reporters, and did not reveal that they were produced by the government.

A federal statute forbids use of taxpayers' money for propaganda purposes without express authorization of Congress. The General Accounting Office said the Department of Health and Human Services violated this statute by distributing to television stations "story packages" touting the Medicare discount cards advocated by the George W. Bush Administration. The GAO said the videos were sent to stations by mail, satellite, or syndicated services and were used by at least 40 stations. HHS contended the material was not covert propaganda because the stations could have identified them as government-sponsored, but the GAO said in some instances even the news directors of stations that ran the videos claimed they did not know the material was government-produced. The GAO said viewers were likely to be misled even if news directors were not. See Ruling Says White House's Medicare Videos Were Illegal, N.Y. Times, May 20, 2004, at A23.

The few limitations imposed so far on the government's freedom to proselytize are almost all legislative limits on spending, like the statute mentioned above. Can an argument be made that government speech masquerading as journalism violates the First Amendment?

CHAPTER III

CONTENT–NEUTRAL REGULATION OF MEDIA

Media are subject to a great deal of content-neutral regulation. Most mass media are businesses, and as corporations, landowners, employers, manufacturers, polluters, and taxpayers they are subject to extensive regulation, as are other businesses. Insofar as those regulations apply no differently to media than to other businesses, they are beyond the scope of this book. But these regulations may not always be content-neutral, and even if they are, they have the potential to interfere with media speech. Here, we consider a few areas in which business regulations and other ostensibly content-neutral regulations have been thought—at least by media litigants—to raise First Amendment questions.

The distinction between content-neutral and content-based regulations is imperfect; a tax that appears to draw a content-neutral line between large and small newspapers may in fact be content-based if it turns out that the large papers all favor one political party and most of the small ones support another. Whether a particular restriction is content-neutral is often hotly contested, as the following case indicates, and may go a long way toward determining the outcome. As you consider the problems covered in this chapter and the next, you should ask why a particular regulation is classified as it is, what is the significance of the classification, and what additional facts might persuade the courts to analyze the regulation differently.

A. PRESERVING MULTIPLE VOICES

Whether government should try to promote diversity and competition in the media has long been a contentious issue. The debate has intensified in recent years as a few large conglomerates acquired many media outlets that previously were separately owned. Historically there have been few restrictions on ownership of print media; even the usual restraints of antitrust law are largely absent from the newspaper business, for reasons we shall see later in this section. Newspaper ownership has been concentrated in a few chains for many years. Regulation of ownership of broadcasting stations limited the concentration in that industry, however.

For many years an FCC rule preventing an entity from owning a newspaper and television station in the same market tended to keep those two types of media outlets in different hands locally. However, media conglomerates often acquired newspapers in markets in which they did not own broadcasting outlets, or vice versa. More importantly, the FCC in recent years has sometimes waived the cross-ownership rule to facilitate mergers, for example, to permit the Tribune Company to acquire other companies that gave it ownership of newspapers as well as television stations in the three largest markets—New York, Chicago, and Los Angeles.

In 1996 Congress abolished the rule that limited a single owner to 12 local televisions stations. In the next six years, the number of stations owned by the ten largest owners (the four major networks plus the Tribune, Gannett, Hearst, Sinclair, Belo, and Cox groups) tripled, to an average of more than 30 each. See State of the News Media 2004, available on-line at Journalism.org.

1. Cable

We have already seen that regulation of broadcasters (including the requirement that they obtain a license before broadcasting) has been justified largely as an attempt to ensure that a variety of voices have access to the spectrum. The two *Turner* cases which follow involve only a narrow aspect of the media concentration issue, but they provide the Supreme Court's most extensive consideration so far of government's role in promoting media diversity. The issue is the constitutionality of must-carry rules, which require cable operators to carry the signals of local over-the-air broadcasters. The rules had been relaxed for a time in the 1980s but were reinstated by Congress in 1992.

Turner Broadcasting System, Inc. v. Federal Communications Commission [*Turner I*]

Supreme Court of the United States, 1994.
512 U.S. 622, 114 S.Ct. 2445, 129 L.Ed.2d 497, 22 Med.L.Rptr. 1865.

Justice Kennedy announced the judgment of the Court and delivered the opinion of the Court, except as to Part III–B.

Sections 4 and 5 of the Cable Television Consumer Protection and Competition Act of 1992 require cable television systems to devote a portion of their channels to the transmission of local broadcast television stations. The case [brought by cable system operators and cable program providers] presents the question whether these provisions abridge the freedom of speech or of the press, in violation of the First Amendment.

The United States District Court for the District of Columbia granted summary judgment for the United States, holding that the challenged provisions are consistent with the First Amendment. Because issues of material fact remain unresolved in the record developed thus far, we vacate the District Court's judgment and remand the case for further proceedings.

[The Court reviewed the history and characteristics of cable television, discussed the 1992 Act in detail, and rejected the government's contention that regulation of cable should be analyzed under the same standard that applies to regulation of broadcast television.]

II [B]

[T]he First Amendment, subject only to narrow and well-understood exceptions, does not countenance governmental control over the content of messages expressed by private individuals. [*R.A.V., supra* p. 42]; Texas v. Johnson, 491 U.S. 397, 414 (1989). Our precedents thus apply the most exacting scrutiny to regulations that suppress, disadvantage, or impose differential burdens upon speech because of its content. [ ]. Laws that compel speakers to utter or distribute speech bearing a particular message are subject to the same rigorous scrutiny. [ ]. In contrast, regulations that are unrelated to the content of speech are subject to an intermediate level of scrutiny, [ ], because in most cases they pose a less substantial risk of excising certain ideas or viewpoints from the public dialogue.

Deciding whether a particular regulation is content based or content neutral is not always a simple task. We have said that the "principal inquiry in determining content neutrality . . . is whether the government has adopted a regulation of speech because of [agreement or] disagreement with the message it conveys." [ ] See *R.A.V.*, [ ] ("The government may not regulate [speech] based on hostility—or favoritism—towards the underlying message expressed"). The purpose, or justification, of a regulation will often be evident on its face. [ ] But while a content-based purpose may be sufficient in certain circumstances to show that a regulation is content based, it is not necessary to such a showing in all cases. [ ] Nor will the mere assertion of a content-neutral purpose be enough to save a law which, on its face, discriminates based on content. [ ]

As a general rule, laws that by their terms distinguish favored speech from disfavored speech on the basis of the ideas or views expressed are content based. [ ] By contrast, laws that confer benefits or impose burdens on speech without reference to the ideas or views expressed are in most instances content neutral. [ ]

C

Insofar as they pertain to the carriage of full power broadcasters, the must-carry rules, on their face, impose burdens and confer benefits without reference to the content of speech. Although the provisions interfere with cable operators' editorial discretion by compelling them to offer carriage to a certain minimum number of broadcast stations, the extent of the interference does not depend upon the content of the cable operators' programming. The rules impose obligations upon all operators, save those with fewer than 300 subscribers, regardless of the programs or stations they now offer or have offered in the past. Nothing in the Act imposes a restriction, penalty, or burden by reason of the views, programs, or stations the cable operator has selected or will select. The number of channels a cable operator must set aside depends only on the operator's channel capacity [ ]; hence, an operator cannot avoid or mitigate its obligations under the Act by altering the programming it offers to subscribers. Cf. [*Tornillo*].

The must-carry provisions also burden cable programmers by reducing the number of channels for which they can compete. But, again, this burden is unrelated to content, for it extends to all cable programmers irrespective of the programming they choose to offer viewers. [ ] And finally, the privileges conferred by the must-carry provisions are also unrelated to content. The rules benefit all full power broadcasters who request carriage—be they commercial or noncommercial, independent or network-affiliated, English or Spanish language, religious or secular. The aggregate effect of the rules is thus to make every full power commercial and noncommercial broadcaster eligible for must-carry, provided only that the broadcaster operates within the same television market as a cable system.

It is true that the must-carry provisions distinguish between speakers in the television programming market. But they do so based only upon the manner in which speakers transmit their messages to viewers, and not upon the messages they carry: Broadcasters, which transmit over the airwaves, are favored, while cable programmers, which do not, are disfavored. Cable operators, too, are burdened by the carriage obligations, but only because they control access to the cable conduit. So long as they are not a subtle means of exercising a content preference, speaker distinctions of this nature are not presumed invalid under the First Amendment.

That the must-carry provisions, on their face, do not burden or benefit speech of a particular content does not end the inquiry. Our cases have recognized that even a regulation neutral on its face may be content-based if its manifest purpose is to regulate speech because of the message it conveys. [ ]

Appellants contend, in this regard, that the must-carry regulations are content-based because Congress' purpose in enacting them was to promote speech of a favored content. We do not agree. Our review of the Act and its various findings persuades us that Congress' overriding objective in enacting must-carry was not to favor programming of a particular subject matter, viewpoint, or format, but rather to preserve access to free television programming for the 40 percent of Americans without cable.

In unusually detailed statutory findings, [ ], Congress explained that because cable systems and broadcast stations compete for local advertising revenue, [ ], and because cable operators have a vested financial interest in favoring their affiliated programmers over broadcast stations, [ ], cable operators have a built-in "economic incentive . . . to delete, reposition, or not carry local broadcast signals." [ ]. Congress concluded that absent a requirement that cable systems carry the signals of local broadcast stations, the continued availability of free local broadcast television would be threatened. . . .

. . .

Appellants and the dissent make much of the fact that, in the course of describing the purposes behind the Act, Congress referred to the value of broadcast programming. In particular, Congress noted that broadcast television is "an important source of local news[,] public affairs programming and other local broadcast services critical to an informed electorate," [ ], and that noncommercial television "provides educational and informational programming to the Nation's citizens." [ ]. We do not think, however, that such references cast any material doubt on the content-neutral character of must-carry. That Congress acknowledged the local orientation of broadcast programming and the role that noncommercial stations have played in educating the public does not indicate that Congress regarded broadcast programming as more valuable than cable programming. Rather, it reflects nothing more than the recognition that the services provided by broadcast television have some intrinsic value and, thus, are worth preserving against the threats posed by cable. . . .

. . .

We likewise reject the suggestion . . . that the must-carry rules are content-based because the preference for broadcast stations "automatically entails content requirements." [ ] It is true that broadcast programming, unlike cable programming, is subject to certain limited content restraints imposed by statute and FCC regulation. But it does not follow that Congress mandated cable carriage of broadcast television stations as a means of ensuring that particular programs will be shown, or not shown, on cable systems.

. . .

D

Appellants advance three additional arguments to support their view that the must-carry provisions warrant strict scrutiny. In brief, appellants contend that the provisions (1) compel speech by cable operators, (2) favor broadcast programmers over cable programmers, and (3) single out certain members of the press for disfavored treatment. None of these arguments suffices to require strict scrutiny in the present case.

1

. . .

Tornillo and [Pacific Gas & Electric Co. v. Public Utilities Comm'n of Cal., 475 U.S. 1, 11 (plurality opinion) (invalidating a rule requiring a privately owned utility to include with its bills "an editorial newsletter published by a consumer group critical of the utility's ratemaking practices")] do not control this case for the following reasons. First, unlike the access rules struck down in those cases, the must-carry rules are content-neutral in application. . . .

Second, appellants do not suggest, nor do we think it the case, that must-carry will force cable operators to alter their own messages to respond to the broadcast programming they are required to carry. [ ] Given cable's long history of serving as a conduit for broadcast signals, there appears little risk that cable viewers would assume that the broadcast stations carried on a cable system convey ideas or messages endorsed by the cable operator. . . .

Finally, the asserted analogy to *Tornillo* ignores an important technological difference between newspapers and cable television. Although a daily newspaper and a cable operator both may enjoy monopoly status in a given locale, the cable operator exercises far greater control over access to the relevant medium. A daily newspaper, no matter how secure its local monopoly, does not possess the power to obstruct readers' access to other competing publications—whether they be weekly local newspapers, or daily newspapers published in other cities. Thus, when a newspaper asserts exclusive control over its own news copy, it does not thereby prevent other newspapers from being distributed to willing recipients in the same locale.

The same is not true of cable. When an individual subscribes to cable, the physical connection between the television set and the cable network gives the cable operator bottleneck, or gatekeeper, control over most (if not all) of the television programming that is channeled into the subscriber's home. Hence, simply by virtue of its ownership of the essential pathway for cable speech, a cable operator can prevent its subscribers from obtaining access to programming it chooses to exclude. A cable operator, unlike speakers in other media, can thus silence the voice of competing speakers with a mere flick of the switch.

The potential for abuse of this private power over a central avenue of communication cannot be overlooked. [ ] The First Amendment's command that government not impede the freedom of speech does not disable the government from taking steps to ensure that private interests not restrict, through physical control of a critical pathway of communication, the free flow of information and ideas. . . .

2

Second, appellants urge us to apply strict scrutiny because the must-carry provisions favor one set of speakers (broadcast programmers) over another (cable programmers). Appellants maintain that as a consequence of this speaker preference, some cable programmers who would have secured carriage in the absence of must-carry may now be dropped. Relying on language in *Buckley v. Valeo*, [infra p. 134], appellants contend that such a regulation is presumed invalid under the First Amendment because the government may not "restrict the speech of some elements of our society in order to enhance the relative voice of others." [ ]

To the extent appellants' argument rests on the view that all regulations distinguishing between speakers warrant strict scrutiny, [ ], it is mistaken. . . .

Our holding in *Buckley* does not support appellants' broad assertion that all speaker-partial laws are presumed invalid. Rather, it stands for the proposition that speaker-based laws demand strict scrutiny when they reflect the Government's preference for the substance of what the favored speakers have to say (or aversion to what the disfavored speakers have to say). [ ] Because the expenditure limit in *Buckley* was designed to ensure that the political speech of the wealthy not drown out the speech of others, we found that it was concerned with the communicative impact of the regulated speech. . . .

The question here is whether Congress preferred broadcasters over cable programmers based on the content of programming each group offers. The answer, as we explained above, [ ], is no. Congress granted must-carry privileges to broadcast stations on the belief that the broadcast television industry is in economic peril due to the physical characteristics of cable transmission and the economic incentives facing the cable industry. Thus, the fact that the provisions benefit broadcasters and not cable programmers does not call for strict scrutiny under our precedents.

3

[The Court rejected the argument that strict scrutiny was required by the line of cases that apply strict scrutiny to taxation schemes that single out one medium or a subset thereof (see infra p. 225). Although the must-carry rules applied only to cable and not to other video delivery systems such as satellite systems, the Court said this discrimination against the cable medium was justified by the bottleneck monopoly power exercised by cable operators and the dangers this posed to the viability of broadcast television. It also said the must-carry provisions applied to all cable systems and therefore did not create as much risk of undermining First Amendment interests as narrowly targeted tax schemes.]

III [A]

In sum, the must-carry provisions do not pose such inherent dangers to free expression, or present such potential for censorship or manipulation, as to justify application of the most exacting level of First Amendment scrutiny. We agree with the District Court that the appropriate standard by which to evaluate the constitutionality of must-carry is the intermediate level of scrutiny applicable to content-neutral restrictions that impose an incidental burden on speech. See Ward v. Rock Against Racism, 491 U.S. 781 (1989); United States v. O'Brien, 391 U.S. 367 (1968).

Under *O'Brien*, a content-neutral regulation will be sustained if

> "it furthers an important or substantial governmental interest; if the governmental interest is unrelated to the suppression of free expression; and if the incidental restriction on alleged First Amendment freedoms is no greater than is essential to the furtherance of that interest." [ ]

To satisfy this standard, a regulation need not be the least speech-restrictive means of advancing the Government's interests. "Rather, the requirement of narrow tailoring is satisfied 'so long as the . . . regulation promotes a substantial government interest that would be achieved less effectively absent the regulation.' " [ ] Narrow tailoring in this context requires, in other words, that the means chosen do not "burden substantially more speech than is necessary to further the government's legitimate interests." [ ]

Congress declared that the must-carry provisions serve three interrelated interests: (1) preserving the benefits of free, over-the-air local broadcast television, (2) promoting the widespread dissemination of information from a multiplicity of sources, and (3) promoting fair competition in the market for television programming. [ ] None of these interests is related to the "suppression of free expression," [ ], or to the content of any speakers' messages. And viewed in the abstract, we have no difficulty concluding that each of them is an important governmental interest. [ ]

. . . The interest in maintaining the local broadcasting structure does not evaporate simply because cable has come upon the scene. Although cable and other technologies have ushered in alternatives to broadcast television, nearly 40 percent of American households still rely on broadcast stations as their exclusive source of television programming. . . .

Likewise, assuring that the public has access to a multiplicity of information sources is a governmental purpose of the highest order, for it promotes values central to the First Amendment. . . . Finally, the Government's interest in eliminating restraints on fair competition is always substantial, even when the individuals or entities subject to particular regulations are engaged in expressive activity protected by the First Amendment. [ ]

B

That the Government's asserted interests are important in the abstract does not mean, however, that the must-carry rules will in fact advance those interests. When the Government defends a regulation on speech as a means to redress past harms or prevent anticipated harms, it must do more than simply "posit the existence of the disease sought to be cured." [ ] It must demonstrate that the recited harms are real, not merely conjectural, and that the regulation will in fact alleviate these harms in a direct and material way. [ ]

. . . On the state of the record developed thus far, and in the absence of findings of fact from the District Court, we are unable to conclude that the Government has [demonstrated either].

In sum, because there are genuine issues of material fact still to be resolved on this record, we hold that the District Court erred in granting summary judgment in favor of the Government. . . . [W]e think it necessary to permit the parties to develop a more thorough factual record, and to allow the District Court to resolve any factual disputes remaining, before passing upon the constitutional validity of the challenged provisions.

[The dissenters thought it clear that the provisions were content-based and that strict scrutiny was required. In the view of Justice O'Connor, joined by Justices Scalia, Ginsburg, and Thomas, the content-based nature of the regulation at issue was a congressional preference for the types of programs that broadcast stations provide to the public. She cited legislative findings that broadcast television stations continue to be an important source of local news and public affairs programming. This emphasis on localism amounted to legislative favoritism based on the content of broadcasters' speech. Since it was content-based, the regulation had to pass the exacting strict scrutiny standard and could not do so.]

Notes and Questions

1. The Court acknowledges that one of Congress's purposes, in addition to preserving access to free television, was to protect local programming. Is the latter a content-based purpose? How can the Court know that the former was Congress's "overriding objective"? Is it meaningful to talk of the "benefits of free, over-the-air local broadcasting" without considering the content of that broadcasting? Is the "widespread dissemination of information from a multiplicity of sources" a worthy goal of government regulation if the content of that expression is similar or identical?

2. Should strict scrutiny apply if Congress acts for both content-neutral and content-based reasons? Although the Court has defined content-neutral restrictions as those that "are justified without reference to the content of the regulated speech," see City of Renton v. Playtime Theatres, Inc., 475 U.S. 41, 48 (1986) it has also made clear that a restriction can be treated as content-neutral despite evidence of legislative hostility to the content, if the "predominate" purpose is content-neutral. Id. at 47–48.

3. Having concluded that the must-carry rules do not warrant review under strict scrutiny, the Court applies instead "the intermediate level of scrutiny applicable to content-neutral restrictions that impose an incidental burden on speech." Is it reasonable to characterize must-carry rules as imposing only an "incidental" burden on speech? Do all content-neutral regulations impose only "incidental" burdens on speech?

4. *Tornillo* [supra p. 69] said a newspaper's choice of material to publish constituted the exercise of editorial control and judgment that couldn't be regulated consistently with the First Amendment. Why doesn't that apply to a cable operator's choice of material to carry on its channels? Is the argument that must-carry rules are content-neutral a sufficient basis for distinguishing *Tornillo*? The Court suggests two additional distinctions. One is that viewers aren't likely to assume that cable operators endorse the programming of the local broadcasters they carry. Would newspaper readers be likely to believe the Miami Herald endorsed Tornillo's response? The other suggested distinction is that "the cable operator exercises far greater control over access to the relevant medium." But that is true only if the relevant medium is the local cable system in the first case and all competing publications in the other. Is that the right comparison?

5. Does the *Turner* Court's refusal to apply the editorial judgment rationale to cable narrow the applicability of *Tornillo* to instances in which the regulation operates as a content-based penalty?

6. Justice Stevens did not join in Part III–B of Justice Kennedy's opinion because he thought the must-carry rules should be sustained without further proceedings. That left the Court evenly divided between the four dissenters who would have held the rules invalid without further proceedings and the four justices who voted to remand. Justice Stevens concurred in the judgment to remand in order to provide a disposition.

————

Antitrust rationale. In an omitted portion of the majority opinion, the Court rejects the government's claim that "the must-carry provisions are nothing more than industry-specific antitrust legislation, and thus warrant rational-basis scrutiny under this Court's 'precedents governing legislative efforts to correct market failure in a market whose commodity is speech'."

This contention is unavailing. . . . [W]hile the enforcement of a generally applicable law may or may not be subject to heightened scrutiny under the First Amendment, compare Cohen v. Cowles Media Co., 501 U.S. 663, 670 (1991), with Barnes v. Glen Theatre, Inc., 501 U.S. 560, 566–567 (1991), laws that single out the press, or certain elements thereof, for special treatment "pose a particular danger of abuse by the State," Arkansas Writers' Project, Inc. v. Ragland, 481 U.S. 221, 228 (1987), and so are always subject to at least some degree of heightened First Amendment scrutiny. See Preferred Communications, 476 U.S., at 496, ("Where a law is subjected to a colorable First Amendment challenge, the rule of rationality which will sustain legislation against other constitutional challenges typically does not have the same controlling force"). Because the must-carry provisions impose special obligations upon cable operators and special burdens upon cable programmers, some measure of heightened First Amendment scrutiny is demanded. See [*Minneapolis Star*, infra p. 226].

O'Brien. The Court applied the test for judging the constitutionality of the must-carry rules that it created in United States v. O'Brien, 391 U.S. 367, 369 (1968). That case involved the conviction of David Paul O'Brien for burning his draft card on the steps of the South Boston Courthouse to protest the U.S. military establishment. O'Brien had been convicted under the federal Military Training and Service Act of 1948, which had been amended in 1965 to add the phrases "knowingly destroys" and "knowingly mutilates" to the section which previously applied only to one "who forges, alters, or in any manner changes" his draft card. O'Brien argued before the Court that the 1965 amendment was unconstitutional as applied to him because his act of burning his registration certification was protected "symbolic speech" within the First Amendment. It was in this context that the Court created the four-part *O'Brien* test, under which it found that the law under which O'Brien was convicted passed First Amendment scrutiny.

Professor Rodney Smolla has referred to *O'Brien* as a "pernicious precedent," arguing that the only reason for enacting the 1965 amendments, in the words of the report of the Senate Armed Services Committee, was to silence "the defiant destruction and mutilation of draft cards by dissident persons who disapprove of national policy." "For the Supreme Court to whitewash this law by pretending it was passed for reasons unrelated to expression was sheer hypocrisy—this was one of the most content-based laws the Congress had ever passed and the Court knew it." As we will see, the *O'Brien* test is used extensively to evaluate regulations applicable to electronic media. See Rodney A. Smolla, Free Speech in an Open Society 54–64 (1992).

Having concluded that the "must-carry" provisions of the Cable Television Consumer Protection and Competition Act of 1992 were content-neutral restrictions on speech, subject to intermediate First Amendment scrutiny under *O'Brien*, the Supreme Court remanded the case to the District Court for the District of Columbia for additional fact-finding. After extensive pretrial discovery, both parties moved for summary judgment. The three-judge court voted 2–1 to uphold the must-carry rules. The Supreme Court again accepted direct review. The only change in the Court's makeup since the earlier decision was that Justice Breyer had replaced Justice Blackmun, who had voted with the majority. The Court's decision in *Turner II* follows.

Turner Broadcasting System, Inc. v. Federal Communications Commission [*Turner II*]

Supreme Court of the United States, 1997.
520 U.S. 180, 117 S.Ct. 1174, 137 L.Ed.2d 369, 25 Med.L.Rptr. 1449.

JUSTICE KENNEDY delivered the opinion of the Court, except as to a portion of Part II–A–1.

. . .

[II] A

On our earlier review, we were constrained by the state of the record to assessing the importance of the Government's asserted interests when "viewed in the abstract." [ ] The expanded record now permits us to consider whether the must-carry provisions were designed to address a real harm, and whether those provisions will alleviate it in a material way. [ ] We turn first to the harm or risk which prompted Congress to act. The Government's assertion that "the economic health of local broadcasting is in genuine jeopardy and in need of the protections afforded by must-carry," [ ] rests on two component propositions: First, "significant numbers of broadcast stations will be refused carriage on cable systems" absent must-carry. [ ] Second, "the broadcast stations denied carriage will either deteriorate to a substantial degree or fail altogether." [ ] In reviewing the constitutionality of a statute, "courts must accord substantial deference to the predictive judgments of Congress." [ ] Our sole obligation is "to assure that, in formulating its judgments, Congress has drawn reasonable inferences based on substantial evidence." . . .

1

We have no difficulty in finding a substantial basis to support Congress' conclusion that a real threat justified enactment of the must-carry provisions. . . .

. . . Cable served at least 60 percent of American households in 1992, [ ] and evidence indicated cable market penetration was projected to grow beyond 70 percent. [ ] As Congress noted [ ], cable operators possess a local monopoly over cable households. Only one percent of communities are served by more than one cable system. [ ] Even in communities with two or more cable systems, in the typical case each system has a local monopoly over its subscribers. . . .

Evidence indicated the structure of the cable industry would give cable operators increasing ability and incentive to drop local broadcast stations from their systems, or reposition them to a less-viewed channel. Horizontal concentration was increasing as a small number of multiple system operators (MSO's) acquired large numbers of cable systems nationwide. [ ] The trend was accelerating, giving the MSO's increasing market power. In 1985, the 10 largest MSO's controlled cable systems serving slightly less than 42 percent of all cable subscribers; by 1989, the figure was nearly 54 percent. [ ]

Vertical integration in the industry also was increasing. . . .

. . .

Cable systems also have more systemic reasons for seeking to disadvantage broadcast stations: Simply stated, cable has little interest in assisting, through carriage, a competing medium of communication. . . .

The dissent contends Congress could not reasonably conclude cable systems would engage in such predation because cable operators, whose primary source of revenue is subscriptions, would not risk dropping a widely viewed broadcast station in order to capture advertising revenues. [ ] However, if viewers are faced with the choice of sacrificing a handful of broadcast stations to gain access to dozens of cable channels (plus network affiliates), it is likely they would still subscribe to cable even if they would prefer the dropped television stations to the cable programming that replaced them. Substantial evidence introduced on remand bears this out: With the exception of a handful of very popular broadcast stations (typically network affiliates), a cable system's choice between carrying a cable programmer or broadcast station has little or no effect on cable subscriptions, and subscribership thus typically does not bear on carriage decisions. [ ]

It was more than a theoretical possibility in 1992 that cable operators would take actions adverse to local broadcasters; indeed, significant numbers of broadcasters had already been dropped. [The Court cited evidence indicating that after the must-carry rules were repealed, between 19 and 31 percent of all local broadcast stations, 47 percent of local independent commercial stations, and 36 percent of noncommercial stations, were not carried by the typical cable system. It concluded that the problem was likely to grow worse if cable operators were relieved of the threat that must-carry rules might be reinstated. The Court said ratings data refuted the dissent's claim that many dropped broadcasters were stations with few viewers.]

The evidence on remand also indicated that the growth of cable systems' market power proceeded apace. The trend towards greater horizontal concentration continued, driven by "enhanced growth prospects for advertising sales." By 1994, the 10 largest MSO's controlled 63 percent of cable systems, [ ] a figure projected to have risen to 85 percent by the end of 1996. [ ] MSO's began to gain control of as many cable systems in a given market as they could, in a trend known as "clustering." [ ] Cable systems looked increasingly to advertising (and especially local advertising) for revenue growth [ ], and cable systems had increasing incentives to drop local broadcasters in favor of cable programmers (whether affiliated or not). [ ] The vertical integration of the cable industry also continued, so by 1994, MSO's serving about 70 percent of the Nation's cable subscribers held equity interests in cable programmers. . . .

2

The harm Congress feared was that stations dropped or denied carriage would be at a "serious risk of financial difficulty," [ ] and would "deteriorate to a substantial degree or fail altogether." [ ] Congress had before it substantial evidence to support its conclusion. . . .

. . .

. . . We think it apparent must-carry serves the Government's interests "in a direct and effective way." [ ] Must-carry ensures that a number of local broadcasters retain cable carriage, with the concomitant audience access and advertising revenues needed to support a multiplicity of stations. . . .

B

The second portion of the *O'Brien* inquiry concerns the fit between the asserted interests and the means chosen to advance them. Content-neutral regulations do not pose the same "inherent dangers to free expression," [ ] that content-based regulations do, and thus are subject to a less rigorous analysis, which affords the Government latitude in designing a regulatory solution. [ ] Under intermediate scrutiny, the Government may employ the means of its choosing " 'so long as the . . . regulation promotes a substantial governmental interest that would be achieved less effectively absent the regulation,' " and does not " 'burden substantially more speech than is necessary to further' " that interest. [*Turner I*]

The must-carry provisions have the potential to interfere with protected speech in two ways. First, the provisions restrain cable operators' editorial discretion in creating programming packages by "reducing the

number of channels over which [they] exercise unfettered control." [ ]
Second, the rules "render it more difficult for cable programmers to
compete for carriage on the limited channels remaining." [ ]

Appellants say the burden of must-carry is great, but the evidence
adduced on remand indicates the actual effects are modest. Significant
evidence indicates the vast majority of cable operators have not been
affected in a significant manner by must-carry. Cable operators have been
able to satisfy their must-carry obligations 87 percent of the time using
previously unused channel capacity, [ ]; 94.5 percent of the 11,628 cable
systems nationwide have not had to drop any programming in order to
fulfill their must-carry obligations; the remaining 5.5 percent have had to
drop an average of only 1.22 services from their programming, [ ]; and cable
operators nationwide carry 99.8 percent of the programming they carried
before enactment of must-carry. [ ]. Appellees note that only 1.18 percent of
the approximately 500,000 cable channels nationwide is devoted to channels added because of must-carry, [ ]; weighted for subscribership, the
figure is 2.4 percent. [ ] Appellees contend the burdens of must-carry will
soon diminish as cable channel capacity increases, as is occurring nationwide. [ ].

. . .

While the parties' evidence is susceptible of varying interpretations, a
few definite conclusions can be drawn about the burdens of must-carry. It
is undisputed that broadcast stations gained carriage on 5,880 channels as
a result of must-carry. . . .

Because the burden imposed by must-carry is congruent to the benefits
it affords, we conclude must-carry is narrowly tailored to preserve a
multiplicity of broadcast stations for the 40 percent of American households
without cable. . . . Congress took steps to confine the breadth and burden
of the regulatory scheme. For example, the more popular stations (which
appellants concede would be carried anyway) will likely opt to be paid for
cable carriage under the "retransmission consent" provision* of the Cable
Act; those stations will nonetheless be counted towards systems' must-
carry obligations. Congress exempted systems of 12 or fewer channels, and
limited the must-carry obligation of larger systems to one-third of capacity,
[ ]; allowed cable operators discretion in choosing which competing and
qualified signals would be carried, [ ]; and permitted operators to carry
public stations on unused public, educational, and governmental channels
in some circumstances, [ ].

[Finally, Justice Kennedy rejected appellants' contention that Congress
could have achieved its goals through less speech-restrictive alternatives.
Appellants raised five alternatives to the must-carry rules that were
claimed to be less restrictive: (1) a more limited version of the must-carry
rules that were in effect briefly in the late 1980s; (2) the use of so-called

---

* This provision gave broadcasters the
option of declining cable carriage unless the
cable operator paid them a fee, an option that
obviously would be available only to stations
that didn't need cable coverage as much as
the cable operator needed them.—eds.

A/B switches "which, in combination with antennas, would permit viewers to switch between cable and broadcast input, allowing cable subscribers to watch broadcast programs not carried on cable"; (3) the use of "a leased-access regime, under which both broadcasters and cable programmers would have equal access to cable channels at regulated rates"; (4) a system of subsidies for financially weak broadcast stations; and (5) "a system of antitrust enforcement or an administrative complaint procedure to protect broadcasters from cable operators' anticompetitive conduct."

After noting that the Court had never accepted a "least-restrictive-alternative" analysis for content-neutral regulations or speech, Justice Kennedy rejected each of the five proffered alternatives. In brief, the first failed because the Court "must defer" to the demonstration that Congress wanted more extensive protection. The second failed because of technical flaws in the A/B switches and their cumbersome features. Also, only 11.7 percent of all cable-connected television sets had antennas and A/B switches attached. Only 38% of these set owners had ever used the switch. The third failed because Congress had indicated that charging for cable carriage was inimical to the interests of small broadcasters. The fourth failed because a system of subsidies "would serve a very different purpose than must-carry." Also, the proposal "would require the Government to develop other criteria for giving subsidies and to establish a potentially elaborate administrative structure to make subsidy determinations." With regard to the fifth, the Court found that "Congress could conclude, however, that the considerable expense and delay inherent in antitrust litigation, and the great disparities in wealth and sophistication between the average independent broadcast station and average cable system operator, would make these remedies inadequate substitutes for guaranteed carriage."]

III

Judgments about how competing economic interests are to be reconciled in the complex and fast-changing field of television are for Congress to make. Those judgments "cannot be ignored or undervalued simply because [appellants] cas[t] [their] claims under the umbrella of the First Amendment." *CBS v. DNC*, supra p. 141. Appellants' challenges to must-carry reflect little more than disagreement over the level of protection broadcast stations are to be afforded and how protection is to be attained. We cannot displace Congress' judgment respecting content-neutral regulations with our own, so long as its policy is grounded on reasonable factual findings supported by evidence that is substantial for a legislative determination. Those requirements were met in this case, and in these circumstances the First Amendment requires nothing more. The judgment of the District Court is affirmed.

––––––––

Justice Breyer disagreed with the argument in Part II–A–1 of Justice Kennedy's opinion that the rules could be sustained as an attempt to prevent cable operators from using their position to disadvantage broadcasters as competitors, but believed they could be justified as measures "(1) preserving the benefits of free, over-the-air local broadcast television," and "(2) promoting the widespread dissemination of information from a multiplicity of sources." He wrote:

> With important First Amendment interests on both sides of the equation, the key question becomes one of proper fit. That question, in my view, requires a reviewing court to determine both whether there are significantly less restrictive ways to achieve Congress' over-the-air programming objectives, and also to decide whether the statute, in its effort to achieve those objectives, strikes a reasonable balance between potentially speech-restricting and speech-enhancing consequences. [ ] The majority's opinion analyzes and evaluates those consequences, and I agree with its conclusions in respect to both of these matters. [ ]

———

Justice O'Connor again wrote the dissent, joined by Justices Scalia, Ginsburg, and Thomas. Although she adhered to her earlier view that strict scrutiny should apply, she sought to show here that the provisions did not survive even intermediate scrutiny. First, "the principal opinion simply assumes that most adverse carriage decisions are anticompetitively motivated, and that must-carry is therefore a measured response to a problem of anticompetitive behavior. [ ] We ordinarily do not substitute unstated and untested assumptions for our independent evaluation of the facts bearing upon an issue of constitutional law." Then:

> In my view, the statute is not narrowly tailored to serve a substantial interest in preventing anticompetitive conduct. I do not understand Justice Breyer to disagree with this conclusion. [ ] Congress has commandeered up to one third of each cable system's channel capacity for the benefit of local broadcasters, without any regard for whether doing so advances the statute's alleged goals. To the extent that Congress was concerned that anticompetitive impulses would lead vertically integrated operators to prefer those programmers in which the operators have an ownership stake, the Cable Act is overbroad, since it does not impose its requirements solely on such operators.

Justice O'Connor also asserted that alternatives, principally leased access regimes, could serve the state's interests without burdening as much speech: "a leased access regime would respond directly to problems of vertical integration and problems of predatory behavior. Must-carry quite clearly does not respond to the problem of vertical integration." If Congress were concerned "that a leased access scheme would impose a burden on 'small broadcasters' forced to pay for access, subsidies would eliminate the problem."

She also expressed deep skepticism about the majority's "multiplicity of broadcasting services" interest and argued that the must-carry rules were not well tailored to achieve this interest:

Perhaps because of the difficulty of defending the must-carry provisions as a measured response to anticompetitive behavior, the Court asserts an "independent" interest in preserving a "multiplicity" of broadcast programming sources. [citing Justices Kennedy and Breyer]. In doing so, the Court posits existence of "conduct that threatens" the availability of broadcast television outlets, quite apart from anticompetitive conduct. [ ] We are left to wonder what precisely that conduct might be. Moreover, when separated from anticompetitive conduct, this interest in preserving a "multiplicity of broadcast programming sources" becomes poorly defined. Neither the principal opinion nor the partial concurrence offers any guidance on what might constitute a "significant reduction" in the availability of broadcast programming. The proper analysis, in my view, necessarily turns on the present distribution of broadcast stations among the local broadcast markets that make up the national broadcast "system." Whether cable poses a "significant" threat to a local broadcast market depends first on how many broadcast stations in that market will, in the absence of must-carry, remain available to viewers in noncable households. It also depends on whether viewers actually watch the stations that are dropped or denied carriage. The Court provides some raw data on adverse carriage decisions, but it never connects that data to markets and viewership.

Even assuming that the Court is correct that the 5,880 channels occupied by added broadcasters "represent the actual burden of the regulatory scheme," [ ], the Court's leap to the conclusion that must-carry "is narrowly tailored to preserve a multiplicity of broadcast stations," [ ], is nothing short of astounding. The Court's logic is circular. Surmising that most of the 5,880 channels added by the regulatory scheme would be dropped in its absence, the Court concludes that the figure also approximates the "benefit" of must-carry. . . . The "evi[l] the Government seeks to eliminate," [ ], is not the failure of cable operators to carry these 5,880 stations. Rather, to read the first half of the principal opinion, the "evil" is anticompetitive behavior by cable operators. As a factual matter, we do not know whether these stations were not carried because of anticompetitive impulses. Positing the effect of a statute as the governmental interest "can sidestep judicial review of almost any statute, because it makes all statutes look narrowly tailored." [ ] Without a sense whether most adverse carriage decisions are anticompetitively motivated, it is improper to conclude that the statute is narrowly tailored simply because it prevents some adverse carriage decisions. [ ]

Notes and Questions

1.   The dissenters and Justice Breyer reject the argument that must-carry is justified to prevent anticompetitive behavior by cable operators. If that is not the "substantial" interest required under *O'Brien,* what is?

2. Must-carry rules require cable operators to carry the expression of existing broadcasters. How can expanding the reach of these broadcasters' signals increase the diversity of electronic media voices? How else might must-carry rules contribute to enhancing a multiplicity of voices? If must-carry rules cannot be shown to expand the number and variety of voices in the electronic media, would this affect their constitutionality?

3. The majority cites the statistic that "cable operators nationwide carry 99.8 percent of the programming they carried before enactment of must-carry" to demonstrate that the burden of must-carry rules is not very great. Does this figure also suggest that the impact of must-carry was also not very great? Is this relevant to evaluating the constitutionality of the rules?

4. The dissent focuses primarily on the fit between the must-carry rules and the government's interest. What less restrictive means might the government have used? How much deference should a court give to Congress when considering the availability of less restrictive means? How do the majority and dissenting opinions resolve the question of how much overbreadth may be tolerated under the *O'Brien* test?

Satellite must-carry. Direct broadcast satellite (DBS) systems are also required to carry certain stations in the interest of diversity of information sources. A statute requiring them to reserve 4 to 7 percent of their channel capacity for noncommercial programming was upheld in Time Warner Entertainment Co. v. Federal Communications Comm'n, 93 F.3d 957 (D.C. Cir. 1996). Citing *Turner II*, the court said the government's interest in "assuring that the public has access to a multiplicity of informational sources is a governmental purpose of the highest order, for it promotes values central to the First Amendment." A rule requiring DBS systems that carry one local channel to carry all other requesting channels in that market was upheld in Satellite Broadcasting and Communications Ass'n v. FCC, 275 F.3d 337, 30 Med. L. Rptr. 1097 (4th Cir. 2001).

Cable ownership. Rules designed to prevent concentration of ownership in the cable industry have not fared well in court. FCC rules prohibited a single entity from owning cable systems that reached more than 30 percent of the nation's subscribers, prevented cable system owners from devoting more than 40 percent of their channels to their own programming affiliates, and banned ownership of a television station and a cable system in the same market. These were all struck down as violations of the First Amendment in Time Warner Entertainment Co. v. FCC, 240 F.3d 1126, 29 Med. L. Rptr. 1658 (D.C. Cir. 2001). The court left open the possibility that a higher limit, such as 60 percent, might be permissible as a limit on audience reach.

2.   BROADCASTING

Broadcasters have historically been subject to restrictions on ownership designed to ensure the availability of local programming and maintain diversity of voices on the airwaves. These included limits on the number of outlets a single entity could own in one market and nationally. A one-to-a-market rule restricted one person from owning or controlling more than one broadcast license in any geographic market, another rule prohibited cross-ownership of newspaper and broadcast facilities in the same market; and a national audience cap provided that no person could own or control TV stations reaching more than 25 percent of the U.S. population.

Beginning with passage of the Telecommunications Act of 1996, Pub. L. 104–104, 110 Stat. 56, many of these rules have been scrapped. Today, the national ownership limits for radio have been eliminated and the local limits have been significantly relaxed. The statutory limits on broadcast-cable cross-ownership in the same market have been eliminated. In August 1999, the FCC amended its local duopoly rule that had prevented joint ownership of two VHF stations in the same market to allow such combinations in many markets. One immediate response was the merger of CBS and Viacom, which each owned a station in several major markets and would have had to give up one had they merged under the old rule. The FCC also relaxed its radio-television cross-ownership rule to permit such combinations.

In 2003 the FCC announced a massive relaxation of the remaining limits on media ownership, which set off a firestorm of protest among public interest groups and in Congress. As a result, some of the FCC's proposals were thwarted, at least temporarily.

The FCC initially raised the national ownership cap from 12 television stations reaching 25 percent of the audience to 35 percent with no limit on the number of stations. Aggressive acquisition campaigns by Viacom and News Corp. soon bumped up against that new limit, however, and in 2003 the FCC proposed to raise it to 45 percent. (The limits are actually higher than stated because an owner's UHF stations count only fractionally.) The 45 percent limit encountered substantial public opposition and Congress intervened, forbidding the FCC to raise that limit higher than 39 percent, a figure that allowed Viacom and News Corp. to keep all the stations they had acquired.

The intervention by Congress insulated the audience cap from judicial review, but many of the other provisions in the 2003 FCC order were successfully challenged by public interest and consumer groups in Prometheus Radio Project v. FCC, 373 F.3d 372 (3d Cir. 2004). The most significant of those was the ban on cross-ownership of a newspaper and a television station in the same market. Media corporations have long owned newspapers and television stations in different markets, and most media conglomerates do. But the cross-ownership rule is a major obstacle to mergers among those conglomerates because the merged entity would often end up owning both in the same market. Under intense pressure from the media industry, the FCC proposed to abolish the ban on cross-ownership in markets with at least nine TV stations, retain it in markets with no more than three stations, and permit it on a case-by-case basis in medium-sized markets.

In the *Prometheus* case the Third Circuit held, 2–1, that the FCC's decision that cross-ownership could be permitted without loss of diversity employed several "irrational assumptions and inconsistencies." For example, the "diversity index" used by the FCC to measure the effect of the change assigned to the Duchess County Community College television station the same weight as the ABC station in New York and more weight than the New York Times and its New York radio station combined. The majority said the FCC gave too much weight to the Internet as a media outlet and irrationally assumed that all media of the same type should count equally regardless of their actual contribution to diversity of viewpoints. The court agreed, however, that the complete ban on cross-ownership was no longer justified and that the FCC had authority to change it. The court remanded for further fact-finding and rule-making proceedings.

Cross-ownership of radio and television stations in the same market was previously covered by a different set of rules, but the 2003 FCC order proposed to bring those under the same regulations as newspaper cross-ownership, and the Third Circuit decision applied to both.

The 2003 FCC order proposed to raise the number of television stations a single entity can own in a single market from two stations in the largest markets (at least 18 stations) to three and from one to two in medium-sized markets (at least five stations), as long as no more than one of the commonly-owned stations was in the top four in local ratings. The Third Circuit approved the top-four limitation but remanded for reconsideration of the numerical limits.

The dissenter, Judge Anthony J. Sirica, accused the majority of substituting its judgment for that of the FCC and said the court should have deferred to the FCC's determinations even if it considered them ill-advised. FCC Chairman Michael K. Powell, who had made deregulation of ownership the centerpiece of his tenure, said the decision would make it difficult for the FCC to set any kind of bright-line rules on ownership because the standards of justification the court set were too high.

The arguments for deregulation are that it will enable media to operate more efficiently, facilitate the development of new technologies, and be more competitive in the world. Arguments against it are that it may allow a single corporation to control much of the flow of information locally and a handful of media conglomerates to dominate the media nationally. Does the development of the Internet and other communications technologies alleviate the risks of concentration of ownership in the conventional media? Has the fight for local ownership and diversity of viewpoints already been lost?

3. NEWSPAPERS

Concentration of ownership in the media industries, whether caused by anticompetitive practices or by natural economic forces, has created a body of law peculiar to media businesses. In the case of newspapers, head-to-head competition between daily newspapers has been declining in America through most of this century. Today, the vast majority of readers are served by a monopoly newspaper owned by a national chain or group. As of 2004, only 22 cities in the U.S. had truly competing dailies (i.e. papers not owned by the same owner or operating under a joint operating agreement). Newspaper Association of America, Facts about Newspapers (2004). In 1945 groups owned 21 percent of the dailies in the United States; in 2003 the 22 largest groups controlled 69 percent of the daily circulation and 73 percent of Sunday circulation. See State of the News Media 2004, available on-line at Journalism.org.

It was settled long ago that the First Amendment does not exempt newspapers from antitrust laws. During World War II the government challenged bylaws that enabled the Associated Press to deny its services to its members' competitors. The Supreme Court unanimously rejected AP's First Amendment defense:

> Freedom to publish is guaranteed by the Constitution, but freedom to combine to keep others from publishing is not. Freedom of the press from governmental interference under the First Amendment does not sanction repression of that freedom by private interests. The First Amendment affords not the slightest support for the contention that a combination to restrain trade in news and views has any constitutional immunity.

Associated Press v. United States, 326 U.S. 1, 1 Med. L. Rptr. 2269 (1945).

Before and after this decision, a number of competing newspapers entered into joint operating agreements. The newspapers retained their separate identities and separate news departments, but combined their business operations, agreed upon circulation and advertising prices, and shared profits. One of these agreements was challenged in Citizen Publishing Co. v. United States, 394 U.S. 131, 1 Med. L. Rptr. 2704 (1969). The Supreme Court upheld the trial court's determination that the profit-pooling and price-fixing arrangements violated section 1 of the Sherman Act and that the overall effect was to lessen competition in violation of the Clayton Act.

The decision raised questions about the validity of similar agreements in 22 other cities, and the newspaper industry promptly sought relief from Congress. The result was the "Newspaper Preservation Act," 15 U.S.C. §§ 1801 et seq., passed in 1970. It retroactively validated the existing joint operating agreements and permitted the formation of new ones upon a finding by the Attorney General "that not more than one of the newspaper publications involved in the arrangement is a publication other than a failing newspaper." A "failing newspaper" was defined as one which, "regardless of its ownership or affiliation, is in probable danger of financial failure." Since passage of the Act, 29 JOAs have been approved, but only 12 are currently in effect. See http://www.freep.com/jobspage/links/joa.htm. In theory, at least, a JOA keeps the editorial voice of the failing newspaper alive and spares the dominant newspaper a long and costly battle with an increasingly desperate competitor for readers and advertisers.

Qualifying for a JOA. The Detroit Free Press and the Detroit News are owned, respectively, by Knight–Ridder, Inc. and Gannett Co., the two largest newspaper groups in the country. They began negotiating a JOA immediately upon Gannett's purchase of the News in 1985, and in 1986 executed a 100–year agreement. For a number of years the two newspapers had been locked in a price war. Newsstand prices for the daily editions were twenty cents for the News and fifteen cents for the Free Press—far below the norm for metropolitan dailies. Advertising rates were also abnormally low, and executives of both papers said they were afraid to raise prices unilaterally. In circulation the papers were about even, but the News led by about 60–40 in advertising.

The newspapers sought the Attorney General's approval of their JOA on the ground that the Free Press was "in probable danger of financial failure." Both papers were losing money at a rate of more than $10 million a year. Gannett executives testified they would not raise prices if the JOA were denied, and Knight–Ridder said it would close down the Free Press if the JOA were denied and Gannett did not raise prices.

The administrative law judge recommended disapproval, finding that the Free Press was not in danger of financial failure and that both papers' losses were due not to irreversible market factors, but to "their strategies of seeking market dominance and future profitability at any cost along with the expectation that failure to achieve these goals would result in favorable consideration of a JOA application." The Attorney General nevertheless approved the JOA. He concluded that the News had the power to outlast the Free Press by continuing the price war and that the Free Press had no way to extricate itself unilaterally from this predicament.

Various public interest groups sued to prevent implementation of the agreement, alleging that the two parent groups were using their deep pockets to artificially depress prices, thereby creating losses to justify approval of a JOA that would produce large profits for both in the future. The district court upheld the JOA, and the court of appeals affirmed. Michigan Citizens for an Independent Press v. Thornburgh, 868 F.2d 1285, 16 Med. L. Rptr. 1065 (D.C. Cir. 1989). The majority said:

> The real difficulty with this case . . . is the effect that the prospect of a JOA has on the behavior of competing newspapers. [ ] It is feared that a statute authorizing a JOA creates a self-fulfilling prophecy. Newspapers in two newspaper towns will compete recklessly because of a recognition that the loser will be assured a soft landing.

> . . . [But] the record of years of fierce competition and consequent losses to both papers led the Attorney General reasonably to conclude that both papers were principally pursuing market domination and that their strategies had been followed before any mutual discussion of a JOA. Nevertheless, the Attorney General implicitly recognized that it would be impossible completely to preclude competing newspapers from factoring into their business strategy the prospect of a JOA. As he laconically put it, "newspapers cannot be faulted for considering and acting upon an alternative that Congress has created."

We can envision a perfectly rational different policy, one that would require a showing that the weaker paper was more bloodied before approving a JOA and therefore *might* discourage the sort of competition we saw in Detroit. Congress, however, delegated to the Attorney General, and not to us, the delicate and troubling responsibility of putting content into the ambiguous phrase "probable danger of financial failure." . . .

Judge (now Justice) Ruth Bader Ginsburg, dissenting, said the Attorney General's interpretation "allows parties situated as Gannett and Knight–Ridder are artificially to generate and maintain the conditions that will yield them a passing JOA. I remain unpersuaded that, with passage of the Newspaper Preservation Act, Congress opened the door to this sort of self-serving, competition-quieting arrangement." She urged that the case be remanded to the Attorney General to give him an opportunity to show why his approval should not be deferred until "the results of the current competition afford a firmer basis for predicting whether the Free Press, profitably for itself, for readers, and for advertisers, can survive."

Rehearing en banc was denied by a 5–4 vote. 868 F.2d 1300, 16 Med. L. Rptr. 1315. The Supreme Court, 4–4, affirmed without opinion, Justice White not participating, 492 U.S. 936 (1989).

The effects of JOAs. It is impossible to know what would have happened in the absence of a JOA, but the agreements sometimes seem to facilitate rather than prevent the closure of a competing newspaper. Cox Enterprises, owner of the Miami News, and Knight–Ridder, owner of the Miami Herald, had a 30–year JOA which expired in 1996. It required the Herald to absorb the News's operating losses and to give the News 15 percent of the Herald's profits. In 1988 the parties renegotiated a new JOA to extend to 2021. It required Cox to absorb the News's losses, and gradually reduced its share of the Herald's profits to 10 percent. Immediately upon execution of the new agreement, Cox announced that the News would be closed unless a buyer was found. None was, and the paper closed at the end of 1988. One analyst estimated the deal saved Knight–Ridder $70 million it would have lost if it had had to continue absorbing the News's operating losses over the remainder of the original JOA term, and that Cox's 10 percent share of the Herald's profits over the next 30 years should amount to at least $165 million. See John Morton, The Miami News' Profitable Death, Wash. J. Rev., Dec. 1988, at 46. It was later learned that Cox had bought $100 million in Knight–Ridder stock before the deal as an apparent takeover threat. Cox consented to a $1.75 million fine for failing to disclose the stock purchase.

In 1999 Hearst Newspapers, owner of the San Francisco Examiner, ended a 34–year-old JOA between the Examiner and the San Francisco Chronicle, when it bought out the Chronicle. At the time of the sale, the Chronicle's circulation was more than four times greater than the Examiner's. The Justice Department's announced policy is that a newspaper may not be sold to its competitor if another buyer is willing to pay any price above liquidation value. But papers have gained monopolies by buying their rivals in Dallas, Little Rock, Pittsburgh, and San Antonio with no intervention by the Justice Department to solicit offers from other bidders.

As a result of these and other experiences, important questions have been raised about the Justice Department's scrutiny (or lack thereof) of JOAs and the economic conditions necessary for approving them; the likely anticompetitive impact, particularly on smaller papers, of JOAs; the role of chains in JOAs; and the potential economic benefits of JOAs for participating papers and their owners.

Although antitrust law has rarely impeded consolidation in the newspaper business since the 1980s, it still intervenes occasionally. An antitrust suit by a smaller competing newspaper and an advertiser prevented one of the two dominant dailies in northwest Arkansas from acquiring the other. The court rejected the defendants' argument that national and statewide newspapers, as well as radio, television, and direct mail were part of the relevant market. It approved the trial judge's finding that "it was reasonably probable the acquisition of the Times by NAT would substantially lessen competition in violation of Section 7." See Community Publishers, Inc. v. DR Partners, 139 F.3d 1180, 26 Med. L. Rptr. 1569 (8th Cir. 1998).

New competitors. The major source of new competition in the newspaper business is from suburban weeklies, alternative papers, and ethnic newspapers, especially Spanish-language newspapers. Circulation of alternative papers increased from three million in 1990 to 7.5 million in 2002 and circulation of Spanish-language newspapers more than tripled during that period. See State of the News Media 2004, available online at Journalism.org.

These newspapers have long complained that metropolitan dailies' exclusive rights to comics, syndicated features, and supplemental news services are a major obstacle to competition in the cities. They say the entrenched dailies often tie up the most popular features, even if they rarely or never publish them, to make them unavailable to potential competitors. The Daily Herald, a distant third in Chicago as a competitor of the Tribune and Sun–Times, sued the Tribune alleging that the pattern of exclusive contracts between the Tribune and distributors of these features violated the Sherman Act by making it impossible for smaller papers to attract readers who demand those features. The Seventh Circuit affirmed dismissal of the suit. It said the contracts are terminable upon relatively short notice, usually a year or less, and that freedom to compete for the contract is all that antitrust principles require. "The Herald has never tried to make a better offer, and we conclude that it has come to the wrong forum. It should try to outbid the Tribune and Sun–Times in the marketplace, rather than to outmaneuver them in court." Paddock Publications, Inc. v. Chicago Tribune Co., 103 F.3d 42, 25 Med. L. Rptr. 1187 (7th Cir. 1996), cert. denied 520 U.S. 1265 (1997).

4. COMPETITION AMONG MEDIA

New technologies have blurred the lines between different types of media, leading to the creation of new media altogether, and facilitating the move of many nonmedia businesses into traditional media activities. The principal media response to the prospects of new competition has not been litigation, however, but horizontal (and sometimes vertical) integration. Through mergers and acquisitions, many media companies have become multimedia conglomerates, with interests in newspapers, magazines, cable, broadcasting, films, program production, and home video.

One example was the merger in 2000 of Time Warner, Inc. with America Online, Inc. Time Warner, already one of the largest of the "old media" conglomerates with ownership of cable systems, magazines, books, CNN, and movies, brought about 80 percent of the existing revenues to the merger but Time Warner agreed to give AOL shareholders 55 percent of the stock in the merged company because it thought the "new media" world of AOL brought most of the future value to the deal. That promise was slow to materialize. By 2003 AOL/Time Warner stock had lost $214 billion in value, the entire AOL management team put in place at the time of the merger had been ousted, and industry observers were calling the merger "an unmitigated disaster." See The Typical Guy Who Became an Accidental Media Titan, Times (London), June 27, 2003, at Bus. 33.

Nevertheless, "old" and "new" media continue to converge. Some believe these developments are reshaping the media more dramatically than all the developments of First Amendment law, but so far the government has shown little interest in their antitrust implications and there has been little litigation to provide a forum for the First Amendment implications.

B. TAXATION

Concern about taxation of the press has played a role in American constitutional thought from the beginning. The Stamp Act of 1765, imposed upon the colonies by Parliament to help pay the cost of maintaining a British army on American soil, levied a tax on newspapers, books, pamphlets, and documents. It was one of the most hated of all the measures imposed on the colonies by England, and helped to catalyze American demands for independence. It forced American printers to take sides in the growing conflict between Tories and Patriots and thus helped mold the press into a powerful voice for independence.

It cannot be said that the First Amendment was specifically intended to prevent special taxes on the press, because the Framers left no record that they ever discussed the matter. But it is clear that the First Amendment was enacted against a historical background that saw such taxes as a potential threat to freedom of the press. That history is fully developed in Randall P. Bezanson, Taxes on Knowledge in America (1994). Beginning in the 1980s the Supreme Court decided a series of tax challenges by the media. The decisions are summarized in the case that follows.

Leathers v. Medlock

Supreme Court of the United States, 1991.

499 U.S. 439, 111 S.Ct. 1438, 113 L.Ed.2d 494, 18 Med.L.Rptr. 1953.

[Arkansas applied its general sales tax to cable television services but exempted newspapers, magazines, and home antenna satellite services.

Cable interests challenged the tax on First Amendment grounds. While the litigation was pending, the legislature amended the tax statute to bring satellite services under the tax but continued to exempt newspapers and magazines. The Arkansas Supreme Court held that the discrimination that had existed between cable services and satellite services violated the First Amendment because those were substantially the same medium, but the continuing discrimination between different media, such as cable and print, was constitutional.

The Supreme Court granted both sides' petitions for certiorari and held that the tax system did not violate the First Amendment when it taxed only cable and satellite services, or even when it taxed cable alone. The case was remanded to the Arkansas Supreme Court, however, for consideration of the cable operators' claim that the tax statute violated the equal protection clause during the period when it taxed cable operators but exempted satellite services.]

JUSTICE O'CONNOR delivered the opinion of the Court.

. . .

Cable television provides to its subscribers news, information, and entertainment. It is engaged in "speech" under the First Amendment, and is, in much of its operation, part of the "press." [ ] That it is taxed differently from other media does not by itself, however, raise First Amendment concerns. Our cases have held that a tax that discriminates among speakers is constitutionally suspect only in certain circumstances.

In Grosjean v. American Press Co., 297 U.S. 233 (1936), the Court considered a First Amendment challenge to a Louisiana law that singled out publications with weekly circulations above 20,000 for a 2% tax on gross receipts from advertising. The tax fell exclusively on 13 newspapers. Four other daily newspapers and 120 weekly newspapers with weekly circulations of less than 20,000 were not taxed. The Court discussed at length the pre-First Amendment English and American tradition of taxes imposed exclusively on the press. This invidious form of censorship was intended to curtail the circulation of newspers and thereby prevent the people from acquiring knowledge of government activities. [ ] The Court held that the tax at issue in *Grosjean* was of this type, and was therefore unconstitutional. [ ]

In Minneapolis Star & Tribune Co. v. Minnesota Comm'r of Revenue, 460 U.S. 575 (1983), we noted that it was unclear whether the result in *Grosjean* depended on our perception in that case that the State had imposed the tax with the intent to penalize a selected group of newspapers or whether the structure of the tax was sufficient to invalidate it. [ ] *Minneapolis Star* resolved any doubts about whether direct evidence of improper censorial motive is required in order to invalidate a differential tax on First Amendment grounds: "Illicit legislative intent is not the *sine qua non* of a violation of the First Amendment." [ ]

At issue in *Minneapolis Star* was a Minnesota special use tax on the cost of paper and ink consumed in the production of publications. The tax exempted the first $100,000 worth of paper and ink consumed annually. Eleven publishers, producing only 14 of the State's 388 paid circulation newspapers, incurred liability under the tax in its first year of operation. The Minneapolis Star and Tribune Company (Star Tribune) was responsible for roughly two-thirds of the total revenue raised by the tax. The following year, 13 publishers, producing only 16 of the State's 374 paid circulation papers, paid the tax. Again, the Star Tribune bore roughly two-thirds of the tax's burden. We found no evidence of impermissible legislative motive in the case apart from the structure of the tax itself.

We nevertheless held the Minnesota tax unconstitutional for two reasons. First, the tax singled out the press for special treatment. We noted that the general applicability of any burdensome tax law helps to ensure that it will be met with widespread opposition. When such a law applies only to a single constituency, however, it is insulated from this political constraint. [ ] Given "the basic assumption of our political system that the press will often serve as an important restraint on government," we feared that the threat of exclusive taxation of the press could operate "as effectively as a censor to check critical comment." [ ] "Differential taxation of the press, then, places such a burden on the interests protected by the First Amendment," that it is presumptively unconstitutional. [ ]

Beyond singling out the press, the Minnesota tax targeted a small group of newspapers—those so large that they remained subject to the tax despite its exemption for the first $100,000 of ink and paper consumed annually. The tax thus resembled a penalty for certain newspapers. Once again, the scheme appeared to have such potential for abuse that we concluded that it violated the First Amendment: "[W]hen the exemption selects such a narrowly defined group to bear the full burden of the tax, the tax begins to resemble more a penalty for a few of the largest newspapers than an attempt to favor struggling smaller enterprises." [ ]

Arkansas Writers' Project, Inc. v. Ragland, 481 U.S. 221 (1987), reaffirmed the rule that selective taxation of the press through the narrow targeting of individual members offends the First Amendment. In that case, Arkansas Writers' Project sought a refund of state taxes it had paid on sales of the Arkansas Times, a general interest magazine, under Arkansas' Gross Receipts Act of 1941. Exempt from the sales tax were receipts from sales of religious, professional, trade and sports magazines. [ ] We held that Arkansas' magazine exemption, which meant that only "a few Arkansas magazines pay any sales tax," operated in much the same way as did the $100,000 exemption in *Minneapolis Star* and therefore suffered from the same type of discrimination identified in that case. [ ] Moreover, the basis on which the tax differentiated among magazines depended entirely on their content. [ ]

These cases demonstrate that differential taxation of First Amendment speakers is constitutionally suspect when it threatens to suppress the expression of particular ideas or viewpoints. Absent a compelling justification, the government may not exercise its taxing power to single out the press. See *Grosjean,* [ ]; *Minneapolis Star,* [ ]. The press plays a unique role as a check on government abuse, and a tax limited to the press raises concerns about censorship of critical information and opinion. A tax is also suspect if it targets a small group of speakers. See *Minneapolis Star*, [ ]; *Arkansas Writers'*, [ ]. Again, the fear is censorship of particular ideas or viewpoints. Finally, for reasons that are obvious, a tax will trigger heightened scrutiny under the First Amendment if it discriminates on the basis of the content of taxpayer speech. [ ]

The Arkansas tax at issue here presents none of these types of discrimination. The Arkansas sales tax is a tax of general applicability. It applies to receipts from the sale of all tangible personal property and a broad range of services, unless within a group of specific exemptions. Among the services on which the tax is imposed are natural gas, electricity, water, ice, and steam utility services; telephone, telecommunications, and telegraph service; the furnishing of rooms by hotels, apartment hotels, lodging houses, and tourist camps; alteration, addition, cleaning, refinishing, replacement, and repair services; printing of all kinds; tickets for admission to places of amusement or athletic, entertainment, or recreational events; and fees for the privilege of having access to or use of amusement, entertainment, athletic, or recreational facilities. [ ] The tax does not single out the press and does not therefore threaten to hinder the press as a watchdog of government activity. We have said repeatedly that a State may impose on the press a generally applicable tax. [ ]

Furthermore, there is no indication in this case that Arkansas has targeted cable television in a purposeful attempt to interfere with its First Amendment activities. Nor is the tax one that is structured so as to raise suspicion that it was intended to do so. Unlike the taxes involved in *Grosjean* and *Minneapolis Star*, the Arkansas tax has not selected a narrow group to bear fully the burden of the tax.

The tax is also structurally dissimilar to the tax involved in *Arkansas Writers'*. In that case, only "a few" Arkansas magazines paid the State's sales tax. [ ] Arkansas Writers' Project maintained before the Court that the Arkansas Times was the only Arkansas publication that paid sales tax. The Commissioner contended that two additional periodicals also paid the tax. We responded that, "[w]hether there are three Arkansas magazines paying tax or only one, the burden of the tax clearly falls on a limited group of publishers." [ ] In contrast, [the statute in question] extended Arkansas' sales tax uniformly to the approximately 100 cable systems then operating in the State. [ ] While none of the seven scrambled satellite broadcast services then available in Arkansas [ ] was taxed until [the amendment] became effective, Arkansas' extension of its sales tax to cable television hardly resembles a "penalty for a few." [ ]

The danger from a tax scheme that targets a small number of speakers is the danger of censorship; a tax on a small number of speakers runs the risk of affecting only a limited range of views. The risk is similar to that from content-based regulation: it will distort the market for ideas. "The constitutional right of free expression is . . . intended to remove governmental restraints from the arena of public discussion, putting the decision as to what views shall be voiced largely into the hands of each of us . . . in the belief that no other approach would comport with the premise of individual dignity and choice upon which our political system rests." *Cohen v. California*, 403 U.S. 15, 24 (1971). There is no comparable danger from a tax on the services provided by a large number of cable operators offering a wide variety of programming throughout the State. That the Arkansas Supreme Court found cable and satellite television to be the same medium does not change this conclusion. Even if we accept this finding, the fact remains that the tax affected approximately 100 suppliers of cable television services. This is not a tax structure that resembles a penalty for particular speakers or particular ideas.

Finally, Arkansas' sales tax is not content based. There is nothing in the language of the statute that refers to the content of mass media communications. Moreover, the record establishes that cable television offers subscribers a variety of programming that presents a mixture of news, information, and entertainment. It contains no evidence, nor is it contended, that this material differs systematically in its message from that communicated by satellite broadcast programming, newspapers, or magazines.

Because the Arkansas sales tax presents none of the First Amendment difficulties that have led us to strike down differential taxation in the past, cable petitioners can prevail only if the Arkansas tax scheme presents "an additional basis" for concluding that the State has violated petitioners First Amendment rights. See *Arkansas Writers'*, [ ]. Petitioners argue that such a basis exists here: Arkansas' tax discriminates among media and, if the Arkansas Supreme Court's conclusion regarding cable and satellite television is accepted, discriminated for a time within a medium. Petitioners argue that such intermedia and intramedia discrimination, even in the absence of any evidence of intent to suppress speech or of any effect on the expression of particular ideas, violates the First Amendment. Our cases do not support such a rule.

. . .

[D]ifferential taxation of speakers, even members of the press, does not implicate the First Amendment unless the tax is directed at, or presents the danger of suppressing, particular ideas. That was the case in *Grosjean, Minneapolis Star,* and *Arkansas Writers'*, but it is not the case here. The Arkansas Legislature has chosen simply to exclude or exempt certain media from a generally applicable tax. Nothing about that choice has ever suggested an interest in censoring the expressive activities of cable television. Nor does anything in this record indicate that Arkansas' broad-based, content-neutral sales tax is likely to stifle the free exchange of ideas. We conclude that the State's extension of its generally applicable sales tax to cable television services alone, or to cable and satellite services, while exempting the print media, does not violate the First Amendment.

. . .

JUSTICE MARSHALL, with whom JUSTICE BLACKMUN joins, dissenting.

. . .

Our decisions on selective taxation establish a nondiscrimination principle for like-situated members of the press. Under this principle, "differential treatment, unless justified by some special characteristic of the press, . . . is presumptively unconstitutional," and must be struck down "unless the State asserts a counterbalancing interest of compelling importance that it cannot achieve without differential taxation." *Minneapolis Star,* [ ].

The nondiscrimination principle is an instance of government's general First Amendment obligation not to interfere with the press as an institution. As the Court explained in *Grosjean,* the purpose of the Free Press Clause "was to preserve an untrammeled press as a vital source of public information." [ ] Reviewing both the historical abuses associated with England's infamous " 'taxes on knowledge' " and the debates surrounding ratification of the Constitution, [ ] our decisions have recognized that the Framers viewed selective taxation as a distinctively potent "means of abridging the freedom of the press." [ ]

. . .

. . . If *Minneapolis Star, Arkansas Writers' Project,* and *Grosjean* stand for anything, it is that the "power to tax" does *not* include "the power to discriminate" when the press is involved. Nor is it the case under these decisions that a tax regime that singles out individual members of the press implicates the First Amendment *only* when it is "directed at, or presents the danger of suppressing, *particular* ideas." [ ] Even when structured in a manner that is content-neutral, a scheme that imposes differential burdens on like-situated members of the press violates the First Amendment because it poses *the risk* that the State might abuse this power. See *Minneapolis Star* [ ].

At a minimum, the majority incorrectly conflates our cases on selective taxation of the press and our cases on the selective taxation (or subsidization) of speech generally. *Regan* [v. Taxation With Representation, 461 U.S. 540 (1983)] holds that the government does not invariably violate the Free Speech Clause when it selectively subsidizes one group of speakers according to content-neutral criteria. This power, when exercised with appropriate restraint, inheres in government's legitimate authority to tap the energy of expressive activity to promote the public welfare. See *Buckley v. Valeo,* [ ].

But our cases on the selective taxation of the *press* strike a different posture. Although the Free Press Clause does not guarantee the press a preferred position over other speakers, the Free Press Clause does "protec[t] [members of the press] from invidious discrimination." L. Tribe, American Constitutional Law § 12–20, p. 963 (2d ed. 1988). Selective taxation is precisely that. In light of the Framers' specific intent "to preserve an untrammeled press as a vital source of public information," [*Grosjean, Minneapolis Star*], our precedents recognize that the Free Press

Clause imposes a special obligation on government to avoid disrupting the integrity of the information market. As Justice Stewart explained:

> "[T]he Free Press guarantee is, in essence, a *structural* provision of the Constitution. Most of the other provisions in the Bill of Rights protect specific liberties or specific rights of individuals: freedom of speech, freedom of worship, the right to counsel, the privilege against compulsory self-incrimination, to name a few. In contrast, the Free Press Clause extends protection to an institution." Stewart, "Or of the Press," [supra p. 57]

Because they distort the competitive forces that animate this institution, tax differentials that fail to correspond to the social cost associated with different information media, and that are justified by nothing more than the State's desire for revenue, violate government's obligation of evenhandedness. Clearly, this is true of disproportionate taxation of cable television. Under the First Amendment, government simply has no business interfering with the process by which citizens' preferences for information formats evolve.

Notes and Questions

1. If a distinction between general interest magazines and sports magazines is content-based and a distinction between cable television and home satellite television is content-neutral, how would courts classify a statute that taxed newspapers distributed by home delivery and exempted those delivered by mail?

2. Why was it significant in *Minneapolis Star* that the tax targeted a few large newspapers? Is the potential for abuse greater there than where the tax targets a particular medium?

3. Would *Leathers v. Medlock* (and the cases preceding it) come out differently if the First Amendment contained the speech clause but no press clause? If they are press clause cases, how broadly does the concept of "press" reach? Would it reach discriminatory taxation of movies?

4. In an omitted portion of the majority opinion, Justice O'Connor writes that "Inherent in the power to tax is the power to discriminate." At least where speech is not involved, it is true that legislatures are allowed to discriminate without much explanation: railroads can be taxed differently than trucking companies, farm owners differently than small business owners, beer differently than wine. These differences unquestionably affect the competitive positions of the taxpayers, and in some instances that is no doubt their purpose. May the legislature exempt a particular medium from taxation for the very purpose of enhancing its competitive position vis-à-vis competing media?

5. Under the dissenters' "nondiscrimination principle for like-situated members of the press," which media would be considered like-situated? Might the state be required to justify such discrimination on the basis of differing social costs created by the media in question? Would the legisla-

ture be allowed to discriminate on the basis of asserted social costs or benefits that are content-related—for example, social costs and benefits of pornography as compared with those of news?

———

Discrimination among different types of media. The most common form of intermedia tax discrimination is between newspapers, which often are exempted from sales taxes, and magazines, which usually are not. *Leathers v. Medlock* seems to permit that distinction, and some courts have so interpreted it. But just a few days after deciding *Leathers,* the Supreme Court denied certiorari in a Tennessee case holding that it is unconstitutional to exempt newspapers from a sales tax but not magazines. See Newsweek, Inc. v. Celauro, 789 S.W.2d 247, 18 Med. L. Rptr. 1134 (Tenn. 1990), cert. denied 499 U.S. 983 (1991) (Blackmun, J., dissenting).

The Pennsylvania Supreme Court, 4–2, affirmed a decision allowing magazines to be taxed when newspapers were not, but a dissenting opinion argued that the distinction violated the free press clause of the state constitution. The majority interpreted *Leathers v. Medlock* as permitting some media to be exempted from sales taxes when others are not, as long as the distinction is based on format rather than content. The dissenters did not address this First Amendment analysis, but said the Pennsylvania constitution provides broader protection for the press. That document, which was adopted in 1776 and thus predates the First Amendment, states that "the printing press shall be free to every person who may undertake to examine the proceedings of the Legislature or any branch of government, and no law shall ever be made to restrain the right thereof." The dissenters said "A tax on magazines that discourages one form of expression, magazines, in favor of another, newspapers, clearly operates to restrain the use of the printing press to examine the proceedings of government." The majority, however, said that because the distinction between magazines and newspapers is based on format rather than content, it satisfies the state constitution as well as *Leathers v. Medlock*. Magazine Publishers of America v. Commonwealth, 539 Pa. 563, 654 A.2d 519, 23 Med. L. Rptr. 1337 (1995).

Questions of this sort promise to become even more vexing as conventional means of delivery of media give way to technological change. If newspapers are delivered electronically, for example, will differential taxation of newspapers and cable be defensible then? In response to lobbying from Newsday, which planned to launch an electronic newspaper, the New York legislature redefined that state's sales tax exemption for newspapers. The language was carefully crafted in an attempt to avoid exempting other providers of on-line information services. See Jerome L. Wilson, New York gives a tax break to electronic newspapers, Editor and Publisher, Aug. 27, 1994, at 15. Is it possible to distinguish these kinds of information services sufficiently to avoid unconstitutionality?

C. DISTRIBUTION

The extent to which the First Amendment protects the sales and distribution activities of publications has divided the courts sharply. One view is that distribution is as essential to free expression as the right to publish and is therefore entitled to as much constitutional protection. Another is that newspapers, magazines, and books are products, the sale of which can be subjected to reasonable regulation so long as it is content-neutral.

In 1938 the Supreme Court unanimously overturned a Griffin, Georgia, ordinance forbidding the distribution of "circulars, handbooks, advertising, or literature of any kind . . . without first obtaining the written permission from the City Manager. . . ." Chief Justice Hughes wrote for the Court: "Whatever the motive which induced its adoption, [the ordinance's] character is such that it strikes at the very foundation of the freedom of the press by subjecting it to license and censorship." Lovell v. City of Griffin, 303 U.S. 444 (1938).

In Martin v. Struthers, 319 U.S. 141 (1943), the Court ruled 5–4 that an ordinance forbidding door-to-door distribution of religious literature was unconstitutional. For the majority, Justice Black wrote:

The dangers of distribution can so easily be controlled by traditional legal methods, leaving to each householder the full right to decide whether he will receive strangers as visitors, that stringent prohibition can serve no purpose but that forbidden by the Constitution, the naked restriction of the dissemination of ideas.

For the dissenters, Justice Reed wrote:

While I appreciate the necessity of watchfulness to avoid abridgments of our freedom of expression, it is impossible for me to discover in this trivial town police regulation a violation of the First Amendment. No ideas are being suppressed. No censorship is involved. The freedom to teach or preach by word or book is unabridged, save only the right to call a householder to the door of his house to receive the summoner's message. I cannot expand this regulation to a violation of the First Amendment.

These issues are complicated by the fact that distribution often involves the use of public property, which means that government may assert proprietary as well as regulatory interests. Since *Martin v. Struthers*, the right of newspapers to deliver their products door-to-door and use human vendors to sell them on the streets has rarely been questioned. The advent of coin-operated newsracks, however, touched off a new round of conflicts between newspapers and governmental authorities.

The issue reached the Supreme Court in City of Lakewood v. Plain Dealer Publishing Co., 486 U.S. 750, 15 Med. L. Rptr. 1481 (1988). A Cleveland suburb enacted an ordinance requiring permits for newsracks located on public streets and sidewalks and giving the mayor power to grant or deny permit applications. The ordinance required the mayor to state reasons for denying a permit, and subjected the grant of a permit to various conditions, including approval of newsrack designs by the city's Architectural Review Board, provision of a $100,000 liability insurance policy by the newspaper, and "other terms and conditions deemed necessary and reasonable by the Mayor."

The publisher of the Cleveland Plain Dealer, without attempting to secure a permit under the ordinance, attacked it as unconstitutional on its face. By a 4–3 vote, the Supreme Court held unconstitutional "those portions of the Lakewood ordinance giving the Mayor unfettered discretion to deny a permit application and unbounded authority to condition the permit on any additional terms he deems 'necessary and reasonable.'"

In an opinion by Justice Brennan, the majority cited the cases recognizing a First Amendment right to distribute leaflets and said those cannot be dismissed by "the meaningless distinction that here the newspapers are ultimately distributed by a machine rather than by hand. . . . The effectiveness of the newsrack as a means of distribution, especially for low-budget, controversial neighborhood newspapers, means that the twin threats of self-censorship and detectable censorship are, if anything, greater for newsracks than for pamphleteers."

In dissent, Justice White, joined by Justices Stevens and O'Connor, said the Plain Dealer had a right to distribute its newspapers on the streets, "as others have a right to leaflet, solicit, speak, or proselytize in this same public forum area," but that this "does not encompass the right to take city property . . . and appropriate it for its own exclusive use, on a semi-permanent basis, by means of the erection of a newsbox. . . . There is no constitutional right to place newsracks on city sidewalks over the objections of the city." The dissenters said a city could constitutionally ban newsracks from sidewalks altogether; the majority did not address that question. Because Chief Justice Rehnquist and Justice Kennedy did not participate, the 4–3 decision is a fragile precedent for a First Amendment right to locate newsracks on public property.

The government's powers as property owner received fuller treatment in the case that follows.

Atlanta Journal and Constitution v. The City of Atlanta Department of Aviation

United States Court of Appeals, Eleventh Circuit, en banc, 2003.
322 F.3d 1298, 31 Med. L. Rptr. 1842.

[In preparation for the 1996 Olympics, the City of Atlanta renovated Hartsfield Atlanta International Airport and adopted a new plan (the "Plan") for airport concessions designed to make the airport more customer-friendly and reduce visual clutter. Previously, newspapers had been allowed to install their own newsracks at specified locations in the airport for the payment of fees ranging from 20 to 30 percent of gross revenues. Under the new plan only standard city-provided newsracks were permitted.

Newspapers were required to apply to the Department of Aviation for a permit to use them and were charged $20 per month per newsstand. The airport was required by federal and state law to be self-supporting; to meet those requirements the city counted on profits from the airport concessions. The newsrack fee was calculated to amortize the cost of the racks and give the city a 7 percent annual return on its investment. Publishers of the Atlanta Journal and Constitution, USA Today, and the New York Times objected to the new plan and obtained an injunction prohibiting the city from implementing the plan or charging any newsrack fee in excess of administrative costs. A panel of the court of appeals affirmed, but the court granted rehearing en banc.]

Before EDMONDSON, CHIEF JUDGE, AND TJOFLAT, ANDERSON, BIRCH, DUBINA, BLACK, CARNES, BARKETT, MARCUS, WILSON AND HILL, CIRCUIT JUDGES.

BIRCH, CIRCUIT JUDGE:

. . .

II. DISCUSSION

A. *First Amendment Scrutiny*

The distribution of newspapers, no less than the publication of the newspapers themselves, is an activity protected by the First Amendment. Lovell v. City of Griffin, 303 U.S. 444 (1938). Accordingly, a government (here, the City) is subject to certain limitations on the type and content of the restrictions it may place on this activity.

. . . If the property is a public forum or a designated public forum, then any content-based restrictions on speech within that forum are highly scrutinized: the restrictions must be narrowly drawn to serve a compelling state interest. See Int'l Soc. for Krishna Consciousness, Inc. v. Lee ("*ISKCON*"), 505 U.S. 672, 678 (1992).[9] "In a public forum, by definition, all parties have a constitutional right of access and the state must demonstrate compelling reasons for restricting access to a single class of speakers, a single viewpoint, or a single subject." Perry Educ. Ass'n v. Perry Local Educators' Ass'n, 460 U.S. 37, 55 (1983).

When the City seeks to regulate speech on government-owned property which is not a public forum or a designated public forum, the standard is modified, becoming more deferential to regulation. If the property is a nonpublic forum, then the City "ha[s] 'no constitutional obligation per se to let any organization use the [forum].' " Id. at 48, . . . "[O]n government property that has not been made a public forum, not all speech is equally situated, and the state may draw distinctions which relate to the special purpose for which the property is used." [Id.]

---

9. Based on *ISKCON,* [ ] there are three cognizable types of government property: (1) the public forum, which is property of a type "traditionally . . . available for public expression"; (2) a designated public forum, which is property specifically designated by the State for expressive activity; and (3) a nonpublic forum, which is all government-owned property not traditionally or explicitly designated as a public forum. [Footnote relocated.]

Therefore, in a nonpublic forum, the City may properly restrict exercise of expression that is inconsistent with the intended use or function of that property through reasonable, viewpoint-neutral regulations. *See ISK-CON,* [ ]. That is, even content-based restrictions, which in other venues would be subject to strict scrutiny, are constitutional so long as they are a reasonable, viewpoint-neutral attempt to ensure that the facility serves its intended purpose. "Implicit in the concept of the nonpublic forum is the right to make distinctions in access on the basis of subject matter and speaker identity. These distinctions may be impermissible in a public forum but are inherent and inescapable in the process of limiting a nonpublic forum to activities compatible with the intended purpose of the property." [ ] This deferential standard is a "much more limited review" than that applicable in a public or designated public forum. [*ISKCON*]

In this case, the forum in question is the Airport, which is City-owned. Government-owned commercial airports, such as Hartsfield, are not public fora. Id. at 680–82. There is no argument from the parties that the airport is a designated public forum under the circumstances of this case, and, accordingly, we will employ the more deferential standard appropriate for regulation of nonpublic forum expressive activity.

Our examination of the Plan is restricted to two major bases that led the district court and our panel to declare the scheme unconstitutional: first, the profit-conscious fee for rental of the newsracks, and, second, the unrestrained discretion vested in a government official responsible for setting that fee and choosing which publications could use the newsracks. Though the Department has proffered numerous reasons to support its newsrack regulation, we need discuss only one, its interest as a proprietor, to resolve the first issue before us. The regulations are constitutionally valid if they are reasonable and viewpoint-neutral. We find no question that the regulations are viewpoint-neutral, and, therefore, we focus on their reasonableness below.

B. *Reasonableness*

. . .

We examine the City's restrictions for reasonableness given the surrounding circumstances. Restrictions must only be reasonable; "[they] need not be the most reasonable or the only reasonable limitation[s]." [*ISK-CON*] The contours of the allowed distribution are not dictated by the publishers' preferences; the First Amendment does not guarantee the least expensive method of distribution, and the City is free to approve an alternative scheme that results in higher costs for the publishers, assuming that such scheme is reasonable overall. Kovacs v. Cooper, 336 U.S. 77, 88–89 (1949) (plurality opinion). Thus, we apply this reasonableness standard to the two issues before us, the profit-conscious fee and the discretion granted to the responsible official.

1. Profit–Conscious Fee

The central thrust of the publishers' argument concerns the ability of the Department to charge a profit-conscious fee for use of the Airport's newsracks. A profit-conscious fee cannot be justified by reference to any of the Airport's stated concerns about security, or aesthetics, or traffic flow. Rather, to support a profit-conscious fee, the Department must point to its interest in maintaining the Airport as a business.

According to the publishers, *any* fee charged on an activity protected by the First Amendment must be limited to the recoupment of administrative costs associated with that activity; the fee cannot be a method of enhancing general government revenue. In advancing this argument, the publishers point to a line of Supreme Court cases that makes this very point. *See* Murdock v. Pennsylvania, 319 U.S. 105, 113–14 (1943); [ ].

This line of cases does not control the instant case. The Airport is operated as a self-sufficient business by the City, as mandated by statute and required by federal regulation, and the Plan at issue here is an outgrowth of its role as a business proprietor rather than its ordinary role as a regulator. "Where the government is acting as a proprietor, managing its internal operations, rather than acting as a lawmaker with the power to regulate or license, its action will not be subjected to the heightened review to which its actions as a lawmaker may be subject." [*ISKCON*]. However, "[t]he Government, even when acting in its proprietary capacity, does not enjoy absolute freedom from First Amendment constraints, as does a private business, but its action is valid in these circumstances unless it is unreasonable. . . ."

a. Reasonableness of fee

The proprietor capacity distinction suggests that reasonableness, for purposes of forum analysis, includes a commercial component. In a proprietary capacity, the City has a substantial interest in the "bottom line," and, when the City acts as a proprietor, reasonable regulations may include profit-conscious fees for access for expressive conduct, in a manner similar to fees that would be charged if the forum was owned by a private party (i.e., a fee for a[n] auditorium for a dance recital, or a fee for displaying advertisements in a newspaper).

Here, the fee is facially reasonable; it does not appear that the Department is applying monopolistic muscle to the publishers. It would be different if the Department set a prohibitively high fee for use of the newsracks. However, the charges imposed do not strike us as outside the reasonable bounds for this alternative distribution channel granted to the publishers. In addition, the history of regulation at the Airport and the availability of alternative distribution methods for the publishers bolsters the Plan's reasonableness. [The court said the fee was not out of line with the fees newspapers had paid previous to the Plan, which also presumably included a profit, and the newspapers had an alternative distribution channel through the airport newsstands, which were required by contract to carry all three of the newspapers in question.]

b. Special fee

The publishers contend that the imposition of this rent for the newsracks creates a special fee imposed on the press in violation of [*Minneapolis*

Star]. The First Amendment provides the press no protection from government's generally applicable economic regulation, but does prevent government from treating the press in a special manner. [ ]

In *Minneapolis Star*, the State of Minnesota enacted a use tax on the materials necessary for newspaper publication, including paper and ink. [ ] In comparison to the general taxation scheme of the state, this particular use tax possessed several unique qualities: first, it did not complement the sales tax, as most use taxes do, but rather applied even to those products bought in-state and subject to sales tax; and, second, it was the only use tax imposed on goods that would eventually be made into retail products, that is, the only use tax on "an intermediate transaction." [ ]

Because of these unique characteristics, the Court found that the use tax was "without parallel in the State's tax scheme," and "single[s] out the press for special treatment." [ ] It was this targeted, unique tax that presented and particularized the constitutional problem. . . .

The fees imposed by the Department on the publishers are not a special tax on the press, and the *Minneapolis Star* line of cases has no application here. Instead, these fees are part of the general scheme of the Airport to "tax" those vendors who are granted space in the facility. Every vendor, no matter the type of goods sold, must remit to the Airport compensation for the granted right of access to the Airport's customers. Calling the newsrack fee a "special tax" is unduly formalistic. True, the contracts made by the Department with the publishers involve a different method of computing the fee due than the contracts with other Airport vendors. Moreover, the amount of the fee is not linked by some mathematical scale to the fees imposed on other vendors in the Airport. However, this is not a fee, like that involved in *Minneapolis Star*, that has no analogue in the general scheme of regulation. All vendors remit to the Airport a fee for the space they lease or a portion of profits from the goods they sell, or a combination of the two. None of these fees imposed on other vendors is limited to recovery of the Airport's administrative costs. The newsrack Plan is not an aberration within this scheme of vendor regulation.

2.   Unrestrained Discretion

A grant of unrestrained discretion to an official responsible for monitoring and regulating First Amendment activities is facially unconstitutional. See City of Lakewood v. Plain Dealer Publ'g Co., 486 U.S. 750, 755–56 (1988) (stating that the Supreme Court "ha[s] long held that when a licensing statute allegedly vests unbridled discretion in a government official over whether to permit or deny expressive activity, one who is subject to the law may challenge it facially without the necessity of first applying for, and being denied, a license" (footnote and citations omitted)). Here, we believe that the district court and our panel correctly identified the boundless discretion granted to the Department official responsible for administering the newsrack Plan as exceeding the bounds of constitutionality. None of the Department's proffered reasons for regulation, including its interest as a proprietor, can justify this grant of discretion.

While market forces, *ceteris paribus,** might constrain the fees charged the publishers to reasonable levels, the City, even acting as a proprietor, retains its power to censor. Such power must be cabined by some standard of First Amendment reasonableness over and above the invisible hand of the marketplace. Structural and procedural safeguards can reduce the possibility that an official will use her power to corrupt the protections of the First Amendment. The official charged with administering the Plan should have clear standards by which to accept or reject a publisher's request to use the newsracks at the Airport. Perhaps a first-come, first-served system, a lottery system, or a system in which each publisher is limited to a percentage of available newsracks would be appropriate vehicles for limiting the official's discretion. We leave the intricacies of the safeguards to the Department, whose knowledge of the practicalities, including consumer demand, can be applied.[13] The official in charge must be constrained in some form in her exercise of discretion.

Therefore, though we find that the Department could impose a profit-conscious fee on publishers who wished to distribute newspapers through newsracks, we also find that the manner in which the Department is able to exercise this prerogative runs afoul of the Constitution's concern over unbridled official discretion in the First Amendment arena. . . .

C. *Profit-Making Fees on First Amendment Expression*

In Sentinel Communications v. Watts, 936 F.2d 1189 (11th Cir. 1991), we held that Florida was prohibited from charging publishers five cents per paper sold at newsracks placed at state-run highway rest stops. According to the *Sentinel* court, the problem with this fee arose from its revenue-raising character:

> [I]t is well established that a licensing fee is permissible, but a state or municipality may charge no more than the amount needed to cover administrative costs. The government may not profit by imposing licensing or permit fees on the exercise of first amendment rights, and

---

* All other things being equal—eds.

13. The official may be charged with considering market forces, such as consumer demand, in making his decisions, in keeping with the coexisting interest of the Airport in generating a profit. These decisions as a business are permissible; the regulations exist to constrain the temptation of discriminating among publications on viewpoint grounds, not the temptation of discriminating against publications based on whether they are likely to grant a greater return on investment to the Airport.

The line between denial of a permit for business-related reasons, such as consumer demand, and for unconstitutional reasons, such as viewpoint, is admittedly blurry. Consumer demand may be low for papers that espouse unpopular viewpoints. Therefore, the effect of making decisions based on consumer demand may be to deny all unpopular viewpoints from the Airport's newsracks. Especially given that the newsrack fees in this case are a flat fee—that is, the publishers pay a set fee per month for rental of the newsrack, rather than a percentage of gross receipts from sale of their papers through the newsracks—the denial of a permit for business-related reasons harbors a greater risk that the decision is but a mask for censorship of unpopular viewpoints in contravention of the First Amendment. This risk may be addressed by future regulations concerning newsracks at the Airport.

is prohibited from raising revenue in the guise of defraying its administrative costs.

Id. at 1205 (citations omitted).

While a government acting facially or impliedly in its capacity as regulator or licensor cannot profit from the exercise of First Amendment rights, it is not the law that a government, universally, is prohibited from imposing profit-making or revenue-raising fees on First Amendment expression. We hold that when a government acts in a proprietary capacity, that is, in a role functionally indistinguishable from a private business, then commercially reasonable, profit-conscious contracts may be negotiated for distribution space in a non-public forum for First Amendment activities, subject to structural protections that reduce or eliminate the possibility of viewpoint discrimination.[14]

III. CONCLUSION

Based on the foregoing discussion, we find that the Department can impose a profit-conscious fee on the use of newsracks in the Airport, but that the discretion surrounding such fee must be restrained through procedures or instructions designed to reduce or eliminate the possibility of viewpoint discrimination. . . .

[Concurring opinions of Judges Tjoflat, Anderson, Carnes, and Barkett are omitted.]

Notes and Questions

1. In the *ISKCON* case the Supreme Court rejected the argument that airports should be viewed as public fora like streets and parks. The Court said they historically had not been places that had as a principal purpose the free exchange of ideas, and public access to them is regulated in the interest of security.

2. The court in the principal case says speech in a nonpublic forum may be restricted "to ensure that the facility serves its intended purpose." The city did not contend that allowing the newspapers to maintain their own newsracks would interfere with the intended purpose of the airport except to the extent that it would deprive the airport of a source of revenue. Is that the kind of interest that justifies restricting speech in a nonpublic forum?

3. In Multimedia Publishing Co. v. Greenville–Spartanburg Airport District, 991 F.2d 154, 21 Med. L. Rptr. 1369 (4th Cir. 1993), the court said that even if airports are not public fora, expressive activity on public property is nevertheless entitled to "special solicitude" and it is not enough that the regulation is rationally related to a legitimate governmental objective. The court said the airport authority had not shown that the

---

14. We note that at least two other circuits are in accord. See Jacobsen v. City of Rapid City, S.D., 128 F.3d 660, 664 n. 2 (8th Cir. 1997); Gannett Satellite Info. Network, Inc. v. Metropolitan Transp. Auth., 745 F.2d 767, 774 (2d Cir. 1984); [ ].

placement of newsracks was incompatible with the airport's primary purpose. The airport asserted aesthetic, economic, security, and safety reasons for the ban, but those reasons were found to be "post hoc, pretextual creations."

4. If the government could not charge a revenue-raising fee for newsracks at highway rest stops, why is it permitted to do so in airports? If the government was acting as regulator or licensor in the rest stop case, why is it considered to be acting in a proprietary capacity in the airport case? If the government's purpose is to raise revenue, is it ipso facto acting in a proprietary capacity?

5. As long as regulations are content-neutral and decisions are not left to an official's unfettered discretion, courts give local governments substantial leeway to regulate placement of newsracks. An ordinance requiring publishers to apply for a permit, pay a fee, and provide liability insurance, and restricting the size, type, and location of newsracks, was upheld in Jacobsen v. Harris, 869 F.2d 1172, 16 Med. L. Rptr. 1380 (8th Cir. 1989). Courts seem to be deferential even when the city's objectives are purely aesthetic. See, e.g Globe Newspaper Co. v. Beacon Hill Architectural Comm'n, 100 F.3d 175, 24 Med. L. Rptr. 2537 (1st Cir. 1996), upholding the authority of Boston's Beacon Hill Architectural Commission to ban newsracks in its historical neighborhood, and Gold Coast Publications, Inc. v. Corrigan, 42 F.3d 1336, 23 Med. L. Rptr. 1353 (11th Cir. 1994), upholding an ordinance requiring all newsracks in Coral Gables, Florida, to have "gloss brown pedestals, gloss beige sides and door and gloss brown coin box" to help the city carry out a "Mediterranean theme" in its public places.

––––––––

Newsstands. Street-corner buildings from which a variety of newspapers, magazines, and snacks are sold raise a different set of issues. An en banc decision by the Seventh Circuit in a newsstand case illustrates the breadth of disagreement over the proper analytical framework for distribution cases generally. By a vote of 9–3, the court upheld a Chicago ordinance requiring operators of newsstands located on public sidewalks to obtain city permits. Judge Manion and four other judges argued that the ordinance regulated only the conduct of building structures on public property, not speech. They distinguished the *Lakewood* case on the ground that newsstands are larger and more permanent than newsracks, and normally carry many publications with diverse viewpoints; this meant they were a more serious interference with the normal use of streets and sidewalks and were less likely to be targeted for viewpoint-based discrimination. The other seven judges did not find the distinction between newsracks and newsstands persuasive, however.

Four concurring judges did not share the plurality's view that the case involved conduct rather than speech, but thought the ordinance could be upheld as a reasonable time, place, and manner restriction and did not give an administrator the kind of "unbridled discretion" that was found objectionable in *Lakewood*.

Three dissenting judges argued that *Lakewood* and FW/PBS v. City of Dallas, 493 U.S. 215 (1990) (striking down parts of an ordinance licensing adult businesses) required that the Chicago ordinance be analyzed as a prior restraint. It could not be sustained under this analysis, they said, because it lacked provisions requiring prompt action on license applications and speedy judicial review of denials. They rejected the argument that newsstand operators would not be discriminated against on the basis of content; city officials might target newsstands that sold legal pornography or smaller offbeat weeklies that offended certain officials.

The author of one of the concurring opinions, Judge Flaum, said "There is a great need for clarification of standards in this area, and I respectfully suggest that this case is deserving of further review in the Supreme Court of the United States." The Supreme Court denied certiorari. See Graff v. City of Chicago, 9 F.3d 1309 (7th Cir. 1993) (en banc), cert. denied 511 U.S. 1085 (1994).

Note that in this case, views as to the appropriate level of First Amendment protection range from none, to time-place-and-manner analysis, to prior-restraint analysis. What seems most appropriate here?

Non-news publications. If newspapers have a First Amendment right to place vending machines on public sidewalks, why not vendors of videos or compact discs? And if the media have a right to attach a locked newsrack permanently to the sidewalk, does a sidewalk orator have a right to build a permanent platform for his or her exclusive use so he or she does not have to compete with other speakers for a choice location? Is this an instance where the First Amendment gives the media more protection than other speakers?

Sometimes municipalities are willing to permit newsracks for daily newspapers but not for every vendor of a printed product. May they discriminate between different types of publications on the basis of frequency of distribution?

In Cincinnati v. Discovery Network, Inc., 507 U.S. 410, 21 Med. L. Rptr. 1161 (1993), plaintiffs were companies that promoted their businesses with free magazines distributed through newsracks on sidewalks. They lost their newsrack permits when the city began enforcing an ordinance that forbade such distribution of commercial handbills but not newspapers.

The Court assumed that the publications in question were commercial speech and that the city had a substantial interest in controlling the number of newsracks on public property. But the effect of the city's action was to remove only 62 of 1,500 to 2,000 newsracks, and the Court found this insufficient to meet the fit between the regulation and its asserted purpose that the Court had established in its commercial speech cases (see *Central Hudson* and *Fox* infra pp. 170–71). Indeed, because the forbidden newsracks were no more harmful to safety and aesthetics than those permitted, the distinction between commercial and noncommercial speech "bears no relationship *whatsoever* to the particular interests the state has asserted."

The Court rejected 6–3 the city's argument that commercial speech could be singled out to bear all of the burden of the safety and aesthetic concerns simply because it was speech of lesser value. "[T]he city's argument attaches more importance to the distinction between commercial and noncommercial speech than our cases warrant and seriously underestimates the value of commercial speech." The majority declined to decide, however, whether discrimination against commercial speech is permissible only when it relates to the commercial nature of the speech.

Justice Blackmun, concurring, argued that truthful, noncoercive commercial speech about lawful activities should enjoy full First Amendment protection, and that the *Central Hudson* analysis should be abandoned. Chief Justice Rehnquist, joined by Justices White and Thomas, dissented. He argued that the city's decision to place all of the burden on a less-protected form of speech was a better result in First Amendment terms than accomplishing the goals by restricting all newsracks, and was a reasonable fit with those goals even if it reduced the number of newsracks only marginally.

Disrupting distribution. Newspapers that are distributed without charge have a special vulnerability—their circulation can be disrupted merely by removing the papers from distribution boxes. When the interference with newspaper distribution is by private actors—vandals, thieves, or protesters—it raises no First Amendment issue, of course, but it is still a significant problem for those who distribute their publications free. Destruction of newsracks and theft of papers that are offered for sale are punishable as ordinary property crimes, but what is the crime if someone removes supplies of free newspapers? Publishers of "shoppers" sometimes allege that their publications are being removed by competitors, and on some college campuses supplies of free student newspapers have been taken by persons protesting the paper's policies.

In 1994, 10,000 copies of the University of Maryland at College Park free daily student newspaper, the Diamondback, were stolen and replaced with flyers that read: "Due to its racist nature, the Diamondback will not be available today—read a book!" The Maryland General Assembly responded by passing a statute making it a misdemeanor to exert "unauthorized control over newspapers with the intent to prevent other individuals from reading the newspapers." 27 Md. Code Ann. § 345. Some "free" newspapers have responded with initiatives of their own, for example, specifying that a customer's first copy is free but that there is a charge for subsequent copies. Michael Koster, The New Campus Censors, Colum. Journalism Rev., Sept.–Oct. 1994, at 19.

If the disrupters are public officials, they may be liable for civil rights violations. For example, an alternative newspaper won a jury verdict for $35,600 plus attorneys' fees against the City of San Francisco after police officers seized 2,000 copies of an edition that criticized the police chief. See

Jury Finds Police Violated a Newspaper's Rights, N.Y. Times, Sept. 18, 1994 at A14.

Even buying up copies of a newspaper may be a violation of the publisher's First Amendment rights if the purpose is to keep the paper out of the hands of readers. See Rossignol v. Voorhaar, 316 F.3d 516, 31 Med. L.Rptr. 1417 (4th Cir. 2003). Sheriff's deputies, anticipating that a local alternative weekly newspaper would publish election-day articles critical of the sheriff and the state's attorney, spent the night before the election buying 1,300 copies of the paper from 40 stores and 40 newsracks. Many readers were unable to obtain the paper. The deputies were off-duty and used their own money to buy the papers, but the court said they acted under color of law because their plan was approved by the sheriff, their status as law enforcement officers gave them assurance they would not be prosecuted under the Maryland Newspaper Theft Act, and the knowledge that they were law enforcement officers intimidated store clerks who otherwise might have refused to sell them their entire supply of papers. Because the purpose of the scheme was to suppress criticism of public officials, the sheriff and the deputies could be found liable for violating the publisher's civil rights.

D. LABOR RELATIONS

As employers, media are subject to the National Labor Relations Act and other employment regulations. When these regulations are applied to editorial employees, they can interfere with the employer's autonomy. The argument that the NLRA could not be applied to the press for this reason was rejected in Associated Press v. National Labor Relations Board, 301 U.S. 103, 1 Med. L. Rptr. 2689 (1937). The Court held that the First Amendment did not preclude inquiry into AP's reasons for discharging an employee who claimed he was fired for engaging in union organizing activity. As the following case indicates, however, that holding does not dispose of all the First Amendment issues in regulation of labor relations of media businesses.

Nelson v. McClatchy Newspapers, Inc.
Supreme Court of Washington, 1997.
131 Wash.2d 523, 936 P.2d 1123, 25 Med. L. Rptr. 1703.

[Defendant newspaper, The News Tribune (TNT), reassigned plaintiff reporter Sandra Nelson from her duties as education reporter to a swing shift copy editor post (maintaining her prior salary, benefits and seniority, but working nights and weekends and no longer reporting stories) after she refused to abandon her offhours political activity to comply with the newspaper's ethics code. That activity consisted of "highly visible support for gay and lesbian rights, feminist issues, and abortion rights." Nelson filed suit, asserting a variety of claims, including that her reassignment violated the state Fair Campaign Practices Act, RCW 42.17.680(2), which provides:

No employer or labor organization may discriminate against an officer or employee in the terms or conditions of employment for (a) the failure to contribute to, (b) the failure in any way to support or oppose, or (c) in any way supporting or opposing a candidate, ballot proposition, political party, or political committee.

Nelson demanded reinstatement or employment in another reporting job. The trial court granted summary judgment for the newspaper. The Washington Supreme Court, hearing the case en banc, agreed that this statute applied to Nelson, and then addressed the newspaper's claim that RCW 42.17.680(2) unconstitutionally infringed its First Amendment rights by interfering with its ability to exercise editorial discretion and protect its credibility.]

SANDERS, J.

. . .

When addressing whether a governmental regulation or action affecting the press is violative of its constitutional free press protection, we begin by noting the two governing polar principles and then consider where the complained action falls. On one extreme is the general principle that a newspaper has "no special immunity from the application of general laws" simply because it is the press. [*Associated Press v. N.L.R.B.*] On the opposite side is the principle that the government absolutely may not regulate the content of a newspaper. [*Miami Herald Publishing Co. v. Tornillo*, supra p. 69]

Miami Herald Publishing is the seminal case on the issue. In *Miami Herald* the United States Supreme Court held that the state absolutely may not regulate the content of a newspaper. [ ] At issue was the constitutionality of a Florida "right-of-access" statute which forced newspapers to publish responses of politicians who had been criticized by the paper. At the heart of *Miami Herald* is the notion that in order to uphold the circulation of ideas the editors of a newspaper must be free to exercise editorial control and discretion. [ ] The Court held that " 'liberty of the press is in peril as soon as the government tries to compel what is to go into a newspaper.' " [ ] The Court concluded because the state law deprived the paper of its editorial discretion, it was necessarily unconstitutional as applied to the newspaper. Thus, *Miami Herald* clearly establishes that editorial control is a necessary component of the free press and a state law infringing thereon will be unconstitutional as applied.

Following *Miami Herald* was Passaic Daily News v. N.L.R.B., 736 F.2d 1543 (D.C. Cir. 1984). *Passaic* held a newspaper could not be constitutionally required to publish a reporter's column as a remedy for unlawful termination because it would interfere with the paper's editorial function. [ ] If a newspaper cannot be required to publish a particular reporter's work, how can it be constitutionally required to employ the individual as a reporter? Perhaps the paper could be ordered to employ the reporter for noneditorial services, but that is exactly what TNT is presently doing.

Editorial integrity and credibility are core objectives of editorial control and thus merit protection under the free press clauses. This conclusion is illustrated by a well-worded opinion by Chief Justice Burger: "The power of a privately owned newspaper to advance its own political, social, and economic views is bounded only by two factors: first, the acceptance of a sufficient number of readers and hence advertisers to assure financial success; and, second, the journalistic integrity of its editors and publishers." Columbia Broadcasting Sys., Inc. v. Democratic Nat'l Comm., 412 U.S. 94 (1973) (Burger, C.J., plurality op.). Our conclusion is also supported by academic texts showing credibility to be crucial to a paper's ability to operate. For example, a piece chronicling the development of the print media indicates that by 1900 "impartial gathering and reporting of the news were generally recognized to be the basic obligation of newspapers." Warren K. Agee et al., Introduction to Mass Communications 57 (7th ed. 1982).

In Newspaper Guild of Greater Philadelphia v. N.L.R.B., 636 F.2d 550, 560 (D.C. Cir. 1980), the circuit court wrote that editorial integrity is to a newspaper what machinery is to a manufacturer. The court stated that "protection of the editorial integrity of a newspaper lies at the core of publishing control." [ ] The court continued: "At least with respect to most news publications, credibility is central to their ultimate product and to the conduct of the enterprise." Accordingly, the court noted that a newspaper's ability to control its credibility falls within the sphere of First Amendment protection and laws infringing thereon must be scrutinized. [ ]

The *Newspaper Guild* court continued that

In order to preserve [its managerial prerogative to control its editorial integrity,] a news publication must be free to establish without interference, reasonable rules designed to prevent its employees from engaging in activities which may directly compromise their standing as responsible journalists and that of the publication for which they work as a medium of integrity. [ ]

This is directly on point. The no-conflict-of-interest policy employed by TNT was expressly designed for the exact purpose of upholding TNT's credibility. This policy therefore merits protection under the free press clauses of the state and federal constitutions.

Nelson claims [*Associated Press*] supports her position that codes of ethics regulating high profile employee activity do not go to a newspaper's core function and hence are not protected under the free press clauses. There the Associated Press fired one of its editors for attempting to unionize the work force. [ ] Firing the editor violated the National Labor Relations Act's specific grant to workers to form, join, and participate in labor unions. [ ] The Court, by a five to four vote with a strong dissent by Justice Sutherland, found the NLRA constitutional, [ ], but also concluded the true motivation for the firing related to union membership, not editorial prerogative.

The Court rested its decision on a finding that unionizing had "no relation whatever" to Associated Press's news distributing function. Thus, *Associated Press* must be distinguished from this case. While internally unionizing a small work force may not impinge on a news publication's credibility and integrity vis-à-vis the outside world, high profile politicized activities of a reporter arguably do. The *Associated Press* case affirmatively supports this view. In particular, the decision unambiguously noted that it was not commenting on whether Associated Press could discharge the editor if or when his continued activity led Associated Press to believe its appearance of impartiality was subverted. [ ] On the contrary, the *Associated Press* decision itself noted that Associated Press could still publish the news as it desired and could still create and enforce policies of its own choosing. [ ] The Court also stated that Associated Press would be free to discharge the editor or any editorial employee who fails to comply with the policies it may adopt. If a publisher may discharge an employee for failing to comply with its editorial policies, it should be equally entitled to transfer an employee to an equal-paying position which has less public exposure. *Associated Press* does not hold that freedom of the press may be violated by any general law but only *that* general law (the NLRA) did not.

. . .

Nelson also points to Hausch v. Donrey of Nevada, Inc., 833 F. Supp. 822 (1993), to support her assertion that TNT's attempt to protect its editorial integrity and credibility did not fall within the zone of free press protections. In *Hausch* the United States District Court for Nevada held the press is not immune from suit under the antidiscrimination laws of Title VII of the Civil Rights Act of 1964 simply because it is the press. [ ] However, the court there noted that the paper had not alleged that its ability to control the integrity and credibility of the paper had been affected by the antidiscrimination laws. [ ] Accordingly *Hausch* is not on point.

Here, TNT implemented a code of ethics which it designed in good faith to foster the newspaper's integrity and credibility. Case law unambiguously allows a news publication to follow a code designed to limit conflicts of interest which may diminish publication credibility. TNT adopted such a code. Freedom of the press leaves such decisions to the press, not the legislature or the courts. The code is facially designed to uphold the appearance of impartiality. Indeed, the code seems representative of those in place at 75 percent of our nation's newspapers. In fact, as stated earlier, it is nearly identical to those employed by the Associated Press, The Washington Post, and the Society of Professional Journalists.

IV. CONCLUSION

We recognize Nelson's statutory right to avoid workplace discrimination based on her politics. Since this right is established by the statute we need not consider whether it is also established by the state constitution. However, the First Amendment freedom of the press is the constitutional minimum regardless of the legal source of government abridgment. Choosing an editorial staff is a core press function, at least when that choice is based on editorial considerations. That is the case here. This statute has been unconstitutionally applied.

DOLLIVER, J., dissenting.

. . .

The majority asserts that this case illustrates a conflict between two "polar principles" in First Amendment jurisprudence. [ ] The majority acknowledges, on the one hand, "that a newspaper has 'no special immunity from the application of general laws' simply because it is the press." [*Associated Press*] On the other hand, the majority reasons, the government may not regulate the content of a newspaper. [*Miami Herald v. Tornillo*] I see no conflict between these principles in this case because there has been no showing that the government would be regulating content by enforcing this statute. No one has alleged that Ms. Nelson's reporting was influenced in any way by her political views. Nor has anyone alleged that application of the statute would impinge upon the newspaper's exclusive right to determine what to print.

The First Amendment prohibits the government from regulating what a newspaper prints. [ ] The majority cites this principle to support its holding that the First Amendment also prohibits government regulation of a newspaper's employment decisions. However, there is a distinction between regulation of content and regulation of employment decisions, as is illustrated in [*Passaic Daily News*].

In *Passaic Daily News*, the District of Columbia Circuit held that the defendant newspaper had improperly demoted a columnist due to his outside labor union activities. [ ] The court stated that the First Amendment did not insulate the press from application of a federal statute prohibiting employers from discharging employees for labor union activity. Yet, at the same time, the court held that the newspaper could not be forced to print the reporter's weekly editorial column as a remedy for the illegal demotion. [ ] *Passaic Daily News* makes it clear that there is a distinction under the First Amendment between government regulation of the press's labor practices and government regulation of editorial control. Whereas the former is allowed, the latter is prohibited by the First Amendment.

Referring to *Passaic Daily News*, the majority states, "if a newspaper cannot be required to publish a particular reporter's work, how can it be constitutionally required to employ the individual as a reporter?" [ ] Yet, this was precisely what happened in *Passaic Daily News*: The newspaper was not required to publish the reporter's weekly editorial column, but it was also prohibited from demoting him due to his activities. The reporter was still allowed to report on local stories; he was just not allowed to write a controversial editorial column. For the court to have ordered the newspaper to continue to publish the column would have been to completely usurp its editorial control. In contrast, the reporter here writes only unbiased stories. There has been no showing that the newspaper's editorial control would be threatened by her continued employment as a reporter.

The majority relies upon [*Newspaper Guild of Greater Philadelphia*] to buttress its holding that the First Amendment gives the newspaper the right to adopt internal policies protecting its credibility. [ ] Although *Newspaper Guild* addressed the type of policy at issue here, it did so as a means to concluding that a labor union does not have the right to bargain on all aspects of a newspaper's ethics code. The court was not deciding whether an individual employee's statutory and constitutional rights to political expression were trumped by a newspaper's First Amendment right to enforce its ethics code. The case thus provides limited precedential value.

In contrast, the Supreme Court considered whether an individual employee's statutory rights were trumped by a newspaper's First Amendment rights in [*Associated Press*]. There the Court held that the newspaper could not claim First Amendment immunity from provisions of the National Labor Relations Act protecting an employee's right to organize. [ ] The Court noted that there had been no allegation that the reporter's work was biased, and held that the discharge had been on behalf of the reporter's outside union activity, which was specifically protected by federal law. [ ] Just as those statutory provisions protect outside labor activity, the provisions of the Fair Campaign Practices Act protect outside political activity. Absent a showing of bias in Ms. Nelson's work, and a consequent interference with The News Tribune's right to editorial control from the application of the statute, the newspaper cannot claim First Amendment immunity here.

Notes and Questions

1. The Court concludes that *Tornillo*, supra p. 69, controls this case. However, *Tornillo* involved a direct regulation of newspaper content that was triggered by the content of the paper and that then compelled the newspaper to print content that it otherwise would not have. Can *Tornillo* be distinguished from the present case? Does *Tornillo* preclude the enforcement of other laws of general application against the press? Both the majority and the dissent interpret *Tornillo* to mean that the government "may not regulate the content of a newspaper." Is this an accurate reading of *Tornillo*? If not, should the court in *Nelson* have reached a different result? Would the majority's analysis be the same if Nelson had sought damages rather than reinstatement?

2. Recall that in *Tornillo*, Justice Brennan insisted that the decision did not preclude mandatory retraction of defamatory speech. If that is correct, might violation of the NLRA create another exception to the principle that a newspaper cannot be compelled to publish material it would prefer to omit?

3. The majority distinguished the Supreme Court's decision in *Associated Press v. N.L.R.B.* on the basis that the internal unionizing activity in that case did not compromise the Associated Press' credibility and integrity vis-à-vis the outside world, while "high profile politicized activities of a reporter arguably do." Is this reasoning correct? Is there any reason to

think that pro-union activities would not run as much risk of compromising a news organization's image of impartiality as pro-feminist, pro-lesbian, or pro-choice activities?

4.   Suppose a newspaper demotes an editorial writer for union organizing activity; can it be ordered to reinstate the writer? The answer probably is no, because the editorial writer will be held to be a managerial or confidential employee not subject to the NLRA. See, e.g., Wichita Eagle & Beacon Publishing Co. v. NLRB, 480 F.2d 52 (10th Cir. 1973), cert. denied 416 U.S. 982 (1974) (editorial writers were "so closely aligned with the newspaper's management in the formulation, determination, and effectuation, not to mention expression, of the newspaper management's policies through its editorials as to be properly excluded. . . .")

———

Sex discrimination. Do the anti-discrimination provisions of Title VII limit a newspaper's freedom to choose editorial employees? In *Hausch v. Donrey of Nevada,* cited in *Nelson* supra, the court applied Title VII to a newspaper's decision regarding hiring and promotion decisions for editorial positions, despite the First Amendment concerns expressed by the defendant. The defendant newspaper argued that its decision not to promote the managing editor, a woman, to editor was part of the "process of editorial control" and affected the content of the newspaper. The court held that unlike the statute in *Tornillo,* which required the newspaper to publish "certain specific material," applying Title VII does not amount to the regulation of the content of a newspaper. Any indirect effect on content caused by nondiscrimination in the selection of editors is not a "burden on the First Amendment." Whether a magazine targeted toward minority groups or women could be forced to hire a more qualified white male for its editorial staff over a member of the target group would pose a harder question, the court said. Recall that the majority in *Nelson* concluded that *Hausch* was not on point because "the paper [in *Hausch*] had not alleged that its ability to control the integrity and credibility of the paper had been affected by the antidiscrimination laws." Is selection of an editor less closely related to editorial control than restricting reporters' outside activities?

LEGAL ISSUES ARISING FROM PUBLICATION

CHAPTER IV

Defamation

In Part One we considered various forms of direct government regulation of media. In Part Two we turn to the impact on media of tort law. Within the tort world, the law of defamation, which comprises the distinct but related torts of libel and slander, has had the most pronounced impact on media historically. These are the oldest of the tort actions brought against media, and it is in defamation that the constitutional limitations on tort liability for speech are most fully developed.

For the most part, the constitutional rules have been superimposed over the common law framework, which was already complex and confusing. As a result, the current law of defamation is an amalgam of state law (both statutory and common law) and constitutional law (mainly federal, but occasionally derived from state constitutions). In this chapter we try to synthesize these different strands to the extent that the present state of the law permits. This decision reflects a belief that lawyers can understand the modern law of defamation without knowing all the details of its past or all the artifacts of its transformation.

Of course the source of a legal rule—statute, common law, or constitution—often has important procedural, jurisdictional, and substantive consequences. It is important throughout this chapter (indeed, throughout all the chapters on civil liabilities) to pay close attention to such matters. But it is also important to observe the interplay of constitutional, statutory, and common law concepts. It is often worth asking, for example, whether a different statutory or common law rule would permit a different constitutional response. And different rules come into play at different stages of litigation. Specific common law or statutory rules, for example, may provide grounds for a motion to dismiss for failure to state a cause of action when constitutional grounds would not be available until the motion for summary judgment.

At common law a defamation plaintiff made out a prima facie case by showing that the defendant published a defamatory statement concerning the plaintiff. (That formula is deceptively simple because, as we shall see, "published," "defamatory," and "concerning the plaintiff" are all terms of art.) Today, at least in the kinds of cases that are brought against media, the plaintiff must prove that defendant published a *false* defamatory statement *of fact* concerning the plaintiff and was guilty of some level of *fault* with respect to the falsity of the statement. The plaintiff may also have to show that he or she has complied with a retraction statute and has suffered some demonstrable harm. We attempt in the following sections to treat each of these requirements separately. They are closely interrelated, however, and each can be fully appreciated only in connection with the others.

A.   WHAT IS DEFAMATION?

The first question to be answered in every libel or slander case is whether the statement complained about is defamatory. Although reputation is the interest protected by these torts, whether a statement is actionable as defamation cannot be determined simply by asking whether it harmed the plaintiff's reputation. Many statements that harm reputation are not defamatory, and a defamatory statement may be actionable without any proof that it actually harmed the plaintiff's reputation. But defamatory statements are not necessarily actionable; for example they are not actionable unless they are also false. Whether a statement is "defamatory" depends upon the answers to several different inquiries.

Romaine v. Kallinger

Supreme Court of New Jersey, 1988.
109 N.J. 282, 537 A.2d 284, 15 Med. L. Rptr. 1209.

[This case arose out of a non-fiction book, "The Shoemaker," written about a man who went on a criminal rampage. One of the episodes involved events at the Romaine house. Part of that discussion included the following:

> A militant women's libber, Maria Fasching was famous among her friends for her battles on behalf of the weak and downtrodden. She would always try to rescue someone a bully had attacked, and she could not tolerate racists.
>
> Maria thought of herself as a "free spirit." She resisted anything that she considered a restriction on her freedom. She cared for cats that had been hit by cars and for birds with broken wings.
>
> Today, Maria Fasching was on the four-to-midnight shift at Hackensack Hospital, and she wore her nurse's uniform under her coat. In the morning Maria's friend Randi Romaine, who lived in the stucco house, had called Maria and asked her to drop over for coffee. The two women had not seen each other for a long time, for between hospital duties and preparations for her wedding, Maria's schedule was full.
>
> At first Maria said that she couldn't visit because she had to go to a wake. This wake, however, was only for an acquaintance. Randi and her twin sister, Retta, had been Maria's friends since they were all in the first grade. Besides, Maria was eager for news from Randi about a junkie they both knew who was doing time in prison. Finally, Maria changed her mind. She didn't go to the wake, but drove her Volkswagen to the two-story tan stucco house at 124 Glenwood Avenue, the house of Mr. and Mrs. Dewitt Romaine.

While at the Romaine house Maria was murdered by the man whose rampage was the subject of the book. Among the variety of claims pressed by several plaintiffs in this suit, we concern ourselves with Randi Romaine's libel claim against the publisher and author. The trial court granted defendants' motion for summary judgment and the Appellate Division affirmed.]

HANDLER, J.

. . .

According to plaintiffs, one sentence in the passage falsely depicts the reason for Ms. Fasching's visit: "Besides, Maria was eager for news from Randi about a junkie they both knew who was doing time in prison." . . .

Plaintiff Randi Romaine asserts that the particular sentence is defamatory as a matter of law, or alternatively, that the statement's defamatory content was at least a question for the jury. She claims this sentence falsely accuses her of criminality or associations with criminals. Plaintiff also contends that the false accusation was particularly damaging because it injured Ms. Romaine's professional reputation as a drug counselor and a social worker, interfering with her ability to obtain future employment.

A defamatory statement is one that is false and "injurious to the reputation of another" or exposes another person to "hatred, contempt or ridicule" or subjects another person to "a loss of the good will and confidence" in which he or she is held by others. [ ]; see W. Keeton, D. Dobbs, R. Keeton & D. Owen, Prosser and Keeton on the Law of Torts, § 111 at 773–78 (5th ed. 1984); see also Restatement (Second) of Torts § 559 (1977) (a defamatory communication is one that "tends so to harm the reputation of another as to lower him in the estimation of the community or to deter third persons from associating or dealing with him.")

The threshold issue in any defamation case is whether the statement at issue is reasonably susceptible of a defamatory meaning. [ ] This question is one to be decided first by the court. [ ] In making this determination, the court must evaluate the language in question "according to the fair and natural meaning which will be given it by reasonable persons of ordinary intelligence." Herrmann v. Newark Morning Ledger Co., 48 N.J. Super. 420, 431 (App. Div.), aff'd on rehearing 49 N.J.Super. 551 (App. Div. 1958), [ ]. In assessing the language, the court must view the publication as a whole and consider particularly the context in which the statement appears. [ ]

If a published statement is susceptible of one meaning only, and that meaning is defamatory, the statement is libelous as a matter of law. [ ] Conversely, if the statement is susceptible of only a non-defamatory meaning, it cannot be considered libelous, justifying dismissal of the action. [ ] However, in cases where the statement is capable of being assigned more than one meaning, one of which is defamatory and another not, the question of whether its content is defamatory is one that must be resolved by the trier of fact. [ ]

Certain kinds of statements denote such defamatory meaning that they are considered defamatory as a matter of law. A prime example is the false attribution of criminality. [ ] Lawrence v. Bauer Publishing & Printing Ltd. [89 N.J. 451, 446 A.2d 469, 8 Med. L. Rptr. 1536 (1982)] (statement that plaintiff might be charged with criminal conduct defamatory as a matter of law). Relying essentially on this example of defamation, plaintiff Randi Romaine contends in this case that the published offending statement must be considered libelous per se. According to Ms. Romaine, the sentence has only a defamatory meaning, in that it accuses her of having engaged in criminal conduct or having associated with criminals relating to drugs.

The trial court concluded, and the Appellate Division agreed, that only the most contorted reading of the offending language could lead to the conclusion that it accuses plaintiff of illegal drug use or criminal associations. We concur in the determinations of the courts below. "[A]ccording to the fair and natural meaning which will be given [this statement] by reasonable persons of ordinary intelligence," [ ] it does not attribute any kind of criminality to plaintiff. A reasonable and fair understanding of the statement simply does not yield an interpretation that the plaintiff was or had been in illegal possession of drugs or otherwise engaging in any illegal drug-related activity. See Valentine v. C.B.S., Inc., 698 F.2d 430, 432 (11th Cir. 1983) ("The Plaintiff's interpretation does not construe the words as the common mind would understand them but is tortured and extreme."); Forsher v. Bugliosi, 26 Cal.3d 792, 805, 698 P.2d 716, 723, 163 Cal. Rptr. 628, 635 (1980) ("the claimed defamatory nature of the book as it relates to appellant is so obscure and attenuated as to be beyond the realm of reasonableness").

At most, the sentence can be read to imply that plaintiff knew a junkie. Even if we assume that a commonly accepted and well-understood meaning of the term "junkie" is "a narcotics peddler or addict," [citing dictionaries], the statement still does not suggest either direct or indirect involvement by plaintiff herself in any criminal drug-related activities. Absent exceptional circumstances, the mere allegation that plaintiff knows a criminal is not defamatory as a matter of law. See, e.g., Gonzales v. Times Herald Printing Company, 513 S.W.2d 124 (Tex. Civ. App. 1974) (statement that plaintiff's husband was engaged in the sale and importation of narcotics did not defame her); Rose v. Daily Mirror, Inc., 284 N.Y. 335, 31 N.E.2d 182 (1940) [ ] (plaintiff not defamed by being mistakenly described as the widow of a mobster); cf. Bufalino v. Associated Press, 692 F.2d 266 (2d Cir. 1982) (mere imputation of family relationship with Mafia leader not defamatory; characterization of plaintiff as a political contributor with alleged mob ties found to have a potentially defamatory meaning), [ ].

Beyond the language itself, we are satisfied that the statement in its contextual setting cannot fairly and reasonably be invested with any defamatory meaning. Maria Fasching, we note, is described in the chapter as a person who had compassion for others and who would care for less fortunate persons. The reasonable meaning of the critical sentence that is implied from this context is that Ms. Fasching's interest in the "junkie" stemmed from sympathy and compassion, not from any predilection toward or involvement in criminal drug activity. As extended to Randi Romaine, the only fair inference to be drawn from the larger context is that Ms. Romaine shared her friend's feelings, attitudes and interests, and that her own interest in the junkie was similar to that of Ms. Fasching's.

We note the further contention that this statement had a defamatory meaning because it implied that the only reason for Ms. Fasching's visit to the Romaine home was her "interest" in news about a "junkie." A review of the full text, however, indicates that there were several reasons for the visit, only one of which was Ms. Fasching's interest in the "junkie." The lower courts soundly rejected this contention.

We conclude that the statement is not defamatory as a matter of law and accordingly uphold the ruling of the lower court on this point.

. . .

[Justice O'Hern dissented on this point, contending that the passage was ambiguous and "reasonably susceptible of a defamatory meaning" and thus presented a jury question.]

Notes and Questions

1. In a negligence case, there would be no cause of action unless the plaintiff could show that he or she had been injured. Here the court shows no interest in that question. The initial question is not whether the statement caused injury, but whether it is defamatory. Note that none of the definitions the court quotes asks whether the statement actually caused injury. The explanation may be that libel and slander were crimes before they were torts, or it may be that at the time they became torts, tort law focused more on wrongs than on injuries. Would it be better to begin the analysis of a defamation case by asking whether the statement caused harm instead of asking whether the words are of a sort that tend to cause harm? Keep this question in mind as we see more of the consequences of this peculiarity of defamation law.

2. The case is decided on the basis of hypothetical questions: How "could" or "would" the statement have been interpreted. The court alludes to no evidence as to how the statement actually *was* interpreted by those who read it. Again, this is typical of the way this issue is usually framed. Why is it unnecessary at this stage to know how the statement was actually understood?

3. Whether the statement complained of is defamatory often requires two quite different inquiries: What does the statement mean, and is the imputation (i.e., the meaning ascribed to the statement by the outcome of the first inquiry) one the law makes actionable? As in the principal case, courts usually collapse these into a single issue: Is the statement capable of a defamatory meaning? The court does this in the principal case, even though both parts of the issue are contested. The court avoids deciding the meaning issue by holding that even if the words are interpreted as the plaintiff suggests, the law does not make them actionable. The following

discussion attempts to keep these two inquiries separate, but jury instructions and judicial opinions often collapse them into one.

1.   WHAT DO THE WORDS MEAN?

Evaluating the language. The opinion says "the court must evaluate the language in question 'according to the fair and natural meaning which will be given it by reasonable persons of ordinary intelligence.'" Why is that the standard—as opposed, say, to the "most impressionable" readers? Or the "most intelligent" readers? Or the type of readers at whom the book was aimed? Is the court employing a type of "reasonable person" test, or is this a test that allows the court to make its own substantive judgment about the meaning of the statement?

Implications. Note that neither of the defamatory meanings that the plaintiff alleges is explicit. If the sentence accuses her of criminality or of associating with criminals, those are implications arising from the assertion that she knew a junkie. "Libel by implication" is sometimes discussed as if it were a special or unusual subspecies of defamation, but in fact it is quite common. Words rarely do their work without the assistance of inferences. As in the principal case, courts usually do not distinguish between the explicit and implicit messages that a statement conveys. Implications do require special consideration, however, when the defendant says it did not recognize or intend the implication that the plaintiff claims. That problem is addressed later in this chapter when we consider fault issues.

Extrinsic information. Sometimes a statement innocent on its face takes on a defamatory meaning because of extrinsic information known to recipients of the statement. For example, suppose an article stated only that the plaintiff had often been seen at "123 Hay Road," but some (or all) of the readers knew that there was a brothel at that address. A plaintiff is allowed to show extrinsic facts that would explain why the statement would be understood in a defamatory sense by those who knew the unstated facts—e.g., that 123 Hay Road is known to be a brothel. Such extrinsic information is called the "inducement" and the inference that may be drawn by those who know the facts (in this example, the inference that plaintiff patronizes prostitutes) is called the "innuendo." In England libel plaintiffs must specifically plead the inducement and innuendo if they wish to claim a defamatory meaning not apparent on the face of the publication. In the United States those formalities are rarely required (although analysis might be clearer if they were), but reliance on extrinsic facts does have one consequence that we shall consider shortly.

Ambiguity. Words often have more than one meaning, and one of those may be defamatory while other meanings of the same word are not. A classic example is the word "gay," which once meant (and still can mean) "exuberant," but now more often means homosexual. In *Romaine* the court says it is for the trier of fact to decide whether ambiguous statements would be understood in a defamatory or non-defamatory sense, and most courts agree. A few states, however, embrace an "innocent construction rule," which holds that if the statement can reasonably be construed in an innocent sense when the words are given their natural and obvious meaning, it is not actionable. See, e.g., Anderson v. Vanden Dorpel, 172 Ill.2d 399, 667 N.E.2d 1296, 217 Ill.Dec. 720 (1996), in which the court held that a former employer's statement in a job reference that the plaintiff-employee failed to follow up on assignments was not actionable because it could mean only that "the plaintiff did not fit in with the organization of the employer making the assessment and failed to perform well in that particular job setting."

Context. The *Romaine* court said "the court must view the publication as a whole." If the recipients can be assumed to have read the entire publication, that makes obvious sense. A single passage should not be actionable if it is surrounded by material that removes the defamatory sting of the pinpointed passage. But often it cannot be assumed that every recipient received the exculpating information. Headlines, captions, and teasers, for example, cannot tell the full story, and sometimes the truncated message they convey is defamatory. In what is probably a concession to the practical needs of journalism, courts usually deny recovery unless the juxtaposition of headline and text makes it difficult to indulge the fiction that recipients will ingest the publication whole.

One of the few cases allowing a plaintiff to pursue a claim for a defamatory headline is Kaelin v. Globe Communications Corp., 162 F.3d 1036, 27 Med. L. Rptr. 1142 (9th Cir. 1998).

A week after O. J. Simpson was acquitted of murder in 1995, the National Examiner carried a page one headline that read, "COPS THINK KATO DID IT!" A subhead said ". . . he fears they want him for perjury, pals say." A story on page 17 said that friends of Kato Kaelin, Simpson's houseguest at the time of the murders, feared that police would try to prove that Kaelin did not tell the truth about events the night of the murders. Kaelin sued on the theory that the headline implied that he was suspected of committing the murders, which the newspaper conceded was false. Defendants argued that that implication was negated by the subhead on page one or by the story on page 17.

The court held that the subhead did not remove the defamatory implication of the headline because readers could have understood that Kaelin was suspected of both murder and perjury. As to the text of the story,

> The Kaelin story was located 17 pages away from the cover. In this respect, the National Examiner's front page headline is unlike a conventional headline that immediately precedes a newspaper story, and nowhere does the cover headline reference the internal page where readers could locate the article. A reasonable juror could conclude that the Kaelin article was too far removed from the cover headline to have the salutary effect that [the defendant] claims.

Tabloids often print cover headlines that refer to stories located inside. Is the effect of this decision to create one rule for "conventional headlines" and another for the headlines that are typical of tabloids?

2.   IS THE ASCRIBED MEANING DEFAMATORY?

Once the meaning of the statement has been determined, there remains the question: is the statement of a sort that the law makes actionable as defamation? As a matter of policy, the law refuses to make actionable many statements that harm reputation. "Defamatory" is a term of art that encompasses social, practical, and jurisprudential considerations as well as free speech values.

Opprobrium. Recall the definitions of "defamatory" that were quoted in *Romaine.* One suggested that a statement is defamatory if it subjects a person to loss of good will or confidence. Another included statements that would deter third persons from associating or dealing with the person. These definitions must be viewed with some skepticism. It is not defamatory to state erroneously that a person is dead or that a professional person is battling cancer, even though such statements might well cause loss of good will or confidence and seem quite likely to deter third parties from dealing with the plaintiff. See Decker v. Princeton Packet, Inc., 116 N.J. 418, 561 A.2d 1122, 16 Med. L. Rptr. 2194 (1989) (death); Golub v. Enquirer/Star Group, Inc., 89 N.Y.2d 1074, 681 N.E.2d 1282, 659 N.Y.S.2d 836, 25 Med. L. Rptr. 1863 (1997) (cancer).

Some older definitions suggest that words are defamatory if they subject a person to scorn, ridicule, or obloquy, but those too seem inaccurate. Epithets and insults are not actionable, and obloquy is not necessarily so. For example, in Ward v. Zelikovsky, 136 N.J. 516, 643 A.2d 972 (N.J. 1994), the court held that it was not defamatory to call a woman a "bitch" or to say that she hated Jews. The same is true of non-specific accusations of racism or bigotry. See, e.g., Stevens v. Tillman, 855 F.2d 394 (7th Cir. 1988). The rationale of these decisions is not that such accusations are incapable of harming reputation, but that making them actionable would unduly inhibit speech. As the *Ward* court said, "The most important reason [for denying a cause of action] is the chilling effect such a holding would cast over a person's freedom of expression."

Today a statement is not likely to be actionable as defamation unless it suggests some moral opprobrium. A more accurate definition than those mentioned above might be one used in New York: a defamatory statement is one that "tends to expose a person to hatred, contempt or aversion, or to induce an evil or unsavory opinion of him in the minds of a substantial number in the community." See Nichols v. Item Publishers, Inc., 309 N.Y. 596, 132 N.E.2d 860 (1956).

Divergent values. Whether a statement is defamatory is a value-laden inquiry, and moral values are not universally shared. Some people, perhaps most, would think it laudable for a prisoner to inform prison authorities about illegal activities by other inmates. But the prison population may view the matter very differently—indeed, so differently that a false accusation that a prisoner was an informer might prove fatal. The definition quoted in the preceding paragraph contains one response to this problem: does the statement induce an unsavory opinion of the plaintiff *in the minds of a substantial number in the community.* But that of course depends on how the community is defined. If it means the prison community (as it might if the charge is made in the prison newspaper), the "substantial number" requirement might be met.

But the law imposes an additional requirement. Traditionally the courts said the matter must be viewed from the perspective of "right-thinking" people. See, e.g., Kimmerle v. New York Evening Journal, Inc., 262 N.Y. 99, 186 N.E. 217 (1933). A more modern expression of the same idea is that a statement is not defamatory unless it would tend to prejudice the plaintiff "in the eyes of a substantial and respectable minority of the community." See Restatement (Second) of Torts § 559, comment *e.* This has allowed the courts to hold that it is not defamatory to call a prison inmate an informer. See Robert D. Sack, Sack on Defamation 2–22 n. 86 (3d ed. 1999). We shall explore this issue further in Matherson v. Marchello, infra p. 263.

Humor. Can a person be defamed by a joke, satire, or parody? As in the cases involving defamatory headlines, it is not enough to show that the statement was understood in a defamatory sense by some recipients. See New Times Inc. v. Isaacks, 146 S.W.3d 144, 32 Med. L. Rptr. 2480 (Tex. 2004). A seventh-grader was arrested and held in a juvenile detention center for five days after he wrote an assigned Halloween story that the principal thought contained terroristic threats. An alternative newspaper spoofed the episode with a story called "Stop the Madness" which depicted the fictitious jailing of a six-year-old for writing a book report about cannibalism and fanaticism. It attributed made-up quotes to the juvenile judge who had jailed the seventh-grader and the district attorney who had defended the judge's action.

The judge and the district attorney sued, claiming some readers believed they had actually jailed the six-year-old and said the things attributed to them. Lower courts denied the newspaper's summary judgment motion on the ground that the story failed to provide adequate notice that it was satire or parody. The Texas Supreme Court reversed:

> The court of appeals has underestimated the "reasonable reader." As the relevant cases show, the hypothetical reasonable person—the mythic Cheshire cat who darts about the pages of the tort law—is no dullard. He or she does not represent the lowest common denominator, but reasonable intelligence and learning. He or she can tell the difference between satire and sincerity. . . .
>
> The appropriate inquiry is objective, not subjective. Thus, the question is not whether some actual readers were mislead, as they inevitably will be, but whether the hypothetical reasonable reader could be. [ ] Thus, we focus on a single objective inquiry: whether the satire can be reasonably understood as stating actual fact. . . .
>
> This is not the same as asking whether all readers actually understood the satire, or "got the joke." Intelligent, well-read people act unreasonably from time to time, while the hypothetical reasonable

reader, for purposes of defamation law, does not. In a case of parody or satire, courts must analyze the words at issue with detachment and dispassion, considering them in context and as a whole, as a reasonable reader would consider them.

The court said although readers who read only the first few sentences of the spoof might think it recounted actual facts, those who read the entire story would realize it was satire.

Compare Mitchell v. Globe International Publishing Co., 773 F. Supp. 1235, 19 Med. L. Rptr. 1405 (W.D. Ark. 1991). Under the headline "World's oldest newspaper carrier, 101, quits because she's pregnant!" the Sun, a supermarket tabloid, published a story saying that a woman who had been delivering papers in Australia for 94 years became pregnant by a man she met on her paper route. The story was accompanied by a photo of plaintiff, a 96–year old newsstand operator in Mountain Home, Arkansas. The defendant argued that the story could not be understood in a defamatory sense because "every one is well aware that it is physically impossible for a 101– or 96–year-old woman to be pregnant," but the court disagreed. Even if the facts stated in the headline could not be believed, the implication of sexual promiscuity could, the judge said. "The articles are written in a purportedly factual manner. . . . The Sun apparently intends for the readers to determine which articles are fact and which are fiction or what percentage of a given article is fact or fiction." The case proceeded to trial and a jury returned a general verdict for the newspaper on the libel claim but awarded Mitchell substantial damages on the alternate theory of false light invasion of privacy. This is discussed in Chapter V.

Sometimes the question in these cases is merely one of meaning: could it be taken seriously or not? More often, as in *Mitchell v. Globe*, the issue is how much of it could be taken seriously. Satire and parody work only if the recipients believe there is *some* truth in what's said. In these cases the question is not so much whether the meaning is defamatory as whether the law should subject these forms of expression to the same straight-faced analysis that it applies to news reporting and other more literal forms of expression.

Figurative speech. A statement is not actionable if it cannot reasonably be interpreted as stating actual facts about a person. This rule immunizes several different types of statements. One is statements too fantastic or improbable to be believed. See, e.g., Pring v. Penthouse International Ltd., 695 F.2d 438, 8 Med. L. Rptr. 2409 (10th Cir. 1982) (denying liability for implication that Miss America contestant was able to levitate men by oral sex). Another is words used in "a loose figurative sense." Thus, it was not actionable to use Jack London's famous definition of a scab—"a traitor to his God, his country, his family and his class"—to describe plaintiff. See Letter Carriers v. Austin, 418 U.S. 264 (1974).

Yet another type of speech immunized by this rule is rhetorical hyperbole. A newspaper published a citizen's charge that plaintiff was "blackmailing" the city in connection with pending real estate negotiations. The Supreme Court held that the First Amendment precluded the state from treating this as actionable defamation. Although in some contexts a charge of "blackmail" might be understood as charging a specific crime, that was not true in this case. The word was "no more than rhetorical hyperbole, a vigorous epithet used by those who considered Bresler's vigorous negotiating position extremely unreasonable." Greenbelt Cooperative Publishing Ass'n v. Bresler, 398 U.S. 6, 1 Med. L. Rptr. 1589 (1970). The actual holding may have been only that such a statement could not meet the constitutional fault requirements that the Court had imposed in certain kinds of defamation cases. But the decision generally has been treated as having established an independent First Amendment rule that rhetorical hyperbole is not actionable, and eventually the Court itself seemed to endorse that reading. See Milkovich v. Lorain Journal Co., 497 U.S. 1, 17 Med. L. Rptr. 2009 (1990). These cases and their significance are discussed in further detail in Section F.

For an extensive consideration of the nature of defamation and the interests the law might seek to vindicate, see Robert C. Post, The Social Foundations of Defamation Law: Reputation and the Constitution, 74 Cal. L. Rev. 691 (1986).

3.   ROLES OF JUDGE AND JURY

The *Romaine* court suggests that the court's role is only to determine whether the statement is "clearly defamatory" or "clearly not defamatory," and that all other questions are for the jury. As the preceding notes indicate, the matter is not quite that simple. Is it "clearly not defamatory" to say that a person is dead or has cancer or hates Jews? Reasonable people might well disagree as to whether those imputations are harmful to reputation. Similarly, reasonable people might well disagree as to how "right-thinking people" feel about communism or homosexuality. Yet the courts typically make these decisions themselves instead of submitting them to a jury. The reasons for this judicial assertiveness are rarely articulated. Perhaps it is because judges believe that they are at least as well equipped as jurors to determine the meaning of words and assess their effect; that is, after all, what judges spend most of their time doing. It may also reflect a belief that what is actionable as defamation is freighted with policy considerations. The law could treat epithets and insults as defamation, but judges may believe they have better things to do. It could make humor or hyperbole actionable when someone fails to get the joke or misunderstands the nonliteral use of language, but that would exact a price in terms of richness and diversity of expression. Whatever the reasons, the inquiry usually made in determining whether a question is for the jury—could reasonable minds differ?—is of limited help in determining the jury's role here.

It is clear, however, that the judge and jury are answering different questions. The first question, always for the judge, is whether the statement is "capable of a defamatory meaning," that is, whether it is one the law allows a defamation plaintiff to complain about. The answer here may be "no" because the judge believes no reasonable person could interpret the statement as the plaintiff urges, or it may be "no" for any of the more complex reasons suggested above. In either event, the case goes no further;

if the statement is held to be incapable of a defamatory meaning, the case is dismissed. The second question is reached only if the judge's answer to the first question is "yes." If the judge holds that the statement is capable of a defamatory meaning, then the jury decides whether it was in fact defamatory under all the circumstances of the case. This determination may involve interpretation of ambiguous language or evaluation of context or community mores. Or it may simply reflect the jury's disagreement with the judge. Having already held that the statement is capable of a defamatory meaning, there is little room for the judge to overturn such a determination.

Because so many factors can remove the sting of an apparently defamatory statement, judges infrequently hold that a statement is defamatory as a matter of law. On the other hand, they often hold that a particular allegation is "not defamatory as a matter of law." Note that this phrase could mean that the court is declaring as a matter of law that the statement is not defamatory, or that the court is declining to hold that the statement is defamatory as a matter of law. Which meaning of this phrase did the court intend in *Romaine*?

B. SPECIAL DAMAGES, SLANDER PER SE, AND LIBEL PER QUOD

1. SLANDER PER SE

In most cases, the principles outlined in the preceding section determine whether the statement is within the ambit of the law of defamation, and courts make that decision without inquiring into the nature or extent of the plaintiff's harm. In a few subsets of defamation cases, however, the courts hold that even if a plaintiff establishes that the statement is defamatory under these principles, recovery is barred unless the plaintiff shows "special harm." Up to this point it has been unnecessary to distinguish between libel and slander, but now we must do so, because whether a plaintiff must show special harm depends largely on whether the case is classified as libel or slander.

In slander, the general rule is that a plaintiff has no cause of action unless the statement is (1) defamatory, and (2) causes demonstrable pecuniary loss, or "special harm." An exception (which nearly swallows the rule) allows recovery without proof of special harm if the statement is "slanderous per se." The concepts of "special harm" and "per se" are generally relevant only in slander cases, but occasionally they creep into libel cases. How the distinction between libel and slander is drawn, and the effect of that distinction on the special harm requirement, are issues in the following case.

Matherson v. Marchello

New York Appellate Division, Second Department, 1984.
100 A.D.2d 233, 473 N.Y.S.2d 998.

TITONE, J.P.

. . .

On October 28, 1980, radio station WBAB conducted an interview with the members of a singing group called "The Good Rats." Following a commercial which advertised a Halloween party at an establishment known as "OBI", a discussion ensued in which various members of the group explained that they are no longer permitted to play at OBI South because:

> "Good Rat #1: Well, you know, we had that law suit with Mr. Matherson.
>
> "A Good Rat: And we used to fool around with his wife.
>
> "Good Rat #1: And we won.
>
> "A Good Rat: One of us used to fool around with his wife. He wasn't into that too much.
>
> "D. J.: Oh yea.
>
> "Good Rat #1: (interrupted and joined by another Good Rat) We used to start off our gigs over there with the National Anthem, and he was very upset about that, now all of a sudden he's very patriotic and he's using it in his commercials.
>
> "A Good Rat: I don't think it was his wife that he got so upset about, I think it was when somebody started messing around with his boyfriend that he really freaked out. Really.
>
> (Laughter)
>
> "That did it man."

Plaintiffs, who are husband and wife, subsequently commenced this action against "The Good Rats" (as individuals and against their record company), alleging that the words "we used to fool around with his wife" and "I don't think it was his wife that he got upset about, I think it was when somebody started messing around with his boyfriend that he really freaked out" were defamatory. They seek compensatory and punitive damages for humiliation, mental anguish, loss of reputation and injury to their marital relationship as well as for the loss of customers, business opportunities and good will allegedly suffered by Mr. Matherson. [The lower court] granted defendants' motion to dismiss. . . .

Preliminarily, we observe that if special damages are a necessary ingredient of plaintiffs' cause of action, Special Term properly found the allegations of the complaint to be deficient.

Special damages consist of "the loss of something having economic or pecuniary value" (Restatement, Torts 2d, § 575, comment *b*) which "must flow directly from the injury to reputation caused by the defamation; not from the [emotional] effects of defamation" (Sack, Libel, Slander, and Related Problems, § VII.2.2, 345–346; [ ]) and it is settled law that they must be fully and accurately identified "with sufficient particularity to identify actual losses" [ ]. When loss of business is claimed, the persons who ceased to be customers must be named and the losses itemized [ ]. "Round figures" or a general allegation of a dollar amount as special damages do not suffice [ ]. Consequently, plaintiffs' non-specific conclusory allegations do not meet the stringent requirements imposed for pleading special damages [ ].

We must, therefore, determine whether an allegation of special damages is necessary. In large measure, this turns on which branch of the law of defamation is involved. As a result of historical accident, which, though not sensibly defensible today, is so well settled as to be beyond our ability to uproot it [ ], there is a schism between the law governing slander and the law governing libel [ ].[1]

A plaintiff suing in slander must plead special damages unless the defamation falls into any one of four per se categories [ ]. Those categories consist of allegations (1) that the plaintiff committed a crime [ ], (2) that tend to injure the plaintiff in his or her trade, business or profession [ ], (3) that plaintiff has contracted a loathsome disease [ ], and (4) that impute unchastity to a woman [ ].[2] The exceptions were established apparently for no other reason than a recognition that by their nature the accusations encompassed therein would be likely to cause material damage [ ].

On the other hand, a plaintiff suing in libel need not plead or prove special damages. . . .[3] Thus, unlike the law of slander, in the law of libel the existence of damage is conclusively presumed from the publication itself and a plaintiff may rely on general damages. . . .

. . .

Traditionally, the demarcation between libel and slander rested upon whether the words were written or spoken [ ]. Written defamations were considered far more serious because, at the time the distinction arose, few persons could read or write and, therefore, anything which was written would carry a louder ring of purported truth [ ]. In addition, a written defamation could be disseminated more widely and carried a degree of permanence.

With the advent of mass communication, the differential was blurred. Motion pictures were held to be libel [ ]. No set rule developed with respect

---

1. . . . The distinction has . . . not gone unchallenged. As early as 1812, a defendant urged that a libel read by one person should not be treated more harshly than a slander spoken to hundreds in a crowd. While the Judge conceded the merits of the argument, he refused to overturn the firmly rooted contrary precedents. Thorley v. Lord Kerry [4 Taunt. 355, 128 Eng. Rep. 367 (1812)].

2. The first three categories were established relatively early. The fourth is of more recent vintage, having first been put into effect in England by the Slander of Women Act of 1891. . . . We do not view these categories as fixed or rigid and, in appropriate circumstances, a new category may be judicially established [ ].

3. We have avoided the use of the terms libel per se and libel per quod because, as explained in this footnote, the cases and commentators are divided on the question of whether any meaningful distinction exists between the two. It is clear that when the defamatory import is apparent from the face of the publication itself without resort to any other source, the libel, often referred to as libel per se, is actionable without proof of special harm [ ]. Libel per quod, on the other hand, has been traditionally defined as an encompassing libel in which the defamatory import can only be ascertained by reference to facts not set forth in the publication [ ].

to radio and television [ ]. In some cases, distinction was drawn between [extemporaneous] speech, which was classified as slander, and words read from a script, which were classified as libel [ ]. This distinction was the subject of considerable criticism. [ ]

We today hold that defamation which is broadcast by means of radio or television should be classified as libel. As we have noted, one of the primary reasons assigned to justify the imposition of broader liability for libel than for slander has been the greater capacity for harm that a writing is assumed to have because of the wide range of dissemination consequent upon its permanence in form. Given the vast and far-flung audiences reached by the broadcasting media today, it is self-evident that the potential harm to a defamed person is far greater than that involved in a single writing (see Hartmann v. Winchell, [296 N.Y. 296, 304, 73 N.E.2d 30 (1947)], Fuld, J. concurring). Section 568A of the Restatement of Torts, Second, and the more recent decisions in sister States [ ] opt for holding such defamation to be libel and we perceive no basis for perpetuating a meaningless, outmoded, distinction.

On the question of whether the allegedly defamatory statements are actionable, our scope of review is limited. . . . Unless we can say, as a matter of law, that the statements could not have had a defamatory connotation, it is for the jury to decide whether or not they did [ ].

Taken in the context of a rock and roll station's interview with musicians, and taking note of contemporary usage, we have no difficulty in concluding that the words "fooling around with his wife" could have been interpreted by listeners to mean that Mrs. Matherson was having an affair with one of the defendants. Such charges are clearly libelous. . . .

The second comment—"I don't think it was his wife that he got upset about, I think it was when somebody started messing around with his boyfriend that he really freaked out"—presents a far more subtle and difficult question (see Imputation of Homosexuality as Defamation, Ann., 3 A.L.R.4th 752). [Defendants] claim that many public officials have acknowledged their homosexuality and, therefore, no social stigma may be attached to such an allegation. We are constrained to reject defendants' position at this time.

It cannot be said that social opprobrium of homosexuality does not remain with us today. Rightly or wrongly, many individuals still view homosexuality as immoral (see Newsweek Aug. 8, 1983, p. 33, containing the results of a Gallup poll; [ ]). Legal sanctions imposed upon homosexuals in areas ranging from immigration (Matter of Longstaff, 716 F.2d 1439) to military service (Watkins v. United States Army, 721 F.2d 687) have recently been reaffirmed despite the concurring Judge's observation in *Watkins* [ ] that it "demonstrates a callous disregard for the progress American law and society have made toward acknowledging that an individual's choice of life style is not the concern of government, but a fundamental aspect of personal liberty" [ ].

In short, despite the fact that an increasing number of homosexuals are publicly expressing satisfaction and even pride in their status, the potential and probable harm of a false charge of homosexuality, in terms of social and economic impact, cannot be ignored. . . .

[Since both statements were to be treated as libel rather than slander, plaintiff was not required to prove special damages, so the judgment of the trial court was reversed.]

THOMPSON, BRACKEN, and RUBIN, JJ., concur.

Notes and Questions

1. Which of the justifications offered for the differing treatment of written and oral defamation is strongest? In addition to those offered by the court, consider the possibility that a writing might be given more weight because it requires more thought and planning than a spontaneous oral utterance, which might simply be tossed off. (California, by statute—Cal. Civil Code §§ 46, 48.5(4)—treats defamations by radio and television as slander.) Defamation on the Internet is generally assumed to be libel. See Lyrissa Barnett Lidsky, Silencing John Doe: Defamation and Discourse in Cyberspace, 49 Duke L.J. 855, 859 n. 7 (2000).

2. Because the court decided to treat broadcast defamation as libel, it was unnecessary to decide whether the defamatory imputations would fit within one of the slander per se categories. The imputation that Mrs. Matherson committed adultery with one of the Good Rats obviously would seem to clearly fall within the "unchastity of a woman" category. (But note that the trial judge thought Mrs. Matherson had to prove special harm; the opinion contains no explanation of this.)

What about the imputation of homosexuality regarding Mr. Matherson? The unspoken assumption of the common law seems to have been that accusing a man of unchastity was not sufficiently likely to cause material damage. But in this era of legal, if not actual, equality in sexual matters, such a distinction is untenable. A few states have responded by redefining the category to make it gender neutral. See, e.g., Nazeri v. Missouri Valley College, 860 S.W.2d 303 (Mo. 1993) (extending the fourth category to any "serious sexual misconduct," following § 569, comment *f* of the Restatement (Second) of Torts). Homosexuality, however, is not synonymous with either unchastity or sexual misconduct. Nevertheless, a number of courts have held that a charge of homosexuality is slanderous per se. Cases so holding are cited in *Nazeri*, supra.

3. Not all charges of crime suffice. In Liberman v. Gelstein, 80 N.Y.2d 429, 605 N.E.2d 344, 590 N.Y.S.2d 857, 21 Med. L. Rptr. 1079 (1992), the court noted that parking violations would not be serious enough. A charge of bribing local police to allow cars to be parked illegally sufficed, but a second charge, that "Liberman . . . threatened to kill me and my family" was not slanderous per se because at the time such threats were not serious crimes under New York law. Do these distinctions make sense?

4. As we saw previously, whether a statement is defamatory is viewed from the perspective of "right-thinking" people, or through "the eyes of a substantial and respectable minority of the community." As the principal case implies, what right-thinking or respectable people think may change over time. "Communist" seems to have gone from being non-defamatory before World War II to being defamatory during the McCarthy era and the Cold War, and perhaps now to being non-defamatory again. See Gottschalk v. State, 575 P.2d 289 (Alaska 1978). Although empirical evidence is relevant, it is not controlling; ultimately it is for the court to decide when a viewpoint is no longer respectable.

2.   LIBEL PER SE

This unfortunate term is used to mean at least three entirely different things. One meaning is parallel to slander per se—a written statement is libel per se if it falls within one of the four categories recognized in slander per se. This use of libel per se is simply erroneous. Historically libel never employed the categories of slander per se, and the reasons for employing those in slander were to avoid in that tort the full range of liabilities that existed in libel.

Those states that use "libel per se" in a sense parallel to "slander per se" also employ the special damages requirement in a parallel way: Plaintiffs whose libel does not fall into one of the four categories must prove special damages.

A second meaning is that the statement is defamatory as a matter of law, i.e., incapable of a non-defamatory meaning. This usage is analytically confused. Whether a statement is libelous depends on a great many issues other than whether it is defamatory—e.g., whether it is false, whether it is privileged, etc. A statement therefore may be defamatory as a matter of law without being libelous as a matter of law.

A third usage is to signify that the defamatory meaning is apparent on the face of the statement. In this usage, the essential meaning of "libel per se" is simply that the plaintiff need not plead and prove extrinsic facts. Courts that employ this usage call written statements that are defamatory on their face "libel per se," and use the term "libel per quod" to describe statements that are not defamatory on their face but may be defamatory because of extrinsic facts. See, e.g., Holtzscheiter v. Thomson Newspapers Inc., 332 S.C. 502, 506 S.E.2d 497, 26 Med. L. Rptr. 2537 (1998), holding that the only consequence of treating a statement as "libel per quod" was to permit the plaintiff to show the defamatory meaning of the statement through extrinsic evidence.

Some courts, however, attach a further consequence when the statement is not defamatory on its face. They hold that some or all cases of "libel per quod" require proof of special damages. Sometimes they require such proof in all cases where the statement is not defamatory on its face. Sometimes they require proof of special damages if the statement is not defamatory on its face *and* its innuendo does not fit within the slander per se categories. See Robert D. Sack, Sack on Defamation 2–98 (3d ed. 1999).

A few states have a special rule called "the single-instance rule" that requires proof of special damages in a narrow category of libel cases. New York courts take the position that accusing a physician or other professional of a single act of malpractice is not defamatory on its face, and therefore is not actionable unless special harm is shown, as long as the statement does not also impute "general ignorance, incompetence or lack of skill." See D'Agrosa v. Newsday, Inc., 158 A.D.2d 229, 558 N.Y.S.2d 961 (1990). This "single instance rule" is formally adopted only in a few states, but something like it probably is at work everywhere, in the sense that an accusation of incompetence or negligence is not *necessarily* actionable; all of us are incompetent in some things, and even the most competent people occasionally make mistakes.

Historically there was no special damages requirement in libel, and some states still do not impose one in libel cases of any kind. The courts that do so appear either to be confused about the relationship between libel and slander, or to have decided not to try to undo the results of previous confusion in their states. Extension of the special damage requirement beyond its historical role has little to commend it, particularly since the requirement functions only as a threshold, not a limit on recovery: even if special damages must be proven, a plaintiff who is able to do so is not limited to those damages, but becomes eligible for all of the damages that any other plaintiff might receive. See, e.g., Schaffer v. Zekman, 196 Ill. App.3d 727, 554 N.E.2d 988, 17 Med. L. Rptr. 1931 (1990).

C. IDENTIFICATION OF PLAINTIFF

The plaintiff must show that he or she was the person defamed or was among a group that was defamed. The early common law asked whether the statement was "of and concerning" the plaintiff, and libel lawyers perpetuate this archaic expression by talking about "the of-and-concerning issue." The question is actually quite straightforward: was the statement understood to refer to the plaintiff? Note that the question is not whether the defendant intended to refer to the plaintiff; that may be relevant on fault issues, but not on the identification issue. In most cases identification is not an issue at all, because the plaintiff is named or is identified visually or by reference to the position he or she holds. Identification of plaintiff becomes an issue principally in the three types of cases discussed below.

Identification by implication. A plaintiff may be identified by implications that arise either from the face of the publication or from extrinsic facts that tell at least some recipients of the message that it refers to the plaintiff. An example of the former is the juxtaposition of words and visual images in such a way that the words are understood to refer to the person pictured. See, e.g., Clark v. American Broadcasting Cos., Inc., 684 F.2d 1208, 8 Med. L. Rptr. 2049 (6th Cir. 1982). The defendant used videotape of street scenes to illustrate a report about prostitution. The plaintiff, who had been photographed without her knowledge while walking on a city street, was shown on the screen while the narrator was describing the prevalence of prostitution in the neighborhood. The implication was that she was a prostitute.

The plaintiff may be identified by physical characteristics or circumstances that are known to viewers or readers. In Bindrim v. Mitchell, 92 Cal.App.3d 61, 155 Cal.Rptr. 29, 5 Med. L. Rptr. 1113 (1979), the publication was a novel about a purportedly fictitious therapist. But although the plaintiff did not share the name or physical characteristics of the fictional character, some readers knew that the author had attended the plaintiff's therapy sessions and that he was the only therapist who used the techniques described in the novel. Proof of such extrinsic facts is sometimes called "colloquium."

For discussions of the special problems of identification of plaintiffs in works of fiction, see Symposium, Defamation in Fiction, 51 Brook. L. Rev. 223 (1985).

Group libel. Different problems arise when the statement is about a group of individuals. In such cases might one member be able to claim that the statement hurt his or her personal reputation? At the extreme, an attack on all lawyers in the United States or on all clergymen would be held to be such a general broadside that no individual lawyer or clergyman could sue.

There are at least two variables in these cases. One is the size of the group, and the other is the inclusiveness of the language. A charge made against a small group may defame all members of that group. For example, a newspaper article may assert that "the officers" of a corporation have embezzled funds. If there are only four officers of the corporation, each of them may be defamed, even though the statement is that "one of the officers of the corporation" had embezzled funds. The group is small enough so that all four officials are put under a shadow, and most states would permit all four to sue.

As the group grows larger the impact of the statement depends on the inclusiveness of the language as well as the size of the group. A book about Dallas stated that "some" Neiman–Marcus department store models were "call girls. . . . The salesgirls are good, too—pretty and often much cheaper. . . ." And "most of the [male] sales staff are fairies, too."

Suits were filed by all nine models, 30 of the 382 saleswomen, and 15 of the 25 salesmen. The defendants did not challenge the right of the nine models to sue. The other two groups were challenged as being too large.

The claim of "the salesgirls" was dismissed. The result would be the same even if the authors had explicitly referred to "all"—and even if all 382 had sued. The judge cited cases rejecting suits when the statements attacked all officials of a statewide union or all the taxicab drivers in Washington, D.C.

On the other hand, the salesmen's case was allowed to proceed. It was close to others involving members of a posse, or the 12 doctors on a hospital's residential staff. Neiman–Marcus v. Lait, 13 F.R.D. 311 (S.D.N.Y.

1952). Would the result have been the same if the authors had referred to "some" or "a few" of the men?

A few states have statutes purporting to make it a crime to defame a class of people because of their race or religion. The Supreme Court, 5–4, upheld the constitutionality of such a statute in Beauharnais v. Illinois, 343 U.S. 250 (1952), but their validity seems questionable after the *R.A.V.* case, supra p. 42.

Entities other than natural persons. Corporations do not have reputations in the full sense that individuals do, but they may sue for the types of reputational harm that they are capable of suffering. Section 561 of the Restatement (Second) of Torts states that a corporation for profit may sue if "the matter tends to prejudice it in the conduct of its business or to deter others from dealing with it." The same is true of partnerships and labor unions. A non-profit organization may sue if it "depends upon financial support from the public, and the matter tends to interfere with its activities by prejudicing it in public estimation."

Defamation of a corporation or other non-natural legal entity may defame the individuals who own or manage it, but only if the accusation implies that the individual was personally involved in or responsible for the matter that is the subject of the defamation. Thus, defamation of a closely held corporation may defame the major stockholder, particularly if the individual and the corporation have the same name. See discussion in Schiavone Construction Co. v. Time Inc., 619 F. Supp. 684, 12 Med. L. Rptr. 1153 (D. N.J. 1985), related appeal, 848 F.2d 43, 15 Med. L. Rptr. 1417 (2d Cir. 1988).

Governmental agencies and subdivisions generally cannot sue for defamation. See, e.g., College Savings Bank v. Florida Prepaid Postsecondary Educ. Expense Bd., 919 F. Supp. 756, 24 Med. L. Rptr. 1558 (D. N.J. 1996). The theory is that such suits would be a form of seditious libel, which was held to have been outlawed by the First Amendment in *New York Times v. Sullivan*, which follows.

D. FAULT

At common law, libel and slander were strict liability torts, in the sense that the plaintiff was not required to show that the defendant had been negligent or guilty of some other form of fault. By the middle of the twentieth century the possibility that liability without fault might be imposed for defamatory speech seemed increasingly troublesome from a First Amendment perspective.

In what became one of the most famous and important cases in all of constitutional jurisprudence, the Court decided that the common law of libel violated the First Amendment, at least when it was used by public officials against the media. The Court's solution to this problem was to require as a matter of First Amendment law a showing of fault—indeed, a high level of fault—with respect to the truth or falsity of the defamatory statement. Although this solution obviously implicated the falsity issue as well as fault, the Court did not focus explicitly on falsity. As we shall see in Section F, the impact on the falsity issue became apparent only later.

1.   ACTUAL MALICE

a. Public Officials

New York Times Co. v. Sullivan
(Together with Abernathy v. Sullivan)

Supreme Court of the United States, 1964.
376 U.S. 254, 84 S. Ct. 710, 11 L. Ed.2d 686, 1 Med. L. Rptr. 1527.

[This action was based on a full-page advertisement in the New York Times on behalf of several individuals and groups protesting a "wave of terror" against blacks involved in non-violent demonstrations in the South. Plaintiff, one of three elected commissioners of Montgomery, the capital of Alabama, was in charge of the police department. When he demanded a retraction, the Times responded that it failed to see how he was defamed, even though it did subsequently publish a retraction at the request of the Alabama governor, whose complaint was similar to Sullivan's. Plaintiff then filed suit against the Times and four clergymen whose names appeared in the ad. Plaintiff alleged that the third and the sixth paragraphs of the advertisement libeled him:

"In Montgomery, Alabama, after students sang 'My Country, 'Tis of Thee' on the State Capitol steps, their leaders were expelled from school, and truckloads of police armed with shotguns and teargas ringed the Alabama State College Campus. When the entire student body protested to state authorities by refusing to re-register, their dining hall was padlocked in an attempt to starve them into submission."

. . .

"Again and again the Southern violators have answered Dr. King's peaceful protests with intimidation and violence. They have bombed his home almost killing his wife and child. They have assaulted his person. They have arrested him seven times—for 'speeding,' 'loitering' and similar 'offenses.' And now they have charged him with 'perjury'—a *felony* under which they could imprison him for *ten years.* . . ."

Plaintiff claimed that he was libeled in the third paragraph by the reference to the police, since his responsibilities included supervision of the Montgomery police. He asserted that the paragraph could be read as charging the police with ringing the campus and seeking to starve the students by padlocking the dining hall. As to the sixth paragraph, he contended that the word "they" referred to his department since arrests are usually made by the police and the paragraph could be read as accusing him of committing the acts charged. Several witnesses testified that they read the statements as referring to plaintiff in his capacity as commissioner.]

[The defendants admitted several inaccuracies in these two paragraphs: the students sang The Star Spangled Banner, not My Country, 'Tis of Thee; nine students were expelled, not for leading the demonstration, but for demanding service at a lunch counter in the county courthouse; the dining hall was never padlocked; police at no time ringed the campus though they were deployed nearby in large numbers; they were not called to the campus in connection with the demonstration; Dr. King had been arrested only four times; and officers disputed his account of the alleged assault. Plaintiff proved that he had not been commissioner when three of the four arrests occurred and that he had nothing to do with procuring the perjury indictment.]

[The trial judge instructed the jury that the statements were libel per se, that the jury should decide whether they were made "of and concerning" the plaintiff and, if so, that general damages were to be presumed. Although noting that punitive damages required more than carelessness, he refused to charge that they required a finding of actual intent to harm or "gross negligence and recklessness." He also refused to order the jury to separate its award of general and punitive damages. The jury returned a verdict for $500,000—the full amount demanded. The Alabama Supreme Court affirmed, holding that malice could be found in several aspects of the Times' conduct.]

Mr. Justice Brennan delivered the opinion of the Court.

. . .

I.

We may dispose at the outset of two grounds asserted to insulate the judgment of the Alabama courts from constitutional scrutiny. The first is the proposition relied on by the State Supreme Court—that "The Fourteenth Amendment is directed against State action and not private action." That proposition has no application to this case. Although this is a civil lawsuit between private parties, the Alabama courts have applied a state rule of law which petitioners claim to impose invalid restrictions on their constitutional freedoms of speech and press. It matters not that that law has been applied in a civil action and that it is common law only, though supplemented by statute. [ ] The test is not the form in which state power has been applied but, whatever the form, whether such power has in fact been exercised. [ ]

The second contention is that the constitutional guarantees of freedom of speech and of the press are inapplicable here, at least so far as the Times is concerned, because the allegedly libelous statements were published as part of a paid, "commercial" advertisement. [The argument was rejected.]

II.

Under Alabama law as applied in this case, a publication is "libelous per se" if the words "tend to injure a person . . . in his reputation" or to "bring [him] into public contempt"; the trial court stated that the standard was met if the words are such as to "injure him in his public office, or impute misconduct to him in his office, or want of official integrity, or want of fidelity to a public trust. . . ." The jury must find that the words were published "of and concerning" the plaintiff, but where the plaintiff is a public official his place in the governmental hierarchy is sufficient evidence to support a finding that his reputation has been affected by statements that reflect upon the agency of which he is in charge. Once "libel per se" has been established, the defendant has no defense as to stated facts unless he can persuade the jury that they were true in all their particulars. [ ] His privilege of "fair comment" for expressions of opinion depends on the truth of the facts upon which the comment is based. [ ] Unless he can discharge the burden of proving truth, general damages are presumed, and may be awarded without proof of pecuniary injury. A showing of actual malice is apparently a prerequisite to recovery of punitive damages, and the defendant may in any event forestall a punitive award by a retraction meeting the statutory requirements. Good motives and belief in truth do not negate an inference of malice, but are relevant only in mitigation of punitive damages if the jury chooses to accord them weight. [ ]

The question before us is whether this rule of liability, as applied to an action brought by a public official against critics of his official conduct, abridges the freedom of speech and of the press that is guaranteed by the First and Fourteenth Amendments.

Respondent relies heavily, as did the Alabama courts, on statements of this Court to the effect that the Constitution does not protect libelous publications. Those statements do not foreclose our inquiry here. None of the cases sustained the use of libel laws to impose sanctions upon expression critical of the official conduct of public officials. . . . In deciding the question now, we are compelled by neither precedent nor policy to give any more weight to the epithet "libel" than we have to other "mere labels" of state law. NAACP v. Button, 371 U.S. 415, 429 (1963). Like insurrection, contempt, advocacy of unlawful acts, breach of the peace, obscenity, solicitation of legal business, and the various other formulae for the repression of expression that have been challenged in this Court, libel can claim no talismanic immunity from constitutional limitations. It must be measured by standards that satisfy the First Amendment.

The general proposition that freedom of expression upon public questions is secured by the First Amendment has long been settled by our decisions. . . . Mr. Justice Brandeis, in his concurring opinion in Whitney v. California, 274 U.S. 357, 375–376 (1927), gave the principle its classic formulation:

> Those who won our independence believed . . . that public discussion is a political duty; and that this should be a fundamental principle of the American government. . . . Believing in the power of reason as applied through public discussion, they eschewed silence coerced by law—the argument of force in its worst form. Recognizing the occa-

sional tyrannies of governing majorities, they amended the Constitution so that free speech and assembly should be guaranteed.

Thus we consider this case against the background of a profound national commitment to the principle that debate on public issues should be uninhibited, robust, and wide-open, and that it may well include vehement, caustic, and sometimes unpleasantly sharp attacks on government and public officials. See Terminiello v. Chicago, 337 U.S. 1, 4 (1949); De Jonge v. Oregon, 299 U.S. 353, 365 (1937). The present advertisement, as an expression of grievance and protest on one of the major public issues of our time, would seem clearly to qualify for the constitutional protection. The question is whether it forfeits that protection by the falsity of some of its factual statements and by its alleged defamation of respondent.

Authoritative interpretations of the First Amendment guarantees have consistently refused to recognize an exception for any test of truth—whether administered by judges, juries, or administrative officials—and especially one that puts the burden of proving truth on the speaker. Cf. Speiser v. Randall, 357 U.S. 513, 525–526 (1958). The constitutional protection does not turn upon "the truth, popularity, or social utility of the ideas and beliefs which are offered." NAACP v. Button, 371 U.S. 415, 445 (1963). As Madison said, "Some degree of abuse is inseparable from the proper use of every thing; and in no instance is this more true than in that of the press." 4 Elliot's Debates on the Federal Constitution (1876), p. 571. In Cantwell v. Connecticut, 310 U.S. 296, 310 (1940), the Court declared:

> In the realm of religious faith, and in that of political belief, sharp differences arise. In both fields the tenets of one man may seem the rankest error to his neighbor. To persuade others to his own point of view, the pleader, as we know, at times, resorts to exaggeration, to vilification of men who have been, or are, prominent in church or state, and even to false statement. But the people of this nation have ordained in the light of history, that, in spite of the probability of excesses and abuses, these liberties are, in the long view, essential to enlightened opinion and right conduct on the part of the citizens of a democracy.

That erroneous statement is inevitable in free debate, and that it must be protected if the freedoms of expression are to have the "breathing space" that they "need . . . to survive," NAACP v. Button, 371 U.S. 415, 433 (1963), was also recognized by the Court of Appeals for the District of Columbia Circuit in Sweeney v. Patterson, 128 F.2d 457, 458 [ ]. Judge Edgerton spoke for a unanimous court which affirmed the dismissal of a Congressman's libel suit based upon a newspaper article charging him with anti-Semitism in opposing a judicial appointment. He said:

> Cases which impose liability for erroneous reports of the political conduct of officials reflect the obsolete doctrine that the governed must not criticize their governors. . . . The interest of the public here outweighs the interest of appellant or any other individual. The protection of the public requires not merely discussion, but information. Political conduct and views which some respectable people approve,

and others condemn, are constantly imputed to Congressmen. Errors of fact, particularly in regard to a man's mental states and processes, are inevitable. . . . Whatever is added to the field of libel is taken from the field of free debate.[13]

Injury to official reputation affords no more warrant for repressing speech that would otherwise be free than does factual error. Where judicial officers are involved, this Court has held that concern for the dignity and reputation of the courts does not justify the punishment as criminal contempt of criticism of the judge or his decision. Bridges v. California, 314 U.S. 252 (1941). This is true even though the utterance contains "half-truths" and "misinformation." Pennekamp v. Florida, 328 U.S. 331, 342, 343, n. 5, 345 (1946). . . . Criticism of their official conduct does not lose its constitutional protection merely because it is effective criticism and hence diminishes their official reputations.

If neither factual error nor defamatory content suffices to remove the constitutional shield from criticism of official conduct, the combination of the two elements is no less inadequate. This is the lesson to be drawn from the great controversy over the Sedition Act of 1798, 1 Stat. § 596, which first crystallized a national awareness of the central meaning of the First Amendment. . . .

Although the Sedition Act was never tested in this Court,[16] the attack upon its validity has carried the day in the court of history. Fines levied in its prosecution were repaid by Act of Congress on the ground that it was unconstitutional. . . . The invalidity of the Act has also been assumed by Justices of this Court. [ ] These views reflect a broad consensus that the Act, because of the restraint it imposed upon criticism of government and public officials, was inconsistent with the First Amendment.

There is no force in respondent's argument that the constitutional limitations implicit in the history of the Sedition Act apply only to Congress and not to the States. It is true that the First Amendment was originally addressed only to action by the Federal Government, and that Jefferson, for one, while denying the power of Congress "to controul the freedom of the press," recognized such a power in the States. [ ] But this distinction was eliminated with the adoption of the Fourteenth Amendment and the application to the States of the First Amendment's restrictions. [ ]

What a State may not constitutionally bring about by means of a criminal statute is likewise beyond the reach of its civil law of libel. The

---

13. See also Mill, On Liberty (Oxford: Blackwell, 1947), at 47:

". . . [T]o argue sophistically, to suppress facts or arguments, to misstate the elements of the case, or misrepresent the opposite opinion . . . all this, even to the most aggravated degree, is so continually done in perfect good faith, by persons who are not considered, and in many other respects may not deserve to be considered, ignorant or incompetent, that it is rarely possible, on adequate grounds, conscientiously to stamp the misrepresentation as morally culpable; and still less could law presume to interfere with this kind of controversial misconduct."

16. The Act expired by its terms in 1801.

fear of damage awards under a rule such as that invoked by the Alabama courts here may be markedly more inhibiting than the fear of prosecution under a criminal statute. [ ] Alabama, for example, has a criminal libel law which subjects to prosecution "any person who speaks, writes, or prints of and concerning another any accusation falsely and maliciously importing the commission by such person of a felony, or any other indictable offense involving moral turpitude," and which allows as punishment upon conviction a fine not exceeding $500 and a prison sentence of six months. [ ] Presumably a person charged with violation of this statute enjoys ordinary criminal-law safeguards such as the requirements of an indictment and of proof beyond a reasonable doubt. These safeguards are not available to the defendant in a civil action. . . . And since there is no double-jeopardy limitation applicable to civil lawsuits, this is not the only judgment that may be awarded against petitioners for the same publication.[18] Whether or not a newspaper can survive a succession of such judgments, the pall of fear and timidity imposed upon those who would give voice to public criticism is an atmosphere in which the First Amendment freedoms cannot survive. Plainly the Alabama law of civil libel is "a form of regulation that creates hazards to protected freedoms markedly greater than those that attend reliance upon the criminal law." Bantam Books, Inc. v. Sullivan, 372 U.S. 58, 70 (1963).

The state rule of law is not saved by its allowance of the defense of truth. . . . Allowance of the defense of truth, with the burden of proving it on the defendant, does not mean that only false speech will be deterred.[19] Even courts accepting this defense as an adequate safeguard have recognized the difficulties of adducing legal proofs that the alleged libel was true in all its factual particulars. See, e.g., Post Publishing Co. v. Hallam, 59 F. 530, 540 (C.A.6th Cir. 1893); see also Noel, Defamation of Public Officers and Candidates, 49 Col. L. Rev. 875, 892 (1949). Under such a rule, would-be critics of official conduct may be deterred from voicing their criticism, even though it is believed to be true and even though it is in fact true, because of doubt whether it can be proved in court or fear of the expense of having to do so. They tend to make only statements which "steer far wider of the unlawful zone." Speiser v. Randall, supra, 357 U.S., at 526. The rule thus dampens the vigor and limits the variety of public debate. It is inconsistent with the First and Fourteenth Amendments.

The constitutional guarantees require, we think, a federal rule that prohibits a public official from recovering damages for a defamatory falsehood relating to his official conduct unless he proves that the statement

18. The Times states that four other libel suits based on the advertisement have been filed against it by others who have served as Montgomery City Commissioners and by the Governor of Alabama; that another $500,000 verdict has been awarded in the only one of these cases that has yet gone to trial; and that the damages sought in the other three total $2,000,000.

19. Even a false statement may be deemed to make a valuable contribution to public debate, since it brings about "the clearer perception and livelier impression of truth, produced by its collision with error." Mill, On Liberty (Oxford: Blackwell, 1947), at 15; see also Milton, Areopagitica, in Prose Works (Yale, 1959), Vol. II, at 561.

was made with "actual malice"—that is, with knowledge that it was false or with reckless disregard of whether it was false or not. An oft-cited statement of a like rule, which has been adopted by a number of state courts, is found in the Kansas case of Coleman v. MacLennan, 78 Kan. 711, 98 P. 281 (1908). . . .

Such a privilege for criticism of official conduct is appropriately analogous to the protection accorded a public official when *he* is sued for libel by a private citizen. In Barr v. Matteo, 360 U.S. 564, 575 (1959), this Court held the utterance of a federal official to be absolutely privileged if made "within the outer perimeter" of his duties. The States accord the same immunity to statements of their highest officers, although some differentiate their lesser officials and qualify the privilege they enjoy. But all hold that all officials are protected unless actual malice can be proved. The reason for the official privilege is said to be that the threat of damage suits would otherwise "inhibit the fearless, vigorous, and effective administration of policies of government" and "dampen the ardor of all but the most resolute, or the most irresponsible, in the unflinching discharge of their duties." Barr v. Matteo, supra, 360 U.S., at 571. Analogous considerations support the privilege for the citizen-critic of government. It is as much his duty to criticize as it is the official's duty to administer. . . . As Madison said, [ ], "the censorial power is in the people over the Government, and not in the Government over the people." It would give public servants an unjustified preference over the public they serve, if critics of official conduct did not have a fair equivalent of the immunity granted to the officials themselves.

We conclude that such a privilege is required by the First and Fourteenth Amendments.

III.

We hold today that the Constitution delimits a State's power to award damages for libel in actions brought by public officials against critics of their official conduct. Since this is such an action, the rule requiring proof of actual malice is applicable. While Alabama law apparently requires proof of actual malice for an award of punitive damages, where general damages are concerned malice is "presumed." Such a presumption is inconsistent with the federal rule. . . . Since the trial judge did not instruct the jury to differentiate between general and punitive damages, it may be that the verdict was wholly an award of one or the other. But it is impossible to know, in view of the general verdict returned. Because of this uncertainty, the judgment must be reversed and the case remanded.

Since respondent may seek a new trial, we deem that considerations of effective judicial administration require us to review the evidence in the present record to determine whether it could constitutionally support a judgment for respondent. . . .

Applying these standards, we consider that the proof presented to show actual malice lacks the convincing clarity which the constitutional standard demands, and hence that it would not constitutionally sustain the judgment for respondent under the proper rule of law. The case of the individual petitioners requires little discussion. Even assuming that they could constitutionally be found to have authorized the use of their names on the advertisement, there was no evidence whatever that they were aware of any erroneous statements or were in any way reckless in that regard. The judgment against them is thus without constitutional support.

As to the Times, we similarly conclude that the facts do not support a finding of actual malice. [The testimony of the Secretary of the Times that he believed the advertisement to be "substantially correct" was "at least a reasonable one, and there was no evidence to impeach the witness' good faith in holding it." Nor was the later retraction for the governor evidence of actual malice toward plaintiff. Leaving open the question of whether failure to retract "may ever constitute such evidence," it could not suffice here because the letter showed reasonable doubt whether the ad referred to plaintiff at all, and also because the letter was not a final refusal. As to evidence that the Times published the ad without first checking news stories in its own files, the Court stated that the "mere presence" of such stories "does not, of course, establish that the Times 'knew' the advertisement was false, since the state of mind required for actual malice would have to be brought home to the persons in the Times' organization having responsibility for the publication of the advertisement." Those persons relied on the "good reputation of many of those whose names were listed as sponsors of the advertisement, and upon the letter from A. Philip Randolph, known to them as a responsible individual, certifying that the use of the names was authorized."]

We also think the evidence was constitutionally defective in another respect: it was incapable of supporting the jury's finding that the allegedly libelous statements were made "of and concerning" respondent. Respondent relies on the words of the advertisement and the testimony of six witnesses to establish a connection between it and himself. . . . There was no reference to respondent in the advertisement, either by name or official position. A number of the allegedly libelous statements—the charges that the dining hall was padlocked and that Dr. King's home was bombed, his person assaulted, and a perjury prosecution instituted against him—did not even concern the police; despite the ingenuity of the arguments which would attach this significance to the word "They," it is plain that these statements could not reasonably be read as accusing respondent of personal involvement in the acts in question. The statements upon which respondent principally relies as referring to him are the two allegations that did concern the police or police functions: that "truckloads of police . . . ringed the Alabama State College Campus" after the demonstration on the State Capitol steps, and that Dr. King had been "arrested . . . seven times." These statements were false only in that the police had been "deployed near" the campus but had not actually "ringed" it and had not gone there in connection with the State Capitol demonstration, and in that Dr. King had been arrested only four times. The ruling that these discrepancies between what was true and what was asserted were sufficient to injure respondent's reputation may itself raise constitutional problems, but we need not consider them here. Although the statements may be taken as referring to the police, they did not on their face make even an oblique reference to respondent as an individual. Support for the asserted reference must, therefore, be sought in the testimony of respondent's witnesses. But none of them suggested any basis for the belief that respondent himself was attacked in the advertisement beyond the bare fact that he was in overall charge of the Police Department and thus bore official responsibility for police conduct; to the extent that some of the witnesses thought respondent to have been charged with ordering or approving the conduct or otherwise being personally involved in it, they based this notion not on any statements in the advertisement, and not on any evidence that he had in fact been so involved, but solely on the unsupported assumption that, because of his official position, he must have been. This reliance on the bare fact of respondent's official position was made explicit by the Supreme Court of Alabama. . . .

This proposition has disquieting implications for criticism of governmental conduct. For good reason, "no court of last resort in this country has ever held, or even suggested, that prosecutions for libel on government have any place in the American system of jurisprudence." City of Chicago v. Tribune Co., 307 Ill. 595, 601, 139 N.E. 86, 88 (1923). The present proposition would sidestep this obstacle by transmuting criticism of government, however impersonal it may seem on its face, into personal criticism, and hence potential libel, of the officials of whom the government is composed. There is no legal alchemy by which a State may thus create the cause of action that would otherwise be denied for a publication which, as respondent himself said of the advertisement, "reflects not only on me but on the other Commissioners and the community." Raising as it does the possibility that a good-faith critic of government will be penalized for his criticism, the proposition relied on by the Alabama courts strikes at the very center of the constitutionally protected area of free expression.[30] We hold that such a proposition may not constitutionally be utilized to establish that an otherwise impersonal attack on governmental operations was a libel of an official responsible for those operations. Since it was relied on exclusively here, and there was no other evidence to connect the statements with respondent, the evidence was constitutionally insufficient to support a finding that the statements referred to respondent.

The judgment of the Supreme Court of Alabama is reversed and the case is remanded to that court for further proceedings not inconsistent with this opinion.

Reversed and remanded.

---

30. Insofar as the proposition means only that the statements about police conduct libeled respondent by implicitly criticizing his ability to run the Police Department, recovery is also precluded in this case by the doctrine of fair comment. See American Law Institute, Restatement of Torts (1938) § 607. Since the Fourteenth Amendment requires recognition of the conditional privilege for honest misstatements of fact, it follows that a defense of fair comment must be afforded for honest expression of opinion based upon privileged, as well as true, statements of fact. Both defenses are of course defeasible if the public official proves actual malice, as was not done here.

MR. JUSTICE BLACK, with whom MR. JUSTICE DOUGLAS joins, concurring.

I concur in reversing this half-million-dollar judgment against the New York Times Company and the four individual defendants. In reversing the Court holds that "the Constitution delimits a State's power to award damages for libel in actions brought by public officials against critics of their official conduct." I base my vote to reverse on the belief that the First and Fourteenth Amendments not merely "delimit" a State's power to award damages to "public officials against critics of their official conduct" but completely prohibit a State from exercising such a power. The Court goes on to hold that a State can subject such critics to damages if "actual malice" can be proved against them. "Malice," even as defined by the Court, is an elusive, abstract concept, hard to prove and hard to disprove. The requirement that malice be proved provides at best an evanescent protection for the right critically to discuss public affairs and certainly does not measure up to the sturdy safeguard embodied in the First Amendment. Unlike the Court, therefore, I vote to reverse exclusively on the ground that the Times and the individual defendants had an absolute unconditional constitutional right to publish in the Times advertisement their criticisms of the Montgomery agencies and officials. . . .

The half-million-dollar verdict does give dramatic proof, however, that state libel laws threaten the very existence of an American press virile enough to publish unpopular views on public affairs and bold enough to criticize the conduct of public officials. . . . In fact, briefs before us show that in Alabama there are now pending eleven libel suits by local and state officials against the Times seeking $5,600,000 and five such suits against the Columbia Broadcasting System seeking $1,700,000. Moreover, this technique for harassing and punishing a free press—now that it has been shown to be possible—is by no means limited to cases with racial overtones; it can be used in other fields where public feelings may make local as well as out-of-state newspapers easy prey for libel verdict seekers. . . . This record certainly does not indicate that any different verdict would have been rendered here whatever the Court had charged the jury about "malice," "truth," "good motives," "justifiable ends," or any other legal formulas which in theory would protect the press. Nor does the record indicate that any of these legalistic words would have caused the courts below to set aside or to reduce the half-million-dollar verdict in any amount.

. . .

. . . An unconditional right to say what one pleases about public affairs is what I consider to be the minimum guarantee of the First Amendment.[6]

I regret that the Court has stopped short of this holding indispensable to preserve our free press from destruction.

MR. JUSTICE GOLDBERG, with whom MR. JUSTICE DOUGLAS joins, concurring in the result.

. . .

6. Cf. Meiklejohn, Free Speech and Its Relation to Self–Government (1948).

In my view, the First and Fourteenth Amendments to the Constitution afford to the citizen and to the press an absolute, unconditional privilege to criticize official conduct despite the harm which may flow from excesses and abuses. . . .

. . .

. . . It may be urged that deliberately and maliciously false statements have no conceivable value as free speech. That argument, however, is not responsive to the real issue presented by this case, which is whether that freedom of speech which all agree is constitutionally protected can be effectively safeguarded by a rule allowing the imposition of liability upon a jury's evaluation of the speaker's state of mind. If individual citizens may be held liable in damages for strong words, which a jury finds false and maliciously motivated, there can be little doubt that public debate and advocacy will be constrained. And if newspapers, publishing advertisements dealing with public issues, thereby risk liability, there can also be little doubt that the ability of minority groups to secure publication of their views on public affairs and to seek support for their causes will be greatly diminished. . . .

. . .

This is not to say that the Constitution protects defamatory statements directed against the private conduct of a public official or private citizen. Freedom of press and of speech insures that government will respond to the will of the people and that changes may be obtained by peaceful means. Purely private defamation has little to do with the political ends of a self-governing society. The imposition of liability for private defamation does not abridge the freedom of public speech or any other freedom protected by the First Amendment.[4] . . .

. . .

Notes and Questions

1. What is the problem with strict liability? Would a negligence standard raise the same problems? Would the absolute privilege suggested by the concurring opinions be preferable?

2. Justice Brennan's concern lest speakers be induced to "steer far wider of the unlawful zone" than legally necessary has been articulated by others as the concern that fear of liability has the potential to "chill" speech. In the passage from *Speiser v. Randall* that is cited in the principal case, the Court said that where speech is close to the line between lawful and unlawful,

---

4. In most cases, as in the case at bar, there will be little difficulty in distinguishing defamatory speech relating to private conduct from that relating to official conduct. I recognize, of course, that there will be a gray area. The difficulties of applying a public-private standard are, however, certainly of a different genre from those attending the differentiation between a malicious and non-malicious state of mind. . . .

the possibility of mistaken fact-finding—inherent in all litigation—will create the danger that the legitimate utterance will be penalized. The man who knows that he must bring forth proof and persuade another of the lawfulness of his conduct necessarily must steer far wider of the unlawful zone than if the state must bear these burdens.

How is this concern relevant to the problems raised by libel law?

3. Why did the Court see the introduction of "actual malice" as the solution to the constitutional problem? The Court ascribed the "chilling effect" to the burdens and risks of proving truth. Might the problem have been solved by shifting to the plaintiff the burden of proving falsity? Does the Court's definition of "actual malice"—as proof that the statement was made with "knowledge that it was false or with reckless disregard of whether it was false or not"—implicitly shift the burden on the issue of truth or falsity? We shall consider this further in Section F.

4. Toward the end, the opinion discusses whether the libel was of and concerning the plaintiff. Why isn't that a jury question? For a discussion of how the Times' argument that the article was not about the plaintiff expanded during the oral argument, see Arthur Selwyn Miller and Jerome A. Barron, The Supreme Court, The Adversary System, and the Flow of Information to the Justices: A Preliminary Inquiry, 61 Va. L. Rev. 1187 (1975). For a discussion of the opinion drafting process, see Bernard Schwartz, Super Chief: Earl Warren and his Supreme Court—A Judicial Biography 531–41 (1983). The story of the Supreme Court's deliberation in the *Sullivan* case is told in intriguing detail in Anthony Lewis, "Make No Law" (1991). For extensive later commentary on the case, see Special Issue: *New York Times v. Sullivan* Forty Years Later: Retrospective, Perspective, Prospective, 9 Comm. L. & Pol'y No. 4 (Autumn 2004).

5. The majority in the *New York Times* case did not say why it rejected the absolute privilege proposed by the concurring opinions, but the Court did so a few months later, in Garrison v. Louisiana, 379 U.S. 64, 1 Med. L. Rptr. 1548 (1964):

Although honest utterance, even if inaccurate, may further the fruitful exercise of the right of free speech, it does not follow that the lie, knowingly and deliberately published about a public official, should enjoy a like immunity. At the time the First Amendment was adopted, as today, there were those unscrupulous enough and skillful enough to use the deliberate or reckless falsehood as an effective political tool to unseat the public servant or even topple an administration. [ ] That speech is used as a tool for political ends does not automatically bring it under the protective mantle of the Constitution. For the use of the known lie as a tool is at once at odds with the premises of democratic government and with the orderly manner in which economic, social, or political change is to be effected. Calculated falsehood falls into that class of utterances which "are no essential part of any exposition of ideas, and are of such slight social value as a step to truth that any benefit that may be derived from them is clearly outweighed by the social interest in order and morality. . . ." [*Chaplinsky*]. Hence the knowingly false statement and the false statement made with reckless disregard of the truth, do not enjoy constitutional protection.

b. Public Figures

Three years after *New York Times*, the Court considered two cases together: Curtis Publishing Co. v. Butts, and Associated Press v. Walker, 388 U.S. 130, 1 Med. L. Rptr. 1568 (1967).

In *Butts* the defendant magazine had accused the plaintiff athletic director of disclosing his game plan to an opposing coach before their game. Although he was on the staff of a state university, Butts was paid by a private alumni organization. In *Walker,* the defendant news service reported that the plaintiff, a former United States Army general who resigned to engage in political activity, had personally led students in an attack on federal marshals who were enforcing a desegregation order at the University of Mississippi.

In both cases, lower courts affirmed substantial jury awards against the defendants and refused to apply the *Times* doctrine on the ground that public officials were not involved. The Supreme Court divided several ways, affirming *Butts,* 5–4, and reversing *Walker,* 9–0. Chief Justice Warren wrote the pivotal opinion in which he concluded that both men were "public figures" and that the standard developed in *New York Times* should apply to "public figures" as well.

> To me, differentiation between "public figures" and "public officials" and adoption of separate standards of proof for each has no basis in law, logic, or First Amendment policy. Increasingly in this country, the distinctions between governmental and private sectors are blurred. Since the depression of the 1930's and World War II there has been a rapid fusion of economic and political power, a merging of science, industry, and government, and a high degree of interaction between the intellectual, governmental, and business worlds. Depression, war, international tensions, national and international markets, and the surging growth of science and technology have precipitated national and international problems that demand national and international solutions. While these trends and events have occasioned a consolidation of governmental power, power has also become much more organized in what we have commonly considered to be the private sector. In many situations, policy determinations which traditionally were channeled through formal political institutions are now originated and implemented through a complex array of boards, committees, commissions, corporations, and associations, some only loosely connected with the Government. This blending of positions and power has also occurred in the case of individuals so that many who do not hold public office at the moment are nevertheless intimately involved in the resolution of important public questions or, by reason of their fame, shape events in areas of concern to society at large.

Viewed in this context then, it is plain that although they are not subject to the restraints of the political process, "public figures," like "public officials," often play an influential role in ordering society. And surely as a class these "public figures" have as ready access as "public officials" to mass media of communication, both to influence policy and to counter criticism of their views and activities. Our citizenry has a legitimate and substantial interest in the conduct of such persons, and freedom of the press to engage in uninhibited debate about their involvement in public issues and events is as crucial as it is in the case of "public officials." The fact that they are not amenable to the restraints of the political process only underscores the legitimate and substantial nature of the interest, since it means that public opinion may be the only instrument by which society can attempt to influence their conduct.

He found that on the merits the standard had not been met in *Walker*. In *Butts* he found that defendant's counsel had deliberately waived the *Times* doctrine and he also found evidence establishing reckless disregard of the truth. He thus voted to reverse *Walker* and affirm *Butts*.

Justice Harlan, joined by three others, argued that something less than the *Times* standard should apply to public figures because criticism of government was not involved:

> We consider and would hold that a "public figure" who is not a public official may also recover damages for a defamatory falsehood whose substance makes substantial danger to reputation apparent, on a showing of highly unreasonable conduct constituting an extreme departure from the standards of investigation and reporting ordinarily adhered to by responsible publishers.

Applying that standard, Justice Harlan concluded that Walker had failed to establish a case, but that Butts had shown that the Saturday Evening Post ignored elementary precautions in preparing a potentially damaging story. Together with the Chief Justice's vote, there were five votes to affirm *Butts*. Justices Brennan, White, Black, and Douglas voted to reverse both cases.

Does it make sense to treat public figures the same as public officials? For an argument that it does not, see Frederick Schauer, Public Figures, 25 Wm. & Mary L. Rev. 905 (1984).

Later in this chapter we will explore the methods courts use to distinguish "public figures" from "private figures." In the meantime, we turn to the consequences that flow from labeling a person "public" for defamation law purposes. Most of those arise from the actual malice requirement.

c.   *The Actual Malice Standard*

If the Court had left it to the jury to decide whether "actual malice" was present, *New York Times v. Sullivan* would have had a limited effect on the law of libel. But the Court did not stop there, and most of the impact of the decision resulted from the Court's subsequent refinements of the "actual malice" concept and its adoption of ancillary procedural rules that greatly restricted the jury's power. Together, these have made actual malice an obstacle that few plaintiffs can overcome.

i. Substantive issues

What must a plaintiff show to satisfy the "actual malice" standard? The Supreme Court has addressed that question several times since *New York Times*.

Garrison v. Louisiana. The Court extended New York Times to criminal libel, holding that "only those false statements made with the high degree of awareness of their probable falsity demanded by *New York Times* may be the subject of either civil or criminal sanctions." 379 U.S. 64, 1 Med. L. Rptr. 1548 (1965). This signaled that the standard was to focus on subjective awareness of falsity, and therefore bore little resemblance to the tort law concept of recklessness.

St. Amant v. Thompson. The defendant repeated false charges against plaintiff without checking the charges or investigating the source's reputation for veracity. The Supreme Court concluded that "reckless disregard" had not been shown. 390 U.S. 727, 1 Med. L. Rptr. 1586 (1968). Actual malice

> is not measured by whether a reasonably prudent man would have published, or would have investigated before publishing. There must be sufficient evidence to permit the conclusion that the defendant in fact entertained serious doubts as to the truth of his publication. . . .
>
> . . .
>
> The defendant in a defamation action brought by a public official cannot, however, automatically insure a favorable verdict by testifying that he published with a belief that the statements were true. The finder of fact must determine whether the publication was indeed made in good faith. Professions of good faith will be unlikely to prove persuasive, for example, where a story is fabricated by the defendant, is a product of his imagination, or is based wholly on an unverified anonymous telephone call. Nor will they be likely to prevail when the publisher's allegations are so inherently improbable that only a reckless man would have put them in circulation. Likewise, recklessness may be found where there are obvious reasons to doubt the veracity of the informant or the accuracy of his reports.

Harte–Hanks Communications, Inc. v. Connaughton. A newspaper accused a judicial candidate of having used "dirty tricks" to smear his opponent, the incumbent. A unanimous Court upheld an award of $5,000 compensatory and $195,000 punitive damages. 491 U.S. 657, 16 Med. L. Rptr. 1881 (1989).

The evidence of "dirty tricks" relied heavily on a source whose credibility had been seriously impugned by other witnesses and whose version of the episode was essentially unconfirmed. Reviewing the record extensively, the Court concluded that actual malice could be found from (1) the newspaper's failure to interview "the one witness that both [the plaintiff and the source] claimed would verify their conflicting accounts of the relevant events," a failure that the Court found "utterly bewildering"; (2) the paper's failure to listen to a tape that the paper had been told exonerated plaintiff, which plaintiff had delivered to the paper at the paper's request; (3) an earlier editorial on the election, which "could be taken to indicate that [the editor] had already decided to publish [the source's] allegations, regardless of how the evidence developed and regardless of whether or not [the source's] story was credible upon ultimate reflection"; (4) discrepancies in testimony of defendant's witnesses which the Court said would support a finding that "the failure to conduct a complete investigation involved a deliberate effort to avoid the truth."

Accepting the jury's implicit determination that the newspaper's explanations for not interviewing the crucial witness and for not listening to the tape "were not credible, it is likely that the newspaper's inaction was a product of a deliberate decision not to acquire knowledge of facts that might confirm the probable falsity of [the source's] charges. Although failure to investigate will not alone support a finding of actual malice [*St. Amant*], the purposeful avoidance of the truth is in a different category."

In a footnote at that point, the Court noted that it was not suggesting that a newspaper must accept or be shaken by vehement "denials." These are "so commonplace in the world of polemical charge and countercharge that, in themselves, they hardly alert the conscientious reporter to the likelihood of error."

In passing, the Court observed that a "newspaper's motive in publishing the story—whether to promote an opponent's candidacy or to increase its circulation—cannot provide a sufficient basis for finding actual malice."

Masson v. New Yorker Magazine, Inc. Plaintiff alleged that a magazine article written by Janet Malcolm had attributed to plaintiff fabricated quotations that hurt his reputation. The lower courts had upheld summary judgment for the defendants. The Supreme Court reversed, holding that Masson was entitled to a jury finding on the issue of actual malice. 501 U.S. 496, 18 Med. L. Rptr. 2241 (1991).

The plaintiff argued that "excepting corrections of grammar or syntax, publication of a quotation with knowledge that it does not contain the words the public figure used demonstrates actual malice." The Court was unwilling to go that far. Interviewers often must reconstruct interviews from notes. Use of language that the subject did not use does not amount to actual malice in that situation. Even if an interview is tape recorded, the "full and exact statement will be reported in only rare circumstances."

> We conclude that a deliberate alteration of the words uttered by a plaintiff does not equate with knowledge of falsity for purposes of [*Times*] unless the alteration results in a material change in the meaning conveyed by the statement. The use of quotation to attribute

words not in fact spoken bears in a most important way on that inquiry, but it is not dispositive in every case.

On remand in the *Masson* case, the Ninth Circuit concluded that although a publisher who has no "obvious reasons to doubt" the accuracy of a story "is not required to initiate an investigation that might plant such doubt," once "doubt exists, the publisher must act reasonably in dispelling it." Although this approach puts publishers who fact-check stories "at somewhat of a disadvantage compared to other publisher such as newspapers and supermarket tabloids that cannot or will not engage in thorough fact-checking," the different treatment "makes considerable sense":

> Readers of reputable magazines such as the New Yorker are far more likely to trust the verbatim accuracy of the stories they read than are the readers of supermarket tabloids or even daily newspapers, where they understand the inherent limitations in the fact-finding process. The harm inflicted by a misstatement in a publication known for scrupulously investigating the accuracy of its stories can be far more serious than a similar misstatement in a publication known not to do so.

Masson v. New Yorker Magazine, Inc., 960 F.2d 896, 20 Med. L. Rptr. 1009 (9th Cir. 1992). The court did, however, dismiss the case against the publisher of the book into which the New Yorker articles were converted. The publisher was entitled to rely on the New Yorker's reputation for accuracy and on its rejection of the plaintiff's complaints about the series. The book publisher had no "obvious reasons to doubt" the story's accuracy and thus no obligation to investigate.

A jury eventually ruled in favor of Malcolm, finding that one of the quotations was not defamatory, one was not published with actual malice, and the rest were not false. The Ninth Circuit affirmed. See 85 F.3d 1394, 24 Med. L. Rptr. 1787 (9th Cir. 1996).

Notes and Questions

1. *St. Amant* says failure to investigate, without more, does not constitute actual malice. Yet in *Connaughton* the defendant's failure to conduct a thorough investigation helped persuade the Court that the newspaper had made a "deliberate decision not to acquire knowledge of facts that might confirm the probable falsity" of the statement? What, if anything, makes *Connaughton* something more than a failure-to-investigate case?

2. In *Garrison v. Louisiana*, supra p. 283, the Court suggested that the reason for permitting public figures to recover if they can show actual malice is that calculated falsehoods deserve no First Amendment protection. Does that imply that courts should employ the "reckless disregard" branch of the test only when they believe the defendant was deliberately avoiding the truth? Is *Connaughton* a reckless disregard case or a case of knowing falsity?

3. If Malcolm knew Masson did not say the defamatory things she attributed to him, why does this constitute actual malice only if the alteration "results in a material change in the meaning conveyed by the statement"? Does this treatment of deliberate falsification imply anything about knowing but inadvertent falsehoods, e.g., a mental lapse that causes a writer to name Jones as the murder when she intended to name Smith?

Actual malice in the lower courts. Many important questions about actual malice have been addressed only by lower courts.

A. *Connaughton* suggests that bits of evidence, insufficient by themselves, can be cumulated to show actual malice. But courts do this very cautiously. See, e.g., Tavoulareas v. Piro, 817 F.2d 762, 13 Med. L. Rptr. 2377 (D.C. Cir. en banc 1987). A panel decision had added up "bricks" of evidence to build a "wall" of actual malice. The en banc court, reversing the panel, 7–1, acknowledged that individual bits of evidence could be accumulated, but suggested caution and rejected two of the panel's "bricks." The en banc court said evidence of the reporter's "ill will or bad motives will support a finding of actual malice only when combined with other, more substantial evidence of a defendant's bad faith."

It also ruled that evidence that the management of the Washington Post urged reporters to find sensational stories "cannot, as a matter of law, constitute evidence of actual malice. We agree with the Post that the First Amendment forbids penalizing the press for encouraging its reporters to expose wrongdoing by public corporations and public figures."

B. Is failure to retract admissible to show the defendant's indifference to the truth? Yes, said Schwartz v. Worrall Publications Inc., 258 N.J.Super. 493, 610 A.2d 425, 20 Med. L. Rptr. 1661 (App. Div. 1992). In *Connaughton*, however, the Supreme Court warned that "courts must be careful not to put too much reliance on such factors."

C. Does proof that the article is unfair establish actual malice? In Westmoreland v. CBS, Inc., 601 F. Supp. 66, 11 Med. L. Rptr. 1703 (S.D.N.Y. 1984), the court said no. Judge Leval had ordered CBS to give plaintiff a copy of CBS's in-house report on the production of the program that led to the suit. Later, he held the report to be inadmissible at trial because it dealt only with the fairness of the CBS program:

> The fairness of the broadcast is not at issue in the libel suit. Publishers and reporters do not commit a libel in a public figure case by publishing unfair one-sided attacks. . . . The fact that a commentary is one sided and sets forth categorical accusations has no tendency to prove that the publisher believed it to be false. The libel law does not require the publisher to grant his accused equal time or fair reply. . . . A publisher who honestly believes in the truth of his accusations . . . is under no obligation under the libel law to treat the subject of his accusations fairly or evenhandedly.

D. Can malice be inferred from evidence that the defendant acted with undue haste? In Meisler v. Gannett Co., 12 F.3d 1026, 22 Med. L. Rptr. 1214 (11th Cir. 1994), the defendant carried an article based on an Associated Press wire service story marked "URGENT" even though AP indicated that "MORE" would be coming on this story. The additional material, which removed the defamatory sting of the first installment, arrived before the deadline, but the author never saw it. Plaintiff sought to show "actual malice" from the paper's failure to wait to learn the complete story. An expert testified that "urgent" means the story has been rushed and that "more" alerts the newspaper to expect additional information. But the court said this was insufficient to show that the writer knew of the first article's falsity, had serious doubt about its accuracy, or had a high degree of awareness of falsity.

E. Can actual malice be inferred from evidence that the defendant knew readers might interpret a publication in a false and defamatory sense? Recall Kaelin v. Globe Communications Corp., supra p. 258, in which a tabloid's page one headline stated "COPS THINK KATO DID IT!" while a story on page 17 made clear that "IT" referred not to the murders for which Kaelin's friend O. J. Simpson was tried, but to the possibility that Kaelin committed perjury. The editor testified that "the front page of the tabloid paper is what we sell the paper on, not what's inside it," and admitted that he had been "a bit concerned" that readers might understand the cover headline to mean that Kaelin was suspected of murder. Since the defendant admitted it never believed Kaelin to be a murder suspect, the Ninth Circuit held that a jury could find actual malice by inferring that the newspaper acted with a "high degree of awareness . . . of probable falsity." 162 F.3d 1036, 27 Med. L. Rptr. 1142 (9th Cir. 1998).

Actual malice and implications. We have already seen that the defamatory sting of a statement is often implicit rather than explicit, supra p. 257. Can actual malice be shown when the implication alleged by the plaintiff is one the defendant knew was false (or seriously doubted) but claims it did not intend to convey? Courts have offered a variety of answers to this question. Some have held that there can be no finding of actual malice unless the defendant intended to convey the defamatory meaning, see Dodds v. American Broadcasting Co., 145 F.3d 1053, 26 Med. L. Rptr. 1705 (9th Cir. 1998), or endorsed that meaning, see White v. Fraternal Order of Police, 909 F.2d 512, 17 Med. L. Rptr. 2137 (D.C. Cir. 1990). Some say the plaintiff must prove "that the alleged implication is the principal inference a reasonable reader or viewer will draw from the publication as having been intended by the publisher." See Sassone v. Elder, 626 So.2d 345, 22 Med. L. Rptr. 1049 (La. 1993). It has also been suggested that there can be no recovery for false implications as long as the explicit statements are true. See, e.g., Schaefer v. Lynch, 406 So.2d 185, 7 Med. L. Rptr. 2302 (La. 1981).

For a thorough discussion of implied libel, see C. Thomas Dienes and Lee Levine, Implied Libel, Defamatory Meanings, and State of Mind: The Promise of *New York Times Co. v. Sullivan*, 78 Iowa L. Rev. 2337 (1992).

Imputing actual malice. Rarely will a plaintiff be able to show that the *corporation* that published or broadcast the defamation knew or had serious doubts about its falsity. Is it enough to show that an employee did? Generally the courts say yes. They sometimes describe this as vicarious liability, but strictly speaking it is not. Under the common law rules about publication (see infra p. 337), the employee who writes or speaks the defamation and the corporation that prints or broadcasts it are both publishers and the liability of both is primary, not vicarious. The corporation is liable for the employee's defamation for the same reason it is liable for defamation by the author of a letter to the editor. But the employer's liability is similar to vicarious liability in the sense that the actual malice of the employee acting within the scope of employment is imputed to the employer.

Freelance writers usually are treated as independent contractors and their actual malice is not imputed to the publisher. In the *Masson* case, supra p. 287, the New Yorker magazine was dismissed from the case because the jury found that Malcolm was an independent contractor and the jury did not find actual malice on the part of New Yorker editors. See 832 F. Supp. 1350 (N.D. Cal. 1993).

ii. Procedural issues

Convincing clarity. The *New York Times* opinion said "the proof presented to show actual malice lacks the convincing clarity which the constitutional standard demands." Why is the standard convincing clarity rather than the usual preponderance of evidence? The Court did not explain its insistence on this heightened standard, but its applicability, at least to the actual malice issue, is now unquestioned.

In Long v. Arcell, 618 F.2d 1145, 6 Med. L. Rptr. 1430 (5th Cir. 1980), after a jury finding for the public-figure plaintiff, the trial court granted the defendant newspaper a judgment notwithstanding the verdict. The trial court's ruling was affirmed on appeal. The only evidence for the jury involved conflicting accounts of conversations:

> If the applicable burden of proof had been a preponderance of the evidence, a jury verdict either way would have to stand. Similarly, if liability could be imposed on a clear and convincing showing of negligence, we would be hard pressed to disregard the jury's verdict. We repeat, however, that the plaintiff's burden was to prove actual malice by clear and convincing evidence. This record simply does not contain clear and convincing evidence that the defendants knew that their information was incorrect or had a "high degree of awareness of . . . [its] probable falsity." [*Garrison*]

Independent review. The requirement of clear and convincing evidence has been bolstered by the corollary requirement that appellate courts must exercise "independent review" to assure that the required proof has been presented with the required clarity. In Bose Corp. v. Consumers Union, 466 U.S. 485, 10 Med. L. Rptr. 1625 (1984), a federal judge sitting as fact-finder found actual malice and entered judgment against defendant magazine. The court of appeals understood its obligation to be to "independently examin[e] the record to ensure that the district court has applied properly the governing constitutional law and that the plaintiff has indeed satisfied its burden of proof." Using that standard the court of appeals reversed.

The Court, 6–3, upheld the court of appeals. It analogized libel cases to others in which the unprotected character of particular communications depends upon "judicial evaluation of special facts that have been deemed to have constitutional significance":

> The rule of independent appellate review . . . emerged from the exigency of deciding concrete cases; it is law in its purest form under our common law heritage. It reflects a deeply held conviction that judges—and particularly members of this Court—must exercise such review in order to preserve the precious liberties established and ordained by the Constitution. The question whether the evidence in the record in a defamation case is of the convincing clarity required to strip the utterance of First Amendment protection is not merely a question for the trier of fact. Judges, as expositors of the Constitution, must independently decide whether the evidence in the record is sufficient to cross the constitutional threshold that bars the entry of any judgment that is not supported by clear and convincing proof of "actual malice."

In the *Connaughton* case, supra p. 286, the Supreme Court neither embraced nor rejected this bifurcated approach. The Court said that in "determining whether the constitutional standard has been satisfied, the reviewing court must consider the factual record in full. Although credibility determinations are reviewed under the clearly erroneous standard because the trier of fact has had the 'opportunity to observe the demeanor of the witnesses,'" the reviewing court must examine for itself "the statements in issue and the circumstances under which they were made to see . . . whether they are of a character which the principles of the First Amendment . . . protect."

The independent-review requirement is criticized in Henry P. Monaghan, Constitutional Fact Review, 85 Colum. L. Rev. 229 (1985). See also, Randall P. Bezanson, Fault, Falsity and Reputation in Public Defamation Law: An Essay on Bose Corporation v. Consumers Union, 8 Hamline L. Rev. 105 (1985).

The summary judgment standard. In Anderson v. Liberty Lobby, Inc., 477 U.S. 242, 12 Med. L. Rptr. 2297 (1986), the Court held, 6–3, that the standard for considering summary judgment motions under Federal Rule 56 must take into account the burden plaintiff will have to meet at trial. For public plaintiffs, then, on a summary judgment motion the judge must decide "whether the evidence in the record could support a reasonable jury finding either that the plaintiff has shown actual malice by clear and convincing evidence or that the plaintiff has not."

Several states, noting that the *Liberty Lobby* case was decided on nonconstitutional grounds, have declined to follow it. In Dairy Stores, Inc. v. Sentinel Publishing Co., 104 N.J. 125, 516 A.2d 220, 13 Med. L. Rptr. 1594 (1986), the court used its own summary judgment standards that required denial upon finding a "genuine issue of material fact." The "clear-and-convincing test inevitably implicates a weighing of the evidence, an exercise that intrudes into the province of the jury." See Moffatt v. Brown, 751 P.2d 939, 15 Med. L. Rptr. 1601 (Alaska 1988) (following New Jersey).

The interaction of substantive and procedural requirements at the summary judgment stage. When the requirements of actual malice, clear and convincing proof, and independent review intersect in motions for summary judgment, courts continue to struggle over the appropriate method of appellate review.

Such a determination produced profound disagreement within the Court of Appeals for the Ninth Circuit. Suzuki brought a product disparagement case against Consumers Union for rating the Suzuki Samurai SUV "Not Acceptable" because of an alleged propensity to roll over in emergency maneuvers. The district court granted Consumers Union's motion for summary judgment on the ground there was no clear and convincing evidence of actual malice. The Ninth Circuit reversed. 292 F.3d 1192 (2002).

Two judges held that there was evidence from which a reasonable jury could find actual malice, but they disagreed as to how to reach that conclusion. Judge Tashima said evidence that Consumers Union rigged tests of the vehicle was adequate to permit a reasonable jury "to find by clear and convincing evidence that CU sought to produce a predetermined result in the Samurai test," which could support an inference of awareness of probable falsity. He also believed CU's failure to investigate the validity of its testing procedures after they were questioned by the National Highway Transportation Safety Administration could support a finding that CU purposely avoided discovering the falsity of its allegations. In his view, either of these would support a conclusion that CU acted with reckless disregard with respect to the claims that the Samurai had a dangerous tendency to roll over. He conceded there was contrary evidence on both points, but believed that on summary judgment the court was required to draw all reasonable inferences in favor of Suzuki.

Judge Graber believed that only two more specific allegations were actionable. One was a statement that CU had devised one particular test procedure after discovering the Samurai's propensity to roll over; she said a jury could find that CU developed the test in order to create a rollover propensity. The other was CU's claim that the Samurai "easily rolls over;" she said the evidence showed that CU had to work hard to make the vehicle roll over.

Judge Ferguson, dissenting, said both members of the majority failed to exercise the vigorous independent review demanded by *Bose*, supra p. 292, because they viewed the evidence in the light most favorable to the plaintiff. Independent review requires the court to consider all the evidence and decide for itself whether subjecting the defendant to liability would inhibit protected expression.

The full court voted 12–11 to deny CU's motion for rehearing, but issued a new opinion. The 11 dissenters joined in an opinion in which they endorsed the accuracy of CU's reporting and said the panel majority had rendered the independent review requirement meaningless. See Suzuki Motor Corp. v. Consumers Union of the United States, Inc., 330 F.3d 1110, 31 Med. L. Rptr. 2089 (9th Cir. 2003). The suit was eventually settled with a statement from CU saying it never intended to say the Samurai rolled over easily in routine driving conditions. See Suzuki and Consumers Union Agree on Dismissal of Lawsuit, July 2004, http://www.consumer reports.org/static/0707suz0.html

iii. Defendants' refusal to disclose evidence

Because actual malice is defined in terms of subjective awareness of falsity, it invites inquiry into the defendant's journalistic decision processes. Media defendants often resist disclosing these matters.

Herbert v. Lando. The plaintiff, Colonel Anthony Herbert, sued the producer and reporter of the television program "60 Minutes" and the CBS network for remarks on the program about his conduct while in military service in Vietnam. During his deposition, Lando, the producer, generally responded but he refused to answer some questions about why he made certain investigations and not others; what he concluded about the honesty of certain people he interviewed for the program; and about conversations he had with Mike Wallace, the reporter, in the preparation of the program segment. Lando contended that these thought processes and internal editorial discussions were protected from disclosure by the First Amendment. The Supreme Court disagreed. 441 U.S. 153, 4 Med. L. Rptr. 2575 (1979).

Justice White, for the Court, understood the defendants to be arguing that "the defendant's reckless disregard of truth, a critical element, could not be shown by direct evidence through inquiry into the thoughts, opinions and conclusions of the publisher but could be proved only by objective evidence from which the ultimate fact could be inferred." This was a barrier of some substance, "particularly when defendants themselves are prone to assert their good-faith belief in the truth of their publications, and libel plaintiffs are required to prove knowing or reckless falsehood with 'convincing clarity.'"

Although pretrial discovery techniques had led to "mushrooming litigation costs," this was happening in all areas of litigation. Until major changes in pretrial procedures were developed for all cases, the Court would rely on "what in fact and in law are ample powers of the district judge to prevent abuse."

Confidential sources. Media do enjoy more limited privileges to withhold information, however. As we shall discuss at length in Chapter IX, most courts recognize a "reporter's privilege" under the First Amendment or a state shield statute. These usually permit a reporter or editor to refuse to disclose confidential sources, and in some instances they also prevent forced disclosure of non-confidential information, such as notes and out-takes. If the libel defendant is held to be protected by such a privilege, disclosure cannot be compelled and the plaintiff must proceed without the information, as would be the case with any other privileged evidence.

This can be a serious, if not fatal, obstacle to a plaintiff who must prove actual malice. The plaintiff may suspect that the source is one that the defendant knew was unreliable (or that there was no independent source), but that will be difficult to prove if the defendant cannot be required to identify the source.

One solution is to allow the defendant to refuse to disclose, but instruct the jury that it may infer that the information withheld would support the plaintiff's theory. Another is to preclude the defendant from relying on the existence of evidence that it refuses to present, e.g., prevent it from claiming that it had a source whom it refuses to identify. But courts rarely take such steps. See, e.g, Sprague v. Walter, 518 Pa. 425, 543 A.2d 1078, 15 Med. L. Rptr. 1625 (1988), holding that where the refusal to identify the source is privileged, the defendant nevertheless may introduce evidence obtained from the source and is entitled to an instruction telling the jury not to draw any adverse inference from the refusal to disclose.

In most instances the reporter's privilege is not absolute, and can be overcome if the plaintiff meets certain tests of materiality and necessity. If no privilege is available in the jurisdiction, or if the court decides that the balance of interests requires disclosure despite the privilege, the libel defendant can be ordered to reveal the source. Refusal can lead to contempt proceedings or sanctions of the sort normally imposed on defendants who refuse to comply with valid discovery orders. In Downing v. Monitor Pub. Co., 120 N.H. 383, 415 A.2d 683, 6 Med. L. Rptr. 1193 (1980), the court decided that something more than the threat of contempt was needed:

> [W]e hold that when a defendant in a libel action brought by a plaintiff who is required to prove actual malice under *New York Times,* refuses to declare his sources of information upon a valid order of the court, there shall arise a presumption that the defendant had no source. This presumption may be removed by a disclosure of the sources a reasonable time before trial. Because such a disclosure may, for the press, be similar to the disclosure of a "trade secret," there may be circumstances under which an appropriate order limiting outside access to the informant's name when disclosed would not be improper.

A jury awarded $1.7 million in damages in a defamation case against the Boston Globe after the judge entered a default judgment against the newspaper for failing to disclose its source for the allegedly defamatory article. The jury awarded $420,000 in damages against the reporter who wrote the story. Both awards were affirmed on appeal. See Ayash v. Dana

Farber Cancer Institute, ____ N.E.2d ____, 443 Mass. 367, 2005 WL 289185 (2005).

Such extreme sanctions are unusual, however. Usually the courts hold that the sanction must be no more severe than necessary to offset the disadvantage placed on the plaintiff by the refusal to disclose. See Sierra Life Ins. Co. v. Magic Valley Newspapers, 101 Idaho 795, 623 P.2d 103, 6 Med. L. Rptr. 1769 (1980). In Oak Beach Inn Corp. v. Babylon Beacon, Inc., 62 N.Y.2d 158, 464 N.E.2d 967, 476 N.Y.S.2d 269, 10 Med. L. Rptr. 1761 (1984), striking the defendant's answer was held to be excessive where the defendant had agreed to defend against the allegation of actual malice by relying on proof of its own independent investigation rather than placing any reliance on its source.

Confidential source problems in the libel area are reviewed in Robert G. Berger, The "No–Source" Presumption: The Harshest Remedy, 36 Am. U. L. Rev. 603 (1987). We defer all other aspects of the reporter's privilege issue to Chapter IX.

2. NEGLIGENCE

a. Private Plaintiffs

The foregoing discussion of public officials, public figures, and actual malice implies that the constitutional limitations on defamation law might be different for private plaintiffs. Indeed they are, but perhaps not as different as they seem at first.

Gertz v. Robert Welch, Inc.

Supreme Court of the United States, 1974.
418 U.S. 323, 94 S. Ct. 2997, 41 L. Ed.2d 789, 1 Med. L. Rptr. 1633.

[Plaintiff, an attorney, was retained to represent the family of a youth killed by Nuccio, a Chicago policeman. In that capacity, plaintiff attended the coroner's inquest and filed an action for damages but played no part in a criminal proceeding in which Nuccio was convicted of second degree murder. Respondent published American Opinion, a monthly outlet for the views of the John Birch Society. As part of its efforts to alert the public to an alleged nationwide conspiracy to discredit local police, the magazine's editor engaged a regular contributor to write about the Nuccio episode. The article that appeared charged a frame-up against Nuccio and portrayed plaintiff as a "major architect" of the plot. It also falsely asserted that he had a long police record, was an official of the Marxist League for Industrial Democracy, and was a "Leninist" and a "Communist-fronter." The editor said he had no reason to doubt the charges and made no effort to verify them.]

[Gertz filed an action for libel in District Court because of diversity of citizenship. The trial judge first ruled that Gertz was not a public official or public figure and that under Illinois law there was no defense. The jury awarded $50,000. On further reflection, the judge granted the defendant judgment notwithstanding the jury's verdict on the theory that the *Times* rule should be extended to all defamation relating to matters of public concern. While the appeal was pending, a plurality of the Supreme Court embraced that theory in Rosenbloom v. Metromedia, Inc., 403 U.S. 29, 1 Med. L. Rptr. 1597 (1971). The court of appeals, relying on the plurality opinion in *Rosenbloom,* affirmed because of the absence of clear and convincing evidence of actual malice. Gertz appealed, arguing that plaintiffs who were not public figures or public officials should not have to show actual malice.]

MR. JUSTICE POWELL delivered the opinion of the Court.

. . .

III.

We begin with the common ground. Under the First Amendment there is no such thing as a false idea. However pernicious an opinion may seem, we depend for its correction not on the conscience of judges and juries but on the competition of other ideas. But there is no constitutional value in false statements of fact. Neither the intentional lie nor the careless error materially advances society's interest in "uninhibited, robust, and wide-open" debate on public issues. . . .

Although the erroneous statement of fact is not worthy of constitutional protection, it is nevertheless inevitable in free debate. . . . And punishment of error runs the risk of inducing a cautious and restrictive exercise of the constitutionally guaranteed freedoms of speech and press. Our decisions recognize that a rule of strict liability that compels a publisher or broadcaster to guarantee the accuracy of his factual assertions may lead to intolerable self-censorship. Allowing the media to avoid liability only by proving the truth of all injurious statements does not accord adequate protection to First Amendment liberties. . . . The First Amendment requires that we protect some falsehood in order to protect speech that matters.

The need to avoid self-censorship by the news media is, however, not the only societal value at issue. If it were, this Court would have embraced long ago the view that publishers and broadcasters enjoy an unconditional and indefeasible immunity from liability for defamation. . . .

The legitimate state interest underlying the law of libel is the compensation of individuals for the harm inflicted on them by defamatory falsehood. We would not lightly require the State to abandon this purpose, for, as Mr. Justice Stewart has reminded us, the individual's right to the protection of his own good name

> "reflects no more than our basic concept of the essential dignity and worth of every human being—a concept at the root of any decent system of ordered liberty. The protection of private personality, like the protection of life itself, is left primarily to the individual States under the Ninth and Tenth Amendments. But this does not mean that the right is entitled to any less recognition by this Court as a basic of

our constitutional system." Rosenblatt v. Baer, 383 U.S. 75, 92 (1966) (concurring opinion).

Some tension necessarily exists between the need for a vigorous and uninhibited press and the legitimate interest in redressing wrongful injury. . . .

The *New York Times* standard defines the level of constitutional protection appropriate to the context of defamation of a public person. Those who, by reason of the notoriety of their achievements or the vigor and success with which they seek the public's attention, are properly classed as public figures and those who hold governmental office may recover for injury to reputation only on clear and convincing proof that the defamatory falsehood was made with knowledge of its falsity or with reckless disregard for the truth. This standard administers an extremely powerful antidote to the inducement to media self-censorship of the common-law rule of strict liability for libel and slander. And it exacts a correspondingly high price from the victims of defamatory falsehood. Plainly many deserving plaintiffs, including some intentionally subjected to injury, will be unable to surmount the barrier of the *New York Times* test. Despite this substantial abridgment of the state law right to compensation for wrongful hurt to one's reputation, the Court has concluded that the protection of the *New York Times* privilege should be available to publishers and broadcasters of defamatory falsehood concerning public officials and public figures. [ ] We think that these decisions are correct, but we do not find their holdings justified solely by reference to the interest of the press and broadcast media in immunity from liability. Rather, we believe that the *New York Times* rule states an accommodation between this concern and the limited state interest present in the context of libel actions brought by public persons. For the reasons stated below, we conclude that the state interest in compensating injury to the reputation of private individuals requires that a different rule should obtain with respect to them.

Theoretically, of course, the balance between the needs of the press and the individual's claim to compensation for wrongful injury might be struck on a case-by-case basis. As Mr. Justice Harlan hypothesized, "it might seem, purely as an abstract matter, that the most utilitarian approach would be to scrutinize carefully every jury verdict in every libel case, in order to ascertain whether the final judgment leaves fully protected whatever First Amendment values transcend the legitimate state interest in protecting the particular plaintiff who prevailed." [*Rosenbloom*]. But this approach would lead to unpredictable results and uncertain expectations, and it could render our duty to supervise the lower courts unmanageable. Because an *ad hoc* resolution of the competing interests at stake in each particular case is not feasible, we must lay down broad rules of general application. Such rules necessarily treat alike various cases involving differences as well as similarities. Thus it is often true that not all of the considerations which justify adoption of a given rule will obtain in each particular case decided under its authority.

With that caveat we have no difficulty in distinguishing among defamation plaintiffs. The first remedy of any victim of defamation is self-help— using available opportunities to contradict the lie or correct the error and thereby to minimize its adverse impact on reputation. Public officials and public figures usually enjoy significantly greater access to the channels of effective communication and hence have a more realistic opportunity to counteract false statements than private individuals normally enjoy.[9] Private individuals are therefore more vulnerable to injury, and the state interest in protecting them is correspondingly greater.

More important than the likelihood that private individuals will lack effective opportunities for rebuttal, there is a compelling normative consideration underlying the distinction between public and private defamation plaintiffs. An individual who decides to seek governmental office must accept certain necessary consequences of that involvement in public affairs. He runs the risk of closer public scrutiny than might otherwise be the case. And society's interest in the officers of government is not strictly limited to the formal discharge of official duties. As the Court pointed out in [*Garrison v. Louisiana*], the public's interest extends to "anything which might touch on an official's fitness for office. . . . Few personal attributes are more germane to fitness for office than dishonesty, malfeasance, or improper motivation, even though these characteristics may also affect the official's private character."

Those classed as public figures stand in a similar position. Hypothetically, it may be possible for someone to become a public figure through no purposeful action of his own, but the instances of truly involuntary public figures must be exceedingly rare. For the most part those who attain this status have assumed roles of especial prominence in the affairs of society. Some occupy positions of such persuasive power and influence that they are deemed public figures for all purposes. More commonly, those classed as public figures have thrust themselves to the forefront of particular public controversies in order to influence the resolution of the issues involved. In either event, they invite attention and comment.

Even if the foregoing generalities do not obtain in every instance, the communications media are entitled to act on the assumption that public officials and public figures have voluntarily exposed themselves to increased risk of injury from defamatory falsehood concerning them. No such assumption is justified with respect to a private individual. He has not accepted public office or assumed an "influential role in ordering society." *Curtis Publishing Co. v. Butts*, [ ], (Warren, C. J., concurring in result). He has relinquished no part of his interest in the protection of his own good name, and consequently he has a more compelling call on the courts for redress of injury inflicted by defamatory falsehood. Thus, private individu-

---

9. Of course, an opportunity for rebuttal seldom suffices to undo harm of defamatory falsehood. Indeed, the law of defamation is rooted in our experience that the truth rarely catches up with a lie. But the fact that the self-help remedy of rebuttal, standing alone, is inadequate to its task does not mean that it is irrelevant to our inquiry.

als are not only more vulnerable to injury than public officials and public figures; they are also more deserving of recovery.

For these reasons we conclude that the States should retain substantial latitude in their efforts to enforce a legal remedy for defamatory falsehood injurious to the reputation of a private individual. The extension of the *New York Times* test proposed by the *Rosenbloom* plurality would abridge this legitimate state interest to a degree that we find unacceptable. And it would occasion the additional difficulty of forcing state and federal judges to decide on an *ad hoc* basis which publications address issues of "general or public interest" and which do not—to determine, in the words of Mr. Justice Marshall, "what information is relevant to self-government." [*Rosenbloom*] We doubt the wisdom of committing this task to the conscience of judges. Nor does the Constitution require us to draw so thin a line between the drastic alternatives of the *New York Times* privilege and the common law of strict liability for defamatory error. The "public or general interest" test for determining the applicability of the *New York Times* standard to private defamation actions inadequately serves both of the competing values at stake. On the one hand, a private individual whose reputation is injured by defamatory falsehood that does concern an issue of public or general interest has no recourse unless he can meet the rigorous requirements of *New York Times*. This is true despite the factors that distinguish the state interest in compensating private individuals from the analogous interest involved in the context of public persons. On the other hand, a publisher or broadcaster of a defamatory error which a court deems unrelated to an issue of public or general interest may be held liable in damages even if it took every reasonable precaution to ensure the accuracy of its assertions. And liability may far exceed compensation for any actual injury to the plaintiff, for the jury may be permitted to presume damages without proof of loss and even to award punitive damages.

We hold that, so long as they do not impose liability without fault, the States may define for themselves the appropriate standard of liability for a publisher or broadcaster of defamatory falsehood injurious to a private individual. This approach provides a more equitable boundary between the competing concerns involved here. It recognizes the strength of the legitimate state interest in compensating private individuals for wrongful injury to reputation, yet shields the press and broadcast media from the rigors of strict liability for defamation. At least this conclusion obtains where, as here, the substance of the defamatory statement "makes substantial danger to reputation apparent." [*Butts*] This phrase places in perspective the conclusion we announce today. Our inquiry would involve considerations somewhat different from those discussed above if a State purported to condition civil liability on a factual misstatement whose content did not warn a reasonably prudent editor or broadcaster of its defamatory potential. Cf. Time, Inc. v. Hill, 385 U.S. 374 (1967). Such a case is not now before us, and we intimate no view as to its proper resolution.

IV.

Our accommodation of the competing values at stake in defamation suits by private individuals allows the States to impose liability on the publisher or broadcaster of defamatory falsehood on a less demanding showing than that required by *New York Times*. This conclusion is not based on a belief that the considerations which prompted the adoption of the *New York Times* privilege for defamation of public officials and its extension to public figures are wholly inapplicable to the context of private individuals. Rather, we endorse this approach in recognition of the strong and legitimate state interest in compensating private individuals for injury to reputation. But this countervailing state interest extends no further than compensation for actual injury. For the reasons stated below, we hold that the States may not permit recovery of presumed or punitive damages, at least when liability is not based on a showing of knowledge of falsity or reckless disregard for the truth.

The common law of defamation is an oddity of tort law, for it allows recovery of purportedly compensatory damages without evidence of actual loss. Under the traditional rules pertaining to actions for libel, the existence of injury is presumed from the fact of publication. Juries may award substantial sums as compensation for supposed damage to reputation without any proof that such harm actually occurred. The largely uncontrolled discretion of juries to award damages where there is no loss unnecessarily compounds the potential of any system of liability for defamatory falsehood to inhibit the vigorous exercise of First Amendment freedoms. Additionally, the doctrine of presumed damages invites juries to punish unpopular opinion rather than to compensate individuals for injury sustained by the publication of a false fact. More to the point, the States have no substantial interest in securing for plaintiffs such as this petitioner gratuitous awards of money damages far in excess of any actual injury.

We would not, of course, invalidate state law simply because we doubt its wisdom, but here we are attempting to reconcile state law with a competing interest grounded in the constitutional command of the First Amendment. It is therefore appropriate to require that state remedies for defamatory falsehood reach no farther than is necessary to protect the legitimate interest involved. It is necessary to restrict defamation plaintiffs who do not prove knowledge of falsity or reckless disregard for the truth to compensation for actual injury. We need not define "actual injury," as trial courts have wide experience in framing appropriate jury instructions in tort actions. Suffice it to say that actual injury is not limited to out-of-pocket loss. Indeed, the more customary types of actual harm inflicted by defamatory falsehood include impairment of reputation and standing in the community, personal humiliation, and mental anguish and suffering. Of course, juries must be limited by appropriate instructions, and all awards must be supported by competent evidence concerning the injury, although there need be no evidence which assigns an actual dollar value to the injury.

We also find no justification for allowing awards of punitive damages against publishers and broadcasters held liable under state-defined standards of liability for defamation. In most jurisdictions jury discretion over the amounts awarded is limited only by the gentle rule that they not be excessive. Consequently, juries assess punitive damages in wholly unpredictable amounts bearing no necessary relation to the actual harm caused. And they remain free to use their discretion selectively to punish expressions of unpopular views. Like the doctrine of presumed damages, jury discretion to award punitive damages unnecessarily exacerbates the danger of media self-censorship, but, unlike the former rule, punitive damages are wholly irrelevant to the state interest that justifies a negligence standard for private defamation actions. They are not compensation for injury. Instead, they are private fines levied by civil juries to punish reprehensible conduct and to deter its future occurrence. In short, the private defamation plaintiff who establishes liability under a less demanding standard than that stated by *New York Times* may recover only such damages as are sufficient to compensate him for actual injury.

V.

Notwithstanding our refusal to extend the *New York Times* privilege to defamation of private individuals, respondent contends that we should affirm the judgment below on the ground that petitioner is either a public official or a public figure. There is little basis for the former assertion. Several years prior to the present incident, petitioner had served briefly on housing committees appointed by the mayor of Chicago, but at the time of publication he had never held any remunerative governmental position. Respondent admits this but argues that petitioner's appearance at the coroner's inquest rendered him a "de facto public official." Our cases recognize no such concept. Respondent's suggestion would sweep all lawyers under the *New York Times* rule as officers of the court and distort the plain meaning of the "public official" category beyond all recognition. We decline to follow it.

Respondent's characterization of petitioner as a public figure raises a different question. That designation may rest on either of two alternative bases. In some instances an individual may achieve such pervasive fame or notoriety that he becomes a public figure for all purposes and in all contexts. More commonly, an individual voluntarily injects himself or is drawn into a particular public controversy and thereby becomes a public figure for a limited range of issues. In either case such persons assume special prominence in the resolution of public questions.

Petitioner has long been active in community and professional affairs. He has served as an officer of local civic groups and of various professional organizations, and he has published several books and articles on legal subjects. Although petitioner was consequently well known in some circles, he had achieved no general fame or notoriety in the community. None of the prospective jurors called at the trial had ever heard of petitioner prior to this litigation, and respondent offered no proof that this response was atypical of the local population. We would not lightly assume that a citizen's participation in community and professional affairs rendered him a public figure for all purposes. Absent clear evidence of general fame or notoriety in the community, and pervasive involvement in the affairs of society, an individual should not be deemed a public personality for all aspects of his life. It is preferable to reduce the public-figure question to a more meaningful context by looking to the nature and extent of an individual's participation in the particular controversy giving rise to the defamation.

In this context it is plain that petitioner was not a public figure. He played a minimal role at the coroner's inquest, and his participation related solely to his representation of a private client. He took no part in the criminal prosecution of Officer Nuccio. Moreover, he never discussed either the criminal or civil litigation with the press and was never quoted as having done so. He plainly did not thrust himself into the vortex of this public issue, nor did he engage the public's attention in an attempt to influence its outcome. We are persuaded that the trial court did not err in refusing to characterize petitioner as a public figure for the purpose of this litigation.

We therefore conclude that the *New York Times* standard is inapplicable to this case and that the trial court erred in entering judgment for respondent. Because the jury was allowed to impose liability without fault and was permitted to presume damages without proof of injury, a new trial is necessary. We reverse and remand for further proceedings in accord with this opinion.

It is so ordered.

[Justice Blackmun joined the Court's opinion, providing the deciding vote. He had joined the plurality opinion in *Rosenbloom* and said he would have adhered to that view if his vote were not needed to create a majority, but believed it was important for the Court "to have a clearly defined majority position that eliminates the unsureness engendered by *Rosenbloom*'s diversity." He predicted *Gertz* would have "little, if any, practical effect on the functioning of responsible journalism."]

Mr. Chief Justice Burger, dissenting.

. . .

Agreement or disagreement with the law as it has evolved to this time does not alter the fact that it has been orderly development with a consistent basic rationale. . . . I would prefer to allow this area of law to continue to evolve as it has up to now with respect to private citizens rather than embark on a new doctrinal theory which has no jurisprudential ancestry.

The petitioner here was performing a professional representative role as an advocate in the highest tradition of the law, and under that tradition the advocate is not to be invidiously identified with his client. The important public policy which underlies this tradition—the right to counsel—would be gravely jeopardized if every lawyer who takes an "unpopular" case, civil or criminal, would automatically become fair game for irresponsible reporters and editors who might, for example, describe the lawyer as a "mob mouthpiece" for representing a client with a serious prior criminal record, or as an "ambulance chaser" for representing a claimant in a personal injury action.

I would reverse the judgment of the Court of Appeals and remand for reinstatement of the verdict of the jury and the entry of an appropriate judgment on that verdict.

MR. JUSTICE BRENNAN, dissenting.

I agree with the conclusion, expressed in Part V of the Court's opinion, that, at the time of publication of respondent's article, petitioner could not properly have been viewed as either a "public official" or "public figure"; instead, respondent's article, dealing with an alleged conspiracy to discredit local police forces, concerned petitioner's purported involvement in "an event of public or general interest." . . .

. . .

Although acknowledging that First Amendment values are of no less significance when media reports concern private persons' involvement in matters of public concern, the Court refuses to provide, in such cases, the same level of constitutional protection that has been afforded the media in the context of defamation of public persons. The accommodation that this Court has established between free speech and libel laws in cases involving public officials and public figures—that defamatory falsehood be shown by clear and convincing evidence to have been published with knowledge of falsity or with reckless disregard of truth—is not apt, the Court holds, because the private individual does not have the same degree of access to the media to rebut defamatory comments as does the public person and he has not voluntarily exposed himself to public scrutiny.

While these arguments are forcefully and eloquently presented, I cannot accept them, for the reasons I stated in *Rosenbloom:*

> The *New York Times* standard was applied to libel of a public official or public figure to give effect to the [First] Amendment's function to encourage ventilation of public issues, not because the public official has any less interest in protecting his reputation than an individual in private life. While the argument that public figures need less protection because they can command media attention to counter criticism may be true for some very prominent people, even then it is the rare case where the denial overtakes the original charge. Denials, retractions, and corrections are not 'hot' news, and rarely receive the prominence of the original story. When the public official or public figure is a minor functionary, or has left the position that put him in the public eye . . ., the argument loses all of its force. In the vast majority of libels involving public officials or public figures, the ability to respond through the media will depend on the same complex factor on which the ability of a private individual depends: the unpredictable event of the media's continuing interest in the story. Thus the unproved, and highly improbable, generalization that an as yet [not fully defined] class of 'public figures' involved in matters of public concern will be better able to respond through the media than private individu-

als also involved in such matters seems too insubstantial a reed on which to rest a constitutional distinction. [ ]

. . .

. . . Under a reasonable-care regime, publishers and broadcasters will have to make prepublication judgments about juror assessment of such diverse considerations as the size, operating procedures, and financial condition of the news-gathering system, as well as the relative costs and benefits of instituting less frequent and more costly reporting at a higher level of accuracy. [ ] Moreover, in contrast to proof by clear and convincing evidence required under the *Times* test, the burden of proof for reasonable care will doubtless be the preponderance of the evidence. . . .

Mr. Justice White, dissenting.

. . .

The Court evinces a deep-seated antipathy to "liability without fault." But this catch-phrase has no talismanic significance and is almost meaningless in this context where the Court appears to be addressing those libels and slanders that are defamatory on their face and where the publisher is no doubt aware from the nature of the material that it would be inherently damaging to reputation. He publishes notwithstanding, knowing that he will inflict injury. With this knowledge, he must intend to inflict that injury, his excuse being that he is privileged to do so—that he has published the truth. But as it turns out, what he has circulated to the public is a very damaging falsehood. Is he nevertheless "faultless"? Perhaps it can be said that the mistake about his defense was made in good faith, but the fact remains that it is he who launched the publication knowing that it could ruin a reputation.

In these circumstances, the law has heretofore put the risk of falsehood on the publisher where the victim is a private citizen and no grounds of special privilege are invoked. The Court would now shift this risk to the victim, even though he has done nothing to invite the calumny, is wholly innocent of fault, and is helpless to avoid his injury. . . . The press today is vigorous and robust. To me, it is quite incredible to suggest that threats of libel suits from private citizens are causing the press to refrain from publishing the truth. I know of no hard facts to support that proposition, and the Court furnishes none.

The communications industry has increasingly become concentrated in a few powerful hands operating very lucrative businesses reaching across the Nation and into almost every home. Neither the industry as a whole nor its individual components are easily intimidated, and we are fortunate that they are not. Requiring them to pay for the occasional damage they do to private reputation will play no substantial part in their future performance or their existence.

In any event, if the Court's principal concern is to protect the communications industry from large libel judgments, it would appear that its new requirements with respect to general and punitive damages would be ample protection. . . .

It is difficult for me to understand why the ordinary citizen should himself carry the risk of damage and suffer the injury in order to vindicate First Amendment values by protecting the press and others from liability for circulating false information. This is particularly true because such statements serve no purpose whatsoever in furthering the public interest or the search for truth but, on the contrary, may frustrate that search and at the same time inflict great injury on the defenseless individual. The owners of the press and the stockholders of the communications enterprises can much better bear the burden. And if they cannot, the public at large should somehow pay for what is essentially a public benefit derived at private expense.

. . .

For the foregoing reasons, I would reverse the judgment of the Court of Appeals and reinstate the jury's verdict.

[Justice Blackmun concurred and Justice Douglas dissented.]

Notes and Questions

1. Why did the majority adhere to the *Times* rule for public officials? For public figures?

2. Why did the majority in *Gertz* reject the argument embraced by the plurality in *Rosenbloom?*

3. After this decision, what could Gertz hope to recover if he was able to show negligence but not actual malice? Did he suffer "actual injury"?

His strategy when his case was retried under the new rules may give some clues. He continued to claim presumed and punitive damages, and he offered evidence of actual malice. The jury awarded him $100,000 compensatory damages and $300,000 punitive damages. On appeal, the court affirmed. It concluded that the jury could find "actual malice" because the editor of the magazine had solicited an author with a "known and unreasonable propensity to label persons or organizations as Communist, to write the article; and after the article was submitted, made virtually no effort to check the validity of statements that were defamatory *per se* of Gertz, and in fact added further defamatory material based on [the writer's] 'facts.' " It also held that the actual malice of the writer could be imputed to the magazine. Gertz v. Robert Welch, Inc., 680 F.2d 527, 8 Med. L. Rptr. 1769 (7th Cir. 1982).

4. Even if a plaintiff shows actual malice, state law may preclude or limit punitive damages. Some states require a showing of some further element, such as animosity toward plaintiff, in addition to actual malice. Some states do not permit punitive damages at all, and some do not permit them in libel cases. Many tort reform statutes limit the amount of punitive damages; although these statutes were written primarily with physical injury cases in mind, they may apply also to defamation actions.

5. Justice Powell said negligence-based liability is permissible "at least . . . where, as here, the substance of the defamatory statement 'makes substantial danger to reputation apparent.' . . . Our inquiry would involve considerations somewhat different from those discussed above if a State purported to condition civil liability on a factual misstatement whose content did not warn a reasonably prudent editor or broadcaster of its defamatory potential." Is he suggesting that that actual malice might be required for statements that are defamatory only by virtue of extrinsic facts? That such statements are not actionable at all? These questions remain unresolved.

———

State law alternatives. Gertz establishes only a federal constitutional minimum, leaving the states free to adopt other rules that are more protective of speech. Most of these require private plaintiffs to prove actual malice. New York requires private plaintiffs to prove "that the publisher acted in a grossly irresponsible manner without due consideration for the standards of information gathering and dissemination ordinarily followed by responsible parties." Chapadeau v. Utica Observer–Dispatch, Inc., 38 N.Y.2d 196, 341 N.E.2d 569, 379 N.Y.S.2d 61, 1 Med. L. Rptr. 1693 (1975). This rule applies only to defamations that occur "within the sphere of legitimate public concern," but media decisions as to what are matters of public concern "will not be second-guessed as long as they are sustainable." Gaeta v. New York News, Inc., 62 N.Y.2d 340, 465 N.E.2d 802, 477 N.Y.S.2d 82, 10 Med. L. Rptr. 1966 (1984).

For an extensive discussion of the strict liability aspects of common law defamation, see Paul C. Weiler, Defamation, Enterprise Liability, and Freedom of Speech, 17 U. Toronto L. J. 278 (1967) and Harry Kalven, Jr., The Reasonable Man and the First Amendment: *Hill, Butts,* and *Walker,* 1967 Sup. Ct. Rev. 267. See also David A. Anderson, Libel and Press Self–Censorship, 53 Tex. L. Rev. 422, 432 n. 52 (1975), arguing that strict liability is especially pernicious in defamation because the other enterprises "have no choice but to accept the additional risk of liability if they are to continue their profitmaking activities, while most broadcasters and publishers can avoid liability, without discontinuing their activities or reducing their profits, by ceasing to carry material that creates the risk of liability—i.e., by increasing their self-censorship." Can a sound argument be made for strict liability in this area? Note that unlike potential personal injury victims, who can protect themselves with medical and income-protection insurance, such first party insurance is not generally available for potential libel victims.

b. Administering the Negligence Standard

Before we explore the many questions raised by the private plaintiff rules adopted in *Gertz*, it is important to note that most cases do not present these questions. Most reported cases against media (and we would expect unreported cases as well) are litigated as "actual malice" cases and not as negligence cases, for reasons that are fairly obvious. First, plaintiffs mentioned in the media are likely to be either admittedly public or found to be public. Second, unless a private plaintiff is willing to forgo presumed and punitive damages, he or she must prove actual malice anyway. If the plaintiff succeeds in doing so, there is no occasion to focus on the meaning of "actual injury." Conversely, a plaintiff who cannot establish "actual injury"—no matter what that is held to encompass—also must prove actual malice. As a result, negligence-based liability for defamation is of minor importance in media cases. It plays a larger role in business litigation, perhaps because pecuniary losses in those cases are likely to be large enough to be worth litigating over.

The standard. Justice Powell phrased the permissible standard in private-plaintiff cases negatively: states may use whatever standard they wish "so long as they do not impose liability without fault." No state has adopted a fault standard lower than negligence.

If negligence is the standard, the first question is whether the standard is professional negligence or ordinary care. This may be significant both in formulating the standard and in determining whether expert testimony is required (or permitted) to show the standard and the deviation. The states that have addressed this question have split. Compare Troman v. Wood, 62 Ill.2d 184, 340 N.E.2d 292 (1975) (rejecting the professional negligence approach because it would make prevailing newspaper practices controlling and might lead toward a progressive depreciation of the standard of care) with Gobin v. Globe Pub. Co., 216 Kan. 223, 531 P.2d 76 (1975) (adopting a variation on the medical malpractice standard: "the conduct of the reasonably careful publisher or broadcaster in the community or in similar communities under the existing circumstances").

Evidence of negligence. The Restatement (Second) of Torts § 580B, comment *h*, suggests that the reasonableness of the investigation varies with the following factors: 1. "The time element"—investigations may be shorter for topical news than for a story that has no time pressure. 2. "The nature of the interest promoted by publication"—a story informing the public of matters important in a democracy may warrant quicker publication than a story involving "mere gossip." 3. "Potential damage to plaintiff if the communication proves to be false"—whether the statement is defamatory on its face; how many readers will understand the defamation; how harmful is the charge.

One court has stated two other factors: the nature and reliability of the source of the information and the "reasonableness in checking the veracity of the information, considering its cost in terms of money, time, personnel, urgency of the publication, nature of the news and any other pertinent element." Torres–Silva v. El Mundo, 3 Med. L. Rptr. 1508 (P.R. 1977). See generally Lackland H. Bloom, Jr., Proof of Fault in Media Defamation Litigation, 38 Vand. L. Rev. 247 (1985).

Some have questioned the emphasis on time pressure. In Walter V. Schaefer, Defamation and the First Amendment, 52 Colo. L. Rev. 1 (1980), the former Chief Justice of Illinois said:

> It has been suggested that the press, television, and radio all operate under severe time constraints and that this consideration should excuse or justify defamatory statements. It should not be forgotten, however, that these time constraints are entirely self-imposed. Apparently the media people believe that for competitive reasons it is desirable to be first with a particular news story. My own impression is that the public is massively unconcerned about that question. But if my impression is wrong, deadline pressures afford no more justification for harm caused by negligent attacks upon reputation than for harm caused by a reporter's negligent driving in his haste to cover a story. Both negligent acts are and have been insurable.

Procedural issues. Most courts refuse to apply independent appellate review in cases in which the negligence standard controls. See Levine v. CMP Publications, Inc., 738 F.2d 660, 10 Med. L. Rptr. 2337 (5th Cir. 1984). There is also a split over whether to require "clear and convincing" evidence of negligence. Although most courts have declined to do so, a few have reached the opposite result as a matter of state law. The issue is discussed in Lansdowne v. Beacon Journal Publishing Co., 32 Ohio St.3d 176, 512 N.E.2d 979, 14 Med. L. Rptr. 1801 (1987).

c. *Actual Injury*

As we have already seen, the subject of damages was complicated enough at common law. Whether a plaintiff needed to show "special" damages and, if so, what constituted "special" damages produced much litigation. The Supreme Court's introduction, in *Gertz,* of "actual injury damages" did not purport to track any pre-existing concept of damages. Indeed, the Court went out of its way to use examples that showed that the new term was not the equivalent of "special" damages. Aside from these few sentences in *Gertz,* the Court's only guidance as to what "actual injury" means comes from Time, Inc. v. Firestone, 424 U.S. 448, 1 Med. L. Rptr. 1665 (1976). The plaintiff withdrew her claim for reputational harm on the eve of trial. Defendant argued that this barred her from recovering under *Gertz.* The Court disagreed. If Florida permitted recoveries in defamation actions that did not claim harm to reputation, *Gertz* did not forbid it:

> In [*Gertz*] we made it clear that States could base awards on elements other than injury to reputation, specifically listing "personal humiliation, and mental anguish and suffering" as examples of injuries which might be compensated consistently with the Constitution upon a showing of fault.

In *Firestone,* the plaintiff had presented evidence from her minister, her attorney, and several friends and neighbors. One of the latter was a physician who testified to "having to administer a sedative to respondent in an attempt to reduce discomfort wrought by her worrying about the article." Plaintiff also testified that she feared the effect that the false report of her adultery might have on her young son when he grew older. "The jury decided these injuries should be compensated by an award of $100,000. We have no warrant for re-examining this determination."

Gobin v. Globe Publishing Co., 232 Kan. 1, 649 P.2d 1239, 8 Med. L. Rptr. 2191 (1982), held that there could be no recovery for defamation without proof of harm to reputation. See also Richie v. Paramount Pictures Corp., 544 N.W.2d 21, 24 Med. L. Rptr. 1897 (Minn. 1996) and Schlegal v. Ottumwa Courier, 585 N.W.2d 217, 27 Med. L. Rptr. 1178 (Iowa 1998).

Hearst Corporation v. Hughes, 297 Md. 112, 466 A.2d 486, 9 Med. L. Rptr. 2504 (1983), chose to follow Florida's path in *Firestone* by permitting recovery of proven "personal humiliation and mental anguish" in the absence of reputational harm, though it noted that other state courts had disagreed. The Maryland court asserted that the contrary view failed to "respect the centuries of human experience which led to a presumption of harm flowing from words actionable per se. One reason for that common law position was the difficulty a defamation plaintiff has in proving harm to reputation." Since victims of defamation "can reasonably become genuinely upset as a result of the publication," the court saw "no social purpose to be served by requiring the plaintiff additionally to prove actual impairment of reputation."

Some courts have embraced the actual injury concept as a replacement for the common law special harm requirement discussed supra in Section B. For example, in *Nazeri v. Missouri Valley College*, supra p. 267, the court held that plaintiffs in libel and slander cases alike "need not concern themselves with whether the defamation was per se or per quod, nor with whether special damages exist, but must prove actual damages in all cases."

3. LIABILITY WITHOUT FAULT

Has *Gertz* occupied the entire field of defamation? Are there any categories of cases left in which states are free to impose strict liability in libel cases? In which they may award presumed or punitive damages without a showing of "actual malice"?

Dun & Bradstreet v. Greenmoss Builders. Justice Powell's opinion in *Gertz* did not speak of all defendants, but of "publishers and broadcasters." Many thought this meant non-media defendants would not receive the benefit of the *Gertz* limitations. But in Dun & Bradstreet, Inc. v. Greenmoss Builders, Inc., 472 U.S. 749, 11 Med. L. Rptr. 2417 (1985) a majority of the justices rejected any distinction between media and non-media defendants, although that was not the basis of decision. Justice White said it "makes no sense to give the most protection to those publishers who reach the most readers and therefore pollute the channels of communication with the most misinformation and do the most damage to private reputation."

Justice Brennan, joined by Justices Marshall, Blackmun, and Stevens, also rejected the distinction. First, in light of the growing power of mass media and their growing concentration, "protection for the speech of non-media defendants is essential to ensure a diversity of perspectives." In addition, "transformations in the technological and economic structure of the communications industry [have produced] an increasing convergence of what might be labeled 'media' and 'nonmedia.'"

Since this case, non-media defendants have not been stripped of *Gertz* protection solely because they are not media.

The *Dun & Bradstreet* case was decided on a different rationale. A different majority held that states may award presumed and punitive damages without proof of actual malice to private plaintiffs who are defamed in "speech on matters of purely private concern."

> While such speech is not totally unprotected by the First Amendment, [ ], its protections are less stringent. In *Gertz,* we found that the state interest in awarding presumed and punitive damages was not "substantial" in view of their effect on speech at the core of First Amendment concern. [ ] This interest, however, *is* "substantial" relative to the incidental effect these remedies may have on speech of significantly less constitutional interest. The rationale of the common law rules has been the experience and judgment of history that "proof of actual damage will be impossible in a great many cases where, from the character of the defamatory words and the circumstances of publication, it is all but certain that serious harm has resulted in fact." [ ] As a result, courts for centuries have allowed juries to presume that some damage occurred from many defamatory utterances and publications. [ ] This rule furthers the state interest in providing remedies for defamation by ensuring that those remedies are effective. In light of the reduced constitutional value of speech involving no matters of public concern, we hold that the state interest adequately supports awards of presumed and punitive damages—even absent a showing of "actual malice." . . .

> In addition, the speech here, like advertising, is hardy and unlikely to be deterred by incidental state regulation. See [*Virginia Pharmacy*]. It is solely motivated by the desire for profit, which, we have noted, is a force less likely to be deterred than others. [ ] Arguably, the reporting here was also more objectively verifiable than speech deserving of greater protection. [ ] In any case, the market provides a powerful incentive to a credit reporting agency to be accurate, since false credit reporting is of no use to creditors. Thus, any incremental "chilling" effect of libel suits would be of decreased significance.

Justices White and Chief Justice Burger concurred in the judgment. They agreed that *Gertz* should not protect Dun & Bradstreet from presumed and punitive damages, but they would have gone further and repudiated *Gertz* as to all private plaintiffs.

The dissenters believed the majority was cutting away the protective mantle of *Gertz.* "Without explaining what *is* a 'matter of public concern,' the plurality opinion proceeds to serve up a smorgasbord of reasons why the speech at issue here is not, [ ], and on this basis affirms" the award. Any standard that can be gleaned from the opinions is "impoverished" and "irreconcilable with First Amendment principles. The credit reporting at issue here surely involves a subject matter of sufficient public concern to require the comprehensive protections of *Gertz.*"

The case involved a credit report that erroneously said the plaintiff corporation had filed for bankruptcy. The dissenters argued that such a report would clearly be a matter of public concern if reported in the local newspaper, and they said it should make no difference that Dun & Bradstreet sent the report only to five subscribers.

Justice Brennan asserted in a footnote that, since the subject matter "would clearly receive the comprehensive protections of *Gertz* were the speech publicly disseminated, [the] factor of confidential circulation to a limited number of subscribers is perhaps properly understood as the linchpin" of Justice Powell's analysis.

Initially, media expressed concern that *Dun & Bradstreet* might lead courts to second-guess editorial judgments and deny the protection of *Gertz* for media defamation arising out of matters the courts decided were not of "public concern." But so far courts have not done so, and media defendants have not been held liable without at least the *Gertz* requirements being met.

Defamation in commercial speech. It is possible—though not yet authoritatively established—that the constitutional protections of *Times* and *Gertz* are not applicable when the defamation occurs in commercial speech. In Procter & Gamble Co. v. Amway Corp., 242 F.3d 539, 29 Med. L. Rptr. 1449 (2001), Procter & Gamble sued Amway Corporation under a variety of federal and state unfair competition and product disparagement laws for harm allegedly caused when an Amway employee distributed a voice mail message repeating a rumor linking P & G with Satanism. The trial court had dismissed the suit in part because P & G was unable to prove that the Amway employee acted with actual malice. The Fifth Circuit reversed on this point, finding that the voice mail could constitute commercial speech and that because commercial speech is not protected from government regulation when the speech is false, there is no reason to protect false commercial speech from civil liability:

> *Central Hudson* [supra p. 170, and other commercial speech decisions], combined with the Court's plain statements that false commercial speech receives no protection, foreclose us from importing the actual-malice standard from defamation into the law of false commercial speech. Thus, if the trier of fact determines that the Amway distributors' motives in spreading the Satanism rumor were economic and that the speech therefore was commercial, this false commercial

speech cannot qualify for the heightened protection of the First Amendment, so P & G is not required to show actual malice in proving its Lanham Act claim.

The court rejected a suggestion that a negligence standard be adopted for such cases, arguing that it would blur the line the Supreme Court has drawn between protected and unprotected speech.

E. THE PUBLIC–PRIVATE DISTINCTION

Although comparatively few media libel cases are actually tried as negligence-based private-plaintiff cases, there continue to be numerous opinions addressing the public-private distinction. Most involve summary judgment motions, either granted or denied, in which the defendant claims the plaintiff is public and cannot show actual malice. Plaintiffs who cannot show actual malice at that stage are doomed unless they can persuade the judge that they are private and therefore need not need not do so. If they can survive these motions, they can at least get to trial and they therefore have some chance of obtaining a settlement, even if their chances of ultimately succeeding under the *Gertz* rules are slim. This may help to explain why so many plaintiffs seek to be treated as "private" and so few actually go to trial under that scheme. (On average, only seven of twenty media libel cases per year went to trial on a negligence theory from 1980 to 1998. See Libel Defense Resource Center, 1999 Report on Trials and Damages, Jan. 31, 1999, at 17.)

Because the decision processes are different, we treat the issue of identifying public figures separately from the issue of public officials.

1. WHO IS A PUBLIC OFFICIAL?

In Rosenblatt v. Baer, 383 U.S. 75, 1 Med. L. Rptr. 1558 (1966), plaintiff Baer had been hired by the three elected county commissioners to supervise a public recreation facility owned by the county. When he sued over a newspaper attack on the management of the facility, Justice Brennan's majority opinion held that Baer appeared to be a "public official" under criteria suggested by the rationale for the *Times* rule:

> There is, first, a strong interest in debate on public issues, and, second, a strong interest in debate about those persons who are in a position significantly to influence the resolution of those issues. Criticism of government is at the very center of the constitutionally protected area of free discussion. . . . It is clear, therefore, that the "public official" designation applies at the very least to those among the hierarchy of government employees who have, or appear to the public to have, substantial responsibility for or control over the conduct of government affairs.
>
> . . . Where a position in government has such apparent importance that the public has an independent interest in the qualifications and performance of the person who holds it, beyond the general public interest in the qualifications and performance of all government em-

ployees, both elements we identified in *New York Times* are present and the *New York Times* malice standards apply.[13]

Rosenblatt remains the Court's definitive articulation of the test for determining whether a person is a public official. A dictum in Hutchinson v. Proxmire, 443 U.S. 111, 5 Med. L. Rptr. 1279 (1979), discussed infra p. 317, noted that the Court had not "provided precise boundaries for the category of 'public official'; it cannot be thought to include all public employees, however."

Kassel v. Gannett Co., Inc., 875 F.2d 935, 16 Med. L. Rptr. 1814 (1st Cir. 1989) proposed a more elaborate process of decision. That court suggested that the test rests on a "tripodal base." The first leg is the recognition that discussion of issues of public importance must be "uninhibited, robust, and wide-open." Thus, "[p]olicymakers, upper-level administrators, and supervisors" are public officials because they "occupy niches of 'apparent importance' sufficient to give the public an independent interest in the qualifications and performances of the persons who hold them." If, as stated in a *Rosenblatt* footnote, "a night watchman accused of stealing state secrets" is not a public official, then the "inherent attributes of the position, not the occurrence of random events, must signify the line of demarcation."

The second leg focuses on the plaintiff's access to media to counteract the impact of false and injurious statements (building on *Gertz*). The court explained that "government workers who, by virtue of their employment, may easily defuse erroneous or misleading reports without judicial assistance should more likely be ranked as 'public officials' for libel law purposes. Conversely, those who work for the sovereign, but who enjoy little or no sway over, or 'special' access to, the news media are less likely to be trapped within the seine" of that label.

The final leg, again drawing on *Gertz*, involves the degree to which the plaintiff has assumed the risk of exposure to criticism by the media: "[p]ersons who actively seek positions of influence in public life do so with the knowledge that, if successful in attaining their goals, diminished privacy will result." On the other hand, there are public employees who have not assumed an influential role in government and cannot be said to have "exposed themselves to increasing risk of injury from defamatory falsehood concerning them."

The court identified these as "instructive policy concerns," not independent requirements. Is *Kassel* consistent with the two alternative approaches suggested in *Rosenblatt*? Do the self-help and assumed risk analyses make sense in the context of public officials?

---

13. It is suggested that this test might apply to a night watchman accused of stealing state secrets. But a conclusion that the *New York Times* malice standards apply could not be reached merely because a statement defamatory of some person in government employ catches the public's interest: that conclusion would virtually disregard society's interest in protecting reputation. The employee's position must be one which would invite public scrutiny and discussion of the person holding it, apart from the scrutiny and discussion occasioned by the particular charges in controversy.

Candidates. Not surprisingly, the Court quickly and unanimously extended the *Times* rationale to candidates on the ground that "it can hardly be doubted that the constitutional guarantee has its fullest and most urgent application precisely to the conduct of campaigns for political office." Monitor Patriot Co. v. Roy, 401 U.S. 265, 1 Med. L. Rptr. 1619 (1971), and Ocala Star–Banner Co. v. Damron, 401 U.S. 295, 1 Med. L. Rptr. 1624 (1971).

Perhaps less inevitably, the Court decided in *Roy* that the *Times* rule should include "anything which might touch on an official's fitness for office" when a candidate's behavior is being discussed:

> A candidate who, for example, seeks to further his cause through the prominent display of his wife and children can hardly argue that his qualities as a husband or father remain of "purely private" concern. And the candidate who vaunts his spotless record and sterling integrity cannot convincingly cry "Foul!" when an opponent or an industrious reporter attempts to demonstrate the contrary. Any test adequate to safeguard First Amendment guarantees in this area must go far beyond the customary meaning of the phrase "official conduct."

> Given the realities of our political life, it is by no means easy to see what statements about a candidate might be altogether without relevance to his fitness for the office he seeks. The clash of reputations is the staple of election campaigns, and damage to reputation is, of course, the essence of libel. But whether there remains some exiguous area of defamation against which a candidate may have full recourse is a question we need not decide in this case.

In *Roy*, a newspaper column, published three days before the election, falsely accused a candidate for the U.S. Senate of criminal activity many years earlier. The Court concluded that a "charge of criminal conduct, no matter how remote in time or place, can never be irrelevant to an official's or a candidate's fitness for office" for purposes of applying the *Times* rule.

In *Damron*, a newspaper reported two weeks before a local election that a candidate had been charged with perjury, when in fact his brother was the one charged. Again, the *Times* rule applied.

Public employees. There is virtual unanimity that police officers are public officials for defamation purposes. See Britton v. Koep, 470 N.W.2d 518, 19 Med. L. Rptr. 1208 (Minn. 1991), asserting that other states "unanimously have held that police officers, undercover agents, and deputy sheriffs are public officials. The rationale appears to be that, even for those who work undercover or anonymously, [ ], those officers possess significant powers granted by the government." But see Madsen v. United Television Inc., 797 P.2d 1083, 17 Med. L. Rptr. 1942 (Utah 1990), in which the court refused to decide whether a "police officer is *ipso facto* a public official."

As to other categories of public employees, whether they are treated as public figures depends on the nature of their powers and duties. A firefighter who sued over a newscast about his termination for inability to pass the EMT examination was held not to be a public official. The court thought it "strain[ed] credibility to say that [plaintiff], as a low-ranking fire fighter, had substantial responsibility over the conduct of governmental affairs." Jones v. Palmer Communications Inc., 440 N.W.2d 884, 16 Med. L. Rptr. 2137 (Iowa 1989).

Former public officials. Former officials remain public officials for purposes of commentary on their performance while in office. In Milgroom v. News Group Boston Inc., 412 Mass. 9, 586 N.E.2d 985, 20 Med. L. Rptr. 1097 (1992), a former judge criticized for conduct during her tenure on the bench was held to remain a public official for commentary on that performance since the "administration of justice" is a "subject of continuing public interest." See also Zerangue v. TSP Newspapers, Inc., 814 F.2d 1066, 13 Med. L. Rptr. 2438 (5th Cir. 1987) (officials who lost their jobs six years earlier remain in public official category for purposes of coverage of their activities while in office).

A former head of the Justice Department organized crime strike force was a public official with respect to charges that he "avoided prosecuting certain organized crime figures." But he was a private person as to charges that after leaving office, as an attorney he exploited personal contacts in the department to seek favorable treatment for his clients. Crane v. The Arizona Republic, 972 F.2d 1511, 20 Med. L. Rptr. 1649 (9th Cir. 1992).

For an extended examination of public official case law, see David Elder, Defamation, Public Officialdom, and the *Rosenblatt v. Baer* Criteria—A Proposal for Revivification Two Decades after *New York Times Co. v. Sullivan,* 33 Buff. L. Rev. 572 (1984). Elder argues that lower courts have misconstrued Supreme Court public official cases and that courts should restrict the scope of that concept.

2. WHO IS A PUBLIC FIGURE?

In *Gertz* the Court said it had "no difficulty distinguishing among defamation plaintiffs" on the basis of their public or private status. In fact, in subsequent cases members of the Supreme Court have not been able to agree among themselves as to who is a public figure. We briefly summarize the Supreme Court's public figure cases, and then turn to the efforts of the lower courts.

The Firestone case. In Time Inc. v. Firestone, 424 U.S. 448, 1 Med. L. Rptr. 1665 (1976), Time Magazine incorrectly reported that a member of "one of America's wealthier industrial families" had received a divorce because of his wife's adultery. A five-member majority held plaintiff to be private: "Respondent did not assume any role of especial prominence in the affairs of society, other than perhaps Palm Beach society, and she did not thrust herself to the forefront of any particular public controversy in order to influence the resolution of the issues involved in it." The fact that the case may have been of great public interest, did not make plaintiff a public figure. Moreover, the Court observed, plaintiff was compelled to go to court to seek relief in a marital dispute and her involvement was not voluntary. The fact that she held "a few" press conferences during the case did not change her otherwise private status. She did not attempt to use them to influence the outcome of the trial or to thrust herself into an unrelated dispute.

The Wolston case. In Wolston v. Reader's Digest Ass'n, 443 U.S. 157, 5 Med. L. Rptr. 1273 (1979), defendant's 1974 book incorrectly listed plaintiff as one of a group "who were convicted of espionage or falsifying information or perjury and/or contempt charges following espionage indictments or who fled to the Soviet bloc to avoid prosecution." In fact, he had been indicted for and convicted of contempt of court.

During the six weeks in 1958 between his failure to appear and his sentencing, plaintiff's case was the subject of 15 stories in Washington and New York newspapers. "This flurry of publicity subsided" following the sentencing, and plaintiff "succeeded for the most part in returning to the private life he had led" prior to the subpoena. A six-member majority held plaintiff private because he had neither "voluntarily thrust" nor "injected" himself into the forefront of the controversy surrounding the investigation of Soviet espionage in the United States. Wolston had not "engaged the attention of the public in an attempt to influence the resolution of the issues involved. . . . He did not in any way seek to arouse public sentiment in his favor and against the investigation. Thus, this is not a case where a defendant invites a citation for contempt in order to use the contempt citation as a fulcrum to create public discussion about the methods being used in connection with an investigation or prosecution."

The Hutchinson case. In Hutchinson v. Proxmire, 443 U.S. 111, 5 Med. L. Rptr. 1279 (1979), decided the same day as *Wolston*, defendant, a United States Senator, had criticized government grants to certain scientists, including plaintiff, on the grounds that the grants were examples of wasteful government spending on unjustifiable scientific research. (Absolute privilege, discussed infra p. 347, did not apply because the claimed defamations were in press releases and newsletters.)

The eight-member majority held plaintiff to be private. Neither the fact that plaintiff had successfully applied for federal funds nor that he had access to media to respond to Senator Proxmire's charges, "demonstrates that Hutchinson was a public figure prior to the controversy." Rather, his "activities and public profile are much like those of countless members of his profession. His published writings reach a relatively small category of professionals concerned with research in human behavior." Those charged with defamation "cannot, by their own conduct, create their own defense by making the claimant a public figure. See [*Wolston*]." Nor had plaintiff "assumed any role of public prominence in the broad question of concern about expenditures."

Although *Gertz, Firestone, Wolston,* and *Hutchinson* all reject the defendant's claim that the plaintiff is a public figure, in fact a great many plaintiffs are treated as public figures. Frequently they do not contest the issue, and when they do they often lose. *Gertz* suggested that some plaintiffs are public figures for all purposes and some for more limited purposes. We employ that distinction, but courts sometimes do not.

a. General–Purpose Public Figures

According to one definition,

> [A] general public figure is a well-known "celebrity," his name a "household word." The public recognizes him and follows his words and deeds, either because it regards his ideas, conduct, or judgment as worthy of the attention or because he actively pursues that consideration.

Waldbaum v. Fairchild Publications, Inc., 627 F.2d 1287, 5 Med. L. Rptr. 2629 (D.C. Cir. 1980). Is that definition consistent with *Gertz*? Is it a useful way to approach the question? See also Buckley v. Littell, 539 F.2d 882 (2d Cir. 1976) (William F. Buckley, Jr.); Carson v. Allied News Co., 529 F.2d 206 (7th Cir. 1976) (Johnny Carson); Chuy v. Philadelphia Eagles Football Club, 595 F.2d 1265, 4 Med. L. Rptr. 2537 (3d Cir. en banc 1979) (a professional football player who is alleged to have a career-ending disease is a public figure). All except *Waldbaum* were decided before *Hutchinson* and *Wolston*. Which of the following might meet the quoted standard: Ralph Reed? William Kristol? Michael Jordan? Barry Bonds? Dan Rather? Robert Redford? Michael Moore? J.K. Rowling? Oprah Winfrey? To what segment of the public must the person be known? Is recognition by law students a fair gauge of "celebrity"?

Although there are few contested cases holding plaintiffs to be general-purpose public figures, many plaintiffs do not challenge the defendant's characterization of them as public figures. See, e.g., Kaelin v. Globe Communications Corp., 162 F.3d 1036, 27 Med. L. Rptr. 1142 (9th Cir. 1998), supra p. 258 (houseguest of O. J. Simpson); Church of Scientology International v. Time Warner Inc., 26 Med. L. Rptr. 2394 (S.D.N.Y. 1998) (religious group). In these it is of course impossible to know whether the plaintiffs considered themselves general- or limited-purpose public figures, or whether they even took note of the distinction.

b. Limited–Purpose Public Figures

WFAA–TV, Inc. v. McLemore

Supreme Court of Texas, 1998.
978 S.W.2d 568, 26 Med. L. Rptr. 2385, certiorari denied 526 U.S. 1051.

HANKINSON, Justice, delivered the opinion for a unanimous Court.

In this defamation suit arising out of the 1993 Bureau of Alcohol, Tobacco and Firearms (ATF) raid on the Branch Davidian compound at Mount Carmel, we decide whether a media plaintiff, one of only a few journalists to report live from the scene of the raid, whose reports were rebroadcast worldwide, and who willingly gave numerous interviews about his role in the failed raid, is a public figure. The plaintiff sued WFAA–TV Channel 8 in Dallas alleging that its news reports concerning his role in the failed raid damaged his reputation in the community. The trial court denied WFAA's motion for summary judgment, and the court of appeals affirmed. [ ]. Because we conclude that the plaintiff in this case became a limited-purpose public figure after thrusting himself to the forefront of the controversy surrounding the failed ATF assault, we reverse the court of appeals' judgment and render judgment that the plaintiff take nothing.

On February 28, 1993, ATF agents approached the Mount Carmel compound occupied by the Branch Davidians, a small religious sect that had amassed an arsenal of illegal weaponry. Two local media outlets, KWTX–TV Channel 10 in Waco and the Waco Tribune–Herald, learned from various sources that a major law enforcement operation would proceed at Mount Carmel that morning. KWTX–TV dispatched reporter John McLemore and cameraman Dan Mullony to report on the event.

When the ATF agents attempted to enter one of the buildings on the compound, they became involved in a gunfight with the Davidians. During the battle, four ATF agents and three Davidians were killed, and twenty ATF agents were wounded. McLemore and Mullony, the only media representatives to follow the agents onto the compound, reported live from the midst of the firefight.

[Two days after the gunfight, media reports began to focus on why the ATF raid had failed and what sparked the gunfight. A Houston newspaper reporter interviewed on ABC's "Nightline" said ATF agents believed they were set up by reporters for the local newspaper and television station, "who were already at the compound, some of whom were reporters for, I believe, the TV station, allegedly were already hiding in the trees when federal agents arrived." The next day WFAA in Dallas picked up the story and repeated the report that ATF agents saw local media hiding in trees at the compound before the attack began. During these broadcasts WFAA showed video footage of McLemore while apparently on the compound grounds and named McLemore as one of three or four local news personnel whose presence had tipped off the Davidians. In fact no news people were on the premises before the agents arrived, no one was hiding in the trees, and the Davidians been alerted to the impending raid earlier when a different television reporter asked directions from a motorist on a nearby road who happened to be a member of the sect. Soon after the reports aired, McLemore sued WFAA–TV and other media defendants. The trial court granted summary judgment to the other defendants on various grounds. WFAA–TV moved for summary judgment on the ground that McLemore was a public figure and could not show actual malice. The trial court denied that motion, concluding that McLemore was not a public figure, and the court of appeals affirmed.]

Because a defamation plaintiff's status dictates the degree of fault he or she must prove to render the defendant liable, the principal issue in this case is whether McLemore is a public figure. The question of public-figure status is one of constitutional law for courts to decide. See Rosenblatt v. Baer [supra p. 313]; Trotter v. Jack Anderson Enters., Inc., 818 F.2d 431, 433 (5th Cir. 1987). . . .

To determine whether an individual is a limited-purpose public figure, the Fifth Circuit has adopted a three-part test:

(1) the controversy at issue must be public both in the sense that people are discussing it and people other than the immediate participants in the controversy are likely to feel the impact of its resolution;

(2) the plaintiff must have more than a trivial or tangential role in the controversy; and

(3) the alleged defamation must be germane to the plaintiff's participation in the controversy.

Trotter, 818 F.2d at 433 (citing Tavoulareas v. Piro, 817 F.2d 762, 772–73 (D.C. Cir. 1987) (en banc)); see also Waldbaum v. Fairchild Pub., Inc. 627 F.2d 1287, 1296–98 (D.C. Cir. 1980). Although the *Trotter/Waldbaum* test does not distinguish between plaintiffs who have voluntarily injected themselves into a controversy and those who are involuntarily drawn into a controversy, some courts have held that plaintiffs who are drawn into a controversy cannot be categorized as limited-purpose public figures.[1] Because, as we explain below, McLemore clearly voluntarily injected himself into the controversy at issue, we need not decide in this case whether "voluntariness" is a requirement under the limited-purpose public-figure test we apply. Nevertheless, the *Trotter/Waldbaum* elements provide a "generally accepted test" to determine limited-purpose public-figure status. [ ]

Applying the *Trotter/Waldbaum* limited-purpose public-figure elements to this case, we must first determine the controversy at issue. [ ] In *Waldbaum*, the D.C. Circuit elaborated on how to determine the existence and scope of a public controversy:

> To determine whether a controversy indeed existed and, if so, to define its contours, the judge must examine whether persons actually were discussing some specific question. A general concern or interest will not suffice. The court can see if the press was covering the debate, reporting what people were saying and uncovering facts and theories to help the public formulate some judgment.

[ ] In this case, numerous commentators, analysts, journalists, and public officials were discussing the raid and the reasons why the ATF raid failed. . . . [T]he press was actively covering the debate over why the ATF raid failed. Many such discussions focused on the role of the local media in the ATF's failure to capture the Davidian compound. The controversy surrounding the Branch Davidian raid was public, both in the sense that people were discussing it and people other than the immediate participants in the controversy were likely to feel the impact of its resolution. [ ] While the court of appeals defined the controversy as limited to "McLemore's

---

1. See, e.g., Lerman v. Flynt Distrib. Co., Inc., 745 F.2d 123, 136–37 (2d Cir. 1984) (adopting four-part limited public-figure test, requiring defendant to prove plaintiff: (1) "successfully invited public attention to his views in an effort to influence others prior to the incident that is the subject of litigation (2) voluntarily injected himself into a public controversy related to the subject of the litigation; (3) assumed a position of prominence in the public controversy; and (4) maintained regular and continuing access to the media"). . . .

personal ethical standards as a journalist," we do not view it so narrowly. Based on the facts outlined above, we conclude that the public controversy at issue is the broader question of why the ATF agents failed to accomplish their mission.

To determine that an individual is a public figure for purposes of the public controversy at issue, the second *Trotter/Waldbaum* element requires the plaintiff to have had more than a trivial or tangential role in the controversy. [ ] In considering a libel plaintiff's role in a public controversy, several inquiries are relevant and instructive: (1) whether the plaintiff actually sought publicity surrounding the controversy, Brewer v. Memphis Pub. Co., 626 F.2d 1238, 1254 (5th Cir. 1980); (2) whether the plaintiff had access to the media, see, e.g., *Gertz*, [ ] *Curtis* [*Publishing Co. v. Butts*, supra p. 284]; and (3) whether the plaintiff "voluntarily engag[ed] in activities that necessarily involve[d] the risk of increased exposure and injury to reputation," [ ]. "By publishing your views you invite public criticism and rebuttal; you enter voluntarily into one of the submarkets of ideas and opinions and consent therefore to the rough competition in the marketplace." Dilworth v. Dudley, 75 F.3d 307, 309 (7th Cir. 1996).

The record reflects that McLemore acted voluntarily to invite public attention and scrutiny on several occasions and in several different ways during the course of the public debate on the failed ATF raid. For example, McLemore was the only journalist to go onto the grounds of the compound, while other reporters assigned to cover the raid did not. By reporting live from the heart of the controversial raid, McLemore assumed a risk that his involvement in the event would be subject to public debate. Following the battle, McLemore spoke to other members of the press about the attempted raid, conveying his pride in his coverage from the midst of the gunfight, and portraying himself as a hero in assisting wounded ATF agents when he remarked that his role in the raid was "at considerable personal risk" and in contrast to other journalists who "were pinned down in a ditch" outside the compound. As a journalist, McLemore had ready, continual access to the various media sources. To one group of reporters, he explained that "as a journalist, I was . . . pleased to see that my coverage of this story was being broadcast to a wide audience." Thus, by choosing to engage in activities that necessarily involved increased public exposure and media scrutiny, McLemore played more than a trivial or tangential role in the controversy and, therefore, bore the risk of injury to his reputation. [ ]

The third and final element we consider—that the alleged defamation is germane to the plaintiff's participation in the controversy—is also satisfied in this case. [ ] McLemore alleges that WFAA defamed him by displaying footage of his coverage from the scene of the compound during the raid, while reporting that federal officials believed a member of the local media informed the Branch Davidians about the ATF raid. Therefore, the alleged defamation directly relates to McLemore's participation in the controversy. He was on the scene in his role as a journalist, as conveyed by the footage WFAA broadcast, and WFAA's alleged defamatory comments are indeed germane to McLemore's participation in the controversy over the media's role in the failed attack. See Waldbaum, 627 F.2d at 1298–1300 (explaining that a public figure's talents, education, experience, and motives were relevant to the public's decision to listen to him). Accordingly, McLemore reached limited-purpose public-figure status through his employment-related activities when he voluntarily injected himself into the Branch Davidian raid.

[The summary judgment motion was supported by an affidavit in which the WFAA–TV reporter stated that her reporting was based on "public allegations by responsible, respected and well-informed journalists and news organizations" which she believed to be accurate. The court said this, in the absence of controverting evidence from McLemore, negated actual malice.]

Notes and Questions

1. If McLemore had not spoken to other media about his role in the raid, would his coverage of it have been enough to make him a public figure? Note that the court says "he voluntarily injected himself into the Branch Davidian raid" even though he was assigned to cover it by his employer. Did he voluntarily inject himself into it by covering it better (or at least more aggressively) than others?

2. Could McLemore have been found a public figure under the test set out by the Second Circuit in footnote 1? The court says the public controversy is "why the ATF agents failed to accomplish their mission." How did McLemore participate in that controversy?

3. Although it is not mentioned in the opinion, McLemore was in fact something of a hero. When the shooting began, he ran to his news vehicle under fire and called for ambulances. When a cease-fire was negotiated, he used the vehicle to carry several wounded agents out of range of the Davidians' guns. Against orders from his newsroom, he did not go on air with his dramatic eyewitness account of the raid until he had delivered the wounded agents to the medical triage area. The next day the director of the ATF called to thank him for his bravery and assistance. See Ann Zimmerman, Caught in the crossfire, Dallas Observer Oct. 29, 1998, at 19. Do these additional facts strengthen the claim that he became a public figure?

4. Most courts share this court's view that the public-private issue is a question for the judge to decide. The First Circuit, in Kassel v. Gannett Co., supra p. 314, concluded that the issue "must be decided by the trial judge even where disputed fact questions prevent the resolution of the issue on a motion for summary judgment." Why is this so? The issue may involve classic factual questions: how widely known was the plaintiff? Did the plaintiff have media access? Was there a pre-existing public controversy? Was the plaintiff's participation voluntary? If the issue were submitted to the jury, how would the jury be instructed on other issues, such as fault and damages? Is avoidance of complicated conditional instructions a sufficient reason for treating the question as one of law?

c. *Involuntary Public Figures*

As the principal case indicates, some of the tests for public figure status seem to require that the plaintiff's participation be voluntary; others do not. Involuntary public figures have been very rare. Among the few that have been found so far are Meeropol v. Nizer, 560 F.2d 1061, 2 Med. L. Rptr. 2269 (2d Cir. 1977) (children of convicted spies Julius and Ethel Rosenberg); Carson v. Allied News Co., 529 F.2d 206 (7th Cir. 1976) (Johnny Carson's wife—unless she is "voluntary" because she married a famous person); Street v. National Broadcasting Co., 645 F.2d 1227, 7 Med. L. Rptr. 1001 (6th Cir. 1981) (main prosecution witness in famous Scottsboro case of 1931, in which nine black youths in Alabama were accused of raping plaintiff and another white woman; alleged defamation occurred 40 years after trial). Are these cases consistent with *Gertz* and *Wolston?*

In Dameron v. Washington Magazine, Inc., 779 F.2d 736, 12 Med. L. Rptr. 1508 (D.C. Cir. 1985), plaintiff had been the only air traffic controller on duty in 1974 when a plane approaching Dulles Airport crashed into Mt. Weather. Plaintiff testified in administrative and judicial proceedings that followed. In that case claims based on controller negligence were dismissed. In 1982 a plane crashed into the Potomac River. The story on the 1982 crash in defendant's city magazine included a sidebar on earlier local plane crashes and their causes. In that list the 1974 crash was attributed to "controller" failure. Plaintiff sued for libel. The district judge granted the magazine summary judgment.

The court of appeals held that persons "can become involved in public controversies and affairs without their consent or will. Air-controller Dameron, who had the misfortune to have a tragedy occur on his watch, is such a person" and became an involuntary public figure for the limited purpose of discussions of the Mt. Weather crash. The court acknowledged that the test set out in *Waldbaum* [cited in the principal case], which was controlling in the District of Columbia, required an "inquiry into the plaintiff's voluntary actions that have caused him to become embroiled in a public controversy." But the court said:

> This analysis clearly must be modified somewhat to accommodate the possibility of a potentially involuntary limited-purpose public figure that is presented here. We think, however, that the facts here satisfy the Supreme Court's definition of a public figure and an appropriately modified *Waldbaum* inquiry. There was indisputably a public controversy here. Nor can it be doubted that the alleged defamation was germane to the question of controller responsibility for air safety in general and the Mt. Weather crash in particular. There is no question that Dameron played a central, albeit involuntary, role in this controversy.

The case was distinguishable from *Wolston* because Dameron was "a central figure, however involuntarily, in the discrete and specific public controversy with respect to which he was allegedly defamed—the controversy over the cause of the Mt. Weather crash." *Wolston* was tangential to the investigation of Soviet espionage in general. If Dameron can prove that he was not a cause of the Mt. Weather crash, might he still be a central figure in the "controversy" over the cause of that crash? Would this amount to permitting the defendant to make Dameron a public figure by falsely accusing him?

In the principal case, the court said it need not decide whether persons can become public figures involuntarily because McLemore was a voluntary public figure. Might the case have been more appropriately analyzed as an involuntary plaintiff case, along the lines of *Dameron*?

One court has said that under the reasoning of *Dameron*, anyone caught up in a matter of public concern must prove actual malice if defamed in that context. "In light of the Supreme Court's repeated rejection of *Rosenbloom* [supra p. 297] we are unwilling to adopt an approach that returns us to an analysis that is indistinguishable." Wells v. Liddy, 186 F.3d 505, 539 (4th Cir. 1999). The court said the involuntary public figure category ought to be limited to "exceedingly rare" cases in which the plaintiff had become a central figure in a significant public controversy and had assumed the risk of publicity.

Plaintiffs who are involved with organized crime figures may be found to be involuntary public figures. See, e.g., Marcone v. Penthouse International, Ltd., 754 F.2d 1072, 11 Med. L. Rptr. 1577 (3d Cir. 1985). So too a person whose job brought him into constant contact, socially and officially, with a group of high ranking public officials, some of whom were involved in drugs. When one of them died of a drug overdose, plaintiff became a limited-purpose public figure:

> One may hobnob with high officials without becoming a public figure, but one who does so runs the risk that personal tragedies that for less well-connected people would pass unnoticed may place him at the heart of a public controversy. Clyburn engaged in conduct that he knew markedly raised the chances that he would become embroiled in a public controversy.

Clyburn v. News World Communications, Inc., 903 F.2d 29, 17 Med. L. Rptr. 1888 (D.C. Cir. 1990).

F. FALSITY

1. BURDEN OF PROOF

During the period when the English government rigorously used the law of criminal libel, truth was not a defense on the theory that unfavorable truths about government or officials were even more likely to stir up anti-government attitudes and actions than were falsehoods. But in civil libel, the common law long ago recognized truth as a defense provided the defendant published with good motives and for justifiable ends, and eventually the proviso was dropped, making truth a complete defense. *New York Times v. Sullivan*, supra p. 272, implied that treating truth as a defense might not be enough, but the Supreme Court did not address the matter explicitly until it decided the following case.

Philadelphia Newspapers, Inc. v. Hepps

Supreme Court of the United States, 1986.
475 U.S. 767, 106 S. Ct. 1558, 89 L. Ed.2d 783, 12 Med. L. Rptr. 1977.

[The Philadelphia Inquirer published a series of five investigative articles the thrust of which was that a chain of "Thrifty" stores, whose principal owner was Hepps, was "connected with underworld figures and organized crime." Hepps and his corporation and franchisees brought a libel suit against the corporate parent of the newspaper and the individual staffers who wrote the series. A state statute gave the defendants the burden of proving truth, but the trial judge believed that was unconstitutional and instructed the jury that the plaintiff bore the burden of proving falsity. The jury found for defendants. The Pennsylvania Supreme Court reversed, holding that the statute controlled the burden of proof issue and was not unconstitutional.]

JUSTICE O'CONNOR delivered the opinion of the Court. . . .

. . . As to falsity, Pennsylvania follows the common law's presumption that an individual's reputation is a good one. Statements defaming that person are therefore presumptively false, although a publisher who bears the burden of proving the truth of the statements has an absolute defense. [ ]

[The opinion interpreted *New York Times Co. v. Sullivan*, and subsequent cases as having already required that public-figure plaintiffs prove falsity, although the decisions had not said so explicitly. The issue in this case was whether the constitution also requires that private plaintiffs bear the burden of proving falsity.]

. . . We believe that the common law's rule on falsity—that the defendant must bear the burden of proving truth—must . . . fall here to a constitutional requirement that the plaintiff bear the burden of proving falsity, as well as fault, before recovering damages.

There will always be instances when the fact-finding process will be unable to resolve conclusively whether the speech is true or false; it is in those cases that the burden of proof is dispositive. Under a rule forcing the plaintiff to bear the burden of showing falsity, there will be some cases in which plaintiffs cannot meet their burden despite the fact that the speech is in fact false. The plaintiff's suit will fail despite the fact that, in some abstract sense, the suit is meritorious. Similarly, under an alternative rule placing the burden of showing truth on defendants, there would be some cases in which defendants could not bear their burden despite the fact that the speech is in fact true. Those suits would succeed despite the fact that, in some abstract sense, those suits are unmeritorious. Under either rule, then, the outcome of the suit will sometimes be at variance with the outcome that we would desire if all speech were either demonstrably true or demonstrably false.

This dilemma stems from the fact that the allocation of the burden of proof will determine liability for some speech that is true and some that is false, but all of such speech [as] is unknowably true or false. Because the burden of proof is the deciding factor only when the evidence is ambiguous, we cannot know how much of the speech affected by the allocation of the burden of proof is true and how much is false. In a case presenting a configuration of speech and plaintiff like the one we face here, and where the scales are in such an uncertain balance, we believe that the Constitution requires us to tip them in favor of protecting true speech. To ensure that true speech on matters of public concern is not deterred, we hold that the common-law presumption that defamatory speech is false cannot stand when a plaintiff seeks damages against a media defendant for speech of public concern.[4]

In the context of governmental restriction of speech, it has long been established that the government cannot limit speech protected by the First Amendment without bearing the burden of showing that its restriction is justified. [ ] It is not immediately apparent from the text of the First Amendment, which by its terms applies only to governmental action, that a similar result should obtain here: a suit by a private party is obviously quite different from the government's direct enforcement of its own laws. Nonetheless, the need to encourage debate on public issues that concerned the Court in the governmental-restriction cases is of concern in a similar manner in this case involving a private suit for damages: placement by state law of the burden of proving truth upon media defendants who publish speech of public concern deters such speech because of the fear that liability will unjustifiably result. [ ] Because such a "chilling" effect would be antithetical to the First Amendment's protection of true speech on matters of public concern, we believe that a private-figure plaintiff must bear the burden of showing that the speech at issue is false before recovering damages for defamation from a media defendant. To do otherwise could "only result in a deterrence of speech which the Constitution makes free." [ ]

We recognize that requiring the plaintiff to show falsity will insulate from liability some speech that is false, but unprovably so. Nonetheless, the Court's previous decisions on the restrictions that the First Amendment places upon the common law of defamation firmly support our conclusion here with respect to the allocation of the burden of proof. In attempting to resolve related issues in the defamation context, the Court has affirmed

---

4. We . . . have no occasion to consider the quantity of proof of falsity that a private-figure plaintiff must present to recover damages. Nor need we consider what standards would apply if the plaintiff sues a non-media defendant, see Hutchinson v. Proxmire, 443 U.S. 111, 133, n.16, 99 S. Ct. 2675, 2687, n.16, 61 L. Ed.2d 411 (1979), or if a State were to provide a plaintiff with the opportunity to obtain a judgment that declared the speech at issue to be false but did not give rise to liability for damages. [Footnote relocated].

that "[t]he First Amendment requires that we protect some falsehood in order to protect speech that matters." . . .

We note that our decision adds only marginally to the burdens that the plaintiff must already bear as a result of our earlier decisions in the law of defamation. The plaintiff must show fault. A jury is obviously more likely to accept a plaintiff's contention that the defendant was at fault in publishing the statements at issue if convinced that the relevant statements were false. As a practical matter, then, evidence offered by plaintiffs on the publisher's fault in adequately investigating the truth of the published statements will generally encompass evidence of the falsity of the matters asserted. See Keeton, Defamation and Freedom of the Press, 54 Texas L. Rev. 1221, 1236 (1976). See also Franklin & Bussel, The Plaintiff's Burden in Defamation: Awareness and Falsity, 25 Wm. & Mary L. Rev. 825, 856–857 (1984).

For the reasons stated above, the judgment of the Pennsylvania Supreme Court is reversed, and the case is remanded for further proceedings not inconsistent with this opinion.

JUSTICE BRENNAN, with whom JUSTICE BLACKMUN joins, concurring.

. . . I write separately only to note that, while the Court reserves the question whether the rule it announces applies to non-media defendants, [ ] I adhere to my view that such a distinction is "irreconcilable with the fundamental First Amendment principle that '[t]he inherent worth of . . . speech in terms of its capacity for informing the public does not depend upon the identity of the source, whether corporation, association, union, or individual.' " [ ]

. . .

JUSTICE STEVENS, with whom THE CHIEF JUSTICE, JUSTICE WHITE, and JUSTICE REHNQUIST join, dissenting.

. . .

In my opinion deliberate, malicious character assassination is not protected by the First Amendment to the United States Constitution. That Amendment does require the target of a defamatory statement to prove that his assailant was at fault, and I agree that it provides a constitutional shield for truthful statements. I simply do not understand, however, why a character assassin should be given an absolute license to defame by means of statements that can be neither verified nor disproved. The danger of deliberate defamation by reference to unprovable facts is not a merely speculative or hypothetical concern. Lack of knowledge about third parties, the loss of critical records, an uncertain recollection about events that occurred long ago, perhaps during a period of special stress, the absence of eyewitnesses—a host of factors may make it impossible for an honorable person to disprove malicious gossip about his past conduct, his relatives, his friends, or his business associates.

The danger of which I speak can be illustrated within the confines of this very case. Appellants published a series of five articles proclaiming that "Federal authorities . . . have found connections between Thrifty and underworld figures," [ ]; that "Federal agents have evidence of direct financial involvement in Thrifty by [Joseph] Scalleat," a "leader of organized crime in northeastern Pennsylvania," [ ]; and that "the Thrifty Beverage beer chain . . . had connections itself with organized crime," [ ]. The defamatory character of these statements is undisputed. Yet the factual basis for the one specific allegation contained in them is based on an admitted relationship between [plaintiffs] and a third party. The truth or falsity of that statement depends on the character and conduct of that third party—a matter which the jury may well have resolved against the plaintiffs on the ground that they could not disprove the allegation on which they bore the burden of proof.[8]

Despite the obvious blueprint for character assassination provided by the decision today, the Court's analytical approach—by attaching little or no weight to the strong state interest in redressing injury to private reputation—provides a wholly unwarranted protection for malicious gossip. As I understand the Court's opinion, its counterintuitive result is derived from a straightforward syllogism. The major premise seems to be that "the First Amendment's protection of true speech on matters of public concern," is [ ] tantamount to a command that no rule of law can stand if it will exclude any true speech from the public domain. The minor premise is that although "we cannot know how much of the speech affected by the allocation of the burden of proof is true and how much is false," [ ] at least some unverifiable gossip is true. From these premises it necessarily follows that a rule burdening the dissemination of such speech would contravene the First Amendment. Accordingly, "a private-figure plaintiff must bear the burden of showing that the speech at issue is false before recovering damages for defamation from a media defendant." [ ]

The Court's result is plausible however, only because it grossly undervalues the strong state interest in redressing injuries to private reputations. The error lies in its initial premise, with its mistaken belief that doubt regarding the veracity of a defamatory statement must invariably be resolved in favor of constitutional protection of the statement and against vindication of the reputation of the private individual. . . .

. . .

[In a footnote, the dissenters said they would hold that public plaintiffs also need not prove falsity, if that issue were before the Court.]

Notes and Questions

1. How might Hepps disprove the allegation that he or his business interests had underworld connections? Would his own testimony denying such connections be sufficient if the jury believed him?

2. The plaintiffs' proof problems were complicated by the fact that the newspaper refused to disclose the sources of its information. A state statute

---

8. At trial, the individual plaintiff simply denied knowledge of Joseph Scalleat's employment with Beer Sales Consultants and of BSC's employment by three Thrifty Stores. [ ]

protected the newspaper's right to keep sources confidential. The trial judge refused the plaintiffs' request to instruct the jury that it could draw inferences adverse to the defendants from their failure to present affirmative evidence as to the truthfulness of their sources. Plaintiffs did not appeal that decision, and the Court rejected plaintiffs' suggestion that these circumstances should affect the decision on burden of proof.

3. Note that the decision leaves the states free to treat truth as a defensive matter when the defamatory matter is not of public concern, and perhaps when the defendant is not media. But the Supreme Court has not treated non-media defendants differently, and lower courts generally apply *Hepps* to non-media cases. See, e.g., Burroughs v. FFP Operating Partners, L.P., 28 F.3d 543 (5th Cir. 1994). Virtually all of the statements media are sued over are treated as matters of public concern, as are many of the statements at issue in non-media litigation. Some states require all plaintiffs to prove falsity. See, e.g., Savage v. Pacific Gas & Electric Co., 21 Cal.App.4th 434, 26 Cal.Rptr.2d 305, 22 Med. L. Rptr. 1737 (1993). Whether the majority will do so remains to be seen.

4. Some courts have concluded that falsity must be shown with convincing clarity. Compare Steaks Unlimited, Inc. v. Deaner, 623 F.2d 264, 6 Med. L. Rptr. 1129 (3d Cir. 1980) and Buckley v. Littell, 539 F.2d 882, 1 Med. L. Rptr. 1762 (2d Cir. 1976) (requiring convincing clarity on falsity element) with Liberty Lobby, Inc. v. Dow Jones & Co., 838 F.2d 1287, 14 Med. L. Rptr. 2249 (D.C. Cir. 1988) and In re Standard Jury Instructions, 575 So.2d 194, 18 Med. L. Rptr. 1703 (Fla. 1991) (use "fair preponderance of the evidence").

5. Lower courts also disagree as to whether the First Amendment requires independent appellate review of the falsity element. Compare Liberty Lobby, Inc. v. Dow Jones & Co., 838 F.2d 1287, 14 Med. L. Rptr. 2249 (D.C. Cir. 1988) and Rouch v. Enquirer & News of Battle Creek, 440 Mich. 238, 487 N.W.2d 205, 20 Med. L. Rptr. 2265 (1992) (independent review on falsity) with Hinerman v. The Daily Gazette Co., 188 W.Va. 157, 423 S.E.2d 560, 20 Med. L. Rptr. 2169 (1992) (no independent review on falsity).

Material falsity. At common law, defendants were not required to prove literal truth of the charge but only to show that it was "substantially" true. Thus, if the defendant charged the plaintiff with stealing $25,000 from a bank, truth was established even if the actual amount was only $12,000. This idea has survived the switch in burden of proof. In *Masson v. New Yorker Magazine*, supra p. 287, the Court captured the common law's spirit in observing that the law of libel "overlooks minor inaccuracies and concentrates upon substantial truth." Thus, the test was whether what was published "would have had a different effect upon the mind of the reader from that which the pleaded truth would have produced." See also Haynes v. Alfred A. Knopf, Inc., infra p. 367 (the law protects false "details that, while not trivial, would not if corrected have altered the picture that the true facts paint").

On the other hand, if the evidence shows that the plaintiff did not commit any theft whatever but was a bigamist, the evidence of bigamy would not prevent the plaintiff from establishing the falsity of the published statement. The defendant might be able to mitigate damages by showing that the plaintiff's reputation was already in low esteem because of the bigamy and that he therefore suffered less harm than might otherwise have occurred.

After *Hepps*, the "substantial truth" doctrine has become one of "material falsity:" the statement must be not merely technically false, but materially so. See, e.g., Rouch v. Enquirer & News of Battle Creek, 440 Mich. 238, 487 N.W.2d 205, 20 Med. L. Rptr. 2265 (1992).

2. FALSITY AND OPINION

If the constitution requires plaintiffs to prove falsity, it would seem to follow that it does not permit liability for statements that by their nature are incapable of being proved false. This implication of *Hepps* was not immediately appreciated, but it has turned out to be as important as the explicit holding of the case. Before *Hepps*, lower courts wrestled with the problem of defamation by statements couched as opinion. Many of them recognized a constitutional defense for "opinion." A good example is Ollman v. Evans, 750 F.2d 970, 11 Med. L. Rptr. 1433 (D.C. Cir. en banc 1984). Syndicated columnists Evans and Novak argued against the proposed appointment of a Marxist political science professor to head the Department of Government and Politics at the University of Maryland. Among other statements, the column quoted a political scientist who, refusing to be identified, was said to have asserted that "Ollman has no status within the profession, but is a pure and simple activist." The president of the University of Maryland rejected the appointment.

The trial judge's dismissal was affirmed by a split court that produced seven opinions. The lead opinion emphasized four factors for analysis: (1) "the common usage or meaning of the specific language of the challenged statements itself"; (2) "the statement's verifiability—is the statement capable of being objectively characterized as true or false?"; (3) "the full context of the statement—the entire article or column"; and (4) "the broader context or setting in which the statement appears. Different types of writing have . . . widely varying social conventions which signal to the reader the likelihood of a statement's being either fact or opinion." This quickly became the most popular method of analyzing opinion cases.

After lower courts spent some years arguing over the *Ollman* approach, and four years after *Hepps*, the Supreme Court addressed the issue.

Milkovich v. Lorain Journal Co.

Supreme Court of the United States, 1990.
497 U.S. 1, 110 S. Ct. 2695, 111 L. Ed.2d 1, 17 Med. L. Rptr. 2009.

[Milkovich was coach of the Maple Heights high school wrestling team, which was involved in a brawl with a competing team. After a hearing, the

Ohio High School Athletic Association (OHSAA) censured Milkovich and placed his team on probation. Parents of some of the team members sued to enjoin OHSAA from enforcing the probation, contending OHSAA's investigation and hearing violated due process. Milkovich and Scott, the superintendent, testifying at a judicial hearing on the suit, both denied that Milkovich had incited the brawl through his behavior toward the crowd and a meet official. The judge granted the restraining order sought by the parents. A sports columnist who had attended the meet, but not the judicial hearing, wrote about the hearing in a column published the next day in the defendant newspaper. The headline was "Maple beat the law with the 'big lie.' " The theme of the column was that at the judicial hearing Milkovich and Scott misrepresented Milkovich's role in the altercation and thereby prevented the team from receiving the punishment it deserved. The concluding paragraphs of the column were as follows:

> "Anyone who attended the meet, whether he be from Maple Heights, Mentor [the opposing school] or impartial observer, knows in his heart that Milkovich and Scott lied at the hearing after each having given his solemn oath to tell the truth.

> "But they got away with it."

> "Is that the kind of lesson we want our young people learning from their high school administrators and coaches?"

> "I think not."

Milkovich and Scott both sued the newspaper, alleging that the column accused them of perjury. After 15 years of litigation and several appeals, the Ohio Court of Appeals held in Milkovich's case that the column was constitutionally protected opinion and granted the newspaper's motion for summary judgment. The Supreme Court reversed.]

CHIEF JUSTICE REHNQUIST delivered the opinion of the Court.

[The opinion reviewed the various constitutional limitations imposed on state libel law in the series of cases beginning with *New York Times v. Sullivan,* supra p. 272. The Court also mentioned *Hepps, Bresler,* supra p. 262, *Letter Carriers,* supra p. 261, and *Hustler Magazine, Inc. v. Falwell,* infra p. 417, which held that an ad parody "could not reasonably have been interpreted as stating actual facts about the public figure involved."]

Respondents would have us recognize, in addition to the established safeguards discussed above, still another First Amendment-based protection for defamatory statements which are categorized as "opinion" as opposed to "fact." For this proposition they rely principally on the following dictum from our opinion in *Gertz:*

> Under the First Amendment there is no such thing as a false idea. However pernicious an opinion may seem, we depend for its correction not on the conscience of judges and juries but on the competition of other ideas. But there is no constitutional value in false statements of fact.[ ]

Judge Friendly appropriately observed that this passage "has become the opening salvo in all arguments for protection from defamation actions on the ground of opinion, even though the case did not remotely concern the question." [Cianci v. New Times Publishing Co., 639 F.2d 54, 6 Med. L. Rptr. 1625, 2145 (2d Cir. 1980)] Read in context, though, the fair meaning of the passage is to equate the word "opinion" in the second sentence with the word "idea" in the first sentence. Under this view, the language was merely a reiteration of Justice Holmes' classic "marketplace of ideas" concept. [ ]

Thus we do not think this passage from *Gertz* was intended to create a wholesale defamation exemption for anything that might be labeled "opinion." Not only would such an interpretation be contrary to the tenor and the context of the passage, but it would also ignore the fact that expressions of "opinion" may often imply an assertion of objective fact.

If a speaker says, "In my opinion John Jones is a liar," he implies a knowledge of facts which lead to the conclusion that Jones told an untruth. Even if the speaker states the facts upon which he bases his opinion, if those facts are either incorrect or incomplete, or if his assessment of them is erroneous, the statement may still imply a false assertion of fact. Simply couching such statements in terms of opinion does not dispel these implications; and the statement, "In my opinion Jones is a liar," can cause as much damage to reputation as the statement, "Jones is a liar." As Judge Friendly aptly stated: "[It] would be destructive of the law of libel if a writer could escape liability for accusations of [defamatory conduct] simply by using, explicitly or implicitly, the words 'I think,' " See *Cianci* [ ]. . . .

Apart from their reliance on the *Gertz* dictum, respondents do not really contend that a statement such as, "In my opinion John Jones is a liar," should be protected by a separate privilege for "opinion" under the First Amendment. But they do contend that in every defamation case the First Amendment mandates an inquiry into whether a statement is "opinion" or "fact," and that only the latter statements may be actionable. They propose that a number of factors developed by the lower courts (in what we hold was a mistaken reliance on the *Gertz* dictum) be considered in deciding which is which. But we think the " 'breathing space' ", which " 'freedoms of expression require to survive' " [ ] is adequately secured by existing constitutional doctrine without the creation of an artificial dichotomy between "opinion" and fact.

Foremost, we think *Hepps* stands for the proposition that a statement on matters of public concern must be provable as false before there can be liability under state defamation law, at least in situations, like the present, where a media defendant is involved.[1] Thus, unlike the statement, "In my opinion Mayor Jones is a liar," the statement, "In my opinion Mayor Jones shows his abysmal ignorance by accepting the teachings of Marx and

---

1. In *Hepps* the Court reserved judgment on cases involving non-media defendants, [ ] and accordingly we do the same. Prior to *Hepps,* of course, where public-official or public-figure plaintiffs were involved, the *New York Times* rule already required a showing of falsity before liability could result. [ ]

Lenin," would not be actionable. *Hepps* ensures that a statement of opinion relating to matters of public concern which does not contain a provably false factual connotation will receive full constitutional protection.

Next, the *Bresler–Letter Carriers–Falwell* line of cases provide protection for statements that cannot "reasonably [be] interpreted as stating actual facts" about an individual. [ ] This provides assurance that public debate will not suffer for lack of "imaginative expression" or the "rhetorical hyperbole" which has traditionally added much to the discourse of our nation. [ ]

The [constitutional fault] requirements further ensure that debate on public issues remains "uninhibited, robust, and wide-open." . . .

We are not persuaded that, in addition to these protections, an additional separate constitutional privilege for "opinion" is required to ensure the freedom of expression guaranteed by the First Amendment. The dispositive question in the present case then becomes whether or not a reasonable fact-finder could conclude that the statements [in the column] imply an assertion that petitioner Milkovich perjured himself in a judicial proceeding. We think this question must be answered in the affirmative. . . . This is not the sort of loose, figurative or hyperbolic language which would negate the impression that the writer was seriously maintaining petitioner committed the crime of perjury. Nor does the general tenor of the article negate this impression.

We also think the connotation that petitioner committed perjury is sufficiently factual to be susceptible of being proved true or false. A determination of whether petitioner lied in this instance can be made on a core of objective evidence by comparing, inter alia, petitioner's testimony before the trial court. As the [Ohio Supreme Court noted in the case of the superintendent] "[w]hether or not H. Don Scott did indeed perjure himself is certainly verifiable by a perjury action with evidence adduced from the transcripts and witnesses present at the hearing. Unlike a subjective assertion the averred defamatory language is an articulation of an objectively verifiable event." [ ] So too with petitioner Milkovich.

The numerous decisions discussed above establishing First Amendment protection for defendants in defamation actions surely demonstrate the Court's recognition of the Amendment's vital guarantee of free and uninhibited discussion of public issues. But there is also another side to the equation; we have regularly acknowledged the "important social values which underlie the law of defamation," . . . .

We believe our decision in the present case holds the balance true. The judgment of the Ohio Court of Appeals is reversed and the case remanded for further proceedings not inconsistent with this opinion.

[Justice Brennan, joined by Justice Marshall, dissented. He said the Court addressed the opinion issue "cogently and almost entirely correctly," and agreed that the lower courts had been under a "misimpression that there is a so-called opinion privilege wholly in addition to the protections we have already found to be guaranteed by the First Amendment." But he disagreed with the application of agreed principles to the facts: "I find that the challenged statements cannot reasonably be interpreted as either stating or implying defamatory facts about petitioner. Under the rule articulated in the majority opinion, therefore, the statements are due 'full constitutional protection.' "

He characterized the columnist's assumption that Milkovich lied as "patently conjecture" and asserted that conjecture is as important to the free flow of ideas and opinions as "imaginative expression" and "rhetorical hyperbole," which the majority agreed are protected. He offered several examples:

> Did NASA officials ignore sound warnings that the Challenger Space Shuttle would explode? Did Cuban–American leaders arrange for John Fitzgerald Kennedy's assassination? Was Kurt Waldheim a Nazi officer? Such questions are matters of public concern long before all the facts are unearthed, if they ever are. Conjecture is a means of fueling a national discourse on such questions and stimulating public pressure for answers from those who know more.

The dissent argued that the language of the column itself made clear to readers that the columnist was engaging in speculation, personal judgment, emotional rhetoric, and moral outrage. "No reasonable reader could understand [the columnist] to be impliedly asserting—as fact—that Milkovich had perjured himself."]

Notes and Questions

1. Is it for the judge or jury to decide whether a statement "is sufficiently factual to be susceptible of being proved true or false"? In the principal case, did the Court decide as a matter of law that the statement was sufficiently factual, or did it merely hold that a jury should be allowed to decide that question? Lower courts are sharply divided as to whether there is any jury role in connection with this issue. Compare Piersall v. Sportsvision of Chicago, 230 Ill.App.3d 503, 595 N.E.2d 103, 20 Med. L. Rptr. 1223 (1992) (judge decides) with Yetman v. English, 168 Ariz. 71, 811 P.2d 323 (1991) (jury decides).

2. The majority says "the statement, 'In my opinion Mayor Jones shows his abysmal ignorance by accepting the teachings of Marx and Lenin,' would not be actionable." If the mayor does not accept the teachings of Marx and Lenin, might the statement be actionable? Does the Court mean only that the statement that the mayor is abysmally ignorant is not actionable if the rest of the statement is true?

3. The procedural history of the *Milkovich* case, described at length in omitted portions of the majority opinion, illustrates the persistence and endurance that libel litigation sometimes demands of its participants. The column was published in 1974. The case settled shortly after this opinion.

4. Is this approach to the opinion problem likely to produce different results than the *Ollman* approach? Does the context in which the defama-

tory statement is used play any role in the Milkovich analysis? As the following cases indicate, that question has generated much discussion since *Milkovich*.

————

The Phantom of the Opera. In Phantom Touring Inc. v. Affiliated Publications, 953 F.2d 724, 19 Med. L. Rptr. 1786 (1st Cir. 1992), two competing stage versions of "Phantom of the Opera," both derived from a public domain novel, were playing in the United States. The earlier version was Kenneth Hill's; the later was the much more popular version by Andrew Lloyd Webber. Just before ticket sales were to begin in Boston for the Hill version the Boston Globe published two articles by its critic Kelly suggesting that readers be wary of Hill's "Fake Phantom" which it said had been "thriving off the confusion created by the two productions." One article quoted a Washington Post critic to the effect that Hill's version "bears as much resemblance to its celebrated counterpart as Jell–O does to Baked Alaska," and that described Hill's version as "a rip-off, a fraud, a scandal, a snake-oil job." Other statements are discussed below. The lower court dismissed the libel case, and the First Circuit affirmed.

The court of appeals recognized that since *Milkovich* there was no longer a "wholesale defamation exemption for anything that might be labeled opinion." Nonetheless, *Milkovich* had reaffirmed three major propositions. First, the challenged statements "must be provably false." Thus, " 'That's the worst play I've ever seen' would be protected not because it is labeled an opinion but because it is so subjective that it is not 'susceptible of being proved true or false.' " (What if the plaintiff playwright has proof that the speaker in fact really liked the play but wrote what he did solely because he held a personal grudge against the plaintiff?)

Second, *Milkovich* had protected speech that could not reasonably be interpreted as stating "actual facts" about a person: those involving parody, "loose figurative speech," or "rhetorical hyperbole." Thus, following the *Greenbelt* case, a critic writing that the "producer who decided to charge admission for that show is committing highway robbery," would be protected because no reasonable reader could understand this to be an accusation of robbery. Context was all-important in determining how readers might understand the crucial words.

Third, the court thought *Bose Corp. v. Consumers Union* (supra p. 291) required the court to make an independent examination of the whole record on this issue, instead of deferring to the jury.

The court concluded that the rip off-fraud-scandal-snake oil passage was "not only figurative and hyperbolic, but we also can imagine no objective evidence to disprove it." The same applied to assertions that Hill's version was "fake" or "phony."

The most serious issue involved passages that could be read on their face to assert that the confusion was intentional—even though the advertising stated that there was no connection between the two shows. Arguably a charge of "deliberate deception" could be proven false by showing, for example, longstanding plans to tour the Hill show before Webber's version rose to prominence. But the "sum effect of the format, tone and entire content of the articles is to make it unmistakably clear that Kelly was expressing a point of view only." The language appeared in a column generally understood to be more opinionated than a typical news report. (Although this was given no weight in *Milkovich*, the *Phantom* court thought that was only because of the facts of that case—not because context was never relevant.)

The court thought Kelly's language was subjective by design. His "snide, exasperated language indicated that his comments represented his personal appraisal of the factual information contained in the article." Of "greatest importance" was the breadth of the articles "which not only discussed all the facts underlying his views, but also gave information from which readers might draw contrary conclusions. In effect, the articles offered a self-contained give-and-take, a kind of verbal debate between Kelly and those persons responsible for booking and marketing" plaintiff's version. The "assertion of deceit reasonably could be understood only as Kelly's personal conclusion about the information presented, not as a statement of fact." Kelly had noted that others did not share his negative view of the merit of Hill's version, that it had had some lengthy runs, and its producer was quoted to the effect that "critics may not like us, but audiences do." This "full disclosure of the facts underlying his judgment—none of which have been challenged as false—makes this case fundamentally different" from *Milkovich*.

Is the court's approach compromised if the plaintiff can present ten witnesses who say they read the column and understood that the author "must have had more facts" than he stated?

State law. By interpreting state constitutions to be more protective of speech than the federal constitution, some state courts give opinion more protection than *Milkovich* requires. New York has gone furthest in this regard. In Immuno AG. v. Moor–Jankowski, 77 N.Y.2d 235, 567 N.E.2d 1270, 566 N.Y.S.2d 906, 18 Med. L. Rptr. 1625 (1991), the New York Court of Appeals held that the state constitution requires that more attention be paid to the context of the defamatory statement than does the federal constitution after *Milkovich*. It said its own pre-*Milkovich* decisions continue to provide the appropriate means of determining whether a statement is actionable under the state constitution. "[W]e believe an analysis that begins by looking at the content of the whole communication, its tone and apparent purpose [ ] better balances the values at stake than an analysis that first examines the challenged statements for express and implied factual assertions, and finds them actionable unless couched in loose, figurative or hyperbolic language in charged circumstances."

Conjecture. Justice Brennan's suggestion that conjecture deserves to be constitutionally protected seems to have been followed in at least one case. A book (and a magazine article excerpted from the book) enumerated five different scenarios of how a mysterious death might have occurred and stated that the truth was not known. The plaintiff, who was the person implicated in two of the scenarios, sued for defamation. The court, interpreting New York law, concluded that readers could not reasonably have understood the publications as accusations of murder when the various scenarios were stated to be only conjecture: "Though the overall content of the book generally informs the readers that the book describes factual and historical accounts of real events, [the author] uses a number of clear signals to indicate to the reader that the versions of the events surrounding the studio fire were nothing more than conjecture and speculation." Among these devices were statements that, in the court's words, conveyed the idea that the studio fire "remains shrouded in mystery even to the present day" and the fact that the five scenarios were presented as "versions" told by different people all lacking first-hand knowledge and each inconsistent with the versions of others. What if four of the five scenarios implicated the plaintiff? See Levin v. McPhee, 119 F.3d 189, 25 Med. L. Rptr. 1946 (2d Cir. 1997).

G. PUBLICATION AND REPUBLICATION

Publication is a term of art in the law of defamation. It is the communication of the allegedly defamatory material to a third person. Generally, that means anyone other than the defamer and the person defamed. It can be accomplished by any means—written, oral, broadcast, printed, photographic, etc. A defamatory accusation made only to the person defamed normally is not actionable because it is not "published." But if it is foreseeable that the person defamed will be required to pass it along to a third person (e.g. an employer or supervisor), the original defamer may be liable even though the person defamed is the only true "publisher" of the defamation. See, e.g., Purcell v. Seguin State Bank, 999 F.2d 950 (5th Cir. 1993).

Republication, strictly speaking, is not a term of art. It simply refers to the repetition of defamatory material originated by someone else. Such repetition is actually a new "publication" and the repeater is a "publisher," liable as if he or she originated the defamatory statement. Thus, a broadcaster that merely reports as news someone else's defamatory accusation is as fully liable, potentially at least, as the accuser. A newspaper that publishes a defamatory letter to the editor, or a radio station that broadcasts the defamatory comments of a call-in guest on a talk show, is similarly liable. The rationale for this rule is that otherwise media and others could defame at will merely by finding someone to whom they can attribute the defamatory statements. The rule that treats the repeater the same as the originator seems surprising to some people. Perhaps for that reason, it is sometimes called the "republication rule," but it means only that republication is treated the same as publication.

The "republication rule" is seriously at odds with the expectations and practices of some new communications technologies, especially the Internet. A culture of more or less uninhibited repetition developed on the Internet, apparently oblivious to the effects of the republication rule. When the expectations of that culture clashed with the traditional assumptions embodied in the republication rule, Congress intervened.

1. PUBLISHERS AND DISTRIBUTORS

Zeran v. America Online, Inc.

United States Court of Appeals, Fourth Circuit, 1997.
129 F.3d 327, 25 Med. L. Rptr. 2526, certiorari denied 524 U.S. 937.

Before WILKINSON, CHIEF JUDGE, RUSSELL, CIRCUIT JUDGE, and BOYLE, CHIEF UNITED STATES DISTRICT JUDGE for the Eastern District of North Carolina, sitting by designation.

WILKINSON, Chief Judge:

Kenneth Zeran brought this action against America Online, Inc. ("AOL"), arguing that AOL unreasonably delayed in removing defamatory messages posted by an unidentified third party, refused to post retractions of those messages, and failed to screen for similar postings thereafter. The district court granted judgment for AOL on the grounds that the Communications Decency Act of 1996 ("CDA")—47 U.S.C. § 230—bars Zeran's claims. Zeran appeals, arguing that § 230 leaves intact liability for interactive computer service providers who possess notice of defamatory material posted through their services. He also contends that § 230 does not apply here because his claims arise from AOL's alleged negligence prior to the CDA's enactment. Section 230, however, plainly immunizes computer service providers like AOL from liability for information that originates with third parties. Furthermore, Congress clearly expressed its intent that § 230 apply to lawsuits, like Zeran's, instituted after the CDA's enactment. Accordingly, we affirm the judgment of the district court.

I.

"The Internet is an international network of interconnected computers," currently used by approximately 40 million people worldwide. [ ] One of the many means by which individuals access the Internet is through an interactive computer service. These services offer not only a connection to the Internet as a whole, but also allow their subscribers to access information communicated and stored only on each computer service's individual proprietary network. [ ] AOL is just such an interactive computer service. Much of the information transmitted over its network originates with the company's millions of subscribers. They may transmit information privately via electronic mail, or they may communicate publicly by posting messages on AOL bulletin boards, where the messages may be read by any AOL subscriber.

[Zeran's allegations were as follows. A few days after the 1995 bombing of the federal building in Oklahoma City, which killed more than 160 people, someone posted a message on an AOL bulletin board advertising

"Naughty Oklahoma T–Shirts" featuring offensive and tasteless slogans related to the bombing of the Alfred P. Murrah Federal Building in Oklahoma City. Those interested in purchasing the shirts were instructed to call "Ken" at Zeran's home phone number in Seattle. Zeran received many angry and derogatory messages, including death threats. He could not change his phone number because he relied on its availability to the public in running his business out of his home. Later that day, Zeran called AOL and informed a company representative of his predicament. The employee assured Zeran that the posting would be removed from AOL's bulletin board but explained that as a matter of policy AOL would not post a retraction.

Over the next few days additional messages were posted advertising additional shirts, bumper stickers, and key chains with new tasteless slogans, asking interested buyers to call Zeran's phone number, and advising them to "please call back if busy." The angry, threatening phone calls intensified. During this time period, Zeran called AOL repeatedly and was told by company representatives that the individual account from which the messages were posted would soon be closed. Zeran was receiving an abusive phone call approximately every two minutes. An Oklahoma City radio station, KRXO, received a copy of the first AOL posting, related the message's contents on the air, attributed them to "Ken" at Zeran's phone number, and urged the listening audience to call the number. After this radio broadcast, Zeran was inundated with death threats and other violent calls from Oklahoma City residents. The number of calls to Zeran's residence finally subsided to fifteen per day after an Oklahoma City newspaper exposed the AOL posting as a hoax.

Suits against KRXO and AOL were transferred to Eastern District of Virginia. The district court granted AOL judgment on the pleadings under Federal Rule 12(c), based on the claim that section 230 was a complete defense. This appeal followed.]

Zeran did not bring any action against the party who posted the offensive messages.[4]

II.

A.

. . . Zeran seeks to hold AOL liable for defamatory speech initiated by a third party. He argued to the district court that once he notified AOL of the unidentified third party's hoax, AOL had a duty to remove the defamatory posting promptly, to notify its subscribers of the message's false nature, and to effectively screen future defamatory material. . . .

The relevant portion of § 230 states: "No provider or user of an interactive computer service shall be treated as the publisher or speaker of any information provided by another information content provider." 47

---

4. Zeran maintains that AOL made it impossible to identify the original party by failing to maintain adequate records of its users. The issue of AOL's record keeping practices, however, is not presented by this appeal.

U.S.C. § 230(c)(1). By its plain language, § 230 creates a federal immunity to any cause of action that would make service providers liable for information originating with a third-party user of the service. Specifically, § 230 precludes courts from entertaining claims that would place a computer service provider in a publisher's role. Thus, lawsuits seeking to hold a service provider liable for its exercise of a publisher's traditional editorial functions—such as deciding whether to publish, withdraw, postpone or alter content—are barred.

The purpose of this statutory immunity is not difficult to discern. Congress recognized the threat that tort-based lawsuits pose to freedom of speech in the new and burgeoning Internet medium. The imposition of tort liability on service providers for the communications of others represented, for Congress, simply another form of intrusive government regulation of speech. Section 230 was enacted, in part, to maintain the robust nature of Internet communication and, accordingly, to keep government interference in the medium to a minimum. In specific statutory findings, Congress recognized the Internet and interactive computer services as offering "a forum for a true diversity of political discourse, unique opportunities for cultural development, and myriad avenues for intellectual activity." Id. § 230(a)(3). . . .

None of this means, of course, that the original culpable party who posts defamatory messages would escape accountability. While Congress acted to keep government regulation of the Internet to a minimum, it also found it to be the policy of the United States "to ensure vigorous enforcement of Federal criminal laws to deter and punish trafficking in obscenity, stalking, and harassment by means of computer." Id. § 230(b)(5). Congress made a policy choice, however, not to deter harmful online speech through the separate route of imposing tort liability on companies that serve as intermediaries for other parties' potentially injurious messages.

Another important purpose of § 230 was to encourage service providers to self-regulate the dissemination of offensive material over their services. In this respect, § 230 responded to a New York state court decision, Stratton Oakmont, Inc. v. Prodigy Servs. Co., 1995 WL 323710 (N.Y.Sup. May 24, 1995). There, the plaintiffs sued Prodigy—an interactive computer service like AOL—for defamatory comments made by an unidentified party on one of Prodigy's bulletin boards. The court held Prodigy to the strict liability standard normally applied to original publishers of defamatory statements, rejecting Prodigy's claims that it should be held only to the lower "knowledge" standard usually reserved for distributors. The court reasoned that Prodigy acted more like an original publisher than a distributor both because it advertised its practice of controlling content on its service and because it actively screened and edited messages posted on its bulletin boards.

Congress enacted § 230 to remove the disincentives to self regulation created by the Stratton Oakmont decision. Under that court's holding, computer service providers who regulated the dissemination of offensive material on their services risked subjecting themselves to liability, because such regulation cast the service provider in the role of a publisher. Fearing that the specter of liability would therefore deter service providers from blocking and screening offensive material, Congress enacted § 230's broad immunity "to remove disincentives for the development and utilization of blocking and filtering technologies that empower parents to restrict their children's access to objectionable or inappropriate online material." 47 U.S.C. § 230(b)(4). In line with this purpose, § 230 forbids the imposition of publisher liability on a service provider for the exercise of its editorial and self-regulatory functions.

B.

Zeran argues, however, that the § 230 immunity eliminates only publisher liability, leaving distributor liability intact. Publishers can be held liable for defamatory statements contained in their works even absent proof that they had specific knowledge of the statement's inclusion. W. Page Keeton et al., Prosser and Keeton on the Law of Torts § 113, at 810 (5th ed. 1984). According to Zeran, interactive computer service providers like AOL are normally considered instead to be distributors, like traditional news vendors or book sellers. Distributors cannot be held liable for defamatory statements contained in the materials they distribute unless it is proven at a minimum that they have actual knowledge of the defamatory statements upon which liability is predicated. [ ] Zeran contends that he provided AOL with sufficient notice of the defamatory statements appearing on the company's bulletin board. This notice is significant, says Zeran, because AOL could be held liable as a distributor only if it acquired knowledge of the defamatory statements' existence.

Because of the difference between these two forms of liability, Zeran contends that the term "distributor" carries a legally distinct meaning from the term "publisher." Accordingly, he asserts that Congress' use of only the term "publisher" in § 230 indicates a purpose to immunize service providers only from publisher liability. He argues that distributors are left unprotected by § 230 and, therefore, his suit should be permitted to proceed against AOL. We disagree. Assuming arguendo that Zeran has satisfied the requirements for imposition of distributor liability, this theory of liability is merely a subset, or a species, of publisher liability, and is therefore also foreclosed by § 230.

The terms "publisher" and "distributor" derive their legal significance from the context of defamation law. Although Zeran attempts to artfully plead his claims as ones of negligence, they are indistinguishable from a garden variety defamation action. Because the publication of a statement is a necessary element in a defamation action, only one who publishes can be subject to this form of tort liability. Restatement (Second) of Torts § 558(b) (1977); [ ]. Publication does not only describe the choice by an author to include certain information. In addition, both the negligent communication of a defamatory statement and the failure to remove such a statement when first communicated by another party—each alleged by Zeran here under a negligence label—constitute publication. Restatement (Second) of

Torts § 577; see also Tacket v. General Motors Corp., 836 F.2d 1042, 1046–47 (7th Cir. 1987). In fact, every repetition of a defamatory statement is considered a publication. [ ]

In this case, AOL is legally considered to be a publisher. "[E]very one who takes part in the publication . . . is charged with publication." [ ] Even distributors are considered to be publishers for purposes of defamation law:

> Those who are in the business of making their facilities available to disseminate the writings composed, the speeches made, and the information gathered by others may also be regarded as participating to such an extent in making the books, newspapers, magazines, and information available to others as to be regarded as publishers. They are intentionally making the contents available to others, sometimes without knowing all of the contents—including the defamatory content—and sometimes without any opportunity to ascertain, in advance, that any defamatory matter was to be included in the matter published.

[Prosser & Keeton] at 803. AOL falls squarely within this traditional definition of a publisher and, therefore, is clearly protected by § 230's immunity.

Zeran contends that decisions like *Stratton Oakmont* and Cubby, Inc. v. CompuServe Inc., 776 F. Supp. 135, 19 Med. L. Rptr. 1525 (S.D.N.Y. 1991), recognize a legal distinction between publishers and distributors. He misapprehends, however, the significance of that distinction for the legal issue we consider here. It is undoubtedly true that mere conduits, or distributors, are subject to a different standard of liability. As explained above, distributors must at a minimum have knowledge of the existence of a defamatory statement as a prerequisite to liability. But this distinction signifies only that different standards of liability may be applied within the larger publisher category, depending on the specific type of publisher concerned. See Keeton et al., [ ] at 799–800 (explaining that every party involved is charged with publication, although degrees of legal responsibility differ). To the extent that decisions like *Stratton* and *Cubby* utilize the terms "publisher" and "distributor" separately, the decisions correctly describe two different standards of liability. *Stratton* and *Cubby* do not, however, suggest that distributors are not also a type of publisher for purposes of defamation law.

Zeran simply attaches too much importance to the presence of the distinct notice element in distributor liability. The simple fact of notice surely cannot transform one from an original publisher to a distributor in the eyes of the law. To the contrary, once a computer service provider receives notice of a potentially defamatory posting, it is thrust into the role of a traditional publisher. The computer service provider must decide whether to publish, edit, or withdraw the posting. In this respect, Zeran seeks to impose liability on AOL for assuming the role for which § 230 specifically proscribes liability—the publisher role.

. . .

Zeran next contends that interpreting § 230 to impose liability on service providers with knowledge of defamatory content on their services is consistent with the statutory purposes outlined in Part IIA. Zeran fails, however, to understand the practical implications of notice liability in the interactive computer service context. Liability upon notice would defeat the dual purposes advanced by § 230 of the CDA. Like the strict liability imposed by the *Stratton Oakmont* court, liability upon notice reinforces service providers' incentives to restrict speech and abstain from self-regulation.

If computer service providers were subject to distributor liability, they would face potential liability each time they receive notice of a potentially defamatory statement—from any party, concerning any message. Each notification would require a careful yet rapid investigation of the circumstances surrounding the posted information, a legal judgment concerning the information's defamatory character, and an on-the-spot editorial decision whether to risk liability by allowing the continued publication of that information. Although this might be feasible for the traditional print publisher, the sheer number of postings on interactive computer services would create an impossible burden in the Internet context. [ ] Because service providers would be subject to liability only for the publication of information, and not for its removal, they would have a natural incentive simply to remove messages upon notification, whether the contents were defamatory or not. [ ] Thus, like strict liability, liability upon notice has a chilling effect on the freedom of Internet speech.

. . .

III.

[The court rejected Zeran's argument that his suit was not covered by the statute because it was enacted after the postings in question. His suit had been filed after the effective date of the act, and the statute said "No cause of action may be brought and no liability may be imposed under any State or local law that is inconsistent with this section."]

Affirmed.

Notes and Questions

1. Is this decision based on the relationship between "publisher" and "distributor" at common law or on the court's reading of the statute?

2. If Internet service providers like AOL need immunity from liability for republishing defamation, why not radio stations that use live call-in formats? Newspapers that publish letters to the editor?

3. What arguments justify the court's analysis of AOL's situation after it received notice from Zeran? Was there reason to doubt Zeran's complaint when it came in? Should that be relevant?

4. Might Zeran have a cause of action based on either (1) AOL's refusal to help him identify the person who posted the statements (if that person is

identifiable) or (2) AOL's claim that its operating structure does not permit it to identify such posters?

5.   If the potential liability of the originator offers sufficient protection for reputation in this context (where the practices of the medium make it especially difficult to identify that person), is there any reason to retain the republication rule in any context?

———

Applicability of Section 230. Renting computers with Internet access to customers was found to constitute the provision of an "interactive computer service" and therefore qualify for immunity under section 230 of the CDA. See PatentWizard, Inc. v. Kinko's, Inc., 163 F. Supp. 2d 1069, 29 Med. L. Rptr. 2530 (D.S.D. 2001). Operating a Web-based chat room has also been found to fit within section 230. Schneider v. Amazon.com, Inc., 31 P.3d 37, 29 Med. L. Rptr. 2421 (Wash. App. 2001).

The statute may apply even when the ISP is actively involved in obtaining the defamatory material. See Blumenthal v. Drudge, 992 F. Supp. 44, 26 Med. L. Rptr. 1717 (D.D.C. 1998). AOL employed Matt Drudge to prepare and provide online the "Drudge Report." In one of its messages, the report charged that a White House aide and former journalist, Sidney Blumenthal, had a history of abusing his wife. Within hours, after Blumenthal complained, Drudge removed the item. Blumenthal and his wife sued Drudge and AOL for defamation.

A federal district judge "reluctantly" dismissed the case against AOL on the ground that section 230 was intended to protect Internet service providers in this situation. Drudge was not an anonymous contributor, but had a contract with AOL under which AOL paid him $3,000 a month, promoted his report to its subscribers, and reserved the right to edit his material. The judge said he personally believed these arrangements should make AOL responsible for Drudge's defamation, but

> Congress has made a different policy choice by providing immunity even where the interactive service provider has an active, even aggressive, role in making available content prepared by others. In some sort of tacit quid pro quo arrangement with the service provider community, Congress has conferred immunity from tort liability as an incentive to Internet service providers to self-police the Internet for obscenity and other offensive material, even where the self-policing is unsuccessful or not even attempted.

Because the repeater and the originator are both treated as publishers in their own right, either may be liable even if the other is not. Thus, at common law, AOL could be liable even if Drudge was not (e.g., even if he enjoyed some privilege not available to AOL), and Drudge may be liable even though AOL is immune under the statute. And Drudge is potentially liable not only for the harm caused by his own publication of the defamation but also for all repetitions that are foreseeable or "natural and probable" consequences of the original. Because of joint and several liability, Drudge could be liable for harm caused by AOL's republication even if AOL were also liable for that harm.

The Seventh Circuit suggested that *Zeran*'s (and *Drudge*'s) reading of § 230 is inconsistent with the statute's title, "Protection for 'Good Samaritan' blocking and screening of offensive material." The court said the purpose suggested by the title would be better served by holding that the statute creates immunity only for claims arising from the ISP's attempts to screen communications for indecency, leaving them liable for torts that protect the interests of third parties. "Why should a law designed to eliminate ISP's liability to creators of offensive material end up defeating claims by the victims of tortious or criminal conduct?" See Doe v. GTE Corp., 347 F.3d 655 (7th Cir. 2003).

2. NEUTRAL REPORTAGE

Much of the law of defamation operates to soften the impact of the republication rule. The statute applied in *Zeran* is a legislative abrogation of the rule. As a matter of common law, media and other defendants often avoid liability by claiming a privilege to defame, and most of these are privileges to republish someone else's defamation. We shall see the operation of these privileges in Section H. The republication rule is also mitigated by a constitutional privilege recognized by some courts.

In Edwards v. National Audubon Society, Inc., 556 F.2d 113 (2d Cir. 1977), the court said "[W]hen a responsible, prominent organization . . . makes serious charges against a public figure, the First Amendment protects the accurate and disinterested reporting of those charges, regardless of the reporter's private views regarding their validity." [ ] That principle has come to be called the neutral report privilege. *Edwards* held that the New York Times could not be held liable for having reported the Audubon Society's defamatory accusations against a group of prominent scientists. The court said the evidence did not support a jury finding the reporter acted with actual malice because he had serious doubts about the truth of the charges, but said that even if he did, the publication was protected by the neutral report principle. Another court explained the rationale as follows:

> The theory underlying the privilege is that the reporting of defamatory allegations relating to an existing public controversy has significant informational value for the public regardless of the truth of the allegations: If the allegations are true, their reporting provides valuable information about the target of the accusation; if the allegations are false, their reporting reflects in a significant way on the character of the accuser. In either event, according to the theory, the very making of the defamatory allegations sheds valuable light on the character of the controversy (its intensity and perhaps viciousness). As we understand it, the theory also rests on a distinction between publication and republication. Applying this distinction, proponents of the neutral reportage privilege urge that the reporting of a false and

defamatory accusation should be deemed neither defamatory nor false if the report accurately relates the accusation, makes it clear that the republisher does not espouse or concur in the accusation, and provides enough additional information (including, where practical, the response of the defamed person) to allow the readers to draw their own conclusions about the truth of the accusation.

Khawar v. Globe International, Inc., 19 Cal.4th 254, 965 P.2d 696, 79 Cal.Rptr.2d 178, 26 Med. L. Rptr. 2505 (1998).

The neutral report privilege is by no means universally recognized. Some state and federal appellate courts have rejected it entirely, see Dickey v. CBS, Inc., 583 F.2d 1221 (3d Cir. 1978); McCall v. Courier–Journal & Louisville Times, 623 S.W.2d 882 (Ky. 1981); Postill v. Booth Newspapers, Inc., 118 Mich.App. 608, 325 N.W.2d 511 (1982); Hogan v. Herald Co., 84 A.D.2d 470, 446 N.Y.S.2d 836 (1982), while some that have adopted it have disagreed as to its elements. Compare, e.g., Martin v. Wilson Pub. Co., 497 A.2d 322 (R.I. 1985) (stating that privilege applies "only in the extremely limited situation in which the publication accurately attributes such statements to an identified and responsible source") with Barry v. Time, Inc., 584 F. Supp. 1110 (N.D.Cal. 1984) (applying privilege to report of accusations made by other than a "responsible" person or organization). The Supreme Court has never held that the First Amendment mandates a neutral report privilege; in Harte–Hanks Communications v. Connaughton, supra p. 286, the Court declined to decide the issue. See 491 U.S. at 660, fn. 1 (1989). After reviewing this history, the Pennsylvania Supreme Court predicted the Supreme Court will not adopt the neutral report privilege, and on that basis refused to recognize it. See Norton v. Glenn, 860 A.2d 48, 32 Media L. Rep. 2409 (Pa. 2004)

Despite the lack of consensus about the existence or scope of the privilege, there may be situations that cry out for some such protection. Suppose the president of the United States told an interviewer that the vice president was plotting to kill him; should a media defendant that reported the president's statement without endorsing its truth be potentially liable? Note that if the defendant believed the president's statement was false, *New York Times v. Sullivan* would offer no protection.

In view of the extent to which the republication rule is vitiated by exceptions such as Section 230 and the neutral report privilege, would it be wise to abandon the rule? In *Zeran* the court ascribes to Congress the view that liability under the republication rule is "simply another form of intrusive government regulation of speech." Is that an accurate view? Would abandonment of the rule release a flood of republished defamation? Considering the success of Internet service providers in getting Congress to solve *their* problem with the republication rule, should the media seek a statutory solution? If so, what should they ask for? A statute adopting the neutral report privilege? Some broader immunity from republication liability?

H.   COMMON-LAW PRIVILEGES

1.   THE NATURE OF PRIVILEGES

Over the centuries the law of defamation has developed numerous privileges to protect those who make defamatory statements. Privileges are defenses; it is up to the defendant to plead privilege and prove facts necessary to establish the applicability of the privilege. Some privileges are "absolute" in the sense that if the occasion gives rise to an absolute privilege, there will be no liability even if the speaker deliberately lied about the plaintiff. High executive officials, judges, and participants in judicial proceedings have an absolute privilege to speak freely on matters relevant to their obligations. No matter how such a speaker abuses the privilege by lying, no tort liability will flow. See Barr v. Matteo, 360 U.S. 564 (1959). The federal constitution and most state constitutions create a similar privilege for legislators, immunizing them from liability for defamatory statements made during debate.

Few absolute privileges are available to media. One protects broadcasters who are required by federal statute to grant equal opportunity on the air to all candidates for the same office. If a candidate allowed to broadcast under this statute commits defamation, the broadcaster is not liable. See Farmers Educational & Cooperative Union of America v. WDAY, Inc., 360 U.S. 525 (1959), discussed in Chapter II, supra p. 138. Cable operators are immune from liability for defamation presented by others on access channels. See 47 U.S.C. § 558.

Most privileges are "conditional" or "qualified" (the terms mean the same). The defendant who can establish the applicability of such a privilege will prevail unless the plaintiff can show that the speaker "abused" the privilege. The plaintiff shows abuse by proving that the defendant did not honestly believe what he said or that defendant published more information or published it more widely than was justified by the occasion that provided the privilege. Most courts have defined abuse in terms of the defendant's using the occasion for purposes other than what was intended by the creation of the privilege. For example, under the common law conditional privilege for communications between persons having a mutual interest, one may malign a third party to one's partner if one honestly believes the statement and if it relates to the affairs of the partnership. But one may not lie or gratuitously discuss the third party's personal affairs with that partner, or discuss even appropriate matters with the partner if others are present. Efforts to extend this type of privilege to reports by mass media have failed.

Most common law privileges primarily benefit non-media speakers. For example, privileges similar to the mutual interest privilege discussed above protect employers who talk to other employers about prospective employees, businesses that exchange credit information, and discussions among family members. Another protects a person who defames someone to protect his or her own interests (e.g., by erroneously accusing someone of stealing the speaker's property), and another protects defamatory statements made to law enforcement officers.

2.   FAIR COMMENT

The fair comment privilege protects literary, artistic, and similar kinds of criticism, regardless of its merit, as long as it is made honestly, with honesty being measured by the accuracy of the critic's descriptive observations. If the critic describing the work gives the "facts" accurately and fairly, the critic's honest conclusions are privileged as "fair comment." Classic cases discussing the privilege are Triggs v. Sun Printing & Pub. Co., 179 N.Y. 144, 71 N.E. 739 (1904), Adolf Philipp Co. v. New Yorker Staats–Zeitung, 165 A.D. 377, 150 N.Y.S. 1044 (1914), and Cherry v. Des Moines Leader, 114 Iowa 298, 86 N.W. 323 (1901).

Originally this privilege was confined to literary and artistic criticism, but eventually defendants began claiming the privilege of fair comment with regard to other matters of public interest, including the conduct of politicians. The privilege claimed would permit citizens—and media—to criticize and argue about the conduct of their officials. Most courts greatly restricted this use of the privilege by holding that criticism of officials was not privileged unless it was based upon true underlying facts. The leading case was Post Publishing Co. v. Hallam, 59 F. 530 (6th Cir. 1893), in which Judge Taft said:

> The existence and extent of privilege in communications are determined by balancing the needs and good of society against the right of an individual to enjoy a good reputation when he has done nothing which ought to injure it. The privilege should always cease where the sacrifice of the individual right becomes so great that the public good to be derived from it is outweighed. . . . But, if the privilege is to extend to cases like that at bar, then a man who offers himself as a candidate must submit uncomplainingly to the loss of his reputation, not with a single person or a small class of persons, but with every member of the public, whenever an untrue charge of disgraceful conduct is made against him, if only his accuser honestly believes the charge upon reasonable ground. . . . [T]he danger that honorable and worthy men may be driven from politics and public service by allowing too great latitude in attacks upon their characters outweighs any benefit that might occasionally accrue to the public from charges of corruption that are true in fact, but are incapable of legal proof. . . .

A few courts interpreted the fair comment privilege more broadly. They held that false assertions of facts relating to matters of public interest were themselves privileged if they were honestly believed to be true, and that comments based on those facts were also privileged if honestly believed. See Coleman v. MacLennan, 78 Kan. 711, 98 P. 281 (1908), in which the court rejected *Hallam*'s fears with the observation that "men of unimpeachable character from all political parties continually present themselves as candidates in sufficient numbers to fill the public offices and manage the public institutions" in Kansas despite the broader interpretation of the fair report privilege.

In *New York Times v. Sullivan*, supra p. 272, the Supreme Court eventually embraced the *Coleman v. MacLennon* view as a matter of constitutional law. That development, together with the controversy over the neutral report privilege discussed in the preceding section, have largely mooted the argument over extending the fair report privilege to public affairs.

3.   FAIR AND ACCURATE REPORT

Of all the state law privileges, the one most important to media is the privilege to publish a fair and accurate report of official proceedings. Much of the day-to-day content of media consists of reporting on the activities of government, and this privilege covers most of that. In its classic application, the privilege protects media when they report someone else's defamatory statements in a court proceedings, a city council meeting, or a legislative hearing. Those applications of the privilege are so well established and so expansively interpreted that few cases now arise from those settings. Today the fair report privilege is more likely to be contested when media invoke it in connection with reporting based on documents, informal government disclosures, or other matters that do not fit the classic description of "official proceedings." The following is such a case.

Medico v. Time Inc.

United States Court of Appeals for the Third Circuit, 1981.
643 F.2d 134, 6 Med. L. Rptr. 2529.
Certiorari denied, 454 U.S. 836 (1981).

Before ADAMS, GARTH and SLOVITER, CIRCUIT JUDGES.

ADAMS, CIRCUIT JUDGE.

This appeal from a summary judgment in favor of the defendant presents an important question concerning the law of defamation. We must review the district court's determination that a news magazine enjoys a privilege, under the common law of Pennsylvania, to publish a summary of FBI documents identifying the plaintiff as a member of an organized crime "family." We affirm.

I.

In its March 6, 1978 issue, Time magazine published an article describing suspected criminal activities of then-Congressman Daniel J. Flood. . . .

As an example of suspected misconduct, the Time article listed the following:

> Among the matters under scrutiny: Ties between Flood and Pennsylvania Rackets Boss Russell Bufalino. The suspected link: the Wilkes–Barre firm of Medico Industries, controlled by President Philip

Medico and his brothers. The FBI discovered more than a decade ago that Flood steered Government business to the Medicos and traveled often on their company jet. Investigators say Bufalino frequently visited the Medico offices; agents tape-recorded Bufalino's description of Philip as a capo (chief) in his Mafia family. [Testimony by a former Flood aide] has sparked new investigative interest in the Flood–Medico–Bufalino triangle.

. . .

[Time moved for summary judgment based on the substantial truth of its publication. It submitted FBI documents and affidavits of two FBI agents. The district court granted Time's motion for summary judgment, but not on the basis of the truth defense. It held that to succeed on the ground of truth, Time had to prove that Medico *was* a Mafia capo, not merely that the FBI believed that to be so.]

After declining to hold for Time on the truth theory, the district court considered whether the Time article fell within the common law privilege accorded the press to report on official proceedings. The judge seemed troubled because Pennsylvania courts apparently had so far extended the privilege only to reports of proceedings open to the public, whereas Time had summarized reports which the FBI had kept secret and whose release to Time evidently had been unauthorized. But after an exhaustive analysis of Pennsylvania precedents, the court concluded that Pennsylvania courts, if presented with the question, would find summaries of non-public government reports within the privilege. The district judge then ascertained that the Time article represented a fair and accurate account of the FBI documents. Accordingly he held that the publication was privileged, and awarded summary judgment in favor of Time.

On appeal, Medico argues that the district court incorrectly determined that Time's publication was privileged under Pennsylvania law. Time counters that the district judge accurately construed the applicable state law on privilege, and contends further that the defense of truth applies and affords an alternate basis for affirming the district court. . . .

II.

The fair report privilege on which the district court relied developed as an exception to the common law rule that the republisher of a defamation was subject to liability similar to that risked by the original defamer. . . . The common law regime created special problems for the press. When a newspaper published a newsworthy account of one person's defamation of another, it was, by virtue of the republication rule, charged with publication of the underlying defamation. Thus, although the common law exonerated one who published a defamation as long as the statement was true, a newspaper in these circumstances traditionally could avail itself of the truth defense only if the truth of the underlying defamation were established.

To ameliorate the chilling effect on the reporting of newsworthy events occasioned by the combined effect of the republication rule and the truth defense, the law has long recognized a privilege for the press[9] to publish accounts of official proceedings or reports even when these contain defamatory statements. So long as the account presents a fair and accurate summary of the proceedings, the law abandons the assumption that the reporter adopts the defamatory remarks as his own. The privilege thus permits a newspaper or other press defendant to relieve itself of liability without establishing the truth of the substance of the statement reported. The fair report privilege has a somewhat more limited scope than the truth defense, however. So long as the speaker establishes the truth of his statement, he is shielded from liability, regardless of his motives: the fair report privilege, on the other hand, can be defeated in most jurisdictions by a showing that the publisher acted for the sole purpose of harming the person defamed.

Unlike many states, Pennsylvania has never codified the fair report privilege. . . . We believe it appropriate to accept as the law of Pennsylvania the version of the fair report privilege embodied in the current Restatement.

Section 611 of Restatement (Second) provides:

Report of Official Proceeding or Public Meeting

The publication of defamatory matter concerning another in a report of an official action or proceeding or of a meeting open to the public that deals with a matter of public concern is privileged if the report is accurate and complete or a fair abridgement of the occurrence reported.

With respect to the present controversy, the basic inquiry is whether Time's summary of FBI documents concerning Philip Medico is "a report of an official action or proceeding."[17]

The district court examined and rejected the possibility that the FBI reports in question are not "official" because they are not generally available to the public. Medico does not challenge this reasoning on appeal, and we perceive no need to rehearse arguments that the district court has already canvassed. Medico contends before this Court that the FBI documents should not be deemed "official" because they express only tentative and preliminary conclusions that the FBI has never adopted as accurate. He points out that the title page to the FBI report on La Cosa Nostra bears the following legend: "This document contains neither recommendations nor conclusions of the FBI. It is the property of the FBI and is loaned to

---

9. There is some dispute whether the privilege is available to non-press defendants. The *Restatement* [covers] "any person who makes an oral, written or printed report" on an official proceeding should have access to the defense. . . .

17. Although the Time article did not explicitly credit the FBI Report on La Cosa

Nostra or the FBI personal file card on Medico as the Magazine's sources of information, the statements about Medico, taken in context, may reasonably be understood to inform the reader that the story was based on FBI materials. . . .

your agency; it and its contents are not to be distributed outside your agency."

Neither the text of Section 611 nor the accompanying comments dispose of the issue Medico raises. Section 611 itself speaks only of "official" action or proceedings, without elaborating on when a statement is made in an official capacity. [The court notes that two comments to that section point in different ways on whether the report is within the scope of the privilege. Nor did case law resolve it. The closest case protected a news report that summarized a defamatory civil complaint that had formed the basis for a temporary restraining order. Hanish v. Westinghouse Broadcasting Co., 487 F. Supp. 397 (E.D. Pa. 1980)].[21]

Assuming the court in *Hanish* correctly predicted Pennsylvania law, we think that decision supports application of the Section 611 privilege to the present case. FBI files seem at least as "official" as the pleadings in civil cases. Although civil complaints are instituted, for the most part, by private parties, the FBI documents concerning Medico were compiled by government agents acting in their official capacities. Moreover, the danger that a civil litigant will willfully insert defamatory assertions in his complaint generally would appear at least as great as the risk that a criminal investigatory agency will knowingly include false or malicious statements in its files. If Pennsylvania courts would grant the privilege to newspaper accounts of civil complaints on which a court has acted ex parte, we think it likely that they would grant the privilege to republication of defamatory items from the FBI materials on Medico.

III.

Three policies underlie the fair report privilege, and an examination of them provides further guidance for our decision today. Initially, an agency theory was offered to rationalize a privilege of fair report: one who reports what happens in a public, official proceeding acts as an agent for persons who had a right to attend, and informs them of what they might have seen for themselves. The agency rationale, however, cannot explain application of the privilege to proceedings or reports not open to public inspection.

A theory of public supervision also informs the fair report privilege. Justice Holmes, applying the privilege to accounts of courtroom proceedings, gave the classic formulation of this principle:

> [The privilege is justified by] the security which publicity gives for the proper administration of justice. . . . It is desirable that the trial of causes should take place under the public eye, not because the controversies of one citizen with another are of public concern, but because it is of the highest moment that those who administer justice should always act under the sense of public responsibility and that every citizen should be able to satisfy himself with his own eyes as to the mode in which a public duty is performed.

21. Considerable controversy surrounds republication of defamations contained in pleadings on which no official action has been taken. . . .

Cowley v. Pulsifer, 137 Mass. 392, 394 (1884). The supervisory rationale has been invoked in the context of executive action as well.

We believe the public supervision rationale applies to the present case. As public inspection of courtroom proceedings may further the just administration of the laws, public scrutiny of the proceedings and records of criminal investigatory agencies may often have the equally salutary effect of fostering among those who enforce the laws "the sense of public responsibility." For example, exposing the content of agency records may, in some cases, help ensure impartial enforcement of the laws.

[We need not] decide, however, whether the supervisory rationale is relevant to every republication of documents found in FBI files. For any general supervisory concern with respect to the FBI is heightened in the present case by the public's interest in examining the conduct of individuals it elects to positions of civic trust. Elected officials derive their authority from, and are answerable to, the public. If the citizenry is effectively and responsibly to discharge its obligation to monitor the conduct of its government, there can be no penalty for exposing to general view the possible wrongdoing of government officials. Because the alleged defamation of Medico occurred in an article analyzing the conduct of former Congressman Flood, we believe it implicates this aspect of the supervisory rationale. Moreover, even though Time's publication arguably may have tarnished the reputation of Medico, a private individual, as well as that of Representative Flood, the public has a lively interest in considering the relationships formed by elected officials.

A third rationale for the fair report privilege rests, somewhat tautologically, on the public's interest in learning of important matters.[27] While "mere curiosity in the private affairs of others is of insufficient importance to warrant granting the privilege," the present case does not involve such idle probing. The Time article discussed two topics of legitimate public interest. First, for the same reasons that support the supervisory rationale, examination of the affairs of elected officials is obviously a matter of legitimate public concern. In addition, as various federal courts have already recognized, there is significant public importance to reports on investigations of organized criminal activities, whether or not these implicate government officials.

Because the Time article focused on organized crime, we think the informational rationale is especially relevant. The district court in the case at hand commented on the difficulty of gathering information pertaining to organized criminal activity: "Due to the size, sophistication and secrecy of most organized criminal endeavors, only the largest and most sophisticated intelligence-gathering entities can monitor them effectively. In practice this task has been taken up primarily by the Justice Department of the federal government and, in particular, by the FBI." Indeed, the documents that

---

27. . . . Some jurisdictions rely on the informational rationale to extend the privilege to accounts of the proceedings of public meetings of private, non-governmental organizations, as long as the meeting deals with matters of concern to the public.

Time summarized had been compiled by a government agency. In light of the difficulty in obtaining independent corroboration of FBI information, the press may often have to rely on materials the government acquires if it is to report on organized crime at all. We believe Time's publication of FBI materials mentioning Medico served a legitimate public interest in learning about organized crime.

Care must be taken, of course, to ensure that the supervisory and informational rationales not expand into justifications for reporting any defamatory matter maintained in any government file. Personal interests in privacy are not to be taken lightly, and are not to be overborne by mere invocation of a public need to know.[30] But we believe that the public interest is involved when, as here, information compiled by an enforcement agency may help shed light on a Congressman's alleged criminal or unethical behavior.

. . .

V.

Once the libel defendant establishes the existence of a "privileged occasion" for the publication of a defamatory article, the burden returns to the plaintiff to prove that the defendant abused its privilege. [ ] Pennsylvania recognizes two forms of "abuse": the account of an official report may fail to be fair and accurate,[40] as when the publisher overly embellishes the account, [ ] or the defamatory material may be published for the sole purpose of causing harm to the person defamed. [ ]. Inasmuch as Medico does not allege that Time published its article for the purpose of harming him, the sole issue with respect to abuse of privilege is whether the district court erred in concluding that there was no genuine question whether Time's publication fairly and accurately summarized the FBI materials concerning Medico.

We agree with the district court that nothing in the record suggests that the Time article unfairly or inaccurately reported on the FBI materials. . . .

. . . Time has accurately portrayed the FBI records as indicating that Medico has been identified as part of the Bufalino crime family.

VI.

Medico further contends that Time can avail itself of the fair report privilege only if it actually based its article on the FBI materials; if the report reflects the contents of the official materials merely by coincidence, the privilege does not attach. Medico maintains there is a genuine issue of

---

30. The excesses of the McCarthy era, for example, prompted some commentators to point out the reputational injury the republication of official defamation can cause, and to advocate restricting the fair report privilege. [ ]

40. Placement on the plaintiff of the burden of demonstrating that a privileged report was not fair and accurate traditionally distinguished the fair report privilege from the truth defense, in which defendant bore the burden of proving truth. . . .

fact whether Time employees worked with the FBI materials in preparing the article.

Pennsylvania law squarely contradicts this argument. . . .

VII.

. . .[42]

The judgment of the district court granting Time's motion for summary judgment will be affirmed.

Notes and Questions

1. The court discusses three theories that have been asserted to support the fair report privilege. Which is most persuasive? Will one support a broader protective net than the others?

2. Note that *Medico* interprets Pennsylvania law as not requiring actual reliance on the official report or proceeding. The Second Circuit disagreed with this reading of Pennsylvania law on the ground that the privilege could not be "divorced from its underlying policy of encouraging the broad dissemination of public records." Protecting a defendant who did not actually rely on an official report "does nothing to encourage the initial reporting of public records and proceedings. Certainly, § 611 should not be interpreted to protect unattributed, defamatory statements supported only after-the-fact through a frantic search of official records." Bufalino v. Associated Press, 692 F.2d 266, 8 Med. L. Rptr. 2385 (2d Cir. 1982). In a footnote, the *Bufalino* court observed that "even where the reporter has actually relied on official records, the privilege can be lost through failure to make proper attribution." Would the *Medico* court agree? What do the three theories have to say on this point?

Truth, privilege, and republication. Not all courts are as insistent as the *Medico* court was in maintaining distinctions between truth and accuracy and between publishers and republishers. For example, a series of Texas decisions state that the law "only requires proof that allegations

---

42. The possible interpretations of Time's publication about Medico may be used to illustrate the different approaches to the truth defense. The Time article is subject to at least three constructions:

A. Medico is a Mafia *capo.*

B. Government agents overheard Bufalino describe Medico as a Mafia *capo.*

C. FBI records indicate that government agents overheard Bufalino describe Medico as a Mafia *capo.*

Under the fair report privilege, the accuracy of C relieves Time of liability. If the privilege did not apply, however, we would have to ascertain whether Pennsylvania law would exonerate Time on the basis of the truth defense if Time established the truth of B, or whether Time would have to prove A. In light of our holding that Time's publication comes under the fair report privilege, we need not dispose of this question. In addition, we need not review the district court's determination that Time has failed to demonstrate the truth of either A or B.

were in fact made and under investigation in order to prove substantial truth." KTRK Television v. Felder, 950 S.W.2d 100 (Tex. App. 1997), citing McIlvain v. Jacobs, 794 S.W.2d 14 (Tex. 1990). *Medico*, however, represents the generally accepted approach. If Time reports that "the FBI says Medico is a Mafioso," it can succeed on the ground of truth only if Medico *is* a Mafioso (more precisely, after *Hepps*, only if Medico cannot prove he is not). This is because the republication rule treats Time as having adopted the FBI's statement as its own. For purposes of truth or falsity, Time is treated as if it were the original publisher of the statement that Medico is a Mafioso. On the other hand, the fair report privilege by definition is available only to republishers—those who are reporting someone else's defamation. For purposes of the privilege, Time is treated as a republisher and the issue is the *accuracy* of its report (i.e., whether the FBI said Medico was a Mafioso), not the truth of it (i.e., whether Medico was a Mafioso).

These distinctions in turn require careful identification of precisely what is defamatory. If Time reports that the FBI "suspects" or "believes" Medico is a Mafioso, the report might be treated not as a repetition of the FBI's defamatory statement, but as an assertion of a different matter, one that can be proved true or false independently of whether Medico really is a Mafioso. As footnote 42 indicates, such language could be parsed in quite different ways. Generally, though, the courts treat such statements as republication despite use of expressions like "believes," "suspects," "charges," and treat them as false unless the underlying accusation is true.

Thus, even a report that plaintiff was arrested and charged with a crime may be treated as republication of the accusation that he or she committed the crime. In Rouch v. Enquirer & News of Battle Creek, Mich., 427 Mich. 157, 398 N.W.2d 245, 13 Med. L. Rptr. 2201 (1986), the newspaper reported the plaintiff's arrest for rape. After plaintiff, who was never charged, was exonerated, he sued the newspaper. The court treated the issue as one of privilege rather than truth, and rejected the paper's reliance on the state's privilege for fair report privilege on the ground that an "arrest that amounts to no more than an apprehension" was not a "proceeding." The statute was not intended to create a "government action," "arrest record," or "public records" privilege.

The legislature reacted by amending the privilege statute, Mich. Comp. Laws § 600.2911, to extend protection to "a fair and true report of matters of public record, a public and official proceeding, or of a governmental notice, announcement, written or recorded report or record generally available to the public, or act or action of a public body."

Fairness and accuracy. In most states the fair report privilege is not "qualified" in the usual sense; the defendant need not believe the truth of the defamation and does not lose the privilege by publishing too widely. See, e.g., Rosenberg v. Helinski, 328 Md. 664, 616 A.2d 866, 20 Med. L. Rptr. 2233 (1992). It can be lost, however, if the report is not "fair and accurate." These are necessarily terms of art, since few media reports of complex proceedings are entirely fair or accurate. See, e.g., Holy Spirit

Ass'n for the Unification of World Christianity v. New York Times Co., 49 N.Y.2d 63, 399 N.E.2d 1185, 424 N.Y.S.2d 165, 5 Med. L. Rptr. 2219 (1979):

> [N]ewspaper accounts of legislative or other official proceedings must be accorded some degree of liberality. . . . This is so because a newspaper article is, by its very nature, a condensed report of events which must, of necessity, reflect to some degree the subjective view of its author. Nor should a fair report which is not misleading, composed and phrased in good faith under the exigencies of a publication deadline, be thereafter parsed and dissected on the basis of precise denotative meanings which may literally, although not contextually, be ascribed to the words used.

See also Gurda v. Orange County Publications, 56 N.Y.2d 705, 436 N.E.2d 1326, 451 N.Y.S.2d 724, 9 Med. L. Rptr. 1120 (1982), in which the court applied the privilege to benefit a newspaper that used "fraud" and "fine" to describe what had happened in a civil case in which the judge had ruled that plaintiff had defrauded someone and awarded damages and attorney's fees.

Most courts adopt a test of accuracy that is similar to the test for "substantial truth," discussed at p. 329 supra. Thus, in Koniak v. Heritage Newspapers, Inc., 198 Mich.App. 577, 499 N.W.2d 346, 20 Med. L. Rptr. 2286 (1993), the defendant reported that plaintiff had been charged with assaulting someone 30 to 55 times when in fact he had been charged with eight assaults. The court observed that "whether plaintiff assaulted his stepdaughter once, eight times or thirty times would have little effect on the reader."

When questions of fairness arise, it is usually in connection with the condensation or summary of a report. The Restatement (Second) of Torts, § 611 Comment *f*, states that "although it is unnecessary that the report be exhaustive and complete, it is necessary that nothing be omitted or misplaced in such a manner as to convey an erroneous impression to those who hear or read it, as for example a report of the discreditable testimony in a judicial proceeding and a failure to publish the exculpatory evidence." It probably would be more accurate to confine this statement to deliberate or unnecessary omission of exculpatory or discrediting material; often such omissions are excused by deadline pressures or space constraints.

The matter is discussed in Schiavone Construction Co. v. Time, Inc., 735 F.2d 94, 10 Med. L. Rptr. 1831 (3d Cir. 1984), in which the magazine reported that an individual's name appeared several times in FBI reports concerning the disappearance of Jimmy Hoffa, but failed to quote the passage in the report that said that none of the references "suggested any criminality or organized crime associations" on plaintiff's part. This raised a fact question about fairness that barred summary judgment.

As noted in *Medico* and in the discussion of the *Rouch* case, many states have adopted legislation to codify this privilege. These may vary from the common law in the scope of coverage and other limitations.

For extensive discussion of this privilege, see David Elder, The Fair Report Privilege (1988).

Expansion of the fair report privilege. In some jurisdictions the privilege seems to have been expanded far beyond its origins as shield for the reporting of official proceedings to cover a report of a proceeding that is not open to the public. Dorsey v. National Enquirer, Inc., 952 F.2d 250, 19 Med. L. Rptr. 1673 (9th Cir. 1991), involved the singer Arnold Dorsey, whose stage name is Engelbert Humperdinck. The National Enquirer ran a story headlined "Mom of Superstar Singer's Love Child Claims in Court . . . Engelbert has AIDS Virus." The story was based on an affidavit filed by the mother in family court in New York seeking to force Dorsey to buy life insurance naming the child as beneficiary. It stated the mother's "information and belief" that Dorsey "has AIDS related syndrome."

The Enquirer conceded the falsity of the allegation but won summary judgment on the basis of the California statute which recognizes a privilege for a fair and true report "of (1) a judicial, (2) a legislative, or (3) other public official proceeding, or (4) anything said in the course thereof. . . ." Dorsey argued that the wording of subsection (3) implied that subsection (1) covered only public judicial proceedings. But the court construed the statute as applicable to closed judicial proceedings, citing previous decisions applying the privilege to an internal agency report, an FBI "rap sheet," and grand jury proceedings. The court then held that in the absence of disputed facts and where all reasonable inferences from the evidence pointed in the same direction summary judgment should be granted to the defendant. The addition to the article of some out-of-court remarks did not go beyond the gist or sting of the affidavit.

The "wire service defense." The common law recognizes a variation of the fair report privilege that protects republication of stories provided by reputable wire services—at least in the absence of some information that casts doubt on the accuracy of the wire service's story. For a recent example, citing the earlier history of the doctrine, see Howe v. Detroit Free Press, Inc., 219 Mich.App. 150, 555 N.W.2d 738, 25 Med. L. Rptr. 1602 (1996), aff'd 586 N.W.2d 85 (Mich. 1998). A newspaper published a wire service story that said a major league baseball pitcher was a member of a family that was a "prisoner of his father's drinking problems." In the father's libel suit, the court concluded that the newspaper had a privilege to publish the wire service story unless it "knows the story is false or . . . the release itself contains unexplained inconsistencies." To require the newspaper to "independently verify the accuracy of every wire-service release it desires to reproduce would force smaller publishers to confine themselves to stories about purely local events, and would make it difficult for smaller, local news organizations to compete with publishers who could afford to either verify every story or assume the risk of litigation."

Should this privilege be extended to material obtained from other media generally? New York law recognizes a qualified privilege that protects a media entity when it republishes defamatory material obtained from any other media unless the republisher "had, or should have had, substantial reason to question the accuracy of the articles or the bona fides of (the) reporter." The New York Post invoked this privilege when it was sued by Richard Jewell over its coverage of the Olympic Bombing in Atlanta. Based on the reporting of other news organizations, the Post published a column and several articles depicting Jewell, the person who found the bomb at the Olympics, as a "Rambo," "fat, failed," "disaster," "desperate to stand out as a hero," "disgraced former deputy," and "home-grown failure." The Post moved for summary judgment, claiming it relied on reports from the Associated Press and CNN that named Jewell as a suspect in the bombing. A federal district court denied the motion. The Post's writers could not remember which reports they used, and the judge said this made it impossible to determine as a matter of law whether they had reason to doubt the accuracy of those reports. See Jewell v. NYP Holdings Inc., 23 F. Supp.2d 348 (S.D.N.Y. 1998). This case was eventually settled, along with suits by Jewell against NBC, CNN, WABC, for a total of more than $2 million.

I. OTHER ISSUES

1. RETRACTION

At common law a defendant who retracts the defamatory statement may offer the evidence of retraction in mitigation of damages. The promptness, prominence, and forthrightness of the retraction will affect the extent to which it is effective in undoing or minimizing the harm, and therefore are factors (usually for the jury to weigh) in determining the extent to which the retraction reduces the damages.

Most of the states have retraction statutes, which may or may not abrogate the common law rule. Some of these seem to do no more than the common law, but most go further. Some apply even if the defamation is intentional. Most limit the type or amount of damages a plaintiff may recover unless the plaintiff gives the defendant an opportunity to retract and the defendant fails to do so. Many are available only to media defendants.

In a few states retraction statutes have been held unconstitutional. See Boswell v. Phoenix Newspapers, Inc., 152 Ariz. 9, 730 P.2d 186, 13 Med. L. Rptr. 1785 (1986) (statute violated state constitutional provision that right of action "to recover damages for injuries shall never be abrogated") and Madison v. Yunker, 180 Mont. 54, 589 P.2d 126, 4 Med. L. Rptr. 1337 (1978) (statute violated state constitutional provision that courts be "open to every person, and speedy remedy afforded for every injury to person, property, or character").

One of the most elaborate retraction statutes is that of California, Cal.Civ.Code § 48a. It provides that in any action for libel against a newspaper or slander in a broadcast, the plaintiff may recover only special damages unless a correction is demanded and not published or broadcast. The prospective plaintiff's demand must be written, must specify the statements claimed to be defamatory, and must be served on the defendant within 20 days after the plaintiff learns of the publication or broadcast. If the defendant fails to publish or broadcast a retraction "in substantially as conspicuous a manner in said newspaper or on said broadcasting station as were the statements claimed to be libelous, in a regular issue thereof published or broadcast within three weeks after such service, plaintiff . . . may recover general, special, and exemplary damages."

Statutes of this type put considerable pressure on both the plaintiff and the defendant. A defendant may have to decide whether to retract before it has had a full opportunity to determine whether the statement in question is false. A plaintiff who is unaware of the need to request a retraction or the deadline for doing so may inadvertently forfeit a good cause of action. And since many plaintiffs are unable to prove substantial amounts of economic loss, they may be effectively barred from recovery even if the retraction fails to undo all the harm. Courts sometimes strain to construe the statutes in a way that will avoid these results.

For example, in Burnett v. National Enquirer, Inc., 144 Cal.App.3d 991, 193 Cal.Rptr. 206, 9 Med. L. Rptr. 1921 (1983), entertainer Carol Burnett demanded, and the Enquirer published, a retraction of a gossip item that falsely accused her of drunken and boorish behavior in public. Burnett had no special damages, but the trial court awarded her $50,000 in general compensatory damages and $750,000 in punitive damages on the ground that the Enquirer was not a newspaper and therefore not entitled to the benefits of the California retraction statute. The court of appeals affirmed on the ground that the Enquirer did not operate under the deadline constraints that the legislature had in mind when it named newspapers as beneficiaries of the statute. The appeals court reduced the total award to $200,000.

An unusually sweeping retraction statute has been proposed by the National Conference of Commissioners on Uniform State Laws. It is called the "Uniform Correction or Clarification of Defamation Act." It would apply to all defendants and all communications, and would limit recovery to proven economic losses unless the prospective plaintiff requested a retraction within 90 days and the defendant refused to make a "timely and sufficient" retraction. A retraction would be "timely" if published within 45 days. It would be "sufficient" if published in a manner reasonably likely to reach the same audience as the defamation and if it either corrected the error, disclaimed any intent to communicate any defamatory meaning claimed to be implied, or disclaimed any intent to assert the truth of a statement attributed to a third person. A defendant who failed or refused to retract initially could still do so anytime before trial, and by doing so could limit its liability to proven economic loss plus the plaintiff's litigation expenses, including attorney's fees, up to the time the defendant offered to retract. The proposed uniform statute has been adopted only in North Dakota.

2. LIABILITY ABROAD

The Supreme Court has held that the First Amendment does not exempt libel defendants from general rules regarding jurisdiction in distant places. See Keeton v. Hustler Magazine, Inc., 465 U.S. 770, 10 Med. L. Rptr. 1405 (1984) (allowing a state to assert jurisdiction based on defendant's minimal circulation there even though neither plaintiff nor defendant was domiciled there and most of the damage to reputation occurred elsewhere). Since people (and media) who communicate via Internet have little power to prevent access to their material, they are potentially subject to suit in any jurisdiction.

A few courts have proposed special rules for the Internet to limit defendants' exposure to distant jurisdictions. Several have embraced a "sliding scale" approach in which a state's ability to exercise jurisdiction over a nonresident Internet defendant depends on the degree of interactivity of the site. Internet users who actively do business with customers in the forum state are subject to jurisdiction there. Those who only passively make information available there are not. Those who engage in some interactivity with their readers, as by providing an open forum, are subject to jurisdiction in a state only if they "manifest an intent to target and focus on" readers in that state, Young v. New Haven Advocate, 315 F.3d 256 (4th Cir. 2002), or if the publication "is directed at" the state, Revell v. Lidov, 317 F.3d 467, 31 Med. L. Rptr. 1521 (5th Cir. 2002).

Many countries have jurisdictional rules that allow foreign defendants to be sued in their courts and under their law. Since other countries' defamation laws are considerably less protective of defendants than those of the United States, the prospect of having to defend abroad is generally an unwelcome one for American media. The problem is exacerbated by the widespread use of the Internet, by conventional media as well as others. Material posted on the Internet can be accessed in any country, and therefore is arguably "published" there and thus subject to jurisdiction in any country in which it is received.

In a case that attracted much attention in the United States, the Australian High Court held that the New York publisher of Barron's magazine could be sued in Australia under Australian law for statements made on Barron's website about an Australian businessman. See Dow Jones & Co. v. Gutnick [2002] HCA 56, 194 ALR 433. Gutnick sued only for the damage he had suffered in Victoria, his state of residence. The website had several hundred paid subscribers in Victoria, but Dow Jones had no physical presence there.

Victorian law allowed the courts of that state to exercise jurisdiction only if the tort was committed there, and defined the place of tort as the place of publication. The High Court said the law of defamation has always defined publication as not merely the physical act, but the communication of the material to a recipient with resulting harm to reputation, and that occurred in Victoria. Dow Jones argued that the global nature of Internet communication required a new rule for Internet defamation that would deem publication to have occurred where the material is uploaded onto a server (in this instance, New Jersey). Recognizing that this rule might permit publishers to choose jurisdiction by locating their servers in havens that would protect them from liability, Dow Jones proposed an exception that would permit jurisdiction elsewhere if the choice of server location were shown to be "merely adventitious or opportunistic." The defendant also argued that the Australian courts should decline to exercise jurisdiction under their version of forum non conveniens.

The High Court declined to adopt new rules for Internet defamation. The judges said the proposed rule would make U.S. courts and U.S. law dominant, because a disproportionate number of servers are located there, to the detriment of other legal systems that have proper concerns about defamatory speech originated elsewhere and different ideas about how to deal with it. Defamed persons might have difficulty determining where the publisher's server was located, and the exception for "adventitious or opportunistic" location of servers was like to generate much disagreement.

Having held that jurisdiction was proper in Victoria, the court said Victorian choice of law principles applied, and those rules specified the same place of tort-place of publication analysis as the jurisdictional issue.

Unless the defendant has assets in the forum jurisdiction, a plaintiff who wins a libel case abroad can collect it only by getting a U.S. court to enforce the foreign judgment. Under the Uniform Foreign–Money Judgments Recognition Act states agree to enforce judgments from other jurisdictions without re-examining the merits, but they need not recognize a foreign judgment if the "cause of action on which the judgment is based is repugnant to the public policy of the State." In Telnikoff v. Matusevitch, 347 Md. 561, 702 A.2d 230, 25 Med. L. Rptr. 2473 (1997), the court announced that it would refuse to enforce an English libel judgment. The court found that English libel law was so unprotective of speech that the judgment was repugnant to the public policy of Maryland and would not be recognized.

Among the differences between U.S. and English law where: English law required no showing of fault; defamatory statements were presumed to be false with the defendant having to prove them true; a qualified privilege could be overcome by proof of "spite or ill-will or some other wrong or improper motive;" punitive or exemplary damages were available under numerous circumstances in defamation actions and were not, as in Maryland, limited to cases in which there was actual malice; proof of ill-will or spite would vitiate the fair comment defense; and "context appears to be eliminated from a court's determination of whether a statement is considered fact or comment." Finally, English law "flatly reject[ed] the principles set forth in" *Times* and *Gertz*. The dissenter objected that

> Public policy should not require us to give First Amendment protection . . . to English residents who defame other English residents in publications distributed only in England. Failure to make our constitutional provisions relating to defamation applicable to wholly internal English defamation would not seem to violate fundamental notions of what is decent and just and should not undermine public confidence in the administration of law. The court does little or no analysis of the global public policy considerations and seems inclined to

make Maryland libel law applicable to the rest of the world by providing a safe haven for foreign libel judgment debtors.

See also Bachchan v. India Abroad Publications Inc., 154 Misc. 2d 228, 585 N.Y.S.2d 661, 20 Med. L. Rptr. 1051 (1992), declining to enforce an English libel judgment.

Three of the seven judges who decided the *Gutnick* case suggested that Australia might recognize a common-law defense that would protect a nonresident publisher if its conduct was "reasonable" and would take the legal rules of the publisher's home jurisdiction into account in determining reasonableness. If such a defense were available, could American courts refuse to enforce Australian judgments?

3.   SLAPP MOTIONS

Some states have enacted anti-SLAPP statutes, which originally were designed to protect citizens (e.g., environmentalists) against groundless libel suits filed by their adversaries (e.g., polluting industries) to discourage them from exercising their right to protest. (SLAPP is an acronym for "Strategic Lawsuit Against Public Participation.") Typically the statutes permit a defendant to file an early motion to strike the complaint. If the defendant can show that the suit arises out of an act of free speech about a public issue, the complaint will be dismissed unless the plaintiff can demonstrate, through pleadings and affidavits, a probability of prevailing. Claims that this violates plaintiff's right to jury trial generally have been unsuccessful. See, e.g., Lee v. Pennington, 830 So.2d 1037 (La. App. 2002).

In a few states, most notably California, SLAPP motions have become an important line of defense for media. See Lafayette Morehouse, Inc. v. Chronicle Pub. Co., 37 Cal.App.4th 855, 44 Cal.Rptr.2d 46 (1995) (holding that a newspaper was entitled to invoke the SLAPP procedure). Under the California statute, the grant or denial of a SLAPP motion is immediately appealable, with the result that many questions of defamation law are now resolved in SLAPP proceedings in that state. The California statute also provides for the award of attorneys fees to a prevailing party. See, e.g., Braun v. Chronicle Publishing Co., 52 Cal.App.4th 1036, 61 Cal.Rptr.2d 58, 25 Med. L. Rptr. 1594 (1997) (awarding the San Francisco Chronicle $17,000 in attorneys fees against a medical director who had alleged that the newspaper libeled her in an investigative series about the training center she managed).

4.   REFORM

A generation ago there was much agitation to reform libel law. Reformers argued that its complexity imposed significant restraints on free speech without doing much to protect reputation. Some proposed dramatic changes, such as overruling *New York Times* or substituting declaratory relief for awards of damages. See Richard A. Epstein, Was *New York Times v. Sullivan* Wrong? 53 U.Chi. L. Rev. 782 (1986); Marc A. Franklin, A Declaratory Judgment Alternative to Current Libel Law, 74 Cal. L. Rev.

809 (1986); Pierre N. Leval, The No–Money, No–Fault Libel Suit: Keeping *Sullivan* in its Proper Place, 101 Harv. L. Rev. 1287 (1988); Randall P. Bezanson, The Libel Tort Today, 45 Wash. & Lee L. Rev. 535 (1988); David A. Anderson, Is Libel Law Worth Reforming, 140 U. Pa. L. Rev. 487 (1991).

Others suggested modest changes, such as limiting damages or assessing legal fees against parties who are not proceeding in good faith. See Paul A. LeBel, Reforming the Tort of Defamation: An Accommodation of the Competing Interests Within the Current Constitutional Framework, 66 Neb. L. Rev. 249 (1987). For an elaborate empirical study of libel litigation and a proposal that libel cases be removed from the damage context and placed in the setting of some alternative mode of dispute resolution, see Randall P. Bezanson, Gilbert Cranberg, and John Soloski, Libel Law and the Press: Myth and Reality (1987).

The reform movement now seems moribund, perhaps because the burden of libel litigation has diminished greatly for most media. To be sure, there are occasional large judgments. As of this writing, the largest affirmed on appeal was $24 million in Sprague v. Walter, 441 Pa.Super. 1, 656 A.2d 890 (1995). The case was settled for an undisclosed amount in 1996 while defendant's petition for certiorari was pending. A judgment of $10 million was affirmed in Prozeralik v. Capital Cities Communications Inc., 222 App. Div. 2d 1020, 635 N.Y.S.2d 913 (1995), appeal denied, 88 N.Y.2d 843, 667 N.E.2d 334, 644 N.Y.S.2d 683 (1996).

In the aggregate, however, libel is not a significant financial burden on media. From 1983 to 2003, 73 percent of the libel, privacy, and other content-related cases against media were disposed of by the grant of the defendant's motion to dismiss. See Media Law Resource Center, 2004 Motion to Dismiss Study, October 2004. According to the MLRC's 2004 Report of Trials and Damages, February 2004, only seventeen libel cases against media went to trial in the entire U.S. in 2002–2003, and defendants won at trial in all but five of those. From 1980–2003, judgments in favor of plaintiffs were reversed or reduced on appeal 46 percent of the time. Over the same period, the median award in cases in which plaintiffs were ultimately successful was $90,500. The average final award was much higher ($632,722) because of a few very large verdicts. The total of all final awards from 1980–2003 was $77 million. To put this in perspective, the total of final libel awards for 24 years were equal to 0.0004 percent of combined revenues of newspapers, magazines, and broadcasting for a single year ($200 billion in fiscal 2001). See Leo Troy, Almanac of Business and Industrial Financial Ratios 253, 255, 265 (2004).

Libel insurance is available at rates that seem inexpensive compared with other types of insurance. Nonetheless, media often assert that libel law has a chilling effect, at least on smaller outlets. The most timid or financially insecure media are subject to the same rules of libel law as the richest and most aggressive of media. Is it possible for the law to achieve the right level of deterrence for all types of media? If we must choose between overprotection of the most powerful media or underprotection of the weakest, which should we choose?

CHAPTER V

PROTECTING PRIVACY

The law first began recognizing a distinct cause of action for invasion of privacy about a century ago. The initial impetus came from one of the most famous of all law review articles, The Right to Privacy, by Louis D. Brandeis and his law partner Samuel Warren, published in the Harvard Law Review in 1890. Journalism for the masses was just beginning to flourish, and conflicted sharply with Victorian notions of propriety, modesty, and morality. Brandeis and Warren, appalled by the growth of photojournalism and the practices of the Boston newspapers, wrote:

The press is overstepping in every direction the obvious bounds of propriety and of decency. Gossip is no longer the resource of the idle and of the vicious, but has become a trade, which is pursued with industry as well as effrontery. To satisfy a prurient taste the details of sexual relations are spread broadcast in the columns of the daily papers. To occupy the indolent, column upon column is filled with idle gossip, which can only be procured by intrusion upon the domestic circle. . . . When personal gossip attains the dignity of print, and crowds the space available for matters of real interest to the community, what wonder that the ignorant and thoughtless mistake its relative importance. Easy of comprehension, appealing to that weak side of human nature which is never wholly cast down by the misfortunes and frailties of our neighbors, no one can be surprised that it usurps the place of interest in brains capable of other things. Triviality destroys at once robustness of thought and delicacy of feelings. No enthusiasm can flourish, no generous impulse can survive under its blighting influence.

Working with a variety of rather remote precedents from other areas of law, the authors developed an argument that courts should recognize an action for invasion of privacy by media publication. See Samuel D. Warren and Louis D. Brandeis, The Right to Privacy, 4 Harv. L. Rev. 193 (1890). Although the courts were initially unreceptive to the proposed cause of action, gradually they accepted it and broadened it to include several different interests. By 1960, Professor Prosser was able to identify four distinct privacy torts. One is a remedy for publicly disclosing private facts. Another is for depicting a person in a false light. A third is for commercial exploitation of a person's name or likeness. A fourth is for intruding—physically or technologically—into a person's solitude. See William L. Prosser, Privacy, 48 Cal. L. Rev. 383 (1960).

Although the various privacy actions are primarily common law creations, they are quite different from most other common law torts. Unlike libel and slander, which were well developed long before there was a First

Amendment, privacy law has developed along with expansive modern notions of freedom of expression. As a result, the tort of privacy is heavily infused with First Amendment thinking, to the point that it is not always clear whether a particular piece of privacy doctrine is tort law or constitutional law.

Second, privacy law has been influenced to an unusual extent by extrajudicial thinking. As noted above, the remedy originated from a law review article. Privacy law was given its modern form by Prosser. The Restatement (Second) of Torts, for which Prosser was Reporter, adopted not only his four-branch division of the subject, but also, to a large extent, his description of each branch of the tort. Since the privacy torts were not yet solidified in most states, the Restatement had great influence on the development of privacy law. Judicial decisions reflect the views of Prosser and the Restatement at least as much as the Restatement reflects judicial thinking.

Many of the major developments in U.S. privacy law in the past 30 years have come about as a result of new statutes enacted to address specific privacy issues, rather than application of the four privacy torts. The 1970s witnessed considerable activity on the federal level—prompted largely by the growing use of computers within the federal government—including enactment of the Privacy Act of 1974 and appointment of a blue-ribbon Privacy Protection Study Commission to examine the government's use of personal data. After comparatively little activity during the 1980s, the latter half of the 1990s witnessed a tremendous upsurge in privacy-related legislative activity at both the federal and state level. In 1998, for example, 2,367 privacy bills were introduced or carried over in state legislatures; 42 states enacted a total of 786 bills. This recent surge in activity appears to be prompted by another new technology—the Internet—as well as by the adoption of significant new privacy laws by European and other countries. These new laws reflect two important developments. First, many of these laws focus on controlling access to and use of routine information about individuals—name, address, telephone number, social security number, credit card number, etc.—rather than providing for recovery of damages for the disclosure of embarrassing or intimate information or the creation of a false impression. In this sense, many of these laws may be characterized as data protection laws. Second, many of these laws protect privacy from invasion by private organizations rather than by the government. Whether the same principles apply to threats to privacy originating from government as apply to those emanating from private information-collection and use remains to be seen.

We consider in this book only the tort law of privacy and recent statutory developments that concern the mass media. There are many other types of privacy law, such as the constitutional right of privacy that protects certain personal rights involving contraception and abortion, and statutory rights of privacy that are designed to limit acquisition and use of personal information by government agencies or regulated commercial entities, such as banks or utilities. Those privacy laws are beyond the scope of this book, but they nevertheless form an important part of the context in which courts evaluate privacy claims and interpret privacy statutes affecting the media.

Even when limited only to those issues that concern the mass media, however, privacy issues are too diverse to be confined to a single chapter. In this chapter, we examine the three torts and statutory developments applicable to the *publication* of information by the mass media. In Chapter VIII, we address the fourth privacy tort—intrusion—together with other torts arising from *news-gathering*. Laws affecting the media's *access* to information and institutions—public and private—are covered in Chapter X. We treat the special situation of access to courts and judicial information in Chapter XI.

We begin with the three privacy torts applicable to publication.

A.   PUBLIC DISCLOSURE OF PRIVATE FACTS

1.   THE TORT

This branch of the tort protects far less privacy than its name might suggest. As a matter of tort law, there is no cause of action unless the disclosure would be highly offensive to a person of reasonable sensibilities and is of no legitimate public concern. Some courts substitute the term "newsworthiness" for "legitimate public concern," but the latter is probably more accurate, because it suggests that the issue has a normative as well as a descriptive aspect. What is highly offensive is of course a matter of contemporary mores, which are themselves influenced by media practices in disclosing personal facts. In a society that values openness, courts find it difficult to say that people have no legitimate concern in receiving information they apparently wish to receive. In addition to these tort limitations the constitutional law imposes further restrictions on the cause of action, as we shall see shortly. As the effect of these limitations becomes clear, you may wish to consider whether this tort protects enough privacy to justify its continued existence in its present form.

Haynes v. Alfred A. Knopf, Inc.

United States Court of Appeals, Seventh Circuit, 1993.
8 F.3d 1222, 21 Med. L. Rptr. 2161.

[The book, "The Promised Land: The Great Black Migration and How it Changed America," by Nicholas Lemann, used the life of Ruby Lee Daniels to illustrate its themes about the social, political, and economic effects of the movement of blacks from the rural South to the cities of the North between 1940 and 1970. The author switched back and forth between discussion of that migration in general, and its personal dimensions as reflected in Ms. Daniels's descriptions of her life and experiences, beginning when she was a sharecropper in Mississippi and progressing through her move to Chicago and her life there over the next 40 years.

Among the things she discussed was her relationship with her ex-husband, Luther Haynes. She depicted him as a heavy-drinking ne'er-do-well who neglected their children, could not keep a job, was unfaithful, and eventually left her for another woman. The court quoted one excerpt:

> Luther began to drink too much. When he drank he got mean, and he and Ruby would get into ferocious quarrels. He was still working but he wasn't always bringing his paycheck home. . . . It got to the point where [Luther] would go out on Friday evenings after picking up his paycheck and Ruby would hope he wouldn't come home, because she knew he would be drunk. On the Friday evenings when he did come home—over the years Ruby developed a devastating imitation of Luther, and could recreate the scene quite vividly—he would walk into the apartment, put on a record and turn up the volume, and saunter into their bedroom, a bottle in one hand and a cigarette in the other, in the mood for love. On one such night, Ruby's last child, Kevin, was conceived. Kevin always had something wrong with him—he was very moody, he was scrawny, and he had a severe speech impediment. Ruby was never able to find out exactly what the problem was, but she blamed it on Luther; all that alcohol must have gotten into his sperm, she said.

Haynes admitted many of the incidents in the book, but they had all occurred 25 years earlier, and since then he had reformed, remarried, and lived an exemplary life. He and his present wife, Dorothy, sued the author and publisher for libel and invasion of privacy. The trial court granted summary judgment for the defendants, and the Court of Appeals affirmed. The court held that the Hayneses had no cause of action for libel because the defamatory statements about them were substantially true.]

Before POSNER, CHIEF JUDGE, and MANION and WOOD, CIRCUIT JUDGES.

POSNER, CHIEF JUDGE:

. . .

Even people who have nothing rationally to be ashamed of can be mortified by the publication of intimate details of their life. Most people in no way deformed or disfigured would nevertheless be deeply upset if nude photographs of themselves were published in a newspaper or a book. They feel the same way about photographs of their sexual activities, however "normal," or about a narrative of those activities, or about having their medical records publicized. Although it is well known that every human being defecates, no adult human being in our society wants a newspaper to show a picture of him defecating. The desire for privacy illustrated by these examples is a mysterious but deep fact about human personality. It deserves and in our society receives legal protection. The nature of the injury shows, by the way, that the defendants are wrong to argue that this branch of the right of privacy requires proof of special damages. [ ]

But this is not the character of the depictions of the Hayneses in The Promised Land. Although the plaintiffs claim that the book depicts their "sex life" and "ridicules" Luther Haynes's lovemaking (the reference is to the passage we quoted in which the author refers to Ruby's "devastating imitation" of Luther's manner when he would come home Friday nights in an amorous mood), these characterizations are misleading. No sexual act is described in the book. No intimate details are revealed. Entering one's bedroom with a bottle in one hand and a cigarette in the other is not foreplay. Ruby's speculation that Kevin's problems may have been due to Luther's having been a heavy drinker is not the narration of a sexual act.

. . .

. . . The revelations in the book are not about the intimate details of the Hayneses' life. They are about misconduct, in particular Luther's. (There is very little about Dorothy in the book, apart from the fact that she had an affair with Luther while he was still married to Ruby and that they eventually became and have remained lawfully married.) The revelations are about his heavy drinking, his unstable employment, his adultery, his irresponsible and neglectful behavior toward his wife and children. So we must consider cases in which the right of privacy has been invoked as a shield against the revelation of previous misconduct.

Two early cases illustrate the range of judicial thinking. In *Melvin v. Reid*, 297 Pac. 91 (Cal. App. 1931), the plaintiff was a former prostitute, who had been prosecuted but acquitted of murder. She later had married and (she alleged) for seven years had lived a blameless respectable life in a community in which her lurid past was unknown—when all was revealed in a movie about the murder case which used her maiden name. The court held that these allegations stated a claim for invasion of privacy. The Hayneses' claim is similar although less dramatic. They have been a respectable married couple for two decades. Luther's alcohol problem is behind him. He has steady employment as a doorman. His wife is a nurse, and in 1990 he told Lemann that the couple's combined income was $60,000 a year. He is not in trouble with the domestic relations court. He is a deacon of his church. He has come a long way from sharecropping in Mississippi and public housing in Chicago and he and his wife want to bury their past just as Mrs. Melvin wanted to do and in *Melvin v. Reid* was held entitled to do. [ ] In Luther Haynes's own words, from his deposition, "I know I haven't been no angel, but since almost 30 years ago I have turned my life completely around. I stopped the drinking and all this bad habits and stuff like that, which I deny, some of [it] I didn't deny, because I have changed my life. It take me almost 30 years to change it and I am deeply in my church. I look good in the eyes of my church members and my community. Now, what is going to happen now when this public reads this garbage which I didn't tell Mr. Lemann to write? Then all this is going to go down the drain. And I worked like a son of a gun to build myself up in a good reputation and he has torn it down."

But with *Melvin v. Reid* compare *Sidis v. F–R Publishing Corp.*, 113 F.2d 806 [1 Med. L. Rptr. 1775] (2d Cir. 1940), another old case but one more consonant with modern thinking about the proper balance between the right of privacy and the freedom of the press. A child prodigy had flamed out; he was now an eccentric recluse. The New Yorker ran a "where is he now" article about him. The article, entitled "April Fool," did not reveal any misconduct by Sidis but it depicted him in mocking tones as a comical failure, in much the same way that the report of Ruby's "devastating imitation" of the amorous Luther Haynes could be thought to have depicted him as a comical failure, albeit with sinister consequences absent from Sidis's case. The invasion of Sidis's privacy was palpable. But the publisher won. No intimate physical details of Sidis's life had been revealed; and on the other side was the undoubted newsworthiness of a child prodigy, as of a woman prosecuted for murder. Sidis, unlike Mrs. Melvin, was not permitted to bury his past.

. . .

. . . People who do not desire the limelight and do not deliberately choose a way of life or course of conduct calculated to thrust them into it nevertheless have no legal right to extinguish it if the experiences that have befallen them are newsworthy, even if they would prefer that those experiences be kept private. The possibility of an involuntary loss of privacy is recognized in the modern formulations of this branch of the privacy tort, which require not only that the private facts publicized be such as would make a reasonable person deeply offended by such publicity but also that they be facts in which the public has no legitimate interest. [ ]

The two criteria, offensiveness and newsworthiness, are related. An individual, and more pertinently perhaps the community, is most offended by the publication of intimate personal facts when the community has no interest in them beyond the voyeuristic thrill of penetrating the wall of privacy that surrounds a stranger. The reader of a book about the black migration to the North would have no legitimate interest in the details of Luther Haynes's sex life; but no such details are disclosed. Such a reader does have a legitimate interest in the aspects of Luther's conduct that the book reveals. For one of Lemann's major themes is the transposition virtually intact of a sharecropper morality characterized by a family structure "matriarchal and elastic" and by an "extremely unstable" marriage bond to the slums of the northern cities, and the interaction, largely random and sometimes perverse, of that morality with governmental programs to alleviate poverty. Public aid policies discouraged Ruby and Luther from living together, public housing policies precipitated a marriage doomed to fail. No detail in the book claimed to invade the Hayneses' privacy is not germane to the story that the author wanted to tell, a story not only of legitimate but of transcendent public interest.

The Hayneses question whether the linkage between the author's theme and their private life really is organic. They point out that many social histories do not mention individuals at all, let alone by name. That is true. Much of social science, including social history, proceeds by abstraction, aggregation, and quantification rather than by case studies. . . . But it would be absurd to suggest that cliometric or other aggregative, impersonal methods of doing social history are the only proper way to go about it and presumptuous to claim even that they are the best way. Lemann's book has been praised to the skies by distinguished scholars, among them black scholars covering a large portion of the ideological spectrum—Henry Louis Gates, Jr., William Junius Wilson, and Patricia Williams. Lemann's methodology places the individual case history at center stage. If he cannot tell the story of Ruby Daniels without waivers from every person who she thinks did her wrong, he cannot write this book.

Well, argue the Hayneses, at least Lemann could have changed their names. But the use of pseudonyms would not have gotten Lemann and Knopf off the legal hook. The details of the Hayneses' lives recounted in the book would identify them unmistakably to anyone who has known the Hayneses well for a long time (members of their families, for example), or who knew them before they got married; and no more is required. . . . Lemann would have had to change some, perhaps many, of the details. But then he would no longer have been writing history. He would have been writing fiction. The non-quantitative study of living persons would be abolished as a category of scholarship, to be replaced by the sociological novel. That is a genre with a distinguished history punctuated by famous names, such as Dickens, Zola, Stowe, Dreiser, Sinclair, Steinbeck, and Wolfe, but we do not think that the law of privacy makes it (or that the First Amendment would permit the law of privacy to make it) the exclusive format for a social history of living persons that tells their story rather than treating them as data points in a statistical study. Reporting the true facts about real people is necessary to "obviate any impression that the problems raised in the [book] are remote or hypothetical." [ ] And surely a composite portrait of ghetto residents would be attacked as racial stereotyping.

The Promised Land does not afford the reader a titillating glimpse of tabooed activities. The tone is decorous and restrained. Painful though it is for the Hayneses to see a past they would rather forget brought into the public view, the public needs the information conveyed by the book, including the information about Luther and Dorothy Haynes, in order to evaluate the profound social and political questions that the book raises. . . . [A]ll the discreditable facts about the Hayneses that are contained in judicial records are beyond the power of tort law to conceal; and the disclosure of those facts alone would strip away the Hayneses' privacy as effectively as The Promised Land has done. (This case, it could be argued, has stripped them of their privacy, since their story is now part of a judicial record—the record of this case.) We do not think it is an answer that Lemann got his facts from Ruby Daniels rather than from judicial records. The courts got the facts from Ruby. We cannot see what difference it makes that Lemann went to the source.

Ordinarily the evaluation and comparison of offensiveness and newsworthiness would be, like other questions of the application of a legal standard to the facts of a particular case, matters for a jury, not for a judge on a motion for summary judgment. But summary judgment is properly granted to a defendant when on the basis of the evidence obtained in pretrial discovery no reasonable jury could render a verdict for the plaintiff, [ ], and that is the situation here. . . .

. . .

Does it follow, as the Hayneses' lawyer asked us rhetorically at oral argument, that a journalist who wanted to write a book about contemporary sexual practices could include the intimate details of named living persons' sexual acts without the persons' consent? Not necessarily, although the revelation of such details in the memoirs of former spouses and lovers is common enough and rarely provokes a lawsuit even when the former spouse or lover is still alive. The core of the branch of privacy law with which we deal in this case is the protection of those intimate physical details the publicizing of which would be not merely embarrassing and painful but deeply shocking to the average person subjected to such exposure. The public has a legitimate interest in sexuality, but that interest may be outweighed in such a case by the injury to the sensibilities of the person made use of by the author in such a way. [ ] At least the balance would be sufficiently close to preclude summary judgment for the author and publisher. [ ]

The judgment for the defendants is AFFIRMED.

Notes and Questions

1. If Ms. Daniels had discussed her life with her ex-husband not with the author of a serious book, but on a tabloid TV show, would that make a difference in evaluating the offensiveness or newsworthiness of the disclosures? Would it matter whether her tone was scandalous instead of decorous?

2. Judge Posner's assertion that offensiveness and newsworthiness are related criteria is unusual. Courts usually analyze them as independent variables. Is it true that disclosures are more offensive if they are of no legitimate public concern? That the public concern is less likely to be legitimate if the disclosure is especially offensive? There is no liability in any event unless the disclosure is "highly offensive." Is there room within that concept for the kind of sliding scale that Posner seems to envision?

3. The court gives assurances that its decision does not necessarily mean that authors are free to give intimate details of people's sex lives. If the author had been writing a book on race and sexuality, why wouldn't he be free to quote Ms. Daniels's descriptions of Haynes's sex life on the same theory that enables him to quote her descriptions of Haynes's job history and drinking habits? Is the court suggesting that some disclosures would be actionable no matter how legitimate the public concern?

In most public disclosure cases, the publication discusses some matter of public concern; the issue is whether the private facts in question are sufficiently related to that matter. How does this court decide that the private facts revealed about Luther Haynes are "germane" to a story "of transcendent public interest"?

4. Passage of time between the occurrence of an event and publication might be relevant to the offensiveness of the disclosure, the legitimacy of

the public concern, or to whether the information is truly private. What role did it play in *Haynes*? In the *Melvin* and *Sidis* cases (both described in the principal case)? This issue probably also has a constitutional dimension. See p. 379 infra.

————

Evaluating public concern. In many cases, the key issue is whether the private facts are sufficiently related to a subject of conceded public concern to justify their disclosure. In the *Haynes* case, for example, the plaintiffs did not question the legitimacy of the public's concern about the larger themes of the book; they only questioned the relevance to those themes of the specific facts about them. Who decides how strong the relevance must be?

In Gilbert v. Medical Economics Co., 665 F.2d 305, 7 Med. L. Rptr. 2372 (10th Cir. 1981), the plaintiff was an anesthesiologist who had been involved in two alleged instances of malpractice. The magazine Medical Economics used her photograph and facts about her personal and professional life to illustrate a story headlined "Who Let This Doctor In The O.R.? The Story Of A Fatal Breakdown In Medical Policing." The article discussed the plaintiff's psychiatric history and marital problems. She contended there was no evidence that these matters had any connection with the alleged malpractice.

Upholding summary judgment for the magazine, the court held that the disclosures were "substantially relevant to the newsworthy topic of policing the medical profession." The court said editors should be free to draw an inference that the personal matters had a causal relationship with the malpractice, even if no court or other tribunal had so found. "Because the inferences of causation drawn in this case are not, as a matter of law, so purely conjectural that no reasonable editor could draw them other than through guesswork and speculation, we hold that defendants did not abuse their editorial discretion in this case. . . . Although application of the newsworthiness standard to undisputed facts may well present a jury question in some cases, here objective and reasonable minds could not differ in finding the article in question to be privileged in its entirety. . . ."

A California court appeared to reject the "reasonable editor" standard in Diaz v. Oakland Tribune, Inc., 139 Cal. App.3d 118, 188 Cal. Rptr. 762, 9 Med. L. Rptr. 1121 (1983). A newspaper columnist wrote: "The students at the College of Alameda will be surprised to learn that their student body president, Toni Diaz, is no lady, but is in fact a man whose real name is Antonio. Now, I realize, that in these times, such a matter is no big deal, but I suspect his classmates in P.E. 97 may wish to make other showering arrangements." Diaz, who had had a sex change operation, won a verdict of $250,000 compensatory and $525,000 punitive damages. The court of appeals reversed because of errors in the jury instructions, but rejected the defendants' argument that the newsworthiness issue should not have been submitted to the jury. The court then went on to analyze the newsworthiness of the article without reference to editorial judgment:

> [W]e find little if any connection between the information disclosed and Diaz's fitness for office. The fact that she is a transsexual does not adversely reflect on her honesty or judgment. . . . Nor does the fact that she was the first woman student body president, in itself, warrant that her entire private life be open to public inspection. . . . Nor is there merit to defendants' claim that the changing roles of women in society make this story newsworthy. . . . Therefore we conclude that the jury was the proper body to answer the question whether the article was newsworthy or whether it extended beyond the bounds of decency.

The court held that the evidence was sufficient to support an award of punitive damages, although it cautioned the trial judge to scrutinize any such award on retrial to be sure it was not excessive. It held that the award of $250,000 compensatory damages, almost all for emotional distress, was not excessive as a matter of law. After this decision the parties settled for a sum reported to be substantial.

The Virgil case. Sports Illustrated decided to do a story about body surfing, focusing on plaintiff, who was reputed to be the most daredevil of all body surfers. Plaintiff was interviewed and photographed at the beach. To verify the accuracy of the article, a checker for the magazine called plaintiff's home. Plaintiff claimed he learned then for the first time that the article would deal not only with his prominence as a surfer but also with "some rather bizarre incidents in his life that were not directly related to surfing." These included the facts (apparently true) that he had once dived head first down a flight of stairs, sometimes ate "spiders and other insects," had never learned to read, and was considered "abnormal" by other surfers. When plaintiff learned of the scope of the proposed article, he "revoked his consent" to any mention of his name or use of his photograph in the article. When the article appeared with the information about plaintiff and photographs of him, he sued for invasion of privacy.

The trial court's denial of summary judgment for the magazine was affirmed on interlocutory appeal. Virgil v. Time, Inc., 527 F.2d 1122 (9th Cir. 1975). The court adopted the view of the Restatement (Second) of Torts, that liability may be imposed if the matter published is "not of legitimate concern to the public." Then the court quoted from what later became section 652D comment *h*:

> In determining what is a matter of legitimate public interest, account must be taken of the customs and conventions of the community; and in the last analysis what is proper becomes a matter of the community mores. The line is to be drawn when the publicity ceases to be the giving of information to which the public is entitled, and becomes a morbid and sensational prying into private lives for its own sake, with which a reasonable member of the public, with decent standards, would say that he had no concern. . . .

On remand, the trial judge granted the magazine summary judgment. First, he concluded that the facts were "generally unflattering and perhaps embarrassing, but they are simply not offensive to the degree of morbidity or sensationalism. In fact, they connote nearly as strong a positive image as they do a negative one. On the one hand Mr. Virgil can be seen as a juvenile exhibitionist, but on the other hand he also comes across as the tough, aggressive maverick, an archetypal character occupying a respected place in the American consciousness. Given this ambiguity . . . no reasonable juror could conclude that [the facts] were highly offensive."

Even if offensiveness were found, the magazine was entitled to summary judgment because the parties "agree that body surfing at the Wedge is a matter of legitimate public interest, and it cannot be doubted that Mike Virgil's unique prowess at the same is also of legitimate public interest. Any reasonable person . . . would have to conclude that the personal facts concerning Mike Virgil were included as a legitimate journalistic attempt to explain Virgil's extremely daring and dangerous style of body surfing at the Wedge. There is no possibility that a juror could conclude that the personal facts were included for any inherent morbid, sensational, or curiosity appeal they might have." Virgil v. Sports Illustrated, 424 F. Supp. 1286 (S.D.Cal. 1976).

Naming names. An argument frequently offered to justify naming a person about whom embarrassing private facts are disclosed is that identifying the person strengthens the credibility and impact of the article. The Tenth Circuit accepted this argument in *Gilbert,* saying the plaintiff's name and photograph "obviate any impression that the problems raised in the article are remote or hypothetical, thus providing an aura of immediacy and even urgency. . . ." Are these considerations sufficient by themselves to make a disclosure "of legitimate public concern?" Is there any circumstance in which identifying the person *would not* enhance the credibility and impact of the story?

Public figures. There is no formal distinction between public figures and private persons in the law of privacy, as there is in the law of libel. In privacy the same basic rules apply to all types of plaintiffs. But it is clear that the scope of legitimate public curiosity is wider when the subject is a public figure.

A district judge held that Pamela Anderson Lee's sex life was a matter of legitimate public concern because "[s]he is famous as a sex symbol." The tabloid TV program "Hard Copy" broadcast an item about a company's plan to release on the Internet a 45–minute videotape of the actress having sex with her then-boyfriend Bret Michaels. The "Hard Copy" broadcast included eight short excerpts from the tape. Michaels obtained a temporary restraining order prohibiting the Internet company from distributing the tape, and Anderson sued Paramount, the producers of "Hard Copy," for disclosure of private facts and violation of her right of publicity. The court rejected both claims on the ground that her sex life was a matter of legitimate public concern. " '[P]urported romantic involvements' of celebrities are matters of public concern," the judge said. In Anderson's case, since the reason for her fame is that she is a sex symbol, "the private facts depicted in the Hard Copy broadcast have a substantial nexus to a matter of legitimate public interest." See Michaels v. Internet Entertainment Group, Inc., 5 F. Supp.2d 823, 27 Med. L. Rptr. 1097 (C.D.Cal. 1998).

During an assassination attempt on President Ford in San Francisco, Oliver Sipple knocked the arm of the assailant, Sara Jane Moore, as she sought to aim a second shot at the President. Sipple was the object of extensive media attention, including stories that disclosed his homosexuality and suggested that because of it Ford had not expressed appropriate gratitude to Sipple. Sipple, asserting that relatives who lived in the Midwest did not know of his sexual preference, sued the San Francisco Chronicle. The newspaper defended in part on the argument that privacy was not involved because Sipple had marched in gay parades and had acknowledged that at least 100 to 500 people in San Francisco knew he was a homosexual.

Summary judgment for the paper was affirmed on appeal. First, the facts were not private. Second, they were newsworthy. The article was prompted by "legitimate political considerations, i.e., to dispel the false public opinion that gays were timid, weak and unheroic figures and to raise the equally important political question whether the President of the United States entertained a discriminatory attitude or bias against a minority group such as homosexuals." Sipple v. Chronicle Publishing Co., 154 Cal. App.3d 1040, 201 Cal. Rptr. 665, 10 Med. L. Rptr. 1690 (1984).

Privacy rights of survivors. The cause of action for invasion of privacy, like that for defamation, is usually considered personal. That means it does not survive the death of the victim and does not give rise to any cause of action by survivors. Occasionally, however, courts permit survivors to recover for what appear to be invasions of a decedent's privacy. In Reid v. Pierce County, 136 Wash.2d 195, 961 P.2d 333 (1998), employees of the county medical examiner allegedly displayed autopsy photos at cocktail parties and in scrapbooks compiled for their own amusement. Surviving relatives were held to have a cause of action for invasion of their common law right of privacy. Citing a long line of cases recognizing a cause of action for mutilating or mishandling corpses, the court said misuse of photos differed only in degree. The existence of a statute making autopsy records confidential and a county policy forbidding employees from taking autopsy photos for personal purposes reinforced the court's conclusion that "the immediate relatives of a decedent have a protectable privacy interest in the autopsy records of the decedent."

In the context of exempting private matters from disclosure under the federal Freedom of Information Act, the Supreme Court has held that survivors have cognizable privacy interests. See National Archives and Records Administration v. Favish, infra p. 606.

Rejecting the privacy action. All but a handful of states recognize the "private facts" tort action. The most notable of the states that have rejected the action is New York, where the Court of Appeals rejected the idea of common law remedies for invasion of privacy in 1902 and has not retreated from that position. See Roberson v. Rochester Folding Box Co., 171 N.Y. 538, 64 N.E. 442 (1902). In New York the only remedy for any of the four types of tortious invasion of privacy is a statute that permits actions for damages and injunctions for unauthorized use of a person's name or likeness, but only if the use is "for advertising purposes, or for the purposes of trade." N.Y. Civ. Rts. Law §§ 50–51. We will see this statute, and its effect on privacy jurisprudence, several times in later sections of this chapter.

In Anderson v. Fisher Broadcasting Companies, Inc., 300 Or. 452, 712 P.2d 803, 12 Med. L. Rptr. 1604 (1986), the court on state law grounds rejected the privacy action brought by an accident victim against a television station that used film of him, bleeding and in pain, in promotional spots for a forthcoming special news report on emergency medical treatment. In so doing, the court observed:

> What is "private" so as to make its publication offensive likely differs among communities, between generations, and among ethnic, religious, or other social groups, as well as among individuals. Likewise, one reader's or viewer's "news" is another's tedium or trivia. The editorial judgment of what is "newsworthy" is not so readily submitted to the ad hoc review of a jury as [the lower court] believed. It is not properly a community standard. Even when some editors themselves vie to tailor "news" to satisfy popular tastes, others may believe that the community should see or hear facts or ideas that the majority finds uninteresting or offensive.

The court said Oregon does not recognize a cause of action for public disclosure "unless the manner or purpose of defendant's conduct is wrongful in some respect apart from causing the plaintiff's hurt feelings."

See also Hall v. Post, 323 N.C. 259, 372 S.E.2d 711, 15 Med. L. Rptr. 2329 (1988), rejecting the action largely because it will generally duplicate the action for intentional infliction of emotional distress.

Before he became a judge, the author of the *Haynes* opinion suggested that a person who seeks to withhold some part of his or her past is trying to present a misrepresentation to the public. Although the individual is free to try to hide this information, Professor Posner argued that the law should not impose sanctions on those who tell the public the truth about such a person. Richard Posner, The Right of Privacy, 12 Ga. L. Rev. 393 (1978). Is that consistent with the view of privacy he took in *Haynes*? Five comments on the article immediately follow it.

2.   CONSTITUTIONAL LIMITATIONS

We turn now to cases in which the issue is not the tort law of privacy, but constitutional limitations on that law. In fact, that distinction is hard to maintain. In many of the cases we considered above, discussions of tort law were intermingled with discussions about constitutional ramifications. In the *Haynes* case, for example, the opinion discusses the constitutional cases in this section for guidance in interpreting the offensiveness and newsworthiness elements of the tort. Although we separate the tort and constitutional aspects for the sake of analytical clarity, it is important to recognize that courts often intermingle them.

In 1975, the Supreme Court decided its first "private facts" case. Cox Broadcasting Corp. v. Cohn, 420 U.S. 469, 1 Med. L. Rptr. 1819 (1975). A 17–year–old had been raped in Georgia and did not survive. A Georgia criminal statute made it a misdemeanor for "any news media or any other person to print and publish, broadcast, televise or disseminate through any other medium of public discussion . . . the name or identity of any female who may have been raped." During a recess in a criminal hearing in the case, a television reporter was allowed to inspect the indictment, which named the victim. Cox Broadcasting used the victim's name in reporting on the case that night.

The victim's father brought a tort action for disclosure of his daughter's name. The state supreme court held that the complaint stated a common law action for damages. A First Amendment defense was rejected on the ground that the statute was an authoritative declaration that Georgia considered a rape victim's name not to be a matter of public concern. The court could discern "no public interest or general concern about the identity of the victim of such a crime as will make the right to disclose the identity of the victim rise to the level of First Amendment protection."

The Supreme Court reversed. Cox Broadcasting argued for a "broad holding that the press may not be made criminally or civilly liable for publishing information that is neither false nor misleading but absolutely accurate, however damaging it may be to reputation or individual sensibilities." Justice White's majority opinion avoided the broad question by addressing the narrower question of "whether the State may impose sanctions on the accurate publication of the name of a rape victim obtained from public records—more specifically, from judicial records which are maintained in connection with a public prosecution and which themselves are open to public inspection. We are convinced that the State may not do so."

Justice White noted that the public relies on the press to bring them facts about the operation of government in a convenient form. Without such information "most of us and many of our representatives would be unable to vote intelligently or to register opinions on the administration of government generally." The "commission of crime, prosecutions resulting from it, and judicial proceedings arising from the prosecutions . . . are without question events of legitimate concern to the public and consequently fall within the responsibility of the press to report the operations of government."

Justice White noted that the developing law of privacy afforded the press a privilege to report the events of judicial proceedings. "By placing the information in the public domain on official court records, the State must be presumed to have concluded that the public interest was thereby being served. Public records by their very nature are of interest to those concerned with the administration of government, and a public benefit is performed by the reporting of the true contents of the records by the media." Freedom to publish material released by government is of "critical importance to our type of government in which the citizenry is the final judge of the proper conduct of public business." In such situations, "the States may not impose sanctions on the publication of truthful information contained in official court records open to public inspection."

The Court was "reluctant to embark on a course that would make public records generally available to the media but forbid their publication if offensive to the sensibilities of the supposed reasonable man. Such a rule would make it very difficult for the media to inform citizens about the public business and yet stay within the law. The rule would invite timidity and self-censorship and very likely lead to the suppression of many items that would otherwise be published and that should be made available to the public. . . . If there are privacy interests to be protected in judicial proceedings, the States must respond by means which avoid public documentation or other exposure of private information. Once true information is disclosed in public court documents open to public inspection, the press cannot be sanctioned for publishing it." The Court noted that it was implying nothing about any constitutional questions that might arise from a state policy of closing judicial proceedings or records to public access.

Chief Justice Burger concurred only in the judgment. Justice Rehnquist dissented on the ground that the state courts had not rendered a final judgment.

Old court records. Does *Cox Broadcasting* protect the disclosure of privacy-invading information from court records indefinitely? Before that decision, some courts thought matters of public record could become private with the passage of time. In Briscoe v. Reader's Digest Association, 4 Cal.3d 529, 93 Cal. Rptr. 866, 483 P.2d 34, 1 Med. L. Rptr. 1845 (1971), an article reported that 11 years earlier plaintiff had hijacked a truck in Kentucky, for which he had served time. The subject sued for invasion of privacy, alleging that he had been rehabilitated and was living in California with family and friends who did not know of his past. Although the conviction was a matter of public record, the court held that the complaint stated a cause of action. "Ideally, his neighbors should recognize his present worth and forget his past life of shame. But men are not so divine as to forgive the past trespasses of others, and plaintiff therefore endeavored to reveal as little as possible of his past life."

The California Supreme Court eventually overruled *Briscoe*, however, holding that *Cox Broadcasting* and subsequent Supreme Court cases had established an absolute right of the press to publish information from open court records regardless of the passage of time. Any state interest in the rehabilitation of offenders falls short of the "state interest of the highest order" that would be necessary to overcome the presumption of openness recognized by *Florida Star*. Gates v. Discovery Communications, Inc., 34 Cal.4th 679, 21 Cal. Rptr.3d 663, 101 P.3d 552 (2004). The plaintiff in *Gates* was a man who had served a three-year prison term as an accessory to murder but had led a lawful, productive, and obscure life after his release. Thirteen years after the murder the defendants broadcast a television documentary about the crime, including the name and photo of the plaintiff. The court said "Neither that the defendants' documentary was of an historical nature nor that it involved 'reenactments,' rather than first-hand coverage, of the events reported diminishes any constitutional protection it enjoys."

———

After *Cox Broadcasting* the Court decided three cases which, though not themselves tort actions for invasion of privacy, were destined to affect the Court's response to the public disclosure tort. We saw two of these cases in Chapter I: *Landmark Communications,* in which the Court held that a state could not fine a newspaper for reporting that a judge was under investigation, and *Daily Mail,* which held that the state could not prosecute a newspaper for identifying a juvenile suspect in a homicide case. The third case was Oklahoma Publishing Co. v. District Court, 430 U.S. 308, 2 Med. L. Rptr. 1456 (1977), in which a judge after admitting the press and public to a juvenile hearing, ordered the press not to publish the offender's name or photograph. The Court held that because the information had been publicly revealed at the hearing, the judge could not prohibit the media from publishing it.

Florida Star v. B.J.F.

Supreme Court of the United States, 1989.
491 U.S. 524, 109 S. Ct. 2603, 105 L. Ed.2d 443, 16 Med. L. Rptr. 1801.

JUSTICE MARSHALL delivered the opinion of the Court.

Florida Stat. section 794.03 (1987) makes it unlawful to "print, publish, or broadcast . . . in any instrument of mass communication" the name of the victim of a sexual offense. Pursuant to this statute, appellant The Florida Star was found civilly liable for publishing the name of a rape victim which it had obtained from a publicly released police report. The issue presented here is whether this result comports with the First Amendment. We hold that it does not.

I

The Florida Star is a weekly newspaper which serves the community of Jacksonville, Florida, and which has an average circulation of approximately 18,000 copies. A regular feature of the newspaper is its "Police Reports" section. The section, typically two to three pages in length, contains brief articles describing local criminal incidents under police investigation. On October 20, 1983, appellee B.J.F. reported to the Duval County, Florida, Sheriff's Department (the Department) that she had been robbed and sexually assaulted by an unknown assailant. The Department prepared a report on the incident which identified B.J.F., by her full name. The Department then placed the report in its press room. The Department does not restrict access either to the press room or to the reports made available therein.

A Florida Star reporter-trainee sent to the press room copied the police report verbatim, including B.J.F.'s full name, on a blank duplicate of the Department's forms. A Florida Star reporter then prepared a one-paragraph article about the crime, derived entirely from the trainee's copy of the police report. The article included B.J.F.'s full name. It appeared in the "Robberies" subsection of the "Police Reports" section on October 29, 1983, one of fifty-four police blotter stories in that day's edition. . . .

In printing B.J.F.'s full name, The Florida Star violated its internal policy of not publishing the names of sexual offense victims.

[B.J.F. sued the newspaper on the theory that the newspaper violated the portion of the statute quoted above and the Sheriff's Department on the theory that it violated another provision making it a crime "to cause or allow" information identifying a victim of a sexual offense to be published or broadcast. The Sheriff's Department settled for $2,500. The Star's motion to dismiss was denied.]

At the ensuing day-long trial, B.J.F. testified that she had suffered emotional distress from the publication of her name. She stated that she had heard about the article from fellow workers and acquaintances; that her mother had received several threatening phone calls from a man who stated that he would rape B.J.F. again; and that these events had forced B.J.F. to change her phone number and residence, to seek police protection, and to obtain mental health counseling. In defense, The Florida Star put forth evidence indicating that the newspaper had learned B.J.F.'s name from the incident report released by the Department, and that the newspaper's violation of its internal rule against publishing the names of sexual offense victims was inadvertent.

At the close of B.J.F.'s case, and again at the close of its defense, The Florida Star moved for a directed verdict. On both occasions, the trial judge denied these motions. He ruled from the bench that section 794.03 was constitutional because it reflected a proper balance between the First Amendment and privacy rights, as it applied only to a narrow set of "rather sensitive . . . criminal offenses." [ ] At the close of the newspaper's defense, the judge granted B.J.F.'s motion for a directed verdict on the issue of negligence, finding the newspaper per se negligent based upon its violation of section 794.03. [ ] This ruling left the jury to consider only the questions of causation and damages. The judge instructed the jury that it could award B.J.F. punitive damages if it found that the newspaper had "acted with reckless indifference to the rights of others." [ ] The jury awarded B.J.F. $75,000 in compensatory damages and $25,000 in punitive damages. Against the actual damage award, the judge set off B.J.F.'s settlement with the Department.

The First District Court of Appeal affirmed in a three-paragraph per curiam opinion. . . . The Supreme Court of Florida denied discretionary review.

The Florida Star appealed to this Court. We noted probable jurisdiction, [ ], and now reverse.

II

The tension between the right which the First Amendment accords to a free press, on the one hand, and the protections which various statutes and common-law doctrines accord to personal privacy against the publication of truthful information, on the other, is a subject we have addressed several times in recent years. Our decisions in cases involving government attempts to sanction the accurate dissemination of information as invasive of privacy, have not, however, exhaustively considered this conflict. On the contrary, although our decisions have without exception upheld the press' right to publish, we have emphasized each time that we were resolving this conflict only as it arose in a discrete factual context.

The parties to this case frame their contentions in light of a trilogy of cases which have presented, in different contexts, the conflict between truthful reporting and state-protected privacy interests. [The Court briefly reviewed *Cox Broadcasting, Oklahoma Publishing,* and *Daily Mail.*]

Appellant takes the position that this case is indistinguishable from *Cox Broadcasting.* [ ] Alternatively, it urges that our decisions in the above trilogy, and in other cases in which we have held that the right of the press to publish truth overcame asserted interests other than personal privacy, can be distilled to yield a broader First Amendment principle that the press may never be punished, civilly or criminally, for publishing the truth. [ ] Appellee counters that the privacy trilogy is inapposite, because in each case the private information already appeared on a "public record," [ ] and because the privacy interests at stake were far less profound than in the present case. [ ] In the alternative, appellee urges that *Cox Broadcasting* be overruled and replaced with a categorical rule that publication of the name of a rape victim never enjoys constitutional protection. [ ]

We conclude that imposing damages on appellant for publishing B.J.F.'s name violates the First Amendment, although not for either of the reasons appellant urges. Despite the strong resemblance this case bears to *Cox Broadcasting,* that case cannot fairly be read as controlling here. The name of the rape victim in that case was obtained from courthouse records that were open to public inspection, a fact which Justice White's opinion for the Court repeatedly noted, [ ] (noting "special protected nature of accurate reports of *judicial* proceedings") (emphasis added). Significantly, one of the reasons we gave in *Cox Broadcasting* for invalidating the challenged damages award was the important role the press plays in subjecting trials to public scrutiny and thereby helping guarantee their fairness. [ ] That role is not directly compromised where, as here, the information in question comes from a police report prepared and disseminated at a time at which not only had no adversarial criminal proceedings begun, but no suspect had been identified.

Nor need we accept appellant's invitation to hold broadly that truthful publication may never be punished consistent with the First Amendment.

Our cases have carefully eschewed reaching this ultimate question, mindful that the future may bring scenarios which prudence counsels our not resolving anticipatorily. [ ] Indeed, in *Cox Broadcasting*, we pointedly refused to answer even the less sweeping question "whether truthful publications may ever be subjected to civil or criminal liability" for invading "an area of privacy" defined by the State. [ ] Respecting the fact that press freedom and privacy rights are both "plainly rooted in the traditions and significant concerns of our society," we instead focused on the less sweeping issue of "whether the State may impose sanctions on the accurate publication of the name of a rape victim obtained from public records— more specifically, from judicial records which are maintained in connection with a public prosecution and which themselves are open to public inspection." [ ] We continue to believe that the sensitivity and significance of the interests presented in clashes between First Amendment and privacy rights counsel relying on limited principles that sweep no more broadly than the appropriate context of the instant case.

In our view, this case is appropriately analyzed with reference to such a limited First Amendment principle. It is the one, in fact, which we articulated in *Daily Mail* in our synthesis of prior cases involving attempts to punish truthful publication: "[I]f a newspaper lawfully obtains truthful information about a matter of public significance then state officials may not constitutionally punish publication of the information, absent a need to further a state interest of the highest order." [ ] According the press the ample protection provided by that principle is supported by at least three separate considerations, in addition to, of course, the overarching "public interest, secured by the Constitution, in the dissemination of truth." [ ] The cases on which the *Daily Mail* synthesis relied demonstrate these considerations.

First, because the *Daily Mail* formulation only protects the publication of information which a newspaper has "lawfully obtain[ed]," [ ], the government retains ample means of safeguarding significant interests upon which publication may impinge, including protecting a rape victim's anonymity. To the extent sensitive information rests in private hands, the government may under some circumstances forbid its non-consensual acquisition, thereby bringing outside of the *Daily Mail* principle the publication of any information so acquired. To the extent sensitive information is in the government's custody, it has even greater power to forestall or mitigate the injury caused by its release. The government may classify certain information, establish and enforce procedures ensuring its redacted release, and extend a damages remedy against the government or its officials where the government's mishandling of sensitive information leads to its dissemination. Where information is entrusted to the government, a less drastic means than punishing truthful publication almost always exists for guarding against the dissemination of private facts. [ ][5]

5. The *Daily Mail* principle does not settle the issue of whether, in cases where information has been acquired *unlawfully* by a newspaper or by a source, government may ever punish not only the unlawful acquisition, but the ensuing publication as well.

A second consideration undergirding the *Daily Mail* principle is the fact that punishing the press for its dissemination of information which is already publicly available is relatively unlikely to advance the interests in the service of which the State seeks to act. It is not, of course, always the case that information lawfully acquired by the press is known, or accessible, to others. But where the government has made certain information publicly available, it is highly anomalous to sanction persons other than the source of its release. . . .

A third and final consideration is the "timidity and self-censorship" which may result from allowing the media to be punished for publishing certain truthful information. [ ] *Cox Broadcasting* noted this concern with overdeterrence in the context of information made public through official court records, but the fear of excessive media self-suppression is applicable as well to other information released without qualification, by the government. A contrary rule, [denying] protection to those who rely on the government's implied representations of the lawfulness of dissemination, would force upon the media the onerous obligation of sifting through government press releases, reports, and pronouncements to prune out material arguably unlawful for publication. This situation could inhere even where the newspaper's sole object was to reproduce, with no substantial change, the government's rendition of the event in question.

Applied to the instant case, the *Daily Mail* principle clearly commands reversal. The first inquiry is whether the newspaper "lawfully obtain[ed] truthful information about a matter of public significance." [ ] It is undisputed that the news article describing the assault on B.J.F. was accurate. In addition, appellant lawfully obtained B.J.F.'s name. Appellee's argument to the contrary is based on the fact that under Florida law, police reports which reveal the identity of the victim of a sexual offense are not among the matters of "public record" which the public, by law, is entitled to inspect. [ ] But the fact that the state officials are not required to disclose such reports does not make it unlawful for a newspaper to receive them when furnished by the government. Nor does the fact that the Department apparently failed to fulfill its obligation under section 794.03 not to "cause or allow to be . . . published" the name of a sexual offense victim make the newspaper's ensuing receipt of this information unlawful. Even assuming the Constitution permitted a State to proscribe *receipt* of information, Florida has not taken this step. It is clear, furthermore, that the news article concerned "a matter of public significance," [ ] in the sense in which the *Daily Mail* synthesis of prior cases used that term. That is, the article generally, as opposed to the specific identity contained within it, involved a matter of paramount public import: the commission, and investigation, of a violent crime which had been reported to authorities. [ ]

The second inquiry is whether imposing liability on appellant pursuant to section 794.03 serves "a need to further a state interest of the highest

This issue was raised but not definitively resolved in New York Times Co. v. United States, 403 U.S. 713 (1971), and reserved in [*Landmark Communications*]. We have no occasion to address it here.

order." [*Daily Mail*] Appellee argues that a rule punishing publication furthers three closely related interests: the privacy of victims of sexual offenses; the physical safety of such victims, who may be targeted for retaliation if their names become known to their assailants; and the goal of encouraging victims of such crimes to report these offenses without fear of exposure. [ ]

At a time in which we are daily reminded of the tragic reality of rape, it is undeniable that these are highly significant interests, a fact underscored by the Florida Legislature's explicit attempt to protect these interests by enacting a criminal statute prohibiting much dissemination of victim identities. We accordingly do not rule out the possibility that, in a proper case, imposing civil sanctions for publication of the name of a rape victim might be so overwhelmingly necessary to advance these interests as to satisfy the *Daily Mail* standard. For three independent reasons, however, imposing liability for publication under the circumstances of this case is too precipitous a means of advancing these interests to convince us that there is a "need" within the meaning of the *Daily Mail* formulation for Florida to take this extreme step. [ ]

First is the manner in which appellant obtained the identifying information in question. As we have noted, where the government itself provides information to the media, it is most appropriate to assume that the government had, but failed to utilize, far more limited means of guarding against dissemination than the extreme step of punishing truthful speech. That assumption is richly borne out in this case. B.J.F.'s identity would never have come to light were it not for the erroneous, if inadvertent, inclusion by the Department of her full name in an accident report made available in a press room open to the public. Florida's policy against disclosure of rape victims' identities, reflected in section 794.03, was undercut by the Department's failure to abide by this policy. Where, as here, the government has failed to police itself in disseminating information, it is clear under *Cox Broadcasting, Oklahoma Publishing,* and *Landmark Communications* that the imposition of damages against the press for its subsequent publication can hardly be said to be a narrowly tailored means of safeguarding anonymity. [ ] Once the government has placed such information in the public domain, "reliance must rest upon the judgment of those who decide what to publish or broadcast," [*Cox Broadcasting*] and hopes for restitution must rest upon the willingness of the government to compensate victims for their loss of privacy, and to protect them from the other consequences of its mishandling of the information which these victims provided in confidence.

That appellant gained access to the information in question through a government news release makes it especially likely that, if liability were to be imposed, self-censorship would result. Reliance on a news release is a paradigmatically "routine newspaper reporting techniqu[e]." [*Daily Mail*] The government's issuance of such a release, without qualification, can only convey to recipients that the government considered dissemination lawful, and indeed expected the recipients to disseminate the information further. Had appellant merely reproduced the news release prepared and released by the Department, imposing civil damages would surely violate the First Amendment. The fact that appellant converted the police report into a news story by adding the linguistic connecting tissue necessary to transform the report's facts into full sentences cannot change this result.

A second problem with Florida's imposition of liability for publication is the broad sweep of the negligence per se standard applied under the civil cause of action implied from section 794.03. Unlike claims based on the common law tort of invasion of privacy, [ ], civil actions based on section 794.03 require no case-by-case findings that the disclosure of a fact about a person's private life was one that a reasonable person would find highly offensive. On the contrary, under the per se theory of negligence adopted by the courts below, liability follows automatically from publication. This is so regardless of whether the identity of the victim is already known throughout the community; whether the victim has voluntarily called public attention to the offense; or whether the identity of the victim has otherwise become a reasonable subject of public concern—because, perhaps, questions have arisen whether the victim fabricated an assault by a particular person. Nor is there a scienter requirement of any kind under section 794.03, engendering the perverse result that truthful publications challenged pursuant to this cause of action are less protected by the First Amendment than even the least protected defamatory falsehoods: those involving purely private figures, where liability is evaluated under a standard, usually applied by a jury, of ordinary negligence. See *Gertz v. Robert Welch, Inc.*, [ ]. We have previously noted the impermissibility of categorical prohibitions upon media access where important First Amendment interests are at stake. See Globe Newspaper Co. v. Superior Court, 457 U.S. 596, 608 (1982) (invalidating state statute providing for the categorical exclusion of the public from trials of sexual offenses involving juvenile victims.) More individualized adjudication is no less indispensable where the State, seeking to safeguard the anonymity of crime victims, sets its face against publication of their names.

Third, and finally, the facial underinclusiveness of section 794.03 raises serious doubts about whether Florida is, in fact, serving, with this statute, the significant interests which appellee invokes in support of affirmance. Section 794.03 prohibits the publication of identifying information only if this information appears in an "instrument of mass communication," a term the statute does not define. Section 794.03 does not prohibit the spread by other means of the identities of victims of sexual offenses. An individual who maliciously spreads word of the identity of a rape victim is thus not covered, despite the fact that the communication of such information to persons who live near, or work with, the victim may have consequences equally devastating as the exposure of her name to large numbers of strangers. [ ]

When a State attempts the extraordinary measure of punishing truthful publication in the name of privacy, it must demonstrate its commitment to advancing this interest by applying its prohibition evenhandedly, to the smalltime disseminator as well as the media giant. Where important First Amendment interests are at stake, the mass scope of disclosure is not an acceptable surrogate for injury. A ban on disclosures effected by "instrument[s] of mass communication" simply cannot be defended on the ground that partial prohibitions may effect partial relief. [ ] Without more careful and inclusive precautions against alternative forms of dissemination, we cannot conclude that Florida's selective ban on publication by the mass media satisfactorily accomplishes its stated purpose.

III

Our holding today is limited. We do not hold that truthful publication is automatically constitutionally protected, or that there is no zone of personal privacy within which the State may protect the individual from intrusion by the press, or even that a State may never punish publication of the name of a victim of a sexual offense. We hold only that where a newspaper publishes truthful information which it has lawfully obtained, punishment may lawfully be imposed, if at all, only when narrowly tailored to a state interest of the highest order, and that no such interest is satisfactorily served by imposing liability . . . under the facts of this case. The decision below is therefore reversed.

JUSTICE SCALIA, concurring in part and concurring in the judgment.

I think it sufficient to decide this case to rely upon the third ground set forth in the Court's opinion [ ]: that a law cannot be regarded as protecting an interest "of the highest order" [ ], and thus as justifying a restriction upon truthful speech, when it leaves appreciable damage to that supposedly vital interest unprohibited. I would anticipate that the rape victim's discomfort at the dissemination of news of her misfortune among friends and acquaintances would be at least as great as her discomfort at its publication by the media to people to whom she is only a name. Yet the law in question does not prohibit the former in either oral or written form. Nor is it clear, as I think it must be to validate this statute, that Florida's general privacy law would prohibit such gossip. Nor, finally, is it credible that the interest meant to be served by the statute is the protection of the victim against a rapist still at large—an interest that arguably would extend only to mass publication. There would be little reason to limit a statute with that objective to rape alone; or to extend it to all rapes, whether or not the felon has been apprehended and confined. In any case, the instructions here did not require the jury to find that the rapist was at large.

This law has every appearance of a prohibition that society is prepared to impose upon the press but not upon itself. Such a prohibition does not protect an interest "of the highest order." For that reason, I agree that the judgment of the court below must be reversed.

[Justice White, joined by Chief Justice Rehnquist and Justice O'Connor, dissented. He objected to the reliance on *Daily Mail* on the ground that its holding was introduced "with the cautious qualifier that such a rule was 'suggest[ed]' by our prior cases, 'none of [which] directly control[led]' in *Daily Mail*. The rule the Court takes as a given was thus offered only as a hypothesis in *Daily Mail:* it should not be so uncritically accepted as constitutional dogma." Moreover, that case involved disclosure of the name of the perpetrator of a murder. "Surely the rights of those accused of crimes and those who are their victims must differ with respect to privacy concerns. That is, whatever rights alleged criminals have to maintain their anonymity pending an adjudication of guilt—the rights of crime victims must be infinitely more substantial." Finally, in *Daily Mail* the Court noted that the case involved "no issue of privacy." "But in this case, there is an issue of privacy—indeed, this is the principal issue—and therefore, this case falls outside of *Daily Mail's* 'rule' (which, as I suggest above, was perhaps not even meant as a rule in the first place)."

Justice White then turned to the Court's "independent" reasons for its result. First, the government's release of the information was "inadvertent." When the state makes a mistake in its efforts to protect privacy "it is not too much to ask the press, in instances such as this, to respect simple standards of decency and refrain from publishing a victim's name, address, and/or phone number." In a footnote at this point, Justice White noted that the Court's proper concern for a free press should "be balanced against rival interests in a civilized and humane society. An absolutist view of the former leads to insensitivity as to the latter."

As to the Court's second reason—that Florida was judging the Star by too strict a liability standard—Justice White thought the point unavailable on this record because the jury found the Star reckless. In any event, it was permissible for the standard of care to be set by the legislature rather than the courts.

As to the third point—underinclusiveness—Justice White read the earlier cases to be concerned about singling out "one segment of the news media or press for adverse treatment"—print media as opposed to broadcast media or large newspapers as opposed to small newspapers. He was willing to accept the apparent legislative conclusion that "neighborhood gossips do not pose the danger and intrusion to rape victims that 'instrument[s] of mass communication' do. Simply put: Florida wanted to prevent the widespread distribution of rape victims' names, and therefore enacted a statute tailored almost as precisely as possible to achieving that end." Finally, it was entirely possible that Florida's common law of privacy would apply against neighborhood gossips in an appropriate case.

Justice White then turned to "more general principles at issue here to see if they recommend the Court's result." Justice White feared that the result would "obliterate one of the most noteworthy legal inventions of the 20th-century: the tort of the publication of private facts." If the plaintiff here could not prevail it was hard to imagine who could win such a case. The problem with the majority opinion was not that it tried to strike a balance but that it accorded too little weight to B.J.F.'s interests. There was no public interest in identifying the plaintiff here and "no public interest in immunizing the press from liability in the rare cases where a State's efforts to protect a victim's privacy have failed."]

Notes and Questions

1.   The Court seems to agree that the state interests advanced by the plaintiff in support of liability "are highly significant." When the state interest is sufficient but the remedy suppresses more speech than is necessary, the Court usually condemns it on the ground that it is "not narrowly tailored." But notice that in this case the Court does not separate the two inquiries; instead it says the statute is "too precipitous a means of advancing these interests to convince us that there is a 'need' within the meaning of the *Daily Mail* formulation. . . ." Elsewhere the court says the state's interests are not "satisfactorily served" by imposing liability. Is this something different from "not narrowly tailored"?

2.   Do the views of rape victims (or the public at large) count in assessing the importance of the state interests? Justice Marshall asserts that word-of-mouth discussion of the rape "may have consequences equally devastating" to the victim as media dissemination. Justice Scalia speculates that dissemination among the victim's friends and acquaintances causes discomfort "at least as great." Suppose victims disagree; suppose they complained to the legislature only about media dissemination, and the legislature decided it could attack that problem without taking on the enforcement difficulties that would be encountered in trying to deal with gossip, which (by hypothesis) victims do not view as a problem anyway. In deciding whether the remedy is underinclusive, is a court free to define for itself the problem being addressed by the legislature?

   Is the scope of the problem defined by the state interests advanced to support the restriction? Here the interests identified by the plaintiff were preserving victims' privacy, protecting them from retaliation, and encouraging the reporting of rape. Are these inconsistent with the view that the problem is media publicity, not word of mouth?

3.   Suppose B.J.F. had sued for the common law tort of public disclosure of private facts instead of negligence per se. Would a judgment in her favor still have been unconstitutional because of the state's failure to prevent the sheriff's office from disclosing her name? Note that the Court's opinion describes each of the Court's three objections to liability as "independent."

4.   In *Haynes*, supra p. 367, the court concluded that the plaintiffs' claim failed as a matter of tort law. If it had met the tort law requirements, would it have been barred by *Florida Star*? Is preventing disclosure of information of the sort at issue in *Haynes* a state interest of the highest order? Would tort liability on those facts be a narrowly tailored remedy? The *Haynes* opinion said *Florida Star* "was careful not to hold that states can never provide a tort remedy to a person about whom truthful, but intensely private, information of some interest to the publish is published."

5.   One court held that if a particular rape is a matter of public concern, then so is the identity of the victim, as a matter of state law. "If a person, whether willingly or not, becomes an actor in an event of public or general interest, then the publication of his connection with such an occurrence is not an invasion of his right to privacy." The plaintiff's rape by another

inmate in the county jail was a matter of public significance as a matter of law, and therefore disclosure of the plaintiff's name was not actionable. See Doe v. Berkeley Publishers, 496 S.E.2d 636 (S.C. 1998), cert. denied 525 U.S. 963 (1998).

6. Recall that in *Philadelphia Newspapers, Inc. v. Hepps*, supra p. 325, the Supreme Court held that "a private-figure [defamation] plaintiff cannot recover damages without also showing that the statements at issue are false" and wrote that punishing true speech was "antithetical to the First Amendment's protection. . . ." Professor Susan Gilles has argued that "[i]f the constitutional requirement of proof of falsity articulated in libel cases is extended to privacy cases, then the private-facts tort is unconstitutional." Does it make sense to extend that requirement to this tort action? How can the privacy tort be distinguished from the defamation tort? Is the former unconstitutional? See Susan M. Gilles, Promises Betrayed: Breach of Confidence as a Remedy for Invasions of Privacy, 43 Buf. L. Rev. 1, 8 (1995).

7. When the State of Florida attempted to prosecute the Globe supermarket tabloid under Sec. 794.03 for publishing the name of the woman who accused William Kennedy Smith of raping her in 1991, the Florida Supreme Court held the statute unconstitutional on its face, largely in reliance on *Florida Star*. See State v. Globe Communications Corp., 648 So.2d 110 (Fla. 1994).

8. B.J.F. might have had a federal civil rights claim against the sheriff's department. In Bloch v. Ribar, 156 F.3d 673 (6th Cir. 1998), the court held that a sheriff's disclosure at a news conference of details about the plaintiff's rape violated her constitutional right of privacy. Because that constitutional right had not been previously established, the court said the sheriff was immune from liability under 42 U.S.C. § 1983. "In light of our ruling in the present case, however, public officials in this circuit will now be on notice that such a privacy right exists" and therefore will not be able in the future to claim the defense of qualified immunity. The court said the constitutional right does not extend to all privacy interests, but only those that implicate "a fundamental right or one implicit in the concept of ordered liberty." It added "a rape victim has a fundamental right of privacy in preventing government officials from gratuitously and unnecessarily releasing the intimate details of the rape where no penological purpose is being served."

———

Lawfully obtained. Note that the sheriff's department settled B.J.F.'s claim that releasing her name to the newspaper was unlawful, yet the Court says the information was "lawfully obtained" because there was no statute forbidding the newspaper from receiving it. Does "lawfully obtained" refer only to the publisher? In *Bartnicki v. Vopper*, infra p. 537, the Supreme Court said the First Amendment does not necessarily protect publication of information lawfully obtained by the publisher from sources that the publisher knows obtained it unlawfully, but the Court protected the publication in that case on the ground that the privacy interests were weak and the public interest in disclosure was strong. The meaning of "lawfully obtained" is explored further in connection with *Bartnicki* in Chapter VIII.

————

Florida Star was the Court's first application of a case-by-case balancing methodology to a tort case. The *"Daily Mail* principle" arose from a criminal proceeding where the party defending the restriction on speech was the state. When that methodology is applied to a tort action it is a private litigant who must identify the state's interests and defend the means that the state has chosen, whether through a statute or the courts' development of its common law, to protect those interests. B.J.F. lost because she was unable to defend the state's choice of means: its failure to prevent the police from releasing her name, its failure to impose liability on individuals as well as media, and its failure to require her to make out a common-law case for invasion of privacy. The implications of this are discussed in the excerpt that follows.

Tortious Speech
David A. Anderson
47 Wash. & Lee L. Rev. 71, 102–04 (1990).

When a court concludes that tort rules are insufficient to protect first amendment interests, it has essentially two options. The first is simply to hold the challenged tort law unconstitutional, leaving the state to guess how or whether the tort can be modified to make it constitutional. The other option is to prescribe what the constitution requires.

. . .

The first option is attractive to courts for several reasons. It keeps courts' constitutional role separate from their common-law role. It leaves the states some room to experiment with their own solutions to speech-tort conflicts. Perhaps most important, it enables courts to identify problems without having to provide solutions. For example, it has allowed the Supreme Court to recognize the collision between the private-facts branch of privacy law and first amendment interests, and to resolve those conflicts on an ad hoc basis in favor of the speech interests, without having to decide how or whether the underlying conflict can be resolved. This aspect of the non-prescriptive approach is especially valuable when there is little consensus among members of the Court; obtaining five votes to hold a particular recovery unconstitutional is no doubt easier than reaching agreement as to what would be constitutional.

Use of this option in the tort context, however, is profoundly unfair to private litigants. In the regulatory context, the legislature or an agency must decide how to respond, if at all, to a decision holding a statute or regulation unconstitutional. These bodies have the power and the responsibility to decide the state's interests. If they choose to experiment with solutions that may or may not prove sufficient, they do so at public expense. If the first solution fails, their institutional continuity enables them to follow up with alternatives.

When a court provides no solution to a constitutional problem in tort law, however, these burdens fall on private litigants. The plaintiff whose case identifies the constitutional problem may get no opportunity to suggest a solution; even if the decision has little to do with the merits of the case, as in *Florida Star*, it usually disposes of the plaintiff's claim. The burden of proposing a solution to the tort-speech conflict falls to those future litigants who are willing to gamble on their own (or their lawyers') ability to predict whether a particular solution will be constitutionally acceptable. Because not every potential litigant will be able or willing to take that gamble, some deserving claims will not be brought, and some defendants will settle improvidently.

This non-prescriptive approach also exacts a price from the public. Whether the speech-tort conflict is ever revisited—and if it is, the thoroughness with which the competing interests are identified and articulated—is entirely at the mercy of private litigants. The Court in *Florida Star* conceded that the state has strong interests in protecting the privacy of rape victims, and said that those interests might justify imposition of tort liability in some circumstances. But the matter will get no further consideration until some future rape victim whose name is published is willing to gamble that her case will seem more compelling to a court than B.J.F.'s. There is always the possibility that the legislature will intervene to vindicate the state's interest, but insofar as tort liability is concerned, legislatures are accustomed to deferring to the courts.

When a court holds a recovery for tortious speech unconstitutional, it shirks its responsibility if it fails to say what, if anything, can be changed to make the rules of the tort constitutionally acceptable. . . . [H]ere as elsewhere the power to proclaim is more likely to be exercised judiciously if it is accompanied by the responsibility to resolve.

———

Is the privilege in *Cox Broadcasting* and *Florida Star* so broad that it bars exceptions such as one that would facilitate the rehabilitation of criminals? Numerous statutes, both federal and in every state, permit—and occasionally even mandate—the expungement of juvenile convictions when the juvenile reaches a certain age. See T. Markus Funk, A Mere Youthful Indiscretion? Re-examining the Policy of Expunging Juvenile Delinquency Records, 29 U. Mich. J. L. Ref. 885 (1996). Many states also have expungement statutes applicable to adult offenders. These statutes generally require that the petitioner demonstrate rehabilitation, which may be shown by the petitioner having reentered society for a prescribed period of time without committing additional offenses. See Michael D. Mayfield, Revisiting

Expungement: Concealing Information in the Information Age, 1997 Utah L. Rev. 1057. Should disclosure of expunged records be constitutionally protected under *Cox Broadcasting* and *Florida Star?*

Enjoining invasions of privacy. Although injunctions in defamation cases have long been impermissible for non-constitutional reasons, the situation in privacy is not so clear. In defamation a verdict for the plaintiff can at least in theory undo some of the damage. An award of damages cannot recapture lost privacy; indeed, as the *Haynes* opinion noted, the litigation is likely to cause a further loss of privacy. The traditional equity requirement of "no adequate remedy at law" therefore seems to be met.

Twice the Supreme Court has been prepared to address the issue. The first case involved an unauthorized biography of a sports star. The Supreme Court asked the parties specifically to address the propriety of injunctive relief. Julian Messner, Inc. v. Spahn, 393 U.S. 818 (1968). Then the parties settled the case. 393 U.S. 1046 (1969). The second time the Court heard argument in a case in which a patient was trying to prevent her analyst from publishing a book about the therapy. Plaintiff claimed that the disguises used in the book were too thin to protect her privacy and that an implied covenant barred such a book. The state courts had enjoined publication of the book pending the outcome of the litigation. The Supreme Court granted certiorari, Roe v. Doe, 417 U.S. 907 (1974), heard arguments, and then dismissed the writ as having been "improvidently granted." 420 U.S. 307 (1975). On remand, the state court found liability and ordered all of the books, except for 220 that had been distributed early, destroyed. Doe v. Roe, 93 Misc.2d 201, 400 N.Y.S.2d 668 (1977).

In a case involving the movie "Titticut Follies" the state courts had enjoined the general distribution of the movie because it invaded the privacy of inmates of a state institution for the criminally insane. The Supreme Court denied certiorari over a long dissent by Justice Harlan, joined by Justice Brennan. Justice Douglas also dissented. Wiseman v. Massachusetts, 398 U.S. 960 (1970). A petition for rehearing was denied over the dissents of Justices Harlan, Brennan, and Blackmun. Justice Douglas did not participate. 400 U.S. 860 (1970).

Injunctions to protect privacy are rare, however. For example, a court rejected an actress's attempt to enjoin her former husband from revealing—and the National Enquirer from publishing—aspects of her personal life, such as her alleged use of drugs and alcohol and her sexual relationships. Instead, plaintiff's remedy was a possible damages action for defamation or privacy. Gilbert v. National Enquirer, 43 Cal. App.4th 1135, 51 Cal. Rptr.2d 91, 24 Med. L. Rptr. 2377 (1996).

B.   FALSE LIGHT PRIVACY

The conventional idea of invasion of privacy as conceived by Warren and Brandeis involved true statements about aspects of plaintiff's life that others had no business knowing. But along the way, a few cases involved false charges that placed the plaintiff in a false light but did not harm his "reputation" so as to permit an action for defamation. As one example, a group used the plaintiff's name without authorization on a petition to the governor to veto a bill. Although falsely stating that plaintiff had signed the petition would not have been defamatory, the court found the situation actionable because it cast plaintiff in a false light. See Hinish v. Meier & Frank Co., 166 Or. 482, 113 P.2d 438 (1941).

Time, Inc. v. Hill. The false light action was significantly limited by Time, Inc. v. Hill, 385 U.S. 374, 1 Med. L. Rptr. 1791 (1967). In September 1952, James Hill and his family were held hostage in their home for 19 hours by three escaped convicts who apparently treated them decently. The incident received extensive nationwide coverage. Thereafter the Hills moved to another state, sought seclusion and refused to make public appearances. A novel modeled in general on the event was published the following year. In 1955, Life magazine in a short article and photo spread announced that a play and a motion picture were being made from the novel, which they said was "inspired" by the Hill episode. The play, "a heart-stopping account of how a family rose to heroism in a crisis," would enable the public to see the Hill story "reenacted." Photographs in the magazine showed actors performing scenes from the play at the house at which the original events had occurred.

Suit was brought in New York under that state's peculiar privacy statute (supra pp. 376–77). The New York statute provides a remedy only for uses "for advertising purposes or for the purposes of trade." Case law in New York held that falsification could be evidence that the use was for trade purposes rather than for public information. The Hills alleged that the story was false because the novel and the play included fictitious incidents of the convicts committing violence on the father and uttering a "verbal sexual insult" at the daughter. The state courts allowed recovery after lengthy litigation.

The Supreme Court, by a very fragile majority, decided that the privilege to comment on matters of public interest had constitutional protection. The Court used the defamation analogy that was then being developed in the wake of the *New York Times* case and applied it to this false light privacy case, holding that there could be no liability unless the falsity was either deliberate or reckless. (The Court had not yet decided what fault standard governed defamation actions by private citizens.)

The opinions in the *Hill* case give little clue as to whether the falsity of the magazine's account made it more objectionable to the Hills than a truthful account would have been. Leonard Garment, the lawyer who originally represented the Hills, later wrote that two psychiatrists testified that Mrs. Hill "had come through the original hostage incident fairly well but had fallen apart when the Life article brought back her memories transformed into her worst nightmares and presented them to the world as reality." Garment eventually turned the case over to his law partner, Richard Nixon, who argued the case in the Supreme Court. See Leonard Garment, Annals of Law: The Hill Case, The New Yorker, Apr. 17, 1989 at 90. Garment also asserted that the "blood and gore" and "leering sexuality" depicted by the magazine caused Mrs. Hill distress above that caused by the truthful parts of the article. See Gary T. Schwartz, Explaining and Justifying a Limited Tort of False Light Invasion of Privacy, 41 Case W. Res. L. Rev. 885 (1991).

The preliminary vote of the Court in *Time, Inc. v. Hill* favored the Hills. For the story and the opinions in that first stage, see Bernard Schwartz, The Unpublished Opinions of the Warren Court 240–303 (1985). See also Harry Kalven, Jr., The Reasonable Man and the First Amendment: *Hill, Butts,* and *Walker,* 1967 Sup. Ct. Rev. 267.

Cantrell v. Forest City Publishing Co.

Supreme Court of the United States, 1974.
419 U.S. 245, 95 S.Ct. 465, 42 L.Ed.2d 419, 1 Med.L.Rptr. 1815.

MR. JUSTICE STEWART delivered the opinion of the Court.

Margaret Cantrell and four of her minor children brought this diversity action in a Federal District Court for invasion of privacy against the Forest City Publishing Co., publisher of a Cleveland newspaper, the Plain Dealer, and against Joseph Eszterhas, a reporter formerly employed by the Plain Dealer, and Richard Conway, a Plain Dealer photographer. The Cantrells alleged that an article published in the Plain Dealer Sunday Magazine unreasonably placed their family in a false light before the public through its many inaccuracies and untruths. The District Judge struck the claims relating to punitive damages as to all the plaintiffs and dismissed the actions of three of the Cantrell children in their entirety, but allowed the case to go to the jury as to Mrs. Cantrell and her oldest son, William. The jury returned a verdict [for $60,000] against all three of the respondents for compensatory money damages in favor of these two plaintiffs.

The Court of Appeals for the Sixth Circuit reversed, holding that, in the light of the First and Fourteenth Amendments, the District Judge should have granted the respondents' motion for a directed verdict as to all the Cantrells' claims. . . .

I.

In December 1967, Margaret Cantrell's husband Melvin was killed along with 43 other people when the Silver Bridge across the Ohio River at Point Pleasant, West Virginia, collapsed. The respondent Eszterhas was assigned by the Plain Dealer to cover the story of the disaster. He wrote a "news feature" story focusing on the funeral of Melvin Cantrell and the impact of his death on the Cantrell family.

Five months later, after conferring with the Sunday Magazine editor of the Plain Dealer, Eszterhas and photographer Conway returned to the Point Pleasant area to write a follow-up feature. The two men went to the Cantrell residence, where Eszterhas talked with the children and Conway took 50 pictures. Mrs. Cantrell was not at home at any time during the 60 to 90 minutes that the men were at the Cantrell residence.

Eszterhas' story appeared as the lead feature in the August 4, 1968, edition of the Plain Dealer Sunday Magazine. The article stressed the family's abject poverty; the children's old, ill-fitting clothes and the deteriorating condition of their home were detailed in both the text and accompanying photographs. As he had done in his original prize-winning article on the Silver Bridge disaster, Eszterhas used the Cantrell family to illustrate the impact of the bridge collapse on the lives of the people in the Point Pleasant area.

It is conceded that the story contained a number of inaccuracies and false statements. Most conspicuously, although Mrs. Cantrell was not present at any time during the reporter's visit to her home, Eszterhas wrote, "Margaret Cantrell will talk neither about what happened nor about how they are doing. She wears the same mask of non-expression she wore at the funeral. She is a proud woman. Her world has changed. She says that after it happened, the people in town offered to help them out with money and they refused to take it." Other significant misrepresentations were contained in details of Eszterhas' descriptions of the poverty in which the Cantrells were living and the dirty and dilapidated conditions of the Cantrell home.

The case went to the jury on a so-called "false light" theory of invasion of privacy. In essence, the theory of the case was that by publishing the false feature story about the Cantrells and thereby making them the objects of pity and ridicule, the respondents damaged Mrs. Cantrell and her son William by causing them to suffer outrage, mental distress, shame, and humiliation.

II.

. . .

The District Judge in the case before us, in contrast to the trial judge in *Time, Inc. v. Hill,* did instruct the jury that liability could be imposed only if it concluded that the false statements in the Sunday Magazine feature article on the Cantrells had been made with knowledge of their falsity or in reckless disregard of the truth. No objection was made by any of the parties to this knowing-or-reckless-falsehood instruction. Consequently, this case presents no occasion to consider whether a State may constitutionally apply a more relaxed standard of liability for a publisher or broadcaster of false statements injurious to a private individual under a false-light theory of invasion of privacy, or whether the constitutional standard announced in *Time, Inc. v. Hill* applies to all false-light cases. Cf. [*Gertz*]. Rather, the sole question that we need decide is whether the Court of Appeals erred in setting aside the jury's verdict.

III.

At the close of the petitioners' case-in-chief, the District Judge struck the demand for punitive damages. He found that Mrs. Cantrell had failed to present any evidence to support the charges that the invasion of privacy "was done maliciously within the legal definition of that term." The Court of Appeals interpreted this finding to be a determination by the District Judge that there was no evidence of knowing falsity or reckless disregard of the truth introduced at the trial. Having made such a determination, the Court of Appeals held that the District Judge should have granted the motion for a directed verdict for respondents as to all the Cantrells' claims. [ ]

. . .

Although the verbal record of the District Court proceedings is not entirely unambiguous, the conclusion is inescapable that the District Judge was referring to the common-law standard of malice rather than to the *New York Times* "actual malice" standard when he dismissed the punitive damages claims. . . .

Moreover, the District Judge was clearly correct in believing that the evidence introduced at trial was sufficient to support a jury finding that the respondents Joseph Eszterhas and Forest City Publishing Co. had published knowing or reckless falsehoods about the Cantrells.[6] There was no dispute during the trial that Eszterhas, who did not testify, must have known that a number of the statements in the feature story were untrue. In particular, his article plainly implied that Mrs. Cantrell had been present during his visit to her home and that Eszterhas had observed her "wear[ing] the same mask of non-expression she wore [at her husband's] funeral." These were "calculated falsehoods," and the jury was plainly justified in finding that Eszterhas had portrayed the Cantrells in a false light through knowing or reckless untruth.

The Court of Appeals concluded that there was no evidence that Forest City Publishing Co. had knowledge of any of the inaccuracies contained in Eszterhas' article. However, there was sufficient evidence for the jury to find that Eszterhas' writing of the feature was within the scope of his employment at the Plain Dealer and that Forest City Publishing Co. was therefore liable under traditional doctrines of *respondeat superior.* . . .

For the foregoing reasons, the judgment of the Court of Appeals is reversed and the case is remanded to that court with directions to enter a judgment affirming the judgment of the District Court as to the respondents Forest City Publishing Co. and Joseph Eszterhas.

It is so ordered.

MR. JUSTICE DOUGLAS, dissenting.

. . .

A bridge accident catapulted the Cantrells into the public eye and their disaster became newsworthy. To make the First Amendment freedom to report the news turn on subtle differences between common-law malice and actual malice is to stand the Amendment on its head. Those who write the

---

6. Although we conclude that the jury verdicts should have been sustained as to Eszterhas and Forest City Publishing Co., we agree with the Court of Appeals' conclusion that there was insufficient evidence to support the jury's verdict against the photographer Conway. . . .

current news seldom have the objective, dispassionate point of view—or the time—of scientific analysts. They deal in fast-moving events and the need for "spot" reporting. The jury under today's formula sits as a censor with broad powers—not to impose a prior restraint, but to lay heavy damages on the press. The press is "free" only if the jury is sufficiently disenchanted with the Cantrells to let the press be free of this damages claim. That regime is thought by some to be a way of supervising the press which is better than not supervising it at all. But the installation of the Court's regime would require a constitutional amendment. Whatever might be the ultimate reach of the doctrine Mr. Justice Black and I have embraced, it seems clear that in matters of public import such as the present news reporting, there must be freedom from damages lest the press be frightened into playing a more ignoble role than the Framers visualized.

I would affirm the judgment of the Court of Appeals.

Notes and Questions

1. How would the courts analyze a defamation action brought by the Cantrells? A public disclosure privacy action?

2. What is the nature of the *respondeat superior* problem in *Cantrell?* Might this point be significant in future defamation cases in determining whose behavior to evaluate in considering liability? Recall the second appeal in *Gertz,* supra p. 306.

3. Justice Stewart readily analyzes this case as involving the "false light" category of privacy. Might it also be analyzed as a public disclosure privacy case in which the media claimed the defense of newsworthiness but lost because the defense is not available when the material reported is deliberately or recklessly false? What are the differences between the two analyses?

4. How are compensatory damages to be measured in this case? Is the falsity relevant in that calculation?

5. One of the elements of the false light tort at common law is that the depiction must be one that would be highly offensive to a person of reasonable sensibilities. Might this requirement, rigorously applied, preclude recovery in cases like *Hill* and *Cantrell?*

———

Actual malice or negligence? In a footnote to his concurring opinion in *Cox Broadcasting,* supra p. 378, Justice Powell observed:

The Court's abandonment of the "matter of general or public interest" standard as the determinative factor for deciding whether to apply the *New York Times* malice standard to defamation litigation brought by private individuals, [ ], calls into question the conceptual basis of *Time Inc. v. Hill.* In neither *Gertz* nor our more recent decision in [*Cantrell*], however, have we been called upon to determine whether a State may constitutionally apply a more relaxed standard of liability under a false-light theory of invasion of privacy. [ ]

Is *Hill* still good law?

The question of actual malice or negligence in false light cases has persisted. The situation is summarized in Lovgren v. Citizens First National Bank of Princeton, 126 Ill.2d 411, 534 N.E.2d 987, 16 Med. L. Rptr. 1214 (1989), in which the court upheld such a claim in favor of a plaintiff whose property was advertised without his consent as being up for sale at a forthcoming public auction. After summarizing the *Hill–Cantrell* sequence, the court concluded that it would, as a matter of state law, insist on "actual malice." It quoted from the Prosser & Keeton treatise on Torts:

> It is suggested that virtually all actionable invasions of privacy have been intentional invasions or invasions of a kind that defendant knew or had reason to know would not only be offensive but rightly so and are therefore examples of outrageous conduct that was committed with knowledge or with reason to know that it would cause severe mental stress. Recovery for an invasion of privacy on the ground that the plaintiff was depicted in a false light makes sense only when the account, if true, would not have been actionable as an invasion of privacy. In other words, the outrageous character of the publicity comes about in part by virtue of the fact that some part of the matter reported was false and deliberately so.

False light and defamation. A few years after *Cantrell,* in *Zacchini v. Scripps–Howard Broadcasting Co.,* infra p. 408, the Court approvingly quoted Dean Prosser's statement that the interest protected in false light actions "is clearly that of reputation, with the same overtones of mental distress as in defamation." Under this view, why might a state permit liability for errors that do not harm reputation? Might the *Masson* case, supra p. 287, be better analyzed as a false light case?

Some courts explain the false light action as a remedy for cases in which the falsehood causes emotional distress without causing harm to reputation. In Flowers v. Carville, 310 F.3d 1118 (9th Cir. 2002), the court held that Gennifer Flowers could maintain separate false light and defamation claims against the publisher of James Carville's book accusing her of lying about her relationship with President Clinton. It said the false light action could compensate for emotional injuries not covered by the defamation claim.

Should all the common law and statutory limitations on defamation, such as retraction statutes, special damage requirements, and statutes of limitations, apply as well to false light privacy?

In Fellows v. National Enquirer, Inc., 42 Cal.3d 234, 721 P.2d 97, 228 Cal. Rptr. 215, 13 Med. L. Rptr. 1305 (1986), defendant's article asserted that "Gorgeous Angie Dickinson's all smiles about the new man in her life—TV producer Arthur Fellows. Angie's steady-dating Fellows all over TinselTown, and happily posed for photographers with him as they exited the swanky Spago restaurant in Beverly Hills." Accompanying the article was a photograph of Dickinson and Fellows over the caption stating that Dickinson was "Dating a Producer."

Fellows demanded a retraction under Cal. Civil Code § 48a, asserting that plaintiff "has never dated Miss Dickinson, is not 'the new man in her life,' and has been married to Phyllis Fellows for the last 18 years." Defendant refused retraction and plaintiff sued for libel and false light privacy. Plaintiff withdrew his libel claim and proceeded solely on a false light claim with no allegation of special damages.

Under California law, libel that relied on extrinsic facts had to be supported by special damages. Cal. Civil Code § 45a. Plaintiff's privacy claim asserted that he had been falsely portrayed as the "new man" in Dickinson's life and as "steady-dating" her. The trial judge dismissed the privacy claim for lack of special damages and was affirmed on appeal.

The clear purpose of section 45a was to provide additional protection to libel defendants. Since "virtually every published defamation would support an action for false light invasion of privacy, exempting such actions from the requirement of proving special damages would render the statute a nullity." Under this rationale is there any state requirement that protects libel defendants that would not also be applied to plaintiffs who sue on a false light theory? What should happen if a false light claim is based on language that does not rise to the level of being defamatory? The court went out of its way to announce that its ruling did not apply to false light claims "that would be actionable as a public disclosure of private facts had the representation made in the publication been true."

Plaintiffs lawyers often plead false light in the alternative with a libel claim, and it often fails for the same reason that the defamation claim fails. If the latter survives, the false light claim is often dropped. One of the rare examples of a case in which a false light claim succeeded when a libel action failed is Peoples Bank and Trust Co. v. Globe International Pub., Inc., 978 F.2d 1065, 20 Med. L. Rptr. 1925 (8th Cir. 1992).

Plaintiff was the estate of a 96–year–old woman whose photo was used in a supermarket tabloid, the Sun, to illustrate a story about a 101–year-old Australian newspaper carrier who the Sun said became pregnant by one of her customers. The woman sued for both libel and false light but died before final judgment. The jury found for the newspaper on the libel claim but for the plaintiff on the false light claim. Since both verdicts were general, they provided no explanation of the jury's reasoning.

The newspaper said the story was intended as fiction and could not have been understood otherwise. But the court of appeals said the Sun comingled factual and fictional stories so thoroughly that "At trial even its own writers could not tell which stories were true and which were completely fabricated." The jury could find that readers could reasonably have believed that the story portrayed actual facts, and that the newspaper "recklessly failed to anticipate that result." The court upheld an award of $850,000 in punitive damages, but held that an award of $650,000 compensatory damages was excessive because there was no evidence of lost earning capacity, permanent injury, medical expenses, or future pain and suffering. On remand the district judge reduced the compensatory award to $150,000. 817 F. Supp. 72 (W.D.Ark. 1993).

An Illinois appellate court applied *Lovgren*, supra, to determine that, despite the similarities between the two actions, the public/private distinction among plaintiffs in defamation actions was not relevant in a suit for false light invasion of privacy. See Dubinsky v. United Airlines Master Executive Council, 303 Ill.App.3d 317, 708 N.E.2d 441 (1999).

False light by association. A few cases have permitted a false light recovery to persons whose photographs have appeared in certain magazines without their consent. One involved a model whose nude photographs appeared in Hustler magazine. Douglass v. Hustler Magazine, Inc., 769 F.2d 1128, 11 Med. L. Rptr. 2264 (7th Cir. 1985). After the court described the magazine's contents, it concluded that a jury could reasonably find that the magazine was offensive and that "to be depicted as voluntarily associated with [Hustler] . . . is unquestionably degrading to a normal person, especially if the depiction is erotic." For other reasons, plaintiff's judgment was reversed and a new trial ordered.

In Braun v. Flynt, 726 F.2d 245, 10 Med. L. Rptr. 1497 (5th Cir. 1984), plaintiff was employed at an amusement park. Part of her job included working in a novelty act with "Ralph, the Diving Pig." "Treading water in a pool, plaintiff would hold out a bottle of milk with a nipple on it. Ralph would dive into the pool and feed from the bottle." Publicity photographs of the act were used without authorization in Chic Magazine in a section entitled "Chic Thrills," a collection of vignettes, most of which "either concerned sex overtly or were accompanied by a photograph or cartoon of an overtly sexual nature." According to the court, the "particular issue of the magazine with which the case is involved contained numerous explicit photographs of female genitalia. Suffice it to say that *Chic* is a glossy, oversized, hardcore men's magazine."

From that base, the court concluded that the jury had implicitly found that "the ordinary reader automatically will form an unfavorable opinion about the character of a woman whose picture appears in *Chic* magazine." Even if no reader thought plaintiff unchaste, the jury "might have found that the publication implied Mrs. Braun's approval of the opinions expressed in *Chic* or that it implied Mrs. Braun had consented to having her picture in *Chic*. Either of these findings would support the jury verdict that the publication placed Mrs. Braun in a false light highly offensive to a reasonable person." A judgment for $65,000 was upheld.

In Faloona v. Hustler Magazine, Inc., 799 F.2d 1000, 13 Med. L. Rptr. 1353 (5th Cir. 1986), plaintiffs had consented to be photographed nude for two books on human sexuality. Hustler published the photos in connection with an excerpt from one book and a review of the other. Plaintiffs' false light theory was rejected on the ground that "no reasonable person could consider the photographs as indicating plaintiffs' approval of *Hustler,* or that they were willing to pose nude for *Hustler.* It is obvious that the photographs were reproductions from the books being reviewed or excerpted. No tie to *Hustler* is claimed or suggested. It is this sharp definition of context which distinguishes this case from" *Douglass* and *Braun*.

In Dempsey v. National Enquirer, 702 F. Supp. 927, 16 Med. L. Rptr. 1396 (D.Me. 1988), the court refused to apply the *Douglass* and *Braun* cases to an article that appeared in the National Enquirer. Plaintiff, a pilot, had fallen out of a light plane in flight but had clung to the open boarding ladder on the side and survived his co-pilot's emergency landing with only a few scratches. He sued the Enquirer on the theory that its story implied that he had willingly told his story to the Enquirer. The court doubted that article implied this, but said "even if the article could imply that the plaintiff consented to the publication," the complaint failed to show that "association per se with the [National Enquirer] would be highly objectionable to a reasonable person." *Douglass* and *Braun* did not apply because there was no allegation here that the Enquirer was a magazine like the ones involved in those cases.

The same plaintiff had more success in a separate suit against the Enquirer's sibling, the Star. The Star presented the pilot's story under his byline, with an introduction saying "Here, Dempsey . . . tells in his own words how he found himself suddenly thrust into the ultimate daredevil stunt." The article was a dramatic first-person account, even though Dempsey said he had never been interviewed by the Star, had not given them information, and had not written the story. The court refused to dismiss his false light claim. The judge said the article "unequivocally attributed authorship to the plaintiff," thereby portraying him falsely in a way that could be found to be highly offensive to a reasonable person. Dempsey v. National Enquirer, 702 F. Supp. 934 (D.Me. 1989).

Rejecting the tort. A few states have doubted the utility of the false light tort and have rejected it. See, e.g., Renwick v. The News and Observer Publishing Co., 310 N.C. 312, 312 S.E.2d 405, 10 Med. L. Rptr. 1443 (1984). The court noted that in states that recognize the action "the false light need not necessarily be a defamatory light. [ ] In many if not most cases, however, the false light is defamatory and an action for libel or slander will also lie." The court relied on language from *Hill* to explain that it would "create a grave risk of serious impairment of the indispensable service of a free press in a free society if we saddle the press with the impossible burden of verifying to a certainty the facts associated in news articles with a person's name, picture or portrait, particularly as related to non-defamatory matter." The court thought the action "constitutionally suspect" and thought it "would not differ significantly" from the existing defamation action. (Recall that after *Renwick* the same court decided not to adopt the public disclosure action either, *Hall v. Post,* supra p. 377.)

The Texas Supreme Court, 5–4, rejected the false light action even though lower courts and federal district courts applying Texas law had recognized it for a decade. See Cain v. Hearst Corp., 878 S.W.2d 577, 22 Med. L. Rptr. 2161 (Tex. 1994). The case was brought by a prisoner serving a life term for murder. He did not challenge portions of a newspaper story that said he murdered his lawyer to marry the widow and murdered another man for his money, but he objected to passages saying he was a member of the "Dixie mafia" and was believed to have killed as many as eight people. He filed his false light suit six months after the statute of limitations for libel had run.

The majority said false light often overlaps with defamation or intentional infliction of emotional distress, and its potential to chill speech is too great to justify retaining the tort for the few instances where it would offer the only remedy. The dissenters noted that many tort remedies overlap. They said the chilling effect could be controlled by limiting the tort to serious and harmful falsehoods and applying fault and procedural limitations similar to those applied to defamation.

About two-thirds of states recognize the false-light privacy tort. For contrasting views of the tort, see Diane Zimmerman, False Light Invasion of Privacy: The Light That Failed, 64 N.Y.U. L. Rev. 364 (1989), and Gary T. Schwartz, Explaining and Justifying a Limited Tort of False Light Invasion of Privacy, 41 Case W. Res. L. Rev. 885 (1991).

C. APPROPRIATION

1. NATURE OF THE TORT

"Appropriation" claims involve the attempts of people to control the exploitation of their names, likenesses, and fame and any pecuniary value resulting therefrom. The claim was explicitly recognized for the first time in Haelan Laboratories v. Topps Chewing Gum, Inc., 202 F.2d 866 (2d Cir. 1953), in which the court spoke of the need to protect the proprietary interest of celebrities in their names and likenesses. *Haelan* involved a famous baseball player who had assigned the right to the use of his name and likeness to a bubblegum manufacturer for the promotion of its products. A competing manufacturer subsequently induced the ballplayer to enter into a similar contract with full knowledge of the pre-existing agreement. The court recognized the ballplayer's right to control commercial use of his name and likeness as a method through which such misappropriation could be prevented.

This tort is often described in broad terms as a remedy for unauthorized use of a person's name or likeness. For example, the Restatement (Second) of Torts § 652C provides: "One who appropriates to his own use or benefit the name or likeness of another is subject to liability to the other for invasion of privacy." A Texas statute, known colloquially as "The Buddy Holly Act" because it was passed to prevent unauthorized exploitation of his memory, prohibits unconsented use of "a deceased individual's name, voice, signature, photograph, or likeness in any manner. . . ." Tex. Prop. Code Ch. 4 (Actions & Remedies) § 26.011.

If the tort were really this broad, it would indeed be a major problem for media. But in fact the remedy is confined almost entirely to commercial exploitation, such as unauthorized use of a person's likeness in an advertisement or endorsement of a product or service. The Texas statute quoted above goes on to exempt any use in a play, book, film, radio or television program, magazine or newspaper article, political material, or work of art, or even in an advertisement for any of the foregoing. The common law tort usually provides no remedy when a person's name or likeness is appropriated for purposes of journalism, entertainment, or satire.

For example, in the first *Dempsey* case, supra p. 402, the court rejected claims that the publication of the article had been an appropriation of the plaintiff's name and physical features for commercial purposes. Simply because a publication hopes that its contents will increase revenues does not make its articles all commercial appropriations. Plaintiff relied on section 652C of the Restatement, quoted above.

The court, however, quoted from comment *d* to that section: "No one has the right to object merely because his name or his appearance is brought before the public, since neither is in any way a private matter and both are open to public observation. . . . The fact that the defendant is engaged in the business of publication, for example of a newspaper, out of which he makes or seeks to make a profit, is not enough to make the incidental publication a commercial use of the name or likeness. Thus a newspaper, although it is not a philanthropic institution, does not become liable under the rule stated in this Section to every person whose name or likeness it publishes."

As a result, this branch of privacy law is usually of little concern to media outside of their advertising departments. We briefly consider it here to round out our discussion of privacy and to touch on the few areas where it may affect media more directly.

Since *Haelan,* similar claims have been recognized by most states. Although some states have adopted the action as a separate common law remedy, most have developed it as an offshoot of either the common law right of privacy or of a privacy statute. "Rights of publicity" statutes, like the California statute below, are increasingly common.

Unauthorized Commercial Use of Name, Voice, Signature, Photograph or Likeness
Cal. Civil Code § 3344 (1999).

(a) Any person who knowingly uses another's name, voice, signature, photograph, or likeness, in any manner, on or in products, merchandise, or goods, or for purposes of advertising or selling, or soliciting purchases of, products, merchandise, goods or services, without such person's prior consent . . . shall be liable for any damages sustained by the person or persons injured as a result thereof. In addition, in any action brought under this section, the person who violated the section shall be liable to the injured party or parties in an amount equal to the greater of seven hundred fifty dollars ($750) or the actual damages suffered by him or her as a result of the unauthorized use, and any profits from the unauthorized use that are attributable to the use and are not taken into account in computing the actual damages.

(b) As used in this section, "photograph" means any photograph or photographic reproduction, still or moving, or any videotape or live television transmission, of any person, such that the person is readily identifiable.

. . .

(c) Where a photograph or likeness of an employee of the person using the photograph or likeness appearing in the advertisement or other publication prepared by or in behalf of the user is only incidental, and not essential, to the purpose of the publication in which it appears, there shall arise a rebuttable presumption affecting the burden of producing evidence that the failure to obtain the consent of the employee was not a knowing use of the employee's photograph or likeness.

(d) For purposes of this section, a use of a name, voice, signature, photograph, or likeness in connection with any news, public affairs, or sports broadcast or account, or any political campaign, shall not constitute a use for which consent is required under subdivision (a).

(e) The use of a name, voice, signature, photograph, or likeness in a commercial medium shall not constitute a use for which consent is required under subdivision (a) solely because the material containing such use is commercially sponsored or contains paid advertising. Rather it shall be a question of fact whether or not the use of the person's name, voice, signature, photograph, or likeness was so directly connected with the commercial sponsorship or with the paid advertising as to constitute a use for which consent is required under subdivision (a).

––––––––

Courts have imposed two important limitations on actions under this statute. One appears to limit the statute's application to purely "commercial speech or at least to speech that does not contribute significantly to a matter of public interest." In Hoffman v. Capital Cities/ABC, 255 F.3d 1180, 29 Med. L. Rptr. 1993 (9th Cir. 2001), Los Angeles Magazine had combined the face and head of actor Dustin Hoffman with a photo of the body of a male model wearing a silk gown and high heels designed by contemporary fashion designers. The illustration was part of a fashion spread called "Grand Illusions," and the copy read: "By using state-of-the-art digital magic, we clothed some of cinema's most enduring icons in fashions by the hottest designers." The Hoffman composite was an allusion to his title role in the movie "Tootsie," in which he dressed as a woman.

The court reversed an award to Hoffman of over $3 million. It found that the use of Hoffman's photo was not "pure commercial speech," noting that the magazine "did not use Hoffman's image in a traditional advertisement printed merely for the purpose of selling a particular product" nor "did the article simply advance a commercial message."

"Grand Illusions" appears as a feature article on the cover of the magazine and in the table of contents. It is a complement to and a part of the issue's focus on Hollywood past and present. Viewed in context, the article as a whole is a combination of fashion photography, humor, and visual and verbal editorial comment on classic films and famous actors. Any commercial aspects are "inextricably entwined" with expressive elements, and so they cannot be separated out "from the fully protected whole." . . . [C]ommon sense tells us this is not a simple advertisement.

As a result, the Ninth Circuit concluded that the article was entitled to "full First Amendment protection" unless the altered photograph was defamatory and published with *New York Times* actual malice, and it said the record would not support such a claim.

In Downing v. Abercrombie & Fitch, 265 F.3d 994, 29 Med. L. Rptr. 2390 (9th Cir. 2001), the Ninth Circuit distinguished *Hoffman* in a subsequent case brought by a group of surfers for the uncompensated use of their names and photographs in clothing retailer Abercrombie & Fitch's catalog. Even though the photograph was accompanied by an article about surfing culture and locations, the appellate court found that the plaintiffs' photograph did not "contribute significantly to a matter of the public interest" and that as a result Abercrombie cannot "avail itself of the First Amendment defense."

Even if the speech is purely commercial, there may be a First Amendment defense if the use of the name or likeness is "transformative". See Comedy III Productions, Inc. v. Gary Saderup, Inc., 21 P.3d 797, 29 Med. L. Rptr. 1897 (Cal. 2001). Borrowing a concept from intellectual property law, the court said "when an artist is faced with a right of publicity challenge to his or her work, he or she may raise as affirmative defense that the work is protected by the First Amendment inasmuch as it contains significant transformative elements or that the value of the work does not derive primarily from the celebrity's fame." The court pointed to the celebrity images of Andy Warhol, which it said were "able to convey a message that went beyond the commercial exploitation of celebrity images and became a form of ironic social comment on the dehumanization of celebrity itself." But the held that in the case at bar, the sale of lithographs and t-shirts bearing images of the Three Stooges were not protected by the First Amendment because they made "no significant transformative or creative contribution" to those images.

Notes and Questions

1. Does subsection (d) of the California statute eliminate the possibility that this statute will be applied to the media? Would the statute likely be constitutional without this subsection? Does this subsection eliminate whatever constitutional concerns the statute might otherwise raise?

2. Does the statute protect privacy interests or property interests? As applied in many states, this tort seems to protect both. A person may wish to prevent exploitation of his or her personality altogether; such a person seems to be asserting a privacy interest. But a person might also be

perfectly willing to have his or personality exploited, if the price is right. In this setting the interest looks more like a property right. All professional models and many athletes, actors, and musicians make a business of selling rights to exploit their names or likenesses. Some courts use the term "right of publicity" (effectively the opposite of a "right of privacy") to describe this interest in preserving the pecuniary value of one's personality.

Whether appropriation is considered as a subset of privacy rights has important implications for its judicial development. For example, does the right survive the death of the celebrity in whom the right is based? That is, can a celebrity's heirs or assigns prevent unauthorized exploitation after the famous person has died? Courts that have found the right to be descendible have analogized it to an ordinary property right or a copyright, both of which are inheritable. Courts that have found no descendible right have analogized it to privacy rights, which are personal in nature, and have stressed the line-drawing difficulties inherent in any development of a right that survives the death of the celebrity.

3. At least twelve states protect the right of publicity after the death of the person involved. In California, the right of "deceased personality" is provided for in Cal. Civil Code § 990:

> (a) Any person who uses a deceased personality's name, voice, signature, photograph, or likeness, in any manner, on or in products, merchandise, or goods, or for purposes of advertising or selling, or soliciting purchases of, products, merchandise, goods, or services, without prior consent from the person or persons specified in subdivision (c), shall be liable for any damages sustained by the person or persons injured as a result thereof.

The statute defines "deceased personality" to mean "any natural person whose name, voice, signature, photograph, or likeness has commercial value at the time of his or her death, whether or not during the lifetime of that natural person the person used his or her name, voice, signature, photograph, or likeness on or in products, merchandise or goods, or for purposes of advertising or selling, or solicitation of purchase of, products, merchandise, goods or service." Why restrict the law only to people whose "personality" had commercial value during their lifetime? Why protect the commercial value of the "personality" of someone who never sought to exploit that value while alive?

The statute exempts not only the "use of a name, voice, signature, photograph, or likeness in connection with any news, public affairs, or sports broadcast or account, or any political campaign," but also the use in a "play, book, magazine, newspaper, musical composition, film, radio or television program," in "[m]aterial that is of political or newsworthy value," and in "[s]ingle and original works of fine art."

The California law makes clear that the rights of "deceased personality" are "property rights, freely transferable, in whole or in part, by contract or by means of trust or testamentary documents, whether the transfer occurs before the death of the deceased personality, by the deceased personality or his or her transferees, or, after the death of the deceased personality, by the person or persons in whom the rights vest under this section or the transferees of that person or persons."

4.   What are the implications for digital technology that makes it possible to create "virtual actors" who look, sound, and move on the screen like the real people they recreate? In 1992, the U.S. Court of Appeals for the Ninth Circuit allowed a suit by Vanna White, who appeared on the television game show "Wheel of Fortune," to proceed against Samsung Electronics for an advertisement for Samsung VCRs featuring a "robot, dressed in a wig, gown, and jewelry . . . consciously selected to resemble White's hair and dress. The robot was posed next to a game board which is instantly recognizable as the Wheel of Fortune game show set, in a stance for which White is famous." White claimed a violation of California's right of publicity statute, Cal. Civil Code § 3344, and federal trademark law, 15 U.S.C. § 1125(a). The appellate court found that White's suit presented sufficient questions of fact to overturn the trial's court grant of summary judgment against her. See White v. Samsung Electronics America, Inc., 971 F.2d 1395, 1397 (9th Cir. 1992), rehearing en banc denied, 989 F.2d 1512 (9th Cir. 1993).

For a critique of the right of publicity, particularly its application to digital images, see Harvey L. Zuckman, The Ninth Circuit's Invasion of the Tort of Invasion of Privacy, 11 CommLaw Conspectus 237 (2003).

2.   UNAUTHORIZED COVERAGE OF ENTERTAINMENT ACTS

The Zacchini Case. Hugo Zacchini performed a human cannonball act at a county fair. Persons attending the fair were not charged a separate admission to see Zacchini's act. A television reporter covering the fair with the permission of fair officials filmed Zacchini's act over Zacchini's objection, and the 15–second segment was shown on the local news that night with favorable commentary.

Zacchini sued the station for, among other things, "unlawful appropriation of plaintiff's professional property." The trial court granted the station's motion for summary judgment. The Ohio Supreme Court held that one may not use the name or likeness of another for the taker's own benefit even if the use was not commercial. That court nevertheless granted judgment for the station, on the ground that the film was about a matter of legitimate public interest and its use in a newscast was privileged.

The Supreme Court reversed 5–4, holding that the Ohio Supreme Court mistakenly believed such a privilege was required by the First Amendment:

> It is evident, and there is no claim here to the contrary, that petitioner's state-law right of publicity would not serve to prevent respondent from reporting the newsworthy facts about petitioner's act. Wherever the line in particular situations is to be drawn between media reports that are protected and those that are not, we are quite sure that the

First and Fourteenth Amendments do not immunize the media when they broadcast a performer's entire act without his consent. The Constitution no more prevents a State from requiring respondent to compensate petitioner for broadcasting his act on television than it would privilege respondent to film and broadcast a copyrighted dramatic work without liability to the copyright owner. . . .

The Court said that by protecting Zacchini's performance from unauthorized broadcast, "Ohio has recognized what may be the strongest case for a 'right of publicity'—involving not the appropriation of an entertainer's reputation to enhance the attractiveness of a commercial product, but the appropriation of the very activity by which the entertainer acquired the reputation in the first place."

Justice Powell, joined by Justices Brennan and Marshall, dissented, arguing that use of the film was part of routine news coverage protected by the First Amendment "absent a strong showing by the plaintiff that the news broadcast was a subterfuge or cover for private or commercial exploitation." Justice Powell said the majority's "repeated incantation of a single formula: 'a performer's entire act' " was not a sufficiently clear standard to resolve even the case at hand. "One may assume that the actual firing was preceded by some fanfare, possibly stretching over several minutes, to heighten the audience's anticipation. . . . If this is found to have been the case on remand, then respondent could not be said to have appropriated the 'entire act' in its 15–second newsclip—and the Court's opinion then would afford no guidance for the resolution of the case."

Justice Stevens dissented on the ground that the case should have been remanded to the Ohio Supreme Court to clarify whether its decision rested on state law or First Amendment principles. Zacchini v. Scripps–Howard Broadcasting Co., 433 U.S. 562, 2 Med. L. Rptr. 2089 (1977).

Although the decision clearly indicates that a state need not confine its remedies for misappropriation to instances where the use is commercial, the states have not been eager to abandon that limitation. Moreover, the Court's use of the "entire act" rubric does not encourage reliance on *Zacchini* because media rarely make unauthorized use of a performer's entire act.

Promoters of entertainment and sports events normally protect their rights by controlling access to the event. Terms of admission often prohibit use of cameras or tape recorders entirely, or specify portions of performances that may be recorded or photographed. Broadcasting rights are protected by allowing only those who have contracted with the promoters to set up their broadcasting equipment. Performers, in turn, protect their interests through their contracts with the promoters; whether the promoter has a right to authorize live broadcast of a concert, for example, is determined by the terms of the contract between the performer and the promoter.

If Zacchini did not protect his rights contractually, why should the courts provide him a remedy through tort law? The television station was permitted—probably even encouraged—by the fair officials to broadcast film of various events at the fair. Should they be entitled to rely on that invitation without inquiring into the officials' authority to extend it?

Plaintiffs generally have been unsuccessful when they have tried to invoke *Zacchini* to create a cause of action not otherwise provided by the law of copyright or the tort of commercial exploitation of name or likeness. Actress Ginger Rogers relied on *Zacchini* in an attempt to prevent Federico Fellini from using the title "Ginger and Fred" for his 1986 movie about an Italian dancing couple. The district court characterized *Zacchini* as a "narrowly drawn opinion effectively limited to its facts," and distinguished it on the ground that "Ginger and Fred" did not threaten Rogers' economic viability. Rogers v. Grimaldi, 695 F. Supp. 112, 15 Med. L. Rptr. 2097 (S.D.N.Y. 1988), affirmed 875 F.2d 994, 16 Med. L. Rptr. 1648 (2d Cir. 1989).

3.   SELF-PROMOTION

Media sometimes encounter this branch of the law when they use photos or film of people to promote their publications or programs.

A publication's use of an earlier story to advertise its own product does not come within "advertising purposes" under the New York privacy statute, supra pp. 376–77. In Booth v. Curtis Publishing Co., 15 A.D.2d 343, 223 N.Y.S.2d 737, aff'd without opinion 11 N.Y.2d 907, 182 N.E.2d 812, 228 N.Y.S.2d 468 (1962), Holiday magazine published a photograph of actress Shirley Booth in a story about a prominent resort. The color photograph was "a very striking one, show[ing] Miss Booth in the water up to her neck, but wearing a brimmed, high-crowned street hat of straw." Several months after the story appeared, Holiday took out full-page advertisements in the New Yorker and Advertising Age magazines. Both reprinted the Booth photograph as a sample of the content of Holiday magazine. "Because of the photograph's striking qualities it would be quite effective in drawing attention to the advertisements; but it was also a sample of magazine content."

The court found the use of the photograph to be an "incidental" mentioning of plaintiff in the course of advertising itself. "It stands to reason that a publication can best prove its worth and illustrate its content by submission of complete copies of or extraction from past editions. . . . And, of course, it is true that the publisher must advertise in other public media, just as it must by poster, circular, cover, or soliciting letter. This is a practical necessity which the law may not ignore in giving effect to the purposes of the statute."

Although the court recognized that "realistically" the use of the photograph attracted the attention of the reader, that use was outweighed by the magazine's need to demonstrate its content. Finally, nothing in the advertisement suggested that plaintiff endorsed defendant's magazine.

This case was followed in Namath v. Sports Illustrated, 48 A.D.2d 487, 371 N.Y.S.2d 10 (1975), affirmed 39 N.Y.2d 897, 386 N.Y.S.2d 397, 352 N.E.2d 584 (1976).

4. FALSE OR MISLEADING PROMOTIONAL MATERIAL

Celebrities have had considerable success with appropriation claims over false or misleading promotional material. The line between the false light and appropriation branches of privacy law is often blurred in these cases.

The actor Jose Solano, Jr., brought suit against Playgirl magazine for its use without his consent of his picture on its front cover. He made claims for both false light and appropriation under the California statute. The district court granted the magazine summary judgment, finding that the picture, showing Solano bare-chested, and the headline "TV Guys. Prime-time's Sexy Young Stars Exposed" did not create a false impression and that, in any event, Solano could not prove actual malice. But the Ninth Circuit ruled that the use of a photograph in which Solano was only partially clothed and the word "exposed" in the headline could have given readers the false impression that Solano appeared nude within the magazine. The court pointed to evidence from depositions of Playgirl staff indicating that they were aware that some people might be misled by the cover and held that that was sufficient to allow a jury to conclude that Playgirl acted with actual malice. The court distinguished *Hoffman* (supra p. 405), on the basis that the text of that article made clear that digital techniques had been used to alter the actor's photograph. See Solano v. Playgirl, Inc., 292 F.3d 1078, 30 Med. L. Rptr. 1878 (9th Cir. 2002).

Cher's case. In Cher v. Forum International, Ltd., 692 F.2d 634, 8 Med. L. Rptr. 2484 (9th Cir. 1982), the entertainer Cher had agreed to give an interview to US Magazine, reserving the right to bar publication if she did not like the results. She exercised that right. The interviewer, however, then sold the interview to Star and Forum magazines, each of which published excerpts. Cher alleged that she would not have given either of the defendants an interview because she did not approve of them. She sued and won judgments against both magazines.

The court of appeals reversed the judgment against Star. Star had put on its cover "Exclusive Series" followed by "Cher: My life, my husbands and my many, many men." The court concluded that Star "was entitled to inform its readers that the issue contained an article about Cher, that the article was based on an interview with Cher herself, and that the article had not previously appeared elsewhere." The words used to convey that information "cannot support a finding of the knowing or reckless falsity required under *Time, Inc. v. Hill.*" Nor did the words convey the false claim that Cher endorsed the magazine. The then-existing version of the California "right of publicity" statute had an express exception for news accounts that was held to cover this case.

A judgment of $269,000 against Forum and its parent, Penthouse International, was upheld, however. Forum had changed the text to make it appear that Forum was posing the questions to Cher in an interview— "apparently a common practice in the industry." The cover said "Exclusive: Cher Talks Straight." Forum also used Cher's name on a subscription pull-out card that asserted that things Cher would not tell US Magazine she was telling Forum. The card also stated "So join Cher and Forum's hundreds of thousands of other adventurous readers today." The claim that Cher was telling Forum readers things she would not tell US was "patently false. This kind of mendacity is not protected by the First Amendment. . . ." The falsity was particularly clear here because US was a magazine to which Cher *was* willing to give an interview.

The trial court had also found liability for the "join Cher" language on the card. Although the court of appeals thought the language somewhat ambiguous, it was willing to accept the trial court's reading that this was an implied endorsement of Forum and its conclusion that the falsity of that reading showed a reckless disregard for the truth. The court of appeals concluded that "no matter how carefully the editorial staff of Forum may have trod the border between the actionable and the protected, the advertising staff engaged in the kind of knowing falsity that strips away the protection of the First Amendment."

The Eastwood cases. Eastwood v. Superior Court, 149 Cal. App.3d 409, 198 Cal. Rptr. 342, 10 Med. L. Rptr. 1073 (1983), involved a claim by Clint Eastwood against the National Enquirer for the unauthorized use of his likeness on the cover and in related television advertisements about a false non-defamatory story inside the issue. The story involved allegations that Eastwood was romantically involved with two female celebrities. The court concluded that the use was commercial exploitation and was not privileged under state or federal law. The trial court had improperly sustained a demurrer to the complaint. The court of appeal saw no reason why Eastwood should have to show that he was being falsely depicted as endorsing the National Enquirer. This was one way to impose liability but was not essential. The court also concluded that the article was not necessarily protected as a news account because of an allegation that the story was a calculated falsehood.

Eastwood won more than $800,000 in a different suit against the Enquirer. In Eastwood v. National Enquirer, Inc., 123 F.3d 1249, 25 Med. L. Rptr. 2198 (9th Cir. 1997), defendant magazine featured an "exclusive interview" with plaintiff actor, who alleged that the interview was a total fabrication. The Enquirer had bought the "interview" from a non-employee. Plaintiff sued under section 43(a) of the Lanham Act for misrepresentation of the article's origin, for invasion of privacy, and for misappropriation of his name, likeness and personality under California statute (Civil Code § 3344) and common law. "The gist of the complaint is that Eastwood's reputation was damaged by the suggestion that he would grant an interview to a sensationalist tabloid." All three theories were submitted to the jury, which awarded $75,000 for harm to reputation and $75,000 for profits unjustly obtained by the defendant, without specifying which theory it based its verdict on. The judge awarded plaintiff $653,000 in attorney's fees under the Lanham Act and the California statute. The Ninth Circuit affirmed.

The court apparently believed the actual malice standard applied because Eastwood was a public figure claiming harm to reputation. Reviewing the record at length for clear and convincing evidence of actual malice, the court concluded that only a preponderance supported the finding that the Enquirer knew that the interview had not occurred. But there was clear and convincing evidence on a second theory: even if the defendant thought an interview had occurred, it knew its designation on the cover and elsewhere that the interview was "exclusive" was false. The Enquirer asserted that "exclusive" meant only that "no one else is publishing this article in our market." But the court noted that the magazine published the "interview" under the byline of one of its own assistant editors, "inserted scene-setting phrases," and used the style "Eastwood said" rather than "Eastwood has said" to indicate that his quotes were given directly to the Enquirer writer. The totality of these devices showed clearly and convincingly that "the editors intended to convey the impression—known to them to be false—that Eastwood willfully submitted to an interview by the Enquirer. This intentional conduct satisfies the 'actual malice' standard, permitting a verdict for Eastwood." The court noted that it would not have been enough to show that Enquirer readers would think the interview took place. The showing that the editors intentionally conveyed an impression they knew to be false was crucial; otherwise, according to *Bose*, supra p. 291, "any individual using a malapropism might be liable . . . even though he did not realize his folly at the time."

In Lee v. Penthouse Intl., Ltd., 25 Med. L. Rptr. 1651 (C.D. Cal. 1997), defendant published sexually explicit photographs of a well-known married couple—Pamela Anderson Lee and Tommy Lee (an actress and a musician). The photos were allegedly made by the couple during their honeymoon and later stolen from their house by persons unknown. On the cover of the issue, Pamela Lee was shown in a tight fitting dress. Plaintiffs sued, alleging appropriation because of the cover, and appropriation and invasion of privacy because of publication of the intimate photos.

The district court granted summary judgment on all claims. Under California common law and statute, there was no requirement that the advertising suggest an endorsement or association with the plaintiffs. But the law did require a use for advertising. The court analyzed the second *Eastwood* case, supra, at length and concluded that the same analysis applied here in that the publication had used the cover and the article to attract readers, exploiting the use of the famous names. But *Eastwood* was distinguished on the ground that there the plaintiff alleged that the story was a complete fabrication, while the Lees did not allege that the Penthouse article was false. Falsity was crucial to determining whether the article was to be protected as newsworthy, because a fabricated story cannot be newsworthy. In this case, the story and photos accurately reported the events, and the state statute (Cal. Civil Code § 3344, supra) provided that use of a "name, photograph or likeness in connection with any news" shall not constitute commercial appropriation. Pamela Lee had previously revealed a variety of details about the couple's sexual activities and these photos clearly related to those revelations. The intimate nature of the photos did not make them less newsworthy. The other claims similarly failed.

———

Consider this series of hypotheticals from Steven Shiffrin, The First Amendment and Economic Regulation: Away from a General Theory of the First Amendment, 78 Nw. U. L. Rev. 1212, 1257 n. 275 (1983):

> A magazine may have a profit motive in taking a particular position on a particular subject, but the courts will ordinarily not count that motivation as significant. In thinking about profit motive and the dissemination of truth consider these examples: (1) Without his consent, Mercedes Benz *truthfully* advertises that Frank Sinatra drives a Mercedes. Sinatra sues for misappropriation. Does it make a difference if Mercedes in its ad says, "We didn't ask Sinatra's permission to tell you this" or "Sinatra doesn't want us to tell you this but . . ."? (2) Suppose *Time* magazine writes a story on Mercedes Benz and puts Sinatra on the cover with a picture of his Mercedes. Suppose they put Sinatra on the cover purely for reasons of profit. (3) Suppose Time Inc. advertises: "Get the recent issue of *Time* with Frank Sinatra on the cover with his Mercedes." (4) Suppose *Time* truthfully advertises: "Sinatra doesn't want us to tell you this, but he is one of our regular readers."

Are any of these uses actionable?

———

On the development of the tort law of privacy generally, see Ken Gormley, One Hundred Years of Privacy, 1992 Wis. L. Rev. 1335 (1992). Randall P. Bezanson, The Right to Privacy Revisited: Privacy, News, and Social Change, 1890–1990, 80 Cal. L. Rev. 1133 (1992). Robert C. Post, The Social Foundations of Privacy: Community and Self in the Common Law Tort, 77 Cal. L. Rev. 957 (1989).

Professor Cass Sunstein has argued that states should do more—whether through statutes or common law—to protect privacy:

> [T]he law could do more [to protect privacy]. Some states might build on their existing laws to create a firmer wall of privacy around people who do not want to be exploited, harassed or humiliated. States might, for example, try specifically forbidding photographers to invade

a private domain through the use of long-distance photographic equipment. They might allow people to recover damages if they have been repeatedly harassed about a personal tragedy. They might make it a misdemeanor to publish photographs taken without permission in a home or other private domain.

In such experiments, however, a good deal of creativity and care is required. Broadly drawn laws would create problems. For example, the First Amendment would almost certainly bar any law that might have been used to forbid the publication of the famous photographs of Gary Hart with Donna Rice. These kinds of hurdles, though, should not discourage experimentation, because it is perfectly legitimate for states to experiment with new ways to adapt to social and technological change.

Cass R. Sunstein, Reinforce the Walls of Privacy, N.Y. Times, Sept. 6, 1997, at 23.

D. DATA PROTECTION STATUTES

Much of the recent debate about privacy has focused on the collection and use of personal information in electronic databases. Concern about this has intensified with the development of technologies that allow the automatic collection of such information from Internet users by means of "cookies", "spyware," and other unnoticed data collection methods. For the most part, this affects only the business aspects of media and so far has only marginally affected journalism.

The collection and use of personal information in the United States is regulated by a growing array of statutes beyond those we have already seen. Although these statutes rarely act on the media directly, they may limit the availability of information on which the press may draw. For example, the federal Driver Privacy Protection Act, 18 U.S.C. § 2721, restricts the availability of previously public information that journalists use to identify and locate sources and other people involved in news stories. The DPPA and other laws affecting the ability of the press to collect information are discussed in Chapter X.

In 1995 the European Union adopted a Data Protection Directive that caused considerable consternation among American media. The Directive required members of the EU to adopt legislation protecting individuals' privacy from various uses of information in databases and specified what such legislation must do. It required businesses that compile databases to notify individuals as to the uses to which the information might be put, allow them to forbid some uses, and give them rights to see and correct the information relating to them. See Directive 95/46 of the European Parliament and of the Council, Oct. 24, 1995.

The Directive did not apply to the United States, of course, but it contained a provision prohibiting the transfer of personally identifiable information from EU countries into or out of non-EU countries that did not have similar data protection policies. Data-protection policies in the U.S. are much less protective of personal information.

American companies in general feared that the restrictions on transfer of data into and out of EU countries would interfere with the internationalization of banking, credit, and marketing, and media organizations feared that it might inhibit the use of information for journalistic purposes.

The media fears seem to have been largely unrealized. For one thing, the directive contains an exception for "journalistic purposes." More important, under intense lobbying by American companies, the U.S. and the EU negotiated an agreement that allows transfer of information to or from U.S. businesses if they voluntarily adopt one of several alternative methods of protecting individuals' privacy. See European Commission, Art. 25.6 Decision, available at http://www.export.gov.safeharbor/Art256DecisionJune 2000.htm. As a result, the impact on U.S. journalism has been minimal, but many Europeans remain dissatisfied with the U.S. response, and many in the U.S. remain wary of future attempts to strengthen international restraints on use of personal information. See generally Jane E. Kirtley, Privacy and the Press in the New Millenium: How International Standards are Driving the Privacy Debate in the United States and Abroad, 23 U.Ark.–Little Rock L. Rev. 69 (2000).

CHAPTER VI

LIABILITY FOR EMOTIONAL, ECONOMIC, AND PHYSICAL HARM

As we saw in the two preceding chapters, defamation and invasion of privacy are well-defined torts, and the First Amendment jurisprudence that limits them is fairly extensive. In this chapter, we consider other types of harms caused by mass communication. Here the tort doctrines are less fully developed. The courts, including the Supreme Court, seem undecided in these cases as to the seriousness of the threat to free speech and unsure as to the appropriate First Amendment response. Because First Amendment doctrine in these areas is to a great extent a work in progress, it may be helpful to think of these materials as a study in the formulation of a First Amendment response to problems that are either new or had not previously been thought to raise free speech issues. The Supreme Court's only major contributions to this process, as we shall see in the following two principal cases, seem to point in very different directions.

A. EMOTIONAL DISTRESS

1. INTENTIONAL INFLICTION

The tort action for intentional infliction of emotional distress, developed in the last century, is closely related to the privacy torts. It has spread rapidly and is generally recognized. Most states tend to follow some version of the Restatement (Second) of Torts § 46, with its focus on extreme and outrageous behavior by the defendant that produces serious emotional consequences to the plaintiff. Actionable instances often involve conduct that has no purpose other than to inflict emotional distress, or conduct that has another purpose but goes beyond the pale of tolerable conduct, such as harassment by a debt collector. We begin with the leading Supreme Court case.

Hustler Magazine, Inc. v. Falwell

Supreme Court of the United States, 1988.
485 U.S. 46, 108 S.Ct. 876, 99 L.Ed.2d 41, 14 Med.L.Rptr. 2281.

CHIEF JUSTICE REHNQUIST delivered the opinion of the Court.

Petitioner Hustler Magazine, Inc., is a magazine of nationwide circulation. Respondent Jerry Falwell, a nationally known minister who has been active as a commentator on politics and public affairs, sued petitioner and its publisher, petitioner Larry Flynt. . . .

The inside front cover of the November 1983 issue of Hustler Magazine featured a "parody" of an advertisement for Campari Liqueur that contained the name and picture of respondent and was entitled "Jerry Falwell talks about his first time." This parody was modeled after actual Campari ads that included interviews with various celebrities about their "first times." Although it was apparent by the end of each interview that this meant the first time they sampled Campari, the ads clearly played on the sexual double entendre of the general subject of "first times." Copying the form and layout of these Campari ads, Hustler's editors chose respondent as the featured celebrity and drafted an alleged "interview" with him in which he states that his "first time" was during a drunken incestuous rendezvous with his mother in an outhouse. The Hustler parody portrays respondent and his mother as drunk and immoral, and suggests that respondent is a hypocrite who preaches only when he is drunk. In small print at the bottom of the page, the ad contains the disclaimer, "ad parody—not to be taken seriously." The magazine's table of contents also lists the ad as "Fiction; Ad and Personality Parody."

Soon after the November issue of Hustler became available to the public, respondent brought this diversity action in the United States District Court for the Western District of Virginia against Hustler Magazine, Inc., Larry C. Flynt, and Flynt Distributing Co. Respondent stated in his complaint that publication of the ad parody in Hustler entitled him to recover damages for libel, invasion of privacy, and intentional infliction of emotional distress. The case proceeded to trial. At the close of the evidence, the District Court granted a directed verdict for petitioners on the invasion of privacy claim. The jury then found against respondent on the libel claim, specifically finding that the ad parody could not "reasonably be understood as describing actual facts about [respondent] or actual events in which [he] participated." [ ] The jury ruled for respondent on the intentional infliction of emotional distress claim, however, and stated that he should be awarded $100,000 in compensatory damages, as well as $50,000 each in punitive damages from petitioners [Hustler Magazine and Flynt]. Petitioners' motion for judgment notwithstanding the verdict was denied.

On appeal, the [Fourth Circuit] affirmed the judgment against petitioners. [ ] The court rejected petitioners' argument that the "actual malice" standard of *New York Times Co. v. Sullivan*, [ ], must be met before respondent can recover for emotional distress. The court agreed that because respondent is concededly a public figure, petitioners are "entitled to the same level of first amendment protection in the claim for intentional infliction of emotional distress that they received in [respondent's] claim for libel." [ ] But this does not mean that a literal application of the actual malice rule is appropriate in the context of an emotional distress claim. In the court's view, the *New York Times* decision emphasized the constitutional importance not of the falsity of the statement or the defendant's disregard for the truth, but of the heightened level of culpability embodied in the requirement of "knowing . . . or reckless" conduct. Here, [in the view of the Fourth Circuit] the *New York Times* standard is satisfied by the state-law requirement, and the jury's finding, that the defendants have acted intentionally or recklessly.[3] The Court of Appeals then went on to reject the contention that because the jury found that the ad parody did not describe actual facts about respondent, the ad was an opinion that is protected by the First Amendment. As the court put it, this was "irrelevant," as the issue is "whether [the ad's] publication was sufficiently outrageous to constitute intentional infliction of emotional distress." [ ] Petitioners then filed a petition for rehearing en banc, but this was denied by a divided court. Given the importance of the constitutional issues involved, we granted certiorari.

This case presents us with a novel question involving First Amendment limitations upon a State's authority to protect its citizens from the intentional infliction of emotional distress. We must decide whether a public figure may recover damages for emotional harm caused by the publication of an ad parody offensive to him, and doubtless gross and repugnant in the eyes of most. Respondent would have us find that a State's interest in protecting public figures from emotional distress is sufficient to deny First Amendment protection to speech that is patently offensive and is intended to inflict emotional injury, even when that speech could not reasonably have been interpreted as stating actual facts about the public figure involved. This we decline to do.

At the heart of the First Amendment is the recognition of the fundamental importance of the free flow of ideas and opinions on matters of public interest and concern. "[T]he freedom to speak one's mind is not only an aspect of individual liberty—and thus a good unto itself—but also is essential to the common quest for truth and the vitality of society as a whole." [*Bose*] We have therefore been particularly vigilant to ensure that individual expressions of ideas remain free from governmentally imposed sanctions. The First Amendment recognizes no such thing as a "false" idea. [*Gertz*] As Justice Holmes wrote, "[W]hen men have realized that time has upset many fighting faiths, they may come to believe even more than they believe the very foundations of their own conduct that the ultimate good desired is better reached by free trade in ideas—that the best test of truth is the power of the thought to get itself accepted in the competition of the market. . . ." [*Abrams*]

The sort of robust political debate encouraged by the First Amendment is bound to produce speech that is critical of those who hold public office or those public figures who are "intimately involved in the resolution of important public questions or, by reason of their fame, shape events in areas of concern to society at large." [*Walker* and *Butts*] (Warren, C.J., concurring in result). Justice Frankfurter put it succinctly in Baumgartner

---

3. Under Virginia law, in an action for intentional infliction of emotional distress a plaintiff must show that the defendant's conduct (1) is intentional or reckless; (2) offends generally accepted standards of decency or morality; (3) is causally connected with the plaintiff's emotional distress; and (4) caused emotional distress that was severe. [ ]

v. United States, 322 U.S. 665, 673–674 (1944), when he said that "[o]ne of the prerogatives of American citizenship is the right to criticize public men and measures." Such criticism, inevitably, will not always be reasoned or moderate; public figures as well as public officials will be subject to "vehement, caustic, and sometimes unpleasantly sharp attacks," [*New York Times*]. "[T]he candidate who vaunts his spotless record and sterling integrity cannot convincingly cry 'Foul!' when an opponent or an industrious reporter attempts to demonstrate the contrary." [*Monitor Patriot Co.*]

Of course, this does not mean that any speech about a public figure is immune from sanction in the form of damages. Since [*New York Times*] we have consistently ruled that a public figure may hold a speaker liable for the damage to reputation caused by publication of a defamatory falsehood, but only if the statement was made "with knowledge that it was false or with reckless disregard of whether it was false or not." [ ] False statements of fact are particularly valueless; they interfere with the truth-seeking function of the marketplace of ideas, and they cause damage to an individual's reputation that cannot easily be repaired by counterspeech, however persuasive or effective. See [*Gertz*] n.9. But even though falsehoods have little value in and of themselves, they are "nevertheless inevitable in free debate," [*Gertz*], and a rule that would impose strict liability on a publisher for false factual assertions would have an undoubted "chilling" effect on speech relating to public figures that does have constitutional value. "Freedoms of expression require 'breathing space.'" [*Hepps*, quoting *New York Times*] This breathing space is provided by a constitutional rule that allows public figures to recover for libel or defamation only when they can prove both that the statement was false and that the statement was made with the requisite level of culpability.

Respondent argues, however, that a different standard should apply in this case because here the State seeks to prevent not reputational damage, but the severe emotional distress suffered by the person who is the subject of an offensive publication. Cf. Zacchini v. Scripps–Howard Broadcasting Co., 433 U.S. 562 (1977) (ruling that the "actual malice" standard does not apply to the tort of appropriation of a right of publicity). In respondent's view, and in the view of the Court of Appeals, so long as the utterance was intended to inflict emotional distress, was outrageous, and did in fact inflict serious emotional distress, it is of no constitutional import whether the statement was a fact or an opinion, or whether it was true or false. It is the intent to cause injury that is the gravamen of the tort, and the State's interest in preventing emotional harm simply outweighs whatever interest a speaker may have in speech of this type.

Generally speaking the law does not regard the intent to inflict emotional distress as one which should receive much solicitude, and it is quite understandable that most if not all jurisdictions have chosen to make it civilly culpable where the conduct in question is sufficiently "outrageous." But in the world of debate about public affairs, many things done with motives that are less than admirable are protected by the First Amendment. In *Garrison v. Louisiana*, [ ], we held that even when a speaker or writer is motivated by hatred or ill-will his expression was protected by the First Amendment:

"Debate on public issues will not be uninhibited if the speaker must run the risk that it will be proved in court that he spoke out of hatred; even if he did speak out of hatred, utterances honestly believed contribute to the free interchange of ideas and the ascertainment of truth." [ ]

Thus while such a bad motive may be deemed controlling for purposes of tort liability in other areas of the law, we think the First Amendment prohibits such a result in the area of public debate about public figures.

Were we to hold otherwise, there can be little doubt that political cartoonists and satirists would be subjected to damages awards without any showing that their work falsely defamed its subject. Webster's defines a caricature as "the deliberately distorted picturing or imitating of a person, literary style, etc. by exaggerating features or mannerisms for satirical effect." [ ] The appeal of the political cartoon or caricature is often based on exploration of unfortunate physical traits or politically embarrassing events—an exploration often calculated to injure the feelings of the subject of the portrayal. The art of the cartoonist is often not reasoned or evenhanded, but slashing and one-sided. One cartoonist expressed the nature of the art in these words:

"The political cartoon is a weapon of attack, of scorn and ridicule and satire; it is least effective when it tries to pat some politician on the back. It is usually as welcome as a bee sting and is always controversial in some quarters." Long, The Political Cartoon: Journalism's Strongest Weapon, The Quill, 56, 57 (Nov. 1962).

Several famous examples of this type of intentionally injurious speech were drawn by Thomas Nast, probably the greatest American cartoonist to date, who was associated for many years during the post-Civil War era with Harper's Weekly. In the pages of that publication Nast conducted a graphic vendetta against William M. "Boss" Tweed and his corrupt associates in New York City's "Tweed Ring." It has been described by one historian of the subject as "a sustained attack which in its passion and effectiveness stands alone in the history of American graphic art." M. Keller, The Art and Politics of Thomas Nast 177 (1968). Another writer explains that the success of the Nast cartoon was achieved "because of the emotional impact of its presentation. It continuously goes beyond the bounds of good taste and conventional manners." C. Press, The Political Cartoon 251 (1981).

Despite their sometimes caustic nature, from the early cartoon portraying George Washington as an ass down to the present day, graphic depictions and satirical cartoons have played a prominent role in public and political debate. Nast's castigation of the Tweed Ring, Walt McDougall's characterization of presidential candidate James G. Blaine's banquet with the millionaires at Delmonico's as "The Royal Feast of Belshazzar," and numerous other efforts have undoubtedly had an effect on the course and outcome of contemporaneous debate. Lincoln's tall, gangling posture, Teddy Roosevelt's glasses and teeth, and Franklin D. Roosevelt's jutting jaw and cigarette holder have been memorialized by political cartoons with an effect that could not have been obtained by the photographer or the portrait artist. From the viewpoint of history it is clear that our political discourse would have been considerably poorer without them.

Respondent contends, however, that the caricature in question here was so "outrageous" as to distinguish it from more traditional political cartoons. There is no doubt that the caricature of respondent and his mother published in Hustler is at best a distant cousin of the political cartoons described above, and a rather poor relation at that. If it were possible by laying down a principled standard to separate the one from the other, public discourse would probably suffer little or no harm. But we doubt that there is any such standard, and we are quite sure that the pejorative description "outrageous" does not supply one. "Outrageousness" in the area of political and social discourse has an inherent subjectiveness about it which would allow a jury to impose liability on the basis of the jurors' tastes or views, or perhaps on the basis of their dislike of a particular expression. An "outrageousness" standard thus runs afoul of our longstanding refusal to allow damages to be awarded because the speech in question may have an adverse emotional impact on the audience. See NAACP v. Claiborne Hardware Co., 458 U.S. 886, 910 (1982) ("Speech does not lose its protected character . . . simply because it may embarrass others or coerce them into action"). And, as we stated in FCC v. Pacifica Foundation, 438 U.S. 726 (1978):

> "[T]he fact that society may find speech offensive is not a sufficient reason for suppressing it. Indeed, if it is the speaker's opinion that gives offense, that consequence is a reason for according it constitutional protection. For it is a central tenet of the First Amendment that the government must remain neutral in the marketplace of ideas." [ ]

See also Street v. New York, 394 U.S. 576, 592 (1969) ("It is firmly settled that . . . the public expression of ideas may not be prohibited merely because the ideas are themselves offensive to some of their hearers").

Admittedly, these oft-repeated First Amendment principles, like other principles, are subject to limitations. We recognized in *Pacifica Foundation*, that speech that is " 'vulgar,' 'offensive,' and 'shocking' " is "not entitled to absolute constitutional protection under all circumstances." [ ]In Chaplinsky v. New Hampshire, 315 U.S. 568 (1942), we held that a state could lawfully punish an individual for the use of insulting " 'fighting' words— those which by their very utterance inflict injury or tend to incite an immediate breach of the peace." [ ]These limitations are but recognition of the observation in [*Dun & Bradstreet*] that this Court has "long recognized that not all speech is of equal First Amendment importance." But the sort of expression involved in this case does not seem to us to be governed by any exception to the general First Amendment principles stated above.

We conclude that public figures and public officials may not recover for the tort of intentional infliction of emotional distress by reason of publications such as the one here at issue without showing in addition that the publication contains a false statement of fact which was made with "actual malice," i.e., with knowledge that the statement was false or with reckless disregard as to whether or not it was true. This is not merely a "blind application" of the *New York Times* standard, [ ], it reflects our considered judgment that such a standard is necessary to give adequate "breathing space" to the freedoms protected by the First Amendment.

Here it is clear that respondent Falwell is a "public figure" for purposes of First Amendment law.[5] The jury found against respondent on his libel claim when it decided that the Hustler ad parody could not "reasonably be understood as describing actual facts about [respondent] or actual events in which [he] participated." [ ]The Court of Appeals interpreted the jury's finding to be that the ad parody "was not reasonably believable," [ ], and in accordance with our custom we accept this finding. Respondent is thus relegated to his claim for damages awarded by the jury for the intentional infliction of emotional distress by "outrageous" conduct. But for reasons heretofore stated this claim cannot, consistently with the First Amendment, form a basis for the award of damages when the conduct in question is the publication of a caricature such as the ad parody involved here. The judgment of the Court of Appeals is accordingly

Reversed.

JUSTICE KENNEDY took no part in the consideration or decision of this case.

JUSTICE WHITE, concurring in the judgment.

As I see it, the decision in [*New York Times*] has little to do with this case, for here the jury found that the ad contained no assertion of fact. But I agree with the Court that the judgment below, which penalized the publication of the parody, cannot be squared with the First Amendment.

Notes and Questions

1. Why are the limitations imposed by tort law insufficient to protect free speech? Is the First Amendment implicated any time state law imposes liability for speech? Speech on matters of public concern? Or is it implicated in this case only because the tort employs the test of "outrageousness"?

2. In a deposition Flynt testified that his objective in publishing the parody was to "assassinate" Falwell's integrity. See 797 F.2d 1270, 1273 (4th Cir. 1986). Is that relevant to whether the publication was tortious? To whether it was protected by the First Amendment?

3. Falsity is not an issue in the tort of intentional infliction of emotional distress, yet this decision permits recovery only if the plaintiff can prove

---

5. Neither party disputes this conclusion. Respondent is the host of a nationally syndicated television show and was the founder and president of a political organization formerly known as the Moral Majority. He is also the founder of Liberty University in Lynchburg, Virginia, and is the author of several books and publications. [ ]

that the distress-inflicting statement contains a false statement of fact. Is this to prevent truthful statements from being held tortious, or is it merely to make the actual malice test available in a tort where it otherwise would not work?

4. Is there any reason to limit the rationale of this case to public plaintiffs? What about private plaintiffs in cases that involve matters of public concern? Is there any parallel to the *Dun & Bradstreet* analysis? See Dworkin v. Hustler Magazine, Inc., 867 F.2d 1188, 16 Med. L. Rptr. 1113 (9th Cir. 1989).

————

Howell v. New York Post. Might the means by which information is obtained be so outrageous as to support a claim for intentional infliction of emotional distress? In a much-publicized case in New York, Hedda Nussbaum and her lover were charged in connection with the death of her adopted daughter. Nussbaum was committed to a private psychiatric hospital. A photographer for the New York Post trespassed onto the grounds and used a telephoto lens to get a photo of Nussbaum with another patient, which the newspaper published. The other patient, whose psychiatric treatment had been unknown to all but her immediate family, sued for, among other things, intentional infliction of emotional distress.

The court disposed of the claim on tort law grounds, concluding that the photographer's conduct was not "such atrocious, indecent, and utterly despicable conduct as to meet the rigorous requirements of an intentional infliction of emotional distress claim." Howell v. New York Post Co., 81 N.Y.2d 115, 612 N.E.2d 699, 596 N.Y.S.2d 350, 21 Med. L. Rptr. 1273 (1993).

Esposito-Hilder v. SFX Broadcasting. In another New York case, the Appellate Division held that a bride singled out by a radio station's "Ugliest Bride" contest stated a cause of action for intentional infliction of emotional distress. See Esposito–Hilder v. SFX Broadcasting, Inc., 236 A.D.2d 186, 665 N.Y.S.2d 697, 26 Med. L. Rptr. 1541 (1997). The complaint alleged that on the day the plaintiff's bridal photograph was published in a local newspaper, the station's disk jockeys engaged in a routine in which they made derogatory and disparaging comments about plaintiff's appearance and invited their listening audience to do the same. She alleged that because she worked for a rival station, defendants deviated from the ordinary routine of this "contest" by disclosing her full name, place of employment, and job supervisors. She said she and her supervisors and colleagues heard this broadcast and that it caused her extreme emotional distress, exacerbated by the fact that it happened when she was a newly-wed.

The court held that plaintiff could maintain a claim for emotional distress even though a defamation claim on the same facts would be barred by the special protection that the New York constitution provides for opinion:

[W]e observe that the tort of intentional infliction of emotional distress has received very little judicial solicitude (see, [*Falwell*]). Indeed, Chief Judge Kaye noted in *Howell v. New York Post Co.*, that of those claims considered by the Court of Appeals, "every one has failed because the alleged conduct was not sufficiently outrageous" [ ]. Emphasizing that we decide this question in the narrow context in which it occurs, i.e., whether the complaint should be dismissed for failure to state a cause of action, we conclude that under the unique factual circumstances herein presented, [the trial court] properly denied defendants' motion [to dismiss], and we affirm.

[W]e attach particular significance to several factors. First, plaintiff is a private individual and not a "public figure." Second, the nature of the communications made by defendants involved a matter of virtually no "public interest"; there is an inference that defendants' conduct represented a deliberate intent to inflict injury upon plaintiff based upon the claimed unprecedented expansion of its standard "routine" of the "Ugliest Bride" contest to include particulars concerning plaintiff's name, employer, supervisors and the like, and the fact that the parties are business competitors in the radio broadcast industry.

We are not unmindful of the constitutional issues implicated in this case and in our resolution thereof. In the quest for the proper accommodation between the right of redress for infliction of injury and the freedoms of speech and expression protected by the First Amendment, we have determined that the State's relatively strong interest in compensating individuals for harm outweighs the relatively weak First Amendment protection to be accorded defendants. It is elementary that not all speech or expression is to be accorded equal First Amendment protection; the most jealously protected speech is that which advances the free, uninhibited flow of ideas and opinions on matters of public interest and concern; that which is addressed to matters of private concern, or focuses upon persons who are not "public figures", is less stringently protected (see, [*Falwell*]; *Dun & Bradstreet v. Greenmoss Bldrs.*, [supra p. 310]; [*Gertz*]. Moreover, among the forms of communication, broadcasting enjoys the most limited 1st Amendment protection (see, *FCC v. Pacifica Found.*, [supra p. 149].

Why is it significant that the plaintiff worked for the defendant's competitor? Is animosity toward a competitor different in any legally relevant way from Hustler's admitted animosity for Falwell? Is the court's determination that the "Ugliest Bride" contest deserves only "weak" First Amendment protection consistent with *Falwell*?

Should the law protect some minimal level of "civility" in public discourse? See generally Paul A. LeBel, Emotional Distress, the First Amendment, and "This Kind of Speech": A Heretical Perspective on Hustler Magazine v. Falwell, 60 Colo. L. Rev. 315 (1989), and Rodney A. Smolla, Emotional Distress and the First Amendment, 20 Ariz. St. L.J. 423 (1988). The relationship between civility norms and privacy law is explored more broadly in Robert Post, The Social Foundations of Privacy: Community and Self in the Common Law Tort, 77 Cal. L. Rev. 957 (1989).

Roach v. Stern. Plaintiff gave half of the cremated remains of her sister, Debbie Tay, to defendant Hayden who had been a close friend. Tay had been a topless dancer, a cable TV host, and a frequent guest on the Howard Stern show. Hayden phoned Stern and talked on the air about Tay's death. Stern invited him to appear on the show the next day. Before the show the plaintiff complained. Nevertheless, Hayden appeared with a box containing Tay's remains. The court said that what followed was an "irreverent and rather tasteless" tribute to Tay. Stern shook and rattled the box, removed bone fragments, and speculated as to what parts of the body they were. He suggested that one guest chew on a fragment, and asked "What's it taste like?" Closing credits said that the show was dedicated to the decedent.

The court concluded that the complaint stated a cause of action for intentional infliction of emotional distress. Roach v. Stern, 252 A.D.2d 488, 675 N.Y.S.2d 133 (App. Div. 1998).

The trial court had held that although vulgar and disrespectful, the program was not beyond all bounds of decency, and therefore was not sufficiently outrageous to be actionable. The Appellate Division disagreed. "[I]n light of Stern's reputation for vulgar humor and Tay's actions during her guest appearances on his program, a jury might reasonably conclude that the manner in which Tay's remains were handled, for entertainment purposes and against the express wishes of her family, went beyond the bounds of decent behavior." A dissenter said the conduct was not extreme and outrageous "in light of who Debbie Tay was. Debbie Tay rose to fame by spinning outrageous tales of sexual encounters with female aliens on the Howard Stern show, and used the notoriety she had achieved to launch her own cable access show."

Is the source of Tay's fame relevant in determining whether the defendants' conduct was sufficiently outrageous?

Identifying crime victims, witnesses, or potential targets. What is the appropriate analytical framework for claims by witnesses or victims who say that their identification by media has subjected them to threats, or at least a risk, of physical harm? Some of these are brought as invasion of privacy claims, some as intentional infliction of emotional distress, and some as negligence cases.

In Times Mirror Co. v. Superior Court (Doe), 198 Cal. App.3d 1420, 244 Cal. Rptr. 556, 15 Med. L. Rptr. 1129 (1988), the complaint alleged that plaintiff Doe returned home at midnight to find her roommate dead on the floor. She looked up to confront a man. She then fled the apartment and called the police. The newspaper published a story that identified the plaintiff by name as having discovered the body. After several intervening paragraphs, the article stated that "one witness" had given police a description of a man seen fleeing the apartment.

Plaintiff's suit for invasion of privacy centered on the claim that the story had told the murderer the identity of the only witness in the case and had thus subjected her to an increased risk of harm. The trial court's denial of summary judgment was affirmed, 2–1. The majority rejected an "absolute" First Amendment defense for printing the name of a witness. (There was a dispute whether the name had come from an official source or from the reporter's work.) Next, the newspaper argued that the fact reported was not private because plaintiff had told some friends, neighbors, and relatives that she had discovered the body and confronted the murderer. The court responded that "[t]alking to selected individuals does not render private information public. . . . On the record before us we cannot say Doe rendered otherwise private information public by cooperating in the criminal investigation and seeking solace from friends and relatives."

Next, the defendant contended that the publication was newsworthy. The court relied on privacy cases for the proposition that community mores controlled and that jurors could find that Doe's name was not newsworthy by balancing the public benefit of knowing the name against the effect publication of her name might have on her safety and emotional well-being. The jury must also "consider the seriousness of the intrusion and the extent to which Doe voluntarily exposed herself to notoriety."

Finally, the newspaper relied on cases like *Smith v. Daily Mail*, supra p. 36, for the proposition that absent an interest of the highest order the state may not punish a defendant for publishing lawfully obtained truthful information. The court rejected the claim: "The state must investigate violent crimes and protect witnesses. Already reluctant witnesses will be more hesitant to provide information if their names will appear in the morning paper. The state's interest is particularly strong when the criminal is still at large. The state's interest is reflected in the regular police policy not to release the identity of witnesses. . . . The interest of the state to protect witnesses and to conduct criminal investigations is sufficient to overcome the Times' First Amendment right to publish Doe's name."

The dissenter contended that plaintiff "unhappily, became an involuntary public figure. As a matter of law, the publication of Doe's name was newsworthy." Nor did the mention of Doe in the story offend community notions of decency. The majority was rejecting the reactions of the reasonable person and substituting the "subjective reaction" of the plaintiff. "The reporter and the editor are now hostage to the paranoiac, the psychotic, the schizophrenic, whose reactions to publication now determine the scope to First Amendment media immunity."

When the defendant sought certiorari, *Florida Star v. B.J.F.*, supra p. 380, was already before the Court. Defendant contended that its case was also worthy of certiorari or that the state court action should be stayed until the Court decided *Florida Star*. The Court denied the stay although it had not yet decided the *Florida Star* case. The *Doe* case was settled shortly after the stay was denied. Editor & Publisher, Mar. 18, 1989, at 22. See also Hyde v. City of Columbia, 637 S.W.2d 251 (Mo.App. 1982) (relying on *Gertz* to uphold a negligence action based on an article identifying a woman who escaped from an abductor who was still at large); Sanchez Duran v. Detroit News, Inc., 200 Mich.App. 622, 504 N.W.2d 715, 21 Med. L. Rptr. 1891 (1993) (denying action to Colombian judge who had fled to the United States after death threats and whose local residence was reported by defendant papers). In *Sanchez Duran* plaintiff sought to live a low-profile but not secret life. What if the papers assert that they published the story to warn plaintiff's neighbors of the danger?

A person who actually threatens another with physical harm cannot claim the protection of the First Amendment. See NAACP v. Claiborne Hardware Co., 458 U.S. 886 (1982). What about those who transmit others' threats or make it easier for others to carry out their threats? An anti-abortion group that distributed "Wanted" posters of doctors who performed abortions and facilitated their publication on a Web site was held liable for subjecting the doctors to a risk that they would be killed by third parties. See Planned Parenthood v. American Coalition of Life Activists, 290 F.3d 1058 (9th Cir. 2002) (en banc). The 6–5 majority said because doctors who had been identified in prior posters had in fact been killed, under the circumstances the posters and Web postings amounted to "true threats" not protected by the First Amendment. The dissenters said because the defendants had not made threats themselves, their speech was fully protected.

2. NEGLIGENT INFLICTION

Liability for negligent infliction of emotional distress is still very limited and uncertain. Some courts allow recovery in certain special cases, such as negligent delivery of death messages or negligent handling of corpses. Some states permit recovery by persons who are present when close family members suffer physical injury or death from defendant's negligent conduct. Some courts have flirted with the possibility of broader recovery for negligently inflicted emotional distress, limited only by foreseeability and causation. This possibility seems to have faded, however, with decisions in several states backing away from such a broad cause of action. See, e.g., Thing v. La Chusa, 48 Cal.3d 644, 771 P.2d 814, 257 Cal. Rptr. 865 (1989).

Nonetheless, in a few cases media have been held potentially liable for negligently inflicting emotional distress.

Doe v. ABC. In Doe v. American Broadcasting Cos., 152 A.D.2d 482, 543 N.Y.S.2d 455, 16 Med. L. Rptr. 1958 (1989), two rape victims agreed to be interviewed on a television program if they were not identifiable. The station repeatedly assured them that neither their faces nor their voices would be recognizable. A Saturday night promo was aired for the Monday night program. On Monday morning the employer of one of the two told her that he and his wife had seen the promo and recognized plaintiff. On Monday night, the plaintiff's "outline, shape, and facial features were clear enough to identify her to those who knew her. Her voice was 'an absolute, instantaneous, positive identification.'" The plaintiff was called by people who recognized her. She called defendant to complain and was assured that she would be unidentifiable in future broadcasts. The next portion of the series was shown on Thursday night. Both plaintiffs "were recognizable to those who knew them and there appeared to be no attempt to disguise their voices. At one point during the broadcast the face of one of the plaintiffs was entirely visible. The plaintiffs, one of whom had never told her family of the rape, described the many comments from people who had recognized them on television and detailed the great distress which this had caused." (The facts are taken from the dissent because none appear in the majority opinion.)

The plaintiffs sued for breach of contract and for negligent and intentional infliction of emotional distress. The court held, 3–2, that the claims for intentional infliction could not proceed because defendant's actions did not amount to the "intentional, deliberate and outrageous conduct necessary." But the court held unanimously that the plaintiffs stated valid claims for breach of contract and negligent infliction of emotional distress.

In Decker v. The Princeton Packet, Inc., 116 N.J. 418, 561 A.2d 1122, 16 Med. L. Rptr. 2194 (1989), the defendant newspaper inadvertently printed an obituary announcing the death of plaintiff. The court held that although it had begun to allow recovery for emotional injury without accompanying or resulting physical injury, in negligence cases the emotional harm must be foreseeably severe. What was foreseeable here were "the subjective reactions of ordinary persons who feel victimized by the false report of death, namely, annoyance, embarrassment, and irritation." As a matter of law these were not severe enough to ground a negligence action.

Should there be some action for a negligently false obituary? Will the false light claim work? What if the plaintiff owned a business and claimed that the obituary led customers to stop frequenting the business? Recall that no cause of action lies in defamation for falsely stating that a person is dead. Should that influence the answers to these questions?

B. ECONOMIC HARM

1. BREACH OF PROMISE

Cohen v. Cowles Media Co.

Supreme Court of the United States, 1991.
501 U.S. 663, 111 S.Ct. 2513, 115 L.Ed.2d 586, 18 Med.L.Rep. 2273.

[Cohen was a public relations consultant employed in a Republican gubernatorial campaign. On condition that he not be identified as the source, he offered reporters documents (public court records) showing that the Democratic candidate for lieutenant governor had been convicted 12 years earlier of shoplifting. Reporters for two newspapers accepted the information on Cohen's terms, but their editors decided the source of the leak was part of the story and included Cohen's name over the protests of the reporters. Cohen lost his job and sued the newspapers. The Minnesota

Supreme Court held that (1) the reporters' arrangement with Cohen did not amount to a contract, (2) he might have a cause of action for breach of the promise of confidentiality on a theory of promissory estoppel, but (3) permitting such a judgment would violate the First Amendment. Cohen appealed.]

JUSTICE WHITE delivered the opinion of the Court.

. . .

Respondents rely on the proposition that "if a newspaper lawfully obtains truthful information about a matter of public significance then state officials may not constitutionally punish publication of the information, absent a need to further a state interest of the highest order." *Smith v. Daily Mail*, [supra p. 36]. That proposition is unexceptionable, and it has been applied in various cases that have found insufficient the asserted state interests in preventing publication of truthful, lawfully obtained information. See, e.g., *Florida Star v. B.J.F.*, [supra p. 380]; *Smith v. Daily Mail*, supra; *Landmark Communications*, [supra p. 32].

This case, however, is not controlled by this line of cases but, rather, by the equally well-established line of decisions holding that generally applicable laws do not offend the First Amendment simply because their enforcement against the press has incidental effects on its ability to gather and report the news. As the cases relied on by respondents recognize, the truthful information sought to be published must have been lawfully acquired. The press may not with impunity break and enter an office or dwelling to gather news. Neither does the First Amendment relieve a newspaper reporter of the obligation shared by all citizens to respond to a grand jury subpoena and answer questions relevant to a criminal investigation, even though the reporter might be required to reveal a confidential source. *Branzburg v. Hayes*, [infra p. 561]. The press, like others interested in publishing, may not publish copyrighted material without obeying the copyright laws [ ]. Similarly, the media must obey the National Labor Relations Act [ ] and the Fair Labor Standards Act [ ]; may not restrain trade in violation of the antitrust laws [ ]; and must pay non-discriminatory taxes [ ]. It is, therefore, beyond dispute that "[t]he publisher of a newspaper has no special immunity from the application of general laws. He has no special privilege to invade the rights and liberties of others." [ ] Accordingly, enforcement of such general laws against the press is not subject to stricter scrutiny than would be applied to enforcement against other persons or organizations.

There can be little doubt that the Minnesota doctrine of promissory estoppel is a law of general applicability. It does not target or single out the press. Rather, insofar as we are advised, the doctrine is generally applicable to the daily transactions of all the citizens of Minnesota. The First Amendment does not forbid its application to the press.

Justice Blackmun suggests that applying Minnesota promissory estoppel doctrine in this case will "punish" respondents for publishing truthful information that was lawfully obtained. [ ] This is not strictly accurate because compensatory damages are not a form of punishment, as were the criminal sanctions at issue in *Smith v. Daily Mail*, supra. If the contract between the parties in this case had contained a liquidated damages provision, it would be perfectly clear that the payment to petitioner would represent a cost of acquiring newsworthy material to be published at a profit, rather than a punishment imposed by the State. The payment of compensatory damages in this case is constitutionally indistinguishable from a generous bonus paid to a confidential news source. In any event, as indicated above, the characterization of the payment makes no difference for First Amendment purposes when the law being applied is a general law and does not single out the press. Moreover, Justice Blackmun's reliance on cases like *Florida Star v. B.J.F.*, supra, and *Smith v. Daily Mail* is misplaced. In those cases, the State itself defined the content of publications that would trigger liability. Here, by contrast, Minnesota law simply requires those making promises to keep them. The parties themselves, as in this case, determine the scope of their legal obligations, and any restrictions that may be placed on the publication of truthful information are self-imposed.

Also, it is not at all clear that respondents obtained Cohen's name "lawfully" in this case, at least for purposes of publishing it. Unlike the situation in *Florida Star*, where the rape victim's name was obtained through lawful access to a police report, respondents obtained Cohen's name only by making a promise that they did not honor. The dissenting opinions suggest that the press should not be subject to any law, including copyright law for example, which in any fashion or to any degree limits or restricts the press' right to report truthful information. The First Amendment does not grant the press such limitless protection.

Nor is Cohen attempting to use a promissory estoppel cause of action to avoid the strict requirements for establishing a libel or defamation claim. As the Minnesota Supreme Court observed here, "Cohen could not sue for defamation because the information disclosed [his name] was true." [ ] Cohen is not seeking damages for injury to his reputation or his state of mind. He sought damages in excess of $50,000 for breach of a promise that caused him to lose his job and lowered his earning capacity. Thus, this is not a case like *Hustler Magazine, Inc. v. Falwell*, [supra p. 417], where we held that the constitutional libel standards apply to a claim alleging that the publication of a parody was a state-law tort of intentional infliction of emotional distress.

Respondents and amici argue that permitting Cohen to maintain a cause of action for promissory estoppel will inhibit truthful reporting because news organizations will have legal incentives not to disclose a confidential source's identity even when that person's identity is itself newsworthy. Justice Souter makes a similar argument. But if this is the case, it is no more than the incidental, and constitutionally insignificant, consequence of applying to the press a generally applicable law that requires those who make certain kinds of promises to keep them. . . .

[The Court remanded to the Minnesota Supreme Court, which decided that Cohen had a valid claim for promissory estoppel and affirmed an award of $200,000.]

JUSTICE BLACKMUN, with whom JUSTICE MARSHALL and JUSTICE SOUTER join, dissenting.

. . .

Contrary to the majority, I regard our decision in *Hustler Magazine, Inc. v. Falwell*, [ ] to be precisely on point. There, we found that the use of a claim of intentional infliction of emotional distress to impose liability for the publication of a satirical critique violated the First Amendment. There was no doubt that Virginia's tort of intentional infliction of emotional distress was "a law of general applicability" unrelated to the suppression of speech. Nonetheless, a unanimous Court found that, when used to penalize the expression of opinion, the law was subject to the strictures of the First Amendment. In applying that principle, we concluded, [ ] that "public figures and public officials may not recover for the tort of intentional infliction of emotional distress by reason of publications such as the one here at issue without showing in addition that the publication contains a false statement of fact which was made with 'actual malice,' " as defined by *New York Times Co. v. Sullivan* [ ]. In so doing, we rejected the argument that Virginia's interest in protecting its citizens from emotional distress was sufficient to remove from First Amendment protection a "patently offensive" expression of opinion. [ ][3]

As in *Hustler*, the operation of Minnesota's doctrine of promissory estoppel in this case cannot be said to have a merely "incidental" burden on speech; the publication of important political speech is the claimed violation. Thus, as in *Hustler*, the law may not be enforced to punish the expression of truthful information or opinion.[4] In the instant case, it is undisputed that the publication at issue was true.

---

3. The majority attempts to distinguish *Hustler* on the ground that there the plaintiff sought damages for injury to his state of mind whereas the petitioner here sought damages "for a breach of a promise that caused him to lose his job and lowered his earning capacity." [ ] I perceive no meaningful distinction between a statute that penalizes published speech in order to protect the individual's psychological well being or reputational interest and one that exacts the same penalty in order to compensate the loss of employment or earning potential. Certainly, our decision in *Hustler* recognized no such distinction.

4. The majority argues that, unlike the criminal sanctions we considered in *Smith v. Daily Mail* [ ], the liability at issue here will not "punish" respondents in the strict sense of that word. [ ] While this may be true, we have long held that the imposition of civil liability based on protected expression constitutes "punishment" of speech for First Amendment purposes. See, e.g., Pittsburgh Press Co. v. Pittsburgh Comm'n on Human Relations, 413 U.S. 376, 386, 93 S. Ct. 2553, 2559, 37 L. Ed.2d 669 (1973) ("In the context of a libelous advertisement . . . this Court has held that the First Amendment does not shield a newspaper from *punishment* for libel when with actual malice it publishes a falsely defamatory advertisement") (emphasis added), citing *New York Times Co. v. Sullivan*, [ ]; *Gertz v. Robert Welch, Inc.*, [ ]. . . . Though they be civil, the sanctions we review in this case are no more justifiable as "a cost of acquiring newsworthy material," [ ] than were the libel damages at issue in *New York Times Co.*, a permissible cost of disseminating newsworthy material.

To the extent that truthful speech may ever be sanctioned consistent with the First Amendment, it must be in furtherance of a state interest "of the highest order." *Smith*,[ ]. Because the Minnesota Supreme Court's opinion makes clear that the State's interest in enforcing its promissory estoppel doctrine in this case was far from compelling [ ], I would affirm that court's decision.

I respectfully dissent.

[JUSTICE SOUTER also dissented, in an opinion in which JUSTICE MARSHALL, JUSTICE BLACKMUN, and JUSTICE O'CONNOR joined. He argued that "the State's interest in enforcing a newspaper's promise of confidentiality [is] insufficient to outweigh the interest in unfettered publication of the information revealed in this case. . . ."]

Notes and Questions

1. The Court's assertion that "generally applicable laws do not offend the First Amendment simply because their enforcement against the press has incidental effects on its ability to gather and report the news" could be a major retreat from the practice of looking carefully at the actual effects of innocuous-sounding restrictions on freedom of the press. But the result in *Cohen* could be explained by a much narrower principle: that the First Amendment does not protect the press from enforcement of self-imposed restrictions. Which is the more appropriate reading of the case?

2. Is the majority in *Cohen* interpreting *Falwell* as a case aimed only at preventing endruns around the constitutional law of defamation? Does the fact that Cohen was seeking damages for economic harm, namely the loss of his job, provide a basis for distinguishing his case from *Falwell*?

3. If he lost his job because of a false statement, he would have a cause of action for defamation only if he could overcome some serious constitutional obstacles. Why should he face no constitutional obstacles when he loses his job because of a true statement? Is it accurate to say that it was a broken promise, not just a true statement, that cost him his job?

4. If the state's application of its law of promissory estoppel raises no First Amendment problem because it does not "target or single out the press," how far does that principle extend? Are the media targeted or singled out by the law of defamation? Invasion of privacy? Intentional infliction of emotional distress? Negligent misrepresentation?

5. In Chapter III, we saw that government regulations may be unconstitutional, even though they do not single out the press, if they interfere with editorial autonomy (e.g., *Nelson v. McClatchy Newspapers,* supra p. 244) or burden speech unnecessarily (e.g., *Cincinnati v. Discovery Network*, supra p. 242). Are those cases reconcilable with *Cohen*?

2. NEGLIGENCE

Cohen is atypical in two respects. Most cases against media for economic harm involve loss suffered by a reader or viewer who relied on the content of a report to his or her detriment; Cohen was harmed by what was printed about him. And the harm in *Cohen* was intentionally inflicted, while in most economic harm cases the media defendant is at most negligent.

The general tort rule that one owes no duty to avoid negligently causing purely economic harm protects media along with other potential defendants. For example, when an error in the Wall Street Journal caused financial loss to a reader who traded in bonds in reliance on the Journal's information, the court held that the reader's complaint against the newspaper failed to state a cause of action. The court relied on the general tort rule that one who negligently supplies false information for use by others in business transactions is liable only to members of a limited group whose transactions the speaker intends to influence. The opinion added: "[T]he competing public policy and constitutional concerns tilt decidedly in favor of the press when mere negligence is alleged." Gutter v. Dow Jones, Inc., 22 Ohio St.3d 286, 490 N.E.2d 898, 12 Med. L. Rptr. 1999 (1986).

3.   DISPARAGEMENT

Injurious falsehood, disparagement, and trade libel are different names for very similar torts. In each, the harm is not to the reputation of a person, but to the commercial value of a product or other property. The owner of the disparaged property has a cause of action for pecuniary loss caused by a falsehood that the defendant (1) should recognize is likely to harm the value of the property, and (2) makes with reckless disregard (or knowledge) of its falsity. See Restatement (Second) of Torts § 623A. These principles typically are invoked by the manufacturer of a product against a competitor (or other person) who uses falsehoods to interfere with the sale of the product, but they may also be invoked against media. See, e.g, *Bose v. Consumers Union*, supra p. 291.

Blatty v. New York Times. Plaintiff, author of a novel, sued the newspaper for omitting his book from its best seller list. He alleged that his book had sold more copies than several of the books listed, and that the Times either knew this or negligently failed to ascertain it. He contended this amounted to disparagement of his book. The court unanimously affirmed dismissal of his suit. Blatty v. New York Times Co., 42 Cal.3d 1033, 728 P.2d 1177, 232 Cal. Rptr. 542, 13 Med. L. Rptr. 1928 (1986).

The majority relied on an analogy to the "of and concerning" requirement of defamation law. Since the plaintiff had not been named at all, the publication was not "of and concerning" him or his book. The majority thought this requirement should be applied by analogy to other torts such as injurious falsehood or disparagement. The majority suggested that without such a limit cases barred under group libel principles (see supra p. 270) might be brought on injurious falsehood grounds or disparagement instead. The "of and concerning" requirement, though it might immunize some statements that can harm an individual, is "too important to the vigor and openness of public discourse in a free society to be discouraged." The majority thought the state constitution required this result.

Three concurring justices rejected the emphasis on "of and concerning" because of the ease with which harm could be done by fraudulent omission. Nonetheless, the concurrers concluded that the allegations at most claimed negligence on the newspaper's part—and that this was insufficient for liability.

Was the alleged disparagement "of and concerning" Blatty's book? Should that be sufficient in a disparagement action? Is it significant that there might have been other books also "disparaged" by the Times's method of compiling its best seller lists? Should that preclude Blatty from recovering?

Auvil v. CBS. A trial judge rejected an argument based on the *Blatty* rationale in a case resulting from a health scare over apples. In 1989, "60 Minutes" presented a segment on the dangers of Washington State apples that had been treated with the chemical Alar. CBS quoted a report that described Alar as the "most potent" carcinogen in the nation's food supply, and said children faced the greatest risk. The program aired at the height of the apple season in Washington, and consumer reaction made it impossible for many growers to sell their crops. A number of the growers sued CBS for disparagement.

In Auvil v. CBS "60 Minutes," 836 F. Supp. 740, 21 Med. L. Rptr. 2059 (E.D.Wash. 1993), the district court said the plaintiffs' apples were sufficiently identified as a dangerous commodity, even if the growers were not named. But the judge granted CBS summary judgment on the ground that even if the statements were false, "they were about an issue that mattered, cannot be proven as false and therefore must be protected. . . . A news reporting service is not a scientific testing lab and these services should be able to rely on a scientific government report when they are relaying the report's results." The Ninth Circuit affirmed on this ground without considering the validity of the *Blatty* argument. See 67 F.3d 816, 23 Med. L. Rptr. 2454 (9th Cir. 1995).

"Veggie libel statutes." The Alar episode caused great concern among producers of perishable agricultural products, who saw it as confirmation that a consumer panic touched off by a false health scare could cause them to lose their year's revenue before the fears could be alleviated. As a result of their lobbying, at least 13 states adopted statutes to make clear that such product disparagement suits are permitted. The Florida version, for example, permits producers of perishable products to sue anyone who damages the producer by "wilfully or maliciously" disseminating "false information" that a food product is not safe for human consumption. "False information" is defined as "not based on reliable, scientific facts and reliable, scientific data which the disseminator knows or should have known to be false." Fla. Stat. Ann. § 865.065 (1995). The statutes and related information are collected on the Center for Science in the Public Interest's website: www.cspinet.org/foodspeak/.

When the so-called "veggie libel statutes" were enacted, many in the media were concerned that they would threaten aggressive reporting about health risks from food. But the statutes have generally been construed narrowly and have not become important sources of media liability. See, e.g., Texas Beef Group v. Winfrey, 201 F.3d 680, 28 Med. L. Rptr. 1481 (5th Cir. 2000) The Texas "False Disparagement of Perishable Food Products Act" allows producers of perishable food products to recover damages against a person who knowingly disseminates false information stating or implying that the product is unsafe. The Oprah Winfrey show broadcast a segment on "mad cow disease," which is believed to have killed a number of humans in Great Britain. A guest on the show asserted that there was a risk of a similar outbreak in the United States that would be worse than the AIDS syndrome. Winfrey responded by saying "I'll never eat another hamburger."

A group of cattle producers in the business of fattening cattle for slaughter filed suit, alleging that the broadcast caused a crash in the market for cattle ready for slaughter. The district judge granted Winfrey's motion for directed verdict on the ground that cattle on the hoof were not a "perishable" food product within the meaning of the statute, and also on the ground that there was no evidence that any of the defendants knew the falsity of the statements made about mad cow disease. The Fifth Circuit affirmed on the latter ground: "Stripped to its essentials, the cattlemen's complaint is that the [Winfrey] show did not present the Mad Cow issue in the light most favorable to United States beef. . . . So long as the factual underpinnings remained accurate, as they did here, the editing did not give rise to an inference that knowingly false information was being disseminated."

Most of the statutes require a showing of knowing falsity or reckless disregard of falsity. Is that constitutionally required? Most states define falsity in terms of "reasonable and reliable scientific data." Does that give insufficient protection to reporting on health concerns that are rejected by mainstream scientific thought?

For a thoughtful discussion of the role of the market in evaluating scientific expression, see Martin Redish, Product Health Claims and the First Amendment: Scientific Expression and the Twilight Zone of Commercial Speech, 43 Vand. L. Rev. 1433 (1990).

C. Physical Harm

The cases in which media cause physical harm seem quite irreconcilable. There are many variables in these cases. Sometimes a reader or viewer causes harm by a "copycat" act emulating some action portrayed by the media. Sometimes the harm is caused by children, who may or may not appreciate the danger. Sometimes the media defendant has not merely provided an example, but has directed or suggested or advocated the harmful act. These are sometimes referred to loosely as "how-to" cases. In any of these types of cases, the injury is sometimes self-inflicted and sometimes inflicted on a third person. The nature of the speech that causes the injury varies widely: it may be news, an advertisement, pornography, a movie or a television show. It may be true or false. The defendant may have advocated or even incited the harmful act, or it may have been merely negligent, or even innocent. (See, e.g., Saloomey v. Jeppesen & Co., 707 F.2d 671 (2d Cir. 1983), affirming recovery in both negligence and strict liability for erroneous aeronautical flight charts).

The courts have not developed any consistent scheme for evaluating these variables. Each of these variables seems to influence the result in one case or another, but a variable that seems important in one case may recede into the background in the next. That means that any method of organizing this section will bear scant resemblance to the approaches taken in some of the cases. We have organized it according to the theory of liability employed, and that tends to focus on the defendant's purpose, state of mind, or degree of fault. It must be noted that because the courts have not consistently employed this focus, the lines between different bases of liability are often fuzzy or inarticulate. And as the following cases indicate, there is considerable substantive disagreement as to the amount of protection speech requires in physical harm cases.

1. INCITEMENT

Herceg v. Hustler Magazine, Inc.

United States Court of Appeals, Fifth Circuit, 1987.
814 F.2d 1017, 13 Med. L. Rptr. 2345, certiorari denied, 485 U.S. 959 (1988).

Before RUBIN, JOHNSON and JONES, CIRCUIT JUDGES.

ALVIN B. RUBIN, CIRCUIT JUDGE:

An adolescent read a magazine article that prompted him to commit an act that proved fatal. The issue is whether the publisher of the magazine may be held liable for civil damages.

I.

In its August 1981 issue, as part of a series about the pleasures—and dangers—of unusual and taboo sexual practices, Hustler Magazine printed "Orgasm of Death," an article discussing the practice of autoerotic asphyxia. This practice entails masturbation while "hanging" oneself in order to temporarily cut off the blood supply to the brain at the moment of orgasm. The article included details about how the act is performed and the kind of physical pleasure those who engage in it seek to achieve. The heading identified "Orgasm of Death" as part of a series on "Sexplay," discussions of "sexual pleasures [that] have remained hidden for too long behind the doors of fear, ignorance, inexperience and hypocrisy" and are presented "to increase [readers'] sexual knowledge, to lessen [their] inhibitions and—ultimately—to make [them] much better lover[s]."

An editor's note, positioned on the page so that it is likely to be the first text the reader will read, states: "Hustler emphasizes the often-fatal dangers of the practice of 'autoerotic asphyxia,' and recommends that readers seeking unique forms of sexual release DO NOT ATTEMPT this method. The facts are presented here solely for an educational purpose."

The article begins by presenting a vivid description of the tragic results the practice may create. It describes the death of one victim and discusses research indicating that such deaths are alarmingly common: as many as 1,000 United States teenagers die in this manner each year. Although it describes the sexual "high" and "thrill" those who engage in the practice seek to achieve, the article repeatedly warns that the procedure is "neither healthy nor harmless," "it is a serious—and often fatal—mistake to believe that asphyxia can be controlled" and "beyond a doubt—. . . auto-asphyxiation is one form of sex play you try only if you're anxious to wind up in cold storage, with a coroner's tag on your big toe." The two-page article warns readers at least ten different times that the practice is dangerous, self-destructive and deadly. It states that persons who successfully perform the technique can achieve intense physical pleasure, but the attendant risk is that the person may lose consciousness and die of strangulation.

Tragically, a copy of this issue of Hustler came into the possession of Troy D., a fourteen-year-old adolescent, who read the article and attempted the practice. The next morning, Troy's nude body was found, hanging by its neck in his closet, by one of Troy's closest friends, Andy V. A copy of Hustler Magazine, opened to the article about the "Orgasm of Death," was found near his feet.

[Troy's mother and Andy V. brought this diversity case alleging incitement, negligence, products liability, dangerous instrumentality, and attractive nuisance. The trial judge dismissed all but incitement, which was the sole theory at trial. The jury found incitement and awarded each plaintiff compensatory and punitive damages. Hustler appealed from the denial of judgment n.o.v. or a new trial. Plaintiffs did not cross-appeal from dismissal of their other claims.]

II.

The constitutional protection accorded to the freedom of speech and of the press is not based on the naive belief that speech can do no harm but on the confidence that the benefits society reaps from the free flow and exchange of ideas outweigh the costs society endures by receiving reprehensible or dangerous ideas. Under our Constitution, as the Supreme Court has reminded us, "there is no such thing as a false idea. However pernicious an opinion may seem we depend for its correction not on the conscience of judges and juries but on the competition of other ideas." [*Gertz*] We rely on a reverse Gresham's law, trusting to good ideas to drive out bad ones and forbidding governmental intervention into the free market of ideas. One of our basic constitutional tenets, therefore, forbids the state to punish protected speech, directly or indirectly, whether by criminal penalty or civil liability.

The Supreme Court has recognized that some types of speech are excluded from, or entitled only to narrowed constitutional protection. Freedom of speech does not protect obscene materials, child pornography, fighting words, incitement to imminent lawless activity, and purposefully-made or recklessly-made false statements of fact such as libel, defamation, or fraud. Whatever the problems created in attempting to categorize speech in such fashion, the Hustler article fits none of them.

Even types of speech protected generally by the first amendment may be subject to government regulation. Freedom of speech is not an absolute. If the state interest is compelling and the means of regulation narrowly tailored to accomplish a proper state purpose, regulation of expression is not forbidden by the first amendment. The extent of the danger created by a publication therefore is not immaterial in determining the state's power to penalize that publication for harm that ensues, but first amendment protection is not eliminated simply because publication of an idea creates a potential hazard. Whether the Hustler article, therefore, placed a dangerous idea into Troy's head is but one factor in determining whether the state may impose damages for that consequence. Against the important social goal of protecting the lives of adolescents like Troy, the Constitution requires us to balance more than Hustler's right to publish the particular article, subject to the possibility of civil liability should harm ensue, but also the danger that unclear or diminished standards of first amendment protection may both inhibit the expression of protected ideas by other speakers and constrict the right of the public to receive those ideas.

[The court emphasized that the only question before the court was the applicability of the incitement theory on these facts.]

III.

Appellate review of jury findings in cases implicating first amendment rights must remain faithful both to the substantial evidence standard set forth in Rule 52(a) and the constitutional obligation of appellate courts "to 'make an independent examination of the whole record' in order to make sure 'that the judgment does not constitute a forbidden intrusion on the field of free expression.' " [*Bose*] Although we must accept the jury's fact findings if they are fairly supported by the record, that requirement "does not inhibit an appellate court's power to correct errors of law, including those that may infect a so-called mixed finding of law and fact, or a finding of fact that is predicated on a misunderstanding of the governing rule of law."

The text of the Hustler article provides the best basis for deciding whether the article may be held to have incited Troy's behavior. The jury was also entitled to consider evidence concerning whether Troy read the article immediately prior to attempting the autoerotic asphyxiation procedure, the psychiatric testimony about the likely effect such an article would have on normal adolescent readers, and the evidence about the probable state of his mind at the time he entered upon the experiment that resulted in his death. Although the jury was not asked to answer special interrogatories establishing what evidence they credited or discredited, it is apparent from the verdict that the jurors believed the testimony leading to the conclusion that Troy had read the article immediately before he entered in the acts that proved fatal and that his reaction to the article was not the result of any clinical psychological abnormality. Because these conclusions are adequately supported by evidence in the record, we accept them as true.

[The court stated that *Bose* also applied to the "jury's mixed finding of fact and law that the article culpably incited Troy's behavior."]

Although we are doubtful that a magazine article that is no more direct than "Orgasm of Death" can ever constitute an incitement in the sense in which the Supreme Court—in cases we discuss below—has employed that term to identify unprotected speech the states may punish without violating the first amendment, we first analyze the evidence on the theory that it might satisfy doctrinal tests relating to incitement, for that was the theory under which the case was tried and submitted. Substituting our judgment for the jury's, as we must, we hold that liability cannot be imposed on Hustler on the basis that the article was an incitement to attempt a potentially fatal act without impermissibly infringing upon freedom of speech.

[The court reviewed the *Brandenburg* discussion of incitement, supra p. 561, concluding that plaintiff would have to prove (1) Autoerotic asphyxiation is a lawless act; (2) Hustler advocated this act; (3) Hustler's publication went even beyond "mere advocacy" and amounted to incitement; (4) the incitement was directed to imminent action. The court also noted that in Hess v. Indiana, 414 U.S. 105 (1973), the Supreme Court emphasized that the "lawless action" had to be "imminent."]

We need not decide whether Texas law made autoerotic asphyxiation illegal or whether *Brandenburg* is restricted to the advocacy of criminal conduct. Even if the article paints in glowing terms the pleasures supposedly achieved by the practice it describes, as the plaintiffs contend, no fair reading of it can make its content advocacy, let alone incitement to engage in the practice.

Herceg and Andy V. complain that the article provides unnecessary detail about how autoerotic asphyxiation is accomplished. The detail is adapted from an article published by a psychiatrist in the Journal of Child Psychiatry. Although it is conceivable that, in some instances, the amount of detail contained in challenged speech may be relevant in determining whether incitement exists, the detail in "Orgasm of Death" is not enough to permit breach of the first amendment. The manner of engaging in autoerotic asphyxiation apparently is not complicated. To understand what the term means is to know roughly how to accomplish it. Furthermore, the article is laden with detail about all facets of the practice, including the physiology of how it produces a threat to life and the seriousness of the danger of harm.

Under *Brandenburg*, therefore, the article was entitled to first amendment protection. But the parties' and, apparently, the district court's effort to apply the Brandenburg analysis to the type of "incitement" with which Hustler was charged appears inappropriate. Incitement cases usually concern a state effort to punish the arousal of a crowd to commit a criminal action. The root of incitement theory appears to have been grounded in concern over crowd behavior. As John Stuart Mill stated in his dissertation, On Liberty, "An opinion that corn-dealers are starvers of the poor, or that private property is robbery ought to be unmolested when simply circulated through the press, but may justly incur punishment when delivered orally to an excited mob assembled before the house of a corn-dealer." In Noto v. United States [367 U.S. 290 (1961)], the Supreme Court expressed similar views about incitement: "the mere abstract teaching . . . of the moral propriety or even moral necessity for a resort to force and violence, is not the same as preparing a group for violent action and steering it to such action." Whether written material might ever be found to create culpable incitement unprotected by the first amendment is, however, a question that we do not now reach.

IV.

[The court, relying on the language from *Sullivan* about the potential impact of civil damages, rejected a purported distinction between civil and criminal liability. If the state could not punish Hustler criminally it could not permit the award of damages against it.]

V.

In the alternative, Herceg and Andy suggest that a less stringent standard than the Brandenburg test be applied in cases involving non-political speech that has actually produced harm. Although political speech is at "the core of the First Amendment," [N.A.A.C.P. v. Claiborne Hardware Co., 458 U.S. 886, 926–27 (1982)], the Supreme Court generally has not attempted to differentiate between different categories of protected speech for the purposes of deciding how much constitutional protection is required. Such an endeavor would not only be hopelessly complicated but would raise substantial concern that the worthiness of speech might be judged by majoritarian notions of political and social propriety and morality. If the shield of the first amendment can be eliminated by proving after publication that an article discussing a dangerous idea negligently helped bring about a real injury simply because the idea can be identified as "bad," all free speech becomes threatened. An article discussing the nature and danger of "crack" usage—or of hang-gliding—might lead to liability just as easily. As is made clear in the Supreme Court's decision in Hess, the "tendency to lead to violence" is not enough. Mere negligence, therefore, cannot form the basis of liability under the incitement doctrine any more than it can under libel doctrine.[38]

VI.

Finally, even if this court were to determine that the plaintiffs may establish a cause of action under a theory of negligence, that theory could not form the basis of affirming the decision below [because the plaintiffs

---

38. Accord, Walt Disney Productions, Inc. v. Shannon, 247 Ga. 402, 276 S.E.2d 580 (1981).

tried the case solely on an incitement theory after defendant won summary judgment on the various other claims].

. . .

For the reasons stated above, the judgment of the district court is reversed.

Edith H. Jones, Circuit Judge, concurring and dissenting:

I concur in the result in this case only because I am persuaded that plaintiffs had an obligation to cross-appeal the court's dismissal of their claims based on negligence, attractive nuisance, and strict liability or dangerous instrumentality. . . .

What disturbs me to the point of despair is the majority's broad reasoning which appears to foreclose the possibility that any state might choose to temper the excesses of the pornography business by imposing civil liability for harms it directly causes. Consonant with the first amendment, the state can protect its citizens against the moral evil of obscenity, the threat of civil disorder or injury posed by lawless mobs and fighting words, and the damage to reputation from libel or defamation, to say nothing of the myriad dangers lurking in "commercial speech." Why cannot the state then fashion a remedy to protect its children's lives when they are endangered by suicidal pornography? To deny this possibility, I believe, is to degrade the free market of ideas to a level with the black market for heroin. Despite the grand flourishes of rhetoric in many first amendment decisions concerning the sanctity of "dangerous" ideas, no federal court has held that death is a legitimate price to pay for freedom of speech.

In less emotional terms, I believe the majority has critically erred in its analysis of this case under existing first amendment law. . . . I agree that "Orgasm of Death" does not conveniently match the current categories of speech defined for first amendment purposes. Limiting its constitutional protection does not, however, disserve any of these categories and is more appropriate to furthering the "majoritarian" notion of protecting the sanctity of human life. Finally, the "slippery slope" argument that if Hustler is held liable here, Ladies Home Journal or the publisher of an article on hang-gliding will next be a casualty of philistine justice simply proves too much: This case is not a difficult one in which to vindicate Troy's loss of life.

I.

Proper analysis must begin with an examination of Hustler generally and this article in particular. Hustler is not a bona fide competitor in the "marketplace of ideas." It is largely pornographic, whether or not technically obscene. One need not be male to recognize that the principal function of this magazine is to create sexual arousal. Consumers of this material so partake for its known physical effects much as they would use tobacco, alcohol or drugs for their effects. By definition, pornography's appeal is therefore non-cognitive and unrelated to, in fact exactly the opposite of, the transmission of ideas.

Not only is Hustler's appeal non-cognitive, but the magazine derives its profit from that fact. If Hustler stopped being pornographic, its readership would vanish.

According to the trial court record, pornography appeals to pubescent males. Moreover, although sold in the "adults only" section of newsstands, a significant portion of its readers are adolescent. Hustler knows this. Such readers are particularly vulnerable to thrill-seeking, recklessness, and mimicry. Hustler should know this. Hustler should understand that to such a mentality the warnings "no" or "caution" may be treated as invitations rather than taboos.

"Orgasm of Death" provides a detailed description how to accomplish autoerotic asphyxiation. The article appears in the "Sexplay" section of the magazine which, among other things, purports to advise its readers on "how to make you a much better lover." The warnings and cautionary comments in the article could be seen by a jury to conflict with both the explicit and subliminal message of Hustler, which is to tear down custom, explode myths and banish taboos about sexual matters. The article trades on the symbiotic connection between sex and violence. In sum, as Hustler knew, the article is dangerously explicit, lethal, and likely to be distributed to those members of society who are most vulnerable to its message. "Orgasm of Death," in the circumstances of its publication and dissemination, is not unlike a dangerous nuisance or a stick of dynamite in the hands of a child. Hustler's publication of this particular article bears the seeds of tort liability although, as I shall explain, the theory on which the case was tried is incorrect.

II.

First Amendment analysis is an exercise in line-drawing between the legitimate interests of society to regulate itself and the paramount necessity of encouraging the robust and uninhibited flow of debate which is the life-blood of government by the people. That some of the lines are blurred or irregular does not, however, prove the majority's proposition that it would be hopelessly complicated to delineate between protected and unprotected speech in this case. Such a formulation in fact begs the critical question in two ways. First, a hierarchy of first amendment speech classifications has in fact developed largely in the last few years, and there is no reason to assume the hierarchy is ineluctable. Second, the essence of the judicial function is to judge. If it is impossible to judge, there is no reason for judges to pretend to perform their role, and it is a non sequitur for them to conclude that society's or a state's judgment is "wrong." Hence, in novel cases like this one, the reasons for protecting speech under the first amendment must be closely examined to properly evaluate Hustler's claim to unlimited constitutional protection.

[Judge Jones cited the *Greenmoss* case as an example of one in which negligence was used to ground a damage recovery after the Court "evaluated the interest sought to be protected by the state against the level of first amendment interest embodied in the communication at issue."]

. . .

. . . Because of the solely commercial and pandering nature of the magazine neither Hustler nor any other pornographic publication is likely to be deterred by incidental state regulation. No sensitive first amendment genius is required to see that, as the Court concluded in *Dun & Bradstreet*, "[t]here is simply no credible argument that this type of [speech] requires special protection to insure that 'debate on public issues [will] be uninhibited, robust, and wide-open.' " [ ]

To place Hustler effectively on a par with *Dun & Bradstreet*'s "private speech" or with commercial speech, for purposes of permitting tort lawsuits against it hardly portends the end of participatory democracy, as some might contend. First, any given issue of Hustler may be found legally obscene and therefore entitled to no first amendment protection. Second, tort liability would result after-the-fact, not as a prior restraint, and would be based on harm directly caused by the publication in issue. [ ] Third, to the extent any chilling effect existed from the exposure to tort liability this would, in my view, protect society from loss of life and limb, a legitimate, indeed compelling, state interest. Fourth, obscenity has been widely regulated by prior restraints for over a century. Before Roth v. United States, 354 U.S. 476 (1957), there was no Hustler magazine and it would probably have been banned. Despite such regulation, it does not appear that the pre-*Roth* era was a political dark age. Conversely, increasing leniency on pornography in the past three decades has allowed pornography to flourish, but it does not seem to have corresponded with an increased quality of debate on "public" issues. These observations imply that pornography bears little connection to the core values of the first amendment and that political democracy has endured previously in the face of "majoritarian notions of social propriety."

. . .

The foregoing analysis immediately differentiates this case from *Brandenburg v. Ohio*, which addressed prior restraints on public advocacy of controversial political ideas. Placing Hustler on the same analytical plane with *Brandenburg* represents an unwarranted extension of that holding, which, unlike *Dun & Bradstreet* and the commercial speech cases, rests in the core values protected by the first amendment. Even *Brandenburg*, however, recognized that the state's regulatory interest legitimately extends to protecting the lives of its citizens from violence induced by speech. . . .

III.

Texas courts have never been called upon to assess a claim like this one. Since there is no cross-appeal, we should not speculate on the precise nature of the theory of liability a Texas court might accept, although negligence and attractive nuisance seem theoretically appropriate. [Citing *Weirum v. RKO General*, discussed infra].

. . .

Notes and Questions

1. What does the majority find wrong with the plaintiffs' reliance on an incitement theory? What does Judge Jones find wrong with it?

2. Is there a difference between (a) a pure news story about someone being killed by attempting autoerotic asphyxia, (b) a story that tells about the practice and suggests that it is erotically satisfying though very dangerous, and (c) an article that explicitly discusses the benefits and accurately conveys the dangers of the practice, and then instructs readers step-by-step on how to do it if they should wish to try it?

Might the idea of "unnecessary detail" apply to a news article that detailed how a plane hijacker avoided airport security? What if the article had appeared in Hustler? Recall Judge Jones's statement that Hustler "is not a bona fide competitor in the 'marketplace of ideas.' "

3. Is the nature of the publication relevant or only the nature of the article? What if Hustler had reproduced an article from the Journal of Child Psychiatry and added warnings against emulation? What if the issue of the Journal with the article (with no admonitions against emulation) had found its way into the hands of a psychiatrist's child who died as did Troy?

———

The Weirum case. A Los Angeles rock radio station with a predominantly teenage audience ran a contest involving a roaming disc jockey. The station announced the disc jockey's location on air and gave money to the listener who was the first to arrive at that location. In an effort to be first, a listener forced another car off the road, killing the elderly driver. The court noted that the jury could have found that the station was trying to "generate a competitive pursuit on public streets, accelerated by repeated importuning by radio to be the very first to arrive at a particular destination" and win the money. A wrongful death judgment against the station was upheld on appeal. Weirum v. RKO, 15 Cal.3d 40, 539 P.2d 36, 123 Cal. Rptr. 468 (1975).

The majority in *Herceg* distinguished *Weirum* by noting that the speech there "was merely a promotional device to encourage listeners to continue listening to the radio station," entitled to only limited protection as commercial speech. Moreover, the station had "included light-hearted warnings to listeners 'to get your kids out of the street' because of the reckless driving that the announcement might incite, and no warning of any kind was given to urge listeners who sought to win the prizes to use discretion in driving."

See David A. Anderson, Tortious Speech, 47 Wash. & Lee L. Rev. 71 (1990), arguing that "If the incitement standard can ever permit liability for tortious speech causing physical injury, it should be satisfied by defendants' exhorting a teenage audience to engage in reckless driving that the station knew would be dangerous to others." The article argues that courts should not require, as the *Herceg* majority did, that the act causing injury be a "lawless" one: showing that "the act was foreseeably dangerous should be enough; if the incitement test, which was developed to deal with criminal speech, is to be applied to tortious speech, it should at least be adapted to the new setting."

Copycat cases. In some cases the media are alleged to have urged, instructed, or stimulated someone to cause physical harm. In others the allegation is merely that the media depicted something that the actor emulated. The latter are sometimes called "copycat" cases. Was *Herceg* such a case? Even if it was not, does its reasoning preclude liability in copycat cases generally?

An early and influential copycat case was Olivia N. v. National Broadcasting Co., 126 Cal. App.3d 488, 178 Cal. Rptr. 888, 7 Med. L. Rptr. 2359 (1981), involving a made-for-television film presented nationally by the network at 8 p.m. The subject "was the harmful effect of a state-run home upon an adolescent girl who had become a ward of the state." In one scene the girl is attacked in the shower by a group of girls, one of whom is waving a plumber's helper "suggestively by her side." The film strongly suggests, though does not explicitly show, that the implement was used to rape the girl. A few days later, some juveniles who had seen the movie raped plaintiff with a soda bottle.

The court upheld a non-suit entered after plaintiff's opening statement when it became clear that plaintiff would rely on a negligence theory and not try to prove "incitement." This standard was necessary because the speech did not fall into any unprotected category and did not "advocate or encourage violent acts." Plaintiff's efforts to distinguish fiction from (implicitly more valuable or protected) "news programs and documentaries" failed because the distinction "was too blurred to protect adequately First Amendment values." The court quoted Winters v. New York, 333 U.S. 507 (1948): "Everyone is familiar with instances of propaganda through fiction. What is one man's amusement, teaches another's doctrine." If news and fiction could not be separated, and if a negligence theory were used, "a television network or local station could be liable when a child imitates activities portrayed in a news program or documentary." The court thought *Gertz v. Robert Welch, Inc.*, supra p. 296, was limited to defamation and did not justify the use of negligence in other areas of tort law.

The *Olivia N.* court, forced to confront the *Weirum* case decided by its supreme court, said that although *Weirum* had used "broad" language (including a statement that the First Amendment "does not sanction the infliction of physical injury merely because achieved by word, rather than act"), the case had to be read in light of the fact that the defendant there had "actively and repeatedly encouraged listeners to speed to announced locations." No such urging was found in *Olivia N.*

Inability to show incitement defeated the wrongful death action brought by parents of a 15–year–old girl who was kidnapped, tortured, raped, and murdered by three young men who allegedly said they were emulating acts described in the lyrics of the musical group "Slayer." The court said the group and the producers and distributors of its music could not be held liable because the lyrics were not specifically intended to bring about the imminent ritual murder of a young woman. See Pahler v. Slayer, 2001 WL 1736476, 29 Med. L. Rptr. 2627 (Cal. Super. 2001).

It is often difficult to tell whether a program merely inspires emulation, or does something more. Consider DeFilippo v. National Broadcasting Co., Inc., 446 A.2d 1036, 8 Med. L. Rptr. 1872 (R.I. 1982), in which plaintiff's 13–year–old son was watching the Tonight Show with Johnny Carson and his guest, a professional stuntman named Robinson. Carson announced that after the commercial break he would attempt a stunt that involved dropping through a trapdoor with a noose around his neck. Robinson then said "Believe me, it's not something that you want to go and try. This is a stunt. . . ." The audience began to laugh, producing the following dialogue:

Robinson: I've got to laugh—you know, you're all laughing. . . .

Carson: Explain that to me.

Robinson: I've seen people try things like this. I really have. I happen to know somebody who did something similar to it, just fooling around, and almost broke his neck. . . .

The commercial break followed. After the break, Carson did the stunt accompanied by comic dialogue. Carson came through unscathed. Several hours after the broadcast, plaintiffs' son was found hanging from a noose in front of the television set which was still on and tuned to the station that had presented the Tonight Show.

The plaintiffs asserted a variety of theories, all of which were rejected. The only theory that would permit liability was incitement and it failed because the son was apparently the only person alleged to have "emulated the action portrayed" on the show. Moreover, the quoted dialogue indicated that those on the show tried to prevent emulation—and certainly did not invite it. To permit recovery here "on the basis of one minor's action would invariably lead to self-censorship by broadcasters in order to remove any matter that may be emulated and lead to a law suit."

Which case is stronger on its facts for the plaintiff—*Herceg* or *DeFilippo*? In her opinion in *Herceg*, Judge Jones observed that *DeFilippo* and *Olivia N.* used "first amendment analysis with which I differ." Was *Herceg* a how-to-do-it case?

Pornography. One of the reasons courts refuse to permit the suppression of pornography may be doubt as to the nature and extent of the harm it causes. In cases where pornography can be shown to have caused physical harm, should courts be less protective of pornography? Recall that the dissenter in *Herceg* asserted that the content of the speech should be considered in these cases. Why did the majority disagree? Recall also that the Supreme Court has upheld legislation barring the promotion of sexual performances by a child or the distribution of material depicting such performances even if the speech is not obscene or actionably indecent. See *New York v. Ferber*, supra p. 148.

In American Booksellers Ass'n. v. Hudnut, 771 F.2d 323, 11 Med. L. Rptr. 2465 (7th Cir. 1985), aff'd without opinion 475 U.S. 1001 (1986), the court overturned an Indianapolis ordinance seeking to bar speech that presents women as sexual objects or in positions of sexual subordination. The court rejected the city's argument that pornography, like obscenity, is low-value speech that can be regulated without infringing important First Amendment values:

> True, pornography and obscenity have sex in common. But Indianapolis left out of its definition any reference to literary, artistic, political, or scientific value. The ordinance applies to graphic sexually explicit subordination in works great and small. The Court sometimes balances the value of speech against the costs of its restriction, but it does this by category of speech and not by the content of particular works. [ ] Indianapolis has created an approved point of view and so loses the support of these cases.

But the court said a section of the ordinance creating civil remedies for injuries and assaults attributable to pornography, although not severable, appeared "salvageable in principle" should the city choose to revise the ordinance. After discussing remedies in libel law, the court stated that "if immediately after the Klan's rally in *Brandenburg*, a mob had burned to the ground the house of a nearby black person, that person could have recovered damages from the speaker who whipped the crowd into a frenzy." But:

> A law awarding damages for assaults caused by speech also has the power to muzzle the press, and again courts would place careful limits on the scope of the right. Certainly no damages could be awarded unless the harm flowed directly from the speech and there was an element of intent on the part of the speaker, as in *Sullivan* and *Brandenburg*.
>
>   . . . Unless the [civil] remedy is very closely confined, it could be more dangerous to speech than all the libel judgments in history. The constitutional requirement for a valid recovery for assault caused by speech might turn out to be too rigorous for any plaintiff to meet. But the Indianapolis ordinance requires the complainant to show that the attack was 'directly caused by specific pornography' [ ], and it is not beyond the realm of possibility that a state court could construe this limitation in a way that would make the statute constitutional.

Would the article in *Herceg* be actionable under the *Hudnut* approach? See generally Marianne Wesson, Girls Should Bring Lawsuits Everywhere . . . Nothing Will Be Corrupted: Pornography as Speech and Product, 60 U. Chi. L. Rev. 845 (1993); Note, Pornographer Liability for Physical Harms Caused by Obscenity and Child Pornography: A Tort Analysis, 27 Ga. L. Rev. 789 (1993).

2. AIDING AND ABETTING

Rice v. Paladin Enterprises, Inc.

United States Court of Appeals, Fourth Circuit, 1997.
128 F.3d 233, 25 Med. L. Rptr. 2441, certiorari denied 523 U.S. 1074 (1998).

Before WILKINS, LUTTIG, AND WILLIAMS, Circuit Judges.

LUTTIG, Circuit Judge:

[Plaintiffs brought wrongful death and survival actions claiming that James Perry bought two books by mail order from defendant publisher: "Hit Man: A Technical Manual for Independent Contractors" and "How to Make a Disposable Silencer"; that Perry read both books and, one year later, followed them in many respects when he killed three people. Perry was hired by a man to kill the man's ex-wife, his eight-year-old quadriplegic son, and the son's nurse so the man could collect $2 million that the son had received as a settlement for his injuries. The case was in federal court on diversity grounds. Defendant moved for summary judgment, which the district court granted. The court of appeals began its opinion with some four pages of quotations from the book. In those, the author argues that "the professional hit man fills a need in society" and assures readers that "if my advice and the proven methods in this book are followed, certainly no one will ever know." The book gives detailed instructions about how to obtain assignments and arrange payments, and how to prepare for, execute, and cover up a murder. It assures readers that they will not be troubled by what they have done: "By the time you collect the balance of your contract fee, the doubts and fears of discovery have faded. Those feelings have been replaced by cockiness, a feeling of superiority, a new independence and self-assurance."]

[After reviewing the stipulated facts in detail, the court concluded that "In soliciting, preparing for, and committing these murders, Perry meticulously followed countless of Hit Man's 130 pages of detailed factual instructions on how to murder and to become a professional killer." The opinion is severely truncated here; only a reading of the full 34–page opinion can convey the depth of the court's antipathy toward Paladin's position.]

For reasons that are here of no concern to the court, Paladin has stipulated to a set of facts which establish as a matter of law that the publisher is civilly liable for aiding and abetting James Perry in his triple murder, unless the First Amendment absolutely bars the imposition of liability upon a publisher for assisting in the commission of criminal acts. As the parties stipulate: "The parties agree that the sole issue to be decided by the Court . . . is whether the First Amendment is a complete defense, as a matter of law, to the civil action set forth in the plaintiffs' Complaint. . . ."

Paladin, for example, has stipulated for purposes of summary judgment that Perry followed the above-enumerated instructions from Hit Man, as well as instructions from another Paladin publication, "How to Make a Disposable Silencer, Vol. II" in planning executing, and covering up the murders. . . . Paladin has stipulated not only that, in marketing Hit Man, Paladin "intended to attract and assist criminals and would-be criminals who desire information and instructions on how to commit crimes," [ ], but also that it "intended and had knowledge" that Hit Man actually "would be used, upon receipt, by criminals and would-be criminals to plan and execute the crime of murder for hire." [ ]. Indeed, the publisher has even stipulated that, through publishing and selling Hit Man, it assisted Perry in particular in the perpetration of the very murders for which the victims' families now attempt to hold Paladin civilly liable. [ ]

[These stipulations were made for purposes of the summary judgment motion only and Paladin reserved the right to contest at trial all of the facts stipulated to here. Apparently the defendant's objective was to obtain an early decision that the First Amendment protected the book without submitting to extensive discovery as to the publisher's intentions or knowledge.]

Because long-established caselaw provides that speech—even speech by the press—that constitutes criminal aiding and abetting does not enjoy the protection of the First Amendment, and because we are convinced that such caselaw is both correct and equally applicable to speech that constitutes civil aiding and abetting of criminal conduct (at least where, as here, the defendant has the specific purpose of assisting and encouraging commission of such conduct and the alleged assistance and encouragement takes a form other than abstract advocacy), we hold, as urged by the Attorney General and the Department of Justice, that the First Amendment does not pose a bar to a finding that Paladin is civilly liable as an aider and abetter of Perry's triple contract murder. We also hold that the plaintiffs have stated against Paladin a civil aiding and abetting claim under Maryland law sufficient to withstand Paladin's motion for summary judgment. For these reasons, which we fully explain below, the district court's grant of summary judgment in Paladin's favor is reversed and the case is remanded for trial.

II.

A.

. . .

[E]very court that has addressed the issue, including this court, has held that the First Amendment does not necessarily pose a bar to liability for aiding and abetting a crime, even when such aiding and abetting takes the form of the spoken or written word.

[The court reviewed a line of cases sustaining convictions of tax protesters for aiding and abetting tax evasion even though the defendants were motivated by a political belief that the federal income tax is unconstitutional.]

Indeed, as the Department of Justice recently advised Congress, the law is now well established that the First Amendment, and *Brandenburg*'s "imminence" requirement in particular, generally poses little obstacle to the punishment of speech that constitutes criminal aiding and abetting, because "culpability in such cases is premised, not on defendants' 'advocacy' of criminal conduct, but on defendants' successful efforts to assist others by detailing to them the means of accomplishing the crimes." [ ] And, while there is considerably less authority on the subject, we assume that those speech acts which the government may criminally prosecute with little or no concern for the First Amendment, the government may likewise subject to civil penalty or make subject to private causes of action. Compare *Garrison v. Louisiana* [supra p. 283] (applying the same "actual malice" standard to both criminal libel prosecutions and private defamation actions) with *New York Times v. Sullivan* [supra p. 272]. . . .

[The court acknowledged that the constitution might limit the state's power to impose liability for aiding and abetting in two ways. First, speech that in itself does not deserve protection is sometimes protected to prevent chilling valuable speech (citing *New York Times v. Sullivan*). But the court said this "poses no bar to the imposition of civil (or criminal) liability for speech acts which the plaintiff (or prosecution) can establish with specific, if not criminal, intent." Second, the states' power to impose liability for aiding and abetting might be limited to protect speech that amounted to "mere advocacy," but the court said Hit Man was far more.]

Here, it is alleged, and a jury could reasonably find [ ], that Paladin aided and abetted the murders at issue through the quintessential speech act of providing step-by-step instructions for murder (replete with photographs, diagrams, and narration) so comprehensive and detailed that it is as if the instructor were literally present with the would-be murderer not only in the preparation and planning, but in the actual commission of, and follow-up to, the murder; there is not even a hint that the aid was provided in the form of speech that might constitute abstract advocacy. As the district court itself concluded, Hit Man "merely teaches what must be done to implement a professional hit." [ ] Moreover, although we do not believe such would be necessary, we are satisfied a jury could readily find that the provided instructions not only have no, or virtually no, non-instructional communicative value, but also that their only instructional communicative "value" is the indisputably illegitimate one of training persons how to murder and to engage in the business of murder for hire. [The court quoted the district judge: "This Court, quite candidly, personally finds Hit Man to be reprehensible and devoid of any significant redeeming social value"].

Aid and assistance in the form of this kind of speech bears no resemblance to the "theoretical advocacy," [ ], the advocacy of "principles divorced from action," [ ], the "doctrinal justification," [ ] "the mere abstract teaching [of] the moral propriety or even moral necessity for a resort to force and violence," [ ], or any of the other forms of discourse critical of government, its policies, and its leaders, which have always animated, and to this day continue to animate, the First Amendment. Indeed, this detailed, focused instructional assistance to those contemplating or in the throes of planning murder is the antithesis of speech protected under *Brandenburg*. It is the teaching of the "techniques" of violence, [ ], the "advocacy and teaching of concrete action," [ ], the "prepar[ation] . . . for violent action and [the] steeling . . . to such action," [ ]. It is the instruction in the methods of terror of which Justice Douglas spoke in *Dennis v. United States*, when he said, "If this were a case where those who claimed protection under the First Amendment were teaching the techniques of sabotage . . . I would have no doubts. The freedom to speak is not absolute; the teaching of methods of terror . . . should be beyond the pale. . . ." 341 U.S. 494, 581 (1951) (Douglas, J., dissenting). As such, the murder instructions in Hit Man are, collectively, a textbook example of the type of speech that the Supreme Court has quite purposely left unprotected, and the prosecution of which, criminally or civilly, has historically been thought subject to few, if any, First Amendment constraints. Accordingly, we hold that the First Amendment does not pose a bar to the plaintiffs' civil aiding and abetting cause of action against Paladin Press. If, as precedent uniformly confirms, the states have the power to regulate speech that aids and abets crime, then certainly they have the power to regulate the speech at issue here.

III.

A.

[After reviewing Maryland cases, the court concluded, contrary to the holding of the district judge, that the state recognizes a civil action for aiding and abetting.]

Especially in light of the case law discussed above, we are satisfied not only that the Maryland courts would conclude that an aiding and abetting cause of action would lie in the circumstances of this case, but also that plaintiffs have, by way of stipulation and otherwise, established a genuine issue of material fact as to each element of that cause of action . . . even assuming that the First Amendment erects a heightened standard from that required under Maryland state law.

Even without these express stipulations of assistance, however, a reasonable jury could conclude that Paladin assisted Perry in those murders, from the facts that Perry purchased and possessed Hit Man and that the methods and tactics he employed in his murders . . . so closely paralleled those prescribed in the book. . . . Without repeating these in detail here, Perry faithfully followed the book's instructions in making a home-made silencer, using a rental car with stolen out-of-state tags, murdering the victims in their own home, using an AR–7 rifle to shoot the victims in the eyes from point blank range, and concealing his involvement in the murders. The number and extent of these parallels to the instructions in Hit Man cannot be consigned, as a matter of law, to mere coincidence; the correspondence of techniques at least creates a jury issue as to whether the book provided substantial assistance, if it does not conclusively establish such assistance.

A jury likewise could reasonably find that Perry was encouraged in his murderous acts by Paladin's book. Hit Man does not merely detail how to commit murder and murder for hire; through powerful prose in the second person and imperative voice, it encourages its readers in their specific acts of murder. . . .

Furthermore, even if the stipulation only established knowledge, summary judgment was yet inappropriate because a trier of fact could still conclude that Paladin acted with the requisite intent to support civil liability. Wholly apart from Paladin's stipulations, there are four bases upon which, collectively, if perhaps not individually, a reasonable jury could find that Paladin possessed the intent required under Maryland law, as well as the intent required under any heightened First Amendment standard. [ ]

[The four bases were as follows: (1) the jury could conclude from statements in the book itself that the publisher intended to assist in the achievement of criminal purposes; (2) the book's overt promotion of murder "is more than sufficient to crate a triable issue of fact as to Paladin's intent in publishing and selling the manual." (3) the publisher's promotional material would permit a jury to conclude that "Paladin marketed Hit Man directly and even primarily to murderers and would-be criminals; and (4) intent to aid and abet murder could be inferred because 'Hit Man's only genuine use is the unlawful one of facilitating such murders." The court said a jury would not be unreasonable in dismissing, and might be unreasonable in accepting, Paladin's suggestions that Hit Man had value as entertainment or as information for law enforcement personnel.]

. . .

B.

Any argument that Hit Man is abstract advocacy entitling the book, and therefore Paladin, to heightened First Amendment protection under *Brandenburg* is, on its face, untenable. Although the district court erred in its alternative conclusion that the speech of Hit Man is protected advocacy, [ ], even that court expressly found that "the book merely teaches what must be done to implement a professional hit." [ ] Indeed, Paladin's protests notwithstanding, this book constitutes the archetypal example of speech which, because it methodically and comprehensively prepares and steels its audience to specific criminal conduct through exhaustively detailed instructions on the planning, commission, and concealment of criminal conduct, finds no preserve in the First Amendment. To the extent that confirmation of this is even needed, given the book's content and declared purpose to be "an instruction book on murder," [ ], that confirmation is found in the stark contrast between this assassination manual and the speech heretofore held to be deserving of constitutional protection.

. . .

. . . Hit Man is, pure and simple, a step-by-step murder manual, a training book for assassins. There is nothing even arguably tentative or recondite in the book's promotion of, and instruction in, murder.[3] To the contrary, the book directly and unmistakably urges concrete violations of the laws against murder and murder for hire and coldly instructs on the commission of these crimes. The Supreme Court has never protected as abstract advocacy speech so explicit in its palpable entreaties to violent crime.

2.

. . .

IV.

Paladin, joined by a spate of media amici, including many of the major networks, newspapers, and publishers, contends that any decision recognizing even a potential cause of action against Paladin will have far-reaching chilling effects on the rights of free speech and press. [ ] That the national media organizations would feel obliged to vigorously defend Paladin's assertion of a constitutional right to intentionally and knowingly assist murderers with technical information which Paladin admits it intended and knew would be used immediately in the commission of murder and other crimes against society is, to say the least, breathtaking. But be that as it may, it should be apparent from the foregoing that the indisputably important First Amendment values that Paladin and amici argue would be imperiled by a decision recognizing potential liability under the peculiar facts of this case will not even arguably be adversely affected by allowing plaintiffs' action against Paladin to proceed. In fact, neither the extensive briefing by the parties and the numerous amici in this case, nor the exhaustive research which the court itself has undertaken, has revealed even a single case that we regard as factually analogous to this case.

Paladin and amici insist that recognizing the existence of a cause of action against Paladin predicated on aiding and abetting will subject broadcasters and publishers to liability whenever someone imitates or "copies" conduct that is either described or depicted in their broadcasts, publications, or movies. This is simply not true. In the "copycat" context, it will presumably never be the case that the broadcaster or publisher actually intends, through its description or depiction, to assist another or

---

3. The several brief "disclaimers" and "warnings" in Hit Man's advertisement description and on its cover, that the book's instructions are "for informational purposes only!" and "for academic study only!," and that "[n]either the author nor the publisher assumes responsibility for the use or misuse of the information contained in this book," are plainly insufficient in themselves to alter the objective understanding of the hundreds of thousands of words that follow, which, in purely factual and technical terms, tutor the book's readers in the methods and techniques of killing. These "disclaimers" and "warnings" obviously were affixed in order to titillate, rather than "to dissuade readers from engaging in the activity [the book] describes," as the district court suggested they might be understood, [ ].

others in the commission of violent crime; rather, the information for the dissemination of which liability is sought to be imposed will actually have been misused *vis-a-vis* the use intended, not, as here, used precisely as intended. It would be difficult to overstate the significance of this difference insofar as the potential liability to which the media might be exposed by our decision herein is concerned.

And, perhaps most importantly, there will almost never be evidence proffered from which a jury even could reasonably conclude that the producer or publisher possessed the actual intent to assist criminal activity. In only the rarest case, as here where the publisher has stipulated in almost taunting defiance that it intended to assist murderers and other criminals, will there be evidence extraneous to the speech itself which would support a finding of the requisite intent; surely few will, as Paladin has, "stand up and proclaim to the world that because they are publishers they have a unique constitutional right to aid and abet murder." [ ] Moreover, in contrast to the case before us, in virtually every "copycat" case, there will be lacking in the speech itself any basis for a permissible inference that the "speaker" intended to assist and facilitate the criminal conduct described or depicted. Of course, with few, if any, exceptions, the speech which gives rise to the copycat crime will not directly and affirmatively promote the criminal conduct, even if, in some circumstances, it incidentally glamorizes and thereby indirectly promotes such conduct.

Additionally, not only will a political, informational, educational, entertainment, or other wholly legitimate purpose for the description or depiction be demonstrably apparent; but the description or depiction of the criminality will be of such a character that an inference of impermissible intent on the part of the producer or publisher would be unwarranted as a matter of law. So, for example, for almost any broadcast, book, movie, or song that one can imagine, an inference of unlawful motive from the description or depiction of particular criminal conduct therein would almost never be reasonable, for not only will there be (and demonstrably so) a legitimate and lawful purpose for these communications, but the contexts in which the descriptions or depictions appear will themselves negate a purpose on the part of the producer or publisher to assist others in their undertaking of the described or depicted conduct. [ ]

Paladin contends that exposing it to liability under the circumstances presented here will necessarily expose broadcasters and publishers of the news, in particular, to liability when persons mimic activity either reported on or captured on film footage and disseminated in the form of broadcast news. [ ] This contention, as well, is categorically wrong. News reporting, we can assume, no matter how explicit it is in its description or depiction of criminal activity, could never serve as a basis for aiding and abetting liability consistent with the First Amendment. It will be self-evident in the context of news reporting, if nowhere else, that neither the intent of the reporter nor the purpose of the report is to facilitate repetition of the crime or other conduct reported upon, but, rather, merely to report on the particular event, and thereby to inform the public.

A decision that Paladin may be liable under the circumstances of this case is not even tantamount to a holding that all publishers of instructional manuals may be liable for the misconduct that ensues when one follows the instructions which appear in those manuals. Admittedly, a holding that Paladin is not entitled to an absolute defense to the plaintiffs' claims here may not bode well for those publishers, if any, of factually detailed instructional books, similar to Hit Man, which are devoted exclusively to teaching the techniques of violent activities that are criminal per se. But, in holding that a defense to liability may not inure to publishers for their dissemination of such manuals of criminal conduct, we do not address ourselves to the potential liability of a publisher for the criminal use of published instructions on activity that is either entirely lawful, or lawful or not depending upon the circumstances of its occurrence. Assuming, as we do, that liability could not be imposed in these circumstances on a finding of mere foreseeability or knowledge that the instructions might be misused for a criminal purpose, the chances that claims arising from the publication of instructional manuals like these can withstand motions for summary judgment directed to the issue of intent seem to us remote indeed, at least absent some substantial confirmation of specific intent like that that exists in this case.

. . .

The judgment of the district court is hereby reversed, and the case remanded for trial.

Notes and Questions

1. On the eve of trial, Paladin agreed to a "multimillion-dollar" settlement with the plaintiffs and agreed to stop distributing the book. See David G. Savage, Publisher of "Hit Man" Manual Agrees to Settle Suit Over Triple Slaying, L.A. Times, May 22, 1999, at A10.

2. If a jury in this case could infer intent from the publisher's stated purposes, the book's promotion of murder, the publisher's marketing strategy, and the absence of legitimate uses for the book, is it clear that liability in the Hit Man case would be no precedent for "copycat" cases?

3. Why did the court find the defendant's stipulations "astonishing"? Was the court unduly influenced by them, given their tentative and tactical nature? Did the defendant's strategy backfire when the court decided that the facts would support liability even without the stipulations?

4. *Rice* reportedly marked the first time a U.S. publisher had been held financially liable for a crime committed by a reader. Is the decision precedent for: (a) Liability only on facts that satisfy *Brandenburg*? (b) Reinterpretation of *Brandenburg* to eliminate its "imminence" requirement? (c) Liability for aiding and abetting the commission of a crime even if the speech does not amount to incitement? (d) Liability under any

generally applicable theory for speech that is "tantamount to legitimately proscribable non-expressive conduct"?

––––––––

Natural Born Killers. A closely watched case after *Rice* was Byers v. Edmondson, 826 So.2d 551 (La. App. 2002). Two teenagers who said they were emulating the 1994 Oliver Stone movie Natural Born Killers, about two serial killers who become celebrities, went on a crime spree during which they shot and seriously wounded a store clerk. In a suit alleging that the movie incited imminent lawless activity, a state court initially denied the defendants' motion for summary judgment. Relying heavily on *Rice*, an intermediate appellate court affirmed. The court held that the First Amendment would not bar recovery if the makers of the movie intended to incite people to commit crimes. As evidence of such an intent, the plaintiffs noted that Stone had said in a 1996 interview, "The most pacifistic people in the world said they came out of this movie and wanted to kill somebody."

On remand, however, the trial judge granted the media defendants summary judgment on the ground that the plaintiffs would not be able to prove that the movie makers intended to stimulate violence. The Court of Appeal affirmed on the ground that the First Amendment barred recovery unless the plaintiffs proved incitement, and as a matter of law that could not be found. The court said whether Stone intended for viewers to commit violent acts was irrelevant so long as the movie did not amount to incitement.

Does this case vindicate the *Rice* opinion's assurances that the decision there would not support recovery in copycat cases? Could evidence that a movie-maker knew the movie might inspire copycat crimes support an inference that she or he had the kind of "specific intent" that the court found in *Rice*?

Other courts have held that the First Amendment precludes liability even when the defendant was aware of the risk of copycat crimes. See, e.g., Yakubowicz v. Paramount Pictures Corp., 404 Mass. 624, 536 N.E.2d 1067 (1989). That case involved a movie that depicted teen-age gang violence and was released during a school break to maximize attendance by high school students. After learning of several killings that were allegedly inspired by the movie, Paramount released theaters from their contractual obligations to show the film, but did not withdraw it. Plaintiff's decedent was killed by a youth who saw the film after these events. Despite the defendant's awareness of the risk, the court said the First Amendment precluded liability in the absence of incitement.

3.   NEGLIGENCE

As we have seen, tort law itself severely restricts liability for negligently causing emotional distress or economic harm. When the harm is physical, however, negligence law is generally applicable. The First Amendment therefore is likely to be the only protection for media who negligently cause physical harm. The use of incitement theory, at least when it is applied as rigorously as in *Herceg*, would seem to imply that the First Amendment permits no recovery under lesser standards of liability. The *Rice* court assumed that liability could not be imposed "on a finding of mere foreseeability or knowledge." But in fact there are a few cases imposing liability (or entertaining the possibility) on the basis of negligence, some enhanced version of negligence, or recklessness. Identifying the variables that persuade courts that they need not insist on proof of incitement (or some close relative such as aiding and abetting) is the challenge in these cases.

Braun v. Soldier of Fortune Magazine, Inc.

United States Court of Appeals, Eleventh Circuit, 1992.
968 F.2d 1110, 20 Med. L. Rptr. 1777, certiorari denied 506 U.S. 1071 (1993).

[Michael Savage placed the following personal service advertisement in Soldier of Fortune magazine:

GUN FOR HIRE: 37 year old professional mercenary desires jobs. Vietnam veteran. Discrete [sic] and very private. Body guard, courier, and other special skills. All jobs considered. [Telephone number and address].

The ad ran for ten months and Savage said he received thirty to forty responses a week, most of them seeking his help in perpetrating criminal acts such as murder, kidnapping, and assault. One call was from an Atlanta man seeking to murder his business partner, Richard Braun. Savage and two other men went to Braun's home where one of the other men shot Braun to death and wounded his son Michael.

Michael Braun and his brother brought a wrongful death action in Alabama under Georgia law against the magazine for the death of their father. Michael also sued for his own personal injuries.

The publisher, managing editor, and advertising manager of Soldier of Fortune testified that they did not understand Savage's ad as referring to illegal activity and that they were unaware of criminal activity associated with any Soldier of Fortune ads prior to Braun's murder. The plaintiffs introduced evidence showing that a number of newspapers and magazines had carried stories describing links between other Soldier of Fortune ads and convictions for murder, kidnapping, extortion, and other crimes.

A jury awarded the sons $2,375,000 in compensatory and $10 million in punitive damages. The district court ordered remittitur reducing the punitive award to $2 million. The magazine and its parent corporation, collectively referred to as "SOF" in the opinion, appealed.]

Before ANDERSON and DUBINA, CIRCUIT JUDGES, and ESCHBACH, SENIOR CIRCUIT JUDGE.

ANDERSON, CIRCUIT JUDGE:

. . .

A. *Duty Under Georgia Law*

. . .

Georgia courts recognize a "general duty one owes to all the world not to subject them to an unreasonable risk of harm." [ ] Accordingly, the district court properly found that SOF had a legal duty to refrain from publishing advertisements that subjected the public, including appellees, to a clearly identifiable unreasonable risk of harm from violent criminal activity. . . .

1.   Risk–Utility Balancing

To determine whether the risk to others that an individual's actions pose is "unreasonable," Georgia courts generally apply a risk-utility balancing test. [ ] A risk is unreasonable if it is "of such magnitude as to outweigh what the law regards as the utility of the defendant's alleged negligent conduct." [ ] Simply put, liability depends upon whether the burden on the defendant of adopting adequate precautions is less than the probability of harm from the defendant's unmodified conduct multiplied by the gravity of the injury that might result from the defendant's unmodified conduct. [ ]

For the reasons stated below, we find that the district court properly struck the risk-utility balance when it instructed that the jury could hold SOF liable for printing Savage's advertisement only if the advertisement on its face would have alerted a reasonably prudent publisher to the clearly identifiable unreasonable risk of harm to the public that the advertisement posed. . . .

SOF relies heavily on Eimann v. Soldier of Fortune Magazine, Inc., 880 F.2d 830, [16 Med. L. Rptr. 2148] (5th Cir. 1989), to support its contention that the district court erred in its application of risk-utility balancing to this case. In *Eimann*, the son and mother of a murder victim brought a wrongful death action under Texas law against SOF, seeking to hold SOF liable for publishing a personal service ad through which the victim's husband hired an assassin to kill her. The advertisement in question read:

> EX–MARINES—67–69 'Nam Vets, Ex–DI, weapons specialist-jungle warfare, pilot, M.E., high risk assignments, U.S. or overseas. . . .

The district court instructed the jury that it could find SOF liable if "(1) the relation to illegal activity appears on the ad's face; or (2) 'the advertisement, embroidered by its context, would lead a reasonable publisher of ordinary prudence under the same or similar circumstances to conclude that the advertisement could reasonably be interpreted' as an offer to commit crimes." [ ] The jury found for plaintiffs and awarded them $1.9 million in compensatory damages and $7.5 million in punitive damages. [ ]

The Fifth Circuit reversed the jury's verdict. After applying Texas risk-utility balancing principles similar to Georgia's, the court concluded that "[t]he standard of conduct imposed by the district court against SOF is too high. . . ." . . . .

SOF's reliance on *Eimann* is misplaced. We distinguish *Eimann* from this case based on the instructions to the respective juries. In *Eimann*, the district court violated risk-utility balancing principles when it allowed the jury to impose liability on SOF if a reasonable publisher would conclude "that the advertisement could reasonably be interpreted" as an offer to commit crimes. [ ] (emphasis added). The Fifth Circuit correctly observed that virtually anything might involve illegal activity, [ ], and that applying the district court's standard would mean that a publisher "must reject all [ambiguous] advertisements," [ ] (emphasis in original), or risk liability for any "untoward consequences that flow from his decision to publish" them. [ ]

In this case, the district court stressed in its instructions that the jury could hold SOF liable only if the ad on its face contained a "clearly identifiable unreasonable risk" of harm to the public. We are convinced that the district court's use of phrases like "clear and present danger" and "clearly identifiable unreasonable risk" properly conveyed to the jury that it could not impose liability on SOF if Savage's ad posed only an unclear or insubstantial risk of harm to the public and if SOF would bear a disproportionately heavy burden in avoiding this risk. The jury instructions in *Eimann*, in contrast, did not preclude the jury from imposing liability on the basis of an ambiguous advertisement that presented only an unclear risk of harm to the public.

. . .

2. First Amendment Limitations

SOF further argues that the district court erred in instructing the jury to apply a negligence standard because the First Amendment forbids imposing liability on publishers for publishing an advertisement unless the ad openly solicits criminal activity. . . .

. . .

Imposing tort liability for publishing advertisements that result in injury directly implicates the First Amendment interest in commercial speech. It is well-settled that the First Amendment does not protect commercial speech "related to illegal activity," *Central Hudson*, [supra p. 170] and, thus, there is no constitutional interest in publishing personal service ads that solicit criminal activity, [ ]. However, if state tort law places too heavy a burden on publishers with respect to the advertisements they print, the fear of liability might impermissibly impose a form of self-censorship on publishers. [ ] Such a chilling effect would compromise the First Amendment interest in commercial speech by depriving protected speech "of a legitimate and recognized avenue of access to the public." [ ]

This case poses a greater risk than one finds in ordinary commercial speech cases that a state's regulatory regime or tort law will impermissibly chill publishers from printing commercial speech that enjoys First Amendment protection. Most cases involving regulation of commercial speech present only a minor risk that overly broad speech regulation will chill protected commercial speech because, generally speaking, "advertising is linked to [the] commercial well-being" of the speaker. [ ] The advertiser's strong economic interest helps ensure that its particular message reaches the public, even in the face of restrictive regulations. However, "in the advertising context, a publisher only provides a forum for the actual speaker as a means of communicating with the listener." [ ] Accordingly, since "[p]ublishers do not tout their own products or services," they "have a far smaller financial interest than advertisers in the advancement of any one particular product or service." [ ]

SOF further argues that imposing liability on publishers for the advertisements they print indirectly threatens core, non-commercial speech to which the Constitution accords its full protection. Cf., *Central Hudson* [supra p. 170]. In *Eimann* [ ] the Fifth Circuit agreed that "the publication's editorial content would surely feel the economic crunch from loss of revenue that would result if publishers were required to reject all ambiguous advertisements." [ ] SOF also alleges that payment of the jury's verdict would force the magazine to close and, consequently, would deprive public debate of SOF's protected, non-commercial speech. [ ]

The district court was sensitive to the need to reconcile Georgia's interest in imposing liability on publishers for printing advertisements related to criminal activity with the First Amendment's concern that state law not chill protected expression. Accordingly, the court instructed the jury to apply a "modified" negligence standard under which SOF had no legal duty to investigate the ads it printed. . . . For the reasons set out below, we conclude that the district court's "modified" negligence standard satisfied the First Amendment's interests in protecting the commercial and core speech at issue in this case.

Supreme Court cases discussing the limitations the First Amendment places on state defamation law indicate that there is no constitutional infirmity in Georgia law holding publishers liable under a negligence standard with respect to the commercial advertisements they print. . . . In *Gertz v. Robert Welch, Inc.*, [supra p. 296] the Court held that, as long as a state does not impose liability without fault, it may constitutionally hold a publisher liable for "defamatory falsehood injurious to the reputation of a private individual." In light of the fact that the Court has found that a negligence standard satisfies the First Amendment's concern for the non-commercial, core speech at issue in *Gertz*, we see no constitutional infirmity in Georgia tort law holding publishers liable under a negligence standard with respect to the commercial advertisements they print. [ ]

Past Supreme Court decisions indicate, however, that the negligence standard that the First Amendment permits is a "modified" negligence standard. The Court's decisions suggest that Georgia law may impose tort liability on publishers for injury caused by the advertisements they print only if the ad on its face, without the need to investigate, makes it apparent that there is a substantial danger of harm to the public. In *Gertz*, for example, the Court held that a state could impose liability on a publisher who negligently printed a defamatory statement whose substance made "substantial danger to reputation apparent." [ ] Significantly, the Court noted that its inquiry would be different "if a State purported to condition civil liability on a factual misstatement whose content did not warn a reasonably prudent editor or broadcaster of its defamatory potential." [ ]

Based upon the foregoing authorities, we conclude that the First Amendment permits a state to impose upon a publisher liability for compensatory damages for negligently publishing a commercial advertisement where the ad on its face, and without the need for investigation, makes it apparent that there is a substantial danger of harm to the public. . . . Furthermore, these limitations on tort liability ensure that the burden imposed on publishers will have a minimal impact on their advertising revenue, and, consequently, on their ability to publish non-commercial speech. [ ][8]

. . .

3.   Independent First Amendment Review

. . . In order to guarantee that the jury imposed no greater burden on SOF than the Constitution permits, we subject to independent examination the jury's finding that Savage's ad, on the face, would convey to a reasonably prudent publisher that it created a clearly identifiable unreasonable risk that the advertiser was available to commit serious violent crimes.

Our review of the language of Savage's ad persuades us that SOF had a legal duty to refrain from publishing it. Savage's advertisement (1) emphasized the term "Gun for Hire," (2) described Savage as a "professional mercenary," (3) stressed Savage's willingness to keep his assignments confidential and "very private," (4) listed legitimate jobs involving the use of a gun—bodyguard and courier—followed by a reference to Savage's "other special skills," and (5) concluded by stating that Savage would consider "[a]ll jobs." The ad's combination of sinister terms makes it apparent that there was a substantial danger of harm to the public. The ad expressly solicits all jobs requiring the use of a gun. When the list of legitimate jobs—i.e., body guard and courier—is followed by "other special skills" and "all jobs considered," the implication is clear that the advertiser would consider illegal jobs. We agree with the district court that "the language of this advertisement is such that, even though couched in terms not explicitly offering criminal services, the publisher could recognize the offer of criminal activity as readily as its readers obviously did." [ ]

We emphasize that we are not adopting a per se rule that all advertisements using terms such as "Gun for Hire" present a clearly identifiable unreasonable risk of harm to the public from violent criminal activity. An

---

8. As for SOF's argument that the district court's judgment would force the magazine out of business and, thus, silence its protected speech, we observe that the Supreme Court has squarely rejected the notion that the First Amendment interest in protected speech requires that "publishers and broadcasters enjoy an unconditional and indefeasible immunity from [tort] liability." *Gertz* [ ]

advertiser certainly could use such terms in a metaphoric or humorous manner that would not indicate a clear risk of substantial danger to the public. However, viewing the advertisement that Savage submitted to SOF in its entirety, we conclude that the ad on its face makes it apparent that there was a substantial danger that Savage was soliciting illegal jobs involving the use of a gun. Thus, the First Amendment standard articulated above was satisfied.

. . .

For the foregoing reasons, we AFFIRM the district court's judgment.

ESCHBACH, SENIOR CIRCUIT JUDGE, dissenting: . . .

I differ with the majority's application of the law to the facts of this case. Specifically, in discharging our duty of independent First Amendment review of the language of Savage's ad, [ ] I remain convinced that the language of the advertisement is ambiguous, rather than patently criminal as the majority believes. And although the majority has carefully culled the legal standards it applies from the jury instructions, I remain concerned over whether the instructions were clear enough that the jury could have done so as well. Because of the confluence of these two concerns—the ambiguity of both the advertisement and the jury instructions—I am not confident that the jury actually found that this advertisement was a clear solicitation for criminal activity. Under these circumstances, I am unable to uphold the crushing third-party liability the jury has imposed on Soldier of Fortune Magazine. I respectfully dissent.

Notes and Questions

1. If the jury in the *Eimann* case had been given the same instructions as the jury in *Braun*, could it properly have imposed liability?

2. In *Central Hudson*, supra p. 170, the Supreme Court said "For commercial speech to come within [the First Amendment] it must at least concern lawful activity. . . ." Why isn't that a sufficient answer to Soldier of Fortune's First Amendment argument?

3. Is the basis of liability in *Braun* applicable only in commercial speech cases? Is an ad commercial speech when the advertiser is sued, but "core" speech when the publisher is sued? Should the speech be analyzed as something in between when the publisher is sued? Recall that the defamation in *Sullivan*, supra p. 272, occurred in an advertisement.

4. The court analogizes to *Gertz*, supra p. 296, to hold that a "modified" negligence standard is sufficient to overcome First Amendment protections. In *Gertz*, however, the speech at issue was false; here it was not false (the advertiser apparently had whatever skills, capabilities, and willingness he advertised). Is the requirement of "defamatory, false and negligently so" more protective of the press than the negligence approach developed in *Braun*? Might the difference between harm to reputation and physical harm justify the difference?

5. The plaintiffs in *Braun* apparently accepted a $200,000 settlement in satisfaction of the $4.375 million judgment. See James Brooke, For Soldier of Fortune, Bosnia Is Latest Front, N.Y. Times, Dec. 11, 1995, at D7.

————

The Jenny Jones case. During the taping of an episode of the "Jenny Jones Show" that was to be about "men who have secret crushes on men," Scott Amedure surprised another participant, Jonathan Schmitz, by announcing that he had a crush on Schmitz. Schmitz knew the show was to be about secret admirers but claimed he had been told that his secret admirer would be a woman. Three days after the taping Schmitz killed Amedure. The segment was not broadcast. The decedent's survivors sued Warner Brothers, which produced the show, on the theory that the producers negligently created the risk that Schmidt would react violently to the encounter. The trial judge rejected the argument that the First Amendment precluded recovery and a jury awarded the plaintiffs $25 million. The Michigan Court of Appeals reversed on state law grounds, however, holding that the producers had no duty to anticipate a criminal act by Schmidt. See Graves v. Warner Bros., Inc., 656 N.W.2d 195, 31 Med. L. Rptr. 1255 (Mich. App. 2002). A dissenter argued that the producers' negligence was in creating a volatile situation in which it was foreseeable that a psychologically unstable or criminally dangerous person might react violently, and that the producers therefore should be subject to the rule that holds defendants liable for third-party crimes when those are the very risk that makes the conduct negligent.

A state court held that a newspaper owed no duty to refrain from negligently publishing information that allegedly caused the plaintiff's decedent to be murdered. The Dallas Morning News published the street name and block (but not the house number) of a suspect in a gang-related drive-by shooting. On the day the information was published, persons unknown came to the suspect's house and murdered his sister. Dismissal of a negligence claim against the newspaper was affirmed on the ground that there is no duty under Texas law "to refrain from publishing what is a true, public, facially harmless, and newsworthy fact." Although it reached this result as a matter of tort law, the court said its risk-utility analysis was influenced by First Amendment concerns. "We conclude that the risk, foreseeability, and likelihood of injury in this case are outweighed by the social utility of crime reporting, the burden that would be borne by the News to prevent injury, and the consequences of placing that burden on the News." See Orozco v. Dallas Morning News, Inc., 975 S.W.2d 392, 27 Med. L. Rptr. 1343 (Tex.App. 1998).

Recall that the plaintiff in *Florida Star*, supra p. 380, also alleged that the publication of her name resulted in threats of physical harm. If she had actually been physically harmed as a result of the publication of her name and had sued for that injury rather than invasion of privacy, would the result have been the same?

Physical harm cases against against Internet service providers may be restricted by the Communications Decency Act. Recall that the *Zeran* case [supra p. 338] held that the CDA gives ISPs absolute immunity for publishing defamatory statements of third parties, even if the ISP has notice of the defamatory content. Although Zeran was brought as a negligence claim, the court treated it as if it were a defamation claim. A sharply divided Florida Supreme Court held that the same logic applies to state law claims that cannot be considered defamation. See Doe v. America Online, Inc., 783 So.2d 1010 (Fla. 2001). The complaint alleged that an anonymous AOL subscriber induced an 11–year–old boy to engage in sex acts which the subscriber videotaped and marketed through an AOL chat room. Answering certified questions in a negligence suit brought against AOL on behalf of the boy, the court relied heavily on *Zeran* to hold, 4–3, that the CDA applied to tort actions generally, thereby preempting all state common law remedies against ISPs for injuries resulting from material not originated by the ISP. The dissenters said *Zeran*'s interpretation of the CDA, and the majority's extension of it to other torts, "frustrates the core concepts explicitly furthered by the Act and contravenes its express purposes."

Video games. In several highly publicized mass murder sprees, there have been claims that the perpetrators were influenced by repeated exposure to violent video games. Wrongful death claims against the manufacturers or distributors of the games sometimes fail on tort law grounds. In James v. Meow Media, Inc., 300 F.3d 683, 30 Med. L. Rptr. 2185 (6th Cir. 2002), the court held that state law imposed no duty on video game makers to guard against the possibility that their products might cause minors who play them to commit crimes. The case arose from the 1997 shooting spree in Paducah, Kentucky, in which a high school student killed three schoolmates and injured many others. Subsequent investigation revealed that the perpetrator regularly played a number of interactive computer games that involved shooting virtual opponents. The court said if the shooting was triggered by the games, that result "was simply too idiosyncratic to expect the defendants to have anticipated it." The court found it unnecessary to decide First Amendment questions, but said liability under state law would raise significant First Amendment problems, which it said provided "yet another policy reason not to impose a duty of care."

Courts that have reached the First Amendment issue have generally held that video games are fully protected speech. See Sanders v. Acclaim Entertainment, Inc., 188 F. Supp. 2d 1264 (D. Colo. 2002) (denying liability for the Columbine High School murders in Colorado); Wilson v. Midway Games, Inc., 198 F. Supp. 2d 167 (D. Conn. 2002) (denying liability for a stabbing death caused by a 13–year–old allegedly addicted to the game Mortal Kombat).

How-to communications. Frequently print and broadcast media communicate information that they intend the audience to act on. *Rice* involved a how-to-do-it publication, but the decision there is of little help in the more typical instances, such as columns or programs about cooking or home repairs, where the defendant neither intended nor counseled any illegal act. People who respond by trying the recipe or by trying to make something pursuant to instructions are only doing what the author expected them to do, and if an error causes injury it can hardly be said to be unforeseeable. But might tort law concerns about crushing burdens creep in if a careless proofreading error causes hundreds or thousands of upset stomachs that night? If tort liability does not bar recovery, might First Amendment arguments do so? There is obviously no "incitement" to "imminent" lawless action. Should that be necessary in this type of case?

The issue arises most frequently with books—but books present a special problem because the suits are against the publishers. The courts are uniform in finding that the publisher has no duty to check on or warn about the quality of work done by outside authors. See, e.g., Winter v. G.P. Putnam's Sons, 938 F.2d 1033, 19 Med. L. Rptr. 1053 (9th Cir. 1991) (publisher not liable for negligence to readers who, relying on The Encyclopedia of Mushrooms, picked and ate poisonous mushrooms). Although a publisher may assume a duty of fact checking, "there is nothing inherent in the role of publisher or the surrounding legal doctrines to suggest that such a duty should be imposed." If the court had decided as a matter of tort law to require publishers to use reasonable care to avoid such errors, would the First Amendment prohibit it from doing so?

Is there a difference between a physician who gives a patient incorrect diet advice during an office visit and a physician who writes that same incorrect advice in a general book or newspaper health column advocating the diet? See Note, Media Liability for Physical Injury Resulting from the Negligent Use of Words, 72 Minn. L. Rev. 1193 (1988).

Plaintiffs have argued that the how-to-do-it cases resemble the flight chart cases. The *Winter* court distinguished them by asserting that the charts were highly technical tools similar to a compass, while the Encyclopedia of Mushrooms was like a book on how to use a compass or a chart.

Alternatives to negligence. In Walt Disney Productions, Inc. v. Shannon, 247 Ga. 402, 276 S.E.2d 580, 7 Med. L. Rptr. 1209 (1981), the court applied a "clear and present danger" standard. Defendant's "Mickey Mouse Club" television program announced that a "special feature on today's show is all about the magic you can create with sound effects." A participant showed the audience how to reproduce the sound of a tire coming off an automobile by "putting a BB pellet inside a 'large, round balloon,' filling the balloon with air, and rotating the BB inside the balloon. Craig, who was 11 years old, undertook to repeat what he had seen on television. He put a piece of lead almost twice the size of a BB into a 'large, skinny balloon.' He blew up the balloon and the balloon burst, impelling the lead into Craig's eye and partially blinding him."

Although the court could "envision situations in which an adult could be held liable in tort solely on the ground that statements uttered by him constituted an invitation to a child to do something causing the child injury," no such liability should flow unless "what the adult invited the child to do presented a clear and present danger that injury would in fact result. Although it can be said that what the defendants allegedly invited the child to do in this case posed a foreseeable risk of injury, it cannot be said that it posed a clear and present danger of injury." In a footnote, the court noted that "of an estimated 16 million children watching this program, only the plaintiff in this case reported an injury."

Why apply "clear and present danger" here? How might the judges in *Herceg* analyze this case? Would a negligence standard be appropriate? Can *Herceg* be analyzed as speech aimed at children? If children should have actions in any of these cases, should any defense be available to reduce damages?

Most discussion has centered around negligence as the alternative to incitement or other rigorous standards. In Note, Publisher Liability For Material that Invites Reliance, 66 Tex. L. Rev. 1155 (1988), the author proposes an intermediate position:

> (1) One who recklessly publishes false or misleading material that invites reliance is subject to liability for physical harm caused by the user's reasonable reliance on such material, when such harm results
>
>> (a) to the user, or
>>
>> (b) to such third persons as the actor should reasonably expect to be put in peril by use of the material.
>
> (2) Recklessness consists of
>
>> (a) the failure to test procedures or instructions that reasonably might cause physical injury if false or misleading, if the predominant purpose of the material and the central inducement to its purchase is the intended reliance on those procedures or instructions by users, or
>>
>> (b) the failure to investigate or otherwise examine procedures or instructions that the publisher knows or should know are defective or dangerous, if the intended reliance upon it by users is an incidental purpose of the material taken as a whole.

How would this differ from negligence? Would it change the result in *Herceg*? In any of the cases discussed above?

Postscript. Even if one agrees that the social values protected by the First Amendment should cause courts in all or most of these cases to protect publishers or broadcasters from liability for what might otherwise be actionable under tort law, some have asked why the injured plaintiff should be left bearing the loss. The argument is vigorously made in Frederick Schauer, Uncoupling Free Speech, 92 Colum. L. Rev. 1321 (1992). Although most of the article is addressed to compensating victims of defamation, even those who are skeptical that many plaintiffs suffer severe damages in defamation will be hard pressed to deny the reality of the harm suffered in cases like *Olivia N.* and *Herceg*. In these situations he suggests that a victim compensation scheme is "worth contemplating."

Schauer's core hypothetical is a combination of two cases in which a group of boys injure a girl as detailed in a magazine that the boys have in their possession when apprehended. Schauer asks: "If it is 'our' First Amendment, then why don't we and not Olivia N. pay for it?" The plaintiff's award under state tort law could be paid by a special fund. Even if "full" tort compensation were not forthcoming, the payment of medical and other out-of-pocket expenses "can be viewed as improving the existing model rather than as falling short of an ideal." How should such a fund be financed?

One advantage Schauer sees is that if the plaintiff recovered only, say, one fourth of what tort law would provide, society "would then understand, as it probably does not now, both the costs of a free speech system, and that the [smaller award] is the result not of necessity but of a conscious choice about where society wishes the immediate burden of its rights to fall." Even if the final decision should be against setting up such a fund, "going through the steps focuses us much more sharply on the costs of the First Amendment, and on the identity of those who are paying for them."

CHAPTER VII

COPYRIGHT

The law of copyright is important to media in many ways. Authors and others sometimes sue media for infringement of their copyrights. This aspect of copyright bears some resemblance to the torts considered in the preceding chapters: Media are being sued for economic harm they allegedly cause by their publications or broadcasts, and the risk of such liability raises First Amendment questions similar to those raised by liability for other publication torts.

But media also are among the principal beneficiaries of copyright law. It prevents competitors from appropriating their articles, photos, features, newscasts, and other expression. It allows them to control and exploit ancillary uses of their product in electronic databases, online services, anthologies, and retrospectives. It gives them control over the work produced by their employees and enables them to gain control over the work of freelancers. Media therefore are copyright plaintiffs as well as defendants, and they may find themselves trying to use copyright law to suppress someone else's speech instead of defending their own right to speak.

The most important reason for including a brief look at copyright in a mass media law course is that copyright law reflects assumptions about the system of freedom of expression that are quite at odds with those seen elsewhere in media law. The underlying premise of copyright law is that speech interests in the long run are best served by a system of regulation, even though that system may operate to suppress speech in the short run. Within its limited sphere, it is a system by which government grants and protects exclusive rights to speak in the belief that this will ultimately produce more (or better) speech than a laissez faire approach. In other areas of this book we have seen such arguments rejected. Advocates of a right of access to media, for example, argued that "The government can lay down rules of the game that will promote rather than restrict free speech." But the Supreme Court, in *Tornillo*, supra p. 69, said the editorial choice as to what to publish in a newspaper cannot be regulated consistently with the First Amendment. Copyright law does exactly that—it tells editors what they may or may not print—but the courts do not see that as raising similar First Amendment problems.

Copyright law also provides remedies that are rarely permitted elsewhere in law when the matter at issue is speech. Copyright infringement under some circumstances is punishable as a felony. Seizure and destruction of infringing works is a remedy which, if not routine, is not uncommon. Statutory damages of up to $100,000 may be awarded without proof of harm. (Compare *Gertz v. Robert Welch Inc.*, supra p. 296, limiting the

469

states' power to award defamation damages in excess of actual injury.) Prior restraints are not disfavored in copyright law; a plaintiff who establishes "a reasonable likelihood of success" in an infringement case is presumed to be entitled to at least a preliminary injunction. (Compare *New York Times Co. v. United States*, supra p. 98: "Any system of prior restraints of expression comes to this Court bearing a heavy presumption against its constitutional validity.")

This chapter is a highly selective exploration of a vast and complex body of law. It treats the aspects of copyright law that most directly affect the operations of media. It also raises important questions about the nature of free speech. Does the operation of copyright law undermine the pervasive First Amendment argument that government regulation (or tort liability) is inimical to freedom of speech? Does copyright law call into question the traditional hostility to prior restraints on speech? Are copyright questions so different from the other issues considered in this course that both approaches can be correct?

A.   A BRIEF SURVEY OF COPYRIGHT LAW

The laws of copyright are among the most conspicuous but least condemned restraints on freedom of expression. Article I, section 8, of the Constitution gives Congress the power "to promote the progress of science and useful arts by securing for limited times to authors and inventors the exclusive right to their respective writings and discoveries. . . ." The first Congress used that authority to adopt copyright legislation, and it has been with us in some form ever since.

In 1976, Congress concluded more than a decade of hearings and debate by passing a new Copyright Act that substantially rewrote U.S. copyright law (codified as amended at 17 U.S.C. §§ 101 et seq.). Copyright law today applies to all works of authorship—including literature, music, drama, pantomime, choreography, photography, graphic art, sculpture, film, computer software, sound recordings, and architecture—provided that they are "fixed" and "original," regardless of whether they were published. 17 U.S.C. § 102. A work is "fixed" when it is embodied, by or with the permission of its creator, in "any tangible medium of expression," such as paper, computer disk, or video tape. A work is "original" if it "was independently created by the author" as opposed to being copied. 17 U.S.C. § 101. These requirements are deliberately broad and easy to satisfy. As a result, copyright law now protects every letter, memo, note, home video, photograph, answering machine message, and e-mail.

The protection of copyright law extends, however, only to expression, not the underlying facts or ideas expressed. 17 U.S.C. § 102(b). In *Feist Publications, Inc. v. Rural Telephone Service Company*, a unanimous Supreme Court wrote: "The most fundamental axiom of copyright law is that '[n]o author may copyright his ideas or the facts he narrates. . . .' [C]opyright assures authors the right to their original expression, but encourages others to build freely upon the ideas and information conveyed by a work." 499 U.S. 340, 344–45 (1991). Expression includes not only the words, code, sounds, or visual elements which are used to actually depict a work, but also certain elements of plot, structure, character, and other elements that "lie beneath the work's surface." See Paul Goldstein, Copyright (2d ed.) § 2.3 (1996).

Copyright law no longer requires compliance with statutory formalities or application to the government as a condition for protection (although there are still good reasons, relating primarily to litigation strategy, to register works with the Library of Congress and put a copyright notice on them). Protection begins as soon as the work is "fixed" and lasts for 70 years past the life of the author. If the author is an organization, protection lasts for 120 years after creation or 95 years after publication, whichever expires first.

The law gives a creator, or, in some circumstances, a creator's employer (see below), five exclusive rights: the right to reproduce, adapt, distribute, publicly perform, and publicly display a copyrighted work. For the period covered by the copyright, the law permits only the copyright holder to engage in, or authorize someone else to engage in, any activity covered by the five exclusive rights. The exclusive rights may be transferred or licensed, individually or collectively, for use by others. 17 U.S.C. § 106.

Courts have interpreted copyright law's infringement provisions very broadly. Individuals and institutions are liable not only for their own conduct, but also for the conduct of employees (under the doctrine of respondeat superior); the conduct of anyone whom they supervise and in whose work they have a financial interest (vicarious infringement); and the conduct of anybody whose infringing activity they knowingly induce, cause, or to which they materially contribute (contributory infringement). The law does not require that the defendant intend to infringe, or, except in the case of contributory infringement, even have knowledge of the infringing conduct. Innocent intent or lack of knowledge may affect damages, but it does not affect liability.

Copyright law provides significant penalties for violating the exclusive rights, including injunctions, impoundment and destruction of infringing copies, actual damages and lost profits, statutory damages up to $100,000 per infringement, court costs, and attorneys' fees. The Act also provides criminal penalties for "[a]ny person who infringes a copyright willfully and for purposes of commercial advantage or private financial gain." 17 U.S.C. §§ 502–506.

B. COPYRIGHT LAW AND THE MASS MEDIA

Copyright law affects the activities of the media in many ways. This section addresses three of the most important.

1. COPYRIGHT OWNERSHIP

For media, the most important ownership question is the status of work created by their agents, including employees and freelancers. As noted above, copyright ownership initially vests in the creator of the work.

There is one exception, however, and that is when a work is "made for hire." When the work is "made for hire," the copyright owner is not the actual creator, but rather the employer or other person for whom the work was prepared. A work "made for hire" is either:

(1) a work prepared by an employee within the scope of his or her employment; or

(2) a work specially ordered or commissioned for use as a contribution to a collective work, as a part of a motion picture or other audiovisual work, as a translation, as a supplementary work, as a compilation, as an instructional text, as a test, as answer material for a test, or as an atlas, if the parties expressly agree in a written instrument signed by them that the work shall be considered a work made for hire.

17 U.S.C. § 101. Thus a media organization normally is the initial owner of copyright in publications or broadcasts created by its employees. (Ownership may be transferred, of course, and specific rights may be granted by license without actual transfer of ownership.) When the material is created by non-employees—such as freelancers—however, those persons often hold the copyright. Copyright in their work belongs to the publishing or broadcasting organization only if it meets all three requirements of section 101(2): it was specially ordered or commissioned (e.g., not received unsolicited); it was created as a contribution to one of the kinds of work described in the statute; and the parties agreed in writing that it was to be considered a work for hire.

Publishers or broadcasters who use the work of freelancers without meeting these conditions hold only whatever rights they have contractually obtained, explicitly or implicitly, from the circumstances of the freelancer's submission of the work. Often this amounts to no more than a license to make first publication of the work. The freelancer retains all other rights, making the publisher or broadcaster liable for infringement if it should make any further use of the work, as in an anthology, a year-end recapitulation, or a database.

In Community for Creative Non–Violence v. Reid, 490 U.S. 730, 16 Med. L. Rptr. 1769 (1989), the Supreme Court was asked to avoid the rigors of section 101(2) by expansively interpreting the term "employee" in section 101(1). It declined. Reid had created a sculpture for CCNV in conformance with CCNV's concept and general design ideas. The parties did not discuss copyright ownership in advance. After the sculpture was finished, each filed a competing copyright claim. The trial judge held that CCNV owned the copyright, but the Court of Appeals for the District of Columbia reversed, holding that it was not a work for hire and therefore copyright was owned by Reid.

The Supreme Court unanimously affirmed. CCNV did not claim the sculpture was a specially commissioned work under subsection (2); there was no written agreement to that effect, and even if there had been, a sculpture is not one of the types of works to which that subsection applies. Instead, CCNV argued that Reid should be considered an "employee" for purposes of subsection (1), on the ground that CCNV had retained the right to control Reid's product and had actually exercised such control. The Court, however, held that the legislative history of the Act required the term to be understood in light of the general common law of agency, which takes into account many factors in addition to control of the work. It concluded Reid was not an employee because he was engaged in a skilled occupation, supplied his own tools, worked in his own studio, was retained for a brief time for the project in question and no others, had control of his own working hours and the employment and compensation of assistants, and was not treated as an employee for purposes of benefits, social security and payroll taxes, worker's compensation, or unemployment taxes.

If a contribution is neither the work of an employee nor a work for hire, its author retains the copyright. In the absence of an agreement to the contrary, the publisher of a collective work gets only "the privilege of reproducing and distributing the contribution as part of that particular collective work, any revision of that collective work, and any later collective work in the same series." 17 U.S.C. § 201(c). Moreover, the authors or their survivors may terminate such licenses after 35 years. 17 U.S.C. § 203. As a consequence, publishers may be unable to reuse those articles or illustrations in future works such as books, calendars, and special anniversary editions, and may lose their rights altogether after 35 years. Apparently many publishers failed to obtain contractual assignments from their freelance contributors in the past. Some industry sources said the *CCNV* decision put in question the ownership of millions of dollars in literary and entertainment properties, and might affect 40 percent of all existing copyrights. See Albert Scardino, The Media Business: A Copyright Ruling Opens a Costly Can of Worms, N.Y. Times, June 12, 1989, at D12.

The same rules apply to freelance work when the publisher attempts to make it available in electronic databases. The New York Times and other newspaper and magazine publishers attempted to place their periodicals in publicly available databases without securing copyright permissions from freelance writers whose work was included. When the authors sued for copyright infringement, the publishers claimed inclusion of the works in databases were "revisions" within the meaning of § 201(c). The district court accepted the publishers' theory, but the Second Circuit reversed and the Supreme Court affirmed.

The Court emphasized the fact that the databases in question (NEXIS, New York Times OnDisc, and General Periodicals on Disc) permitted retrieval on an article-by-article basis. They did not merely convert intact periodicals from one medium to another, but were functionally equivalent to a vast file room in which "an inhumanly speedy librarian would search the room and provide copies of the articles matching patron-specified criteria. . . . Such a storage and retrieval system effectively overrides the Authors' exclusive right to control the individual reproduction and distribution of each article. . . ." New York Times Co. v. Tasini, 533 U.S. 483, 29 Med. L. Rptr. 1865 (2001). Justice Stevens, joined by Justice Breyer, dissented, arguing that "the decision to convert the single collective work newspaper into a collection of individual ASCII files can be explained as little more than a decision that reflects the different nature of the electronic medium," and the conversion therefore should be considered a revision within the meaning of the statute.

By the time *Tasini* was decided, most publishers had adopted a practice of acquiring from all freelance contributors permission to place works in electronic databases, but the decision exposed them to liability for infringing the copyrights of all the earlier freelance contributors from whom they had not obtained permissions. The Times approached this problem by announcing that it would remove such articles from the Times' database unless the authors agreed to give up their rights with respect to electronic publication, and would not accept future contributions from them unless they agreed to give up their rights to compensation for electronic use of previous contributions. Tasini attempted to challenge those policies but his complaint was dismissed on standing grounds. See 184 F. Supp.2d 350, 30 Med. L. Rptr. 1407 (S.D.N.Y. 2002).

2. FAIR USE

The grant of rights to the owner of the copyright is conditioned on a series of defenses set forth in 17 U.S.C. §§ 107–118. The most important of these defenses is found in section 107, dealing with the problem of fair use:

> Notwithstanding the provisions of section 106, the fair use of a copyrighted work, including such use by reproduction in copies or phonorecords or by any other means specified by that section, for purposes such as criticism, comment, news reporting, teaching (including multiple copies for classroom use), scholarship, or research, is not an infringement of copyright. In determining whether the use made of a work in any particular case is a fair use the factors to be considered shall include—
>
> (1) the purpose and character of the use, including whether such use is of a commercial nature or is for non-profit educational purposes;
>
> (2) the nature of the copyrighted work;
>
> (3) the amount and substantiality of the portion used in relation to the copyrighted work as a whole; and
>
> (4) the effect of the use upon the potential market for or value of the copyrighted work.

In its most common application to media, copyright law helps them protect the commercial value of their publications or broadcasts. Media use it to keep others, including other media, from pirating their product. In *Pacific and Southern Co. v. Duncan*, 744 F.2d 1490, 11 Med. L. Rptr. 1135 (11th Cir. 1984), the defendant, doing business as TV News Clips, taped the news programs of television stations—including the plaintiff's—and sold copies of the clips to those persons or groups covered by the news reports. The copies were sold "for personal use only not for rebroadcast" and the service did not claim any copyright in them. It erased tapes after one month.

The court of appeals rejected defendant's claims that this was a fair use. The commercial nature of defendant's practices "militates quite strongly against a finding of fair use." Moreover, defendant's use "is neither productive nor creative in any way. It does not analyze the broadcast or improve it at all. . . . TV News Clips only copies and sells." Since the court treated each story on the news as a "coherent narrative," it found that the defendant had taken the entire work. The fourth factor also cut against defendant since it "uses the broadcasts for a purpose that WXIA might use for its own benefit." The potential market is undermined.

The second factor might be seen to favor defendant because of the importance to society of access to the news. "But the courts should also take care not to discourage authors from addressing important topics for fear of losing their copyright protections." The court also rejected the defendant's claims that its taping preserved evidence that might be of possible use in defamation cases brought against it, and that enforcing copyright law in this case would deny public access to broadcast material

a. Fair Use and the News

Copyright law is a double-edged sword, however, and media sometimes find it an obstacle to their own journalistic objectives. In the following case, the publication of former President Ford's book was itself the news event being covered. Nonetheless, the Supreme Court held that a magazine violated copyright by quoting excerpts from the forthcoming book.

Harper & Row Publishers, Inc. v. Nation Enterprises

Supreme Court of the United States, 1985.
471 U.S. 539, 105 S. Ct. 2218, 85 L. Ed.2d 588, 11 Med. L. Rptr. 1969.

JUSTICE O'CONNOR delivered the opinion of the Court.

This case requires us to consider to what extent the "fair use" provision of the Copyright Revision Act of 1976, 17 U.S.C. § 107 (hereinafter the Copyright Act), sanctions the unauthorized use of quotations from a public figure's unpublished manuscript. In March 1979, an undisclosed source provided The Nation magazine with the unpublished manuscript of "A Time to Heal: The Autobiography of Gerald R. Ford." Working directly from the purloined manuscript, an editor of The Nation produced a short piece entitled "The Ford Memoirs—Behind the Nixon Pardon." The piece was timed to "scoop" an article scheduled shortly to appear in Time magazine. Time had agreed to purchase the exclusive right to print prepublication excerpts from the copyright holders, Harper & Row Publishers, Inc. (hereinafter Harper & Row) and Reader's Digest Association, Inc. (hereinafter Reader's Digest). As a result of The Nation article, Time canceled its agreement. Petitioners brought a successful copyright action [for $12,500] against The Nation. On appeal, the Second Circuit reversed the lower court's finding of infringement, holding that The Nation's act was sanctioned as a "fair use" of the copyrighted material. We granted certiorari, [ ], and we now reverse.

. . .

II

We agree with the Court of Appeals that copyright is intended to increase and not to impede the harvest of knowledge. But we believe the Second Circuit gave insufficient deference to the scheme established by the Copyright Act for fostering the original works that provide the seed and substance of this harvest. The rights conferred by copyright are designed to assure contributors to the store of knowledge a fair return for their labors. [ ]

. . .

As we noted last Term, "[The Constitution's] limited grant is a means by which an important public purpose may be achieved. It is intended to motivate the creative activity of authors and inventors by the provision of a special reward, and to allow the public access to the products of their genius after the limited period of exclusive control has expired." Sony Corp. of America v. Universal City Studios, 464 U.S. 417 (1984). "The monopoly created by copyright thus rewards the individual author in order to benefit the public." Id., at 477 (dissenting opinion). This principle applies equally to works of fiction and non-fiction. The book at issue here, for example, was two years in the making, and began with a contract giving the author's copyright to the publishers in exchange for their services in producing and marketing the work. In preparing the book, Mr. Ford drafted essays and word portraits of public figures and participated in hundreds of taped interviews that were later distilled to chronicle his personal viewpoint. It is evident that the monopoly granted by copyright actively served its intended purpose of inducing the creation of new material of potential historical value.

Section 106 of the Copyright Act confers a bundle of exclusive rights to the owner of the copyright. Under the Copyright Act, these rights—to publish, copy, and distribute the author's work—vest in the author of an original work from the time of its creation. In practice, the author commonly sells his rights to publishers who offer royalties in exchange for their services in producing and marketing the author's work. The copyright owner's rights, however, are subject to certain statutory exceptions. Among these is § 107 which codifies the traditional privilege of other authors to make "fair use" of an earlier writer's work. In addition, no author may copyright facts or ideas. The copyright is limited to those aspects of the work—termed "expression"—that display the stamp of the author's originality.

Creation of a non-fiction work, even a compilation of pure fact, entails originality. . . . The copyright holders of "A Time to Heal" complied with the relevant statutory notice and registration procedures. [ ] Thus there is no dispute that the unpublished manuscript of "A Time to Heal," as a whole, was protected by 106 from unauthorized reproduction. Nor do respondents dispute that verbatim copying of excerpts of the manuscript's original form of expression would constitute infringement unless excused as fair use. [ ] Yet copyright does not prevent subsequent users from copying from a prior author's work those constituent elements that are not original—for example, quotations borrowed under the rubric of fair use from other copyrighted works, facts, or materials in the public domain—as long as such use does not unfairly appropriate the author's original contributions. [ ] Perhaps the controversy between the lower courts in this case over copyrightability is more aptly styled a dispute over whether The Nation's appropriation of unoriginal and uncopyrightable elements encroached on the originality embodied in the work as a whole. Especially in the realm of factual narrative, the law is currently unsettled regarding the ways in which uncopyrightable elements combine with the author's original contributions to form protected expression. . . .

We need not reach these issues, however, as The Nation has admitted to lifting verbatim quotes of the author's original language totaling between 300 and 400 words and constituting some 13% of [the 2,250 words in] The Nation article. In using generous verbatim excerpts of Mr. Ford's unpublished manuscript to lend authenticity to its account of the forthcoming memoirs, The Nation effectively arrogated to itself the right of first publication, an important marketable subsidiary right. For the reasons set forth below, we find that this use of the copyrighted manuscript, even stripped to the verbatim quotes conceded by the Nation to be copyrightable expression, was not a fair use within the meaning of the Copyright Act.

III

A

Fair use was traditionally defined as "a privilege in others than the owner of the copyright to use the copyrighted material in a reasonable manner without his consent." [ ] The statutory formulation of the defense of fair use in the Copyright Act of 1976 reflects the intent of Congress to codify the common-law doctrine. Section 107 requires a case-by-case determination whether a particular use is fair, and the statute notes four nonexclusive factors to be considered. This approach was "intended to restate the [pre-existing] judicial doctrine of fair use, not to change, narrow, or enlarge it in any way." H.R.Rep. No. 94–1476, p. 66 (1976) (hereinafter House Report). [ ]

"[T]he author's consent to a reasonable use of his copyrighted works ha[d] always been implied by the courts as a necessary incident of the constitutional policy of promoting the progress of science and the useful arts, since a prohibition of such use would inhibit subsequent writers from attempting to improve upon prior works and thus . . . frustrate the very ends sought to be attained." . . .

. . .

Perhaps because the fair use doctrine was predicated on the author's implied consent to "reasonable and customary" use when he released his work for public consumption, fair use traditionally was not recognized as a defense to charges of copying from an author's as yet unpublished works. Under common-law copyright, "the property of the author . . . in his intellectual creation [was] absolute until he voluntarily part[ed] with the same." [ ] This absolute rule, however, was tempered in practice by the equitable nature of the fair use doctrine. In a given case, factors such as implied consent through *de facto* publication or performance or dissemination of a work may tip the balance of equities in favor of prepublication use. [ ] But it has never been seriously disputed that "the fact that the plaintiff's work is unpublished . . . is a factor tending to negate the defense of fair use." . . .

The [1976 revision of the] Copyright Act represents the culmination of a major legislative re-examination of copyright doctrine. [ ] Among its other innovations, it eliminated publication "as a dividing line between common law and statutory protection," [ ], extending statutory protection to all works from the time of their creation. It also recognized for the first time a distinct statutory right of first publication, which had previously been an element of the common-law protections afforded unpublished works. The Report of the House Committee on the Judiciary confirms that "Clause (3) of section 106, establishes the exclusive right of publications. . . . Under this provision the copyright owner would have the right to control the first public distribution of an authorized copy . . . of his work." [ ]

Though the right of first publication, like the other rights enumerated in § 106, is expressly made subject to the fair use provision of § 107, fair use analysis must always be tailored to the individual case. [ ] The nature of the interest at stake is highly relevant to whether a given use is fair. From the beginning, those entrusted with the task of revision recognized the "overbalancing reasons to preserve the common law protection of undisseminated works until the author or his successor chooses to disclose them." [ ] The right of first publication implicates a threshold decision by the author whether and in what form to release his work. First publication is inherently different from other § 106 rights in that only one person can be the first publisher; as the contract with Time illustrates, the commercial value of the right lies primarily in exclusivity. Because the potential damage to the author from judicially enforced "sharing" of the first publication right with unauthorized users of his manuscript is substantial, the balance of equities in evaluating such a claim of fair use inevitably shifts.

. . .

. . . The author's control of first public distribution implicates not only his personal interest in creative control but his property interest in exploitation of prepublication rights, which are valuable in themselves and serve as a valuable adjunct to publicity and marketing. See Belushi v. Woodward, 598 F. Supp. 36 (D.D.C. 1984) (successful marketing depends on coordination of serialization and release to public); Marks, Subsidiary

Rights and Permissions, in What Happens in Book Publishing, 230 (C. Grannis ed. 1967) (exploitation of subsidiary rights is necessary to financial success of new books). Under ordinary circumstances, the author's right to control the first public appearance of his undisseminated expression will outweigh a claim of fair use.

B

Respondents, however, contend that First Amendment values require a different rule under the circumstances of this case. The thrust of the decision below is that "[t]he scope of [fair use] is undoubtedly wider when the information conveyed relates to matters of high public concern." . . . Respondents explain their copying of Mr. Ford's expression as essential to reporting the news story it claims the book itself represents. In respondents' view, not only the facts contained in Mr. Ford's memoirs, but "the precise manner in which [he] expressed himself was as newsworthy as what he had to say." [ ] Respondents argue that the public's interest in learning this news as fast as possible outweighs the right of the author to control its first publication.

The Second Circuit noted, correctly, that copyright's idea/expression dichotomy "strike[s] a definitional balance between the First Amendment and the Copyright Act by permitting free communication of facts while still protecting an author's expression." 723 F.2d, at 203. No author may copyright his ideas or the facts he narrates. . . . As this Court long ago observed: "[T]he news element—the information respecting current events contained in the literary production—is not the creation of the writer, but is a report of matters that ordinarily are *publici juris;* it is the history of the day." International News Service v. Associated Press, 248 U.S. 215, 234 (1918). But copyright assures those who write and publish factual narratives such as "A Time to Heal" that they may at least enjoy the right to market the original expression contained therein as just compensation for their investment. [ ]

. . . The promise of copyright would be an empty one if it could be avoided merely by dubbing the infringement a fair use "news report" of the book. [ ]

Nor do respondents assert any actual necessity for circumventing the copyright scheme with respect to the types of works and users at issue here. Where an author and publisher have invested extensive resources in creating an original work and are poised to release it to the public, no legitimate aim is served by preempting the right of first publication. . . .

. . .

It is fundamentally at odds with the scheme of copyright to accord lesser rights in those works that are of greatest importance to the public. Such a notion ignores the major premise of copyright and injures author and public alike. "[T]o propose that fair use be imposed whenever the 'social value [of dissemination] . . . outweighs any detriment to the artist,' would be to propose depriving copyright owners of their right in the property precisely when they encounter those users who could afford to pay for it." . . .

. . .

IV

Fair use is a mixed question of law and fact. Pacific and Southern Co. v. Duncan, 744 F.2d 1490, 1495, n.8 ([11th Cir.] 1984). Where the District Court has found facts sufficient to evaluate each of the statutory factors, an appellate court "need not remand for further fact-finding . . . [but] may conclude as a matter of law that [the challenged use] do[es] not qualify as a fair use of the copyrighted work." Id., at 1495. Thus whether The Nation article constitutes fair use under 107 must be reviewed in light of the principles discussed above. The factors enumerated in the section are not meant to be exclusive: "[S]ince the doctrine is an equitable rule of reason, no generally applicable definition is possible, and each case raising the question must be decided on its own facts." [ ] The four factors identified by Congress as especially relevant in determining whether the use was fair are: (1) the purpose and character of the use; (2) the nature of the copyrighted work; (3) the substantiality of the portion used in relation to the copyrighted work as a whole; (4) the effect on the potential market for or value of the copyrighted work. We address each one separately.

Purpose of the Use. The Second Circuit correctly identified news reporting as the general purpose of The Nation's use. News reporting is one of the examples enumerated in § 107 to "give some idea of the sort of activities the courts might regard as fair use under the circumstances." . . . The fact that an article arguably is "news" and therefore a productive use is simply one factor in a fair use analysis.

. . . The Nation has every right to seek to be the first to publish information. But The Nation went beyond simply reporting uncopyrightable information and actively sought to exploit the headline value of its infringement, making a "news event" out of its unauthorized first publication of a noted figure's copyrighted expression.

The fact that a publication was commercial as opposed to non-profit is a separate factor that tends to weigh against a finding of fair use. "[E]very commercial use of copyrighted material is presumptively an unfair exploitation of the monopoly privilege that belongs to the owner of the copyright." [*Sony*] In arguing that the purpose of news reporting is not purely commercial, The Nation misses the point entirely. The crux of the profit/nonprofit distinction is not whether the sole motive of the use is monetary gain but whether the user stands to profit from exploitation of the copyrighted material without paying the customary price. [ ]

In evaluating character and purpose we cannot ignore The Nation's stated purpose of scooping the forthcoming hardcover and Time abstracts. [ ] The Nation's use had not merely the incidental effect but the *intended purpose* of supplanting the copyright holder's commercially valuable right of first publication. Also relevant to the "character" of the use is "the propriety of the defendant's conduct." . . . The trial court found that The Nation knowingly exploited a purloined manuscript. [ ] Unlike the typical claim of fair use, The Nation cannot offer up even the fiction of consent as justification. Like its competitor newsweekly, it was free to bid for the right of abstracting excerpts from "A Time to Heal." . . .

Nature of the copyrighted work. Second, the Act directs attention to the nature of the copyrighted work. "A Time to Heal" may be characterized as an unpublished historical narrative or autobiography. The law generally recognizes a greater need to disseminate factual works than works of fiction or fantasy. . . . Some of the briefer quotes from the memoir are arguably necessary adequately to convey the facts; for example, Mr. Ford's characterization of the White House tapes as the "smoking gun" is perhaps so integral to the idea expressed as to be inseparable from it. [ ] But The Nation did not stop at isolated phrases and instead excerpted subjective descriptions and portraits of public figures whose power lies in the author's individualized expression. Such use, focusing on the most expressive elements of the work, exceeds that necessary to disseminate the facts.

The fact that a work is unpublished is a critical element of its "nature." [ ] Our prior discussion establishes that the scope of fair use is narrower with respect to unpublished works. . . .

In the case of Mr. Ford's manuscript, the copyright holders' interest in confidentiality is irrefutable; the copyright holders had entered into a contractual undertaking to "keep the manuscript confidential" and required that all those to whom the manuscript was shown also "sign an agreement to keep the manuscript confidential." [ ] While the copyright holders' contract with Time required Time to submit its proposed article seven days before publication, The Nation's clandestine publication afforded no such opportunity for creative or quality control. [ ] It was hastily patched together and contained "a number of inaccuracies." [ ] A use that so clearly infringes the copyright holder's interests in confidentiality and creative control is difficult to characterize as "fair."

Amount and Substantiality of the Portion Used. Next, the Act directs us to examine the amount and substantiality of the portion used in relation to the copyrighted work as a whole. In absolute terms, the words actually quoted were an insubstantial portion of "A Time to Heal." The district court, however, found that "[T]he Nation took what was essentially the heart of the book." [ ] We believe the Court of Appeals erred in overruling the district judge's evaluation of the qualitative nature of the taking. See, e.g., *Roy Export Co. Establishment v. Columbia Broadcasting System, Inc.,* [672 F.2d 1095, 8 Med. L. Rptr. 1637 (2d Cir. 1982)] (taking of 55 seconds out of one hour and 29 minute film deemed qualitatively substantial). A Time editor described the chapters on the pardon as "the most interesting and moving parts of the entire manuscript." . . .

As the statutory language indicates, a taking may not be excused merely because it is insubstantial with respect to the *infringing* work. As Judge Learned Hand cogently remarked, "[N]o plagiarist can excuse the wrong by showing how much of his work he did not pirate." *Sheldon v. Metro–Goldwyn Pictures Corp.*, 81 F.2d 49, 56 ([2d Cir.]), [ ]. Conversely, the fact that a substantial portion of the infringing work was copied verbatim is evidence of the qualitative value of the copied material, both to the originator and to the plagiarist who seeks to profit from marketing someone else's copyrighted expression.

Stripped to the verbatim quotes,[8] the direct takings from the unpublished manuscript constitute at least 13% of the infringing article. See *Meeropol v. Nizer*, 560 F.2d 1061, 1071 ([2d Cir.] 1977) (copyrighted letters constituted less than 1% of infringing work but were prominently featured). The Nation article is structured around the quoted excerpts which serve as its dramatic focal points. [ ] In view of the expressive value of the excerpts and their key role in the infringing work, we cannot agree with the Second Circuit that the "magazine took a meager, indeed an infinitesimal amount of Ford's original language." [ ]

Effect on the Market. Finally, the Act focuses on "the effect of the use upon the potential market for or value of the copyrighted work." This last factor is undoubtedly the single most important element of fair use. . . . [O]nce a copyright holder establishes with reasonable probability the existence of a causal connection between the infringement and a loss of revenue, the burden properly shifts to the infringer to show that this damage would have occurred had there been no taking of copyrighted expression. [ ] Petitioners established a prima facie case of actual damage that respondent failed to rebut. [ ] The trial court properly awarded actual damages and accounting of profits. [ ]

. . .

It is undisputed that the factual material in the balance of The Nation's article, besides the verbatim quotes at issue here, was drawn exclusively from the chapters on the pardon. The excerpts were employed as featured episodes in a story about the Nixon pardon—precisely the use petitioners had licensed to Time. The borrowing of these verbatim quotes from the unpublished manuscript lent The Nation's piece a special air of authenticity—as Navasky [The Nation's editor] expressed it, the reader would know it was Ford speaking and not The Nation. Thus it directly competed for a share of the market for prepublication excerpts. . . .

V

. . . In sum, the traditional doctrine of fair use, as embodied in the Copyright Act, does not sanction the use made by The Nation of these

---

8. . . . The Court of Appeals found that only "approximately 300 words" were copyrightable but did not specify which words. The court's discussion, however, indicates it excluded from consideration those portions of The Nation's piece that, although copied verbatim from Ford's manuscript, were quotes attributed by Ford to third persons and quotations from government documents. At oral argument, counsel for The Nation did not dispute that verbatim quotes and very close paraphrase could constitute infringement. [ ] Thus the Appendix identifies as potentially infringing only verbatim quotes or very close paraphrase and excludes from consideration government documents and words attributed to third persons. The Appendix is not intended to endorse any particular rule of copyrightability but is intended merely as an aid to facilitate our discussion.

copyrighted materials. Any copyright infringer may claim to benefit the public by increasing public access to the copyrighted work. [ ] But Congress has not designed, and we see no warrant for judicially imposing, a "compulsory license" permitting unfettered access to the unpublished copyrighted expression of public figures.

The Nation conceded that its verbatim copying of some 300 words of direct quotation from the Ford manuscript would constitute an infringement unless excused as a fair use. Because we find that The Nation's use of these verbatim excerpts from the unpublished manuscript was not a fair use, the judgment of the Court of Appeals is reversed and remanded for further proceedings consistent with this opinion.

It is so ordered.

[Justice Brennan, joined by Justices Marshall and White, dissented. They would have held that The Nation's quotation of 300 words from the Ford book was fair use. They viewed the purpose of the copying as news reporting rather than commercial use and rejected the majority's "categorical presumption against prepublication fair use." The amount of material copied would not have been considered excessive if used in a book review and could not be considered less favorably because it appeared in a news report instead. Finally, Time's cancellation of its contract could not be accepted as proof of the negative effect of the copying on the serialization market, because that cancellation might have been the result of The Nation's protected publication of information and ideas from the manuscript, rather than the few quoted passages. "The Court's exceedingly narrow approach to fair use permits Harper & Row to monopolize information. . . . The Court imposes liability on The Nation for no other reason than that The Nation succeeding in being first to provide certain information to the public."

The dissenters also rejected Harper & Row's claim that even if copying of the quotations was protected, the article as a whole was an infringement. The article did not track the structure and language of the original closely enough support that theory, they said.]

Notes and Questions

1.   Would the analysis change if The Nation's article had appeared a week after the book was published? A week after the Time publication?

2.   During oral argument, counsel for The Nation asserted that "There are two words to describe what The Nation was doing: news reporting." Why does the majority reject that view?

3.   The Court makes much of the "right of first publication." Where is this right found? Given its importance in the Court's view, can any use of an unpublished work constitute fair use?

4.   The Court refers several times to how much of The Nation's article was taken from President Ford's memoir. Why is this relevant? Recall that section 107 requires the reviewing court to consider "the amount and

substantiality of the portion used in relation to the copyrighted work as a whole.''

During the Los Angeles riots that followed the acquittal of police officers accused of beating Rodney King, a mob pulled Reginald Denny from his truck and beat him. The episode was captured on videotape from a helicopter by Los Angeles News Service (LANS), an independent news organization that sells photos, videos, and news stories to media. Several television stations broadcast the video under license from LANS. Another station, KCAL–TV asked for a license to broadcast the footage but was turned down. KCAL then obtained a copy of the tape from another station and broadcast it several times in its news coverage without LANS's permission.

LANS sued for copyright infringement and KCAL defended on the ground of fair use, arguing that the tape was not merely a news report, but was news in itself. The Ninth Circuit rejected that argument on the ground that the station had not treated the tape as a news event, but had run it as if it were the station's own coverage. The court held that summary judgment for KCAL was improper. Although KCAL's use did not deprive LANS of its right of first publication, as in the *Harper & Row* case, "we cannot say that KCAL's use of the Denny tape had neither the effect nor purpose of depriving LANS of its also valuable right of licensing its original videotape which creatively captured the Denny beating in a way that no one else did." The court said the fact-finder could find against the station on all of the fair use factors except nature of the copyrighted work; because the tape was informational and factual, that factor weighed substantially in KCAL's favor. See Los Angeles News Service v. KCAL–TV Channel 9, 108 F.3d 1119, 25 Med. L. Rptr. 1506 (9th Cir.), cert. denied 522 U.S. 823 (1997).

b. Unpublished Material

Copyright exists not only in material prepared for publication, but also (since the 1976 Copyright Act) in communications never intended to be published, such as letters, memoranda, and tape recordings of a person's conversations or ruminations. This creates a potential problem for media: Do they violate copyright when they quote such material in news reports? In other contexts, the copyright owner's objection to unauthorized use usually is commercial—the owner wants to be paid, or wants to prevent the use in question in order to preserve the future commercial value of the work. Here it is to avoid publicity or prevent embarrassment or exposure of wrongdoing; can copyright law be used to suppress information? In some circumstances at least, the answer is yes.

The Salinger case. The Second Circuit held that J.D. Salinger, author of "Catcher in the Rye" and other novels and short stories, could prevent a biographer from quoting his unpublished letters even though Salinger had no intention of publishing them himself and had objected to their use primarily because he did not want a biography of him to be written at all. See Salinger v. Random House, Inc., 811 F.2d 90, 13 Med. L. Rptr. 1954 (2d Cir. 1987). The biographer, Ian Hamilton, literary critic of the Sunday Times of London, had read the letters in various university libraries to which they had been donated by the friends and associates to whom Salinger had sent them. Hamilton tried to meet Salinger's objections by paraphrasing most of the language he had originally quoted, but Salinger nevertheless sued to enjoin publication of the book. The district judge denied the injunction on the ground that the biography was a fair use of the letters, but the Second Circuit reversed and ordered the judge to grant the injunction.

The court thought *The Nation* case required it to place "special emphasis on the unpublished nature of Salinger's letters." Analyzing the fair use issue in that light, it found that only one of the factors favored the biographer, Hamilton. "Hamilton's purpose in using the Salinger letters to enrich his scholarly biography weighs the first fair use factor in Hamilton's favor. . . ."

The other factors all favored Salinger. Since the copyrighted letters were unpublished, the second factor (the nature of the copyrighted work) weighed "heavily" in favor of Salinger. So did the third factor (amount copied). The court said close paraphrases, as well as direct quotes, should be counted in making this determination. Counting paraphrases, the court concluded that Hamilton had used at least 10 percent of 42 letters, and at least one-third of 17 letters. "The taking is significant not only from a quantitative standpoint but from a qualitative one as well. The copied passages, if not the 'heart of the book,' [ ], are at least an important ingredient of the book as it now stands. To a large extent, they make the book worth reading. The letters are quoted or paraphrased on at least 40 percent of the book's 192 pages." [Note that the statute says the issue is the portion used in relation to the *copyrighted* work, not in relation to the infringing use.]

The fourth factor, effect on the market, weighed "slightly" in Salinger's favor, even though the court conceded that the book would not displace the market for the letters. "[T]he need to assess the effect on the market for Salinger's letters is not lessened by the fact that their author has disavowed any intention to publish them during his lifetime. First, the proper inquiry concerns the 'potential market' for the copyrighted work, [ ]. Second, Salinger has the right to change his mind. He is entitled to protect his *opportunity* to sell his letters, an opportunity estimated by his literary agent to have a current value in excess of $500,000." The court concluded:

> To deny a biographer like Hamilton the opportunity to copy the expressive content of unpublished letters is not, as appellees contend, to interfere in any significant way with the process of enhancing public knowledge of history or contemporary events. The facts may be reported. Salinger's letters contain a number of facts that students of his life and writings will no doubt find of interest, and Hamilton is entirely

free to fashion a biography that reports these facts. But Salinger has a right to protect the expressive content of his unpublished writings for the term of his copyright, and that right prevails over a claim of fair use under "ordinary circumstances," [*Harper & Row*]. Public awareness of the expressive content of the letters will have to await either Salinger's decision to publish or the expiration of his copyright, save for such special circumstances as might fall within the "narrower" scope of fair use available for unpublished works, [ ]. Evidently, public interest in the expressive content of the letters of a well-known writer remains substantial even fifty years after his death. [ ]

Is protection of an author's privacy within the purposes of the copyright system? Which elements of the fair use analysis are affected if an author's objective in invoking copyright law is not to protect his or her own right to profit from the work, but to prevent anyone from publishing it? The author of the *Salinger* opinion endorses the use of copyright law to protect privacy in Jon O. Newman, Copyright Law and the Protection of Privacy, 12 Colum.-VLA J.L. & Arts 459 (1988).

The New Era cases. The Second Circuit again addressed the issue of use of copyright law to suppress information in two cases involving unflattering biographies of L. Ron Hubbard, the founder of the Church of Scientology. The first case produced some sharp debate among the judges of the Second Circuit, but did not squarely decide the proper role of fair use analysis in this context. That case was New Era Publications International v. Henry Holt & Co., 873 F.2d 576, 16 Med. L. Rptr. 1559 (2d Cir. 1989). It involved a biography by Russell Miller entitled "Bare–Faced Messiah: The True Story of L. Ron Hubbard." The book contended that Hubbard and the Church of Scientology had glorified his image over a period of 30 years through various embellished and distorted accounts of Hubbard's life and activities in Hubbard's own writings and in information put out by the church.

Miller relied in part on information from court records, official documents, interviews, and newspaper stories, but in many instances the evidence of alleged discrepancies and distortions came from Hubbard's own unpublished works, such as letters and diaries. Copyright in these works was held by New Era under license from the Church of Scientology, to which Hubbard had bequeathed the rights upon his death.

New Era sought to enjoin publication of the biography in the United States. The case was decided at the trial level by Judge Leval, who had tried the *Salinger* case (and later was promoted to the bench of the Second Circuit). He believed the book, Bare–Faced Messiah, should be protected as fair use, but conceded that "given *Salinger*'s strong presumption against fair use for unpublished materials, I cannot conclude that the Court of Appeals would accord fair use protection to all of Miller's quotations, or that the biography as a whole would be considered non-infringing." He concluded that the book contained 44 passages that would not qualify as fair use under *Salinger*.

Nevertheless, Judge Leval exercised his equitable discretion to deny the injunction. He conceded that injunctive relief is common in copyright cases, but said those typically involve "piracy of artistic creations motivated exclusively by greed." This case was different:

> [A]n injunction would . . . suppress an interesting, well-researched, provocative study of a figure who, claiming both scientific and religious credentials, has wielded enormous influence over millions of people. . . . The abhorrence of the First Amendment to prior restraint is so powerful a force in shaping so many areas of our law, it would be anomalous to presume casually its appropriateness for all cases of copyright infringement. . . .
>
> In the past, efforts to suppress critical biography through the copyright injunction have generally not succeeded because courts (sometimes straining) have found fair use. [ ] The conflict between freedom of speech and the injunctive remedy was thus avoided. Since *Salinger,* however, the issue is inescapable.

He concluded that New Era's damage remedy was adequate to protect its copyright interests with far less harm to First Amendment interests. 695 F. Supp. 1493 (S.D.N.Y. 1988).

The Second Circuit affirmed, but only on the ground of laches. New Era had taken no steps to protect its rights until the book was in print, even though it had known for several years that it was being prepared. "The prejudice suffered by Holt as the result of New Era's unreasonable and inexcusable delay in bringing action invokes the bar of laches." Judge Miner wrote an extended opinion, however, in which the majority rejected Judge Leval's analysis on both the fair use and First Amendment points.

As to fair use, the court said Judge Leval's analysis was too generous to Holt, and as a result the book was a more serious infringement than Leval had concluded. Leval had suggested that use of an author's words to make a point about his character ought to be viewed more favorably than use of an author's words to display the distinctiveness of his writing style. He also urged a distinction between uses to merely "enliven" the text and uses that are necessary to communicate significant points about the subject. The court of appeals rejected both of those suggestions, and also disagreed with Leval's conclusion that Miller's book would not affect the market for an authorized biography of Hubbard, which New Era said it planned to commission.

As for Judge Leval's First Amendment concerns, the court was not persuaded "that any first amendment concerns not accommodated by the Copyright Act are implicated in this action. Our observation that the fair use doctrine encompasses all claims of first amendment in the copyright field [ ] has never been repudiated. See, e.g., [*Harper & Row*]. An author's expression of an idea, as distinguished from the idea itself, is not considered subject to the public's 'right to know.' [ ]."

Chief Judge Oakes concurred, but would have affirmed on the merits as well as on the laches ground. He believed there was no proof that Bare–

Faced Messiah would impair the future market value of Hubbard's writings, that the public interest in encouraging biographical work justified denying the injunction, and that "a non-injunctive remedy provides the best balance between the copyright interests and the First Amendment interests at stake in this case."

Although Henry Holt Co. had prevailed on the laches ground, it took the unusual step of requesting rehearing en banc to challenge the panel's conclusions on the fair use issue. The request was denied, 7–5, but it provoked a heated exchange of opinions among the judges of the Second Circuit. 884 F.2d 659, 16 Med. L. Rptr. 2224 (2d Cir. 1989). This exchange is well worth reading.

The second *New Era* case involved a different biography which used only Hubbard's published writings. The district court found 103 infringing passages in the biography and enjoined its publication, but the Second Circuit said all were fair use. The four factors all favored the biographer, the court said. The author's purpose was not to appropriate Hubbard's work, but "for the entirely legitimate purpose of making his point that Hubbard was a charlatan and the Church a dangerous cult." The court (an entirely different panel from the one that decided *New Era I*) said *New Era I* did not reject the idea that quotation to show character flaws could be fair use, but only held that such a purpose entitled the infringer to "no special consideration." None of the works copied was unpublished, and most were viewed as being factual rather than creative, so the nature of the copyrighted work favored the biographer. The book used only a small percentage of any of Hubbard's works, and the court did not view the quoted passages as containing the "heart" of the copyrighted material. The biography might dissuade the public from buying Hubbard's works, but only because it depicted him unfavorably, and the court said copyright law does not protect against that sort of injury.

New Era argued that the first *New Era* case held that copying for the purpose of demonstrating character defects is not fair use. But the court read the previous decision as holding only that such a purpose entitled the copier to no special consideration in fair use analysis. See New Era Publications v. Carol Publishing Group, 904 F.2d 152, 17 Med. L. Rptr. 1913 (2d Cir. 1990).

Congress responded to these cases in 1992 by adding the following to section 107: "The fact that a work is unpublished shall not itself bar a finding of fair use if such finding is made upon consideration of all of the above factors."

c. *Letters to the Editor*

Since the writer of a letter owns the copyright in it, he or she may impose conditions on the right to publish it, just as any other copyright holder may grant a conditional license to use of the copyrighted work. What implications does this have for publication of letters-to-the-editor?

In Diamond v. Am–Law Publishing Corp., 745 F.2d 142 (2d Cir. 1984), defendant American Lawyer published a story reporting that a formal grievance had been filed against the plaintiff, a lawyer. He wrote defendant demanding an apology and a retraction. The editor invited the plaintiff to write a letter stating that no grievance had been filed. Plaintiff then sent a long letter making that point and also attacking the reporting practices of the defendant. The letter stated that "You are authorized to publish this letter but only it its entirety." Defendant published excerpts from the letter that made the point about the grievance but omitted, without showing any deletions, the parts attacking the defendant.

The lawyer sued for infringement but lost because although the newspaper had no license to print the letter as edited, it could do so as a matter of fair use. The trial court's grant of summary judgment for the newspaper and its award of $15,000 in attorney's fees and costs were affirmed on appeal. Fair use was established as a matter of law. The non-use or editing of the letter did not put the copyrighted work in an unfair or distorted light. The omissions involved an unrelated matter and did not mislead the public about the contents of the entire letter. (Even if it did, it was not clear that this made it a copyright violation.) In any event, the use here was for comment or news reporting, uses protected under section 107. Finally, plaintiff could show no present or future use of the letter that had been adversely affected by defendant's use.

3. FIRST AMENDMENT IMPLICATIONS OF COPYRIGHT ENFORCEMENT

First Amendment challenges to copyright restrictions traditionally have been rejected on the ground that copyright law itself contains sufficient protections for free speech. The Court gave this answer to the First Amendment argument in the *Nation* case, supra. Many commentators vigorously dispute this proposition, however. See, e.g., Lawrence Lessig, Free Culture (2004), arguing that copyright has become a means by which a few large media companies, holding thousands of copyrights, monopolize the culture, stifle creativity, and thwart development of new technologies.

Professor Netanel argues that "the conflict between copyright and free speech falls solidly within the province of First Amendment doctrine." Judicial immunization of copyright law from First Amendment scrutiny has become "a peculiar and pernicious anomaly" because of the rampant expansion of copyright law in the past half-century at the same time that the First Amendment was becoming more protective of speech in other areas. Courts should subject copyright restrictions to the kind of intermediate scrutiny employed in Turner Broadcasting, supra p. 202, should require copyright holders to bear the burden of disproving fair use, and should award damages rather than injunctive relief when a user invokes a colorable but unsuccessful fair use defense. See Neil Weinstock Netanel, Locating Copyright Within the First Amendment Skein, 54 Stan. L. Rev. 1, 85–86 (2001).

Professor Baker argues that under a proper understanding of the First Amendment, existing copyright doctrines such as fair use and non-protection of facts and ideas make copyright restrictions on commercial copying constitutionally acceptable, but such restrictions generally should not be applied to non-commercial copying. "Copyright legislation that restricts an individual's expressive choices and copyright rules that limit the media's capacity to perform the democratic roles of a free press should be found unconstitutional under the First Amendment." C. Edwin Baker, First Amendment Limits on Copyright, 55 Vand. L. Rev. 891, 951 (2002).

Despite these and other criticisms, a majority of the Supreme Court remains unpersuaded. In Eldred v. Ashcroft, 537 U.S. 186 (2003), the Court rejected claims that the Copyright Term Extension Act of 1998, which extended the term of copyright from 50 to 70 years beyond the death of the author, violated both the Commerce Clause and the First Amendment. As for the claim that the term was now so long that it exceeded the Copyright Clause's authorization to protect copyright for "limited times," the Court said it was within Congress's power to fix the limit. As for the First Amendment claim:

> [T]he Copyright Clause and the First Amendment were adopted close in time. This proximity indicates that, in the Framers' view, copyright's limited monopolies are compatible with free speech principles. . . . [C]opyright law contains built-in First Amendment accommodations. [ ] First, it distinguishes between ideas and expression and makes only the latter eligible for copyright protection. . . . Second, the "fair use" defense allows the public to use not only facts and ideas contained in a copyrighted work, but also expression itself in certain circumstances.

The Court said copyrights are not "categorically immune from challenges under the First Amendment. . . . But when, as in this case, Congress has not altered the traditional contours of copyright protection, further First Amendment scrutiny is unnecessary."

Justice Stevens dissented on Copyright Clause grounds, and Justice Breyer on First Amendment grounds. Justice Breyer said the statute required closer constitutional analysis, though not necessarily intermediate scrutiny:

> This statute will cause serious expression-related harm. It will likely restrict traditional dissemination of copyrighted works. It will likely inhibit new forms of dissemination through the use of new technology. It threatens to interfere with efforts to preserve our Nation's historical and cultural heritage and efforts to use that heritage, say, to educate our Nation's children. It is easy to understand how the statute might benefit the private financial interests of corporations or heirs who own existing copyrights. But I cannot find any constitutionally legitimate, copyright-related way in which the statute will benefit the public. Indeed, in respect to existing works, the serious public harm and the virtually nonexistent public benefit could not be more clear.

[T]he statute cannot be understood rationally to advance a constitutionally legitimate interest. The statute falls outside the scope of legislative power that the Copyright Clause, read in light of the First Amendment, grants to Congress. I would hold the statute unconstitutional.

In what circumstances might enforcement of the Copyright Act violate the First Amendment? Time Inc. v. Bernard Geis Associates, 293 F. Supp. 130 (S.D.N.Y. 1968), involved the Zapruder film of the assassination of President Kennedy. Plaintiff bought and copyrighted Zapruder's film. Defendant wanted to produce a study of the assassination but could not come to terms with plaintiff on getting a license to use the photographs. Instead, defendant prepared sketches that were admittedly copied very closely from published copies of the Zapruder film. The court found the need for copying the expression very strong here because of the difficulty of paraphrasing photographs and the central importance of the film. The court found fair use after concluding that the defendant's book would not be likely to hurt the sales of plaintiff's possible future books or motion pictures incorporating the film.

If it were shown that the book had indeed seriously hurt plaintiff's sales of the copyrighted material, then fair use might not have been available. In such a case the copyright statute would permit Time, Inc. to seek compensatory damages or the defendant's profits for the infringement, and perhaps an injunction and punitive damages. Would the First Amendment permit these remedies?

In Twin Peaks Productions, Inc. v. Publications Int'l, Ltd., 996 F.2d 1366, 21 Med. L. Rptr. 1545 (2d Cir. 1993), the court mentioned the Zapruder film as a possible example of a case in which the non-protectable information that the defendant seeks to disseminate is inseparable from the copyrighted information. The court believed such a case might present a distinct First Amendment question not forestalled by the fair use doctrine.

If copyright is "not categorically immune" from First Amendment scrutiny, one might expect that prior restraints, at least, would be difficult to sustain. But as the *Salinger* case makes clear, injunctions are not disfavored in copyright law. Media attempts to bring the "heavy presumption of unconstitutionality" to bear on injunctions in this area have met with little success. See, e.g., In re Capital Cities/ABC, Inc., 918 F.2d 140, 18 Med. L. Rptr. 1450 (11th Cir. 1990). A plaintiff claiming to own exclusive rights to the story sought to enjoin ABC from broadcasting a movie about a Vietnam War POW who collaborated with the enemy. The court said the trial judge could view the film, decide which portions violated the plaintiff's copyright, and enjoin the broadcast of those portions of the movie. ABC argued that this would be a classic exercise of judicial censorship in violation of the First Amendment. But the court said it was a proper way of balancing ABC's First Amendment rights against the plaintiff's copyright interests. "Such a 'surgical' restraint does not 'give directives as to the content of expression,' only the manner of expression."

The readiness of courts to employ prior restraints in copyright cases was made clear in the case of Napster, a music software company that was enjoined from operating, and eventually put out of business, on the ground that it helped others infringe copyrights. A & M Records Inc. v. Napster, Inc., 239 F.3d 1004 (9th Cir. 2001).

The availability of preliminary injunctions poses one of the most significant conflicts between copyright law and traditional First Amendment law, and has become increasingly controversial. The Supreme Court has said the goals of copyright law are "not always best served by automatically granting injunctive relief." Campbell v. Acuff–Rose Music, Inc., 510 U.S. 569, 578 n. 10, 22 Med. L. Rptr. 1353 (1994). In the *Tasini* case, supra p. 473, the Court said its holding that the publishers were infringing the copyrights of freelancers did not necessarily mean that an injunction should issue.

The principle that courts will not enjoin a libel was well established as a matter of common law, and is now reinforced by the First Amendment's heavy presumption against prior restraints generally, which we saw in Chapter II, supra. The following excerpt considers why that traditional disdain for content-based prior restraints does not extend to copyright actions and questions the validity of treating copyright injunctions differently.

Freedom of Speech and Injunctions in Intellectual Property Cases

Mark A. Lemley and Eugene Volokh
48 Duke L.J. 147, 147–198 (1998).

Say we think a new book is going to libel us, and we ask a court for a preliminary injunction against the book's publication. We argue that we're likely to succeed on the merits of our libel claim, and that failure to enjoin the speech would cause us irreparable harm.

Too bad, the court will certainly say; a content-based preliminary injunction of speech would be a blatantly unconstitutional prior restraint. Maybe after a trial on the merits and a judicial finding that the speech is in fact constitutionally unprotected libel, we could get a permanent injunction, though even that's not clear. But we definitely could not get a preliminary injunction, based on mere likelihood of success. Likewise for preliminary injunctions against obscenity and other kinds of speech, despite the fact that such speech, if ultimately found to be unprotected at trial, could be criminally or civilly punished.

In copyright cases, though, preliminary injunctions are granted pretty much as a matter of course, even when the defendant has engaged in creative adaptation, not just literal copying. How can this be? True, the Supreme Court has held that copyright law is a constitutionally permissible speech restriction; though copyright law restricts what we can write or record or perform, the First Amendment doesn't protect copyright-infringing speech against such a restraint. But libel law and obscenity law are likewise constitutionally valid restrictions on speech, and yet courts refuse to allow preliminary injunctions there. The "First Amendment due process" rule against prior restraints applies even to speech that's alleged to be constitutionally unprotected. Why, then, not to allegedly infringing speech?

. . .

. . . . [C]ould it be that copyright law is somehow specially immune from the normal concerns surrounding other speech restrictions? We've often heard this view among copyright lawyers. While copyright law is clearly a speech restriction, to many it lacks that speech restriction flavor. It doesn't sound like censorship, just people enforcing their lawful property rights. Still, while many have this intuition, is there some specific reason underlying it, some reason that can justify setting aside the normal First Amendment procedural guarantees?

1. Property Rights. The argument that copyright law should be exempted from standard First Amendment procedural rules because it protects property rights strikes us as a non sequitur. Free speech guarantees can't be avoided simply by characterizing a speech restriction as an "intellectual property law." After all, one could plausibly view libel law as protecting a person's property interest in his reputation, or a company's property interest in its product's reputation—some courts have indeed done so. . . .

. . .

2. Private Enforcement. Because copyright law is largely enforced by private litigation rather than government prosecution, some argue that it's much less likely to turn into an engine of government censorship. But of course libel law is also enforced almost exclusively by private litigation. Despite this, courts correctly ban preliminary injunctions in libel cases, even those brought by people who aren't public officials.

. . .

3. Content–Neutrality. It's also incorrect to argue that intellectual property law is content-neutral and should therefore be subject to laxer rules. Copyright liability turns on the content of what is published.

. . .

4. Subject Matter of the Jeopardized Speech. Some suggest that injunctions in copyright cases pose less of a threat to free speech because they typically involve non-political matters; after all, would it be such a big deal if a court erroneously concluded that Battlestar Galactica infringes the plot of Star Wars? When the risk of error or chill falls only on such non-political material, the argument goes, there's no need for special procedural protections.

This argument, though, runs counter to fifty years of First Amendment precedents that give art, entertainment, comedy, and the like the same level of protection that is given to political speech. The Court has never suggested that the risk of erroneous restriction is less important as to these materials than as to political advocacy. . . .

. . .

5.   Copyright Law Furthers Free Speech Values. Nor can copyright law be exempted from the general prior restraint rules on the grounds that "copyright itself [can] be the engine of free expression." Copyright law's speech-enhancing effect, coupled with the specific constitutional authorization for copyright law, may justify holding copyright law to be a substantively valid speech restriction, though even this is in large part true because copyright law is limited in the powers it gives copyright owners. But the point of procedural rules, such as the prior restraint doctrine, is precisely to make sure that even substantively valid speech restrictions don't end up restricting speech that should remain protected.

Preliminary injunctions may be entered without a final adjudication that the speech is unprotected, and thus may restrict speech that is not in fact infringing, frustrating free expression rather than furthering it. And there's no reason to think that applying the prior restraint doctrine would substantially diminish copyright law's benefits to the marketplace of ideas: damages remedies and permanent injunctions entered after a final adjudication would still be available, and would give creators plenty of incentive.

. . .

6.   The Copyright and Patent Clause. Unlike libel and obscenity law, copyright laws have a specific textual hook in the Constitution. . . . In *Harper & Row*, the Court mentioned this as one reason why copyright law is a constitutionally permissible speech restriction. But the existence of the congressional power can't exempt copyright law from all First Amendment scrutiny. The Copyright and Patent Clause grants power to Congress, but the point of the Bill of Rights is to restrain the federal government in the exercise of its enumerated powers. In exercising its other powers, Congress is subject to First Amendment constraints: For instance, the government has the enumerated power to run the post office, but this doesn't mean it can refuse to carry communist propaganda; the government has power to regulate interstate commerce, but this doesn't mean it can impose content-based restrictions on the interstate distribution of newspapers. Likewise, in exercising its copyright power, Congress is bound by the Fourth, Fifth, and Sixth Amendments. Copyright law must be bound by the First Amendment too.

. . .

7.   Importance of the Government Interest. The interest promoted by copyright law—the interest in providing an incentive for the dissemination of ideas—is, even without regard to its constitutional status, quite important. One might even go so far as to call it "compelling," a term of constitutional significance.

But many speech restrictions—for instance, those aimed at protecting individual reputation, preventing harms caused by the distribution of child pornography, protecting national security, and preventing violent acts incited by violent advocacy—are justified by important (perhaps even compelling) interests, too. The requirement that speech be finally adjudicated to be unprotected before it can be enjoined doesn't prevent these important interests from being served; it just requires that they be served through a certain set of procedures. True, the procedures might in some cases make the process of vindicating these interests a bit less effective. But the general First Amendment judgment underlying the prior restraint doctrine is that this extra burden is justified by the interest in preventing the punishment of constitutionally protected speech.

8.   Irreparable Harm. Courts often stress that copyright infringements presumptively cause "irreparable injury," harm that can't be remedied by an eventual damages award. And to a certain extent that's true: preventing illegal behavior is generally more effective than is trying to compensate for the harms after they have occurred.

But this is true for virtually all kinds of harmful speech; for some kinds, such as libel, it's even more true than for copyright infringement. Copyright law is aimed primarily at ensuring that authors are economically rewarded so that they and others will continue to create new works of authorship—damages can generally reward authors relatively adequately and are often not terribly hard to estimate. Reputation, on the other hand, once sullied can never be perfectly repaired. Damages are only a highly imperfect palliative, may be impossible to get from an indigent defendant, and in any event are very hard to estimate, even roughly. Further, one might reasonably contend that enriching plaintiffs is not really the point of libel law, as it is with copyright: certainly one sees many cases of copyright owners licensing their rights in exchange for money, while it is harder to imagine people regularly selling others the right to defame them. Yet despite all this, libels may not be preliminarily enjoined.

. . .

9.   Ideas Can Be Expressed in Another Way. Copyright law, properly applied, generally restricts expression and not ideas or facts. Even a preliminarily enjoined speaker may be able to communicate the gist of his message, so long as he expresses it differently enough. Thus, some have suggested that copyright law is not a speech restriction because it leaves open adequate alternate channels of communication by allowing defendants to choose different words to express their ideas.

But obscenity law likewise restricts expression more than idea. . . .

Furthermore, while a damages award or a permanent injunction should by definition punish or restrict only copying of expression, preliminary injunctions may well enjoin even speech that will ultimately turn out to copy only facts or ideas. This is the nature of preliminary relief: because the test for entering a preliminary injunction turns on a reasonable likelihood of success on the merits, some fraction of preliminary injunctions will eventually prove to have enjoined speech that's not infringing—speech that copies only facts or ideas, or speech that's a fair use. So preliminary injunctions in copyright cases, like preliminary injunctions in libel cases, may often suppress facts and ideas, and not just particular modes of expression.

10. "The Only Question Is Who Gets to Do the Publishing." Some might argue that copyright law is unlike other restrictions because it doesn't actually suppress speech: the expression involved will in due course be published, but by the copyright owner and to his financial benefit. An injunction won't deprive the public of the speech; it will just cause the speech to come from a different person. As with the right of publicity, the argument would go, "the only question is who gets to do the publishing."

In cases of non-literal copying, though, this factual claim will often be wrong. Non-literal copiers, even when they use another's expression, are by definition creating something different from (albeit in some ways similar to) the copyright owner's work. . . . And when the expression is enjoined, the public will only see what the copyright owner is saying, not what the would-be copier wanted to say.

What's more, even if the copying is literal or close to it, a copyright injunction may well prevent the expression from reaching the public altogether, at least for the many decades that the copyright lasts; some copyright owners use copyright law precisely for this purpose. The whole point of a copyright injunction, as opposed to a suit for damages, is not merely to redistribute the profits, but to prevent dissemination of defendant's work. . . .

11. No Need for Timeliness. Some might argue that brief, temporary injunctions of movies or books pose little danger to free speech because such media, unlike newspapers or demonstrations, aren't particularly time-sensitive: it doesn't much matter whether you see a movie or read a book today or a week or two later.

This is a plausible argument, and is perhaps the best defense (though maybe still not an adequate defense) of the Court's toleration of prescreening systems for books and movies, so long as such systems really do create only a brief delay. It might justify some preliminary injunctions in copyright cases, and perhaps even libel cases, involving non-time-sensitive media.

But even for these injunctions, *Freedman v. Maryland* imposes certain requirements which copyright injunctions don't now satisfy—preliminary injunctions in copyright cases can last for many months, hardly the brief restraint that Freedman contemplates. And the timeliness argument can't justify any preliminary injunctions of more time-sensitive publications, such as newspaper articles or television programs or even articles in weekly magazines.

12. Tradition: "A Copyright Question, Not a Free Speech Question." Finally, we've heard some people argue that it's a mistake—a form of "constitutional law imperialism"—to disrupt, on recently discovered First Amendment grounds, a balance carefully established over 200 years. Whether preliminary injunctions should be available in copyright cases

should be seen, the argument goes, as a copyright law question, not as a free speech question.

Constitutional law imperialism, however, isn't our invention. The theory of *Marbury v. Madison* is that all U.S. laws are subject to the U.S. Constitution; and as the Court has clearly held, no "formulae for the repression of expression" can claim "talismanic immunity from constitutional limitations." Tradition alone cannot prevent constitutional scrutiny, as the Court made clear with respect to obscenity law and libel law, which had long been seen as not "raising any Constitutional problem" but which were ultimately held to be restrained by free speech principles. Sometimes, as in *Harper & Row*, the Court will conclude that a speech restriction passes constitutional muster; but all speech restrictions, regardless of their historical provenance, must be tested by First Amendment standards.

. . .

We thus see no compelling normative reason to treat copyright differently from other speech restrictions, restrictions that are likewise substantively valid but that nonetheless require certain procedural safeguards. And we see a good reason not to treat copyright more favorably than other speech restraints.

The First Amendment demands sacrifices from many who earnestly believe in the legitimacy of their favorite speech restrictions. Exempting restrictions such as copyright law—which is largely identified with rich and powerful interests—from the "normal" rules of the First Amendment throws the legitimacy of free speech protection into question. Partisans of restrictions on bigoted speech, for instance, routinely defend the restrictions they propose by pointing out that not all speech restrictions are looked upon with disfavor; while we disagree with their substantive proposals, they are right to demand that existing exceptions to the First Amendment get the same scrutiny as the proposed ones. Likewise, libel victims who are denied preliminary injunctions in their lawsuits against publishers deserve an explanation for why the same publishers routinely get preliminary injunctions in their lawsuits against supposed infringers.

Any special preference for copyright law must thus be justified by some substantial difference between copyright and other speech restrictions. Where, as here, no such difference exists, favoritism for a particular kind of speech restriction risks corroding public respect for First Amendment law more generally. And, ironically, publishers and producers—the very people who often benefit from the way copyright law now ignores First Amendment protections—have the most to lose from any corrosion of First Amendment protection outside copyright.

Notes and Questions

1. Professors Lemley and Volokh identify and then reject twelve distinctions between preliminary injunctions in copyright infringement cases and

other prior restraints. Is the authors' rejection of these twelve convincing? Are there other more viable distinctions?

2.   If there are no credible distinctions between preliminary injunctions in copyright infringement cases and other prior restraints, does that suggest that the traditional disfavor with which courts view prior restraints should be applied to copyright injunctions? Or does it suggest that preliminary injunctions in contexts other than copyright infringement cases should be more widely permitted? Or both?

PART THREE

LEGAL ISSUES ARISING FROM NEWSGATHERING

CHAPTER VIII

Newsgathering Torts

In the 1990s the aggressiveness of newsgatherers, especially television magazine and "reality" shows, set off an explosion of litigation complaining not about what the media publish or broadcast, but the tactics they use to acquire information and images. As we have seen in the preceding chapters, once the media obtain information, their right to publish it is generally protected by the First Amendment. But courts generally take the view that the First Amendment provides little or no protection for torts (or crimes) committed in the course of gathering news. At some point that surely is the case: few would expect the First Amendment to protect a reporter's right to commit burglary or a photographer's right to trespass into a person's home to gather news. But is it clear that liability for torts committed in the course of newsgathering is of no First Amendment concern? Suppose a state made it a tort to engage in uninvited telephone solicitation and subjected news media to liability for telephoning people at their homes to solicit their comments about newsworthy matters; would courts dismiss a constitutional challenge merely by branding the conduct as tortious? In *Branzburg v. Hayes*, infra p. 561, the Supreme Court recognized that "without some protection for seeking out the news, freedom of the press could be eviscerated." Nevertheless, the level of protection the media receive diminishes sharply when the tort occurs in the process of gathering information rather than publication.

Although the cases considered in this chapter all begin with a complaint about something the media did in the course of gathering information, they often also include claims for harm caused by publication of the information so obtained. Such claims cloud the distinction between publishing torts and newsgathering torts.

A disproportionate number of these cases originated in California. Whether the courts in the rest of the country will respond as the California Supreme Court and the Ninth Circuit have remains to be seen.

A. TRESPASS

A person commits a trespass when he enters property in the possession of another without authorization or consent. The media sometimes enter private property to gather information about newsworthy events. The First Amendment does not insulate them from trespass liability when they do, but as the following cases illustrate, courts will sometimes adapt tort law to accommodate unique issues presented when reporters trespass to gather news.

The Fletcher case. A 17–year–old girl perished in a fire at her home. News media representatives, including a photographer for the local newspaper, were invited into the badly damaged home by the fire marshal. The fire marshal ran out of film for his own camera and asked the newspaper photographer to take a picture of a "silhouette" left on the floor after the victim's body was removed, to demonstrate that the body was already on the floor before the heat from the fire damaged the floor. The photographer complied and gave a copy of the photo to police and fire officials. This photo and others were published in the newspaper the next day. The victim's mother, who had been out of town at the time of the fire, first learned of the facts surrounding her daughter's death from the newspaper story and accompanying photos.

The mother sued the newspaper for trespass, invasion of privacy, and intentional infliction of emotional distress. The trial court and the court of appeal granted judgment for defendant on the last two counts, but the court of appeal held that Mrs. Fletcher had a cause of action for trespass. The Florida Supreme Court reversed this determination, holding (4–1) that the landowner impliedly consented to entry by news personnel under these circumstances, by virtue of longstanding custom and practice. The newspaper had presented affidavits of news editors and law enforcement officials stating that it had been longstanding practice in Florida for representatives of news media to enter upon private premises where a disaster of great public interest has occurred, as long as they do so at the invitation of law enforcement officials and cause no physical damage to the premises. The case therefore came within the broader rule that there is no trespass where the entry is under circumstances from which the consent of the owner may be implied. Florida Publishing Co. v. Fletcher, 340 So.2d 914, 2 Med. L. Rptr. 1088 (Fla.1976).

Whether because it turned on peculiar facts, or because courts have little enthusiasm for its result, *Fletcher* has not been widely followed. Even in Florida, it has not been interpreted expansively. In Green Valley School Inc. v. Cowles Florida Broadcasting, Inc., 327 So.2d 810 (Fla.App.1976), television reporters had been invited to accompany officers on a midnight raid in search of evidence of sexual misbehavior and drug use at a controversial boarding school. The station's "custom and practice" defense to the school's trespass suit was rejected by the court of appeals. "In this jurisdiction, a law enforcement officer is not as a *matter of law* endowed with the right or authority to invite people of his choosing to invade private property and participate in a midnight raid of the premises." The Florida Supreme Court dismissed the station's appeal on the ground that the court of appeals decision was not in conflict with the principle endorsed in *Fletcher.* 340 So.2d 1154 (Fla.1976).

The Le Mistral case. In *Le Mistral v. Columbia Broadcasting System,* CBS, as owner and operator of WCBS–TV in New York City, directed reporter Rich and a camera crew to visit restaurants that had been cited for health code violations. Plaintiff's restaurant was one of those filmed. The jury found CBS liable for trespass and awarded plaintiff $1,200 in compensatory damages and $250,000 in punitive damages. After verdict (in a passage approved on appeal), the trial judge stated:

> The instructions given to the crew, whether specific to this event or as standing operating procedure, were to avoid seeking an appointment or permission to enter any of the premises where a story was sought, but to enter unannounced catching the occupants by surprise; "with cameras rolling" in the words of CBS' principal witness, Rich. From the evidence the jury was entitled to conclude that following this procedure the defendant's employees burst into plaintiff's restaurant in noisy and obtrusive fashion and following the loud commands of the reporter, Rich, to photograph the patrons dining, turned their lights and camera upon the dining room. Consternation, the jury was informed, followed. Patrons waiting to be seated left the restaurant. Others who had finished eating, left without waiting for their checks. Still others hid their faces behind napkins or table cloths or hid themselves beneath tables. (The reluctance of the plaintiff's clientele to be video taped was never explained, and need not be. Patronizing a restaurant does not carry with it an obligation to appear on television). [The] president of the plaintiff and manager of its operations, refused to be interviewed, and as the camera continued to "roll" he pushed the protesting Miss Rich and her crew from the premises. All told, the CBS personnel were in the restaurant not more than ten minutes, perhaps as little as one minute, depending on the testimony the jury chose to credit. The jury by its verdict clearly found the defendant guilty of trespass and from the admissions of CBS' own employees they were guilty of trespass. The witness Rich sought to justify her crew's entry into the restaurant by calling it, on a number of occasions, a "place of public accommodation," but, as she acknowledges, they did not seek to avail themselves of the plaintiff's "accommodation"; they had no intention of purchasing food or drink.

On appeal, the court held that the compensatory damage award was justified, but that there should be a new trial on the amount of punitive damages because the trial judge erroneously excluded testimony from a defense witness as to CBS's motive and purpose in entering the restaurant. Le Mistral, Inc. v. Columbia Broad. Sys., 61 A.D.2d 491, 402 N.Y.S.2d 815, 3 Med. L. Rptr. 1913 (1978). Apparently the restaurant ultimately did not receive any punitive damages. See TV Guide, May 3, 1980, at 6.

B. INTRUSION

Intrusion is a branch of the law of privacy, which we considered in Chapter V. Section 652B of the Restatement (Second) of Torts sets forth the elements of intrusion: "One who intentionally intrudes, physically or otherwise, upon the solitude or seclusion of another or his private affairs or concerns, is subject to liability to the other for invasion of his privacy, if the intrusion would be highly offensive to a reasonable person." Notice that while the other privacy torts deal with harm caused by publication, intrusion deals with the harm caused by conduct, including newsgathering activities.

Dietemann v. Time, Inc.

United States Court of Appeals, Ninth Circuit, 1971.
449 F.2d 245, 1 Med. L. Rptr. 2417.

[Plaintiff, "a disabled veteran with little education, was engaged in the practice of healing with clay, minerals, and herbs." He did not advertise, and he made no charges for his diagnoses or his prescriptions. Two employees of defendant's Life Magazine, Mrs. Metcalf and Mr. Ray, arranged with the office of the District Attorney of Los Angeles County to go to plaintiff's home. On the day in question they rang the bell outside plaintiff's locked gate. When he appeared they falsely stated that they had been sent by a certain person. Plaintiff unlocked the gate, admitted them to his house and brought them to his den. After using some equipment and holding what appeared to be a wand, plaintiff told Metcalf that she had a lump in her breast from having eaten rancid butter 11 years, 9 months and 7 days earlier. While plaintiff was examining Metcalf, Ray took photographs with a hidden camera. A radio transmitter hidden in Metcalf's purse transmitted the entire conversation to another Life employee and two government officials parked nearby. Life subsequently ran a story on plaintiff's activities, including a photograph and reference to the recorded conversation. Thereafter, when plaintiff was arrested for practicing medicine without a license, Life and newspaper photographers accompanied the police and took photographs. Plaintiff sued for damages on the ground that his privacy had been invaded by the intrusion. The district judge concluded that California would hold plaintiff entitled to damages and he awarded $1,000 general damages for injury to plaintiff's "feelings and peace of mind." Defendant appealed.]

Before CARTER and HUFSTEDLER, CIRCUIT JUDGES, and VON DER HEYDT, DISTRICT JUDGE.

HUFSTEDLER, CIRCUIT JUDGE.

. . .

The appeal presents three ultimate issues: (1) Under California law, is a cause of action for invasion of privacy established upon proof that defendant's employees, by subterfuge, gained entrance to the office portion of plaintiff's home wherein they photographed him and electronically recorded and transmitted to third persons his conversation without his consent as a result of which he suffered emotional distress? (2) Does the First Amendment insulate defendant from liability for invasion of privacy because defendant's employees did those acts for the purpose of gathering material for a magazine story and a story was thereafter published utilizing some of the material thus gathered? (3) Were the defendant's employees acting as special agents of the police and, if so, did their acts violate the First, Fourth, and Fourteenth Amendments of the Federal Constitution, thereby subjecting defendant to liability under the Civil Rights Act (42 U.S.C. § 1983)? Because we hold that plaintiff proved a cause of action under California law and that the First Amendment does not insulate the defendant from liability, we do not reach the third issue.

. . .

In jurisdictions other than California in which a common law tort for invasion of privacy is recognized, it has been consistently held that surreptitious electronic recording of a plaintiff's conversation causing him emotional distress is actionable. Despite some variations in the description and the labels applied to the tort, there is agreement that publication is not a necessary element of the tort, that the existence of a technical trespass is immaterial, and that proof of special damages is not required. [ ]

Although the issue has not been squarely decided in California, we have little difficulty in concluding that clandestine photography of the plaintiff in his den and the recordation and transmission of his conversation without his consent resulting in his emotional distress warrants recovery for invasion of privacy in California. . . .

. . .

We are convinced that California will "approve the extension of the tort of invasion of privacy to instances of intrusion, whether by physical trespass or not, into spheres from which an ordinary man in plaintiff's position could reasonably expect that the particular defendant should be excluded." [Citing Pearson v. Dodd, 410 F.2d 701 (D.C. Cir. 1969)].

Plaintiff's den was a sphere from which he could reasonably expect to exclude eavesdropping newsmen. He invited two of defendant's employees to the den. One who invites another to his home or office takes a risk that the visitor may not be what he seems, and that the visitor may repeat all he hears and observes when he leaves. But he does not and should not be required to take the risk that what is heard and seen will be transmitted by photograph or recording, or in our modern world, in full living color and hi-fi to the public at large or to any segment of it that the visitor may select. A different rule could have a most pernicious effect upon the dignity of man and it would surely lead to guarded conversations and conduct where candor is most valued, e.g., in the case of doctors and lawyers.

The defendant claims that the First Amendment immunizes it from liability for invading plaintiff's den with a hidden camera and its concealed electronic instruments because its employees were gathering news and its instrumentalities "are indispensable tools of investigative reporting." We agree that newsgathering is an integral part of news dissemination. We strongly disagree, however, that the hidden mechanical contrivances are "indispensable tools" of newsgathering. Investigative reporting is an ancient art; its successful practice long antecedes the invention of miniature cameras and electronic devices. The First Amendment has never been construed to accord newsmen immunity from torts or crimes committed during the course of newsgathering. The First Amendment is not a license to trespass, to steal, or to intrude by electronic means into the precincts of another's home or office.[2] It does not become such a license simply because the person subjected to the intrusion is reasonably suspected of committing a crime.

Defendant relies upon the line of cases commencing with *New York Times Co. v. Sullivan,* [ ] . . . to sustain its contentions that (1) publication of news, however tortiously gathered, insulates defendant from liability for the antecedent tort, and (2) even if it is not thus shielded from liability, those cases prevent consideration of publication as an element in computing damages.

As we previously observed, publication is not an essential element of plaintiff's cause of action. Moreover, it is not the foundation for the invocation of a privilege. Privilege concepts developed in defamation cases and to some extent in privacy actions in which publication is an essential component are not relevant in determining liability for intrusion conduct antedating publication. [ ] Nothing in *New York Times* or its progeny suggests anything to the contrary. Indeed, the Court strongly indicates that there is no First Amendment interest in protecting news media from calculated misdeeds. [ ]

No interest protected by the First Amendment is adversely affected by permitting damages for intrusion to be enhanced by the fact of later publication of the information that the publisher improperly acquired. Assessing damages for the additional emotional distress suffered by a plaintiff when the wrongfully acquired data are purveyed to the multitude chills intrusive acts. It does not chill freedom of expression guaranteed by the First Amendment. A rule forbidding the use of publication as an ingredient of damages would deny to the injured plaintiff recovery for real harm done to him without any countervailing benefit to the legitimate interest of the public in being informed. The same rule would encourage conduct by news media that grossly offends ordinary men.

The judgment is affirmed.

JAMES M. CARTER, CIRCUIT JUDGE (concurring and dissenting).

I concur in all of the majority opinion except that portion refusing to meet the issue of the liability of defendants' agents, acting as agents of the police. . . .

Notes and Questions

1.   The court says one "who invites another to his home or office takes a risk that the visitor may not be what he seems, and that the visitor may repeat all he hears and observes when he leaves." If that is true, why does Dietemann have a cause of action? Is it relevant that his premises were not open to the public?

2.   In this respect the facts of this case are different from those in *Pearson v. Dodd,* [ ]. In *Pearson,* the defendant received documents knowing that they had been removed by the donor without the plaintiff's consent. But the donor was not the defendant's agent, and the defendant did not participate in purloining the documents.

2. Is there a legally significant distinction to be drawn between one who discloses the substance of a communication and the taping of the communication itself? Is there a difference between a tape recorder, which preserves the words actually spoken, and a camera, which creates and preserves visual images that the reporters could have described afterward only from memory?

3. Could this case be analyzed as a trespass, with the defendants claiming consent and the plaintiff arguing that the consent was obtained by fraud? How would the damages be measured? On the court's theory what damages would be recoverable if the article had never been published? We defer discussion of the effect of fraud in inducing consent to the *Food Lion* case, infra p. 547.

4. If damages may be assessed here for the harm done by publication, what basis is there for according newsgathering torts less First Amendment protection than publication torts?

———

Galella v. Onassis. Photographer Ron Galella was the first prominent "paparazzo" in the United States. He won fame largely by photographing Jacqueline Kennedy Onassis and her children. Eventually Onassis caused Galella to be arrested, he sued her for violation of his civil rights and she counterclaimed for injunctive relief against Galella's continuous efforts to photograph her and her children. At trial she showed that Galella jumped in the path of John F. Kennedy Jr. as he was riding his bicycle in Central Park across the way from his home, interrupted Caroline Kennedy at tennis, invaded the children's private schools, and came uncomfortably close in a power boat to Onassis swimming. He bribed doormen and romanced a family servant to keep him advised of the movements of the family. The government intervened on Onassis's side in its capacity as protector of the children's safety.

The district court found the photographer guilty of harassment, intentional infliction of emotional distress, assault and battery, commercial exploitation of defendant's personality, and invasion of privacy. It found that Galella had on occasion intentionally physically touched Onassis and her daughter, caused fear of physical contact in his frenzied attempts to get their pictures, followed Onassis and her children too closely in an automobile, and endangered the safety of the children while they were swimming, water skiing and horseback riding.

Galella was enjoined from (1) keeping Onassis and her children under surveillance or following any of them; (2) approaching within 100 yards of their home, or within 100 yards of either child's school or within 75 yards of either child or 50 yards of defendant; (3) using the name, portrait or picture of Onassis or her children for advertising; and (4) attempting to communicate with them except through their attorney.

The court of appeals affirmed but modified the injunction. It agreed with the district court that Galella had "insinuated himself into the very fabric of Mrs. Onassis' life . . .," and said such conduct might or might not be an invasion of privacy under New York law, but was clearly proscribable under New York's statute prohibiting harassment:

> Of course legitimate countervailing social needs may warrant some intrusion despite an individual's reasonable expectation of privacy and freedom from harassment. However the interference allowed may be no greater than that necessary to protect the overriding public interest. Mrs. Onassis was properly found to be a public figure and thus subject to news coverage. [ ] Nonetheless, Galella's action went far beyond the reasonable bounds of news gathering. When weighed against the *de minimis* public importance of the daily activities of [Onassis], Galella's constant surveillance, his obtrusive and intruding presence, was unwarranted and unreasonable. If there were any doubt in our minds, Galella's inexcusable conduct toward [the] children would resolve it.

As for Galella's claim that his activity was protected by the First Amendment, the court said:

> There is no such scope to the First Amendment right. Crimes and torts committed in news gathering are not protected. Branzburg v. Hayes, 408 U.S. 665 (1972); [ ]; Dietemann v. Time Inc., 449 F.2d 245 (9th Cir. 1971) [ ] There is no threat to a free press in requiring its agents to act within the law.

But the court found that the injunction went too far and "unnecessarily infringe[d] on reasonable efforts to 'cover' defendant." The court therefore modified the lower court's order to prevent the defendant from coming within 25 feet of Jacqueline Onassis, from impeding "her movement in public places, from acting in a way that would place her life and safety [ ] in jeopardy," and from engaging in "any conduct which would reasonably be foreseen to harass, alarm, or frighten the defendant." The court also affirmed the injunction regarding Onassis' children, albeit with modifications:

> . . . Galella thus may be enjoined from (a) entering the children's schools or play areas; (b) engaging in action calculated or reasonably foreseen to place the children's safety or well being in jeopardy, or which would threaten or create physical injury; (c) taking any action which could reasonably be foreseen to harass, alarm, or frighten the children; and (d) from approaching within thirty (30) feet of the children.
>
> . . .
>
> As modified, the relief granted fully allows Galella the opportunity to photograph and report on Mrs. Onassis' public activities. Any prior restraint on news gathering is miniscule and fully supported by the findings.

A dissenting judge thought the district court's injunction should have been affirmed without modification. Galella v. Onassis, 487 F.2d 986, 1

Med. L. Rptr. 2425 (2d Cir. 1973). How did the court determine that 25 feet was the correct distance to safeguard Mrs. Onassis' privacy and safety?

Nine years later, Galella was found guilty of 12 violations of the injunction by taking photographs within 25 feet of Mrs. Onassis. The judge suspended a fine of $120,000 when Galella agreed to pay the $10,000 in legal fees incurred by Onassis and agreed never again to photograph her. Galella v. Onassis, 533 F. Supp. 1076, 8 Med. L. Rptr. 1321 (S.D.N.Y.1982).

Why didn't Onassis sue for trespass? Can a person pursue a claim for a trespass on a third person's property? In states other than New York, the plaintiff would be able to invoke the common law tort of intrusion. In such states, would it ever make sense to sue for trespass instead of suing for intrusion? How might the intrusion tort apply to the *Galella* case?

Anti-paparazzi legislation. Accusations that photographers pursuing her car contributed to the death of Princess Diana in Paris in 1997 created a wave of public concern about press treatment of celebrities, particularly by freelance photographers who sell their photos to tabloids. California enacted a statute making it a tort to trespass on the premises of third parties to get pictures or recordings of "personal or familial activity" or to use visual or auditory enhancing devices to obtain photos or recordings of such activities under circumstances that give the subject a reasonable expectation of privacy. Violators are liable for up to three times the amount of compensatory damages, and also for punitive damages and disgorgement of profits. The statute also attempts to reach the media who use paparazzi by exposing them to liability for causing a violation of the statute, "regardless of whether there is an employer-employee relationship." Cal. Civ. Code. § 1708.8. Would this statute cover anything that is not already covered by the common law tort of intrusion? Paparazzi and the tabloids that are the main buyers of their images argue that they are trying to break through the carefully crafted images that celebrities cultivate and expose the truth about them. Should that justification be taken into account in deciding whether paparazzi deserve First Amendment protection?

———

It has been common for law enforcement and emergency services to permit media to accompany them and observe, photograph, and film rescues, arrests, and raids. Often these events occur in public places, but sometimes the media have accompanied officers into homes and other places where people might have expectations of privacy. Beginning in the 1990s, "reality television" shows presenting these activities as entertainment produced a rash of suits by people unwillingly portrayed in these situations. Some suits were against the media, some against the officers or agencies that permitted the "ride-alongs," and some against both. So far as unconsented media presence in homes is concerned, the following decision appears likely to end the practice.

Wilson v. Layne

Supreme Court of the United States, 1999.
526 U.S. 603, 119 S. Ct. 1692, 143 L. Ed.2d 818, 27 Med. L. Rptr. 1705.

[Deputy federal marshals and local police invited a reporter and photographer from the Washington Post to accompany them when they conducted a raid to arrest a fugitive named Dominic Wilson. The officers, wearing street clothes, broke into a residence at 6:45 a.m. The residents, Charles and Geraldine Wilson, were sleeping. When he heard the commotion, Charles ran into the living room, wearing only briefs. He confronted the officers, demanded to know their business, and cursed them. They wrestled him to the floor. Geraldine Wilson, dressed only in a nightgown, emerged from the bedroom. The reporter observed the events and the photographer took pictures. Dominic Wilson was not present and no one was arrested. The Post did not publish the photos. The Wilsons sued the officers on the theory that the officers had violated their Fourth Amendment rights by bringing the reporter and photographer into their home. The Court of Appeals held that the defendants were entitled to summary judgment on the ground of qualified immunity, because the presence of the news personnel did not violate any constitutional right that was clearly established at the time.]

CHIEF JUSTICE REHNQUIST delivered the opinion of the Court.

. . .

The Fourth Amendment embodies [the] centuries-old principle of respect for the privacy of the home: "The right of the people to be secure in their persons, houses, papers, and effects, against unreasonable searches and seizures, shall not be violated, and no warrants shall issue, but upon probable cause, supported by oath or affirmation, and particularly describing the place to be searched, and the persons or things to be seized." U.S. Const. Amend. IV, [ ].

[T]he common-law tradition at the time of the drafting of the Fourth Amendment was ambivalent on the question of whether police could enter a home without a warrant. We were ultimately persuaded that the "overriding respect for the sanctity of the home that has been embedded in our traditions since the origins of the Republic" meant that absent a warrant or exigent circumstances, police could not enter a home to make an arrest. [ ] We decided that "an arrest warrant founded on probable cause implicitly carries with it the limited authority to enter a dwelling in which the suspect lives when there is reason to believe the suspect is within." [ ]

Here, of course, the officers had such a warrant, and they were undoubtedly entitled to enter the Wilson home in order to execute the arrest warrant for Dominic Wilson. But it does not necessarily follow that they were entitled to bring a newspaper reporter and a photographer with them. . . . [T]he Fourth Amendment does require that police actions in execution of a warrant be related to the objectives of the authorized intrusion, [ ].

Certainly the presence of reporters inside the home was not related to the objectives of the authorized intrusion. Respondents concede that the reporters did not engage in the execution of the warrant, and did not assist the police in their task. The reporters therefore were not present for any reason related to the justification for police entry into the home—the apprehension of Dominic Wilson.

. . .

Respondents argue that the presence of the Washington Post reporters in the Wilsons' home nonetheless served a number of legitimate law enforcement purposes. They first assert that officers should be able to exercise reasonable discretion about when it would "further their law enforcement mission to permit members of the news media to accompany them in executing a warrant." [ ] But this claim ignores the importance of the right of residential privacy at the core of the Fourth Amendment. It may well be that media ride-alongs further the law enforcement objectives of the police in a general sense, but that is not the same as furthering the purposes of the search. Were such generalized "law enforcement objectives" themselves sufficient to trump the Fourth Amendment, the protections guaranteed by that Amendment's text would be significantly watered down.

Respondents next argue that the presence of third parties could serve the law enforcement purpose of publicizing the government's efforts to combat crime, and facilitate accurate reporting on law enforcement activities. There is certainly language in our opinions interpreting the First Amendment which points to the importance of "the press" in informing the general public about the administration of criminal justice. [The Court cited *Cox Broadcasting Corp. v. Cohn*, supra p. 378, and *Richmond Newspapers, Inc. v. Virginia*, infra p. 673.]

Surely the possibility of good public relations for the police is simply not enough, standing alone, to justify the ride-along intrusion into a private home. And even the need for accurate reporting on police issues in general bears no direct relation to the constitutional justification for the police intrusion into a home in order to execute a felony arrest warrant.

Finally, respondents argue that the presence of third parties could serve in some situations to minimize police abuses and protect suspects, and also to protect the safety of the officers. While it might be reasonable for police officers to themselves videotape home entries as part of a "quality control" effort to ensure that the rights of homeowners are being respected, or even to preserve evidence, [ ], such a situation is significantly different from the media presence in this case. The Washington Post reporters in the Wilsons' home were working on a story for their own purposes. They were not present for the purpose of protecting the officers, much less the Wilsons. A private photographer was acting for private purposes, as evidenced in part by the fact that the newspaper and not the police retained the photographs. Thus, although the presence of third parties during the execution of a warrant may in some circumstances be constitutionally permissible, [ ], the presence of these third parties was not.

The reasons advanced by respondents, taken in their entirety, fall short of justifying the presence of media inside a home. We hold that it is a violation of the Fourth Amendment for police to bring members of the media or other third parties into a home during the execution of a warrant when the presence of the third parties in the home was not in aid of the execution of the warrant.

III

Since the police action in this case violated the petitioners' Fourth Amendment right, we now must decide whether this right was clearly established at the time of the search. [The majority held it was not unreasonable for a police officer in April 1992 to have believed that bringing media observers along during the execution of an arrest warrant (even in a home) was lawful; it was not obvious from the general principles of the Fourth Amendment that such conduct violated the Amendment, there were no judicial opinions holding the practice unlawful, and in the absence of other authority the officers were entitled to rely on the official Marshal's Service ride-along policy which explicitly contemplated that media who engaged in ride-alongs might enter private homes with their cameras as part of fugitive apprehension arrests. The judgment of the Court of Appeals ordering summary judgment for the defendants was affirmed.]

[Justice Stevens agreed that the presence of members of the media violated the Fourth Amendment rights of the plaintiffs, but he dissented from the holding that the officers were nevertheless immune.] . . . The clarity of the constitutional rule, a federal statute (18 U.S.C. § 3105), common-law decisions, and the testimony of [a] senior law enforcement officer all support my position that it has long been clearly established that officers may not bring third parties into private homes to witness the execution of a warrant. . . .

Notes and Questions

1. Is it now "clearly established" that it is unconstitutional for officers to allow media to accompany them into a home to make an arrest? Into a home for any purpose? Onto private premises of any kind? Into any situation where unwilling participants have reasonable expectations of privacy?

2. When might media presence serve a legitimate law enforcement purpose? Does this decision mean that media presence cannot be constitutionally permissible if it has any journalistic purpose, even if it also serves some law enforcement purpose?

3. If media presence is "unreasonable" for Fourth Amendment purposes, what implications does that have for media defenses to state law torts such as trespass or intrusion? Does it help establish the "offensiveness" require-

ment of the intrusion tort? Does it preclude a "custom and practice" defense to a trespass action?

––––––––

Media liability for participating in ride-alongs. Wilson did not address media liability, but several other decisions do. One of the most important is Berger v. Hanlon, 129 F.3d 505, 25 Med. L. Rptr. 2505 (9th Cir. 1997). In *Berger*, federal agents with a search warrant entered plaintiffs' Montana ranch looking for evidence that the rancher had been killing eagles. Under a contract with the federal agency, CNN went along to get footage for a show it was doing on the poisoning of eagles. A federal agent was wired with a secret CNN microphone that transmitted to a nearby CNN crew. CNN produced eight hours of tape.

The rancher later was convicted on one misdemeanor count of misusing pesticide but was acquitted of three felony counts of killing eagles. The rancher and his wife sued the federal agents and CNN for various federal and state torts. The federal claim was under Bivens v. Six Unknown Agents, 403 U.S. 388 (1971), alleging that the agents violated plaintiffs' constitutional rights by inviting CNN along and that CNN did so by acting in concert with the agents so as to become federal actors themselves. The trial judge granted summary judgment for all the defendants, but the court of appeals reversed.

The raid violated the Fourth Amendment, the court of appeals said, and CNN could be held liable along with the agents for violating the landowners' constitutional rights because CNN's involvement was so extensive that they became state actors. "This was no ordinary search. It was jointly planned by law enforcement officials and the media, as memorialized by a written contract, so that the officials could assist in the media obtaining material for their commercial programming. . . . This search stands out as one that at all times was intended to serve a major purpose other than law enforcement." The Magistrate who granted the search warrant did not know of CNN's deal with the federal agents.

The court said videotaping for law enforcement purposes would not render a search unreasonable, but characterized this taping as for "entertainment purposes." The court found that taping a residential search for commercial television purposes is unreasonable. The court relied on *Dietemann*, supra p. 503, to reject the media argument that the plaintiffs consented to the entry by the agents and CNN crew and thereby also consented to the possibility that they might be secretly taping. Plaintiffs had an expectation of privacy in their dealings with the wired agent.

Because of the written agreement and the sharing of information, the media were government actors for *Bivens* purposes. There was "inextricable" media involvement in planning and executing the search. But for this same reason CNN could not be held liable under the federal wiretap statute, which the court said does not apply to those acting under color of law.

In the state-based claim of trespass, CNN relied on the *Fletcher* case, supra p. 501, for the existence of a privilege for the media to accompany officers onto private premises. But the court distinguished *Fletcher* on the ground that it involved a calamity and great public interest, neither of which were present here. It remanded the trespass claim for further consideration of Montana law. The court also concluded that an action might lie for intentional infliction of emotional distress under Montana law. The court rejected conversion claims on the ground that "recorded sounds and images cannot be the subject of a conversion claim."

Both the officers and CNN applied for certiorari. The Supreme Court denied CNN's petition, 575 U.S. 961 (1998), but granted that of the officers and then vacated the appellate court's decision and ruled against the plaintiffs on the basis of the qualified immunity recognized by *Wilson v. Layne*. Nevertheless, the Court in its per curiam opinion said the Bergers "alleged a Fourth Amendment violation under our decision today in *Wilson v. Layne*." Hanlon v. Berger, 526 U.S. 808, 27 Med. L. Rptr. 1716 (1999). Should that be understood as meaning *Wilson v. Layne* is not confined to intrusions into homes? Does it make a difference that the federal agent who entered the Bergers' home was wearing a secret microphone transmitting to CNN?

On remand, despite the Supreme Court's holding that the officers were entitled to qualified immunity, the Ninth Circuit held that the media defendants were not, citing cases holding that private actors who conspire with federal officers do not share the immunity granted to the latter. The court held that the Bergers' state-law claims against CNN for trespass and intentional infliction of emotional distress also could proceed to trial. It affirmed summary judgment for the defendants on the federal wiretap claim. See Berger v. Hanlon, 188 F.3d 1155, 27 Med. L. Rptr. 2213 (9th Cir. 1999). CNN eventually settled with the Bergers after the district court rejected CNN's renewed motion to dismiss. The settlement included a confidentiality clause preventing the parties from revealing the amount of the settlement. See CNN Settles Privacy Suit over Involvement in Search of Ranch, http://www.rcfp.org/news/2001/0608cablen.html.

Parker v. Boyer. In another case involving media participating in a search, the Eighth Circuit rejected the argument that a television crew's involvement was state action sufficient to subject the television station to liability under 42 U.S.C. § 1983. Parker v. Boyer, 93 F.3d 445, 24 Med. L. Rptr. 2307 (8th Cir. 1996), cert. denied 519 U.S. 1148 (1997). The court held that since the camera crew and the police did not assist each other in performing their separate missions, the television crew was not acting under the color of state law and therefore did not violate section 1983. The court rejected an argument that the reporter became an agent of the state by exercising a right or privilege created by the state when it gave the media permission to accompany the officers. "Seizing an opportunity is not the same as invoking a right or privilege." A dissenter argued that the news crew was a state actor because it acted in concert with the police in entering the home. "The news crew came to the location with the police and could not have entered if the police had not done so first."

For a comprehensive listing of "ride-along" cases and a discussion of the various factors that influence their outcomes, see Karen M. Markin, An "Unholy Alliance": The Law of Media Ride–Alongs, 12 CommLaw Conspectus 33 (2004).

———

The ride-along cases discussed above involved media coverage of events on private premises. Are the media safe when they cover arrests, rescues, or disasters in public places?

Shulman v. Group W Productions, Inc.

Supreme Court of California, 1998.
18 Cal.4th 200, 955 P.2d 469, 74 Cal. Rptr.2d 843, 26 Med. L. Rptr. 1737.

As Modified on Denial of Rehearing.

WERDEGAR, JUSTICE.

. . .

In the present case, we address the balance between privacy and press freedom in the commonplace context of an automobile accident. Plaintiffs, two members of a family whose activities and position did not otherwise make them public figures, were injured when their car went off the highway, overturning and trapping them inside. A medical transport and rescue helicopter crew came to plaintiffs' assistance, accompanied on this occasion by a video camera operator employed by a television producer. The cameraman filmed plaintiffs' extrication from the car, the flight nurse and medic's efforts to give them medical care during the extrication, and their transport to the hospital in the helicopter. The flight nurse wore a small microphone that picked up her conversations with other rescue workers and with one of the plaintiffs. This videotape and sound track were edited into a segment that was broadcast, months later, on a documentary television show, *On Scene: Emergency Response*. Plaintiffs, who consented neither to the filming and recording nor to the broadcasting, allege the television producers thereby intruded into a realm of personal privacy and gave unwanted publicity to private events of their lives.

The trial court granted summary judgment for the producers on the ground that the events depicted in the broadcast were newsworthy and the producers' activities were therefore protected under the First Amendment to the United States Constitution. The Court of Appeal reversed, finding triable issues of fact exist as to one plaintiff's claim for publication of private facts and legal error on the trial court's part as to both plaintiffs' intrusion claims. Agreeing with some, but not all, of the Court of Appeal's analysis, we conclude summary judgment was proper as to plaintiffs' cause of action for publication of private facts, but not as to their cause of action for intrusion.[2]

I. Publication of Private Facts

[The majority held that the broadcast of plaintiffs' words and images was "newsworthy as a matter of law and, therefore, cannot be the basis for tort liability under a private facts claim." The dissenting justices thought this issue should be left to the jury to determine.]

II. Intrusion

Of the four privacy torts identified by Prosser, the tort of intrusion into private places, conversations or matters is perhaps the one that best captures the common understanding of an "invasion of privacy." It encompasses unconsented-to physical intrusion into the home, hospital room or other place the privacy of which is legally recognized, as well as unwarranted sensory intrusions such as eavesdropping, wiretapping, and visual or photographic spying. (See Rest.2d Torts, § 652B, com. b., pp. 378–379, and illustrations.) It is in the intrusion cases that invasion of privacy is most clearly seen as an affront to individual dignity. . . .

. . . [T]he action for intrusion has two elements: (1) intrusion into a private place, conversation or matter, (2) in a manner highly offensive to a reasonable person. We consider the elements in that order.

We ask first whether defendants "intentionally intrude[d], physically or otherwise, upon the solitude or seclusion of another," that is, into a place or conversation private to Wayne or Ruth. (Rest.2d Torts, § 652B; *Miller, supra,* 187 Cal. App.3d at p. 1482, 232 Cal. Rptr. 668.) "[T]here is no liability for the examination of a public record concerning the plaintiff. . . . [Or] for observing him or even taking his photograph while he is walking on the public highway." [ ]. To prove actionable intrusion, the plaintiff must show the defendant penetrated some zone of physical or sensory privacy surrounding, or obtained unwanted access to data about, the plaintiff. The tort is proven only if the plaintiff had an objectively reasonable expectation of seclusion or solitude in the place, conversation or data source. [ ]

Cameraman Cooke's mere presence at the accident scene and filming of the events occurring there cannot be deemed either a physical or sensory intrusion on plaintiffs' seclusion. Plaintiffs had no right of ownership or possession of the property where the rescue took place, nor any actual control of the premises. Nor could they have had a reasonable expectation that members of the media would be excluded or prevented from photo-

---

2. Five justices (Chief Justice George, Justice Mosk, Justice Kennard, Justice Chin and myself) conclude summary judgment was proper on the cause of action for publication of private facts. Five justices (Chief Justice George, Justice Kennard, Justice Baxter, Justice Brown and myself) conclude summary judgment was improper on the cause of action for intrusion. Part I of this opinion's discussion expresses the views of a majority of the court's members. [ ] Part II expresses a majority's views except for the reservations stated by Justice Brown. [ ]

graphing the scene; for journalists to attend and record the scenes of accidents and rescues is in no way unusual or unexpected. [ ]

Two aspects of defendants' conduct, however, raise triable issues of intrusion on seclusion. First, a triable issue exists as to whether both plaintiffs had an objectively reasonable expectation of privacy in the interior of the rescue helicopter, which served as an ambulance. Although the attendance of reporters and photographers at the scene of an accident is to be expected, we are aware of no law or custom permitting the press to ride in ambulances or enter hospital rooms during treatment without the patient's consent. [ ] Other than the two patients and Cooke, only three people were present in the helicopter, all Mercy Air staff. As the Court of Appeal observed, "[i]t is neither the custom nor the habit of our society that any member of the public at large or its media representatives may hitch a ride in an ambulance and ogle as paramedics care for an injured stranger." [ ]

Second, Ruth was entitled to a degree of privacy in her conversations with Carnahan and other medical rescuers at the accident scene, and in Carnahan's conversations conveying medical information regarding Ruth to the hospital base. Cooke, perhaps, did not intrude into that zone of privacy merely by being present at a place where he could hear such conversations with unaided ears. But by placing a microphone on Carnahan's person, amplifying and recording what she said and heard, defendants may have listened in on conversations the parties could reasonably have expected to be private.

The Court of Appeal held plaintiffs had no reasonable expectation of privacy at the accident scene itself because the scene was within the sight and hearing of members of the public. The summary judgment record, however, does not support the Court of Appeal's conclusion; instead, it reflects, at the least, the existence of triable issues as to the privacy of certain conversations at the accident scene, as in the helicopter. The videotapes (broadcast and raw footage) show the rescue did not take place "on a heavily traveled highway," as the Court of Appeal stated, but in a ditch many yards from and below the rural superhighway, which is raised somewhat at that point to bridge a nearby crossroad. From the tapes it appears unlikely the plaintiffs' extrication from their car and medical treatment at the scene could have been observed by any persons who, in the lower court's words, "passed by" on the roadway. Even more unlikely is that any passersby on the road could have heard Ruth's conversation with Nurse Carnahan or the other rescuers.

Whether Ruth expected her conversations with Nurse Carnahan or the other rescuers to remain private and whether any such expectation was reasonable are, on the state of the record before us, questions for the jury. We note, however, that several existing legal protections for communications could support the conclusion that Ruth possessed a reasonable expectation of privacy in her conversations with Nurse Carnahan and the other rescuers. A patient's conversation with a provider of medical care in the course of treatment including emergency treatment, carries a traditional and legally well-established expectation of privacy. [ ]

. . .

We turn to the second element of the intrusion tort, offensiveness. . . .

[A]ll the circumstances of an intrusion, including the motives or justification of the intruder, are pertinent to the offensiveness element. Motivation or justification becomes particularly important when the intrusion is by a member of the print or broadcast press in the pursuit of news material. Although, as will be discussed more fully later, the First Amendment does not immunize the press from liability for torts or crimes committed in an effort to gather news [ ], the constitutional protection of the press does reflect the strong societal interest in effective and complete reporting of events, an interest that may—as a matter of tort law—justify an intrusion that would otherwise be considered offensive. While refusing to recognize a broad privilege in newsgathering against application of generally applicable laws, the United States Supreme Court has also observed that "without some protection for seeking out the news, freedom of the press could be eviscerated." (*Branzburg v. Hayes* (1972) [infra p. 561]; [ ]).

In deciding, therefore, whether a reporter's alleged intrusion into private matters (i.e., physical space, conversation or data) is "offensive" and hence actionable as an invasion of privacy, courts must consider the extent to which the intrusion was, under the circumstances, justified by the legitimate motive of gathering the news. Information collecting techniques that may be highly offensive when done for socially unprotected reasons— for purposes of harassment, blackmail or prurient curiosity, for example— may not be offensive to a reasonable person when employed by journalists in pursuit of a socially or politically important story. Thus, for example, "a continuous surveillance which is tortious when practiced by a creditor upon a debtor may not be tortious when practiced by media representatives in a situation where there is significant public interest [in discovery of the information sought]." (Hill, *Defamation and Privacy Under the First Amendment* (1976) 76 Colum. L.Rev. 1205, 1284.)

The mere fact the intruder was in pursuit of a "story" does not, however, generally justify an otherwise offensive intrusion; offensiveness depends as well on the particular method of investigation used. At one extreme, " 'routine . . . reporting techniques,' " such as asking questions of people with information ("including those with confidential or restricted information") could rarely, if ever, be deemed an actionable intrusion. [ ] At the other extreme, violation of well-established legal areas of physical or sensory privacy—trespass into a home or tapping a personal telephone line, for example—could rarely, if ever, be justified by a reporter's need to get the story. Such acts would be deemed highly offensive even if the information sought was of weighty public concern; they would also be outside any protection the Constitution provides to newsgathering. (*Cohen v. Cowles Media Co.*, [supra p. 429]; *Dietemann,* [supra p. 503].)

Between these extremes lie difficult cases, many involving the use of photographic and electronic recording equipment. Equipment such as hidden cameras and miniature cordless and directional microphones are powerful investigative tools for newsgathering, but may also be used in ways that severely threaten personal privacy. California tort law provides no bright line on this question; each case must be taken on its facts.

On this summary judgment record, we believe a jury could find defendants' recording of Ruth's communications to Carnahan and other rescuers, and filming in the air ambulance, to be " 'highly offensive to a reasonable person.' " [ ] With regard to the depth of the intrusion [ ], a reasonable jury could find highly offensive the placement of a microphone on a medical rescuer in order to intercept what would otherwise be private conversations with an injured patient. In that setting, as defendants could and should have foreseen, the patient would not know her words were being recorded and would not have occasion to ask about, and object or consent to, recording. Defendants, it could reasonably be said, took calculated advantage of the patient's "vulnerability and confusion." [ ] Arguably, the last thing an injured accident victim should have to worry about while being pried from her wrecked car is that a television producer may be recording everything she says to medical personnel for the possible edification and entertainment of casual television viewers.

For much the same reason, a jury could reasonably regard entering and riding in an ambulance—whether on the ground or in the air—with two seriously injured patients to be an egregious intrusion on a place of expected seclusion. . . .

Nor can we say as a matter of law that defendants' motive—to gather usable material for a potentially newsworthy story—necessarily privileged their intrusive conduct as a matter of common law tort liability. A reasonable jury could conclude the producers' desire to get footage that would convey the "feel" of the event—the real sights and sounds of a difficult rescue—did not justify either placing a microphone on Nurse Carnahan or filming inside the rescue helicopter. . . . A reasonable jury could find that defendants, in placing a microphone on an emergency treatment nurse and recording her conversation with a distressed, disoriented and severely injured patient, without the patient's knowledge or consent, acted with highly offensive disrespect for the patient's personal privacy . . .

Turning to the question of constitutional protection for newsgathering, one finds the decisional law reflects a general rule of *nonprotection:* the press in its newsgathering activities enjoys no immunity or exemption from generally applicable laws. [ ]

"It is clear that the First Amendment does not invalidate every incidental burdening of the press that may result from the enforcement of civil and criminal laws of general applicability. Under prior cases, otherwise valid laws serving substantial public interests may be enforced against the press as against others, despite the possible burden that may be imposed." (*Branzburg v. Hayes,* [ ]) California's intrusion tort and section 632 [the

California eavesdropping statute] are both laws of general applicability. They apply to all private investigative activity, whatever its purpose and whoever the investigator, and impose no greater restrictions on the media than on anyone else. . . .

. . . The conduct of journalism does not depend, as a general matter, on the use of secret devices to record private conversations. *Dietemann*, [ ] More specifically, nothing in the record or briefing here suggests that reporting on automobile accidents and medical rescue activities depends on secretly recording accident victims' conversations with rescue personnel or on filming inside an occupied ambulance. Thus, if any exception exists to the general rule that "the First Amendment does not guarantee the press a constitutional right of special access to information not available to the public generally" *Branzburg v. Hayes*, [ ], such exception is inapplicable here.

. . .

[The court reversed the grant of summary judgment for the defense on the intrusion claim and remanded for trial.]

CHIN, JUSTICE, concurring and dissenting.

[After discussing the private facts claims, Justice Chin explained why he dissented from the holding that the intrusion claims should be remanded.]

Ruth's expectations notwithstanding, I do not believe that a reasonable trier of fact could find that defendants' conduct in this case was "highly offensive to a reasonable person," the test adopted by the plurality. Plaintiffs do not allege that defendants, though present at the accident rescue scene and in the helicopter, interfered with either the rescue or medical efforts, elicited embarrassing or offensive information from plaintiffs, or even tried to interrogate or interview them. Defendants' news team evidently merely recorded newsworthy events "of legitimate public concern" [ ] as they transpired. Defendants' apparent motive in undertaking the supposed privacy invasion was a reasonable and nonmalicious one: to obtain an accurate depiction of the rescue efforts from start to finish. The event was newsworthy, and the ultimate broadcast was both dramatic and educational, rather than tawdry or embarrassing.

. . .

In short, to turn a jury loose on the defendants in this case is itself "highly offensive" to me. I would reverse the judgment of the Court of Appeal with directions to affirm the summary judgment for defendants on all causes of action.

BROWN, JUSTICE, concurring and dissenting.

I concur in the plurality's conclusion that summary judgment should not have been granted as to the cause of action for intrusion, and I generally concur in its analysis of that cause of action.[1] I respectfully

---

1. I decline to join the plurality opinion's discussion of the intrusion cause of action in its entirety. As the plurality notes, "[t]he conduct of journalism does not depend,

dissent, however, from the conclusion that summary judgment was proper as to plaintiff Ruth Shulman's cause of action for publication of private facts. [Justice Brown's extensive discussion of the private facts claim is omitted.]

Notes and Questions

1.   After this decision the parties reached a settlement that included an agreement not to disclose its terms. The plaintiffs' lawyer asserted that it was hypocritical of the defendants to insist on confidentiality. "For eight years these defendants maintained that what happened to Ruth was in the public domain, and now they insist the settlement be top secret. Don't you think the resolution of this case is of greater public interest than her ordeal ever was?" See National Law Journal, Sept. 14, 1999, at A6. Is there merit in this complaint about confidential settlements?

2.   Assume a bystander at the accident scene purposely placed himself close enough so that he could overhear conversations between Ruth and Nurse Carnahan. Would Ruth have a cause of action against the bystander for intrusion? Would the fact that a bystander was able to overhear these conversations defeat Ruth's claim against the producers of *On Scene: Emergency Response*? Would it at least defeat that portion of the claim based on the filming and audiotaping at the accident scene?

3.   What is the basis of Wayne's intrusion claim? Is the possibility that his conversations could have been recorded enough to form the basis of a claim?

4.   Should newsworthiness be a defense to an intrusion claim? Why or why not?

C.   EAVESDROPPING AND WIRETAPPING

Deteresa v. American Broadcasting Companies, Inc.
United States Court of Appeals, Ninth Circuit, 1997.
121 F.3d 460, 25 Med. L. Rptr. 2038.

Cert. denied 523 U.S. 1137 (1998).

Before: O'SCANNLAIN and TASHIMA, CIRCUIT JUDGES; WHALEY, DISTRICT JUDGE.

O'SCANNLAIN, CIRCUIT JUDGE:

We must decide whether a television producer violated laws against eavesdropping when he surreptitiously taped his conversation with a woman who refused to appear on his show.

as a general matter, on the use of secret devices to record private conversations." [ ] Therefore, I do not share the view that "[e]quipment such as hidden cameras and miniature cordless and directional microphones are powerful investigative tools for newsgathering." [ ] On a more fundamental level, I disagree with the artificial barrier the plurality erects between the publication of private facts and the intrusion causes of action. Unlike the plurality, for instance, I would hold that the depth of the intrusion into private affairs and the lawfulness of the news media's conduct are relevant to *both* causes of action.

I

On June 12, 1994, Nicole Brown Simpson and Ronald Goldman were murdered at Ms. Simpson's Los Angeles home. Shortly after the murders, O.J. Simpson, Ms. Simpson's ex-husband, traveled from Los Angeles to Chicago on American Airlines flight 668. Beverly Deteresa was an attendant on that flight.

On June 19, 1994, Anthony Radziwill, a producer for American Broadcasting Companies, Inc. ("ABC"), came to the door of Deteresa's condominium in Irvine, California. Radziwill told Deteresa that he worked for ABC and wanted to speak with her about appearing on a television show to discuss the flight. Deteresa asked for identification, and Radziwill showed her an ABC picture I.D. Deteresa initially told Radziwill that she was not interested in appearing on the show. She did reveal, however, that she was "frustrated" to hear news reports about the flight that she knew were false. She informed Radziwill, for instance, that contrary to the reports she had heard, Simpson had not kept his hand in a bag during the flight. She also told Radziwill how many passengers had sat in first class and in which seat Simpson had sat. Before Radziwill left, Deteresa told him that she would "think about" appearing on his show.

Radziwill called Deteresa the next morning, June 20, 1994. He asked her again if she would go on camera. When Deteresa declined, Radziwill told her that he had audiotaped their entire conversation the previous day. He also had directed a cameraperson to videotape them from a public street adjacent to Deteresa's home. Deteresa hung up on Radziwill and told her husband, Matthew Deteresa, what had happened. Matthew Deteresa called Radziwill and told him that his wife did not want ABC to broadcast the videotape. Radziwill replied that ABC did not need consent to broadcast the videotape. Matthew then spoke with someone at ABC named "Doc." Matthew asked either Doc or Radziwill not to broadcast the Deteresas' address, Beverly's name, or the audiotape.

That night, ABC broadcast a five-second clip of the videotape on a program called "Day One." Simultaneous to the clip, an ABC announcer stated that "the flight attendant who served Simpson in the first class section told 'Day One' that she did not, as widely reported, see him wrap his hand in a bag of ice." ABC did not broadcast any portion of the audiotape.

[The district court granted the defendants summary judgment.]

II

Deteresa's first cause of action alleges that ABC and Radziwill violated the California eavesdropping statute when Radziwill audiotaped his conversation with Deteresa.

California Penal Code section 632(a) provides:

Every person who, intentionally and without the consent of all parties to a confidential communication, by means of any electronic amplifying or recording device, eavesdrops upon or records the confidential communication, whether the communication is carried on among the parties in the presence of one another or by means of a telegraph, telephone or other device, except a radio, shall be punished. . . .

Cal. Penal Code § 632(a). Section 637.2(a) permits a civil action against a person who violates the eavesdropping statute. [ ]

What the parties dispute is whether Radziwill audiotaped a "confidential communication." If the communication between Radziwill and Deteresa was not confidential, section 632(a) does not apply. Section 632(c) [states:

The term "confidential communication" includes] any communication carried on in circumstances as may reasonably indicate that any party to the communication desires it to be confined to the parties thereto, but excludes a communication made in a public gathering or in any legislative, judicial, executive or administrative proceeding open to the public, or in any other circumstance in which the parties to the communication may reasonably expect that the communication may be overheard or recorded.

Id. § 632(c).

[The court concluded that the California Supreme Court would construe the term "confidential communication" to require "a reasonable expectation that the content of the communication has been entrusted privately to the listener," as opposed to merely a reasonable expectation that the conversation was not being overheard.]

[W]e must ask whether Deteresa had an objectively reasonable expectation that the conversation would not be divulged to anyone else. ABC and Radziwill contend that there is no triable issue as to the fact that Deteresa had no such expectation—Radziwill immediately revealed that he worked for ABC and wanted Deteresa to appear on television to discuss the flight; Deteresa did not tell Radziwill that her statements were in confidence; Deteresa did not tell Radziwill that the conversation was just between them; and Deteresa did not request that Radziwill not share the information with anyone else. Radziwill, for his part, did not promise to keep what Deteresa told him in confidence. We agree, from these undisputed facts, that no one in Deteresa's shoes could reasonably expect that a reporter would not divulge her account of where Simpson had sat on the flight and where he had or had not kept his hand.

Deteresa and Radziwill also chatted about Radziwill's famous relatives, including John F. Kennedy, Jr. At some point they discussed what ABC could do to make Deteresa more comfortable about coming down to the studio to be taped for an interview. Deteresa contends that Radziwill's casual demeanor led her to believe that the conversation was "off the record." Casual or not, these parts of conversation were about Radziwill's famous relatives and about what ABC was willing to do to make Deteresa more comfortable. No reasonable juror could find that Deteresa reasonably expected that a reporter would not divulge these parts of the conversation to anyone else.

The district court thus properly granted summary judgment as to Deteresa's section 632(a) cause of action.

III

Deteresa's second cause of action alleges that ABC and Radziwill tortiously invaded her privacy by intrusion into seclusion.

. . .

This is not, contrary to Deteresa's contention, a case in which a news team entered someone's bedroom without authorization to film a rescue attempt by paramedics. [ ] Nor is it a case in which someone gained entrance into another's home by subterfuge. *Dietemann v. Time, Inc.*, [supra p. 503]. Nor is it a case in which a private investigator obtained entrance into a hospital room by deception. Noble v. Sears, Roebuck & Co., 33 Cal. App. 3d 654, 109 Cal. Rptr. 269 (1973).

Rather, Deteresa spoke voluntarily and freely with an individual whom she knew was a reporter. He did not enter her home, let alone did he enter by deception or trespass. There is no evidence that any intimate details of anyone's life were recorded. No portion of what was recorded was ever broadcast.

The district court properly concluded from these undisputed facts that the intrusion was not sufficiently offensive to state a common law intrusion into seclusion privacy claim.

[The court denied Deteresa's claim under the federal eavesdropping statute, 18 U.S.C. § 2511, because there was no evidence that Radziwill's purpose in taping the conversation was to commit a crime or tort. See infra p. 527. A fraud claim was rejected on the ground that Radziwill had no duty under California law to disclose to Deteresa that he was taping. Deteresa's claim that ABC committed an unfair business practice by engaging in widespread tortious or criminal use of hidden cameras failed for lack of any proof of that allegation.]

Affirmed.

WHALEY, DISTRICT JUDGE, concurring in part and dissenting in part:

[Judge Whaley dissented on the question of liability under the California eavesdropping statute. He thought a communication should be treated as confidential when one of the parties has a reasonable expectation that no one is eavesdropping.]

There are a number of reasons why the Legislature might decide to place control over confidentiality in the hands of the speaker rather than the listener or solicitor of the communication. One is the distinction between the privacy interests that are implicated by secondhand repetition of a communication as opposed to surreptitious recording or monitoring.

See, e.g., *Ribas v. Clark*, [infra p. 528] (Privacy Act creates distinction between the risk that private comments will be betrayed by the listener and the infringement on privacy that attends their secret taping). As the Court of Appeal has explained:

> In the former situation [i.e., secondhand repetition] the speaker retains control over the extent of his immediate audience. Even though that audience may republish his words, it will be done secondhand, after the fact, probably not in its entirety, and the impact will depend on the credibility of the teller. Where electronic monitoring is involved, however, the speaker is deprived of the right to control the extent of his own firsthand dissemination. . . . In this regard participant monitoring . . . den[ies] the speaker a most important aspect of privacy of communication, the right to control the extent of first instance dissemination of his statements. [ ]

The [majority's interpretation] reduces this "important aspect of privacy of communication" to a nullity when one of the parties to a communication is a reporter. The result is a de facto rule that individuals who talk to reporters presumptively consent to the secret recording of those conversations. In some circumstances, such as [a tabloid reporter notorious for breaking promises of confidentiality], this presumption is effectively irrebuttable. It is difficult, if not impossible, to reconcile this result with the Legislature's clearly expressed intent to "protect the right of privacy of the people of this state." Cal. Penal Code § 630. . . .

. . . In my view, the focus of our inquiry should be whether Deteresa had a reasonable expectation that Radziwill knew she did not want her statements divulged, not whether she had a reasonable expectation he would actually keep her confidence.

II.

[Judge Whaley argued that even under the majority's interpretation of the statute, a genuine issue remained for trial.] The majority's analysis looks to the circumstances surrounding the Deteresa—Radziwill conversation but appears to give dispositive weight to the fact that Radziwill identified himself to Deteresa as an employee of ABC. While a plaintiff certainly has a more difficult case . . . when her confidant is a member of the news media, it is not impossible to prove a reasonable expectation of confidentiality in a conversation with a reporter.[3] Certainly, news correspondents' family members can have such an expectation as to intimate matters, and it is an accepted convention in the news media that the contents of a communication made "off the record" or on "deep background" cannot be divulged unless gained from another source. That said, the fact that Deteresa's statements were not expressly conditioned on nondissemination, and the fact that she assumed Radziwill was a reporter, work to her disadvantage.

---

3. Although Radziwill was a producer, not a reporter, the record indicates Deteresa assumed he was a reporter.

The nature of the conversation obviously is also important. As the majority notes, Deteresa's discussion of previously unknown information about one of the top news stories of the day certainly cuts against the reasonableness of an expectation those comments would not be divulged. There was more to the conversation than these statements, however. At the outset of the conversation, for example, Radziwill told Deteresa that he was approaching her to see if she would be willing to appear on his television program, not that he wanted interview her at that time. Deteresa refused this invitation and a conversation ensued that focused principally on whether Radziwill and ABC could overcome this refusal. Deteresa contends that she was lulled by Radziwill's "casual demeanor" into believing that her subsequent comments about her flight were "off the record," emphasizing that Radziwill did not attempt to interview her, was not attended by a visible camera crew or recording device, and that he did not take any notes of their conversation. Additionally, Deteresa points to the fact that their conversation included a discussion of the importance of individual privacy, including a general conversation relating to the invasions of privacy experienced by Radziwill's famous relatives. While these factors do not amount to a compelling case, the conversational context in which Deteresa made her comments to Radziwill, viewed in the light most favorable to her, supports the position that she reasonably expected those comments would not be disseminated.

The location of the conversation is also relevant. Here the conversation occurred on Deteresa's doorstep after she was unexpectedly called to the door. There is certainly a distinction between the comments that one may make to a reporter in a public forum as opposed to those that are made on the threshold of one's home. Moreover, the final clause of § 632(c) expressly recognizes that whether a statement is likely to be overheard is a relevant consideration in the determination of whether the statement is confidential. While the majority correctly concludes in Part III supra that Deteresa did not have a reasonable expectation of privacy as to her image because she could be readily seen from the street, the record does not support a conclusion that her comments could be overheard from a public place. Because of the greater expectation of privacy that inheres from the home, and the fact that the record does not establish that Deteresa's comments could be heard from the street, this factor weighs in Deteresa's favor.

Additionally, it is undisputed that Deteresa's comments were secretly recorded from the very moment she opened her door. Thus, the privacy interest that California recognizes as inhering in the surreptitious recording of statements was infringed before Deteresa was given an opportunity to determine whether her comments were on the record. Unless § 632 countenances a presumption that all communications made from one's doorstep to a media representative may be secretly recorded, Radziwill's taping of Deteresa's statements comments violated § 632 at least until the circumstances indicated she reasonably expected her comments would be reported.

In sum, though Deteresa's case is not particularly strong, there is sufficient evidence in the record to permit a reasonable juror to infer from the circumstances of her conversation with Radziwill that she desired and reasonably expected her communications would not be disseminated.

III.

The purpose of California's Privacy Act was to sharply restrict the legality of wiretapping, eavesdropping, and surreptitious recording, thereby remedying "a serious threat to the free exercise of personal liberties" and "protect[ing] the right of privacy of the people of this state." Cal. Penal Code § 630. The majority's interpretation and application of § 632 frustrates that intent by allowing media representatives to approach persons at their homes, uninvited, and secretly record their statements without attempting to secure permission. Because I believe that a genuine issue remains for trial on the question of whether such conduct was permissible in this case, I respectfully dissent.

Notes and Questions

1. What are the respective merits of the majority and dissenting views as to the meaning of "confidential communication"? In an omitted portion of the opinion the majority explained the difference with this hypothetical:

> Suppose X and Y are hiking in the woods. Y offers to pay X the $5.00 that Y owes X. X tells Y to pay the money to Z, because X owes Z $5.00. When X finds out that Y had taped the conversation, he sues Y. Under [the dissent's view] X wins because in the wilderness he had a reasonable expectation that no one overheard their conversation. Under [the majority's view] Y wins, because X had a reasonable expectation that Y would divulge the conversation to Z.

2. Under this decision, can a person ever have a reasonable expectation that a conversation with a reporter will not be disclosed? Is not being taped?

3. Accepting the majority's view on that issue, what are the merits of the two opinions as to whether a jury question exists?

4. What is the significance of the majority's reference to the *Dietemann* case as one involving subterfuge in gaining access? What role did that play in *Dietemann*?

"Consent." Some statutes, like the one at issue in *Deteresa*, require the consent of all parties. Others permit eavesdropping or wiretapping with the "consent" of any party, thus permitting anyone to record a conversation to which he or she is a party. (This of course is not consent in the usual sense; a tortfeasor cannot consent on behalf of the victim.) Most of the state statutes are of the so-called "one-party consent" variety, as is the federal

Electronic Communications Privacy Act, 18 U.S.C. § 2510 et seq. The federal act permits a participant to eavesdrop or wiretap or authorize a third party to do so, so long as the recording is not "for the purpose of committing any criminal or tortious act. . . ." 18 U.S.C. § 2511(2)(d). This phrase precludes liability in most newsgathering situations, because journalists usually are a party to the conversations they record.

Even if the recording itself is tortious, it does not violate the federal statute unless it is done for a tortious or criminal *purpose*. "Where the taping is legal, but is done for the purpose of facilitating some further impropriety, such as blackmail, section 2511 applies. Where the purpose is not illegal or tortious, but the means are, the victims must seek redress elsewhere." See Sussman v. American Broadcasting Cos., 186 F.3d 1200, 27 Med. L. Rptr. 2337 (9th Cir. 1999), cert. denied 528 U.S. 1131 (2000). This appeal involved the same clandestine videotaping found to be actionable in *Sanders v. ABC*, infra p. 530. In *Sussman,* the court said "Athough ABC's taping may well have been a tortious invasion of privacy under state law [as indicated by *Sanders*], plaintiffs have produced no probative evidence that ABC had an illegal or tortious purpose when it made the tape," and summary judgment for ABC on the federal claims therefore was proper. (Their state law claims were not at issue in this appeal.)

One court read into the federal statute a blanket exemption for journalists, on the theory that "Congress never intended, at least in cases involving media defendants and giving rise to First Amendment considerations, to provide a cause of action for conduct relative to the gathering and disseminating of news which does not rise to the level of a crime or a tort. . . ." See Boddie v. American Broadcasting Cos., 694 F. Supp. 1304, 16 Med. L. Rptr. 1100 (N.D.Ohio 1988).

Sussman rejected this interpretation. "Congress could have drafted the statute so as to exempt all journalists from its coverage, but did not. Instead, it treated journalists just like any other party who tapes conversations surreptitiously." The court said a news organization that secretly videotaped bedroom activities for a legitimate newsgathering purpose (e.g., listening for "pillow talk" about some newsworthy event) could be liable under the federal statute if the use of the tape also had a purpose such as tortious disclosure of private facts. "The existence of the lawful purpose would not sanitize a tape that was also made for an illegitimate purpose; the taping would violate 2511." Nevertheless, media have rarely been sued under the federal statute or the state statutes that follow the "one-party consent" model.

Statutes that follow the California model, requiring consent of all parties, are of far greater concern to the media. Many journalists apparently had been unaware of their potential liabilities under these statutes until Linda Tripp was indicted in 1999 under a Maryland statute of this type. Tripp's surreptitious recordings of her conversations with Monica Lewinsky led to the impeachment of President Clinton.

The Maryland statute is particularly strict, making it a felony to intercept any wire, oral, or electronic communication, even if the communication is not private or confidential. It is also a felony under the statute to disclose or use a communication known to have been illegally intercepted. See Md. Cts. & Jud. Proc. § 10–401. Tripp was indicted for intercepting (by taping Lewinsky's conversations) and for disclosing the tapes to Newsweek. See Tripp Indicted on Charges of Wiretapping; Maryland Law Prohibits Taping Without Consent, Wash. Post, July 31, 1999, at A1. The prosecution was dropped after the judge excluded Lewinsky's testimony that the prosecutor said would establish that Tripp continued to tape conversations after her lawyer told her it was illegal. The judge said Lewinsky's recollection of the date of the conversation was tainted by her discussion of the matter with Kenneth Starr's special prosecutors. See Maryland Is Dropping Wiretap Case Against Tripp, N.Y. Times, May 25, 2000, at A12.

Constitutionality of "all-party consent" statutes: Reporters and others challenged a Florida statute that forbade taping without the consent of all parties. They claimed the use of concealed recording equipment was essential to investigative reporting for three reasons: it aided accuracy of reporting; persons being interviewed would not be candid if they knew they were being recorded; and the recording provided corroboration in case of suit for defamation.

The Florida Supreme Court rejected the challenge. The statute allows "each party to a conversation to have an expectation of privacy from interception by another party to the conversation. It does not exclude any source from the press, intrude upon the activities of the news media in contacting sources, prevent the parties to the communication from consenting to the recording, or restrict the publication of any information gained from the communication. First Amendment rights do not include a constitutional right to corroborate news gathering activities when the legislature has statutorily recognized the private rights of individuals." In response to the argument that secret recording may be the only way to get credible information about crime, the court stated that protection against intrusion might extend even to a person "reasonably suspected of committing a crime." Shevin v. Sunbeam Television Corp., 351 So.2d 723, 3 Med. L. Rptr. 1312 (Fla.1977).

The Supreme Court dismissed the media appeal for want of a substantial federal question, 435 U.S. 920 (1978). Justices Brennan, White and Blackmun would have noted probable jurisdiction and set the case for oral argument.

Expectations of privacy. Like the statute at issue in *Deteresa*, many of the statutes (of both types) make the wiretapping or eavesdropping actionable only if it violated the plaintiff's reasonable expectation of privacy. In view of the widespread availability of technology that makes spying relatively easy, when do people have reasonable expectations that their conversations are private? Do the following cases provide any guidance?

The California Supreme Court has said a party to a telephone conversation can have a reasonable expectation that no one is listening on an extension line. See Ribas v. Clark, 38 Cal.3d 355, 696 P.2d 637, 212 Cal. Rptr. 143 (1985). A wife asked the defendant to listen in on an extension phone as she talked to her estranged husband. The defendant then testified in an arbitration hearing about matters she overheard. The husband sued for violation of a different section of the same statute that was invoked in *Deteresa*. The court read the statute broadly to bar "far more than illicit wiretapping," including the recording of a conversation without the other's consent:

> While one who imparts private information risks the betrayal of his confidence by the other party, a substantial distinction has been recognized between the secondhand repetition of the contents of a conversation and its simultaneous dissemination to an unannounced second auditor, whether that auditor be a person or mechanical device. [ ]
>
> As one commentator has noted, such secret monitoring denies the speaker an important aspect of privacy of communication—the right to control the nature and extent of the firsthand dissemination of his statement. [ ] Partly because of this factor, the Privacy Act has been read to require the assent of all parties to a communication before another may listen.

Does the interpretation given this statute cast doubt on the result reached in *Deteresa*? Is *Deteresa* inconsistent with this interpretation of the statute? The majority in *Deteresa* ignored *Ribas*.

The Michigan Supreme Court held that Sally Jessy Raphael and others could be liable for the surreptitious taping and broadcast of a conversation between the plaintiff and her daughter in a public park. Plaintiff was a staff member of the Church of Scientology. Her daughter became concerned that the church was dominating her mother and causing her to sever ties with her family. The daughter requested a "heart-to-heart" conversation with her mother to discuss these concerns and arranged with Raphael's producers to secretly film and record the encounter. The producers equipped the daughter with a hidden microphone that transmitted the conversation to a nearby van, from which the producers filmed the meeting and taped the conversation.

Michigan statutes make it a crime to use a device to eavesdrop on a private conversation without the consent of all parties thereto, or to use or divulge information obtained by such eavesdropping. The defendants contended the conversation was not private because it took place in a park, because the mother should have expected it to be repeated to others, and because it was being transmitted on an FM frequency by a participant (the daughter). The jury found for the defendants, but an appeals court held that the plaintiff was entitled to a directed verdict on the liability question. The supreme court reversed that decision but held that plaintiff was entitled to a new trial with more favorable jury instructions:

> Plaintiff was not entitled to a directed verdict because reasonable minds could differ on the question whether the conversation at issue was "private." The trial court should have instructed the jury that the question whether plaintiff's conversation was private depends on

whether she intended and reasonably expected it to be private at the time and under the circumstances involved. Also, the court improperly instructed the jury that "where one reasonably expects the substance of a private conversation to be communicated to others and not remain confidential, it is not a private conversation within the meaning of the eavesdropping statute." This instruction was erroneous because it focused on the "substance" of the plaintiff's conversation. The proper question is whether plaintiff intended and reasonably expected that the *conversation* was private, not whether the subject matter was intended to be private. Finally, the trial court improperly instructed the jury that "a conversation knowingly broadcast by a participant into the public airwaves is not private." Again, this is not an accurate statement of the law—a participant may not unilaterally nullify other participants' expectations of privacy by secretly recording the conversation.

See Dickerson v. Raphael, 601 N.W.2d 108, 27 Med. L. Rptr. 2215 (Mich. 1999).

Are statutes of the Maryland type, which forbid eavesdropping and wiretapping without regard to expectations of privacy, preferable?

Eavesdropping and wiretapping may be actionable under state or federal statutes, as in the cases discussed above, but they also may be actionable as the common law tort of intrusion. In the following case the California Supreme Court considers the effect of its earlier eavesdropping decisions on the intrusion tort.

Sanders v. American Broadcasting Companies, Inc.

Supreme Court of California, 1999.
20 Cal.4th 907, 978 P.2d 67, 85 Cal. Rptr.2d 909, 27 Med. L. Rptr. 2025.

WERDEGAR, J.

Defendant Stacy Lescht, a reporter employed by defendant American Broadcasting Companies, Inc. (ABC), obtained employment as a "telepsychic" with the Psychic Marketing Group (PMG), which also employed plaintiff Mark Sanders in that same capacity. While she worked in PMG's Los Angeles office, Lescht, who wore a small video camera hidden in her hat, covertly videotaped her conversations with several coworkers, including Sanders.

Sanders sued Lescht and ABC for, among other causes of action, the tort of invasion of privacy by intrusion. Although a jury found for Sanders on the intrusion cause of action, the Court of Appeal reversed the resulting judgment in his favor on the ground that the jury finding for the defense on another cause of action, violation of Penal Code section 632, established Sanders could have had no reasonable expectation of privacy in his workplace conversations because such conversations could be overheard by others in the shared office space. We granted review to determine whether the fact a workplace interaction might be witnessed by others on the premises necessarily defeats, for purposes of tort law, any reasonable expectation of privacy the participants have against covert videotaping by a journalist. We conclude it does not: In an office or other workplace to which the general public does not have unfettered access, employees may enjoy a limited, but legitimate, expectation that their conversations and other interactions will not be secretly videotaped by undercover television report-ers, even though those conversations may not have been completely private from the participants' coworkers. For this reason, contrary to the Court of Appeal's holding, the jury's finding as to Penal Code section 632 did not require the trial court to enter nonsuit on, or otherwise dispose of, Sanders' cause of action for tortious intrusion. Nor, we also conclude, were the jury instructions on the intrusion cause of action prejudicially erroneous.

Although we reverse, for these reasons, the Court of Appeals' judgment for defendants, we do not hold or imply that investigative journalists necessarily commit a tort by secretly recording events and conversations in offices, stores or other workplaces. Whether a reasonable expectation of privacy is violated by such recording depends on the exact nature of the conduct and all the surrounding circumstances. In addition, liability under the intrusion tort requires that the invasion be highly offensive to a reasonable person, considering, among other factors, the motive of the alleged intruder. (*Shulman v. Group W Productions, Inc.* [supra p. 514]; Miller v. National Broadcasting Co., 187 Cal. App. 3d 1463, 232 Cal. Rptr. 668 (1986).) The scope of our review in this case does not include any question regarding the offensiveness element of the tort, and we therefore express no view on the offensiveness or inoffensiveness of defendants' conduct. We hold only that, where the other elements of the intrusion tort are proven, the cause of action is not defeated as a matter of law simply because the events or conversations upon which the defendant allegedly intruded were not completely private from all other eyes and ears.

. . .

In 1992, plaintiff Mark Sanders was working as a telepsychic in PMG's Los Angeles office, giving "readings" to customers who telephoned PMG's 900 number (for which they were charged a per-minute fee). The psychics' work area consisted of a large room with rows of cubicles, about 100 total, in which the psychics took their calls. Each cubicle was enclosed on three sides by five-foot-high partitions. The facility also included a separate lunch room and enclosed offices for managers and supervisors. During the period of the claimed intrusion, the door to the PMG facility was unlocked during business hours, but PMG, by internal policy, prohibited access to the office by nonemployees without specific permission. An employee testified the front door was visible from the administration desk and a supervisor greeted any nonemployees who entered.

[Defendant Lescht obtained employment as a telepsychic in PMG's Los Angeles office. While on the job, Lescht secretly videotaped and audiotaped conversations she had with her co-workers, including two conversations with Sanders. The first conversation took place in an aisle outside Lescht's cubicle. It was conducted in moderate tones, and other co-workers passing by joined in. The second conversation took place in Sanders' cubicle, with Sanders and Lescht speaking "in relatively soft voices. . . . During this second, longer conversation, Sanders discussed his personal aspirations and beliefs and gave Lescht a psychic reading."]

Sanders pled two causes of action against Lescht and ABC based on the videotaping itself: violation of Penal Code section 632 (hereafter section 632) and the common law tort of invasion of privacy by intrusion. The court ordered trial on these counts bifurcated, with the section 632 count tried first. In a special verdict form, the jury was asked whether the conversation upon which defendants allegedly intruded was conducted "in circumstances in which the parties to the communication may reasonably have expected that the communications may have been overheard." Based on the jury's affirmative answer to this question, the trial court ordered judgment entered for defendants on the section 632 cause of action.

Defendants then moved to dismiss the remaining cause of action for intrusion, for an order of nonsuit, and to reopen their earlier motion for summary judgment on this cause of action. After receiving written submissions and hearing argument, the court denied these motions, allowing trial to go forward on the issue of liability for photographic intrusion. In reliance on *Dietemann v. Time, Inc.*, [supra p. 503], which the trial court viewed as articulating a "subtort with regard to invasion of privacy by photographing," the trial court ruled plaintiff could proceed on the theory he had a limited right of privacy against being covertly videotaped by a journalist in his workplace, even though his interaction with that journalist may have been witnessed, and his conversations overheard, by coworkers. At the conclusion of the second phase of trial, the jury found defendants liable on the cause of action for invasion of privacy by intrusion. In subsequent trial phases, the jury fixed compensatory damages at $335,000; found defendants had acted with malice, fraud or oppression; and awarded exemplary damages of about $300,000.

[The Court of Appeals reversed and ordered judgment for the defendants, holding that] the jury finding on the section 632 action barred any recovery for intrusion.

. . .

While *Shulman* reiterated the requirement that an intrusion plaintiff have a reasonable expectation of privacy, neither in *Shulman* nor in any other case have we stated that an expectation of privacy, in order to be reasonable for purposes of the intrusion tort, must be of absolute or complete privacy. . . .

. . .

This case squarely raises the question of an expectation of limited privacy. On further consideration, we adhere to the view suggested in *Shulman*: privacy, for purposes of the intrusion tort, is not a binary, all-or-nothing characteristic. There are degrees and nuances to societal recognition of our expectations of privacy: the fact the privacy one expects in a given setting is not complete or absolute does not render the expectation unreasonable as a matter of law. Although the intrusion tort is often defined in terms of "seclusion" [ ] the seclusion referred to need not be absolute. "Like 'privacy,' the concept of 'seclusion' is relative. The mere fact that a person can be seen by someone does not automatically mean that he or she can legally be forced to be subject to being seen by everyone." [ ]

Dietemann v. Time, Inc. [ ], upon which the trial court relied, does, indeed, exemplify the idea of a legitimate expectation of limited privacy. Reporters for a news magazine deceitfully gained access to a quack doctor's home office, where they secretly photographed and recorded his examination of one of them. [ ] The court held the plaintiff could, under California law, reasonably expect privacy from press photography and recording, even though he had invited the reporters—unaware of their true identity—into his home office: "Plaintiff's den was a sphere from which he could reasonably expect to exclude eavesdropping newsmen. He invited two of defendant's employees to the den. One who invites another to his home or office takes a risk that the visitor may not be what he seems, and that the visitor may repeat all he hears and observes when he leaves. But he does not and should not be required to take the risk that what is heard and seen will be transmitted by photograph or recording, or in our modern world, in full living color and hi-fi to the public at large. . . ." Id. at p. 249; see also *Boddie v. American Broadcasting Companies, Inc.* [supra p. 527] (Journalists' covert recording of interview may violate federal anti-wiretapping statute even though plaintiff knew her interlocutors were journalists: "it remains an issue of fact for the jury whether [plaintiff] had an expectation that the interview was not being recorded and whether that expectation was justified under the circumstances.")

. . .

Defendants' claim, that a "complete expectation of privacy" is necessary to recover for intrusion, thus fails as inconsistent with case law as well as with the common understanding of privacy. Privacy for purposes of the intrusion tort must be evaluated with respect to the identity of the alleged intruder and the nature of the intrusion. As seen below, moreover, decisions on the common law and statutory protection of workplace privacy show that the same analysis applies in the workplace as in other settings; consequently, an employee may, under some circumstances, have a reasonable expectation of visual or aural privacy against electronic intrusion by a stranger to the workplace, despite the possibility the conversations and interactions at issue could be witnessed by coworkers or the employer.

. . .

Finally, defendants rely on . . . Desnick v. American Broadcasting Companies, Inc., 44 F.3d 1345, 23 Med. L. Rptr. 1161 (7th Cir. 1995)[which held that there was no actionable invasion of privacy when agents of ABC, posing as patients, covertly recorded or videotaped doctors' conversations with the "patients" in the doctors' offices.]

In *Desnick*, the question was whether the covert videotaping by "testers" posing as patients was a tortious invasion of privacy. The appellate court held it was not, partly because "the only conversations that were recorded were conversations with the testers themselves." [ ] "The test patients entered offices that were open to anyone expressing a desire for ophthalmic services and videotaped physicians engaged in professional, not personal, communications with strangers (the testers themselves)." [ ]

The *Desnick* court characterized the doctor-patient relationship as one between a service provider and a customer and therefore viewed these parties' conversations in the medical office as essentially public conversations between strangers. We need not agree or disagree with this characterization in order to see that it renders the decision's reasoning inapplicable to the question before us. We are concerned here with interactions between coworkers rather than between a proprietor and customer. As the briefed question is framed, the interactions at issue here could not have been witnessed by the general public, although they could have been overheard or observed by other employees in the shared workplace.

. . .

To summarize, we conclude that in the workplace, as elsewhere, the reasonableness of a person's expectation of visual and aural privacy depends not only on who might have been able to observe the subject interaction, but on the identity of the claimed intruder and the means of intrusion. [*Shulman*; *Dietemann*; . . .] For this reason, we answer the briefed question affirmatively: a person who lacks a reasonable expectation of complete privacy in a conversation, because it could be seen and overheard by coworkers (but not the general public), may nevertheless have a claim for invasion of privacy by intrusion based on a television reporter's covert videotaping of that conversation.

Defendants warn that "the adoption of a doctrine of per se workplace privacy would place a dangerous chill on the press' investigation of abusive activities in open work areas, implicating substantial First Amendment concerns." We adopt no such per se doctrine of privacy. We hold only that the possibility of being overheard by coworkers does not, as a matter of law, render unreasonable an employee's expectation that his or her interactions within a nonpublic workplace will not be videotaped in secret by a journalist. In other circumstances, where, for example, the workplace is regularly open to entry or observation by the public or press, or the interaction that was the subject of the alleged intrusion was between proprietor (or employee) and customer, any expectation of privacy against press recording is less likely to be deemed reasonable. Nothing we say here prevents a media defendant from attempting to show, in order to negate the offensiveness element of the intrusion tort, that the claimed intrusion, even if it infringed on a reasonable expectation of privacy, was "justified by the legitimate motive of gathering the news." [ ] As for possible First Amendment defenses, any discussion must await a later case, as no constitutional issue was decided by the lower courts or presented for our review here.

[The jury's finding that Sanders might reasonably have expected his conversations to be overheard precluded liability under section 632 because the statute was inapplicable if "the parties to the communication may reasonably expect that the communication may be overheard or recorded." But because he could have a "reasonable expectation of privacy" even if the privacy was not complete, "the jury's finding as to an expectation of being overheard by coworkers did not as a matter of law preclude imposing of liability for common law intrusion." The court rejected defendants' claims that the jury had been erroneously instructed, and remanded for consideration of other procedural and evidentiary questions, issues involving the types and amounts of damages awarded, and "any of defendants' appellate claims other than those we have expressly addressed."]

Notes and Questions

1. What exactly were Sanders' reasonable expectations of privacy? That his conversations would not become known to anyone other than coworkers? That they would not be secretly recorded? That they would not be broadcast to the general public?

2. Suppose the employer had covertly (in the interest of candor or verisimilitude) videotaped him and used the scenes in a training video for new telepsychics. Would Sanders have a cause of action for intrusion?

3. If the concept of privacy is relative, in the sense that reasonable expectations may vary depending on "the identity of the claimed intruder and the means of intrusion," what implications does that have for the other tort branches of privacy law? In private facts cases, like *Haynes,* supra p. 367, and *Florida Star*, supra p. 380, does whether the matter disclosed is "private" depend on the identity of the discloser and/or the means by which it is disclosed?

4. Does this interpretation of "reasonable expectations of privacy" indicate that the dissenter in *Deteresa* was right about the California Supreme Court's likely interpretation of "confidential communication"? Are the two phrases sufficiently different to permit the latter to be interpreted as the majority in *Deteresa* did?

5. The opinion notes that no First Amendment issue was involved in this decision. How should those issues be framed? Is it unconstitutional to recognize reasonable expectations of privacy in information that is not completely private?

6. The opinion suggests that ABC could still win on the ground that the intrusion was not highly offensive because its purpose was newsgathering. Might the fact that Sanders' expectations of privacy were incomplete also be relevant on the offensiveness issue?

7. On remand of the *Sanders* case, the California court of appeal rejected ABC's claim that the damage award could not include damages resulting from the broadcast. "The argument assumes that it is only the wrongful intrusion, not the broadcast, that causes damage. Here, however, the

damages from the intrusion were increased by the fact that the intrusion was broadcast." The court held that ABC had failed to preserve its claim that the intrusion did not meet the offensiveness requirement of California law. It denied Sanders' claim for over $500,000 in attorneys fees on the ground that Sanders had not "demonstrated why the interests of justice demand that his fees be paid out of something other than his substantial [$635,000] judgment." The court added a footnote saying, "The large size of the award adequately compensates Sanders for being secretly taped twice, despite being a self-professed psychic who nonetheless was unable to divine that Lescht secreted a camera in her hat and a microphone in her brassiere." See Sanders v. American Broadcasting Cos., 1999 WL 1458129, 28 Med. L. Rptr. 1183 (Cal. App. 1999) (unpublished opinion).

8. The Ninth Circuit refused to apply the rationale of *Sanders* and *Shulman* to an Arizona case, saying it did not believe Arizona courts would interpret privacy rights as broadly as California courts have done. See Medical Laboratory Management Consultants v. American Broadcasting Cos., Inc., 306 F.3d 806, 31 Med. L. Rptr. 1001 (9th Cir. 2002). ABC representatives posing as potential customers obtained a tour of plaintiff's laboratories during which they used hidden cameras to record what ABC said were failures to detect cancer cells in pap smears being analyzed by the lab. The court conceded that the proprietor of the lab could have "a reasonable expectation of limited privacy" against secret recording under the California conception of privacy, but predicted Arizona would not protect that interest. The court said the fact that the Arizona eavesdropping statute permits secret recording by a party to a conversation while California requires consent of all parties indicated that Arizona's conception of privacy was narrower. Even if Arizona followed *Shulman* and *Sanders*, the court said, this case would be distinguishable because it involved conversations with strangers about business matters, not intimate matters or conversations with co-workers about personal matters.

D. USING TORTIOUSLY OBTAINED INFORMATION

The cases discussed so far have involved defendants who were alleged to have behaved tortiously in gathering information. But one of the early cases in this area involved the receipt of information obtained as a result of tortious behavior of others. In Pearson v. Dodd, 410 F.2d 701, 1 Med. L. Rptr. 1809 (D.C. Cir. 1969), aides to Senator Thomas Dodd secretly removed documents from his files, made copies of them, and then delivered them to columnists Drew Pearson and Jack Anderson, who published them.

Dodd claimed invasion of privacy and conversion. Assuming that the Senator's aides committed tortious intrusions, the court nonetheless concluded that no liability attached to the defendant even though they received the documents "knowing" they "had been removed without authorization:"

> . . . [A]ppellants did more than receive and peruse the copies of the documents taken from appellee's files; they published excerpts from them in the national press. But in analyzing a claimed breach of

privacy, injuries from intrusion and injuries from publication should be kept clearly separate. Where there is intrusion, the intruder should generally be liable whatever the content of what he learns. An eavesdropper to the marital bedroom may hear marital intimacies, or he may hear statements of fact or opinion of legitimate interest to the public; for purposes of liability that should make no difference. On the other hand, where the claim is that private information concerning plaintiff has been published, the question of whether that information is genuinely private or is of public interest should not turn on the manner in which it has been obtained. Of course, both forms of invasion may be combined in the same case.

Here we have separately considered the nature of appellants' publications concerning appellee, and have found that the matter published was of obvious public interest. The publication was not itself an invasion of privacy. Since we have also concluded that appellants' role in obtaining the information did not make them liable to appellee for intrusion, their subsequent publication, itself no invasion of privacy, cannot reach back to render that role tortious.

The court then concluded that no action lay for conversion.

One author states that Anderson convinced one of Dodd's aides "to carry thousands of documents from Dodd's files to Anderson's home, where he and [the aide] went over them night after night, weekend after weekend, for nearly a year. . . ." Leonard Downie, Jr., The New Muckrakers 142 (1976). If the *Pearson* opinion had reflected this, would the *Dietemann* court have been able to distinguish it (as the court attempted to do in the footnote on p. 505)?

In the next case, the Supreme Court addresses whether the media may be held liable for using information tortiously or unlawfully obtained by a third party.

Bartnicki v. Vopper

Supreme Court of the United States, 2001.
532 U.S. 514, 29 Med. L. Rptr. 1737.

[During contentious negotiations between a Pennsylvania school board and a teachers' union, Bartnicki, the union's chief negotiator, used the cellular phone in her car to call Kane, the president of the local union. The two discussed the timing of a proposed strike, difficulties created by public comment on the negotiations, and the need for a dramatic response to the board's intransigence. At one point, Kane said: " 'If they're not gonna move for three percent, we're gonna have to go to their, their homes. . . . To blow off their front porches, we'll have to do some work on some of those guys. (PAUSES). Really, uh, really and truthfully because this is, you know, this is bad news. (UNDECIPHERABLE).' "]

[Someone who was never identified intercepted and recorded this conversation. Jack Yocum, the head of a local taxpayers' organization that opposed the union's demands, testified that he found a tape of the conversation in his mailbox and recognized the voices of Bartnicki and Kane. He gave the tape to Vopper, host of a local radio talk show. Vopper, who had been critical of the union, played the tape on his talk show. Another station also broadcast the tape, and local newspapers published its contents.]

[Bartnicki and Kane filed suit in federal court against Vopper, his radio station, Yocum, and other representatives of the media, alleging that each of the defendants "knew or had reason to know" that the recording of the private telephone conversation was illegal under both federal and Pennsylvania wiretapping statutes. The federal act, 18 U.S.C. § 2511(1)(a), forbids interception by a person not a party to the conversation, and subsection (c) provides that any person who "intentionally discloses, or endeavors to disclose, to any other person the contents of any wire, oral, or electronic communication, knowing or having reason to know that the information was obtained through the interception of a wire, oral, or electronic communication in violation of this subsection; . . . shall be punished. . . ." The Pennsylvania Act contains a similar provision. Both statutes also authorize suits for damages.]

[In answer to certified questions from the District Court, the Court of Appeals held that the federal and Pennsylvania wiretapping statutes were content-neutral and therefore subject to intermediate scrutiny. 200 F.3d 109, 121 (3d Cir. 1999). Applying that standard, the majority in the Court of Appeals concluded that the statutes were invalid because they deterred significantly more speech than necessary to protect the privacy interests at stake.]

JUSTICE STEVENS delivered the opinion of the Court.

. . .

IV

The constitutional question before us concerns the validity of the statutes as applied to the specific facts of these cases. Because of the procedural posture of these cases, it is appropriate to make certain important assumptions about those facts. We accept petitioners' submission that the interception was intentional, and therefore unlawful, and that, at a minimum, respondents "had reason to know" that it was unlawful. Accordingly, the disclosure of the contents of the intercepted conversation by Yocum to school board members and to representatives of the media, as well as the subsequent disclosures by the media defendants to the public, violated the federal and state statutes. Under the provisions of the federal statute, as well as its Pennsylvania analog, petitioners are thus entitled to recover damages from each of the respondents. The only question is whether the application of these statutes in such circumstances violates the First Amendment.[8]

---

8. In answering this question, we draw no distinction between the media respondents and Yocum. See, *e.g., New York Times* *Co. v. Sullivan,* 376 U.S. 254, 265–266, 84 S. Ct. 710, 11 L. Ed.2d 686 (1964); *First Nat.*

In answering that question, we accept respondents' submission on three factual matters that serve to distinguish most of the cases that have arisen under § 2511. First, respondents played no part in the illegal interception. Rather, they found out about the interception only after it occurred, and in fact never learned the identity of the person or persons who made the interception. Second, their access to the information on the tapes was obtained lawfully, even though the information itself was intercepted unlawfully by someone else. [ ] Third, the subject matter of the conversation was a matter of public concern. If the statements about the labor negotiations had been made in a public arena—during a bargaining session, for example—they would have been newsworthy. This would also be true if a third party had inadvertently overheard Bartnicki making the same statements to Kane when the two thought they were alone.

V

We agree with petitioners that § 2511(1)(c), as well as its Pennsylvania analog, is in fact a content-neutral law of general applicability. . . .

On the other hand, the naked prohibition against disclosures is fairly characterized as a regulation of pure speech. [S]ubsection (c) is not a regulation of conduct. It is true that the delivery of a tape recording might be regarded as conduct, but given that the purpose of such a delivery is to provide the recipient with the text of recorded statements, it is like the delivery of a handbill or a pamphlet, and as such, it is the kind of "speech" that the First Amendment protects.[11] . . .

VI

As a general matter, "state action to punish the publication of truthful information seldom can satisfy constitutional standards." [*Daily Mail,* casebook p. 62] More specifically, this Court has repeatedly held that "if a newspaper lawfully obtains truthful information about a matter of public significance then state officials may not constitutionally punish publication of the information, absent a need . . . of the highest order." *Id.;* see also *Florida Star* [casebook p. 380]; *Landmark Communications,* [casebook p. 32].

Accordingly, in *New York Times Co. v. United States,* [casebook p. 48], the Court upheld the right of the press to publish information of great public concern obtained from documents stolen by a third party. In so doing, that decision resolved a conflict between the basic rule against prior restraints on publication and the interest in preserving the secrecy of information that, if disclosed, might seriously impair the security of the Nation. In resolving that conflict, the attention of every Member of this

---

Bank of Boston v. Bellotti, 435 U.S. 765, 777, 98 S. Ct. 1407, 55 L. Ed.2d 707 (1978).

11. Put another way, what gave rise to statutory liability in this suit was the information communicated on the tapes. See *Boehner v. McDermott,* 191 F.3d 463, 484 (C.A.D.C.1999) (Sentelle, J., dissenting) ("What . . . is being punished . . . here is not conduct dependent upon the nature or origin of the tapes; it is speech dependent upon the nature of the contents").

Court was focused on the character of the stolen documents' contents and the consequences of public disclosure. Although the undisputed fact that the newspaper intended to publish information obtained from stolen documents was noted in Justice Harlan's dissent,[ ], neither the majority nor the dissenters placed any weight on that fact.

However, *New York Times v. United States* raised, but did not resolve, the question "whether, in cases where information has been acquired *unlawfully* by a newspaper or by a source, government may ever punish not only the unlawful acquisition, but the ensuing publication as well." [ ] The question here, however, is a narrower version of that still-open question. Simply put, the issue here is this: "Where the punished publisher of information has obtained the information in question in a manner lawful in itself but from a source who has obtained it unlawfully, may the government punish the ensuing publication of that information based on the defect in a chain?"[ ]

. . .

The Government identifies two interests served by the statute—first, the interest in removing an incentive for parties to intercept private conversations, and second, the interest in minimizing the harm to persons whose conversations have been illegally intercepted. We assume that those interests adequately justify the prohibition in § 2511(1)(d) against the interceptor's own use of information that he or she acquired by violating § 2511(1)(a), but it by no means follows that punishing disclosures of lawfully obtained information of public interest by one not involved in the initial illegality is an acceptable means of serving those ends.

The normal method of deterring unlawful conduct is to impose an appropriate punishment on the person who engages in it. If the sanctions that presently attach to a violation of § 2511(1)(a) do not provide sufficient deterrence, perhaps those sanctions should be made more severe. But it would be quite remarkable to hold that speech by a law-abiding possessor of information can be suppressed in order to deter conduct by a non-law-abiding third party. . . .

[P]etitioners cite no evidence that Congress viewed the prohibition against disclosures as a response to the difficulty of identifying persons making improper use of scanners and other surveillance devices and accordingly of deterring such conduct, and there is no empirical evidence to support the assumption that the prohibition against disclosures reduces the number of illegal interceptions.

Although this suit demonstrates that there may be an occasional situation in which an anonymous scanner will risk criminal prosecution by passing on information without any expectation of financial reward or public praise, surely this is the exceptional case. Moreover, there is no basis for assuming that imposing sanctions upon respondents will deter the unidentified scanner from continuing to engage in surreptitious interceptions. Unusual cases fall far short of a showing that there is a "need . . . of the highest order" for a rule supplementing the traditional means of deterring antisocial conduct. The justification for any such novel burden on expression must be "far stronger than mere speculation about serious harms."[ ] Accordingly, the Government's first suggested justification for applying § 2511(1)(c) to an otherwise innocent disclosure of public information is plainly insufficient.

The Government's second argument, however, is considerably stronger. Privacy of communication is an important interest. . . .

"In a democratic society privacy of communication is essential if citizens are to think and act creatively and constructively. Fear or suspicion that one's speech is being monitored by a stranger, even without the reality of such activity, can have a seriously inhibiting effect upon the willingness to voice critical and constructive ideas." President's Commission on Law Enforcement and Administration of Justice, The Challenge of Crime in a Free Society 202 (1967).

Accordingly, it seems to us that there are important interests to be considered on *both* sides of the constitutional calculus. In considering that balance, we acknowledge that some intrusions on privacy are more offensive than others, and that the disclosure of the contents of a private conversation can be an even greater intrusion on privacy than the interception itself. As a result, there is a valid independent justification for prohibiting such disclosures by persons who lawfully obtained access to the contents of an illegally intercepted message, even if that prohibition does not play a significant role in preventing such interceptions from occurring in the first place.

We need not decide whether that interest is strong enough to justify the application of § 2511(c) to disclosures of trade secrets or domestic gossip or other information of purely private concern. [ ] In other words, the outcome of these cases does not turn on whether § 2511(1)(c) may be enforced with respect to most violations of the statute without offending the First Amendment. The enforcement of that provision in these cases, however, implicates the core purposes of the First Amendment because it imposes sanctions on the publication of truthful information of public concern.

In these cases, privacy concerns give way when balanced against the interest in publishing matters of public importance. As Warren and Brandeis stated in their classic law review article: "The right of privacy does not prohibit any publication of matter which is of public or general interest." The Right to Privacy, 4 Harv. L.Rev. 193, 214 (1890). One of the costs associated with participation in public affairs is an attendant loss of privacy. . . .

Our opinion in *New York Times Co. v. Sullivan*, 376 U.S. 254, 84 S. Ct. 710, 11 L. Ed.2d 686 (1964), reviewed many of the decisions that settled the "general proposition that freedom of expression upon public questions is secured by the First Amendment." [ ]

We think it clear that parallel reasoning requires the conclusion that a stranger's illegal conduct does not suffice to remove the First Amendment shield from speech about a matter of public concern. The months of negotiations over the proper level of compensation for teachers at the Wyoming Valley West High School were unquestionably a matter of public concern, and respondents were clearly engaged in debate about that concern. That debate may be more mundane than the Communist rhetoric that inspired Justice Brandeis' classic opinion in *Whitney v. California,* [supra p. 7], but it is no less worthy of constitutional protection.

The judgment is affirmed.

JUSTICE BREYER, with whom JUSTICE O'CONNOR joins, concurring.

I join the Court's opinion. I agree with its narrow holding limited to the special circumstances present here: (1) the radio broadcasters acted lawfully (up to the time of final public disclosure); and (2) the information publicized involved a matter of unusual public concern, namely, a threat of potential physical harm to others. I write separately to explain why, in my view, the Court's holding does not imply a significantly broader constitutional immunity for the media.

. . .

As a general matter, despite the statutes' direct restrictions on speech, the Federal Constitution must tolerate laws of this kind because of the importance of these privacy and speech-related objectives. [ ] Rather than broadly forbid this kind of legislative enactment, the Constitution demands legislative efforts to tailor the laws in order reasonably to reconcile media freedom with personal, speech-related privacy.

Nonetheless, looked at more specifically, the statutes, as applied in these circumstances, do not reasonably reconcile the competing constitutional objectives. Rather, they disproportionately interfere with media freedom. For one thing, the broadcasters here engaged in no unlawful activity other than the ultimate publication of the information another had previously obtained. They "neither encouraged nor participated directly or indirectly in the interception."[ ] No one claims that they ordered, counseled, encouraged, or otherwise aided or abetted the interception, the later delivery of the tape by the interceptor to an intermediary, or the tape's still later delivery by the intermediary to the media. . . .

For another thing, the speakers had little or no *legitimate* interest in maintaining the privacy of the particular conversation. That conversation involved a suggestion about "blow[ing] off . . . front porches" and "do[ing] some work on some of those guys,"[ ], thereby raising a significant concern for the safety of others. Where publication of private information constitutes a wrongful act, the law recognizes a privilege allowing the reporting of threats to public safety. [ ] Even where the danger may have passed by the time of publication, that fact cannot legitimize the speaker's earlier privacy expectation. Nor should editors, who must make a publication decision quickly, have to determine present or continued danger before publishing this kind of threat.

Further, the speakers themselves, the president of a teacher's union and the union's chief negotiator, were "limited public figures," for they voluntarily engaged in a public controversy. They thereby subjected themselves to somewhat greater public scrutiny and had a lesser interest in privacy than an individual engaged in purely private affairs. [ ]

This is not to say that the Constitution requires anyone, including public figures, to give up entirely the right to private communication, *i.e.,* communication free from telephone taps or interceptions. But the subject matter of the conversation at issue here is far removed from that in situations where the media publicizes truly private matters. [ ]

Thus, in finding a constitutional privilege to publish unlawfully intercepted conversations of the kind here at issue, the Court does not create a "public interest" exception that swallows up the statutes' privacy-protecting general rule. Rather, it finds constitutional protection for publication of intercepted information of a special kind. Here, the speakers' legitimate privacy expectations are unusually low, and the public interest in defeating those expectations is unusually high. Given these circumstances, along with the lawful nature of respondents' behavior, the statutes' enforcement would disproportionately harm media freedom.

. . .

Chief JUSTICE REHNQUIST, with whom JUSTICE SCALIA and JUSTICE THOMAS join, dissenting.

. . .

These laws are content neutral; they only regulate information that was illegally obtained; they do not restrict republication of what is already in the public domain; they impose no special burdens upon the media; they have a scienter requirement to provide fair warning; and they promote the privacy and free speech of those using cellular telephones. It is hard to imagine a more narrowly tailored prohibition of the disclosure of illegally intercepted communications, and it distorts our precedents to review these statutes under the often fatal standard of strict scrutiny. These laws therefore should be upheld if they further a substantial governmental interest unrelated to the suppression of free speech, and they do.

Congress and the overwhelming majority of States reasonably have concluded that sanctioning the knowing disclosure of illegally intercepted communications will deter the initial interception itself, a crime which is extremely difficult to detect. It is estimated that over 20 million scanners capable of intercepting cellular transmissions currently are in operation,[ ] notwithstanding the fact that Congress prohibited the marketing of such devices eight years ago,[ ] As Congress recognized, "[a]ll too often the invasion of privacy itself will go unknown. Only by striking at all aspects of the problem can privacy be adequately protected."[ ]

. . .

[T]he incidental restriction on alleged First Amendment freedoms is no greater than essential to further the interest of protecting the privacy of individual communications. Were there no prohibition on disclosure, an unlawful eavesdropper who wanted to disclose the conversation could anonymously launder the interception through a third party and thereby avoid detection. Indeed, demand for illegally obtained private information would only increase if it could be disclosed without repercussion. The law against interceptions, which the Court agrees is valid, would be utterly ineffectual without these antidisclosure provisions.

. . .

. . . The Court concludes that the private conversation between Gloria Bartnicki and Anthony Kane is somehow a "debate . . . worthy of constitutional protection."[ ] Perhaps the Court is correct that "[i]f the statements about the labor negotiations had been made in a public arena—during a bargaining session, for example—they would have been newsworthy."[ ] The point, however, is that Bartnicki and Kane had no intention of contributing to a public "debate" at all, and it is perverse to hold that another's unlawful interception and knowing disclosure of their conversation is speech "worthy of constitutional protection."[ ] The Constitution should not protect the involuntary broadcast of personal conversations. Even where the communications involve public figures or concern public matters, the conversations are nonetheless private and worthy of protection. Although public persons may have forgone the right to live their lives screened from public scrutiny in some areas, it does not and should not follow that they also have abandoned their right to have a private conversation without fear of it being intentionally intercepted and knowingly disclosed.

. . .

Notes and Questions

1.   Although the Court concedes that the wiretapping statutes are content neutral, it applies a form of strict scrutiny, apparently on the ground that the statutes regulate "pure speech." Do they? If so, does this case announce a new First Amendment principle—that content-neutral regulation of pure speech triggers strict scrutiny? In footnote 11, the Court suggests that the statutes punish speech because of "the nature of its contents." If that is true, aren't they content-based? Does the fact that the statutes impose liability for broadcasting the tape only if the contents of the tape were illegally recorded make them content-based?

2.   What exactly is the matter of public concern? To Justices Breyer and O'Connor, it was the "threat of potential physical harm to others" that made the tape "a matter of unusual public concern." This, together with the facts that the plaintiffs were public figures and the defendants did not participate in the eavesdropping, seem to be the "special circumstances" that convinced them that the decision is a narrow one that does not broadly immunize media from liability for using illegally obtained information.

3.   If the other members of the majority do not view the holding that narrowly, what do they consider to be the matter of public concern? Is it the teachers' dispute? If so, does Justice Stevens' opinion indicate that a

person's (or at least a public figure's) *views* about a matter of public concern are themselves a matter of public concern? Or is he saying that the views themselves may be private, but because they relate to a matter of public concern, the interest in protecting their privacy isn't strong enough to overcome the First Amendment interest in publication of truthful information?

4. After *Bartnicki*, what should media conclude about the risks of using information that they know was unlawfully obtained by someone else? That they can safely use such information as long as they were not involved in the illegal acquisition? That they may be liable for such use unless there are special circumstances sufficient to convince a court that liability would "disproportionately interfere with media freedom"? In this connection, note that the vote of at least one of the two concurring justices was necessary to make a majority.

5. The Court in *Bartnicki* explicitly distinguished Peavy v. WFAA–TV, Inc., 221 F.3d 158 (5th Cir. 2000), on the ground that the media defendant in that case may have participated in the interceptions. The Fifth Circuit in *Peavy* reversed a summary judgment for the defendants, holding that state and federal wiretap acts were subject only to intermediate scrutiny where there was evidence that the media defendant had encouraged and given instructions regarding the illegal taping. The governmental interests that were found insufficient in *Bartnicki* to overcome strict scrutiny—eliminating incentives to wiretap and protecting the privacy of electronic communications—were sufficient in the Fifth Circuit's view to survive intermediate scrutiny. The television station had not broadcast the tapes in question, but the court held that it could be liable for disclosing the substance of the tapes unless it had also acquired the information by other, nonprohibited means. The court also held that other language of the federal statute, prohibiting "use" of illegally taped conversations, might also have been violated even though the station did not broadcast the tapes. The station eventually settled the case on terms it refused to disclose. See Texas television station settles federal wiretapping lawsuit, The News Media and the Law, Spring 2002, at 33.

6. The federal Electronic Communications Privacy Act, supra pp. 526–27, makes it a crime to disclose a conversation known to have been recorded in violation of the act and creates a damage action against those who do so. Does this apply to a source who gives an illegally recorded tape to the media? Does the First Amendment permit the statute to be so interpreted? A federal court of appeals answered yes to both questions. See Boehner v. McDermott, 191 F.3d 463, 27 Med. L. Rptr. 2345 (D.C. Cir. 1999). Congressman Boehner, chairman of the House Republican Conference, while driving his car in Florida participated in a telephone conference call with then-Speaker Newt Gingrich and other Republican leaders to discuss Gingrich's agreement to accept a reprimand from the House Ethics Committee if the committee would agree not to hold a hearing on his alleged ethics violation. John and Alice Martin, Florida residents listening on a radio scanner, recorded the conversation and discussed it with their Democratic

congresswoman. She suggested that they give the tape to Congressman McDermott, a Democrat and co-chair of the House Ethics Committee. McDermott gave copies of the tape to the New York Times and two other newspapers. The papers all published reports based on the contents of the tape, which they said showed Gingrich violated his agreement with the ethics committee. The papers honored their promise not to identify McDermott as the source, but when the stories came out the Martins revealed that they had given the tape to McDermott.

The Martins were fined $500 each for eavesdropping, McDermott resigned from the ethics committee, and Gingrich eventually resigned from the House. McDermott was not prosecuted, but Boehner sued him for damages under the section of the statute prohibiting intentional disclosure of a communication that the discloser knows was recorded in violation of the statute. The district court dismissed the complaint on the ground that imposing liability for "disclosure of truthful and lawfully obtained information on a matter of substantial public concern" would violate the First Amendment. The Court of Appeals reversed, 2–1.

The majority and the dissent agreed that the case turned on "whether, in cases where information has been acquired unlawfully by a newspaper or by a source, government may ever punish not only the unlawful acquisition, but the ensuing publication as well." The majority held that McDermott did not lawfully obtain the tape, even though no statute forbade him from receiving contents of illegal eavesdropping, because he knew the Martins had obtained it illegally and that it was illegal for the Martins to give it to him. The majority therefore applied the intermediate scrutiny of *United States v. O'Brien*. supra p. 210. It held that the statute was only an incidental restriction on speech, unrelated to the content of the speech, and advanced the government's substantial interest in preventing use and disclosure of illegally intercepted communications. The majority said McDermott was in no different position than if he had accepted the tape knowing it had been obtained by burglarizing Boehner's office.

The dissenter argued that McDermott himself had obtained the tape lawfully within the meaning of *Daily Mail* and *Florida Star* even if it had been "unlawfully obtained somewhere in the chain." Holding him liable under the statute could not withstand the strict scrutiny required by those precedents. The dissenter conceded that the government had a compelling interest in protecting the privacy of electronic communications and that punishing the person who intercepted such communications might be a narrowly tailored remedy. But he said the government had not established that "an undifferentiated burden on the speech of anyone who acquires the information contained in the communication from the unlawful interceptor is necessary to accomplish the state's legitimate goal or narrowly tailored to serve that end. I do not see how we can draw a line today that would punish McDermott and not hold liable for sanctions every newspaper, every radio station, every broadcasting network that obtained the same information from McDermott's releases and published it again."

Under the majority's reasoning, could the newspapers be held liable for disclosing the tape they received from McDermott? Could the papers avoid liability by not finding out how the Martins obtained the tape?

After deciding *Bartnicki,* the Supreme Court vacated the judgment in *Boehner v. McDermott* and remanded for reconsideration in light of *Bartnicki.* 532 U.S. 1050 (2001). The Court of Appeals then remanded to the district court to allow Boehner to amend his complaint and to allow the district court to address the constitutional issues in light of *Bartnicki.* The district court granted partial summary judgment for the plaintiff, holding that the First Amendment did not protect McDermott from liability under the federal wiretapping statute. Boehner v. McDermott, 332 F. Supp.2d 149 (2004). The district court distinguished *Bartnicki* on the grounds that it "did not present a knowing acceptance scenario such as is alleged here." Id. at 164. The court stressed that at the time Congressman McDermott received the tape, he knew both the source's identity and the illegal means by which the source had obtained the tape.

E. OTHER TORTS

1. FRAUD AND BREACH OF FIDUCIARY DUTY

Food Lion, Inc. v. Capital Cities/ABC, Inc.
United States Court of Appeals for the Fourth Circuit, 1999.
194 F.3d 505, 27 Med. L. Rptr. 2409.

[Producers of ABC's PrimeTime Live decided to conduct an undercover investigation of allegations of unsanitary meat handling practices at Food Lion stores. They authorized ABC reporters Lynne Dale (Lynne Litt at the time) and Susan Barnett to apply for jobs with the grocery chain, submitting applications with false identities and references and fictitious local addresses. The applications failed to mention the reporters' concurrent employment with ABC and otherwise misrepresented their educational and employment experiences. Based on these applications, a South Carolina Food Lion store hired Barnett as a deli clerk and a North Carolina Food Lion store hired Dale as a meat wrapper trainee. Barnett worked for Food Lion for two weeks, and Dale for one week. They used tiny cameras ("lipstick" cameras, for example) and microphones concealed on their bodies to secretly record 45 hours of footage of Food Lion employees treating, wrapping and labeling meat, cleaning machinery, and discussing the practices of the meat department.

PrimeTime Live eventually broadcast a program including videotape that appeared to show Food Lion employees repackaging and redating fish that had passed the expiration date, grinding expired beef with fresh beef, and applying barbeque sauce to chicken past its expiration date in order to mask the smell and sell it as fresh in the gourmet food section. The program included statements by former Food Lion employees alleging even more serious mishandling of meat at Food Lion stores in several states. The truth of the PrimeTime Live broadcast was not an issue in the litigation.

Food Lion sued ABC and the PrimeTime Live producers and reporters (the "ABC defendants") for fraud, breach of the duty of loyalty, trespass, and unfair trade practices. It sought to recover (1) administrative costs and wages paid in connection with the employment of Dale and Barnett, (2) broadcast (publication) damages for matters such as loss of good will, lost sales and profits, and diminished stock value, and (3) punitive damages. The jury found all of the ABC defendants liable to Food Lion for fraud and violation of the North Carolina Unfair and Deceptive Trade Practices Act (UTPA). It found Dale and Barnett liable for trespass and breach of the duty of loyalty. The district court ruled that damages allegedly incurred by Food Lion as a result of ABC's broadcast of PrimeTime Live—"lost profits, lost sales, diminished stock value or anything of that nature"—could not be recovered because these damages were not proximately caused by the tortious acts of the defendants. The jury awarded Food Lion $1,400 in compensatory damages on its fraud claim, $1.00 each on its duty of loyalty and trespass claims, and $1,500 on its UTPA claim. The jury awarded $5,545,750 in punitive damages on the fraud claim against ABC and its two producers, Kaplan and Rosen, but did not award punitive damages against the reporters. In post-trial proceedings the district court ruled that the punitive damages award was excessive, and Food Lion accepted a remittitur to a total of $315,000. After trial the ABC defendants moved for judgment as a matter of law on all claims, the motion was denied, and the defendants appealed. Food Lion cross-appealed, contesting the district court's ruling that the damages the grocery chain sought as a result of the PrimeTime Live broadcast were not recoverable in this action.]

MICHAEL, CIRCUIT JUDGE:

    . . .

II.

A.

1.

[The court held 2–1 that Food Lion could not recover for fraud. Food Lion alleged that it spent money hiring and training the ABC employees in reliance on implied representations that they were bona fide applicants who would work more than a week or two. The majority said Food Lion could not have expected Litt and Barnett to work for any particular length of time because they were at-will employees, and Food Lion therefore could not claim to have reasonably relied on their resume misrepresentations when it incurred these costs. Food Lion also alleged that it was fraudulently induced to pay them wages on their implied representations that they were loyal employees working in Food Lion's interests. But the majority said Food Lion paid the employees because they did the work, not because of statements on their applications, and the misrepresentations therefore were not the proximate cause of the wages paid.]

2.

ABC argues that Dale and Barnett cannot be held liable for a breach of duty of loyalty to Food Lion under existing tort law in North and South Carolina. . . .

. . . Up to now, disloyal conduct by an employee has been considered tortious in North and South Carolina in three circumstances. First, the tort of breach of duty of loyalty applies when an employee competes directly with her employer, either on her own or as an agent of a rival company. [ ] Second, the tort applies when the employee misappropriates her employer's profits, property, or business opportunities. [ ] Third, the tort applies when the employee breaches her employer's confidences. [ ]

Because Dale and Barnett did not compete with Food Lion, misappropriate any of its profits or opportunities, or breach its confidences, ABC argues that the reporters did not engage in any disloyal conduct that is tortious under existing law. Indeed, the district court acknowledged that it was the first court to hold that the conduct in question "would be recognized by the Supreme Courts of North Carolina and South Carolina" as tortiously violating the duty of loyalty. [ ] We believe the district court was correct to conclude that those courts would decide today that the reporters' conduct was sufficient to breach the duty of loyalty and trigger tort liability.

What Dale and Barnett did verges on the kind of employee activity that has already been determined to be tortious. The interests of the employer (ABC) to whom Dale and Barnett gave complete loyalty were adverse to the interests of Food Lion, the employer to whom they were unfaithful. ABC and Food Lion were not business competitors but they were adverse in a fundamental way. ABC's interest was to expose Food Lion to the public as a food chain that engaged in unsanitary and deceptive practices. Dale and Barnett served ABC's interest, at the expense of Food Lion, by engaging in the taping for ABC while they were on Food Lion's payroll. In doing this, Dale and Barnett did not serve Food Lion faithfully, and their interest (which was the same as ABC's) was diametrically opposed to Food Lion's. In these circumstances, we believe that the highest courts of North and South Carolina would hold that the reporters—in promoting the interests of one master, ABC, to the detriment of a second, Food Lion—committed the tort of disloyalty against Food Lion.

. . .

3.

. . .

In North and South Carolina, as elsewhere, it is a trespass to enter upon another's land without consent. [ ] Accordingly, consent is a defense to a claim of trespass. [ ] Even consent gained by misrepresentation is sometimes sufficient. See *Desnick*, [supra p. 533.] The consent to enter is canceled out, however, "if a wrongful act is done in excess of and in abuse of authorized entry." [ ]

We turn first to whether Dale and Barnett's consent to be in nonpublic areas of Food Lion property was void from the outset because of the resume misrepresentations. "Consent to an entry is often given legal effect" even though it was obtained by misrepresentation or concealed intentions. [*Desnick*]. Without this result,

> a restaurant critic could not conceal his identity when he ordered a meal, or a browser pretend to be interested in merchandise that he could not afford to buy. Dinner guests would be trespassers if they were false friends who never would have been invited had the host known their true character, and a consumer who in an effort to bargain down an automobile dealer falsely claimed to be able to buy the same car elsewhere at a lower price would be a trespasser in a dealer's showroom. [Id.]

We like *Desnick*'s thoughtful analysis about when a consent to enter that is based on misrepresentation may be given effect. In *Desnick* ABC sent persons posing as patients needing eye care to the plaintiffs' eye clinics, and the test patients secretly recorded their examinations. Some of the recordings were used in a PrimeTime Live segment that alleged intentional misdiagnosis and unnecessary cataract surgery. *Desnick* held that although the test patients misrepresented their purpose, their consent to enter was still valid because they did not invade "any of the specific interests[relating to peaceable possession of land] the tort of trespass seeks to protect:" the test patients entered offices "open to anyone expressing a desire for ophthalmic services" and videotaped doctors engaged in professional discussions with strangers, the testers; the testers did not disrupt the offices or invade anyone's private space; and the testers did not reveal the "intimate details of anybody's life." [ ] *Desnick* supported its conclusion with the following comparison:

> "Testers" who pose as prospective home buyers in order to gather evidence of housing discrimination are not trespassers even if they are private persons not acting under color of law. The situation of [ABC's] "testers" is analogous. Like testers seeking evidence of violation of anti-discrimination laws, [ABC's] test patients gained entry into the plaintiffs' premises by misrepresenting their purposes (more precisely by a misleading omission to disclose those purposes). But the entry was not invasive in the sense of infringing the kind of interest of the plaintiffs that the law of trespass protects; it was not an interference with the ownership or possession of land. [ ]

We return to the jury's first trespass finding in this case, which rested on a narrow ground. The jury found that Dale and Barnett were trespassers because they entered Food Lion's premises as employees with consent given because of the misrepresentations in their job applications. Although the consent cases as a class are inconsistent, we have not found any case suggesting that consent based on a resume misrepresentation turns a successful job applicant into a trespasser the moment she enters the employer's premises to begin work. Moreover, if we turned successful resume fraud into trespass, we would not be protecting the interest underlying the tort of trespass—the ownership and peaceable possession of land. See [*Desnick*]. Accordingly, we cannot say that North and South Carolina's highest courts would hold that misrepresentation on a job application alone nullifies the consent given to an employee to enter the employer's property, thereby turning the employee into a trespasser. The jury's finding of trespass therefore cannot be sustained on the grounds of resume misrepresentation.

There is a problem, however, with what Dale and Barnett did after they entered Food Lion's property. The jury also found that the reporters committed trespass by breaching their duty of loyalty to Food Lion "as a result of pursuing [their] investigation for ABC." We affirm the finding of trespass on this ground because the breach of duty of loyalty—triggered by the filming in non-public areas, which was adverse to Food Lion—was a wrongful act in excess of Dale and Barnett's authority to enter Food Lion's premises as employees. [ ]

. . .

. . . [T]he South Carolina courts make clear that the law of trespass protects the peaceable enjoyment of property. [ ] It is consistent with that principle to hold that consent to enter is vitiated by a wrongful act that exceeds and abuses the privilege of entry.

Here, both Dale and Barnett became employees of Food Lion with the certain consequence that they would breach their implied promises to serve Food Lion faithfully. They went into areas of the stores that were not open to the public and secretly videotaped, an act that was directly adverse to the interests of their second employer, Food Lion. Thus, they breached the duty of loyalty, thereby committing a wrongful act in abuse of their authority to be on Food Lion's property.

. . .

4.

[The court reversed the finding of liability under the North Carolina Unfair and Deceptive Trade Practices Act on the ground that the statute, the primary purpose of which was to protect consumers, was available to business plaintiffs only if they were competitors of the defendant or were engaged in business dealings with the defendant.]

B.

ABC argues that even if state tort law covers some of Dale and Barnett's conduct, the district court erred in refusing to subject Food Lion's claims to any level of First Amendment scrutiny. ABC makes this argument because Dale and Barnett were engaged in newsgathering for PrimeTime Live. It is true that there are "First Amendment interests in newsgathering." In re Shain, 978 F.2d 850, 855 (4th Cir. 1992) (Wilkinson

J., concurring). See also *Branzburg v. Hayes*, [infra p. 561] ("without some protection for seeking out the news, freedom of the press could be eviscerated."). However, the Supreme Court has said in no uncertain terms that "generally applicable laws do not offend the First Amendment simply because their enforcement against the press has incidental effects on its ability to gather and report the news." *Cohen v. Cowles Media Co.*, [supra p. 429]; see also *Desnick*, [ ] ("the media have no general immunity from tort or contract liability").

. . .

The key inquiry in *Cowles* was whether the law of promissory estoppel was a generally applicable law. The Court began its analysis with some examples of generally applicable laws that must be obeyed by the press, such as those relating to copyright, labor, antitrust, and tax. [ ] More relevant to us, "the press may not with impunity break and enter an office or dwelling to gather news." [ ] In analyzing the doctrine of promissory estoppel, the Court determined that it was a law of general applicability because it "does not target or single out the press," but instead applies "to the daily transactions of all the citizens of Minnesota." [ ] The Court concluded that "the First Amendment does not confer on the press a constitutional right to disregard promises that would otherwise be enforced under state law." [ ] The Court thus refused to apply any heightened scrutiny to the enforcement of Minnesota's promissory estoppel law against the newspapers.

The torts Dale and Barnett committed, breach of the duty of loyalty and trespass, fit neatly into the *Cowles* framework. Neither tort targets or singles out the press. Each applies to the daily transactions of the citizens of North and South Carolina. If, for example, an employee of a competing grocery chain hired on with Food Lion and videotaped damaging information in Food Lion's non-public areas for later disclosure to the public, these tort laws would apply with the same force as they do against Dale and Barnett here. Nor do we believe that applying these laws against the media will have more than an "incidental effect" on newsgathering. See *Cowles*, [ ]. We are convinced that the media can do its important job effectively without resort to the commission of run-of-the-mill torts.[5]

ABC argues that *Cowles* is not to be applied automatically to every "generally applicable law" because the Supreme Court has since said that "the enforcement of [such a] law may or may not be subject to heightened scrutiny under the First Amendment." [*Turner I*, supra p. 202] (contrasting Barnes v. Glen Theatre, Inc., 501 U.S. 560 [ ] (1991), and *Cowles*). In *Glen Theatre* nude dancing establishments and their dancers challenged a generally applicable law prohibiting public nudity. Because the general ban on public nudity covered nude dancing, which was expressive conduct, the Supreme Court applied heightened scrutiny. [ ] In *Cowles* a generally applicable law (promissory estoppel) was invoked against newspapers who

---

5. Indeed, the ABC News Policy Manual states that "news gathering of whatever sort does not include any license to violate the law."

broke their promises to a source that they would keep his name confidential in exchange for information leading to a news story. There, the Court refused to apply heightened scrutiny, concluding that application of the doctrine of promissory estoppel had "no more than [an] incidental" effect on the press's ability to gather or report news. [ ] There is arguable tension between the approaches in the two cases. The cases are consistent, however, if we view the challenged conduct in *Cowles* to be the breach of promise and not some form of expression. In *Glen Theatre*, on the other hand, an activity directly covered by the law, nude dancing, necessarily involved expression, and heightened scrutiny was applied. Here, as in *Cowles*, heightened scrutiny does not apply because the tort laws (breach of duty of loyalty and trespass) do not single out the press or have more than an incidental effect upon its work.

C.

For the foregoing reasons, we affirm the judgment that Dale and Barnett breached their duty of loyalty to Food Lion and committed trespass. We likewise affirm the damages award against them for these torts in the amount of $2.00. We have already indicated that the fraud claim against all of the ABC defendants must be reversed. Because Food Lion was awarded punitive damages only on its fraud claim, the judgment awarding punitive damages cannot stand.

III.

In its cross-appeal Food Lion argues that the district court erred in refusing to allow it to use its non-reputational tort claims (breach of duty of loyalty, trespass, etc.) to recover compensatory damages for ABC's broadcast of the PrimeTime Live program that targeted Food Lion. The publication damages Food Lion sought (or alleged) were for items relating to its reputation, such as loss of good will and lost sales. The district court determined that the publication damages claimed by Food Lion "were the direct result of diminished consumer confidence in the store" and that "it was [Food Lion's] food handling practices themselves—not the method by which they were recorded or published—which caused the loss of consumer confidence." [ ] The court therefore concluded that the publication damages were not proximately caused by the non-reputational torts committed by ABC's employees. We do not reach the matter of proximate cause because an overriding (and settled) First Amendment principle precludes the award of publication damages in this case, as ABC has argued to the district court and to us. Food Lion attempted to avoid the First Amendment limitations on defamation claims by seeking publication damages under non-reputational tort claims, while holding to the normal state law proof standards for these torts. This is precluded by *Hustler Magazine v. Falwell*, [supra p. 417].

Food Lion acknowledges that it did not sue for defamation because its "ability to bring an action for defamation [ ] required proof that ABC acted with actual malice." [ ] Food Lion thus understood that if it sued ABC for defamation it would have to prove that the PrimeTime Live broadcast contained a false statement of fact that was made with "actual malice," that is, with knowledge that it was false or with reckless disregard as to whether it was true or false. See *New York Times Co. v. Sullivan*, [supra p. 272]. It is clear that Food Lion was not prepared to offer proof meeting the *New York Times* standard under any claim that it might assert. What Food Lion sought to do, then, was to recover defamation-type damages under non-reputational tort claims, without satisfying the stricter (First Amendment) standards of a defamation claim. We believe that such an end-run around First Amendment strictures is foreclosed by *Hustler*.

. . .

Food Lion argues that *Cowles*, supra, and not *Hustler* governs its claim for publication damages. According to Food Lion, *Cowles* allowed the plaintiff to recover—without satisfying the constitutional prerequisites to a defamation action—economic losses for publishing the plaintiff's identity in violation of a legal duty arising from generally applicable law. Food Lion says that its claim for damages is like the plaintiff's in *Cowles*, and not like Falwell's in *Hustler*. This argument fails because the Court in *Cowles* distinguished the damages sought there from those in *Hustler* in a way that also distinguishes Food Lion's case from *Cowles*:

> Cohen is not seeking damages for injury to his reputation or his state of mind. He sought damages . . . for breach of a promise that caused him to lose his job and lowered his earning capacity. Thus, this is not a case like *Hustler* . . . where we held that the constitutional libel standards apply to a claim alleging that the publication of a parody was a state-law tort of intentional infliction of emotional distress. [ ]

Food Lion, in seeking compensation for matters such as loss of good will and lost sales, is claiming reputational damages from publication, which the *Cowles* Court distinguished by placing them in the same category as the emotional distress damages sought by Falwell in *Hustler*. In other words, according to *Cowles*, "constitutional libel standards" apply to damage claims for reputational injury from a publication such as the one here.

Food Lion also argues that because ABC obtained the videotapes through unlawful acts, that is, the torts of breach of duty of loyalty and trespass, it (Food Lion) is entitled to publication damages without meeting the *New York Times* standard. The Supreme Court has never suggested that it would dispense with the Times standard in this situation, and we believe *Hustler* indicates that the Court would not. In *Hustler* the magazine's conduct would have been sufficient to constitute an unlawful act, the intentional infliction of emotional distress, if state law standards of proof had applied. Indeed, the Court said, "generally speaking the law does not regard the intent to inflict emotional distress as one which should receive much solicitude." *Hustler*, [ ]. Notwithstanding the nature of the underlying act, the Court held that satisfying *New York Times* was a prerequisite to the recovery of publication damages. That result was "necessary," the Court concluded, in order "to give adequate 'breathing space' to the freedoms protected by the First Amendment." [ ]

In sum, Food Lion could not bypass the *New York Times* standard if it wanted publication damages. The district court therefore reached the correct result when it disallowed these damages, although we affirm on a different ground.

IV.

To recap, we reverse the judgment to the extent it provides that the ABC defendants committed fraud and awards compensatory damages of $1,400 and punitive damages of $315,000 on that claim; we affirm the judgment to the extent it provides that Dale and Barnett breached their duty of loyalty to Food Lion and committed a trespass and awards total damages of $2.00 on those claims; we reverse the judgment to the extent it provides that the ABC defendants violated the North Carolina UTPA; and we affirm the district court's ruling that Food Lion was not entitled to prove publication damages on its claims.

NIEMEYER, CIRCUIT JUDGE, concurring in part and dissenting in part:

[Judge Niemeyer dissented only from the portion of the opinion denying recovery for fraud (and hence for punitive damages). He argued that Food Lion had relied to its detriment on the ABC employees' misrepresentations.]

. . .

Applicants for employment, even at-will employment, present themselves representing by implication: (1) that they want to become employees; (2) that they intend to work indefinitely, until a change in circumstances leads them or their employer to terminate the arrangement; (3) that there is a possibility that they would become long-term employees; and (4) that they will be loyal employees as long as they work, prepared to work at the promotion of their employer's business. ABC's undercover reporters presented themselves to Food Lion, representing all of these matters falsely. . . .

. . .

. . . Food Lion had less of a chance—indeed, no chance—of developing experienced, long-term, and loyal employees because the likelihood of that possibility was misrepresented. If these employees had disclosed their true identities and intentions accurately, Food Lion would never have hired them and incurred expenses to train them on the chance that they would stay because the employees had already determined there was no such chance. . . .

Notes and Questions

1. Neither party sought Supreme Court review of the *Food Lion* decision.

2. What types of undercover newsgathering operations can be undertaken without potential liability under this decision? Can a reporter pose as an employee without breaching the duty of loyalty? Surreptitiously tape without exceeding the scope of consent and thereby becoming a trespasser?

3. Does the duty of loyalty preclude bona fide employees from giving media information adverse to the interests of the employer?

4. Consent obtained through misrepresentation normally is ineffective. What policies support the exception recognized in *Desnick* and applied here? Would similar policies support an exception to the employee's duty of loyalty?

5. What was the "wrongful act" that exceeded the scope of the ABC employees' consent to enter Food Lion's nonpublic areas? Is surreptitious newsgathering itself a "wrongful act"? Would an undercover journalist commit a wrongful act for these purposes by taking notes for a story adverse to the landowner? By making mental notes for that purpose?

6. Why is the First Amendment inapplicable to these torts as long as the recovery does not include damages resulting from the broadcast? Can *Cowles* be properly viewed as a case in which the challenged conduct was "breach of promise and not some form of expression?" The newspapers in that case breached their promise to Cohen by publishing his name; why is that not "some form of expression"?

7. The trial court avoided the constitutional issue by denying publication damages on the ground of proximate cause. The court of appeals avoided the proximate cause issue by denying publication damages on First Amendment grounds. Which approach is better?

––––––––

Measuring damages. In *Food Lion* the court held that the First Amendment precludes recovery for publication damages (or at least "defamation-type damages") in a newsgathering torts case unless the constitutional libel requirements are met. Might such damages also be precluded as a matter of tort law? In *Dietemann*, the court held that damages for the instrusion could include the harm resulting from subsequent publication. The *Prahl* case held the same in a trespass case, citing section 162 of the Restatement, which provides that recoverable trespass damages include any "physical harm to the possessor of the land . . ., or to the land or to his things, or to members of his household or to their things . . ." that result from the trespass. Does this language support liability for harm resulting from subsequent publication?

In Costlow v. Cusimano, 34 A.D.2d 196, 311 N.Y.S.2d 92 (1970), the court took a narrower view of trespass damages. Plaintiffs alleged that their two children suffocated in a refrigerator located at the family's residence; that defendant, hoping to sell an article about the deaths, arrived at the scene and photographed the premises and the bodies of the children; and that the photographs were published, causing plaintiffs intense emotional distress. The court held that since the articles were newsworthy, no claim could be based on their publication. It then held that the only remedies for any trespass to the premises were nominal and punitive damages: "There is no support for plaintiffs' argument that damages for injury to reputation and for emotional disturbance are recoverable on the alleged facts as the natural consequence of the trespass. . . . [D]amages for trespass are limited to consequences flowing from the interference with possession and not for separable acts more properly allocated under other categories of liability."

Which is the better view? See James E. King and Frederick T. Muto, Compensatory Damages for Newsgatherer Torts: Toward a Workable Standard, 14 U.C. Davis L. Rev. 919 (1981); Rex S. Heinke, Added Damages for Publication Should Not Be Available in Intrusion—Trespass Cases without Independent Justification, Comm. Lawyer (Summer 1983), at 6.

2.   NEGLIGENCE

Clift v. Narragansett Television: Clift v. Narragansett Television L.P., 688 A.2d 805, 25 Med. L. Rptr. 1417 (R.I. 1996) held that "everyone, including the press, should be answerable for unprivileged negligent actions that proximately result in suicide." *Clift* involved an unusual set of facts. A mentally ill man who was threatening to kill himself became involved in a stand-off with police. Without informing the police, a reporter for a television station called the man's home and interviewed him on air. A few minutes after the interview, the man killed himself. The man's wife and children brought suit against the television station, alleging various causes of action, including negligence. The trial judge granted summary judgment on the negligence claim in favor of the television station, and the plaintiff appealed.

The Supreme Court of Rhode Island reversed. The court recognized that the case raised "fundamental First Amendment considerations," but stated that those considerations could be adequately addressed by applying to the press the same standard of liability applied to other citizens. Under that standard, the so-called "uncontrollable impulse" rule, defendants may be held liable if their negligence causes a person to suffer delirium or insanity resulting in an "uncontrollable impulse" to commit suicide. The court found that the plaintiff had alleged facts "that suggest that the decedent's suicide resulted from an uncontrollable impulse that was brought about by a delirium or insanity caused by [the reporter's] negligence." As a result, the court reinstated not only the plaintiffs' negligence claim, but also the derivative claims for wrongful death, loss of consortium and loss of companionship.

The court held that the television station was entitled to summary judgment on plaintiffs' invasion of privacy claims. The decedent's claim did not survive his death, and the family members could claim no invasion based on a single call to which the decedent consented or on the broadcast of the "newsworthy" interview. The court also held that the trial court had properly dismissed plaintiffs' intentional infliction of emotional distress claims. There was no evidence that defendants intended to cause injury nor that they were a substantial factor in bringing it about, a requirement in suicide cases. Moreover, the plaintiffs had alleged no physical symptoms of emotional distress. A dissenting judge would have reinstated the intentional infliction claim; he argued that plaintiffs should not be required to allege physical symptoms in intentional tort cases.

The Branch Davidian case. A federal district judge held that media could be liable for deaths and injuries of federal agents if the media negligently alerted the Branch Davidians to an impending raid on the sect's compound near Waco, Texas. A suit filed by agents injured in the raid and survivors of four agents killed in the raid alleged that members of the sect learned from local television and newspaper staffers that federal officers were about to raid the compound. A television station employee allegedly inadvertently tipped off the Davidians by asking directions of a motorist he encountered in the vicinity of the compound just before the raid; the motorist happened to be a member of the sect. The suit also alleged that the newspaper and the television station were negligent in failing to conceal their presence as they drove back and forth on the road in front of the compound in anticipation of a raid they knew was supposed to be a surprise. (An accusation that a newspaper reporter was responsible for tipping off the Davidians was the basis of the libel case, *WFAA–TV v. McLemore*, supra p. 318.)

Although he acknowledged that there were no precedents holding journalists liable for such negligence, the judge denied the media motions for summary judgment. "It was arguably foreseeable to the newspaper and KWTX that the failure to provide any guidelines or instructions to the reporters sent to the scene could result in the Davidians being alerted to the impending raid." It was a jury question whether the decision of the law enforcement agency to proceed after it knew that the surprise element had been lost meant that any media negligence was not the proximate cause of the harm. Risenhoover v. England, 936 F. Supp. 392, 24 Med. L. Rptr. 1705 (W.D.Tex.1996). After their summary judgment motions were denied the newspaper, the television station, and an ambulance service that allegedly tipped the media settled for an undisclosed amount. See Waco paper, TV station settle over Branch Davidian Raid, L.A. Times, Oct. 19, 1996, at A4.

As we saw in Chapter VI, courts rarely permit liability for harms caused by publication or broadcast unless something more than ordinary negligence is shown. Are the free speech implications of liability in cases like the Branch Davidian case sufficiently weak to make ordinary negligence a permissible basis of liability here?

3.   INDUCING BREACH OF CONTRACT

Might media be liable for tortiously inducing a source to violate a confidentiality agreement? The question arose when CBS planned to air a segment of its "60 Minutes" show in which Mike Wallace was to have interviewed Dr. Jeffrey Wigand, a former employee of Brown & Williamson Tobacco Corp., about cigarette industry practices. The network apparently knew that Wigand had signed a severance agreement that barred him from revealing the practices he was planning to discuss. In addition, the network had agreed to indemnify Wigand against legal expenses that he might incur in defending himself against any action brought against him for breach of that contract. CBS decided not to present the program as planned but did present it some months later after the Wall Street Journal had published the substance of Wigand's comments.

There was substantial disagreement about whether CBS might have been liable in tort had it been the first to reveal Wigand's allegations. See the wide-ranging discussions in the symposium on Undercover Newsgathering Techniques: Issues and Concerns, 4 Wm. & Mary Bill Rts. J. 1005 (1996).

For more general discussions of newsgathering torts, see John W. Wade, The Tort Liability of Investigative Reporters, 37 Vand. L. Rev. 301 (1984); Lyrissa Lidsky, Prying, Spying, and Lying: Intrusive Newsgathering and What the Law Should Do About It, 73 Tul. L. Rev. 173 (1998), and David A. Logan, Masked Media: Judges, Juries, and the Law of Surreptitious Newsgathering, 83 Iowa L. Rev. 161 (1997).

For an argument that courts should adopt categorical rules stating what types of media deception are permissible, see Bernard W. Bell, Secrets and Lies: News Media and Law Enforcement Use of Deception as an Investigative Tool, 60 U. Pitt.L.Rev. 745 (1999). The author suggests that media should not be relieved of liability if they impersonate professionals, befriend individuals to gain their confidence, or become household or other "intimate" employees, but should be free to impersonate members of the general public, customers, or employees generally.

CHAPTER IX

SUBPOENAS AND SEARCHES

Reporters may possess information that would be useful to the litigants in a civil case, the prosecution or defense in a criminal trial, a grand jury, or a legislative committee. In the absence of some special protection, they may be subpoenaed to testify and turn over physical evidence such as notes, tapes, and photos, or their premises may be searched pursuant to a properly issued warrant. They often resist these attempts to compel disclosure, particularly when they believe the disclosure would violate an obligation of confidentiality. We have already seen some of the consequences of refusal to disclose in the chapter on defamation.

To resist such compelled disclosures, reporters ("reporter" is used here as shorthand; the person subpoenaed may be an editor, a broadcaster, a photographer, or even a biographer or historian) sometimes claim a privilege like those that protect communications to physicians, clergy, and attorneys.

Maryland recognized such a privilege by statute in 1896, and since then more than half of the states have enacted privilege statutes. For many years these statutes—and perhaps informal accommodations between the press and the authorities—seem to have averted most confrontations over compulsory disclosure.

In the late 1960s and early 1970s the number of confrontations multiplied rapidly, primarily because the U.S. Department of Justice began to subpoena reporters frequently. Since there was no federal privilege statute, reporters were forced to articulate First Amendment objections to these subpoenas. The issue reached the Supreme Court in 1972 in the three cases decided as *Branzburg v. Hayes,* infra.

Although the Supreme Court has not addressed a reporter's privilege case since *Branzburg*, a handful of high-profile subpoenas issued in 2004 has raised alarm within the media and reinvigorated the debate on whether reporters can be forced to turn over information to serve the needs of law enforcement or private litigants. Most of these confrontations stemmed from investigations to discover and punish those who leak sensitive government information. Given the federal government's announced intention to aggressively pursue future leaks, even more confrontations seem likely. Even if these confrontations do not reshape the law, the aggressive pursuit of government employees who leak information is certain to have an effect on reporters' newsgathering efforts.

The jurisprudence protecting journalists from compelled disclosure has expanded steadily since 1972 and is now exceedingly complex. Sometimes protection is based on the First Amendment, sometimes on a statute or state constitutional law, and sometimes on the common law. Another important variable is the nature of the disclosure sought—confidential or nonconfidential, published or unpublished, personal observation or second-hand account. Another is the type of proceeding in which disclosure is sought—grand jury investigation, criminal prosecution, criminal defense, civil litigation, or other proceeding. Yet another is whether the reporter (or his or her employer) is a party to the proceeding in which disclosure is sought. Should a reporter be forced to betray the confidence of a whistle-blower who exposes corruption in government? The source of a false and defamatory gossip item? To testify as to what he or she saw at the site of a disaster? To give testimony that might exonerate a criminal defendant? To reveal, as a defendant in a libel case, the source of the defamatory material? These variables may be treated differently from state to state, and even from one federal circuit to another.

This chapter does not attempt to segregate these variables. Rather, it is organized around substantive issues that tend to recur in different types of compelled disclosure cases. Section A deals with issues relating to the conceptual basis for the claim of privilege: how compelled disclosure may infringe on free speech values, whether (and how) an evidentiary privilege can prevent those infringements, and how much courts should assume about the behavior of sources and journalists. This section also explores the problems that arise when reporters violate promises of confidentiality. Section B looks at issues surrounding the application of the privilege. It includes issues of coverage: who is to be exempted from compulsory disclosure; what kinds of information are protected, and in what kinds of proceedings? It also addresses conditions under which the reporter may be compelled to disclose despite the applicability of a privilege. Section C assesses the future of shield statutes. Section D deals with an entirely different kind of compelled disclosure, arising from searches rather than subpoenas.

A. REPORTER'S PRIVILEGE: THE CONCEPT

1. THE NATURE OF THE CLAIM

The arguments against compelled disclosure by reporters are rarely spelled out in the "shield" statutes or in cases applying the statutes. Lawyers for reporters who had no statutory protection were forced to articulate those arguments, however, when they first asked the Supreme Court to find protection in the First Amendment.

Branzburg v. Hayes (Together With In Re Pappas and United States v. Caldwell)

Supreme Court of the United States, 1972.
408 U.S. 665, 92 S. Ct. 2646, 33 L. Ed.2d 626, 1 Med. L. Rptr. 2617.

[This was a consolidation of separate cases involving demands on three reporters by grand juries. One was a federal grand jury, and there was (and still is) no federal shield statute. The others were state grand juries, one in Massachusetts, which had no shield statute, the other in Kentucky, whose statute was held inapplicable to the particular disclosures sought.

One of the reporters, Branzburg, was involved in two cases. In the first, he had written a newspaper article about persons supposedly using a chemical process to change marijuana into hashish. In response to a subpoena, he appeared before a grand jury but refused to identify the individuals he had observed. The judge rejected his claims of privilege and ordered him to answer. The Kentucky Court of Appeals denied relief, construing the Kentucky shield statute to protect the identity of a person who supplied information to a reporter in confidence, but not of a person whose activities the reporter had observed personally.

Branzburg's second case arose out of a later story he wrote after interviewing drug users and observing them smoke marijuana. Subpoenaed again by the grand jury, he filed a motion to quash, arguing that he should not be required even to enter the grand jury room because "[o]nce Mr. Branzburg is required to go behind the closed doors of the Grand Jury room, his effectiveness as a reporter in these areas is totally destroyed." The trial court issued an order protecting him from revealing "confidential associations, sources or information" but requiring that he "answer any questions which concern or pertain to any criminal act" he had personally observed. The Kentucky Court of Appeals again denied relief.

In *Pappas,* a Massachusetts television reporter recorded and photographed statements of local Black Panther Party officials during a period of racial turmoil. He was allowed to enter the party's headquarters to cover an expected police raid in return for his promise to disclose nothing he observed within. He stayed three hours, no raid occurred, and he broadcast no story. He was summoned before the county grand jury but refused to answer any questions about what had taken place while he was there. When he was recalled, he moved to quash the second summons. The motion was denied by the trial judge, who noted the absence of a statutory newsman's privilege in Massachusetts and denied the existence of a constitutional privilege. The Supreme Judicial Court of Massachusetts affirmed.

In the third case, Caldwell had been assigned by the New York Times to cover the Black Panther Party and other black militant groups. He was subpoenaed to testify before a federal grand jury in connection with alleged crimes by the militants, including mail fraud and threats to assassinate the President. The district court denied his motion to quash the subpoena but issued a protective order limiting the questioning to information given to Caldwell for publication and prohibiting questions that would require him to reveal confidential associations, sources, or information. Caldwell still refused to testify on the ground that requiring him to appear in secret before the grand jury would destroy his working relationship with the Black Panthers. He was held in contempt, but the court of appeals reversed, holding that he had a First Amendment privilege to refuse to appear before the grand jury in the absence of some special showing of necessity.]

Opinion of the Court by JUSTICE WHITE. . . .

II.

. . . Although the newsmen in these cases do not claim an absolute privilege against official interrogation in all circumstances, they assert that the reporter should not be forced either to appear or to testify before a grand jury or at trial until and unless sufficient grounds are shown for believing that the reporter possesses information relevant to a crime the grand jury is investigating, that the information the reporter has is unavailable from other sources, and that the need for the information is sufficiently compelling to override the claimed invasion of First Amendment interests occasioned by the disclosure. Principally relied upon are prior cases emphasizing the importance of the First Amendment guarantees to individual development and to our system of representative government, decisions requiring that official action with adverse impact on First Amendment rights be justified by a public interest that is "compelling" or "paramount," and those precedents establishing the principle that justifiable governmental goals may not be achieved by unduly broad means having an unnecessary impact on protected rights of speech, press, or association. The heart of the claim is that the burden on news gathering resulting from compelling reporters to disclose confidential information outweighs any public interest in obtaining the information.

We do not question the significance of free speech, press, or assembly to the country's welfare. Nor is it suggested that news gathering does not qualify for First Amendment protection; without some protection for seeking out the news, freedom of the press could be eviscerated. But these cases involve no intrusions upon speech or assembly, no prior restraint or restriction on what the press may publish, and no express or implied command that the press publish what it prefers to withhold. No exaction or tax for the privilege of publishing, and no penalty, civil or criminal, related to the content of published material is at issue here. The use of confidential sources by the press is not forbidden or restricted; reporters remain free to seek news from any source by means within the law. No attempt is made to require the press to publish its sources of information or indiscriminately to disclose them on request.

The sole issue before us is the obligation of reporters to respond to grand jury subpoenas as other citizens do and to answer questions relevant to an investigation into the commission of crime. . . .

It has generally been held that the First Amendment does not guarantee the press a constitutional right of special access to information not available to the public generally. Zemel v. Rusk, 381 U.S. 1, 16–17 (1965); [ ]. In *Zemel v. Rusk,* supra, for example, the Court sustained the Government's refusal to validate passports to Cuba even though that restriction "render[ed] less than wholly free the flow of information concerning that country." Id., at 16. The ban on travel was held constitutional, for "[t]he right to speak and publish does not carry with it the unrestrained right to gather information." [ ][22]

Despite the fact that news gathering may be hampered, the press is regularly excluded from grand jury proceedings, our own conferences, the meetings of other official bodies gathered in executive session, and the meetings of private organizations. Newsmen have no constitutional right of access to the scenes of crime or disaster when the general public is excluded, and they may be prohibited from attending or publishing information about trials if such restrictions are necessary to assure a defendant a fair trial before an impartial tribunal. In *Sheppard v. Maxwell,* [ ], for example, the Court reversed a state court conviction where the trial court failed to adopt "stricter rules governing the use of the courtroom by newsmen, as Sheppard's counsel requested," neglected to insulate witnesses from the press, and made no "effort to control the release of leads, information, and gossip to the press by police officers, witnesses, and the counsel for both sides." [ ] "[T]he trial court might well have proscribed extrajudicial statements by any lawyer, party, witness, or court official which divulged prejudicial matters." [ ] See also *Estes v. Texas,* [ ].

It is thus not surprising that the great weight of authority is that newsmen are not exempt from the normal duty of appearing before a grand jury and answering questions relevant to a criminal investigation. At common law, courts consistently refused to recognize the existence of any privilege authorizing a newsman to refuse to reveal confidential information to a grand jury. . . .

The prevailing constitutional view of the newsman's privilege is very much rooted in the ancient role of the grand jury that has the dual function of determining if there is probable cause to believe that a crime has been committed and of protecting citizens against unfounded criminal prosecutions. . . . Because its task is to inquire into the existence of possible criminal conduct and to return only well-founded indictments, its investigative powers are necessarily broad. . . .

A number of States have provided newsmen a statutory privilege of varying breadth, but the majority have not done so, and none has been provided by federal statute. Until now the only testimonial privilege for unofficial witnesses that is rooted in the Federal Constitution is the Fifth Amendment privilege against compelled self-incrimination. We are asked to create another by interpreting the First Amendment to grant newsmen a testimonial privilege that other citizens do not enjoy. This we decline to do. Fair and effective law enforcement aimed at providing security for the person and property of the individual is a fundamental function of government, and the grand jury plays an important, constitutionally mandated role in this process. On the records now before us, we perceive no basis for

---

22. "There are few restrictions on action which could not be clothed by ingenious argument in the garb of decreased data flow. For example, the prohibition of unauthorized entry into the White House diminishes the citizen's opportunities to gather information he might find relevant to his opinion of the way the country is being run, but that does not make entry into the White House a First Amendment right." 381 U.S., at 16–17.

holding that the public interest in law enforcement and in ensuring effective grand jury proceedings is insufficient to override the consequential, but uncertain, burden on news gathering that is said to result from insisting that reporters, like other citizens, respond to relevant questions put to them in the course of a valid grand jury investigation or criminal trial.

This conclusion itself involves no restraint on what newspapers may publish or on the type or quality of information reporters may seek to acquire, nor does it threaten the vast bulk of confidential relationships between reporters and their sources. Grand juries address themselves to the issues of whether crimes have been committed and who committed them. Only where news sources themselves are implicated in crime or possess information relevant to the grand jury's task need they or the reporter be concerned about grand jury subpoenas. Nothing before us indicates that a large number or percentage of *all* confidential news sources falls into either category and would in any way be deterred by our holding that the Constitution does not, as it never has, exempt the newsman from performing the citizen's normal duty of appearing and furnishing information relevant to the grand jury's task.

The preference for anonymity of those confidential informants involved in actual criminal conduct is presumably a product of their desire to escape criminal prosecution, and this preference, while understandable, is hardly deserving of constitutional protection. It would be frivolous to assert—and no one does in these cases—that the First Amendment, in the interest of securing news or otherwise, confers a license on either the reporter or his news sources to violate valid criminal laws. Although stealing documents or private wiretapping could provide newsworthy information, neither reporter nor source is immune from conviction for such conduct, whatever the impact on the flow of news. Neither is immune, on First Amendment grounds, from testifying against the other, before the grand jury or at a criminal trial. The Amendment does not reach so far as to override the interest of the public in ensuring that neither reporter nor source is invading the rights of other citizens through reprehensible conduct forbidden to all other persons. . . .

Thus, we cannot seriously entertain the notion that the First Amendment protects a newsman's agreement to conceal the criminal conduct of his source, or evidence thereof, on the theory that it is better to write about crime than to do something about it. . . .

There remain those situations where a source is not engaged in criminal conduct but has information suggesting illegal conduct by others. Newsmen frequently receive information from such sources pursuant to a tacit or express agreement to withhold the source's name and suppress any information that the source wishes not published. Such informants presumably desire anonymity in order to avoid being entangled as a witness in a criminal trial or grand jury investigation. They may fear that disclosure will threaten their job security or personal safety or that it will simply result in dishonor or embarrassment.

The argument that the flow of news will be diminished by compelling reporters to aid the grand jury in a criminal investigation is not irrational, nor are the records before us silent on the matter. But we remain unclear how often and to what extent informers are actually deterred from furnishing information when newsmen are forced to testify before a grand jury. The available data indicate that some newsmen rely a great deal on confidential sources and that some informants are particularly sensitive to the threat of exposure and may be silenced if it is held by this Court that, ordinarily, newsmen must testify pursuant to subpoenas, but the evidence fails to demonstrate that there would be a significant constriction of the flow of news to the public if this Court reaffirms the prior common-law and constitutional rule regarding the testimonial obligations of newsmen. Estimates of the inhibiting effect of such subpoenas on the willingness of informants to make disclosures to newsmen are widely divergent and to a great extent speculative.[23] It would be difficult to canvass the views of the informants themselves; surveys of reporters on this topic are chiefly opinions of predicted informant behavior and must be viewed in the light of the professional self-interest of the interviewees.[24] Reliance by the press on confidential informants does not mean that all such sources will in fact dry up because of the later possible appearance of the newsman before a grand jury. The reporter may never be called and if he objects to testifying, the prosecution may not insist. . . . Moreover, grand juries characteristically conduct secret proceedings, and law enforcement officers are themselves experienced in dealing with informers, and have their own methods for protecting them without interference with the effective administration of justice. . . .

Accepting the fact, however, that an undetermined number of informants not themselves implicated in crime will nevertheless, for whatever reason, refuse to talk to newsmen if they fear identification by a reporter in an official investigation, we cannot accept the argument that the public interest in possible future news about crime from undisclosed, unverified sources must take precedence over the public interest in pursuing and

---

23. Cf. e.g., the results of a study conducted by Guest & Stanzler, which appears as an appendix to their article, [64 Nw. U. L. Rev. 18]. A number of editors of daily newspapers of varying circulation were asked the question, "Excluding one-or two-sentence gossip items, on the average how many stories based on information received in confidence are published in your paper each year? Very rough estimate." Answers varied significantly, e.g., "Virtually innumerable," Tucson Daily Citizen (41,969 daily circ.), "Too many to remember," Los Angeles Herald–Examiner (718,221 daily circ.), "Occasionally," Denver Post (252,084 daily circ.), "Rarely," Cleveland Plain Dealer (370,499 daily circ.), "Very rare, some politics," Oregon Journal (146,403 daily circ.). This study did not purport to measure the extent of deterrence of informants caused by subpoenas to the press.

24. In his Press Subpoenas: An Empirical and Legal Analysis, Study Report of the Reporters' Committee on Freedom of the Press 6–12, Prof. Vince Blasi discusses these methodological problems. Prof. Blasi's survey found that slightly more than half of the 975 reporters questioned said that they relied on regular confidential sources for at least 10% of their stories. Id., at 21. Of this group of reporters, only 8% were able to say with some certainty that their professional functioning had been adversely affected by the threat of subpoena; another 11% were not certain whether or not they had been adversely affected. Id., at 53.

prosecuting those crimes reported to the press by informants and in thus deterring the commission of such crimes in the future.

We note first that the privilege claimed is that of the reporter, not the informant, and that if the authorities independently identify the informant, neither his own reluctance to testify nor the objection of the newsman would shield him from grand jury inquiry, whatever the impact on the flow of news or on his future usefulness as a secret source of information. More important, it is obvious that agreements to conceal information relevant to commission of crime have very little to recommend them from the standpoint of public policy. . . . Such conduct deserves no encomium, and we decline now to afford it First Amendment protection by denigrating the duty of a citizen, whether reporter or informer, to respond to grand jury subpoena and answer relevant questions put to him.

. . .

We are admonished that refusal to provide a First Amendment reporter's privilege will undermine the freedom of the press to collect and disseminate news. But this is not the lesson history teaches us. As noted previously, the common law recognized no such privilege, and the constitutional argument was not even asserted until 1958. From the beginning of our country the press has operated without constitutional protection for press informants and the press has flourished. The existing constitutional rules have not been a serious obstacle to either the development or retention of confidential news sources by the press.

It is said that currently press subpoenas have multiplied, that mutual distrust and tension between press and officialdom have increased, that reporting styles have changed, and that there is now more need for confidential sources, particularly where the press seeks news about minority cultural and political groups or dissident organizations suspicious of the law and public officials. These developments, even if true, are treacherous grounds for a far-reaching interpretation of the First Amendment fastening a nationwide rule on courts, grand juries, and prosecuting officials everywhere. . . .

. . .

The privilege claimed here is conditional, not absolute; given the suggested preliminary showings and compelling need, the reporter would be required to testify. Presumably, such a rule would reduce the instances in which reporters could be required to appear, but predicting in advance when and in what circumstances they could be compelled to do so would be difficult. Such a rule would also have implications for the issuance of compulsory process to reporters at civil and criminal trials and at legislative hearings. If newsmen's confidential sources are as sensitive as they are claimed to be, the prospect of being unmasked whenever a judge determines the situation justifies it is hardly a satisfactory solution to the problem. For them it would appear that only an absolute privilege would suffice.

We are unwilling to embark the judiciary on a long and difficult journey to such an uncertain destination. The administration of a constitutional newsman's privilege would present practical and conceptual difficulties of a high order. Sooner or later, it would be necessary to define those categories of newsmen who qualified for the privilege, a questionable procedure in light of the traditional doctrine that liberty of the press is the right of the lonely pamphleteer who uses carbon paper or a mimeograph just as much as of the large metropolitan publisher who utilizes the latest photocomposition methods. . . . The informative function asserted by representatives of the organized press in the present cases is also performed by lecturers, political pollsters, novelists, academic researchers, and dramatists. Almost any author may quite accurately assert that he is contributing to the flow of information to the public, that he relies on confidential sources of information, and that these sources will be silenced if he is forced to make disclosures before a grand jury.

In each instance where a reporter is subpoenaed to testify, the courts would also be embroiled in preliminary factual and legal determinations with respect to whether the proper predicate had been laid for the reporter's appearance: Is there probable cause to believe a crime has been committed? Is it likely that the reporter has useful information gained in confidence? Could the grand jury obtain the information elsewhere? Is the official interest sufficient to outweigh the claimed privilege?

Thus, in the end, by considering whether enforcement of a particular law served a "compelling" governmental interest, the courts would be inextricably involved in distinguishing between the value of enforcing different criminal laws. By requiring testimony from a reporter in investigations involving some crimes but not in others, they would be making a value judgment that a legislature had declined to make since in each case the criminal law involved would represent a considered legislative judgment, not constitutionally suspect, of what conduct is liable to criminal prosecution. The task of judges, like other officials outside the legislative branch, is not to make the law but to uphold it in accordance with their oaths.

At the federal level, Congress has freedom to determine whether a statutory newsman's privilege is necessary and desirable and to fashion standards and rules as narrow or broad as deemed necessary to deal with the evil discerned and, equally important, to refashion those rules as experience from time to time may dictate. There is also merit in leaving state legislatures free, within First Amendment limits, to fashion their own standards in light of the conditions and problems with respect to the relations between law enforcement officials and press in their own areas. It goes without saying, of course, that we are powerless to bar state courts from responding in their own way and construing their own constitutions so as to recognize a newsman's privilege, either qualified or absolute.

In addition, there is much force in the pragmatic view that the press has at its disposal powerful mechanisms of communication and is far from helpless to protect itself from harassment or substantial harm. . . .

Finally, as we have earlier indicated, news gathering is not without its First Amendment protections, and grand jury investigations if instituted or conducted other than in good faith, would pose wholly different issues for resolution under the First Amendment. Official harassment of the press undertaken not for purposes of law enforcement but to disrupt a reporter's relationship with his news sources would have no justification. Grand juries are subject to judicial control and subpoenas to motions to quash. We do not expect courts will forget that grand juries must operate within the limits of the First Amendment as well as the Fifth.

III.

[The Court reversed *Caldwell*, rejecting the claim that the Government must show a "compelling need" before a reporter can be forced to appear before a grand jury. The Court affirmed *Branzburg v. Hayes* and *Branzburg v. Meigs* on the grounds that Branzburg "had direct information to provide the grand jury concerning the commission of serious crimes." Finally the Court affirmed *In re Pappas*, and held that the reporter was required to testify before the grand jury "subject, of course, to the supervision of the presiding judge as to 'the propriety, purposes, and scope of the grand jury inquiry and the pertinence of the probable testimony.' [ ]"]

JUSTICE POWELL, concurring.

I add this brief statement to emphasize what seems to me to be the limited nature of the Court's holding. The Court does not hold that newsmen, subpoenaed to testify before a grand jury, are without constitutional rights with respect to the gathering of news or in safeguarding their sources. Certainly, we do not hold, as suggested in Mr. Justice Stewart's dissenting opinion, that state and federal authorities are free to "annex" the news media as "an investigative arm of government." The solicitude repeatedly shown by this Court for First Amendment freedoms should be sufficient assurance against any such effort, even if one seriously believed that the media—properly free and untrammeled in the fullest sense of these terms—were not able to protect themselves.

As indicated in the concluding portion of the opinion, the Court states that no harassment of newsmen will be tolerated. If a newsman believes that the grand jury investigation is not being conducted in good faith he is not without remedy. Indeed, if the newsman is called upon to give information bearing only a remote and tenuous relationship to the subject of the investigation, or if he has some other reason to believe that his testimony implicates confidential source relationships without a legitimate need of law enforcement, he will have access to the court on a motion to quash and an appropriate protective order may be entered. The asserted claim to privilege should be judged on its facts by the striking of a proper balance between freedom of the press and the obligation of all citizens to give relevant testimony with respect to criminal conduct. The balance of these vital constitutional and societal interests on a case-by-case basis accords with the tried and traditional way of adjudicating such questions.*

In short, the courts will be available to newsmen under circumstances where legitimate First Amendment interests require protection.

JUSTICE DOUGLAS, dissenting in *United States v. Caldwell* [and the other two cases].

.   .   .

It is my view that there is no "compelling need" that can be shown which qualifies the reporter's immunity from appearing or testifying before a grand jury, unless the reporter himself is implicated in a crime. . . .

JUSTICE STEWART, with whom JUSTICE BRENNAN and JUSTICE MARSHALL join, dissenting.

The Court's crabbed view of the First Amendment reflects a disturbing insensitivity to the critical role of an independent press in our society. The question whether a reporter has a constitutional right to a confidential relationship with his source is of first impression here, but the principles that should guide our decision are as basic as any to be found in the Constitution. While Justice Powell's enigmatic concurring opinion gives some hope of a more flexible view in the future, the Court in these cases holds that a newsman has no First Amendment right to protect his sources when called before a grand jury. The Court thus invites state and federal authorities to undermine the historic independence of the press by attempting to annex the journalistic profession as an investigative arm of government. Not only will this decision impair performance of the press' constitutionally protected functions, but it will, I am convinced, in the long run harm rather than help the administration of justice.

I respectfully dissent.

I.

The reporter's constitutional right to a confidential relationship with his source stems from the broad societal interest in a full and free flow of information to the public. . . .

.   .   .

---

* It is to be remembered that Caldwell asserts a constitutional privilege not even to appear before the grand jury unless a court decides that the Government has made a showing that meets the three pre-conditions specified in the dissenting opinion of Mr. Justice Stewart. To be sure, this would require a "balancing" of interests by the court, but under circumstances and constraints significantly different from the balancing that will be appropriate under the court's decision. The newsman witness, like all other witnesses, will have to appear; he will not be in a position to litigate at the threshold the State's very authority to subpoena him. Moreover, absent the constitutional pre-conditions that Caldwell and that [the] dissenting opinion would impose as heavy burdens of proof to be carried by the State, the court—when called upon to protect a newsman from improper or prejudicial questioning—would be free to balance the competing interests on their merits in the particular case. The new constitutional rule endorsed by [the] dissenting opinion would, as a practical matter, defeat such a fair balancing and the essential societal interest in the detection and prosecution of crime would be heavily subordinated.

A.

In keeping with this tradition, we have held that the right to publish is central to the First Amendment and basic to the existence of constitutional democracy. [ ]

. . .

No less important to the news dissemination process is the gathering of information. News must not be unnecessarily cut off at its source, for without freedom to acquire information the right to publish would be impermissibly compromised. Accordingly, a right to gather news, of some dimensions, must exist. . . .

B.

The right to gather news implies, in turn, a right to a confidential relationship between a reporter and his source. This proposition follows as a matter of simple logic once three factual predicates are recognized: (1) newsmen require informants to gather news; (2) confidentiality—the promise or understanding that names or certain aspects of communications will be kept off the record—is essential to the creation and maintenance of a news-gathering relationship with informants; and (3) an unbridled subpoena power—the absence of a constitutional right protecting, in *any* way, a confidential relationship from compulsory process—will either deter sources from divulging information or deter reporters from gathering and publishing information.

It is obvious that informants are necessary to the news-gathering process as we know it today. If it is to perform its constitutional mission, the press must do far more than merely print public statements or publish prepared handouts. Familiarity with the people and circumstances involved in the myriad background activities that result in the final product called "news" is vital to complete and responsible journalism, unless the press is to be a captive mouthpiece of "newsmakers."

It is equally obvious that the promise of confidentiality may be a necessary prerequisite to a productive relationship between a newsman and his informants. An officeholder may fear his superior; a member of the bureaucracy, his associates; a dissident, the scorn of majority opinion. All may have information valuable to the public discourse, yet each may be willing to relate that information only in confidence to a reporter whom he trusts, either because of excessive caution or because of a reasonable fear of reprisals or censure for unorthodox views. The First Amendment concern must not be with the motives of any particular news source, but rather with the conditions in which informants of all shades of the spectrum may make information available through the press to the public. [ ]

. . .

Finally, and most important, when governmental officials possess an unchecked power to compel newsmen to disclose information received in confidence, sources will clearly be deterred from giving information, and reporters will clearly be deterred from publishing it, because uncertainty about exercise of the power will lead to "self-censorship." [ ] The uncertainty arises, of course, because the judiciary has traditionally imposed virtually no limitations on the grand jury's broad investigatory powers. [ ]

After today's decision, the potential informant can never be sure that his identity or off-the-record communications will not subsequently be revealed through the compelled testimony of a newsman. A public-spirited person inside government, who is not implicated in any crime, will now be fearful of revealing corruption or other governmental wrongdoing, because he will now know he can subsequently be identified by use of compulsory process. The potential source must, therefore, choose between risking exposure by giving information or avoiding the risk by remaining silent.

The reporter must speculate about whether contact with a controversial source or publication of controversial material will lead to a subpoena. In the event of a subpoena, under today's decision, the newsman will know that he must choose between being punished for contempt if he refuses to testify, or violating his profession's ethics and impairing his resourcefulness as a reporter if he discloses confidential information.

. . .

II.

Posed against the First Amendment's protection of the newsman's confidential relationships in these cases is society's interest in the use of the grand jury to administer justice fairly and effectively. The grand jury serves two important functions: "to examine into the commission of crimes" and "to stand between the prosecutor and the accused, and to determine whether the charge was founded upon credible testimony or was dictated by malice or personal ill will." Hale v. Henkel, 201 U.S. 43, 59. And to perform these functions the grand jury must have available to it every man's relevant evidence. [ ]

Yet the longstanding rule making every person's evidence available to the grand jury is not absolute. The rule has been limited by the Fifth Amendment, the Fourth Amendment, and the evidentiary privileges of the common law. . . . And in United States v. Bryan, 339 U.S. 323, the Court observed that any exemption from the duty to testify before the grand jury "presupposes a very real interest to be protected." Id., at 332.

Such an interest must surely be the First Amendment protection of a confidential relationship that I have discussed above in Part I. As noted there, this protection does not exist for the purely private interests of the newsman or his informant, nor even, at bottom, for the First Amendment interests of either partner in the news-gathering relationship. Rather, it functions to insure nothing less than democratic decisionmaking through the free flow of information to the public, and it serves, thereby, to honor the "profound national commitment to the principle that debate on public issues should be uninhibited, robust, and wide-open." *New York Times Co. v. Sullivan*, [ ].

In striking the proper balance between the public interest in the efficient administration of justice and the First Amendment guarantee of the fullest flow of information, we must begin with the basic proposition that because of their "delicate and vulnerable" nature, NAACP v. Button, 371 U.S., at 433, and their transcendent importance for the just functioning of our society, First Amendment rights require special safeguards.

A.

This Court has erected such safeguards when government, by legislative investigation or other investigative means, has attempted to pierce the shield of privacy inherent in freedom of association. In no previous case have we considered the extent to which the First Amendment limits the grand jury subpoena power. . . .

. . .

Thus, when an investigation impinges on First Amendment rights, the government must not only show that the inquiry is of "compelling and overriding importance" but it must also "convincingly" demonstrate that the investigation is "substantially related" to the information sought.

Governmental officials must, therefore, demonstrate that the information sought is *clearly* relevant to a *precisely* defined subject of governmental inquiry. [ ] They must demonstrate that it is reasonable to think the witness in question has that information. [ ] And they must show that there is not any means of obtaining the information less destructive of First Amendment liberties. [ ]

. . .

Accordingly, when a reporter is asked to appear before a grand jury and reveal confidences, I would hold that the government must (1) show that there is probable cause to believe that the newsman has information that is clearly relevant to a specific probable violation of law; (2) demonstrate that the information sought cannot be obtained by alternative means less destructive of First Amendment rights; and (3) demonstrate a compelling and overriding interest in the information.

This is not to say that a grand jury could not issue a subpoena until such a showing were made, and it is not to say that a newsman would be in any way privileged to ignore any subpoena that was issued. Obviously, before the government's burden to make such a showing were triggered, the reporter would have to move to quash the subpoena, asserting the basis on which he considered the particular relationship a confidential one.

B.

The crux of the Court's rejection of any newsman's privilege is its observation that only "where news sources themselves are implicated in crime or possess information *relevant* to the grand jury's task need they or the reporter be concerned about grand jury subpoenas." [ ] But this is a most misleading construct. For it is obviously not true that the only persons about whom reporters will be forced to testify will be those "confidential informants involved in actual criminal conduct" and those having "information suggesting illegal conduct by others." [ ] As noted above, given the grand jury's extraordinarily broad investigative powers and the weak standards of relevance and materiality that apply during such inquiries, reporters, if they have no testimonial privilege, will be called to give information about informants who have neither committed crimes nor have information about crime. It is to avoid deterrence of such sources and thus to prevent needless injury to First Amendment values that I think the government must be required to show probable cause that the newsman has information that is clearly relevant to a specific probable violation of criminal law.

. . .

Notes and Questions

1. Note that four members of the Court would recognize a privilege in these cases, and a fifth, Justice Powell, seems to indicate that he might do so under other circumstances. Is there a majority for the proposition that compulsory disclosure raises First Amendment issues? That there is a First Amendment privilege that must be balanced case-by-case against the need for disclosure? What is the disagreement between Justices Powell and Stewart? Does Justice Powell's decision to write separately imply that Justice White and the three others who join his opinion are ruling out the possibility of a privilege under any circumstances?

2. The purpose of the privilege claimed by the reporters and endorsed by the dissenters is to assure sources that their confidences will be kept. Do sources rely on the applicable privilege law in deciding whether to disclose to reporters? Do they ascertain for themselves what the law is? Do they rely on reporters' promises of confidentiality, without regard to the law of privilege?

3. If the privilege works because the source relies on it in deciding whether to disclose, or because the reporter relies on it in deciding whether to promise confidentiality, it will be effective only to the extent that it enables the decision-maker—whether source or reporter—to predict in advance whether the reporter can be ordered to disclose. Does the qualified privilege proposed by Justice Stewart permit such a prediction to be made with reasonable confidence?

4. Suppose empirical evidence showed that the existence or absence of a reporter's privilege had little effect on sources' willingness to cooperate with reporters, but that reporters usually would go to jail rather than comply with disclosure orders. In that event, a privilege would have little effect on the flow of information to the public, but would avoid sending reporters to jail for adhering to what they believe are professional obligations. Is that a sufficient reason for recognizing a privilege?

2. PRIVILEGE LAW AFTER BRANZBURG
a. Recognizing a Constitutional Privilege

Branzburg of course had no effect on the 17 state shield statutes already in existence. Since *Branzburg*, at least 14 additional states have enacted such laws. The statutes are collected in Sack on Defamation (3d ed. 1999). The most significant development, however, was that many state and federal courts read the dissenting and concurring opinions in *Branzburg* as creating a federal constitutional privilege. With little encouragement from the Supreme Court, a large body of constitutional reporter's privilege law has grown up. As of 2002, all but one of the federal circuit courts of appeal appeared to recognize some form of qualified constitutional privilege against compelled disclosure by reporters. See Anthony L. Fargo, The Journalist's Privilege for Nonconfidential Information in States Without Shield Laws, 7 Comm. L. & Policy 241, 252 n.74 (2002) (collecting cases).

Whether *Branzburg* leaves room for any First Amendment privilege is still in some doubt. In University of Pennsylvania v. EEOC, 493 U.S. 182 (1990), a unanimous Court rejected a university's claim that First Amendment principles of academic freedom gave it a qualified privilege to resist a subpoena for tenure review materials. The opinion said *Branzburg* "rejected the notion that under the First Amendment a reporter could not be required to appear or testify as to information obtained in confidence without a special showing that the reporter's testimony was necessary."

In Jaffee v. Redmond, 518 U.S. 1 (1996), the Court expressed skepticism about the efficacy of qualified privileges. Discussing a "psychotherapists' privilege," the Court said, "Making the promise of confidentiality contingent upon a trial judge's later evaluation of the relative importance of the patient's interest in privacy and the evidentiary need for disclosure would eviscerate the effectiveness of the privilege." Does that bode ill for the chances of the Court's adopting the qualified privilege advocated by the dissent in *Branzburg*? Or does it suggest that the Court might go further and make the privilege absolute?

Several of the federal appellate courts have rejected the argument that Justice Powell's concurrence provided the fifth vote for a general qualified privilege for news reporters. They note that Powell joined in Justice White's opinion, and they read his separate concurrence as applying only to instances in which the subpoena power is used in bad faith or for harassment. See United States v. Smith, 135 F.3d 963, 26 Med. L. Rptr. 1457 (5th Cir. 1998); In re Grand Jury Proceedings, 5 F.3d 397, 21 Med. L. Rptr. 1972 (9th Cir. 1993); In re Grand Jury Proceedings, 810 F.2d 580, 13 Med. L. Rptr. 2049 (6th Cir. 1987). Citing these decisions, the Indiana Supreme Court said "We cannot read *Branzburg* to find the United States Constitution to require the very test that was rejected in that case." See In re WTHR–TV, 693 N.E.2d 1, 26 Med. L. Rptr. 1961 (Ind.1998).

As to grand jury proceedings, *Branzburg* leaves little room for any expansive notion of privilege. In *Cohen v. Cowles Media Co.*, supra p. 429, the Court read *Branzburg* for the proposition that "the First Amendment [does not] relieve a newspaper reporter of the obligation shared by all citizens to respond to a grand jury subpoena and answer questions relevant to a criminal investigation, even though the reporter might be required to reveal a confidential source." See also In re Grand Jury Proceedings, 5 F.3d

397, 21 Med. L. Rptr. 1972 (9th Cir. 1993), holding that decisions in other circuits recognizing a qualified constitutional privilege have no application to grand jury proceedings. The Fourth Circuit seems to embrace the view that any privilege in connection with grand jury proceedings is limited to the situations of grand jury abuse mentioned in Justice Powell's concurrence in *Branzburg*. See In re Grand Jury 87–3 Subpoena, 955 F.2d 229, 19 Med. L. Rptr. 1953 (4th Cir. 1992).

The Fifth Circuit also refuses to apply the privilege to grand jury subpoenas absent prosecutorial abuse. Vanessa Leggett, a professor and freelance writer, served 168 days in jail for refusing to hand over notes, tape recordings, and transcripts of interviews to a federal grand jury investigating a murder. Leggett had obtained the material during a series of interviews with a prisoner who subsequently committed suicide, leaving a note claiming responsibility for the murder. She had previously provided copies of some of the material to state investigators, subject to an agreement limiting their use and disclosure. When federal investigators sought the originals without any limit as to their use, Leggett refused and was jailed for contempt. She was not released until the grand jury's term expired.

The Fifth Circuit refused to order Leggett's release. The court expressed skepticism as to whether Leggett was a "journalist," but even assuming for purposes of its decision that she was, found that while "the strength of this journalist's privilege is at its apex in the context of civil cases where the disclosure of confidential information is at issue . . . the privilege is far weaker in criminal cases, reaching its nadir in grand jury proceedings." The court concluded that the privilege is "ineffectual against a grand jury subpoena absent evidence of governmental harassment or oppression," neither of which, the court asserted, had Leggett demonstrated. See In re Grand Jury Subpoenas, 29 Med. L. Rptr. 2301 (5th Cir. 2001) (unpublished opinion). The Supreme Court declined to review the case. See Leggett v. United States, 535 U.S. 1011 (2002).

Press groups disagreed sharply with the Fifth Circuit's decision, noting that there was ample evidence of "government harassment or oppression." They noted, for example, that the U.S. Attorney (the prosecutor rather than the FBI appeared to be calling the shots in this case) failed to follow the Justice Department's own guidelines for seeking information intended for publication and sought the material only after Leggett declined a request to serve as an FBI informant; the material requested concerned a suspect who was dead and who had been in police custody and therefore subject to police questioning; the prosecutor was unwilling to negotiate limits on the material sought or uses to which it would be put as state officials had, and the fact that a second grand jury met only 16 days before bringing indictments, apparently without need for Leggett's material. See Guillermo X. Garcia, The Vanessa Leggett Saga, Am. Journ. Rev., Mar. 2002 at 20.

Most jurisdictions recognize some form of reporter's privilege, although the enthusiasm with which the privilege is embraced varies from one jurisdiction to another. At one extreme, the Florida courts have made the privilege all but absolute (except as to reporters who are actual eyewitnesses to crime); although they describe the privilege as qualified, they rarely find sufficient reason to override it. At the other extreme, the Massachusetts Supreme Judicial Court has gone only so far as to hold that "it was not improper for the judge to consider the investigative purpose of and the public interest in [the reporter's] use of confidential sources" in deciding not to compel the reporter to testify. Sinnott v. Boston Retirement Board, 402 Mass. 581, 524 N.E.2d 100, 15 Med. L. Rptr. 1608 (1988).

b.   *Other Sources of Privilege*

Some courts have found a privilege in sources other than the First Amendment. In both California and New York, for example, reporters are protected both under their state constitutions and under shield statutes. Washington bases its version of the privilege on state common law. After the New Mexico Court of Appeals declared that state's shield statute unconstitutional as an infringement on the courts' rule-making power, the New Mexico Supreme Court created a privilege by rule.

The federal courts sometimes speak of the privilege as emanating from "federal common law." See, e.g., *Gonzales v. NBC, infra.* This is a reference to Rule 501 of the Federal Rules of Evidence, which provides that questions of privilege in federal courts "shall be governed by the principles of the common law as they may be interpreted by the courts of the United States in the light of reason and experience." An exception in Rule 501 provides that state privilege law controls "with respect to an element of a claim or defense as to which State law supplies the rule of decision." Other federal courts treat the privilege as deriving directly from the First Amendment. Those that employ "federal common law" draw on the same constitutional policies, however, and the method of analysis seems to be roughly the same under either approach. Are there other consequences of treating it as a common law, rather than constitutional, privilege?

c.   *How the Privilege Works*

The courts have rejected the proposition that reporters should not be compelled to appear even to invoke the privilege. Reporters must respond, either by appearing or by moving to quash the subpoena. Usually the reporter must supply some information to lay the foundation for the privilege. Sometimes an affidavit setting out the basis for the reporter's objections to disclosure is sufficient to support the motion to quash. On other occasions, courts have insisted that the reporter testify as to the circumstances from which the claim of confidentiality arises. Other courts have allowed the privilege to be invoked only on a question-by-question basis.

Like other privileges, a reporter's privilege can be waived. Some reporters have been spared the burden of litigating a privilege claim by sources who agreed to waive the obligation of confidentiality. Still others have been spared from going to jail by sources who agreed to waive confidentiality after the privilege claim was rejected by the courts.

This does not necessarily mean the reporter *must* disclose if the source waives. Attorney-client and physician-patient privileges are viewed as "belonging" to the client or patient, and can be waived by them. Reporter's privilege, however, is sometimes treated as belonging to the reporter. See United States v. Cuthbertson, 630 F.2d 139, 6 Med. L. Rptr. 1545 (3d Cir. 1980), which held that the privilege could only be waived by the reporter.

On the other hand, once the source has destroyed the confidentiality, the claim of privilege is weakened. In jurisdictions that recognize a qualified privilege like that described in Justice Stewart's dissent, destruction of the confidentiality may tip the balance in favor of disclosure even though the privilege is not considered waived.

Occasionally courts hold that reporters have inadvertently waived any claim of privilege by disclosing part of the information sought. This pitfall usually can be avoided by objecting to all disclosure before making any; after the objection is overruled, the reporter cannot be said to have voluntarily waived the privilege.

Judges sometimes demand to inspect *in camera* the material claimed to be privileged. Such demands can create difficult choices for reporters. If *in camera* inspection is properly ordered, the reporter can be held in contempt for refusing to comply even though the material might ultimately have been found privileged and thus shielded from further disclosure. See In re Selcraig, 705 F.2d 789, 9 Med. L. Rptr. 1705 (5th Cir. 1983). But if the information in question is confidential, its surrender to the judge may itself be a breach of the reporter's promise to the source.

Suppose the reporter is willing to go to jail rather than disclose, but believes the judge, after inspecting the material, will not require disclosure. Can the reporter turn the material over (or testify) *in camera* without giving up the right to go to jail to prevent public disclosure? Should a judge agree to an *in camera* inspection in which his or her only choices are to hold the material nondisclosable or give it back to the reporter and hold the reporter in contempt?

Demands to submit to *in camera* inspection usually are subjected to at least some of the requirements the privilege imposes on compulsory disclosure generally. In the *Farber* case, infra p. 595, the court held that in the future, reporters could not be compelled to disclose even *in camera* until the court had held a hearing and made a preliminary determination that there was a reasonable likelihood that the information would be relevant and not available from other sources.

d.   *Leaks, Investigations, and Government Secrecy*

Subpoena controversies tend to become especially intense when they involve attempts to learn who leaked information to the media. If the leaking was illegal, the reporter has evidence of a crime. At the same time, leaks are a fact of life in newsgathering and in government. This issue was raised in a highly publicized case involving grand jury subpoenas issued in 2004 to reporters Judith Miller of the New York Times and Matthew Cooper of Time magazine. Miller and Cooper were subpoenaed as part of an investigation into who leaked the name of undercover CIA agent Valerie Plame to syndicated columnist Robert Novak. Novak, citing "two senior officials" in the Bush administration, disclosed Plame's identity in a column questioning the credibility of her husband, former ambassador Joseph Wilson IV. Wilson had criticized President George W. Bush for providing faulty evidence of weapons of mass destruction in Iraq. Wilson claimed that the Bush administration "outed" his wife in retaliation for his criticisms.

A special prosecutor was appointed to investigate who disclosed Plame's identity, since intentionally "outing" an undercover CIA agent may be a crime. As part of the investigation, the prosecutor issued grand jury subpoenas to Cooper, who had written about the Plame controversy, and Miller, who had researched the story but never written about it. Several other prominent reporters were subpoenaed and gave depositions in the case after their key source, Vice President Cheney's Chief of Staff Lewis "Scooter" Libby, waived confidentiality. Although Cooper gave deposition testimony regarding Libby, he resisted a second subpoena for information about an additional source. Miller, who provided no information to the special prosecutor, also filed a motion to quash. See James C. Goodale, Why Reporters Go to Jail, 231 New York L. J, Dec. 3, 2004, at 3; Allan Wolper, Ethics Corner: Robert Novak plays "I've got a secret", Editor & Publisher, Dec. 1, 2004.

The district court rejected the journalists' motions to quash the subpoenas and ordered the journalists to comply. Cooper and Miller were then held in contempt, with possible sentences of up to 18 months in jail. The court of appeals affirmed, agreeing unanimously that even if a First Amendment privilege existed, it was not absolute and had been overcome by the special prosecutor's showing of need, and holding 2-1 that there was no federal common law privilege. See In re Grand Jury Subpoena, Judith Miller, 397 F.3d 964 (D.C.Cir. 2005).

A federal district judge in another high profile case also rejected reporters' attempts to protect confidential sources who had improperly revealed government information. Wen Ho Lee v. U.S. Dep't of Justice, 287 F. Supp. 2d 15 (D.D.C. 2003). The judge ordered five prominent reporters to comply with a subpoena issued by a plaintiff suing the Justice Department, the Department of Energy, and the FBI. The plaintiff, Wen Ho Lee, was a former government scientist who had been investigated and ultimately exonerated of providing nuclear secrets to the Chinese.

Lee's suit alleged that, while he was being investigated, government employees leaked personal information about him to the media in violation of the Privacy Act, causing him to lose his job and suffer harm to his reputation and severe emotional distress. Lee sought the identity of those government employees from the reporters who had written articles about him during the investigation. The district court held that whatever First

Amendment privilege the reporters might enjoy had been overcome. Specifically, the court found that the identity of the leaker was critical to plaintiff's claim and that plaintiff had exhausted alternative sources for discovering who leaked the information before subpoenaing the reporters. More significantly, the judge expressed "doubt that a truly worthy First Amendment interest resides in protecting the identity of government personnel who disclose to the press information that the Privacy Act says they may not reveal." Thus, the judge intimated that cases in which reporters "conceal[ ] from the plaintiff possible government complicity" might be subject to a lower standard of protection than other types of civil cases. See also Wen Ho Lee v. U.S. Dep't of Justice, 327 F. Supp.2d 26 (D.D.C. 2004) (holding journalists in contempt and ordering them to pay $500 per day until they complied with order to reveal confidential sources)

The First Circuit held that *Branzburg* extended to a contempt proceeding arising out of a leak. A television reporter obtained a videotape made by the FBI showing a city official accepting a bribe. A federal judge overseeing a grand jury investigation of the matter had barred release of the videotapes. In pursuit of a possible contempt charge against the leaker, the judge appointed a special prosecutor to investigate the leak, and held the reporter in civil contempt when he refused to reveal who gave him the tape. The reporter argued that *Branzburg* was limited to grand jury subpoenas, but the appellate court said it applied to investigations by special prosecutors as well. The court acknowledged that its own decisions required heightened sensitivity when First Amendment interests were at stake, but said this requires no more than a showing that the information is directly relevant to a good faith claim and is not available elsewhere. See In re special Proceedings, 373 F.3d 37, 32 Med. L. Rptr. 1897 (1st Cir. 2004). The reporter was convicted of criminal contempt. A week after his conviction, his source, a lawyer who had violated the protective order, came forward and revealed himself but said that he had never requested confidentiality. The district judge sentenced the reporter to six months' home confinement, during which he was barred from media appearances, Internet use, or any discussion of his sentence. Elizabeth Mehren, Home Confinement for Journalist, L.A. Times, Dec. 10, 2004, at A22.

Lucy Dalglish, Executive Director of the Reporters Committee for Freedom of the Press, described the subpoena situation in 2004 as " 'the worst it has ever been,' " and media attorney Bruce Sanford claimed that the situation " 'has changed with a velocity that would make your head spin faster than Linda Blair in the Exorcist.' " See Joe Strupp, Reporters Face Jail, Fines, Dates in Court, Editor & Publisher, Oct. 1, 2004.

The federal government's increasing use of subpoenas against journalists to investigate leaks is part of a broader pattern of government secrecy that could have significant effects on newsgathering. As we shall see in Chapter 10, the executive branch has increased its resistance to disclosure of information under the Freedom of Information Act. Meanwhile, the number of classified documents has increased dramatically since 2001. See Jack Nelson, Government Secrecy: What Leaks are Good Leaks, L.A.

Times, Jan. 5, 2003, at H3 (noting that document classification increased by 44% over the previous year in fiscal year 2001); see also Information Security Oversight Office, Report to the President 2003, available at http://www.fas.org/sgp/isoo/2003rpt.pdf (noting an increase in classification and a decrease in declassification "over the past several years"). This raises the stakes for those who might give this information to reporters because unauthorized disclosure of classified information may be a criminal offense.

In 2002, the Justice Department announced its intention to aggressively pursue and punish those who leak classified government information. See Office of the Attorney General, Report to Congress on Unauthorized Disclosures of Classified Information (2002), available at http://www.fas.org/sgp/othergov/dojleaks.html. Leak investigations resulted in hundreds of government employees being asked to sign affidavits that they did not leak classified information. Potential sources were also asked to waive any confidentiality agreement they may have entered into with reporters.

Although the Bush administration is not the first to use confidentiality waivers to pressure reporters to give up their confidential sources, media observers fear that the widespread use of such waivers threatens newsgathering to an unprecedented extent. See Edward Fitzpatrick and Mike Stanton, Use of waivers feeds press debate, Providence J.-Bulletin, Dec. 12, 2004, at A1. See also Irina Dmitrieva, Stealing Information: Application of a Criminal Anti–Theft Statute to Leaks of Confidential Government Information, 55 Fla. L. Rev. 1043 (2003) (discussing the prosecution and conviction of a DEA employee for leaking confidential but unclassified information to the London Times).

e. Consequences of Noncompliance

What happens if the privilege claim is rejected and the reporter still refuses to disclose? As we saw in the defamation chapter, when the reporter (or his or her employer) is a party to the proceeding in which disclosure is sought, the judge has available an array of sanctions. Under the Federal Rules of Civil Procedure, for example, a party's failure to comply with a discovery order may result in striking a claim or defense, default judgment, and/or an award of attorney's fees.

When the reporter is not a party, contempt is usually the only sanction available. Typically, the sanction is civil contempt—the reporter is committed to jail until he or she complies with the disclosure order. Occasionally the reporter is sentenced to a specific term (or fine) for criminal contempt. The defendant in a criminal contempt case has the same constitutional rights as any other criminal defendant.

If it appears that the reporter will remain in jail indefinitely rather than comply, some courts hold that the sanction becomes penal rather than coercive, and thus subject to maximum sentence provisions of the criminal contempt law. In Rosato v. Superior Court, 51 Cal. App.3d 190, 124 Cal. Rptr. 427, 1 Med. L. Rptr. 2560 (1975), after four reporters and editors had served fifteen days in jail, the court held a hearing, determined that they would not testify, sentenced them to five-day terms for criminal contempt (with credit for time already served), and released them.

Can reporters avoid subpoena problems by routinely destroying notes or erasing tapes? There is no universal answer. If the material is not available to be subpoenaed, neither is it available for future journalistic uses, or for use by the reporter or his or her employer as evidence in libel suits or other legal proceedings. Even if it would not have been helpful to the media defendant, the suspicions aroused when the jury is told that notes are routinely destroyed may do more harm than the evidence would have done. See generally Betty Holcomb, Should reporters torch their notes? Colum. Journalism Rev., Jan./Feb. 1986, at 42.

In any event, material must not be destroyed after litigation is commenced, or after the reporter learns that litigation is likely. Such destruction may be a crime, and a jury may be instructed that it can infer that the destroyed material must have contained evidence supporting the plaintiff's claims. In one libel case, an employee's destruction of documents was held to be evidence supporting a finding of actual malice. See Brown & Williamson Tobacco Corp. v. Jacobson, 827 F.2d 1119, 14 Med. L. Rptr. 1497 (7th Cir. 1987).

f. Violating Confidences

In *Branzburg* the reporters argued, and dissent agreed, that respecting confidentiality "is essential to the creation and maintenance of a news-gathering relationship with informants." Does that argument leave any room for media to break their promises of confidentiality when their journalistic judgment tells them they should? In *Cohen v. Cowles Media Co.*, supra p. 429, we saw one case in which media did so. Is the First Amendment argument that the newspapers made in that case consistent with the rationale for a reporter's privilege?

Since the *Cohen* case, other instances of "burning sources" have come to light. A reporter for the Cincinnati Enquirer disclosed as part of a plea bargain the source who had assisted him in illegally accessing the voice mail system of Chiquita Brands International, a Cincinnati-based company. As a result of the disclosure, the source was convicted of four misdemeanor counts of attempting unauthorized access to computer files. The source sued the Enquirer for breaking its promise of confidentiality. The trial court dismissed the suit on the ground that Ohio law provided absolute immunity from tort liability for anyone providing information to a prosecutor or grand jury and the court of appeals affirmed. Ventura v. Cincinnati Enquirer, 396 F.3d 784, 33 Med. L. Rptr. 1225 (6th Cir. 2005).

The investigative report based on the illegally accessed voice mails accused Chiquita Brands of bribing foreign officials, mistreating foreign workers, and illegally circumventing laws against foreign ownership of land. When the reporter's illegal tapping of the voice mails came to light, the Enquirer fired him, paid Chiquita more than $10 million, and published a front page apology renouncing the series. See Douglas Frantz, Chiquita Still Under Cloud After Newspaper's Retreat, N.Y. Times, July 17, 1998, at A1; Laurence Zuckerman, Paper Forced to Apologize for Articles About Chiquita, N.Y. Times, June 29, 1998, at A10. Chiquita eventually paid a $100,000 penalty and agreed to a cease and desist order in response to an SEC finding that its employees had paid a $30,000 bribe to a Colombian official. See SEC v. Chiquita Brands International, Inc., Civ. Action NO. 1:01CV02079 (D.D.C.) (filed October 3, 2001), http://www.sec.gov/litigation/litreleases/lr17169.htm.

A reporter for the Austin American–Statesman promised in writing that he would not identify a man who volunteered information about the mother of two murdered infants. The newspaper published a story based on the information, then set up a meeting with the district attorney, told him how they had obtained the information, and told him "that we would follow the law." The prosecutor immediately obtained a subpoena, a hearing was convened at which the newspaper's objections were overruled, and the newspaper revealed the name without appealing. The editor noted that "the promise of nondisclosure was given without the approval of editors" and the source had reneged on his promise to go to the authorities voluntarily after disclosing his information to the newspaper. See Rich Oppel, When we become part of the story, Austin American–Statesman, April 27, 1999, at A9.

B. APPLYING THE PRIVILEGE

If a reporter's privilege is recognized, numerous questions remain to be answered. Some have to do with the scope, or coverage, of the privilege, and some with the circumstances under which the privilege can be defeated. Most scope questions fall into one of two categories: (1) what kinds of materials are shielded, and (2) what kinds of "reporters" may claim the privilege? In addition, the type of proceeding—whether civil, criminal or administrative—may affect the scope of the privilege.

Even if a court decides that a privilege applies, the court may still order disclosure if the privilege has been overcome. Most evidentiary privileges are absolute, in the sense that once they are determined to be applicable to the communication in question, they cannot be defeated no matter how great the need for the disclosure. About half of the state reporter's privilege statutes are absolute in this sense. The rest of the statutes—and the First Amendment privilege that many courts have recognized since *Branzburg*—are qualified. That means that even though they are applicable to the disclosure sought, by their own terms they may be overcome if certain showings are made.

In deciding whether a qualified privilege should be set aside, courts usually draw heavily on the analysis suggested by the dissent in *Branzburg*. This is true whether the source of the privilege is the First Amendment or federal common law. It is generally true even when the source is a state statute or state constitution, although a few of these contain narrower grounds for defeasance (the Michigan statute, for example, can be defeated only in an inquiry into a crime punishable by life in prison).

1. WHAT MATERIAL IS COVERED?

The typical case is one in which the source has authorized the reporter to use the information provided but insisted that his or her identity be kept confidential, or that the information itself be kept confidential. But often media organizations also resist disclosure of material that was not obtained in confidence. These problems arise most frequently in connection with subpoenas for reporters' notes, unpublished photos, or portions of video or audio tapes not broadcast. Media lawyers tend to refer to all of these loosely as "outtakes cases."

In these cases the analogy to other privileges, such as attorney-client, breaks down, because those typically apply only when the information is given in confidence. More importantly, the rationale advanced by the reporters in *Branzburg*—that compelled disclosure will cause sources to cease talking to reporters—is not fully applicable, because no promise of confidentiality to a source is at issue.

a. Statutory Coverage

Though some statutes by their terms protect only confidences, many others explicitly cover nonconfidential materials. For example, the Maryland shield statute applies to notes, outtakes, photos, video and sound tapes, and film, as long as they have not been disseminated to the public. Other statutes seem to protect the reporter from being compelled to testify about even published material. The New Jersey statute, for example, protects "Any news or information obtained in the course of pursuing [the reporter's] professional activities whether or not it is disseminated." It has been construed to prevent the reporter from being asked in court to verify the accuracy of quotes in a published story. In re Schuman, 114 N.J. 14, 552 A.2d 602, 16 Med. L. Rptr. 1092 (1989). What First Amendment interests might be jeopardized by requiring a reporter to give such testimony, or to produce originals of published photographs?

Some statutes seem to recognize a rationale other than maintaining confidences. The Delaware statute applies if the reporter swears "that the disclosure of the information would violate an express or implied understanding with the source under which the information was originally obtained *or would substantially hinder the reporter in the maintenance of existing source relationships or the development of new source relationships.*" Del. Code tit. X, § 4322. (Emphasis added). Could a conscientious reporter swear in good faith that disclosure of unaired videotape was eligible for protection under this provision? How might such a disclosure interfere with source relationships?

b. Does the First Amendment Privilege Cover Outtakes?

The following case addresses whether the First Amendment privilege applies to nonconfidential material as well as whether the privilege has been overcome.

Gonzales v. National Broadcasting Company, Inc.

U.S. Court of Appeals, Second Circuit, 1999.
194 F.3d 29; 27 Med. L. Rptr. 2459.

Before MCLAUGHLIN and LEVAL, CIRCUIT JUDGES, and SPATT, DISTRICT JUDGE.

LEVAL, CIRCUIT JUDGE.

[A civil rights action for "racial profiling" was filed in federal district court in Louisiana under 42 U.S.C. § 1983. The plaintiffs alleged that they had been pulled over and detained by Louisiana Deputy Sherifff Darrell Pierce without any basis because they were Hispanic. They contended that Pierce pulled them over as part of a pattern of harassing and extorting valuable property from minority citizens. Plaintiffs sought compensatory and punitive damages and an injunction.]

[While plaintiffs' suit was pending,] NBC aired a segment on its "Dateline" television program reporting on what it described as pervasive abuses by law enforcement officers in Louisiana who conduct unwarranted stops of motorists, particularly of out-of-state travelers. According to the report, these stops often lead to harassment and seizure of property. The report included a videotaped stop of one of its employees, Pat Weiland, by Deputy Pierce. Weiland, a Dateline producer and a cameraman, rented a car, equipped it with hidden cameras, and traveled incognito on Louisiana roadways to investigate allegations of malfeasance by Louisiana highway patrolmen. In May, 1996, six months after the [plaintiffs] were pulled over, Deputy Pierce stopped Weiland, claiming Weiland had been slowing down and speeding up. The Dateline report asserted that the car had in fact been on cruise control below the posted speed limit. The report also maintained that footage recorded by hidden cameras demonstrated that no traffic laws had been violated, and that the car had been stopped without probable cause. . . .

. . . [The plaintiffs] served NBC with a subpoena seeking the original, unedited camera footage of Deputy Pierce's stop of Weiland, as well as deposition testimony from NBC representatives about the events recorded on the videotape. Approximately one month later, Deputy Pierce served NBC with a similar subpoena. NBC objected to both subpoenas in part on the grounds that they sought materials protected from disclosure by the qualified privilege for journalists. Both the Plaintiffs and the Defendant filed motions in the Southern District of New York to compel NBC's compliance with their respective subpoenas in September, 1997. [The district court granted the motions to compel. The court of appeals first affirmed on the ground that no qualified privilege exists for nonconfidential information, but granted NBC's motion for rehearing and issued this opinion.]

. . .

II. DISCUSSION

We agree with NBC that the qualified privilege protecting press materials from disclosures applies to nonconfidential as well as to confidential materials. We agree with Plaintiffs, however, that litigants seeking to subpoena nonconfidential press materials need make a less demanding showing than those who seek confidential press resources, and that the parties to the Louisiana Action have made the requisite showing in this dispute.

A. *The nature of the qualified privilege for nonconfidential press materials.*

This circuit has long recognized the existence of a qualified privilege for journalistic information. In Baker v. F. & F. Inv., 470 F.2d 778 (2d Cir. 1972), the first case to recognize such a privilege, we affirmed the district court's denial of a motion to compel a reporter to disclose the name of a "blockbuster" whom the reporter had interviewed while preparing an article on housing discrimination. [ ]. The source's identity was sought by plaintiffs in a civil rights action. [ ]. We explained that

> federal law [does not] require disclosure of [journalists'] confidential sources in each and every case, both civil and criminal, in which the issue is raised. Absent a federal statute to provide specific instructions, courts which must attempt to divine the contours of non-statutory federal law governing the compelled disclosure of confidential journalistic sources must rely on both judicial precedent and well-informed judgment as to the proper federal public policy to be followed in each case.

Id. at 781. While our reasoning in *Baker* focused on the importance of protecting journalists' confidential sources, we also grounded the qualified privilege in a broader concern for the potential harm to the "paramount public interest in the maintenance of a vigorous, aggressive and independent press capable of participating in robust, unfettered debate over controversial matters." *Id.* at 782.

In *McGraw-Hill, Inc. v. Arizona* (In re Petroleum Prods. Antitrust Litig.), 680 F.2d 5 (2d Cir. 1982), our next decision to address this area of doctrine, we reaffirmed the existence of the journalists' privilege, vacating a district court's order compelling an editor of a news service to produce a document containing the names of confidential sources sought by certain state governments in an antitrust action. *Id.* at 6–7. In language that has since been characterized as the Second Circuit's "test" for overcoming the journalists' privilege, we explained that

> The law in this Circuit is clear that to protect the important interests of reporters and the public in preserving the confidentiality of journalists' sources, disclosure may be ordered only upon a clear and specific showing that the information is: highly material and relevant, necessary or critical to the maintenance of the claim, and not obtainable from other available sources.

Id. at 7 (internal citations omitted). Although our reasoning in *Petroleum Products* again focused on the importance of maintaining the confidentiality of press sources, we also invoked other factors. We quoted with approval, for instance, Justice Department Guidelines discouraging any attempt to subpoena the press to appear before grand juries, and stipulating that "all reasonable attempts should be made to obtain information from non-press sources before there is any consideration of subpoenaing the press." *Id.* at 8 (internal citations omitted).

While *Baker* and *Petroleum Products* established the existence of a journalists' privilege for confidential materials, subsequent decisions of this court have repeatedly stated that the privilege also extends to nonconfidential materials, and have enforced the privilege in that context. . . . In the course of the foregoing rulings, our court has not expressed in detail the reasons for applying the journalists' privilege to nonconfidential materials. As earlier mentioned, both *Petroleum Products* and *Baker* focused on the public policy interest in safeguarding the confidentiality of those who convey information to the press. [ ]. Indeed, the requirements for overcoming the privilege that we elucidated in *Petroleum Products* were designed "to protect the important interests of reporters and the public in preserving the confidentiality of journalists' sources." [ ] Yet *Petroleum Products* and *Baker* alike implied that there were also broader concerns undergirding the qualified privilege for journalists—such as the "pivotal function of reporters to collect information for public dissemination." . . . .

These broader concerns, we believe, are relevant regardless whether the information sought from the press is confidential. If the parties to any lawsuit were free to subpoena the press at will, it would likely become standard operating procedure for those litigating against an entity that had been the subject of press attention to sift through press files in search of information supporting their claims. The resulting wholesale exposure of press files to litigant scrutiny would burden the press with heavy costs of subpoena compliance, and could otherwise impair its ability to perform its duties—particularly if potential sources were deterred from speaking to the press, or insisted on remaining anonymous, because of the likelihood that they would be sucked into litigation. Incentives would also arise for press entities to clean out files containing potentially valuable information lest they incur substantial costs in the event of future subpoenas. And permitting litigants unrestricted, court-enforced access to journalistic resources would risk the symbolic harm of making journalists appear to be an investigative arm of the judicial system, the government, or private parties.[5]

---

5. We are not the only circuit that has taken note of the foregoing concerns; others also have recognized a privilege for nonconfidential press materials. *See, e.g.,* Shoen v. Shoen, 48 F.3d 412, 415–16 (9th Cir. 1995) (reasoning that "routine court-compelled disclosure of [nonconfidential journalistic] research materials poses a serious threat to the vitality of the newsgathering process," and positing that the absence of a privilege for nonconfidential information would result in numerous adverse effects); United States v. Cuthbertson, 630 F.2d 139, 147 (3d Cir. 1980) (reasoning that "compelled production of a reporter's resource materials can constitute a significant intrusion into the newsgathering and editorial processes," and "may substantially undercut the public policy favoring the free flow of information to the public that is the foundation for the [journalists'] privilege"); see also United States v. LaRouche Campaign, 841 F.2d 1176, 1182 (1st Cir. 1988) (reasoning that "[w]e discern a lurking and subtle threat to journalists and their employers if disclosure of outtakes,

For these reasons, we reaffirm that the qualified privilege for journalists applies to nonconfidential, as well as to confidential, information.[6] However, it is important to recognize that, where the protection of confidential sources is not involved, the nature of the press interest protected by the privilege is narrower. Cf. Shoen v. Shoen, 5 F.3d 1289, 1295–96 (9th Cir. 1993) (reasoning that " 'the lack of a confidential source may be an important element in balancing the defendant's need for the material sought against the interest of the journalist in preventing production in a particular case' ") ([ ]). The stringent test we enunciated in *Petroleum Products* for overcoming the qualified privilege was designed "to protect . . . the confidentiality of journalists' sources." 680 F.2d at 7. We believe that when protection of confidentiality is not at stake, the privilege should be more easily overcome. Accordingly, we now hold that, while nonconfidential press materials are protected by a qualified privilege, the showing needed to overcome the privilege is less demanding than the showing required where confidential materials are sought. Where a civil litigant seeks nonconfidential materials from a nonparty press entity, the litigant is entitled to the requested discovery notwithstanding a valid assertion of the journalists' privilege if he can show that the materials at issue are of likely relevance to a significant issue in the case, and are not reasonably obtainable from other available sources.

B.   *Whether the privilege has been overcome in this case.*

. . . As noted above, because the outtakes were not materials obtained by NBC in confidence, the *Petroleum Products* test is not applicable. We need only determine whether the parties to the Louisiana Action have established that the outtakes are of likely relevance to a significant issue in the case, and contain information not reasonably obtainable from other available sources. We answer both questions affirmatively.

The outtakes are clearly relevant to a significant issue in the case. The District Court reasonably found they may assist the trier of fact in assessing whether Deputy Pierce had probable cause to stop the NBC vehicle and might help determine whether he engaged in a pattern or practice of stopping vehicles without probable cause, as the Plaintiffs allege. [ ]. We are also persuaded that the outtakes contain information that is not reasonably obtainable from other available sources, because they

notes, and other unused information, even if nonconfidential, becomes routine and casually, if not cavalierly, compelled," and discussing the nature of this threat at length).

6. Previous decisions of our court have expressed differing views on whether the journalists' privilege is constitutionally required, or rooted in federal common law. *Compare* Baker, 470 F.2d at 781 (reasoning that "[a]bsent a federal statute to provide specific instructions, courts which must attempt to divine the contours of non-statutory federal law governing the compelled dis-

closure of confidential journalistic sources must rely on both judicial precedent and well-informed judgment as to the proper federal public policy to be followed in each case") with von Bulow, 811 F.2d at 142 (reasoning that "the process of newsgathering is a protected right under the First Amendment, albeit a qualified one," and that "[t]his qualified right . . . results in the journalist's privilege"). Until Congress legislates to modify the privilege or do away with it, however, we need not decide whether the privilege is founded in the Constitution.

can provide unimpeachably objective evidence of Deputy Pierce's conduct. We agree with the district court that in this instance a deposition is not an adequate substitute for the information that may be obtained from the videotapes. [ ].

We conclude that (i) NBC's videotapes are protected by a qualified journalists' privilege applicable to nonconfidential press materials; (ii) the privilege applicable to nonconfidential press information is overcome on a showing that the materials sought are of likely relevance to a significant issue in the case and are not reasonably obtainable through other available sources; and (iii) the parties to the Louisiana action, who subpoenaed the tapes, have satisfied the test to overcome NBC's privilege.

CONCLUSION

The orders of the district court granting the motions to compel production of the outtakes, and holding NBC in contempt, are hereby AFFIRMED.

Notes and Questions

1.   If burdens imposed on NBC by compulsory disclosure of outtakes raise First Amendment concerns, would similar concerns be raised if comparable burdens were imposed by other legal requirements (e.g., FCC regulations requiring preservation of outtakes, or discovery rules requiring employees to spend time responding to libel suits)?

2.   Does this court believe that a federal common law reporter's privilege is necessarily weaker than a First Amendment privilege? Cf. In re Special Counsel Investigation, 338 F. Supp.2d 16, 19 (D.D.C. 2004) (stating that "the arguments in favor of protection of the press are weaker in [the] context" of a common law privilege than in the context of the First Amendment)

3.   Not all courts have accepted the argument that a First Amendment privilege ought to apply to nonconfidential sources. In McKevitt v. Pallasch, 339 F.3d 530, 31 Med. L. Rptr. 2141 (7th Cir. 2003), the Seventh Circuit criticized cases, including *Gonzales*, that extend the privilege to nonconfidential sources based on "concern with harassment, burden, using the press as an investigative arm of government, and so forth," noting that "these considerations were rejected by *Branzburg* even in the context of a confidential source." The Seventh Circuit questioned "what possible bearing the First Amendment could have on the question of compelled disclosure" when the information sought comes from a nonconfidential source. The court noted, however, that rejecting a First Amendment privilege would not leave reporters without protection: "It seems to us that rather than speaking of privilege, courts should simply make sure that a subpoena duces tecum directed to the media, like any other subpoena duces tecum, is reasonable in the circumstances, which is the general criterion for judicial review of subpoenas. Fed.R.Crim.P. 17(c); [ ]. We do not see why there need to be special criteria merely because the possessor of the documents or

other evidence sought is a journalist." Under this approach, could a court take into account the fact that the media, particularly broadcasters, are subpoenaed more frequently than many other types of businesses? For further discussion of outtakes cases, see Anthony L. Fargo, The Journalist's Privilege for Nonconfidential Information in States Without Shield Laws, 7 Comm. L. & Policy 241 (2002).

———

Voluntary compliance. If production of outtakes has the adverse First Amendment consequences that NBC asserts in the principal case, should media feel free to turn them over voluntarily? Several news organizations quietly acquiesced in subpoenas issued by independent counsel Kenneth Starr during the Whitewater investigation and the White House sex scandal. CBS News, ABC News, the Wall Street Journal, the New Yorker, and local television stations in Florida and Pennsylvania all supplied information in response to subpoenas issued by special prosecutors. Some said they only released published material, and all said they divulged no confidential sources. See Felicity Barringer, In a New Atmosphere, Press is Silent on Subpoena Flurry, N.Y. Times, April 24, 1998, at A1.

ABC went along with the sealing of all documents related to its subpoena; the existence of the ABC subpoena came to light when a court clerk mistakenly placed in the press box a document that was supposed to be sealed. When media think voluntary compliance with subpoenas is in their best interest, are the First Amendment interests asserted in the principal case better served by publicizing the incidents or keeping them secret? Are those interests inevitably compromised by voluntary compliance?

Some non-news organizations resisted Starr's subpoenas. One was William Morrow & Co., publisher of a book by Whitewater figure Webster Hubbell. The publisher challenged the subpoena and made the fight public. The day that a story about the subpoena appeared on page one of the New York Times, Starr dropped his attempt to obtain editorial material from the publisher. See Florence George Graves, Starr Struck, Am. J. Rev., April 1998, at 19.

Starr also subpoenaed sales records of two bookstores from which Monica Lewinsky was believed to have purchased books. The stores moved to quash, and the district court held that the subpoenas would violate First Amendment rights of Lewinsky and the booksellers unless the special prosecutor could show a compelling need for the records and a sufficient relationship to the grand jury investigation. See In re Grand Jury Subpoena to Kramerbooks & Afterwords, Inc., 26 Med. L. Rptr. 1599 (D.D.C.1998). Lewinsky subsequently agreed to voluntarily provide the records of her purchases. See Lewinsky's Lawyers to Turn Over Records of Book Purchases, N.Y. Times, June 23, 1998, at A13. If news media are less inclined than booksellers to resist subpoenas, does that undercut the argument that journalism has a special need for protection?

c. Reporter as Eyewitness

No matter how broad the purposes of the privilege may be thought to be, there are some circumstances in which the reporter cannot avoid testifying. In Pinkard v. Johnson, 118 F.R.D. 517, 14 Med. L. Rptr. 2195 (M.D.Ala.1987), a reporter was subpoenaed to testify about a conversation, notes, and his observations at a public meeting. The district court held that a First Amendment privilege protected the notes, that the reporter had waived the privilege with respect to the conversation, and that no privilege attached to his observations at the public meeting.

The Florida Supreme Court held that the First Amendment privilege "extends to both confidential and nonconfidential information gathered in the course of a reporter's employment" but "does not apply to eyewitness observations or physical evidence, including recordings, of a crime." See State v. Davis, 720 So.2d 220, 26 Med. L. Rptr. 2457 (Fla.1998). Likewise, the Florida shield statute "applies only to information or eyewitness observations obtained within the normal scope of employment and does not apply to physical evidence, eyewitness observations, or visual or audio recording of crimes." See Fla. Stat. § 90.5015(2). As a result, no privilege is available in Florida to a reporter who witnesses a police search and arrest, Miami Herald Publishing Co. v. Morejon, 561 So.2d 577, 17 Med. L. Rptr. 1920 (Fla.1990), or for outtakes depicting an arrest, CBS, Inc. v. Jackson, 578 So.2d 698, 18 Med. L. Rptr. 2110 (Fla.1991).

When the reporter has witnessed the commission of a crime, the courts may hold the privilege inapplicable even when the observation occurred pursuant to a promise of confidentiality.

2. WHO MAY CLAIM THE PRIVILEGE?

a. Statutory Definitions of "Reporter"

Most of the statutes define quite narrowly the class of persons who may claim the privilege. The California statute, for example, applies to a "publisher, editor, reporter, or other person connected with or employed upon a newspaper, magazine, or other periodical publication, or by a press association or wire service" or "a radio or television news reporter or other person connected with or employed by a radio or television station." Cal. Evid. Code § 1070. In In re Van Ness, 8 Med. L. Rptr. 2563 (Cal. Super. Ct. 1982), a trial court held that a freelance is not sufficiently "connected" until he or she has a contractual arrangement with a specific publisher.

Occasionally the statutory definition is expansive. The Delaware statute, for example, defines "reporter" as "any journalist, scholar, educator, polemicist, or other individual" who spends at least 20 hours a week in "obtaining or preparing information for dissemination with the aid of facilities for the mass reproduction of words, sounds, or images in a form available to the general public. . . ." Del. Code tit. X § 4320 (1974). Would this cover a motion picture producer? A songwriter? A painter? A contributor to an Internet forum?

b. First Amendment Privilege Claimants

Employers. The First Amendment privilege obviously covers the reporter or photographer who obtained the information. Courts normally hold that it also covers their employers. Thus, when notes or outtakes are sought from the publisher or broadcaster, the privilege may be invoked just as if the subpoena were directed at the individual who obtained the material. One court even allowed the employer to invoke the privilege *against* its reporter. When former Wall Street Journal columnist Foster Winans was charged with criminal violations of the securities laws, he subpoenaed his former employer to produce his own diary and notes, which were in the Journal's possession and contained references to Winans's confidential sources. The court permitted the Journal to invoke the privilege and held that Winans had not met "the heavy burden of showing that disclosure of the identity of confidential sources is required." Carpenter v. United States, 484 U.S. 19, 14 Med. L. Rptr. 1853 (1987). Another district judge, however, has questioned whether the employer has standing to assert the privilege if the reporter whose notes are in the employer's possession is willing to have them produced. See Bauer v. Brown, 11 Med. L. Rptr. 2168 (W.D.Va. 1985).

Scholars. Historians, biographers, sociologists, and other academic researchers may rely on confidences much as reporters do. The Second Circuit suggested that a scholar's privilege might be recognized "where a serious academic inquiry is undertaken pursuant to a considered research plan in which the need for confidentiality is tangibly related to the accuracy or completeness of the study." In re Grand Jury Subpoena, 750 F.2d 223, 11 Med. L. Rptr. 1224 (2d Cir. 1984).

In a later case the same court said the privilege should not be limited to news media but should be available if the person seeking to invoke the privilege had "the intent to use material—sought, gathered or received—to disseminate information to the public and such intent existed at the inception of the newsgathering process." See von Bulow v. von Bulow, 811 F.2d 136, 13 Med. L. Rptr. 2041 (2d Cir. 1987). Compare the Leggett case, supra p. 576, in which the Fifth Circuit expressed skepticism as to whether a professor and freelance writer conducting interviews for a book was really a "journalist" for purposes of the privilege.

Unconventional media. The privilege is not necessarily limited to traditional sources of news. A district judge held that online gossip reporter Matt Drudge was entitled to invoke a qualified First Amendment privilege. See Blumenthal v. Drudge, 186 F.R.D. 236, 27 Med. L. Rptr. 2004 (D.D.C. 1999). A trade publication was accorded a First Amendment privilege for technical information gathered from its members on the theory that it was no less dependent than news organizations on its ability to gather information in confidence. See In re Photo Marketing International, 120 Mich.App. 527, 327 N.W.2d 515, 9 Med. L. Rptr. 1087 (1982).

3. Overcoming a Qualified Privilege

One widely accepted version of the requirements for defeating the privilege is that quoted in *Gonzales*, supra: "disclosure may be ordered only upon a clear and specific showing that the information is: highly material and relevant, necessary or critical to the maintenance of the claim, and not obtainable from other available sources." Some courts condense this three-part test into two parts, omitting the first element on the ground that it is subsumed by the second. See, e.g., Zerilli v. Smith, 656 F.2d 705, 7 Med. L. Rptr. 1121 (D.C. Cir. 1981).

Whether the test has three parts or two, it is clear that "materiality and relevance" in the usual evidentiary sense is not enough: there must be some specific showing of need to outweigh the sacrifice of First Amendment values that disclosure entails. The court is unlikely to see sufficient need for disclosure when the evidence sought would be only cumulative. Suppose the evidence sought would corroborate testimony that otherwise might be discounted?

What should be the standard of necessity when the disclosure is sought by a criminal defendant, for whom any bit of evidence that might create a reasonable doubt could be dispositive? The California Supreme Court said "a criminal defendant must show a *reasonable possibility* the information will materially assist his defense." The court said this would include not only evidence tending to exculpate, but also evidence establishing a lesser offense or mitigating circumstances, or impeachment evidence. See Delaney v. Superior Court, 50 Cal.3d 785, 789 P.2d 934, 268 Cal. Rptr. 753, 17 Med. L. Rptr. 1817 (1990).

Alternative sources. In In re Special Grand Jury Investigation, 104 Ill.2d 419, 472 N.E.2d 450, 11 Med. L. Rptr. 1142 (1984), a reporter had obtained leaked copies of transcripts of a judicial inquiry board. A grand jury investigating the leaks called three members of the board, each of whom invoked a state constitutional privilege not to testify. The prosecutor then sought to compel the reporter to testify under provisions of the Illinois shield statute that allow the privilege to be set aside when "all other available sources of information have been exhausted and disclosure of the information sought is essential to the protection of the public interest involved." The court held that "all other available sources" had not been exhausted, because there were other board members and staff members who had access to transcripts and had not been questioned. "We think it clear that the statute requires more than a showing of inconvenience to the investigator before a reporter can be compelled to disclose his sources. . . ."

But if there are so many other possible sources that it is impractical to try to eliminate each of them, the exhaustion requirement is not likely to be interpreted literally. In Carey v. Hume, 492 F.2d 631, 638–39 (D.C. Cir. 1974), where the potential sources included "a very substantial list of employees," the undisclosed source could have been "anyone from an office boy to a top officer," and the reporter was unwilling to provide any information to narrow the field, the court held that requiring exhaustion of alternative sources would impose too great a burden on the party seeking disclosure.

4. DEFEATING THE PRIVILEGE IN LIBEL CASES

In most of the cases we have considered so far, the reporter was not a party to the proceeding in which he or she was asked to supply evidence. In some cases, however, the reporter or the reporter's employer is a party, and therefore subject to the discovery rules that apply to litigants themselves. The most common examples are libel cases in which plaintiffs seek information for use in their suits against reporters and/or their employers. In the defamation chapter, we saw that because the reporter in this situation is a litigant (or a person subject to the control of a litigant), the court can impose sanctions for nondisclosure that would not be available against a nonparty reporter. These include striking defenses, default judgment, and/or attorney's fees.

In general, the privilege rules we have seen so far apply equally to libel cases (a few state statutes contain special provisions for libel cases, however). If the privilege is absolute, it cannot be ignored merely because it is invoked by a party to a libel suit. If it is qualified, it can be defeated only by meeting the requirements discussed in this section. Attempts to defeat it seem to succeed somewhat more often in the libel field, however. For one thing, the materiality of the information is often obvious. If the plaintiff can prove that the source was not credible, or that the defendant is invoking the privilege to conceal the fact that it fabricated the defamatory allegation, the plaintiff has important evidence on the issue of actual malice.

The need for the disclosure may be equally obvious. The actual malice standard requires the plaintiff to prove that the defendant had serious doubts as to the truth of its publication. To the extent that the disclosure might illuminate the defendant's state of mind, it goes to the heart of the plaintiff's case, and it is evidence that is not likely to be available elsewhere.

On the other hand, compelled disclosure in libel cases also poses special risks to the newsgathering process. If the privilege can be easily overcome by filing a libel suit, it does little good to uphold the privilege in other contexts. For this reason, some courts have suggested that discovery should not be ordered until the plaintiff has presented substantial evidence that the statement is false and defamatory, or at least has established that the case is not frivolous. In Downing v. Monitor Pub. Co., 120 N.H. 383, 415 A.2d 683, 6 Med. L. Rptr. 1193 (1980), the court refused to require advance proof of falsity, but said the plaintiff must "satisfy the trial court that he has evidence to establish that there is a genuine issue of fact regarding" falsity before disclosure can be compelled.

California, through statutory and constitutional privileges, gives reporters absolute protection from contempt, but these provisions do not protect them from the other sanctions that may be imposed on parties to litigation. To fill this gap, the California courts recognize a qualified constitutional privilege in addition to the absolute privileges against contempt. See Mitchell v. Superior Court, 37 Cal.3d 268, 690 P.2d 625, 208

Cal. Rptr. 152, 11 Med. L. Rptr. 1076 (1984). This case identified the source of the qualified privilege as both the federal and state constitutions.

Despite all these protections, the Ninth Circuit, applying California law, upheld an order requiring the national tabloid Star to disclose confidential sources in a libel suit by Rodney Dangerfield. See Star Editorial, Inc. v. District Court, 7 F.3d 856, 21 Med. L. Rptr. 2281 (9th Cir. 1993).

The Star quoted unnamed employees of Caesar's Palace in a story headlined "Vegas casino accuses Caddyshack funnyman: Rodney Dangerfield 'Swills Vodka By The Tumblerful, Smokes Pot All Day and Uses Cocaine.' " The court held that the California qualified privilege had been overcome. The privilege was being invoked by a party in civil litigation, and the evidence sought went to the heart of Dangerfield's claim. "Actual malice would be extremely difficult to prove without knowing whether the confidential sources existed and, if so, what they said and whether they were credible." There were no alternative sources. Dangerfield's lawyers had deposed all of the 20 nonconfidential sources identified by the Star (all denied knowledge of the incidents recounted in the article). They did not depose the reporter who conducted the interviews, but the court said it would be futile to do so because the reporter had absolute immunity from contempt and as a nonparty would be subject to no other sanctions. Finally, the plaintiff had made a prima facie showing that the article was false through his own testimony, that of the nonconfidential sources, and the Star's admission that one incident in the story was false.

Rhode Island is one of the states whose shield statute makes special provision for libel cases. The statutory privilege does not apply to "the source of any allegedly defamatory information in any case where the defendant, in a civil action for defamation, asserts a defense based on the source of such information." A newspaper resisted disclosing the source while invoking the defense that it had published the defamatory material in good faith in reliance on the source. The Rhode Island Supreme Court held the statutory privilege inapplicable. It also rejected cases recognizing a First Amendment or common law privilege on the ground that it is unrealistic to demand that a libel plaintiff exhaust other possible means of discovering the sources relied on by the newspaper before being allowed to seek the information directly from the defendant. See Capuano v. Outlet Co., 579 A.2d 469, 18 Med. L. Rptr. 1030 (R.I.1990).

5.   DEFEATING AN ABSOLUTE PRIVILEGE

Even if the privilege is in terms absolute, it may have to yield when it conflicts with other constitutional rights. The most frequent conflict is with the Sixth Amendment rights of compulsory process and fair trial.

The most famous clash between the privilege and a defendant's fair trial interests occurred in Matter of Farber, 78 N.J. 259, 394 A.2d 330, 4 Med. L. Rptr. 1360 (1978). Farber, a reporter for the New York Times, wrote an investigative series that led to murder indictments against a physician for a number of deaths years earlier in New Jersey. The defense subpoenaed the reporter and the newspaper demanding that they produce certain documents relating to interviews with witnesses. The trial judge ordered the documents delivered to him for *in camera* inspection. Farber and the Times refused to comply and were held in civil and criminal contempt. The civil contempt involved a fine of $5,000 per day on the Times and a flat $1,000 on Farber, who was sentenced to jail until he complied. The criminal penalties were $100,000 on the newspaper, and $1,000 on Farber plus six months in jail.

On review, the New Jersey Supreme Court affirmed, 5–2. The court rejected the journalists' constitutional arguments on the ground that *Branzburg* "squarely held that no such First Amendment right exists."

The court conceded, however, that Farber and the newspaper clearly were covered by the state shield law, which was absolute, containing no provision for defeasance. But the majority concluded that the state constitution afforded a criminal defendant the right to compel witnesses to attend and to compel the production of documents "for which he may have, or may believe he has, a legitimate need in preparing or undertaking his defense." This "prevails over" the shield statute, "but in recognition of the strongly expressed legislative viewpoint favoring confidentiality, we prescribe the imposition" of some procedural safeguards.

The court directed that in similar cases in the future the reporter would be "entitled to a preliminary determination before being compelled to submit the subpoenaed materials to a trial judge." In such a hearing, the defendant would have to show "by a fair preponderance of the evidence, including all reasonable inferences, that there was a reasonable probability or likelihood that the information sought by the subpoena was material and relevant to his defense, that it could not be secured from any less intrusive source, and that the defendant had a legitimate need to see and otherwise use it."

Both the civil and criminal contempt penalties were upheld. Farber spent a total of 40 days in jail. He was released after the jury received the murder case since he could no longer effectively comply with the court's order to turn over the documents. After the criminal trial ended in the acquittal of the physician, several other pending citations for contempt of court against Farber were dismissed and the sentence for criminal contempt was suspended without probation.

Just before leaving office in early 1982, New Jersey Governor Brendan Byrne pardoned the New York Times and Farber and ordered return of $101,000 collected in fines for criminal contempt. Another $185,000 imposed for civil contempt was not affected by the pardon. The Governor stated that the defendants had been "attempting to uphold a principle they believed in. They should not be burdened by a record of criminal contempt any longer." Editor & Publisher, Jan. 23, 1982, at 16.

Is it proper for a court to convert an absolute privilege into a qualified one to save it from unconstitutionality? If the court had held that the statute was unconstitutional because it gave the defendant no opportunity to secure the information, but that a qualified First Amendment privilege existed, would the result have been any different? For an argument that a court should honor the absolute privilege even if it means that the state cannot prosecute the accused, see Alfred Hill, Testimonial Privileges and Fair Trial, 80 Colum. L. Rev. 1173 (1980).

In a later case, the New Jersey Supreme Court refused to subordinate the shield statute to a plaintiff's right to sue for libel, rejecting the plaintiff's claim that this right was protected by the state constitution. See Maressa v. New Jersey Monthly, 89 N.J. 176, 445 A.2d 376, 8 Med. L. Rptr. 1473 (1982). Cf. Delaney, supra p. 593 (holding that California's absolute privilege must yield when it conflicts with a defendant's due process right to a fair trial).

C. SHIELD LEGISLATION

There remains substantial disagreement about whether a statutory privilege is desirable, and, if so, its appropriate extent and nature. Some scholars of the law of evidence oppose all privileges as obstacles to the search for truth. At its February 1974 meeting, the House of Delegates of the American Bar Association voted 157–122 to reject the proposition that a reporter's privilege is essential "to protect the public interest . . . in the free dissemination of news and information to the American people on matters of public importance." 99 A.B.A. Ann. Rept. 162 (1974). Privilege legislation has even been opposed by some members of the media who would prefer to rely solely on the First Amendment as a shield. They reason that if it is conceded that Congress has the power to help the press now it may later be assumed to have power to enact legislation hostile to the press. See Editor & Publisher, Mar. 30, 1974, at 15.

A media lawyer considered and refuted objections to legislation in Dan Paul, Why a Shield Law?, 29 U. Miami L. Rev. 459 (1975):

> There is, however, [an] argument which frets about compromising a basic constitutional right by allowing the legislature to tinker. This problem could be solved by adding two sentences to any shield legislation: "No provision of this act shall be construed to create or imply any limitations upon or otherwise affect any rights secured by the Constitution of the United States. The rights provided by this Act shall be in addition to any rights provided by the Constitution." . . .

> [Some] theorists are also worried about putting reporters in a special class. This ignores what the first amendment is all about. Gatherers and disseminators of information are already in a special class under the first amendment, as are people who insist on religious freedom. The founding fathers put them there. Of course it would be a terrible mistake to draw shield legislation so narrowly that it would apply only to reporters. A broad, one sentence shield law might serve the purpose:

> No person shall be required in any federal or state proceeding to disclose either the source of any published or unpublished information

obtained for any medium offering communication to the public, or any unpublished information obtained or prepared in gathering or processing information for any public medium of communication.

A shield law should be short, simple, and absolute because it must be a badge which a reporter can carry and completely understand without having to hire a lawyer or go to court. Some individuals, however, have argued that other factors should be balanced against the first amendment to justify shield law exceptions when: (1) the only way to prove that the defendant is innocent is to have the reporter testify; (2) the reporter is the only source concerning a committed crime; or (3) national security is involved. I do not accept any of these exceptions. They would create loopholes which would destroy the privilege and bring us back to the case-by-case method. While this might result in some miscarriages of justice, so does the privilege against self-incrimination. The fact that a person is the only witness to a crime does not mean he is required to waive his privilege against self-incrimination.

Is an absolute statute desirable? If not, in which of the situations we discussed should reporters be fully protected? Partially protected? Most media representatives, particularly those from smaller newspapers and broadcasters, appear to believe a limited statute would help avoid expensive litigation without creating new dangers.

More than 100 bills to enact a federal shield law have been filed in Congress in the years since *Branzburg*. All have failed, mostly because of inability of the media to agree as to the terms of such legislation. After the subpoena crises of 2004, some observers were predicting that media were more likely to agree on a federal statutory solution. See Back to square one, 34 years later, The News Media and the Law, Fall 2004, at 1.

At the state level, new shield legislation has usually been enacted in response to court decisions restricting application of existing shield laws or denying broad protection under the First Amendment. In New Jersey, for example, the courts held that the statutory privilege was waived when the reporter made a partial disclosure; the legislature then amended the statute to negate this holding. After the courts subordinated the statute to a criminal defendant's Sixth Amendment rights, the legislature again amended the statute to make such abrogation more difficult. The history of this interplay between the New Jersey courts and legislature is recounted in In re Schuman, 114 N.J. 14, 552 A.2d 602, 16 Med. L. Rptr. 1092 (1989).

After the New York Court of Appeals interpreted that state's statute to cover only material obtained in confidence, see Knight–Ridder Broadcasting, Inc. v. Greenberg, 70 N.Y.2d 151, 511 N.E.2d 1116, 518 N.Y.S.2d 595, 14 Med. L. Rptr. 1299 (1987), the legislature amended the statute to create a new qualified privilege for nonconfidential "unpublished news." The legislature retained the absolute statutory privilege for confidential information. See N.Y. Civ. Rts. Law § 79–h(2)(c) (1990).

The North Carolina legislature enacted a shield statute for the first time in 1999 after an appellate court ordered a television reporter to disclose a confidential source. See Governor signs NC shield law, Publisher's Auxiliary, Aug. 9, 1999, at 1.

For further reading, see Patrick M. Garry, The Trouble With Confidential Sources: A Criticism of the Supreme Court's Interest–Group View of the First Amendment in Cohen v. Cowles Media Co., 14 Comm/Ent. L.J. 403 (1992); Paul Marcus, The Reporter's Privilege: An Analysis of the Common Law, Branzburg v. Hayes, and Recent Statutory Developments, 25 Ariz. L. Rev. 815 (1983); Carl C. Monk, Evidentiary Privilege for Journalists' Sources: Theory and Statutory Protection, 51 Mo. L. Rev. 1 (1986); John E. Osborn, The Reporter's Confidentiality Privilege: Updating the Empirical Evidence After a Decade of Subpoenas, 17 Colum. Hum. Rts. L. Rev. 57 (1985); Monica Langley and Lee Levine, Branzburg Revisited: Confidential Sources and First Amendment Values, 57 Geo. Wash. L. Rev. 13 (1988).

D. SEARCH WARRANTS

The protections of the preceding sections may be circumvented if authorities are free to obtain warrants to search newsrooms and seize notes, memoranda, photos, tapes, or other evidence described in the warrants. After a Supreme Court decision holding that such searches were permissible, the practice seemed for a time to pose a serious threat to confidential relationships and editorial autonomy. Congress and many state legislatures quickly passed laws restricting newsroom searches, however, and the threat dissipated.

The problem erupted when investigators searched the offices of the campus newspaper at Stanford. Police believed that Stanford Daily photographers had taken photographs that would aid in identifying persons who had assaulted policemen during a violent campus demonstration. The police obtained a search warrant and served it on the Daily. The affidavits accompanying the request for the warrant indicated no reason why a subpoena might not have sufficed.

After the search, the Daily brought an action under 42 U.S.C. § 1983 against the chief of police and other local officials for a determination that the search had violated the Daily's First, Fourth, and Fourteenth Amendment rights. The district judge granted declaratory relief, concluding that no search warrant could issue against any person not suspected of a crime unless a subpoena was shown to be impracticable. Where the object of the search was a newspaper, the judge ruled that a warrant could issue only "where there is a *clear showing* that (1) important materials will be destroyed or removed from the jurisdiction; *and* (2) a restraining order would be futile." The court of appeals adopted the trial judge's opinion and affirmed.

The Supreme Court reversed 5–3, with Justices Stewart, Marshall, and Stevens dissenting. Zurcher v. Stanford Daily, 436 U.S. 547, 3 Med. L. Rptr. 2377 (1978). Justice White, for the majority, first rejected a Fourth Amendment claim that search warrants could not be directed at any third parties, i.e., persons not themselves suspected of criminal activity. He then turned to the narrower argument that the First Amendment forbade searches directed at the press:

> The District Court held, and respondents assert here, that, whatever may be true of third-party searches generally, where the third party is a newspaper, there are additional factors derived from the First Amendment that justify a nearly *per se* rule forbidding the search warrant and permitting only the subpoena *duces tecum*. The general submission is that searches of newspaper offices for evidence of crime reasonably believed to be on the premises will seriously threaten the ability of the press to gather, analyze, and disseminate news. This is said to be true for several reasons: First, searches will be physically disruptive to such an extent that timely publication will be impeded. Second, confidential sources of information will dry up, and the press will also lose opportunities to cover various events because of fears of the participants that press files will be readily available to the authorities. Third, reporters will be deterred from recording and preserving their recollections for future use if such information is subject to seizure. Fourth, the processing of news and its dissemination will be chilled by the prospects that searches will disclose internal editorial deliberations. Fifth, the press will resort to self-censorship to conceal its possession of information of potential interest to the police.

But the Court held that these risks required no greater protection than that provided to all by the Fourth Amendment proscription against unreasonable searches and seizures. Even where the materials sought to be seized may be protected by the First Amendment, that meant only that the requirements of the Fourth Amendment must be applied with "scrupulous exactitude." Nothing in the Fourth Amendment barred searches of newspaper offices. They were subject to the same procedures, including the approval of "neutral magistrates." Few searches of newspaper premises had occurred recently. "This reality hardly suggests abuse; and if abuse occurs, there will be time enough to deal with it. Furthermore, the press is not only an important, critical, and valuable asset to society, but it is not easily intimidated—nor should it be."

The media turned to the legislatures for relief and within a few months they received it. Congress passed a statute, 42 U.S.C. § 2000aa, that applies to state as well as federal searches. It forbids any official from searching or seizing documentary materials or "any work product material possessed by a person reasonably believed to have a purpose to disseminate to the public a newspaper, book, broadcast, or other similar form of public communication. . . ." Documentary materials include photos, film, tapes, discs, and punch cards. Work product includes notes and drafts, but also mental impressions, conclusions, opinions, or theories of the person who prepared, produced, authored, or created the material.

The statute does not apply where the person possessing the materials is a suspect in the offense to which the materials relate. Documentary materials other than work product may be seized if necessary to prevent death or serious injury or to prevent the material from being destroyed, or if the subject has failed to produce them in response to a subpoena duces tecum after exhausting all appellate remedies. The statute also contains exceptions for national security information and child pornography.

State statutes restricting searches were passed in California, Connecticut, Illinois, Nebraska, New Jersey, Oregon, Texas, Washington, and Wisconsin. Searches by state authorities are controlled by these statutes to the extent that they are more restrictive than the federal statute, and some are. The Texas statute, for example, bans all newsroom searches except for weapons, drugs, or other contraband. Tex. Code Crim. Proc. § 18.02.

There have been a few newsroom searches since *Zurcher,* but the legislation successfully headed off any threat that searches might become a commonplace method of obtaining material from reporters. When authorities do undertake newsroom searches in violation of the statute, they may be liable to the news organization for attorney's fees even when the damages are nominal. For example, the Minneapolis Star and Tribune and a local television station won $80,000 in attorney's fees for an illegal knock-and-enter search by the FBI, even though the search did not preclude them from using the photos and film seized or even cause them to miss deadlines. See Sandra Davidson Scott, Police Are Still Storming Newsrooms With Search Warrants, Editor & Publisher, Sept. 17, 1994, at 48.

Telephone records. The government may learn about reporters' sources and activities in ways that do not involve search warrants or subpoenas. Reporters Committee for Freedom of the Press v. American Tel. & Tel. Co., 593 F.2d 1030, 4 Med. L. Rptr. 1177 (D.C. Cir. 1978), involved government requests to the telephone company for records of long distance calls charged to reporters' telephone numbers. Reporters asserted that the First and Fourth Amendments required that subscribers be given notice before AT & T honored the government's request for toll-call records. The court, 2–1, concluded that balancing was not appropriate because "Government access to third-party evidence in the course of a good faith felony investigation in no sense 'abridges' plaintiffs' information-gathering activities." The possibility of bad-faith investigations (to harass reporters) did not warrant prior judicial intervention unless the reporter could establish "a clear and imminent threat of such future misconduct." The dissenter would have afforded reporters the opportunity to have judicial decisions on such requests made in advance on a case-by-case basis. Certiorari was denied, 440 U.S. 949 (1979), Brennan, Marshall, and Stewart, JJ., dissenting.

After the Department of Justice, in 1979, obtained records of a reporter's toll calls from the local telephone company, the press urged government attention to the problem. The result was the promulgation of amendments to the subpoena guidelines to provide that discussions with the reporter should precede any subpoena to the telephone company where the appropriate Assistant Attorney General concludes that such disclosure would not jeopardize the investigation. Before any subpoena is issued, the "express authorization of the Attorney General" is required. Such authorization should not be requested from the Attorney General unless there is reason to believe a crime has been committed, the need is clear, and alternative investigative steps have been unsuccessfully explored. The reporter should be informed within forty-five days (though that may be delayed another forty-five days) and the information obtained shall be closely held to prevent unauthorized persons from learning what the records reveal. The amended guidelines are codified in 28 C.F.R. § 50.10, and are reprinted in 6 Med. L. Rptr. 2153 (1980).

These guidelines of course do not inhibit a private litigant who seeks to learn the identity of a reporter's sources by subpoenaing the reporter's telephone and travel records. Does the First Amendment furnish a basis for refusing to comply? This issue was raised in a libel suit by the Philip Morris Companies against ABC News over the network's reports that the company added extra nicotine to cigarettes. In an apparent attempt to learn the identity of a former tobacco industry manager who appeared in silhouette in the reports, the company obtained 13 subpoenas aimed at tracing the movements of the correspondent and producer during the period they were researching the programs. After first ordering ABC to turn over the records, the judge vacated the order pending further discovery, which he said might show that the tobacco company had no compelling need for the information. See Philip Morris Cos. v. ABC Inc., 23 Med. L. Rptr. 2438 (Va. Cir. Ct. 1995). Should subpoenas of this sort be analyzed as if they were requests for the journalists to name their sources?

In drafting legislation involving search warrants or telephone records, how broadly would you define the group to be protected? Are these definitions of the same breadth as those that might be appropriate for the shield legislation?

CHAPTER X

ACCESS TO INFORMATION

"[W]ithout some protection for seeking out the news, freedom of the press could be eviscerated," Justice White wrote in *Branzburg v. Hayes*, supra p. 561. For most journalists and most news organizations, barriers to the seeking out of news are the most frequent source of contact (and perhaps frustration) with the law. By far the largest body of media law is that dealing with access to records, meetings, institutions, courtrooms, disaster sites, and private premises where news is being made. Most of this law is statutory or administrative and takes the form of freedom of information acts, open meetings statutes, and rules of courts and legislatures. Moreover, much of access law is state law, which means that its texture and variety are difficult to capture in a casebook.

The First Amendment plays only a limited role in access disputes. Although the Supreme Court has recognized a constitutional right of access, it has done so almost exclusively in the context of disputes over access to judicial proceedings and judicial records. Because this body of law has developed more or less independently of the rest of access law, and because the Supreme Court has not extended its principles to other access questions, we treat courtroom access separately, in the next chapter. After reading that chapter, however, you should consider whether constitutional rights to gather news about judicial proceedings might not also apply to some of the matters discussed in this chapter.

Access laws emerged out of a broad consensus that citizens in a democracy are entitled to know what their governments are up to. Giving citizens unfettered access to government documents and processes, however, threatens other important values, such as privacy, national security, and administrative efficiency. Historically, many of the major developments in access law have come about as the result of statutes enacted to address specific privacy issues. More recently, the terrorist attacks of September 11, 2001 have had an effect on access laws. Both Congress and state legislatures have attempted to amend access laws to prevent terrorist from using them to exploit American vulnerabilities, and since 2001 judges appear to have shown greater deference to the executive branch when it has refused to release information on the grounds that release would jeopardize national security.

In this chapter we consider primarily access to *public* institutions and information, with some attention to the rapidly expanding array of statutes and regulations that limit access to information about private citizens, whether held by the government or others. It is important to keep in mind that the media's legal claims for access to information and the government's ability to restrict access will differ considerably depending upon whether the information is considered "public" or "private." In addition, although this chapter focuses primarily on media access issues, the media often rely on broadly available, commercial information sources and are subject to the same laws that affect the access of other citizens. For example, many larger media organizations access public records through commercial service providers, such as LexisNexis and Westlaw. Similarly, many journalists rely on information in credit reports to identify and locate sources.

We first examine access to public records and public meetings, where the relevant law is primarily statutory. We then consider access to public institutions such as prisons, where claims of a constitutional right of access are raised. Next we take up access to disaster sites and other news scenes; the relevant law in these cases is usually common law. We then turn to the impact of criminal law on access. Finally, we examine questions that arise when access is offered to some but not others. (Recall that the special problems of access to voters and other restrictions related to elections were discussed in Chapter III.)

A. ACCESS TO RECORDS

1. FREEDOM OF INFORMATION ACT

James Madison wrote in 1822 that "[a] popular Government, without popular information, or the means of acquiring it, is but a Prologue to a Farce or a Tragedy; or perhaps both. Knowledge will forever govern ignorance: And a people who mean to be their own Governors, must arm themselves with the power which knowledge gives."

As long as legislatures were the preeminent sources of law in the country, persons concerned with government actions could keep track of the process. With the New Deal, however, vast numbers of administrative agencies and organizations emerged. Congress empowered most to promulgate their own internal rules, to issue substantive regulations, to enforce laws, to adjudicate some controversies, and take other actions of great importance to citizens. The sheer number of regulations and orders being promulgated made it difficult to keep track of the process. In addition, some of the agencies were not open about their operations.

In 1946, Congress passed the Administrative Procedure Act to require all administrative agencies to follow certain procedures in the adoption of regulations and in their adjudicative hearings. Congress also sought to make the internal rules and procedures of agencies more readily available to the public. The APA stated that all public records could be inspected by "persons properly and directly concerned" with the subject matter unless the records were held to be confidential "for good cause." But "good cause" was a simple standard which allowed federal agencies sufficient discretion to circumvent even the minimal inspection principle. As a result, this first effort at openness was not notably successful.

In 1967, Congress responded to growing criticism by adopting the first version of the Freedom of Information Act. The 1967 Act required notice of agency actions, including organization, procedures, and policies, as well as final opinions rendered, and permitted "any person" to request records from "each agency." The Act also provided nine categories of information that was exempt from disclosure. These exemptions soon proved so broad that requesters believed an agency could force any record into one of the exemptions. The 1967 Act also lacked an effective enforcement mechanism. The culture of secrecy in Washington that was aroused by the Cold War remained largely untouched by the FOIA.

In 1974, with the Watergate scandal still lingering, Congress passed a bill amending the FOIA and then easily overrode President Gerald Ford's veto. As amended, the FOIA (codified at 5 U.S.C. § 552) applies to all federal government agencies except Congress, the courts, the government of the District of Columbia, and courts martial or the military during wartime. The Act requires each agency to publish in the Federal Register a description of its organization and a list of its personnel through whom the public can obtain information. Each agency must also explain the procedures by which it will furnish information, and must make available to the public staff manuals and internal instructions that affect members of the public, final opinions in adjudicated cases, and current indexes. Records must be segregated so that agencies cannot classify entire categories of records as exempt. Under the FOIA, "any person" may request information from an agency and the agency must supply it unless the information fits within one of the exceptions described below.

Should the agency refuse, the requester may ask a federal district court to enforce the request. The court may review in private the material the agency wishes to withhold, but it is the agency that bears the burden of showing that the material may be withheld under one of the exemptions to the Act discussed below. If the court decides the information should be released, it can order the government to pay all costs associated with the court action. The 1974 amendments also provided for uniform fee schedules (and fee waivers if the information "benefits the general public"), timetables for responses to requests, fee-shifting to prevailing litigants whose requests are denied, and disciplinary legal action against officials found to be "arbitrarily and capriciously" withholding requested records, although this rarely happens.

The FOIA contains nine exemptions—categories of material that need not be made available to the public. The list of exemptions has been amended several times, sometimes at the behest of agencies and sometimes in response to complaints from the press and other requesters. The current list exempts (1) properly classified national defense and foreign matters, (2) information related solely to internal agency personnel rules and practices, (3) disclosures forbidden by other statutes, (4) trade secrets and certain financial information, (5) some inter- and intra-agency memoranda, (6) "personnel and medical files and similar files the disclosure of which would constitute a clearly unwarranted invasion of personal privacy," (7) many categories of law enforcement records, (8) records of bank examinations, and (9) geological information relating to oil and gas wells. If exempt material can be segregated from the rest of the record, the latter is to be made available.

The FOIA generates millions of requests and hundreds of lawsuits each year. The Supreme Court has decided numerous FOIA cases, most of them not involving media. Even the media cases are too numerous for full treatment here; a few illustrative examples must suffice.

National Archives and Records Administration v. Favish et al.

Supreme Court of the United States, 2004.
541 U.S. 157, 124 S. Ct. 1570, 158 L. Ed.2d 319, 32 Med. L. Rptr. 1545.

KENNEDY, J., delivered the opinion for a unanimous Court.

This case requires us to interpret the Freedom of Information Act (FOIA), 5 U.S.C. § 552. FOIA does not apply if the requested data fall within one or more exemptions. Exemption 7(C) excuses from disclosure "records or information compiled for law enforcement purposes" if their production "could reasonably be expected to constitute an unwarranted invasion of personal privacy." § 552(b)(7)(C).

In Department of Justice v. Reporters Comm. for Freedom of Press, 489 U.S. 749 (1989), we considered the scope of Exemption 7(C) and held that release of the document at issue would be a prohibited invasion of the personal privacy of the person to whom the document referred. The principal document involved was the criminal record, or rap sheet, of the person who himself objected to the disclosure. Here, the information pertains to an official investigation into the circumstances surrounding an apparent suicide. The initial question is whether the exemption extends to the decedent's family when the family objects to the release of photographs showing the condition of the body at the scene of death. If we find the decedent's family does have a personal privacy interest recognized by the statute, we must then consider whether that privacy claim is outweighed by the public interest in disclosure.

I

Vincent Foster, Jr., deputy counsel to President Clinton, was found dead in Fort Marcy Park, located just outside Washington, D. C. The United States Park Police conducted the initial investigation and took color photographs of the death scene, including 10 pictures of Foster's body. The investigation concluded that Foster committed suicide by shooting himself with a revolver. Subsequent investigations by the Federal Bureau of Investigation, committees of the Senate and the House of Representatives, and independent counsels Robert Fiske and Kenneth Starr reached the same conclusion. Despite the unanimous finding of these five investigations, a citizen interested in the matter, Allan Favish, remained skeptical. Favish is now a respondent in this proceeding. . . .

. . . Favish filed the present FOIA request in his own name, seeking, among other things, 11 pictures, 1 showing Foster's eyeglasses and 10 depicting various parts of Foster's body. Like the National Park Service, the Office of Independent Counsel (OIC) refused the request under Exemption 7(C). [Favish brought suit in the District Court for the Central District of California, and the court granted partial summary judgment to OIC.]

. . . [T]he court held, first, that Foster's surviving family members enjoy personal privacy interests that could be infringed by disclosure of the photographs. It then found, with respect to the asserted public interest, that "[Favish] has not sufficiently explained how disclosure of these photographs will advance his investigation into Foster's death." Any purported public interest in disclosure, moreover, "is lessened because of the exhaustive investigation that has already occurred regarding Foster's death." Balancing the competing interests, the court concluded that "the privacy interests of the Foster family members outweigh the public interest in disclosure." [ ]

[The Ninth Circuit Court of Appeals reversed and remanded; it found that the statute did not require the requesting party to show evidence of government misfeasance and that Favish had made arguments "which, if believed, would justify his doubts" about the government investigation of Foster's death. The court found that FOIA exemption 7(C) did protect the privacy interests of Foster's family, but held that the District Court did not properly balance the relevant interests because it relied only on agency affidavits describing the photos instead of the photos themselves.]

[On remand, the District Court ordered release of a photograph of Foster's body looking down from the top of a nearby berm; a photo of the right side of Foster's shoulder; a photo of Foster's right hand; a photo of Foster's right side and arm; and a photo of the top of Fosters head. The Ninth Circuit then affirmed the release of all photos except for the photo of the body from the top of the berm.]

. . .

II

It is common ground among the parties that the death-scene photographs in OIC's possession are "records or information compiled for law enforcement purposes" as that phrase is used in Exemption 7(C). This leads to the question whether disclosure of the four [disputed] photographs "could reasonably be expected to constitute an unwarranted invasion of personal privacy."

Favish contends the family has no personal privacy interest covered by Exemption 7(C). His argument rests on the proposition that the information is only about the decedent, not his family. FOIA's right to personal privacy, in his view, means only "the right to control information about oneself." He quotes from our decision in *Reporters Committee*, where, in holding that a person has a privacy interest sufficient to prevent disclosure of his own rap sheet, we said "the common law and the literal understandings of privacy encompass the individual's control of information concerning his or her person." [ ] This means, Favish says, that the individual who is the subject of the information is the only one with a privacy interest.

We disagree. The right to personal privacy is not confined, as Favish argues, to the "right to control information about oneself." Favish misreads the quoted sentence in *Reporters Committee* and adopts too narrow an interpretation of the case's holding. To say that the concept of personal privacy must "encompass" the individual's control of information about himself does not mean it cannot encompass other personal privacy interests as well. *Reporters Committee* had no occasion to consider whether individuals whose personal data are not contained in the requested materials also have a recognized privacy interest under Exemption 7(C).

Reporters Committee explained, however, that the concept of personal privacy under Exemption 7(C) is not some limited or "cramped notion" of that idea. [ ] Records or information are not to be released under the Act if disclosure "could reasonably be expected to constitute an unwarranted invasion of personal privacy." 5 U.S.C. § 552(b)(7). This provision is in marked contrast to the language in Exemption 6, pertaining to "personnel and medical files," where withholding is required only if disclosure "would constitute a clearly unwarranted invasion of personal privacy." § 552(b)(6). The adverb "clearly," found in Exemption 6, is not used in Exemption 7(C). In addition, "whereas Exemption 6 refers to disclosures that 'would constitute' an invasion of privacy, Exemption 7(C) encompasses any disclosure that 'could reasonably be expected to constitute' such an invasion." *Reporters Committee*, [ ] Exemption 7(C)'s comparative breadth is no mere accident in drafting. We know Congress gave special consideration to the language in Exemption 7(C) because it was the result of specific amendments to an existing statute. [ ].

Law enforcement documents obtained by Government investigators often contain information about persons interviewed as witnesses or initial suspects but whose link to the official inquiry may be the result of mere happenstance. There is special reason, therefore, to give protection to this intimate personal data, to which the public does not have a general right of access in the ordinary course. [ ] In this class of cases where the subject of the documents "is a private citizen," "the privacy interest . . . is at its apex."[ ].

. . . The family does not invoke Exemption 7(C) on behalf of Vincent Foster in its capacity as his next friend for fear that the pictures may reveal private information about Foster to the detriment of his own posthumous reputation or some other interest personal to him. If that were the case, a different set of considerations would control. Foster's relatives instead invoke their own right and interest to personal privacy. They seek to be shielded by the exemption to secure their own refuge from a sensation-seeking culture for their own peace of mind and tranquility, not for the sake of the deceased.

In a sworn declaration filed with the District Court, Foster's sister, Sheila Foster Anthony, stated that the family had been harassed by, and deluged with requests from, "[p]olitical and commercial opportunists" who sought to profit from Foster's suicide. In particular, she was "horrified and devastated by [a] photograph [already] leaked to the press." "Every time I see it," Sheila Foster Anthony wrote, "I have nightmares and heart-pounding insomnia as I visualize how he must have spent his last few minutes and seconds of his life." She opposed the disclosure of the disputed pictures because "I fear that the release of [additional] photographs certainly would set off another round of intense scrutiny by the media. Undoubtedly, the photographs would be placed on the Internet for world consumption. Once again my family would be the focus of conceivably unsavory and distasteful media coverage." "[R]eleasing any photographs," Sheila Foster Anthony continued, "would constitute a painful unwarranted invasion of my privacy, my mother's privacy, my sister's privacy, and the privacy of Lisa Foster Moody (Vince's widow), her three children, and other members of the Foster family." [ ]

As we shall explain below, we think it proper to conclude from Congress' use of the term "personal privacy" that it intended to permit family members to assert their own privacy rights against public intrusions long deemed impermissible under the common law and in our cultural traditions. This does not mean that the family is in the same position as the individual who is the subject of the disclosure. We have little difficulty, however, in finding in our case law and traditions the right of family members to direct and control disposition of the body of the deceased and to limit attempts to exploit pictures of the deceased family member's remains for public purposes.

Burial rites or their counterparts have been respected in almost all civilizations from time immemorial. See generally 26 Encyclopaedia Britannica 851 (15th ed. 1985) (noting that "[t]he ritual burial of the dead" has been practiced "from the very dawn of human culture and . . . in most parts of the world"); [ ]. They are a sign of the respect a society shows for the deceased and for the surviving family members. The power of Sophocles' story in Antigone maintains its hold to this day because of the universal acceptance of the heroine's right to insist on respect for the body of her brother. See Antigone of Sophocles, 8 Harvard Classics: Nine Greek Dramas 255 (C. Eliot ed. 1909). The outrage at seeing the bodies of American soldiers mutilated and dragged through the streets is but a modern instance of the same understanding of the interests decent people have for those whom they have lost. Family members have a personal stake in honoring and mourning their dead and objecting to unwarranted public exploitation that, by intruding upon their own grief, tends to degrade the rites and respect they seek to accord to the deceased person who was once their own.

In addition this well-established cultural tradition acknowledging a family's control over the body and death images of the deceased has long been recognized at common law. Indeed, this right to privacy has much deeper roots in the common law than the rap sheets held to be protected from disclosure in *Reporters Committee*. [Here the Court cited several cases and the Restatement (Second) of Torts § 652D Illus. 7 for the proposition that a family has a privacy interest in controlling photos of a deceased relative.]

. . .

We have observed that the statutory privacy right protected by Exemption 7(C) goes beyond the common law and the Constitution. See *Reporters Committee*, [ ] (contrasting the scope of the privacy protection under FOIA with the analogous protection under the common law and the Constitution); see also Marzen v. Department of Health and Human Servs., 825 F.2d 1148, 1152 (7th Cir. 1987) ("[T]he privacy interest protected under FOIA extends beyond the common law"). It would be anomalous to hold in the instant case that the statute provides even less protection than does the common law.

The statutory scheme must be understood, moreover, in light of the consequences that would follow were we to adopt Favish's position. As a general rule, withholding information under FOIA cannot be predicated on the identity of the requester. See *Reporters Committee*, [ ]. We are advised by the Government that child molesters, rapists, murderers, and other violent criminals often make FOIA requests for autopsies, photographs, and records of their deceased victims. Our holding ensures that the privacy interests of surviving family members would allow the Government to deny these gruesome requests in appropriate cases. We find it inconceivable that Congress could have intended a definition of "personal privacy" so narrow that it would allow convicted felons to obtain these materials without limitations at the expense of surviving family members' personal privacy.

. . . [W]e hold that FOIA recognizes surviving family members' right to personal privacy with respect to their close relative's death-scene images. Our holding is consistent with the unanimous view of the Courts of Appeals and other lower courts that have addressed the question. See, e.g., New York Times Co. v. National Aeronautics and Space Admin., 782 F. Supp. 628, 631, 632 (CADC 1991) (sustaining a privacy claim under the narrower Exemption 6 with respect to an audiotape of the Space Shuttle Challenger astronauts' last words, because "[e]xposure to the voice of a beloved family member immediately prior to that family member's death . . . would cause the Challenger families pain" and inflict "a disruption [to] their peace of mind every time a portion of the tape is played within the hearing") . . .; Katz v. National Archives and Records Admin., 862 F. Supp. 476, 485 (DC 1994) (exempting from FOIA disclosure autopsy X-rays and photographs of President Kennedy on the ground that their release would cause "additional anguish" to the surviving family) . . .; Lesar v. United States Dep't of Justice, 204 U.S. App. D.C. 200, 636 F.2d 472, 487 (CADC 1980) (recognizing, with respect to the assassination of Dr. Martin Luther King, Jr., his survivors' privacy interests in avoiding "annoyance or harassment"). Neither the deceased's former status as a public official, nor the fact that other pictures had been made public, detracts from the weighty privacy interests involved.

III

Our ruling that the personal privacy protected by Exemption 7(C) extends to family members who object to the disclosure of graphic details surrounding their relative's death does not end the case. Although this privacy interest is within the terms of the exemption, the statute directs nondisclosure only where the information "could reasonably be expected to constitute an unwarranted invasion" of the family's personal privacy. The term "unwarranted" requires us to balance the family's privacy interest against the public interest in disclosure. See *Reporters Committee*, [ ].

FOIA is often explained as a means for citizens to know "what the Government is up to." *Id.,* [ ]. This phrase should not be dismissed as a convenient formalism. It defines a structural necessity in a real democracy. The statement confirms that, as a general rule, when documents are within FOIA's disclosure provisions, citizens should not be required to explain why they seek the information .... The information belongs to citizens to do with as they choose. Furthermore, as we have noted, the disclosure does not depend on the identity of the requester. As a general rule, if the information is subject to disclosure, it belongs to all.

When disclosure touches upon certain areas defined in the exemptions, however, the statute recognizes limitations that compete with the general interest in disclosure, and that, in appropriate cases, can overcome it. In the case of Exemption 7(C), the statute requires us to protect, in the proper degree, the personal privacy of citizens against the uncontrolled release of information compiled through the power of the state. The statutory direction that the information not be released if the invasion of personal privacy could reasonably be expected to be unwarranted requires the courts to balance the competing interests in privacy and disclosure. To effect this balance and to give practical meaning to the exemption, the usual rule that the citizen need not offer a reason for requesting the information must be inapplicable.

Where the privacy concerns addressed by Exemption 7(C) are present, the exemption requires the person requesting the information to establish a sufficient reason for the disclosure. First, the citizen must show that the public interest sought to be advanced is a significant one, an interest more specific than having the information for its own sake. Second, the citizen must show the information is likely to advance that interest. Otherwise, the invasion of privacy is unwarranted.

We do not in this single decision attempt to define the reasons that will suffice, or the necessary nexus between the requested information and the asserted public interest that would be advanced by disclosure. On the other hand, there must be some stability with respect to both the specific category of personal privacy interests protected by the statute and the specific category of public interests that could outweigh the privacy claim. Otherwise, courts will be left to balance in an ad hoc manner with little or no real guidance. [ ]. In the case of photographic images and other data pertaining to an individual who died under mysterious circumstances, the justification most likely to satisfy Exemption 7(C)'s public interest requirement is that the information is necessary to show the investigative agency or other responsible officials acted negligently or otherwise improperly in the performance of their duties.

The Court of Appeals was correct to rule that the family has a privacy interest protected by the statute and to recognize as significant the asserted public interest in uncovering deficiencies or misfeasance in the Government's investigations into Foster's death. It erred, however, in defining the showing Favish must make to substantiate his public interest claim. It stated that "[n]othing in the statutory command conditions [disclosure] on the requesting party showing that he has knowledge of misfeasance by the agency" and that "[n]othing in the statutory command shields an agency from disclosing its records because other agencies have engaged in similar investigations." [ ] The court went on to hold that, because Favish has "tender[ed] evidence and argument which, if believed, would justify his doubts," the FOIA request "is in complete conformity with the statutory purpose that the public know what its government is up to." [ ] This was insufficient. The Court of Appeals required no particular showing that any evidence points with credibility to some actual misfeasance or other impropriety. The court's holding leaves Exemption 7(C) with little force or content. By requiring courts to engage in a state of suspended disbelief with regard to even the most incredible allegations, the panel transformed Exemption 7(C) into nothing more than a rule of pleading. The invasion of privacy under its rationale would be extensive. It must be remembered that once there is disclosure, the information belongs to the general public. There is no mechanism under FOIA for a protective order allowing only the requester to see whether the information bears out his theory, or for proscribing its general dissemination.

We hold that, where there is a privacy interest protected by Exemption 7(C) and the public interest being asserted is to show that responsible officials acted negligently or otherwise improperly in the performance of their duties, the requester must establish more than a bare suspicion in order to obtain disclosure. Rather, the requester must produce evidence that would warrant a belief by a reasonable person that the alleged Government impropriety might have occurred. In United States Dep't of State v. Ray, 502 U.S. 164 (1991), we held there is a presumption of legitimacy accorded to the Government's official conduct. [ ]. The presumption perhaps is less a rule of evidence than a general working principle. However the rule is characterized, where the presumption is applicable, clear evidence is usually required to displace it. [ ]; United States v. Chemical Foundation, Inc., 272 U.S. 1, 14–15 [ ] (1926) ("The presumption of regularity supports the official acts of public officers and, in the absence of clear evidence to the contrary, courts presume that they have properly discharged their official duties"). Given FOIA's prodisclosure purpose, however, the less stringent standard we adopt today is more faithful to the statutory scheme. Only when the FOIA requester has produced evidence sufficient to satisfy this standard will there exist a counterweight on the FOIA scale for the court to balance against the cognizable privacy interests in the requested records. Allegations of government misconduct are " 'easy to allege and hard to disprove,' " [ ] so courts must insist on a meaningful evidentiary showing. It would be quite extraordinary to say we must ignore the fact that five different inquiries into the Foster matter reached the same conclusion. As we have noted, the balancing exercise in some other case might require us to make a somewhat more precise determination regarding the significance of the public interest and the historical importance of the events in question. We might need to consider the nexus required between the requested documents and the purported public interest served by disclosure. We need not do so here, however. Favish has not produced any evidence that would warrant a belief by a reasonable person that the alleged Government impropriety might have occurred to put the balance into play.

The Court of Appeals erred in its interpretation of Exemption 7(C). The District Court's first order in March 1998—before its decision was set aside by the Court of Appeals and superseded by the District Court's own order on remand—followed the correct approach. The judgment of the Court of Appeals is reversed, and the case is remanded with instructions to grant OIC's motion for summary judgment with respect to the four photographs in dispute.

It is so ordered.

Notes and Questions

1. What evidence must a requester produce to show the government agency performed its duties negligently? How can the requester obtain this information? Is requiring the requester to produce evidence of governmental negligence or impropriety consistent with FOIA's placement of the burden on the agency to justify nondisclosure? Would a tip from an insider suffice?

2. Does whether a disclosure would amount to an unwarranted invasion of privacy depend on the purpose for which the request for information is made? Can a court determine whether a claimed invasion of privacy would be "unwarranted" without knowing what the requester expects the information to show?

3. Would family members have a legitimate privacy interest in preventing the release of a detailed written report on the final moments of a relative's life? Would it matter how the relative died?

4. The Department of Justice has instructed agencies to consider, in light of *Favish*, "both what the requester might do with the information at hand and also what any other requester (or ultimate recipient) might do with it as well." See U.S. Dep't of Justice, Office of Information and Privacy, FOIA Post, "Supreme Court Rules for 'Survivor' Privacy," http://www.us-

doj.gov/oip/foiapost12.htm. Is this too broad an interpretation of the *Favish* decision?

5.   After *Favish*, must an agency consider a deceased's status as a public figure before releasing information about him?

6.   Does the Court apply categorical or ad hoc balancing to decide this case?

————

Confidential law enforcement sources. FOIA Exemption 7(D) allows agencies to withhold information in law enforcement records if its release could reasonably be expected to disclose the identity of a confidential source. How much does the government have to reveal to establish the applicability of this exception? In Department of Justice v. Landano, 508 U.S. 165, 21 Med. L. Rptr. 1513 (1993), the Supreme Court rejected the FBI's arguments that all its sources of law enforcement information should be presumed to be confidential. It also rejected the requestor's argument that the FBI had to show that it had actually promised the source complete anonymity. The Court agreed that Congress' intent requires that exceptions to the FOIA be construed narrowly, but said whether a source is confidential usually can be inferred from the nature of the crime and the source's relation to it. Such inferences can be drawn when the source is a witness in a gang-related murder or is a paid informant, for example. When the government finds this method of establishing confidentiality insufficient, it can furnish the judge with affidavits to be considered in camera.

Personnel and medical files. The exemption most often invoked to protect privacy interests is Exemption 6, for "personnel and medical files and similar files the disclosure of which would constitute a clearly unwarranted invasion of personal privacy." Litigation under this exemption tends to focus on what constitutes a "similar file" and whether the privacy invasion resulting from disclosure would be "clearly unwarranted."

Exemption 6 is not limited to medical and personnel records but extends " 'to cover detailed Government records on an individual which can be identified as applying to that individual.' " United States Department of State v. Washington Post Co., 456 U.S. 595, 8 Med. L. Rptr. 1521 (1982) (holding that Exemption 6 shielded from disclosure information held by the State Department about whether certain Iranian nationals held valid U.S. passports).

In deciding whether a particular disclosure would cause an unwarranted or clearly unwarranted invasion of privacy, courts engage in a balancing of the privacy interest and the public interest in disclosure—a process that to the media often seems like the substitution of a judge's news judgment for that of an editor. In Strassmann v. Justice Department, 792 F.2d 1267, 12 Med. L. Rptr. 2261 (4th Cir. 1986), a television reporter asserted that attorneys for former West Virginia governor Arch A. Moore Jr. had responded to a request for Moore to testify before a federal grand jury by writing a letter to the U.S. Attorney advising that Moore would invoke the Fifth Amendment if forced to appear before the grand jury. The reporter requested release of the letter. The Justice Department refused to release the letter or acknowledge whether such a letter existed. The district court granted the government's motion for summary judgment and the court of appeals affirmed:

> In balancing the public and private interests, the district court reasoned that an individual should not be stigmatized for exercising his constitutional rights, and the divulgence of the letter, if it existed, could lead the public to infer a link between Governor Moore and criminal wrongdoing. . . . The court found that the most the letter would amount to would be to make "political hay." The court concluded that under these facts the disclosure of the letter, if it existed, would be an unwarranted invasion of Mr. Moore's privacy. . . . We are of the opinion that the findings of fact of the district court are supported by the record, that its legal conclusions are free from error, and that it was justified in its refusal to order disclosure.

Waiver of fees. The FOIA allows agencies to collect "reasonable standard charges for document search, duplication, and review" when material is requested for commercial purposes. When information is sought by a news media representative for noncommercial purposes the agency may charge for duplication only. Documents are to be furnished at reduced cost or at no charge "if disclosure of the information is in the public interest because it is likely to contribute significantly to the public understanding of the operations or activities of the government and is not primarily in the commercial interest of the requester."

The fee waiver provision is a significant source of friction between the media and government agencies. Reporters complain that the language invites agencies to deny fee waivers on the basis of their own assessment of the public's interest in the information. A reporter who asked the State Department what it knew about billions of dollars in gold bullion supposedly buried by former Philippine president Ferdinand Marcos was denied a fee waiver. The letter from the State Department said, "Unfortunately it does not appear the processing of your request will primarily benefit the general public since there is no evidence of a general public interest in the subject matter." James Popkin, Running the New, "Improved" FOIA Obstacle Course, Colum. Journ. Rev. July/Aug. 1989, at 45.

FOIA "misuse" and delay. Some observers have argued that the FOIA is being misused and that such misuse is contributing significantly to the costs and delays associated with FOIA requests. In a 1982 article, written prior to his appointment to the Court, then-Professor Scalia called FOIA "the Taj Mahal of the Doctrine of Unanticipated Consequences, the Sistine Chapel of Cost Benefit Analysis Ignored." Antonin Scalia, The Freedom of Information Act Has No Clothes, Regulation, Mar./Apr. 1982, at 14.

In the first years following passage of the FOIA in 1967, the early principal users were historians and journalists; the costs of administering the FOIA in 1967 were estimated at only $50,000. Now federal agencies spend millions responding to FOIA requests. For example, in 2003, the Department of Health and Human Services processed over 146,257 FOIA requests at a cost of over $15.2 million, not including the cost of litigating appeals of denials. In 2003 the Federal Bureau of Investigation processed more than 11,089 FOIA requests at a cost of over 521 employee *years*. See www.usdoj.gov/oip/annual_report/2003/03foiapg5.htm.

The majority of these requests did not come from journalists or scholars, but rather from "commercial use" requesters. The General Accounting Office reported that "only one out of every twenty FOIA requests were [sic] made by a journalist, scholar or author. In contrast, four out of five requests were made by business executives or their lawyers . . ." In 1988, Assistant Attorney General Stephen J. Markman testified before the Subcommittee on Technology and the Law of the Senate Committee on the Judiciary:

> Today, a typical FOIA scenario is not, as originally envisioned by Congress, the journalist who seeks information about the development of public policy which he intends to publish for the edification of the public.
>
> Rather, it is the corporate lawyer seeking business secrets of a client's competitors, the felon attempting to learn who informed against him, the bored inmate, the drug trafficker trying to evade the law, the foreign requester seeking a subsidized benefit that our citizens cannot obtain from his country, and the private litigant who, constrained by discovery rules, turns to FOIA to give him what a trial court would not. And as if these uses do not diverge enough from the Act's original purpose, it is the public—the intended beneficiary of the whole scheme—who bears nearly the entire financial burden of honoring those requests while often reaping virtually none of the benefits from them.

The burgeoning number of commercial user requests has contributed to significant delays in agency responses to disclosure requests. For example, in 2003 the Central Intelligence Agency, responding to FOIA requests, on average took 8 days to process what it called simple requests and 60 days to process complex requests, which was six times the ten-day limit then set forth in the FOIA. The median time it took the Office of the Attorney General to process simple requests was 19 days; complex requests took 361 days. However, an audit by George Washington University's National Security Archive found that the oldest FOIA requests still pending go back as far as 1987. See http://www2.gwu.edu/?nsarchiv/NSAEBB102/press.htm. Today FOIA litigation typically takes years. Moreover, officials often can avoid disclosure, practically though not literally, by delaying the release of information until it is no longer newsworthy.

Despite concerns about the delays and costs associated with FOIA, thousands of requests, including many by the press, are routinely granted, and the very existence of the statute probably induces many officials to disclose even without a formal request. A scandal over influence-peddling in the Department of Housing and Urban Development was exposed largely through successful FOIA requests for the office files of the former secretary of HUD, Samuel R. Pierce Jr. In response to various requests, 48 boxes of Pierce's correspondence and memoranda were turned over to reporters by his successor, Jack F. Kemp. The disclosures were described as "arguably the most important demonstration in years of the power of the 23–year–old Freedom of Information Act." The same report noted that two of the 1989 Pulitzer Prizes for journalism went to reporters who had used the FOIA or similar state statutes to obtain information for their stories. Philip Shenon, Public Record: The Freedom of Information Act and its role in disclosing influence peddling at H.U.D., N.Y. Times, Aug. 28, 1989, at 7.

For two different perspectives on FOIA, see Christopher P. Beall, The Exaltation of Privacy Doctrines Over Public Information Law, 45 Duke L.J. 1249 (1996), and Fred H. Cate, D. Annette Fields, and James K. McBain, The Right to Privacy and the Public's Right to Know: The "Central Purpose" of the Freedom of Information Act, 46 Admin. L. Rev. 41 (1994).

Access to electronic records. With the widespread computerization of government records, FOIA requesters have raised many important issues. Must an agency search its computerized files when responding to FOIA requests? If information that is responsive to a FOIA request is available electronically, must the agency supply it in electronic format (thereby facilitating subsequent use of that information by the requester)? May an agency supply records in a format that requires proprietary software (for example, a commercial database program) to access?

Congress took the first step toward answering these and related questions in the "Electronic Freedom of Information Act Amendments of 1996." The new law:

(1) Clarifies that the definition of "record" includes any information maintained by an agency, without regard for medium or format.

(2) Requires agencies to make reasonable efforts to search for requested records in electronic format, except when such efforts significantly interfere with the agency's operation.

(3) Requires agencies to provide records in any format requested if the record can be readily reproduced by the agency in that format, and requires agencies to make reasonable efforts to maintain records in a manner that allows them to be reproduced in popularly requested formats.

(4) Requires each agency to make those records available for public inspection and copying, regardless of format, that the agency determines are likely to be subject to subsequent requests, unless the materials are published and offered for sale. In addition, the law specifies that agencies must maintain a general index of these records and, by January 1, 2000, make that index available on a web site or dial-up bulletin board.

(5) Extends the time in which an agency must respond to a proper FOIA request from ten business days to 20, and provides for extensions in unusual circumstances.

Electronic Freedom of Information Act Amendments of 1996, Pub. L. No. 104–231, 110 Stat. 3048 (codified at 5 U.S.C. § 552).

ACCESS TO INFORMATION IN THE WAR ON TERRORISM

In the wake of the terrorist attacks of September 11, 2001, both federal and state governments have adopted new restrictions on access to previously open public records.

One of the earliest actions by federal agencies was to remove information from their websites. The Nuclear Regulatory Commission took down its entire website and removed thousands of documents, while many other federal agencies removed portions of their websites.

FOIA Interpretation. The war on terror also prompted then-Attorney General John Ashcroft to announce a new approach to FOIA compliance. On October 12, 2001, Ashcroft issued a memorandum to the heads of all federal departments and agencies that read as follows:

> As you know, the Department of Justice and this Administration are committed to full compliance with the Freedom of Information Act (FOIA), 5 U.S.C. § 552 (2000). It is only through a well-informed citizenry that the leaders of our nation remain accountable to the governed and the American people can be assured that neither fraud nor government was is concealed.

> The Department of Justice and this Administration are equally committed to protecting other fundamental values that are held by our society. Among them are safeguarding our national security, enhancing the effectiveness of our law enforcement agencies, protecting sensitive business information and, not least, preserving personal privacy.

> Our citizens have a strong interest as well in a government that is fully functional and efficient. . . .

> I encourage your agency to carefully consider protection of all such values and interests when making disclosure determinations under the FOIA. Any discretionary decision by your agency to disclose information protected under the FOIA should be made only after full and deliberate consideration of the institutional, commercial, and personal privacy interests that could be implicated by disclosure of the information.

> . . . When you carefully consider FOIA requests and decide to withhold records, in whole or in part, you can be assured that the Department of Justice will defend your decisions unless they lack a sound legal basis or present an unwarranted risk of adverse impact on the ability of other agencies to protect other important records. . . .

The Ashcroft memorandum's "sound legal basis" standard represented a change in policy. The previous policy had been for agencies not to use discretionary exemptions to withhold information unless disclosure would cause "foreseeable harm." In a Government Accountability Office survey, 25 percent of agencies indicated that the Ashcroft memo had changed the way they handled FOIA requests. For additional information regarding the Ashcroft memorandum, see www.usdoj.gov/oip/foiapost/2001foiapost19.htm.

Exemption 1 of FOIA specifically addresses information that has been classified to protect national security. A district court relied on this exemption to allow the Department of Justice to shield statistics about the number of times it had used the surveillance and investigatory methods authorized by the USA Patriot Act. American Civil Liberties Union v. United States Dep't of Justice, 265 F. Supp.2d 20 (D.D.C. 2003) ("ACLU I"). The court continued to shield the information even after the Justice Department declassified statistics indicating that the FBI had not used one of the most controversial types of surveillance under the Act. American Civil Liberties Union v. United States Dep't of Justice, 321 F. Supp.2d 24 (D.D.C. 2004) ("ACLU II").

Agencies have also used other exemptions to protect information deemed to be a threat to national security. In Coastal Delivery Corp. v. U.S. Customs Service, 272 F. Supp.2d 958 (C.D. Cal. 2003), a district court upheld the U.S. Customs Service's decision to withhold information on its inspections of seaports under Exemption 2, which protects information related "to the internal personnel rules and practices of an agency." The basis for the decision was that "terrorists and others could use the information to discover the rate of inspection and then direct their containers to vulnerable ports." Similarly, in Living Rivers, Inc. v. the U.S. Bureau of Reclamation, 272 F. Supp.2d 1313 (D.Utah 2003), a district court allowed "inundation maps" of flood areas below the Glen Canyon and Hoover dams to be withheld under Exemption 7(F) on the grounds that terrorist could use the maps to cause destruction. The executive director of Living Rivers, the group requesting the maps, stated: "If we had gone forward on this [FOIA request] prior to 9/11 it would have been a slam dunk." The group sought the maps in order to argue that the dams were inherently unsafe and should be decommissioned. See www.rcfp.org/news/mag/27–4/foi-securing.html.

Other district courts have not been as deferential in the face of arguments for withholding documents based on security concerns. In Gordon v. Federal Bureau of Investigation, 2004 WL 1368858, 32 Med. L. Rptr. 2288 (N.D. Cal. 2004), a district court ordered the government to produce information about "no-fly" lists and admonished the government for making "frivolous claims of exemptions." The court cautioned the government that it could not satisfy the burden necessary to withhold documents based merely on "general statements that . . . the information is sensitive security information. . . ." Another district court accused the government of "indifference to the commands of FOIA" after several agencies failed to respond for more than a year to requests for production of documents about the treatment of individuals detained abroad. The court stated: "Merely raising national security concerns can not justify unlimited delay." American Civil Liberties Union v. Dep't of Defense, 339 F. Supp.2d 501, 32 Med. L. Rptr. 2420 (S.D.N.Y. 2004)

———

Identities of detainees. National security concerns shaped a noteworthy decision of the District of Columbia Court of Appeals examining the scope of FOIA Exemption 7(A)'s protection for law enforcement records. In that case, Center for National Security Studies v. U.S. Department of Justice, 331 F.3d 918 (D.C. Cir. 2003), cert. denied 540 U.S. 1104 (2004), several public interest groups requested the Department of Justice to release information about the more than 1,000 foreigners detained by the government as part of the investigation of the September 11 terrorist attacks. The detainees fell into three categories. Some of them were questioned and then detained for immigration violations; some were questioned and then held on federal criminal charges; and some were detained on material witness warrants pending their appearances before grand juries. Most of the detainees (more than 700) were INS detainees, and many were ultimately deported. The information sought by plaintiffs included the names of the detainees, their attorneys, the dates and locations of their arrests, and the location of and reasons for their detention. The government refused to release this information, and the plaintiffs brought suit in district court. The government moved for summary judgment, asserting that the requested information was covered by several FOIA exemptions, including Exemption 7(A), which exempts "records or information compiled for law enforcement purposes . . . to the extent that the production" of them "could reasonably be expected to interfere with enforcement proceedings." 5 U.S.C. § 552(b)(7)(A) (2000). The district court held that the government could withhold detention information except for the names of the detainees and their attorneys. [ ]

On appeal, a panel of the D.C. Circuit held, 2–1, that the government was entitled to withhold all of the requested information under Exemption 7(A) and that neither the First Amendment nor the common law gave a right of access to the information.

The court first addressed the issue of whether Exemption 7(A) shielded the names of the detainees. The court noted that law enforcement records could be withheld under Exemption 7(A) only to the extent that their release " 'could reasonably be expected to interfere with law enforcement proceedings.' " Id. at 920 (quoting 5 U.S.C. § 552(b)(7)(A).) The court found that the government's investigation was "likely to lead to such [enforcement] proceedings."

The court then rejected the argument that the requested documents fell outside Exemption 7 because they were traditional public records such as arrest warrants, INS charging documents, and jail records:

> Plaintiffs are seeking a comprehensive listing of individuals detained during the post-September 11 investigation. The names have been compiled for the "law enforcement purpose" of successfully

prosecuting the terrorism investigation. As compiled, they constitute a comprehensive diagram of the law enforcement investigation after September 11. Clearly this is information compiled for law enforcement purposes.

Next, plaintiffs urge that Exemption 7(A) does not apply because disclosure is not "reasonably likely to interfere with enforcement proceedings." 5 U.S.C. § 552(b)(7)(A). We disagree. Under Exemption 7(A), the government has the burden of demonstrating a reasonable likelihood of interference with the terrorism investigation. The government's declarations, viewed in light of the appropriate deference to the executive on issues of national security, satisfy this burden.

It is well-established that a court may rely on government affidavits to support the withholding of documents under FOIA exemptions, [ ], and that we review the government's justifications therein *de novo,* 5 U.S.C. § 552(a)(4)(B); [ ]. It is equally well-established that the judiciary owes some measure of deference to the executive in cases implicating national security, a uniquely executive purview. *See, e.g.,* Zadvydas v. Davis, 533 U.S. 678 (2001) (noting that "terrorism or other special circumstances" might warrant "heightened deference to the judgments of the political branches"); Dep't of the Navy v. Egan, 484 U.S. 518, 530 (1988) ("courts traditionally have been reluctant to intrude upon the authority of the executive in military and national security affairs"). Indeed, both the Supreme Court and this Court have expressly recognized the propriety of deference to the executive in the context of FOIA claims which implicate national security.

. . .

The need for deference in this case is just as strong as in earlier cases. America faces an enemy just as real as its former Cold War foes, with capabilities beyond the capacity of the judiciary to explore. Exemption 7(A) explicitly requires a predictive judgment of the harm that will result from disclosure of information, permitting withholding when it "could reasonably be expected" that the harm will result. 5 U.S.C. § 552(b)(7)(A). It is abundantly clear that the government's top counterterrorism officials are well-suited to make this predictive judgment. Conversely, the judiciary is in an extremely poor position to second-guess the executive's judgment in this area of national security. . . .

In light of the deference mandated by the separation of powers and Supreme Court precedent, we hold that the government's expectation that disclosure of the detainees' names would enable al Qaeda or other terrorist groups to map the course of the investigation and thus develop the means to impede it is reasonable. A complete list of names informing terrorists of every suspect detained by the government at any point during the September 11 investigation would give terrorist organizations a composite picture of the government investigation, and since these organizations would generally know the activities and locations of its members on or about September 11, disclosure would inform terrorists of both the substantive and geographic focus of the investigation. Moreover, disclosure would inform terrorists which of their members were compromised by the investigation, and which were not. This information could allow terrorists to better evade the ongoing investigation and more easily formulate or revise counter-efforts. In short, the "records could reveal much about the focus and scope of the [agency's] investigation, and are thus precisely the sort of information exemption 7(A) allows an agency to keep secret." [ ] . . . Importantly, plaintiffs here do not request "bits and pieces" of information, but rather seek the names of every single individual detained in the course of the government's terrorism investigation. It is more than reasonable to expect that disclosing the name of every individual detained in the post-September 11 terrorism investigation would interfere with that investigation.

Similarly, the government's judgment that disclosure would deter or hinder cooperation by detainees is reasonable. The government reasonably predicts that if terrorists learn one of their members has been detained, they would attempt to deter any further cooperation by that member through intimidation, physical coercion, or by cutting off all contact with the detainee. A terrorist organization may even seek to hunt down detainees (or their families) who are not members of the organization, but who the terrorists know may have valuable information about the organization.

On numerous occasions, both the Supreme Court and this Court have found government declarations expressing the likelihood of witness intimidation and evidence tampering sufficient to justify withholding of witnesses' names under Exemption 7(A). . . . Consequently, we hold that disclosure of detainees' names could "reasonably be expected to interfere" with the ongoing terrorism investigation.

. . .

. . . [I]n undertaking a deferential review we [ ] recognize the different roles underlying the constitutional separation of powers. It is within the role of the executive to acquire and exercise the expertise of protecting national security. It is not within the role of the courts to second-guess executive judgments made in furtherance of that branch's proper role. The judgment of the district court ordering the government to disclose the names of the detainees is reversed.

The court further held that Exemption 7(A) protected both the names of the attorneys for the detainees and the other detention information sought by plaintiffs.

Judge Tatel's dissenting opinion criticized the majority for giving undue deference to the DOJ's assessment of the potential threat that releasing the information posed to law enforcement purposes. Although Judge Tatel conceded that investigating terrorism and preventing future attacks were compelling governmental interest, he also identified another "compelling interest at stake in this case: the public's interest in knowing whether the government, in responding to the attacks, is violating the constitutional rights of the hundreds of persons whom it has detained in connection with its terrorism investigation—by, as the plaintiffs allege, detaining them mainly because of their religion or ethnicity, holding them in custody for extended periods without charge, or preventing them from seeking or communicating with legal counsel."

Judge Tatel questioned the level of deference accorded the government by the majority opinion, noting that while heightened deference was appropriate with respect to Exemption 1 and "Exemption 3 as it incorporates the National Security Act," it was not clear that such deference was appropriate in Exemption 7 cases. He further noted:

> In any event, the government's case fails even under the heightened deference we have applied in Exemption 1 and National Security Act cases. No matter the level of deference, our review is not "vacuous." [ ] Even when reviewing Exemption 1's applicability to materials classified in the interest of national security, we have made clear that no amount of deference can make up for agency allegations that display, for example, a "lack of detail and specificity, bad faith, [or] failure to account for contrary record evidence," since "deference is not equivalent to acquiescence." [ ]. By accepting the government's vague, poorly explained allegations, and by filling in the gaps in the government's case with its own assumptions about facts absent from the record, this court has converted deference into acquiescence.

Judge Tatel specifically pointed out the government's failure to make an adequate showing that the release of the information would threaten its investigation.

> . . . As of November 5, 2001, the last time the government released a tally, there were 1,182 detainees. [ ] Nothing in the record tells us how many of those 1,182 detainees have been charged with federal terrorism crimes or held as enemy combatants. What little information the record does contain, however, suggests that the number may be relatively small. A list of federally charged detainees attached to the government's motion for summary judgment reports that as of the time this suit was filed, only one detainee had been criminally charged in the September 11 attacks and only 108 detainees had been charged with any federal crime—primarily violations of antifraud statutes. [ ].
>
> In any event, the court concedes the point—even if "many" of those "apprehended during the course of a terrorism investigation" have links to terrorism, not *all* of them do. As the court itself notes, the declarations establish that many of the INS detainees were held because law enforcement agents determined in the course of questioning them that they were in violation of federal laws; only " 'in some instances' " did agents "also determine [ ] that they had links to other facets of the investigation." [ ]. Furthermore, although the court assumes that all those detained on material witness warrants "have relevant knowledge about the terrorism investigation" because a feder-

al judge issues such warrants "based on an affidavit stating that the witness has information relevant to an ongoing criminal investigation," that assumption seems unwarranted given the government's concession that "it may turn out that these individuals have no information useful to the investigation," [ ].

The government gives us no reason to think that releasing the names of these innocent detainees could interfere with its investigation. . . . The government can and should rely on [FOIA Exemption 7(D) and the National Security Act] to protect the names of detainees who provide information to law enforcement agents or whom the government believes will be able to provide such information in the future. The government may not, however, preemptively withhold the identities of innocent detainees who do not now, and may never, have any information of use to the terrorism investigation.

The only argument that could conceivably support withholding innocent detainees' names is the assertion that disclosure of the names "*may* reveal details about the focus and scope of the investigation and thereby allow terrorists to counteract it." [quoting Declaration of James Reynolds, Director of the Terrorism and Violent Crime Section of the Justice Department] That Reynolds believes these harms *may* result from disclosure is hardly surprising—anything is possible. But before accepting the government's argument, this court must insist on knowing whether these harms "*could reasonably be expected to*" result from disclosure—the standard Congress prescribed for exemption under 7(A). Nothing in Reynolds's declaration suggests that these harms are in fact reasonably likely to occur.

. . .

. . . If the government thinks that a new, broader FOIA exemption is needed for terrorism cases, it should ask Congress to create one, just as in the wake of September 11 it asked Congress to authorize roving wiretaps of suspected terrorists and to permit detention of non-U.S. citizens suspected of terrorism without specific charges. *See* USA PATRIOT Act [ ]. But this court may not change the law in Congress's stead. For all its concern about the separation-of-powers principles at issue in this case, the court violates those principles by essentially abdicating its responsibility to apply the law as Congress wrote it. I dissent.

———

The war on terror has affected more than the interpretation of existing FOIA exemptions. In November 2002, Congress passed the Homeland Security Act of 2002, 6 U.S.C.A. § 133 (West Supp. 2003). The Act makes "critical infrastructure information" voluntarily submitted by businesses to federal agencies exempt from disclosure under the FOIA. The Act grants businesses immunity from civil liability if the information reveals wrongdoing and also makes it a crime for a federal employee to disclose the information. Senator Patrick Leahy called this provision the "most severe weakening of the Freedom of Information Act in its 36-year history" and characterized it as "a big business wish list gussied up in security garb." See Reporters Committee for Freedom of the Press, Homefront Confidential: How the War on Terrorism Affects Access to Information and the Public's Right to Know (Spring 2003), www.rcfp.org.

State governments have also reduced access to previously public records in the name of security. "[S]tates enacted measures that would make secret any discussions of evacuation plans, emergency response plans, security measures or emergency health procedures in case of a terrorist attack, as well as the security plans and manuals themselves. Another common bill exempted from open records laws architectural drawings of city buildings and infrastructure, including utility plants, bridges, water lines, sewer lines and transportation lines." Homefront Confidential, supra, "The Rollback in State Openness."

An example of this type of legislation is a California law that exempts from public disclosure "[a] document prepared by or for a state or local agency that assesses its vulnerability to terrorist attack or other criminal acts intended to disrupt the public agency's operations and that is for distribution or consideration in a closed session." West's Ann.Cal.Gov.Code § 6254(aa) (2004). What is the likely effect of this statute?

In addition to legislative changes, journalists and access advocates also report "blatant defiance" of federal and state access laws, often justified by national security concerns. See Charles Layton, The Information Squeeze, Am. Journ. Rev., Sept. 2002, at 20.

2. STATE OPEN RECORDS ACTS

Every state has its own access-to-information statute. Some states even protect access rights in their constitutions. In November 2004 Californians voted overwhelmingly in favor of a ballot measure making access to government meetings and the writings of government officials a constitutional right. Although the measure preserved existing limits on the right of access, it provides that existing statutes must be interpreted to maximize access. The measure also requires government officials to justify the need for future limitations on access rights. Florida voters approved an even stronger amendment to the Florida constitution. The amendment requires the legislature to pass new exemptions to Florida's public-records or sunshine laws by a two-thirds vote.

Many state access statutes are patterned after the FOIA, but some follow a quite different model. For example, the Texas Public Information Act, Tex. Govt. Code § 552, uses a quite different enforcement mechanism. Unlike the FOIA, which places most of the burdens of enforcement on the requester, the Texas statute gives the primary enforcement responsibility to the state attorney general. When a request is received, the agency has ten days in which to either comply or seek the attorney general's determination that it need not comply. If it fails to do either, the information is presumed to be disclosable and the agency cannot subsequently contest that issue unless it can make a "compelling demonstration" that the information should not be disclosed.

If the agency refuses to comply with the attorney general's determination that the information is disclosable, either the requester or the attorney general may seek a writ of mandamus to compel disclosure. As a practical matter, most disputes are resolved by the ruling of the attorney general. Over the years, hundreds of such decisions have created a body of precedent that enables the attorney general to answer many requests merely by citing previous decisions.

Even where the state statute is modeled on the FOIA, it may be construed to require disclosure of more (or less) than the FOIA requires. See, for example, Kerr v. Koch, 15 Med. L. Rptr. 1579 (N.Y.Sup. 1988). A reporter for the Daily News demanded appointment calendars identifying luncheon and dinner guests of the mayor of New York, whether official or private, under New York's Freedom of Information Law. The mayor invoked an exemption for material that if disclosed would constitute an unwarranted invasion of personal privacy. The court ordered disclosure: "In an administration that has been sorely afflicted by scandals of one sort or another, it seems quite proper to know the friends of the City's Chief Magistrate and his association with them, especially where a diary of those associations is represented by an appointments calendar kept on the premises of the agency of the Mayor."

Discrimination among requesters: Like the federal FOIA, most state open records statutes do not inquire as to the purpose for which information is sought—if it is available to media, it is also available to direct marketers, business rivals, and even potential criminals. In a few instances, public outcry over these uses of information has led to legislative attempts to discriminate among different types of requesters.

Until 1999, information about motor vehicle registrations and driver's licenses, including license numbers and addresses, was public in most states. Some states sold this information for direct marketing purposes. Responding to complaints about these practices, as well as incidents in which criminals used such information to facilitate stalking, kidnapping, and auto theft, Congress passed the Driver's Privacy Protection Act, 18 U.S.C. § 2721, which forbade any person from disclosing information from such records except for law enforcement and other specified purposes. Journalistic purposes were not among those for which release of the information was authorized, although states were permitted to disclose records for any use provided that citizens were given an opportunity to "opt out" of such disclosure. After several states challenged the Act, the Supreme Court held that the DPPA did not violate the Tenth Amendment's reservation of power to the states or federalism principles. Reno v. Condon, 528 U.S. 141 (2000).

Even before the Supreme Court heard oral argument, however, Congress amended the Driver's Privacy Protection Act to restrict access even further. The new amendments forbade states from releasing personally identifiable information from motor vehicles and driver's license records for marketing or for any other purpose not specifically authorized in the 1994 statute without first obtaining "the express consent of the person to whom such personal information pertains." As a result, the majority of states that had acted under the 1994 law to permit use of these records for marketing and journalism, among other purposes, unless an individual registered his or her *objection*, thereby "opting out" of disclosure, were required to amend their laws to prohibit such uses unless each individual gives *consent* or "opts in." See H.R. 2084, 106th Cong., 1st Sess. (1999). Publ. L. 106–69.

Does the DPPA prohibit the release of the driver's license numbers of school bus drivers to a reporter seeking to write a story about school bus safety? A Wisconsin Court of Appeals held that the DPPA was not intended to conceal information connected to motor vehicle or driver safety. It concluded that the public interest in disclosure outweighed the privacy interests of the drivers and the bus company withholding information. See Atlas Transit, Inc. v. Korte, 249 Wis.2d 242, 638 N.W.2d 625 (Ct.App. 2001), review denied 250 Wis.2d 558, 643 N.W.2d 95 (2002).

The Supreme Court also upheld the constitutionality of a state statute restricting access to information based on the purpose of the request in Los Angeles Police Dept. v. United Reporting Publishing Corp., 528 U.S. 32 (1999). In 1996, the California legislature amended its Government Code to prohibit use of arrest records "to sell a product or service to any individual or group of individuals." Cal. Govt. Code § 6254(f). The statute was challenged by a company that had been furnishing names and addresses of arrestees to clients that included attorneys, insurance companies, drug counselors, religious counselors, and driving schools. The district court and the Ninth Circuit both analyzed the issue as a commercial speech problem, holding that the statute improperly discriminated against the company's dissemination of truthful and nonmisleading speech. The Supreme Court held, 7–2, that the government had no obligation to provide access to anyone under the First Amendment. Justice Stevens, dissenting, contended that "the State's discriminatory ban on access to information—in an attempt to prohibit persons from exercising their constitutional rights to publish it in a truthful and accurate matter—is . . . invalid."

Statutory restraints on access to public records. The FOIA and similar state statutes prescribe only the records that *must* be disclosed. Officials are free to disclose others at their discretion unless some other law forbids it. At the federal level, the outstanding example of such a prohibition is the Privacy Act, 5 U.S.C. § 552a. It forbids release of personal records that the government routinely accumulates on individuals (e.g., Social Security records) unless disclosure is required by the FOIA or permitted by one of several specific exceptions in the Privacy Act (e.g., disclosure to a court or congressional committee). The restrictions of the Privacy Act impose limits on what government officials may disclose, but do not prescribe punishment for media that publish information improperly made public by the government.

Statutory restrictions on access to public records often arise in response to a specific news event. When NASCAR driver Dale Earnhardt was killed in a crash at the Daytona Speedway in 2001, media invoked the Florida open records act in an attempt to obtain the autopsy photos. The requests set off a fury among racing fans who objected to the disclosures, and the Florida legislature quickly passed a bill providing that requesters other than family must obtain a court order to gain access to autopsy photos and videos. In deciding whether to give access, the court is to consider "whether such disclosure is necessary for the public evaluation of governmental performance; the seriousness of the intrusion into the family's right to privacy and whether such disclosure is the least intrusive means available; and the availability of similar information in other public records. . . ." See 29 Med. L. Rptr., News Notes, May 8, 2001. A Florida Circuit Court upheld the law, and a Florida Court of Appeals affirmed. See Campus Communications, Inc. v. Earnhardt, 821 So.2d 388, 30 Med. L. Rptr. 2223 (Fla. App. 2002). The Florida Supreme Court denied review of the case, 848 So.2d 1153 (table), and the U.S. Supreme Court denied certiorari. 540 U.S. 1049 (2003).

Telephone records. A new set of issues is posed by technology that creates records of even local telephone calls. Records of calls made from an official's cellular phone could reveal wrongdoing or suspicious associations; they could also reveal the unlisted phone numbers of the official, family members, informants, or other officials. Such calls are presumptively exempt from disclosure under the New Jersey Right-to-Know statute and are disclosable only upon a showing that the public need outweighs the privacy interests. "We doubt that the Legislature intended that all detailed information a modern computer-based system can generate constitutes records" for purposes of the statute. See North Jersey Newspapers Co. v. Passaic County, 127 N.J. 9, 601 A.2d 693, 19 Med. L. Rptr. 1962 (1992). See also Rogers v. Superior Court, 19 Cal. App.4th 469, 23 Cal. Rptr.2d 412, 21 Med. L. Rptr. 2234 (1993), holding that records of phone calls made from and received on city council members' cellular phones, home offices, and hotel rooms were exempt from disclosure.

But the Georgia Supreme Court held, over two dissents, that records of calls made from cellular phones are disclosable even if they reveal unlisted numbers. Such disclosures would not be sufficiently offensive to be actionable under the tort law of privacy, and the privacy exception in the Georgia Open Records Act requires an analogous analysis, the court said. See Dortch v. Atlanta Journal and Constitution, 261 Ga. 350, 405 S.E.2d 43, 19 Med. L. Rptr. 1024 (1991); DR Partners v. Board of County Comm. Of Clark County, 6 P.3d 465 (Nev. 2000) (finding no expectation of privacy since commissioners knew billing records of their calls were public record).

B. ACCESS TO GOVERNMENTAL MEETINGS

1. FEDERAL LAW

The Sunshine Act. Unlike the FOIA, which preceded most state open records laws and became the model for many of them, the federal Sunshine

Act was a late arrival and was modeled on the highly successful Florida Sunshine Act, Fla. Stat. § 286.011. The federal Sunshine Act, 5 U.S.C. § 552b, was passed in 1976 at the urging of the Florida congressional delegation. The statement of purpose accompanying the Act declares that "the public is entitled to the fullest practicable information regarding the decision-making processes of the Federal Government." The Act sought to "provide the public with such information while protecting the rights of individuals and the ability of the Government to carry out its responsibilities."

Essentially, the act provides that all federal agencies headed by boards of two or more persons appointed by the President—approximately fifty agencies—must hold "every portion of every meeting" open to the public. Adequate advance notice must be given of each meeting. Even if a meeting is closed because it falls within one of the ten exemptions provided by the Act, the agency must make public a transcript or minutes of all parts of the meeting that do not contain exempt material. Meetings may be closed only after a publicly recorded vote of a majority of the full membership of the agency.

The exemptions apply where the agency "properly determines" that a portion of its meeting "is likely to" result in the disclosure of specified information. The exemptions are similar to those of the FOIA. In addition, the Sunshine Act exempts discussions relating to censure or accusations of crime, discussions of proposed agency action that could be frustrated if revealed in advance, and information about an agency's participation in litigation.

The Federal Advisory Committee Act. This statute, 5 U.S.C. App. § 1, provides yet another access tool, containing both an open-records and an open-meetings provision. It covers committees and task forces set up by Congress, the President, or a federal agency, but does not cover a group "composed wholly of full-time officers or employees of the Federal Government."

The open-records provision of the FACA adopts by reference the exemptions contained in the FOIA. In another respect, however, it is broader than the FOIA, requiring advisory committees to make public reports and working papers even without a request. See Food Chemical News v. Department of Health and Human Services, 980 F.2d 1468, 21 Med. L. Rptr. 1057 (D.C. Cir. 1992).

A case involving Vice President Dick Cheney raised the question whether the Federal Advisory Committee Act covers groups that formally include only federal officials but in which private persons participate extensively. Two groups sued to force the federal energy task force that Cheney headed to comply with the FACA on the ground that executives of energy companies were so deeply involved in the task force that they amounted to de facto members. The district court held that the plaintiffs were entitled to enough discovery to determine how extensively the outsiders had been involved, but Cheney said compulsory disclosure would violate separation of powers principles. The D.C. Circuit held that Cheney could resist discovery only by invoking executive privilege. Without deciding the merits, the Supreme Court rejected Cheney's claim that he could not be subjected to pretrial discovery at all, but it remanded the case to the Court of Appeals with instructions to try to resolve the discovery dispute through "avenues short of forcing the executive to invoke privilege." See Cheney v. United States District Court, 124 S. Ct. 2576, 32 Med. L. Rptr. 2121 (2004). Afterward two public interest groups filed FOIA requests with several agencies whose officials participated on the task force. These agencies refused to comply, and the interests groups filed suit. A district judge held that records created by the agencies and submitted to the task force were subject to disclosure under FOIA. Judicial Watch, Inc. v. United States Dept. of Energy, 310 F. Supp.2d 271 (D.D.C. 2004). Disclosure was stayed pending appeal.

Legislative bodies: The federal open meetings acts, like most state open meetings statutes, do not govern meetings of legislative bodies. Most state constitutions require open legislative sessions, but each house usually is free to make its own rules for meetings of its committees. Sessions of the U.S. House of Representatives have been open since the First Congress, but Senate sessions were closed until 1794. The Senate's practice provoked what may have been America's first open-government campaign, led by Philip Freneau, the famed editor of the National Gazette. See Gerald L. Grotta, Philip Freneau's Crusade for Open Sessions of the U.S. Senate, 48 Journ. Q. 667 (1971). The Senate continues to hold occasional closed sessions, usually for discussions of treaties or nominations.

The Senate or House may close their sessions for any purpose by majority vote, though in recent years they have done so infrequently. Senate committee meetings may be closed only for certain enumerated reasons, including discussions about national defense or foreign affairs, committee personnel matters, trade secrets, or matters required to be kept confidential by law, and to protect the identities of informers or the privacy or reputation of individuals. In the House, committee hearings may be closed when the testimony involves national security or "may tend to defame, degrade, or incriminate any person." House committee meetings other than hearings may be closed for any purpose by majority vote. Most Senate and House committee meetings that are not closed may be televised and broadcast on radio.

During the impeachment trial of President Clinton in 1999, although the Senate heard evidence in open session, it met in closed session to deliberate. The decision provoked considerable controversy. The New York Times editorialized that "[i]t seems inconceivable that in 1999 the Senate would hold a secret debate on whether to overturn a Presidential election, one of the gravest decisions it is ever asked to make. The closed-door rules that prevailed 131 years ago in the impeachment trial of President Andrew Johnson, before the principle of open government proceedings was firmly established, have no place in the modern Senate." The Case Goes to the Senate, N.Y. Times, Feb. 9, 1999.

The impeachment of President Clinton also provided many examples of openness of the political process, including the publication of the Special Prosecutor's lengthy and detailed report, the broadcast of President Clinton's and Monica Lewinsky's videotaped testimony, the release of audiotapes of telephone conversations between Monica Lewinsky and Linda Tripp, and the television coverage of the House Judiciary Committee deliberations and of the Senate trial. This level of public and press access was unprecedented; during the consideration of whether to impeach President Nixon, key documents, including the Special Prosecutor's report, were not made public, and the House Judiciary Committee's deliberations were closed. Some observers have suggested that the extensive openness of the process applied to President Clinton disserved the public interest and unnecessarily compromised the privacy of the parties and witnesses. See Anthony Lewis, To the Stake!, N.Y. Times, Sept. 22, 1998, at A31.

2.   STATE LAWS

The most important body of law governing access to meetings of governmental entities is that created by the state open meetings laws. Every state has such a statute. Usually the statute provides that all meetings of governmental bodies shall be preceded by public notice and shall be open to the public, then sets forth detailed exceptions, definitions of such terms as "meeting" and "governmental body," notice requirements, and provisions for enforcement. Typical exceptions are for discussions of pending or anticipated litigation, land acquisitions, and personnel matters. Definitions of "meeting" are often quite broad, usually covering any gathering of a quorum of the members of the governing body and sometimes even conversations between any two of its members.

One relatively recent issue is whether emails exchanged between members of the governing body about public matters constitute "meetings." If not, email can be used to circumvent open meetings laws. In 2004 the Virginia Supreme Court determined that the exchange of emails between several city council members and members-elect was not a meeting because the emails "did not involve virtually simultaneous interaction" but were instead akin to "traditional letters sent by ordinary mail." Beck v. Shelton, 593 S.E.2d 195, 32 Med. L. Rptr. 1759 (Va. 2004) A Washington appeals court took a different approach to the issue. In Wood v. Battle Ground School District, 27 P.3d 1208 (Wash. App. 2001), the court indicated that emails sent between school board members would constitute a meeting where the "active exchange of information and opinions . . ., as opposed to the mere passive receipt of information, suggests a collective intent to deliberate and/or to discuss Board business." Id. at 1218.

Enforcement of open meetings laws varies. In general, the most effective statutes are those that invalidate any action taken in violation of the openness requirements. The least effective are those whose enforcement depends on criminal prosecution of officials who do not comply; prosecutors tend to be unenthusiastic about devoting their time and resources to resolving disputes between their fellow officials and the press. A provision awarding attorneys' fees to persons who successfully challenge the improper closure of a meeting is often effective. See, e.g., Orange County Publications v. Newburgh City Council, 9 Med. L. Rptr. 1405 (N.Y.Sup. 1983) (holding that council's prior violations of New York open meetings statute justified award of attorneys' fees to newspaper for improper closure of meeting to discuss preliminary redevelopment plan). State open meetings statutes normally cover local as well as state agencies, and thus apply to the meetings of thousands of boards, councils, commissions, and departments.

With the rise of privatization and "outsourcing" of some traditional governmental functions, the applicability of open records and open meetings statutes to private governing bodies has become an issue. In Florida, for example, the legislature encouraged local tax-supported hospitals to enter into lease arrangements with private nonprofit agencies. A newspaper sought a declaration that the governing boards of these agencies were subject to the Florida Public Records Act and Sunshine Act. The Florida Supreme Court held that both were applicable. The Records Act contained language extending its application to public bodies "or persons acting on their behalf," which the court said encompassed lessees of the hospitals. The Sunshine Act contained no such language, but the court said that the concept was implicit in that statute too. During the pendency of litigation on the matter, the legislature passed a new statute making confidential the records and meetings of many private companies operating public hospitals. The court declined to rule on the constitutionality of this statute but said it did not operate retroactively on the dispute at hand. See Memorial Hospital–West Volusia Inc. v. News–Journal Corp., 729 So.2d 373, 27 Med. L. Rptr. 1353 (Fla.1999).

3. A Constitutional Right of Access to Meetings?

Might the press (or public) have a constitutional right to be admitted to governmental meetings? There is little case law on this question, perhaps because media usually rely on the statutory remedies, perhaps because until recently there was little indication that the Constitution protected newsgathering at all. An abortive attempt to recognize such a right occurred in Society of Professional Journalists v. Secretary of Labor, 832 F.2d 1180, 14 Med. L. Rptr. 1827 (10th Cir. 1987), which involved media attempts to gain access to a hearing by the federal Mine Safety and Health Administration regarding a mine disaster. You should reconsider the plausibility of a constitutional claim for access to meetings after reading the Supreme Court's cases on access to institutions and courtrooms, which are discussed in the next section and in Chapter XI.

C. Access to Institutions

When the press seeks to report on conditions in public institutions, such as mental hospitals or prisons, a new set of issues arises. From the press point of view, neither access to records nor access to meetings is sufficient; the reporters and photographers want to see conditions for themselves and talk to the inmates personally. From the government's point of view, concerns arise that are not present in access-to-records or access-to-meetings disputes—concerns relating to security, maintenance of discipline, and protection of the privacy of persons who are largely unable to protect it themselves. Perhaps because there were no statutory solutions to these issues, it was in this context that the press first advanced constitutional arguments for access.

In 1974, the Supreme Court decided two companion cases in which the press sought to enter prisons after the warden had imposed limitations on that access. In Pell v. Procunier, 417 U.S. 817, 1 Med. L. Rptr. 2379 (1974), a regulation of the California Department of Corrections provided that "media interviews with specific individual inmates will not be permitted." Saxbe v. Washington Post Co., 417 U.S. 843, 1 Med. L. Rptr. 2314 (1974), involved a similar ban by the federal prison system.

Justice Stewart, writing for the Court in both cases, noted that "this regulation is not part of an attempt by the State to conceal the conditions in its prisons or to frustrate the press investigation and reporting of those conditions." Reporters could visit the institutions and "speak about any subject to any inmates whom they might encounter." Interviews with inmates selected at random were also permitted, and both the press and the public could take tours through the prisons. "In short, members of the press enjoy access to California prisons that is not available to other members of the public." Indeed, the only apparent restriction was the one being challenged.

> The First and Fourteenth Amendments bar government from interfering in any way with a free press. The Constitution does not, however, require government to accord the press special access to information not shared by members of the public generally. It is one thing to say that a journalist is free to seek out sources of information not available to members of the general public, that he is entitled to some constitutional protection of the confidentiality of such sources, cf. *Branzburg v. Hayes,* supra, and that government cannot restrain the publication of news emanating from such sources. Cf. *N.Y. Times v. United States,* supra. It is quite another thing to suggest that the Constitution imposes upon government the affirmative duty to make available to journalists sources of information not available to members of the public generally. That proposition finds no support in the words of the Constitution or in any decision of this Court. Accordingly, since § 415.071 does not deny the press access to sources of information available to members of the general public, we hold that it does not abridge the protections that the First and Fourteenth Amendments guarantee.

Four Justices dissented. Writing in *Saxbe,* Justice Powell, joined by Justices Brennan and Marshall, asserted that the government was not protecting privileged or confidential information. It "has no legitimate interest in preventing newsmen from obtaining the information. . . . Quite to the contrary, federal prisons are public institutions. The administration of these institutions, the effectiveness of their rehabilitative programs, the conditions of confinement that they maintain, and the experiences of the individuals incarcerated therein are all matters of legitimate societal interest and concern.''

Citizens could not undertake to learn this information for themselves. ''In seeking out the news the press therefore acts as an agent of the public at large.'' Justice Powell could not ''follow the Court in concluding that *any* governmental restriction on press access to information, so long as it is nondiscriminatory, falls outside the purview of First Amendment concern. . . . At some point official restraints on access to news sources, even though not directed solely at the press, may so undermine the function of the First Amendment that it is both appropriate and necessary to require the Government to justify such regulations in terms more compelling than discretionary authority and administrative convenience.''

Justice Powell concluded that the total ban on interviews impaired ''a core value of the First Amendment,'' but that it would be permissible to adopt narrower rules, such as rules that barred interviews with prisoners being disciplined or that limited the number of interviews that might be held with any one person.

Justice Douglas, joined by Justices Brennan and Marshall, also dissented.

A few years later, the Supreme Court returned to the prison question in a slightly different context.

Houchins v. KQED, Inc.

Supreme Court of the United States, 1978.
438 U.S. 1, 98 S. Ct. 2588, 57 L. Ed.2d 553, 3 Med. L. Rptr. 2521.

[A suicide occurred at the Alameda County Jail at Santa Rita, California. KQED, licensee of a television station in nearby San Francisco, reported the story and quoted a psychiatrist as saying that conditions at the Little Greystone building were responsible for the illnesses of his patient-prisoners at the jail. In an earlier proceeding, a federal judge had ruled that the conditions at Greystone constituted cruel and unusual punishment. Houchins, the county sheriff, refused to admit a camera crew KQED sent to get the story and to photograph the facilities, including Greystone. At the time, no public tours of the jail were permitted.

KQED and the NAACP filed suit under 42 U.S.C. § 1983 claiming violation of their First Amendment rights. The NAACP claimed that information about the jail was essential to permit public debate on jail conditions in Alameda County. The complaint requested preliminary and permanent injunctions to prevent the sheriff from ''excluding KQED news personnel from the Greystone cells and Santa Rita facilities and generally preventing full and accurate news coverage of the conditions prevailing therein.''

Shortly after suit was filed, the sheriff announced a program of monthly tours. The press received advance notice, and several reporters, including one from KQED, went on the first tour. Each tour was limited to 25 persons and did not include Little Greystone. Cameras and tape recorders were barred, though the sheriff did supply photographs of some parts of the jail. Tour members "were not permitted to interview inmates, and inmates were generally removed from view."

KQED argued that the tours were unsatisfactory because advance scheduling prevented timely access and because photography and interviewing were barred. The sheriff defended his policy on grounds of "inmate privacy," the danger of creating "jail celebrities" who would "undermine jail security," and the concern that unscheduled tours would "disrupt jail operations."

The district judge issued a preliminary injunction barring the sheriff from denying access to "responsible representatives" of the news media "at reasonable times and hours" and "from preventing KQED news personnel and responsible representatives of the news media from utilizing photographic and sound equipment or from utilizing inmate interviews in providing full and accurate coverage of the Santa Rita facilities." He found that a more flexible policy was "both desirable and attainable" without danger to prison discipline. The court of appeals, in three separate opinions, rejected the sheriff's argument that *Pell* and *Saxbe* controlled, and affirmed the injunction.]

Mr. Chief Justice Burger announced the judgment of the Court and delivered an opinion, in which Mr. Justice White and Mr. Justice Rehnquist joined.

The question presented is whether the news media have a constitutional right of access to a county jail, over and above that of other persons, to interview inmates and make sound recordings, films, and photographs for publication and broadcasting by newspapers, radio, and television.

. . .

II.

Notwithstanding our holding in *Pell v. Procunier,* supra, respondents assert that the right recognized by the Court of Appeals flows logically from our decisions construing the First Amendment. They argue that there is a constitutionally guaranteed right to gather news under *Pell v. Procunier,* [ ], and *Branzburg v. Hayes,* [ ]. From the right to gather news and the right to receive information, they argue for an implied special right of access to government controlled sources of information. This right, they contend, compels access as a *constitutional* matter. . . .

III.

We can agree with many of the respondents' generalized assertions; conditions in jails and prisons are clearly matters "of great public importance." [ ] Penal facilities are public institutions which require large amounts of public funds, and their mission is crucial in our criminal justice system. Each person placed in prison becomes, in effect, a ward of the state for whom society assumes broad responsibility. It is equally true that with greater information, the public can more intelligently form opinions about prison conditions. Beyond question, the role of the media is important; acting as the "eyes and ears" of the public, they can be a powerful and constructive force, contributing to remedial action in the conduct of public business. They have served that function since the beginning of the Republic, but like all other components of our society media representatives are subject to limits.

The media are not a substitute for or an adjunct of government, and like the courts, they are "ill-equipped" to deal with problems of prison administration. [ ]. We must not confuse the role of the media with that of government; each has special, crucial functions each complementing—and, sometimes conflicting with—the other.

The public importance of conditions in penal facilities and the media's role of providing information afford no basis for reading into the Constitution a right of the public or the media to enter these institutions, with camera equipment, and take moving and still pictures of inmates for broadcast purposes. This Court has never intimated a First Amendment guarantee of a right of access to all sources of information within government control. Nor does the rationale of the decisions upon which respondents rely lead to the implication of such a right.

. . .

[*Branzburg*] offers even less support for the respondents' position. Its observation, in dictum, that "news gathering is not without its First Amendment protections," [ ] in no sense implied a constitutional right of access to news sources. That observation must be read in context; it was in response to the contention that forcing a reporter to disclose to a grand jury information received in confidence would violate the First Amendment by deterring news sources from communicating information. [ ] There is an undoubted right to gather news "from any source by means within the law," [ ] but that affords no basis for the claim that the First Amendment compels others—private persons or governments—to supply information.

. . .

The right to *receive* ideas and information is not the issue in this case. [ ] The issue is a claimed special privilege of access which the Court rejected in *Pell* and *Saxbe,* a right which is not essential to guarantee the freedom to communicate or publish.

IV.

The respondents' argument is flawed, not only because it lacks precedential support and is contrary to statements in this Court's opinions, but also because it invites the Court to involve itself in what is clearly a legislative task which the Constitution has left to the political processes. Whether the government should open penal institutions in the manner sought by respondents is a question of policy which a legislative body might appropriately resolve one way or the other.

. . .

Petitioner cannot prevent respondents from learning about jail conditions in a variety of ways, albeit not as conveniently as they might prefer. Respondents have a First Amendment right to receive letters from inmates criticizing jail officials and reporting on conditions. See Procunier v. Martinez, 416 U.S. 396 (1974). Respondents are free to interview those who render the legal assistance to which inmates are entitled. See id., at 419. They are also free to seek out former inmates, visitors to the prison, public officials, and institutional personnel, as they sought out the complaining psychiatrist here.

Moreover, California statutes currently provide for a prison Board of Corrections that has the authority to inspect jails and prisons and *must* provide a public report at regular intervals. . . .

Neither the First Amendment nor Fourteenth Amendment mandates a right of access to government information or sources of information within the government's control. Under our holdings in *Pell* [and *Saxbe*], until the political branches decree otherwise, as they are free to do, the media have no special right of access to the Alameda County Jail different from or greater than that accorded the public generally.

The judgment of the Court of Appeals is reversed and the case is remanded for further proceedings.

Reversed.

Mr. Justice Marshall and Mr. Justice Blackmun took no part in the consideration or decision of this case.

Mr. Justice Stewart, concurring in the judgment.

I agree that the preliminary injunction issued against the petitioner was unwarranted, and therefore concur in the judgment. In my view, however, KQED was entitled to injunctive relief of more limited scope.

The First and Fourteenth Amendments do not guarantee the public a right of access to information generated or controlled by government, nor do they guarantee the press any basic right of access superior to that of the public generally. The Constitution does no more than assure the public and the press equal access once government has opened its doors. Accordingly, I agree substantially with what the opinion of The Chief Justice has to say on that score.

We part company, however, in applying these abstractions to the facts of this case. Whereas he appears to view "equal access" as meaning access that is identical in all respects, I believe that the concept of equal access must be accorded more flexibility in order to accommodate the practical distinctions between the press and the general public.

When on assignment, a journalist does not tour a jail simply for his own edification. He is there to gather information to be passed on to others, and his mission is protected by the Constitution for very specific reasons. "Enlightened choice by an informed citizenry is the basic ideal upon which an open society is premised. . . ." *Branzburg v. Hayes,* [ ] (dissenting opinion). Our society depends heavily on the press for that enlightenment. . . .

That the First Amendment speaks separately of freedom of speech and freedom of the press is no constitutional accident, but an acknowledgment of the critical role played by the press in American society. The Constitution requires sensitivity to that role, and to the special needs of the press in performing it effectively. A person touring Santa Rita jail can grasp its reality with his own eyes and ears. But if a television reporter is to convey the jail's sights and sounds to those who cannot personally visit the place, he must use cameras and sound equipment. In short, terms of access that are reasonably imposed on individual members of the public may, if they impede effective reporting without sufficient justification, be unreasonable as applied to journalists who are there to convey to the general public what the visitors see.

Under these principles, KQED was clearly entitled to some form of preliminary injunctive relief. At the time of the District Court's decision, members of the public were permitted to visit most parts of the Santa Rita jail, and the First and Fourteenth Amendments required the Sheriff to give members of the press *effective* access to the same areas. The Sheriff evidently assumed that he could fulfill this obligation simply by allowing reporters to sign up for tours on the same terms as the public. I think he was mistaken in this assumption, as a matter of constitutional law.

The District Court found that the press required access to the jail on a more flexible and frequent basis than scheduled monthly tours if it was to keep the public informed. By leaving the "specific methods of implementing such a policy . . . [to] Sheriff Houchins," the Court concluded that the press could be allowed access to the jail "at reasonable times and hours" without causing undue disruption. The District Court also found that the media required cameras and recording equipment for effective presentation to the viewing public of the conditions at the jail seen by individual visitors, and that their use could be kept consistent with institutional needs. These elements of the Court's order were both sanctioned by the Constitution and amply supported by the record.

In two respects, however, the District Court's preliminary injunction was overbroad. It ordered the Sheriff to permit reporters into the Little Greystone facility and it required him to let them interview randomly encountered inmates. In both these respects, the injunction gave the press access to areas and sources of information from which persons on the public tours had been excluded, and thus enlarged the scope of what the Sheriff and Supervisors had opened to public view. The District Court erred in concluding that the First and Fourteenth Amendments compelled this broader access for the press.

Because the preliminary injunction exceeded the requirements of the Constitution in these respects, I agree that the judgment of the Court of

Appeals affirming the District Court's order must be reversed. But I would not foreclose the possibility of further relief for KQED on remand. In my view, the availability and scope of future permanent injunctive relief must depend upon the extent of access then permitted the public, and the decree must be framed to accommodate equitably the constitutional role of the press and the institutional requirements of the jail.

MR. JUSTICE STEVENS, with whom MR. JUSTICE BRENNAN and MR. JUSTICE POWELL join, dissenting.

. . .

For two reasons, which shall be discussed separately, the decisions in *Pell* and *Saxbe* do not control the propriety of the District Court's preliminary injunction. First, the unconstitutionality of petitioner's policies which gave rise to this litigation does not rest on the premise that the press has a greater right of access to information regarding prison conditions than do other members of the public. Second, relief tailored to the needs of the press may properly be awarded to a representative of the press which is successful in proving that it has been harmed by a constitutional violation and need not await the grant of relief to members of the general public who may also have been injured by petitioner's unconstitutional access policy but have not yet sought to vindicate their rights.

. . .

In *Pell v. Procunier,* [ ], the Court stated that "newsmen have no constitutional right of access to prisons or their inmates beyond that afforded the general public." But the Court has never intimated that a nondiscriminatory policy of excluding entirely both the public and the press from access to information about prison conditions would avoid constitutional scrutiny. Indeed, *Pell* itself strongly suggests the contrary.

. . .

The decision in *Pell*, therefore, does not imply that a state policy of concealing prison conditions from the press, or a policy denying the press any opportunity to observe those conditions, could have been justified simply by pointing to like concealment from, and denial to, the general public. If that were not true, there would have been no need to emphasize the substantial press and public access reflected in the record of that case. What *Pell* does indicate is that the question whether respondents established a probability of prevailing on their constitutional claim is inseparable from the question whether petitioner's policies unduly restricted the opportunities of the general public to learn about the conditions of confinement in Santa Rita jail. As in *Pell*, in assessing its adequacy, the total access of the public and the press must be considered.

Here, the broad restraints on access to information regarding operation of the jail that prevailed on the date this suit was instituted are plainly disclosed by the record. . . . Petitioner's no-access policy, modified only in the wake of respondents' resort to the courts, could survive constitutional scrutiny only if the Constitution affords no protection to the public's right to be informed about conditions within those public institutions where some of its members are confined because they have been charged with or found guilty of criminal offenses.

II.

The preservation of a full and free flow of information to the general public has long been recognized as a core objective of the First Amendment to the Constitution. It is for this reason that the First Amendment protects not only the dissemination but also the receipt of information and ideas.

. . .

In addition to safeguarding the right of one individual to receive what another elects to communicate, the First Amendment serves an essential societal function. Our system of self-government assumes the existence of an informed citizenry. . . . It is not sufficient, therefore, that the channels of communication be free of governmental restraints. Without some protection for the acquisition of information about the operation of public institutions such as prisons by the public at large, the process of self-governance contemplated by the Framers would be stripped of its substance.[21]

For that reason information-gathering is entitled to some measure of constitutional protection. See, e.g., *Branzburg v. Hayes,* [ ]; *Pell v. Procunier,* [ ]. As this Court's decisions clearly indicate, however, this protection is not for the private benefit of those who might qualify as representatives of the "press" but to insure that the citizens are fully informed regarding matters of public interest and importance.

[Justice Stevens argued that in the prison context, unlike other contexts such as executive sessions of official bodies, there was no interest in confidentiality.] While prison officials have an interest in the time and manner of public acquisition of information about the institutions they administer, there is no legitimate, penological justification for concealing from citizens the conditions in which their fellow citizens are being confined.

. . .

Some inmates—in Santa Rita, a substantial number—are pretrial detainees. . . . Society has a special interest in ensuring that unconvicted citizens are treated in accord with their status.

In this case, the record demonstrates that both the public and the press had been consistently denied any access to the inner portions of the Santa Rita jail, that there had been excessive censorship of inmate corre-

---

21. Admittedly, the right to receive or acquire information is not specifically mentioned in the Constitution. But "the protection of the Bill of Rights goes beyond the specific guarantees to protect from . . . abridgment those equally fundamental personal rights necessary to make the express guarantees fully meaningful. . . . The dissemination of ideas can accomplish nothing if otherwise willing adherents are not free to receive and consider them. It would be a barren marketplace of ideas that had only sellers and no buyers." Lamont v. Postmaster General, 381 U.S. at 308 (Brennan, J., concurring). It would be an even more barren marketplace that had willing buyers and sellers and no meaningful information to exchange.

spondence, and that there was no valid justification for these broad restraints on the flow of information. An affirmative answer to the question whether respondent established a likelihood of prevailing on the merits did not depend, in final analysis, on any right of the press to special treatment beyond that accorded the public at large. Rather, the probable existence of a constitutional violation rested upon the special importance of allowing a democratic community access to knowledge about how its servants were treating some of its members who have been committed to their custody. An official prison policy of concealing such knowledge from the public by arbitrarily cutting off the flow of information at its source abridges the freedom of speech and of the press protected by the First and Fourteenth Amendments to the Constitution.

. . .

I would affirm the judgment of the Court of Appeals.

Notes and Questions

1.   What does the Chief Justice see as the crucial question?

2.   Why would Justice Stewart allow access at times other than those at which the public can enter the jail? What would he do if the sheriff were to stop the public tours?

3.   The district court enjoined the sheriff from excluding KQED, but did not give a remedy to other members of the public. Is that impermissible? In an omitted portion of his dissent, Justice Stevens wrote: "[E]ven though the Constitution provides the press with no greater right of access to information than is possessed by the public at large, a preliminary injunction is not invalid simply because it awards special relief to a successful litigant which is a representative of the press."

4.   Two years after *Houchins*, the Court decided a case that Justice Stevens interpreted as repudiating *Houchins* insofar as the latter held that the First Amendment does not guarantee a right of access to information within the government's control. The case was *Richmond Newspapers, Inc. v. Virginia,* a courtroom access case which is discussed in the next chapter. He interpreted *Richmond Newspapers* as holding "that the First Amendment protects the press and public from abridgment of their rights of access to information about the operation of their government, including the Judicial Branch. . . ." You should re-evaluate *Houchins* after considering all of the subsequent courtroom access cases discussed in the next chapter.

5.   Many prisons restrict news media interviews with prisoners. It seems clear after *Houchins* that prisons do not have an obligation to arrange for interviews with specific inmates at the request of the media. But can they prevent inmates from using their telephone, mail, or visitation privileges to communicate with reporters? Attempts by California prison authorities to regulate such interviews have been the subject of a long conflict there. See William Glaberson, Irked by Focus on Inmates, California Bans Interviews,

N.Y. Times, Dec. 29, 1995, at A16. See also M.L. Stein, Clamping Down, Editor & Publisher, Jan. 13, 1996, at 12. In Procunier v. Martinez, 416 U.S. 396 (1974), the Supreme Court upheld a district court decision striking down rules regulating the correspondence of California prisoners, in part because of the First Amendment rights of the recipients of the prisoner's letters: "Whatever the status of a prisoner's claim to uncensored correspondence with an outsider, it is plain that the latter's interest is grounded in the First Amendment's guarantee of freedom of speech. And this does not depend on whether the nonprisoner correspondent is the author or intended recipient of a particular letter, for the addressee as well as the sender of direct personal correspondence derives from the First and Fourteenth Amendments a protection against unjustified governmental interference with the intended communication."

The California Department of Corrections promulgated rules that banned scheduled face-to-face interviews and denied inmates the right to correspond with the media in confidence. The rules allowed reporters to get on inmates' visitors lists and to see prisoners during visiting hours, but disallowed cameras, recorders, and note-taking. At the urging of the Society of Professional Journalists, the California legislature passed a bill aimed at overturning these limitations, but Governor Pete Wilson vetoed it, stating that media interviews made "celebrities" of inmates, thereby interfering with the goal of making them feel remorse for their offenses, and gave them notoriety that encouraged disruptive behavior by other inmates. See Governor vetoes prison interview bill, News Media and the Law, Fall 1997, at 5. Governor Gray Davis vetoed a similar bill in 1999, as did Governor Arnold Schwarzenegger in 2004. See Lynda Gledhill & John M. Hubbell, Governor vetoes most of 121 bills, S.F. Chronicle, Oct. 1., 2004, at B3.

Access to executions: In 1996, media groups covering an execution by lethal injection at California's San Quentin prison complained that all they were allowed to see was a motionless prisoner lying strapped to a gurney. The intravenous tubes were already in place before the curtain shielding him from view was drawn aside, and the fatal drug was administered from a location out of view and out of hearing. After watching the immobilized prisoner through a window for a few minutes, the witnesses were informed that he was dead.

A coalition of media groups sued the warden of San Quentin alleging that these limitations on their access violated the First Amendment. The trial judge agreed and ordered the warden to allow media representatives to view future executions from before the tubes are inserted until after the inmate is pronounced dead, but the Ninth Circuit reversed. The court held that under *Pell*, and the subsequent Supreme Court access cases, the press had no greater right of access than the public. California had a long history of allowing representatives of the public to witness executions and the court said this might give rise to a First Amendment right to do so.

However, the court held that there had been no showing that the limitations on their access violated "Whatever First Amendment protection exists for viewing executions." The court stated that it would defer to prison officials' determinations that allowing the public and press witnesses to see the prisoner being prepared for execution would increase the chances that the personnel involved might be identified, which would threaten "prison security, staff safety, and the orderly operation of the institutional procedure." However, the court reversed and remanded to allow the district court to determine whether the plaintiffs could present "substantial evidence" that the limitations "represent[ ] an exaggerated response to [ ] security and safety concerns." See California First Amendment Coalition v. Calderon, 150 F.3d 976, 26 Med. L. Rptr. 2009 (9th Cir. 1998).

The district court subsequently enjoined California prison officials from enforcing the policy that prevented media representatives from observing executions in their entirety. The judge said they must be allowed an uninterrupted view from the time the condemned enters the execution chamber until he or she is pronounced dead. See California First Amendment Coalition v. Calderon, 88 F. Supp. 2d 1083, 28 Med. L. Rptr. 2505 (N.D. Cal. 2000). The Ninth Circuit affirmed, finding that the public enjoys a First Amendment right to view executions from the moment the condemned is escorted into the execution chamber, including initial procedures that are inextricably intertwined with the process of putting the condemned inmate to death. The court found that the prison regulations under review in the case impermissibly restricted that right. See California First Amendment Coalition v. Woodford, 299 F.3d 868, 30 Med. L. Rptr. 2345 (9th Cir. 2002).

D. ACCESS TO MILITARY OPERATIONS

The technical capacity to provide live television coverage from battle zones has raised new issues involving access to military operations. During the 1970s, a number of military leaders contended that front-line reporting contributed to the weakening of public support for U.S. involvement in Vietnam. Consequently, when the United States began military operations on the island nation of Grenada in 1983, reporters were excluded for two days, after which a limited group was flown to the island by military aircraft. A lawsuit contesting the exclusion was dismissed for mootness, and the dismissal was upheld on appeal. Flynt v. Weinberger, 762 F.2d 134, 11 Med. L. Rptr. 2118 (D.C. Cir. 1985).

The pool system and the Persian Gulf War. Nonetheless, the outcry over the military's total exclusion of the press led the Defense Department to adopt a "pool" system. Under this system, media organizations chosen by the Department were allowed to select specific reporters to be transported to cover the early stages of military operations. These reporters would then "pool" their information, sharing it with other reporters who had not been selected.

The first real test of the pool system was in the 1991 Persian Gulf war, during which the Pentagon outraged the media by carefully controlling and ultimately manipulating their coverage of the war. With the approval of the White House, the Pentagon limited all coverage of combat to press pools escorted by military personnel. The military, rather than the press, determined where the pools would be taken. Reporters and photographers who tried to strike out on their own were subject to detention and disaccreditation, although by the end of the war some correspondents were able to reach battle sites on their own. Media copy was subject to review by military censors for security purposes. Pentagon guidelines said censors were not to delete material because it criticized or embarrassed to the military, but correspondents complained that censors occasionally deleted material in violation of the guidelines, and transmission of copy was often delayed until its news value had passed.

Most news of the progress of the war came from briefings by high-ranking military officers in Washington and Riyadh. Briefings emphasized dramatic military videos of "smart" bombs precisely seeking out and destroying inanimate military targets. Although it later became clear that 90 percent of the bombs dropped on Iraq were less accurate "dumb" bombs, some of which struck civilian targets, the results of those bombings generally were not shown. One field commander showed reporters videotape of helicopters attacking Iraqi troops, but the military subsequently refused to make public that and other footage showing human targets. The military also refused to provide sound tracks of the voices of pilots and others reacting to combat.

Media complaints about the restrictions received little support from the public or the courts. Media groups challenged the Pentagon rules limiting access to pool representatives, but the complaint was dismissed. See The Nation Magazine v. Department of Defense, 762 F. Supp. 1558, 19 Med. L. Rptr. 1257 (S.D.N.Y.1991). The district court said that some First Amendment right of access to military operations might be found in the Supreme Court's decisions concerning access to courtrooms, parks, and prisons, but that it would have to be carefully crafted to protect the legitimate interests of the military. By the time of the decision the war had ended and the Pentagon said any future rules would be tailored to the specific circumstances of that operation. The court said "prudence dictates that we leave the definition of the exact parameters of press access to military operations abroad for a later date when a full record is available."

Images of military coffins. Another case arising out of access restrictions during the 1991 Gulf War was JB Pictures, Inc. v. Department of Defense, 86 F.3d 236, 24 Med. L. Rptr. 2017 (D.C. Cir. 1996). In that case, the D.C. Circuit upheld the Defense Department policy banning the press and public from witnessing the arrival of war dead at Dover Air Force Base, the military's only East Coast mortuary. Until 1991, the return of the bodies of soldiers killed in action overseas had been a public event accompanied by ceremonies open to the press and public. Shortly before Operation Desert Storm the defendant effectively shifted these events to sites closer to the families of the deceased and gave these families veto power over press coverage: "Media coverage of the arrival of the remains at the port of entry or at interim stops will not be permitted but may be permitted at the service member's duty or home station or at the interment site, if the family so desires." Preexisting access to other events at Dover, such as the departure of personnel, was continued.

Plaintiff media and veterans' organizations argued that this was viewpoint discrimination because it allowed the war to be portrayed in a more favorable light. The court disagreed, noting that the policy was applied uniformly "to all members of the press and public, regardless of their views on war or the United States military." Plaintiffs had argued that the the the policy was not viewpoint-neutral because "the return of war dead is an event necessarily laden with anti-war implications." Instead, the court wrote that "One has only to think of Pericles's famous speech honoring the first Athenians killed in the Peloponnesian War, or the Gettysburg Address, to recognize that one cannot easily pigeonhole the meaning of a return of soldiers killed in battle."

The court further found that even if the restrictions had the potential for "differential effects," they would not necessarily be invalid in light of "the law's permissive treatment of restrictions on access to government operations not historically open to the public." The court stated that even under a balancing test the plaintiffs' access claims would fail. The Dover policy imposed only a "relatively modest" burden on newsgathering since the "basic facts" regarding war casualties could still be obtained and reported.

Finally, the court found that the Dover policy was "amply" justified by two government interests. The first was the reduction of hardship on the families of the deceased who no longer felt the need to travel long distances to Dover. The second justification was the "interest in protecting the privacy of families and friends of the dead, who may not want media coverage of the unloading of caskets at Dover. . . . [W]e do not think the government hypersensitive in thinking that the bereaved may be upset at public display of the caskets of their loved ones."

The policy barring photos of military coffins was not followed consistently during the Clinton Administration but the Pentagon reinstituted it at the beginning of the Iraq war. An attempt in Congress to instruct the Pentagon to allow such photography failed. The Senate defeated, 54–39, an amendment to a military spending plan that would have instructed the Defense Department to work out a new policy permitting news media to cover the arrival of coffins from war zones. Senator John McCain, one of those who supported the amendment, said "I think we ought to know the casualties of war." The Bush Administration said the ban was necessary to protect the privacy of dead soldiers' families.

A few weeks before the Senate vote, a civilian contractor took digital photos of coffins lined up in a military plane in Iraq and emailed them to a friend, who passed them along to the Seattle Times, which published them. The contractor was fired. Several hundred photos of coffins arriving at Dover AFB, taken by Air Force photographers and mistakenly released in response to an FOIA request, were subsequently published on a website.

See Senate Backs Ban on Photos of G.I. Coffins, N.Y.Times, June 22, 2004, at A17. The website is available at www.thememoryhole.org.

For a symposium on the press in the 1991 Gulf War, see 66 St. John's L. Rev. 563 (1992).

––––––––

After the 1991 Gulf War, negotiations between the Pentagon and major news organizations produced a new set of Pentagon rules for future military operations. They state that pools "are not to serve as the standard means of covering U.S. military operations," and that reporters and photographers will be provided access to all major military units. Field commanders are to allow journalists to ride on military vehicles and aircraft whenever feasible. Military public affairs officers are not to interfere with independent reporting and are to be given the resources needed to facilitate timely transmission of pool and independent reports. The only guideline not agreed to by the media was one giving the military the right to review articles and broadcasts to prevent disclosure of information that could endanger the safety of troops or the success of a military mission. News organizations said they would challenge that restriction if and when the Pentagon sought to implement it.

Despite the agreement, news organizations complained that during the early stages of the 1999 NATO bombing of Kosovo they were given even less information than during the Gulf War. See Editors decry information lack in Kosovo, Austin American–Statesman April 18, 1999, at A11. After some editors raised the matter directly with President Clinton, the Pentagon began releasing more information, but journalists continued to complain about the lack of daily data on targets attacked, bombing damage, and weapons and aircraft used. They also complained about lack of access to U.S. commanders. See Joe Strupp, Editors Press NATO, Editor & Publisher, May 1, 1999, at 9.

Journalists and news organizations also charged that the Defense Department largely ignored the 1992 agreement on media coverage during the war in Afghanistan ten years later. Despite the fact that the agreement was "to be followed in any future combat situation involving American troops," Stanley Cloud, who participated in negotiating that agreement as Washington bureau chief for Time, wrote that "in the early stages, at least, much of the fighting took place in secret, far beyond journalists' eyes and ears. Once again, reporters from the freeest country on earth were begging the Defense Department for permission to cover a war firsthand." Journalists were excluded from military operations entirely for the first six weeks of the war, and then forced to rely on press pools for the next month. Reporters allege that they were threatened by U.S. troops, denied access to military personnel, and subjected to censorship. In December, U.S. Marines locked reporters in a warehouse to prevent them from covering American troops killed or injured by a stray bomb.

The Defense Department for the most part did not deny these charges, but rather asserted that, in the words of Assistant Secretary Victoria Clarke, "[w]e are in a whole new world here. We're trying to figure out the rules of the road." The Pentagon apologized for the December detention of U.S. journalists. On December 13, Clarke announced the opening of three Coalition press information centers in Afghanistan, designed to help journalists get interviews and other information, and on December 27, the Defense Department ended pool coverage. It was not until February, however, that journalists were allowed to accompany U.S. ground troops in combat, and then only on condition that they submit their reports to military censors.

Two organizations challenged the Pentagon's restrictions on coverage in Afghanistan. One was Getty Images News Services Corp., which supplies images to many publications. Getty alleged that it had been inappropriately excluded from press pools when they existed, and from press flights arranged by the Defense Department to the detention center at Guantanamo Bay Naval Base. The district court granted the Defense Department's motion to dismiss, largely on the basis that the Department had already rectified much of the treatment of which Getty complained. The court was highly deferential to the Defense Department and the needs of the military, but it did note, citing to *Sherrill v. Knight* [infra p. 660], that the Department needed to adopt and follow "reasonable" standards for determining which press outlets were included on the flights to Guantanamo. "Although the Court is reluctant to interfere significantly in the military's conduct of its affairs, the First and Fifth Amendments seem to require, at a minimum, that before determinating [sic] which media organizations receive the limited access available, DOD must not only have some criteria to guide its determinations, but must have a reasonable way of assessing whether the criteria are met." See Getty Images News Services Corp. v. Department of Defense, 193 F. Supp. 2d 112, 30 Med. L. Rptr. 1513 (D.D.C. 2002)

Hustler publisher Larry Flynt also challenged restrictions on Afghanistan war coverage. The appellate court's decision is below.

Flynt v. Rumsfeld

U.S. Court of Appeals, District of Columbia Circuit, 2004.
355 F.3d 697, 32 Med. L. Rptr. 1289, cert. denied ___ U.S. ___, 125 S. Ct. 313.

SENTELLE, CIRCUIT JUDGE:

Larry Flynt and L.F.P., Inc. (the company that publishes *Hustler* magazine) (collectively "Flynt" or "appellants") sued Donald H. Rumsfeld, Secretary of Defense, and the United States Department of Defense ("DOD") seeking, *inter alia,* injunctive relief against interference with its exercise of a claimed First Amendment right of the news media to have access to U.S. troops in combat operations, and claiming that DOD's delay in granting *Hustler'* s reporter access to U.S. troops in Afghanistan infringed that right. They further argued that DOD's Directive controlling media access to military forces facially violates this same constitutional right. The District Court dismissed Flynt's as-applied constitutional claims for lack of ripeness and standing, and refused to exercise its discretion under the Declaratory Judgment Act to declare the pertinent DOD Directive facially unconstitutional. This appeal followed. Because we find that no such constitutional right exists, we will affirm the District Court's decision on other grounds.

I.   Background

A.   *Hustler*'s attempts to gain access

Shortly after the September 11, 2001, terrorist attacks, the United States military began combat operations in Afghanistan in support of the global war on terrorism. On October 30, 2001, Flynt wrote a letter to the Honorable Victoria Clarke, Assistant Secretary of Defense for Public Affairs, requesting that *Hustler* correspondents "be permitted to accompany ground troops on combat missions and that said correspondents be allowed free access to the theater of United States military operations in Afghanistan and other countries where hostilities may be occurring as part of Operation Enduring Freedom.". . . . [O]n November 15, Clarke sent Flynt a fax stating that access to ground operations was not immediately possible because ". . . the only U.S. troops on the ground in Afghanistan are small numbers of servicemen involved in special operations activity." Clarke explained that "[t]he highly dangerous and unique nature of their work makes it very difficult to embed media" with ground troops, but also stated that there had been "extensive" media access to other aspects of military operations. Specifically, "[s]cores of reporters and photographers have covered the [air] strikes, witnessed the humanitarian drops and interviewed dozens of [soldiers]." Clarke then provided Flynt with contact information for the Fifth Fleet Public Affairs Officer so that *Hustler* could have similar access.

[Flynt did not contact the Fifth Fleet Public Affairs Officer but instead filed this lawsuit. He then sent another letter to Clarke requesting access. She responded by sending a letter describing what types of access were available at that point and explaining that media access decisions were controlled by Department of Defense Directive 5122.5. [This directive stems from the agreement discussed supra p. 646.] Ultimately, in May of 2002, a *Hustler* reporter did obtain access to troops searching for al Qaeda operatives.]

B.   The Directive

As stated above, DOD decisions regarding media access to combat troops are guided by Department of Defense Directive 5122.5. . . . At issue in this case is Enclosure 3, entitled "Statement of DOD Principles for News Media." This enclosure begins with the command that "[o]pen and independent reporting shall be the principal means of coverage of U.S. military operations." It then outlines the manner in which such coverage should occur. It allows for media pools, limited numbers of press persons who represent a larger number of news media organizations and share material, but states that pools are not to be the "standard means of covering U.S. military operations." Rather, pools are only to be used when space is limited or areas to be visited are extremely remote. It also directs that "field commanders should be instructed to permit journalists to ride on military vehicles and aircraft when possible." . . . [ ]

II. Analysis

This court reviews *de novo* the District Court's dismissal of a complaint for lack of subject matter jurisdiction. [ ]. In our review, we assume the truth of the allegations made and construe them favorably to the pleader. [ ]. We review the District Court's decision to withhold declaratory relief for an abuse of discretion. [ ].

A. Appellants' Claims

As a threshold matter, it is important to clarify the right appellants seek to protect. In candor, it is not at all clear from appellants' complaint below or briefs in this court precisely what right they believe was violated or contend the courts should vindicate. After some pressing, at oral argument it became clear that they claimed a right, protected under the First Amendment, in their own words, to "go[ ] in [to battle] with the military." This right is different from merely a right to cover war. The Government has no rule—at least so far as Flynt has made known to us— that prohibits the media from generally covering war. Although it would be dangerous, a media outlet could presumably purchase a vehicle, equip it with the necessary technical equipment, take it to a region in conflict, and cover events there. Such action would not violate Enclosure 3 or any other identified DOD rule.

With that distinction made, appellants' claim comes more sharply into focus. They claim that the Constitution guarantees to the media—specifically *Hustler*'s correspondent—the right to travel *with* military units into combat, with all of the accommodations and protections that entails— essentially what is currently known as "embedding." Indeed, at oral argument appellants' counsel stated that the military is "obligated to *accommodate* the press because the press is what informs the electorate as to what our government is doing in war."

. . .

C. Facial Challenge

. . .

The facial challenge is premised on the assertion that there is a First Amendment right for legitimate press representatives to travel with the military, and to be accommodated and otherwise facilitated by the military in their reporting efforts during combat, subject only to reasonable security and safety restrictions. There is nothing we have found in the Constitution, American history, or our case law to support this claim.

To support the position that there is such a constitutional right, appellants first point to cases that discuss the general purposes underlying the First Amendment. *See New York Times Co. v. United States,* [supra at 98,] ("[t]he press was protected so that it could bare the secrets of government and inform the people.") (Black, J., concurring); [ ]. These cases, however, say nothing about media access to the U.S. combat units engaged in battle.

Appellants also cite cases that allow facial challenges to statutes or regulations that vest public officials with unfettered discretion to grant or deny licenses to engage in expressive activity, such as *City of Lakewood v. Plain Dealer Publishing Co.,* [supra p. 233] and Shuttlesworth v. City of Birmingham, 394 U.S. 147 (1969). This is not, however, a "license" decision. This appeal challenges regulations controlling *access* to government information and activity, not governmental limitation of expression. The Supreme Court has noted the difference. *See, e.g., Los Angeles Police Dept. v. United Reporting Publ'g Corp.,* [supra p. 627] (distinguishing government limits on access to information in its possession from a government restriction on disseminating information one already possesses).

Likewise, this Court has held that "freedom of speech [and] of the press do not create any per se right of access to government . . . activities simply because such access might lead to more thorough or better reporting." *JB Pictures, Inc. v. Dep't of Defense,* [supra p. 644]. Appellants admit they face a "dearth of case law concerning press access to battles." From this unenviable position, they ask us to look to *Richmond Newspapers, Inc. v. Virginia,* [infra p. 673], for guidance.

In *Richmond Newspapers,* a plurality of the Supreme Court held that a constitutional right of public access to criminal trials existed based on a long history of such access in the United States and in England at the time our organic laws were created. [ ]. According to appellants, *Richmond Newspapers* established that the First Amendment may be interpreted to provide for a right of access to government operations, and that access is not limited to criminal trials. They assert that we must apply a *Richmond Newspapers* analysis to the facts of this case. We disagree.

In *Center for National Security Studies v. Department of Justice,* [supra p. 620], we held that there was no First Amendment right for plaintiffs to receive the identities of INS detainees and material witnesses who were detained in the wake of the September 11 attacks. Indeed, we made it clear that "[n]either the Supreme Court nor this Court has applied the *Richmond Newspapers* test outside the context of criminal judicial proceedings or the transcripts of such proceedings." [ ] For emphasis, we added that "neither this Court nor the Supreme Court has ever *indicated* that it would" do so. [ ]. Instead, we noted that in all areas other than criminal proceedings, the Supreme Court has applied the general rule of *Houchins v. KQED,* [supra p. 634], not the exception of *Richmond Newspapers.* [ ] 331 F.3d at 935. *Houchins* held that the press have no First Amendment right of access to prisons, and in doing so stated that the First Amendment does not "mandate[ ] a right of access to government information or sources of information within the government's control." *Houchins*, [ ]. To summarize, neither this Court nor the Supreme Court has ever applied *Richmond Newspapers* outside the context of criminal proceedings, and we will not do so today.

Appellants argue that we did, however, use the *analysis* underlying the *Richmond Newspapers* decision in *JB Pictures Inc.* [ ] In that case, several media and veterans organizations challenged a Department of Defense policy. That policy shifted ceremonies for deceased service members arriving from overseas from Dover Air Force base to locations closer to the service members' homes. It also gave the families of deceased military personnel the authority to limit press access to those ceremonies. Contrary to appellants' assertion, the extent of our *Richmond Newspapers* discussion in that case is contained in one sentence: "[i]t is obvious that military bases do not share the tradition of openness on which the Court relied in striking down restrictions on access to criminal court proceedings in . . . *Richmond Newspapers*." [ ]. Thus *J.B. Pictures* not only does not support wholesale adoption of a *Richmond Newspapers* analysis in every case involving requests for access to government activities or information, it rejects such a rule.

Even if we were to apply a *Richmond Newspapers* test, which again, we do not, it would not support appellants' facial challenge to the Directive. As an initial matter, the history of press access to military units is not remotely as extensive as public access to criminal trials. Without going into great historic detail, it is sufficient that in *Richmond Newspapers* the Supreme Court relied on the "unbroken, uncontradicted history" of public access to criminal trials. . . .

No comparable history exists to support a right of media access to U.S. military units in combat. The very article cited by appellants for the proposition that media have traditionally had broad access to soldiers in combat does not support this position. *See* John E. Smith, *From the Front Lines to the Front Page: Media Access to War in the Persian Gulf and Beyond*, 26 Colum. J.L. & Soc. Probs. 291, 292–305 (1993). Beginning with the American Revolution, war reporting was primarily in the form of private letters from soldiers and official reports that were sent home and published in newspapers. [ ] Indeed, the rise of the professional war correspondent did not begin until at least the time of the Civil War. [ ] In addition, it is not entirely clear that in any of our early wars the media was actively embedded into units, which is the right appellants seek. In sum, even if we were to attempt a *Richmond Newspapers* analysis and consider the historical foundations of a right of media access to combat units, appellants' claim would fail miserably.

Even if *Richmond Newspapers* applied in this context, and even if there was a historical basis for media access to troops in combat, the Directive would still not violate the First Amendment. *Richmond Newspapers* expressly stated that "[j]ust as a government may impose reasonable time, place, and manner restrictions" in granting access to public streets, "so may a trial judge . . . impose reasonable limitations on access to a trial." [ ]. These limitations could be based on the need to maintain a "quiet and orderly setting," or "courtrooms' . . . limited capacity." [ ] The Directive appellants challenge is incredibly supportive of media access to the military with only a few limitations. . . . The restrictions contained in the Directive are few, including: special operations restrictions; limited restrictions on media communications owing to electromagnetic operational security concerns; use of media pools when the sheer size of interested media is unworkable, such as at the beginning of an operation; and expulsion for members of the media who violate the ground rules. [ ]. Appellants have offered no reason to conclude that these restrictions are unreasonable. Even if *Richmond Newspapers* did apply, appellants' argument would fail.

. . . In no way did the District Court abuse its discretion in refusing to grant declaratory relief.

D. As-applied Challenges

We now turn to the as-applied challenges. As explained above, the constitutional right appellants assert does not exist, so the as-applied claim could only survive if this otherwise constitutional Directive was applied to them in some unconstitutional way. It was not. At no time has Flynt ever claimed that he, or *Hustler,* was treated differently under the Directive than any other media outlet. Nor has he claimed that the Directive is some sort of a sham that was not followed.

. . .

Because we hold that there is no constitutionally based right for the media to embed with U.S. military forces in combat, and because we further hold that the Directive was not applied to Flynt or *Hustler* magazine in any unconstitutional manner, the District Court's judgment is affirmed.

Notes and Questions

1. What would be the implications of recognizing a constitutional right to accompany troops into battle? Would the right only apply where there had been a formal declaration of war?

———

"Embedding" and public support for military operations. Although the Pentagon remains wary that the media's coverage of battle will undermine public support for military operations or unwittingly aid the enemy, it also appears to have become aware of the power of the media to motivate public support for its operations and budget. Although the court in *Flynt v. Rumsfeld* found no constitutional right of the media to accompany active units into battle, the Pentagon voluntarily chose to allow media "embedding" during the 2003 U.S.-led invasion of Iraq. Reportedly concerned

about foreign propaganda concerning the conduct of the invasion, Secretary of Defense Rumsfeld decided to allow journalists to be assigned to field units and cover virtually every aspect of the military action. More than 700 U.S. and foreign journalists were "embedded" with military units and their live reports became a mainstay of electronic coverage of the war.

Critics have subsequently noted that some embedded journalists became too involved in the stories they were reporting and too attached to their units (reporting, for example, on "our movements" and "our casualties"), suffered a higher percentage of casualties than soldiers, and provided coverage that tended to focus on details concerning specific unit movements (rather than on broader strategic and policy issues). Moreover, embedded journalists were required to sign an agreement that restricted their reporting about ongoing missions, prohibited reporting on the specific results of missions even after they were completed or cancelled, required them to comply with "embargoes" on stories, and acknowledged that the embedded assignments could be terminated at any time and for any reason. See Andrew Bushell and Brent Cunningham, Being There, Colum. Journ. Rev., Mar./Apr. 2003, at 18.

But the coverage put a real face on a distant war, was popular with the public, and gave a greater impression of accountability through journalists' first-hand observations and broad access to combat troops. Moreover, despite a few highly publicized breaches of security, the vast majority of reporting apparently did little to compromise military tactics. See a collection of articles under the series title, The Real–Time War, Colum. Journ. Rev., May/Jun. 2003, at 26;

E.   CRIMINAL LAW RESTRICTIONS ON ACCESS

Although many of the restrictions on access to information provide for criminal as well as civil penalties, criminal penalties are used only infrequently. However, in some situations, such as disaster sites, criminal law is the primary means of controlling access.

City of Oak Creek v. Ah King

Supreme Court of Wisconsin, 1989.
148 Wis.2d 532, 436 N.W.2d 285, 16 Med. L. Rptr. 1273.

[An airliner crashed in what the court called a "non-public area" of a publicly owned airport, General Mitchell Field. The General Mitchell Field Media Guide for Airport Emergencies provided that "no representatives of the media will be permitted to enter non-public/restricted areas of the airport without an authorized escort." Immediately after the crash local law enforcement authorities ordered the crash site secured and stationed officers on streets leading to the site with instructions to keep out all unauthorized persons.

Ah King was a television cameraman who, in a car with others from his station, followed an emergency vehicle through a police roadblock and parked on East College Avenue near the airport. Oak Creek city detective Virgil White, stationed at the roadblock, followed the car and ordered the occupants to leave. As they walked back toward the roadblock, Ah King jumped over a fence separating the street from the airport, ran to the top of a hill, and began taking pictures of the crash site. Detective White pursued Ah King and ordered him to leave the restricted area. Ah King said he would not leave unless he was arrested, which the officer then did. Detective White testified that there were "No Trespassing" signs on the fence Ah King jumped over, and that about five spectators were standing outside the fence.

Ah King was convicted of violating a municipal ordinance prohibiting disorderly conduct, which was defined in relevant part as conduct tending "to cause or provoke a disturbance." The court first held that the statute applied to Ah King because his repeated refusal to obey the detective's order in the presence of other persons was likely to provoke a disturbance, and that the statute was not unconstitutionally vague.]

CECI, JUSTICE:

. . .

The appellant advances two principal arguments why news gatherers as surrogates for the general public should have a right of access to emergency sites. First, the appellant argues that the first amendment to the United States Constitution protects the right to gather information. Second, the appellant argues that art. 1, sec. 3 of the Wisconsin Constitution protects the right of the press to gather information.

We will first address the appellant's first amendment argument. It has generally been held that the first amendment does not guarantee the press a constitutional right of special access to information not available to the public generally. [*Branzburg*]; Zemel v. Rusk, 381 U.S. 1, 17 (1965).

The right to speak and publish does not carry with it the unrestrained right to gather information. [ ] Therefore, in *Zemel,* the United States Supreme Court sustained the government's refusal to validate passports to Cuba even though that restriction rendered less than wholly free the flow of information concerning that country. [ ] The Court noted:

> There are few restrictions on action which could not be clothed by ingenious argument in the garb of decreased data flow. For example, the prohibition of unauthorized entry into the White House diminishes the citizen's opportunities to gather information he might find relevant to his opinion of the way the country is being run, but that does not make entry into the White House a First Amendment right. [ ]

Similarly, in *Branzburg,* the United States Supreme Court stated that "[n]ewsmen have no constitutional right of access to the scenes of crime or disaster when the general public is excluded. . . ." [ ] "Despite the fact that news gathering may be hampered, the press is regularly excluded from grand jury proceedings, our own conferences, the meetings of other official bodies gathered in executive session, and the meetings of private organizations." [ ]

[The court cited *Pell* and *Houchins* for the proposition that the First Amendment does not give the press a "right of special access" to information not available to the public. The court then held that *Richmond Newspapers Inc. v. Virginia* was inapplicable because it dealt with access to courtrooms by press and public alike, whereas Ah King "is seeking to obtain a special access to the scene of an airplane crash beyond the public's right to access simply because he is a 'news gatherer' as opposed to an 'ordinary citizen.' "]

The dissent concedes that the United States Supreme Court has not recognized a constitutional protection for news gatherers' access to an accident scene, yet the dissent notes that in certain circumstances the Court has recognized that particular institutions have allowed the press greater access than the public to serve as a surrogate for the public. [ ] It is interesting to note the particular facts of the two cases the dissent cites as support for its proposition. In *Richmond Newspapers,* as described above, the Court dealt with the issue of the right of access to courtrooms. In [*Saxbe*] the Court was dealing with the right of access to prisons. The dissent fails to note that there is a difference between an institution allowing news gatherers priority of access on its own accord, in a setting in which the institution may closely control and monitor access, and this court mandating access in an emergency situation. Even the appellant concedes that "[a] right of access to trials does not necessarily imply a right of access to emergency scenes."

Our interpretation of the preceding United States Supreme Court cases leads us to the conclusion that under the first amendment, the appellant has an undoubted right to gather news from any source by means within the law.[22] However, the appellant does not have a first amendment right of access, solely because he is a news gatherer, to the scene of this airplane crash when the general public has been reasonably excluded.

The appellant's second argument is that art. 1, sec. 3 of the Wisconsin Constitution provides a basis for a news gatherer's right of access to the scene of an airplane crash beyond the general public's right of access. The appellant, however, has failed to offer any precedent which would support his contention. In addition, on the basis of the record before us, we are not inclined to recognize such a right because news gatherers were not denied access to the crash site of Midwest Express Flight 105 on September 6, 1985.

While the appellant was disregarding Detective White's orders and penetrating into the nonpublic restricted area of the airport, other news gatherers were assembling in the airport director's office at the airport, pursuant to the General Mitchell Field Media Guide. At 4:30 p.m., the airport director held a briefing which lasted approximately 15 minutes.

---

22. The dissenting justices obviously misread this court's decision when they opine that "the majority opinion concludes that the federal constitution does not protect the media's right to gather information." [ ] As we have just indicated, "under the first amendment, the appellant has an undoubted right to gather news from any source by means *within* the law" (emphasis added). See *Houchins* [ ], citing *Branzburg* [ ].

Immediately thereafter, the director took media representatives directly to the crash site to take photographs or film the scene. Therefore, given the fact that news gatherers were given access to the scene of this airplane crash, we are not inclined to rule on the issue of whether a news gatherer has a right of access to the scene of an airplane crash under the Wisconsin Constitution beyond that of the general public's right of access.

Furthermore, the needs and rights of the injured and dying should be recognized by this court as having preference over newly created "rights" that the dissenting justices would give to a "news gatherer" who is simply concentrating on trying to beat out his competition and make his employer's deadline. As the circuit court so aptly noted in its memorandum decision, in an emergency situation "[t]he injured and dying are entitled to receive the immediate and full attention of rescue workers. Law enforcement personnel should not be required to needlessly occupy themselves with persons who have a personal interest not related to restoration of order or with rescue attempts. The defendant, here, chose to disregard the government's efforts to establish order, set himself and his interest above the law, diluted law enforcement efforts to assist those in need, and by so doing elevated his own interest and concerns above the welfare of the persons involved in the tragic accident and the government's efforts in its law enforcement concerns."

. . .

The decision of the circuit court is affirmed.

Shirley S. Abrahamson, Justice (dissenting).

The state has a significant interest in keeping people away from the site of an accident or crime to expedite assisting victims, to preserve evidence or to protect the public from injury. This state interest, however, is not at issue in this case. The record shows that the defendant was not interfering with or obstructing emergency personnel and that neither he nor other observers were in danger.

The issue in this case is whether the defendant's refusing to obey an officer's command to leave the accident scene constitutes the offense of disorderly conduct as defined in the Oak Creek ordinance. I conclude it does not. Moreover, I conclude that this court should acknowledge that a representative of the news media may function as a proxy for the public in certain situations where public access is limited.

I.

[The dissent argued that Ah King's conduct did not violate the statute because it was not disruptive.]

II.

. . .

The majority opinion does not, in my opinion, adequately address the defendant's argument regarding the rights of news gatherers to access to an accident scene.

The defendant does not argue that the government must always allow news gatherers access to an accident scene. Rather the defendant asks this court to hold that governmental personnel must give news gatherers access to a position at an accident from which they can observe emergency personnel in action unless exclusion of news gatherers from all locations is required to enable emergency personnel to perform their tasks. The defendant argues that this standard accommodates two important objectives: It enables the media to inform the public about the accident and governmental operations while it prevents news gatherers from jeopardizing people's lives, health or property.

While the United States Supreme Court has not explicitly recognized a constitutional protection for news gatherers' access to an accident scene, the Court has recognized that media representatives serve as surrogates for the public. Chief Justice Warren Burger, writing in *Richmond Newspapers, Inc. v. Virginia*, [ ], about the right of the public and the press to attend criminal trials observed:

> Instead of acquiring information about trials by firsthand observation or by word of mouth from those who attended, people now acquire it chiefly through the print and electronic media. In a sense, this validates the media claim of functioning as surrogates for the public.

Chief Justice Burger recognized in the *Richmond Newspapers* case that government authorities have allowed priority access to news gatherers in situations where public access is limited by circumstances. The Chief Justice wrote: "While media representatives enjoy the same right of access as the public, they often are provided special seating and priority of entry so that they may report what people in attendance have seen and heard." [ ]

In [*Saxbe*], Justice Potter Stewart, writing for the court, acknowledged that sometimes the press is given greater access to information than the public. The Justice observed that "members of the press are accorded substantial access to the federal prisons in order to observe and report the conditions they find there. Indeed, journalists are given access to the prisons and to prison inmates that in significant respects exceeds that afforded to members of the general public."

This court has itself institutionalized procedures for accommodating media personnel—procedures which do not provide similar rights to private individuals. Chapter 61 of the Supreme Court Rules, entitled Rules Governing Electronic Media and Still Photography Coverage of Judicial Proceedings, concludes with the caveat, "The privileges granted by this chapter to photograph, televise and record court proceedings may be exercised only by persons or organizations which are part of the news media." [ ]

I conclude that, in determining the scope of news gatherers' access to accidents, the court can and should take into consideration the media's role as the "eyes and ears" of the public at large. [ ] Time, place and manner restrictions on access to the site of an accident which are properly applicable to the general public may not be appropriate when applied to the media.

For the reasons set forth I do not join the majority opinion.

I am authorized to state that CHIEF JUSTICE HEFFERNAN and JUSTICE BABLITCH join this dissent.

Notes and Questions

1.   Could Ah King have been charged with trespassing?

2.   The justices also disagreed as to whether Ah King had violated the statute. The majority said the photographer's refusal to obey the officer's order was not in itself disorderly conduct, but became so because of the presence of other people and the importance of crowd control under the circumstances. The dissent said any threat of disruption was speculative and therefore could not support the conclusion that his conduct was disorderly under the statute.

3.   In an omitted section of their opinion, the dissenters noted that other news gatherers who also were taking pictures within the police boundary were not challenged by the police. According to the lawyer who represented Ah King, this evidence was introduced to show that other media representatives were engaging in the same conduct even closer to the site without causing any disruption. Would it also support an argument that the ordinance could not be enforced against Ah King because it was not enforced against others? Must the police arrest all or none?

4.   A California statute authorizes peace officers to close a disaster site and exclude unauthorized persons, but "nothing in this section shall prevent a duly authorized representative of any news service, newspaper, or radio or television station or network from entering the areas closed pursuant to this section." Cal. Penal Code § 409.5(d). A California appellate court has interpreted this statute as barring police from excluding journalists from disaster sites to protect their safety. The court noted that journalists *may* be excluded to prevent interference with emergency operations, but "only so long and only to such an extent as is necessary to prevent actual interference." See Leiserson v. City of San Diego, 184 Cal. App.3d 41, 229 Cal. Rptr. 22 (1986).

———

Durruthy v. Pastor. Several reporters were arrested in 2000 while covering protests against the federal government's seizure of Elian Gonzalez from the house of his Florida relatives. Elian's mother had drowned attempting to escape Cuba with the boy, and the U.S. government returned him to his father in Cuba over the objections of his Florida relatives. One television cameraman, Durruthy, was arrested after he ran into the street during the protests to get footage of the arrest of an NBC cameraman. Durruthy was initially charged with resisting arrest, but the charges were dropped. He then filed suit under 42 U.S.C. § 1983, alleging excessive use of force and unlawful arrest. The district court "found that there was no probable cause, or even arguable probable cause, to arrest Durruthy." The district court also found that the officer had used excessive force in arresting Durruthy. The Eleventh Circuit Court of Appeals reversed. Durruthy v. Pastor, 351 F.3d 1080 (11th Cir. 2003). The Eleventh Circuit found probable cause to arrest Durruthy because he was violating a Florida statute that forbids pedestrians from walking in the streets when sidewalks are available (i.e., because he was jaywalking). [The street was closed to vehicles at the time of the protest.] The court noted that the Florida statute "contains no exception for anyone, including members of the media." Id. at 1090. The court also found that although the officer used some force in arresting Durruthy, it was not excessive. Therefore, the court held that the officer was entitled to qualified immunity and reversed and remanded the case to the district court. A dissenting judge disputed the majority's analysis of the evidence, contending: "[I]t is patently obvious to any observer of the videotape evidence that the sole reason for [the officer's] conduct was that she and the other officers wanted Durruthy to stop filming the arrest of the NBC cameraman." Id. at 1097.

U.S. v. Matthews. A freelance journalist was charged with receiving and transporting child pornography via the Internet. He claimed he was engaged in an investigation to show that law enforcement officials were not effectively policing the distribution of Internet child pornography. The American Civil Liberties Union filed an amicus brief arguing that journalists need a constitutional right to police Internet pornography because law enforcement agencies historically have misunderstood the nature of the Internet and are usually either indifferent or overzealous in the prosecution of Internet pornography. The district court doubted the freelance's story, but said even if his motives were purely journalistic, the First Amendment would provide no defense. See United States v. Matthews, 11 F. Supp. 2d 656, 26 Med. L. Rptr. 2163 (D.Md.1998).

The Fourth Circuit affirmed. See United States v. Matthews, 209 F.3d 338, 28 Med. L. Rptr. 1673 (4th Cir. 2000). Matthews, supported by the ACLU and the Reporters Committee for Freedom of the Press, argued that the First Amendment protects the use of child pornography for educational or other legitimate purposes, including journalism. They contended that *New York v. Ferber* [supra p. 148] implied that child pornography statutes should be analyzed on a case-by-case basis to prevent impermissible applications that would violate the free speech rights of adults. But the court said *Ferber* "rejected even the possibility of a broad First Amendment defense like that proposed by Matthews." As the trial court had done, the Fourth Circuit cited *Branzburg* and *Cohen* as refuting the Reporters Committee's argument that strict application of the statute would violate a First Amendment right to gather news.

F.   DISCRIMINATORY ACCESS

Many access disputes involve discrimination against types of media, particularly broadcasting, and types of reporting tools, such as cameras and tape recorders. This discrimination against categories of news gatherers is one of the issues addressed in this section. (One special variety of categorical discrimination, exclusion of cameras from courtrooms, is considered in Chapter XI.)

But media are often the beneficiaries of discriminatory access. Their representatives routinely are granted entry to press rooms and press galleries, news conferences, conventions, and disaster sites from which the public is excluded, and often get free admission to sports and entertainment events for which others must pay.

This favored treatment requires that some line be drawn between those who are "press" and those who are not, and that process may invite impermissible discrimination against particular individuals. Some of these issues are explored in the following case.

1. DISCRIMINATION AGAINST INDIVIDUALS

Sherrill v. Knight
United States Court of Appeals, District of Columbia Circuit, 1977.
569 F.2d 124, 3 Med. L. Rptr. 1514.

[Sherrill, Washington correspondent for The Nation, had credentials for the House and Senate press galleries, but was denied a White House press pass. Under the procedure in effect at the time, once an applicant showed congressional credentials, residence in Washington, and an editor's verification of the reporter's need to report from the White House regularly, the pass was issued unless the Secret Service objected. Here, it was ultimately learned, the Secret Service had recommended against issuing the pass on the ground that Sherrill posed a security risk because he had assaulted the press secretary to the governor of Florida and also faced assault charges in Texas. In Sherrill's suit to obtain a press pass, the district court had ordered the Secret Service to formulate "narrow and specific" standards for judgment and to institute certain procedures for handling such requests. The Secret Service appealed.]

McGOWAN, CIRCUIT JUDGE.

. . .

We agree with the District Court that both first and fifth amendment concerns are heavily implicated in this case. We conclude, however, that neither of these concerns requires the articulation of detailed criteria upon which the granting or denial of White House press passes is to be based. We further conclude that notice, opportunity to rebut, and a written decision are required because the denial of a pass potentially infringes upon first amendment guarantees. Such impairment of this interest cannot be permitted to occur in the absence of adequate procedural due process.

III.

Appellants argue that because the public has no right of access to the White House, and because the right of access due the press generally is no greater than that due the general public, denial of a White House press pass is violative of the first amendment only if it is based upon the content of the journalist's speech or otherwise discriminates against a class of protected speech. While we agree with appellants that arbitrary or content-based criteria for press pass issuance are prohibited under the first amendment, there exist additional first amendment considerations ignored by appellants' argument.

These considerations can perhaps be best understood by first recognizing what this case does *not* involve. It is not contended that standards relating to the security of the President are the sole basis upon which members of the general public may be refused entry to the White House, or that members of the public must be afforded notice and hearing concerning such refusal. The first amendment's protection of a citizen's right to obtain information concerning "the way the country is being run" does not extend to every conceivable avenue a citizen may wish to employ in pursuing this right. Nor is the discretion of the President to grant interviews or briefings with selected journalists challenged. It would certainly be unreasonable to suggest that because the President allows interviews with some bona fide journalists, he must give this opportunity to all. Finally, appellee's first amendment claim is not premised upon the assertion that the White House must open its doors to the press, conduct press conferences, or operate press facilities.

Rather, we are presented with a situation where the White House has voluntarily decided to establish press facilities for correspondents who need to report therefrom. These press facilities are perceived as being open to all bona fide Washington-based journalists, whereas most of the White House itself, and press facilities in particular, have not been made available to the general public. White House press facilities having been made publicly available as a source of information for newsmen, the protection afforded newsgathering under the first amendment guarantee of freedom of the press, see [*Branzburg* and *Pell*], requires that this access not be denied arbitrarily or for less than compelling reasons. [ ] Not only newsmen and the publications for which they write, but also the public at large have an interest protected by the first amendment in assuring that restrictions on newsgathering be no more arduous than necessary, and that individual newsmen not be arbitrarily excluded from sources of information. [ ]; [ ].

Given these important first amendment rights implicated by refusal to grant White House press passes to bona fide Washington journalists, such refusal must be based on a compelling governmental interest. Clearly, protection of the President is a compelling, "even an overwhelming," interest. . . . However, this standard for denial of a press pass has never been formally articulated or published. Merely informing individual rejected applicants that rejection was for "reasons of security" does not inform the public or other potential applicants of the basis for exclusion of journalists from White House press facilities. Moreover, we think that the phrase "reasons of security" is unnecessarily vague and subject to ambiguous interpretation.

Therefore, we are of the opinion that appellants must publish or otherwise make publicly known the actual standard employed in determining whether an otherwise eligible journalist will obtain a White House press pass. We do agree with appellants that the governmental interest here does not lend itself to detailed articulation of narrow and specific standards or precise identification of all the factors which may be taken into account in applying this standard. It is enough that the Secret Service be guided solely by the principle of whether the applicant presents a potential source of physical danger to the President and/or his immediate family so serious as to justify his exclusion. [ ] This standard is sufficiently circumspect so as to allow the Secret Service, exercising expert judgment which frequently must be subjective in nature, considerable leeway in denying press passes for security reasons. At the same time, the standard does specify in a meaningful way the basis upon which persons will be deemed security risks, and therefore will allow meaningful judicial review of decisions to deny press passes. We anticipate that reviewing courts will be appropriately deferential to the Secret Service's determination of what justifies the inference that an individual constitutes a potential risk to the physical security of the President or his family.

IV.

In our view, the procedural requirements of notice of the factual bases for denial, an opportunity for the applicant to respond to these, and a final written statement of the reasons for denial are compelled by the foregoing determination that the interest of a bona fide Washington correspondent in obtaining a White House press pass is protected by the first amendment. This first amendment interest undoubtedly qualifies as liberty which may not be denied without due process of law under the fifth amendment.[23] The only further determination which this court must make is "what process is due," [ ]. We think that notice to the unsuccessful applicant of the factual bases for denial with an opportunity to rebut is a minimum prerequisite for ensuring that the denial is indeed in furtherance of Presidential protection, rather than based on arbitrary or less than compelling reasons. [ ] The requirement of a final statement of denial and the reasons therefor is necessary in order to assure that the agency has neither taken additional, undisclosed information into account, nor responded irrationally to matters put forward by way of rebuttal or explanation. This requirement also will avoid situations such as occurred in the case before us, where an applicant does not receive official written notification of his status until more than five years after the status decision is made.

Having determined that appellants' failure to articulate and publish an explicit and meaningful standard governing denial of White House press passes for security reasons, and to afford procedural protections to those

---

23. A related and perhaps equally compelling *property* interest may also be said to require the procedural protections of the fifth amendment. . . . However, because appellee's first amendment liberty interest independently requires the standards and procedural protections set forth in this opinion, we do not reach the question of whether appellee also has a property entitlement of constitutional magnitude.

denied passes, violates the first and fifth amendments, we affirm that portion of the District Court's judgment requiring notice, opportunity to be heard, and a final written statement of the bases of denial. We remand that portion of the District Court's judgment requiring appellants to develop "narrow and specific standards" for press pass denials in order that this requirement may be modified in accordance with this opinion.

Notes and Questions

1. What are the First Amendment bases for the reporter's attack? The Fifth Amendment bases?

2. If government is limited in its ability to discriminate among persons similarly situated, what justifies the court's passing observation upholding the President's discretion to grant interviews to selected journalists? Is this because the President is involved? Could the same rule be justified for the Attorney General? The local army base commander? The press officer at the Supreme Court?

3. After this decision, the Secret Service adopted the following standard:

> In granting or denying a request for a security clearance made in response to an application for a White House press pass, officials of the Secret Service will be guided solely by the principle of whether the applicant presents a potential source of physical danger to the President and/or the family of the President so serious as to justify his or her exclusion from White House press privileges. 31 CFR § 409.1.

Procedural regulations give a rejected applicant notice and an opportunity to respond and a personal appearance before a Secret Service official if requested. If that official sustains the denial, those regulations also require written notification setting forth "as precisely as possible and to the extent that security considerations permit, the factual basis for the denial in relation to the standard set forth in § 409.1." If these regulations had been in effect when Sherrill first applied, what difference would they have made?

––––––

Retaliatory exclusion: A reporter's right to be free from governmental retaliation for exercising her First Amendment rights is a "clearly established constitutional right" for purposes of the civil rights laws. In McBride v. Village of Michiana, 100 F.3d 457, 25 Med. L. Rptr. 1020 (6th Cir. 1996), a reporter brought a claim under 42 U.S.C. § 1983 against a municipality and several of its officials alleging that in retaliation for her unfavorable reporting they attempted to have her removed from her beat, tried to prevent her from attending meetings of the village council, overcharged her for copying public documents, and forbade city employees from speaking to her. The Sixth Circuit found that although there was no Supreme Court or Sixth Circuit case recognizing a reporter's right to be free from retaliation, case law in other contexts "made the illegality of such retaliation apparent." The court specifically cited cases finding civil rights violations when public employees were penalized for exercising First Amendment rights.

In Uniontown Newspapers, Inc. v. Roberts, 839 A.2d 185 (Pa. 2003), a newspaper sought access to telephone records for which a state legislator had requested reimbursement. The legislator told the newspaper that he would release them if it assigned a different reporter to examine them. The newspaper declined and continued to seek access to the records. The legislator then released them to a radio station, stating that he was refusing to give the records to the newspaper because it was biased. Finally, the legislator offered to give the records to the newspaper if its "counsel absolved him of wrongdoing in connection with them." Id. at 188. The newspaper and the reporter sued seeking a right of access to the records. They also alleged that the legislator had violated their rights to equal protection by granting selective access to the records and that he had retaliated against them for exercising their First Amendment rights in violation of 42 U.S.C. § 1983.

Although the Pennsylvania Supreme Court rejected the claim that there was a right of access to the legislator's telephone records, the court held that the newspaper and reporter had alleged cognizable violations of their rights under 42 U.S.C. § 1983. Specifically the court found a cognizable equal protection claim based on the reporter's claim that "he was denied access to records given to other similarly situated reporters, based on his membership in a class of reporters whose speech offended appellee." Id. at 197. The court also cited *McBride*, above, for the proposition that the newspaper and the reporter had made out a prima facie case under section 1983 based on the legislator's retaliation against them for exercising their First Amendment rights. The dissenting judge argued that the reporter had failed to state a cause of action because there was "no state action involved in a legislator's release of his protected telephone records; and reporters with hurt feelings are not a protected class. The reporter, who works for a newspaper, which buys ink by the barrel, surely has a more effective avenue of recourse than Section 1983." Id. at 201.

In Borreca v. Fasi, 369 F. Supp. 906 (D.Hawaii 1974), the mayor of Honolulu denied Borreca, a reporter for a local paper, access to press conferences because he had been "irresponsible, inaccurate, biased, and malicious in reporting on the mayor and the city administration." The newspaper sued to gain admission for Borreca. In an action under 42 U.S.C. § 1983, the judge enjoined the mayor from preventing Borreca from attending press conferences "on the same basis and to the same extent that other news reporters attend" them.

If the mayor discontinues press conferences and instead invites all local reporters except Borreca to his office, can anything be done? Suppose two other reporters are also excluded? Is there a difference between inviting one reporter and excluding ten, and inviting ten and excluding one? Are political considerations likely to inhibit this kind of conduct?

Can physical limitations on the size of a meeting hall or office justify limited invitations to the press? Suppose that the mayor decided to hold a meeting in his or her small office with room for only three visitors. Does *Sherrill* suggest any limitations on who may be invited? Or on the mayor's power to decide to meet in a small office?

2. CATEGORICAL DISCRIMINATION

In some cases, reporters or photographers have been denied credentials or otherwise denied access not because of their personal backgrounds or behavior, but because of their employers, their membership in a disfavored category, or their involvement in some situation or issue, such as a labor dispute.

Substantive disagreement with employer. In Times–Picayune Publishing Corp. v. Lee, 1988 WL 36491, 15 Med. L. Rptr. 1713 (E.D.La.1988), the court found that Sheriff Lee believed the Times–Picayune's coverage of him and his office was "inaccurate and systematically biased" and directed his officers not to respond to any questions from its reporters except through written questions and written responses.

The court issued a preliminary injunction forbidding the sheriff and his employees from treating the Times–Picayune differently from other news organizations. It said the First Amendment guarantees a limited right of access to information made available generally to the public or other members of the press, which cannot be abridged unless the policy furthers a compelling state interest and is the least restrictive means available to achieve the asserted purpose. The sheriff's policy was unconstitutional because promoting accuracy or objectivity in reporting is not a compelling governmental interest; indeed, it is "the essence of censorship" when "the official's discriminatory actions seek to promote an interest with which the government may not concern itself at all—control by an official of what is said and written about him."

Sex discrimination. The New York Yankees excluded women reporters from the locker rooms after games. The judge found state action because Yankee Stadium was on property owned by the city, and ordered a woman reporter for Sports Illustrated admitted to the Yankees' dressing room when male reporters are admitted. Ludtke v. Kuhn, 461 F. Supp. 86, 4 Med. L. Rptr. 1625 (S.D.N.Y.1978).

On equal protection grounds, the judge found no justification for excluding women reporters. The players' privacy could be protected in other, less restrictive ways: "the total exclusion of women sports reporters . . . is not substantially related to the privacy protection objective and thus deprives" plaintiff of equal protection. On a due process point, the court concluded that privacy could be protected by means that did not interfere so greatly with plaintiff's liberty of pursuing her profession. "The other two interests asserted by defendants, maintaining the status of baseball as a family sport and conforming to traditional notions of decency and propriety, are clearly too insubstantial to merit serious consideration."

"Private" discrimination and labor disputes. When the discrimination is not by an official governmental body, First Amendment objections will be

unavailing unless the press can establish that the exclusion is nevertheless "state action." Compare National Broadcasting Co., Inc. v. Communications Workers of America, AFL–CIO, 860 F.2d 1022, 16 Med. L. Rptr. 1356 (11th Cir. 1988) (the exclusion of NBC, which was using nonunion crews to replace striking workers, from the Communications Workers of America convention, was not state action) with American Broadcasting Cos. v. Cuomo, 570 F.2d 1080 (2d Cir. 1977) (efforts by the two candidates in a runoff Democratic primary for mayor of New York City to exclude the local ABC station, the employees of which were on strike, found to implicate state action).

Preferring the public to the press. Is there any circumstance in which representatives of the press may be excluded even though members of the public, or selected representatives thereof, are admitted?

State legislation or prison regulations determine who may attend executions. These usually list state officials, members of the clergy, physicians, and a certain number of reporters. If state law barred all reporters, could they mount a successful challenge? See Kearns–Tribune Corp. v. Utah Board of Corrections, 2 Med. L. Rptr. 1353 (D.Utah 1977), rejecting a challenge by the press to a statute that limited attendance to those officially involved plus five "persons, relatives or friends" selected by the condemned prisoner. Two years later Utah amended its statute to require the warden to permit attendance at executions by a press pool.

3.   DISCRIMINATION AMONG TYPES OF MEDIA

A decision to give the press special access that is not available to the public generally requires some definition of "the press," and that may exclude communicators who believe they have an equally strong claim to special treatment. Also, as Justice Stewart observed in *Houchins,* supra, some of those who are defined as "press" will demand access not only for themselves and their pens and notepads, but for their cameras and tape recorders. When those devices are excluded, the broadcasting media are likely to argue that they are being discriminated against by being denied the opportunity to use the tools that make their medium most effective. Those are the issues considered in this section.

a.   Defining "Press"

The Atlanta federal penitentiary had a regulation permitting interviews with inmates by "representatives of the news media whose principal employment is to gather or report news for a radio or television news program of a station holding a Federal Communications Commission license." Jersawitz, self-producer of a show called "Let's Tell It Like It Is," which he aired on the Atlanta cable system's public access channel, wished to interview an inmate for his program. The warden denied permission on the ground Jersawitz was not a member of the press for purposes of the regulation.

Jersawitz sued for declaratory judgment that the regulation was unconstitutional, but the district court and court of appeals agreed that it was not. The latter rejected his First Amendment argument on the ground that neither the press nor the general public had any constitutional right to interview prisoners under *Pell* and *Saxbe*, supra p. 633. As to his equal protection clause claim, the court said the case involved no claim of constitutional magnitude, no suspect class, and no invidious discrimination that would require strict scrutiny, so the regulation was valid as long as it was rationally related to the prison's objectives. The regulation met this test because:

> In clear terms the regulation recognizes the need for the prison to maintain security and order within the prison and allow limited access for interviews by insuring that the representatives of the news media are responsible persons employed by and responsible to recognized media organizations. This permits the prison facility to identify those persons who are not likely to pose any threat to security without the facility having to conduct extensive individual investigations of each applicant. Thus, it provides the public with an objective and accurate news presentation by a person whose profession is gathering and reporting news without the likelihood of breaching the prison's security.

Jersawitz v. Hanberry, 783 F.2d 1532, 12 Med. L. Rptr. 1842 (11th Cir. 1986).

Is the court's treatment of Jersawitz's First Amendment claim consistent with *Sherrill* and the other cases in the preceding sections of this chapter? Could the regulation survive if it were subjected to the tests applied in those cases?

In Los Angeles Free Press, Inc. v. City of Los Angeles, 9 Cal. App.3d 448, 88 Cal. Rptr. 605 (1970), the county sheriff issued 3,000 press cards annually. The city police issued some 1,800. Both refused to issue any passes to specialized publications such as trade or financial papers, college newspapers, or to media "who perform functions other than those directly connected with the regular gathering and distribution of hard core news generated through police and fireman activities." The press cards were used to get behind police lines and to attend press conferences.

In the suit by the Free Press to get press cards, the trial judge found that the newspaper did not cover daily police or fire stories and dismissed the suit. On appeal, the judgment was affirmed. The court found a "reasonable basis" for the classification, though it did recognize that other bases might be used, such as first-come-first-served. The classification was not arbitrary. The Supreme Court denied certiorari over the dissents of Justices Black, Douglas, and Brennan. 401 U.S. 982 (1971).

Questions about the definition of "press" are also being raised in the context of the Internet. In 1996, the Executive Committee of Correspondents, which oversees accreditation to the House and Senate press galleries, refused to accredit Victor Schreibman, publisher of the online Federal

Information News Service (FINS), to the Senate periodical gallery. The Committee justified its refusal on the basis that FINS was distributed without charge and paid Schreibman no salary. Schreibman claimed, however, that the refusal was based on the fact that FINS was published via the Internet; he noted that the Committee had accredited him in 1993, 1994, and 1995 as a correspondent for the Electronic Public Information Newsletter, which was distributed in print. Schreibman's suit against the Committee was dismissed as presenting a nonjusticiable question, because the court found that the accreditation of journalists to the Congressional press galleries was within Congress' discretion and that the members of the Committee, acting under delegated authority from Congress, were immune from suit under the Constitution's speech and debate clause. See Schreibman v. Holmes, 1997 WL 527341 (D.D.C. 1997), aff'd, 203 F.3d 53 (D.C. Cir. 1999).

While the suit was pending, the Committee did accredit its first correspondent from Slate Magazine, which has an entirely online circulation, and the Committee has since accredited correspondents from other Internet publications. The step was noteworthy not only because it appeared to put to rest claims that the Committee was treating online publications differently than the print or broadcast press, but also because accreditation to a congressional press gallery is a prerequisite for obtaining a White House press pass.

Statutes and regulations that give the press preferential treatment tend to define it based on form rather than function. The wisdom of "defining the press in terms of format, method of distribution, or form of organization" has been questioned on the ground that "there is little correlation between those forms and the purposes for which it might make sense to give preferential treatment to some media." See David A. Anderson, Freedom of the Press, 80 Tex. L. Rev. 429, 436, 441 (2002). In the cases above, were the journalists who sought press passes serving these purposes?

b. Excluding Cameras

Exclusion of cameras from courtrooms is considered in the next chapter. The other class of events from which cameras are regularly excluded is executions. The media have had little success in challenging this exclusion. In 1994 NBC petitioned the North Carolina courts for permission to televise the execution of a prisoner who wanted his execution to be shown on the Donahue show. The North Carolina courts refused and the Supreme Court rejected a petition from Donahue and NBC. See Lawson v. Dixon, 512 U.S. 1215 (1994).

In Rice v. Kempker, 374 F.3d 675 (8th Cir. 2004), the Eighth Circuit held that the First Amendment "does not protect the use of video cameras" at executions. New Life, a religious group, sought a declaratory judgment that the Missouri Department of Corrections media policy, which prohibited videotaping or recording executions, violated the First Amendment. The group hoped to sway public opinion against the death penalty by publicly showing videotapes of executions. The court stated:

> Seeking to persuade this Court to go where no court previously has gone, New Life relies on a two-step argument. The first step new Life asks us to take is to rule that the First Amendment, [ ], requires executions to be open to the public. New Life then argues that prohibitions on videotaping are impermissible burdens on its constitional right of access to executions. We find no need to engage in this two-part inquiry and instead address the issue directly and hold that the First Amendment does not protect the use of video cameras or any other cameras or, for that matter, audio recorders in the execution chamber.

The court did not find it necessary to decide whether there is a constitutional right of access to executions but stated that even if there were such a right, "videotaping and the use of cameras would not be necessary to vindicate [it]."

Finally, the court opined that even if the Department of Corrections policy burdened First Amendment rights, it would still be upheld "a content-neutral time, place, and manner restrictions on speech." The Department's safety and security concerns were substantial governmental interests, and the media policy did not prevent dissemination of information about executions. See also Garrett v. Estelle, 556 F.2d 1274, 2 Med. L. Rptr. 2265 (5th Cir. 1977) (holding that there is no First Amendment right to attend or film executions).

See Jef I. Richards and R. Bruce Easter, Televising Executions: The High–Tech Alternative to Public Hangings, 40 UCLA L. Rev. 381 (1992); Note, The Case for Televised Executions, 11 Cardozo Arts & Ent. L.J. 101 (1992); Note, Televising California's Death Penalty: Is There A Constitutional Right to Broadcast Executions? 43 Hastings L.J. 1489 (1992).

c. *Excluding Tape Recorders*

Some states have banned certain reportorial aids for all reporters. Thus, the heads of both houses of the Maryland legislature barred reporters from attending sessions with "tape-recording devices." This was challenged by reporters, who claimed that "speed and accuracy are essential attributes of media news services" and that recorders will ensure accuracy. Their claims were rejected in Sigma Delta Chi v. Speaker, Maryland House of Delegates, 270 Md. 1, 310 A.2d 156 (1973). Conceding that newsgathering was entitled to some First Amendment protection, the court unanimously denied that banning tape recorders infringed such a right—plaintiffs were not prevented from carrying out their usual duties and the recorders were usable anywhere in the State House except in the chambers. Greater accuracy, although desirable, did not merit constitutional protection.

The court also rejected a due process claim that the restriction interfered with reporters' opportunity to earn a livelihood by diminishing the value of their product, "oral news." The reporters relied on Nevens v. City of Chino, 233 Cal. App.2d 775, 44 Cal. Rptr. 50 (1965), in which a similar ban had been upset on the ground that since the recorders were silent and unobtrusive, their exclusion unreasonably deprived reporters of the means to make an accurate record of what transpired. The California court analogized the ban to an attempt to prohibit the use of "pen, or pencil and paper." The Maryland court thought the analogy inappropriate: while "the removal of pen and paper might frustrate *all* effective communication, the prohibition against tape recorders is a mere inconvenience." There was no due process violation in rules that "may tend to exalt the preservation of order and decorum in the legislative chambers over increased efficiency of the press."

Finally, the reporters claimed that they were being denied equal protection of the laws because press members were being singled out by the ban. The court countered that the rules barred everyone, public and press, from bringing tape recorders into the chambers. The ban was against the equipment, not a class of persons.

Other states have taken the opposite approach. See Feldman v. Town of Bethel, 106 A.D.2d 695, 484 N.Y.S.2d 147 (3d Dept. 1984), upholding the award of damages to a reporter who was arrested for using a tape recorder at a town board meeting. The use of the recorder in an unobtrusive manner was protected by state law.

If one were to find a limited First Amendment right to gather news using whatever tools or aids the reporter wishes, what considerations might overcome that incipient right other than those suggested here? What about the contention that tape recorders destroy the free give-and-take of the legislative debate by freezing the words and intonations used by the speakers? Is that good or bad? Is this related to the trend toward greater openness in the legislative process? What about an argument that tape-recorded words will be accepted as accurate by those who hear them no matter how many witnesses testify that the speaker used different words— and that tapes may be altered so that false inferences would be drawn? Are the arguments different when the recorder is being used openly in a public place?

The frailty of the distinction between "pen and paper" reporters and those who use other tools is revealed in cases involving sketching as a substitute for photography. These cases, along with other aspects of access to judicial proceedings, are considered in the next chapter.

CHAPTER XI

ACCESS TO JUDICIAL PROCEEDINGS

Courtrooms and judicial records, of course, are no less important as sources of news than the other governmental meetings and records considered in the preceding chapter. We consider them separately in this chapter for several reasons. First, judicial proceedings and records invariably are exempted from statutory access schemes, making many of the access mechanisms discussed in the preceding chapter unavailable. Second, some of the conflicts that arise in this area implicate not only the First Amendment, but also the Sixth Amendment ("In all criminal prosecutions, the accused shall enjoy the right to a speedy and public trial, by an impartial jury of the State and district wherein the crime shall have been committed. . . ."). Finally, the litigation over access to judicial proceedings differs from other media access litigation in both quantity and quality. There is more of it, it is primarily constitutional rather than statutory, and the constitutional principles being developed in this area may not be fully applicable to nonjudicial access questions.

The rights of access to courts discussed in this chapter developed against a backdrop of assumptions about individual rights: that persons suspected of crime could not be arrested without charges, were entitled to a prompt judicial hearing, generally could not be detained without bail, were entitled to counsel, were presumed innocent, and were entitled to a trial that was speedy, public, and fair. Since September 11, 2001, these assumed rights have not been accorded to some classifications of suspected terrorists. Some of the issues considered in this chapter may seem trivial in comparison with the more fundamental questions raised by the terrorism cases. Likewise, the justifications for secrecy advanced in the wake of September 11 may seem to be of a different order than those considered in earlier cases. The extent to which the "war on terror" has changed the landscape with respect to secrecy in judicial proceedings remains to be seen. We assume that the principles developed in this chapter will provide at least the starting point for rights of access to judicial proceedings in the future. But as you consider these materials, you should evaluate the importance of the various claims of access in light of larger concerns about both individual rights and security.

In Chapter II we saw the courts' efforts to protect criminal defendants' fair trial rights. The *Sheppard* opinion, supra p. 111, was widely interpreted as a mandate to indirectly restrict news coverage before and during trials by restricting what the participants could tell the press. Trial judges issued orders restricting comment by attorneys and sometimes also by parties and witnesses, and bar associations promulgated rules limiting what attorneys were allowed to say. But as we saw in *Gentile*, supra p. 127, the free speech rights of attorneys and other participants limit the extent to which they can be silenced.

Moreover, the effort to control their disclosures was often ineffective. In sensational cases, the press invariably obtained information of the sort that the rules were designed to suppress. Information that police or prosecutors previously would have announced publicly now was leaked to the press and published without attribution. Defense lawyers responded to leaks of information adverse to their clients by leaking favorable information, and they sometimes initiated publicity battles themselves. Occasionally these episodes led to acrimonious battles in which judges attempted to force reporters to identify lawyers who had leaked information in violation of the rules, but as we saw in Chapter IX, these efforts to compel disclosure often fail. As violation of the rules became commonplace, attorneys frequently ignored them, even holding news conferences at which they discussed matters forbidden by the disciplinary rules.

When restraints on trial participants proved ineffective in preventing pretrial publicity, some judges responded by imposing direct restraints on the press itself, prohibiting publication of certain information thought to be especially prejudicial. The constitutionality of that strategy was dubious from the outset, however, and these doubts were quickly confirmed by *Nebraska Press Association v. Stuart,* supra p. 116. Although that case did not rule out the possibility that a prohibition against publication of prejudicial information might be permissible in some situations, the prerequisites it established are so demanding that "gag orders" against the press have become infrequent.

The ineffectiveness of attempts to restrict trial participants and the constitutional barriers to restricting publication left one obvious avenue open to judges seeking to prevent prejudicial publicity: deny the press access to the pretrial proceedings that often are a major source of such information. *Nebraska Press Association v. Stuart* had mentioned that possibility with apparent approval. Not surprisingly, the constitutionality of such closures was the next major area of litigation over press coverage of judicial proceedings. Because courts tend to view the issue of television coverage (and sometimes still photography) differently from the issue of pen-and-paper coverage, we deal first with issues arising from conventional coverage, and then with issues involving cameras.

A.   ACCESS TO COURTROOMS

1.   CRIMINAL PROCEEDINGS

Gannett Co. v. DePasquale. The first courtroom closure case to reach the Supreme Court was Gannett Co. v. DePasquale, 443 U.S. 368, 5 Med. L. Rptr. 1337 (1979). A judge in New York had barred the press and public from a pretrial hearing to determine whether confessions in a murder case should be suppressed on the ground they were involuntary. The publisher of the local newspaper challenged the closure on both First Amendment and Sixth Amendment grounds. The Court rejected the Sixth Amendment argument on the ground that that amendment guarantees a public trial to the defendant, not to the public. The Court did not decide whether the First Amendment created a right of access to the proceeding, but held that even if it did, the trial judge could properly determine that the right was outweighed in the circumstances of the case by the defendant's right to a fair trial. Justices Blackmun, Brennan, White, and Marshall dissented, arguing that the Sixth Amendment gives the public a qualified right of access to judicial proceedings and the accused had failed to make a sufficient showing of potential prejudice to overcome this qualified right.

The decision provoked outrage in the press and uncertainty among the lower courts at a time when many closures were being challenged. The next term the Court agreed to review another courtroom closure case. Although this case involved closure of the trial itself, rather than pretrial proceedings, it had implications for the latter as well, as we shall see in *Press-Enterprise Co. v. Superior Court (II),* infra p. 684.

a.   Trials

Richmond Newspapers, Inc. v. Virginia

Supreme Court of the United States, 1980.
448 U.S. 555, 100 S. Ct. 2814, 65 L. Ed.2d 973, 6 Med. L. Rptr. 1833.

[Stevenson was charged with murder. The first trial produced a conviction, but it was reversed because of improperly admitted evidence. The second and third ended in mistrials. At the beginning of Stevenson's fourth trial, his counsel moved to exclude the press and public, apparently primarily to prevent jurors from being influenced by news coverage of the trial. A state statute authorized the trial court "in its discretion, to exclude from the trial any persons whose presence would impair the conduct of a fair trial." The prosecutor did not object and the judge closed the courtroom, giving several reasons, including "the rights of the defendant" and the possibility that the presence of spectators would distract the jury. Appellant's reporters left but later in the day the newspaper unsuccessfully moved to vacate the closure order. The trial proceeded the next day behind closed doors and at the close of the prosecution's evidence the court struck the evidence, discharged the jury, and acquitted the defendant. The Virginia Supreme Court denied the newspaper's appeal.]

Chief Justice Burger announced the judgment of the Court and delivered an opinion in which Justice White and Justice Stevens joined.

The narrow question presented in this case is whether the right of the public and press to attend criminal trials is guaranteed under the United States Constitution.

. . .

II.

We begin consideration of this case by noting that the precise issue presented here has not previously been before this Court for decision. In [*Gannett*], the Court was not required to decide whether a right of access to trials, as distinguished from hearings on *pretrial* motions, was constitutionally guaranteed. . . .

A.

The origins of the proceeding which has become the modern criminal trial in Anglo–American justice can be traced back beyond reliable historical records. We need not here review all details of its development, but a summary of that history is instructive. What is significant for present purposes is that throughout its evolution, the trial has been open to all who cared to observe.

. . .

We have found nothing to suggest that the presumptive openness of the trial, which English courts were later to call "one of the essential qualities of a court of justice," [ ], was not also an attribute of the judicial systems of colonial America. . . .

. . .

. . . The early history of open trials in part reflects the widespread acknowledgement, long before there were behavioral scientists, that public trials had significant community therapeutic value. Even without such experts to frame the concept in words, people sensed from experience and observation that, especially in the administration of criminal justice, the means used to achieve justice must have the support derived from public acceptance of both the process and its results.

When a shocking crime occurs, a community reaction of outrage and public protest often follows. [ ] Thereafter the open processes of justice serve an important prophylactic purpose, providing an outlet for community concern, hostility, and emotion. Without an awareness that society's responses to criminal conduct are underway, natural human reactions of outrage and protest are frustrated and may manifest themselves in some form of vengeful "self-help," as indeed they did regularly in the activities of vigilante "committees" on our frontiers. . . .

. . .

In earlier times, both in England and America, attendance at court was a common mode of "passing the time." [ ] With the press, cinema, and electronic media now supplying the representations or reality of the real life drama once available only in the courtroom, attendance at court is no longer a widespread pastime. Yet "[i]t is not unrealistic even in this day to believe that public inclusion affords citizens a form of legal education and hopefully promotes confidence in the fair administration of justice." [ ] Instead of acquiring information about trials by firsthand observation or by word of mouth from those who attended, people now acquire it chiefly through the print and electronic media. In a sense, this validates the media claim of functioning as surrogates for the public. While media representatives enjoy the same right of access as the public, they often are provided special seating and priority of entry so that they may report what people in attendance have seen and heard. This "contribute[s] to public understanding of the rule of law and to comprehension of the functioning of the entire criminal justice system. . . ." *Nebraska Press Assn. v. Stuart,* [ ] (Brennan, J., concurring).

C.

From this unbroken, uncontradicted history, supported by reasons as valid today as in centuries past, we are bound to conclude that a presumption of openness inheres in the very nature of a criminal trial under our system of justice. This conclusion is hardly novel; without a direct holding on the issue, the Court has voiced its recognition of it in a variety of contexts over the years. . . .

Despite the history of criminal trials being presumptively open since long before the Constitution, the State presses its contention that neither the Constitution nor the Bill of Rights contains any provision which by its terms guarantees to the public the right to attend criminal trials. Standing alone, this is correct, but there remains the question whether, absent an explicit provision, the Constitution affords protection against exclusion of the public from criminal trials.

III.

. . .

The Bill of Rights was enacted against the backdrop of the long history of trials being presumptively open. Public access to trials was then regarded as an important aspect of the process itself; the conduct of trials "before as many of the people as chose to attend" was regarded as one of "the inestimable advantages of a free English constitution of government." [ ] In guaranteeing freedoms such as those of speech and press, the First Amendment can be read as protecting the right of everyone to attend trials so as to give meaning to those explicit guarantees. "[T]he First Amendment goes beyond protection of the press and the self-expression of individuals to prohibit government from limiting the stock of information from which members of the public may draw." First National Bank of Boston v. Bellotti, 435 U.S. 765, 783 (1978). Free speech carries with it some freedom to listen. "In a variety of contexts this Court has referred to a First Amendment right to 'receive information and ideas.' " [ ] What this means in the context of trials is that the First Amendment guarantees of speech and press, standing alone, prohibit government from summarily closing courtroom doors which had long been open to the public at the time that amendment was adopted. "For the First Amendment does not speak equivocally. . . . It must be taken as a command of the broadest scope that explicit language, read in the context of a liberty-loving society, will allow." [ ]

It is not crucial whether we describe this right to attend criminal trials to hear, see, and communicate observations concerning them as a "right of access," cf. *Gannett,* supra, at 672 (Powell, J., concurring); [*Saxbe* and *Pell*],[11] or a "right to gather information," for we have recognized that "without some protection for seeking out the news, freedom of the press could be eviscerated." *Branzburg v. Hayes,* [ ]. The explicit, guaranteed rights to speak and to publish concerning what takes place at a trial would lose much meaning if access to observe the trial could, as it was here, be foreclosed arbitrarily.[12]

B.

The right of access to places traditionally open to the public, as criminal trials have long been, may be seen as assured by the amalgam of the First Amendment guarantees of speech and press; and their affinity to the right of assembly is not without relevance. From the outset, the right of assembly was regarded not only as an independent right but also as a catalyst to augment the free exercise of the other First Amendment rights with which it was deliberately linked by the draftsmen. "The right of peaceable assembly is a right cognate to those of free speech and free press and is equally fundamental." [ ] People assemble in public places not only to speak or to take action, but also to listen, observe, and learn; indeed, they may "assembl[e] for any lawful purpose." [ ] Subject to the traditional time, place, and manner restrictions, [ ] streets, sidewalks, and parks are places traditionally open, where First Amendment rights may be exercised, [ ]; a trial courtroom also is a public place where the people generally—and representatives of the media—have a right to be present, and where their presence historically has been thought to enhance the integrity and quality of what takes place.

C.

. . .

We hold that the right to attend criminal trials[17] is implicit in the guarantees of the First Amendment; without the freedom to attend such

---

11. [*Pell*] and *Saxbe* are distinguishable in the sense that they were concerned with penal institutions which, by definition, are not "open" or public places. Penal institutions do not share the long tradition of openness, although traditionally there have been visiting committees of citizens, and there is no doubt that legislative committees could exercise plenary oversight and "visitation rights." *Saxbe* [ ] noted that "limitation on visitations is justified by what the Court of Appeals acknowledged as 'the truism that prisons are institutions where public access is generally limited.' . . ." [ ]

12. That the right to attend may be exercised by people less frequently today

when information as to trials generally reaches them by way of print and electronic media in no way alters the basic right. Instead of relying on personal observation or reports from neighbors as in the past, most people receive information concerning trials through the media whose representatives "are entitled to the same rights [to attend trials] as the general public." *Estes v. Texas,* 381 U.S. at 540, 85 S. Ct. at 1631.

17. Whether the public has a right to attend trials of civil cases is a question not raised by this case, but we note that historically both civil and criminal trials have been presumptively open.

trials, which people have exercised for centuries, important aspects of freedom of speech and "of the press could be eviscerated." *Branzburg,* [ ].

D.

Having concluded there was a guaranteed right of the public under the First and Fourteenth Amendments to attend the trial of Stevenson's case, we return to the closure order challenged by appellants. The Court in *Gannett* made clear that although the Sixth Amendment guarantees the accused a right to a public trial, it does not give a right to a private trial. [ ] Despite the fact that this was the fourth trial of the accused, the trial judge made no findings to support closure; no inquiry was made as to whether alternative solutions would have met the need to ensure fairness; there was no recognition of any right under the Constitution for the public or press to attend the trial. In contrast to the pretrial proceeding dealt with in *Gannett,* supra, there exist in the context of the trial itself various tested alternatives to satisfy the constitutional demands of fairness. See, e.g., *Nebraska Press Association v. Stuart,* [ ]; *Sheppard v. Maxwell,* [ ]. There was no suggestion that any problems with witnesses could not have been dealt with by their exclusion from the courtroom or their sequestration during the trial. [ ] Nor is there anything to indicate that sequestration of the jurors would not have guarded against their being subjected to any improper information. All of the alternatives admittedly present difficulties for trial courts, but none of the factors relied on here was beyond the realm of the manageable. Absent an overriding interest articulated in findings, the trial of a criminal case must be open to the public.[18] Accordingly, the judgment under review is reversed.

Reversed.

JUSTICE POWELL took no part in the consideration or decision of this case.

JUSTICE WHITE, concurring.

This case would have been unnecessary had *Gannett* [ ] construed the Sixth Amendment to forbid excluding the public from criminal proceedings except in narrowly defined circumstances. But the Court there rejected the

---

18. We have no occasion here to define the circumstances in which all or parts of a criminal trial may be closed to the public. [ ] [O]ur holding today does not mean that the First Amendment rights of the public and representatives of the press are absolute. Just as a government may impose reasonable time, place, and manner restrictions upon the use of its streets in the interest of such objectives as the free flow of traffic, see, e.g., Cox v. New Hampshire, 312 U.S. 569 (1941), so may a trial judge, in the interest of the fair administration of justice, impose reasonable limitations on access to a trial. "[T]he question in a particular case is whether that control is exerted so as not to deny or unwarrantedly abridge . . . the opportunities for the communication of thought and the discussion of public questions immemorially associated with resort to public places." Id., at 574. It is far more important that trials be conducted in a quiet and orderly setting than it is to preserve that atmosphere on city streets. [ ] Moreover, since courtrooms have limited capacity, there may be occasions when not every person who wishes to attend can be accommodated. In such situations, reasonable restrictions on general access are traditionally imposed, including preferential seating for media representatives. [ ]

submission of four of us to this effect, thus requiring that the First Amendment issue involved here be addressed. On this issue, I concur in the opinion of The Chief Justice.

JUSTICE STEVENS, concurring.

This is a watershed case. Until today the Court has accorded virtually absolute protection to the dissemination of information or ideas, but never before has it squarely held that the acquisition of newsworthy matter is entitled to any constitutional protection whatsoever. An additional word of emphasis is therefore appropriate.

Twice before, the Court has implied that any governmental restriction on access to information, no matter how severe and no matter how unjustified, would be constitutionally acceptable so long as it did not single out the press for special disabilities not applicable to the public at large. [Discussing *Saxbe* and *Houchins*] Today, however, for the first time, the Court unequivocally holds that an arbitrary interference with access to important information is an abridgment of the freedoms of speech and of the press protected by the First Amendment.

. . .

JUSTICE BRENNAN, with whom JUSTICE MARSHALL joins, concurring in the judgment.

[Deciding when the First Amendment requires access to a courtroom] is as much a matter of sensitivity to practical necessities as it is of abstract reasoning. But at least two helpful principles may be sketched. First, the case for a right of access has special force when drawn from an enduring and vital tradition of public entree to particular proceedings or information. [ ] Such a tradition commands respect in part because the Constitution carries the gloss of history. More importantly, a tradition of accessibility implies the favorable judgment of experience. Second, the value of access must be measured in specifics. Analysis is not advanced by rhetorical statements that all information bears upon public issues; what is crucial in individual cases is whether access to a particular government process is important in terms of that very process.

To resolve the case before us, therefore, we must consult historical and current practice with respect to open trials, and weigh the importance of public access to the trial process itself.

II.

[Justice Brennan agreed with Chief Justice Burger that open trials were the practice, historically and currently, throughout the country.]

III.

Publicity serves to advance several of the particular purposes of the trial (and, indeed, the judicial) process. Open trials play a fundamental role in furthering the efforts of our judicial system to assure the criminal defendant a fair and accurate adjudication of guilt or innocence. [ ] But, as a feature of our governing system of justice, the trial process serves other, broadly political, interests, and public access advances these objectives as well. To that extent, trial access possesses specific structural significance.

The trial is a means of meeting "the notion, deeply rooted in the common law, that 'justice must satisfy the appearance of justice.' " . . .

Secrecy is profoundly inimical to this demonstrative purpose of the trial process. Open trials assure the public that procedural rights are respected, and that justice is afforded equally. Closed trials breed suspicion of prejudice and arbitrariness, which in turn spawns disrespect for law. Public access is essential, therefore, if trial adjudication is to achieve the objective of maintaining public confidence in the administration of justice. [ ]

But the trial is more than a demonstrably just method of adjudicating disputes and protecting rights. It plays a pivotal role in the entire judicial process, and, by extension, in our form of government. Under our system, judges are not mere umpires, but, in their own sphere, lawmakers—a coordinate branch of *government.* While individual cases turn upon the controversies between parties, or involve particular prosecutions, court rulings impose official and practical consequences upon members of society at large. Moreover, judges bear responsibility for the vitally important task of construing and securing constitutional rights. Thus, so far as the trial is the mechanism for judicial factfinding, as well as the initial forum for legal decisionmaking, it is a genuine governmental proceeding.

It follows that the conduct of the trial is preeminently a matter of public interest. [ ] More importantly, public access to trials acts as an important check, akin in purpose to the other checks and balances that infuse our system of government. "The knowledge that every criminal trial is subject to contemporaneous review in the forum of public opinion is an effective restraint on possible abuse of judicial power," [ ] an abuse that, in many cases, would have ramifications beyond the impact upon the parties before the court. Indeed " '[w]ithout publicity, all other checks are insufficient: in comparison of publicity, all other checks are of small account.' " [ ]

Finally, with some limitations, a trial aims at true and accurate factfinding. Of course, proper factfinding is to the benefit of criminal defendants and of the parties in civil proceedings. But other, comparably urgent, interests are also often at stake. A miscarriage of justice that imprisons an innocent accused also leaves a guilty party at large, a continuing threat to society. Also, mistakes of fact in civil litigation may inflict costs upon others than the plaintiff and defendant. Facilitation of the trial factfinding process, therefore, is of concern to the public as well as to the parties.

Publicizing trial proceedings aids accurate factfinding. "Public trials come to the attention of key witnesses unknown to the parties." . . .

Popular attendance at trials, in sum, substantially furthers the particular public purposes of that critical judicial proceeding. In that sense, public access is an indispensable element of the trial process itself. Trial access, therefore, assumes structural importance in our "government of laws" [ ].

IV.

. . . What countervailing interests might be sufficiently compelling to reverse this presumption of openness need not concern us now, for the statute at stake here authorizes trial closures at the unfettered discretion of the judge and parties. Accordingly, Va. Code 19.2–266 violates the First and Fourteenth Amendments, and the decision of the Virginia Supreme Court to the contrary should be reversed.

JUSTICE STEWART, concurring in the judgment.

. . .

Whatever the ultimate answer . . . may be with respect to pretrial suppression hearings in criminal cases, the First and Fourteenth Amendments clearly give the press and the public a right of access to trials themselves, civil as well as criminal. . . .

In conspicuous contrast to a military base, [ ]; a jail, [ ]; or a prison, [ ]; a trial courtroom is a public place. Even more than city streets, sidewalks, and parks as areas of traditional First Amendment activity, [ ] a trial courtroom is a place where representatives of the press and of the public are not only free to be, but where their presence serves to assure the integrity of what goes on.

. . .

[JUSTICE BLACKMUN, concurring in the judgment, argued that the right of public access to trials should be found in the Sixth Amendment, as he had urged in *Gannett*, but agreed, "as a secondary position, that the First Amendment must provide some measure of protection for public access to the trial."]

JUSTICE REHNQUIST, dissenting.

. . .

The issue here is not whether the "right" to freedom of the press conferred by the First Amendment to the Constitution overrides the defendant's "right" to a fair trial conferred by other amendments to the Constitution; it is instead whether any provision in the Constitution may fairly be read to prohibit what the trial judge in the Virginia state court system did in this case. Being unable to find any such prohibition in the First, Sixth, Ninth, or any other Amendments to the United States Constitution, or in the Constitution itself, I dissent.

Notes and Questions

1. To the extent that the decision turns on the tradition of open courtrooms it provides little support for a First Amendment right of access to other proceedings or institutions that either have no extended history or traditionally have been closed. How many of the Justices would find a right of access even in the absence of a tradition of openness?

2. How valuable is a principle that protects rights under the First Amendment if they traditionally existed in practice?

3. Are Justice Brennan's reasons for concluding that public attendance furthers the public purposes of trials any less applicable to attendance at other types of governmental meetings?

4. Chief Justice Burger and Justices Stewart and Stevens were in the majority in both *Gannett* and *Richmond Newspapers*. Do their opinions here succeed in distinguishing the two cases?

———

Globe Newspaper Co. v. Superior Court. The next Supreme Court case on access to trials involved a Massachusetts statute that had been interpreted to require that the courtroom be closed during the testimony of minor victims of sexual offenses. A majority concurred in an opinion by Justice Brennan striking the statute. Globe Newspaper Co. v. Superior Court, 457 U.S. 596, 8 Med. L. Rptr. 1689 (1982). Even though trials involving sexual offenses or other sensational aspects had frequently been closed, the "history of openness" criterion of *Richmond Newspapers* was satisfied. The critical question was not the historical openness of a particular type of trial but rather the "state interests assertedly supporting the restriction." To deny access, "it must be shown that the denial is necessitated by a compelling governmental interest, and is narrowly tailored to serve that interest."

In this case those reasons—to protect the victim from further trauma and to encourage such victims to come forward—did not suffice. Although safeguarding the physical and psychological well-being of minors is a compelling state interest, it did not justify mandatory closure. This is best done on a case-by-case basis in which the trial judge considers such matters as the age of the victim, the victim's maturity, the nature of the crime, the desires of the victim, and the interests of parents and relatives. In the case before the Court, for example, the victims were 16 and 17, and may have been willing to testify in public. In deciding whether to close the courtroom, the trial judge might explore the issues in an in camera proceeding.

The state's interest in encouraging victims to come forward did not suffice because the state presented no support for the claim that automatic closure would achieve that result. The Court doubted the connection because the statute only barred public attendance in court—it did not bar press access to the transcript or other ways in which the press might learn and report what occurred in the closed courtroom. Even if the state's interest was effectively advanced by automatic closure, "it is doubtful that the interest would be sufficient to overcome the constitutional attack, for that same interest could be relied on to support an array of mandatory closure rules designed to encourage victims to come forward." To assert that closure would get more victims of all crimes to come forward and encourage more candid testimony would run contrary to "the very foundation of the right of access recognized in *Richmond Newspapers*."

Chief Justice Burger, joined by Justice Rehnquist, dissented on the merits. They stressed the lack of a history of openness in this type of case and that the statute need not be "precisely tailored so long as the state's interest overrides the law's impact on First Amendment rights and the restrictions imposed further that interest." Since the statute only barred access during the victim's testimony and rationally served the state's overriding interest in avoiding serious psychological damage, they would have upheld the statute. They also feared the effect on parents of learning that their child might have to undergo an in camera hearing before it could be known whether the trial would be closed during the child's testimony. The statute had a "relatively minor incidental impact on First Amendment rights and gives effect to the overriding state interest in protecting child rape victims. Paradoxically, the Court today denies the victims the kind of protection routinely given to juveniles who commit crimes."

Justice Stevens dissented on the ground that the order under review was too abstract for decision.

Voir dire. The questioning of prospective jurors is an important part of criminal trials, of course, but judges sometimes believe that part of the trial can be closed even if the rest of the trial has to be open, in the interest of protecting prospective jurors' privacy or encouraging them to answer probing questions candidly. The Supreme Court has given little support to that view. See Press–Enterprise Co. v. Superior Court, 464 U.S. 501, 10 Med. L. Rptr. 1161 (1984) (*Press-Enterprise I*).

In that case, a black defendant was charged with the rape and murder of a white teenage girl in California. When a newspaper sought access to the voir dire, the state objected on the ground that juror responses would lack the candor needed in such a case. The trial judge closed all but three days of the six-week voir dire. When the newspaper sought the transcript of the voir dire, both the state and the defense objected on the ground that this would violate the jurors' right to privacy because they had answered sensitive questions under an "implied promise of confidentiality." After the trial was over, the judge continued to refuse to release the transcript.

The Supreme Court unanimously reversed. Chief Justice Burger observed that the "primacy of the accused's right is difficult to separate from the right of everyone in the community to attend the *voir dire* which promotes fairness." The standard created, building upon language from the *Globe* case, was:

> The presumption of openness may be overcome only by an overriding interest based on findings that closure is essential to preserve higher values and is narrowly tailored to serve that interest. The interest is to be articulated along with findings specific enough that a reviewing court can determine whether the closure order was properly entered.

The trial judge had made no findings and had not considered whether alternatives to closure might have worked. The Court did recognize that when interrogation touches on "deeply personal matters" a juror may have a compelling interest in privacy. Such concern might be met by informing jurors in advance that they may request a meeting in chambers with the judge and counsel and a court reporter if something potentially embarrassing comes up during voir dire. If necessary, that part of the transcript might be sealed, but the rest would be open.

Nevertheless, in exceptional circumstances courts continue to approve the closing of voir dire. In U.S. v. King, 140 F.3d 76, 26 Med. L. Rptr. 1449 (2d Cir. 1998), the court approved the trial judge's closure of voir dire to promote candor by prospective jurors in a racially charged criminal trial involving boxing promoter Don King. The judge found that jurors' knowledge that their answers might be reported in the press "may so inhibit or chill truthful responses that [the] accused is denied the fair trial to which he is entitled." A 2–1 majority of the court of appeals distinguished *Press-Enterprise I* on the ground that it was concerned merely with protecting the privacy interests of jurors, while the interest in the *King* case was the defendant's right to a fair trial. The majority said the trial judge's findings were sufficient to support closure. "[T]his is that unusual case where the fairness of a trial, or at least the voir dire phase, that is usually promoted by public access is seriously at risk of being impaired unless some modest limitation of access is imposed." The dissenter said:

> These findings hardly distinguish this case from many high-profile cases tried in federal district courts across this country every year. Were mere notoriety to be deemed a sufficient basis for courtroom closure, the broad presumption of openness established by the Supreme Court in *Press-Enterprise I* would soon lose all force. Indeed, it is precisely in those cases involving controversial or notorious defendants that the public—and its media proxies—are likely to take an interest in criminal proceedings. It would be perverse to enshrine a constitutional right of public access to criminal proceedings, and then to enforce that right only in cases in which the public has no interest.

The same court later made clear that encouraging jurors to be candid can justify closing voir dire only in unusual circumstances. In the trial of Martha Stewart for securities law violations, the trial judge conducted part of the voir dire in chambers and excluded the press on the ground that some prospective jurors might not give full and frank answers for fear that their responses would be publicly disclosed. The judge believed that *U.S. v. King* authorized her to do so. But the Court of Appeals said "In *King*, the voir dire explored the racial views of potential jurors; given the prevailing national consensus concerning the evils of racism, the district judge recognized that potential jurors were unlikely to admit openly to harboring racist views. No similarly sensitive or contentious lines of questioning were here identified by the district court." See ABC Inc. v. Stewart, 360 F.3d 90, 32 Med. L. Rptr. 1385 (2d Cir. 2004).

The fear that prospective jurors would not be candid about racial prejudice was also invoked by the Fourth Circuit in a political corruption case in South Carolina. The case involved state legislators charged with extortion, and some of the defendants claimed that a disproportionate number of black legislators were among those targeted by the federal sting operation. Prospective jurors were being closely questioned about possible racial prejudice. The media suggested that sensitive questions could be handled in sidebar conferences with the judge and lawyers, or that jurors could be identified only by number. The judge said sidebar conferences would only attract more attention to the jurors who felt uncomfortable answering certain questions, and even if jurors were identified only by number they would still be aware of the press in the courtroom.

The court of appeals agreed that "under the very unusual circumstances of these cases, no reasonable alternatives to closure will adequately protect the fair trial rights of the defendants." In re South Carolina Press Association, 946 F.2d 1037, 19 Med. L. Rptr. 1432 (4th Cir. 1991). The "unusual circumstances" may have included the fact that trial judge, in advance of voir dire, had sent prospective jurors an 18–page questionnaire that promised recipients their responses would be confidential. The judge said questioning would undoubtedly refer to the questionnaire responses, and if the press were present jurors would be understandably skeptical of further promises, such as assurances that they would be identified only by number. *Globe Newspaper* requires that the press and public be given an opportunity to be heard on the question of exclusion, and the judge in the South Carolina case had sent out the questionnaires before any notice or hearing had been given. In a footnote, the court of appeals said judges in the future should observe the notice requirement before sending out such questionnaires.

Is juror candor a more "overriding" interest than juror privacy? Recall that the objective of encouraging jurors' candor was also asserted in *Press Enterprise I*. Is candor the ultimate reason for protecting jurors' privacy? Is the defendant's right to a fair trial the ultimate reason for encouraging candor?

b.   Pretrial Proceedings

In *Richmond Newspapers* the Court seemed to draw a sharp line between the criminal trial itself and pretrial hearings. In the following case the Court returned to the question of a First Amendment right of access to pretrial proceedings.

Press–Enterprise Co. v. Superior Court (II)
Supreme Court of the United States, 1986.
478 U.S. 1, 106 S.Ct. 2735, 92 L.Ed.2d 1, 13 Med.L.Rptr. 1001.

[Robert Diaz, a nurse, was charged with murdering 12 patients by administering a lethal drug. He exercised his right under California law to have a preliminary hearing, rather than grand jury proceedings, to determine whether he should be made to stand trial. He moved to exclude the press and public under a statute that gave him an unqualified right to have a closed hearing. The hearing lasted 41 days and Diaz was bound over for trial on all charges. After the hearing ended the prosecution and the Press–

Enterprise moved to release transcripts of the closed hearing. Diaz objected and the California courts refused to release the transcripts. Later Diaz waived his right to jury trial and the trial court released the transcript. The Supreme Court held that this did not moot the case because the issue was likely to recur and otherwise was likely to evade review.]

CHIEF JUSTICE BURGER delivered the opinion of the Court.

We granted certiorari to decide whether petitioner has a First Amendment right of access to transcripts of a preliminary hearing growing out of a criminal prosecution.

. . .

. . . The California Supreme Court concluded that the First Amendment was not implicated because the proceeding was not a criminal trial, but a preliminary hearing. However, the First Amendment question cannot be resolved solely on the label we give the event, i.e., "trial" or otherwise, particularly where the preliminary hearing functions much like a full scale trial.

In cases dealing with the claim of a First Amendment right of access to criminal proceedings, our decisions have emphasized two complementary considerations. First, because a " 'tradition of accessibility implies the favorable judgment of experience' " [ ] we have considered whether the place and process has historically been open to the press and general public.

. . .

Second, in this setting the Court has traditionally considered whether public access plays a significant positive role in the functioning of the particular process in question. [ ] Although many governmental processes operate best under public scrutiny, it takes little imagination to recognize that there are some kinds of government operations that would be totally frustrated if conducted openly. A classic example is that "the proper functioning of our grand jury system depends upon the secrecy of grand jury proceedings." Douglas Oil Co. v. Petrol Stops Northwest, 441 U.S. 211, 218 (1979). Other proceedings plainly require public access. In *Press-Enterprise I*, we summarized the holdings of prior cases, noting that openness in criminal trials, including the selection of jurors, "enhances both the basic fairness of the criminal trial and the appearance of fairness so essential to public confidence in the system." [ ]

These considerations of experience and logic are, of course, related, for history and experience shape the functioning of governmental processes. If the particular proceeding in question passes these tests of experience and logic, a qualified First Amendment right of public access attaches. But even when a right of access attaches, it is not absolute. [ ] While open criminal proceedings give assurances of fairness to both the public and the accused, there are some limited circumstances in which the right of the accused to a fair trial might be undermined by publicity.[2] In such cases, the trial court must determine whether the situation is such that the rights of the accused override the qualified First Amendment right of access. . . .

IV

A

The considerations that led the Court to apply the First Amendment right of access to criminal trials in *Richmond Newspapers* and *Globe* and the selection of jurors in *Press-Enterprise I* lead us to conclude that the right of access applies to preliminary hearings as conducted in California.

First, there has been a tradition of accessibility to preliminary hearings of the type conducted in California. Although grand jury proceedings have traditionally been closed to the public and the accused, preliminary hearings conducted before neutral and detached magistrates have been open to the public. Long ago in the celebrated trial of Aaron Burr for treason, for example, with Chief Justice Marshall sitting as trial judge, the probable cause hearing was held in the Hall of the House of Delegates in Virginia, the court room being too small to accommodate the crush of interested citizens. United States v. Burr, 25 F. Cas. 1 (CC Va.1807) (No. 14,692). From *Burr* until the present day, the near uniform practice of state and federal courts has been to conduct preliminary hearings in open court.[3] As we noted in *Gannett*, several states following the original New York Field Code of Criminal Procedure published in 1850 have allowed preliminary hearings to be closed on the motion of the accused. [ ] But even in these states the proceedings are presumptively open to the public and are closed only for cause shown. Open preliminary hearings, therefore, have been accorded " 'the favorable judgment of experience.' " [ ]

The second question is whether public access to preliminary hearings as they are conducted in California plays a particularly significant positive role in the actual functioning of the process. We have already determined in *Richmond Newspapers, Globe,* and *Press-Enterprise I* that public access to criminal trials and the selection of jurors is essential to the proper functioning of the criminal justice system. California preliminary hearings are sufficiently like a trial to justify the same conclusion.

In California, to bring a felon to trial, the prosecutor has a choice of securing a grand jury indictment or a finding of probable cause following a preliminary hearing. Even when the accused has been indicted by a grand jury, however, he has an absolute right to an elaborate preliminary hearing before a neutral magistrate. [ ] The accused has the right to personally appear at the hearing, to be represented by counsel, to cross-examine hostile witnesses, to present exculpatory evidence, and to exclude illegally

---

2. Similarly, the interests of those other than the accused may be implicated. The protection of victims of sex crimes from the trauma and embarrassment of public scrutiny may justify closing certain aspects of a criminal proceeding. [ ]

3. The vast majority of States considering the issue have concluded that the same tradition of accessibility that applies to criminal trials applies to preliminary proceedings. [ ]

obtained evidence. [ ] If the magistrate determines that probable cause exists, the accused is bound over for trial; such a finding leads to a guilty plea in the majority of cases.

It is true that unlike a criminal trial, the California preliminary hearing cannot result in the conviction of the accused and the adjudication is before a magistrate or other judicial officer without a jury. But these features, standing alone, do not make public access any less essential to the proper functioning of the proceedings in the overall criminal justice process. Because of its extensive scope, the preliminary hearing is often the final and most important step in the criminal proceeding. [ ] As the California Supreme Court stated in San Jose Mercury–News v. Municipal Court, 30 Cal.3d 498, 511, 638 P.2d 655, 663 (1982), the preliminary hearing in many cases provides "the sole occasion for public observation of the criminal justice system." [ ]

Similarly, the absence of a jury, long recognized as "an inestimable safeguard against the corrupt or overzealous prosecutor and against the compliant, biased, or eccentric judge," Duncan v. Louisiana, 391 U.S. 145, 156 (1968), makes the importance of public access to a preliminary hearing even more significant. "People in an open society do not demand infallibility from their institutions, but it is difficult for them to accept what they are prohibited from observing." [*Richmond Newspapers*]

Denying the transcripts of a 41–day preliminary hearing would frustrate what we have characterized as the "community therapeutic value" of openness. [ ] Criminal acts, especially certain violent crimes, provoke public concern, outrage, and hostility. "When the public is aware that the law is being enforced and the criminal justice system is functioning, an outlet is provided for these understandable reactions and emotions." [ ] In sum,

> "The value of openness lies in the fact that people not actually attending trials can have confidence that standards of fairness are being observed; the sure knowledge that *anyone* is free to attend gives assurance that established procedures are being followed and that deviations will become known. Openness thus enhances both the basic fairness of the criminal trial and the appearance of fairness so essential to public confidence in the system." Press–Enterprise I, 464 U.S., at 508. (emphasis in original).

We therefore conclude that the qualified First Amendment right of access to criminal proceedings applies to preliminary hearings as they are conducted in California.

B

Since a qualified First Amendment right of access attaches to preliminary hearings in California [ ], the proceedings cannot be closed unless specific, on the record findings are made demonstrating that "closure is essential to preserve higher values and is narrowly tailored to serve that interest." [ ] If the interest asserted is the right of the accused to a fair trial, the preliminary hearing shall be closed only if specific findings are made demonstrating that first, there is a substantial probability that the defendant's right to a fair trial will be prejudiced by publicity that closure would prevent and, second, reasonable alternatives to closure cannot adequately protect the defendant's fair trial rights. [ ]

The California Supreme Court, interpreting its access statute, concluded "that the magistrate shall close the preliminary hearing upon finding a reasonable likelihood of substantial prejudice." [ ] As the court itself acknowledged, the "reasonable likelihood" test places a lesser burden on the defendant than the "substantial probability" test which we hold is called for by the First Amendment. [ ] Moreover, the court failed to consider whether alternatives short of complete closure would have protected the interests of the accused.

In *Gannett* we observed that:

> "Publicity concerning pretrial suppression hearings such as the one involved in the present case poses special risks of unfairness. The whole purpose of such hearings is to screen out unreliable or illegally obtained evidence and insure that this evidence does not become known to the jury. Cf. Jackson v. Denno, 378 U.S. 368. Publicity concerning the proceedings at a pretrial hearing, however, could influence public opinion against a defendant and inform potential jurors of inculpatory information wholly inadmissible at the actual trial." [ ]

But this risk of prejudice does not automatically justify refusing public access to hearings on every motion to suppress. Through voir dire, cumbersome as it is in some circumstances, a court can identify those jurors whose prior knowledge of the case would disable them from rendering an impartial verdict. And even if closure were justified for the hearings on a motion to suppress, closure of an entire 41-day proceeding would rarely be warranted. The First Amendment right of access cannot be overcome by the conclusory assertion that publicity might deprive the defendant of [the right to a fair trial]. And any limitation " 'must be narrowly tailored to serve that interest.' " [ ]

The standard applied by the California Supreme Court failed to consider the First Amendment right of access to criminal proceedings. Accordingly, the judgment of the California Supreme Court is reversed.

Justice Stevens, with whom Justice Rehnquist joins as to Part II, dissenting.

. . .

I have long believed that a proper construction of the First Amendment embraces a right of access to information about the conduct of public affairs [quoting from Justice Stevens's dissent in *Houchins*].

. . .

But it has always been apparent that the freedom to obtain information that the Government has a legitimate interest in not disclosing, [ ], is far narrower than the freedom to disseminate information, which is "virtually absolute" in most contexts, [*Richmond Newspapers*, (Stevens, J., concurring)]. In this case, the risk of prejudice to the defendant's right to a fair trial is perfectly obvious. For me, that risk is far more significant than the countervailing interest in publishing the transcript of the preliminary hearing sooner rather than later. Cf. [*Gannett*] (upholding closure of suppression hearing in part because "any denial of access in this case was not absolute but only temporary"). The interest in prompt publication—in my view—is no greater than the interest in prompt publication of grand jury transcripts. As explained more fully below, we have always recognized the legitimacy of the governmental interest in the secrecy of grand jury proceedings, and I am unpersuaded that the difference between such proceedings and the rather elaborate procedure for determining probable cause that California has adopted strengthens the First Amendment claim to access asserted in this case.

II

The Court nevertheless reaches the opposite conclusion by applying the "two complementary considerations" [ ] of "experience and logic" [ ]. In my view, neither the Court's reasoning nor the result it reaches is supported by our precedents.

The historical evidence proffered in this case is far less probative than the evidence adduced in prior cases granting public access to criminal proceedings. In those cases, a common law tradition of openness at the time the First Amendment was ratified suggested an intention and expectation on the part of the Framers and ratifiers that those proceedings would remain presumptively open. Thus, in [*Richmond Newspapers*] The Chief Justice explained that "[w]hat is significant for present purposes is that throughout its evolution, the trial has been open to all who cared to observe." "[T]he historical evidence demonstrates conclusively that *at the time when our organic laws were adopted,* criminal trials both here and in England had long been presumptively open." [ ] (emphasis added). . . .

In this case, however, it is uncontroverted that a common law right of access did not inhere in preliminary proceedings at the time the First Amendment was adopted, and that the Framers and ratifiers of that provision could not have intended such proceedings to remain open. As Justice Stewart wrote for the Court in [*Gannett*]:

> "[T]here exists no persuasive evidence that at common law members of the public had any right to attend pretrial proceedings; indeed, there is substantial evidence to the contrary. By the time of the adoption of the Constitution . . . pretrial proceedings, precisely because of the . . . concern for a fair trial, were never characterized by the same degree of openness as were actual trials. . . ."

. . .

In the final analysis, the Court's lengthy historical disquisition demonstrates only that in many States preliminary proceedings are generally open to the public. . . . The recent common law developments reported by the Court are relevant, if at all, only insofar as they suggest that preliminary proceedings merit the "beneficial effects of public scrutiny." [*Cox Broadcasting*] The Court's historical crutch cannot carry the weight of opening a preliminary proceeding that the State has ordered closed; that determination must stand or fall on whether it satisfies the second component of the Court's test.

If the Court's historical evidence proves too little, the "value of openness," [ ] on which it relies proves too much, for this measure would open to public scrutiny far more than preliminary hearings "as they are conducted in California" (a comforting phrase invoked by the Court in one form or another more than 8 times in its opinion).[7] In brief, the Court's rationale for opening the "California preliminary hearing" is that it "is often the final and most important step in the criminal proceeding"; that it provides " 'the sole occasion for public observation of the criminal justice system' "; that it lacks the protective presence of a jury; and that closure denies an outlet for community catharsis. [ ] The obvious defect in the Court's approach is that its reasoning applies to the traditionally secret grand jury with as much force as it applies to California preliminary hearings. A grand jury indictment is just as likely to be the "final step" in a criminal proceeding and the "sole occasion" for public scrutiny as is a preliminary hearing. Moreover, many critics of the grand jury maintain that the grand jury protects the accused less well than does a legally-knowledgeable judge who personally presides over a preliminary hearing. [ ] Finally, closure of grand juries denies an outlet for community rage. When the Court's explanatory veneer is stripped away, what emerges is the reality that the California preliminary hearing is functionally identical to the traditional grand jury. . . .

The Court's reasoning—if carried to its logical outcome—thus contravenes the "long-established policy that maintains the secrecy of the grand jury proceedings in the federal courts" and in the courts of 19 States. . . .

In fact, the logic of the Court's access right extends even beyond the confines of the criminal justice system to encompass proceedings held on the civil side of the docket as well. . . . Despite the Court's valiant attempt to limit the logic of its holding, the ratio decidendi of today's decision knows no bounds.

By abjuring strict reliance on history and emphasizing the broad value of openness, the Court tacitly recognizes the importance of public access to government proceedings generally. Regrettably, the Court has taken seriously the stated requirement that the sealing of a transcript be justified by

---

7. Given the Court's focus on the history of preliminary proceedings in general, and its reliance on the broad values served by openness, [ ], I do not see the relevance of the fact that preliminary proceedings in California bear an outward resemblance to criminal trials. To the extent that it matters that in California "[t]he accused has the right to personally appear at the hearing, to be represented by counsel, to cross-examine hostile witnesses, to present exculpatory evidence, and to exclude illegally obtained evidence," [ ] it bears mention that many other States have reformed their grand juries to include one or more of these procedural reforms [ ]. After today's decision, one can only wonder whether the public enjoys a right of access to any or all of these proceedings as well.

a "compelling" or "overriding" governmental interest and that the closure order be "narrowly tailored to serve that interest." . . . The cases denying access have done so on a far lesser showing than that required by a compelling governmental interest/least restrictive-means analysis, [ ], and cases granting access have recognized as legitimate grounds for closure interests that fall far short of those traditionally thought to be "compelling" [ ].

The presence of a legitimate reason for closure in this case requires an affirmance. The constitutionally-grounded fair trial interests of the accused if he is bound over for trial, and the reputational interests of the accused if he is not, provide a substantial reason for delaying access to the transcript for at least the short time before trial. By taking its own verbal formulation seriously, the Court reverses—without comment or explanation or any attempt at reconciliation—the holding in *Gannett* that a "reasonable probability of prejudice" is enough to overcome the First Amendment right of access to a preliminary proceeding. It is unfortunate that the Court neglects this opportunity to fit the result in this case into the body of precedent dealing with access rights generally. I fear that today's decision will simply further unsettle the law in this area.

I respectfully dissent.

Notes and Questions

1. What is the status of the *Gannett* case after this case?

2. Does this sequence concerning access to the courtroom suggest any doubt about the cases denying access to prisons and jails?

3. Is the balancing analysis prescribed by this case the same as that set out in *Press-Enterprise I?* In *Globe Newspaper?* Is Chief Justice Burger suggesting that some different analysis might be appropriate if the interest asserted is something other than the defendant's right to a fair trial?

4. The importance of the preliminary hearing procedure in California, much emphasized by the majority in *Press-Enterprise II,* was diminished significantly in 1990 by passage of a voter initiative that made the procedure less attractive to defendants and denied them the option in some cases.

"A tradition of openness." Just what role does this requirement play? Does this decision apply only to proceedings where there is both (1) a history of openness and (2) reason to believe access would play "a significant positive role in the functioning of the process in question"? What about new types of proceedings that have no history of either openness or closure? What if the history is one of closure, but the court believes openness would be beneficial? Most of these questions remain unanswered. It does appear, however, that the requirement is not to be taken too

literally. In El Vocero de Puerto Rico v. Puerto Rico, 508 U.S. 147, 21 Med. L. Rptr. 1440 (1993), the Court struck down a rule closing preliminary hearings unless the defendant requests an open hearing. Puerto Rico pointed out that the tradition of openness cited in *Globe Newspaper* and *Press-Enterprise II* had never existed in Puerto Rico. The Court said what matters is not the experience of any one jurisdiction, but "the established and widespread tradition of open preliminary hearings among the States."

Few courtroom closures survive the scrutiny demanded by these precedents, even in situations where the reasons for closure seem tenable. For example, in two New York cases judges closed courtrooms to conceal the identity of undercover drug agents. The New York Court of Appeals upheld the closing in one case because the officer testified that she regularly operated in a specific area near the courthouse and would return to work that very day. In the other case the court said the closing was unjustified because the officer's description of the territory he worked was more general ("the Bronx area") and his reasons for requesting closure were "unparticularized impressions of the vicissitudes of undercover narcotics work." See People v. Martinez, 82 N.Y.2d 436, 604 N.Y.S.2d 932, 624 N.E.2d 1027, 22 Med. L. Rptr. 1148 (1993). Are there any types of situations in which closure ought to be presumptively justified?

c. Terrorism cases

After September 11, 2001, the government claimed a need to conduct numerous criminal proceedings in secret, presumably reasoning that the *Richmond Newspapers* line of cases created a presumption of openness which could be overcome by the need to deny potential terrorists information they might learn through public proceedings. The government not only sought to exclude the press and public from courtrooms, but in some cases held suspects incommunicado and kept secret the fact that they had been arrested.

In one case an Algerian named Mohamed Kamel Bellahouel, who had come to the U.S. as a student, married an American citizen, and overstayed his visa, was imprisoned in Miami, apparently because he had been seen with three of the September 11 hijackers. He filed a petition for habeas corpus in federal district court. For more than a year, there was no public record that the case even existed—all pleadings were sealed, every hearing was conducted in a closed courtroom, and no mention of the case was made on any docket. After 18 months, a local reporter discovered the existence of the case when a clerk at the Eleventh Circuit inadvertently allowed Bellahouel's name to appear briefly on the court's argument calendar. The case remained sealed even after the reporter published a story about it. When Bellahouel petitioned the Supreme Court for certiorari, the case was docketed as "M.K.B. v. Warden," large portions of the petition for review were redacted from the public record, and the lower courts were not identified. A coalition of 23 media and public interest groups moved to intervene in the Supreme Court proceeding to protest the secrecy, but their motion was denied and the Court denied Bellahouel's petition for certiorari. 124 S. Ct. 1405 (2004).

If the Constitution permits a person to be held incommunicado without charges, counsel, or a hearing, is it plausible to argue that a tradition of openness compels media access? Will the outcome of access challenges depend on the resolution of issues as to the rights of the detainees? Note that the Supreme Court has held that neither U.S. citizens nor aliens can be denied the right of habeas corpus even if they are "enemy combatants," and that citizens, at least, have a due process right to contest their detention. See Hamdi v. Rumsfeld, 124 S. Ct. 2633 (2004), and Rasul v. Bush, 124 S. Ct. 2686 (2004). The extent of detainees' substantive constitutional rights remains to be determined. If it turns out that suspected terrorists somehow have diminished constitutional rights, is it possible that media rights of access to information about them will remain undiminished?

The Moussaoui case. The case of the only person charged in U.S. courts as an actual participant in the September 11 attacks proceeded almost entirely in secret for 20 months. Even the defendant's own pro se pleadings were placed under seal. Eventually the Fourth Circuit ordered the government to review the entire file and make public nonclassified material that could be released without prejudice to national security or foreign relations concerns. United States v. Moussaoui, 31 Med. L. Rptr. 1705 (4th Cir. 2003) (unpublished opinion). Only then did the public learn that Zacarias Moussaoui's defense was that he had nothing to do with the attacks and could not have been scheduled to be among the hijackers, as the government contended, because he was scheduled to participate in later attacks outside the U.S., and that he was seeking the testimony of other captured Al Qaeda operatives who he claimed could confirm that he was not a participant. See Jerry Markon, Moussaoui Says He Was to Aid Later Attack, Wash. Post, May 14, 2003, at A–2. Much of the file remained sealed, however, and the documents released were often heavily redacted.

The district judge ruled—in secret—that Moussaoui was entitled to take the deposition of one captured Al Qaeda suspect because there was a strong possibility that the witness would provide "material favorable testimony on the defendant's behalf—both as to guilt and potential punishment." (Moussaoui could face the death penalty if convicted.) One of the rare open proceedings in the case occurred when the government's appeal of that order was argued in the Fourth Circuit. That court bifurcated the argument, opening to the press and public only the portion relating to the court's jurisdiction, the government's separation of powers arguments, and the scope of the court's power to compel testimony. The court also ordered release of a redacted version of the transcript of the secret portion of the argument. When it acted on this appeal, the Fourth Circuit did not reach the merits, holding that the appeal was premature until the district court attempted to require the government to give Moussaoui access to the witness and the government refused. See United States v. Moussaoui, 333 F.3d 509 (4th Cir. 2003).

The first September 11–related case to go to trial was that of four Michigan men charged with conspiring to help the hijackers. The judge closed the individual voir dire of the jury panel on the ground that closure was necessary to keep jurors' answers from being tainted by their having read or heard about the answers of other prospective jurors and to encourage candid answers on sensitive matters such as their feelings toward Muslims. U.S. v. Koubriti, 252 F. Supp.2d 424, 31 Med. L. Rptr. 1940 (E.D. Mich. 2003). The trial itself was open and resulted in conviction of two of the men on terrorism-related charges. The convictions were vacated, however, when the government admitted that the prosecutor had improperly withheld information from the defense. The Justice Department declined to retry the defendants. After three years in custody, nearly all in solitary confinement, Koubriti was released, although he still faced a lesser charge of document fraud. The co-defendant remained in jail on the document fraud charges, apparently unable to raise bail. See Ex-terror suspect freed, Detroit News, Oct. 13, 2004, at http://www.detnews.com/2004/metro/0410/13/c01–302102. htm.

Portions of the first trials of persons captured in Afghanistan were closed, but most of the proceedings, which were conducted by military tribunals at Guantanamo Bay, Cuba, in 2004, were open to the press on condition that the reporters agree to a five-page list of ground rules which included a promise not to publish anything that the presiding officer decided should be kept secret.

Secret dockets. The practice of maintaining dual docketing systems, one public and one sealed, is not limited to terrorism cases and is said to be widespread in both state and federal courts. The federal district court in Miami allegedly maintains a secret docket for certain federal drug prosecutions. According to one source, 30 to 40 percent of the criminal docket of the U.S. District Court for the District of Columbia is conducted in secret. See "Blackout of Justice," News Media and the Law, Winter 2004, at 7.

The practice persists despite decisions holding it unconstitutional. The Second Circuit held that an extensive secret docketing system used in Connecticut state courts for many years violates the First Amendment. See Hartford Courant Co. v. Pellegrino, 371 F.3d 49 (2d Cir. 2004). The newspaper alleged that thousands of cases were routinely sealed, concealing among other cases divorce proceedings involving public figures such as General Electric chairman Jack Welch. The Second Circuit said "[D]ocket sheets provide a kind of index to judicial proceedings and documents, and endow the public and press with the capacity to exercise their rights guaranteed by the First Amendment." Because it was not clear whether the court administrators named in the newspaper's suit had authority to open the files, the court remanded the case to determine whether the practice of sealing was purely administrative or was mandated by judicial order. See also United States v. Valenti, 987 F.2d 708, 21 Med. L. Rptr. 1236 (11th Cir. 1993).

For analytical purposes we sometimes separate matters that are possibly inseparable. In this chapter we have seen closed judicial proceedings and attempts to keep secret their very existence. In Chapter X we observed denial of access to war zones, prisons, and records, increased classification of information, and attempts to prevent disclosure of even nonclassified information. In Chapter IX we saw attempts to prevent information from being leaked by compelling reporters to identify the leakers. From the government's point of view, these are all part of the same effort to combat terrorism and govern effectively. What is their aggregate effect on open government?

2.   CIVIL TRIALS

The Supreme Court has not decided whether there is a constitutional right of access to civil trials, but it seems to be assumed that the First Amendment right to attend civil trials is at least as strong as the right to attend criminal trials. The leading case recognizing a qualified First Amendment right of access to civil trials is Publicker Industries, Inc. v. Cohen, 733 F.2d 1059, 10 Med. L. Rptr. 1777 (3d Cir. 1984). Other federal courts agree that *Richmond Newspapers* applies and that a First Amendment right exists. See, e.g., Westmoreland v. CBS, 752 F.2d 16, 23 (2d Cir. 1984); Rushford v. New Yorker Magazine, 846 F.2d 249 (4th Cir. 1988); Brown & Williamson Tobacco Co. v. Federal Trade Commission, 710 F.2d 1165 (6th Cir. 1983); In re Continental Illinois Securities Litigation, 732 F.2d 1302 (7th Cir. 1984); Newman v. Graddick, 696 F.2d 796 (11th Cir. 1983).

The California Supreme Court held unanimously that the precedents established in criminal cases from *Richmond Newspapers* through *Press-Enterprise II* are generally applicable to civil cases as well. Concluding that the U.S. Supreme Court would recognize a First Amendment right of access to civil proceedings, the court interpreted the California open court statute to require that before substantive civil proceedings can be closed or transcripts sealed, the judge must give public notice of the proposed closure and

> must hold a hearing and expressly find that (i) there exists an overriding interest supporting closure and/or sealing; (ii) there is a substantial probability that the interest will be prejudiced absent closure and/or sealing; (iii)the proposed closure and/or sealing is narrowly tailored to serve the overriding interest; and (iv) there is no less restrictive means of achieving the overriding interest.

NBC Subsidiary (KNBC–TV), Inc. v. Superior Court, 20 Cal.4th 1178, 980 P.2d 337, 86 Cal. Rptr.2d 778 (1999). The case involved trial of various claims by Sondra Locke against Clint Eastwood. The trial judge had excluded the media and public from the courtroom during all proceedings that were conducted outside the presence of the jury, and he refused to provide transcripts of those proceedings until the end of the trial. He said these steps were necessary to prevent jurors from being prejudiced by inadmissible matters in the highly publicized dispute arising out of business dealings between the two actors. The judge rejected media arguments that they had a First Amendment right of access to the proceedings and transcripts. But the California Supreme Court said "the public has an interest, in all civil cases, in observing and assessing the performance of its public judicial system, and that interest strongly supports a general right of access in ordinary civil cases."

Immigration hearings. Deportation hearings and other cases involving immigration laws are administrative proceedings handled in special courts. After September 11, hundreds of aliens were taken into custody. Attorney General Ashcroft issued additional "security procedures" for the handling of these cases in U.S. Immigration Courts. On September 21, 2001, Chief Immigration Judge Michael Creppy issued an order closing all hearings in cases deemed by the INS to be of "special interest" because of their possible connection to terrorism. Persons detained in such cases were to see "no visitors, no family, no press," and Immigration Court officials were ordered to avoid "disclosing any information" about a case, including even whether a particular case exists on the docket, to anyone outside the Immigration Court. See Memorandum from Michael Creppy to All Immigration Judges [and] Court Administrators re: Cases requiring special procedures (Sept. 21, 2001) (available at <http://archive.aclu.org/court/creppy_memo.pdf>). Immigration judges began opening some proceedings on a case-by-case basis after a few weeks, but many remained closed.

The chief judge's secrecy order was challenged by media groups in Michigan and New Jersey. The district courts held the order unconstitutional in both cases and enjoined its enforcement, but on appeal the circuit courts split. In the Michigan case, the Sixth Circuit held that even though immigration hearings are administrative proceedings conducted by the executive branch, they "exhibit substantial quasi-judicial characteristics" and therefore are properly analyzed under *Richmond Newspapers* [supra p. 673] rather than *Houchins* [supra p. 634]. The court held that deportation hearings traditionally have been open, and that openness "undoubtedly plays a significant positive role in this process." It therefore held that media had a First Amendment right of access which could be defeated only if the closure could survive the form of strict scrutiny specified in *Globe Newspaper* [supra p. 673] and *Press-Enterprise II* [supra p. 684].

The court accepted the government's argument that it had a compelling interest in preventing disclosure of even bits and pieces of information about suspected terrorist activities. But it held the directive unconstitutional nonetheless because the hearing in question had been closed without specific findings of a need to do so, and because case-by-case determination offered a narrowly tailored alternative to Creppy's blanket secrecy order. Detroit Free Press v. Ashcroft, 303 F.3d 681, 30 Med. L. Rptr. 2313 (6th Cir. 2002).

The Third Circuit explicitly rejected this reasoning in the New Jersey case. It agreed that *Richmond Newspapers* provided the correct framework for analysis, but held that neither the history prong of that test nor the logic prong supported the claim of a First Amendment right of access to deportation hearings. North Jersey Media Group, Inc. v. Ashcroft, 308 F.3d 198, 31 Med. L. Rptr. 1065 (3d Cir. 2002).

Despite evidence that Congress had made deportation hearings pre-sumptively open since the end of the nineteenth century, and that Justice Department regulations had made them generally open since 1964, the court said "the tradition of open deportation hearings is too recent and inconsistent to support a First Amendment right of access." The court acknowledged that its own precedents recognized such a right even in the absence of a history of openness at common law, but said those should be limited to the criminal context.

Analyzing the other prong of the test, the Third Circuit said access would advance the general goals of openness, but expressed skepticism about the usefulness of that argument. It said it had found no case in which the logic test operated to *deny* access. Whenever courts find the history prong satisfied, the court said, they usually find also that logic supports openness.

The court said this branch of analysis should include not only the benefits of openness, but also the disadvantages. In this case, the benefits were outweighed by the risks to national security that open hearings might pose. The court cited an FBI official's assertions that even minor pieces of apparently innocuous information, such as name and address of a subject and time and place of arrest, "might allow a terrorist organization to build a picture of the investigation." Information revealed by open hearings might allow terrorists to see which methods of illegal entry into the United States work and which do not, determine what the government does and does not know about terrorist activities, and allow them to shift activities to as-yet-undiscovered terror cells. The court admitted that these were speculative, but said the logic prong of the *Richmond Newspapers* test is unavoidably speculative because it focuses on what the effects of openness will be.

Because the court held that there was no First Amendment right of access to the hearings, it said it need not decide whether case-by-case adjudication offered a narrowly tailored alternative.

A dissenting judge argued that both history and logic supported a First Amendment right of access, and that "national security interests can be accommodated on a case-by-case basis."

The Supreme Court denied certiorari in the Third Circuit case, and certiorari was not sought in the Sixth Circuit case.

3.   JUVENILE PROCEEDINGS

Delinquency proceedings. These are often closed, either by statutory mandate or at the discretion of the judge. The original theory was that publicity was likely to interfere with the rehabilitation of the offender. In recent years, however, there has been increasing skepticism about the rationale for treating juveniles differently from adults, at least when they are charged with serious crimes. Some states allow judges to open juvenile proceedings at their discretion, and others allow juveniles charged with serious offenses to be transferred to the adult criminal justice system, where they enjoy no special secrecy provisions.

Before the decisions in *Globe Newspaper* and *Press-Enterprise II,* there seemed to be little doubt that closure of juvenile proceedings was constitutional. Even if the First Amendment created a qualified right to attend such proceedings, the state was likely to be found to have compelling interests in closure:

> Publication of the youth's name could impair the rehabilitative goals of the juvenile justice system. Confidential proceedings protect the delinquent from the stigma of conduct which may be outgrown and avoids the possibility that the adult is penalized for what he used to be, or worse yet, the possibility that the stigma becomes self-perpetuating, thereby making change and growth impossible. Publication of a delinquent's name may handicap his prospects for adjustment into society, for acceptance by the public, or it may cause him to lose employment opportunities. Public proceedings could so embarrass the youth's family that they withhold their support in rehabilitative efforts. . . . Publicity sometimes serves as a reward for the hardcore juvenile delinquent, thereby encouraging him to commit further antisocial acts to attract attention. [ ] Further, the legislative goals of expunging the juvenile's delinquency record are vitiated if the same information could at any subsequent time be obtained freely from newspaper morgues.

In re J.S., 140 Vt. 458, 438 A.2d 1125, 1129, 7 Med. L. Rptr. 2402 (1981). This view still commands substantial judicial support. Without actually deciding the matter, the First Circuit expressed doubt that the standards established by *Globe Newspaper* and *Press-Enterprise II* are applicable to juvenile proceedings. It said the assumption that "the First Amendment right of public access does apply to some degree to juvenile proceedings [is] a highly dubious assumption, particularly in light of the long, entrenched, and well-founded tradition of confidentiality regarding juvenile proceedings and the compelling rehabilitative purposes behind this tradition." Nevertheless, the court refused to hold that the federal Juvenile Delinquency Act requires closure of juvenile hearings even though it states that "neither the name nor picture of any juvenile shall be made public in connection with a juvenile delinquency proceeding. . . ." The court said "the Act does not mandate across-the-board closure for all juvenile proceedings, but merely authorizes closure, or any other measures designed to ensure confidentiality, to be determined on a case-by-case basis." Public dissemination of the juveniles' pictures could be prevented by banning cameras from the proceedings, and their names could be kept secret by identifying them only through initials or pseudonyms. The court asserted that "this interpretation fully comports with the purpose and language of the statute as a whole, and is far preferable to a strained construction of the Act that mandates complete closure and thus triggers First Amendment concerns." See United States v. Three Juveniles, 61 F.3d 86, 23 Med. L. Rptr. 2262 (1st Cir. 1995).

Courts often construe statutes imaginatively to avoid the constitutional questions. See, e.g, United States v. A.D., 28 F.3d 1353, 22 Med. L. Rptr. 1988 (3d Cir. 1994), construing a provision in the federal act prohibiting disclosure of "information and records relating to the proceeding . . . to anyone other than the judge, counsel for the juvenile, and the Government . . ." as giving the district judge discretion to open hearings and release records on a case-by-case basis.

Similarly, state law is often interpreted to at least give the judge discretion to open the proceeding. In Wideman v. Garbarino, 160 Ariz. 16, 770 P.2d 320, 16 Med. L. Rptr. 1253 (1989), for example, a state constitutional provision requiring that preliminary examining trials for juveniles be held "in chambers" was interpreted to give the juvenile judge discretion to admit news media. In Associated Press v. Bradshaw, 410 N.W.2d 577, 14 Med. L. Rptr. 1566 (S.D. 1987), the court held that a statute providing that the juvenile judge "may" admit news media representatives created a qualified right of access that could not be denied "unless specific supportive findings are made which demonstrate that closure is essential to preserve higher values and the order must be narrowly tailored to serve that interest."

As the statute mentioned above suggests, courtrooms are one place where the press often enjoys access on more favorable terms than the general public. In trials of unusual public interest, specific seats or sections of the courtroom often are reserved for the press, and occasionally closed circuit television is arranged for additional press representatives who cannot be admitted to the courtroom. Recall that Chief Justice Burger in a footnote in his *Richmond Newspapers* opinion, supra p. 673, characterized such preferential arrangements as "reasonable restrictions on general access."

Custody proceedings. Among the types of proceedings that traditionally have not been open are child custody hearings. This tradition occasionally is challenged when prominent people are involved. In a case involving the child actor McCaulay Culkin and his siblings, the court reversed a trial judge's decision to open the courtroom. See P.B. v. C.C., 223 A.D.2d 294, 647 N.Y.S.2d 732, 25 Med. L. Rptr. 1027 (1996), appeal denied 89 N.Y.2d 808 (1997). A 4–1 majority, concluding that the controlling statutory consideration was "the best interest of the children," focused on the fact that of the six minor children, only two had achieved any degree of fame. Reports on the case had already involved allegations of alcohol and drug abuse and domestic violence. Affidavits suggested that most children "use denial as a healthy defense to an acrimonious separation, and that intense media scrutiny would likely cause a child to revert to more destructive alternative defenses." Also, the children had already been "subjected to derision and embarrassment by their peers, and have suffered educational and emotional difficulties as a result of this spectacle."

An added concern was that, although it was not possible to know in advance what would be elicited at trial, "witnesses at trial might constrain themselves from providing the court with the pertinent details for fear that their testimony might be exploited by the press." Closing the courtroom when this fear presented itself would be too late: "The best efforts of a well-intentioned judge cannot adequately protect against devastating revelations or allegations which may be adduced in the course of rapidly unfolding examination and cross-examination in a hotly contested and acrimonious litigation."

The dissenter thought the presumption in favor of open proceedings had not been overcome.

Conditional access. Judges sometimes offer reporters admission to otherwise closed proceedings provided they agree not to report certain matters. The Illinois Supreme Court upheld such a procedure. In two hearings involving children alleged to be the victims of parental abuse, the judge refused to admit reporters unless they signed a pledge not to reveal the identity of the victims. The Illinois Juvenile Court Act gave news media, but not the public, a right to attend such proceedings.

The court rejected the newspaper's argument that both the statute and the First Amendment gave the press a right to report anything it learned in the proceeding. The majority distinguished *Oklahoma Publishing Co. v. District Court*, supra p. 380, which involved delinquency proceedings, on the ground that the state has a stronger interest in protecting the privacy of juvenile victims than alleged delinquents. It distinguished *Smith v. Daily Mail*, supra p. 36, on the ground that the name of the juvenile there was not obtained from attendance at a proceeding closed to the public. Two dissenting justices found the distinctions unpersuasive and viewed the condition imposed by the trial judge as an impermissible prior restraint. See In re a Minor, 149 Ill.2d 247, 595 N.E.2d 1052, 20 Med. L. Rptr. 1372 (1992).

Should this be analyzed under principles applicable to courtroom access generally, prior restraint, or unconstitutional conditions? Or is it merely a question of the scope of preferential media treatment?

4. COURTROOM PHOTOGRAPHY AND BROADCASTING

In all of the preceding material in this chapter, the assumption has been that the media seek access only for pen-and-paper reporting. When they seek to photograph or broadcast courtroom proceedings, the access question usually is treated quite differently.

Judicial hostility to courtroom photography traces back half a century. In the aftermath of the Lindbergh kidnapping case, mentioned in Chapter III, the American Bar Association adopted Canon 35 in 1937. Together with amendments in 1952 and 1963, this ethical stricture bans radio and television broadcasting and still cameras from courtrooms. In 1979, an ABA committee proposed that Canon 3A(7), the successor to Canon 35, be amended to allow televising of trials at the judge's discretion. The ABA rejected the recommendation, but many states eventually adopted it.

In Estes v. Texas, 381 U.S. 532, 1 Med. L. Rptr. 1187 (1965), defendant had been indicted in the Texas state courts for "swindling"—inducing farmers to buy nonexistent fertilizer tanks and then to deliver to him mortgages on the property. The nature of the charges, and the large sums of money involved, attracted nationwide interest. Texas was one of two states that then permitted televised trials. Over defendant's objection, the trial judge permitted televising of a two-day hearing before trial. Estes was convicted.

The Supreme Court, 5–4, reversed the conviction. In his majority opinion Justice Clark concluded that the use of television involved "such a probability that prejudice will result that it is deemed inherently lacking in due process" even without any showing of specific prejudice. He was concerned about the impact on jurors, judges, parties, witnesses, and lawyers.

Justice Harlan, who provided the crucial fifth vote for reversal, joined the majority opinion only to the extent that it applied to televised coverage of "courtroom proceedings of a criminal trial of widespread public interest," "a criminal trial of great notoriety," and "a heavily publicized and highly sensational affair." In such cases he was worried about the impact on jurors.

In Chandler v. Florida, 449 U.S. 560, 7 Med. L. Rptr. 1041 (1981), the Court unanimously rejected the view that televising a criminal trial over the objections of the defendant automatically rendered the trial unfair. The defendants had argued that the impact of television on the participants introduced potentially prejudicial but unidentifiable aspects into the trial. The majority, in an opinion by Chief Justice Burger, first concluded that *Estes* did not stand for the proposition that broadcasting was barred "in all cases and under all circumstances." Because of Justice Harlan's narrow basis for concurring in that case, the ruling in *Estes* should apply only to cases of widespread interest. (On this point, two Justices insisted that *Chandler* overruled *Estes* and should say so.)

The majority said the risk of prejudice from press coverage of a trial was not limited to broadcasting. "The risk of juror prejudice in some cases does not justify an absolute ban on news coverage of trials by the printed media; so also the risk of such prejudice does not warrant an absolute constitutional ban on all broadcast coverage." A case attracts attention because of its intrinsic interest to the public. The "appropriate safeguard" against prejudice in such cases "is the defendant's right to demonstrate that the media's coverage of his case—be it printed or broadcast—compromised the ability of the particular jury that heard the case to adjudicate fairly." The Court also observed that the changes in technology since *Estes* supported the state's argument that it should now be permitted to allow television in the courtroom.

Since the defendants in *Chandler*—two former city policemen accused of burglarizing a restaurant—showed no adverse impact from the televising, the convictions were upheld.

State courts. When *Estes* was decided, most states forbade courtroom photography. Now virtually all permit it under some circumstances. In most states assent of the trial judge is required; in some a criminal defendant has the power to prevent it. Some distinguish between still photography and television, permitting the former but not the latter.

The movement to open courtrooms to cameras has been influenced by events of the moment. The advent of the Court TV cable network proved the popularity of televised proceedings with the viewing public. That popularity reached a peak with the 1995 murder trial of O.J. Simpson, which millions of viewers watched avidly. But that case also touched off something of a backlash against televising trials. Many thought the televising of that trial influenced the behavior of the judge and lawyers, made celebrities of even minor witnesses, and turned the trial into an entertainment spectacle. California had permitted broadcast coverage of all state court proceedings since 1984, but after the Simpson trial the governor and a majority of the state's judges called for a ban on television coverage of trials. The California Judicial Council rejected the proposals for a complete ban, but adopted new rules restricting judges' power to permit television. The new rules forbid televising of jury selection, bench conferences, spectators, and conversations between counsel and clients or witnesses. Guidelines require judges to consider the security and dignity of the court, privacy rights of participants, and potential impact on jurors before authorizing coverage. Judges need not give reasons for denying or authorizing coverage. See Maura Dolan, State Panel Puts Partial Ban on Court Cameras, L.A. Times, May 18, 1996 at 1. California's reaction was not universal, however. In many states judges continued to allow broadcasting, and in some the rights of the electronic media to cover trials were expanded. CourtTV claimed that it televised 33 trials during the nine months of the Simpson trial without any complaint from the judges involved.

Federal courts. There is still substantial resistance to cameras, however, most notably in the federal courts. In criminal proceedings the use of cameras is prohibited altogether. Rule 53 of the Federal Rules of Criminal Procedure provides, "The taking of photographs in the court room during the progress of judicial proceedings . . . shall not be permitted." This is enforced even when a criminal defendant wishes to have the proceedings broadcast. See United States v. Hastings, 695 F.2d 1278, 8 Med. L. Rptr. 2617 (11th Cir. 1983). The defendant, a federal judge charged with bribery, and numerous media intervenors argued that the defendant had a right under the First and Sixth Amendments to have the trial videotaped for broadcast. But the court held that despite the defendant's assent, the prohibition was justified by other interests, such as maintenance of decorum and prevention of any appearance of unfairness that might result.

Federal guidelines allow judges to use electronic sound recording equipment to record proceedings in district courts and authorize the sale of tapes made by this equipment to the public. In the Oklahoma City bombing case, Judge Matsch designated a court reporter to use mechanical stenography to make the official record but also decided to use sound recording equipment as a backup. Speakers connected with the sound system in the courtroom were also placed in an adjacent courtroom to enable the public and members of the press who could not find seating in the courtroom to listen to the proceedings.

During an April, 1996 hearing, tapes were taken from the courtroom while the hearing was still being conducted and were sold to members of the press as they were completed. Shortly after the hearing, members of the press requested that the sound feed from the adjacent courtroom be extended into a nearby press room so that they could make their own recordings. Both the government and defendant Nichols argued that the court should stop the sale of audio tapes and deny an extension of the sound feed. The judge granted both requests, noting that "the ready access to the sound recordings has resulted in the functional equivalent of a broadcast of the court proceedings in violation of Rule 53." He noted that the sound recording system was not being used to make the official record; if it were, production and sale of audio tapes would be required to provide access to the official record, he said. United States v. McVeigh, 931 F. Supp. 753 (D. Colo. 1996). The Court of Appeals rejected a media challenge to this ruling. See 119 F.3d 806 (10th Cir. 1997).

In civil proceedings, the question of access by cameras is controlled by the local rules in each district. The Judicial Conference of the United States has urged the district courts to ban all broadcasting, but it lacks the power to compel such a prohibition. In Katzman v. Victoria's Secret Catalogue, 923 F. Supp. 580 (S.D.N.Y. 1996), the district judge granted Court TV's motion to be allowed to televise arguments in a civil RICO case against the catalog company. A local rule in the Southern District of New York gave trial judges discretion to allow television, and the judge noted that the Judicial Conference had no power to abrogate that rule. He said the Conference's view was not binding, and in his mind it was outweighed by the overwhelmingly positive reactions of the states and the federal courts that have permitted television.

The federal resistance to cameras seemed to be weakening in 1990 when the Judicial Conference approved a pilot program authorizing six district courts and two courts of appeals to experiment with courtroom photography in civil cases. The experiment seemed to go smoothly and the media expected the authorization to be expanded, but when the pilot program expired at the end of 1994, the 27 judges in the Judicial Conference voted down a proposal to make it permanent by a margin of about 2–1. Some of the judges were said to have been influenced by the fact that most of the broadcast images were merely used as background for a reporter's commentary and did not let viewers actually see any significant portion of the proceedings for themselves. See Linda Greenhouse, U.S. Judges Vote Down TV in Courts, N.Y. Times Sept. 21, 1994, at A11.

Judges sometimes express the fear that unless broadcasting is banned completely, judges, criminal defendants, or parties in civil litigation will be unable to resist pressure from media to consent to it against their better judgment. As to judges, does the strength of this argument depend on whether they are elected? As to parties, is there any more reason to spare them this decision than other difficult tactical choices (such as the decision to publicly air the dispute by litigating)?

Sketching. In the states in which cameras are banned, and in the federal courts, television news directors have resorted to having artists sketch in the courtroom. Sweeping bans against the practice have been rejected. United States v. Columbia Broadcasting System, Inc., 497 F.2d 102, 1 Med. L. Rptr. 1351 (5th Cir. 1974). Another case invalidated a restriction on sketching even when it was aimed at preventing jurors from being publicly identified. The judge had told prospective jurors he would attempt to keep their identities concealed. When he saw artists sketching, he ordered them to submit their sketches to him for review. Analyzing the matter as a prior restraint, the Arizona Supreme Court invalidated the order on First Amendment grounds. The record did not show sufficient support for a prior restraint. Of the 150 jurors questioned, "several" expressed fear of being identified but none of these was on the final panel. Using the three-part approach of the *Nebraska Press* case, the court concluded that the danger was not significant or imminent enough to justify the censorship; less restrictive measures (e.g., voir dire) would have sufficed; and the sketch order was likely to have very limited success in meeting the judge's concern. See KPNX Broadcasting Co. v. Superior Court, 139 Ariz. 246, 678 P.2d 431, 10 Med. L. Rptr. 1289 (1984).

Appellate proceedings. Restrictions on photography and broadcasting rest in part on concerns about possible adverse effects on witnesses and jurors. These worries obviously have no application to appellate proceedings, and there has been some tendency to open these to cameras. Each U.S. court of appeals is now free to decide for itself whether to allow photography and broadcasting of appellate arguments in civil cases. The Ninth Circuit announced that it would entertain requests for electronic coverage of all appellate proceedings except direct criminal appeals and extradition proceedings. Requests must be made seven days in advance, counsel may object, and coverage is to be permitted only if the panel unanimously agrees. The panel has the power to refuse, limit, or terminate coverage to protect the rights of parties or the dignity of the court. See Ninth Circuit Agrees to Permit Cameras in Courts, News Notes, Med. L. Rptr. April 16, 1996.

The Supreme Court still prohibits television coverage of its proceedings but in several cases has allowed audio tapes of the arguments to be distributed to the media immediately after the arguments concluded. See Reporters Committee for Freedom of the Press, Supreme Court Allows Audio Taping of Affirmative Action Arguments (2003) http:// www.rcfp.org/news/2003/0401grutte.html; Supreme Court to release audio tapes from terror, Cheney cases, http://www.cnn.com/2004/LAW/04/08/scotus.tapes/.

Some courts routinely make available audio recordings of oral arguments. The Texas Supreme Court began posting links to audio recordings of arguments by the end of the day "as an interim step toward broadcasting all arguments on the internet through streaming audio and video software, assuming the Legislature provides funds for this project." See http://www.supreme.courts.state.tx.us/webrecordings12.3.04.htm.

B.   ACCESS TO JURORS AND WITNESSES

These cases raise two distinct sets of questions. One is whether the media have any right of access to jurors or witnesses. The other is whether jurors or witnesses have a right to speak to the media. Because restrictions are more often challenged by the media than by jurors or witnesses, most of the cases speak (directly, at least) only to the first question. The Supreme Court decisions we encountered in the previous section are the cases cited most frequently in these cases.

A different set of precedents might be relevant if the issue were the First Amendment rights of witnesses and jurors. We saw in *Gentile v. State Bar*, supra p. 127, that attorneys do not forfeit their First Amendment rights when they participate in judicial proceedings. Because the participation of jurors and witnesses is usually involuntary, one might suppose that their right to speak would be protected at least as fully as that of lawyers. The only Supreme Court case addressing the question is *Butterworth v. Smith*, supra p. 132, which held that a reporter's First Amendment right to disclose what he knew about a matter under investigation by a grand jury did not vanish when he was called before the grand jury as a witness. Does that decision support a juror's right to disclose what transpired during deliberations? If a witness or a juror invokes a First Amendment right to disclose, should the issue be analyzed under *Gentile v. State Bar*, Nebraska Press Association v. Stuart, *supra* p. 116, or some other framework?

Identifying jurors. Jurors' identities have traditionally been public, and under the *Richmond Newspapers* series of cases attempts to keep them secret generally have been unsuccessful, at least as to those actually selected as jurors. The Ohio Supreme Court canvassed the decisions and reported that "virtually every court having occasion to address this issue has concluded that [questionnaires answered by prospective jurors] are part of voir dire and thus subject to a presumption of openness." State ex rel. Beacon Journal Pub. Co. v. Bond, 781 N.E.2d 180, 31 Med. L. Rptr. 1424 (Ohio 2002).

The court held that neither juror privacy nor the defendant's fair trial interests justified a blanket order withholding questionnaires. It ordered their release, subject to redaction of personal information such as social security number, driver's license number, and telephone number. It said those were not relevant to the issue of the jurors' impartiality, which the court identified as the key reason why juror information was presumptively open under the First Amendment. The trial judge had promised the prospective jurors that their responses would be confidential, but the court said "Constitutional rights are not superseded by the mere promise of a trial judge to act contrary to those rights."

The trial judge also had refused to disclose the list of prospective jurors. The Ohio Supreme Court said other courts are divided as to whether such lists are presumptively open, but concluded they should be because historically jurors have been known in the community and because knowing their identity allows the public to judge their impartiality.

The Fourth Circuit held that the trial judge may not be required to release names and addresses of members of the venire before the jury is selected and seated, but once that occurs the names of both those seated and those not chosen become part of the public record of the case. "If the district court thinks the dangers of a highly publicized trial are too great, it may always sequester the jury; and change of venue is always possible as a method of obviating pressure or prejudice." In re Baltimore Sun Co., 841 F.2d 74, 14 Med. L. Rptr. 2379 (4th Cir. 1988).

Even when circumstances justify an anonymous jury, the judge may not prohibit the media from revealing jurors' identities if they learn them from independent newsgathering. In a criminal case against former Louisiana Governor Edwin Edwards and others, the district judge granted the government's motion to empanel an anonymous jury to guard against harassment or intimidation of the jurors. The judge ordered the media "not to attempt to circumvent this Court's ruling preserving the jury's anonymity." The Fifth Circuit said the judge had authority to protect the identities of the jurors and to forbid the media from attempting to learn them by obtaining confidential court documents. But insofar as the order attempted to forbid them from attempting to identify the jurors through independent investigation, it could not survive the scrutiny required by *Nebraska Press Association v. Stuart,* supra p. 116. See United States v. Brown, 250 F.3d 907 (5th Cir. 2001).

In trials of suspected Mafia figures where possible retaliation against jurors is feared, or in cases where jurors might be subject to public pressure, judges sometimes keep the names and addresses of jurors secret even from the parties. Is this practice subject to challenge by media on the ground that it denies access to information that historically has been available? How palpable must the risk be before the state's interest in secrecy becomes compelling?

Interviewing jurors. The other major access problem involving jurors arises from judges' desire to protect jurors from harassment, pressure, or embarrassment in post-verdict interviews. In some jurisdictions lawyers connected with the case are forbidden from questioning jurors about their deliberations, or are permitted to do so only with court approval. In others attorneys have uninhibited access to jurors after verdict. In cases of high public interest, reporters often wish to interview jurors for many of the same reasons attorneys wish to do so—for example, to learn why they decided as they did.

But judges may be concerned that disclosures about jury deliberations will affect the candor of future jurors. In United States v. Cleveland, 128 F.3d 267, 25 Med. L. Rptr. 2500 (5th Cir. 1997), after a six-week, high-visibility criminal trial and eight days of deliberation, the trial judge instructed the jurors that they could not be interviewed "concerning the deliberations of the jury" without an order from the court. A media challenge to the order was rejected. The court defined "deliberations of the jury" as referring only to "discussions about the case occurring among jurors within the sanctity of the jury room" and not the juror's "general reactions" to the trial proceedings itself. The order was narrowly tailored to meet a threat to the administration of justice—"namely, the threat presented to freedom of speech within the jury room by the possibility of post-verdict interviews."

It seems clear now that a blanket order banning all contact with jurors by the press cannot survive the scrutiny called for by *Press-Enterprise II*. In Journal Publishing Co. v. Mechem, 801 F.2d 1233, 13 Med. L. Rptr. 1391 (10th Cir. 1986), at the conclusion of a controversial civil rights trial involving the Albuquerque police chief and several other officers the judge admonished the jurors as follows:

> You should not discuss your verdict after you leave here with anyone. If anyone tries to talk to you about it, or wants to talk to you about it, let me know. If they wish [to] take the matter up with me, why, they may do so, but otherwise don't discuss it with anyone.

The court of appeals held the order impermissibly overbroad:

> It contained no time or scope limitations and encompassed every possible juror interview situation. It would have been constitutionally permissible for the court routinely to instruct jurors that they may refuse interviews and seek the aid of the court if the interviewers persist after they express a reluctance to speak. [ ] It could have told the jurors not to discuss the specific votes and opinions of noninterviewed jurors in order to encourage free deliberation in the jury room. [ ] But the court could not issue a sweeping restraint forbidding all contact between the press and former jurors without a compelling reason.

Narrower admonitions along the lines of those suggested in the *Mechem* case have been upheld. In United States v. Harrelson, 713 F.2d 1114, 9 Med. L. Rptr. 2113 (5th Cir. 1983), the judge who had presided over a highly publicized murder trial entered the following order:

> 1. No juror has any obligation to speak to any person about this case, and may refuse all interviews or comment.

> 2. No person may make repeated requests for interviews or questioning after a juror has expressed his or her desire not to be interviewed.

> 3. No interviewer may inquire into the specific vote of any juror other than the juror being interviewed.

> 4. No interview may take place until each juror in this case has received a copy of this order, mailed simultaneously with the entry of this order.

On appeal, the court upheld the order. Quoting an earlier case in that circuit, the court said that "jurors, even after completing their duty, are entitled to privacy and to protection against harassment." Further, the court recognized that "at *some* point repeated importunings of one who has declined to be interviewed become harassment and an improper invasion of privacy." The question then became how many to allow. "The trial judge concluded that one request made after a known refusal to be interviewed was enough to allow and that more—repeated requests—were too many. We cannot say that in so concluding he abused his discretion." A juror who later changed his or her mind was "always free to initiate an interview. The court's order does no more than forbid nagging him into doing so."

But a judge cannot forbid even repeated requests to jurors for interviews "in the absence of any finding by the court that harassing or intrusive interviews are occurring or are intended." United States v. Antar, 38 F.3d 1348, 22 Med. L. Rptr. 2417 (3d Cir. 1994).

In the face of reports that tabloids were offering jurors in the O.J. Simpson case money in exchange for their first-person stories, the California legislature enacted a statute defining such payments as jury tampering. The statute made it a misdemeanor to offer or accept such payment prior to or within 90 days after discharge of the jury. Any payment in violation is forfeited to a Victims Restitution Fund. See Cal. Penal Code § 116.5.

Witnesses. Can judges order witnesses not to talk to the media? In *Sheppard v. Maxwell*, supra p. 111, the court suggested that trial judges had a duty to control the extrajudicial statements of witnesses. On the other hand, *Butterworth v. Smith*, supra p. 132, held that a newspaper reporter called as a witness before a grand jury had a First Amendment right to disclose what he knew about a matter under investigation, and that decision does not suggest that nonjournalist witnesses would have any lesser rights. There are few cases addressing the First Amendment rights of witnesses. It is not clear whether their rights should be analyzed by analogy to those of attorneys (see *Gentile v. State Bar*, supra), those of the media (see *Nebraska Press Association v. Stuart*, supra p. 116), or those of jurors (as described in the preceding section).

The willingness of some media to pay witnesses for information or first-person accounts raises a new set of legal questions. In the O.J. Simpson murder prosecution in 1995, potential witnesses accepted money for telling their stories to television programs. Both the prosecution and the defense expressed concern that the practice would call into question the credibility of witnesses. The prosecution decided not to use a witness whose testimony placed Simpson near the crime scene at about the time of the crime because of fears that her credibility would be impugned by the fact that she had received $5,000 for telling her story to the TV tabloid show Hard Copy.

In response to these incidents, the California legislature passed legislation making it a crime for a person who "reasonably should know" that he or she will be a witness from agreeing to accept money for information relating to the case until after final judgment in the case. Violation was punishable by six months in jail and a fine equal to three times the amount of compensation accepted. A companion provision in the civil code authorized prosecutors to seek injunctions against enforcement of contracts to pay witnesses.

A media coalition challenged the legislation, and a district judge held it unconstitutional. See California First Amendment Coalition v. Lungren, No. C 95–0440–FMS, 1995 WL 482066 (N.D. Cal. 1995) (not officially reported). Citing *Simon & Schuster Inc. v. New York State Crime Victims Board*, supra p. 87, the judge held that the statutes were content-based regulations and therefore were invalid unless they were necessary to serve a compelling state interest and were narrowly drawn to achieve that end. She relied on *Cox Broadcasting v. Cohn*, supra p. 378, for the proposition that witnesses' stories are "at the core of protected expression," and on *Nebraska Press Association v. Stuart*, supra p. 116, for the proposition that the statutes imposed a prior restraint on witness speech. She said these two propositions should be kept in mind in applying the test of *Simon & Schuster*. She rejected the state's argument that *Gentile* and *Nebraska Press* established that the First Amendment rights of trial participants may be restricted in the interest of fair trial. She said both of those decisions require case-by-case evaluation as opposed to the blanket prohibition of the California legislation.

The judge conceded that the state had a compelling interest in insuring a fair trial and that protecting the credibility of witnesses served that interest. But she said the statutes were unnecessary to protect this interest because the state had other mechanisms to discourage witness fabrications, such as prohibitions on perjury and bribery of witnesses, witness competency requirements in the law of evidence, the oath procedure, and cross-examination. She described these as "non-speech-restrictive safeguards." The state contended that these devices were inadequate because they cannot prevent juries from discrediting or rejecting the testimony of a witness whom they believe has been influenced by payment. But the judge said this amounted only to an argument that it would be inconvenient to counter the jury's perception of bias. The state's argument that the interest in protecting a defendant's Sixth Amendment interest in a fair trial was more compelling than the interest in providing victim restitution in the *Simon & Schuster* case was not persuasive because the legislation failed the narrowly tailored test, not the compelling interest test.

Does *Simon & Schuster* provide the right framework for analysis of this case? Does *Gentile* suggest that restrictions designed to protect fair trial need not be as narrowly drawn as other speech restrictions? Do the alternatives mentioned by the district judge address the credibility issue? Is the possibility that payment of witnesses will affect their credibility a real problem? Is it correct (or necessary) to characterize the legislation as a prior restraint?

The state did not appeal the district court decision. This suit did not challenge the California statute, mentioned in the preceding section, forbidding payments to jurors.

C. ACCESS TO JUDICIAL RECORDS AND DISCOVERY MATERIALS

So far we have dealt primarily with efforts of media representatives to attend judicial proceedings and/or photograph or broadcast them. But many other disputes arise over access to records rather than proceedings—access to transcripts, exhibits, tapes, indictments, search warrants, sentencing reports, settlements, or discovery documents. These disputes have generated a tremendous amount of litigation in the last few years, only a sample of which can be mentioned here.

Conflicts over access to records are quite diverse. Access to transcripts of courtroom proceedings is closely related to access to the proceedings themselves and tends to be analyzed similarly. Affidavits in support of search warrants or arrest warrants, sentencing reports, court-ordered psychiatric reports, and laboratory reports all have some of the characteristics of judicial records but may not be part of the actual proceeding. At the other extreme, depositions and documents produced during discovery in civil cases are much further removed from the courtroom; they usually are obtained without judicial supervision and they may never be introduced as evidence. Settlement agreements may be worked out with the active intervention of the judge and filed with the court, or they may be simply contracts between the parties. Not surprisingly, the cases reflect this diversity. In attempting to make sense of the decisions, it may be helpful to think about these questions: What is a "judicial record?" Are there arguments against access to particular records that are not present with respect to proceedings?

1. COMMON LAW ACCESS

Before there was any support for a First Amendment right of access to either judicial proceedings or records, the Supreme Court recognized a common law right of access to records in the federal courts. The case was Nixon v. Warner Communications, Inc., 435 U.S. 589, 3 Med. L. Rptr. 2074 (1978).

During the trial of Watergate conspirator John Mitchell, copies of White House audio tapes were introduced in evidence. Various broadcasting companies sought permission to copy them, both for news purposes and for purposes of marketing the copies commercially. The tapes had been played in open court and transcripts of them had been released and widely published, but the broadcasters argued that the full significance of the conversations could not be appreciated without hearing the inflections and emphasis of President Nixon and others whose voices were captured on the tapes. Nixon objected to their release, and Judge Sirica denied the networks' requests.

The Supreme Court held that there was no constitutional right of access to the tapes. *Richmond Newspapers* had not yet been decided; relying on *Houchins, Saxbe,* and *Pell* (the prison access cases discussed in

Chapter X) the Court said that since the public had no access to the tapes, the press had no First Amendment right of access to them.

But the Court did recognize a common law right of access to judicial records arising from the long-standing practice of allowing inspection of court records by anyone wishing to do so. This was only a qualified right, which normally would have to be balanced against Nixon's property and privacy interests, his claims that the tapes were covered by executive privilege, and his argument that it would be "unseemly" for the court to appear to be facilitating commercial exploitation by making the tapes available.

In this case, however, no such balancing was necessary, because Congress had recently passed the Presidential Recordings Act, requiring the White House to turn over the originals of the tapes to the Administrator of General Services for screening and eventual release to the public of those deemed by him to be of historical value. Because of this alternative means of serving the public interest in disclosure, the common law right of access to judicial records did not require Judge Sirica to release the tapes. Four members of the Court dissented. Justices Marshall and Stevens would have ordered the tapes released, and Justices White and Brennan would have ordered the judge to turn over copies as well as originals of the tapes to the General Services Administration "forthwith." (The GSA made the tapes public in 1980).

Nixon arguably does not require the states to recognize a common law right of access to court records, and some do not. In Virmani v. Presbyterian Health Services Corp., 515 S.E.2d 675, 27 Med. L. Rptr. 2537 (N.C. 1999), the court said a North Carolina statute providing for secrecy in medical peer review committees also applied to civil litigation arising from such review, and the statute trumped any common law right of access. "We do not believe that *Nixon* is controlling authority for the proposition that federal or state common law provides the public a right of access to state courts or their records."

Insofar as the *Nixon* case denied any First Amendment right of access, its authority is questionable in light of the later sequence of courtroom access cases considered in Section A of this chapter. But it has had continuing influence by virtue of its recognition of a common law right of access to judicial records. This at least supports a judge's exercise of discretion to release a record over the objections of a litigant or witness. See, e.g., United States v. Smith, 787 F.2d 111, 12 Med. L. Rptr. 1935 (3d Cir. 1986). The decision has also influenced state courts to find a right of access to judicial records in their own common law or state constitutions.

2. FIRST AMENDMENT ACCESS

Nixon notwithstanding, it is now clear that there is some First Amendment right of access to records. In both *Press Enterprise I* and *Press Enterprise II*, the precise issue was access to transcripts. The Court in both cases decided that question by deciding whether the proceedings themselves should have been open and, concluding that they should have, held that the First Amendment required release of the transcripts. Those decisions thus imply that there is a First Amendment right of access to records of open proceedings or proceedings that should have been open.

Nevertheless, trial judges may be able to effectively reverse the presumption of openness with respect to records once a danger to fair trial rights is shown. In a highly publicized political corruption case involving the mayor of Providence, the First Circuit held that a federal district judge may adopt a procedure that automatically seals all papers filed in the case until the judge determines that a specific document poses no undue risk to the defendant's fair trial rights. In re Providence Journal Co., 293 F.3d 1, 30 Med. L.Rptr. 2025 (1st Cir. 2002). The court agreed that *Press Enterprise II* and *Globe Newspaper* recognized a First Amendment right of access to these records but held that protecting fair trial rights in a case where the dangers of prejudice had been demonstrated is a compelling interest, and under the circumstances of the case "implementation of a general procedure to seal all memoranda temporarily appears narrowly tailored."

Expungement. Some states have statutes providing for the sealing or expungement of records if the defendant is acquitted, no-billed by a grand jury, or meets the conditions of a deferred adjudication. The Ohio Supreme Court upheld the constitutionality of such a statute when it was used to seal the records of a trial after its conclusion. See State ex rel. Cincinnati Enquirer v. Winkler, 101 Ohio St.3d 382, 805 N.E.2d 1094, 32 Med. L.Rptr. 1634 (2004). The trial had been open, and the records had remained open for five weeks.

> The public's ability to attend a criminal trial is not hindered. The media's right to report on the court proceedings is not diminished. The statute does not restrict the media's right to publish truthful information relating to the criminal proceedings that have been sealed. In addition, the public had a right of access to any court record before, during, and for a period of time after the criminal trial. In fact, the public's access to the records is unrestricted until a decision is made to seal records. The statute ensures fairness by balancing the competing concerns of the public's right to know and the defendant's right to keep certain information private.

Most disputes over access to records involve materials further removed from the question of access to proceedings. For example, media sometimes seek access to physical evidence. In Globe Newspaper Co. v. Commonwealth, 570 S.E.2d 809, 31 Med. L. Rptr. 1312 (Va. 2002), several newspapers requested access to fluid specimens in a rape-murder case in which the defendant had been executed ten years previously. The newspapers wanted to conduct DNA tests, using more sophisticated methods than were available at the time of trial, to determine whether the defendant was wrongly identified. The court said there was no historical right of access to evidence for the purpose of testing, and creating one would not have a positive effect on the functioning of the judicial process because of the practical problems of supervising such testing and protecting the integrity of the evidence.

The following case involved materials that are arguably at the farthest remove: discovery materials obtained by the media as litigants, not as disinterested journalists.

Seattle Times Co. v. Rhinehart

Supreme Court of the United States, 1984.
467 U.S. 20, 104 S. Ct. 2199, 81 L. Ed.2d 17, 10 Med. L. Rptr. 1705.

[Rhinehart and the Aquarian Foundation, a controversial religious group he headed, sued two newspapers for libel, claiming harm to the fundraising and recruitment activities of the foundation. During discovery, the newspapers asked for membership lists and names of financial contributors. The plaintiffs refused to produce this information on the ground that it would violate the members' and donors' freedom of religion and rights of privacy and association. The trial court ordered them to disclose, but issued a protective order forbidding the newspapers from publishing the information, divulging it to other media, or otherwise using it for any purposes other than the litigation.]

Justice Powell delivered the opinion of the Court.

This case presents the issue whether parties to civil litigation have a First Amendment right to disseminate, in advance of trial, information gained through the pretrial discovery process.

. . .

Respondents appealed from the trial court's production order, and petitioners appealed from the protective order. The Supreme Court of Washington affirmed both. 98 Wash. 2d 226, 654 P.2d 673 (1982). With respect to the protective order, the court reasoned:

Assuming then that a protective order may fall, ostensibly, at least, within the definition of a "prior restraint of free expression", we are convinced that the interest of the judiciary in the integrity of its discovery processes is sufficient to meet the "heavy burden" of justification. The need to preserve that integrity is adequate to sustain a rule like CR 26(c) which authorizes a trial court to protect the confidentiality of information given for purposes of litigation." [ ][9]

The court noted that "[t]he information to be discovered concerned the financial affairs of the plaintiff Rhinehart and his organization, in which he and his associates had a recognizable privacy interest; and the giving of publicity to these matters would allegedly and understandably result in annoyance, embarrassment and even oppression." [ ] Therefore, the court

9. Although the Washington Supreme Court assumed, arguendo, that a protective order could be viewed as an infringement on First Amendment rights, the court also stated: "A persuasive argument can be made that when persons are required to give information which they would otherwise be entitled to keep to themselves, in order to secure a government benefit or perform an obligation to that government, those receiving that information waive the right to use it for any purpose except those which are authorized by the agency of government which exacted the information." [ ]

concluded, the trial court had not abused its discretion in issuing the protective order.

. . .

III

Most States, including Washington, have adopted discovery provisions modeled on Rules 26 through 37 of the Federal Rules of Civil Procedure. [ ] Rule 26(b)(1) provides that a party "may obtain discovery regarding any matter, not privileged, which is relevant to the subject matter involved in the pending action." It further provides that discovery is not limited to matters that will be admissible at trial so long as the information sought "appears reasonably calculated to lead to the discovery of admissible evidence." [ ]

The Rules do not differentiate between information that is private or intimate and that to which no privacy interests attach. Under the Rules, the only express limitations are that the information sought is not privileged, and is relevant to the subject matter of the pending action. Thus, the Rules often allow extensive intrusion into the affairs of both litigants and third parties. . . .

Petitioners argue that the First Amendment imposes strict limits on the availability of any judicial order that has the effect of restricting expression. They contend that civil discovery is not different from other sources of information, and that therefore the information is "protected speech" for First Amendment purposes. Petitioners assert the right in this case to disseminate any information gained through discovery. They do recognize that in limited circumstances, not thought to be present here, some information may be restrained. They submit, however:

> When a protective order seeks to limit expression, it may do so only if the proponent shows a compelling governmental interest. Mere speculation and conjecture are insufficient. Any restraining order, moreover, must be narrowly drawn and precise. Finally, before issuing such an order a court must determine that there are no alternatives which intrude less directly on expression. [ ]

We think the rule urged by petitioners would impose an unwarranted restriction on the duty and discretion of a trial court to oversee the discovery process.

IV

It is, of course, clear that information obtained through civil discovery authorized by modern rules of civil procedure would rarely, if ever, fall within the classes of unprotected speech identified by decisions of this Court. In this case, as petitioners argue, there certainly is a public interest in knowing more about respondents. This interest may well include most— and possibly all—of what has been discovered as a result of the court's order under Rule 26(b)(1). It does not necessarily follow, however, that a litigant has an unrestrained right to disseminate information that has been obtained through pretrial discovery. . . .

The critical question that this case presents is whether a litigant's freedom comprehends the right to disseminate information that he has obtained pursuant to a court order that both granted him access to that information and placed restraints on the way in which the information might be used. In addressing that question it is necessary to consider whether the "practice in question [furthers] an important or substantial governmental interest unrelated to the suppression of expression" and whether "the limitation of First Amendment freedoms [is] no greater than is necessary or essential to the protection of the particular governmental interest involved." [ ]; [ ].

A

At the outset, it is important to recognize the extent of the impairment of First Amendment rights that a protective order, such as the one at issue here, may cause. As in all civil litigation, petitioners gained the information they wish to disseminate only by virtue of the trial court's discovery processes. As the Rules authorizing discovery were adopted by the state legislature, the processes thereunder are a matter of legislative grace. A litigant has no First Amendment right of access to information made available only for purposes of trying his suit. Zemel v. Rusk, 381 U.S. 1, 16–17, 85 S. Ct. 1271, 1280–1281, 14 L. Ed.2d 179 (1965) ("The right to speak and publish does not carry with it the unrestrained right to gather information"). Thus, continued court control over the discovered information does not raise the same specter of government censorship that such control might suggest in other situations. See In re Halkin, 194 U.S. App. D.C., at 287, 598 F.2d, at 206–207 (Wilkey, J., dissenting).

Moreover, pretrial depositions and interrogatories are not public components of a civil trial. Such proceedings were not open to the public at common law, *Gannett Co. v. DePasquale*, [supra p. 672] and, in general, they are conducted in private as a matter of modern practice. [ ] Much of the information that surfaces during pretrial discovery may be unrelated, or only tangentially related, to the underlying cause of action. Therefore, restraints placed on discovered, but not yet admitted, information are not a restriction on a traditionally public source of information.

Finally, it is significant to note that an order prohibiting dissemination of discovered information before trial is not the kind of classic prior restraint that requires exacting First Amendment scrutiny. See *Gannett Co. v. DePasquale*, [supra p. 672] (Powell, J., concurring). As in this case, such a protective order prevents a party from disseminating only that information obtained through use of the discovery process. Thus, the party may disseminate the identical information covered by the protective order as long as the information is gained through means independent of the court's processes. In sum, judicial limitations on a party's ability to disseminate information discovered in advance of trial implicates the First Amendment rights of the restricted party to a far lesser extent than would restraints on dissemination of information in a different context. Therefore, our consideration of the provision for protective orders contained in the Washington Civil Rules takes into account the unique position that such orders occupy in relation to the First Amendment.

B

Rule 26(c) furthers a substantial governmental interest unrelated to the suppression of expression. [ ] . . . . The Washington Civil Rules enable parties to litigation to obtain information "relevant to the subject matter involved" that they believe will be helpful in the preparation and trial of the case. Rule 26, however, must be viewed in its entirety. Liberal discovery is provided for the sole purpose of assisting in the preparation and trial, or the settlement, of litigated disputes. Because of the liberality of pretrial discovery permitted by Rule 26(b)(1), it is necessary for the trial court to have the authority to issue protective orders conferred by Rule 26(c). It is clear from experience that pretrial discovery by depositions and interrogatories has a significant potential for abuse. This abuse is not limited to matters of delay and expense; discovery also may seriously implicate privacy interests of litigants and third parties. The Rules do not distinguish between public and private information. Nor do they apply only to parties to the litigation, as relevant information in the hands of third parties may be subject to discovery.

There is an opportunity, therefore, for litigants to obtain—incidentally or purposefully—information that not only is irrelevant but if publicly released could be damaging to reputation and privacy. The government clearly has a substantial interest in preventing this sort of abuse of its processes. [ ] The prevention of the abuse that can attend the coerced production of information under a State's discovery rule is sufficient justification for the authorization of protective orders.[22]

C

We also find that the provision for protective orders in the Washington Rules requires, in itself, no heightened First Amendment scrutiny. To be sure, Rule 26(c) confers broad discretion on the trial court to decide when a protective order is appropriate and what degree of protection is required. The Legislature of the State of Washington, following the example of the Congress in its approval of the Federal Rules of Civil Procedure, has determined that such discretion is necessary, and we find no reason to disagree. The trial court is in the best position to weigh fairly the competing needs and interests of parties affected by discovery. The unique character of the discovery process requires that the trial court have substantial latitude to fashion protective orders.

---

22. The Supreme Court of Washington properly emphasized the importance of ensuring that potential litigants have unimpeded access to the courts: "[A]s the trial court rightly observed, rather than expose themselves to unwanted publicity, individuals may well forgo the pursuit of their just claims. The judicial system will thus have made the utilization of its remedies so onerous that the people will be reluctant or unwilling to use it, resulting in frustration of a right as valuable as that of speech itself." [ ]

V

The facts in this case illustrate the concerns that justifiably may prompt a court to issue a protective order. As we have noted, the trial court's order allowing discovery was extremely broad. It compelled respondents—among other things—to identify all persons who had made donations over a 5–year period to Rhinehart and the Aquarian Foundation, together with the amounts donated. In effect the order would compel disclosure of membership as well as sources of financial support. The Supreme Court of Washington found that dissemination of this information would "result in annoyance, embarrassment and even oppression." [ ] It is sufficient for purposes of our decision that the highest court in the State found no abuse of discretion in the trial court's decision to issue a protective order pursuant to a constitutional state law. We therefore hold that where, as in this case, a protective order is entered on a showing of good cause as required by Rule 26(c), is limited to the context of pretrial civil discovery, and does not restrict the dissemination of the information if gained from other sources, it does not offend the First Amendment.

The judgment accordingly is affirmed.

Justice Brennan, with whom Justice Marshall joins, concurring.

The Court today recognizes that pretrial protective orders, designed to limit the dissemination of information gained through the civil discovery process, are subject to scrutiny under the First Amendment. As the Court acknowledges, before approving such protective orders, "it is necessary to consider whether the 'practice in question [furthers] an important or substantial governmental interest unrelated to the suppression of expression' and whether 'the limitation of First Amendment freedoms [is] no greater than is necessary or essential to the protection of the particular governmental interest involved.' " . . . I agree that the respondents' interests in privacy and religious freedom are sufficient to justify this protective order and to overcome the protections afforded free expression by the First Amendment. I therefore join the Court's opinion.

Notes and Questions

1. Why is the protective order in this case "not the kind of classic prior restraint that requires exacting First Amendment scrutiny"? The passage that Justice Powell cites in support of this (from his concurring opinion in *Gannett Co. v. DePasquale*) said that excluding the press from the courtroom "denies access to only one, albeit important, source," while a classic prior restraint, such as the one in *Nebraska Press v. Stuart*, prohibits publication irrespective of the source. Is this answer persuasive?

2. What implications, if any, does *Rhinehart* have for a First Amendment right of access to materials other than discovery documents?

3. Is *Rhinehart* applicable to situations in which media who are not parties to the litigation (a) seek access to discovery materials, or (b) claim a right to publish such materials? Note that neither the Supreme Court nor

the Washington Supreme Court explicitly endorsed the argument that litigants might be considered to have waived their right to publish discovery material they obtained through discovery. Does that preclude a reading of *Rhinehart* that limits it to disclosure of discovery materials by *parties*?

4.   In an omitted portion of the opinion, the Court discussed In re Halkin, 598 F.2d 176 (D.C. Cir. 1979), which held that a similar protective order was a "paradigmatic prior restraint" requiring close scrutiny under the First Amendment, and In re San Juan Star Co., 662 F.2d 108 (1st Cir. 1981), which held that such orders need only meet "a standard of 'good cause' that incorporates a 'heightened sensitivity' to the First Amendment concerns at stake." In *Halkin* the right to disclose was claimed by a party to the underlying litigation; in *San Juan Star* it was claimed by a nonparty newspaper that intervened. The Supreme Court did not mention this difference, and indicated that it viewed the two decisions as being in conflict. Does this imply that *Rhinehart* should be read to apply to nonparty media disclosures of discovery materials?

The *Rhinehart* case is subjected to close analysis in Robert C. Post, Management of Speech: Discretion and Rights, 1984 S. Ct. Rev. 169.

3.   ACCESS TO SPECIFIC TYPES OF DOCUMENTS

In most cases seeking access to documents, media claim both a common law and First Amendment right of access. When courts find a right at common law, they usually decline to address the First Amendment issue. When they find no right under either theory, they often apply similar analyses to both. It is therefore difficult to separate the cases into common law and First Amendment categories. It is equally difficult to categorize types of documents as generally open or generally closed.

One question that runs through many of these cases is whether the materials at issue are judicial records. If the court decides that they are not, there appears to be no right of access under either the common law or the First Amendment. Such a holding may make the records disclosable under freedom of information statutes, however. Recall from Chapter X that judicial records are exempt from the FOIA and most state open records statutes. Rejecting the claim that the documents sought are judicial records may destroy that exemption. In Daily Gazette Co. v. Withrow, 177 W.Va. 110, 350 S.E.2d 738, 14 Med. L. Rptr. 1447 (1986), a civil rights action against a sheriff was settled and the parties agreed to keep the settlement terms confidential. In the absence of any claim that the settlement was a judicial record, the court held that public officials have a common law duty to keep a public record of settlements of lawsuits arising from their official actions, and that such a record is disclosable under the state freedom of information statute.

Conversely, a public entity may be able to insulate itself from disclosure under a state open records act by persuading a federal judge to seal records relating to a settlement. In City of Hartford v. Chase, 942 F.2d 130, 19 Med. L. Rptr. 1172 (2d Cir. 1991), the court held that the confidentiality order, entered at the request of the city and its adversary, permitted the city to refuse to comply with the state statute, not only as to documents filed in the lawsuit but also as to other settlement-related materials in the city's possession. But another court said "It is precisely because courts have the power to trump freedom of information laws that they should exercise this power judiciously and sparingly." See Pansy v. Borough of Stroudsburg, 23 F.3d 772, 22 Med. L. Rptr. 1641 (3d Cir. 1994), holding that "a strong presumption exists against granting or maintaining an order of confidentiality" concerning information that would otherwise be disclosable under a freedom of information statute.

a.   *Documents Related to Criminal Proceedings*

Probable cause affidavits, search warrants, arrest warrants, plea bargains, sentencing reports, and grand jury records are often sought by media because of the details they provide about the crime or the accused. They have few of the characteristics of court records, however, and unless they are introduced in court, they are not necessarily disclosable.

In Times Mirror Co. v. United States, 873 F.2d 1210, 16 Med. L. Rptr. 1513 (9th Cir. 1989), the court held that the First Amendment right of access recognized in *Press-Enterprise II* does not apply to search warrants, at least while the investigation is continuing, because historically they have not generally been public, and because making them available would not serve a positive role in the proceeding for many of the same reasons that grand jury proceedings are kept secret. See also Baltimore Sun Co. v. Goetz, 886 F.2d 60, 16 Med. L. Rptr. 2295 (4th Cir. 1989); Times Mirror Co. v. United States, 873 F.2d 1210 (9th Cir. 1989); Seattle Times v. Eberharter, 105 Wash.2d 144, 713 P.2d 710, 12 Med. L. Rptr. 1794 (1986); and Newspapers of New England, Inc. v. Ware Clerk–Magistrate, 403 Mass. 628, 531 N.E.2d 1261, 16 Med. L. Rptr. 1457 (1988), all denying access to search warrants while investigations were continuing. Once the prosecution is completed, however, the common law right of access may require that search warrants be disclosed. See In re Application of Newsday, Inc., 895 F.2d 74, 17 Med. L. Rptr. 1385 (2d Cir. 1990).

Even if there is a presumptive right of access to such materials, it may be overcome by other interests. The Eighth Circuit recognized a First Amendment right of access to search warrants and supporting affidavits, but held that it may be overcome by the need to protect the privacy and reputational interests of persons who were targets of the search but were not indicted. See Employees of McDonnell Douglas Corp. v. Pulitzer Publishing Co., 895 F.2d 460, 17 Med. L. Rptr. 1364 (8th Cir. 1990). In Utah v. Archuleta, 857 P.2d 234, 21 Med. L. Rptr. 2241 (Utah 1993), the Utah Supreme Court held that the media presumptively had a right of access to probable cause statements, affidavits in support of search warrants, and witness subpoenas that had been filed with the trial court. This right was based on the First Amendment, the state constitution, and the common law. But "the documents sought contained sensitive and inflammatory information that was not necessarily accurate or admissible" and therefore posed a substantial threat to the fair trial rights of a defendant in a "highly publicized and gruesome case" of torture, rape, and murder.

The media in the Utah case also sought to inspect and copy exhibits that were introduced at the preliminary hearing, including the autopsy report; photos of the victim's body; fluid, tissue, and hair samples and bone fragments taken from the victim; various instruments used to torture and kill the victim, bloody clothing, and fingerprints. The court said there was no First Amendment right of access to these because there was no history of the public being allowed to examine such exhibits and allowing them to do so would not play a significant positive role in the functioning of the judicial process. For similar reasons the court found no common law or state constitutional right of access.

Plea agreements generally must be disclosed, perhaps because they are usually dispositive and normally come after the major threats to the defendant's fair trial rights have passed. The Ninth Circuit held that the presumption of openness recognized by the Supreme Court in the two *Press-Enterprise* cases and in *Globe Newspaper* is applicable to plea agreements. The court said these have historically been open and because most criminal cases end with plea agreements, denying access to them "would effectively block the public's access to a significant segment of our criminal justice system." The Oregonian Publishing Co. v. U.S. District Court, 920 F.2d 1462, 18 Med. L. Rptr. 1504 (9th Cir. 1990).

Sentencing reports are more problematic, possibly because they often include unverified or privacy-invading information. See, e.g., United States v. Corbitt, 879 F.2d 224 (7th Cir. 1989), holding that there is no First Amendment right to such reports and finding the common law right outweighed by the privacy interests of the defendant and his associates. But see United States v. Kaczynski, 154 F.3d 930, 26 Med. L. Rptr. 2147 (9th Cir. 1998), holding that the common law required disclosure of results of a psychiatric exam because the public interest in mental state and motivations of the "Unabomber" outweighed his privacy interests.

Grand juries. Rule 6(e) of the Federal Rules of Criminal Procedure requires that hearings on, and records pertaining to, "matters affecting a grand jury proceeding" be closed or sealed "to the extent necessary to prevent disclosure of matters occurring before a grand jury." Most states have similar rules. Grand jury proceedings are invariably secret, and the indictments that the grand jury issues often are sealed until the person named is arrested. Thereafter the indictment usually becomes part of the public record of the case, but the testimony upon which it rests remains secret. If the grand jury does not indict, there apparently is no right of access to the testimony and documents that it considered unless a statute or rule authorizes disclosure. See Daily Journal Corp. v. Superior Court, 20 Cal. 4th 1117, 979 P.2d 982, 86 Cal. Rptr.2d 623, 27 Med. L. Rptr. 2232 (Cal. 1999), rejecting media demands for grand jury evidence to enable the public to determine whether Merrill Lynch had "bought its way out" of a tenable criminal prosecution for its role in the bankruptcy of Orange County by agreeing to a civil settlement.

Even if there is no First Amendment right of access, courts may have discretion to disclose grand jury records if there is no rule forbidding it. In Arizona v. Mecham, 15 Med. L. Rptr. 2151 (Ariz. Super. 1988), the court, exercising its discretion under state law, ordered disclosure of the transcripts of grand jury proceedings that led to the indictment of the governor. The court pointed out that neither the prosecution nor the defendants objected to the disclosure, the criminal proceedings had been concluded, much of the grand jury testimony had already been disclosed at trial, and the case was one of great public interest. The court also pointed out, however, that the case was unique, involving the only governor in the nation's history to simultaneously face a felony charge, impeachment proceedings, and a recall election. For these reasons, the court said "this Order is not to be considered as precedent for future requests for public disclosure of Grand Jury transcripts."

Does grand jury secrecy require that all proceedings ancillary to the grand jury's work (and related documents) be secret too? That question surfaced in connection with the Whitewater special prosecutor's investigation of Monica Lewinsky's relationship with President Clinton. Several witnesses who were subpoenaed in that investigation resisted on grounds of executive privilege or attorney-client privilege, and President Clinton moved to have the special prosecutor held in contempt for leaking grand jury testimony to the press. On order of the chief judge of the district court for the District of Columbia, all hearings on these matters were closed to the press and public and all transcripts, pleadings, and other documents were sealed.

Major newspapers, magazines, and networks complained that hearings on the privilege claims and contempt allegations were not grand jury proceedings and should be open as a matter of common law and First Amendment law. They asked for advance notice of hearings on privilege or contempt matters, opportunity to be heard before such hearings were closed, and public docketing of all motions and orders. The chief judge rejected all the media requests, and the D.C. Circuit upheld her decision in most respects. See In re Motions of Dow Jones & Co., 142 F.3d 496 (D.C. Cir. 1998).

The court of appeals noted that the media did not question the constitutionality of Rule 6(e) and said this rule applies to ancillary proceedings because those will nearly always pose a danger of revealing "matters occurring before a grand jury." The media pointed out that Chief Judge Sirica conducted a famous public hearing on President Nixon's refusal to comply with a grand jury subpoena to turn over the Watergate tapes, but the court said that example "proves too much" because the transcript of the Nixon hearing shows that it disclosed matters that the media in the present case agreed should not be disclosed under Rule 6(e).

The court said: "Recognizing a First Amendment right to force ancillary proceedings to be conducted without referring to grand jury matters would create enormous practical problems in judicial administration, and there is no strong history or tradition in favor of doing so." As to noting hearings, motions, and orders on the public docket, the court said the judge should do so by using captions that would not reveal the nature of matters before the grand jury.

b. Documents Related to Civil Proceedings

Pleadings in civil cases are clearly judicial records and are presumptively open at common law and probably also as a matter of First Amendment law. That doesn't mean they can't be sealed, however. In one of the many civil suits arising out of allegations of sexual abuse by priests, a sharply divided Kentucky Supreme Court held that there was no right of access to allegations that had been stricken as immaterial. Roman Catholic Diocese of Lexington v. Noble, 92 S.W.3d 724, 31 Med. L. Rptr. 1321 (Ky. 2002). The 4–3 majority said there could be no First Amendment right of access because "there is nothing to indicate that the public and the press historically have had access to sham, immaterial, impertinent, redundant, or scandalous material that is without 'legal effect,' " and that access to the material could "only serve to improperly prejudice the populace in general, and potential jurors in particular, against the Diocese's case." It held that whether to allow access as a matter of common law was within the trial court's discretion.

Discovery documents. As the Court noted in *Rhinehart*, most of the fact-finding activity in civil litigation takes place outside the courtroom, in the process of discovery. Although the precise issue in *Rhinehart* was the validity of a protective order restricting a party's use of discovery material, the decision generally has been read to speak to the broader question of public access to discovery material. It has proved to be a powerful obstacle to disclosure, even when the claim for access seems strong.

As to discovery materials that have not been filed in court, there is little basis for either a common law or First Amendment right of access. See, e.g., State ex rel. Mitsubishi Heavy Industries v. Milwaukee County Circuit Court, 605 N.W.2d 868, 28 Med. L. Rptr. 1685 (Wis. 2000), holding that such documents were not public records and newspaper therefore had no claim of access to them. States are free to designate these as public records, however, and some have done so. The state that has gone furthest in this regard is Texas. A procedural rule adopted by the state supreme court in 1990 treats discovery documents and settlement agreements as court records—even if they have not been filed—if they relate to information "concerning matters that have a probable adverse effect upon the general public health or safety, or the administration of public office, or the operation of government." These and all other court records may be sealed only after a public notice is posted and a hearing held, and then only upon a finding that the interest in openness is outweighed by "a specific, serious, and substantial interest" that cannot be protected by alternative means. Nonparties have a right to intervene to contest the sealing or to unseal the records at any future time. Tex. R. Civ. P. 76a. Less far-reaching rules have been adopted in Florida, New York, and a few other states.

The New Jersey Supreme Court said "the universal understanding of the legal community is that unfiled documents in discovery are not subject to public access," but it nevertheless referred the question to the New Jersey Civil Practice Committee to decide whether that position should be changed. Frankl v. Goodyear Tire & Rubber Co., 181 N.J. 1, 853 A.2d 880 (2004).

When discovery materials are filed with the court, usually in connection with pre-trial motions, they become court records subject to the common law and First Amendment rights of access, but the courts generally hold that this only means that the party seeking secrecy must show good cause for maintaining confidentiality under Rule 26 of the Federal Rules of Civil Procedure. See Chicago Tribune Co. v. Bridgestone/Firestone Inc., 263 F.3d 1304 (11th Cir. 2001), holding that the trial judge must balance a manufacturer's trade secrecy claims against the newspaper's claim that disclosure would serve the public's interest in health and safety.

Good cause that existed when a protective order was entered may disappear with the passage of time. In Public Citizen v. Liggett Group Inc., 858 F.2d 775, 15 Med. L. Rptr. 2129 (1st Cir. 1988), the court said dismissal of the underlying case, removing any concerns about the defendant's right to a fair trial, was a change in circumstances sufficient to justify modification of a protective order despite the defendant's argument that it had relied on the order in furnishing the material.

Some courts have suggested that a change in the Federal Rules of Civil Procedure now requires the media to justify all requests for access to unfiled discovery documents. Rule 5(d) formerly required that "all discovery materials must be filed with the district court, unless the court orders otherwise." This created a presumption that such materials would be accessible to the public, unless the court entered a protective order. Rule 5(d) has been amended, however, to prohibit the filing of certain discovery materials unless they are actually used in the trial or the court orders that they be filed. The Second Circuit, in dicta, suggested that the recent amendment to Rule 5(d) "provides no presumption of filing all discovery materials, let alone public access to them." See Securities & Exchange Comm'n v. TheStreet.Com, 273 F.3d 222 (2d Cir. 2001). At least one district court has relied on the change in Rule 5(d) and the Second Circuit's dicta to find that the press must show a "legitimate reason" before a court will order third-party access to discovery materials. See New York v. Microsoft Corp., 206 F.R.D. 19, 30 Med. L Rptr. 1632 (D.D.C. 2002).

Videotapes of depositions. Unless a state rule authorizes it, media generally have no right to attend depositions. Transcripts of depositions are discovery documents subject to the disclosure rules and procedures described above. If a deposition is videotaped and the tape is filed in court, one might assume it becomes a court record subject to disclosure unless good cause for secrecy is established. Some courts so hold. See In re Application of CBS, Inc., 828 F.2d 958, 14 Med. L. Rptr. 1636 (2d Cir. 1987), allowing broadcasters to copy a videotaped deposition given by former Teamsters president Roy L. Williams in a trial in which Williams was identified as an unindicted co-conspirator.

But access to two videotaped depositions given by President Clinton was denied on the ground that they were not judicial records. In the criminal trial of the Whitewater defendant Susan McDougal, Clinton's videotaped deposition was played in open court and the judge made available a transcript but denied requests for permission to copy the tape for broadcast. The testimony and the transcript thereof were admitted in evidence but the videotape itself was not. Relying on *Nixon,* the Eighth Circuit said the videotape was not a judicial record. See United States v. McDougal, 103 F.3d 651, 25 Med. L. Rptr. 1097 (8th Cir. 1996), cert. denied sub nom. Citizens United v. United States, 522 U.S. 809 (1997). Unlike the tapes at issue in *Nixon,* the videotape was not documentary evidence itself, but was merely an electronic recording of a witness's testimony. But even if the videotape were treated as a judicial record, the district judge did not abuse his discretion in applying the common law balancing process suggested by *Nixon.*

The court said the public's interest in having access to the videotape was "only marginal because the testimony has already been made visually and aurally accessible in the courtroom and the transcript has been widely distributed and publicized." As in *Nixon,* there was a potential for "misuse" of the tape, but the court did not say how it might be misused. Noting that the media were denied physical access to the videotape of President Reagan's deposition testimony in the Iran–Contra prosecutions, the court said "there is a strong judicial tradition of proscribing public access to recordings of testimony given by a sitting president. . . ." Without discussing later Supreme Court cases establishing a First Amendment right of access to judicial proceedings, the court said the media's First Amendment right of access was satisfied by allowing them to listen to the testimony in the courtroom and to read the transcript of the deposition.

President Clinton also testified by videotaped deposition in Paula Jones' sexual harassment suit against him. After that suit was dismissed on his motion for summary judgment, news organizations asked the judge to unseal the discovery materials in the case. Relying on the decision of the Eighth Circuit in the *McDougal* case, the judge refused to unseal either the video or transcript of it on the ground that it was not a judicial record. See Jones v. Clinton, 12 F. Supp. 2d 931, 26 Med. L. Rptr. 1979 (E.D. Ark. 1998).

Is there a tenable distinction between videotapes introduced as documentary evidence (e.g., a security camera's tape of a robbery) and a videotaped deposition? Why is the video of the deposition, instead of merely the transcript thereof, shown to the jury? Do those reasons argue for treating the video as evidence?

Settlements. These pose several different types of access problems. If the settlement is no more than a contract between the parties, by which one agrees to dismiss the suit in exchange for something of value from the other, it ordinarily would be no more accessible than any other private contract. Under the Texas rule mentioned above, however, even these agreements may be court records if they meet the public interest standards of that rule. Generally, settlements that are submitted to the court for approval become judicial records subject to the common law and First Amendment rights of access. See Jessup v. Luther, 277 F.3d 926 (7th Cir. 2002).

Frequently the determinative issue is whether good cause for a protective order is established by assertions that secrecy was an essential condition of the settlement. Some courts, however, apply a different analysis. In a personal injury case, the parties reached a settlement, a condition of which was that the entire court file, along with the settlement, was to be sealed. A plaintiff in a different lawsuit against the same company, seeking information for use in his own case, challenged the sealing of the record. The court held the sealing impermissible even assuming the settlement would not have been reached but for the judge's agreement to seal the record. The court said "Once a matter is brought before a court for resolution, it is no longer solely the parties' case, but also the public's case. Absent a showing of extraordinary circumstances . . . the court file must remain accessible to the public." Brown v. Advantage Engineering, Inc., 960 F.2d 1013, 20 Med. L. Rptr. 1252 (11th Cir. 1992). See also Wilson v. American Motors Corp., 759 F.2d 1568, 11 Med. L. Rptr. 2008 (11th Cir. 1985).

If the sealing order includes not only the settlement agreement, but also discovery materials and records of hearings, motions, affidavits, and other materials that were publicly available when filed, it may be possible to unbundle the documents that are subject to the order and disclose at least the settlement. See, e.g., Shenandoah Publishing House v. Fanning, 235 Va. 253, 368 S.E.2d 253, 15 Med. L. Rptr. 1659 (1988), permitting sealing of discovery documents after settlement, but holding that the parties' generalized claims of financial, reputational, and emotional harm were not sufficient to overcome a presumption of openness as to the agreement itself.

Notes and Questions

1. Do the cases described above reflect principles that can be used to predict outcomes in cases seeking access to judicial records, or are they merely ad hoc decisions?

2. The common law right of access contemplates case-by-case balancing of the interests in disclosure against the specific reasons for secrecy. The First Amendment right of access depends on the history and experience inquiries mandated by *Richmond Newspapers, Globe Newspaper,* and *Press-Enterprise I* and *II,* and even if those yield the conclusion that there is a First Amendment right of access, it too can be overcome by a sufficient showing of a need for secrecy. Given those sources of indeterminacy, does the First

Amendment add anything to the common law right of access? Does either approach leave less to the judge's discretion than the other?

———

In reflecting upon the materials covered in this chapter, note the large number of variables. The list of reasons for which restrictions on access are imposed includes fair trial rights; efficient operation of the court system; rehabilitation of offenders; privacy of victims, witnesses, and jurors; effectiveness of law enforcement; and judicial dignity and courtroom decorum, to name a few. The interests in disclosure are also diverse, ranging from mere curiosity about the amount of money someone received in a personal injury settlement to discovery of wrongdoing by police and elected officials.

Access can be a matter as simple as allowing reporters to see pleadings or as complex as arranging procedures to allow copying of videotapes. Enforcing restrictions can be as easy as ordering a photographer to leave the courtroom or as difficult as trying to control the speech of a juror long after he or she has been discharged. And the variety is far greater than it appears here, because we have condensed, synthesized, and simplified this survey of judicial access issues. For an extensive treatment, see Dan Paul, Richard J. Ovelmen, and Enrique D. Arana, Access, 1 Communications Law 65–383 (Practising Law Institute 2004).

If the First Amendment creates certain rights of access to judicial proceedings, why doesn't it also guarantee some rights of access to the other governmental sources of news considered in Chapter X? In that chapter we saw a number of relatively successful statutory solutions to access problems. Would statutory solutions work in the court context? Would they violate separation of powers principles? If courtroom access questions must be left to judges, are they better decided by application of constitutional and common law principles in access litigation than by judicial rulemaking? These questions have emerged only since the courts began recognizing common law and First Amendment rights of access, and many of them have yet to be resolved.

INDEX